# Lecture Notes in Computer Science 13685

More information about this series at https://link.springer.com/bookseries/558

Shai Avidan · Gabriel Brostow ·
Moustapha Cissé · Giovanni Maria Farinella ·
Tal Hassner (Eds.)

# Computer Vision – ECCV 2022

17th European Conference
Tel Aviv, Israel, October 23–27, 2022
Proceedings, Part XXV

 Springer

*Editors*
Shai Avidan
Tel Aviv University
Tel Aviv, Israel

Gabriel Brostow ⓘ
University College London
London, UK

Moustapha Cissé
Google AI
Accra, Ghana

Giovanni Maria Farinella ⓘ
University of Catania
Catania, Italy

Tal Hassner ⓘ
Facebook (United States)
Menlo Park, CA, USA

ISSN 0302-9743          ISSN 1611-3349 (electronic)
Lecture Notes in Computer Science
ISBN 978-3-031-19805-2          ISBN 978-3-031-19806-9 (eBook)
https://doi.org/10.1007/978-3-031-19806-9

This Springer imprint is published by the registered company Springer Nature Switzerland AG
The registered company address is: Gewerbestrasse 11, 6330 Cham, Switzerland

# Foreword

Organizing the European Conference on Computer Vision (ECCV 2022) in Tel-Aviv during a global pandemic was no easy feat. The uncertainty level was extremely high, and decisions had to be postponed to the last minute. Still, we managed to plan things just in time for ECCV 2022 to be held in person. Participation in physical events is crucial to stimulating collaborations and nurturing the culture of the Computer Vision community.

There were many people who worked hard to ensure attendees enjoyed the best science at the 16th edition of ECCV. We are grateful to the Program Chairs Gabriel Brostow and Tal Hassner, who went above and beyond to ensure the ECCV reviewing process ran smoothly. The scientific program includes dozens of workshops and tutorials in addition to the main conference and we would like to thank Leonid Karlinsky and Tomer Michaeli for their hard work. Finally, special thanks to the web chairs Lorenzo Baraldi and Kosta Derpanis, who put in extra hours to transfer information fast and efficiently to the ECCV community.

We would like to express gratitude to our generous sponsors and the Industry Chairs, Dimosthenis Karatzas and Chen Sagiv, who oversaw industry relations and proposed new ways for academia-industry collaboration and technology transfer. It's great to see so much industrial interest in what we're doing!

Authors' draft versions of the papers appeared online with open access on both the Computer Vision Foundation (CVF) and the European Computer Vision Association (ECVA) websites as with previous ECCVs. Springer, the publisher of the proceedings, has arranged for archival publication. The final version of the papers is hosted by SpringerLink, with active references and supplementary materials. It benefits all potential readers that we offer both a free and citeable version for all researchers, as well as an authoritative, citeable version for SpringerLink readers. Our thanks go to Ronan Nugent from Springer, who helped us negotiate this agreement. Last but not least, we wish to thank Eric Mortensen, our publication chair, whose expertise made the process smooth.

October 2022

Rita Cucchiara
Jiří Matas
Amnon Shashua
Lihi Zelnik-Manor

# Preface

Welcome to the proceedings of the European Conference on Computer Vision (ECCV 2022). This was a hybrid edition of ECCV as we made our way out of the COVID-19 pandemic. The conference received 5804 valid paper submissions, compared to 5150 submissions to ECCV 2020 (a 12.7% increase) and 2439 in ECCV 2018. 1645 submissions were accepted for publication (28%) and, of those, 157 (2.7% overall) as orals.

846 of the submissions were desk-rejected for various reasons. Many of them because they revealed author identity, thus violating the double-blind policy. This violation came in many forms: some had author names with the title, others added acknowledgments to specific grants, yet others had links to their github account where their name was visible. Tampering with the LaTeX template was another reason for automatic desk rejection.

ECCV 2022 used the traditional CMT system to manage the entire double-blind reviewing process. Authors did not know the names of the reviewers and vice versa. Each paper received at least 3 reviews (except 6 papers that received only 2 reviews), totalling more than 15,000 reviews.

Handling the review process at this scale was a significant challenge. To ensure that each submission received as fair and high-quality reviews as possible, we recruited more than 4719 reviewers (in the end, 4719 reviewers did at least one review). Similarly we recruited more than 276 area chairs (eventually, only 276 area chairs handled a batch of papers). The area chairs were selected based on their technical expertise and reputation, largely among people who served as area chairs in previous top computer vision and machine learning conferences (ECCV, ICCV, CVPR, NeurIPS, etc.).

Reviewers were similarly invited from previous conferences, and also from the pool of authors. We also encouraged experienced area chairs to suggest additional chairs and reviewers in the initial phase of recruiting. The median reviewer load was five papers per reviewer, while the average load was about four papers, because of the emergency reviewers. The area chair load was 35 papers, on average.

Conflicts of interest between authors, area chairs, and reviewers were handled largely automatically by the CMT platform, with some manual help from the Program Chairs. Reviewers were allowed to describe themselves as senior reviewer (load of 8 papers to review) or junior reviewers (load of 4 papers). Papers were matched to area chairs based on a subject-area affinity score computed in CMT and an affinity score computed by the Toronto Paper Matching System (TPMS). TPMS is based on the paper's full text. An area chair handling each submission would bid for preferred expert reviewers, and we balanced load and prevented conflicts.

The assignment of submissions to area chairs was relatively smooth, as was the assignment of submissions to reviewers. A small percentage of reviewers were not happy with their assignments in terms of subjects and self-reported expertise. This is an area for improvement, although it's interesting that many of these cases were reviewers hand-picked by AC's. We made a later round of reviewer recruiting, targeted at the list of authors of papers submitted to the conference, and had an excellent response which helped provide enough emergency reviewers. In the end, all but six papers received at least 3 reviews.

The challenges of the reviewing process are in line with past experiences at ECCV 2020. As the community grows, and the number of submissions increases, it becomes ever more challenging to recruit enough reviewers and ensure a high enough quality of reviews. Enlisting authors by default as reviewers might be one step to address this challenge.

Authors were given a week to rebut the initial reviews, and address reviewers' concerns. Each rebuttal was limited to a single pdf page with a fixed template.

The Area Chairs then led discussions with the reviewers on the merits of each submission. The goal was to reach consensus, but, ultimately, it was up to the Area Chair to make a decision. The decision was then discussed with a buddy Area Chair to make sure decisions were fair and informative. The entire process was conducted virtually with no in-person meetings taking place.

The Program Chairs were informed in cases where the Area Chairs overturned a decisive consensus reached by the reviewers, and pushed for the meta-reviews to contain details that explained the reasoning for such decisions. Obviously these were the most contentious cases, where reviewer inexperience was the most common reported factor.

Once the list of accepted papers was finalized and released, we went through the laborious process of plagiarism (including self-plagiarism) detection. A total of 4 accepted papers were rejected because of that.

Finally, we would like to thank our Technical Program Chair, Pavel Lifshits, who did tremendous work behind the scenes, and we thank the tireless CMT team.

October 2022

Gabriel Brostow
Giovanni Maria Farinella
Moustapha Cissé
Shai Avidan
Tal Hassner

# Organization

## General Chairs

Rita Cucchiara      University of Modena and Reggio Emilia, Italy
Jiří Matas      Czech Technical University in Prague, Czech
     Republic
Amnon Shashua      Hebrew University of Jerusalem, Israel
Lihi Zelnik-Manor      Technion – Israel Institute of Technology, Israel

## Program Chairs

Shai Avidan      Tel-Aviv University, Israel
Gabriel Brostow      University College London, UK
Moustapha Cissé      Google AI, Ghana
Giovanni Maria Farinella      University of Catania, Italy
Tal Hassner      Facebook AI, USA

## Program Technical Chair

Pavel Lifshits      Technion – Israel Institute of Technology, Israel

## Workshops Chairs

Leonid Karlinsky      IBM Research, Israel
Tomer Michaeli      Technion – Israel Institute of Technology, Israel
Ko Nishino      Kyoto University, Japan

## Tutorial Chairs

Thomas Pock      Graz University of Technology, Austria
Natalia Neverova      Facebook AI Research, UK

## Demo Chair

Bohyung Han      Seoul National University, Korea

## Social and Student Activities Chairs

Tatiana Tommasi            Italian Institute of Technology, Italy
Sagie Benaim               University of Copenhagen, Denmark

## Diversity and Inclusion Chairs

Xi Yin                     Facebook AI Research, USA
Bryan Russell              Adobe, USA

## Communications Chairs

Lorenzo Baraldi            University of Modena and Reggio Emilia, Italy
Kosta Derpanis             York University & Samsung AI Centre Toronto,
                           Canada

## Industrial Liaison Chairs

Dimosthenis Karatzas       Universitat Autònoma de Barcelona, Spain
Chen Sagiv                 SagivTech, Israel

## Finance Chair

Gerard Medioni             University of Southern California & Amazon,
                           USA

## Publication Chair

Eric Mortensen             MiCROTEC, USA

## Area Chairs

Lourdes Agapito            University College London, UK
Zeynep Akata               University of Tübingen, Germany
Naveed Akhtar              University of Western Australia, Australia
Karteek Alahari            Inria Grenoble Rhône-Alpes, France
Alexandre Alahi            École polytechnique fédérale de Lausanne,
                           Switzerland
Pablo Arbelaez             Universidad de Los Andes, Columbia
Antonis A. Argyros         University of Crete & Foundation for Research
                           and Technology-Hellas, Crete
Yuki M. Asano              University of Amsterdam, The Netherlands
Kalle Åström               Lund University, Sweden
Hadar Averbuch-Elor        Cornell University, USA

Matthijs Douze                Facebook AI Research, USA
Mohamed Elhoseiny             King Abdullah University of Science and
                              Technology, Saudi Arabia
Sergio Escalera               University of Barcelona, Spain
Yi Fang                       New York University, USA
Ryan Farrell                  Brigham Young University, USA
Alireza Fathi                 Google, USA
Christoph Feichtenhofer       Facebook AI Research, USA
Basura Fernando               Agency for Science, Technology and Research
                              (A*STAR), Singapore
Vittorio Ferrari              Google Research, Switzerland
Andrew W. Fitzgibbon          Graphcore, UK
David J. Fleet                University of Toronto, Canada
David Forsyth                 University of Illinois at Urbana-Champaign, USA
David Fouhey                  University of Michigan, USA
Katerina Fragkiadaki          Carnegie Mellon University, USA
Friedrich Fraundorfer         Graz University of Technology, Austria
Oren Freifeld                 Ben-Gurion University, Israel
Thomas Funkhouser             Google Research & Princeton University, USA
Yasutaka Furukawa             Simon Fraser University, Canada
Fabio Galasso                 Sapienza University of Rome, Italy
Jürgen Gall                   University of Bonn, Germany
Chuang Gan                    Massachusetts Institute of Technology, USA
Zhe Gan                       Microsoft, USA
Animesh Garg                  University of Toronto, Vector Institute, Nvidia,
                              Canada
Efstratios Gavves             University of Amsterdam, The Netherlands
Peter Gehler                  Amazon, Germany
Theo Gevers                   University of Amsterdam, The Netherlands
Bernard Ghanem                King Abdullah University of Science and
                              Technology, Saudi Arabia
Ross B. Girshick              Facebook AI Research, USA
Georgia Gkioxari              Facebook AI Research, USA
Albert Gordo                  Facebook, USA
Stephen Gould                 Australian National University, Australia
Venu Madhav Govindu           Indian Institute of Science, India
Kristen Grauman               Facebook AI Research & UT Austin, USA
Abhinav Gupta                 Carnegie Mellon University & Facebook AI
                              Research, USA
Mohit Gupta                   University of Wisconsin-Madison, USA
Hu Han                        Institute of Computing Technology, Chinese
                              Academy of Sciences, China

| | |
|---|---|
| Bohyung Han | Seoul National University, Korea |
| Tian Han | Stevens Institute of Technology, USA |
| Emily Hand | University of Nevada, Reno, USA |
| Bharath Hariharan | Cornell University, USA |
| Ran He | Institute of Automation, Chinese Academy of Sciences, China |
| Otmar Hilliges | ETH Zurich, Switzerland |
| Adrian Hilton | University of Surrey, UK |
| Minh Hoai | Stony Brook University, USA |
| Yedid Hoshen | Hebrew University of Jerusalem, Israel |
| Timothy Hospedales | University of Edinburgh, UK |
| Gang Hua | Wormpex AI Research, USA |
| Di Huang | Beihang University, China |
| Jing Huang | Facebook, USA |
| Jia-Bin Huang | Facebook, USA |
| Nathan Jacobs | Washington University in St. Louis, USA |
| C.V. Jawahar | International Institute of Information Technology, Hyderabad, India |
| Herve Jegou | Facebook AI Research, France |
| Neel Joshi | Microsoft Research, USA |
| Armand Joulin | Facebook AI Research, France |
| Frederic Jurie | University of Caen Normandie, France |
| Fredrik Kahl | Chalmers University of Technology, Sweden |
| Yannis Kalantidis | NAVER LABS Europe, France |
| Evangelos Kalogerakis | University of Massachusetts, Amherst, USA |
| Sing Bing Kang | Zillow Group, USA |
| Yosi Keller | Bar Ilan University, Israel |
| Margret Keuper | University of Mannheim, Germany |
| Tae-Kyun Kim | Imperial College London, UK |
| Benjamin Kimia | Brown University, USA |
| Alexander Kirillov | Facebook AI Research, USA |
| Kris Kitani | Carnegie Mellon University, USA |
| Iasonas Kokkinos | Snap Inc. & University College London, UK |
| Vladlen Koltun | Apple, USA |
| Nikos Komodakis | University of Crete, Crete |
| Piotr Koniusz | Australian National University, Australia |
| Philipp Kraehenbuehl | University of Texas at Austin, USA |
| Dilip Krishnan | Google, USA |
| Ajay Kumar | Hong Kong Polytechnic University, Hong Kong, China |
| Junseok Kwon | Chung-Ang University, Korea |
| Jean-Francois Lalonde | Université Laval, Canada |

| | |
|---|---|
| Mathieu Salzmann | École polytechnique fédérale de Lausanne, Switzerland |
| Dimitris Samaras | Stony Brook University, USA |
| Aswin Sankaranarayanan | Carnegie Mellon University, USA |
| Imari Sato | National Institute of Informatics, Japan |
| Yoichi Sato | University of Tokyo, Japan |
| Shin'ichi Satoh | National Institute of Informatics, Japan |
| Walter Scheirer | University of Notre Dame, USA |
| Bernt Schiele | Max Planck Institute for Informatics, Germany |
| Konrad Schindler | ETH Zurich, Switzerland |
| Cordelia Schmid | Inria & Google, France |
| Alexander Schwing | University of Illinois at Urbana-Champaign, USA |
| Nicu Sebe | University of Trento, Italy |
| Greg Shakhnarovich | Toyota Technological Institute at Chicago, USA |
| Eli Shechtman | Adobe Research, USA |
| Humphrey Shi | University of Oregon & University of Illinois at Urbana-Champaign & Picsart AI Research, USA |
| Jianbo Shi | University of Pennsylvania, USA |
| Roy Shilkrot | Massachusetts Institute of Technology, USA |
| Mike Zheng Shou | National University of Singapore, Singapore |
| Kaleem Siddiqi | McGill University, Canada |
| Richa Singh | Indian Institute of Technology Jodhpur, India |
| Greg Slabaugh | Queen Mary University of London, UK |
| Cees Snoek | University of Amsterdam, The Netherlands |
| Yale Song | Facebook AI Research, USA |
| Yi-Zhe Song | University of Surrey, UK |
| Bjorn Stenger | Rakuten Institute of Technology |
| Abby Stylianou | Saint Louis University, USA |
| Akihiro Sugimoto | National Institute of Informatics, Japan |
| Chen Sun | Brown University, USA |
| Deqing Sun | Google, USA |
| Kalyan Sunkavalli | Adobe Research, USA |
| Ying Tai | Tencent YouTu Lab, China |
| Ayellet Tal | Technion – Israel Institute of Technology, Israel |
| Ping Tan | Simon Fraser University, Canada |
| Siyu Tang | ETH Zurich, Switzerland |
| Chi-Keung Tang | Hong Kong University of Science and Technology, Hong Kong, China |
| Radu Timofte | University of Würzburg, Germany & ETH Zurich, Switzerland |
| Federico Tombari | Google, Switzerland & Technical University of Munich, Germany |

Todd Zickler                    Harvard University, USA
Wangmeng Zuo                    Harbin Institute of Technology, China

## Technical Program Committee

Davide Abati
Soroush Abbasi
    Koohpayegani
Amos L. Abbott
Rameen Abdal
Rabab Abdelfattah
Sahar Abdelnabi
Hassan Abu Alhaija
Abulikemu Abuduweili
Ron Abutbul
Hanno Ackermann
Aikaterini Adam
Kamil Adamczewski
Ehsan Adeli
Vida Adeli
Donald Adjeroh
Arman Afrasiyabi
Akshay Agarwal
Sameer Agarwal
Abhinav Agarwalla
Vaibhav Aggarwal
Sara Aghajanzadeh
Susmit Agrawal
Antonio Agudo
Touqeer Ahmad
Sk Miraj Ahmed
Chaitanya Ahuja
Nilesh A. Ahuja
Abhishek Aich
Shubhra Aich
Noam Aigerman
Arash Akbarinia
Peri Akiva
Derya Akkaynak
Emre Aksan
Arjun R. Akula
Yuval Alaluf
Stephan Alaniz
Paul Albert
Cenek Albl

Filippo Aleotti
Konstantinos P.
    Alexandridis
Motasem Alfarra
Mohsen Ali
Thiemo Alldieck
Hadi Alzayer
Liang An
Shan An
Yi An
Zhulin An
Dongsheng An
Jie An
Xiang An
Saket Anand
Cosmin Ancuti
Juan Andrade-Cetto
Alexander Andreopoulos
Bjoern Andres
Jerone T. A. Andrews
Shivangi Aneja
Anelia Angelova
Dragomir Anguelov
Rushil Anirudh
Oron Anschel
Rao Muhammad Anwer
Djamila Aouada
Evlampios Apostolidis
Srikar Appalaraju
Nikita Araslanov
Andre Araujo
Eric Arazo
Dawit Mureja Argaw
Anurag Arnab
Aditya Arora
Chetan Arora
Sunpreet S. Arora
Alexey Artemov
Muhammad Asad
Kumar Ashutosh

Sinem Aslan
Vishal Asnani
Mahmoud Assran
Amir Atapour-Abarghouei
Nikos Athanasiou
Ali Athar
ShahRukh Athar
Sara Atito
Souhaib Attaiki
Matan Atzmon
Mathieu Aubry
Nicolas Audebert
Tristan T.
    Aumentado-Armstrong
Melinos Averkiou
Yannis Avrithis
Stephane Ayache
Mehmet Aygün
Seyed Mehdi
    Ayyoubzadeh
Hossein Azizpour
George Azzopardi
Mallikarjun B. R.
Yunhao Ba
Abhishek Badki
Seung-Hwan Bae
Seung-Hwan Baek
Seungryul Baek
Piyush Nitin Bagad
Shai Bagon
Gaetan Bahl
Shikhar Bahl
Sherwin Bahmani
Haoran Bai
Lei Bai
Jiawang Bai
Haoyue Bai
Jinbin Bai
Xiang Bai
Xuyang Bai

Yang Bai
Yuanchao Bai
Ziqian Bai
Sungyong Baik
Kevin Bailly
Max Bain
Federico Baldassarre
Wele Gedara Chaminda
    Bandara
Biplab Banerjee
Pratyay Banerjee
Sandipan Banerjee
Jihwan Bang
Antyanta Bangunharcana
Aayush Bansal
Ankan Bansal
Siddhant Bansal
Wentao Bao
Zhipeng Bao
Amir Bar
Manel Baradad Jurjo
Lorenzo Baraldi
Danny Barash
Daniel Barath
Connelly Barnes
Ioan Andrei Bârsan
Steven Basart
Dina Bashkirova
Chaim Baskin
Peyman Bateni
Anil Batra
Sebastiano Battiato
Ardhendu Behera
Harkirat Behl
Jens Behley
Vasileios Belagiannis
Boulbaba Ben Amor
Emanuel Ben Baruch
Abdessamad Ben Hamza
Gil Ben-Artzi
Assia Benbihi
Fabian Benitez-Quiroz
Guy Ben-Yosef
Philipp Benz
Alexander W. Bergman

Urs Bergmann
Jesus Bermudez-Cameo
Stefano Berretti
Gedas Bertasius
Zachary Bessinger
Petra Bevandić
Matthew Beveridge
Lucas Beyer
Yash Bhalgat
Suvaansh Bhambri
Samarth Bharadwaj
Gaurav Bharaj
Aparna Bharati
Bharat Lal Bhatnagar
Uttaran Bhattacharya
Apratim Bhattacharyya
Brojeshwar Bhowmick
Ankan Kumar Bhunia
Ayan Kumar Bhunia
Qi Bi
Sai Bi
Michael Bi Mi
Gui-Bin Bian
Jia-Wang Bian
Shaojun Bian
Pia Bideau
Mario Bijelic
Hakan Bilen
Guillaume-Alexandre
    Bilodeau
Alexander Binder
Tolga Birdal
Vighnesh N. Birodkar
Sandika Biswas
Andreas Blattmann
Janusz Bobulski
Giuseppe Boccignone
Vishnu Boddeti
Navaneeth Bodla
Moritz Böhle
Aleksei Bokhovkin
Sam Bond-Taylor
Vivek Boominathan
Shubhankar Borse
Mark Boss

Andrea Bottino
Adnane Boukhayma
Fadi Boutros
Nicolas C. Boutry
Richard S. Bowen
Ivaylo Boyadzhiev
Aidan Boyd
Yuri Boykov
Aljaz Bozic
Behzad Bozorgtabar
Eric Brachmann
Samarth Brahmbhatt
Gustav Bredell
Francois Bremond
Joel Brogan
Andrew Brown
Thomas Brox
Marcus A. Brubaker
Robert-Jan Bruintjes
Yuqi Bu
Anders G. Buch
Himanshu Buckchash
Mateusz Buda
Ignas Budvytis
José M. Buenaposada
Marcel C. Bühler
Tu Bui
Adrian Bulat
Hannah Bull
Evgeny Burnaev
Andrei Bursuc
Benjamin Busam
Sergey N. Buzykanov
Wonmin Byeon
Fabian Caba
Martin Cadik
Guanyu Cai
Minjie Cai
Qing Cai
Zhongang Cai
Qi Cai
Yancheng Cai
Shen Cai
Han Cai
Jiarui Cai

Bowen Cai
Mu Cai
Qin Cai
Ruojin Cai
Weidong Cai
Weiwei Cai
Yi Cai
Yujun Cai
Zhiping Cai
Akin Caliskan
Lilian Calvet
Baris Can Cam
Necati Cihan Camgoz
Tommaso Campari
Dylan Campbell
Ziang Cao
Ang Cao
Xu Cao
Zhiwen Cao
Shengcao Cao
Song Cao
Weipeng Cao
Xiangyong Cao
Xiaochun Cao
Yue Cao
Yunhao Cao
Zhangjie Cao
Jiale Cao
Yang Cao
Jiajiong Cao
Jie Cao
Jinkun Cao
Lele Cao
Yulong Cao
Zhiguo Cao
Chen Cao
Razvan Caramalau
Marlène Careil
Gustavo Carneiro
Joao Carreira
Dan Casas
Paola Cascante-Bonilla
Angela Castillo
Francisco M. Castro
Pedro Castro

Luca Cavalli
George J. Cazenavette
Oya Celiktutan
Hakan Cevikalp
Sri Harsha C. H.
Sungmin Cha
Geonho Cha
Menglei Chai
Lucy Chai
Yuning Chai
Zenghao Chai
Anirban Chakraborty
Deep Chakraborty
Rudrasis Chakraborty
Souradeep Chakraborty
Kelvin C. K. Chan
Chee Seng Chan
Paramanand Chandramouli
Arjun Chandrasekaran
Kenneth Chaney
Dongliang Chang
Huiwen Chang
Peng Chang
Xiaojun Chang
Jia-Ren Chang
Hyung Jin Chang
Hyun Sung Chang
Ju Yong Chang
Li-Jen Chang
Qi Chang
Wei-Yi Chang
Yi Chang
Nadine Chang
Hanqing Chao
Pradyumna Chari
Dibyadip Chatterjee
Chiranjoy Chattopadhyay
Siddhartha Chaudhuri
Zhengping Che
Gal Chechik
Lianggangxu Chen
Qi Alfred Chen
Brian Chen
Bor-Chun Chen
Bo-Hao Chen

Bohong Chen
Bin Chen
Ziliang Chen
Cheng Chen
Chen Chen
Chaofeng Chen
Xi Chen
Haoyu Chen
Xuanhong Chen
Wei Chen
Qiang Chen
Shi Chen
Xianyu Chen
Chang Chen
Changhuai Chen
Hao Chen
Jie Chen
Jianbo Chen
Jingjing Chen
Jun Chen
Kejiang Chen
Mingcai Chen
Nenglun Chen
Qifeng Chen
Ruoyu Chen
Shu-Yu Chen
Weidong Chen
Weijie Chen
Weikai Chen
Xiang Chen
Xiuyi Chen
Xingyu Chen
Yaofo Chen
Yueting Chen
Yu Chen
Yunjin Chen
Yuntao Chen
Yun Chen
Zhenfang Chen
Zhuangzhuang Chen
Chu-Song Chen
Xiangyu Chen
Zhuo Chen
Chaoqi Chen
Shizhe Chen

Xiaotong Chen

Xiaozhi Chen

Dian Chen

Defang Chen

Dingfan Chen

Ding-Jie Chen

Ee Heng Chen

Tao Chen

Yixin Chen

Wei-Ting Chen

Lin Chen

Guang Chen

Guangyi Chen

Guanying Chen

Guangyao Chen

Hwann-Tzong Chen

Junwen Chen

Jiacheng Chen

Jianxu Chen

Hui Chen

Kai Chen

Kan Chen

Kevin Chen

Kuan-Wen Chen

Weihua Chen

Zhang Chen

Liang-Chieh Chen

Lele Chen

Liang Chen

Fanglin Chen

Zehui Chen

Minghui Chen

Minghao Chen

Xiaokang Chen

Qian Chen

Jun-Cheng Chen

Qi Chen

Qingcai Chen

Richard J. Chen

Runnan Chen

Rui Chen

Shuo Chen

Sentao Chen

Shaoyu Chen

Shixing Chen

Shuai Chen

Shuya Chen

Sizhe Chen

Simin Chen

Shaoxiang Chen

Zitian Chen

Tianlong Chen

Tianshui Chen

Min-Hung Chen

Xiangning Chen

Xin Chen

Xinghao Chen

Xuejin Chen

Xu Chen

Xuxi Chen

Yunlu Chen

Yanbei Chen

Yuxiao Chen

Yun-Chun Chen

Yi-Ting Chen

Yi-Wen Chen

Yinbo Chen

Yiran Chen

Yuanhong Chen

Yubei Chen

Yuefeng Chen

Yuhua Chen

Yukang Chen

Zerui Chen

Zhaoyu Chen

Zhen Chen

Zhenyu Chen

Zhi Chen

Zhiwei Chen

Zhixiang Chen

Long Chen

Bowen Cheng

Jun Cheng

Yi Cheng

Jingchun Cheng

Lechao Cheng

Xi Cheng

Yuan Cheng

Ho Kei Cheng

Kevin Ho Man Cheng

Jiacheng Cheng

Kelvin B. Cheng

Li Cheng

Mengjun Cheng

Zhen Cheng

Qingrong Cheng

Tianheng Cheng

Harry Cheng

Yihua Cheng

Yu Cheng

Ziheng Cheng

Soon Yau Cheong

Anoop Cherian

Manuela Chessa

Zhixiang Chi

Naoki Chiba

Julian Chibane

Kashyap Chitta

Tai-Yin Chiu

Hsu-kuang Chiu

Wei-Chen Chiu

Sungmin Cho

Donghyeon Cho

Hyeon Cho

Yooshin Cho

Gyusang Cho

Jang Hyun Cho

Seungju Cho

Nam Ik Cho

Sunghyun Cho

Hanbyel Cho

Jaesung Choe

Jooyoung Choi

Chiho Choi

Changwoon Choi

Jongwon Choi

Myungsub Choi

Dooseop Choi

Jonghyun Choi

Jinwoo Choi

Jun Won Choi

Min-Kook Choi

Hongsuk Choi

Janghoon Choi

Yoon-Ho Choi

Yukyung Choi
Jaegul Choo
Ayush Chopra
Siddharth Choudhary
Subhabrata Choudhury
Vasileios Choutas
Ka-Ho Chow
Pinaki Nath Chowdhury
Sammy Christen
Anders Christensen
Grigorios Chrysos
Hang Chu
Wen-Hsuan Chu
Peng Chu
Qi Chu
Ruihang Chu
Wei-Ta Chu
Yung-Yu Chuang
Sanghyuk Chun
Se Young Chun
Antonio Cinà
Ramazan Gokberk Cinbis
Javier Civera
Albert Clapés
Ronald Clark
Brian S. Clipp
Felipe Codevilla
Daniel Coelho de Castro
Niv Cohen
Forrester Cole
Maxwell D. Collins
Robert T. Collins
Marc Comino Trinidad
Runmin Cong
Wenyan Cong
Maxime Cordy
Marcella Cornia
Enric Corona
Huseyin Coskun
Luca Cosmo
Dragos Costea
Davide Cozzolino
Arun C. S. Kumar
Aiyu Cui
Qiongjie Cui

Quan Cui
Shuhao Cui
Yiming Cui
Ying Cui
Zijun Cui
Jiali Cui
Jiequan Cui
Yawen Cui
Zhen Cui
Zhaopeng Cui
Jack Culpepper
Xiaodong Cun
Ross Cutler
Adam Czajka
Ali Dabouei
Konstantinos M. Dafnis
Manuel Dahnert
Tao Dai
Yuchao Dai
Bo Dai
Mengyu Dai
Hang Dai
Haixing Dai
Peng Dai
Pingyang Dai
Qi Dai
Qiyu Dai
Yutong Dai
Naser Damer
Zhiyuan Dang
Mohamed Daoudi
Ayan Das
Abir Das
Debasmit Das
Deepayan Das
Partha Das
Sagnik Das
Soumi Das
Srijan Das
Swagatam Das
Avijit Dasgupta
Jim Davis
Adrian K. Davison
Homa Davoudi
Laura Daza

Matthias De Lange
Shalini De Mello
Marco De Nadai
Christophe De
    Vleeschouwer
Alp Dener
Boyang Deng
Congyue Deng
Bailin Deng
Yong Deng
Ye Deng
Zhuo Deng
Zhijie Deng
Xiaoming Deng
Jiankang Deng
Jinhong Deng
Jingjing Deng
Liang-Jian Deng
Siqi Deng
Xiang Deng
Xueqing Deng
Zhongying Deng
Karan Desai
Jean-Emmanuel Deschaud
Aniket Anand Deshmukh
Neel Dey
Helisa Dhamo
Prithviraj Dhar
Amaya Dharmasiri
Yan Di
Xing Di
Ousmane A. Dia
Haiwen Diao
Xiaolei Diao
Gonçalo José Dias Pais
Abdallah Dib
Anastasios Dimou
Changxing Ding
Henghui Ding
Guodong Ding
Yaqing Ding
Shuangrui Ding
Yuhang Ding
Yikang Ding
Shouhong Ding

Haisong Ding

Hui Ding

Jiahao Ding

Jian Ding

Jian-Jiun Ding

Shuxiao Ding

Tianyu Ding

Wenhao Ding

Yuqi Ding

Yi Ding

Yuzhen Ding

Zhengming Ding

Tan Minh Dinh

Vu Dinh

Christos Diou

Mandar Dixit

Bao Gia Doan

Khoa D. Doan

Dzung Anh Doan

Debi Prosad Dogra

Nehal Doiphode

Chengdong Dong

Bowen Dong

Zhenxing Dong

Hang Dong

Xiaoyi Dong

Haoye Dong

Jiangxin Dong

Shichao Dong

Xuan Dong

Zhen Dong

Shuting Dong

Jing Dong

Li Dong

Ming Dong

Nanqing Dong

Qiulei Dong

Runpei Dong

Siyan Dong

Tian Dong

Wei Dong

Xiaomeng Dong

Xin Dong

Xingbo Dong

Yuan Dong

Samuel Dooley

Gianfranco Doretto

Michael Dorkenwald

Keval Doshi

Zhaopeng Dou

Xiaotian Dou

Hazel Doughty

Ahmad Droby

Iddo Drori

Jie Du

Yong Du

Dawei Du

Dong Du

Ruoyi Du

Yuntao Du

Xuefeng Du

Yilun Du

Yuming Du

Radhika Dua

Haodong Duan

Jiafei Duan

Kaiwen Duan

Peiqi Duan

Ye Duan

Haoran Duan

Jiali Duan

Amanda Duarte

Abhimanyu Dubey

Shiv Ram Dubey

Florian Dubost

Lukasz Dudziak

Shivam Duggal

Justin M. Dulay

Matteo Dunnhofer

Chi Nhan Duong

Thibaut Durand

Mihai Dusmanu

Ujjal Kr Dutta

Debidatta Dwibedi

Isht Dwivedi

Sai Kumar Dwivedi

Takeharu Eda

Mark Edmonds

Alexei A. Efros

Thibaud Ehret

Max Ehrlich

Mahsa Ehsanpour

Iván Eichhardt

Farshad Einabadi

Marvin Eisenberger

Hazim Kemal Ekenel

Mohamed El Banani

Ismail Elezi

Moshe Eliasof

Alaa El-Nouby

Ian Endres

Francis Engelmann

Deniz Engin

Chanho Eom

Dave Epstein

Maria C. Escobar

Victor A. Escorcia

Carlos Esteves

Sungmin Eum

Bernard J. E. Evans

Ivan Evtimov

Fevziye Irem Eyiokur
Yaman

Matteo Fabbri

Sébastien Fabbro

Gabriele Facciolo

Masud Fahim

Bin Fan

Hehe Fan

Deng-Ping Fan

Aoxiang Fan

Chen-Chen Fan

Qi Fan

Zhaoxin Fan

Haoqi Fan

Heng Fan

Hongyi Fan

Linxi Fan

Baojie Fan

Jiayuan Fan

Lei Fan

Quanfu Fan

Yonghui Fan

Yingruo Fan

Zhiwen Fan

Zicong Fan
Sean Fanello
Jiansheng Fang
Chaowei Fang
Yuming Fang
Jianwu Fang
Jin Fang
Qi Fang
Shancheng Fang
Tian Fang
Xianyong Fang
Gongfan Fang
Zhen Fang
Hui Fang
Jiemin Fang
Le Fang
Pengfei Fang
Xiaolin Fang
Yuxin Fang
Zhaoyuan Fang
Ammarah Farooq
Azade Farshad
Zhengcong Fei
Michael Felsberg
Wei Feng
Chen Feng
Fan Feng
Andrew Feng
Xin Feng
Zheyun Feng
Ruicheng Feng
Mingtao Feng
Qianyu Feng
Shangbin Feng
Chun-Mei Feng
Zunlei Feng
Zhiyong Feng
Martin Fergie
Mustansar Fiaz
Marco Fiorucci
Michael Firman
Hamed Firooz
Volker Fischer
Corneliu O. Florea
Georgios Floros

Wolfgang Foerstner
Gianni Franchi
Jean-Sebastien Franco
Simone Frintrop
Anna Fruehstueck
Changhong Fu
Chaoyou Fu
Cheng-Yang Fu
Chi-Wing Fu
Deqing Fu
Huan Fu
Jun Fu
Kexue Fu
Ying Fu
Jianlong Fu
Jingjing Fu
Qichen Fu
Tsu-Jui Fu
Xueyang Fu
Yang Fu
Yanwei Fu
Yonggan Fu
Wolfgang Fuhl
Yasuhisa Fujii
Kent Fujiwara
Marco Fumero
Takuya Funatomi
Isabel Funke
Dario Fuoli
Antonino Furnari
Matheus A. Gadelha
Akshay Gadi Patil
Adrian Galdran
Guillermo Gallego
Silvano Galliani
Orazio Gallo
Leonardo Galteri
Matteo Gamba
Yiming Gan
Sujoy Ganguly
Harald Ganster
Boyan Gao
Changxin Gao
Daiheng Gao
Difei Gao

Chen Gao
Fei Gao
Lin Gao
Wei Gao
Yiming Gao
Junyu Gao
Guangyu Ryan Gao
Haichang Gao
Hongchang Gao
Jialin Gao
Jin Gao
Jun Gao
Katelyn Gao
Mingchen Gao
Mingfei Gao
Pan Gao
Shangqian Gao
Shanghua Gao
Xitong Gao
Yunhe Gao
Zhanning Gao
Elena Garces
Nuno Cruz Garcia
Noa Garcia
Guillermo
    Garcia-Hernando
Isha Garg
Rahul Garg
Sourav Garg
Quentin Garrido
Stefano Gasperini
Kent Gauen
Chandan Gautam
Shivam Gautam
Paul Gay
Chunjiang Ge
Shiming Ge
Wenhang Ge
Yanhao Ge
Zheng Ge
Songwei Ge
Weifeng Ge
Yixiao Ge
Yuying Ge
Shijie Geng

Zhengyang Geng
Kyle A. Genova
Georgios Georgakis
Markos Georgopoulos
Marcel Geppert
Shabnam Ghadar
Mina Ghadimi Atigh
Deepti Ghadiyaram
Maani Ghaffari Jadidi
Sedigh Ghamari
Zahra Gharaee
Michaël Gharbi
Golnaz Ghiasi
Reza Ghoddoosian
Soumya Suvra Ghosal
Adhiraj Ghosh
Arthita Ghosh
Pallabi Ghosh
Soumyadeep Ghosh
Andrew Gilbert
Igor Gilitschenski
Jhony H. Giraldo
Andreu Girbau Xalabarder
Rohit Girdhar
Sharath Girish
Xavier Giro-i-Nieto
Raja Giryes
Thomas Gittings
Nikolaos Gkanatsios
Ioannis Gkioulekas
Abhiram
  Gnanasambandam
Aurele T. Gnanha
Clement L. J. C. Godard
Arushi Goel
Vidit Goel
Shubham Goel
Zan Gojcic
Aaron K. Gokaslan
Tejas Gokhale
S. Alireza Golestaneh
Thiago L. Gomes
Nuno Goncalves
Boqing Gong
Chen Gong

Yuanhao Gong
Guoqiang Gong
Jingyu Gong
Rui Gong
Yu Gong
Mingming Gong
Neil Zhenqiang Gong
Xun Gong
Yunye Gong
Yihong Gong
Cristina I. González
Nithin Gopalakrishnan
  Nair
Gaurav Goswami
Jianping Gou
Shreyank N. Gowda
Ankit Goyal
Helmut Grabner
Patrick L. Grady
Ben Graham
Eric Granger
Douglas R. Gray
Matej Grcić
David Griffiths
Jinjin Gu
Yun Gu
Shuyang Gu
Jianyang Gu
Fuqiang Gu
Jiatao Gu
Jindong Gu
Jiaqi Gu
Jinwei Gu
Jiaxin Gu
Geonmo Gu
Xiao Gu
Xinqian Gu
Xiuye Gu
Yuming Gu
Zhangxuan Gu
Dayan Guan
Junfeng Guan
Qingji Guan
Tianrui Guan
Shanyan Guan

Denis A. Gudovskiy
Ricardo Guerrero
Pierre-Louis Guhur
Jie Gui
Liangyan Gui
Liangke Gui
Benoit Guillard
Erhan Gundogdu
Manuel Günther
Jingcai Guo
Yuanfang Guo
Junfeng Guo
Chenqi Guo
Dan Guo
Hongji Guo
Jia Guo
Jie Guo
Minghao Guo
Shi Guo
Yanhui Guo
Yangyang Guo
Yuan-Chen Guo
Yilu Guo
Yiluan Guo
Yong Guo
Guangyu Guo
Haiyun Guo
Jinyang Guo
Jianyuan Guo
Pengsheng Guo
Pengfei Guo
Shuxuan Guo
Song Guo
Tianyu Guo
Qing Guo
Qiushan Guo
Wen Guo
Xiefan Guo
Xiaohu Guo
Xiaoqing Guo
Yufei Guo
Yuhui Guo
Yuliang Guo
Yunhui Guo
Yanwen Guo

Akshita Gupta
Ankush Gupta
Kamal Gupta
Kartik Gupta
Ritwik Gupta
Rohit Gupta
Siddharth Gururani
Fredrik K. Gustafsson
Abner Guzman Rivera
Vladimir Guzov
Matthew A. Gwilliam
Jung-Woo Ha
Marc Habermann
Isma Hadji
Christian Haene
Martin Hahner
Levente Hajder
Alexandros Haliassos
Emanuela Haller
Bumsub Ham
Abdullah J. Hamdi
Shreyas Hampali
Dongyoon Han
Chunrui Han
Dong-Jun Han
Dong-Sig Han
Guangxing Han
Zhizhong Han
Ruize Han
Jiaming Han
Jin Han
Ligong Han
Xian-Hua Han
Xiaoguang Han
Yizeng Han
Zhi Han
Zhenjun Han
Zhongyi Han
Jungong Han
Junlin Han
Kai Han
Kun Han
Sungwon Han
Songfang Han
Wei Han

Xiao Han
Xintong Han
Xinzhe Han
Yahong Han
Yan Han
Zongbo Han
Nicolai Hani
Rana Hanocka
Niklas Hanselmann
Nicklas A. Hansen
Hong Hanyu
Fusheng Hao
Yanbin Hao
Shijie Hao
Udith Haputhanthri
Mehrtash Harandi
Josh Harguess
Adam Harley
David M. Hart
Atsushi Hashimoto
Ali Hassani
Mohammed Hassanin
Yana Hasson
Joakim Bruslund Haurum
Bo He
Kun He
Chen He
Xin He
Fazhi He
Gaoqi He
Hao He
Haoyu He
Jiangpeng He
Hongliang He
Qian He
Xiangteng He
Xuming He
Yannan He
Yuhang He
Yang He
Xiangyu He
Nanjun He
Pan He
Sen He
Shengfeng He

Songtao He
Tao He
Tong He
Wei He
Xuehai He
Xiaoxiao He
Ying He
Yisheng He
Ziwen He
Peter Hedman
Felix Heide
Yacov Hel-Or
Paul Henderson
Philipp Henzler
Byeongho Heo
Jae-Pil Heo
Miran Heo
Sachini A. Herath
Stephane Herbin
Pedro Hermosilla Casajus
Monica Hernandez
Charles Herrmann
Roei Herzig
Mauricio Hess-Flores
Carlos Hinojosa
Tobias Hinz
Tsubasa Hirakawa
Chih-Hui Ho
Lam Si Tung Ho
Jennifer Hobbs
Derek Hoiem
Yannick Hold-Geoffroy
Aleksander Holynski
Cheeun Hong
Fa-Ting Hong
Hanbin Hong
Guan Zhe Hong
Danfeng Hong
Lanqing Hong
Xiaopeng Hong
Xin Hong
Jie Hong
Seungbum Hong
Cheng-Yao Hong
Seunghoon Hong

Yi Hong
Yuan Hong
Yuchen Hong
Anthony Hoogs
Maxwell C. Horton
Kazuhiro Hotta
Qibin Hou
Tingbo Hou
Junhui Hou
Ji Hou
Qiqi Hou
Rui Hou
Ruibing Hou
Zhi Hou
Henry Howard-Jenkins
Lukas Hoyer
Wei-Lin Hsiao
Chiou-Ting Hsu
Anthony Hu
Brian Hu
Yusong Hu
Hexiang Hu
Haoji Hu
Di Hu
Hengtong Hu
Haigen Hu
Lianyu Hu
Hanzhe Hu
Jie Hu
Junlin Hu
Shizhe Hu
Jian Hu
Zhiming Hu
Juhua Hu
Peng Hu
Ping Hu
Ronghang Hu
MengShun Hu
Tao Hu
Vincent Tao Hu
Xiaoling Hu
Xinting Hu
Xiaolin Hu
Xuefeng Hu
Xiaowei Hu

Yang Hu
Yueyu Hu
Zeyu Hu
Zhongyun Hu
Binh-Son Hua
Guoliang Hua
Yi Hua
Linzhi Huang
Qiusheng Huang
Bo Huang
Chen Huang
Hsin-Ping Huang
Ye Huang
Shuangping Huang
Zeng Huang
Buzhen Huang
Cong Huang
Heng Huang
Hao Huang
Qidong Huang
Huaibo Huang
Chaoqin Huang
Feihu Huang
Jiahui Huang
Jingjia Huang
Kun Huang
Lei Huang
Sheng Huang
Shuaiyi Huang
Siyu Huang
Xiaoshui Huang
Xiaoyang Huang
Yan Huang
Yihao Huang
Ying Huang
Ziling Huang
Xiaoke Huang
Yifei Huang
Haiyang Huang
Zhewei Huang
Jin Huang
Haibin Huang
Jiaxing Huang
Junjie Huang
Keli Huang

Lang Huang
Lin Huang
Luojie Huang
Mingzhen Huang
Shijia Huang
Shengyu Huang
Siyuan Huang
He Huang
Xiuyu Huang
Lianghua Huang
Yue Huang
Yaping Huang
Yuge Huang
Zehao Huang
Zeyi Huang
Zhiqi Huang
Zhongzhan Huang
Zilong Huang
Ziyuan Huang
Tianrui Hui
Zhuo Hui
Le Hui
Jing Huo
Junhwa Hur
Shehzeen S. Hussain
Chuong Minh Huynh
Seunghyun Hwang
Jaehui Hwang
Jyh-Jing Hwang
Sukjun Hwang
Soonmin Hwang
Wonjun Hwang
Rakib Hyder
Sangeek Hyun
Sarah Ibrahimi
Tomoki Ichikawa
Yerlan Idelbayev
A. S. M. Iftekhar
Masaaki Iiyama
Satoshi Ikehata
Sunghoon Im
Atul N. Ingle
Eldar Insafutdinov
Yani A. Ioannou
Radu Tudor Ionescu

Umar Iqbal
Go Irie
Muhammad Zubair Irshad
Ahmet Iscen
Berivan Isik
Ashraful Islam
Md Amirul Islam
Syed Islam
Mariko Isogawa
Vamsi Krishna K. Ithapu
Boris Ivanovic
Darshan Iyer
Sarah Jabbour
Ayush Jain
Nishant Jain
Samyak Jain
Vidit Jain
Vineet Jain
Priyank Jaini
Tomas Jakab
Mohammad A. A. K.
    Jalwana
Muhammad Abdullah
    Jamal
Hadi Jamali-Rad
Stuart James
Varun Jampani
Young Kyun Jang
YeongJun Jang
Yunseok Jang
Ronnachai Jaroensri
Bhavan Jasani
Krishna Murthy
    Jatavallabhula
Mojan Javaheripi
Syed A. Javed
Guillaume Jeanneret
Pranav Jeevan
Herve Jegou
Rohit Jena
Tomas Jenicek
Porter Jenkins
Simon Jenni
Hae-Gon Jeon
Sangryul Jeon

Boseung Jeong
Yoonwoo Jeong
Seong-Gyun Jeong
Jisoo Jeong
Allan D. Jepson
Ankit Jha
Sumit K. Jha
I-Hong Jhuo
Ge-Peng Ji
Chaonan Ji
Deyi Ji
Jingwei Ji
Wei Ji
Zhong Ji
Jiayi Ji
Pengliang Ji
Hui Ji
Mingi Ji
Xiaopeng Ji
Yuzhu Ji
Baoxiong Jia
Songhao Jia
Dan Jia
Shan Jia
Xiaojun Jia
Xiuyi Jia
Xu Jia
Menglin Jia
Wenqi Jia
Boyuan Jiang
Wenhao Jiang
Huaizu Jiang
Hanwen Jiang
Haiyong Jiang
Hao Jiang
Huajie Jiang
Huiqin Jiang
Haojun Jiang
Haobo Jiang
Junjun Jiang
Xingyu Jiang
Yangbangyan Jiang
Yu Jiang
Jianmin Jiang
Jiaxi Jiang

Jing Jiang
Kui Jiang
Li Jiang
Liming Jiang
Chiyu Jiang
Meirui Jiang
Chen Jiang
Peng Jiang
Tai-Xiang Jiang
Wen Jiang
Xinyang Jiang
Yifan Jiang
Yuming Jiang
Yingying Jiang
Zeren Jiang
ZhengKai Jiang
Zhenyu Jiang
Shuming Jiao
Jianbo Jiao
Licheng Jiao
Dongkwon Jin
Yeying Jin
Cheng Jin
Linyi Jin
Qing Jin
Taisong Jin
Xiao Jin
Xin Jin
Sheng Jin
Kyong Hwan Jin
Ruibing Jin
SouYoung Jin
Yueming Jin
Chenchen Jing
Longlong Jing
Taotao Jing
Yongcheng Jing
Younghyun Jo
Joakim Johnander
Jeff Johnson
Michael J. Jones
R. Kenny Jones
Rico Jonschkowski
Ameya Joshi
Sunghun Joung

Felix Juefei-Xu
Claudio R. Jung
Steffen Jung
Hari Chandana K.
Rahul Vigneswaran K.
Prajwal K. R.
Abhishek Kadian
Jhony Kaesemodel Pontes
Kumara Kahatapitiya
Anmol Kalia
Sinan Kalkan
Tarun Kalluri
Jaewon Kam
Sandesh Kamath
Meina Kan
Menelaos Kanakis
Takuhiro Kaneko
Di Kang
Guoliang Kang
Hao Kang
Jaeyeon Kang
Kyoungkook Kang
Li-Wei Kang
MinGuk Kang
Suk-Ju Kang
Zhao Kang
Yash Mukund Kant
Yueying Kao
Aupendu Kar
Konstantinos Karantzalos
Sezer Karaoglu
Navid Kardan
Sanjay Kariyappa
Leonid Karlinsky
Animesh Karnewar
Shyamgopal Karthik
Hirak J. Kashyap
Marc A. Kastner
Hirokatsu Kataoka
Angelos Katharopoulos
Hiroharu Kato
Kai Katsumata
Manuel Kaufmann
Chaitanya Kaul
Prakhar Kaushik

Yuki Kawana
Lei Ke
Lipeng Ke
Tsung-Wei Ke
Wei Ke
Petr Kellnhofer
Aniruddha Kembhavi
John Kender
Corentin Kervadec
Leonid Keselman
Daniel Keysers
Nima Khademi Kalantari
Taras Khakhulin
Samir Khaki
Muhammad Haris Khan
Qadeer Khan
Salman Khan
Subash Khanal
Vaishnavi M. Khindkar
Rawal Khirodkar
Saeed Khorram
Pirazh Khorramshahi
Kourosh Khoshelham
Ansh Khurana
Benjamin Kiefer
Jae Myung Kim
Junho Kim
Boah Kim
Hyeonseong Kim
Dong-Jin Kim
Dongwan Kim
Donghyun Kim
Doyeon Kim
Yonghyun Kim
Hyung-Il Kim
Hyunwoo Kim
Hyeongwoo Kim
Hyo Jin Kim
Hyunwoo J. Kim
Taehoon Kim
Jaeha Kim
Jiwon Kim
Jung Uk Kim
Kangyeol Kim
Eunji Kim

Daeha Kim
Dongwon Kim
Kunhee Kim
Kyungmin Kim
Junsik Kim
Min H. Kim
Namil Kim
Kookhoi Kim
Sanghyun Kim
Seongyeop Kim
Seungryong Kim
Saehoon Kim
Euyoung Kim
Guisik Kim
Sungyeon Kim
Sunnie S. Y. Kim
Taehun Kim
Tae Oh Kim
Won Hwa Kim
Seungwook Kim
YoungBin Kim
Youngeun Kim
Akisato Kimura
Furkan Osman Kınlı
Zsolt Kira
Hedvig Kjellström
Florian Kleber
Jan P. Klopp
Florian Kluger
Laurent Kneip
Byungsoo Ko
Muhammed Kocabas
A. Sophia Koepke
Kevin Koeser
Nick Kolkin
Nikos Kolotouros
Wai-Kin Adams Kong
Deying Kong
Caihua Kong
Youyong Kong
Shuyu Kong
Shu Kong
Tao Kong
Yajing Kong
Yu Kong

Zishang Kong
Theodora Kontogianni
Anton S. Konushin
Julian F. P. Kooij
Bruno Korbar
Giorgos Kordopatis-Zilos
Jari Korhonen
Adam Kortylewski
Denis Korzhenkov
Divya Kothandaraman
Suraj Kothawade
Iuliia Kotseruba
Satwik Kottur
Shashank Kotyan
Alexandros Kouris
Petros Koutras
Anna Kreshuk
Ranjay Krishna
Dilip Krishnan
Andrey Kuehlkamp
Hilde Kuehne
Jason Kuen
David Kügler
Arjan Kuijper
Anna Kukleva
Sumith Kulal
Viveka Kulharia
Akshay R. Kulkarni
Nilesh Kulkarni
Dominik Kulon
Abhinav Kumar
Akash Kumar
Suryansh Kumar
B. V. K. Vijaya Kumar
Pulkit Kumar
Ratnesh Kumar
Sateesh Kumar
Satish Kumar
Vijay Kumar B. G.
Nupur Kumari
Sudhakar Kumawat
Jogendra Nath Kundu
Hsien-Kai Kuo
Meng-Yu Jennifer Kuo
Vinod Kumar Kurmi

Yusuke Kurose
Keerthy Kusumam
Alina Kuznetsova
Henry Kvinge
Ho Man Kwan
Hyeokjun Kweon
Heeseung Kwon
Gihyun Kwon
Myung-Joon Kwon
Taesung Kwon
YoungJoong Kwon
Christos Kyrkou
Jorma Laaksonen
Yann Labbe
Zorah Laehner
Florent Lafarge
Hamid Laga
Manuel Lagunas
Shenqi Lai
Jian-Huang Lai
Zihang Lai
Mohamed I. Lakhal
Mohit Lamba
Meng Lan
Loic Landrieu
Zhiqiang Lang
Natalie Lang
Dong Lao
Yizhen Lao
Yingjie Lao
Issam Hadj Laradji
Gustav Larsson
Viktor Larsson
Zakaria Laskar
Stéphane Lathuilière
Chun Pong Lau
Rynson W. H. Lau
Hei Law
Justin Lazarow
Verica Lazova
Eric-Tuan Le
Hieu Le
Trung-Nghia Le
Mathias Lechner
Byeong-Uk Lee

Chen-Yu Lee
Che-Rung Lee
Chul Lee
Hong Joo Lee
Dongsoo Lee
Jiyoung Lee
Eugene Eu Tzuan Lee
Daeun Lee
Saehyung Lee
Jewook Lee
Hyungtae Lee
Hyunmin Lee
Jungbeom Lee
Joon-Young Lee
Jong-Seok Lee
Joonseok Lee
Junha Lee
Kibok Lee
Byung-Kwan Lee
Jangwon Lee
Jinho Lee
Jongmin Lee
Seunghyun Lee
Sohyun Lee
Minsik Lee
Dogyoon Lee
Seungmin Lee
Min Jun Lee
Sangho Lee
Sangmin Lee
Seungeun Lee
Seon-Ho Lee
Sungmin Lee
Sungho Lee
Sangyoun Lee
Vincent C. S. S. Lee
Jaeseong Lee
Yong Jae Lee
Chenyang Lei
Chenyi Lei
Jiahui Lei
Xinyu Lei
Yinjie Lei
Jiaxu Leng
Luziwei Leng

Jan E. Lenssen
Vincent Lepetit
Thomas Leung
María Leyva-Vallina
Xin Li
Yikang Li
Baoxin Li
Bin Li
Bing Li
Bowen Li
Changlin Li
Chao Li
Chongyi Li
Guanyue Li
Shuai Li
Jin Li
Dingquan Li
Dongxu Li
Yiting Li
Gang Li
Dian Li
Guohao Li
Haoang Li
Haoliang Li
Haoran Li
Hengduo Li
Huafeng Li
Xiaoming Li
Hanao Li
Hongwei Li
Ziqiang Li
Jisheng Li
Jiacheng Li
Jia Li
Jiachen Li
Jiahao Li
Jianwei Li
Jiazhi Li
Jie Li
Jing Li
Jingjing Li
Jingtao Li
Jun Li
Junxuan Li
Kai Li

Kailin Li
Kenneth Li
Kun Li
Kunpeng Li
Aoxue Li
Chenglong Li
Chenglin Li
Changsheng Li
Zhichao Li
Qiang Li
Yanyu Li
Zuoyue Li
Xiang Li
Xuelong Li
Fangda Li
Ailin Li
Liang Li
Chun-Guang Li
Daiqing Li
Dong Li
Guanbin Li
Guorong Li
Haifeng Li
Jianan Li
Jianing Li
Jiaxin Li
Ke Li
Lei Li
Lincheng Li
Liulei Li
Lujun Li
Linjie Li
Lin Li
Pengyu Li
Ping Li
Qiufu Li
Qingyong Li
Rui Li
Siyuan Li
Wei Li
Wenbin Li
Xiangyang Li
Xinyu Li
Xiujun Li
Xiu Li

Xu Li
Ya-Li Li
Yao Li
Yongjie Li
Yijun Li
Yiming Li
Yuezun Li
Yu Li
Yunheng Li
Yuqi Li
Zhe Li
Zeming Li
Zhen Li
Zhengqin Li
Zhimin Li
Jiefeng Li
Jinpeng Li
Chengze Li
Jianwu Li
Lerenhan Li
Shan Li
Suichan Li
Xiangtai Li
Yanjie Li
Yandong Li
Zhuoling Li
Zhenqiang Li
Manyi Li
Maosen Li
Ji Li
Minjun Li
Mingrui Li
Mengtian Li
Junyi Li
Nianyi Li
Bo Li
Xiao Li
Peihua Li
Peike Li
Peizhao Li
Peiliang Li
Qi Li
Ren Li
Runze Li
Shile Li

Sheng Li
Shigang Li
Shiyu Li
Shuang Li
Shasha Li
Shichao Li
Tianye Li
Yuexiang Li
Wei-Hong Li
Wanhua Li
Weihao Li
Weiming Li
Weixin Li
Wenbo Li
Wenshuo Li
Weijian Li
Yunan Li
Xirong Li
Xianhang Li
Xiaoyu Li
Xueqian Li
Xuanlin Li
Xianzhi Li
Yunqiang Li
Yanjing Li
Yansheng Li
Yawei Li
Yi Li
Yong Li
Yong-Lu Li
Yuhang Li
Yu-Jhe Li
Yuxi Li
Yunsheng Li
Yanwei Li
Zechao Li
Zejian Li
Zeju Li
Zekun Li
Zhaowen Li
Zheng Li
Zhenyu Li
Zhiheng Li
Zhi Li
Zhong Li

Zhuowei Li
Zhuowan Li
Zhuohang Li
Zizhang Li
Chen Li
Yuan-Fang Li
Dongze Lian
Xiaochen Lian
Zhouhui Lian
Long Lian
Qing Lian
Jin Lianbao
Jinxiu S. Liang
Dingkang Liang
Jiahao Liang
Jianming Liang
Jingyun Liang
Kevin J. Liang
Kaizhao Liang
Chen Liang
Jie Liang
Senwei Liang
Ding Liang
Jiajun Liang
Jian Liang
Kongming Liang
Siyuan Liang
Yuanzhi Liang
Zhengfa Liang
Mingfu Liang
Xiaodan Liang
Xuefeng Liang
Yuxuan Liang
Kang Liao
Liang Liao
Hong-Yuan Mark Liao
Wentong Liao
Haofu Liao
Yue Liao
Minghui Liao
Shengcai Liao
Ting-Hsuan Liao
Xin Liao
Yinghong Liao
Teck Yian Lim

Che-Tsung Lin
Chung-Ching Lin
Chen-Hsuan Lin
Cheng Lin
Chuming Lin
Chunyu Lin
Dahua Lin
Wei Lin
Zheng Lin
Huaijia Lin
Jason Lin
Jierui Lin
Jiaying Lin
Jie Lin
Kai-En Lin
Kevin Lin
Guangfeng Lin
Jiehong Lin
Feng Lin
Hang Lin
Kwan-Yee Lin
Ke Lin
Luojun Lin
Qinghong Lin
Xiangbo Lin
Yi Lin
Zudi Lin
Shijie Lin
Yiqun Lin
Tzu-Heng Lin
Ming Lin
Shaohui Lin
SongNan Lin
Ji Lin
Tsung-Yu Lin
Xudong Lin
Yancong Lin
Yen-Chen Lin
Yiming Lin
Yuewei Lin
Zhiqiu Lin
Zinan Lin
Zhe Lin
David B. Lindell
Zhixin Ling

Zhan Ling
Alexander Liniger
Venice Erin B. Liong
Joey Litalien
Or Litany
Roee Litman
Ron Litman
Jim Little
Dor Litvak
Shaoteng Liu
Shuaicheng Liu
Andrew Liu
Xian Liu
Shaohui Liu
Bei Liu
Bo Liu
Yong Liu
Ming Liu
Yanbin Liu
Chenxi Liu
Daqi Liu
Di Liu
Difan Liu
Dong Liu
Dongfang Liu
Daizong Liu
Xiao Liu
Fangyi Liu
Fengbei Liu
Fenglin Liu
Bin Liu
Yuang Liu
Ao Liu
Hong Liu
Hongfu Liu
Huidong Liu
Ziyi Liu
Feng Liu
Hao Liu
Jie Liu
Jialun Liu
Jiang Liu
Jing Liu
Jingya Liu
Jiaming Liu

Jun Liu
Juncheng Liu
Jiawei Liu
Hongyu Liu
Chuanbin Liu
Haotian Liu
Lingqiao Liu
Chang Liu
Han Liu
Liu Liu
Min Liu
Yingqi Liu
Aishan Liu
Bingyu Liu
Benlin Liu
Boxiao Liu
Chenchen Liu
Chuanjian Liu
Daqing Liu
Huan Liu
Haozhe Liu
Jiaheng Liu
Wei Liu
Jingzhou Liu
Jiyuan Liu
Lingbo Liu
Nian Liu
Peiye Liu
Qiankun Liu
Shenglan Liu
Shilong Liu
Wen Liu
Wenyu Liu
Weifeng Liu
Wu Liu
Xiaolong Liu
Yang Liu
Yanwei Liu
Yingcheng Liu
Yongfei Liu
Yihao Liu
Yu Liu
Yunze Liu
Ze Liu
Zhenhua Liu

Zhenguang Liu
Lin Liu
Lihao Liu
Pengju Liu
Xinhai Liu
Yunfei Liu
Meng Liu
Minghua Liu
Mingyuan Liu
Miao Liu
Peirong Liu
Ping Liu
Qingjie Liu
Ruoshi Liu
Risheng Liu
Songtao Liu
Xing Liu
Shikun Liu
Shuming Liu
Sheng Liu
Songhua Liu
Tongliang Liu
Weibo Liu
Weide Liu
Weizhe Liu
Wenxi Liu
Weiyang Liu
Xin Liu
Xiaobin Liu
Xudong Liu
Xiaoyi Liu
Xihui Liu
Xinchen Liu
Xingtong Liu
Xinpeng Liu
Xinyu Liu
Xianpeng Liu
Xu Liu
Xingyu Liu
Yongtuo Liu
Yahui Liu
Yangxin Liu
Yaoyao Liu
Yaojie Liu
Yuliang Liu

Yongcheng Liu
Yuan Liu
Yufan Liu
Yu-Lun Liu
Yun Liu
Yunfan Liu
Yuanzhong Liu
Zhuoran Liu
Zhen Liu
Zheng Liu
Zhijian Liu
Zhisong Liu
Ziquan Liu
Ziyu Liu
Zhihua Liu
Zechun Liu
Zhaoyang Liu
Zhengzhe Liu
Stephan Liwicki
Shao-Yuan Lo
Sylvain Lobry
Suhas Lohit
Vishnu Suresh Lokhande
Vincenzo Lomonaco
Chengjiang Long
Guodong Long
Fuchen Long
Shangbang Long
Yang Long
Zijun Long
Vasco Lopes
Antonio M. Lopez
Roberto Javier
    Lopez-Sastre
Tobias Lorenz
Javier Lorenzo-Navarro
Yujing Lou
Qian Lou
Xiankai Lu
Changsheng Lu
Huimin Lu
Yongxi Lu
Hao Lu
Hong Lu
Jiasen Lu

Juwei Lu
Fan Lu
Guangming Lu
Jiwen Lu
Shun Lu
Tao Lu
Xiaonan Lu
Yang Lu
Yao Lu
Yongchun Lu
Zhiwu Lu
Cheng Lu
Liying Lu
Guo Lu
Xuequan Lu
Yanye Lu
Yantao Lu
Yuhang Lu
Fujun Luan
Jonathon Luiten
Jovita Lukasik
Alan Lukezic
Jonathan Samuel Lumentut
Mayank Lunayach
Ao Luo
Canjie Luo
Chong Luo
Xu Luo
Grace Luo
Jun Luo
Katie Z. Luo
Tao Luo
Cheng Luo
Fangzhou Luo
Gen Luo
Lei Luo
Sihui Luo
Weixin Luo
Yan Luo
Xiaoyan Luo
Yong Luo
Yadan Luo
Hao Luo
Ruotian Luo
Mi Luo

Tiange Luo
Wenjie Luo
Wenhan Luo
Xiao Luo
Zhiming Luo
Zhipeng Luo
Zhengyi Luo
Diogo C. Luvizon
Zhaoyang Lv
Gengyu Lyu
Lingjuan Lyu
Jun Lyu
Yuanyuan Lyu
Youwei Lyu
Yueming Lyu
Bingpeng Ma
Chao Ma
Chongyang Ma
Congbo Ma
Chih-Yao Ma
Fan Ma
Lin Ma
Haoyu Ma
Hengbo Ma
Jianqi Ma
Jiawei Ma
Jiayi Ma
Kede Ma
Kai Ma
Lingni Ma
Lei Ma
Xu Ma
Ning Ma
Benteng Ma
Cheng Ma
Andy J. Ma
Long Ma
Zhanyu Ma
Zhiheng Ma
Qianli Ma
Shiqiang Ma
Sizhuo Ma
Shiqing Ma
Xiaolong Ma
Xinzhu Ma

Gautam B. Machiraju
Spandan Madan
Mathew Magimai-Doss
Luca Magri
Behrooz Mahasseni
Upal Mahbub
Siddharth Mahendran
Paridhi Maheshwari
Rishabh Maheshwary
Mohammed Mahmoud
Shishira R. R. Maiya
Sylwia Majchrowska
Arjun Majumdar
Puspita Majumdar
Orchid Majumder
Sagnik Majumder
Ilya Makarov
Farkhod F.
   Makhmudkhujaev
Yasushi Makihara
Ankur Mali
Mateusz Malinowski
Utkarsh Mall
Srikanth Malla
Clement Mallet
Dimitrios Mallis
Yunze Man
Dipu Manandhar
Massimiliano Mancini
Murari Mandal
Raunak Manekar
Karttikeya Mangalam
Puneet Mangla
Fabian Manhardt
Sivabalan Manivasagam
Fahim Mannan
Chengzhi Mao
Hanzi Mao
Jiayuan Mao
Junhua Mao
Zhiyuan Mao
Jiageng Mao
Yunyao Mao
Zhendong Mao
Alberto Marchisio

Diego Marcos
Riccardo Marin
Aram Markosyan
Renaud Marlet
Ricardo Marques
Miquel Martí i Rabadán
Diego Martin Arroyo
Niki Martinel
Brais Martinez
Julieta Martinez
Marc Masana
Tomohiro Mashita
Timothée Masquelier
Minesh Mathew
Tetsu Matsukawa
Marwan Mattar
Bruce A. Maxwell
Christoph Mayer
Mantas Mazeika
Pratik Mazumder
Scott McCloskey
Steven McDonagh
Ishit Mehta
Jie Mei
Kangfu Mei
Jieru Mei
Xiaoguang Mei
Givi Meishvili
Luke Melas-Kyriazi
Iaroslav Melekhov
Andres Mendez-Vazquez
Heydi Mendez-Vazquez
Matias Mendieta
Ricardo A. Mendoza-León
Chenlin Meng
Depu Meng
Rang Meng
Zibo Meng
Qingjie Meng
Qier Meng
Yanda Meng
Zihang Meng
Thomas Mensink
Fabian Mentzer
Christopher Metzler

Gregory P. Meyer
Vasileios Mezaris
Liang Mi
Lu Mi
Bo Miao
Changtao Miao
Zichen Miao
Qiguang Miao
Xin Miao
Zhongqi Miao
Frank Michel
Simone Milani
Ben Mildenhall
Roy V. Miles
Juhong Min
Kyle Min
Hyun-Seok Min
Weiqing Min
Yuecong Min
Zhixiang Min
Qi Ming
David Minnen
Aymen Mir
Deepak Mishra
Anand Mishra
Shlok K. Mishra
Niluthpol Mithun
Gaurav Mittal
Trisha Mittal
Daisuke Miyazaki
Kaichun Mo
Hong Mo
Zhipeng Mo
Davide Modolo
Abduallah A. Mohamed
Mohamed Afham
Mohamed Aflal
Ron Mokady
Pavlo Molchanov
Davide Moltisanti
Liliane Momeni
Gianluca Monaci
Pascal Monasse
Ajoy Mondal
Tom Monnier

Aron Monszpart
Gyeongsik Moon
Suhong Moon
Taesup Moon
Sean Moran
Daniel Moreira
Pietro Morerio
Alexandre Morgand
Lia Morra
Ali Mosleh
Inbar Mosseri
Sayed Mohammad
   Mostafavi Isfahani
Saman Motamed
Ramy A. Mounir
Fangzhou Mu
Jiteng Mu
Norman Mu
Yasuhiro Mukaigawa
Ryan Mukherjee
Tanmoy Mukherjee
Yusuke Mukuta
Ravi Teja Mullapudi
Lea Müller
Matthias Müller
Martin Mundt
Nils Murrugarra-Llerena
Damien Muselet
Armin Mustafa
Muhammad Ferjad Naeem
Sauradip Nag
Hajime Nagahara
Pravin Nagar
Rajendra Nagar
Naveen Shankar Nagaraja
Varun Nagaraja
Tushar Nagarajan
Seungjun Nah
Gaku Nakano
Yuta Nakashima
Giljoo Nam
Seonghyeon Nam
Liangliang Nan
Yuesong Nan
Yeshwanth Napolean

Dinesh Reddy
   Narapureddy
Medhini Narasimhan
Supreeth
   Narasimhaswamy
Sriram Narayanan
Erickson R. Nascimento
Varun Nasery
K. L. Navaneet
Pablo Navarrete Michelini
Shant Navasardyan
Shah Nawaz
Nihal Nayak
Farhood Negin
Lukáš Neumann
Alejandro Newell
Evonne Ng
Kam Woh Ng
Tony Ng
Anh Nguyen
Tuan Anh Nguyen
Cuong Cao Nguyen
Ngoc Cuong Nguyen
Thanh Nguyen
Khoi Nguyen
Phi Le Nguyen
Phong Ha Nguyen
Tam Nguyen
Truong Nguyen
Anh Tuan Nguyen
Rang Nguyen
Thao Thi Phuong Nguyen
Van Nguyen Nguyen
Zhen-Liang Ni
Yao Ni
Shijie Nie
Xuecheng Nie
Yongwei Nie
Weizhi Nie
Ying Nie
Yinyu Nie
Kshitij N. Nikhal
Simon Niklaus
Xuefei Ning
Jifeng Ning

Yotam Nitzan
Di Niu
Shuaicheng Niu
Li Niu
Wei Niu
Yulei Niu
Zhenxing Niu
Albert No
Shohei Nobuhara
Nicoletta Noceti
Junhyug Noh
Sotiris Nousias
Slawomir Nowaczyk
Ewa M. Nowara
Valsamis Ntouskos
Gilberto Ochoa-Ruiz
Ferda Ofli
Jihyong Oh
Sangyun Oh
Youngtaek Oh
Hiroki Ohashi
Takahiro Okabe
Kemal Oksuz
Fumio Okura
Daniel Olmeda Reino
Matthew Olson
Carl Olsson
Roy Or-El
Alessandro Ortis
Guillermo Ortiz-Jimenez
Magnus Oskarsson
Ahmed A. A. Osman
Martin R. Oswald
Mayu Otani
Naima Otberdout
Cheng Ouyang
Jiahong Ouyang
Wanli Ouyang
Andrew Owens
Poojan B. Oza
Mete Ozay
A. Cengiz Oztireli
Gautam Pai
Tomas Pajdla
Umapada Pal

Simone Palazzo
Luca Palmieri
Bowen Pan
Hao Pan
Lili Pan
Tai-Yu Pan
Liang Pan
Chengwei Pan
Yingwei Pan
Xuran Pan
Jinshan Pan
Xinyu Pan
Liyuan Pan
Xingang Pan
Xingjia Pan
Zhihong Pan
Zizheng Pan
Priyadarshini Panda
Rameswar Panda
Rohit Pandey
Kaiyue Pang
Bo Pang
Guansong Pang
Jiangmiao Pang
Meng Pang
Tianyu Pang
Ziqi Pang
Omiros Pantazis
Andreas Panteli
Maja Pantic
Marina Paolanti
Joao P. Papa
Samuele Papa
Mike Papadakis
Dim P. Papadopoulos
George Papandreou
Constantin Pape
Toufiq Parag
Chethan Parameshwara
Shaifali Parashar
Alejandro Pardo
Rishubh Parihar
Sarah Parisot
JaeYoo Park
Gyeong-Moon Park

Hyojin Park
Hyoungseob Park
Jongchan Park
Jae Sung Park
Kiru Park
Chunghyun Park
Kwanyong Park
Sunghyun Park
Sungrae Park
Seongsik Park
Sanghyun Park
Sungjune Park
Taesung Park
Gaurav Parmar
Paritosh Parmar
Alvaro Parra
Despoina Paschalidou
Or Patashnik
Shivansh Patel
Pushpak Pati
Prashant W. Patil
Vaishakh Patil
Suvam Patra
Jay Patravali
Badri Narayana Patro
Angshuman Paul
Sudipta Paul
Rémi Pautrat
Nick E. Pears
Adithya Pediredla
Wenjie Pei
Shmuel Peleg
Latha Pemula
Bo Peng
Houwen Peng
Yue Peng
Liangzu Peng
Baoyun Peng
Jun Peng
Pai Peng
Sida Peng
Xi Peng
Yuxin Peng
Songyou Peng
Wei Peng

Weiqi Peng
Wen-Hsiao Peng
Pramuditha Perera
Juan C. Perez
Eduardo Pérez Pellitero
Juan-Manuel Perez-Rua
Federico Pernici
Marco Pesavento
Stavros Petridis
Ilya A. Petrov
Vladan Petrovic
Mathis Petrovich
Suzanne Petryk
Hieu Pham
Quang Pham
Khoi Pham
Tung Pham
Huy Phan
Stephen Phillips
Cheng Perng Phoo
David Picard
Marco Piccirilli
Georg Pichler
A. J. Piergiovanni
Vipin Pillai
Silvia L. Pintea
Giovanni Pintore
Robinson Piramuthu
Fiora Pirri
Theodoros Pissas
Fabio Pizzati
Benjamin Planche
Bryan Plummer
Matteo Poggi
Ashwini Pokle
Georgy E. Ponimatkin
Adrian Popescu
Stefan Popov
Nikola Popović
Ronald Poppe
Angelo Porrello
Michael Potter
Charalambos Poullis
Hadi Pouransari
Omid Poursaeed

Christian Richardt
Stephan R. Richter
Benjamin Riggan
Dominik Rivoir
Mamshad Nayeem Rizve
Joshua D. Robinson
Joseph Robinson
Chris Rockwell
Ranga Rodrigo
Andres C. Rodriguez
Carlos Rodriguez-Pardo
Marcus Rohrbach
Gemma Roig
Yu Rong
David A. Ross
Mohammad Rostami
Edward Rosten
Karsten Roth
Anirban Roy
Debaditya Roy
Shuvendu Roy
Ahana Roy Choudhury
Aruni Roy Chowdhury
Denys Rozumnyi
Shulan Ruan
Wenjie Ruan
Patrick Ruhkamp
Danila Rukhovich
Anian Ruoss
Chris Russell
Dan Ruta
Dawid Damian Rymarczyk
DongHun Ryu
Hyeonggon Ryu
Kwonyoung Ryu
Balasubramanian S.
Alexandre Sablayrolles
Mohammad Sabokrou
Arka Sadhu
Aniruddha Saha
Oindrila Saha
Pritish Sahu
Aneeshan Sain
Nirat Saini
Saurabh Saini

Takeshi Saitoh
Christos Sakaridis
Fumihiko Sakaue
Dimitrios Sakkos
Ken Sakurada
Parikshit V. Sakurikar
Rohit Saluja
Nermin Samet
Leo Sampaio Ferraz
    Ribeiro
Jorge Sanchez
Enrique Sanchez
Shengtian Sang
Anush Sankaran
Soubhik Sanyal
Nikolaos Sarafianos
Vishwanath Saragadam
István Sárándi
Saquib Sarfraz
Mert Bulent Sariyildiz
Anindya Sarkar
Pritam Sarkar
Paul-Edouard Sarlin
Hiroshi Sasaki
Takami Sato
Torsten Sattler
Ravi Kumar Satzoda
Axel Sauer
Stefano Savian
Artem Savkin
Manolis Savva
Gerald Schaefer
Simone Schaub-Meyer
Yoni Schirris
Samuel Schulter
Katja Schwarz
Jesse Scott
Sinisa Segvic
Constantin Marc Seibold
Lorenzo Seidenari
Matan Sela
Fadime Sener
Paul Hongsuck Seo
Kwanggyoon Seo
Hongje Seong

Dario Serez
Francesco Setti
Bryan Seybold
Mohamad Shahbazi
Shima Shahfar
Xinxin Shan
Caifeng Shan
Dandan Shan
Shawn Shan
Wei Shang
Jinghuan Shang
Jiaxiang Shang
Lei Shang
Sukrit Shankar
Ken Shao
Rui Shao
Jie Shao
Mingwen Shao
Aashish Sharma
Gaurav Sharma
Vivek Sharma
Abhishek Sharma
Yoli Shavit
Shashank Shekhar
Sumit Shekhar
Zhijie Shen
Fengyi Shen
Furao Shen
Jialie Shen
Jingjing Shen
Ziyi Shen
Linlin Shen
Guangyu Shen
Biluo Shen
Falong Shen
Jiajun Shen
Qiu Shen
Qiuhong Shen
Shuai Shen
Wang Shen
Yiqing Shen
Yunhang Shen
Siqi Shen
Bin Shen
Tianwei Shen

Xi Shen
Yilin Shen
Yuming Shen
Yucong Shen
Zhiqiang Shen
Lu Sheng
Yichen Sheng
Shivanand Venkanna
    Sheshappanavar
Shelly Sheynin
Baifeng Shi
Ruoxi Shi
Botian Shi
Hailin Shi
Jia Shi
Jing Shi
Shaoshuai Shi
Baoguang Shi
Boxin Shi
Hengcan Shi
Tianyang Shi
Xiaodan Shi
Yongjie Shi
Zhensheng Shi
Yinghuan Shi
Weiqi Shi
Wu Shi
Xuepeng Shi
Xiaoshuang Shi
Yujiao Shi
Zenglin Shi
Zhenmei Shi
Takashi Shibata
Meng-Li Shih
Yichang Shih
Hyunjung Shim
Dongseok Shim
Soshi Shimada
Inkyu Shin
Jinwoo Shin
Seungjoo Shin
Seungjae Shin
Koichi Shinoda
Suprosanna Shit

Palaiahnakote
    Shivakumara
Eli Shlizerman
Gaurav Shrivastava
Xiao Shu
Xiangbo Shu
Xiujun Shu
Yang Shu
Tianmin Shu
Jun Shu
Zhixin Shu
Bing Shuai
Maria Shugrina
Ivan Shugurov
Satya Narayan Shukla
Pranjay Shyam
Jianlou Si
Yawar Siddiqui
Alberto Signoroni
Pedro Silva
Jae-Young Sim
Oriane Siméoni
Martin Simon
Andrea Simonelli
Abhishek Singh
Ashish Singh
Dinesh Singh
Gurkirt Singh
Krishna Kumar Singh
Mannat Singh
Pravendra Singh
Rajat Vikram Singh
Utkarsh Singhal
Dipika Singhania
Vasu Singla
Harsh Sinha
Sudipta Sinha
Josef Sivic
Elena Sizikova
Geri Skenderi
Ivan Skorokhodov
Dmitriy Smirnov
Cameron Y. Smith
James S. Smith
Patrick Snape

Mattia Soldan
Hyeongseok Son
Sanghyun Son
Chuanbiao Song
Chen Song
Chunfeng Song
Dan Song
Dongjin Song
Hwanjun Song
Guoxian Song
Jiaming Song
Jie Song
Liangchen Song
Ran Song
Luchuan Song
Xibin Song
Li Song
Fenglong Song
Guoli Song
Guanglu Song
Zhenbo Song
Lin Song
Xinhang Song
Yang Song
Yibing Song
Rajiv Soundararajan
Hossein Souri
Cristovao Sousa
Riccardo Spezialetti
Leonidas Spinoulas
Michael W. Spratling
Deepak Sridhar
Srinath Sridhar
Gaurang Sriramanan
Vinkle Kumar Srivastav
Themos Stafylakis
Serban Stan
Anastasis Stathopoulos
Markus Steinberger
Jan Steinbrener
Sinisa Stekovic
Alexandros Stergiou
Gleb Sterkin
Rainer Stiefelhagen
Pierre Stock

Ombretta Strafforello
Julian Straub
Yannick Strümpler
Joerg Stueckler
Hang Su
Weijie Su
Jong-Chyi Su
Bing Su
Haisheng Su
Jinming Su
Yiyang Su
Yukun Su
Yuxin Su
Zhuo Su
Zhaoqi Su
Xiu Su
Yu-Chuan Su
Zhixun Su
Arulkumar Subramaniam
Akshayvarun Subramanya
A. Subramanyam
Swathikiran Sudhakaran
Yusuke Sugano
Masanori Suganuma
Yumin Suh
Yang Sui
Baochen Sun
Cheng Sun
Long Sun
Guolei Sun
Haoliang Sun
Haomiao Sun
He Sun
Hanqing Sun
Hao Sun
Lichao Sun
Jiachen Sun
Jiaming Sun
Jian Sun
Jin Sun
Jennifer J. Sun
Tiancheng Sun
Libo Sun
Peize Sun
Qianru Sun

Shanlin Sun
Yu Sun
Zhun Sun
Che Sun
Lin Sun
Tao Sun
Yiyou Sun
Chunyi Sun
Chong Sun
Weiwei Sun
Weixuan Sun
Xiuyu Sun
Yanan Sun
Zeren Sun
Zhaodong Sun
Zhiqing Sun
Minhyuk Sung
Jinli Suo
Simon Suo
Abhijit Suprem
Anshuman Suri
Saksham Suri
Joshua M. Susskind
Roman Suvorov
Gurumurthy Swaminathan
Robin Swanson
Paul Swoboda
Tabish A. Syed
Richard Szeliski
Fariborz Taherkhani
Yu-Wing Tai
Keita Takahashi
Walter Talbott
Gary Tam
Masato Tamura
Feitong Tan
Fuwen Tan
Shuhan Tan
Andong Tan
Bin Tan
Cheng Tan
Jianchao Tan
Lei Tan
Mingxing Tan
Xin Tan

Zichang Tan
Zhentao Tan
Kenichiro Tanaka
Masayuki Tanaka
Yushun Tang
Hao Tang
Jingqun Tang
Jinhui Tang
Kaihua Tang
Luming Tang
Lv Tang
Sheyang Tang
Shitao Tang
Siliang Tang
Shixiang Tang
Yansong Tang
Keke Tang
Chang Tang
Chenwei Tang
Jie Tang
Junshu Tang
Ming Tang
Peng Tang
Xu Tang
Yao Tang
Chen Tang
Fan Tang
Haoran Tang
Shengeng Tang
Yehui Tang
Zhipeng Tang
Ugo Tanielian
Chaofan Tao
Jiale Tao
Junli Tao
Renshuai Tao
An Tao
Guanhong Tao
Zhiqiang Tao
Makarand Tapaswi
Jean-Philippe G. Tarel
Juan J. Tarrio
Enzo Tartaglione
Keisuke Tateno
Zachary Teed

Ajinkya B. Tejankar
Bugra Tekin
Purva Tendulkar
Damien Teney
Minggui Teng
Chris Tensmeyer
Andrew Beng Jin Teoh
Philipp Terhörst
Kartik Thakral
Nupur Thakur
Kevin Thandiackal
Spyridon Thermos
Diego Thomas
William Thong
Yuesong Tian
Guanzhong Tian
Lin Tian
Shiqi Tian
Kai Tian
Meng Tian
Tai-Peng Tian
Zhuotao Tian
Shangxuan Tian
Tian Tian
Yapeng Tian
Yu Tian
Yuxin Tian
Leslie Ching Ow Tiong
Praveen Tirupattur
Garvita Tiwari
George Toderici
Antoine Toisoul
Aysim Toker
Tatiana Tommasi
Zhan Tong
Alessio Tonioni
Alessandro Torcinovich
Fabio Tosi
Matteo Toso
Hugo Touvron
Quan Hung Tran
Son Tran
Hung Tran
Ngoc-Trung Tran
Vinh Tran

Phong Tran
Giovanni Trappolini
Edith Tretschk
Subarna Tripathi
Shubhendu Trivedi
Eduard Trulls
Prune Truong
Thanh-Dat Truong
Tomasz Trzcinski
Sam Tsai
Yi-Hsuan Tsai
Ethan Tseng
Yu-Chee Tseng
Shahar Tsiper
Stavros Tsogkas
Shikui Tu
Zhigang Tu
Zhengzhong Tu
Richard Tucker
Sergey Tulyakov
Cigdem Turan
Daniyar Turmukhambetov
Victor G. Turrisi da Costa
Bartlomiej Twardowski
Christopher D. Twigg
Radim Tylecek
Mostofa Rafid Uddin
Md. Zasim Uddin
Kohei Uehara
Nicolas Ugrinovic
Youngjung Uh
Norimichi Ukita
Anwaar Ulhaq
Devesh Upadhyay
Paul Upchurch
Yoshitaka Ushiku
Yuzuko Utsumi
Mikaela Angelina Uy
Mohit Vaishnav
Pratik Vaishnavi
Jeya Maria Jose Valanarasu
Matias A. Valdenegro Toro
Diego Valsesia
Wouter Van Gansbeke
Nanne van Noord

Simon Vandenhende
Farshid Varno
Cristina Vasconcelos
Francisco Vasconcelos
Alex Vasilescu
Subeesh Vasu
Arun Balajee Vasudevan
Kanav Vats
Vaibhav S. Vavilala
Sagar Vaze
Javier Vazquez-Corral
Andrea Vedaldi
Olga Veksler
Andreas Velten
Sai H. Vemprala
Raviteja Vemulapalli
Shashanka
    Venkataramanan
Dor Verbin
Luisa Verdoliva
Manisha Verma
Yashaswi Verma
Constantin Vertan
Eli Verwimp
Deepak Vijaykeerthy
Pablo Villanueva
Ruben Villegas
Markus Vincze
Vibhav Vineet
Minh P. Vo
Huy V. Vo
Duc Minh Vo
Tomas Vojir
Igor Vozniak
Nicholas Vretos
Vibashan VS
Tuan-Anh Vu
Thang Vu
Mårten Wadenbäck
Neal Wadhwa
Aaron T. Walsman
Steven Walton
Jin Wan
Alvin Wan
Jia Wan

Jun Wan

Xiaoyue Wan

Fang Wan

Guowei Wan

Renjie Wan

Zhiqiang Wan

Ziyu Wan

Bastian Wandt

Dongdong Wang

Limin Wang

Haiyang Wang

Xiaobing Wang

Angtian Wang

Angelina Wang

Bing Wang

Bo Wang

Boyu Wang

Binghui Wang

Chen Wang

Chien-Yi Wang

Congli Wang

Qi Wang

Chengrui Wang

Rui Wang

Yiqun Wang

Cong Wang

Wenjing Wang

Dongkai Wang

Di Wang

Xiaogang Wang

Kai Wang

Zhizhong Wang

Fangjinhua Wang

Feng Wang

Hang Wang

Gaoang Wang

Guoqing Wang

Guangcong Wang

Guangzhi Wang

Hanqing Wang

Hao Wang

Haohan Wang

Haoran Wang

Hong Wang

Haotao Wang

Hu Wang

Huan Wang

Hua Wang

Hui-Po Wang

Hengli Wang

Hanyu Wang

Hongxing Wang

Jingwen Wang

Jialiang Wang

Jian Wang

Jianyi Wang

Jiashun Wang

Jiahao Wang

Tsun-Hsuan Wang

Xiaoqian Wang

Jinqiao Wang

Jun Wang

Jianzong Wang

Kaihong Wang

Ke Wang

Lei Wang

Lingjing Wang

Linnan Wang

Lin Wang

Liansheng Wang

Mengjiao Wang

Manning Wang

Nannan Wang

Peihao Wang

Jiayun Wang

Pu Wang

Qiang Wang

Qiufeng Wang

Qilong Wang

Qiangchang Wang

Qin Wang

Qing Wang

Ruocheng Wang

Ruibin Wang

Ruisheng Wang

Ruizhe Wang

Runqi Wang

Runzhong Wang

Wenxuan Wang

Sen Wang

Shangfei Wang

Shaofei Wang

Shijie Wang

Shiqi Wang

Zhibo Wang

Song Wang

Xinjiang Wang

Tai Wang

Tao Wang

Teng Wang

Xiang Wang

Tianren Wang

Tiantian Wang

Tianyi Wang

Fengjiao Wang

Wei Wang

Miaohui Wang

Suchen Wang

Siyue Wang

Yaoming Wang

Xiao Wang

Ze Wang

Biao Wang

Chaofei Wang

Dong Wang

Gu Wang

Guangrun Wang

Guangming Wang

Guo-Hua Wang

Haoqing Wang

Hesheng Wang

Huafeng Wang

Jinghua Wang

Jingdong Wang

Jingjing Wang

Jingya Wang

Jingkang Wang

Jiakai Wang

Junke Wang

Kuo Wang

Lichen Wang

Lizhi Wang

Longguang Wang

Mang Wang

Mei Wang

Min Wang

Peng-Shuai Wang

Run Wang

Shaoru Wang

Shuhui Wang

Tan Wang

Tiancai Wang

Tianqi Wang

Wenhai Wang

Wenzhe Wang

Xiaobo Wang

Xiudong Wang

Xu Wang

Yajie Wang

Yan Wang

Yuan-Gen Wang

Yingqian Wang

Yizhi Wang

Yulin Wang

Yu Wang

Yujie Wang

Yunhe Wang

Yuxi Wang

Yaowei Wang

Yiwei Wang

Zezheng Wang

Hongzhi Wang

Zhiqiang Wang

Ziteng Wang

Ziwei Wang

Zheng Wang

Zhenyu Wang

Binglu Wang

Zhongdao Wang

Ce Wang

Weining Wang

Weiyao Wang

Wenbin Wang

Wenguan Wang

Guangting Wang

Haolin Wang

Haiyan Wang

Huiyu Wang

Naiyan Wang

Jingbo Wang

Jinpeng Wang

Jiaqi Wang

Liyuan Wang

Lizhen Wang

Ning Wang

Wenqian Wang

Sheng-Yu Wang

Weimin Wang

Xiaohan Wang

Yifan Wang

Yi Wang

Yongtao Wang

Yizhou Wang

Zhuo Wang

Zhe Wang

Xudong Wang

Xiaofang Wang

Xinggang Wang

Xiaosen Wang

Xiaosong Wang

Xiaoyang Wang

Lijun Wang

Xinlong Wang

Xuan Wang

Xue Wang

Yangang Wang

Yaohui Wang

Yu-Chiang Frank Wang

Yida Wang

Yilin Wang

Yi Ru Wang

Yali Wang

Yinglong Wang

Yufu Wang

Yujiang Wang

Yuwang Wang

Yuting Wang

Yang Wang

Yu-Xiong Wang

Yixu Wang

Ziqi Wang

Zhicheng Wang

Zeyu Wang

Zhaowen Wang

Zhenyi Wang

Zhenzhi Wang

Zhijie Wang

Zhiyong Wang

Zhongling Wang

Zhuowei Wang

Zian Wang

Zifu Wang

Zihao Wang

Zirui Wang

Ziyan Wang

Wenxiao Wang

Zhen Wang

Zhepeng Wang

Zi Wang

Zihao W. Wang

Steven L. Waslander

Olivia Watkins

Daniel Watson

Silvan Weder

Dongyoon Wee

Dongming Wei

Tianyi Wei

Jia Wei

Dong Wei

Fangyun Wei

Longhui Wei

Mingqiang Wei

Xinyue Wei

Chen Wei

Donglai Wei

Pengxu Wei

Xing Wei

Xiu-Shen Wei

Wenqi Wei

Guoqiang Wei

Wei Wei

XingKui Wei

Xian Wei

Xingxing Wei

Yake Wei

Yuxiang Wei

Yi Wei

Luca Weihs

Michael Weinmann

Martin Weinmann

Congcong Wen
Chuan Wen
Jie Wen
Sijia Wen
Song Wen
Chao Wen
Xiang Wen
Zeyi Wen
Xin Wen
Yilin Wen
Yijia Weng
Shuchen Weng
Junwu Weng
Wenming Weng
Renliang Weng
Zhenyu Weng
Xinshuo Weng
Nicholas J. Westlake
Gordon Wetzstein
Lena M. Widin Klasén
Rick Wildes
Bryan M. Williams
William Williem
Ole Winther
Scott Wisdom
Alex Wong
Chau-Wai Wong
Kwan-Yee K. Wong
Yongkang Wong
Scott Workman
Marcel Worring
Michael Wray
Safwan Wshah
Xiang Wu
Aming Wu
Chongruo Wu
Cho-Ying Wu
Chunpeng Wu
Chenyan Wu
Ziyi Wu
Fuxiang Wu
Gang Wu
Haiping Wu
Huisi Wu
Jane Wu

Jialian Wu
Jing Wu
Jinjian Wu
Jianlong Wu
Xian Wu
Lifang Wu
Lifan Wu
Minye Wu
Qianyi Wu
Rongliang Wu
Rui Wu
Shiqian Wu
Shuzhe Wu
Shangzhe Wu
Tsung-Han Wu
Tz-Ying Wu
Ting-Wei Wu
Jiannan Wu
Zhiliang Wu
Yu Wu
Chenyun Wu
Dayan Wu
Dongxian Wu
Fei Wu
Hefeng Wu
Jianxin Wu
Weibin Wu
Wenxuan Wu
Wenhao Wu
Xiao Wu
Yicheng Wu
Yuanwei Wu
Yu-Huan Wu
Zhenxin Wu
Zhenyu Wu
Wei Wu
Peng Wu
Xiaohe Wu
Xindi Wu
Xinxing Wu
Xinyi Wu
Xingjiao Wu
Xiongwei Wu
Yangzheng Wu
Yanzhao Wu

Yawen Wu
Yong Wu
Yi Wu
Ying Nian Wu
Zhenyao Wu
Zhonghua Wu
Zongze Wu
Zuxuan Wu
Stefanie Wuhrer
Teng Xi
Jianing Xi
Fei Xia
Haifeng Xia
Menghan Xia
Yuanqing Xia
Zhihua Xia
Xiaobo Xia
Weihao Xia
Shihong Xia
Yan Xia
Yong Xia
Zhaoyang Xia
Zhihao Xia
Chuhua Xian
Yongqin Xian
Wangmeng Xiang
Fanbo Xiang
Tiange Xiang
Tao Xiang
Liuyu Xiang
Xiaoyu Xiang
Zhiyu Xiang
Aoran Xiao
Chunxia Xiao
Fanyi Xiao
Jimin Xiao
Jun Xiao
Taihong Xiao
Anqi Xiao
Junfei Xiao
Jing Xiao
Liang Xiao
Yang Xiao
Yuting Xiao
Yijun Xiao

Yan Yan
Yichao Yan
Zhaoyi Yan
Zike Yan
Zhiqiang Yan
Hongliang Yan
Zizheng Yan
Jiewen Yang
Anqi Joyce Yang
Shan Yang
Anqi Yang
Antoine Yang
Bo Yang
Baoyao Yang
Chenhongyi Yang
Dingkang Yang
De-Nian Yang
Dong Yang
David Yang
Fan Yang
Fengyu Yang
Fengting Yang
Fei Yang
Gengshan Yang
Heng Yang
Han Yang
Huan Yang
Yibo Yang
Jiancheng Yang
Jihan Yang
Jiawei Yang
Jiayu Yang
Jie Yang
Jinfa Yang
Jingkang Yang
Jinyu Yang
Cheng-Fu Yang
Ji Yang
Jianyu Yang
Kailun Yang
Tian Yang
Luyu Yang
Liang Yang
Li Yang
Michael Ying Yang

Yang Yang
Muli Yang
Le Yang
Qiushi Yang
Ren Yang
Ruihan Yang
Shuang Yang
Siyuan Yang
Su Yang
Shiqi Yang
Taojiannan Yang
Tianyu Yang
Lei Yang
Wanzhao Yang
Shuai Yang
William Yang
Wei Yang
Xiaofeng Yang
Xiaoshan Yang
Xin Yang
Xuan Yang
Xu Yang
Xingyi Yang
Xitong Yang
Jing Yang
Yanchao Yang
Wenming Yang
Yujiu Yang
Herb Yang
Jianfei Yang
Jinhui Yang
Chuanguang Yang
Guanglei Yang
Haitao Yang
Kewei Yang
Linlin Yang
Lijin Yang
Longrong Yang
Meng Yang
MingKun Yang
Sibei Yang
Shicai Yang
Tong Yang
Wen Yang
Xi Yang

Xiaolong Yang
Xue Yang
Yubin Yang
Ze Yang
Ziyi Yang
Yi Yang
Linjie Yang
Yuzhe Yang
Yiding Yang
Zhenpei Yang
Zhaohui Yang
Zhengyuan Yang
Zhibo Yang
Zongxin Yang
Hantao Yao
Mingde Yao
Rui Yao
Taiping Yao
Ting Yao
Cong Yao
Qingsong Yao
Quanming Yao
Xu Yao
Yuan Yao
Yao Yao
Yazhou Yao
Jiawen Yao
Shunyu Yao
Pew-Thian Yap
Sudhir Yarram
Rajeev Yasarla
Peng Ye
Botao Ye
Mao Ye
Fei Ye
Hanrong Ye
Jingwen Ye
Jinwei Ye
Jiarong Ye
Mang Ye
Meng Ye
Qi Ye
Qian Ye
Qixiang Ye
Junjie Ye

Sheng Ye
Nanyang Ye
Yufei Ye
Xiaoqing Ye
Ruolin Ye
Yousef Yeganeh
Chun-Hsiao Yeh
Raymond A. Yeh
Yu-Ying Yeh
Kai Yi
Chang Yi
Renjiao Yi
Xinping Yi
Peng Yi
Alper Yilmaz
Junho Yim
Hui Yin
Bangjie Yin
Jia-Li Yin
Miao Yin
Wenzhe Yin
Xuwang Yin
Ming Yin
Yu Yin
Aoxiong Yin
Kangxue Yin
Tianwei Yin
Wei Yin
Xianghua Ying
Rio Yokota
Tatsuya Yokota
Naoto Yokoya
Ryo Yonetani
Ki Yoon Yoo
Jinsu Yoo
Sunjae Yoon
Jae Shin Yoon
Jihun Yoon
Sung-Hoon Yoon
Ryota Yoshihashi
Yusuke Yoshiyasu
Chenyu You
Haoran You
Haoxuan You
Yang You

Quanzeng You
Tackgeun You
Kaichao You
Shan You
Xinge You
Yurong You
Baosheng Yu
Bei Yu
Haichao Yu
Hao Yu
Chaohui Yu
Fisher Yu
Jin-Gang Yu
Jiyang Yu
Jason J. Yu
Jiashuo Yu
Hong-Xing Yu
Lei Yu
Mulin Yu
Ning Yu
Peilin Yu
Qi Yu
Qian Yu
Rui Yu
Shuzhi Yu
Gang Yu
Tan Yu
Weijiang Yu
Xin Yu
Bingyao Yu
Ye Yu
Hanchao Yu
Yingchen Yu
Tao Yu
Xiaotian Yu
Qing Yu
Houjian Yu
Changqian Yu
Jing Yu
Jun Yu
Shujian Yu
Xiang Yu
Zhaofei Yu
Zhenbo Yu
Yinfeng Yu

Zhuoran Yu
Zitong Yu
Bo Yuan
Jiangbo Yuan
Liangzhe Yuan
Weihao Yuan
Jianbo Yuan
Xiaoyun Yuan
Ye Yuan
Li Yuan
Geng Yuan
Jialin Yuan
Maoxun Yuan
Peng Yuan
Xin Yuan
Yuan Yuan
Yuhui Yuan
Yixuan Yuan
Zheng Yuan
Mehmet Kerim Yücel
Kaiyu Yue
Haixiao Yue
Heeseung Yun
Sangdoo Yun
Tian Yun
Mahmut Yurt
Ekim Yurtsever
Ahmet Yüzügüler
Edouard Yvinec
Eloi Zablocki
Christopher Zach
Muhammad Zaigham
    Zaheer
Pierluigi Zama Ramirez
Yuhang Zang
Pietro Zanuttigh
Alexey Zaytsev
Bernhard Zeisl
Haitian Zeng
Pengpeng Zeng
Jiabei Zeng
Runhao Zeng
Wei Zeng
Yawen Zeng
Yi Zeng

Yiming Zeng
Tieyong Zeng
Huanqiang Zeng
Dan Zeng
Yu Zeng
Wei Zhai
Yuanhao Zhai
Fangneng Zhan
Kun Zhan
Xiong Zhang
Jingdong Zhang
Jiangning Zhang
Zhilu Zhang
Gengwei Zhang
Dongsu Zhang
Hui Zhang
Binjie Zhang
Bo Zhang
Tianhao Zhang
Cecilia Zhang
Jing Zhang
Chaoning Zhang
Chenxu Zhang
Chi Zhang
Chris Zhang
Yabin Zhang
Zhao Zhang
Rufeng Zhang
Chaoyi Zhang
Zheng Zhang
Da Zhang
Yi Zhang
Edward Zhang
Xin Zhang
Feifei Zhang
Feilong Zhang
Yuqi Zhang
GuiXuan Zhang
Hanlin Zhang
Hanwang Zhang
Hanzhen Zhang
Haotian Zhang
He Zhang
Haokui Zhang
Hongyuan Zhang

Hengrui Zhang
Hongming Zhang
Mingfang Zhang
Jianpeng Zhang
Jiaming Zhang
Jichao Zhang
Jie Zhang
Jingfeng Zhang
Jingyi Zhang
Jinnian Zhang
David Junhao Zhang
Junjie Zhang
Junzhe Zhang
Jiawan Zhang
Jingyang Zhang
Kai Zhang
Lei Zhang
Lihua Zhang
Lu Zhang
Miao Zhang
Minjia Zhang
Mingjin Zhang
Qi Zhang
Qian Zhang
Qilong Zhang
Qiming Zhang
Qiang Zhang
Richard Zhang
Ruimao Zhang
Ruisi Zhang
Ruixin Zhang
Runze Zhang
Qilin Zhang
Shan Zhang
Shanshan Zhang
Xi Sheryl Zhang
Song-Hai Zhang
Chongyang Zhang
Kaihao Zhang
Songyang Zhang
Shu Zhang
Siwei Zhang
Shujian Zhang
Tianyun Zhang
Tong Zhang

Tao Zhang
Wenwei Zhang
Wenqiang Zhang
Wen Zhang
Xiaolin Zhang
Xingchen Zhang
Xingxuan Zhang
Xiuming Zhang
Xiaoshuai Zhang
Xuanmeng Zhang
Xuanyang Zhang
Xucong Zhang
Xingxing Zhang
Xikun Zhang
Xiaohan Zhang
Yahui Zhang
Yunhua Zhang
Yan Zhang
Yanghao Zhang
Yifei Zhang
Yifan Zhang
Yi-Fan Zhang
Yihao Zhang
Yingliang Zhang
Youshan Zhang
Yulun Zhang
Yushu Zhang
Yixiao Zhang
Yide Zhang
Zhongwen Zhang
Bowen Zhang
Chen-Lin Zhang
Zehua Zhang
Zekun Zhang
Zeyu Zhang
Xiaowei Zhang
Yifeng Zhang
Cheng Zhang
Hongguang Zhang
Yuexi Zhang
Fa Zhang
Guofeng Zhang
Hao Zhang
Haofeng Zhang
Hongwen Zhang

Hua Zhang
Jiaxin Zhang
Zhenyu Zhang
Jian Zhang
Jianfeng Zhang
Jiao Zhang
Jiakai Zhang
Lefei Zhang
Le Zhang
Mi Zhang
Min Zhang
Ning Zhang
Pan Zhang
Pu Zhang
Qing Zhang
Renrui Zhang
Shifeng Zhang
Shuo Zhang
Shaoxiong Zhang
Weizhong Zhang
Xi Zhang
Xiaomei Zhang
Xinyu Zhang
Yin Zhang
Zicheng Zhang
Zihao Zhang
Ziqi Zhang
Zhaoxiang Zhang
Zhen Zhang
Zhipeng Zhang
Zhixing Zhang
Zhizheng Zhang
Jiawei Zhang
Zhong Zhang
Pingping Zhang
Yixin Zhang
Kui Zhang
Lingzhi Zhang
Huaiwen Zhang
Quanshi Zhang
Zhoutong Zhang
Yuhang Zhang
Yuting Zhang
Zhang Zhang
Ziming Zhang

Zhizhong Zhang
Qilong Zhangli
Bingyin Zhao
Bin Zhao
Chenglong Zhao
Lei Zhao
Feng Zhao
Gangming Zhao
Haiyan Zhao
Hao Zhao
Handong Zhao
Hengshuang Zhao
Yinan Zhao
Jiaojiao Zhao
Jiaqi Zhao
Jing Zhao
Kaili Zhao
Haojie Zhao
Yucheng Zhao
Longjiao Zhao
Long Zhao
Qingsong Zhao
Qingyu Zhao
Rui Zhao
Rui-Wei Zhao
Sicheng Zhao
Shuang Zhao
Siyan Zhao
Zelin Zhao
Shiyu Zhao
Wang Zhao
Tiesong Zhao
Qian Zhao
Wangbo Zhao
Xi-Le Zhao
Xu Zhao
Yajie Zhao
Yang Zhao
Ying Zhao
Yin Zhao
Yizhou Zhao
Yunhan Zhao
Yuyang Zhao
Yue Zhao
Yuzhi Zhao

Bowen Zhao
Pu Zhao
Bingchen Zhao
Borui Zhao
Fuqiang Zhao
Hanbin Zhao
Jian Zhao
Mingyang Zhao
Na Zhao
Rongchang Zhao
Ruiqi Zhao
Shuai Zhao
Wenda Zhao
Wenliang Zhao
Xiangyun Zhao
Yifan Zhao
Yaping Zhao
Zhou Zhao
He Zhao
Jie Zhao
Xibin Zhao
Xiaoqi Zhao
Zhengyu Zhao
Jin Zhe
Chuanxia Zheng
Huan Zheng
Hao Zheng
Jia Zheng
Jian-Qing Zheng
Shuai Zheng
Meng Zheng
Mingkai Zheng
Qian Zheng
Qi Zheng
Wu Zheng
Yinqiang Zheng
Yufeng Zheng
Yutong Zheng
Yalin Zheng
Yu Zheng
Feng Zheng
Zhaoheng Zheng
Haitian Zheng
Kang Zheng
Bolun Zheng

Haiyong Zheng
Mingwu Zheng
Sipeng Zheng
Tu Zheng
Wenzhao Zheng
Xiawu Zheng
Yinglin Zheng
Zhuo Zheng
Zilong Zheng
Kecheng Zheng
Zerong Zheng
Shuaifeng Zhi
Tiancheng Zhi
Jia-Xing Zhong
Yiwu Zhong
Fangwei Zhong
Zhihang Zhong
Yaoyao Zhong
Yiran Zhong
Zhun Zhong
Zichun Zhong
Bo Zhou
Boyao Zhou
Brady Zhou
Mo Zhou
Chunluan Zhou
Dingfu Zhou
Fan Zhou
Jingkai Zhou
Honglu Zhou
Jiaming Zhou
Jiahuan Zhou
Jun Zhou
Kaiyang Zhou
Keyang Zhou
Kuangqi Zhou
Lei Zhou
Lihua Zhou
Man Zhou
Mingyi Zhou
Mingyuan Zhou
Ning Zhou
Peng Zhou
Penghao Zhou
Qianyi Zhou

Shuigeng Zhou
Shangchen Zhou
Huayi Zhou
Zhize Zhou
Sanping Zhou
Qin Zhou
Tao Zhou
Wenbo Zhou
Xiangdong Zhou
Xiao-Yun Zhou
Xiao Zhou
Yang Zhou
Yipin Zhou
Zhenyu Zhou
Hao Zhou
Chu Zhou
Daquan Zhou
Da-Wei Zhou
Hang Zhou
Kang Zhou
Qianyu Zhou
Sheng Zhou
Wenhui Zhou
Xingyi Zhou
Yan-Jie Zhou
Yiyi Zhou
Yu Zhou
Yuan Zhou
Yuqian Zhou
Yuxuan Zhou
Zixiang Zhou
Wengang Zhou
Shuchang Zhou
Tianfei Zhou
Yichao Zhou
Alex Zhu
Chenchen Zhu
Deyao Zhu
Xiatian Zhu
Guibo Zhu
Haidong Zhu
Hao Zhu
Hongzi Zhu
Rui Zhu
Jing Zhu

Jianke Zhu
Junchen Zhu
Lei Zhu
Lingyu Zhu
Luyang Zhu
Menglong Zhu
Peihao Zhu
Hui Zhu
Xiaofeng Zhu
Tyler (Lixuan) Zhu
Wentao Zhu
Xiangyu Zhu
Xinqi Zhu
Xinxin Zhu
Xinliang Zhu
Yangguang Zhu
Yichen Zhu
Yixin Zhu
Yanjun Zhu
Yousong Zhu
Yuhao Zhu
Ye Zhu
Feng Zhu
Zhen Zhu
Fangrui Zhu
Jinjing Zhu
Linchao Zhu
Pengfei Zhu
Sijie Zhu
Xiaobin Zhu
Xiaoguang Zhu
Zezhou Zhu
Zhenyao Zhu
Kai Zhu
Pengkai Zhu
Bingbing Zhuang
Chengyuan Zhuang
Liansheng Zhuang
Peiye Zhuang
Yixin Zhuang
Yihong Zhuang
Junbao Zhuo
Andrea Ziani
Bartosz Zieliński
Primo Zingaretti

Nikolaos Zioulis

Andrew Zisserman

Yael Ziv

Liu Ziyin

Xingxing Zou

Danping Zou

Qi Zou

Shihao Zou

Xueyan Zou

Yang Zou

Yuliang Zou

Zihang Zou

Chuhang Zou

Dongqing Zou

Xu Zou

Zhiming Zou

Maria A. Zuluaga

Xinxin Zuo

Zhiwen Zuo

Reyer Zwiggelaar

# Contents – Part XXV

# Cross-domain Ensemble Distillation for Domain Generalization

Kyungmoon Lee[1]([✉])(iD), Sungyeon Kim[2](iD), and Suha Kwak[2](iD)

[1] NALBI Inc., Seoul, Korea
kyungmoon@nalbi.ai
[2] POSTECH, Pohang, Korea
{sungyeon.kim,suha.kwak}@postech.ac.kr
http://cvlab.postech.ac.kr/research/XDED/

**Abstract.** Domain generalization is the task of learning models that generalize to unseen target domains. We propose a simple yet effective method for domain generalization, named cross-domain ensemble distillation (XDED), that learns domain-invariant features while encouraging the model to converge to flat minima, which recently turned out to be a sufficient condition for domain generalization. To this end, our method generates an ensemble of the output logits from training data with the same label but from different domains and then penalizes each output for the mismatch with the ensemble. Also, we present a de-stylization technique that standardizes features to encourage the model to produce style-consistent predictions even in an arbitrary target domain. Our method greatly improves generalization capability in public benchmarks for cross-domain image classification, cross-dataset person re-ID, and cross-dataset semantic segmentation. Moreover, we show that models learned by our method are robust against adversarial attacks and unseen corruptions.

**Keywords:** Domain generalization · Knowledge distillation · Flat minima

## 1 Introduction

Deep neural networks (DNNs) have brought remarkable advances in a number of research areas such as image classification [43], image synthesis [24], and reinforcement learning [54]. The huge success of DNNs depends heavily on the assumption that training and test data are sampled under the independent and identically distributed (i.i.d.) condition. However, this assumption often does not hold in real-world scenarios; a large error occurs due to the discrepancy between training and test data, also known as the domain shift problem. As a solution to

---

This work was done when Kyungmoon Lee was at POSTECH.

---

**Supplementary Information** The online version contains supplementary material available at https://doi.org/10.1007/978-3-031-19806-9_1.

S. Avidan et al. (Eds.): ECCV 2022, LNCS 13685, pp. 1–20, 2022.
https://doi.org/10.1007/978-3-031-19806-9_1

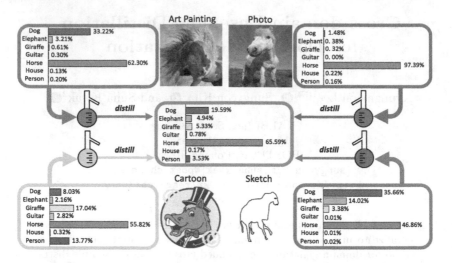

**Fig. 1.** Illustration of cross-domain ensemble distillation (XDED). Although the four images share the same class label, their predictions manifest different inter-class relations due to the visual gap between domains. XDED constructs an ensemble by averaging all predictions and matches it with each prediction.

this problem, domain generalization, the task of learning models that generalize to unseen target domains, is in the spotlight. A key to the success of domain generalization is to learn invariant features across domains. To this end, most previous methods align feature distributions of multiple domains by adversarial training [48,49], minimizing the dissimilarity between the distributions of source domains [55], or contrastive learning [40]. Then, a classifier is trained to predict the labels for the aligned source features in hopes that it will also generalize well for any target domain. However, this approach often drops performance when the target domain differs substantially from the source domains as the model is prone to overfit to the source domains.

Meanwhile, the relationship between the geometry of loss landscapes and generalization ability has attracted increasing attention [18,20,36,38]. In particular, converging to flat minima in loss landscapes is known as a key to achieve robustness against the loss landscape shift between training and test datasets. Inspired by the observation that higher posterior entropy helps a model converge to flat minima [10,60,89], entropy regularization techniques like self-knowledge distillation [87] and entropy maximization [9] have been proposed to increase entropy rather than forcing a model to completely fit training data (*i.e.*, one-hot labels) to induce low entropy. Since the degree of loss landscape shift is generally expected to be bigger in the case of domain generalization, it is more important to converge to flat minima in domain generalization. However, the benefit of flat minima in the context of domain generalization has not been actively studied yet.

In this paper, we propose a novel method, named *cross-domain ensemble distillation* (XDED), that learns domain-invariant features while encouraging convergence to flat minima for domain generalization. Specifically, XDED generates an ensemble of the output logits for the data with the same label but from different domains, and then penalizes each output for the mismatch with the ensemble (Fig. 1). By doing so, it enables a model to learn domain-invariant features by enforcing prediction consistency between the data with the same label but from different domains. Also, XDED increases the posterior entropy of each output distribution, which helps the model converge to flat minima as the entropy regularization does. To the best of our knowledge, XDED is the first to achieve these two objectives simultaneously for domain generalization, and this contribution leads to significant performance improvement.

Since XDED is still limited to exploiting the information of only source domains, there is further room to reduce the domain gap with the target domain. Hence, we also introduce a de-stylization technique well-suited to domain generalization, called UniStyle. UniStyle suppresses domain-specific style bias simply by standardizing intermediate feature maps of input image during both training and test time. Thanks to UniStyle, our model produces style-consistent predictions not only for the source domains but also for the target domain, which greatly reduces the domain gap and boosts the effect of XDED.

Based on the recent theoretical result on the relationship between the domain generalization and the flatness of local minima [8], we first empirically show that the proposed framework can improve generalization capability by achieving two goals: promoting flat minima and reducing the domain gap. Next, we further demonstrate the superiority of our method through extensive experimental results. On the standard public benchmarks for cross-domain image classification, XDED significantly enhances generalization ability in both multi-source and single-source settings. We also validate the effectiveness of our method in various domain generalization scenarios by showing the non-trivial improvement on the DomainBed [26], cross-dataset person re-ID [90,91], and cross-dataset semantic segmentation experiments. Moreover, we demonstrate that models learned by our method also help achieve robustness against adversarial attacks and unseen image corruptions.

## 2   Related Work

**Domain Generalization.** The goal of domain generalization is to learn domain-invariant features that well generalize to unseen target domains. For the purpose, existing methods match feature distributions of different domains by adversarial feature alignment [48,49] or reducing the difference between feature distributions of diverse source domains [55]. Recently, meta-learning frameworks [2,16,47] have been introduced to simulate the domain shift by dividing the meta-train and meta-test domains from source domains. Also, data augmentation methods have been proposed to generate more diverse data beyond those of given source domains [37,41,66,77,93]. Most similar to our framework, ensemble methods for domain generalization have been proposed [65,79,94]. They all train multiple modules such as exemplar SVMs [79], domain-specific BN [34] layers [65] or classifiers [94], and exploit the ensemble of learned modules for prediction in testing. However, we remark that our XDED utilizes the ensemble of model predictions as the soft label and transfers it to the model itself. Therefore, it does not demand any additional module during both training and testing.

**Knowledge Distillation (KD).** KD was originally studied to transfer the knowledge of a deep model to a shallow model for model compression [31]. It has been also used for other purposes such as metric learning [42,59] and network regularization [78,84,87]. In particular for network regularization, self-knowledge distillation (self-KD) has been studied; it distills knowledge from the model itself and enforces prediction consistency between a sample and its perturbed one or other samples. KD has been used for domain adaptation [19,52], and such method trains several teacher models from the source domains and distills the ensemble of their predictions to the student model. It unfortunately requires large memory due to multiple teachers, and are difficult to be extended to domain generalization as they demand target images in training. In contrast, our method improves generalization capability of a model on unseen domains without the need for target images and additional teacher models.

**Flat Minima in Loss Landscapes.** Recent analyses have revealed that finding flat minima is crucial for model generalization [18,20,38]. In this context, multiple methods have been proposed to promote flat minima in loss landscapes since flat minima have an advantage over sharp minima in robustness against the loss landscape shift between training and test data. Among literature on ways of promoting flat minima (*e.g.*, weight averaging [8,35] and training strategies [10,20]), we focus on the high entropy-seeking approaches, on which XDED is based. Maximum Entropy [9,60] maximizes the entropy of an output distribution from a classifier. Similarly, KD-based methods also aim at inducing high entropy of the output distribution by penalizing the mismatch with the output distribution from that of another classifier such as differently initialized peer networks [89] or subnetworks within a network itself [87]. Although SWAD [8] has introduced the importance of flat minima in the area of domain generalization, we remark that SWAD belongs to weight averaging but does not focus on learning domain-invariant features, whereas XDED belongs to entropy regularization as well as is designed for learning domain-invariant features.

**Bias Towards Styles.** Recent studies [6,22] revealed that DNNs overly depend on a strong bias towards styles, and it is also confirmed in the domain generalization literature [12,37,95] that a visual domain is highly correlated to feature statistics. Hence, previous work defines image styles as the bias and attempts to remove the bias by style augmentation in the space of feature statistics [37,95], using another model that is intentionally biased to styles [56], or minimizing a whitening loss [12]. Distinct from these techniques, we show that a simple yet effective de-stylization technique leads to a smaller divergence measure between target and source domains without bells and whistles.

## 3   Our Method

### 3.1   Cross-Domain Ensemble Distillation

**Review of Knowledge Distillation (KD).** The goal of KD [31] is to transfer knowledge of a teacher model $t$ to a student model $s$, usually a wide and deep model to a smaller one, for the purposes of model compression or model regularization. Given input data point $x$ and its label $y \in \{1, \cdots, C\}$, we denote the output logit of model as $z(x) = [z_1(x), \cdots, z_C(x)]$. The posterior predictive distribution of $x$ is then formulated as:

$$P(y|x; \theta, \tau) = \frac{\exp(z_y(x)/\tau)}{\sum_{i=1}^{C} \exp(z_i(x)/\tau)}, \tag{1}$$

where the model is parameterized by $\theta$ and $\tau$ is a temperature scaling parameter. KD enforces to match the predictive distributions of $s$ and $t$. Specifically, it is achieved by minimizing the Kullback-Leibler (KL) divergence between their predictive distributions as follows:

$$\mathcal{L}_{\text{KD}}(X; \theta_s, \tau) = \sum_{x_i \in X} \sum_{c=1}^{C} D_{KL}(P(c|x_i; \theta_t, \tau) \| P(c|x_i; \theta_s, \tau)), \tag{2}$$

where $X$ is a batch of input data, $\theta_t$ and $\theta_s$ are the parameters of a teacher and a student, respectively.

**Cross-domain Ensemble Distillation.** We propose a new KD method for domain generalization, called cross-domain ensemble distillation (XDED). XDED aims to construct the domain-invariant knowledge from the data of multiple domains. Specifically, XDED generates an ensemble of logits from the data with the same label but from different domains. Next, XDED penalizes each logit for the mismatch with the ensemble which is not biased towards a specific domain, which encourages learning domain-invariant features. Unlike the conventional KD, XDED does not require an additional network that increases training complexity (*e.g.*, extra parameters and training time) but distills the ensemble constructed by multiple samples to the model itself in the form of self-KD.

Formally, let $X_y$ denote the set of samples that have the same class label $y$ in a mini-batch. Then, we obtain an ensemble of logits from $X_y$ by simply taking an average as:

$$\bar{z}(X_y) = \sum_{x_i \in X_y} \frac{z(x_i)}{|X_y|}. \tag{3}$$

Then, the predictive distribution for the ensemble created from data $X_y$ is as:

$$\bar{P}(c|X_y; \theta, \tau) = \frac{\exp(\bar{z}_c(X_y)/\tau)}{\sum_{i=1}^{C} \exp(\bar{z}_i(X_y)/\tau)}, \tag{4}$$

The loss function of XDED is defined as follows:

$$\mathcal{L}_{\text{XDED}}(X_y; \theta, \tau) = \sum_{x_i \in X_y} \sum_{c=1}^{C} D_{KL}(\bar{P}(c|X_y; \hat{\theta}, \tau) \| P(c|x_i; \theta, \tau)), \tag{5}$$

where $\hat{\theta}$ is a fixed copy of the parameter $\theta$. Following [53, 84], we stop the gradient to be propagated through $\hat{\theta}$ to prevent the model from falling into some trivial solutions. To sum up, we set our objective function as

$$\min_{\theta} L_{\theta} = \mathcal{L}_{CE}(X, Y; \theta) + \lambda \sum_{y \in Y} \mathcal{L}_{XDED}(X_y; \theta, \tau), \tag{6}$$

where $X$ is a batch of input images, $Y$ is a batch of corresponding class labels, $\mathcal{L}_{CE}$ denotes the vanilla cross-entropy loss, and $\lambda$ is a hyperparameter to balance $\mathcal{L}_{CE}$ and $\mathcal{L}_{XDED}$. $\lambda$ and $\tau$ are 5.0 and 4.0 throughout this paper.

## 3.2   UniStyle: Removing and Unifying Style Bias

To further regularize the model to produce style-consistent predictions, we propose a de-stylization technique that is well-suited to domain generalization. As source domain styles are not expected to appear at test time, we propose UniStyle to prevent the model from being biased towards the domain-specific styles, which reduces the domain gap with the target domain.

More specifically, following existing methods based on style transfer [17, 32, 70], we first represent a neural style as statistics of intermediate feature maps from the feature extractor. Formally, let $F \in \mathbb{R}^{C \times H \times W}$ denote an intermediate feature map of an image. Then, a neural style of the image is represented as the combination of channel-wise mean $\mu(F) \in \mathbb{R}^C$ and standard deviation $\sigma(F) \in \mathbb{R}^C$ of $F$ as:

$$\mu_c(F) = \frac{1}{HW} \sum_{h=1}^{H} \sum_{w=1}^{W} F_{c,h,w}, \tag{7}$$

and

$$\sigma_c(F) = \sqrt{\frac{1}{HW} \sum_{h=1}^{H} \sum_{w=1}^{W} (F_{c,h,w} - \mu_c(F))^2}, \tag{8}$$

where $\mu(F) = [\mu_1(F), \cdots, \mu_C(F)]$ and $\sigma(F) = [\sigma_1(F), \cdots, \sigma_C(F)]$. Next, we simply standardize each feature to have constant channel-wise statistics, $\mu_W$ and $\sigma_W$ as:

$$\text{UniStyle}(F) = \sigma_W \frac{F - \mu(F)}{\sigma(F)} + \mu_W, \tag{9}$$

where $\mu_W = 0$ and $\sigma_W = 1$ (*i.e.*, zero-mean standardization). Technically, UniStyle is a special case of InstanceNorm (IN) [70]. Nevertheless, we remark that UniStyle aims to remove domain-specific information without any learnable parameters to reduce the domain gap while IN learns channel-wise scaling and bias parameters for style transfer. Also, note that we empirically observed that UniStyle is effective when being applied at multiple early layers, which is aligned with recent studies [17, 32] suggesting that the style information is usually captured at the early layers.[1]

---

[1] See the supplementary material for further analyses.

**Table 1.** Comparison of the entropy values. When each model is converged, the entropy value is calculated by averaging over all training samples.

| Methods | OfficeHome (Clipart) | | PACS (Cartoon) | |
|---|---|---|---|---|
| | Entropy | Accuracy | Entropy | Accuracy |
| ResNet-18 | 0.25 | 49.4 | 0.01 | 75.9 |
| MixStyle [95] | 0.35 | 53.4 | 0.03 | 78.8 |
| XDED | **0.92** | **55.2** | **0.38** | **81.7** |

## 3.3 Analysis of Our Method

In this section, we analyze the effectiveness of XDED, especially through the link to the theoretical result and the supporting empirical evidences. We first begin with a theorem related to domain adaptation [3,4], which shows that the expected risk on the target domain is bounded by that on the source domain and the divergence between these domains. To find a model parameter $\theta \in \Theta$ for domain generalization, Cha *et al.* [8] considered a robust empirical loss:

$$\hat{\varepsilon}_S^\gamma(\theta) := \max_{||\Delta|| \leq \gamma} \hat{\varepsilon}_S(\theta + \Delta) \tag{10}$$

where $\hat{\varepsilon}_S(\theta)$ is an empirical risk over source domains $S$ and $\gamma$ is a radius which defines neighbor parameters of $\theta$. Then, Cha *et al.* [8] proved that finding flat minima reduces the domain gap through the theorem below:

**Theorem 1.** *Consider a set of $N$ covers $\{\Theta_k\}_{k=1}^N$ such that the hypothesis space $\Theta \subset \cup_k^N \Theta_k$ where $diam(\Theta) := \sup_{\theta,\theta' \in \Theta} ||\theta - \theta'||_2, N := \lceil (diam(\Theta)/\gamma)^d \rceil$ and $d$ is dimension of $\Theta$. Let $v_k$ be a VC dimension of each $\Theta_k$. Then, for any $\theta \in \Theta$, the following bound holds with probability at least $1 - \delta$,*

$$\varepsilon_T(\theta) < \hat{\varepsilon}_S^\gamma(\theta) + \frac{1}{2I} \sum_{i=1}^I Div(S_i, T) + \max_{k \in [1,N]} \sqrt{\frac{v_k \ln(m/v_k) + \ln(N/\delta)}{m}}, \tag{11}$$

*where $m = nI$ is the number of training samples and $Div(S_i, T)$ is the divergence between the source domain $S_i$ and the target domain $T$.*

We remark that, in Eq. (11), the test loss $\varepsilon_T(\theta)$ is bounded by three terms: (1) the robust empirical loss $\hat{\varepsilon}_S^\gamma(\theta)$, (2) the divergence $Div(S_i, T)$, and (3) a confidence bound depending on the radius $\gamma$ and the number of training samples $m$. In the rest of this section, according to the above theorem, we provide a theoretical interpretation that our method enhances the generalization ability by lowering both $\hat{\varepsilon}_S^\gamma(\theta)$ and $Div(S_i, T)$ with the empirical evidences.

**Promoting Flat Minima.** We remark that XDED is motivated by recent entropy regularization methods [9,87,89] in pursuit of flat minima. It has been empirically demonstrated that these methods promote flat minima by inducing higher posterior entropy. It can be interpreted as relaxing the training procedure

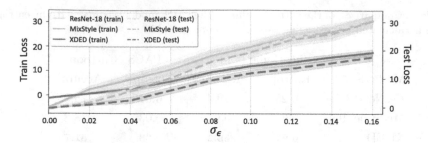

**Fig. 2.** Train/Test losses versus the weight perturbation while varying the standard deviation of the added Gaussian noise. Note that the results are produced with the target domain (Art of PACS) and the rest source domains, and the loss values are log-scaled.

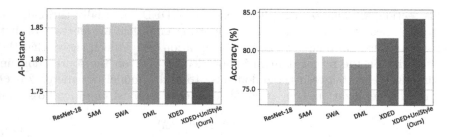

**Fig. 3.** Comparison to existing methods promoting flat minima. Each model is evaluated on Cartoon of PACS after being trained on the rest source domains. **Left:** The divergence ($\mathcal{A}$-distance) between the source domains and the target domain, **Right:** Generalization performance on the target domain.

to learn richer information encoded in soft labels, which helps the model converge to flat minima more than forcing the model to completely fit one-hot labels. In this context, we also demonstrate that XDED clearly induces higher entropy as shown in Table 1. Considering that XDED is motivated by the observation that different domains manifest different inter-class relations due to the domain gap (Fig. 1), this is natural since our ensembles would integrate meaningful inter-class relations from multiple domains and the model learned with them would be led towards high entropy.

Next, to investigate whether the model learned with XDED converges to flat minima indeed, we quantify the flatness of the local minima where the model converged by measuring the increase of loss values between $\theta$ and its neighborhoods, assuming that the model converged in flat minima would have smaller increases. Following [8,9,87,89], we measure the losses of the learned models before and after adding Gaussian noises to model parameters while varying the standard deviation of the noise $\sigma_\epsilon$ (*i.e.*, $\mathcal{L}_{\mathrm{CE}}(X, Y; \theta + \epsilon)$ where $\epsilon \sim N(0, \sigma_\epsilon)$) with 100 runs. As a result, XDED demonstrates its robustness against the weight perturbation with smaller loss increases as shown in Fig. 2.

**Domain-Invariant Feature Learning.** Here, we highlight that XDED also learns domain-invariant features via regularizing the consistency between the predictions from the data with the same label but from different domains and their ensemble. Thus, we compare XDED with existing methods promoting flat minima, which are dedicated to the flatness of local minima only. Specifically, to examine the effectiveness in reducing the divergence $\text{Div}(S_i, T)$, we measure $\mathcal{A}$-distance [3,39]. Due to the computational intractability, we calculated an approximated one [50,56][2] As shown in Fig. 3 (Left), we observe that the existing methods promoting flat minima fail to reduce the distance while XDED clearly lowers the distance and UniStyle further enhances the result. Naturally, that result is connected to the quantitative superiority of our framework over existing flat minima-promoting methods (Fig. 3 (Right)).

## 4    Experiments

### 4.1    Generalization in Image Classification

**Multi-source Domain Generalization.** Specifically, for a fair comparison, we follow the leave-one-domain-out protocol [45] where we train a model on three domains and evaluate it on the remaining domain. For the benchmark datasets, we employ the PACS [45] and OfficeHome [72] that are widely-used benchmarks for domain generalization in image classification. PACS contains 9,991 images of 7 classes over 4 domains: Art Painting, Cartoon, Photo, and Sketch. OfficeHome includes 15,500 images of 65 classes over 4 domains: Artistic, Clipart, Product, and Real. We use ResNet-18 [27] as the backbone, and our UniStyle is applied to output feature maps of the first and second residual blocks for PACS and the first one only for OfficeHome.

**Results.** As summarized in Table. 2, we observe that our method not only significantly enhances the vanilla but also outperforms the latest competing methods. In particular, our method outperforms the second-best method on Cartoon of PACS and Clipart of OfficeHome by about 4.0% and 2.0%, respectively. These results justify the superiority of our method, which is simple yet effective.

**Single-source Domain Generalization.** Thanks to the simple design of our proposed method, which does not explicitly require domain labels, our method can be transparently incorporated with single-source domain generalization where we only have access to a single source domain during training. Therefore, to further evaluate the impact of our method on single-source domain generalization, our model is trained on each single domain of PACS and evaluated on the remaining target domains.

**Results.** As shown in Table. 3, our model, on average, significantly outperforms other baselines by 8.7% in average accuracy. Besides, in all cases except for the case of $C \rightarrow S$, our model shows its superiority in performance. We believe this interesting result stems from the fact that our method is still able to help the model converge to flat minima and exploit the fine-grained relations between intra-domain samples even if only a single source domain is given.

**Table 2.** Leave-one-domain-out generalization results on PACS and OfficeHome.

| Methods | PACS | | | | | OfficeHome | | | | |
|---|---|---|---|---|---|---|---|---|---|---|
| | Art | Cartoon | Photo | Sketch | Avg. | Artistic | Clipart | Product | Real | Avg. |
| ResNet-18 | 77.0 | 75.9 | 96.0 | 69.2 | 79.5 | 58.9 | 49.4 | 74.3 | 76.2 | 64.7 |
| MMD-AE [48] | 75.2 | 72.7 | 96.0 | 64.2 | 77.0 | 56.5 | 47.3 | 72.1 | 74.8 | 62.7 |
| JiGen [7] | 79.4 | 75.3 | 96.0 | 71.6 | 80.5 | 53.0 | 47.4 | 71.4 | 72.7 | 61.2 |
| CrossGrad [66] | 79.8 | 76.8 | 96.0 | 70.2 | 80.7 | 58.4 | 49.4 | 73.9 | 75.8 | 64.4 |
| MASF [16] | 80.2 | 77.1 | 94.9 | 71.6 | 81.0 | – | – | – | – | – |
| Epi-FCR [47] | 82.1 | 77.0 | 93.9 | 73.0 | 81.5 | – | – | – | – | – |
| EISNet [74] | 81.8 | 76.4 | 95.9 | 74.3 | 82.1 | – | – | – | – | – |
| L2A-OT [93] | 83.3 | 78.2 | <u>96.2</u> | 73.6 | 82.8 | <u>60.6</u> | 50.1 | <u>74.8</u> | **77.0** | 65.6 |
| SagNet [56] | 83.5 | 77.6 | 95.4 | 76.3 | 83.2 | 60.2 | 45.3 | 70.4 | 73.3 | 62.3 |
| SelfReg [40] | 82.3 | 78.4 | <u>96.2</u> | 77.4 | 83.6 | – | – | – | – | – |
| MixStyle [95] | 84.1 | 78.8 | 96.1 | 75.9 | 83.7 | 58.7 | 53.4 | 74.2 | 75.9 | 65.5 |
| L2D [75] | 81.4 | 79.5 | 95.5 | 80.5 | 84.2 | – | – | – | – | – |
| FACT [77] | <u>85.3</u> | 78.3 | 95.1 | 79.1 | 84.5 | 60.3 | 54.8 | 74.4 | <u>76.5</u> | <u>66.5</u> |
| DSON [65] | 84.6 | 77.6 | 95.8 | <u>82.2</u> | 85.1 | 59.3 | 45.7 | 71.8 | 74.6 | 62.9 |
| RSC [33] | 83.4 | <u>80.3</u> | 95.9 | 80.8 | 85.1 | 58.4 | 47.9 | 71.6 | 74.5 | 63.1 |
| StyleNeophile [37] | 84.4 | 79.2 | 94.9 | **83.2** | <u>85.4</u> | 59.5 | <u>55.0</u> | 73.5 | 75.5 | 65.8 |
| Ours | **85.6** | **84.2** | **96.5** | 79.1 | **86.4** | **60.8** | **57.1** | **75.3** | <u>76.5</u> | **67.4** |

**Table 3.** Single-source domain generalization accuracy (%) on PACS with a ResNet-18. (A: Art Painting, C: Cartoon, S:Sketch, P:Photo).

| Methods | A→C | A→S | A→P | C→A | C→S | C→P | S→A | S→C | S→P | P→A | P→C | P→S | Avg. |
|---|---|---|---|---|---|---|---|---|---|---|---|---|---|
| ResNet-18 | 62.3 | 49.0 | 95.2 | 65.7 | 60.7 | 83.6 | 28.0 | 54.5 | 35.6 | 64.1 | 23.6 | 29.1 | 54.3 |
| JiGen [7] | 57.0 | 50.0 | 96.1 | 65.3 | 65.9 | 85.5 | 26.6 | 41.1 | 42.8 | 62.4 | 27.2 | 35.5 | 54.6 |
| MixStyle [95] | 65.5 | 49.8 | <u>96.7</u> | 69.9 | 64.5 | 85.3 | 27.1 | 50.9 | 32.6 | 67.7 | <u>38.9</u> | 39.1 | 57.4 |
| RSC [33] | 62.5 | 53.1 | 96.2 | 68.9 | **70.3** | 85.8 | 37.9 | 56.3 | <u>47.4</u> | 66.3 | 26.4 | 32.0 | 58.6 |
| SelfReg [40] | 65.2 | 55.9 | 96.6 | 72.0 | <u>70.0</u> | <u>87.5</u> | 37.1 | 54.0 | 46.0 | 67.7 | 28.9 | 33.7 | 59.5 |
| SagNet [56] | <u>67.1</u> | <u>56.8</u> | 95.7 | <u>72.1</u> | 69.2 | 85.7 | <u>41.1</u> | <u>62.9</u> | 46.2 | <u>69.8</u> | 35.1 | <u>40.7</u> | <u>61.9</u> |
| Ours | **74.6** | **58.1** | **96.8** | **74.4** | 69.6 | **87.6** | **43.3** | **65.6** | **50.3** | **71.4** | **54.3** | **51.5** | **66.5** |

**DomainBed.** We also conduct extensive experiments on the DomainBed [26] which is a testbed for domain generalization to compare state-of-the-art methods across several benchmark datasets. The rationale behind the DomainBed is that the domain generalization performances are too much dependent on the hyperparameter tuning. For a fair comparison, we follow its standard protocols for training and evaluation.

**Results.** As shown in Table. 4, our method generally shows competitive performances and ranks second out of 15 methods on average accuracy. In particular, on CMNIST, our method substantially outperforms other competing methods. Since CMNIST is designed to simulate the domain shift by correlating the digit colors with the class labels, we conjecture that our improvement on CMNIST is attributed to the de-stylization effect of UniStyle, which would help the model decorrelate between the colors and labels.

---

[2] It is defined as $\hat{d}_{\mathcal{A}} = 2(1 - 2\epsilon_{\text{svm}})$ where $\epsilon_{\text{svm}}$ is the generalization error of a SVM-based two-class classifier trained to distinguish between target and source domains.

**Table 4.** Domain generalization accuracy (%) on DomainBed. The column "Terra" stands for TerraIncognita dataset. Note that we adopt leave-one-domain-out cross-validation as a model selection criteria.

| | Model selection: leave-one-domain-out cross-validation | | | | | | |
|---|---|---|---|---|---|---|---|
| Methods | CMNIST | RMNIST | VLCS | PACS | OfficeHome | Terra | Avg. |
| ERM [71] | 36.7 | 97.7 | 77.2 | 83.0 | 65.7 | 41.4 | 66.9 |
| IRM [1] | 40.3 | 97.0 | 76.3 | 81.5 | 64.3 | 41.2 | 66.7 |
| GroupDRO [64] | 36.8 | 97.6 | 77.9 | 83.5 | 65.2 | 44.9 | 66.7 |
| Mixup [86] | 33.4 | 97.8 | 77.7 | 83.2 | 67.0 | **48.7** | 67.9 |
| MLDG [46] | 36.7 | 97.6 | 77.2 | 82.9 | 66.1 | 46.2 | 67.7 |
| CORAL [68] | 39.7 | 97.8 | **78.7** | 82.6 | **68.5** | 46.3 | **68.9** |
| MMD [48] | 36.8 | 97.8 | 77.3 | 83.2 | 60.2 | 46.5 | 66.9 |
| DANN [21] | 40.7 | 97.6 | 76.9 | 81.0 | 64.9 | 44.4 | 67.5 |
| CDANN [49] | 39.1 | 97.5 | 77.5 | 78.8 | 64.3 | 39.9 | 66.1 |
| MTL [5] | 35.0 | 97.8 | 76.6 | 83.7 | 65.7 | 44.9 | 67.2 |
| SagNet [56] | 36.5 | 94.0 | 77.5 | 82.3 | 67.6 | 47.2 | 67.5 |
| ARM [88] | 36.8 | **98.1** | 76.6 | 81.7 | 64.4 | 42.6 | 66.7 |
| VREx [44] | 36.9 | 93.6 | 76.7 | 81.3 | 64.9 | 37.3 | 65.1 |
| RSC [33] | 36.5 | 97.6 | 77.5 | 82.6 | 65.8 | 40.0 | 66.6 |
| Ours | **46.5** | 97.7 | 74.8 | **83.8** | 65.0 | 42.5 | 68.4 |

**Table 5.** Generalization results on the cross-dataset person re-ID.

| | Market → Duke | | Duke → Market | |
|---|---|---|---|---|
| Methods | mAP | R@1 | mAP | R@1 |
| ResNet-50 | 19.3 | 35.4 | 20.4 | 45.2 |
| RandomErase [92] | 14.3 | 27.8 | 16.1 | 38.5 |
| DropBlock [23] | 18.2 | 33.2 | 19.7 | 45.3 |
| MixStyle [95] | 23.4 | 43.3 | 24.7 | 53.0 |
| StyleNeophile [37] | 26.3 | 46.5 | 27.2 | 55.0 |
| Ours | **27.4** | **49.3** | **30.1** | **59.0** |

## 4.2   Generalization in Person Re-ID

In this section, we further evaluate our method on person re-identification (re-ID), which is to match pedestrians across non-overlapping camera views.

**Experimental Setup.** Here, we address domain generalization for person re-ID, where the test data is collected from cameras of the unseen dataset rather than from those of the training dataset. Specifically, the model trained to match people in the source dataset is evaluated by how well it matches pedestrian data of the unseen test set, which are disjoint from the source dataset. For datasets, we adopt two widely-used benchmarks: Market1501 (Market) [90] and DukeMTMC-reID (Duke) [62,91]. We use 32,668 images of 1,501 identities collected from 6 cameras and 36,411 images of 1,812 identities from 8 cameras for Market1501 and Duke, respectively. As for performance measures, we adopt mean average precision (mAP) and Recall@K (R@K). Following the prior work [95], we adopt ResNet-50 [27] as a backbone architecture. In these experiments, we apply UniStyle to the 1st, 2nd, and 3rd residual blocks of a model.

**Table 6.** mIoU (%) results on the cross-dataset semantic segmentation. GTA5 is for training, and Cityscapes, SYNTHIA, BDD, and Mapillary are test sets.

| Methods (GTA5) | Cityscapes | BDD | Mapillary | SYNTHIA |
|---|---|---|---|---|
| DeepLabV3+ [11] | 28.9 | 25.1 | 28.1 | 26.2 |
| SW [58] | 29.9 | 27.4 | 29.7 | 27.6 |
| DRPC [82] | <u>37.4</u> | 32.1 | 34.1 | <u>28.0</u> |
| RobustNet [12] | 36.5 | **35.2** | **40.3** | **28.3** |
| Ours | **39.2** | <u>32.4</u> | <u>37.1</u> | <u>28.0</u> |

**Comparison to Other Regularization Methods.** As shown in Table. 5, our method substantially outperforms other methods in mAP and Recall@1. Although RandomErase and Dropblock are effective for learning discriminative features, they fail to improve performance when encountering unseen domain data. Furthermore, by exploiting inter-class relations provided by different cameras, our method shows its superiority over MixStyle and StyleNeophile which are designed for domain generalization but utilizes one-hot labels only.

### 4.3   Generalization in Semantic Segmentation

**Experimental Setup.** Lastly, to investigate whether our method can be extended to the dense prediction task, evaluation on semantic segmentation is addressed here. Following the mainstream protocol, we train models on a synthetic dataset and evaluate them on several datasets which mainly belong to real-world. Specifically, we adopt GTA5 [61] as a source dataset which consists of 24,966 images. For target datasets, Cityscapes [13], BDD [81], and Mapillary [57] are real-world datasets whose image sizes are 5,000, 10,000, and 25,000, respectively. Lastly, SYNTHIA [63] has 9,400 images. Note that ResNet-50 is used as the backbone and the common 19 classes are used across all datasets.

**Results.** We remark that XDED constructs an ensemble by simply averaging all the logits from the pixels whose gt is the same in a mini-batch. As shown in Table 6, ours outperforms the competing methods overall, even if those are dedicated to this task only. We show that our method can be extended to the pixel-wise classification with little modification on XDED. Also, the results support our claim that our method is simple yet effective in a wide range of tasks.

### 4.4   In-depth Analysis

**Ablation Study.** To investigate the impact of each component in our method, we conduct an ablation study which is summarized in Table 7. The result reveals that two components are complementary and consistently help the model improve the generalization ability. For image classification, XDED contributes most to the performance, and UniStyle boosts the effect of XDED. On both

**Table 7.** Ablation study of the proposed components on cross-domain tasks of image classification (Accuracy) and person re-ID (mAP).

| Methods | Art | Clipart | Market → Duke |
|---------|-----|---------|---------------|
| Vanilla | 77.0 | 49.4 | 19.3 |
| w/UniStyle | 81.2 | 50.4 | <u>26.2</u> |
| w/XDED | <u>83.3</u> | <u>55.2</u> | 24.2 |
| Ours | **85.6** | **57.1** | **27.4** |

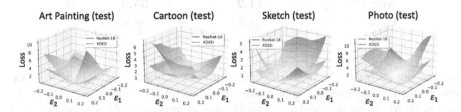

**Fig. 4.** Visualization results of the loss landscapes incorporating the vanilla method and XDED on the PACS dataset. Note that each loss landscape is visualized on the data of source domains, not the data of the marked target domain. Blue and red surfaces are from the vanilla method and XDED, respectively.

**Table 8.** Multi-source domain generalization accuracy (%) on Photo of PACS before and after applying given adversarial attacks.

| Methods | Photo | w/FGSM | w/PGD |
|---------|-------|--------|-------|
| ResNet-18 | 96.0 | 39.6 | 16.3 |
| Label smoothing [69] | 95.6 | 43.5 | 20.2 |
| Mixup [86] | 95.8 | 46.5 | 21.9 |
| Manifold mixup [73] | 93.5 | <u>46.6</u> | <u>23.8</u> |
| MixStyle [95] | <u>96.1</u> | 41.4 | 22.7 |
| Ours | **96.5** | **55.4** | **30.4** |

domains, XDED uniformly improves the vanilla method by about 6%, whereas UniStyle shows different degrees of improvement. It is because the image style discrepancy between domains in OfficeHome is less severe than that in PACS. Interestingly, for the task of person re-ID, UniStyle reveals more impact than does XDED. Due to the inherent characteristics of the task itself, the effect of XDED on collecting meaningful knowledge of the same pedestrian from different cameras may become less significant.

**Loss Surface Visualization.** To further illustrate how XDED leads to flat minima in the loss landscapes, we provide qualitative results that visualize the loss landscapes. Following [9], we plot the loss landscapes on data of source

**Table 9.** Average classification error (%) on the corruption benchmarks.

| Methods | CIFAR-10-C | CIFAR-100-C |
|---|---|---|
| 40-2 WRN [85] | 26.9 | 53.3 |
| Cutout [15] | 26.8 | 53.5 |
| Mixup [86] | 22.3 | 50.4 |
| CutMix [83] | 27.1 | 52.9 |
| AutoAug [14] | 23.9 | 49.6 |
| AugMix [29] | **11.2** | **35.9** |
| Ours | 18.5 | 46.6 |

domains per each case by perturbing the model parameters across the first and second Hessian eigenvectors which are provided by PyHessian [80] which is a framework for Hessian-based analysis of neural networks. As shown in Fig. 4, we observe that the loss landscapes incorporating XDED clearly become flatter than those incorporating the vanilla method for all cases. We argue that these qualitative results also consistently support that XDED promotes flat minima.

**Robustness to Adversarial Examples.** Recent studies have demonstrated that convergence on flat minima strengthens the adversarial robustness [67,76]. To revalidate that our method promotes flat minima, we evaluate the adversarial robustness of learned models. Specifically, we trained models on source domains and added adversarial perturbations on images of the unseen target domain by using existing adversarial attack methods: FGSM [25] and PGD [51]. Table 8 shows that our method outperforms other regularization methods in terms of robustness against both unseen data and adversarial attacks. Considering that adversarial attacks are made to maximize the loss value, we argue that our superiority in adversarial robustness is also attributed to the capability of promoting flat minima as desired, even though our method has no direct connection to adversarial training.

**Results on Corruption Benchmarks.** We further measure the resilience of learned models to unseen corruptions. Following the protocol provided by [28], we trained models on the original training dataset, and evaluated them on the test dataset constructed by corrupting the original test dataset through predefined corruption types. Table. 9 shows that our method outperforms all regularization methods except AugMix [30]. Considering AugMix is a state of the art that is dedicated to corruption robustness while ours is not, we argue that our method still shows its significant robustness against unseen corruptions.

## 5   Conclusion

We have presented a simple yet effective framework for domain generalization. XDED first generates an ensemble of output distributions for the data with the same label but from different domains, and then penalizes each output distribution for the mismatch with the ensemble in the form of self-knowledge distillation. With this approach, our model can learn domain-invariant features and also easily converges to flat minima. Besides, the proposed UniStyle suppresses domain-specific style bias to boost the effect of XDED and encourage style-consistent predictions. Furthermore, we empirically validate the generalization ability of the proposed method from the perspective of flat minima and reduced divergence between source and target. Through extensive experimental results, we demonstrate the superiority of the proposed framework.

**Acknowledgement.** This work was supported by the NRF grant and the NRF grant and the IITP grant funded by Ministry of Science and ICT, Korea (NRF-2021R1A2C3012728, IITP-2019-0-01906, IITP-2022-0-00926, IITP-2022-0-00290).

# References

1. Arjovsky, M., Bottou, L., Gulrajani, I., Lopez-Paz, D.: Invariant risk minimization. arXiv preprint arXiv:1907.02893 (2019)
2. Balaji, Y., Sankaranarayanan, S., Chellappa, R.: Metareg: Towards domain generalization using meta-regularization. In: Proceedings of Neural Information Processing Systems (NeurIPS) (2018)
3. Ben-David, S., Blitzer, J., Crammer, K., Kulesza, A., Pereira, F., Vaughan, J.W.: A theory of learning from different domains. Mach. Learn. **79**, 151–175 (2010)
4. Ben-David, S., et al.: Analysis of representations for domain adaptation. In: Proceedings of Neural Information Processing Systems (NeurIPS) (2007)
5. Blanchard, G., Deshmukh, A.A., Dogan, U., Lee, G., Scott, C.: Domain generalization by marginal transfer learning. J. Mach. Learn. Res. **22** (2021)
6. Brendel, W., Bethge, M.: Approximating CNNs with bag-of-local-features models works surprisingly well on ImageNet. In: Proceedings International Conference on Learning Representations (ICLR) (2019)
7. Carlucci, F.M., D'Innocente, A., Bucci, S., Caputo, B., Tommasi, T.: Domain generalization by solving jigsaw puzzles. In: Proceedings of IEEE Conference on Computer Vision and Pattern Recognition (CVPR) (2019)
8. Cha, J.,et al.: SWAD: domain generalization by seeking flat minima. In: Proceedings of Neural Information Processing Systems (NeurIPS) (2021)
9. Cha, S., Hsu, H., Hwang, T., Calmon, F.P., Moon, T.: CPR: classifier-projection regularization for continual learning. In: Proceedings of International Conference on Learning Representations (ICLR) (2021)
10. Chaudhari, P., et al.: Entropy-SGD: biasing gradient descent into wide valleys. In: Proc. International Conference on Learning Representations (ICLR) (2017)
11. Chen, L.C., Zhu, Y., Papandreou, G., Schroff, F., Adam, H.: Encoder-decoder with atrous separable convolution for semantic image segmentation. In: Proceedings of European Conference on Computer Vision (ECCV) (2018)
12. Choi, S., Jung, S., Yun, H., Kim, J.T., Kim, S., Choo, J.: RobustNet: Improving domain generalization in urban-scene segmentation via instance selective whitening. In: Proceedings of IEEE Conference on Computer Vision and Pattern Recognition (CVPR) (2021)

13. Cordts, M., et al.: The cityscapes dataset for semantic urban scene understanding. In: Proceedings of IEEE Conference on Computer Vision and Pattern Recognition (CVPR) (2016)
14. Cubuk, E.D., Zoph, B., Mane, D., Vasudevan, V., Le, Q.V.: Autoaugment: Learning augmentation policies from data. In: 2019 IEEE/CVF Conference on Computer Vision and Pattern Recognition (CVPR) (2019)
15. DeVries, T., Taylor, G.W.: Improved regularization of convolutional neural networks with cutout. arXiv preprint arXiv:1708.04552 (2017)
16. Dou, Q., Coelho de Castro, D., Kamnitsas, K., Glocker, B.: Domain generalization via model-agnostic learning of semantic features. In: Proceedings of Neural Information Processing Systems (NeurIPS) (2019)
17. Dumoulin, V., Shlens, J., Kudlur, M.: A learned representation for artistic style. In: Proceedings of International Conference on Learning Representations (ICLR) (2017)
18. Dziugaite, G.K., Roy, D.M.: Computing nonvacuous generalization bounds for deep (stochastic) neural networks with many more parameters than training data. In: Proceedings of the Conference on Uncertainty in Artificial Intelligence (UAI) (2017)
19. Feng, H.Z., et al.: KD3A: Unsupervised multi-source decentralized domain adaptation via knowledge distillation. In: Proceedings of International Conference on Machine Learning (ICML) (2021)
20. Foret, P., Kleiner, A., Mobahi, H., Neyshabur, B.: Sharpness-aware minimization for efficiently improving generalization. In: Proceedings of International Conference on Learning Representations (ICLR) (2021)
21. Ganin, Y., et al.: Domain-adversarial training of neural networks. In: Csurka, Gabriela (ed.) Domain Adaptation in Computer Vision Applications. ACVPR, pp. 189–209. Springer, Cham (2017). https://doi.org/10.1007/978-3-319-58347-1_10
22. Geirhos, R., Rubisch, P., Michaelis, C., Bethge, M., Wichmann, F.A., Brendel, W.: ImageNet-trained CNNs are biased towards texture; increasing shape bias improves accuracy and robustness. In: Proceedings of International Conference on Learning Representations (ICLR) (2019)
23. Ghiasi, G., Lin, T.Y., Le, Q.V.: Dropblock: A regularization method for convolutional networks. In: Proceedings of Neural Information Processing Systems (NeurIPS) (2018)
24. Goodfellow, I., et al.: Generative adversarial nets. In: Proceedings of Neural Information Processing Systems (NeurIPS) (2014)
25. Goodfellow, I.J., Shlens, J., Szegedy, C.: Explaining and harnessing adversarial examples. In: Proceedings of International Conference on Learning Representations (ICLR) (2014)
26. Gulrajani, I., Lopez-Paz, D.: In search of lost domain generalization. In: Proceedings of International Conference on Learning Representations (ICLR) (2021)
27. He, K., Zhang, X., Ren, S., Sun, J.: Deep residual learning for image recognition. In: Proceedings of IEEE Conference on Computer Vision and Pattern Recognition (CVPR) (June 2016)
28. Hendrycks, D., Dietterich, T.: Benchmarking neural network robustness to common corruptions and perturbations. In: Proceedings of International Conference on Learning Representations (ICLR) (2019)
29. Hendrycks, D., Mu, N., Cubuk, E.D., Zoph, B., Gilmer, J., Lakshminarayanan, B.: AugMix: a simple data processing method to improve robustness and uncertainty (2020)

30. Hendrycks, D., Mu, N., Cubuk, E.D., Zoph, B., Gilmer, J., Lakshminarayanan, B.: AugMix: a simple data processing method to improve robustness and uncertainty. In: Proceedings of International Conference on Learning Representations (ICLR) (2020)
31. Hinton, G., Vinyals, O., Dean, J.: Distilling the knowledge in a neural network. arXiv preprint arXiv:1503.02531 (2015)
32. Huang, X., Belongie, S.: Arbitrary style transfer in real-time with adaptive instance normalization. In: Proceedings of IEEE International Conference on Computer Vision (ICCV) (2017)
33. Huang, Z., Wang, H., Xing, E.P., Huang, D.: Self-challenging improves cross-domain generalization. In: Proceedings of European Conference on Computer Vision (ECCV) (2020)
34. Ioffe, S., Szegedy, C.: Batch normalization: Accelerating deep network training by reducing internal covariate shift. In: Proceedings of International Conference on Machine Learning (ICML) (2015)
35. Izmailov, P., Podoprikhin, D., Garipov, T., Vetrov, D., Wilson, A.G.: Averaging weights leads to wider optima and better generalization. In: Proceedings of the Conference on Uncertainty in Artificial Intelligence (UAI) (2018)
36. Jiang, Y., Neyshabur, B., Mobahi, H., Krishnan, D., Bengio, S.: Fantastic generalization measures and where to find them. In: Proceedings of International Conference on Learning Representations (ICLR) (2020)
37. Kang, J., Lee, S., Kim, N., Kwak, S.: Style neophile: constantly seeking novel styles for domain generalization. In: Proceedings of IEEE Conference on Computer Vision and Pattern Recognition (CVPR) (2022)
38. Keskar, N.S., Mudigere, D., Nocedal, J., Smelyanskiy, M., Tang, P.T.P.: On large-batch training for deep learning: Generalization gap and sharp minima. In: Proceedings of International Conference on Learning Representations (ICLR) (2017)
39. Kifer, D., Ben-David, S., Gehrke, J.: Detecting change in data streams. In: In Very Large Databases (VLDB) (2004)
40. Kim, D., Park, S., Kim, J., Lee, J.: SelfReg: self-supervised contrastive regularization for domain generalization. In: Proceedings of IEEE International Conference on Computer Vision (ICCV) (2021)
41. Kim, N., Son, T., Lan, C., Zeng, W., Kwak, S.: Wedge: web-image assisted domain generalization for semantic segmentation. arXiv preprint arXiv:2109.14196 (2021)
42. Kim, S., Kim, D., Cho, M., Kwak, S.: Embedding transfer with label relaxation for improved metric learning. In: Proceedings of IEEE Conference on Computer Vision and Pattern Recognition (CVPR) (2021)
43. Krizhevsky, A., Sutskever, I., Hinton, G.E.: ImageNet classification with deep convolutional neural networks. In: Proceedings of Neural Information Processing Systems (NeurIPS) (2012)
44. Krueger, D., et al.: Out-of-distribution generalization via risk extrapolation (rex). In: Proceedings of International Conference on Machine Learning (ICML) (2021)
45. Li, D., Yang, Y., Song, Y.Z., Hospedales, T.M.: Deeper, broader and artier domain generalization. In: Proceedings of IEEE International Conference on Computer Vision (ICCV) (2017)
46. Li, D., Yang, Y., Song, Y.Z., Hospedales, T.M.: Learning to generalize: meta-learning for domain generalization. In: Proceedings of AAAI Conference on Artificial Intelligence (AAAI) (2018)
47. Li, D., Zhang, J., Yang, Y., Liu, C., Song, Y.Z., Hospedales, T.M.: Episodic training for domain generalization. In: Proceedings of IEEE International Conference on Computer Vision (ICCV) (2019)

48. Li, H., Pan, S.J., Wang, S., Kot, A.C.: Domain generalization with adversarial feature learning. In: Proceedings of IEEE Conference on Computer Vision and Pattern Recognition (CVPR) (2018)
49. Li, Y., et al.: Deep domain generalization via conditional invariant adversarial networks. In: Proceedings of European Conference on Computer Vision (ECCV) (2018)
50. Long, M., Cao, Y., Wang, J., Jordan, M.: Learning transferable features with deep adaptation networks. In: Proceedings of International Conference on Machine Learning (ICML) (2015)
51. Madry, A., Makelov, A., Schmidt, L., Tsipras, D., Vladu, A.: Towards deep learning models resistant to adversarial attacks. In: Proceedings of International Conference on Learning Representations (ICLR) (2018)
52. Meng, Z., Li, J., Gong, Y., Juang, B.H.: Adversarial teacher-student learning for unsupervised domain adaptation. In: 2018 IEEE International Conference on Acoustics, Speech and Signal Processing (ICASSP) (2018)
53. Miyato, T., Maeda, S.i., Koyama, M., Ishii, S.: Virtual adversarial training: a regularization method for supervised and semi-supervised learning. In: IEEE Transactions on Pattern Analysis and Machine Intelligence (TPAMI) (2018)
54. Mnih, V., et al.: Playing atari with deep reinforcement learning. In: NeurIPS Deep Learning Workshop (2013)
55. Muandet, K., Balduzzi, D., Schölkopf, B.: Domain generalization via invariant feature representation. In: Proceedings of International Conference on Machine Learning (ICML) (2013)
56. Nam, H., Lee, H., Park, J., Yoon, W., Yoo, D.: Reducing domain gap by reducing style bias. In: Proceedings of IEEE Conference on Computer Vision and Pattern Recognition (CVPR) (2021)
57. Neuhold, G., Ollmann, T., Rota Bulo, S., Kontschieder, P.: The mapillary vistas dataset for semantic understanding of street scenes. In: Proceedings of IEEE International Conference on Computer Vision (ICCV) (2017)
58. Pan, X., Zhan, X., Shi, J., Tang, X., Luo, P.: Switchable whitening for deep representation learning. In: Proceedings of IEEE International Conference on Computer Vision (ICCV) (2019)
59. Park, W., Kim, D., Lu, Y., Cho, M.: Relational knowledge distillation. In: Proceedings of IEEE Conference on Computer Vision and Pattern Recognition (CVPR) (2019)
60. Pereyra, G., Tucker, G., Chorowski, J., Kaiser, Ł., Hinton, G.: Regularizing neural networks by penalizing confident output distributions. In: ICLR Workshop (2017)
61. Richter, S.R., Vineet, V., Roth, S., Koltun, V.: Playing for data: Ground truth from computer games. In: Proceedings of European Conference on Computer Vision (ECCV) (2016)
62. Ristani, E., Solera, F., Zou, R., Cucchiara, R., Tomasi, C.: Performance measures and a data set for multi-target, multi-camera tracking. In: Proceedings of European Conference on Computer Vision (ECCV) (2016)
63. Ros, G., Sellart, L., Materzynska, J., Vazquez, D., Lopez, A.M.: The SYNTHIA dataset: a large collection of synthetic images for semantic segmentation of urban scenes. In: Proceedings of IEEE Conference on Computer Vision and Pattern Recognition (CVPR) (2016)
64. Sagawa, S., Koh, P.W., Hashimoto, T.B., Liang, P.: Distributionally robust neural networks for group shifts: On the importance of regularization for worst-case generalization. In: Proceedings of International Conference on Learning Representations (ICLR) (2020)

65. Seo, S., Suh, Y., Kim, D., Kim, G., Han, J., Han, B.: Learning to optimize domain specific normalization for domain generalization. In: Proceedings of European Conference on Computer Vision (ECCV) (2020)
66. Shankar, S., Piratla, V., Chakrabarti, S., Chaudhuri, S., Jyothi, P., Sarawagi, S.: Generalizing across domains via cross-gradient training. In: Proceedings of International Conference on Learning Representations (ICLR) (2018)
67. Stutz, D., Hein, M., Schiele, B.: Relating adversarially robust generalization to flat minima. In: Proceedings of IEEE International Conference on Computer Vision (ICCV) (2021)
68. Sun, B., Saenko, K.: Deep coral: Correlation alignment for deep domain adaptation. In: Proceedings of European Conference on Computer Vision (ECCV) (2016)
69. Szegedy, C., Vanhoucke, V., Ioffe, S., Shlens, J., Wojna, Z.: Rethinking the inception architecture for computer vision. In: Proceedings of IEEE Conference on Computer Vision and Pattern Recognition (CVPR) (2016)
70. Ulyanov, D., Vedaldi, A., Lempitsky, V.: Instance normalization: The missing ingredient for fast stylization. arXiv preprint arXiv:1607.08022 (2016)
71. Vapnik, V.: Statistical Learning Theory. Wiley, New York (1998)
72. Venkateswara, H., Eusebio, J., Chakraborty, S., Panchanathan, S.: Deep hashing network for unsupervised domain adaptation. In: Proceedings of IEEE Conference on Computer Vision and Pattern Recognition (CVPR) (2017)
73. Verma, V., et al.: Manifold mixup: better representations by interpolating hidden states. In: Proceedings of International Conference on Machine Learning (ICML) (2019)
74. Wang, S., Yu, L., Li, C., Fu, C.W., Heng, P.A.: Learning from extrinsic and intrinsic supervisions for domain generalization. In: Proceedings of European Conference on Computer Vision (ECCV) (2020)
75. Wang, Z., Luo, Y., Qiu, R., Huang, Z., Baktashmotlagh, M.: Learning to diversify for single domain generalization. In: Proceedings of IEEE International Conference on Computer Vision (ICCV) (2021)
76. Wu, D., Xia, S.T., Wang, Y.: Adversarial weight perturbation helps robust generalization. In: Proceedings of Neural Information Processing Systems (NeurIPS) (2020)
77. Xu, Q., Zhang, R., Zhang, Y., Wang, Y., Tian, Q.: A Fourier-based framework for domain generalization. In: Proceedings of IEEE Conference on Computer Vision and Pattern Recognition (CVPR) (2021)
78. Xu, T.B., Liu, C.L.: Data-distortion guided self-distillation for deep neural networks. In: Proc. AAAI Conference on Artificial Intelligence (AAAI) (2019)
79. Xu, Z., Li, W., Niu, L., Xu, D.: Exploiting low-rank structure from latent domains for domain generalization. In: Proceedings of European Conference on Computer Vision (ECCV) (2014)
80. Yao, Z., Gholami, A., Keutzer, K., Mahoney, M.W.: Pyhessian: neural networks through the lens of the hessian. In: 2020 IEEE International Conference on Big Data (Big Data) (2020)
81. Yu, F., et al.: Bdd100k: a diverse driving video database with scalable annotation tooling. arXiv preprint arXiv:1805.04687 (2018)
82. Yue, X., Zhang, Y., Zhao, S., Sangiovanni-Vincentelli, A., Keutzer, K., Gong, B.: Domain randomization and pyramid consistency: simulation-to-real generalization without accessing target domain data. In: Proceedings of IEEE International Conference on Computer Vision (ICCV) (2019)

83. Yun, S., Han, D., Oh, S.J., Chun, S., Choe, J., Yoo, Y.: CutMix: regularization strategy to train strong classifiers with localizable features. In: Proceedings of IEEE International Conference on Computer Vision (ICCV) (2019)
84. Yun, S., Park, J., Lee, K., Shin, J.: Regularizing class-wise predictions via self-knowledge distillation. In: Proceedings of IEEE Conference on Computer Vision and Pattern Recognition (CVPR) (2020)
85. Zagoruyko, S., Komodakis, N.: Wide residual networks. In: Proceedings of British Machine Vision Conference (BMVC) (2016)
86. Zhang, H., Cisse, M., Dauphin, Y.N., Lopez-Paz, D.: mixup: beyond empirical risk minimization. In: Proceedings of International Conference on Learning Representations (ICLR) (2018)
87. Zhang, L., Song, J., Gao, A., Chen, J., Bao, C., Ma, K.: Be your own teacher: Improve the performance of convolutional neural networks via self distillation. In: Proceedings of IEEE International Conference on Computer Vision (ICCV) (2019)
88. Zhang, M.M., Marklund, H., Dhawan, N., Gupta, A., Levine, S., Finn, C.: Adaptive risk minimization: a meta-learning approach for tackling group shift. In: Proceedings of Neural Information Processing Systems (NeurIPS) (2021)
89. Zhang, Y., Xiang, T., Hospedales, T.M., Lu, H.: Deep mutual learning. In: Proceedings of IEEE Conference on Computer Vision and Pattern Recognition (CVPR) (2018)
90. Zheng, L., Shen, L., Tian, L., Wang, S., Wang, J., Tian, Q.: Scalable person re-identification: abenchmark. In: Proceedings of IEEE International Conference on Computer Vision (ICCV) (2015)
91. Zheng, Z., Zheng, L., Yang, Y.: Unlabeled samples generated by GAN improve the person re-identification baseline in vitro. In: Proceedings of IEEE International Conference on Computer Vision (ICCV) (2017)
92. Zhong, Z., Zheng, L., Kang, G., Li, S., Yang, Y.: Random erasing data augmentation. In: Proceedings of AAAI Conference on Artificial Intelligence (AAAI) (2020)
93. Zhou, K., Yang, Y., Hospedales, T., Xiang, T.: Learning to generate novel domains for domain generalization. In: Proceedings of European Conference on Computer Vision (ECCV) (2020)
94. Zhou, K., Yang, Y., Qiao, Y., Xiang, T.: Domain adaptive ensemble learning. In: IEEE Transactions on Image Processing (TIP) (2021)
95. Zhou, K., Yang, Y., Qiao, Y., Xiang, T.: Domain generalization with MixStyle. In: Proceedings of International Conference on Learning Representations (ICLR) (2021)

# Centrality and Consistency: Two-Stage Clean Samples Identification for Learning with Instance-Dependent Noisy Labels

Ganlong Zhao[1,2] , Guanbin Li[1(✉)] , Yipeng Qin[3] , Feng Liu[4] ,
and Yizhou Yu[2(✉)]

[1] Sun Yat-sen University, Guangzhou 510006, China
zhaogl@connect.hku.hk, liguanbin@mail.sysu.edu.cn
[2] The University of Hong Kong, Hong Kong, China
yizhouy@acm.org
[3] Cardiff University, Cardiff, UK
QinY16@cardiff.ac.uk
[4] Deepwise AI Lab, Beijing, China
liufeng@deepwise.com

**Abstract.** Deep models trained with noisy labels are prone to over-fitting and struggle in generalization. Most existing solutions are based on an ideal assumption that the label noise is class-conditional, *i.e.* instances of the same class share the same noise model, and are independent of features. While in practice, the real-world noise patterns are usually more fine-grained as instance-dependent ones, which poses a big challenge, especially in the presence of inter-class imbalance. In this paper, we propose a two-stage clean samples identification method to address the aforementioned challenge. First, we employ a class-level feature clustering procedure for the early identification of clean samples that are near the class-wise prediction centers. Notably, we address the class imbalance problem by aggregating rare classes according to their prediction entropy. Second, for the remaining clean samples that are close to the ground truth class boundary (usually mixed with the samples with instance-dependent noises), we propose a novel consistency-based classification method that identifies them using the consistency of two classifier heads: the higher the consistency, the larger the probability that a sample is clean. Extensive experiments on several challenging benchmarks demonstrate the superior performance of our method against the state-of-the-art. Code is available at https://github.com/uitrbn/TSCSI_IDN.

**Keywords:** Instance-dependent noise · Noisy label · Image classification

## 1 Introduction

Deep learning has shown transformative power in various real-world applications but is notoriously data-hungry [9–11,21,29,45]. There are some other alterna-

© The Author(s), under exclusive license to Springer Nature Switzerland AG 2022
S. Avidan et al. (Eds.): ECCV 2022, LNCS 13685, pp. 21–37, 2022.
https://doi.org/10.1007/978-3-031-19806-9_2

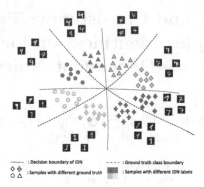

**Fig. 1.** Example of IDN. The different shapes of the markers represent different ground truth classes. The different colors of the markers represent the noisy (IDN) labels. Different from random noise, IDN samples tend to be distributed near the ground truth class boundary, thus confusing the classifier and leading to over-fitted decision boundaries.

tives which try to reduce the cost of human labor for data annotation, such as crawling web images and using machine-generated labels. However, such data are usually noisy, which impedes the generalization of deep learning models due to over-fitting.

Addressing the aforementioned issue, Learning with Noisy Labels (LNL) was proposed as a new topic and has attracted increasing attention in both academia and industry. Existing LNL methods mostly focus on the learning with class-conditional noise (CCN), which aims to recover a noise transition matrix that contains class-dependent probabilities of a clean label flipping into a noisy label. However, CCN is too ideal for real-world LNL as it ignores the dependence of noise on the content of individual images, *a.k.a.* instance-dependent noise (IDN).

Unlike random noise or CCN that can be countered by collecting more (noisy) data [4], IDN has some important characteristic that makes it difficult to be tackled. First, classifiers can easily over-fit to the IDN because the noisy labels are dependent on sample features. As Fig. 1 shows, mislabeled IDN samples (samples with the same shape but with different colors) share similar image features to their mislabeled classes, and thus tend to be distributed near the boundary between their ground truth class and the mislabeled class. As a result, the classifier can easily be confused and over-fits to IDN samples, leading to specious decision boundaries (red lines in Fig. 1). In addition, the challenge of IDN can be further amplified in the presence of inter-class imbalance and differences. Consider Clothing1M [38], an IDN dataset verified by [3], in which the noise is highly imbalanced and asymmetric. In Clothing1M, the IDN samples are unevenly distributed as the samples from similar classes (*e.g.* sweater and knitwear) can be extremely ambiguous, while those from other classes (*e.g.* shawl and underwear) are easily distinguishable. Such unevenly distributed IDN samples can be further

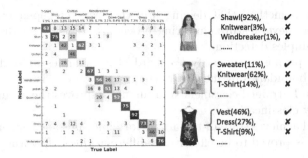

**Fig. 2.** The transition matrix of Clothing1M copied from [38]. The distribution of noisy labels are highly imbalanced. Some classes are almost clean (e.g. Shawl) while some classes has more mislabeled samples than correct labels (e.g. Sweater).

amplified by the class imbalance problem, as there is no guarantee of a balanced dataset due to the absence of ground truth labels.

In this paper, we follow DivideMix [17] that formulates LNL as a semi-supervised learning problem and propose a novel two-stage method to identify clean versus noisy samples in the presence of IDN and the class imbalance problem. In the first stage, we employ a class-level feature-based clustering procedure to identify easily distinguishable clean samples according to their cosine similarity to the corresponding class-wise prediction centers. Specifically, we collect the normalized features of samples belonging to different classes respectively and calculate their class-wise centers located on a unit sphere. Then, we apply Gaussian Mixture Model (GMM) to binarily classify the samples according to their cosine similarity to their corresponding class centers and identify the ones closer to class centers as clean samples. Notably, we propose to augment the GMM classification by aggregating rare classes based on their prediction entropy, thereby alleviating the impact of the class imbalance problem. In the second stage, we propose a consistency-based classification method to identify the hard clean samples that are mixed with IDN samples around the ground truth class boundaries. Our key insight is that such clean samples can be identified by the prediction consistency of two classifiers. Compared to IDN samples, clean samples should produce more consistent predictions. Specifically, we incorporate two regularizers into the training: one applied to the feature extractor to encourage it to facilitate consistent outputs of the two classifiers; one applied to the two classifiers to enforce them generating inconsistent predictions. After training, we use another GMM to binarily classify the samples with smaller GMM means as clean samples. After identifying all clean samples, we feed them into the semi-supervised training as labeled samples, thereby implementing our learning with instance-dependent noisy labels. In summary, our contributions could be summarized as:

– We propose a method that delving into the instance-dependent noise, and design a class-level feature clustering procedure focusing on the imbalanced and IDN samples detection.
– We further propose to identify the hard clean samples around the ground truth class boundaries by measuring the prediction consistency between two in-dependently trained classifiers, and further improves the accuracy of clean versus noisy classification.
– Our method achieves state-of-the-art performance in some challenging benchmarks, and is proved to be effective in different kinds of synthetic IDN.

## 2   Related Work

A large proportion of previous LNL methods focus on the class-conditional noise. With the class-conditional noise assumption, some methods try to correct the loss function with the noise transition matrix [27], which can be estimated through exploiting a noisy dataset [19,27,35,47] or using a clean set of data [12,44]. Such loss correction methods based on noise transition matrix is infeasible for instance-dependent noise, since the matrix is dataset dependent and the number of parameters grows proportionally with the size of training dataset.

Some methods seek to correct the loss by reweighting the noisy samples or selecting the clean data [15,33]. A common solution is to treat the samples with smaller loss as clean data [13,17,31]. However, as pointed out by [3], instance-dependent noise can be more easily over-fitted, and the memorization effect, which indicates that CNN-based models always tend to learn the general simple pattern before over-fitting to the noisy labels, becomes less significant when the model is trained with instance-dependent noise.

Some other methods combat the noisy label with other techniques. For example, Kim et al. [14] combine positive learning with negative learning, which uses the complementary labels of noisy data for model training. Some methods [17,25] formulate LNL as a semi-supervised learning problem. DivideMix [17] divides the dataset into clean and noisy sets, which serve as labeled and unlabeled data for semi-supervised learning. Some methods investigate the influence of augmentation strategy [26] or enforce the prediction consistency between different augmentations [22]. C2D [43] utilizes self-supervised learning to facilitate the learning with noisy labels.

Chen et al. [5] pointed out that for diagonally-dominant class-conditional noise, one can always obtain an approximately optimal classifier by training with a sufficient number of noisy samples. And it raise the significance of learning with IDN. There has been some works for this topic. CORES$^2$ [5] try to progressively sieve out corrupted samples and avoid specifying noise rate. CAL [46] propose a second-order approach with the assistance of additional second-order statistics. Besides, some research work also propose methods for IDN generation [3,36].

# 3   Method

## 3.1   Overview

The classification of noisy versus clean samples by the model outputs and their labels is a prevalent choice in the learning with noisy labels (LNL). Previous studies use the cross-entropy of noisy samples [17] or confidence thresholds [40] for noisy versus clean division. However, as Chen *et al.* [3] point out, samples with instance-dependent noise (IDN) can be more easily over-fitted by neural networks, resulting in less reliable model outputs that confuse the classification of clean versus noisy samples. Such confusion is further amplified when the noisy dataset is imbalanced. For example, the differences between clean and noisy samples might be neglected for rare classes that contribute little to the overall prediction accuracy.

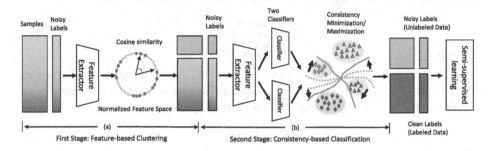

**Fig. 3.** The overview of our proposed method. (a) The first stage. The noisy samples and labels are sent to the feature extractor for calculating the normalized features. The features are clustered with the prediction of samples. Noisy samples are divide to clean set and noisy set according to the cosine similarity between the feature and the center of its labels. (b) The model is train to minimize/maximize the prediction between two classifier heads and samples with smaller consistency are identified as noisy labels. (c) The clean/noisy set serve as labeled/unlabeled data for semi-supervised training.

Therefore, we propose a two-stage method which can effectively address IDN in the presence of class imbalance. In the first stage, we leverage a class-level feature-based clustering process to identify easily distinguishable clean samples that are close to their corresponding class centers in the feature space. Specifically, in this stage, we address the class imbalance by aggregating rare classes identified by their prediction entropy. In the second stage, we address the remaining clean samples, which are close to the ground truth class boundaries and are thus mixed with IDN samples. Our key insight is that such clean samples can be identified by the consistent predictions of two classifiers. Specifically, we propose a mini-max strategy for this consistency-based clean versus noisy classification: we simultaneously regularize the two classifiers to generate inconsistent predictions but enforce the feature extractor to facilitate the two classifiers to generate consistent predictions. After training, we identify the clean samples as the ones that lead to more consistent predictions between the two classifiers. After identifying all clean samples, we follow DivideMix [17] and implement the learning with instance-dependent noisy labels as a semi-supervised learning problem that takes the clean samples as labeled samples, and the rest (noisy) samples as unlabeled samples.

## 3.2 Feature-based Clustering

As common practice, we divide a CNN-based classifier into two parts: a feature extractor $F$ that takes images as input and extracts their features, and the following classifier $G$ that outputs classification probabilities based on the image features extracted by $F$. Given a noisy dataset $\{x_i, \bar{y}_i\}_{i=1}^N$, where $x_i$ is an image sample and $\bar{y}_i$ is its (noisy) label, we denote $\hat{f}_i = \frac{f_i}{\|f_i\|}$ as the normalized feature of $x_i$ extracted by $F$, i.e. $f_i = F(x_i)$, $\hat{y}_i = G(f_i)$ as the predicted label of $x_i$, and calculate the class-wise feature centers $O_c$ according to $\hat{y}_i$ as:

$$O_c = \frac{\sum_{i=1}^{N_c} \hat{f}_i}{\| \sum_{i=1}^{N_c} \hat{f}_i \|}, \tag{1}$$

where $c \in \{1, 2, 3, ..., C\}$ denotes the $C$ classes, $N_c$ is the number of samples $x_i$ whose noisy label $\bar{y}_i = c$. Then, we can obtain the cosine similarity between each sample $x_i$ and its corresponding feature center $O_{\bar{y}_i}$ as:

$$S_i = \hat{f}_i \cdot O_{\bar{y}_i}. \tag{2}$$

Finally, we apply class-wise Gaussian Mixture Model (GMM) to the similarities $S_i$ of samples for each class and performs binary classification. As the cosine similarity of noisy samples tend to be smaller, the component of GMM with a larger mean, i.e. larger similarity, is denoted as the clean set. Thus all the noisy samples is classified as clean or noisy as the preliminary result of first stage.

**Entropy-based Aggregation of Rare Classes.** However, the performance of the proposed feature-based clustering can be unstable when the sizes of some classes are small and not sufficient for binary classification, which often happens in real-world datasets that have large numbers of classes. Addressing this issue, we propose to aggregate rare classes that struggle with the proposed binary classification. Specifically, we set a class aggregate threshold $\theta_{agg}$ and calculate the average prediction entropy of the samples for each class $c$ as:

$$\text{Ent}(c) = -\frac{1}{N_c} \sum_{i=1}^{N_c} \sum_{j=1}^{B} p_i^j \log p_i^j, \tag{3}$$

where $N_c$ is the number of samples for class $c$, $B = 2$ indicates the binary classification of clean versus noisy samples, $p_i^j$ represents the output probability that a sample $x_i$ belongs to class $j$, i.e., clean and noisy probability. Samples of class $c$ that satisfy $\text{Ent}_c > \theta_{agg}$ are aggregated and treated as a single class to facilitate our feature-based clustering.

## 3.3   Consistency-based Classification

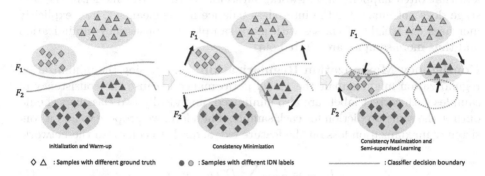

**Fig. 4.** The procedure of the consistency-based classification. At the beginning, two classifiers has different prediction due to different initialization. Then the prediction consistency between two classifiers is minimized to identify the ambiguous noisy samples near the decision boundary. At the third steps, feature extractor is trained to maximize the consistency and the semi-supervised loss further revises both feature extractor and classifiers.

As Fig 1 shows, challenging clean samples are usually near the ground truth class boundaries in the feature space, which can be identified by the consistency between two independently trained classifiers $G_1$ and $G_2$ that have different decision boundaries. Therefore, by replacing the classifier $G$ with $G_1$ and $G_2$ in our network, we can get two corresponding predictions $p_x^1$ and $p_x^2$ of the same sample $x$. Then, we define and calculate the consistency between $G_1$ and $G_2$ on $x$ as:

$$D(p^1, p^2) = \sum_{i=1}^{C} |p_i^1 - p_i^2|, \tag{4}$$

where $x$ is omitted for simplicity and $C$ is the number of classes, *i.e.* the dimension of $p_x^1$ and $p_x^2$. We measure the discrepancy with $L1$ norm following [30].

**Consistency Minimization Regularization.** Although being independently trained, $G_1$ and $G_2$ share the same training dataset and the same loss function, leading to a non-negligible risk that the corresponding two predictions are identical or very similar. To minimize such a risk, we propose to incorporate a regularization loss on $G_1$ and $G_2$ that aims to minimize their consistency:

$$L_{\min} = -\lambda_{\min} \sum_{i=1}^{N} D^*(p_{x_i}^1, p_{x_i}^2), \tag{5}$$

where $N$ is the number of samples and $\lambda_{\min}$ controls the strength,

$$D^*(p_x^1, p_x^2) = w_{C_x} \sum_{i=1}^{C} |p_i^1 - p_i^2|, \tag{6}$$

where $x$ is omitted on the right side for simplicity and $w_{C_x}$ is the frequency of samples $x$'s noisy category $C_x$. $w_{C_x}$ is used to counter the class imbalance problem that often happens in real-world datasets. As the GMM model in the first stage does not guarantee the inter-class balance in the clean set, $w_{C_x}$ explicitly increases the weight of classes with more samples in consistency minimization and thus more samples are filtered out.

**Consistency Maximization Regularization.** Solely using the minimization regularization might impair the model performance because the consistency of samples with correct labels are also minimized, and ideally two classifiers should output the same prediction for each sample. Therefore, we propose to add a consistency maximization loss on the feature extractor $F$ to constrain the network:

$$L_{\max} = \lambda_{\max} \sum_{i=1}^{N} D^*(p_{x_i}^1, p_{x_i}^2), \tag{7}$$

where $\lambda_{\max}$ controls the strength. Furthermore, the maximization of $L_{\max}$ forces the feature extractor to separate the ambiguous features and thus complements semi-supervised training. As shown in the third step of Fig. 4, the feature extractor maximizes the consistency by pushing the samples with small consistency towards clean labeled data, and semi-supervised learning tries to gather the the feature of similar samples.

### 3.4  Training Procedure

Based on the discussions in Sec. 3.2 and Sec. 3.3, we propose to train our model by repeating the following four steps for each epoch.

**Initialization.** Before training, we following [17] and warm up our model including the two classifiers for several epochs with all noisy labels, where steps 1 and 2 belong to our feature-based clustering (Stage 1), and steps 3 and 4 belong to our consistency-based classification (Stage 2).

**Step-1.** We first extract the features of noisy data and calculate the class-wise feature centers according to Eq. 1. Then, we calculate the cosine similarities between features and the center of noisy labels of each sample using Eq. 2.

**Step-2.** We perform a binary (noisy vs. clean) classification to samples by applying class-wise Gaussian Mixture Model (GMM) according to the cosine similarities obtained in Step-1. We label the GMM component with a larger mean as "clean". Then, we select the samples with clean probabilities higher than a threshold $\theta$ as our primary clean set $S_{clean}^1$ and the rest samples as the noisy set $S_{noisy}^1$.

**Step-3.** We first fix the feature extractor and train the two classifiers to minimize their consistency according to Eq. 5 for $N_{\max}$ iterations using $S_{clean}^1$. Then, we evaluate the consistency of all samples in $S_{clean}^1$. Similar to Step-2, we apply a GMM model to the consistencies and select the samples with small mean as clean set $S_{clean}^2$. The rest samples are merged with $S_{noisy}^1$ as $S_{noisy}^2$.

**Step-4** With $S^2_{clean}$ and $S^2_{noisy}$ obtained as above, we optimize our model with a supervised loss on $S^2_{clean}$ and a semi-supervised loss on $S^2_{noisy}$:

$$L = L_{\mathcal{X}} + \lambda_{\mathcal{U}} L_{\mathcal{U}} \tag{8}$$

where $S^2_{clean}$ and $S^2_{noisy}$ are used as labeled set $\mathcal{X}$ and unlabeled set $\mathcal{U}$ respectively, and $\lambda_{\mathcal{U}}$ balances the trade-off between $L_{\mathcal{X}}$ and $L_{\mathcal{U}}$. In addition, we add additional consistency maximization regularization (Eq. 7) to the feature extractor during training.

**Table 1.** Comparison of test accuracies (%) using different methods on CIFAR10 and CIFAR100 with part-dependent label noise. Results of other methods are copied from CAL [46]. Our method outperforms all previous methods in all settings.

| Method | Inst. CIFAR10 | | | Inst. CIFAR100 | | |
|---|---|---|---|---|---|---|
| | $\eta = 0.2$ | $\eta = 0.4$ | $\eta = 0.6$ | $\eta = 0.2$ | $\eta = 0.4$ | $\eta = 0.6$ |
| CE (Standard) | 85.45±0.57 | 76.23±1.54 | 59.75±1.30 | 57.79±1.25 | 41.15±0.83 | 25.68±1.55 |
| Forward $T$ [27] | 87.22±1.60 | 79.37±2.72 | 66.56±4.90 | 58.19±1.37 | 42.80±1.01 | 27.91±3.35 |
| $L_{\text{DMI}}$ [39] | 88.57±0.60 | 82.82±1.49 | 69.94±1.31 | 57.90±1.21 | 42.70±0.92 | 26.96±2.08 |
| $L_q$ [42] | 85.81±0.83 | 74.66±1.12 | 60.76±3.08 | 57.03±0.27 | 39.81±1.18 | 24.87±2.46 |
| Co-teaching [7] | 88.87±0.24 | 73.00±1.24 | 62.51±1.98 | 43.30±0.39 | 23.21±0.57 | 12.58±0.51 |
| Co-teaching+ [41] | 89.80±0.28 | 73.78±1.39 | 59.22±6.34 | 41.71±0.78 | 24.45±0.71 | 12.58±0.51 |
| JoCoR [34] | 88.78±0.15 | 71.64±3.09 | 63.46±1.58 | 43.66±1.32 | 23.95±0.44 | 13.16±0.91 |
| Reweight-R [37] | 90.04±0.46 | 84.11±2.47 | 72.18±2.47 | 58.00±0.36 | 43.83±8.42 | 36.07±9.73 |
| Peer Loss [20] | 89.12±0.76 | 83.26±0.42 | 74.53±1.22 | 61.16±0.64 | 47.23±1.23 | 31.71±2.06 |
| CORES$^2$ [6] | 91.14±0.46 | 83.67±1.29 | 77.68±2.24 | 66.47±0.45 | 58.99±1.49 | 38.55±3.25 |
| DivideMix [17] | 93.33±0.14 | **95.07±0.11** | 85.50±0.71 | 79.04±0.21 | 76.08±0.35 | 46.72±1.32 |
| CAL [46] | 92.01±0.75 | 84.96±1.25 | 79.82±2.56 | 69.11±0.46 | 63.17±1.40 | 43.58±3.30 |
| Ours | **93.68±0.12** | 94.97±0.09 | **94.95±0.11** | **79.61±0.19** | **76.58±0.25** | **59.40±0.46** |

## 4 Experiment

In this section, we will validate the effectiveness of our method on several benchmark datasets with different kinds of IDNs (*i.e.* synthetic and real-world ones) and different numbers of classes.

### 4.1 Datasets

**Synthetic IDN Datasets.** Following previous studies on learning with IDN [46], our synthetic IDN datasets are created by adding two kinds of synthetic noise to CIFAR-10 and CIFAR-100 datasets [16], where CIFAR-10 contains 50,000 training images and 10,000 testing images from 10 different classes, CIFAR-100 contains 50,000 training images and 10,000 testing images from 100 classes. Specifically, we use two kinds of synthetic IDN in our experiment:

- Part-dependent label noise [36], which draws insights from human cognition that humans perceive instances by decomposing them into parts and estimates the IDN transition matrix of an instance as a combination of the transition matrices of different parts of the instance.

– Classification-based label noise [3], which adds noise by i) collecting the predictions of each sample in every epoch during the training of a CNN classifier; ii) averaging the predictions and locate the class label with largest prediction probability other than the ground truth one for each instance as its noisy label; iii) flipping the labels of the samples whose largest probabilities falls in the top $r\%$ of all samples, where $r$ is a user-defined hyper-parameter.

**Table 2.** Classification accuracies on the (clean) test set of Clothing1M. Results of other method are copied from CAL [46]. Our method achieves state-of-the-art performance.

| Method | Accuracy |
|---|---|
| CE (standard) | 68.94 |
| Forward $T$ [27] | 70.83 |
| Co-teaching [7] | 69.21 |
| JoCoR [34] | 70.30 |
| $L_{DMI}$ [39] | 72.46 |
| PTD-R-V [36] | 71.67 |
| DivideMix [17] | 74.76 |
| CORES$^2$ [6] | 73.24 |
| CAL [46] | 74.17 |
| Ours | **75.40** |

**Real-world IDN Datasets.** Following [17], we use Clothing1M [38] and Webvision 1.0 [18] to evaluate our method:

– Clothing1M is a large scale dataset containing more than 1 million images of 14 kinds of clothes. As aforementioned, Clothing1M is highly imbalanced with its noise validated as IDN according to [3]. In our experiments, we use its noisy training set which contains 1 million images and report the performance on test set.
– Webvision is a large scale dataset which contains 2.4 million images from 1000 classes that are crawled from the web as ImageNet ILSVRC12 did. Following previous works [2,17], we compare baseline methods on the first 50 classes of the Google image subset, and report the top-1 and top-5 performance on both Webvision validation set and ImageNet ILSVRC12.

### 4.2   Implementation Details

We follow DivideMix [17] and use MixMatch [1] for semi-supervised learning. For experiments on CIFAR-10 and CIFAR-100, we use ResNet-34 [11] as the feature extractor following [46]. We use similar hyperparameters to [17] across all 3 settings of CIFAR-10 and CIFAR-100 respectively. We train our model using a

SGD optimizer with a momentum of 0.9 and a weight decay parameter of 0.0005. The learning rate is set as 0.02 in the first 150 epochs and reduced to 0.002 in the following 150 epochs. The warm up period is set as 10 epochs for CIFAR-10 and 15 epochs for CIFAR-100 respectively. For Clothing1M, we follow previous studies and use ImageNet pretrained ResNet-50 as the backbone. We train the model for 80 epochs. We set the learning rate as 0.002 in the beginning and reduce it to 0.0002 after 40 epochs of training. For Webvision 1.0, we follow [17] and use the Inception-Resnet v2 [32] as the backbone. We train the model for 120 epochs. We set the learning rate as 0.01 in the first 50 epoch and 0.001 for the rest of the training.

**Table 3.** Classification accuracies (%) on CIFAR-10 with classification-based label noise of different noise ratios. Our method outperforms all previous ones in all settings.

| Method | 10% | 20% | 30% | 40% |
|---|---|---|---|---|
| CE | 91.25 | 86.34 | 80.87 | 75.68 |
| | ±0.27 | ±0.11 | ±0.05 | ±0.29 |
| Forward [27] | 91.06 | 86.35 | 78.87 | 71.12 |
| | ±0.02 | ±0.11 | ±2.66 | ±0.47 |
| Co-teaching [7] | 91.22 | 87.28 | 84.33 | 78.72 |
| | ±0.25 | ±0.20 | ±0.17 | ±0.47 |
| GCE [42] | 90.97 | 86.44 | 81.54 | 76.71 |
| | ±0.21 | ±0.23 | ±0.15 | ±0.39 |
| DAC [33] | 90.94 | 86.16 | 80.88 | 74.80 |
| | ±0.09 | ±0.13 | ±0.46 | ±0.32 |
| DMI [39] | 91.26 | 86.57 | 81.98 | 77.81 |
| | ±0.06 | ±0.16 | ±0.57 | ±0.85 |
| SEAL [3] | 91.32 | 87.79 | 85.30 | 82.98 |
| | ±0.14 | ±0.09 | ±0.01 | ±0.05 |
| Ours | **91.39** | **88.36** | **86.92** | **84.18** |
| | ±0.08 | ±0.11 | ±0.68 | ±0.40 |

### 4.3 Experimental Results

**CIFAR-10 and CIFAR-100.** As aforementioned, we evaluate our method on two kinds of IDN as follows:

– *Part-dependent label noise.* To facilitate a fair comparison, we borrow the noise used in CAL [46] and follow CAL to test the performance of our method against 6 different settings, whose noise ratios vary between 0.2 and 0.6. As

Table 1 shows, our method outperforms previous methods in five in six settings, especially when the noise ratio and class number increase. For example, the improvement of CIFAR-100 with $\eta = 0.6$ is over 10%.

– *Classification-based label noise.* Following [3], we test our method against four different noise ratios, 10%, 20%, 30% and 40%. To facilitate a fair comparison, we borrow the same noise from SEAL [3]. Note that compared to the aforementioned part-dependent label noise, the classification-based label noise used in this experiment is more challenging as it is generated by a CNN-based model. As Table 3 shows, our method still outperforms previous methods in all four different settings. Similar as above, the improvement of our method becomes higher as the noise ratio increases, which demonstrates the effectiveness of our method under different kinds of IDNs.

**Clothing1M.** As aforementioned, Clothing1M contains over 1 million images from 14 classes collected from Internet, which makes it ideal to evaluate how different LNL methods perform against large-scale image datasets. As Table 2 shows, our method outperforms all previous methods and achieves the state-of-the-art performance. Compared to DivideMix [17], we further improve the accuracy by 0.64%.

**Table 4.** Classification accuracies (%) on (mini) Webvision and ILSVRC12. Numbers denote top-1 (top-5) accuracy (%) on the WebVision and the ImageNet ILSVRC12 validation sets.

| Method | WebVision | | ILSVRC12 | |
|---|---|---|---|---|
| | top1 | top5 | top1 | top5 |
| F-correction [28] | 61.12 | 82.68 | 57.36 | 82.36 |
| Decoupling [24] | 62.54 | 84.74 | 58.26 | 82.26 |
| D2L [23] | 62.68 | 84.00 | 57.80 | 81.36 |
| MentorNet [13] | 63.00 | 81.40 | 57.80 | 79.92 |
| Co-teaching [8] | 63.58 | 85.20 | 61.48 | 84.70 |
| Iterative-CV [2] | 65.24 | 85.34 | 61.60 | 84.98 |
| DivideMix [17] | 77.32 | 91.64 | 75.20 | 90.84 |
| NGC [17] | 79.16 | 91.84 | 74.44 | 91.04 |
| Ours | **79.36** | **93.64** | **76.08** | **93.86** |

**Table 5.** Ablation study on our Feature Clustering (Stage 1) and Consistency Classification (Stage 2). The models with neither stages are trained with cross-entropy loss (*i.e.* CE baseline).

| Dataset | Feature Clustering | Consistency Classification | Accuracy |
|---|---|---|---|
| CIFAR-100 ($\mu = 0.6$) | | | 25.68 |
| | ✓ | | 53.60 |
| | | ✓ | 51.41 |
| | ✓ | ✓ | 59.40 |
| Clothing1M | | | 68.94 |
| | ✓ | | 73.32 |
| | | ✓ | 74.26 |
| | ✓ | ✓ | 75.40 |

**Webvision and ImageNet ILSVRC12.** As Table 4 shows, our method achieves better performance on both top-1 and top-5 accuracy on ILSVRC12 and Webvision. The higher improvement on ILSVRC12 suggests that our method is more robust to the domain difference and can generalize better.

### 4.4   Ablation Study

We conduct an ablation study on the two stages of our method. Specifically, we provide the performance of our method on both CIFAR-100, a synthetic IDN dataset with noise ratio $\eta = 0.6$ and Clothing1M, a highly-imbalanced dataset with real-world IDN. We also compare our method to standard CE baseline (*i.e.* neither stages are applied). As Table 5 shows, our method benefits from each stage in terms of the performance on both datasets, and achieves the best results when both stages are employed.

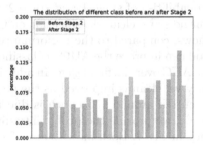

**Fig. 5.** The distributions of different classes in the validation set of Clothing1M before and after the consistency-based classification (Stage 2). After our consistency-based classification, the distribution becomes more balanced.

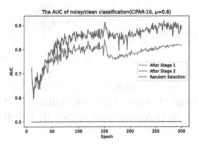

**Fig. 6.** The AUC of noisy vs. clean classification of our method. The second stage steadily improve the AUC of classification. The performance drop at 150 epoch is due to a learning rate change.

## 4.5   Performance Against Class Imbalance

We select the highly-imbalanced Clothing1M to test the performance of our method against class imbalance. Specifically, we are concerned on the distribution (proportion of class-wise sample number w.r.t the whole dataset) changes of all 14 classes within our selected clean samples before and after our consistency-based classification. Since Clothing1M does not contain the ground truth labels for its noisy training set, we mix some samples from its validation set that contains both clean and noisy labels with the original noisy training set, and report the distributions of the validation samples. As Fig. 5 shows, the percentages of most of the rare classes increase after our consistency-based classification, while the percentages of the rich classes decrease. In addition, we observed biggest changes occur in the rarest and richest classes.

## 4.6   AUC of Noisy vs. Clean Classification

Given the prediction probabilities of stage 1 and stage 2, we calculate the area under curve (AUC) of our noisy vs. clean classification on CIFAR-10 with a noise ratio of 0.6. As Fig. 6 shows, compared to the performance of random selection, both stages of our method can improve the AUC of classification, and the second stage further improve the AUC over the first stage. In addition, it can be observed that the accuracy of noisy vs. clean is improved as the training progresses. The performance decrease occurred around 150 epoch is due to a 0.1-fold decrease of the learning rate. Beside, we provide the probability distribution function of similarity and consistency in Fig. 7. Both metrics are effective in distinguishing clean and noisy samples.

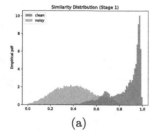 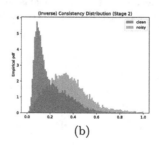

(a)                                      (b)

**Fig. 7.** The probability distribution function of clean/noisy samples respectively for CIFAR-10 ($\mu$=0.6). The range of statistics is normalized to 0 to 1. (a) The similarity distribution of stage 1. (b) The (inverse) consistency distribution of stage 2.

## 5   Conclusion

In this paper, we propose a two-stage method to address the problem of learning with instance-dependent noisy labels in the presence of inter-class imbalance problem. In the first stage, we identify "easy" clean samples that are close to the class-wise prediction centers using a class-level feature clustering procedure. We also address the class imbalance problem by augmenting the clustering with an entropy-based rare class aggregation technique. In the second stage, we further identify the remaining "difficult" clean samples that are close to the ground truth class boundary based on the consistency of two classifier heads. We conducted extensive experiments on several challenging benchmarks to demonstrate the effectiveness of the proposed method.

**Acknowledgements.** This work was supported in part by the Guangdong Basic and Applied Basic Research Foundation (No.2020B1515020048), in part by the National Natural Science Foundation of China (No.61976250, No. U1811463), in part by the Hong Kong Research Grants Council through Research Impact Fund (Grant R-5001-18), and in part by the Guangzhou Science and technology project (No.202102020633).

# References

1. Berthelot, D., Carlini, N., Goodfellow, I., Papernot, N., Oliver, A., Raffel, C.: Mixmatch: a holistic approach to semi-supervised learning. arXiv preprint arXiv:1905.02249 (2019)
2. Chen, P., Liao, B.B., Chen, G., Zhang, S.: Understanding and utilizing deep neural networks trained with noisy labels. In: International Conference on Machine Learning, pp. 1062–1070. PMLR (2019)
3. Chen, P., Ye, J., Chen, G., Zhao, J., Heng, P.A.: Beyond class-conditional assumption: a primary attempt to combat instance-dependent label noise. arXiv preprint arXiv:2012.05458 (2020)
4. Chen, P., Ye, J., Chen, G., Zhao, J., Heng, P.A.: Robustness of accuracy metric and its inspirations in learning with noisy labels. arXiv preprint arXiv:2012.04193 (2020)
5. Cheng, H., Zhu, Z., Li, X., Gong, Y., Sun, X., Liu, Y.: Learning with instance-dependent label noise: a sample sieve approach. arXiv preprint arXiv:2010.02347 (2020)
6. Cheng, H., Zhu, Z., Li, X., Gong, Y., Sun, X., Liu, Y.: Learning with instance-dependent label noise: a sample sieve approach. In: International Conference on Learning Representations (2021)
7. Han, et al.: Co-teaching: robust training of deep neural networks with extremely noisy labels. In: Advances in Neural Information Processing Systems, pp. 8527–8537 (2018)
8. Han, B., et al.: Co-teaching: robust training of deep neural networks with extremely noisy labels. In: Advances in Neural Information Processing Systems, pp. 8536–8546 (2018)
9. He, K., Gkioxari, G., Dollár, P., Girshick, R.: Mask R-CNN. In: Proceedings of the IEEE international conference on computer vision, pp. 2961–2969 (2017)
10. He, K., Zhang, X., Ren, S., Sun, J.: Delving deep into rectifiers: surpassing human-level performance on imagenet classification. In: Proceedings of the IEEE international conference on computer vision, pp. 1026–1034 (2015)
11. He, K., Zhang, X., Ren, S., Sun, J.: Deep residual learning for image recognition. In: Proceedings of the IEEE Conference on Computer Vision and Pattern Recognition, pp. 770–778 (2016)

12. Hendrycks, D., Mazeika, M., Wilson, D., Gimpel, K.: Using trusted data to train deep networks on labels corrupted by severe noise. arXiv preprint arXiv:1802.05300 (2018)
13. Jiang, L., Zhou, Z., Leung, T., Li, L.J., Fei-Fei, L.: MentorNet: learning data-driven curriculum for very deep neural networks on corrupted labels. In: International Conference on Machine Learning, pp. 2304–2313. PMLR (2018)
14. Kim, Y., Yun, J., Shon, H., Kim, J.: Joint negative and positive learning for noisy labels. In: Proceedings of the IEEE/CVF Conference on Computer Vision and Pattern Recognition, pp. 9442–9451 (2021)
15. Konstantinov, N., Lampert, C.: Robust learning from untrusted sources. In: International Conference on Machine Learning, pp. 3488–3498. PMLR (2019)
16. Krizhevsky, A., Hinton, G., et al.: Learning multiple layers of features from tiny images. Tech. rep, Citeseer (2009)
17. Li, J., Socher, R., Hoi, S.C.: DivideMix: learning with noisy labels as semi-supervised learning. In: International Conference on Learning Representations (2020). https://openreview.net/forum?id=HJgExaVtwr
18. Li, W., Wang, L., Li, W., Agustsson, E., Van Gool, L.: WebVision database: visual learning and understanding from web data. arXiv preprint arXiv:1708.02862 (2017)
19. Liu, T., Tao, D.: Classification with noisy labels by importance reweighting. IEEE Trans. Pattern Anal. Mach. Intell. **38**(3), 447–461 (2015)
20. Liu, Y., Guo, H.: Peer loss functions: learning from noisy labels without knowing noise rates. In: Proceedings of the 37th International Conference on Machine Learning, ICML '20 (2020)
21. Long, J., Shelhamer, E., Darrell, T.: Fully convolutional networks for semantic segmentation. In: Proceedings of the IEEE conference on computer vision and pattern recognition, pp. 3431–3440 (2015)
22. Lu, Y., Bo, Y., He, W.: Co-matching: combating noisy labels by augmentation anchoring. arXiv preprint arXiv:2103.12814 (2021)
23. Ma, X., et al.: Dimensionality-driven learning with noisy labels. In: International Conference on Machine Learning, pp. 3355–3364. PMLR (2018)
24. Malach, E., Shalev-Shwartz, S.: Decoupling "when to update" from "how to update". In: Advances in Neural Information Processing Systems, pp. 960–970 (2017)
25. Nguyen, D.T., Mummadi, C.K., Ngo, T.P.N., Nguyen, T.H.P., Beggel, L., Brox, T.: Self: learning to filter noisy labels with self-ensembling. arXiv preprint arXiv:1910.01842 (2019)
26. Nishi, K., Ding, Y., Rich, A., Hollerer, T.: Augmentation strategies for learning with noisy labels. In: Proceedings of the IEEE/CVF Conference on Computer Vision and Pattern Recognition, pp. 8022–8031 (2021)
27. Patrini, G., Rozza, A., Krishna Menon, A., Nock, R., Qu, L.: Making deep neural networks robust to label noise: a loss correction approach. In: Proceedings of the IEEE/CVF Conference on Computer Vision and Pattern Recognition, pp. 1944–1952 (2017)
28. Patrini, G., Rozza, A., Krishna Menon, A., Nock, R., Qu, L.: Making deep neural networks robust to label noise: a loss correction approach. In: Proceedings of the IEEE Conference on Computer Vision and Pattern Recognition, pp. 1944–1952 (2017)
29. Ren, S., He, K., Girshick, R., Sun, J.: Faster R-CNN: towards real-time object detection with region proposal networks. In: Advances in Neural Information Processing Systems, vol. 28 (2015)

30. Saito, K., Watanabe, K., Ushiku, Y., Harada, T.: Maximum classifier discrepancy for unsupervised domain adaptation. In: Proceedings of the IEEE Conference on Computer Vision and Pattern Recognition, pp. 3723–3732 (2018)
31. Shen, Y., Sanghavi, S.: Learning with bad training data via iterative trimmed loss minimization. In: International Conference on Machine Learning, pp. 5739–5748. PMLR (2019)
32. Szegedy, C., Ioffe, S., Vanhoucke, V., Alemi, A.A.: Inception-v4, inception-ResNet and the impact of residual connections on learning. In: Thirty-first AAAI Conference on Artificial Intelligence (2017)
33. Thulasidasan, S., Bhattacharya, T., Bilmes, J., Chennupati, G., Mohd-Yusof, J.: Combating label noise in deep learning using abstention. arXiv preprint arXiv:1905.10964 (2019)
34. Wei, H., Feng, L., Chen, X., An, B.: Combating noisy labels by agreement: a joint training method with co-regularization. In: Proceedings of the IEEE/CVF Conference on Computer Vision and Pattern Recognition, pp. 13726–13735 (2020)
35. Xia, X., et al.: Extended T: learning with mixed closed-set and open-set noisy labels. arXiv preprint arXiv:2012.00932 (2020)
36. Xia, X., et al.: Part-dependent label noise: towards instance-dependent label noise. In: Advances in Neural Information Processing Systems, vol. 33, pp. 7597–7610 (2020)
37. Xia, X., et al.: Are anchor points really indispensable in label-noise learning? In: Advances in Neural Information Processing Systems, pp. 6838–6849 (2019)
38. Xiao, T., Xia, T., Yang, Y., Huang, C., Wang, X.: Learning from massive noisy labeled data for image classification. In: Proceedings of the IEEE Conference on Computer Vision and Pattern Recognition, pp. 2691–2699 (2015)
39. Xu, Y., Cao, P., Kong, Y., Wang, Y.: L_DMI: a novel information-theoretic loss function for training deep nets robust to label noise. In: Advances in Neural Information Processing Systems, pp. 6222–6233 (2019)
40. Yao, Y., et al.: Jo-SRC: a contrastive approach for combating noisy labels. In: Proceedings of the IEEE/CVF Conference on Computer Vision and Pattern Recognition, pp. 5192–5201 (2021)
41. Yu, X., Han, B., Yao, J., Niu, G., Tsang, I.W., Sugiyama, M.: How does disagreement help generalization against label corruption? arXiv preprint arXiv:1901.04215 (2019)
42. Zhang, Z., Sabuncu, M.: Generalized cross entropy loss for training deep neural networks with noisy labels. In: Advances in Neural Information Processing Systems, pp. 8778–8788 (2018)
43. Zheltonozhskii, E., Baskin, C., Mendelson, A., Bronstein, A.M., Litany, O.: Contrast to divide: self-supervised pre-training for learning with noisy labels. arXiv preprint arXiv:2103.13646 (2021)
44. Zheng, G., Awadallah, A.H., Dumais, S.: Meta label correction for noisy label learning. In: Proceedings of the 35th AAAI Conference on Artificial Intelligence (2021)
45. Zhou, H.Y., Chen, X., Zhang, Y., Luo, R., Wang, L., Yu, Y.: Generalized radiograph representation learning via cross-supervision between images and free-text radiology reports. Nature Mach. Intell. 4, 32–40 (2022)
46. Zhu, Z., Liu, T., Liu, Y.: A second-order approach to learning with instance-dependent label noise. In: Proceedings of the IEEE/CVF Conference on Computer Vision and Pattern Recognition, pp. 10113–10123 (2021)
47. Zhu, Z., Song, Y., Liu, Y.: Clusterability as an alternative to anchor points when learning with noisy labels. arXiv preprint arXiv:2102.05291 (2021)

# Hyperspherical Learning in Multi-Label Classification

Bo Ke[1(✉)], Yunquan Zhu[1], Mengtian Li[2], Xiujun Shu[1], Ruizhi Qiao[1], and Bo Ren[1]

[1] Tencent YouTu Lab, Shenzhen, China
{boke,yunquanzhu,ruizhiqiao,timren}@tencent.com, shuxj@mail.ioa.ac.cn
[2] East China Normal University, Shanghai, China
mtli@stu.ecnu.edu.cn

**Abstract.** Learning from online data with noisy web labels is gaining more attention due to the increasing cost of fully annotated datasets in large-scale multi-label classification tasks. Partial (positive) annotated data, as a particular case of data with noisy labels, are economically accessible. And they serve as benchmarks to evaluate the learning capacity of state-of-the-art methods in real scenarios, though they contain a large number of samples with false negative labels. Existing (partial) multi-label methods are usually studied in the Euclidean space, where the relationship between the label embeddings and image features is not symmetrical and thus can be challenging to learn. To alleviate this problem, we propose reformulating the task into a hyperspherical space, where an angular margin can be incorporated into a hyperspherical multi-label loss function. This margin allows us to effectively balance the impact of false negative and true positive labels. We further design a mechanism to tune the angular margin and scale adaptively. We investigate the effectiveness of our method under three multi-label scenarios (single positive labels, partial positive labels and full labels) on four datasets (VOC12, COCO, CUB-200 and NUS-WIDE). In the single and partial positive labels scenarios, our method achieves state-of-the-art performance. The robustness of our method is verified by comparing the performances at different proportions of partial positive labels in the datasets. Our method also obtains more than 1% improvement over the BCE loss even on the fully annotated scenario. Analysis shows that the learned label embeddings potentially correspond to actual label correlation, since in hyperspherical space label embeddings and image features are symmetrical and interchangeable. This further indicates the geometric interpretability of our method. Code is available at https://github.com/TencentYoutuResearch/MultiLabel-HML.

**Keywords:** Multi-label classification · Partial labels · Label correlation

**Supplementary Information** The online version contains supplementary material available at https://doi.org/10.1007/978-3-031-19806-9_3.

# 1    Introduction

Multi-label classification has a wide range of applications in generic scenarios, including medical image processing [2], pedestrian attribute recognition [56] and image retrieval [53]. However, it is not easy to construct a large-scale multi-label dataset by manual annotation. Human annotators need to learn about a large number of nameable labels and assign positive labels accurately. Due to the limitation of human knowledge and fatigue, human annotators tend to skip some positive labels, causing false negatives to occur. In order to alleviate human labour, another effective strategy is to generate datasets from noisy web labels [7]. In this way, the dataset is built by crawling web images by using the labels as queries [26]. Therefore, only one correct label can be obtained for each image; other unknown labels, whether they are actually present or not, are considered as negatives [12]. Those false negatives in annotations inevitably lead to the degradation in the generalization capability of the network. To address the problem of missing positive labels, our work focuses on studying false negative labels under three multi-label scenarios, consisting of single positive labels, partial positive labels and full labels.

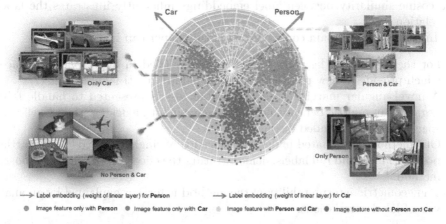

**Fig. 1.** The Overview of learning multi-label with *Person* and *Car* in 3D hyperspherical space. In this case, the cosine similarity between multiple label embeddings and image features is used as the metric for classification. With optimization, images with the same labels are clustered together in a hypersphere. Best viewed in color.

In full labels scenarios, the method on asymmetric loss [38] obtains gains on performance by increasing the weights of hard samples. For noisy data, existing approaches are more concerned with correcting inaccurate labels by pseudo-labeling [1,36,45]. However, there is no unified perspective that can comprehensively handle different proportions of mislabeled samples in the multi-label task. To further explore this issue, we propose to model the multi-label task in the hyperspherical space, as shown in Fig. 1.

The motivation of this hyperspherical reformulation lies in two aspects. First, the relationship between label embedding and image feature is expressed in terms of the angle on the sphere, independent of the magnitude of label embedding or image feature. In multi-label classification, the inter-class distribution is highly imbalanced, which easily leads to poor generalization. With the metric of normalized embeddings and features, the contributions of each class are treated as equal, thus avoiding overfitting [43]. Second, compared to the Euclidean space, the similarity in hyperspherical space is bounded. It is convenient to use metric learning to equalize the weights of samples in bounded space [9]. Especially in noisy data, the weight of the false negatives is amplified during training. These problems can be naturally addressed by incorporating an angular margin based loss function in hyperspherical space. Comprehensively, our work proposes to learn multi-label in hyperspherical space, which is proved to be valid for multi-label datasets with different levels of noisy samples.

It is well known that significant improvement in multi-label classification can be achieved by exploiting label correlations [21]. With the introduction of hyperspherical space, an additional benefit is that the model implicitly learns label correlation. The cosine similarity between label embedding and image feature is used to determine if the label is attached to the image. Since label embeddings and image features are symmetrical and interchangeable in hyperspherical space, the cosine similarity between label embeddings inherently illustrates the label correlation.

In summary, the main contributions in this paper can be concluded as

- For the first time, the multi-label task is modelled in hyperspherical space, which provides a new perspective for the field of multi-label learning.
- A novel angular margin based multi-label loss is presented to handle false negatives in multi-label classification which cannot be dealt with in Euclidean space due to unbounded distance.
- Our method is evaluated under the scenarios of single positive labels, partial positive labels and full labels, demonstrating the effectiveness of the proposed method.
- The geometric interpretability of the method is further explained by an analysis of label correlations.

## 2    Related Works

### 2.1    Learning from Noisy Labels

In multi-label tasks, incompletely labelled data will inevitably be used for training. To analyze the multi-label performance with noisy labels, previous works propose a variety of scenarios [17,20,35]. One of the most commonly used is *weak label*, which assumes the known labels are proper labels while unknown labels are regarded as negatives [10,39,49]. In order to reduce the impact of false negatives in *weak label*, unknown labels are not used for training in the *partial labels* scenario [6,8,12,19]. In *positive-unlabeled learning*, only some positive and unlabeled samples are accessed [13,27]. More strictly, *Single positive labels* proposes the setup that only one single positive label is available for each image at training time [7,51]. Our work mainly investigates learning multi-label models with single and partial positive labels, which is the most practical and economically accessible scenario of noise web labels, as web images are more likely to be published with incomplete correct labels than with completely correct labels or with incorrect labels. In the *single positive labels* scenario, the performance gain of existing methods [7] is only seen on limited datasets, while our proposed method consistently achieves the state-of-the-art performance on multiple datasets, including VOC12 [14], COCO [28], CUB-200 [41] and NUS-WIDE [5]. Our method also obtains significant improvement in the scenarios of partial positive labels and full labels. Moreover, we compare with more noisy single-label classification methods in supplementary material.

## 2.2 Hyperspherical Learning

Hyperspherical learning has made great progress in face recognition in recent years [30,47]. NormFace [43] first introduces training embedding using normalized features in face verification. Sphereface [29] proposes to learn embeddings using large angular margin in open-set face recognition. CosFace [44], Additive margin softmax [42] and ArcFace [9] further improves the form of angular margin to stabilize the training. Learning features in hyperspherical space is also popular in person re-identification. A deep cosine similarity metric is firstly used to achieve better generalization on the test set in person re-identification [48]. Another simple but strong baseline with normalized softmax is also proposed to reduce the difficulty of optimization in person re-identification [15,32,33]. All these works aim to learn representations on hyperspherical space and prove that angular metric is crucial to the generalization in retrieval. Inspired by these observations, we propose to learn multi-label classification in hyperspherical space. Our method differs from existing methods in two aspects. First, while existing methods focus on learning features for retrieval tasks like face recognition and person re-identification, our approach focuses on classification. Second, previous approaches on hyperspherical learning are limited to single class tasks using normalized softmax, while multi-label task, to the best of our knowledge, remains unexplored in hyperspherical learning.

## 2.3 Label Correlation

It is well known that exploiting label correlations is crucial for multi-label classification [21]. Some existing approaches assume that label correlation is shared only in a local group of instances [18], while others deal with missing labels by exploiting both global and local label correlations [52,57]. Graph convolution network (GCN) is naturally suitable to build label correlation, and thus has gained much attention in multi-label tasks [25,34,46]. ML-GCN [4] utilizes graphs to propagate prior label representations, such as word embeddings, in learning classifiers. ADD-GCN [50] learns content-aware category representations without using an external word embedding for graph construction. Recently, vision transformer has gained popularity in the field of image recognition [3,11,31,37,40]. Transformers are also used to construct complementary relationships in multi-label classification by exploring structural relation graph and semantic relation graph [54]. M3TR [55] presents a linguistic guided enhancement method to enhance the high-level semantics. These works demonstrate the potential of transformers for building label correlation [24]. Our approach provides an alternative way to implicitly learn label correlation in multi-label classification by applying constraints in hyperspherical space, where the label embedding should maximize the similarity with corresponding image features and minimize the similarity with other labels if existing label conflicts.

## 3   Method

In this section, we thoroughly introduce multi-label classification into hyperspherical feature space. In Sect. 3.1, the preliminary study demonstrates the multi-label classification in Euclidean space. In Sect. 3.2, normalized sigmoid function is proposed to learn multi-label in hyperspherical space. In Sect. 3.3, a modified variant, named margin based sigmoid function, is proposed to handle false negatives in noisy data. In Sect. 3.4, we enable the hyperparameters to be adaptive to a wide variety of datasets. In Sect. 3.5, label correlation is illustrated in hyperspherical space.

### 3.1   Preliminaries

In multi-label classification, each image needs to be determined whether it belongs to the labels in given sets. Unlike single-label image classification in ImageNet [23], the number of output labels in the multi-label setting may be one, many, or none. The most common practice is to use multiple binary classifiers. Each classifier determines whether the corresponding label exists in the image. Assume that we need to optimize a multi-label classifier with $N$ labels. The multi-label problem could be optimized with binary cross-entropy loss with sigmoid activation $\sigma(z) = 1/(1 + e^{-z})$.

$$\mathcal{L}_{\mathrm{BCE}}(p, \mathcal{Y}) = -(\sum_{i \in \mathcal{Y}}^{N} \log(p_i) + \sum_{i \notin \mathcal{Y}}^{N} \log(1 - p_i)) \qquad (1)$$

where $\mathcal{Y}$ is the set of the true labels in corresponding image, $p$ are the probabilities for the $N$ labels. In Euclidean space, the probabilities are expressed as $p^e$,

$$p^e(W, b, x) = \sigma(Wx + b) \qquad (2)$$

where $W$ are learnable weights of $N$ binary classifiers with the shape of $(N, L)$, $b$ are learnable biases with the shape of $(N,)$ and $x$ is the $L$-dimension feature of the image. In Eq. 2, logits are expressed as the inner product of weights and features in Euclidean space. The sigmoid function then maps the logits into per-class probabilities within the range of $[0, 1]$. With larger probability

$p_i^e$, the sample is more likely to belong to the $i$ class, and vice versa. As $p^e = \sigma(\|W\| \|x\| \cos \angle(W, x) + b)$, the logits are not only related to the angle between classifier weights and features, but also affected by the weights norm and bias of classifiers. We have concerns about learning in Euclidean space in two aspects. First, we suspect that over-optimization of weights norm leads to imbalanced learning between labels. Second, the angle is the better measure of similarity between weights and features compared to the norm. The objective function focusing on the angle is proposed in Sect. 3.2.

## 3.2    Learning in Hyperspherical Space

First, We utilize cosine similarity between the feature and classifier weights to minimize the binary cross-entropy loss. To simplify Eq. 2, we remove the modules that are not cross-correlated between $W$ and $x$, such as bias $b$, weight norm $\|W\|$ and feature norm $\|x\|$, and thus propose normalized sigmoid function,

$$p^n(W, x) = \sigma(s * \frac{Wx}{\|W\| \|x\|}) \tag{3}$$

In Eq. 3, $s$ is the scale factor of the cosine similarity. Different from the norms implicitly used in Eq. 2, the scale $s$ is irrelevant to features $x$ and weights $W$. It is used to rescale the cosine similarity to reach the saturation zone of sigmoid activation. We can treat the weights $W$ as a collection of *label embeddings* in the perspective of the hypersphere. The similarity value ranges from $-1$ to $1$ indicating the confidence of regarding the corresponding label in the given image. The overall loss function minimizes the angle between the feature and the corresponding positive label embedding and maximizes that between the feature and its negative label embedding.

There are two other advantages to learning multi-label in hyperspherical space. First, from the perspective of the hypersphere, we can efficiently conduct metric learning to handle noisy samples in multi-label classification, which is introduced in Sect. 3.3. Second, the correlation value between different label embeddings could be used to estimate the label correlation, which is illustrated in Sect. 3.5.

## 3.3    Learning from Single Positive Labels

To study the impact of noisy samples in multi-label classification, we analyze its simplest form, that is, the single positive labels scenario. In this problem, only one single positive label is known in each image; thus, unknown labels may be positive or negative in fact. A straightforward way is regarding all known labels as positive and all unknown labels as negative during training. We conventionally refer to samples with positive labels as *postives* and samples with negative labels as *negatives*. In this setting, the negatives are composed of true negatives and false negatives according to the ground truth.

We start with an experiment of full labels on VOC12, as shown in the left column of Fig. 2. In this experiment, no noisy labels are added to the training

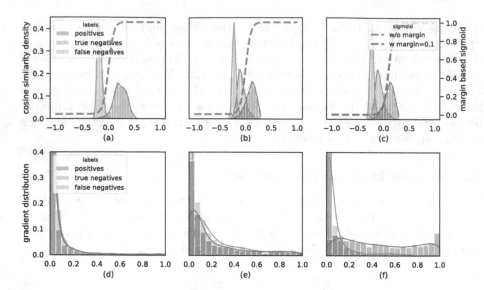

**Fig. 2.** The cosine similarity density (top rows) and the corresponding gradient distribution (bottom rows). The scenarios include normalized sigmoid in full labels (left column), normalized sigmoid in single positive labels (middle column), margin based sigmoid in single positive labels (right column). For the cosine similarity density, the color bar in the Y-axis represents the density in the corresponding similarity (X-axis). For the gradient distribution, the gradient magnitude is attached to the X-axis, while the color bar in the Y-axis represents the density. The actual labels of samples are distinguished by color.

data; thus, all negatives are true negatives. Figure 2 (a) illustrates the cosine similarity distribution of positives and negatives. The result shows less overlap between the distribution of positives and negatives and suggests that positives and negatives are easier to distinguish in the absence of noisy samples.

The middle column of Fig. 2 presents the experiment in single positive labels. The similarity distribution is close to that in full labels except for false negatives, which are partially overlapped with positives and true negatives in distribution, as shown in Fig. 2 (b). There is a conflict for false negatives. On the one hand, these mislabeled samples have visually similar patterns or textures to the positives. However, on the other, these samples are assigned to be negative, making them harder to distinguish. The gradient analysis on single positive labels is illustrated in Fig. 2 (e). Compared to the case of full labels in Fig. 2 (d), the gradients of false negatives still remain at high intensity when the training has converged. These incorrect gradients can mislead the network to converge to a non-optimal solution. We conclude that these hard false negatives cause the generalization gap between the fully-labeled dataset and the dataset with single positive labels.

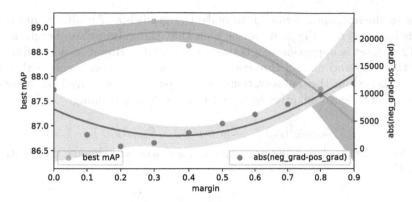

**Fig. 3.** The experiments with fixed margins in the VOC12 dataset. Orange line illustrates the best mAP in different margin. Blue line illustrates the absolute value of the accumulated gradient difference between the positives and negatives. (Color figure online)

The impact of those false negatives should be suppressed while keeping the contribution of the positives. To this end, we introduce angular margin on cosine similarity in our multi-label formulation, also named margin based sigmoid function,

$$p^m(W, x) = \sigma(s * \cos(\arccos(\frac{Wx}{\|W\| \|x\|}) + m))$$  (4)

In Eq. 4, the margin $m$ is added to the angle between classifier weights and features. The dotted lines in Fig. 2 show the variants of margin based sigmoid functions that map the cosine similarity to the probability. We further increase the margin from 0 to 0.1, as shown in the third column in Fig. 2. Observe that the activation function has been shifted to the right by 0.1. From the gradient analysis in Fig. 2 (f), the gradient of positives is enhanced while the gradient of negatives is weakened comparing to Fig. 2 (e). On the one hand, the harmful gradients from the false negatives are partially inhibited. On the other hand, the positives are activated to maximize the cosine similarity between class weights and their features. In multi-label classification, the classifier is the crucial part of both training and testing. To keep the consistency, we use the same activation function as Eq. 4 during training and testing.

### 3.4 Adaptive Learning

As discussed in Sect. 3.3, margin $m$ optimizes the training by adjusting the ratio of positive and negative gradients. The smaller margin would produce a large number of gradients for negatives. Thus the absolute value of the accumulated gradient difference between the positives and negatives is significant as shown in Fig. 3. This imbalance of gradients results in poor performance. A similar degradation also happens when training with a large margin, where the accumulated gradients for positives are more extensive than those for negatives. It is vital to choose the appropriate margin to make the gradients of positives and negatives balanced. From Fig. 3, it can be seen that the appropriate margin in the VOC12 dataset is approximately between 0.2 and 0.4. However, it is tedious to select the scale and margin through a large number of experiments with other datasets. Based on these observations, we further propose a gradient balanced loss function to learn adaptive scale and margin during training.

$$\mathcal{L}_{overall}(p, \mathcal{Y}) = \mathcal{L}_{BCE}(p, \mathcal{Y}) + \mathcal{L}_{adpt}(p, \mathcal{Y}) \tag{5}$$

A constraint on balancing gradients $\mathcal{L}_{adpt}$ works with binary cross-entropy loss in Eq. 5.

$$\mathcal{L}_{adpt}(p, \mathcal{Y}) = \left\| \sum_{i \in \mathcal{Y}}^{N}(1 - p_i) - \sum_{i \notin \mathcal{Y}}^{N} p_i \right\| \tag{6}$$

We aim to minimize the difference of the accumulated gradients between positives and negatives in a mini-batch, as in Eq. 6. Where $\sum_{i \in \mathcal{Y}}^{N}(1 - p_i)$ is the accumulated gradients for positives and the $\sum_{i \notin \mathcal{Y}}^{N} p_i$ is the accumulated gradients for negatives. Note that the probability $p^a$ used in the adaptive loss is slightly different from $p^m$ in BCE loss. In the adaptive loss, the gradients to weights and features are blocked, while the scale $s^*$ and margin $m^*$ are learnable parameters, as shown in Eq. 7.

$$p^a(W, x) = \sigma(s^* * \cos(\arccos(\mathbb{B}(\frac{Wx}{\|W\| \|x\|})) + m^*)) \tag{7}$$

Where $\mathbb{B}$ is the gradient blocking function. The adaptive loss focuses on balancing the gradient by learning the appropriate scale $s^*$ and margin $m^*$ without affecting the model weights $W$. The benefits of adaptive learning are in two aspects. First, adaptive learning removes manual hyperparameters searching on new datasets, such as COCO and NUS. Second, gradient equilibrium provides a better prior for model optimization and thus can boost the performance by adaptive learning.

### 3.5 Label Correlation

As in Fig. 1, the image features with label *person* is around the label embedding of *person* in 3D spherical space. The label embedding could be seen as the cluster center for samples with the same labels. Since label embeddings and image features are symmetrical and interchangeable in hyperspherical space, we could also replace the image features with label embeddings to compute correlation. Similar to Eq. 4, the relation between different label embeddings is formulated as Eq. 8, which could be used to estimate the label correlation.

$$Corr(i, j) = \sigma(s * \cos(\arccos(\frac{w_i w_j}{\|w_i\| \|w_j\|}) + m)) \tag{8}$$

where $w_i$ and $w_j$ are the label embeddings of the $i$th label and $j$th label, respectively. The higher the value, the higher the correlation.

**Table 1.** Statistics of datasets.

| Datasets | #Class | #Pos/Img | #Train Imgs | #Test Imgs |
|----------|--------|----------|-------------|------------|
| VOC12    | 20     | 1.44     | 5,717       | 5,823      |
| COCO     | 80     | 2.92     | 82,081      | 40,137     |
| CUB      | 312    | 31.47    | 5,994       | 5,794      |
| NUS      | 81     | 1.89     | 150,000     | 60,260     |

**Table 2.** Experiments on single positive labels in mAP metric.

| Method     | VOC12 | COCO | CUB  | NUS  |
|------------|-------|------|------|------|
| AN [7]     | 85.1  | 64.1 | 19.1 | 42.0 |
| LS [7]     | 86.7  | _66.9_ | 17.9 | 44.9 |
| WAN [7]    | 86.5  | 64.8 | _20.3_ | _46.3_ |
| EPR [7]    | 85.5  | 63.3 | 20.0 | 46.0 |
| ROLE [7]   | _87.9_ | 66.3 | 15.0 | 43.1 |
| HML (Ours) | **89.1** | **70.7** | **21.1** | **46.7** |

**Table 3.** Experiments on full labels in mAP metric.

| Method     | VOC12 | COCO | CUB  | NUS  |
|------------|-------|------|------|------|
| BCE [7]    | 89.1  | 75.8 | 32.1 | 52.6 |
| LS [7]     | _90.0_ | _76.8_ | _32.6_ | _53.5_ |
| HML (Ours) | **91.3** | **78.6** | **33.6** | **54.1** |

# 4 Experiments

## 4.1 Settings

**Datasets.** We conduct experiments on four datasets on multi-label classification, including VOC12 [14], COCO [28], CUB-200 (CUB) [41] and NUS-WIDE (NUS) [5]. VOC12 is a commonly used dataset on general objects. COCO contains a large number of small objects. CUB focuses on the fine-grained attribute identification of birds. NUS is a large-scale multi-label dataset. The details of datasets are listed in Table 1. For the single positive label setting, we use the same sampled labels from the original dataset as in [7].

**Implementation Details.** We follow the same schedules in [7]. 20% data from the training set is collected for validation. We use ResNet-50 [16] as our backbones in all experiments. For each experiment, the model is trained for 10 epochs with Adam optimizer [22]. We do grid search on learning rates in $\{10^{-2}, 10^{-3}, 10^{-4}, 10^{-5}\}$ and batch sizes in $\{8, 16\}$. The best model is selected by validation sets and used to compare with other methods. We integrated the proposed methods, including hyperspherical learning and adaptive learning, into our model, named hyperspherical multi-label classification (HML). The model is thoroughly evaluated in three scenarios (single positive labels, partial positive labels and full labels).

## 4.2 Single Positive Labels

In Table 2, we evaluate the proposed method in the single positive labels scenario. Our method comprehensively outperforms the methods proposed in [7].

Especially for the COCO dataset, our method has an improvement of 3.8% compared to the WAN [7]. Previous methods do not consistently improve on all the datasets. By comparison, our method exhibits strong generalization on diverse datasets. These experiments verify the effectiveness of suppressing false negatives in single positive labels.

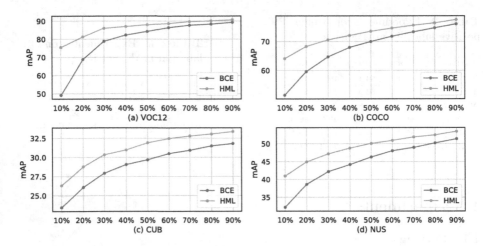

**Fig. 4.** Experiments on partial positive labels. The mAP is reported in different proportions of positive labels.

### 4.3  Partial Positive Labels

In order to further study the impact of false negatives, we conduct experiments on partial positive labels as shown in Fig. 4. In this scenario, impacts of different proportions of positive labels are evaluated. It is not surprising that the performance decreases significantly in very few positives. For general binary cross-entropy loss, the performance drops 40% in the VOC12 dataset with 10% positive labels. Compared to BCE, our method performs better with any proportion of positive labels. Also, the smaller the number of positives, the more significant the improvement. This result illustrates that our method can handle false negatives more effectively than the baseline method.

### 4.4  Full Labels

We also evaluate our method in full labels scenario in Table 3. Label smoothing (LS) [7] is a strong baseline in the full labels scenario compared to BCE, while our method surpasses LS by 1–2%. It shows that our method not only improves performance in datasets with single positive labels, but also generalizes well to datasets with full labels. In hyperspherical space, we could focus on learning positives and suppress the excessive contribution of false negatives.

**Table 4.** Ablation study on hyperspherical learning (HL) and adaptive learning (AL) in mAP metric.

| | | Single Positive Labels | | | | Full Labels | | | |
|---|---|---|---|---|---|---|---|---|---|
| HL | AL | VOC12 | COCO | CUB | NUS | VOC12 | COCO | CUB | NUS |
| ✗ | ✗ | <u>86.9</u> | 66.2 | 19.1 | 42.8 | <u>90.2</u> | 77.6 | 32.1 | 52.6 |
| ✓ | ✗ | **89.1** | <u>70.4</u> | <u>20.6</u> | <u>46.5</u> | **91.3** | <u>78.4</u> | <u>33.5</u> | <u>53.6</u> |
| ✓ | ✓ | **89.1** | **70.7** | **21.1** | **46.7** | **91.3** | **78.6** | **33.6** | **54.1** |

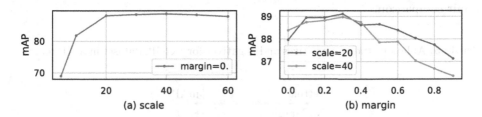

**Fig. 5.** Ablation study on scale and margin for VOC12 dataset in mAP metric.

## 4.5 Ablation Study

**Learning in Hyperspherical Space.** We study the impact of hyperspherical learning in scenarios of single positive labels and full labels in Table 4. In single positive labels scenario, our method significantly improves (up to 4.2%) over the baseline method. Even in the full-labeled dataset, our method has a consistent gain in performance (about 1%) across multiple datasets. It illustrates the strength of our approach in two ways. First, optimizing the cosine similarity facilitates multi-label learning. Second, hyperspherical learning is superior at suppressing the effects of noisy data.

**Adaptive Learning.** The adaptive variant of our method performs slightly better than the fixed variant as shown in Table 4. In the single positive labels scenario, the adaptive variant, in particular, outperforms 0.5 % in the CUB dataset. The CUB dataset is more challenging because more than 95% positive labels are discarded in this scenario. The adaptive variant effectively balances the impact of negatives and positives from the perspective of gradients, which makes the optimization easier.

**Scale and Margin.** The scale and margin are crucial hyperparameters in learning multi-label classification in hyperspherical space. An experimental study on ablation of the scale and margin is shown in Fig. 5. With no margin, the performance gradually converges with the increase of scale. It is because that small scale leads to large gradients even when cosine similarity equals 1. In order to comprehensively investigate the influence of margin, we conduct experiments on scale=20 and scale=40. With the increase of angular margin, the gain of performance is firstly strengthened and then weakened. The best performance is reached at mAP=89.1 with scale=20, margin=0.3. As analyzed in Fig. 3, the balance of gradients between positives and negatives is closely related to the choice of margin. The smaller margin could make the optimization of positives insufficient, while larger margin down weights contribution of negatives. It should be noted that this grid search of scale and margin is only conducted in single positive labels of the VOC12 dataset. The best hyperparameters above with scale=20 and margin=0.3 would also be used in other datasets' experiments for a fair comparison.

**Table 5.** Ablation study on positives and negatives for VOC12 dataset in mAP metric.

| Setting | mAP |
|---|---|
| No Margin | 88.0 |
| Only Positives | 83.4 |
| Only Negatives | 88.2 |
| Positives & Negatives | 89.1 |

**Margin on Positives and Negatives.** The margin is only applied in positives in face verification during training. In our method, the margin is also added to negatives. To explore this difference, we experiment on the four settings of margin on positives and negatives shown in Table 5.

**No Margin.** It is the baseline with no margin on positives and negatives.

**Only Positives.** In this setting, the margin is only added on positives. Since annotations are unknown during testing, there is an inconsistency that the training uses the margin while the testing does not. In testing, the drop of margin reduces the probability of positives, making it difficult to distinguish positives from negatives. As a result, the *Only Positives* is 4.6% worse than *No Margin*. This inconsistency on positives leads to poor generalization.

**Only Negatives.** In this setting, the margin is only added to the negatives. On the one hand, the margin helps to reduce the impact of false negatives. On the other, the reduced probability would not degrade the ability to classify. The *Only Negatives* is slightly better than *No Margin*. It shows the importance of suppressing false negatives.

**Positives & Negatives.** In this setting, the margin is added on all samples and keeps the consistency of training and testing. The margin on positives helps to improve the cosine similarity between the feature and its corresponding positive label embedding, while the margin on negatives suppresses the impact of false negatives. *Positives & Negatives* exceeds *No Margin* 1.1% in mAP. It indicates the necessity to add the margin on both positives and negatives in optimizing multi-label classification in hyperspherical space.

## 4.6  Label Correlation

As discussed in Sect. 3.5, we estimate the label correlation in COCO dataset in Fig. 6. The higher is the correlation value, the stronger is the correlation between the corresponding two labels. We could see some labels sets with strong correlations: {baseball bat, baseball glove}, {fork, knife, spoon, bowl, dinning table}, {apple, orange}, {chair, dinning table}, {laptop, mouse, keyboard} and {microwave, oven}. All these combinations have a higher probability of appearing in the same scene. But the correlations between {apple} and {baseball bat, baseball glove} are weak. It is consistent with the rareness of their co-occurrence in the same scene.

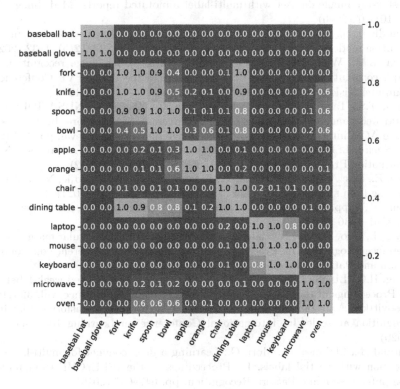

**Fig. 6.** Label correlation in COCO dataset. The labels with correlation value larger than 0.95 with other labels are shown.

## 5   Conclusion

In this paper, we present a novel perspective for learning multi-label classification in hyperspherical space. We thoroughly explore the impact of false positives in noisy multi-label tasks and propose the margin based sigmoid function for multi-label classification. To reduce manual hyperparameters searching, adaptive learning is incorporated into model optimization. Experiments show that our approach significantly improves performance in various scenarios, ranging from single and partial positive labels to full labels. In future work, we intend further to explore the problem of multi-label classification, as it is expected to be extended to the multi-label image retrieval task in hyperspherical space.

# References

1. Akbarnejad, A.H., Baghshah, M.S.: An efficient semi-supervised multi-label classifier capable of handling missing labels. IEEE Trans. Knowl. Data Eng. **31**(2), 229–242 (2018)
2. Bustos, A., Pertusa, A., Salinas, J.M., de la Iglesia-Vayá, M.: PadChest: a large chest x-ray image dataset with multi-label annotated reports. Med. Image Anal. **66**, 101797 (2020)
3. Chaudhari, S., Mithal, V., Polatkan, G., Ramanath, R.: An attentive survey of attention models. ACM Trans. Intell. Syst. Technol. (TIST) **12**(5), 1–32 (2021)
4. Chen, Z.M., Wei, X.S., Wang, P., Guo, Y.: Multi-label image recognition with graph convolutional networks. In: Proceedings of the IEEE/CVF Conference on Computer Vision and Pattern Recognition, pp. 5177–5186 (2019)
5. Chua, T.S., Tang, J., Hong, R., Li, H., Luo, Z., Zheng, Y.: NUS-WIDE: a real-world web image database from national university of Singapore. In: Proceedings of the ACM international conference on image and video retrieval, pp. 1–9 (2009)
6. Cid-Sueiro, J.: Proper losses for learning from partial labels. In: Advances in Neural Information Processing Systems, pp. 1565–1573. Citeseer (2012)
7. Cole, E., Mac Aodha, O., Lorieul, T., Perona, P., Morris, D., Jojic, N.: Multi-label learning from single positive labels. In: CVPR, pp. 933–942 (2021)
8. Cour, T., Sapp, B., Taskar, B.: Learning from partial labels. J. Mach. Learn. Res. **12**, 1501–1536 (2011)
9. Deng, J., Guo, J., Xue, N., Zafeiriou, S.: ArcFace: additive angular margin loss for deep face recognition. In: Proceedings of the IEEE/CVF Conference on Computer Vision and Pattern Recognition, pp. 4690–4699 (2019)
10. Dong, H.C., Li, Y.F., Zhou, Z.H.: Learning from semi-supervised weak-label data. In: Proceedings of the AAAI Conference on Artificial Intelligence, vol. 32 (2018)
11. Dosovitskiy, A., et al.: An image is worth 16 × 16 words: transformers for image recognition at scale. In: International Conference on Learning Representations (2020)
12. Durand, T., Mehrasa, N., Mori, G.: Learning a deep convnet for multi-label classification with partial labels. In: Proceedings of the IEEE/CVF Conference on Computer Vision and Pattern Recognition, pp. 647–657 (2019)
13. Elkan, C., Noto, K.: Learning classifiers from only positive and unlabeled data. In: Proceedings of the 14th ACM SIGKDD international conference on Knowledge discovery and data mining, pp. 213–220 (2008)
14. Everingham, M., Eslami, S.A., Van Gool, L., Williams, C.K., Winn, J., Zisserman, A.: The pascal visual object classes challenge: a retrospective. Int. J. Comput. Vis. **111**(1), 98–136 (2015)
15. Fan, X., Jiang, W., Luo, H., Fei, M.: SphereReID: deep hypersphere manifold embedding for person re-identification. J. Vis. Commun. Image Represent. **60**, 51–58 (2019)
16. He, K., Zhang, X., Ren, S., Sun, J.: Deep residual learning for image recognition. In: Proceedings of the IEEE conference on computer vision and pattern recognition, pp. 770–778 (2016)

17. He, X., Zemel, R.: Learning hybrid models for image annotation with partially labeled data. Adv. Neural. Inf. Process. Syst. **21**, 625–632 (2008)
18. Huang, S.J., Zhou, Z.H.: Multi-label learning by exploiting label correlations locally. In: Proceedings of the AAAI Conference on Artificial Intelligence, vol. 26 (2012)
19. Huynh, D., Elhamifar, E.: Interactive multi-label CNN learning with partial labels. In: Proceedings of the IEEE/CVF Conference on Computer Vision and Pattern Recognition, pp. 9423–9432 (2020)
20. Jin, R., Ghahramani, Z.: Learning with multiple labels. In: NIPS, vol. 2, pp. 897–904. Citeseer (2002)
21. Kang, F., Jin, R., Sukthankar, R.: Correlated label propagation with application to multi-label learning. In: 2006 IEEE Computer Society Conference on Computer Vision and Pattern Recognition (CVPR'06), vol. 2, pp. 1719–1726. IEEE (2006)
22. Kingma, D.P., Ba, J.: Adam: a method for stochastic optimization. In: ICLR (Poster) (2015), http://arxiv.org/abs/1412.6980
23. Krizhevsky, A., Sutskever, I., Hinton, G.E.: ImageNet classification with deep convolutional neural networks. Adv. Neural. Inf. Process. Syst. **25**, 1097–1105 (2012)
24. Lanchantin, J., Wang, T., Ordonez, V., Qi, Y.: General multi-label image classification with transformers. In: Proceedings of the IEEE/CVF Conference on Computer Vision and Pattern Recognition, pp. 16478–16488 (2021)
25. Li, Q., Peng, X., Qiao, Y., Peng, Q.: Learning label correlations for multi-label image recognition with graph networks. Pattern Recogn. Lett. **138**, 378–384 (2020)
26. Li, W., et al.: WebVision challenge: visual learning and understanding with web data. ArXiv preprint arXiv:1705.05640 (2017)
27. Li, X., Liu, B.: Learning to classify texts using positive and unlabeled data. In: IJCAI, vol. 3, pp. 587–592. Citeseer (2003)
28. Lin, T., et al.: Microsoft COCO: common objects in context. In: Fleet, D., Pajdla, T., Schiele, B., Tuytelaars, T. (eds.) ECCV 2014. LNCS, vol. 8693, pp. 740–755. Springer, Cham (2014). https://doi.org/10.1007/978-3-319-10602-1_48
29. Liu, W., Wen, Y., Yu, Z., Li, M., Raj, B., Song, L.: SphereFace: deep hypersphere embedding for face recognition. In: Proceedings of the IEEE conference on computer vision and pattern recognition, pp. 212–220 (2017)
30. Liu, W., et al.: Deep hyperspherical learning. In: Proceedings of the 31st International Conference on Neural Information Processing Systems, pp. 3953–3963 (2017)
31. Liu, Z., et al.: Swin transformer: Hierarchical vision transformer using shifted windows. In: Proceedings of the IEEE/CVF International Conference on Computer Vision (ICCV), pp. 10012–10022 (October 2021)
32. Luo, H., Gu, Y., Liao, X., Lai, S., Jiang, W.: Bag of tricks and a strong baseline for deep person re-identification. In: Proceedings of the IEEE/CVF Conference on Computer Vision and Pattern Recognition Workshops (2019)
33. Luo, H., et al.: A strong baseline and batch normalization neck for deep person re-identification. IEEE Trans. Multimedia **22**(10), 2597–2609 (2019)
34. Meng, Q., Zhang, W.: Multi-label image classification with attention mechanism and graph convolutional networks. In: Proceedings of the ACM Multimedia Asia, pp. 1–6. ACM (2019)
35. Nguyen, N., Caruana, R.: Classification with partial labels. In: Proceedings of the 14th ACM SIGKDD International Conference on Knowledge Discovery and Data Mining, pp. 551–559 (2008)

36. Pham, H., Dai, Z., Xie, Q., Le, Q.V.: Meta pseudo labels. In: Proceedings of the IEEE/CVF Conference on Computer Vision and Pattern Recognition, pp. 11557–11568 (2021)
37. Ranftl, R., Bochkovskiy, A., Koltun, V.: Vision transformers for dense prediction. In: Proceedings of the IEEE/CVF International Conference on Computer Vision, pp. 12179–12188 (2021)
38. Ridnik, T., et al.: Asymmetric loss for multi-label classification. In: Proceedings of the IEEE/CVF International Conference on Computer Vision, pp. 82–91 (2021)
39. Sun, Y.Y., Zhang, Y., Zhou, Z.H.: Multi-label learning with weak label. In: Twenty-fourth AAAI conference on artificial intelligence (2010)
40. Touvron, H., Cord, M., Douze, M., Massa, F., Sablayrolles, A., Jégou, H.: Training data-efficient image transformers & distillation through attention. In: International Conference on Machine Learning, pp. 10347–10357. PMLR (2021)
41. Wah, C., Branson, S., Welinder, P., Perona, P., Belongie, S.: The caltech-UCSD birds-200-2011 dataset. Journal (2011)
42. Wang, F., Cheng, J., Liu, W., Liu, H.: Additive margin softmax for face verification. IEEE Signal Process. Lett. **25**(7), 926–930 (2018)
43. Wang, F., Xiang, X., Cheng, J., Yuille, A.L.: Normface: L2 hypersphere embedding for face verification. In: Proceedings of the 25th ACM International Conference on Multimedia, pp. 1041–1049 (2017)
44. Wang, H., et al.: CosFace: Large margin cosine loss for deep face recognition. In: Proceedings of the IEEE conference on computer vision and pattern recognition, pp. 5265–5274 (2018)
45. Wang, L., Liu, Y., Qin, C., Sun, G., Fu, Y.: Dual relation semi-supervised multi-label learning. In: Proceedings of the AAAI Conference on Artificial Intelligence, vol. 34, pp. 6227–6234 (2020)
46. Wang, Y., He, D., Li, F., Long, X., Zhou, Z., Ma, J., Wen, S.: Multi-label classification with label graph superimposing. In: Proceedings of the AAAI Conference on Artificial Intelligence, vol. 34, pp. 12265–12272 (2020)
47. Wen*, Y., Liu*, W., Weller, A., Raj, B., Singh, R.: Sphereface2: binary classification is all you need for deep face recognition. In: 10th International Conference on Learning Representations (ICLR) (2022). https://openreview.net/forum?id=l3SDgUh7qZO, *equal contribution
48. Wojke, N., Bewley, A.: Deep cosine metric learning for person re-identification. In: 2018 IEEE winter conference on applications of computer vision (WACV), pp. 748–756. IEEE (2018)
49. Xie, M.K., Huang, S.J.: Partial multi-label learning with noisy label identification. IEEE Transactions on Pattern Analysis and Machine Intelligence (2021)
50. Ye, J., He, J., Peng, X., Wu, W., Qiao, Y.: Attention-driven dynamic graph convolutional network for multi-label image recognition. In: Vedaldi, A., Bischof, H., Brox, T., Frahm, J.-M. (eds.) ECCV 2020. LNCS, vol. 12366, pp. 649–665. Springer, Cham (2020). https://doi.org/10.1007/978-3-030-58589-1_39
51. Yu, F., Rawat, A.S., Menon, A., Kumar, S.: Federated learning with only positive labels. In: International Conference on Machine Learning, pp. 10946–10956. PMLR (2020)
52. Yu, Y., Pedrycz, W., Miao, D.: Multi-label classification by exploiting label correlations. Expert Syst. Appl. **41**(6), 2989–3004 (2014)
53. Zhao, F., Huang, Y., Wang, L., Tan, T.: Deep semantic ranking based hashing for multi-label image retrieval. In: Proceedings of the IEEE conference on computer vision and pattern recognition, pp. 1556–1564 (2015)

54. Zhao, J., Yan, K., Zhao, Y., Guo, X., Huang, F., Li, J.: Transformer-based dual relation graph for multi-label image recognition. In: Proceedings of the IEEE/CVF International Conference on Computer Vision, pp. 163–172 (2021)
55. Zhao, J., Zhao, Y., Li, J.: M3tr: Multi-modal multi-label recognition with transformer. In: Proceedings of the 29th ACM International Conference on Multimedia, pp. 469–477 (2021)
56. Zhu, J., Liao, S., Lei, Z., Yi, D., Li, S.: Pedestrian attribute classification in surveillance: Database and evaluation. In: Proceedings of the IEEE international conference on computer vision workshops, pp. 331–338 (2013)
57. Zhu, Y., Kwok, J.T., Zhou, Z.H.: Multi-label learning with global and local label correlation. IEEE Trans. Knowl. Data Eng. **30**(6), 1081–1094 (2017)

# When Active Learning Meets Implicit Semantic Data Augmentation

Zhuangzhuang Chen(ID), Jin Zhang(ID), Pan Wang(ID), Jie Chen(ID),
and Jianqiang Li$^{(\boxtimes)}$(ID)

Shenzhen University, Shenzhen 518060, China
lijq@szu.edu.cn

**Abstract.** Active learning (AL) is a label-efficient technique for training deep models when only a limited labeled set is available and the manual annotation is expensive. Implicit semantic data augmentation (ISDA) effectively extends the limited amount of labeled samples and increases the diversity of labeled sets without introducing a noticeable extra computational cost. The scarcity of labeled instances and the huge annotation cost of unlabelled samples encourage us to ponder on the combination of AL and ISDA. A nature direction is a pipelined integration, which selects the unlabeled samples via acquisition function in AL for labeling and generates virtual samples by changing the selected samples to semantic transformation directions within ISDA. However, this pipelined combination would not guarantee the diversity of virtual samples. This paper proposes diversity-aware semantic transformation active learning, or DAST-AL framework, that looks ahead the effect of ISDA in the selection of unlabeled samples. Specifically, DAST-AL exploits expected partial model change maximization (EPMCM) to consider selected samples' potential contribution of the diversity to the labeled set by leveraging the semantic transformation within ISDA when selecting the unlabeled samples. After that, DAST-AL can confidently and efficiently augment the labeled set by implicitly generating more diverse samples. The empirical results on both image classification and semantic segmentation tasks show that the proposed DAST-AL can slightly outperform the state-of-the-art AL approaches. Under the same condition, the proposed method takes less than 3 min for the first cycle of active labeling while the existing agreement discrepancy selection incurs more than 40 min.

**Keywords:** Active learning · Implicit semantic data augmentation · Expected partial model change maximization · Diversity

## 1 Introduction

In recent years, deep learning has achieved a new height in performing various tasks like image classification, object detection, semantic segmentation *etc.*. However, they suffer from huge annotation labor and incur long time due to the requirement of large-scale labeled data to train the deep models [41]. In some

S. Avidan et al. (Eds.): ECCV 2022, LNCS 13685, pp. 56–72, 2022.
https://doi.org/10.1007/978-3-031-19806-9_4

tasks, it is difficult to accumulate the data and it requires skilled professional to annotate. Therefore, the dependency on large-scale labeled data has become a major bottleneck for deep learning methods [12]. To alleviate this dependency, many methods like, unsupervised learning [6,11,27,43], semi-supervised learning [17,20,34,40], weakly supervised learning [24,28,29,44], active learning [1,2,9,41] *etc.*, have received significant attentions. Although weakly supervised learning and semi-supervised learning have made rapid progresses, active learning remains the foundation of many vision tasks due to its simplicity and better performance [39].

AL is an iterative process. It overcomes the limited labeling budget by selecting a set of samples from an unlabeled pool at each iteration [41] and labels the selected ones. These unlabeled samples will be added to the labeled set after being labeled by an oracle. Different unlabeled samples will yield different results. Therefore, the key question for AL is how to acquire data that can achieve better performance.

To solve this problem, many state-of-the-art works [13,19,41] achieve competitive results by designing the customized modules that make full use of the labeled samples and unlabeled samples. For example, in [32], the authors propose variational adversarial active learning (VAAL) that uses variational autoencoder and a discriminator to learn the uncertainty of the unlabeled samples implicitly. To better leverage both the annotation and the labeled/unlabeled samples' information, state-relabeling adversarial active learning (SRAAL) [41] designs a compact model composed of the unified representation generator and a labeled/unlabeled state discriminator. In [13], the authors propose agreement discrepancy selection (ADS) by designing adversarial classifiers to the convolutional neural network for the selection of informative samples. The above approaches achieve satisfying results by training the customized module with the labeled and unlabeled data in an adversarial manner, involving excessive training time. However, for robots with minimal computing resources and limited runtime, it is hard to get adopted in a new scenario in quick time without extensive training. Hence, enhancing the efficiency of the AL scheme without designing the customized modules remains a critical challenge.

The approaches based on the *expected model change principle*(EMCP) [4,5] address the efficiency challenge by querying the examples that maximally change the current model without designing the customized modules. Specifically, EMCP follows the stochastic gradient descent rule to estimate the ability of a candidate example to change the model by the gradient of the loss at the current candidate example [4,5]. Notably, most of these methods deal with the regression problem with the small model, and as a result, the existing EMCP methods are not directly applicable to classification tasks for the deep networks.

Besides the existing EMCP methods, ISDA [36] is another efficient approach for training the deep networks that provide diverse instances, which can be generated by changing the original instance to semantic transformation directions sampled from the feature covariance matrix. Next, it is straightforward to consider the feasibility of combining EMCP and ISDA. One simple direction is a naive pipelined combination, which selects unlabeled samples by an acquisition function that follows the EMCP, and generates virtual instances from the selected samples by ISDA afterward. However, such an acquisition function fails to consider the potential gain from ISDA with respect to diversity. Hence, without any feedback during the acquisition process, the augmented samples from ISDA would not guarantee diversity (Fig. 1).

To solve the above problem, the assumption in this paper is two-fold: (1) unlabeled samples have an unequal contribution to increasing the diversity of the label set after being labeled and augmented by ISDA, (2) the augmented samples with a higher diversity should have a higher ability to change the classifier. Based on these assumptions, this paper proposes the diversity-aware semantic transformation active learning, or DAST-AL framework. DAST-AL develops EPMCM to look ahead the effect of ISDA in advance of the acquisition process, by selecting unlabeled samples considering the ability of their

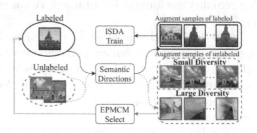

**Fig. 1.** An overview of DAST-AL. DAST-AL looks ahead the effect of ISDA in the process of acquisition while avoiding the costly sampling process. Note that the translated features are mapped to the image space and shown as augment samples in the above figure.

augmented virtual samples to change the current classifier. The proposed EPMCM algorithm of DAST-AL enables us to select the unlabeled samples that have higher gain for increasing the diversity of labeled sets when augmented via ISDA. Furthermore, DAST-AL realizes the previously mentioned gain by labeling and augmenting the selected samples by using ISDA.

Our contributions are summarized as follows:

- Firstly, we propose EPMCM for selecting the unlabeled samples. The augmented samples of these unlabeled samples bring maximum change to the current partial model, and achieve a higher gain from ISDA in the assessment of diversity contributes to the labeled set.
- Then, we propose DAST-AL that overcomes the limited labeling budget by using the proposed EPMCM to efficiently select the unlabeled samples. After labeling and adding these unlabeled samples to the labeled set, DAST-AL efficiently augments the labeled set by using ISDA without the costly burden of explicitly generating the augmented samples.
- Finally, we compare the performance of our proposed method with existing methods in [13,30,32,37,41]. Although we find performances of ADS and DAST-AL are closely comparable, ADS takes 44 minutes in the first iteration of AL which is much higher compared to the proposed DAST-AL.

## 2 Related Work

With a decade's study, AL has proven its superiority over the other methods. Based on the existing methods, we group them into two categories: parameterized sampler and non-parameterized sampler. The difference between the two categories lies in whether the customized modules are introduced for selecting the most informative samples.

The parameterized sampler approaches can further be decomposed into the synthesizing approaches and the pool-based approaches. The synthesizing approaches introduce the generative model to produce new synthetic samples that are informative to the current model [23,26,42]. These approaches introduce or design various generative adversial networks (GAN) [23] or variational auto-encoders (VAE) [33] to enhance the diversity of labeled set by generating diverse data. The pool-based approaches use the customized modules to query the most informative instances from the unlabeled pool. A loss prediction module is designed to select data that is likely to make the target model producing a wrong prediction [37]. VAAL [32] and *task aware* VAAL [19] build a latent space by a VAE that learns together with the ranking conditional GAN. SRAAL [41] build an unsupervised image reconstructor and a supervised target learner to help relabel the state of unlabeled data with different importance. ADS [13] introduces a customized classifier to play the min-max game to select the most informative samples. By introducing the customized modules, these methods achieve the state-of-arts results. However, these approaches suffer from excessive training time during their iterative procedure for selecting the unlabeled samples.

The non-parameterized sampler approaches can also be decomposed into two parts: the uncertainty-based and ECMP-based approaches. The uncertainty-based approaches select the most informative samples by evaluating the uncertainty in the model prediction. To do so, previous works [18,22,35] simply utilize class posterior probabilities to define uncertainty. The probability of a predicted class [22] or an entropy of class posterior probabilities [18,35] defines uncertainty of a data point. To better quantify uncertainty, multiple forward passes with Monte Carlo Dropout are used [15]. However, it involves large computation for large-scale learning, as each data point in the large-scale unlabeled pool needs to be performed with multiple forward passes to measure its uncertainty. The EMCP approaches are based on the decision-theoretic. They select the unlabeled data by estimating expected model changes [4,5] that is based on the current model. These approaches have been well applied on regression tasks. As deep network involves a large number of parameters to estimate their changes, the approaches are hard to be applied to these networks.

Our method fits into the category of EMCP approaches with an exception. We estimate the partial model change for the classification tasks, rather than estimating the expected model change of the full network for regression. Also, our method is different from the synthetic approaches in the sense that we do not design any customized module and have no need to explicitly generate augmented images.

## 3 Method

In this section, we introduce the proposed DAST-AL. We first introduce how to obtain augmented instances in the feature space by following ISDA in Sect. 3.1. Then, we present details of the proposed EPMCM that served as the acquisition function in Sect. 3.2. In each iteration of DAST-AL, the following two steps are successively carried out.

1. Train the backbone network (feature extractor) and classifier on the current labeled set by using ISDA for augmenting this set to introduce more diversity. At the same time, we use the extracted features of the labeled samples at hand to calculate the covariance matrix for each category, where the covariance matrix represents all the feature semantic transformation directions of each category.
2. Use the proposed EPMCM to select the unlabeled sample. Then, the translated feature (i.e., the augmented samples) of these selected samples along infinite semantic transformation directions result in the maximum change to the current partial model. To overcome the limited labeling budget, these selected samples, which are expected to have higher diversity, will be labeled and added to the labeled set for step 1 in the next iteration.

### 3.1 Implicit Data Augmentation via Semantic Transformation

Let $\mathbb{M}^e$ be the feature extractor, $\mathbb{M}^c$ be the classifier, $L$ be the labeled set, $U$ be the unlabeled set, $C$ be the number of classes, and $y_l$ be the label of a sample $x_l$ from $L$.

For a sample $x_l$ in a class $y_l$, we extract its feature with $\boldsymbol{a}_l = \mathbb{M}^e(x_l)$. By following ISDA, the semantic directions for class $y_l$ can then be obtained by sampling random vectors from a zero-mean multi-variate distribution $\mathcal{N}(0, \Sigma_{y_l})$, where $\Sigma_{y_l}$ is the class-conditional covariance matrix estimated from the features of the labeled samples in class $y_l$. As the semantic transformation directions of different categories are different, we use the online estimation algorithm [36] to get the covariance matrixes of all classes $\Sigma = \{\Sigma_1, \Sigma_2, \cdots, \Sigma_C\}$. Referring to ISDA, we can randomly sample along $\mathcal{N}(0, \Sigma_{y_l})$ to generate augmented features with different semantic transformations, i.e., $\tilde{\boldsymbol{a}}_l \sim \mathcal{N}(\boldsymbol{a}_l, \Sigma_{y_l})$.

Consequently, unlimited $\tilde{\boldsymbol{a}}_l$ can be generated to augment the labeled set for diversity by exploiting *expected* cross-entropy loss in ISDA [36]. As for the unlabeled samples, suppose an unlabeled sample $x_u$ can be selected in the AL cycle and labeled by a human expert with the label $y_u$, then it will be added to $L$, and its augmented feature $\tilde{\boldsymbol{a}}_u$ can also be obtained from $\tilde{\boldsymbol{a}}_u \sim \mathcal{N}(\boldsymbol{a}_u, \Sigma_{y_u})$, where $\boldsymbol{a}_u = \mathbb{M}^e(x_u)$. The potential gain from ISDA in the assessment of diversity contributes to the labeled set is up to the diversity of the $\tilde{\boldsymbol{a}}_u$. Therefore, it is crucial to measure the diversity contributing to the labeled set under unlimited $\tilde{\boldsymbol{a}}_u$, so that we can confidently rank the unlabeled samples with the potential gain from ISDA and select the better ones.

## 3.2 The Proposed Expected Partial Model Change Maximization

For selecting samples from the unlabeled set by considering their augmented features, the key is to find a reasonable way to evaluate the diversity contribution of each augmented feature sampling from the multivariate normal distribution. Intuitively, if the augmented feature is useless for the classifier updating, then this feature also has no use to augment the labeled set for more diversity. Inspired by this intuition, we propose EPMCM which is expected to evaluate the diversity contribution of the unlabeled sample under the unlimited augmented features by considering the partial classifier change. A detailed description of EPMCM is given below.

Different from existing EMCP-based methods that deal with regression problems at the instance level [4], we consider training the classifier $\mathbb{M}^c$ under an augmented labeled set $\mathcal{D} = \left\{ \left( \tilde{a}_l^i, y_l \right) \right\}_{i=1}^n$ in the feature space with cross-entropy loss $\mathcal{L}$, where $\tilde{a}_l^i$ is sampled from $\mathcal{N}\left(a_l, \Sigma_{y_l}\right)$ with label $y_l$. Then, following the empirical risk minimization principle [4], $\mathbb{M}^c$ is trained by minimizing the empirical error on $\mathcal{D}$. The corresponding empirical error is shown as follows:

$$\hat{\epsilon}_D = \sum_{i=1}^n \mathcal{L}\left[\mathbb{M}^c\left(a_l^i\right), y_l\right]. \tag{1}$$

Suppose that $\mathbb{M}^c$ is defined by the last fully connected layer, and its parameters consist of the weight matrix $\boldsymbol{W} = [\boldsymbol{w}_1, \ldots, \boldsymbol{w}_C]^T \in \mathcal{R}^{C \times F}$ and biases $\boldsymbol{b} = [b_1, \ldots, b_C]^T \in \mathcal{R}^C$. For learning the best $\boldsymbol{W}$ and $\boldsymbol{b}$, stochastic gradient descent (SGD) [3] can be used to update the parameters iteratively according to the negative gradient of the loss $\mathcal{L}$ with respect to each augment features $a_l^i$ that follows Eq. 2,

$$\{\boldsymbol{W}, \boldsymbol{b}\}_{\text{new}} \leftarrow \{\boldsymbol{W}, \boldsymbol{b}\} - \alpha \frac{\partial \mathcal{L}_{a_l^i}(\{\boldsymbol{W}, \boldsymbol{b}\})}{\partial \{\boldsymbol{W}, \boldsymbol{b}\}}, \quad i = 1, \ldots, n, \tag{2}$$

where the $\alpha$ denotes learning rate.

With the understanding from the discussion above, now we describe the SGD rule in our AL scheme. Let us suppose the augmented feature $\tilde{a}_u$ of unlabeled sample $x_u$ with label $y_u$ is added to the $\mathcal{D}$. The empirical error on the extended $\mathcal{D}^+ = \mathcal{D} \cup (\tilde{a}_u, y_u)$ can be represented in the form of the following equation:

$$\hat{\epsilon}_{\mathcal{D}^+} = \sum_{i=1}^n \mathcal{L}\left[\mathbb{M}^c\left(a_l^i\right), y_l\right] + \underbrace{\mathcal{L}\left[\mathbb{M}^c\left(\tilde{a}_u\right), y_u\right]}_{:=\mathcal{L}_{\tilde{a}_u}(\{\boldsymbol{W}, \boldsymbol{b}\})}. \tag{3}$$

As a consequence of the change in the augmented unlabeled set, the parameters $\boldsymbol{W}$ and $\boldsymbol{b}$ are also get changed. Considering the SGD update rule, as the model change is equivalent to parameters change, the parameters change $C_{\{\boldsymbol{W}, \boldsymbol{b}\}}(\tilde{a}_u)$ can be approximated as the gradient of the $\mathcal{L}$ at the $\tilde{a}_u$, described by Eq. 4,

$$\mathbf{C}_{\{\boldsymbol{W}, \boldsymbol{b}\}}(\tilde{a}_u) = \Delta\{\boldsymbol{W}, \boldsymbol{b}\} \approx \alpha \frac{\partial \mathcal{L}_{\tilde{a}_u}(\{\boldsymbol{W}, \boldsymbol{b}\})}{\partial \{\boldsymbol{W}, \boldsymbol{b}\}}. \tag{4}$$

It should be noted that the dimension of $W$ is $C \times F$ that will lead to a large computational burden with the increasing dimension of the feature. Hence, we only consider estimating the change of the $b$, and then the partial classifier change can be represented as $\mathbf{C}_{\{b\}}(\tilde{a}_u)$. Since the goal of our AL acquisition function is to select the unlabeled sample, the augmented features of which lead to the maximum partial classifier change, we firstly consider an easy implementation that explicitly samples $M$ times from the distribution $\mathcal{N}(a_u, \Sigma_{y_u})$ to compose an limited augmented feature set $\mathcal{D}_{x_u} = \{(\tilde{a}_u^1, y_u), (\tilde{a}_u^2, y_u), \ldots, (\tilde{a}_u^M, y_u)\}$ of size $M$. Here $\tilde{a}_u^k$ denotes $k^{\text{th}}$ sampled augmented features for the unlabeled sample $x_u$. Then, the potential of each $x_u$ to augment the labeled set can be represented by summing the partial classifier change caused by each augmented feature in $\mathcal{D}_{x_u}$. Consequently, the acquisition function in our AL scheme can be formulated as follows:

$$x_u^* = \arg\max_{x_u \in U} \sum_{k=1}^{M} \left\| \mathbf{C}_b\left(\tilde{a}_u^k\right) \right\|, \tilde{a}_u^k \in \mathcal{D}_{x_u}, \tag{5}$$

where $x_u^*$ denotes the selected unlabeled samples.

To calculate Eq. 5, the following two issues must be tackled. **Firstly**, the true label $y_u$ is unknown before querying. Therefore, calculation over all possible labels $y_u$ can be a costly affair for an increasing number of classes. **Secondly**, when considering sampling $M$ times, the sampling variance is unstable and limited. An ideal way is to generate as much data as possible (i.e., set $M$ as large as possible). However the increasing $M$ will incur an excessive time complexity.

To address the first issue, we use a maximum *a-posteriori* approximation by only considering the most likely label $\hat{y}_u$ of $a_u$, predicted by the current $\mathbb{M}^c$. As for the second issue, aiming at simplifying computation while generating more data, we try to implicitly generate the unlimited augmented samples. When $M$ grows to infinity, it is equivalent to considering the expectation of the Eq. 5 under all possible augmented features. Then, the Eq. 5 under the cross-entropy loss can be rewritten as:

$$\begin{aligned}
x_u^* &= \arg\max_{x_u \in U} \left( \mathbb{E}_{\tilde{a}_u \sim \mathcal{N}(a_u, \Sigma_{\hat{y}_u})} \left\| \mathbf{C}_b(\tilde{a}_u) \right\| \right) \\
&= \arg\max_{x_u \in U} \left( \mathbb{E}_{\tilde{a}_u \sim \mathcal{N}(a_u, \Sigma_{\hat{y}_u})} \left\| \frac{\partial \mathcal{L}_{\tilde{a}_u}(b)}{\partial z} \cdot \frac{\partial z}{\partial b} \right\| \right) \\
&= \arg\max_{x_u \in U} \left( \mathbb{E}_{\tilde{a}_u \sim \mathcal{N}(a_u, \Sigma_{\hat{y}_u})} \left[ 1 - \frac{e^{w_{\hat{y}_u}^T \tilde{a}_u + b_{\hat{y}_u}}}{\sum_{j=1}^{C} e^{w_j^T \tilde{a}_u + b_j}} \right] \right) \\
&= \arg\max_{x_u \in U} \left( \mathcal{E}_{x_u}^\infty \right),
\end{aligned} \tag{6}$$

where $z$ is the output of the $\tilde{a}_u$ by using $\mathbb{M}^c$. Specifically speaking, $z$ can be obtained by the formula $z = w^T \tilde{a}_u + b$, and then we have $\frac{\partial z}{\partial b} = 1$, where $1$ represents a vector of dimension $C$ with each value 1. By assuming that the learning rate $\alpha$ is identical for each augmented feature, the third equation is then obtained by unfolding the second equation with the expanded cross-entropy loss.

However, it is infeasible to compute $\mathcal{E}_{x_u}^\infty$ precisely, we derive an upper bound $\overline{\mathcal{E}_{x_u}^\infty}$ as an alternative to that. Although the maximum upper bound is not strictly guaranteed to be numerically maximum, in Sect. 4.1, we demonstrate that the selection of unlabeled samples by the upper bounds is effective. The reason for this effect is that the gap between the upper-bound and $\mathcal{E}_{x_u}^\infty$ will decrease with the increase of sampling times (shown in Table 2). Since we consider the infinite sampling times, the large upper-bound could indicate that $\mathcal{E}_{x_u}^\infty$ would be large too. Moreover, to prove that the selected unlabeled samples are able to augment the labeled set for more diversity, we visualize the augmented features of the selected unlabeled samples (ref. to Sect. 4.3). The corresponding $\overline{\mathcal{E}_{x_u}^\infty}$ is derived in the following manner:

$$
\begin{aligned}
\mathcal{E}_{x_u}^\infty &= \mathbb{E}_{\tilde{a}_u \sim \mathcal{N}(a_u, \Sigma_{\hat{y}_u})} \left[ 1 - \frac{e^{w_{\hat{y}_u}^T \tilde{a}_u + b_{\hat{y}_u}}}{\sum_{j=1}^{C} e^{w_j^T \tilde{a}_u + b_j}} \right] \\
&\leq \mathbb{E}_{\tilde{a}_u \sim \mathcal{N}(a_u, \Sigma_{\hat{y}_u})} \left[ \frac{\sum_{j=1}^{C} e^{w_j^T \tilde{a}_u + b_j}}{e^{w_{\hat{y}_u}^T \tilde{a}_u + b_{\hat{y}_u}}} \right] - 1 \\
&= \mathbb{E}_{\tilde{a}_u \sim \mathcal{N}(a_u, \Sigma_{\hat{y}_u})} \sum_{j=1}^{C} \left( e^{\left(w_j^T - w_{\hat{y}_u}^T\right)\tilde{a}_u + b_j - b_{\hat{y}_u}} \right) - 1 \\
&= \sum_{j=1}^{C} e^{\left(w_j^T - w_{\hat{y}_u}^T\right) a_u + (b_j - b_{\hat{y}_u}) + \frac{1}{2}\left(w_j^T - w_{\hat{y}_u}^T\right) \Sigma_{\hat{y}_u} (w_j - w_{\hat{y}_u})} - 1 \\
&= \overline{\mathcal{E}_{x_u}^\infty}.
\end{aligned}
\tag{7}
$$

where the second inequality is hold by obeying the Jensen's inequality $2 \leq x + \frac{1}{x} \iff 1 - x \leq \frac{1}{x} - 1$, where $x = \frac{e^{w_{\hat{y}_u}^T \tilde{a}_u + b_{\hat{y}_u}}}{\sum_{j=1}^{C} e^{w_j^T \tilde{a}_u + b_j}}, 0 \leq x \leq 1$. Because of $\tilde{a}_u \sim \mathcal{N}(a_u, \Sigma_{\hat{y}_u})$, we can obtain that $\left(w_j^T - w_{\hat{y}_u}^T\right)\tilde{a}_u + b_j - b_{\hat{y}_u}$ is also a Gaussian random variable, i.e., $\left(w_j^T - w_{\hat{y}_u}^T\right)\tilde{a}_u + (b_j - b_{\hat{y}_u}) \sim \mathcal{N}\left(\left(w_j^T - w_{\hat{y}_u}^T\right)a_u + (b_j - b_{\hat{y}_u}), \left(w_j^T - w_{\hat{y}_u}^T\right)\Sigma_{\hat{y}_u}(w_j - w_{\hat{y}_u})\right)$. Then, the fourth equation can be obtained by leveraging the moment-generating function $\mathbb{E}\left[e^{tX}\right] = e^{t\mu + \frac{1}{2}\sigma^2 t^2}$, where $X \sim \mathcal{N}\left(\mu, \sigma^2\right)$ [8]. Finally, by calculating the $\overline{\mathcal{E}_{x_u}^\infty}$, we can select the unlabeled samples more efficiently. Since we do not need to explicit sampling and design the customized modules, the proposed EPMCM can be smoothly integrated into the AL scheme without excessive training time.

## 4 Experiments

Under the scope of this part, we evaluate DAST-AL against state-of-the-art AL approaches on image classification in Sect. 4.1 and segmentation task in

Sect. 4.2. To further verify the efficiency of our method, we perform ablation study in Sect. 4.3 and time analysis in Sect. 4.4.

### 4.1 Active Learning for Image Classification

**Dataset.** To verify our methods, we follow the same experimental settings proposed in [13,32,37,41] that fine-tune the network from the previous cycle if available. We choose commonly used CIFAR-10 and CIFAR-100 datasets for the image classification task. CIFAR-10 consists of 60000 images of $32 \times 32 \times 3$ pixels where 5000 images are used for the training and 1000 images are used for the testing. The CIFAR-10 and CIFAR-100 have 10 categories and 100 categories, respectively, while each category contains 600 images. We also follow the same setting in [32] that uses ImageNet [10] for the validation.

**Compared Methods.** For image classification tasks, we evaluate our method against state-of-the-art AL approaches, including Core-set [30], LL4AL [37], VAAL [32], SRAAL [41], ADS [13]. We also use the random selection method as the baseline. It is important to note that these methods are evaluated by the same target model that consists of feature extractor and classifier.

**Training Settings.** We use ResNet-18 [16] and VGG-16 [31] as the feature extractor in the target model to evaluate the accuracy. By following the experiment setting in [13], we initialize the labeled set $L$ by randomly sampling 1000 data points from the whole unlabeled set $U$ for the CIFAR-10 when using ResNet-18 or VGG-16, and randomly sampling 2500 data points for the CIFAR-100 when using ResNet-18. In the each iteration of AL, the number of labeled samples added to $L$ for CIFAR-10 and CIFAR-100 are 1000 and 2500, respectively. We then re-train the target model. We adopt the same image normalization as reported in the experiment part [13], and the data augmentation strategies including $32 \times 32$ random image crop and horizontal flip. In each AL iteration, according to the previous work experiment setting [13], the training epoch is set to 200, mini-batch size is set to 128, the initial learning rate is set to 0.1 before 160 epochs and it decreases to 0.01 after 160 epochs on CIFAR-10. The momentum and weight decay are set to 0.9 and 0.0005, respectively. To obtain the mean and standard deviation of performance, each experiment is repeated three times.

**Sub-set Sampling.** To make a fair comparison, we adopt the sub-set sampling from [13]. Since the entire training set is considered as the initial unlabeled set $U$, the sample size is very large, _e.g.,_ 50,000 for CIFAR-10 and CIFAR-100. According to the study [25,30], it is less efficient to directly select top-k samples from the $U$, because of the information overlap among the samples [13]. To address this problem, we follow the same settings reported in [2,13] that first selects a random subset $S_R$ and then selects top-k samples from $S_R$ by different methods. Here, the sample size $R$ is set to 10000 based on the study [13].

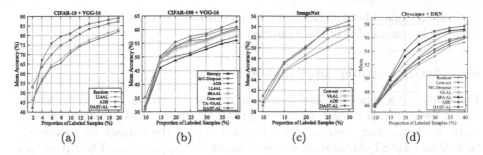

(a) (b) (c) (d)

**Fig. 2.** Comparison of DAST-AL with Core-set [30], LL4AL [37], VAAL [32], SRAAL [41], ADS [13], and random selection method as a baseline: (a) on the CIFAR-10 using the VGG-16 as the target model, (b) on CIFAR-100 using the VGG-16 as the target model, (c) on ImageNet using the same target model in [32], (d) on cityscapes using the DRN as the target model.

**Performance on CIFAR-10.** Figure 2(a) shows the performances on the CIFAR-10 with the VGG-16 as the feature extractor. We can observe that, first, our DAST-AL achieves an accuracy close to 90% by using 20% of the labeled samples. The highest accuracy of the ResNet-18 with full dataset reaches 93.5% as reported in [41], and this is only 3.05% better than DAST-AL with 20% samples. Second, although the state-of-the-art ADS outperforms proposed DAST-AL when using 2% samples, The proposed DAST-AL can outperform ADS when using over 4% samples. The following two are the reasons: (1) At early iterations, ADS can improve feature representation by taking a long time (see the time analysis in Sect. 4.4) to train the customized classifier with a large number of unlabeled samples. (2) Our proposed EPMCM is able to consistently select the unlabeled sample, augmented samples of which have a large diversity contribution for the label set. Notably, the effect of the ADS would decay with the decrease of the unlabeled samples. Moreover, using ResNet-18 as the feature extractor, the proposed DAST-AL has the higher mean accuracy as shown in Table 1, demonstrating the robustness of proposed method comparing the others.

**Performance on CIFAR-100.** Although CIFAR-10 and CIFAR-100 have the same number of training images, CIFAR-100 has 100 categories while CIFAR-10 has 10 categories only. Hence, CIFAR-100 is much more challenging to tackle and needs larger proportions of training samples for achieving gratifying performance. As we can see from Fig. 2(b), at early iteration, DAST-AL outperforms all other methods, except ADS. Meanwhile, when using over 20% samples, our method is marginally better than ADS. The primary reason for the performance improvement of DAST-AL at the above iterations lies in the ability to select the unlabeled samples that can augment the challenging labeled set for more diversity. And, our DAST-AL outperforms the state-of-the-art SRAAL when using the same initial labeled samples. This indicates that DAST-AL can increase the diversity of the labeled samples by using ISDA. In addition, since DAST-AL does not use any unlabeled samples for training, our method does not suffer from the decrease in the number of the unlabeled samples.

## 4.2   Active Learning for Semantic Segmentation

**Dataset.**   Semantic segmentation tasks can be viewed as pixel-level classification tasks, which is more challenging than the image-level classification [41]. Here, we follow the experiment in [41], and choose the dataset Cityscapes [7] to evaluate DAST-AL against state-of-the-art AL approaches. The Cityscapes dataset consists of 3475 frames with instance segmentation annotations. To make a fair comparison, we also modify this dataset into 19 classes following the experiment in [41].

**Compared Methods.**   We evaluate our DAST-AL against a number of existing AL methods that reports performance on the semantic segmentation Cityscapes dataset. These methods contain Core-set [30], MC-Dropout [14], VAAL [32], QBC [21], and SRAAL [41]. As mentioned earlier, we introduce the random selection method as the baseline.

**Training Settings.**   Following the works in [32,41], the target model in our semantic segmentation experiment consists of the dilated residual networks (DRN) [38] as the feature extractor and a convolution layer as a classifier. Similar to the previous image classification setting, we initialize the labeled set $L$ by randomly sampling 348 data points from the whole unlabeled dataset $U$. In the $i^{th}$ iteration of AL, the number of labeled samples added to $L$ is 150, and then re-train the target model. In addition, we only adopt the random horizontal flips as the data augmentation strategy in [32]. In each AL iteration, according to the previous work experiment setting [32,41], the training epoch is set to 50, mini-batch size is 8, the initial learning rate is set to $5 \times 10^{-4}$. To obtain the mean performance, each experiment is repeated 5 times with the same initial labeled pool.

**Performance Comparison.**   For the semantic segmentation task, following the setting in the SRAAL [41], we use the mean intersection over union, denoted as Miou to evaluate the performances of various methods. Since semantic segmentation tasks can be viewed as pixel-level classification tasks, we select the unlabeled samples by averaging $\overline{\mathcal{E}_{x_u}^{\infty}}$ from Eq. 7 of each pixel. In our experiments, we use the same initial labeled set and the same selection budget for different methods.

Figure 2(d) shows our result on various AL methods. We can observe that, first, SRAAL and VAAL obtain better performance than other methods, such as QBC, MC-Dropout, and core-set. This is because both VAAL and SRAAL take a long time to train the VAE module with a large number of unlabeled samples, and then they can select the most informative unlabeled samples. Second, our

DAST-AL outperforms the SRAAL and with a large margin. It verifies that although the maximum upper bound in the Eq. 7 is not strictly guaranteed to be numerically maximum, DAST-AL still can effectively select the unlabeled samples, the augmented samples of which have large diversity shown in Eq. 7. Moreover, our method achieves high performance without being trained with the unlabeled samples and designing any extra modules.

## 4.3 Ablation Study and Discussion

To evaluate the effect of ISDA and EPMCM in DAST-AL, we conduct a series of ablation studies on CIFAR-10 with the ResNet18 as the feature extractor. As we can see from Tab. 1, by using ISDA and EPMCM, DAST-AL significantly boosts the performance at later iterations. By using ISDA only, the accuracy of $Ran^+$ increases close to 2% when compared with Ran under 10% labeled samples. The reason behind the performance improvement of $Ran^+$ is that ISDA can be used to increase the diversity of the labeled set, particularly when the labeled set is small. With the increase of the labeled sample selected by the random method, the accuracy of $Ran^+$ is less than the Ran when using 40% labeled data. This observation firstly verifies that the effect of ISDA is decayed with the random method, and then it proves that the proposed EPMCM can enhance the power of ISDA by selecting the unlabeled samples, augmented samples of which have a larger diversity contribution for the labeled set. For further verifying our remark, we conduct the visualization experiment in Sect. 4.3. Moreover, DAST-AL achieves better results compared to the $Maxp^+$. Notably, it illustrates that ISDA works better with EPMCM as ISDA and EPMCM share the same intuition that how to effectively increase the diversity for the labeled set.

**Table 1.** Comparison of ISDA and EPMCM in DAST-AL on CIFAR-10 under different proportion of labeled samples. Ran denotes DAST-AL random selects the unlabeled samples without ISDA, Maxp denotes DAST-AL select the unlabeled samples by its max prediction probability without ISDA. $(\cdot)^+$ represents the supervision under ISDA. It should be noted that $Maxp^+$ represent the simple pipeline that combines ISDA with existing AL methods.

| Method | Accuracy (%) on labeled proportion (%) | | | | | | |
|---|---|---|---|---|---|---|---|
| | 5 | 10 | 15 | 20 | 25 | 30 | 35 |
| Ran | 67.13 | 80.06 | 85.25 | 87.14 | 89. 25 | 90.36 | 91.21 |
| Maxp | 67.13 | 76.37 | 79.88 | 81.40 | 82.84 | 83.46 | 84.60 |
| $Ran^+$ | 69.27 | 80.76 | 85.60 | 87.82 | 89.30 | 90.67 | 91.15 |
| $Maxp^+$ | 69.27 | 76.35 | 81.13 | 81.72 | 82.85 | 83.24 | 84.03 |
| DAST-AL | **69.27** | 82.98 | **87.84** | **90.42** | **92.10** | **93.06** | **93.32** |

**The Gap Coming from the Upper-Bound Term.** We randomly select 1000 queried samples from CIFAR-10 and get their upper-bound. Meanwhile, we also explicitly generate the different number of augmented samples to compute an acquisition score of the queried sample. Then, we get the mean and std of the gap. The following table shows that the mean of the gap decrease with the increase of the sampling times. Hence, we are allowed to use upper-bound as we are considering the case of infinite augmented samples.

**Table 2.** We compute he gap coming from the upper-bound term with ResNet18.

| Sampling times | 100 | 1000 | 10000 | 100000 |
|---|---|---|---|---|
| Gap (ResNet18) | $0.85 \pm 0.49$ | $0.57 \pm 0.34$ | $0.35 \pm 0.10$ | $0.11 \pm 0.07$ |

**Visualization Results.** To demonstrate that EPMCM can select the unlabeled samples, augmented features of which are able to increase diversity for the labeled set, we obtain the 'Augmented Images' by utilizing the reversing convolutional networks [36] to map the augmented features of the unlabeled samples back to the image space. Specifically speaking, since the ImageNet [10] has a high resolution, we compose a high resolution labeled set by randomly selecting 20000 labeled images from the ImageNet. In our case, 10000 images served as an unlabeled set. Then, we train the labeled set with ISDA to obtain the semantic directions, and select the images from the unlabeled set by random method and EPMCM. For the selected samples, their

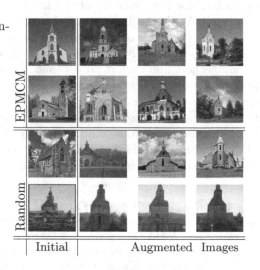

**Table 3.** Visualization of the semantically augmented feature of the selected samples from EPMCM and random. These 'Augmented Images' are generated with features sampled from feature distribution. It should be noted that these 'Augmented Images' are only for visualization.

'Augmented Images' of the corresponding augmented features are shown in right.

In Table 3, the first two pictures from the first column and the last two from the same column represent the unlabeled samples selected by EPMCM and random, respectively. The 'Augmented Images' columns denote the images generated by the augmented features of the unlabeled samples. It can be observed that the unlabeled samples selected by EPMCM are more diverse.

## 4.4   Timing Analysis

Table 4 shows the comparison results including DAST-AL and other methods on CIFAR-10. For a fair comparison, all of these methods are tested in the same torch version using the same NVIDIA TITAN Xp. Table 4 shows the extra params for the customized modules in these methods, the time needed to train for the first iteration in AL, sample a fixed budget of samples from the unlabeled set, and the total time. LL4AL only takes 2.06 min for one iteration in AL but it does not perform as well as DAST-AL considering its achieved mean accuracy. VAAL and SRAAL introduce the customized modules that involve 88.12 M and 90.22 M extra parameters, which need to be trained with the labeled and unlabeled samples in an adversarial manner. This explains why both the methods appear to be very slow in the training steps. ADS is the most competitive baseline to DAST-AL in terms of its achieved accuracy when using the small proportion of the labeled samples. However, DAST-AL takes 128.3 s while ADS requires 2688.6 s for the training in one iteration in AL. This can be explained by the fact that ADS introduces adversarial classifiers with 0.98 M extra parameters to minimize classifiers' prediction discrepancy and maximize prediction agreement with a large number of the unlabeled samples.

**Table 4.** Comparison of the extra params (EP) introduced by DAST-AL and other methods, the sampling time (ST) is taken to select the data from the unlabeled set on the CIFAR-10 dataset, the training time (TT) is taken to train the target model in AL. The total time (ToT) is composed by the training time and sampling time for one iteration in AL.

| Method | EP (M) | TT (s) | ST (s) | ToT (m) |
|---|---|---|---|---|
| Core-set [30] | – | 114.98 | 73.29 | 3.14 |
| LL4AL [37] | 0.2 | 120.72 | 2.97 | 2.06 |
| VAAL [32] | 88.18 | 62855 | 36.12 | 1048 |
| SRAAL [41] | 90.22 | 17897 | 41.67 | 298.9 |
| ADS [13] | 0.98 | 2688.6 | 4.83 | 44.91 |
| DAST-AL | – | 128.30 | 7.59 | 2.26 |

## 5   Conclusion and Future Work

In this paper, we propose a novel diversity-aware semantic transformation active learning method to overcome a limited labeling budget for achieving better performance. By looking ahead the effect of ISDA in the process of acquisition, we can select the unlabeled samples to augment the labeled set for more diversity with ISDA. Since we can not always guarantee that the expected partial model change to be numerically maximum, we will continue our research to calculate this change more accurately. In addition, as our method is able to construct a high-quality label set, we do believe our method can be a complement for existing works i.e., semi-supervised learning which employs unlabeled samples for training. By combining the proposed method with such a method, our method will have much potential for larger-scale datasets.

**Acknowledgements.** This work was supported by the National Nature Science Foundation of China under Grants U2013201, 62073225, 62072315, 61836005 and 62006157, the Natural Science Foundation of Guangdong Province-Outstanding Youth Program under Grant 2019B151502018, the Guangdong "Pearl River Talent Recruitment Program" under Grant 2019ZT08X603, the Guangdong"Pearl River Talent Plan" under Grant 2019JC01X235, and the Shenzhen Science and Technology Innovation Commission R2020A045.

# References

1. Abraham, I., Murphey, T.D.: Active learning of dynamics for data-driven control using Koopman operators. IEEE Trans. Rob. **35**(5), 1071–1083 (2019)
2. Beluch, W.H., Genewein, T., Nürnberger, A., Köhler, J.M.: The power of ensembles for active learning in image classification. In: CVPR, pp. 9368–9377 (2018)
3. Bottou, L.: Stochastic gradient descent tricks. In: Neural Networks: Tricks of the Trade, pp. 421–436 (2012)
4. Cai, W., Zhang, M., Zhang, Y.: Batch mode active learning for regression with expected model change. IEEE Trans. Neural Netw. Learn. Syst. **28**(7), 1668–1681 (2016)
5. Cai, W., Zhang, Y., Zhou, J.: Maximizing expected model change for active learning in regression. In: IEEE International Conference on Data Mining, pp. 51–60 (2013)
6. Caron, M., Bojanowski, P., Joulin, A., Douze, M.: Deep clustering for unsupervised learning of visual features. In: ECCV, pp. 132–149 (2018)
7. Cordts, M., et al.: The cityscapes dataset for semantic urban scene understanding. In: CVPR, pp. 3213–3223 (2016)
8. Curtiss, J.H.: A note on the theory of moment generating functions. Ann. Math. Stat. **13**(4), 430–433 (1942)
9. Dasgupta, S., Hsu, D.: Hierarchical sampling for active learning. In: International Conference on Machine Learning, pp. 208–215 (2008)
10. Deng, J., Dong, W., Socher, R., Li, L.J., Li, K., Fei-Fei, L.: Imagenet: a large-scale hierarchical image database. In: CVPR, pp. 248–255 (2009)
11. Doersch, C., Gupta, A., Efros, A.A.: Unsupervised visual representation learning by context prediction. In: CVPR, pp. 1422–1430 (2015)
12. Ebrahimi, S., Rohrbach, A., Darrell, T.: Gradient-free policy architecture search and adaptation. In: Conference on Robot Learning, pp. 505–514 (2017)
13. Fu, M., Yuan, T., Wan, F., Xu, S., Ye, Q.: Agreement-discrepancy-selection: active learning with progressive distribution alignment. In: AAAI, pp. 7466–7473 (2021)
14. Gal, Y., Ghahramani, Z.: Dropout as a bayesian approximation: representing model uncertainty in deep learning. In: International Conference on Machine Learning, pp. 1050–1059 (2016)
15. Gal, Y., Islam, R., Ghahramani, Z.: Deep bayesian active learning with image data. In: International Conference on Machine Learning, pp. 1183–1192 (2017)

16. He, K., Zhang, X., Ren, S., Sun, J.: Deep residual learning for image recognition. In: CVPR, pp. 770–778 (2016)
17. Jiang, B., Zhang, Z., Lin, D., Tang, J., Luo, B.: Semi-supervised learning with graph learning-convolutional networks. In: CVPR, pp. 11313–11320 (2019)
18. Joshi, A.J., Porikli, F., Papanikolopoulos, N.: Multi-class active learning for image classification. In: CVPR, pp. 2372–2379 (2009)
19. Kim, K., Park, D., Kim, K.I., Chun, S.Y.: Task-aware variational adversarial active learning. In: CVPR, pp. 8166–8175 (2021)
20. Kingma, D.P., Mohamed, S., Rezende, D.J., Welling, M.: Semi-supervised learning with deep generative models. In: NeurIPS, pp. 3581–3589 (2014)
21. Kuo, W., Häne, C., Yuh, E., Mukherjee, P., Malik, J.: Cost-sensitive active learning for intracranial hemorrhage detection. In: Frangi, A.F., Schnabel, J.A., Davatzikos, C., Alberola-López, C., Fichtinger, G. (eds.) MICCAI 2018. LNCS, vol. 11072, pp. 715–723. Springer, Cham (2018). https://doi.org/10.1007/978-3-030-00931-1_82
22. Lewis, D.D., Gale, W.A.: A sequential algorithm for training text classifiers, pp. 3–12 (1994)
23. Li, J., Chen, Z., Chen, J., Lin, Q.: Diversity-sensitive generative adversarial network for terrain mapping under limited human intervention. IEEE Trans. Cybern. **51**, 6029–6040 (2020)
24. Mahajan, D., et al.: Exploring the limits of weakly supervised pretraining. In: ECCV, pp. 181–196 (2018)
25. Making, M.O.D.: Synthesis lectures on artificial intelligence and machine learning (2012)
26. Mayer, C., Timofte, R.: Adversarial sampling for active learning. In: IEEE Winter Conference on Applications of Computer Vision, pp. 3071–3079 (2020)
27. Noroozi, M., Pirsiavash, H., Favaro, P.: Representation learning by learning to count. In: ICCV, pp. 5898–5906 (2017)
28. Peyre, J., Sivic, J., Laptev, I., Schmid, C.: Weakly-supervised learning of visual relations. In: CVPR, pp. 5179–5188 (2017)
29. Saito, S., Yang, J., Ma, Q., Black, M.J.: Scanimate: weakly supervised learning of skinned clothed avatar networks. In: CVPR, pp. 2886–2897 (2021)
30. Sener, O., Savarese, S.: Active learning for convolutional neural networks: a core-set approach. In: ICLR (2018)
31. Simonyan, K., Zisserman, A.: Very deep convolutional networks for large-scale image recognition. In: ICLR (2015)
32. Sinha, S., Ebrahimi, S., Darrell, T.: Variational adversarial active learning. In: ICCV, pp. 5972–5981 (2019)
33. Sohn, K., Lee, H., Yan, X.: Learning structured output representation using deep conditional generative models. NeurIPS **28**, 3483–3491 (2015)
34. Wang, D., Zhang, Y., Zhang, K., Wang, L.: Focalmix: semi-supervised learning for 3D medical image detection. In: CVPR, pp. 3951–3960 (2020)
35. Wang, K., Zhang, D., Li, Y., Zhang, R., Lin, L.: Cost-effective active learning for deep image classification. IEEE TCSVT **27**(12), 2591–2600 (2016)
36. Wang, Y., Huang, G., Song, S., Pan, X., Xia, Y., Wu, C.: Regularizing deep networks with semantic data augmentation. IEEE TPAMI **44**, 3733–3748 (2021)
37. Yoo, D., Kweon, I.S.: Learning loss for active learning. In: CVPR, pp. 93–102 (2019)
38. Yu, F., Koltun, V., Funkhouser, T.: Dilated residual networks. In: CVPR, pp. 472–480 (2017)
39. Yuan, T., et al.: Multiple instance active learning for object detection. In: CVPR, pp. 5330–5339 (2021)

40. Zhai, X., Oliver, A., Kolesnikov, A., Beyer, L.: S4l: self-supervised semi-supervised learning. In: ICCV, pp. 1476–1485 (2019)
41. Zhang, B., Li, L., Yang, S., Wang, S., Zha, Z.J., Huang, Q.: State-relabeling adversarial active learning. In: CVPR, pp. 8756–8765 (2020)
42. Zhu, J.J., Bento, J.: Generative adversarial active learning. arXiv preprint (2017)
43. Zhuang, C., Zhai, A.L., Yamins, D.: Local aggregation for unsupervised learning of visual embeddings. In: ICCV, pp. 6002–6012 (2019)
44. Zhukov, D., Alayrac, J.B., Cinbis, R.G., Fouhey, D., Laptev, I., Sivic, J.: Cross-task weakly supervised learning from instructional videos. In: CVPR, pp. 3537–3545 (2019)

# VL-LTR: Learning Class-wise Visual-Linguistic Representation for Long-Tailed Visual Recognition

Changyao Tian[1], Wenhai Wang[3], Xizhou Zhu[2], Jifeng Dai[2(✉)], and Yu Qiao[3]

[1] Chinese University of Hong Kong, Hong Kong, China
tcyhost@buaa.edu.cn
[2] SenseTime, Hong Kong, China
{zhuwalter,daijifeng}@sensetime.com
[3] Shanghai AI Laboratory, Shanghai, China
{wangwenhai,qiaoyu}@pjlab.org.cn

**Abstract.** Recently, computer vision foundation models such as CLIP and ALI-GN, have shown impressive generalization capabilities on various downstream tasks. But their abilities to deal with the long-tailed data still remain to be proved. In this work, we present a novel framework based on pre-trained visual-linguistic models for long-tailed recognition (LTR), termed VL-LTR, and conduct empirical studies on the benefits of introducing text modality for long-tailed recognition tasks. Compared to existing approaches, the proposed VL-LTR has the following merits. (1) Our method can not only learn visual representation from images but also learn corresponding linguistic representation from noisy class-level text descriptions collected from the Internet; (2) Our method can effectively use the learned visual-linguistic representation to improve the visual recognition performance, especially for classes with fewer image samples. We also conduct extensive experiments and set the new state-of-the-art performance on widely-used LTR benchmarks. Notably, our method achieves 77.2% overall accuracy on ImageNet-LT, which significantly outperforms the previous best method by over 17 points, and is close to the prevailing performance training on the full ImageNet. Code is available at https://github.com/ChangyaoTian/VL-LTR.

**Keywords:** Long-tailed recognition · Vision-language models

## 1 Introduction

Real-world data always presents a long-tailed distribution, where only a few head classes encompass most of the data, and most tail classes have very few

---

C. Tian et al.—Contributed equally.
C. Tian—The work is done when Changyao Tian is an intern at SenseTime Research.

---

**Supplementary Information** The online version contains supplementary material available at https://doi.org/10.1007/978-3-031-19806-9_5.

samples. Such phenomenon is not conducive to the practical application of deep-learning based models. Because of this, a number of works have emerged and tried to alleviate the class imbalance problem from different aspects, such as re-sampling the training data [3,5,41], re-weighting the loss functions [8,22,28], or employing transfer learning methods [29,49,54] (see Fig. 1 (a)). Despite their great contributions, most of these works still restrict themselves to only relying on the image modality for solving this problem.

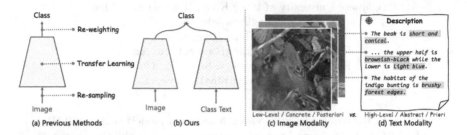

**Fig. 1. Comparison of different long-tailed recognition (LTR) frameworks and different modalities.** (a) Previous LTR methods [3,5,8,22,49,54] mainly focus on the class imbalance problem on the image modality, while (b) our method addresses the LTR task by combining the advantages of image and text modalities. (c) and (d) give intuitive explanations for the correlations and differences between the image and text modalities.

As illustrated in Fig. 1 (c)(d), there are some inner connections between images and text descriptions of the same class, especially when it comes to some visual concepts and attributes. However, different from the image modality that usually presents concrete low-level features (*e.g.*, shape, color, texture) of the object or scene, the text modality typically contains much high-level and abstract information. Furthermore, text descriptions are prior knowledge that can be summarized by experts, which could be useful when there are no sufficient images to learn general class-wise representation for recognition.

Although there have been some visual-linguistic approaches [15,36,58] for visual recognition, their performance is still not satisfactory, due to the gap between image and text representation and the lack of robustness to noisy text. Recently, the rise of visual-linguistic foundation models [19,37,42] has provided an effective way to learn powerful representation that can connect the image and text modalities. Motivated by this, we present a visual-linguistic framework for long-tailed recognition, termed VL-LTR, which can utilize the advantages of both visual and linguistic representation for visual recognition tasks as shown in Fig. 1 (b). Our method mainly consists of two key components, which are (1) a class-wise visual-linguistic pre-training (CVLP) framework for linking images and text descriptions at the class level, and (2) a language-guided recognition (LGR) head designed to perform long-tailed recognition according to the learned visual-linguistic representation.

Overall, the proposed VL-LTR possesses the following merits. (1) Compared to the visual-linguistic pre-training [6,7,21,48,53], our method can learn visual-linguistic representation at the class level, and take the advantages of class-wise linguistic representation to improve visual recognition performance, especially in the long-tailed scenario; (2) Compared to previous visual-linguistic classifiers [15,36,58], our method can not only effectively bridge the gap between visual and linguistic representation, but also be more flexible and robust to noisy text descriptions.

To verify the effectiveness of our method, we conduct extensive experiments on three challenging long-tailed recognition (LTR) benchmarks, including ImageNet-LT [29], Places-LT [29], and iNaturalist 2018 [46]. As shown in Fig. 2, using ResNet-50 [14] as backbone, our method achieves an overall accuracy of 70.1% on ImageNet-LT, which is 10.1 points higher than the previous best method PaCo [7] (ResNeXt-101 [50]). For tail

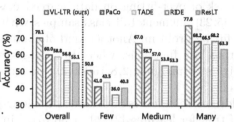

**Fig. 2.** **Performance comparison on ImageNet-LT** [29]. Our VL-LTR (ResNet-50 [14]) significantly outperforms prior arts, including PaCo [7], TADE [53], RIDE (4 Experts) [48], and ResLT [6], which use heavier ResNeXt-50/101 [50] as backbone.

classes, the medium and few-shot accuracy of our method reaches 67.0% and 50.8% respectively, which significantly outperform that of the prior arts [6,7,48,53] as well.

In summary, our main contributions are three-fold.

(1) We provide a detailed analysis on the connection and differences between image and text modalities, and point out that class descriptions can serve as a supplement to images, which is conducive to long-tailed visual recognition.

(2) We present a new visual-linguistic framework for long-tailed visual recognition (VL-LTR), which contains two tailored components, including a class-wise text-image pre-training (CVLP) to bridge the class-level images and text descriptions, and a language-guided recognition (LGR) head to perform classification based on the learned visual-linguistic representation.

(3) The proposed VL-LTR has achieved state-of-the-art performance on prevailing ImageNet-LT, Places-LT, and iNaturalist 2018 datasets. Notably, our method gets the best overall accuracy of 77.2% on ImageNet-LT, outperforming the old record by 17.2 points, and even approaching the performance training on the full ImageNet [9].

# 2    Related Work

## 2.1    Long-Tailed Visual Recognition

Class re-balanced strategy [2,11,13,18,22,49] has been comprehensively studied for long-tailed visual recognition. One type of the class re-balanced strategy is Data Re-sampling [1,3,5,11,13,41], which generates class-balanced data by adjusting the sampling rate of tail classes and head classes, yet they might take the risk of over-fitting on data-scarced classes. Besides that, some recent methods [5,23] augment tail class samples with head classes ones, to alleviate the over-fitting problem. Another kind of class re-balanced strategy is to design re-weighting loss functions, where tail classes would be emphasized by using large weights or margins [2,8,16,22,49], or ignoring negative gradients for tail classes [44].

In addition, researchers also address the long-tailed recognition task from the aspect of transfer learning [21,29,51,56,57]. Liu et al. [29] and Zhu et al. [57] transfer knowledge from head classes's features to tail classes by maintaining memory bank and modeling intra-class variance, respectively. After that, Samuel et al. [39] proposes a late-fusion framework for long-tail learning with class descriptors. Some decoupling methods [21,56] also can be regarded as transferring head classes frozen feature to tail classes when fine-tuning classifiers. Recently, some studies [7,20,40,47,53] also transfer the representation learned by contrastive learning or self-supervised learning for long-tailed problems.

The aforementioned methods mainly focus on addressing the class imbalance problem based on image modalities, while rarely exploring the possibility of integrating text modalities on this problem.

## 2.2    Visual-Linguistic Model

In this section, we mainly discuss visual-linguistic pre-training and classification related to our work.

Visual-linguistic pre-training [4,12,24,25,27,32,33,37,43,52] have achieved great success on a number of downstream vision tasks. Zhang et al. [52] show the importance of visual features in visual-linguistic pre-training and obtain more strong visual representations from large object detectors. Li et al. [27] find that a larger transformer visual-linguistic model can learn more powerful representation from a larger visual-linguistic corpus. In addition, Huang et al. [17,42] proposed a visual-linguistic pre-training model by extracting patch features from the convolutional layers without the proposal computation. Recently, CLIP [37] and ALIGN [19] learns powerful visual-linguistic representation via contrastive learning on large-scale image-text pairs.

Prior to these works, there have been some visual-linguistic approaches [15, 36,58] designed for tasks related to image classification. He et al. [15] propose a two-stream model, which directly combines visual and linguistic representation for fine-grained image classification. Mu et al. [36] present a few-shot visual recognition model that is regularized with text descriptions during training. Similar to He *et al.* [15], Zhuang *et al.* [58] design a multi-modal model for automatic fish classification, with a CNN encoder for images and a RNN encoder for class text. However, these methods (1) cannot effectively model the connection between images and text, leading to a considerable gap between visual and linguistic representation; and (2) require high-quality text annotations, which is usually expensive and thus limits their practical application.

## 3   Methodology

### 3.1   Overall Architecture

In order to make effective use of the linguistic modality in the visual recognition task, we propose a two-stage framework, as depicted in Fig. 3.

(1) The first stage is class-wise visual-linguistic pre-training (CVLP), which is used to link the images and text descriptions of the same class via contrastive learning.
(2) In the second stage, a language-guided recognition (LGR) head is designed to collect the overall linguistic representation of each class to guide the image recognition. As a result, the proposed VL-LTR is able to combine the advantages of visual and linguistic representation and achieve impressive long-tailed recognition performance.

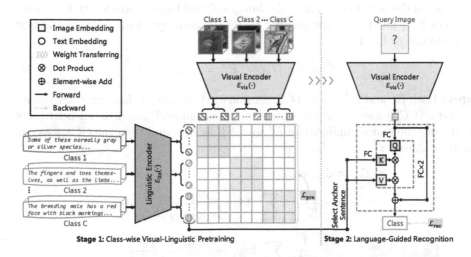

**Fig. 3. Overall architecture of VL-LTR.** The entire model has two stages. In the first stage, class-wise visual-linguistic pre-training (CVLP) takes both the images and text of each class as inputs, learning to connect the representation of the two modalities through class-wise contrastive learning. In the second stage, the language-guided recognition (LGR) head uses the learned visual-linguistic representation to perform image classification.

When training VL-LTR models, we first pre-train the visual and linguistic encoders by class-wise visual-linguistic contrastive learning and the pre-training loss $\mathcal{L}_{\mathrm{pre}}$. During pre-training, an image and a sentence from the same class would be regarded as a positive pair, and otherwise is a negative pair. After pre-training, the weights of the linguistic encoder are frozen, and the anchor sentences of each class are then selected by filtering out the low-scored sentences in text descriptions. The visual encoder and LGR head are fine-tuned by the recognition loss $\mathcal{L}_{\mathrm{rec}}$. Details of the aforementioned loss functions will be introduced in the later sections.

In the inference phase, given a query image and pre-populated text embeddings of anchor sentences, we first feed the image to the visual encoder and obtain an image embedding. Then, the image embedding passes through the LGR head and is categorized into a class according to the image embedding itself as well as the text embeddings of anchor sentences.

## 3.2   Class-Wise Visual-Linguistic Pre-training

The goal of this stage is to learn the visual-linguistic representation of images and text descriptions at the class level. To this end, we design a class-wise visual-linguistic pre-training (CVLP) framework. Unlike previous works [19,37] that use instance-wise image-text pairs for pre-training, our framework is expected to fuse the class-wise linguistic information into the visual space.

During pre-training, as shown in Fig. 3, we first randomly sample a batch of images $\mathcal{I} = \{I_i\}_{i=1}^{N}$, and the corresponding text sentences $\mathcal{T} = \{T_i\}_{i=1}^{N}$, where $N$ denotes the batch size. Then, the images $\mathcal{I}$ and texts $\mathcal{T}$ are fed to the visual encoder $\mathcal{E}_{\mathrm{vis}}(\cdot)$ and linguistic encoder $\mathcal{E}_{\mathrm{lin}}(\cdot)$ respectively, yielding image and text embeddings as Eq. 1:

$$E_i^I = \mathcal{E}_{\mathrm{vis}}(I_i), \quad E_i^T = \mathcal{E}_{\mathrm{lin}}(T_i), \tag{1}$$

where both $E_i^I$ and $E_i^T$ are of $D$ dimensions. After that, a class-wise contrastive learning (CCL) loss is used to optimize the visual and linguistic encoders. Let us denote the cosine similarity of $E_i^I$ and $E_j^T$ as $S_{i,j}$, and then the CCL loss can be formulated as:

$$
\begin{aligned}
\mathcal{L}_{\mathrm{ccl}} =& \mathcal{L}_{\mathrm{vis}} + \mathcal{L}_{\mathrm{lin}} \\
=& -\frac{1}{|\mathcal{T}_i^+|} \sum_{T_j \in \mathcal{T}_i^+} \log \frac{\exp(S_{i,j}/\tau)}{\sum_{T_k \in \mathcal{T}} \exp(S_{i,k}/\tau)} \\
& -\frac{1}{|\mathcal{I}_i^+|} \sum_{I_j \in \mathcal{I}_i^+} \log \frac{\exp(S_{j,i}/\tau)}{\sum_{I_k \in \mathcal{I}} \exp(S_{k,i}/\tau)},
\end{aligned}
\tag{2}
$$

where $\mathcal{L}_{\mathrm{vis}}$ and $\mathcal{L}_{\mathrm{lin}}$ denote the loss of visual and linguistic side respectively, while $\mathcal{T}_i^+$ denotes a subset of $\mathcal{T}$, in which each text shares the same class with the image $I_i$. Correspondingly, all images in $\mathcal{I}_i^+$ share the same class with the text $T_i$. $\tau$ is a learnable parameter with an initial value of 0.07.

In addition to CCL, we also distill the knowledge from the CLIP [37] pre-trained model, to reduce the risk of over-fitting caused by limited text corpus in the pre-training stage. The distillation loss $\mathcal{L}_{\text{dis}}$ can be written as Eq. 3:

$$
\begin{aligned}
\mathcal{L}_{\text{dis}} = &-\frac{\exp(S'_{i,i}/\tau)}{\sum_{T_j \in \mathcal{T}} \exp(S'_{i,j}/\tau)} \log \frac{\exp(S_{i,i}/\tau)}{\sum_{T_k \in \mathcal{T}} \exp(S_{i,k}/\tau)} \\
&-\frac{\exp(S'_{i,i}/\tau)}{\sum_{I_j \in \mathcal{I}} \exp(S'_{j,i}/\tau)} \log \frac{\exp(S_{i,i}/\tau)}{\sum_{I_k \in \mathcal{I}} \exp(S_{k,i}/\tau)}.
\end{aligned}
\tag{3}
$$

Here, $S'$ is the cosine similarity matrix produced by the frozen CLIP model.

Our pre-training framework has two merits as follows: (1) It is convenient to add new training samples for image or text modality in our framework, since the image and text description for a specific class is independent of each other, which greatly reduces the cost of data collection; (2) The text description of each image sample is different in each iteration, which serves as an additional regularization to prevent the model from learning some fixed trivial correlation within a certain image-text pair, and thus our framework is robust to the noisy text from the Internet.

### 3.3    Language-Guided Recognition

In this stage, we design (1) an anchor sentence selection strategy to filter out noise texts, and (2) a language-guided recognition head to effectively use visual and linguistic representation learned in the pre-training stage.

**Anchor Sentence Selection.** Most text descriptions in our corpus are crawled from the Internet, which are noisy and might degrade the recognition performance. To address this problem, we propose an anchor sentence selection (AnSS) strategy to find the most discriminative sentences for each class. Specifically, we first construct a "special" image batch $I'$, which contains at most 50 images (if any) of each class. Then, for each text sentence $T_i$, we score each sentence $T_i$ by computing the $\mathcal{L}_{\text{lin}}$ between the sentence and the image batch $I'$. Finally, we select $M$ text sentences with the smallest $\mathcal{L}_{\text{lin}}$ as the anchor sentences for the follow-up visual recognition.

**Language-Guided Recognition Head.** After obtaining the anchor sentences of each class, we design a language-guided recognition (LGR) head, to adjust the weights of these sentences based on the attention scores with the input image. In this way, visual and linguistic features can be flexibly and dynamically combined according to the query image.

As shown in Fig. 3, given an image embedding $E^I \in \mathbb{R}^D$, as well as the embeddings of all classes' anchor sentences $E^T \in \mathbb{R}^{C \times M \times D}$, where $C$ is the class number, and $M$ is the maximum number of sentences for each class. Then the

LGR head can be formulated as:

$$Q = \text{Linear}(\text{LayerNorm}(E^I)), \tag{4}$$

$$K = \text{Linear}(\text{LayerNorm}(E^T)), \quad V = E^T, \tag{5}$$

$$G = \sigma(\frac{QK^{\mathsf{T}}}{\sqrt{D}})V, \tag{6}$$

$$P = P^I + P^T = \sigma(\text{MLP}(E^I)) + \sigma(\langle E^I, G \rangle / \tau). \tag{7}$$

Here, $Q \in \mathbb{R}^D$, $K \in \mathbb{R}^{C \times M \times D}$, and $V \in \mathbb{R}^{C \times M \times D}$ are query, key and value of the attention operation. $G \in \mathbb{R}^{C \times D}$ is the gather of the $M$ anchor sentence embeddings of each class. $\sigma(\cdot)$ denotes Softmax function. $\text{MLP}(\cdot)$ denotes two linear layers sandwich a ReLU in the middle. $\langle E^I, G \rangle$ is the cosine similarity of $E^I$ and $G$. $P$ is the classification probability of the image $I_q$, $P^I$ and $P^T$ are the classification probabilities based on visual and linguistic representation, respectively.

### 3.4 Loss Function

As mentioned in Sect. 3.1, the training process of our method has two stages, namely pre-training and fine-tuning respectively. In the pre-training stage, the visual encoder and linguistic encoder are jointly optimized by the CCL loss $\mathcal{L}_{\text{ccl}}$ and distillation loss $\mathcal{L}_{\text{dis}}$. So the overall pre-training loss can be written as:

$$\mathcal{L}_{\text{pre}} = \lambda\mathcal{L}_{\text{ccl}} + (1 - \lambda)\mathcal{L}_{\text{dis}}, \tag{8}$$

where $\lambda \in [0, 1]$ is a hyperparameter to balance $\mathcal{L}_{\text{ccl}}$ and $\mathcal{L}_{\text{dis}}$.

In the fine-tuning stage, after computing the classification probabilities $P^I$ and $P^T$, we simply calculate their corresponding CrossEntropy loss $\mathcal{L}_{\text{CE}}$ with the ground truth label $\mathbf{y}$ as Eq. 9:

$$\mathcal{L}_{\text{rec}} = \mathcal{L}_{\text{CE}}(P^I, \mathbf{y}) + \mathcal{L}_{\text{CE}}(P^T, \mathbf{y}). \tag{9}$$

## 4 Experiments

### 4.1 Datasets

We perform extensive experiments on three challenging long-tailed visual recognition benchmarks, namely ImageNet-LT [29], Places-LT [29], and iNaturalist 2018 [46]. Among these benchmarks, ImageNet-LT is constructed from ImageNet-2012 [9] by sampling a subset following the Pareto distribution with the power value $\alpha = 6$, which contains 1,000 classes. The training set has 115.8K images, and the number of images per class ranges from 1,280 to 5 images. Both the validation set and the test set are balanced, containing 20K and 50K images respectively. We select the hyper-parameters on the validation set and report numerical results on the test set. Similar to ImageNet-LT, Places-LT is a long-tailed version of the large-scale scene classification dataset Places [55]. It consists of 62.5K images from 365 categories with class cardinality ranging from 5 to 4,980. iNaturalist 2018 is a real-world, naturally long-tailed dataset, which is composed of 8,142 fine-grained species. The training set contains 437.5K images, and its imbalance factor is equal to 500. We use the official validation set to test our approach, which has 3 images per class.

We also collect the class-level text descriptions for the three datasets. The text descriptions mainly come from Wikipedia[1], an open-source online encyclopedia that contains millions of articles for free. We first use the original class name as an initial query to get the best matching entry on Wikipedia. After cleaning and filtering out some obviously irrelevant sections such as "references" or "external links" of these entries, we split the left into sentences to form the original text candidate set for each class. Noting that some classes have relatively much fewer sentences than others, we also add 80 additional prompt sentences for each class to alleviate the data scarcity problem. These sentences, which are in the form of 'a photo of a {label}', are auto-generated based on the prompt templates provided in [37].

## 4.2  Evaluation Protocol

Following common practices [7,29,56], we evaluate our proposed models on the corresponding balanced validation/test set and report the overall top-1 accuracy. To diagnose the source of improvement, we also report the top-1 accuracy of the three subsets split by the number of training samples in each class, namely many-shot ($\geq$100 samples), medium-shot (20–100 samples), and few-shot ($\leq$20 samples).

## 4.3  Experiments on ImageNet-LT

**Settings.** To verify the effectiveness of our method, we conduct extensive experiments on ImageNet-LT [29]. We use ResNet-50 [14] or ViT-Base/16 [10] as the visual encoder, and a 12-layer Transformer [38] as the linguistic encoder. All models are optimized by AdamW [31] with a momentum of 0.9 and a weight decay of $5 \times 10^{-2}$. We use the same data augmentation as [45] (w/o distillation). In the pre-training phase, the maximum length of text tokens is set to 77 (including [SOS] and [EOS] tokens), and the pre-trained weights of CLIP [37] is loaded. The initial learning rate is set to $5 \times 10^{-5}$ and decays following the cosine schedule [30]. During this phase, models are pre-trained for 50 epochs, with a mini-batch size of 256. In the fine-tuning phase, we select 64 sentences

---

[1] https://en.wikipedia.org/.

for each class and fine-tune models with the mini-batch size of 128 for another 50 epochs. We set the initial learning rate to $1 \times 10^{-3}$ and still decrease it with the cosine schedule. In both stages, we adopt the input size of $224 \times 224$ and the square-root data sampling strategy [34,35] unless specifically mentioned.

For a fair comparison, we also build a baseline that is only based on visual modality while keeping other settings exactly the same as our proposed method, except that the baseline models are directly initialized with CLIP pretrained weights and fine-tuned for 100 epochs. In addition, we re-implement and report the performance of some representative methods as well, such as $\tau$-normalized, cRT, NCM, and LWS [21], which are all initialized with CLIP pre-trained weights.

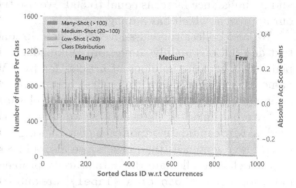

**Fig. 4. Absolute accuracy score of our method over the baseline using ViT-Base/16 [10] as the backbone on ImageNet-LT [29].** Our method enjoys more performance gains on classes with fewer image samples.

**Results.** In Table 1, we can see that our VL-LTR models are superior to conventional vision-based methods with similar visual encoders (*i.e.*, backbones). For example, when using ResNet-50 (R-50) [14] as the backbone, the overall accuracy of our method reaches 70.1%, which outperforms baseline by 9.6 points (70.1% *vs.*60.5%), and 10.1 points better than previous best PaCo [7] (70.1% *vs.*60.0%).

Moreover, from the aspect of few-shot accuracy, the performance of our method is more promising, which is 16.3 points and 7.3 points better than baseline (50.8% *vs.*34.5%) and the second-best method [53] (50.8% *vs.*43.5%). When replacing the backbone with heavy ViT-Base/16 (ViT-B) [10], the overall accuracy of our method can further boost up to 77.2%, which is the current new state-of-the-art of ImageNet-LT, and near the prevailing performance (*i.e.*, 80%) training on the full ImageNet [9].

**Table 1. Results on ImageNet-LT** [29]. Our method outperforms prior arts when using a similar backbone network. "*" indicates the corresponding backbone is initialized with CLIP [37] weights.

| Method | Backbone | Accuracy (%) | | | |
|---|---|---|---|---|---|
| | | Overall | Many | Medium | Few |
| Cross Entropy [26] | ResNeXt-50 | 44.4 | 65.9 | 37.5 | 7.7 |
| OLTR [29] | ResNeXt-50 | 46.3 | - | - | - |
| SSD [26] | ResNeXt-50 | 56.0 | 66.8 | 53.1 | 35.4 |
| RIDE (4 Experts) [48] | ResNeXt-50 | 56.8 | 68.2 | 53.8 | 36.0 |
| TADE [53] | ResNeXt-50 | 58.8 | 66.5 | 57.0 | 43.5 |
| smDRAGON [39] | ResNeXt-50 | 50.1 | - | - | - |
| ResLT [6] | ResNeXt-101 | 55.1 | 63.3 | 53.3 | 40.3 |
| PaCo [7] | ResNeXt-101 | 60.0 | 68.2 | 58.7 | 41.0 |
| NCM [21] | ResNeXt-152 | 51.3 | 60.3 | 49.0 | 33.6 |
| cRT [21] | ResNeXt-152 | 52.4 | 64.7 | 49.1 | 29.4 |
| $\tau$-normalized [21] | ResNeXt-152 | 52.8 | 62.2 | 50.1 | 35.8 |
| LWS [21] | ResNeXt-152 | 53.3 | 63.5 | 50.4 | 34.2 |
| NCM [21] | ResNet-50* | 49.2 | 58.9 | 46.6 | 31.1 |
| cRT [21] | ResNet-50* | 50.8 | 63.3 | 47.2 | 27.8 |
| $\tau$-normalized [21] | ResNet50* | 51.2 | 60.9 | 48.4 | 33.8 |
| LWS [21] | ResNet-50* | 51.5 | 62.2 | 48.6 | 31.8 |
| Zero-Shot CLIP [37] | ResNet-50* | 59.8 | 60.8 | 59.3 | 58.6 |
| Baseline | ResNet-50* | 60.5 | 74.4 | 56.9 | 34.5 |
| VL-LTR (ours) | ResNet-50* | **70.1** | **77.8** | **67.0** | **50.8** |
| VL-LTR (ours) | ViT-Base* | **77.2** | **84.5** | **74.6** | **59.3** |

In Fig. 4, we visualize the class-level performance improvement, which is measured by the absolute accuracy gains of our method against the baseline, both of which use ViT-B as the visual backbone. We see that there is more gains on tail classes, which indicates that our method can help mitigate the data-scarce problem under long-tail settings by introducing class-level text descriptions.

## 4.4    Experiments on Places-LT

**Settings.** We also investigate our method on Places-LT [29], a dataset with a different domain. The experimental setting of Places-LT is the same as Sect. 4.3.

**Results.** As reported in Table 2, using ResNet-50 (R-50) as backbone, our model achieves 48.0% overall accuracy, surpassing counterparts by at least 6.8 points (48.0% *vs.* 41.2%), including state-of-the-art PaCo [7], TADE [53], and ResLT [6], while all of them use ResNet-152 [14] as backbone. The performance are also impressive for the medium- (47.2%) and few-shot (38.4%) classes. Once again, the model with ViT-Base/16 (ViT-B) [10] gives the top overall accuracy of 50.1%, which is a new state-of-the-art on this benchmark.

**Table 2. Results on Places-LT** [29]. "*" indicates the corresponding backbone is initialized with CLIP [37] weights.

| Method | Backbone | Accuracy (%) | | | |
|---|---|---|---|---|---|
| | | Overall | Many | Medium | Few |
| OLTR [29] | ResNet-152 | 35.9 | 44.7 | 37.0 | 25.3 |
| ResLT [6] | ResNet-152 | 39.8 | 39.8 | 43.6 | 31.4 |
| TADE [53] | ResNet-152 | 40.9 | 40.4 | 43.2 | 36.8 |
| PaCo [7] | ResNet-152 | 41.2 | 36.1 | 47.9 | 35.3 |
| NCM [21] | ResNet-152 | 36.4 | 40.4 | 37.1 | 27.3 |
| cRT [21] | ResNet-152 | 36.7 | 42.0 | 37.6 | 24.9 |
| $\tau$-normalized [21] | ResNet-152 | 37.9 | 37.8 | 40.7 | 31.8 |
| LWS [21] | ResNet-152 | 37.6 | 40.6 | 39.1 | 28.6 |
| smDRAGON [39] | ResNet-50 | 38.1 | - | - | - |
| NCM [21] | ResNet-50* | 30.8 | 37.1 | 30.6 | 19.9 |
| cRT [21] | ResNet-50* | 30.5 | 38.5 | 29.7 | 17.6 |
| $\tau$-normalized [21] | ResNet-50* | 31.0 | 34.5 | 31.4 | 23.6 |
| LWS [21] | ResNet-50* | 31.3 | 36.0 | 32.1 | 20.7 |
| Zero-Shot CLIP [37] | ResNet-50* | 38.0 | 37.5 | 37.5 | 40.1 |
| Baseline | ResNet-50* | 39.7 | 50.8 | 38.6 | 22.7 |
| VL-LTR (ours) | ResNet-50* | **48.0** | **51.9** | **47.2** | **38.4** |
| VL-LTR (ours) | ViT-Base* | **50.1** | **54.2** | **48.5** | **42.0** |

### 4.5    iNaturalist 2018

**Settings.** We further test our VL-LTR on iNaturalist 2018, a long-tailed fine-grained benchmark. Following the common practice [45], we adopt a long training schedule. To be specific, our models are pre-trained for 100 epochs, and fine-tuned for 360 epochs. The initial learning rate of the pre-training and fine-tuning phase is set to $5 \times 10^{-4}$ and $2 \times 10^{-5}$, respectively. Correspondingly, the baseline has the same fine-tuning epochs and initial learning rate as the proposed method. All other experimental settings are the same as Sect. 4.3.

**Results.** Table 3 shows the top-1 accuracy on iNaturalist 2018 of different methods. We see that when using ResNet-50 (R-50) [14] as the backbone, our models can achieve a 74.6% overall accuracy, surpassing previous methods with the same backbone by at least 1.4 points. Besides that, when equipped with a strong backbone ViT-Base/16 (ViT-B) [10], our model can have an overall accuracy of 76.8%, which outperforms the state-of-the-art PaCo (ResNet-152) by 1.6 points (76.8% vs.75.2%). Moreover, our model can also benefit from a larger image input size (i.e., 384×384), and achieve 81.0% top-1 accuracy, which is 1.5 points higher than DeiT-B/16-384 [45] (81.0% vs.79.5%).

**Table 3. Results on iNaturalist 2018** [46]. "*" indicates the corresponding backbone is initialized with CLIP weights. "*-384" means the input size of $384 \times 384$.

| Method | Backbone | Accuracy (%) |
|---|---|---|
| CB-Focal [2] | ResNet-50 | 61.1 |
| LDAM+DRW [2] | ResNet-50 | 68.0 |
| BBN [56] | ResNet-50 | 69.6 |
| SSD [26] | ResNet-50 | 71.5 |
| RIDE (4 experts) [48] | ResNet-50 | 72.6 |
| smDRAGON [39] | ResNet-50 | 69.1 |
| ResLT [6] | ResNet-50 | 72.3 |
| TADE [53] | ResNet-50 | 72.9 |
| PaCo [7] | ResNet-50 | 73.2 |
| NCM [21] | ResNet-50 | 63.1 |
| cRT [21] | ResNet-50 | 67.6 |
| $\tau$-normalized [21] | ResNet-50 | 69.3 |
| LWS [21] | ResNet-50 | 69.5 |
| NCM [21] | ResNet-50* | 65.3 |
| cRT [21] | ResNet-50* | 69.9 |
| $\tau$-normalized [21] | ResNet-50* | 71.2 |
| LWS [21] | ResNet-50* | 71.0 |
| Zero-Shot CLIP [37] | ResNet-50* | 3.4 |
| Baseline | ResNet-50* | 72.6 |
| VL-LTR (ours) | ResNet-50* | **74.6** |
| PaCo [7] | ResNet-152 | 75.2 |
| DeiT-B/16 [45] | - | 73.2 |
| DeiT-B/16-384 [45] | - | 79.5 |
| VL-LTR (ours) | ViT-Base* | **76.8** |
| VL-LTR-384 (ours) | ViT-Base* | **81.0** |

## 4.6 Ablation Study

*Settings.* In order to provide a deep analysis of our proposed method, we also conduct ablation studies on the ImageNet-LT dataset. In these experiments, we use ResNet-50 as the default backbone. All other settings remain the same as Sect. 4.3 unless specifically mentioned.

**Class-Wise Visual-Linguistic Pre-training.** To examine the effectiveness of our class-wise visual-linguistic pre-training (CVLP) framework, we remove it by directly performing the fine-tuning process on the pre-trained weights of CLIP [37]. As reported in the #1 and #2 of Table 4, the model with CVLP outperforms the one without CVLP by 7.3 points on the overall accuracy. Such gap might be attributed to the inconsistency between image and text representation, which can be alleviated by our CVLP.

To verify this, we visualize some concepts by retrieving images with the greatest cosine similarity. As shown in Fig. 6, both CLIP and our method can learn common visual concepts, such as the "blue" color, but CLIP [37] fails to capture rare concepts, such as "stick" shape and "spot" texture. More examples are provided in the supplementary material.

**CLIP Pre-trained Weights.** To analyze the influence of CLIP pre-trained weights, we train our method with randomly initialized weights. Comparing the #1 and #3 of Table 4, we can see that initializing with CLIP pre-trained weights benefits our VL-LTR. We also plot the curves of training and validation loss in the fine-tuning stage in Fig. 5, where CLIP pre-trained weights (see red curves) can help alleviate the over-fitting problem. This phenomenon is caused by the limited text corpus for pre-training. There are only 1000 class descriptions (about 127K sentences) for ImageNet-LT, it is easy to overfit an image to a specific set of sentences without a pre-trained linguistic encoder.

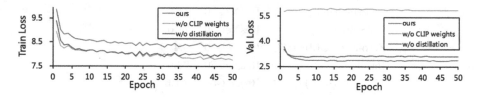

**Fig. 5. Train and validation loss curves of VL-LTR (ResNet-50) on ImageNet-LT [29] under different settings.** Both without CLIP [37] weights (w/o CLIP) and without distillation lead to a certain degree of overfitting. (Color figure online)

**Table 4. Ablation studies on ImageNet-LT [29].** "Head" denotes the recognition head used in the fine-tuning stage, and "SS" denotes the sentence selection strategy.

| # | CLIP Weights | Pre-training w/o $\mathcal{L}_{dis}$ | w/ $\mathcal{L}_{dis}$ | Fine-tuning Head | SS | Accuracy (%) |
|---|---|---|---|---|---|---|
| 1 | ✓ | - | ✓ | LGR | AnSS | **70.1** |
| 2 | ✓ | - | - | LGR | AnSS | 62.8 |
| 3 | - | ✓ | - | LGR | AnSS | 46.8 |
| 4 | ✓ | ✓ | - | LGR | AnSS | 66.2 |
| 5 | ✓ | - | ✓ | FC | - | 62.1 |
| 6 | ✓ | - | ✓ | KNN | - | 63.9 |
| 7 | ✓ | - | ✓ | LGR | Cut Off | 69.7 |

**Distillation Loss.** Similar to the role of pre-trained weights, the distillation loss $\mathcal{L}_{dis}$ is also used to reduce the risk of over-fitting in the pre-training phase. Comparing the red and blue curves in Fig. 5, the over-fitting problem is alleviated in the model with $\mathcal{L}_{dis}$. From the #1 and #4 of Table 4, we also see that the model with $\mathcal{L}_{dis}$ performs better than the one without $\mathcal{L}_{dis}$ (70.1% vs.66.2%).

**Linguistic-Guided Recognition.** We verify the effectiveness of linguistic-guided recognition (LGR) by comparing it with other recognition heads, including FC (vision-based), and KNN (vision-language-based). As reported in #1, #5, and #6 of Table 4, the proposed LGR performs better than FC and KNN by 8.0% and 6.2% points in overall accuracy respectively. It is notable that, as a vision-language-based recognition head, KNN also works better than FC. These results indicate the effectiveness of LGR and the power of visual-linguistic representation.

**Anchor Sentence Selection.** We study the effectiveness of anchor sentence selection (AnSS) by replacing it with "Cut Off" strategy, where we simply select the first $M$ sentences from text descriptions as the anchor sentences for visual recognition. As shown in Table 4, the model with AnSS (see the #1 of Table 4) outperforms the model with "Cut Off" on the overall accuracy, which proves the effectiveness of AnSS to filter out some noisy sentences. Note that, AnSS is a training-free module, which can bring considerable improvements in noisy scenes.

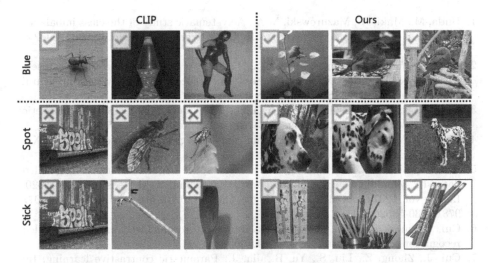

**Fig. 6. Concept visualization**, where "freq" and "rare" mean concepts appear frequently and rarely, respectively. Our method can effectively learn common visual concepts, and even the rare concepts where CLIP [37] makes mistakes, such as "spot" texture and "stick" shape. (Color figure online)

### 4.7   Limitations

Although the proposed VL-LTR achieves good performance on multiple long-tailed recognition benchmarks, it still has some flaws. First, due to the limited text corpus, our method currently relies on existing pre-trained foundation models to learn high-quality linguistic representation. Second, like most LTR works [7,21,26], our VL-LTR is a two-stage method as well, which does not support end-to-end training. But we believe these problems could be well addressed in the future with the enrichment of text data and the development of visual-linguistic model.

## 5   Conclusions

In this work, we introduce VL-LTR, a new visual-linguistic framework for long-tailed recognition. We develop a class-level visual-linguistic pre-training (CVLP) to connect images and text descriptions at class level, and a language-guided recognition (LGR) head to make effective use of visual-linguistic representation for visual recognition. Extensive experiments on various long-tailed recognition benchmarks verify that our method works better than well-designed vision-based methods. We hope this work could provide a strong baseline for vision-language-based long-tailed visual recognition.

## References

1. Buda, M., Maki, A., Mazurowski, M.A.: A systematic study of the class imbalance problem in convolutional neural networks. IEEE Trans. Neural Netw. **106**, 249–259 (2018)
2. Cao, K., Wei, C., Gaidon, A., Aréchiga, N., Ma, T.: Learning imbalanced datasets with label-distribution-aware margin loss. In: Proceedings of Advances in Neural Information Processing System (2019)
3. Chawla, N.V., Bowyer, K.W., Hall, L.O., Kegelmeyer, W.P.: Smote: synthetic minority over-sampling technique. J. Artif. Intell. Res. **16**, 321–357 (2002)
4. Chen, Y.C., et al.: Uniter: learning universal image-text representations. arXiv preprint arXiv:1909.11740 (2019)
5. Chu, P., Bian, X., Liu, S., Ling, H.: Feature space augmentation for long-tailed data. In: Vedaldi, A., Bischof, H., Brox, T., Frahm, J.-M. (eds.) ECCV 2020. LNCS, vol. 12374, pp. 694–710. Springer, Cham (2020). https://doi.org/10.1007/978-3-030-58526-6_41
6. Cui, J., Liu, S., Tian, Z., Zhong, Z., Jia, J.: Result: residual learning for long-tailed recognition. arXiv preprint arXiv:2101.10633 (2021)
7. Cui, J., Zhong, Z., Liu, S., Yu, B., Jia, J.: Parametric contrastive learning. In: Proceedings of IEEE Conference on Computer Vision and Pattern Recognition (2021)
8. Cui, Y., Jia, M., Lin, T.Y., Song, Y., Belongie, S.: Class-balanced loss based on effective number of samples. In: Proceedings of IEEE Conference on Computer Vision and Pattern Recognition (2019)

9. Deng, J., Dong, W., Socher, R., Li, L.J., Li, K., Fei-Fei, L.: ImageNet: a large-scale hierarchical image database. In: Proceedings of IEEE Conference on Computer Vision and Pattern Recognition (2009)

10. Dosovitskiy, A., et al.: An image is worth 16x16 words: transformers for image recognition at scale. In: Proceedings of International Conference on Learning Representations (2021)

11. Drummond, C., Holte, R.C., et al.: C4. 5, class imbalance, and cost sensitivity: why under-sampling beats over-sampling. In: Workshop on Learning from Imbalanced Datasets II, vol. 11, pp. 1–8 (2003)

12. Gan, Z., Chen, Y.C., Li, L., Zhu, C., Cheng, Y., Liu, J.: Large-scale adversarial training for vision-and-language representation learning. In: Proceedings of Advances in Neural Information Processing Systems (2020)

13. Han, H., Wang, W.-Y., Mao, B.-H.: Borderline-SMOTE: a new over-sampling method in imbalanced data sets learning. In: Huang, D.-S., Zhang, X.-P., Huang, G.-B. (eds.) ICIC 2005. LNCS, vol. 3644, pp. 878–887. Springer, Heidelberg (2005). https://doi.org/10.1007/11538059_91

14. He, K., Zhang, X., Ren, S., Sun, J.: Deep residual learning for image recognition. In: Proceedings of the IEEE Conference on Computer Vision and Pattern Recognition (2016)

15. He, X., Peng, Y.: Fine-grained image classification via combining vision and language. In: Proceedings of the IEEE Conference on Computer Vision and Pattern Recognition (2017)

16. Huang, C., Li, Y., Loy, C.C., Tang, X.: Learning deep representation for imbalanced classification. In: Proceedings of the IEEE Conference on Computer Vision and Pattern Recognition (2016)

17. Huang, Z., Zeng, Z., Liu, B., Fu, D., Fu, J.: Pixel-BERT: aligning image pixels with text by deep multi-modal transformers. arXiv preprint arXiv:2004.00849 (2020)

18. Jamal, M.A., Brown, M., Yang, M.H., Wang, L., Gong, B.: Rethinking class-balanced methods for long-tailed visual recognition from a domain adaptation perspective. In: Proceedings of the IEEE Conference on Computer Vision and Pattern Recognition (2020)

19. Jia, C., et al.: Scaling up visual and vision-language representation learning with noisy text supervision. In: Proceedings of International Conference on Machine Learning (2021)

20. Kang, B., Li, Y., Xie, S., Yuan, Z., Feng, J.: Exploring balanced feature spaces for representation learning. In: Proceedings of International Conference on Learning Representations (2020)

21. Kang, B., et al.: Decoupling representation and classifier for long-tailed recognition. In: Proceedings of International Conference on Learning Representations (2019)

22. Khan, S.H., Hayat, M., Bennamoun, M., Sohel, F.A., Togneri, R.: Cost-sensitive learning of deep feature representations from imbalanced data. IEEE Trans. Neural Netw. Learn. Syst. 29(8), 3573–3587 (2017)

23. Kim, J., Jeong, J., Shin, J.: M2M: imbalanced classification via major-to-minor translation. In: Proceedings of the IEEE Conference on Computer Vision and Pattern Recognition (2020)

24. Li, L., Chen, Y., Cheng, Y., Gan, Z., Yu, L., Liu, J.: HERO: hierarchical encoder for video+language omni-representation pre-training. In: Proceedings of the 2020 Conference on Empirical Methods in Natural Language Processing, EMNLP 2020, Online, 16–20 November 2020 (2020)

25. Li, L., Gan, Z., Liu, J.: A closer look at the robustness of vision-and-language pre-trained models. arXiv preprint arXiv:2012.08673 (2020)

26. Li, T., Wang, L., Wu, G.: Self supervision to distillation for long-tailed visual recognition. In: Proceedings of the IEEE Conference on Computer Vision and Pattern Recognition (2021)
27. Li, X., et al.: OSCAR: object-semantics aligned pre-training for vision-language tasks. In: Vedaldi, A., Bischof, H., Brox, T., Frahm, J.-M. (eds.) ECCV 2020. LNCS, vol. 12375, pp. 121–137. Springer, Cham (2020). https://doi.org/10.1007/978-3-030-58577-8_8
28. Lin, T.Y., Goyal, P., Girshick, R., He, K., Dollár, P.: Focal loss for dense object detection. In: Proceedings of the IEEE Conference on Computer Vision (2017)
29. Liu, Z., Miao, Z., Zhan, X., Wang, J., Gong, B., Yu, S.X.: Large-scale long-tailed recognition in an open world. In: Proceedings of the IEEE Conference on Computer Vision and Pattern Recognition (2019)
30. Loshchilov, I., Hutter, F.: SGDR: stochastic gradient descent with warm restarts. In: Proceedings of International Conference on Learning Representations (2017)
31. Loshchilov, I., Hutter, F.: Decoupled weight decay regularization. In: Proceedings of International Conference on Learning Representations (2019)
32. Lu, J., Batra, D., Parikh, D., Lee, S.: VilBERT: pretraining task-agnostic visiolinguistic representations for vision-and-language tasks. In: Proceedings of Advances in Neural Information Processing System (2019)
33. Lu, J., Goswami, V., Rohrbach, M., Parikh, D., Lee, S.: 12-in-1: Multi-task vision and language representation learning. In: Proceedings of the IEEE Conference on Computer Vision and Pattern Recognition (2020)
34. Mahajan, D., et al.: Exploring the limits of weakly supervised pretraining. In: Ferrari, V., Hebert, M., Sminchisescu, C., Weiss, Y. (eds.) ECCV 2018. LNCS, vol. 11206, pp. 185–201. Springer, Cham (2018). https://doi.org/10.1007/978-3-030-01216-8_12
35. Mikolov, T., Sutskever, I., Chen, K., Corrado, G.S., Dean, J.: Distributed representations of words and phrases and their compositionality. In: Proc. Advances in Neural Inf. Process. Syst. (2013)
36. Mu, J., Liang, P., Goodman, N.D.: Shaping visual representations with language for few-shot classification. In: Proceedings of the 58th Annual Meeting of the Association for Computational Linguistics, ACL 2020, Online, 5–10 July 2020 (2020)
37. Radford, A., et al.: Learning transferable visual models from natural language supervision. arXiv preprint arXiv:2103.00020 (2021)
38. Radford, A., et al.: Language models are unsupervised multitask learners. OpenAI blog **1**(8), 9 (2019)
39. Samuel, D., Atzmon, Y., Chechik, G.: From generalized zero-shot learning to long-tail with class descriptors. In: IEEE Winter Conference on Applications of Computer Vision (2021)
40. Samuel, D., Chechik, G.: Distributional robustness loss for long-tail learning. arXiv preprint arXiv:2104.03066 (2021)
41. Shen, L., Lin, Z., Huang, Q.: Relay backpropagation for effective learning of deep convolutional neural networks. In: Leibe, B., Matas, J., Sebe, N., Welling, M. (eds.) ECCV 2016. LNCS, vol. 9911, pp. 467–482. Springer, Cham (2016). https://doi.org/10.1007/978-3-319-46478-7_29
42. Su, W., et al.: Vl-BERT: pre-training of generic visual-linguistic representations. In: Proceedings of International Conference on Learning Representations(2019)

43. Tan, H., Bansal, M.: LXMERT: learning cross-modality encoder representations from transformers. In: Proceedings of the 2019 Conference on Empirical Methods in Natural Language Processing and the 9th International Joint Conference on Natural Language Processing, EMNLP-IJCNLP 2019, Hong Kong, China, 3–7 November 2019 (2019)

44. Tan, J., et al.: Equalization loss for long-tailed object recognition. In: Proceedings of the IEEE Conference on Computer Vision and Pattern Recognition (2020)

45. Touvron, H., Cord, M., Douze, M., Massa, F., Sablayrolles, A., Jégou, H.: Training data-efficient image transformers & distillation through attention. In: Proceedings of International Conference on Machine Learning (2021)

46. Van Horn, G., et al.: The inaturalist species classification and detection dataset. In: Proceedings of the IEEE Conference on Computer Vision and Pattern Recognition (2018)

47. Wang, P., Han, K., Wei, X.S., Zhang, L., Wang, L.: Contrastive learning based hybrid networks for long-tailed image classification. In: Proceedings of the IEEE Conference on Computer Vision and Pattern Recognition (2021)

48. Wang, X., Lian, L., Miao, Z., Liu, Z., Yu, S.X.: Long-tailed recognition by routing diverse distribution-aware experts. In: Proceedings of International Conference on Learning Representations (2020)

49. Wang, Y.X., Ramanan, D., Hebert, M.: Learning to model the tail. In: Proceedings of Advances in Neural Information Processing System (2017)

50. Xie, S., Girshick, R., Dollár, P., Tu, Z., He, K.: Aggregated residual transformations for deep neural networks. In: Proceedings of the IEEE Conference on Computer Vision and Pattern Recognition (2017)

51. Yin, X., Yu, X., Sohn, K., Liu, X., Chandraker, M.: Feature transfer learning for face recognition with under-represented data. In: Proceedings of the IEEE Conference on Computer Vision and Pattern Recognition (2019)

52. Zhang, P., et al.: Vinvl: revisiting visual representations in vision-language models. In: Proceedings of the IEEE Conference on Computer Vision and Pattern Recognition (2021)

53. Zhang, Y., Hooi, B., Hong, L., Feng, J.: Test-agnostic long-tailed recognition by test-time aggregating diverse experts with self-supervision. arXiv preprint arXiv:2107.09249 (2021)

54. Zhong, Y., et al.: Unequal-training for deep face recognition with long-tailed noisy data. In: Proceedings of the IEEE Conference on Computer Vision and Pattern Recognition (2019)

55. Zhou, B., Lapedriza, A., Khosla, A., Oliva, A., Torralba, A.: Places: a 10 million image database for scene recognition. IEEE Trans. Pattern Anal. Mach. Intell. **40**(6), 1452–1464 (2017)

56. Zhou, B., Cui, Q., Wei, X.S., Chen, Z.M.: BBN: bilateral-branch network with cumulative learning for long-tailed visual recognition. In: Proceedings of the IEEE Conference on Computer Vision and Pattern Recognition (2020)

57. Zhu, L., Yang, Y.: Inflated episodic memory with region self-attention for long-tailed visual recognition. In: Proceedings of the IEEE Conference on Computer Vision and Pattern Recognition (2020)

58. Zhuang, P., Wang, Y., Qiao, Y.: Wildfish++: a comprehensive fish benchmark for multimedia research. IEEE Trans. Multimedia **23**, 3603–3617 (2020)

# Class Is Invariant to Context and Vice Versa: On Learning Invariance for Out-Of-Distribution Generalization

Jiaxin Qi[1]([✉]), Kaihua Tang[1], Qianru Sun[2], Xian-Sheng Hua[3], and Hanwang Zhang[1]

[1] Nanyang Technological University, Singapore, Singapore
jiaxin003@e.ntu.edu.sg, {kaihua.tang,hanwangzhang}@ntu.edu.sg
[2] Singapore Management University, Singapore, Singapore
qianrusun@smu.edu.sg
[3] Damo Academy, Alibaba Group, Hangzhou, China

**Abstract.** Out-Of-Distribution generalization (OOD) is all about learning invariance against environmental changes. If the context (In this paper, the word "context" denotes any class-agnostic attributes such as color, texture and background. The formal definition can be found in Appendix, A.2.) in every class is evenly distributed, OOD would be trivial because the context can be easily removed due to an underlying principle: **class is invariant to context**. However, collecting such a balanced dataset is impractical. Learning on imbalanced data makes the model bias to context and thus hurts OOD. Therefore, the key to OOD is context balance. We argue that the widely adopted assumption in prior work—the context bias can be directly annotated or estimated from biased class prediction—renders the context incomplete or even incorrect. In contrast, we point out the ever-overlooked other side of the above principle: **context is also invariant to class**, which motivates us to consider the classes (which are already labeled) as the varying environments (The word "environments" [2] denotes the subsets of training data built by some criteria. In this paper, we take a class as an environment— our key idea.) to resolve context bias (without context labels). We implement this idea by minimizing the contrastive loss of intra-class sample similarity while assuring this similarity to be invariant across all classes. On benchmarks with various context biases and domain gaps, we show that a simple re-weighting based classifier equipped with our context estimation achieves state-of-the-art performance. *We provide the theoretical justifications in Appendix and codes on Github:* https://github.com/simpleshinobu/IRMCon.

## 1 Introduction

The gold standard for collecting a supervised training dataset of quality is to ensure the samples per class are as diverse as possible and the diversities across

**Supplementary Information** The online version contains supplementary material available at https://doi.org/10.1007/978-3-031-19806-9_6.

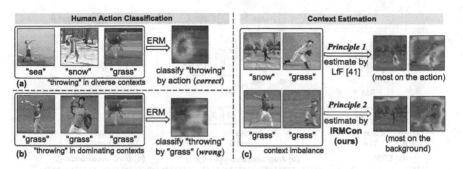

**Fig. 1.** GradCAM [51] visualizations of learned class and context. In (a) and (b): By using ERM, if the context is diverse and balanced within a class, the class feature is accurate—focused on the human's action; if the context dominates in the data, the class feature contains the context feature, e.g., the background "grass". In (c): The conventional context estimation [41] based on Principle 1 is biased to class (focusing on the class of human action "throwing"), while our IRMCon based on Principle 2 estimates better context (focusing on the background).

classes are as evenly distributed as possible [10,34]. For example, the "cat" class should contain cats of varying contexts, such as types, poses, and backgrounds, and the rule also applies in the "dog" class. As illustrated in Fig. 1 (a), on such a dataset, any Empirical Risk Minimization objective (ERM) [59], *e.g.*, the widely used softmax cross-entropy loss [16], can easily keep the class feature by penalizing inter-class similarities, while removing the context feature by favoring intra-class similarities. Thanks to the balanced context, the removal is clean. It can be summarized into the common principle:

**Principle 1.** *Class is invariant to context.*

For example, a "cat" sample is always a cat regardless of types, shapes, and backgrounds.

Given testing samples whose contexts are Out-Of-(training)Distribution (OOD), the above ERM model can still classify correctly thanks to its focus only on the context-invariant class feature[1]—model generalization emerges [17,19,33]. However in practice, due to the limited annotation budget, real-world datasets are far from the "golden" balance, and learning the class invariance on imbalanced datasets is challenging. As shown in Fig. 1 (b), if the context "grass" in class "throwing" dominates the training, the model will use the spurious correlation "most throwing actions happen in the grass" to predict "throwing". Therefore, the obstacle to OOD generalization is context imbalance.

Existing methods for context or context bias estimation fall into two categories (details in Sect. 2). First, they annotate the context directly [2,31], as shown in Fig. 2 (c). This annotation takes additional costs. Besides, it is elusive to annotate complex contexts. For example, it is easy to label the coarse scenes "water" and "grass" but hard to further tell their fine-grained differences. Thus, context supervision is usually incomplete.

---

[1] It is also known as causal or stable feature in literature [49,65,70].

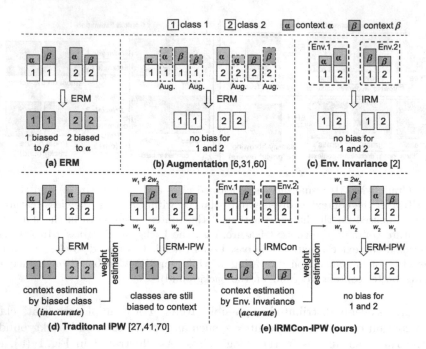

**Fig. 2.** Illustrations of the related approaches [2,6,27,31,41,60,70]. ERM is the baseline. Others and ours aim for mitigating context bias. The components are elaborated below. 1) The length of a context bar indicates the number of samples in that context—longer bar means the context is more prevailing. 2) A sole bar with the mixture of a color and a class number denotes the feature biased to the prevailing context. Our implementation method IRMCon-IPW is based on IRM and IPW, and our technical contribution (over the conventional methods of IRM or IPW) is the approach of disentangling context features not by using but by eliminating class features. We provide a theoretical justification in Sect. 4 and an empirical evaluation in Sect. 5.2.

Second, they estimate context bias by the biased class prediction [4,27,41], as shown in Fig. 2 (d). This relies on the contra-position of Principle 1 which is essentially an *indirect* context estimation.

**Principle 1** *(Complement). If a feature is not invariant to context, it is not class but context.*

Here, the judgment of *"not invariant to context"* is implemented by using the biased prediction of a classifier, *i.e.*, if the classifier predicts wrongly, it is due to that the class invariance is not yet achieved in the classifier. Unfortunately, as the classifier is a combined effect of both class and context, it is ill-posed to disentangle if the bias is from biased context or immature class modeling. The reflection in the result is the incorrect context estimation mixed with class (see the upper part of Fig. 1 (c)). In fact, coinciding with recent findings [14,65], we show in Sect. 5 that existing methods with improper context estimation may even under-perform the ERM baseline. In particular, if the data is less biased, such methods may catastrophically mistake context for class—this limits their applicability only in severely biased training data.

In this paper, we propose a more *direct* and accurate context estimation method without needing any context labels. Our inspiration comes from the other side of Principle 1:

**Principle 2.** *Context is also invariant to class.*

For example, the context "grass" is always grassy regardless of its foreground object class.

Principle 1 implies that the success of learning class invariance is due to the varying context. Similarly, Principle 2 tells us that we can learn context invariance with varying classes, and this is even easier for us to implement because the classes (taken as varying environments [2]) have been labeled and balanced—a common practice for any supervised training data with an equal sample size per class. In Sect. 4, as illustrated in Fig. 2 (e), we propose a context estimator trained by minimizing the contrastive loss of intra-class sample similarity which is invariant to classes (based on Principle 2). In particular, the invariance is achieved by Invariant Risk Minimization (IRM) [2] with our new loss term. We call our method **IRMCon** where **Con** stands for context. Figure 1 (c) illustrates that our IRMCon can capture better context feature. Based on IRMCon, we can simply deploy a re-weighting method, *e.g.*, [35], to generate the balancing weights for different contexts—context balance is achieved.

We follow DOMAINBED [14] for rigorous and reproducible evaluations, including 1) a strong Empirical Risk Minimization (ERM) baseline that is used to be mistakenly poor in OOD, and 2) a fair hyper-parameter tuning validation set. Experimental results in Sect. 5 demonstrate that our IRMCon can effectively learn context variance and eventually improve the context bias estimation, leading to a state-of-the-art OOD performance. Our another contribution in experiments is we propose a non-pretraining setting for OOD. It is known that many conventional experiment settings with pretraining, especially using the ImageNet [10], have data leakage issues as mentioned in related works [62, 66]. We have an in-depth discussion on these issues in Sect. 5.2.

## 2    Related Work

**OOD Tasks.** Traditional machine learning heavily relies on the Independent and Identically Distributed (IID) assumption for training and testing data. Under this assumption, model generalization emerges easily [59]. However, this assumption is often violated by data distribution shift in practice—the Out-of-Distribution (OOD) problem causes the catastrophic performance drop [18, 47]. In general, any test distribution unseen in training can be understood as OOD tasks, such as debiasing [8, 11, 24, 32, 63], long-tailed recognition [23, 37, 56], domain adaptation [5, 12, 58, 69] and domain generalization [28, 40, 52]. In this work, we focus on the most challenging one, where the distribution shift is unlabelled (*e.g.*, different from long-tailed recognition, where the shift of class distribution is known) and even unavailable (*e.g.*, different from domain adaptation, where the OOD data is available). We leave other related tasks as future work.

**Invariant Feature Learning.** The invariant class feature can help the model achieve robust classification when context distribution changes. The prevalent methods are: 1) *Data augmentation* [6,31,60,68]. They pre-define some augmentations for images to enlarge the available context distribution artificially. As the features are only invariant to the augmentation-related contexts, they cannot deal with other contexts out of the augmentation inventory. 2) *Context Annotation* [2,30,54]. They split data by different context annotation into environments, and penalize the model by the feature shifts among different environments. As the features are only invariant to the annotated context, the inaccurate and incomplete annotations will impact their feature invariance. 3) *Causal Learning* [39,44,46,65]. They learn the causal representations to capture the latent data generation process. Then, they can eliminate the context feature and pursue causal effect by intervention. These methods are essentially the re-weighting methods below in a causal perspective. 4) *Reweighting* [27,41,70]. They rebalance the context by re-weighting to help invariance feature learning. But, they improperly estimate the context weights by involving class learning into the context bias estimation. This inaccurate estimation problem severely influences the re-weighting and invariant feature learning. In contrast, IRMCon directly estimates the context without class prediction. The key difference is demonstrated in Fig. 2 (d) and (e): the output of our IRMCon does not contain class feature.

## 3   Common Pipeline: Invariance as Class

Model generalization in supervised learning is based on the fundamental assumption [20,64]: any sample $x$ is generated from the two disentangled features (or independent causal mechanisms [55]), $x = g(\mathbf{x}_c, \mathbf{x}_t)$, where $\mathbf{x}_c$ is the class feature, $\mathbf{x}_t$ is the context feature, $g(\cdot)$ is a generative function that transforms the two features in vector space to sample space (*e.g.*, pixels). In particular, the disentanglement naturally encodes the two principles. To see this for Principle 1, if we only change the context of $x$ and obtain a new image $x'$, we have $\mathbf{x}_c = \mathbf{x}'_c$ but $\mathbf{x}_t \neq \mathbf{x}'_t$—class is invariant to context; Principle 2 can be interpreted in a similar way. Therefore, we'd like to learn a feature extractor $\phi_c(x) = \mathbf{x}_c$ that helps the subsequent classifier to predict robustly across varying contexts.

### 3.1   Empirical Risk Minimization (ERM)

If the training data per class is balanced and diverse, *i.e.*, containing sufficient samples in different contexts, ERM has been theoretically justified that it can learn the class feature extractor $\phi_c(x)$ by minimizing a contrastive based loss such as softmax cross-entropy (CE) loss [64]:

$$\mathcal{L}_{\mathrm{ERM}}(\phi_c, f) = \frac{1}{N} \sum_{i=1}^{N} \mathrm{CE}(y_i, \hat{y}_i = f(\phi_c(x_i))), \tag{1}$$

where $y_i$ is the ground-truth label of $x_i$ and $\hat{y}_i$ is the predicted label by the softmax classifier $f(\cdot)$.

However, when the data is imbalanced and less diverse, ERM cannot learn $\phi_c(x) = \mathbf{x}_c$. We illustrate this in Fig. 2 (a): if more class 1 samples contain context $\beta$ than $\alpha$, the resultant $\phi_c(x)$ will be biased to the prevailing context, e.g., features for classifying class 1 will be entangled with context $\beta$. To this end, augmentation-based methods [6,61] aim to compensate for the imbalance (Fig. 2 (b)). However, as contexts are complex, augmentation will be far from enough to compensate for all of them.

## 3.2    Invariant Risk Minimization (IRM)

If context annotation is available, we can use IRM [2] to learn $\phi_c$ by applying Principle 1 that $\phi_c$ should be invariant to different contexts. Compared to ERM on balanced data that achieves invariance in a passive way via random trials [3], IRM on imbalanced data adopts the active intervention, taking contexts as the environments:

$$\mathcal{L}_{\text{IRM}}(\phi_c, \theta) = \sum_e \frac{1}{|e|} \sum_{(x_i, y_i) \in e} \left[ \text{CE}(y_i, \hat{y}_i) + \lambda \|\nabla_\theta \text{CE}(y_i, \hat{y}_i^\theta)\|^2 \right], \quad (2)$$

where $\hat{y}_i^\theta = f(\phi_c(x_i) \cdot \theta)$, $e$ is one of the environments of the training data according to context labels, and $\lambda > 0$ is a trade-off hyper-parameter for the invariance regularization term. $\theta$ is a dummy classifier, whose gradient is not applied to update itself but to calculate the regularization term in Eq. (2). The regularization term encourages $\phi_c$ to be equally optimal in different environments, i.e., become invariant to environments (contexts). We follow IRM [2] to set $\theta$ as 1.

As illustrated in Fig. 2 (c), if we want to learn a common classifier that discriminates 1 and 2 in both environments, the only way is to remove the context $\alpha$ and $\beta$. However, it has been demonstrated by [36,65] that the context annotation is usually incomplete and using it may even under-perform ERM.

## 3.3    Inverse Probability Weighting (IPW)

When context annotation is unavailable, we can estimate the context and then re-balance data according to context. We begin with the following ERM-IPW loss [22,50]:

$$\mathcal{L}_{\text{ERM-IPW}}(\phi_c, \phi_t, f) = \frac{1}{N} \sum_{i=1}^{N} \text{CE}(y_i, \hat{y}_i = f(\phi_c(x_i))) \cdot \frac{1}{P(x_i \mid \phi_t(x_i))}. \quad (3)$$

We can see that the key difference between ERM-IPW and ERM is the sample-level IPW term $1/P(x_i|\phi_t(x_i))$, where $\phi_t(x) = \mathbf{x}_t$ is the context feature extractor. This IPW implies that if $x$ is more likely associated with its context $\mathbf{x}_t$, i.e., the class feature counterpart $\mathbf{x}_c$ is also more likely associated with $\mathbf{x}_t$, we should under-weight the loss because we need to discourage such a context bias.

However, the context estimation of $\phi_t$ is almost challenging as learning $\phi_c$. Instead, a prevailing strategy is to estimate it by a biased classifier [27,41], $e.g.$,

$$P(x|\phi_t(x)) \propto \frac{\mathrm{CE}(y, \hat{y} = f(\phi_c(x))) + \mathrm{CE}(y, \hat{y} = f_b(\phi_b(x)))}{\mathrm{CE}(y, \hat{y} = f_b(\phi_b(x)))}, \qquad (4)$$

where $\phi_b$ is the bias feature extractor and $f_b$ is the bias classifier. $\phi_b$ and $f_b$ are minimized by ERM equipped with generalized cross entropy (GCE) loss [71]:

$$\mathcal{L}_{\mathrm{ERM}}(\phi_b, f_b) = \frac{1}{N} \sum_{i=1}^{N} \mathrm{GCE}(y_i, \hat{y}_i = f_b(\phi_b(x_i))), \qquad (5)$$

where $\mathrm{GCE}(y, \hat{y}) = \sum_{k=1}^{n} y_k \cdot \frac{1 - \hat{y}_k^q}{q}$ is used to amplify the bias, where $q$ is a constant, $k$ is the index of class and $n$ is the class number. However, the loss in Eq. (5) inevitably includes the effect from the class feature $\mathbf{x}_c$, due to the aforementioned assumption $x = g(\mathbf{x}_c, \mathbf{x}_t)$. In other words, such a combined effect cannot distinguish whether the bias is from class or context, resulting in inaccurate context estimation. We show the illustration in Fig. 2 (d). Specifically, the weights are estimated from class and context, and thus inaccurate to balance the context. In addition, the experimental results in Fig. 6 (Bottom) testify that: inaccurate context estimation will severely hurt the performance, $i.e.$, fail to derive unbiased classifiers.

## 4 Our Approach: Invariance as Context

To tackle the inaccurate context estimation of $\phi_t(x)$, we propose to apply Principle 2 as a way out. As illustrated in Fig. 2 (e), if we consider each class as the environment, we can clearly see that the $unique$ environmental change is the class which has been already labeled. This motivates us to apply IRM to learn invariance as context by removing the environment-equivariant class. The crux is how to design the contrastive based loss—more specifically, how to modify $\theta$ and $\mathrm{CE}(\cdot)$ in Eq. (2). The following is our novel solution.

We design a new contrastive loss based on the intra-class (environment) sample similarity, as follows,

$$\mathcal{L}_{ct}(\phi_t, e, \theta) = \sum_{x_i \in e} -log \frac{exp(\phi_t(x_i)^T \phi_t(\mathrm{Aug}(x_i)) \cdot \theta)}{\sum_{x_i' \in e} exp(\phi_t(x_i)^T \phi_t(x_i') \cdot \theta)}, \qquad (6)$$

where $\mathrm{Aug}(\cdot)$ is the common augmentations, such as flip and Gaussian noise (used in standard contrastive losses [7,13,15]), $e$ is the environment split by class, $e.g.$, under the environment $e_1$, any $x_i \in e_1$ has the class label 1, $\theta$ is the dummy classifier, we add $\theta$ here for the convenience to introduce Eq. (7). The reason for using contrastive loss is that it preserves all the intrinsic features of each sample [43,64]. Yet, without the invariance to class, $\phi_t(x) \neq \mathbf{x}_t$. Then, based on Eq. (2), our proposed IRMCon for learning "invariance as context" is:

$$\mathcal{L}_{\mathrm{IRMCon}}(\phi_t, \theta) = \sum_{e} \frac{1}{|e|} [\mathcal{L}_{ct}(\phi_t, e, \theta) + \lambda |\nabla_\theta \mathcal{L}_{ct}(\phi_t, e, \theta)|], \qquad (7)$$

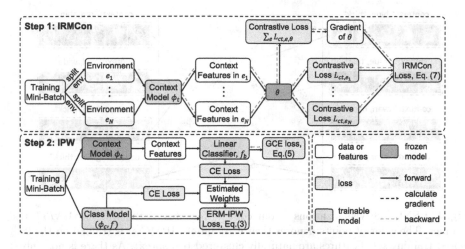

**Fig. 3.** The training pipeline of our IRMCon-IPW. 1) "split env." denotes we split the training samples in mini-batch into subsets based on class labels, i.e., samples of each class in one subset, forming $N$ environments $\{e_i\}_1^N$; 2) $\theta$ is a dummy classifier, whose gradient is for regularizing $\phi_t$ become invariant to classes. See the detailed algorithm in Appendix

where $\theta$ plays the same role in Eq. (2), to regularize $\phi_t$ be invariant to environments (classes). We can prove that solving Eq. (7) achieves $\phi_t(x) = \mathbf{x}_t$, i.e., the context feature is disentangled (see Appendix). As demonstrated in Fig. 4, $\phi_t$ can extract accurate context features. Thanks to $\phi_t$, we can further improve IPW:

$$P(x|\phi_t(x)) \propto \frac{\text{CE}(y, \hat{y} = f(\phi_c(x))) + \text{CE}(y, \hat{y} = f_b(\mathbf{x}_t))}{\text{CE}(y, \hat{y} = f_b(\mathbf{x}_t))}, \quad (8)$$

where $\mathbf{x}_t = \phi_t(x)$. We train $f_b$ by using GCE loss, just replacing $\phi_b(x)$ with $\mathbf{x}_t$ in Eq. (5). $\phi_t$ is trained by IRMCon and then fixed when estimating the context.

As shown in Fig. 5, our biased classifier can estimate more accurate weights to perform better reweighting than the traditional one We streamline the proposed IRMCon-IPW in Fig. 3 and summarize our algorithm in Appendix.

## 5   Experiments

We introduce the benchmarks of two OOD generalization tasks, removing context bias (also called debias) and mitigating domain gaps (also called domain generalization and termed DG), and our implementation details in Sect. 5.1. Then, we evaluate the effectiveness of our approach based on the experimental results in Sect. 5.2.

### 5.1   Datasets and Settings

**Context Biased Datasets.** We follow LfF [41] to use two synthetic datasets,

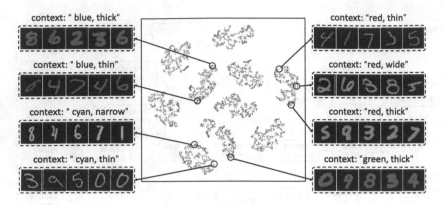

**Fig. 4.** t-SNE [38] visualizations of our context features of the *Colored MNIST* test samples. The color of points denotes their class labels. IRMCon is trained on the 99% biased training set. Features are naturally clustered by context. As there is no context ground-truth, the context labels are interpreted by us.

*Colored MNIST* and *Corrupted CIFAR-10*, and one real-world dataset, *Biased Action Recognition* (*BAR*) [41] for evaluation.

On each dataset, we manually control the context bias ratio by generating (in synthetic datasets) or sampling (in the real-world dataset) training images.

In specific, on *Colored MNIST*, we follow LfF to generate 10 colors as 10 contexts. We connect each digit (class) with a specific color and dye them with the ratio from {99.9%, 99.8%, 99.5%, 99.0%, 98.0%, 95.0%} to construct each biased training set. In the test set, 10 colors are uniformly distributed on the samples of each class. For *Corrupted CIFAR-10*, we follow LfF to use {Saturate, Elastic, Impulse, Brightness, Contrast, Gaussian, Defocus Blur, Pixelate, Gaussian Blur, Frost} as 10 contexts. Similar to *Colored MNIST*, we generate context biased training set by pairing a context and a class with

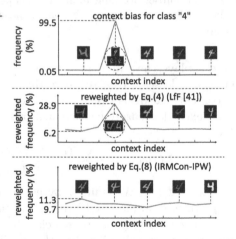

**Fig. 5.** Illustrations of the reweighted sample frequencies for 10 color contexts. All models are trained on the 99.5% biased *Colored MNIST*. The reweighted frequency of a context indicates the normalized sum over the inverse probabilities of the samples in this context. **Top**: Biased context distribution in the training set. **Middle**: Biased context distribution derived by using LfF [41]. **Bottom**: Relatively balanced context distribution by using our method.

a ratio chosen from {99.5%, 99.0%, 98.0%, 95.0%}. In the test set, 10 corruptions are uniformly distributed.

The real-world dataset *BAR* contains six kinds of action-place bias, and each one is between human action and background, e.g., "throwing" always happens with the "grass" background; We choose a bias ratio in {99.0%, 95.0%}.

**Domain Gap Dataset.** We use *PACS* [28] to testify our method. It consists of seven object categories spanning four image domains: *Photo, Art-painting, Cartoon*, and *Sketch*. We follow DOMAINBED [14] to each time select three domains for training and the left one for testing. More details about datasets, *e.g.*, the number and size of the training images, are given in Appendix.

**Table 1.** Accuracy (%) on context biased datasets compared with SOTA methods. We reproduced the methods and averaged the results over three independent trials (mean±std). "*": For reproducing mismatch issues, performance is quoted from the original paper. Our reproduced results are reported in Appendix. "-": no report in that setting.

| Dataset | Bias ratio (%) | Methods | | | | | |
|---|---|---|---|---|---|---|---|
| | | ERM | Rebias [4] | EnD* [57] | LfF [41] | Feat-Aug* [27] | IRMCon-IPW (ours) |
| Colored MNIST | 99.9 | 20.4 ± 1.1 | 20.8 ± 0.6 | - | 56.8 ± 1.6 | - | **66.7 ± 2.3** |
| | 99.8 | 26.4 ± 0.4 | 28.3 ± 0.9 | - | 68.3 ± 1.5 | - | **75.5 ± 1.5** |
| | 99.5 | 42.9 ± 1.1 | 44.4 ± 0.5 | 34.3 ± 1.2 | 77.0 ± 1.5 | 65.2 ± 4.4 | **81.0 ± 0.9** |
| | 99.0 | 59.2 ± 0.5 | 58.6 ± 0.4 | 49.5 ± 2.5 | 82.5 ± 1.7 | 81.7 ± 2.3 | **85.3 ± 0.3** |
| | 98.0 | 72.5 ± 0.2 | 73.5 ± 1.0 | 68.5 ± 2.2 | 84.1 ± 1.5 | 84.8 ± 1.0 | **88.3 ± 0.2** |
| | 95.0 | 85.7 ± 0.5 | 85.5 ± 0.5 | 81.2 ± 1.4 | 86.8 ± 0.5 | 89.7 ± 1.1 | **92.2 ± 0.5** |
| Corrupted Cifar-10 | 99.5 | 22.7 ± 0.5 | 22.7 ± 0.7 | 22.9 ± 0.3 | 26.1 ± 0.7 | 30.0 ± 0.7 | **31.0 ± 0.6** |
| | 99.0 | 25.8 ± 0.6 | 24.9 ± 0.7 | 25.5 ± 0.4 | 31.8 ± 0.7 | 36.5 ± 1.8 | **37.1 ± 0.4** |
| | 98.0 | 28.7 ± 0.1 | 29.1 ± 0.7 | 31.3 ± 0.4 | 38.9 ± 1.0 | 41.8 ± 2.3 | **42.5 ± 1.0** |
| | 95.0 | 39.9 ± 1.6 | 38.9 ± 1.7 | 40.3 ± 0.9 | 51.3 ± 0.9 | 51.1 ± 1.3 | **53.8 ± 1.3** |
| BAR | 99.0 | 52.9 ± 0.7 | 52.1 ± 0.5 | - | 48.1 ± 2.7 | 52.3 ± 1.0 | **55.3 ± 0.6** |
| | 95.0 | 65.2 ± 1.9 | 65.0 ± 1.8 | - | 60.6 ± 2.6 | 63.5 ± 1.5 | **67.9 ± 0.8** |

**Comparing Methods.** As the two types of datasets have their own state-of-the-art (SOTA) methods, we compare with different SOTA methods in context biased benchmark and domain gap benchmark, respectively.

For context biased datasets, we compare with Rebias [4], End [57], LfF [41], and Feat-Aug [27]. For domain gap dataset (DG task), we compare with domain-label based methods, such as DANN [1], fish [53], and TRM [67], as well as domain-label free methods, such as RSC [21] and StableNet [70]. As we claimed at the end of Sect. 3.1, we train all models from scratch. This makes some DG methods (*e.g.*, MMD [30] and CDANN [42]) hard to converge.

**Implementation Details.** We first introduce two implementation details to deal with the implementation issues we met, and then provide training details. 1) *Weighted sample strategy*. This strategy is for the biased dataset. For example, under the 99.9% biased training set, in a mini-batch, all the images may have

**Table 2.** Accuracy (%) on the domain generalization dataset *PACS* [28]. We reproduced all the methods by the DOMAINBED [14] code base without pretraining. Results are averaged over 3 independent trials (mean±std). "-" denotes that methods fail to converge when training from scratch.

| Methods | | PACS | | | | |
|---|---|---|---|---|---|---|
| | | *Art.* | *Cartoon* | *Photo* | *Sketch* | Avg. |
| w/ domain supervision | IRM [2] | $31.1 \pm 1.4$ | $38.7 \pm 2.5$ | - | $44.4 \pm 2.2$ | - |
| | DRO [48] | $39.0 \pm 1.9$ | $53.8 \pm 1.2$ | $63.6 \pm 2.9$ | $\mathbf{62.4 \pm 0.6}$ | 54.7 |
| | InterMix [68] | $42.2 \pm 0.5$ | $52.8 \pm 1.9$ | $61.0 \pm 2.4$ | $58.4 \pm 1.0$ | 53.6 |
| | MLDG [29] | $38.8 \pm 0.7$ | $53.5 \pm 0.7$ | $63.3 \pm 0.1$ | $60.2 \pm 1.2$ | 54.0 |
| | DANN [1] | $31.5 \pm 1.1$ | $48.2 \pm 1.6$ | $58.1 \pm 1.5$ | $44.9 \pm 0.7$ | 45.7 |
| | V-REx [26] | $33.9 \pm 1.2$ | $40.9 \pm 1.2$ | - | $55.1 \pm 2.9$ | - |
| | Fish [53] | $\mathbf{43.1 \pm 2.1}$ | $\mathbf{57.4 \pm 0.4}$ | $\mathbf{64.8 \pm 2.7}$ | $61.1 \pm 0.8$ | $\mathbf{56.6}$ |
| | TRM [67] | $41.8 \pm 1.8$ | $54.9 \pm 0.8$ | - | $61.3 \pm 2.3$ | - |
| w/o domain supervision | ERM | $40.4 \pm 0.7$ | $54.3 \pm 0.3$ | $63.7 \pm 0.4$ | $58.9 \pm 2.6$ | 54.3 |
| | SD [45] | $39.1 \pm 0.8$ | $54.4 \pm 1.4$ | $61.7 \pm 3.8$ | $51.3 \pm 3.2$ | 51.6 |
| | RSC [21] | $40.7 \pm 1.1$ | $49.8 \pm 6.0$ | $58.0 \pm 1.9$ | $53.3 \pm 4.3$ | 50.5 |
| | LfF [41] | $38.2 \pm 1.4$ | $50.4 \pm 0.9$ | $58.0 \pm 0.6$ | $60.4 \pm 1.2$ | 51.8 |
| | IRMCon-IPW | $\mathbf{40.9 \pm 1.7}$ | $\mathbf{56.0 \pm 2.9}$ | $\mathbf{64.9 \pm 0.7}$ | $\mathbf{61.1 \pm 2.5}$ | $\mathbf{55.7}$ |

the same context in a class, unless we can sample over 1,000 images per class to get 1 sample with non-biased context. To solve this issue, we use the bias model from LfF [41] to learn an inaccurate context estimator, and based on its inverse probability we sample a relative context-balanced mini-batch. This strategy frees us from sampling a very large batch to learn Eq. (6).

2) *Strategy for learning augmentation-related context.* It is hard to learn augmentation related context, when using contrastive loss. To minimize contrastive loss, the model needs to learn invariance on augmentations, *i.e.*, augmentation related features will be removed. On *Corrupted Cifar-10*, we add the classification loss in Eq. (5) to our IRMCon loss to train the context extractor. Please note that we use this strategy only for *Corrupted Cifar-10* as context on this dataset is dominated by augmentation-related context, such as 95% "car" has augmentation-related context 'Gaussian noise". Due to space limits, we put other details in Appendix.

3) *Training details.* On the *Colored MNIST*, we use 3-layers MLPs to model $\phi_c, \phi_b$ and $\phi_t$. On the *Corrupted Cifar-10*, we use ResNet-18 for $\phi_c$ and 3-layers CNNs for $\phi_b$ and $\phi_t$. On the *BAR* and *PACS*, we use ResNet-18 for $\phi_c, \phi_b$ and $\phi_t$. For optimization in context biased datasets, we follow LfF [41] to use Adam [25] optimizer with the learning rate as 0.001. Other detailed settings, *e.g.*batch size, epochs, and $\lambda$ in each setting, can be found in Appendix.

On all datasets, we follow DOMAINBED [14] to randomly split the original unbiased test set into 20% and 80% as the validation set and test set, respectively, and select the best model based on validation results. We average the results of three independent runs, and report them in the format of "mean accuracy ± standard deviation".

## 5.2   Results and Analyses

**IRMCon-IPW Achieves SOTA.** We show our results of context biased datasets in Table 1 and domain gap dataset in Table 2.

1) Table 1 presents that our IRMCon-IPW achieves very clear margins over the related methods.

In particular, the improvements are more obvious in the settings of higher bias ratios. The possible reason is when the bias ratio is higher, the "rare" context samples become less. Reweighting methods are more sensitive to the accuracy of context weights estimation. Therefore, accurate context estimation plays a more essential role. Compared to related methods, our IRMCon can estimate more accurate context, *i.e.*, extract high-quality context features like the illustration in Fig. 4, whose gain over others is more obvious when increasing the context bias ratio.

2) Table 2 presents that on the domain gap dataset, our method outperforms ERM and also achieves the best average performance over all the domain label-free methods. In addition, it achieves comparable results to the other DG methods (in the upper block) which need domain labels.

**Why does ERM perform so well in most cases?** On *PACS*, we follow the DOMAINBED [14] to implement a strong ERM baseline. On *BAR*, we use the strong augmentation strategy, Random Augmentation [9], which can be considered as an OOD method as shown in Fig. 2 (b). If we do not apply such strong augmentations, ERM performance drops significantly. We show the corresponding results in Appendix.

**Why do we train models from scratch for OOD problems?** We challenge the traditional pretraining

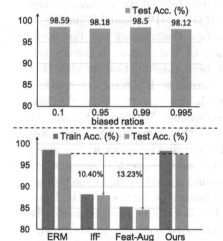

**Fig. 6.** Accuracy (%) of models when training on *Colored MNIST* context-balance set. **Top**: ERM is stable in test sets with varying context biases; **Bottom**: due to the incorrect context estimation, traditional reweighting methods degenerate significantly compared to ERM when training on context-balance set. Thanks to the correct context estimation, our IRMCon-IPW achieves comparable performance to ERM.

settings in some OOD tasks, such as Domain Generalization, because we are concerned that the data or knowledge of the test set has been leaked to the model when pretrained on large-scale image datasets. Data leakage is a usual problem in pretraining settings, such as ImageNet [10] leaks to CUB [62]. Such problem will severely destroy the validity of the OOD task [66]. Empirically, we provide an observation in Domain Generalization to justify our challenge. In pretraining settings, ERM achieves the "impressive" 98% test accuracy [14] when *Photo* domain is used for testing. This number is significantly higher (around 20% higher) than using *Cartoon* and *Sketch* in testing. However, this is not the case if there is no pretraining on ImageNet, see Table 2, bottom block first line, ERM method. The reason is that ImageNet, collected from the real world, leaks more real images in *Photo*, compare to artificial images in *Cartoon* and *Sketch*. Therefore, we propose the non-pretraining setting for all OOD benchmarks to prevent the leakage problem.

**How to evaluate the context feature learned in IRMCon-IPW?** We visualize the comparisons between the context features learned by IRMCon-IPW and LfF in Fig. 7. We show the training and test accuracies of the linear classifiers (we call bias classification heads) that are trained with context features and class labels, *i.e.*, to learn the bias intentionally. We can see from the figures that ours shows the almost same learning behavior as the upper bound case: context is invariant to class and should predict class by random chance. It means that IRMCon-IPW is able to recover the oracle distribution of contexts in the image. This can be taken as a support to the bottom illustration in Fig. 5 where using our weights can achieve a balanced context distribution—the ground truth distribution.

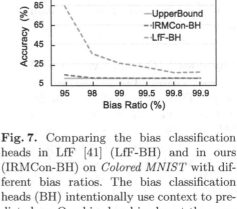

**Fig. 7.** Comparing the bias classification heads in LfF [41] (LfF-BH) and in ours (IRMCon-BH) on *Colored MNIST* with different bias ratios. The bias classification heads (BH) intentionally use context to predict class. Our bias head is almost the same as the upper bound case in test set—random class prediction (10%).

**How does IRMCon-IPW tackle domain gap issues?** Compared to the datasets with pre-defined context distribution in training (*e.g.*, set color distribution in each class in *Colored MNIST* dataset [41]), the domain gap dataset such as *PACS* does not have such explicit context settings. While it has implicit context distribution related to the domain. This distribution is often imbalanced which leads to context bias problems (similar to context biased datasets such as *BAR*). Therefore, our method can help *PACS* to "debias". We notice that, compared to ERM, our improvement for *PACS* is not as significant as that on the context biased datasets. This might be because the context bias in *PACS* is not as severe as that in context biased datasets.

**Failure Cases.** We show some failure cases of our IRMCon in Fig. 8. The failure cases are selected if their IRMCon-IPW classification results are wrong. As expected, we see that the key reasons for failure are the incorrect context estimation, *e.g.*, the contexts are mixed with the foreground or wrongly attended to the foreground. By inspecting the *BAR* dataset, we find that some contexts, *e.g.*, "pool" for the class "diving", are relatively unique for certain classes. This implies that the context is NOT invariant to class. To resolve this, we conjecture that this is a dataset failure and the only way out is to bring external knowledge.

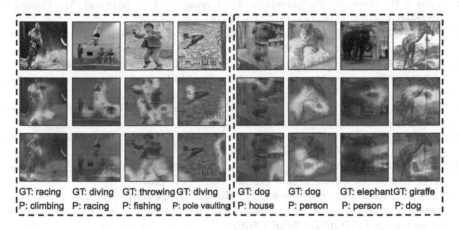

| GT: racing | GT: diving | GT: throwing | GT: diving | GT: dog | GT: dog | GT: elephant | GT: giraffe |
| P: climbing | P: racing | P: fishing | P: pole vaulting | P: house | P: person | P: person | P: dog |

**Fig. 8.** GradCAM [51] visualizations of IRMCon-IPW failure cases. **Top**: input test images; **Middle**: context visualization by bias classifier of IRMCon; **Bottom**: class visualization. Left four columns are selected from *BAR* test set, the model is trained on the 99% biased training set; right four are selected from the *Photo* domain of *PACS*, model is trained on the other three domains. GT: ground-truth label; P: predicted label.

# 6   Conclusions

Context imbalance is the main challenge in learning class invariance for OOD generalization. Prior work tackles this challenge in two ways: 1) relying on context supervision and 2) estimating context bias by classifier failures. We showed how they fail and hence proposed a novel approach called IRM for Context (IRMCon) that directly learns the context feature without context supervision. The success of IRMCon is based on: *context is invariant to class*, which is the overlooked other side of the common principle—class is invariant to context.

Thanks to the class supervision which has been already provided as environments in training data, IRMCon can achieve context invariance by using IRM on the intra-class sample similarity contrastive loss. We used the context feature for Inverse Probability Weighting (IPW): a method for context balancing, to learn the final classifier that generalizes to OOD. IRMCon-IPW achieves state-of-the-art results on several OOD benchmarks.

**Acknowledgements.** This research was supported by the Alibaba-NTU Singapore Joint Research Institute (JRI), and Artificial Intelligence Singapore (AISG), Alibaba Innovative Research (AIR) programme, A*STAR under its AME YIRG Grant (Project No. A20E6c0101).

# References

1. Ajakan, H., Germain, P., Larochelle, H., Laviolette, F., Marchand, M.: Domain-adversarial neural networks. In: NIPS (2014)
2. Arjovsky, M., Bottou, L., Gulrajani, I., Lopez-Paz, D.: Invariant risk minimization. arXiv preprint arXiv:1907.02893 (2019)
3. Austin, P.C.: An introduction to propensity score methods for reducing the effects of confounding in observational studies. In: Multivariate Behavioral Research (2011)
4. Bahng, H., Chun, S., Yun, S., Choo, J., Oh, S.J.: Learning de-biased representations with biased representations. In: ICML (2020)
5. Ben-David, S., Blitzer, J., Crammer, K., Pereira, F., et al.: Analysis of representations for domain adaptation. In: NIPS (2007)
6. Carlucci, F.M., D'Innocente, A., Bucci, S., Caputo, B., Tommasi, T.: Domain generalization by solving Jigsaw puzzles. In: CVPR (2019)
7. Chen, T., Kornblith, S., Norouzi, M., Hinton, G.: A simple framework for contrastive learning of visual representations. In: International Conference on Machine Learning, pp. 1597–1607. PMLR (2020)
8. Clark, C., Yatskar, M., Zettlemoyer, L.: Don't take the easy way out: ensemble based methods for avoiding known dataset biases. arXiv preprint arXiv:1909.03683 (2019)
9. Cubuk, E.D., Zoph, B., Shlens, J., Le, Q.V.: RandAugment: practical automated data augmentation with a reduced search space. In: Proceedings of the IEEE/CVF Conference on Computer Vision and Pattern Recognition Workshops, pp. 702–703 (2020)
10. Deng, J., Dong, W., Socher, R., Li, L.J., Li, K., Fei-Fei, L.: ImageNet: a large-scale hierarchical image database. In: CVPR (2009)
11. Geirhos, R., Rubisch, P., Michaelis, C., Bethge, M., Wichmann, F.A., Brendel, W.: ImageNet-trained CNNs are biased towards texture; increasing shape bias improves accuracy and robustness. arXiv preprint arXiv:1811.12231 (2018)
12. Gong, M., Zhang, K., Liu, T., Tao, D., Glymour, C., Schölkopf, B.: Domain adaptation with conditional transferable components. In: ICML (2016)
13. Grill, J.B., et al.: Bootstrap your own latent - a new approach to self-supervised learning. Adv. Neural. Inf. Process. Syst. **33**, 21271–21284 (2020)
14. Gulrajani, I., Lopez-Paz, D.: In search of lost domain generalization. In: ICLR (2021)

15. He, K., Fan, H., Wu, Y., Xie, S., Girshick, R.: Momentum contrast for unsupervised visual representation learning. In: CVPR (2020)
16. He, K., Zhang, X., Ren, S., Sun, J.: Deep residual learning for image recognition. In: CVPR (2016)
17. He, Y., Shen, Z., Cui, P.: Towards non-IID image classification: a dataset and baselines. Pattern Recogn. **110**, 107383 (2021)
18. Hendrycks, D., Dietterich, T.: Benchmarking neural network robustness to common corruptions and perturbations. In: ICLR (2019)
19. Hendrycks, D., Gimpel, K.: A baseline for detecting misclassified and out-of-distribution examples in neural networks. In: ICLR (2017)
20. Higgins, I., et al.: Towards a definition of disentangled representations. arXiv preprint arXiv:1812.02230 (2018)
21. Huang, Z., Wang, H., Xing, E.P., Huang, D.: Self-challenging improves cross-domain generalization. In: Vedaldi, A., Bischof, H., Brox, T., Frahm, J.-M. (eds.) ECCV 2020. LNCS, vol. 12347, pp. 124–140. Springer, Cham (2020). https://doi.org/10.1007/978-3-030-58536-5_8
22. Jung, Y., Tian, J., Bareinboim, E.: Learning causal effects via weighted empirical risk minimization. In: NIPS (2020)
23. Khan, S.H., Hayat, M., Bennamoun, M., Sohel, F.A., Togneri, R.: Cost-sensitive learning of deep feature representations from imbalanced data. IEEE Trans. Neural Netw. Learn. Syst. (2017)
24. Kim, B., Kim, H., Kim, K., Kim, S., Kim, J.: Learning not to learn: training deep neural networks with biased data. In: CVPR, pp. 9012–9020 (2019)
25. Kingma, D.P., Ba, J.: Adam: a method for stochastic optimization. arXiv preprint arXiv:1412.6980 (2014)
26. Krueger, D., et al.: Out-of-distribution generalization via risk extrapolation (rex). In: International Conference on Machine Learning (2021)
27. Lee, J., Kim, E., Lee, J., Lee, J., Choo, J.: Learning debiased representation via disentangled feature augmentation. In: NIPS (2021)
28. Li, D., Yang, Y., Song, Y.Z., Hospedales, T.M.: Deeper, broader and artier domain generalization. In: Proceedings of the IEEE International Conference on Computer Vision, pp. 5542–5550 (2017)
29. Li, D., Yang, Y., Song, Y.Z., Hospedales, T.M.: Learning to generalize: meta-learning for domain generalization. In: Thirty-Second AAAI Conference on Artificial Intelligence (2018)
30. Li, H., Pan, S.J., Wang, S., Kot, A.C.: Domain generalization with adversarial feature learning. In: CVPR (2018)
31. Li, Y., et al.: Deep domain generalization via conditional invariant adversarial networks. In: Ferrari, V., Hebert, M., Sminchisescu, C., Weiss, Y. (eds.) ECCV 2018. LNCS, vol. 11219, pp. 647–663. Springer, Cham (2018). https://doi.org/10.1007/978-3-030-01267-0_38
32. Li, Y., Vasconcelos, N.: Repair: removing representation bias by dataset resampling. In: CVPR, pp. 9572–9581 (2019)
33. Liang, S., Li, Y., Srikant, R.: Enhancing the reliability of out-of-distribution image detection in neural networks. In: ICLR (2018)
34. Lin, T.-Y., et al.: Microsoft COCO: common objects in context. In: Fleet, D., Pajdla, T., Schiele, B., Tuytelaars, T. (eds.) ECCV 2014. LNCS, vol. 8693, pp. 740–755. Springer, Cham (2014). https://doi.org/10.1007/978-3-319-10602-1_48
35. Little, R.J., Rubin, D.B.: Statistical Analysis with Missing Data, vol. 793. Wiley, Hoboken (2019)

36. Liu, J., Hu, Z., Cui, P., Li, B., Shen, Z.: Heterogeneous risk minimization. In: ICML (2021)
37. Liu, Z., Miao, Z., Zhan, X., Wang, J., Gong, B., Yu, S.X.: Large-scale long-tailed recognition in an open world. In: CVPR (2019)
38. Van der Maaten, L., Hinton, G.: Visualizing data using t-SNE. J. Mach. Learn. Res. **9**(11) (2008)
39. Mahajan, D., Tople, S., Sharma, A.: Domain generalization using causal matching. In: International Conference on Machine Learning, pp. 7313–7324. PMLR (2021)
40. Muandet, K., Balduzzi, D., Schölkopf, B.: Domain generalization via invariant feature representation. In: ICML (2013)
41. Nam, J., Cha, H., Ahn, S., Lee, J., Shin, J.: Learning from failure: training debiased classifier from biased classifier. In: NIPS (2020)
42. Okumura, R., Okada, M., Taniguchi, T.: Domain-adversarial and-conditional state space model for imitation learning. In: 2020 IEEE/RSJ International Conference on Intelligent Robots and Systems (IROS). IEEE (2020)
43. Oord, A.v.d., Li, Y., Vinyals, O.: Representation learning with contrastive predictive coding. arXiv preprint arXiv:1807.03748 (2018)
44. Peters, J., Bühlmann, P., Meinshausen, N.: Causal inference by using invariant prediction: identification and confidence intervals. J. Roy. Stat. Soc. Ser. B (Stat. Methodol.) 947–1012 (2016)
45. Pezeshki, M., Kaba, S.O., Bengio, Y., Courville, A., Precup, D., Lajoie, G.: Gradient starvation: a learning proclivity in neural networks. In: NIPS (2021)
46. Pfister, N., Bühlmann, P., Peters, J.: Invariant causal prediction for sequential data. J. Am. Stat. Assoc. **114**(527), 1264–1276 (2019)
47. Recht, B., Roelofs, R., Schmidt, L., Shankar, V.: Do imagenet classifiers generalize to imagenet? In: ICML (2019)
48. Sagawa, S., Koh, P.W., Hashimoto, T.B., Liang, P.: Distributionally robust neural networks for group shifts: on the importance of regularization for worst-case generalization. In: ICLR (2020)
49. Schölkopf, B., et al.: Toward causal representation learning. Proc. IEEE **109**(5), 612–634 (2021)
50. Seaman, S.R., Vansteelandt, S.: Introduction to double robust methods for incomplete data. Stat. Sci. Rev. J. Inst. Math. Stat. (2018)
51. Selvaraju, R.R., Cogswell, M., Das, A., Vedantam, R., Parikh, D., Batra, D.: Grad-CAM: visual explanations from deep networks via gradient-based localization. In: ICCV (2017)
52. Shen, Z., et al.: Towards out-of-distribution generalization: a survey. arXiv preprint arXiv:2108.13624 (2021)
53. Shi, Y., et al.: Gradient matching for domain generalization. arXiv preprint arXiv:2104.09937 (2021)
54. Sun, B., Saenko, K.: Deep CORAL: correlation alignment for deep domain adaptation. In: Hua, G., Jégou, H. (eds.) ECCV 2016. LNCS, vol. 9915, pp. 443–450. Springer, Cham (2016). https://doi.org/10.1007/978-3-319-49409-8_35
55. Suter, R., Miladinovic, D., Schölkopf, B., Bauer, S.: Robustly disentangled causal mechanisms: validating deep representations for interventional robustness. In: ICML (2019)
56. Tang, K., Huang, J., Zhang, H.: Long-tailed classification by keeping the good and removing the bad momentum causal effect. In: NIPS (2020)
57. Tartaglione, E., Barbano, C.A., Grangetto, M.: End: entangling and disentangling deep representations for bias correction. In: CVPR (2021)

58. Tzeng, E., Hoffman, J., Saenko, K., Darrell, T.: Adversarial discriminative domain adaptation. In: CVPR (2017)
59. Vapnik, V.: Principles of risk minimization for learning theory. In: Advances in Neural Information Processing Systems (1992)
60. Volpi, R., Murino, V.: Addressing model vulnerability to distributional shifts over image transformation sets. In: ICCV (2019)
61. Volpi, R., Namkoong, H., Sener, O., Duchi, J., Murino, V., Savarese, S.: Generalizing to unseen domains via adversarial data augmentation. In: NIPS (2018)
62. Wah, C., Branson, S., Welinder, P., Perona, P., Belongie, S.: The Caltech-UCSD birds-200-2011 dataset. California Institute of Technology (2011)
63. Wang, H., He, Z., Lipton, Z.C., Xing, E.P.: Learning robust representations by projecting superficial statistics out. arXiv preprint arXiv:1903.06256 (2019)
64. Wang, T., Yue, Z., Huang, J., Sun, Q., Zhang, H.: Self-supervised learning disentangled group representation as feature. In: NIPS (2021)
65. Wang, T., Zhou, C., Sun, Q., Zhang, H.: Causal attention for unbiased visual recognition. In: ICCV (2021)
66. Xian, Y., Lampert, C.H., Schiele, B., Akata, Z.: Zero-shot learning-a comprehensive evaluation of the good, the bad and the ugly. IEEE Trans. Pattern Anal. Mach. Intell. (2018)
67. Xu, Y., Jaakkola, T.: Learning representations that support robust transfer of predictors. arXiv preprint arXiv:2110.09940 (2021)
68. Yan, S., Song, H., Li, N., Zou, L., Ren, L.: Improve unsupervised domain adaptation with mixup training. arXiv preprint arXiv:2001.00677 (2020)
69. Yue, Z., Sun, Q., Hua, X.S., Zhang, H.: Transporting causal mechanisms for unsupervised domain adaptation. In: ICCV (2021)
70. Zhang, X., Cui, P., Xu, R., Zhou, L., He, Y., Shen, Z.: Deep stable learning for out-of-distribution generalization. In: CVPR (2021)
71. Zhang, Z., Sabuncu, M.R.: Generalized cross entropy loss for training deep neural networks with noisy labels. In: NIPS (2018)

# Hierarchical Semi-supervised Contrastive Learning for Contamination-Resistant Anomaly Detection

Gaoang Wang[1], Yibing Zhan[2], Xinchao Wang[3], Mingli Song[1(✉)],
and Klara Nahrstedt[4]

[1] Zhejiang University, Hangzhou, China
gaoangwang@intl.zju.edu.cn, brooksong@zju.edu.cn
[2] JD Explore Academy, Beijing, China
zhanyibing@jd.com
[3] National University of Singapore, Singapore, Singapore
xinchao@nus.edu.sg
[4] University of Illinois at Urbana-Champaign, Champaign, USA
klara@illinois.edu

**Abstract.** Anomaly detection aims at identifying deviant samples from the normal data distribution. Contrastive learning has provided a successful way to sample representation that enables effective discrimination on anomalies. However, when contaminated with unlabeled abnormal samples in training set under semi-supervised settings, current contrastive-based methods generally 1) ignore the comprehensive relation between training data, leading to suboptimal performance, and 2) require fine-tuning, resulting in low efficiency. To address the above two issues, in this paper, we propose a novel hierarchical semi-supervised contrastive learning (HSCL) framework, for contamination-resistant anomaly detection. Specifically, HSCL hierarchically regulates three complementary relations: sample-to-sample, sample-to-prototype, and normal-to-abnormal relations, enlarging the discrimination between normal and abnormal samples with a comprehensive exploration of the contaminated data. Besides, HSCL is an end-to-end learning approach that can efficiently learn discriminative representations without fine-tuning. HSCL achieves state-of-the-art performance in multiple scenarios, such as one-class classification and cross-dataset detection. Extensive ablation studies further verify the effectiveness of each considered relation. The code is available at https://github.com/GaoangW/HSCL.

**Keywords:** Anomaly detection · Contrastive learning · Contamination

**Supplementary Information** The online version contains supplementary material available at https://doi.org/10.1007/978-3-031-19806-9_7.

# 1 Introduction

Anomaly detection aims to distinguish outliers from in-distribution samples. In addition to the basic image classification task that aims at identifying abnormal visual samples from the base class [14,59], anomaly detection is also widely exploited in other fields, such as defect detection [1,9,21,27] and abnormal event detection [10,34,37,64]. Some works focus on designing anomaly scores and anomaly classifiers, such as [43,47]. Some methods combine reinforcement learning [44] and knowledge distillation [38] in the anomaly detection. Some self-supervised anomaly detection methods [21,53,59] use clean normal data in training and achieve much progress. Recently, more and more works [11,14,23,52] focus on the contaminated setting, where unlabeled abnormal samples are included in the training set, following the semi-supervised framework. This setting is much closer to the real situations that training data may be contaminated by abnormal samples, while a small labeled set can be easily acquired.

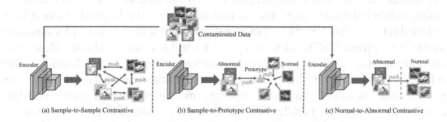

**Fig. 1.** Hierarchical contrastive relations with contaminated data for anomaly detection. Light red, purple, and light pink colors represent labeled normal, abnormal, and unlabeled data, respectively. The green triangle represents the class prototype of normal samples. Current contrastive learning-based anomaly detection approaches only consider (a) sample-to-sample relation and largely overlook the discrimination between normal and abnormal samples. Our proposed method jointly accounts for (a) sample-to-sample, (b) sample-to-prototype, and (c) normal-to-abnormal contrastive relations with both labeled and unlabeled data.

With limited labeled information under the semi-supervised setting, a good representation learning strategy is always crucial to identify the abnormal samples. Inspired by the recent success of contrastive learning for visual representation [5,8,13,15,29,84], much progress of contrastive learning has been made in anomaly detection, and contrastive learning-based approaches [14,48,56,59] have significantly outperformed the conventional reconstruction-based approaches [1,10,21,34,53,83,85].

However, current contrastive learning-based approaches only consider the intuitively instance-level relationship among samples [14,29,59,84], and ignore other potential relations, such as the contrastive relations between samples and prototypes of normal samples, and the discrimination between normal and abnormal samples. The above relations are shown in Fig. 1. Consequently, current contrastive learning-based approaches are prone to errors when distinguishing between normal and abnormal samples on the large contaminated set. Besides, when contaminated with anomalies, a fine-tuning or an adaptation step [14,56] is usually required for obtaining better representations. These multi-stage training schemes often result in low efficiency with additional training tricks like early-stop strategy [14], therefore not suitable for practice.

To address the above issues, we propose a novel Hierarchical Semi-supervised Contrastive Learning framework, termed HSCL, to identify anomalies with contaminated data under the semi-supervised setting. Specifically, HSCL jointly learns sample-to-sample, sample-to-prototype, and normal-to-abnormal relations to better distinguish anomalies over contaminated training data. The sample-to-sample relationship is learned following the basic InfoNCE loss [42] that enlarges the dissimilarities among different samples. Then, the similarities between prototypes and normal/abnormal samples are maximized/minimized, respectively, to regulate the sample-to-prototype contrastive relationship, where the prototypes [37] are defined as the representative features for normal samples. Afterward, the soft weighting on the unlabeled samples is incorporated and is further used for sampling unlabeled data to learn the normal-to-abnormal relationship along with the labeled set. The framework is shown in Fig. 2. With the proposed hierarchical contrastive relations, HSCL achieves 1) end-to-end learning without offline clustering and fine-tuning that has high computational complexity, 2) discriminative learning from a limited number of labels, and 3) contaminated data mining from large unlabeled samples. Extensive experiments are conducted under multiple contamination scenarios. HSCL achieves state-of-the-art (SOTA) results on 1) CIFAR-10, CIFAR-100 [26], and LSUN (FIX) [30,59] for the one-class classification, and 2) ImageNet (FIX) [17,59] and SVHN [40] for cross-dataset anomaly detection. Our main contributions are summarized as follows:

- We present a novel end-to-end contamination-resistant anomaly detection framework using contaminated training data for discriminative representation learning.
- We propose a hierarchical semi-supervised contrastive learning approach that jointly optimizes the complementary sample-to-sample, sample-to-prototype, and normal-to-abnormal relation in an online manner to enlarge the discrimination between normal and abnormal samples.
- We conduct extensive experiments with systematic analysis. The SOTA performance of HSCL on multiple scenarios and datasets validates the effectiveness of our HSCL.

## 2    Related Work

***Reconstruction-Based Anomaly Detection.*** Reconstruction-based approaches assume that abnormal samples cannot be well represented and reconstructed with the model learned from clean normal data. The reconstruction error can be treated as an indicator of anomalies. The commonly used reconstruction-based techniques include the PCA methods [20], sparse representation methods [36], and recent auto-encoder-based methods [10,83,85]?. For example, [10] introduces a memory module that can retrieve the most relevant memory items for reconstruction. However, studies have found that anomalies do not always yield a high reconstruction error when classes are similar [57,78]. Some studies employ generative adversarial networks (GAN) [1,21,34,53] as the complement of the reconstruction loss. For example, [34] adopts the U-Net [50] architecture and leverages the adversarial training to distinguish whether the predicted frame is real or fake after reconstruction. [21] proposes a novel GAN-based anomaly detection model, which consists of one auto-encoder generator and two separate discriminators for normal and anomalous inputs, respectively. However, it has been reported that GAN-based models easily generate suboptimal solutions and hence are inapplicable for complex datasets [33,45].

***Contrastive-Based Anomaly Detection.*** The recent success of contrastive learning [5,8,13,15,29,65] provides a potential manner for visual representations in anomaly detection [14,48,56,59]. These contrastive learning-based approaches significantly outperform the conventional reconstruction-based approaches. For example, [59] proposes distributionally-shifted augmentations in contrastive learning, serving as a solid SOTA method in anomaly detection trained with clean normal data. A fine-tuning stage is employed to adapt the pre-trained features with mean-shifted contrastive loss in [48]. To better address the contaminated data issue, [14] adopts a three-stage training scheme that fine-tunes the representations learned from contrastive loss with pseudo labels. However, existing contrastive learning-based approaches still suffer from the sensitivity to the contaminated abnormal samples or require multi-stage pre-training and fine-tuning, leading to low efficiency and suboptimal performance.

***Visual Representation Learning.*** Recent works explore the visual representation learning [15,24,25,68] based on designing various tasks [49,70,71,73,79–82], such as image inpainting [46], permutation [39], predicting jigsaw puzzles [19], and contrastive learning [8,74]. These learning strategies are also successfully extended to video representation learning, such as [2,7,60,69]. With much progress made recently, visual representation learning is employed in many real-world applications, such as anomaly detection [76,77], and human-based perception [61–63,65]. However, the complex hierarchical relationships among instances are seldom explored in the existing works.

***Semi-supervised and Noisy Label Approaches.*** Several approaches have been proposed for semi-supervised classification in recent years, such as Mix-Match [4], EnAET [67], FixMatch [55], SelfMatch [18], VPU [6] and Active-Match [75]. For example, FixMatch [55] uses the pseudo label generated from weakly augmented data to guide the prediction on strongly augmented data and achieves SOTA performance; VPU [6] learns from positive and unlabeled data. Due to the effectiveness of semi-supervised approaches that take account of both the labeled set and the large unlabeled set, many works have been proposed for anomaly detection under the semi-supervised setting [11,14,23,52]. For example, [52] modifies the one-class classifier that incorporates the negative abnormal samples in the training objective. To deal with contaminated training data, we can treat anomaly detection as a noisy label problem. Since we assume that normal samples are dominant, we can regard all unlabeled samples as normal with noisy labels. Some progress has been made for noisy label classification, such as [28,32,41,72]. For example, DivideMix [28] leverages semi-supervised learning techniques with noisy labels. [41] studies the effectiveness of several augmentation strategies. However, these semi-supervised learning and noisy label approaches usually generate biased solutions when training data is imbalanced, particularly for the anomaly detection task where the normal data is always dominant.

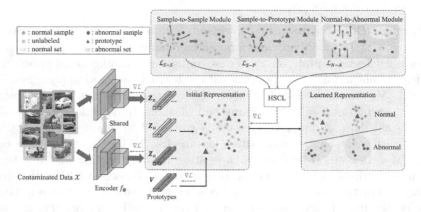

**Fig. 2.** The framework of hierarchical semi-supervised contrastive learning for anomaly detection. Given a mixture of contaminated training data, three complementary sample-to-sample, sample-to-prototype, and normal-to-abnormal relations are learned in a hierarchical way. Specifically, the sample-to-sample relation is learned to enlarge the dissimilarities among different samples. Then, the prototypes are optimized for representing normal samples and pushing away anomalies to learn the sample-to-prototype relations. The normal-to-abnormal module further enlarges the discrimination between normal and abnormal samples. More details are demonstrated in Sect. 3.2.

## 3    Method

### 3.1    Problem Description

We consider the semi-supervised anomaly detection as the same as [14]. Let $\mathcal{X} = \{\mathbf{x}_i\}_{i=1}^N$ denote the training set, where $\mathcal{X}$ contains three disjoint sets, *i.e.*, an unlabeled set $\mathcal{X}_u$, a labeled normal $\mathcal{X}_n$, and an abnormal set $\mathcal{X}_a$, respectively. Assume $\mathcal{X}_u$ is a contaminated set with a majority of normal samples and a small portion of abnormal samples. With the combination of these three sets $\mathcal{X} = \mathcal{X}_u \cup \mathcal{X}_n \cup \mathcal{X}_a$ in training, we aim at learning discriminative representations that can distinguish the anomalies in the testing data.

## 3.2   Hierarchical Semi-Supervised Contrastive Learning

To detect anomalies with the contaminated training set, we propose a hierarchical semi-supervised contrastive learning approach that jointly learns sample-to-sample, sample-to-prototype, and normal-to-abnormal contrastive relations of instances, as shown in Fig. 2. We demonstrate the details as follows.

**Sample-to-Sample Module.** The goal of this module is to learn the sample-to-sample relations and enlarge the dissimilarity among different samples. With only a few labeled samples, it is easy to get overfitting and collapse in trivial solutions. The learned representations of samples should include rich semantic information that can distinguish anomalies in unseen samples. To achieve this goal, we employ the InfoNCE-like loss [8,42,59] as follows,

$$
\mathcal{L}_{\text{InfoNCE}}(\mathbf{x}, \mathcal{X}_+, \mathcal{X}_-)
$$
$$
= -\frac{1}{N} \log \frac{\sum_{\mathbf{x}' \in \mathcal{X}_+} \exp\left(\text{sim}(f_\Theta(\mathbf{x}), f_\Theta(\mathbf{x}'))/\tau\right)}{\sum_{\mathbf{x}' \in (\mathcal{X}_+ \cup \mathcal{X}_-)} \exp\left(\text{sim}(f_\Theta(\mathbf{x}), f_\Theta(\mathbf{x}'))/\tau\right)},
\tag{1}
$$

where $\mathcal{X}_+$ and $\mathcal{X}_-$ represent the set of positive and negative samples to $\mathbf{x}$, respectively; "sim" stands for a similarity measure, $e.g.$, cosine similarity; $\tau$ is the temperature parameter; and $f_\Theta(\cdot)$ is the sample representation from the embedding network. We use the above InfoNCE loss as the training loss for the sample-to-sample module, $i.e.$, $\mathcal{L}_{\text{S-S}} = \mathcal{L}_{\text{InfoNCE}}(\mathbf{x}, \mathcal{X}_+, \mathcal{X}_-)$. Following the typical framework of contrastive learning [8], various augmented copies from the same instance are treated as positive samples, and copies from different instances are negative samples, $i.e.$,

$$
\begin{aligned}
\mathcal{X}_+ &= \{\mathbf{x}' | \text{ID}(\mathbf{x}') = \text{ID}(\mathbf{x})\}, \\
\mathcal{X}_- &= \{\mathbf{x}' | \text{ID}(\mathbf{x}') \neq \text{ID}(\mathbf{x})\}.
\end{aligned}
\tag{2}
$$

Here, ID stands for the sample identity. In addition, following CSI [59], we adopt the shifting transformation (rotation) to generate more out-of-distribution samples that are treated as negative copies of the original samples.

**Sample-to-Prototype Module.** The sample-to-sample module enlarges the dissimilarity among samples and learns neutral representations. However, using the sample-to-sample module alone lacks the discrimination on anomalies. To this end, we propose a prototype learning scheme to learn discriminative representations with sample-to-prototype relations with the assistance of prototypes to represent normal samples. Unlike previous prototype-based approaches [14,37] that use either the reconstruction constraint or offline clustering and omit the relations among labeled samples, we directly model the contrastive relations between samples and the prototypes. As shown in Fig. 2, we aim at generating prototypes that are close to normal samples and away from abnormal samples. The prototypes are differentiable and can be optimized in an online manner. With prototypes, it is easier to generate the sample weight for distinguishing abnormal samples, which will be demonstrated in Eq. (5) and Eq. (7). Additionally, the learned prototypes are used as indicators in the inference stage to distinguish anomalies, as shown in Eq. (9). The details of the sample-to-prototype module is explained as follows.

Denote the prototypes of normal samples as $\mathbf{V} \in \mathbb{R}^{D \times K}$, where $D$ is the feature dimension, and $K$ is the number of prototypes. Since the sample representation is updated for each batch data, $\mathbf{V}$ is also learned simultaneously in batch with the designed sample-to-prototype loss $\mathcal{L}_{\text{S-P}}$ defined as follows,

$$\mathcal{L}_{\text{S-P}}(\mathcal{X}_n^{\tilde{B}} \cup \mathcal{X}_a^{\tilde{B}}) = \frac{1}{N_n}\|\mathbf{b}_n - \max_k(\mathbf{Z}_n^T \mathbf{V}_k)\|_2^2 + \frac{1}{N_a}\|[\max_k(\mathbf{Z}_a^T \mathbf{V}_k)]_+\|_2^2, \quad (3)$$

where $\tilde{B}$ represents the augmented batch data. The subscripts "$n$" and "$a$" represent normal and abnormal samples, respectively. $\mathbf{Z}_n = [\mathbf{z}_1, \mathbf{z}_2, ..., \mathbf{z}_{N_n}] \in \mathbb{R}^{D \times N_n}$ are the normal sample embeddings, $i.e.$, $\mathbf{z}_i = f_{\Theta}(\mathbf{x}_i)$; $\mathbf{b}_n = [1, 1, ..., 1]^T$ is an all-one vector to represent the targeted similarity between normal samples to the closest prototype; $N_n = |\mathcal{X}_n^{\tilde{B}}|$ and $N_a = |\mathcal{X}_a^{\tilde{B}}|$ are the number of normal samples and abnormal samples in the augmented batch data, respectively. The loss function contains two parts. The first part pushes normal samples to be close to the learned prototypes $\mathbf{V}$, where $\max(\cdot)$ takes the maximum similarity between each normal sample representation to the prototypes, constraining that normal samples should be close to at least one prototype. The second part is the constraint of the relationship between prototypes and abnormal samples, where $[\cdot]_+$ clamps negative values to zeros, thus pushing the prototypes to have non-positive cosine similarity scores to abnormal samples. However, the above loss does not consider the large contaminated unlabeled samples. Instead, we consider the modified version with the sample weighting as follows,

$$\mathcal{L}_{\text{S-P}}(\mathcal{X}_n^{\tilde{B}} \cup \mathcal{X}_u^{\tilde{B}} \cup \mathcal{X}_a^{\tilde{B}})$$
$$= \frac{1}{\|\mathbf{w}\|_1}\|\mathbf{w}^T \left(\mathbf{b}_{n \cup u} - \max_k \left(\mathbf{Z}_{n \cup u}^T \mathbf{V}_k\right)\right)\|_2^2 + \frac{1}{N_a}\|[\max_k(\mathbf{Z}_a^T \mathbf{V}_k)]_+\|_2^2, \quad (4)$$

where $\mathbf{Z}_{n \cup u}$ and $\mathbf{b}_{n \cup u}$ include both normal and unlabeled samples; and $\mathbf{w} \in \mathbb{R}^{N_{n \cup u}}$ is the sample weight defined as follows,

$$\mathbf{w}_i = \begin{cases} 1, & \text{if } \mathbf{x}_i \in \mathcal{X}_n; \\ \left(\max_k(\mathbf{z}_i^T \mathbf{V}_k) + 1\right)/2, & \text{if } \mathbf{x}_i \in \mathcal{X}_u. \end{cases} \quad (5)$$

We assume both $\mathbf{V}$ and $\mathbf{z}_i$ are already normalized. Therefore, $\mathbf{w}_i$ is in the range $[0, 1]$. If the representation of an unlabeled sample is closer to the learned prototypes, it is more likely to be a normal sample. Thus, the sample weight $\mathbf{w}_i$ is closer to 1. With the soft weighting strategy incorporated in the loss, the learned prototypes can better represent the normal samples.

**Normal-to-Abnormal Module.** As a complement to the previous two modules, the normal-to-abnormal module directly models the relation between normal and abnormal samples. Along with the assistance of the contamination-resistant sampling strategy, we aim at separating the abnormal representations from normal ones as much as possible. To better utilize the unlabeled set $\mathcal{X}_u$ and the anomalies $\mathcal{X}_a$, we further employ the normal-to-abnormal contrastive relations in the training. To incorporate unlabeled data, we use sampling strategy and propose the normal-to-abnormal contrastive loss as follows,

$$\mathcal{L}_{\text{N-A}} = \mathcal{L}_{\text{InfoNCE}}(\mathbf{x}_{\mathbf{x} \sim p_{\mathbf{w}}}, \{\mathbf{x}'\}_{\mathbf{x}' \sim p_{\mathbf{w}}}, \mathcal{X}_a), \tag{6}$$

**Table 1.** Experiment results of anomaly detection in Scenario-1 over CIFAR-10 with different labeled ratios $\gamma_l$. The best performance of each experiment is shown in bold.

| $\gamma_l$ | .00 | .01 | .05 | .10 |
|---|---|---|---|---|
| CSI [59] | **94.3** | – | – | – |
| SS-DGM [23] | – | 49.7 | 50.8 | 52.0 |
| SSAD [11] | 62.0 | 73.0 | 71.5 | 70.1 |
| DeepSAD [52] | 62.9 | 72.6 | 77.9 | 79.8 |
| Elsa [14] | – | 80.0 | 85.7 | 87.1 |
| Elsa+ [14] | – | 94.3 | 95.2 | 95.5 |
| **HSCL (Ours)** | – | **96.4** | **97.9** | **98.5** |

where we treat abnormal samples $\mathcal{X}_a$ as negatives and draw positive samples from the distribution $p_{\mathbf{w}}$ defined by the sample weight $\mathbf{w}$, i.e.,

$$p_{\mathbf{w}}(\mathbf{x}_i) = \frac{\mathbb{1}_{[\mathbf{w}_i > \mathbf{w}_\delta]} \mathbf{W}_i}{\sum_i \mathbb{1}_{[\mathbf{w}_i > \mathbf{w}_\delta]} \mathbf{W}_i}, \tag{7}$$

where the indicator function $\mathbb{1}_{[\mathbf{w}_i > \mathbf{w}_\delta]} = 1$ if and only if $\mathbf{w}_i$ is greater than a pre-defined threshold $\mathbf{w}_\delta$. This is to avoid sampling false positives as much as possible. Based on the definition of $\mathbf{w}$, normal samples are more likely to have larger weights than abnormal samples. Therefore, the normal instances have higher chances of being sampled.

### 3.3    Training and Inference

Combined with sample-to-sample, sample-to-prototype, and normal-to-abnormal hierarchical learning, the unified total loss is defined as follows,

$$\mathcal{L} = \mathcal{L}_{\text{S-S}} + \lambda_1 \mathcal{L}_{\text{S-P}} + \lambda_2 \mathcal{L}_{\text{N-A}}, \tag{8}$$

where $\lambda_1$ and $\lambda_2$ are the weights to balance the contributions of different losses.

In the inference stage, we define a normality score with the assistance of learned prototypes to distinguish anomalies as follows,

$$s(\tilde{\mathbf{x}}_i | \hat{\Theta}, \hat{\mathbf{V}}) = \max_k \left( f_{\hat{\Theta}}(\tilde{\mathbf{x}}_i)^T \hat{\mathbf{V}}_k \right), \tag{9}$$

where $\tilde{\mathbf{x}}_i$ represents a testing sample; $\hat{\Theta}$ and $\hat{\mathbf{V}}$ represent the learned encoder parameters and prototypes, respectively. The normality score is measured as the maximum similarity between the testing sample and the learned prototypes.

## 4    Experiments

To verify the effectiveness of our proposed HSCL, we consider three anomaly detection scenarios on several commonly used public datasets and compared HSCL with recent anomaly detection methods. Our HSCL significantly outperforms the general semi-supervised and noisy label approaches on the anomaly detection task with both quantitative and visualization results. Moreover, we also show the importance of each component of HSCL in the ablation study.

**Table 2.** Experiment results of anomaly detection in Scenario-2 over CIFAR-10 with different pollution ratios $\gamma_p$. The best performance of each experiment is shown in bold.Experiment results of anomaly detection in Scenario-2 over CIFAR-10 with different pollution ratios $\gamma_p$. The best performance of each experiment is shown in bold.

| Self-supervised/Unsupervised | | | | Supervised/Semi-supervised | | | |
|---|---|---|---|---|---|---|---|
| $\gamma_p$ | .00 | .05 | .10 | $\gamma_p$ | .00 | .05 | .10 |
| OC-SVM [54] | 62.0 | 61.4 | 60.8 | SSAD [11] | 73.8 | 71.5 | 69.8 |
| IF [31] | 60.0 | 59.6 | 58.8 | SS-DGM [23] | 50.8 | 50.1 | 50.5 |
| KDE [51] | 59.9 | 58.1 | 57.3 | DeepSAD [52] | 77.9 | 74.0 | 71.8 |
| DeepSVDD [51] | 60.9 | 59.6 | 58.6 | Elsa [14] | 85.7 | 83.5 | 81.6 |
| $E^3$Outlier [66] | 86.6 | 83.5 | 81.7 | Elsa+ [14] | 95.2 | 93.0 | 91.1 |
| GOAD [3] | 88.2 | 85.2 | 83.0 | **HSCL (Ours)** | **97.9** | **97.6** | **97.3** |
| CSI [59] | 94.3 | 88.2 | 84.5 | | | | |

### 4.1    Scenario Setup

In the experiments, we consider three representative scenarios following the prior work [1,14,33,52] with CIFAR-10 [26], CIFAR-100 [26], ImageNet (FIX) [17], SVHN [40], and LSUN (FIX) [30] public datasets. Note that we use the fixed version of ImageNet and LSUN following the same process as mentioned in [14,59]. The details of each scenario are described as follows.

*(Scenario-1) Semi-supervised One-Class Classification* [1,14,52]. We assume we can access a small subset of labeled normal samples $\mathcal{X}_n$ and abnormal samples $\mathcal{X}_a$ during training. We treat one class as the normal set while the remaining classes as anomalies. Both $\mathcal{X}_n$ and $\mathcal{X}_a$ are randomly sampled. Denote the labeled ratio of $\mathcal{X}_n$ and $\mathcal{X}_a$ both as $\gamma_l$. We report the results on the testing set over 90 experiments (10 normal × 9 abnormal) for a given $\gamma_l$.

*(Scenario-2) Contaminated One-Class Classification* [14,52]. In this setting, in addition to a small labeled subset of normal and abnormal samples, we assume the normal training set is contaminated with anomalies with a pollution ratio $\gamma_p$. This is done by sampling images from every anomalous class and

adding them into the unlabeled set $\mathcal{X}_u$. We report results with each pollution ratio $\gamma_p \in \{0.00, 0.05, 0.10\}$. $\gamma_l$ is fixed to 0.05 for all experiments.

*(Scenario-3) Cross-Dataset Anomaly Detection* [14,33]. In this setting, we use all images in CIFAR-10 as normal samples and the down-sampled ImageNet dataset as labeled anomalies. We test the detection performance on the other four datasets, *i.e.*, CIFAR-100, SVHN, LSUN, and ImageNet, as anomalies over the normal samples from the CIFAR-10 testing set. This setting tests the capability of the proposed method that leverages a large-scaled external dataset as an abnormal auxiliary set.

**Table 3.** Experiment results of anomaly detection in Scenario-2 compared with general semi-supervised learning and noisy label approaches over CIFAR-10 (C-10), CIFAR-100 (C-100), and LSUN. The best performance of each experiment is shown in bold.

| Method | C-10 | | C-100 | | LSUN | |
|---|---|---|---|---|---|---|
| | .05 | .10 | .05 | .10 | .05 | .10 |
| CSI [59] | 88.2 | 84.5 | 82.4 | 80.4 | 73.5 | 71.3 |
| DivideMix [28] | 83.9 | 83.2 | 66.8 | 66.3 | 67.8 | 66.9 |
| Aug-LNL [41] | 84.1 | 83.6 | 66.6 | 67.1 | 68.0 | 64.9 |
| FixMatch [55] | 93.5 | 94.3 | 71.8 | 78.5 | 76.0 | 73.2 |
| **HSCL (Ours)** | **97.6** | **97.3** | **93.0** | **92.2** | **88.6** | **88.9** |

*Evaluation Metrics.* Following [14,59], we use the area under the receiver operating characteristics (AUROC) score as the evaluation metric. The ROC represents the true positive rate against the false-positive rate, while AUROC is the area under the curve. It is a common statistic for the goodness of a predictor in a binary classification task. The higher the score, the better the performance.

## 4.2    Implementation Details

*Training Details.* Following [14,59], we use ResNet-18 [16] as the base encoder network and project images to representations with 128 dimensions. The temperature $\tau$ is set to 0.5 in the InfoNCE loss. $\lambda_1$ and $\lambda_2$ are set to 1. The number of prototypes $K$ is set to 1 for simplicity, and a more thorough analysis of the selection of $K$ is made in the ablation study. The batch size is set to 256. For the optimization, we train the proposed method with 250 epochs under Adam [22] optimizer with an initial learning rate 1e−3. For the learning rate scheduler, we use the linear warmup [12] for the early 10 epochs, followed by the cosine decay schedule [35]. The model is learned from scratch without any large-dataset pre training. We use one Nvidia RTX 3090 GPU for training.

*Augmentation Details.* We use augmentations as the same with SimCLR [8], including Inception crop [58], horizontal flip, color jitter, and gray-scale transform. We also adopt rotation with $\{90°, 180°, 270°\}$ as shifting instances as defined in CSI [59].

## 4.3  Performance Comparison

***Results on Scenario-1.*** We report the AUROC score for scenario-1 in Table 1. Several SOTA methods are adopted for comparison, including CSI [59], SS-DGM [23], SSAD [11], DeepSAD [52], and Elsa [14]. Here, CSI presents a novel detection method based on contrastive learning with shifting instances; SS-DGM proposes a semi-supervised generative model that allows for effective generalization from small labeled datasets to large unlabeled ones; SSAD makes a detailed analysis of supervised anomaly detection with active learning strategy; DeepSAD presents a deep end-to-end methodology for general semi-supervised anomaly detection method; and Elsa is a novel semi-supervised anomaly detection approach that unifies the concept of energy-based models with contrastive learning. Except for CSI that belongs to self-supervised anomaly detection, the proposed HSCL achieves the best performance among all the compared semi-supervised methods, with more than 2% improvement over the second-best method, Elsa+.

**Table 4.** Experiment results of anomaly detection in Scenario-3, where we use CIFAR-10 as in-distribution samples and other datasets as out-of-distribution samples. The best performance of each experiment is shown in bold type.

| Dataset | GOAD | CSI | ELSA+ | **HSCL** |
|---------|------|-----|-------|----------|
| ImageNet | 83.3 | 93.3 | 96.4 | **99.8** |
| LSUN | 78.8 | 90.3 | 95.0 | **95.8** |
| C-100 | 77.2 | **89.2** | 86.3 | 88.4 |
| SVHN | 96.3 | 99.8 | 99.4 | **99.8** |

***Results on Scenario-2.*** Different from Scenario-1 that we have clean labels for anomalies, we have a large unlabeled set contaminated with anomaly samples. In this scenario, we keep the labeled ratio fixed with $\gamma_l = 0.05$ and conduct experiments with the contamination ratio $\gamma_p \in \{0.00, 0.05, 0.10\}$. The results are reported in Table 2. Except for CSI, SS-DGM, SSAD, DeepSAD, and Elsa used in Scenario-1, we also compare with OC-SVM [54], IF [31], KDE [51], DeepSVDD [51], $E^3$Outlier [66], and GOAD [3] methods. Specifically, OC-SVM is a method that estimates a function to distinguish from different distributions; IF is a fundamentally different model-based method that explicitly isolates anomalies instead of profiles normal points; DeepSVDD introduces a new anomaly detection method for one-class classification based on deep support vector data description, which is trained on an anomaly detection based objective; $E^3$Outlier first-time leverages a discriminative deep neural network for representation learning by using surrogate supervision to create multiple pseudo-classes from original data; and GOAD presents a unifying view and proposes an open-set method to relax generalization assumptions. From Table 2, we can see our HSCL achieves the best performance, demonstrating the effectiveness of HSCL in semi-supervised settings. With the increase of $\gamma_p$, the performance degrades largely for most of the compared methods, while HSCL still roughly keeps the similar performance as the situation without contaminated samples. Compared with Elsa+, there is 2.7%, 4.6%, and 6.2% significant improvement with $\gamma_p \in \{0.00, 0.05, 0.10\}$, respectively. This demonstrates the capability of contamination resistance of HSCL when dealing with a large number of unlabeled samples.

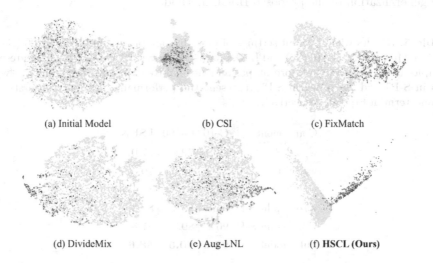

(a) Initial Model          (b) CSI          (c) FixMatch

(d) DivideMix          (e) Aug-LNL          (f) **HSCL (Ours)**

**Fig. 3.** Visualization of learned representation for anomaly detection on CIFAR-10 using t-SNE. From (a) to (f): initial model, CSI, FixMatch, DivideMix, Aug-LNL, and HSCL. Normal samples (from class 0) are in pink color, while abnormal samples (from other classes) are in other colors. (Color figure online)

***Comparison with General Semi-supervised and Noisy Label Approaches.*** The contaminated scenario can be treated as a special case of the general semi-supervised learning setting. The main difference between contaminated anomaly detection and general semi-supervised learning is that the normal sample is dominant in the unlabeled set in anomaly detection, which is an imbalanced data problem. We compare one of the SOTA methods, FixMatch [55], under the anomaly detection setting and report the results on CIFAR-10, CIFAR-100, and LSUN datasets in Table 3. Our proposed HSCL outperforms FixMatch with a large margin, validating the effectiveness of our method for anomaly detection. Note that FixMatch achieves higher performance with $\gamma_p = .10$ than $\gamma_p = .05$ on CIFAR-10 and CIFAR-100. This is reasonable since using $\gamma_p = .05$ suffers from a more severe imbalanced problem, resulting in a larger degeneration on the performance. In addition, the contaminated setting can also be treated as a special case of noisy-label classification. We assume all samples from the contaminated set are from the normal class with some noisy labels. We also compare our proposed HSCL with two recent SOTA methods dealing with noisy label classification, *i.e.*, DivideMix [28] and Aug-LNL [41]. As shown in Table 3, HSCL also outperforms both the methods on CIFAR-10, CIFAR-100, and LSUN datasets.

***Results on Scenario-3.*** The cross-dataset validation is shown in Table 4, where we treat CIFAR-10 as the normal set, while four other datasets, *i.e.*, ImageNet, LSUN, CIFAR-100, and SVHN, as the abnormal set. HSCL outperforms other methods like GOAD, CSI, and Elsa+ in most of the cases. This further verifies the generalization of the proposed HSCL method.

**Table 5.** Results with different settings of module components on C-10, C-100 (short for CIFAR-10 and CIFAR-100) and LSUN datasets. "S-S", "S-P" and "N-A" represent sample-to-sample, sample-to-prototype, and normal-to-abnormal, respectively. "w/o pos in S-P" and "w/o neg in S-P" represent the performance without the first and second term in Eq. (4), respectively.

| Component | C-10 | C-100 | LSUN |
|---|---|---|---|
| w/o S-S | 89.8 | 72.9 | 67.0 |
| w/o S-P | 82.9 | 85.5 | 70.3 |
| w/o N-A | 94.1 | 85.3 | 87.1 |
| w/o pos in S-P | 96.5 | 88.4 | 87.3 |
| w/o neg in S-P | 96.1 | 89.4 | 87.8 |
| Full model | **97.1** | **90.5** | **88.6** |

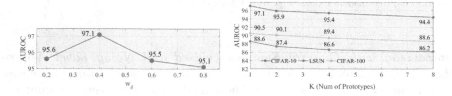

**Fig. 4.** Left: AUROC with variant sampling threshold $\mathbf{w}_\delta$ on CIFAR-10. Right: AUROC with variant number of prototypes on CIFAR-10, CIFAR-100 and LSUN datasets.

***Visualizations.*** To verify the effectiveness of the proposed hierarchical contrastive learning strategy, We draw the sample representations on CIFAR-10 with t-SNE as the dimension reduction method and compare with the initial model, CSI, FixMatch, DivideMix, and Aug-LNL, as shown in Fig. 3. All the models are trained using mixed contaminated data with $\gamma_l = 0.05$ and $\gamma_p = 0.05$.

In this example, the *plane* class is treated as the normal class while samples from other classes are regarded as anomalies. In each sub-figure, we use light pink color to represent the normal class while other colors represent abnormal classes. As shown in the figure, the anomalies can be better distinguished using HSCL compared with other methods.

### 4.4 Ablation Study

***Importance of Different Modules.*** To validate the effect of individual modules, we conduct experiments with the removal of each module. For simplicity, we use "S-S", "S-P", and "N-A" to represent sample-to-sample, sample-to-prototype, and normal-to-abnormal modules, respectively. Note that we use k-NN to distinguish anomalies as the same as [59] when removing the sample-to-prototype module since prototypes are not available at this configuration. We further verify the importance of individual terms of the prototype learning in Eq. (4). We report the results on CIFAR-10, CIFAR-100, and LSUN datasets, as shown in Table 5. As expected, the full model generates the best performance. The drop of "w/o S-P" is due to two facts: 1) prototypes are replaced with k-NN in the normality score and 2) the soft-weighting strategy has to be discarded since prototypes are unavailable. The above changes make the method sensitive to unlabeled abnormal samples, causing the degradation. Prototype learning remains even though we discard only one term in Eq. (4). That is why the degradation of "w/o pos in S-P" and "w/o neg in S-P" is not significant.

***Varying Sampling Threshold.*** To optimize the normal-to-abnormal contrastive learning loss, we sample the data from the unlabeled set according to the sampling strategy with a pre-defined weight threshold $\mathbf{w}_\delta$ in Eq. (7). To learn the effect and sensitivity of the threshold, we vary $\mathbf{w}_\delta$ from 0.2 to 0.8 and report the AUROC of *plane* class on CIFAR-10 dataset in the left of Fig. 4. From the result, when $\mathbf{w}_\delta = 0.4$, we achieve the best performance with AUROC = 97.1%. With different choices of thresholds, the result does not change much, showing the robustness of the sampling strategy.

***Analysis of Prototypes.*** We vary the prototype number $K$ from 1 to 8 on CIFAR-10, CIFAR-100, and LSUN datasets. The results of AUROC are shown in the right of Fig. 4. We achieve the best performance with $K = 1$. With the increase of $K$, the performance slightly degrades. This phenomenon is reasonable for the contamination setting. Since the learned prototypes need to represent normal samples (not abnormal samples), using one prototype to represent the normal class is good enough. However, when we increase the number of prototypes, some prototypes may become closer to unlabeled abnormal samples in the training set, resulting in slightly poorer performance for anomaly detection.

## 5   Conclusion

In this paper, we tackle anomaly detection in a semi-supervised setting with contaminated samples. We learn the discriminative sample representations based on hierarchical contrastive relations among samples, prototypes, and classes in an end-to-end manner. The proposed method, HSCL, achieves the SOTA performance in several different scenarios and outperforms recent general semi-supervised learning and noisy-label approaches. Furthermore, the ablation study, including the analysis of components of individual modules, the sampling strategy with soft weighting, and the number of prototypes, also demonstrates the effectiveness and robustness of the proposed method. In our future work, we plan to conduct anomaly detection with contaminated data in unsupervised settings.

**Acknowledgements.** This work is supported by National Natural Science Foundation of China (62106219, U20B2066, 61976186), the Fundamental Research Funds for the Central Universities (226-2022-00087), NUS Advanced Research and Technology Innovation Centre (Project Reference: ECT-RP2), and NUS Faculty Research Committee Grant (WBS: A-0009440-00-00).

# References

1. Akcay, S., Atapour-Abarghouei, A., Breckon, T.P.: GANomaly: semi-supervised anomaly detection via adversarial training. In: Jawahar, C.V., Li, H., Mori, G., Schindler, K. (eds.) ACCV 2018. LNCS, vol. 11363, pp. 622–637. Springer, Cham (2019). https://doi.org/10.1007/978-3-030-20893-6_39
2. Benaim, S., et al.: SpeedNet: learning the speediness in videos. In: Proceedings of the IEEE Conference on Computer Vision and Pattern Recognition, pp. 9922–9931 (2020)
3. Bergman, L., Hoshen, Y.: Classification-based anomaly detection for general data. arXiv preprint arXiv:2005.02359 (2020)
4. Berthelot, D., Carlini, N., Goodfellow, I., Papernot, N., Oliver, A., Raffel, C.: Mixmatch: a holistic approach to semi-supervised learning. arXiv preprint arXiv:1905.02249 (2019)
5. Caron, M., Misra, I., Mairal, J., Goyal, P., Bojanowski, P., Joulin, A.: Unsupervised learning of visual features by contrasting cluster assignments. arXiv preprint arXiv:2006.09882 (2020)
6. Chen, H., Liu, F., Wang, Y., Zhao, L., Wu, H.: A variational approach for learning from positive and unlabeled data. In: Advances in Neural Information Processing Systems, vol. 33, pp. 14844–14854 (2020)
7. Chen, P., et al.: RspNet: relative speed perception for unsupervised video representation learning. In: Proceedings of the AAAI Conference on Artificial Intelligence, vol. 35, pp. 1045–1053 (2021)
8. Chen, T., Kornblith, S., Norouzi, M., Hinton, G.: A simple framework for contrastive learning of visual representations. In: International conference on machine learning, pp. 1597–1607. PMLR (2020)
9. Chen, Y., Tian, Y., Pang, G., Carneiro, G.: Unsupervised anomaly detection with multi-scale interpolated gaussian descriptors. arXiv preprint arXiv:2101.10043 (2021)
10. Gong, D., et al.: Memorizing normality to detect anomaly: memory-augmented deep autoencoder for unsupervised anomaly detection. In: Proceedings of the IEEE/CVF International Conference on Computer Vision, pp. 1705–1714 (2019)
11. Görnitz, N., Kloft, M., Rieck, K., Brefeld, U.: Toward supervised anomaly detection. J. Artif. Intell. Res. **46**, 235–262 (2013)

12. Goyal, P., et al.: Accurate, large minibatch SGD: training ImageNet in 1 hour. arXiv preprint arXiv:1706.02677 (2017)
13. Grill, J.B., et al.: Bootstrap your own latent: a new approach to self-supervised learning. arXiv preprint arXiv:2006.07733 (2020)
14. Han, S., Song, H., Lee, S., Park, S., Cha, M.: Elsa: Energy-based learning for semi-supervised anomaly detection. arXiv preprint arXiv:2103.15296 (2021)
15. He, K., Fan, H., Wu, Y., Xie, S., Girshick, R.: Momentum contrast for unsupervised visual representation learning. In: Proceedings of the IEEE/CVF Conference on Computer Vision and Pattern Recognition, pp. 9729–9738 (2020)
16. He, K., Zhang, X., Ren, S., Sun, J.: Deep residual learning for image recognition. In: Proceedings of the IEEE Conference on Computer Vision and Pattern Recognition, pp. 770–778 (2016)
17. Hendrycks, D., Mazeika, M., Kadavath, S., Song, D.: Using self-supervised learning can improve model robustness and uncertainty. arXiv preprint arXiv:1906.12340 (2019)
18. Kim, B., Choo, J., Kwon, Y.D., Joe, S., Min, S., Gwon, Y.: SelfMatch: combining contrastive self-supervision and consistency for semi-supervised learning. arXiv preprint arXiv:2101.06480 (2021)
19. Kim, D., Cho, D., Yoo, D., Kweon, I.S.: Learning image representations by completing damaged jigsaw puzzles. In: 2018 IEEE Winter Conference on Applications of Computer Vision, pp. 793–802. IEEE (2018)
20. Kim, J., Grauman, K.: Observe locally, infer globally: a space-time MRF for detecting abnormal activities with incremental updates. In: 2009 IEEE Conference on Computer Vision and Pattern Recognition, pp. 2921–2928. IEEE (2009)
21. Kim, J., Jeong, K., Choi, H., Seo, K.: GAN-based anomaly detection in imbalance problems. In: Bartoli, A., Fusiello, A. (eds.) ECCV 2020. LNCS, vol. 12540, pp. 128–145. Springer, Cham (2020). https://doi.org/10.1007/978-3-030-65414-6_11
22. Kingma, D.P., Ba, J.: Adam: a method for stochastic optimization. arXiv preprint arXiv:1412.6980 (2014)
23. Kingma, D.P., Mohamed, S., Rezende, D.J., Welling, M.: Semi-supervised learning with deep generative models. In: Advances in Neural Information Processing Systems, pp. 3581–3589 (2014)
24. Kolesnikov, A., et al.: Big transfer (BiT): general visual representation learning. In: Vedaldi, A., Bischof, H., Brox, T., Frahm, J.-M. (eds.) ECCV 2020. LNCS, vol. 12350, pp. 491–507. Springer, Cham (2020). https://doi.org/10.1007/978-3-030-58558-7_29
25. Kolesnikov, A., Zhai, X., Beyer, L.: Revisiting self-supervised visual representation learning. In: Proceedings of the IEEE/CVF Conference on Computer Vision and Pattern Recognition, pp. 1920–1929 (2019)
26. Krizhevsky, A., Hinton, G., et al.: Learning multiple layers of features from tiny images (2009)
27. Li, C.L., Sohn, K., Yoon, J., Pfister, T.: CutPaste: self-supervised learning for anomaly detection and localization. In: Proceedings of the IEEE/CVF Conference on Computer Vision and Pattern Recognition, pp. 9664–9674 (2021)
28. Li, J., Socher, R., Hoi, S.C.: DivideMix: learning with noisy labels as semi-supervised learning. In: International Conference on Learning Representations (2019)
29. Li, Y., Hu, P., Liu, Z., Peng, D., Zhou, J.T., Peng, X.: Contrastive clustering. In: 2021 AAAI Conference on Artificial Intelligence (AAAI) (2021)
30. Liang, S., Li, Y., Srikant, R.: Enhancing the reliability of out-of-distribution image detection in neural networks. arXiv preprint arXiv:1706.02690 (2017)

31. Liu, F.T., Ting, K.M., Zhou, Z.H.: Isolation forest. In: 2008 eighth IEEE International Conference on Data Mining, pp. 413–422. IEEE (2008)
32. Liu, S., Niles-Weed, J., Razavian, N., Fernandez-Granda, C.: Early-learning regularization prevents memorization of noisy labels. In: Advances in Neural Information Processing Systems 33 (2020)
33. Liu, W., Wang, X., Owens, J.D., Li, Y.: Energy-based out-of-distribution detection. arXiv preprint arXiv:2010.03759 (2020)
34. Liu, W., Luo, W., Lian, D., Gao, S.: Future frame prediction for anomaly detection-a new baseline. In: Proceedings of the IEEE Conference on Computer Vision and Pattern Recognition, pp. 6536–6545 (2018)
35. Loshchilov, I., Hutter, F.: SGDR: stochastic gradient descent with warm restarts. arXiv preprint arXiv:1608.03983 (2016)
36. Lu, C., Shi, J., Jia, J.: Abnormal event detection at 150 FPS in MATLAB. In: Proceedings of the IEEE International Conference on Computer Vision, pp. 2720–2727 (2013)
37. Lv, H., et al.: Learning normal dynamics in videos with meta prototype network. In: Proceedings of the IEEE/CVF Conference on Computer Vision and Pattern Recognition, pp. 15425–15434 (2021)
38. Ma, R., Pang, G., Chen, L., van den Hengel, A.: Deep graph-level anomaly detection by glocal knowledge distillation. In: Proceedings of the Fifteenth ACM International Conference on Web Search and Data Mining, pp. 704–714 (2022)
39. Misra, I., van der Maaten, L.: Self-supervised learning of pretext-invariant representations. In: Proceedings of the IEEE Conference on Computer Vision and Pattern Recognition, pp. 6707–6717 (2020)
40. Netzer, Y., Wang, T., Coates, A., Bissacco, A., Wu, B., Ng, A.Y.: Reading digits in natural images with unsupervised feature learning (2011)
41. Nishi, K., Ding, Y., Rich, A., Hollerer, T.: Augmentation strategies for learning with noisy labels. In: Proceedings of the IEEE/CVF Conference on Computer Vision and Pattern Recognition, pp. 8022–8031 (2021)
42. van den Oord, A., Li, Y., Vinyals, O.: Representation learning with contrastive predictive coding. arXiv preprint arXiv:1807.03748 (2018)
43. Pang, G., Ding, C., Shen, C., van den Hengel, A.: Explainable deep few-shot anomaly detection with deviation networks. arXiv preprint arXiv:2108.00462 (2021)
44. Pang, G., van den Hengel, A., Shen, C., Cao, L.: Toward deep supervised anomaly detection: reinforcement learning from partially labeled anomaly data. In: Proceedings of the 27th ACM SIGKDD Conference on Knowledge Discovery & Data Mining, pp. 1298–1308 (2021)
45. Pang, G., Shen, C., Cao, L., Hengel, A.V.D.: Deep learning for anomaly detection: a review. ACM Comput. Surv. (CSUR) 54(2), 1–38 (2021)
46. Pathak, D., Krahenbuhl, P., Donahue, J., Darrell, T., Efros, A.A.: Context encoders: feature learning by inpainting. In: Proceedings of the IEEE Conference on Computer Vision and Pattern Recognition, pp. 2536–2544 (2016)
47. Qiu, C., Li, A., Kloft, M., Rudolph, M., Mandt, S.: Latent outlier exposure for anomaly detection with contaminated data. arXiv preprint arXiv:2202.08088 (2022)
48. Reiss, T., Hoshen, Y.: Mean-shifted contrastive loss for anomaly detection. arXiv preprint arXiv:2106.03844 (2021)
49. Ren, S., Zhou, D., He, S., Feng, J., Wang, X.: Shunted self-attention via multi-scale token aggregation. In: Proceedings of the IEEE/CVF Conference on Computer Vision and Pattern Recognition (2022)

50. Ronneberger, O., Fischer, P., Brox, T.: U-Net: convolutional networks for biomedical image segmentation. In: Navab, N., Hornegger, J., Wells, W.M., Frangi, A.F. (eds.) MICCAI 2015. LNCS, vol. 9351, pp. 234–241. Springer, Cham (2015). https://doi.org/10.1007/978-3-319-24574-4_28
51. Ruff, L., et al.: Deep one-class classification. In: International Conference on Machine Learning, pp. 4393–4402. PMLR (2018)
52. Ruff, L., et al.: Deep semi-supervised anomaly detection. arXiv preprint arXiv:1906.02694 (2019)
53. Salehi, M., et al.: ARAE: adversarially robust training of autoencoders improves novelty detection. arXiv preprint arXiv:2003.05669 (2020)
54. Schölkopf, B., Platt, J.C., Shawe-Taylor, J., Smola, A.J., Williamson, R.C.: Estimating the support of a high-dimensional distribution. Neural Comput. **13**(7), 1443–1471 (2001)
55. Sohn, K., et al.: FixMatch: simplifying semi-supervised learning with consistency and confidence. In: Advances in Neural Information Processing Systems vol. 33, pp. 596–608 (2020)
56. Sohn, K., Li, C.L., Yoon, J., Jin, M., Pfister, T.: Learning and evaluating representations for deep one-class classification. arXiv preprint arXiv:2011.02578 (2020)
57. Somepalli, G., Wu, Y., Balaji, Y., Vinzamuri, B., Feizi, S.: Unsupervised anomaly detection with adversarial mirrored autoencoders. arXiv preprint arXiv:2003.10713 (2020)
58. Szegedy, C., et al.: Going deeper with convolutions. In: Proceedings of the IEEE Conference on Computer Vision and Pattern Recognition, pp. 1–9 (2015)
59. Tack, J., Mo, S., Jeong, J., Shin, J.: CSI: novelty detection via contrastive learning on distributionally shifted instances. In: Advances in Neural Information Processing Systems, vol. 33, pp. 11839–11852 (2020)
60. Tian, Y., Krishnan, D., Isola, P.: Contrastive multiview coding. In: Vedaldi, A., Bischof, H., Brox, T., Frahm, J.-M. (eds.) ECCV 2020. LNCS, vol. 12356, pp. 776–794. Springer, Cham (2020). https://doi.org/10.1007/978-3-030-58621-8_45
61. Wang, G., Gu, R., Liu, Z., Hu, W., Song, M., Hwang, J.N.: Track without appearance: learn box and tracklet embedding with local and global motion patterns for vehicle tracking. In: Proceedings of the IEEE/CVF International Conference on Computer Vision, pp. 9876–9886 (2021)
62. Wang, G., Song, M., Hwang, J.N.: Recent advances in embedding methods for multi-object tracking: a survey. arXiv preprint arXiv:2205.10766 (2022)
63. Wang, G., Wang, Y., Gu, R., Hu, W., Hwang, J.N.: Split and connect: a universal tracklet booster for multi-object tracking. IEEE Trans. Multimedia (2022)
64. Wang, G., Yuan, X., Zheng, A., Hsu, H.M., Hwang, J.N.: Anomaly candidate identification and starting time estimation of vehicles from traffic videos. In: CVPR Workshops, pp. 382–390 (2019)
65. Wang, G., Lu, K., Zhou, Y., He, Z., Wang, G.: Human-centered prior-guided and task-dependent multi-task representation learning for action recognition pre-training. arXiv preprint arXiv:2204.12729 (2022)
66. Wang, S., et al.: Effective end-to-end unsupervised outlier detection via inlier priority of discriminative network (2019)
67. Wang, X., Kihara, D., Luo, J., Qi, G.J.: EnAET: a self-trained framework for semi-supervised and supervised learning with ensemble transformations. IEEE Trans. Image Process. **30**, 1639–1647 (2020)
68. Wang, X., Zhang, R., Shen, C., Kong, T., Li, L.: Dense contrastive learning for self-supervised visual pre-training. In: Proceedings of the IEEE/CVF Conference on Computer Vision and Pattern Recognition, pp. 3024–3033 (2021)

69. Xu, D., Xiao, J., Zhao, Z., Shao, J., Xie, D., Zhuang, Y.: Self-supervised spatiotemporal learning via video clip order prediction. In: Proceedings of the IEEE Conference on Computer Vision and Pattern Recognition, pp. 10334–10343 (2019)
70. Xu, Y., Zhang, Q., Zhang, J., Tao, D.: ViTAE: vision transformer advanced by exploring intrinsic inductive bias. In: Advances in Neural Information Processing Systems 34 (2021)
71. Yang, Y., Qiu, J., Song, M., Tao, D., Wang, X.: Distilling knowledge from graph convolutional networks. In: Proceedings of the IEEE/CVF Conference on Computer Vision and Pattern Recognition (2020)
72. Yi, K., Wu, J.: Probabilistic end-to-end noise correction for learning with noisy labels. In: Proceedings of the IEEE/CVF Conference on Computer Vision and Pattern Recognition, pp. 7017–7025 (2019)
73. Yu, W., et al.: MetaFormer is actually what you need for vision. In: Proceedings of the IEEE/CVF Conference on Computer Vision and Pattern Recognition (2022)
74. Yuan, X., et al.: Multimodal contrastive training for visual representation learning. In: Proceedings of the IEEE/CVF Conference on Computer Vision and Pattern Recognition, pp. 6995–7004 (2021)
75. Yuan, X., Li, Z., Wang, G.: Activematch: end-to-end semi-supervised active representation learning. arXiv preprint arXiv:2110.02521 (2021)
76. Zaheer, M.Z., Mahmood, A., Khan, M.H., Segu, M., Yu, F., Lee, S.I.: Generative cooperative learning for unsupervised video anomaly detection. In: Proceedings of the IEEE/CVF Conference on Computer Vision and Pattern Recognition, pp. 14744–14754 (2022)
77. Zaheer, M.Z., Mahmood, A., Astrid, M., Lee, S.-I.: CLAWS: clustering assisted weakly supervised learning with normalcy suppression for anomalous event detection. In: Vedaldi, A., Bischof, H., Brox, T., Frahm, J.-M. (eds.) ECCV 2020. LNCS, vol. 12367, pp. 358–376. Springer, Cham (2020). https://doi.org/10.1007/978-3-030-58542-6_22
78. Zenati, H., Romain, M., Foo, C.S., Lecouat, B., Chandrasekhar, V.: Adversarially learned anomaly detection. In: 2018 IEEE International conference on data mining (ICDM), pp. 727–736. IEEE (2018)
79. Zhan, Y., Yu, J., Yu, T., Tao, D.: On exploring undetermined relationships for visual relationship detection. In: Proceedings of the IEEE/CVF Conference on Computer Vision and Pattern Recognition, pp. 5128–5137 (2019)
80. Zhan, Y., Yu, J., Yu, T., Tao, D.: Multi-task compositional network for visual relationship detection. Int. J. Comput. Vis. **128**(8), 2146–2165 (2020)
81. Zhan, Y., Yu, J., Yu, Z., Zhang, R., Tao, D., Tian, Q.: Comprehensive distance-preserving autoencoders for cross-modal retrieval. In: Proceedings of the 26th ACM International Conference on Multimedia, pp. 1137–1145 (2018)
82. Zhang, Q., Xu, Y., Zhang, J., Tao, D.: VSA: learning varied-size window attention in vision transformers. arXiv preprint arXiv:2204.08446 (2022)
83. Zhao, Y., Deng, B., Shen, C., Liu, Y., Lu, H., Hua, X.S.: Spatio-temporal autoencoder for video anomaly detection. In: Proceedings of the 25th ACM International Conference on Multimedia, pp. 1933–1941 (2017)
84. Zhong, H., et al.: Graph contrastive clustering. arXiv preprint arXiv:2104.01429 (2021)
85. Zhou, C., Paffenroth, R.C.: Anomaly detection with robust deep autoencoders. In: Proceedings of the 23rd ACM SIGKDD International Conference on Knowledge Discovery and Data Mining, pp. 665–674 (2017)

# Tracking by Associating Clips

Sanghyun Woo[1], Kwanyong Park[1], Seoung Wug Oh[2], In So Kweon[1],
and Joon-Young Lee[2(✉)]

[1] KAIST, Daejeon, South Korea
[2] Adobe Research, San Jose, USA
jolee@adobe.com

**Abstract.** The tracking-by-detection paradigm today has become the dominant method for multi-object tracking and works by detecting objects in each frame and then performing data association across frames. However, its sequential *frame-wise matching* property fundamentally suffers from the intermediate interruptions in a video, such as object occlusions, fast camera movements, and abrupt light changes. Moreover, it typically overlooks temporal information beyond the two frames for matching. In this paper, we investigate an alternative by treating object association as **clip-wise matching**. Our new perspective views a single long video sequence as multiple short clips, and then the tracking is performed both within and between the clips. The benefits of this new approach are two folds. First, our method is robust to tracking error accumulation or propagation, as the video chunking allows bypassing the interrupted frames, and the short clip tracking avoids the conventional error-prone long-term track memory management. Second, the multiple frame information is aggregated during the clip-wise matching, resulting in a more accurate long-range track association than the current frame-wise matching. Given the state-of-the-art tracking-by-detection tracker, QDTrack, we showcase how the tracking performance improves with our new tracking formulation. We evaluate our proposals on two tracking benchmarks, TAO and MOT17 that have complementary characteristics and challenges each other.

**Keywords:** Clip-based tracking · Long-term video modeling

## 1 Introduction

Discriminating the identity of multiple objects in a scene and providing individual trajectories of their movements over time, namely multi-object tracking, is one of the fundamental computer vision problems, imperative to tackle many real-world problems, *e.g.* autonomous driving and surveillance. Despite being a rather classical vision task, it is still challenging to design a robust multi-object tracker capable of tracking a time-varying number of objects moving through unconstrained environments in the presence of many other complexities.

Early studies approached the multi-object tracking problem by breaking it into multiple sub-problems that could be tackled individually, typically starting

© The Author(s), under exclusive license to Springer Nature Switzerland AG 2022
S. Avidan et al. (Eds.): ECCV 2022, LNCS 13685, pp. 129–145, 2022.
https://doi.org/10.1007/978-3-031-19806-9_8

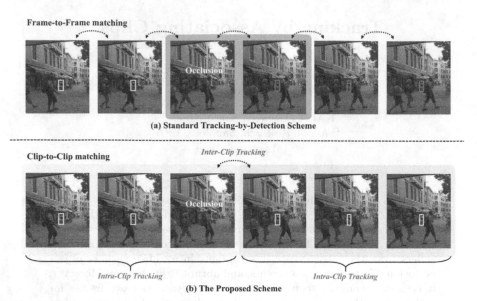

Fig. 1. The proposed clip-to-clip matching. (a) The current tracking paradigm sequentially matches the object instances frame-by-frame, which is vulnerable to intermediate interruptions in a video and cannot faithfully exploit the temporal information during the matching, resulting in tracker drifting. (b) Unlike the standard frame-wise matching scheme, we introduce a new clip-wise tracking method. Our approach is robust to random interference in a video, as we can skip those frames by chunking the video into multiple clips. Moreover, the multiple frame information is exploited during the clip-wise matching. With our proposal, the object can be seamlessly tracked over time.

with object detection, followed by association, track management, and post-processing [1,2,6,14,35,39]. Ever since, this tracking-by-detection paradigm has become the standard approach for multi-object tracking, and most of the state-of-the-art trackers follow this scheme [4,23,28,44,49,51,52].

The tracking-by-detection scheme is essentially a sequential frame-by-frame association approach (see Fig. 1(a)). In practice, it is achieved by matching the temporally smoothed history, which can be either new locations based on the past motion records [51] or moving averaged RE-ID features of the trajectories [28], with the current predictions. However, this sequential frame-based matching fundamentally suffers from two prominent limitations. First, the error accumulation or propagation cannot be handled properly. For example, sudden object motion pattern changes or fast camera movements significantly disturb the previous motion records. Also, object deformation such as occlusion or blur corrupts the moving averaged RE-ID features, leading to track drifting. The phenomenon becomes even more severe when the input video frame rate is low. Second, it does not consider the overall temporal context during matching. Looking at only two frames for matching essentially has ambiguity, resulting in track fragmentation.

To effectively utilize the temporal information and make the tracker robust to intermediate interruptions in a video, we reformulate the standard tracking-by-detection scheme as a clip-to-clip matching problem (see Fig. 1(b)). In particular, we chunk a video into multiple short clips and perform the tracking at the clip level. The video chunking allows skipping challenging frames for tracking, and the short-clip tracking avoids long-term track memory management such as long sequence temporal smoothing of RE-ID features along the video. Furthermore, the association between clips utilizes multi-frame information, which is more robust than the previous frame-based association. While not being sensitive to any specific design of tracker, we build our proposal upon the state-of-the-art RE-ID-based tracking-by-detection paradigm, QDTrack [28], as it can handle both the low [11] and high frame rate [27] video inputs better than the motion-based trackers [23,47,51,52,55].

We define two new basic tracking operations to implement the clip-wise tracker: intra- (within-) and inter- (between-) clip tracking. We target *semi-online scenarios* throughout this paper. Thus we only allow the intra-clip association to perform matching irrespective of the frame order. Meanwhile, inter-clip tracking incrementally merges the clip predictions until the complete video-level object trajectories are all retrieved. It requires associating objects at a track level, and thus the temporal information plays an important role here.

We investigate various viable implementations for both intra- and inter- clip tracking. Specifically, for the intra-clip tracking, we explore two feasible association approaches, directional and direction-free matching [53]. For the inter-clip tracking, we consider the IoU-based chaining [31] and temporal averaged feature matching. We further improve the inter-clip matching by designing a novel transformer-based clip tracker. It learns to temporally attend to all the past track embeddings of each object and predicts representative embeddings. These temporally attended embeddings are matched to associate the clip-level predictions. To make the model more robust at test time, we simulate hard positives and negatives during training: mislocalization and track drifting. We apply our inter-clip tracker recursively over time and merge the clip predictions into global object tracks incrementally.

With our proposals, we achieve state-of-the-art results on the challenging large vocabulary object tracking benchmark, TAO. We also validate our approach on the MOT17 benchmark to focus on the tracking performance more thoroughly. Compared to the baseline, we observe clear improvement in the association performance. Finally, we conduct extensive ablation studies and confirm that the proposals are effective and generic.

## 2    Related Work

**Multi-object Tracking.** The tracking-by-detection paradigm [32] dominates the current state-of-the-art multi-object tracking frameworks [22]. It detects objects first and associates them frame-by-frame across time [1,2,6,14,35, 39]. Recently, deep learning has contributed significantly to improving the performance of multi-object tracking approaches by focusing on designing better detectors [33,34] or developing more effective association objectives [18,21, 28,37,44,46]. Several works also have shown advances regarding detection and tracking as a joint learning task [13,41,47,55]. Nonetheless, these methods often formulate the multi-object tracking problem only with two consecutive frames and dismiss long-term temporal information, which is crucial for tackling various challenges in tracking.

While sequential frame-based matching is efficient and has shown promising results, they are fundamentally vulnerable to intermediate interruptions in a video and miss rich temporal information during matching. Unlike these methods, we target a semi-online scenario where we allow slight lagging and utilize several consecutive frames (*i.e.* clip) as a whole for the association. We show that our proposal is robust to intermediate interruptions in a video and produces better association quality.

**Clip-Level Modeling in Video.** The simultaneous process of multiple frames (*i.e.* clip-level modeling) is a promising research direction in many video tasks including video instance segmentation [3,19,43,48], video object segmentation [29], optical flow estimation [20], and depth estimation [45]. Per-clip models enjoy the opportunities to extract rich temporal information from multiple frames, leading to effectively tackle ambiguities in videos (*e.g.* occlusions or blur). Most existing methods focus on extracting temporal information to improve recognition or segmentation quality, and there has been little consideration to the association part.

Here, we present to associate objects at clip-level, performing the tracking both within and in-between the clips. The clip-level matching provides two clear advantages. First, by chunking, the matching within the clips essentially becomes short-term tracking, avoiding long-term history averaging or memory management. Second, the matching in-between the clips allows exploiting the temporal context, resolving the temporally-local ambiguities of matching between the two consecutive frames. To achieve better long-term association with accurate inter-clip matching, we design a novel transformer architecture.

**Transformers for Tracking.** Recently, transformers [42] have shown impressive results in many computer vision tasks, such as image classification [12,24], object detection [7,56], segmentation [54], and image generation [30]. There are also several methods [26,40,49] adopting the transformers for multi-object tracking by extending DETR frameworks [7]. However, these methods are still limited at utilizing short-term temporal information and rather adopt conventional heuristics such as Intersection over Union (IoU) matching [40], formulate the problem as a two frames task [26], or rely on the frame-by-frame evolving track quries [49].

Apart from the previous works, we set up the clip-based tracking scenario. We see that the key to accurate inter-clip matching is to generate discriminative clip-level representations. Our main idea is to use a Transformer as a track history summarizer. In practice, given a short track sequence of object instance (*i.e.* intra-clip tracking results), we input this track sequence to the transformer

---

**Algorithm 1:** Tracking by Associating Clips

---

    **Input**: A video sequence $V = (f_1, \ldots, f_N)$; object detector Det; clip size $C_S$;
        clip interval $C_I$;
    **Output**: Tracks $T$ of the video

```
1  begin
2  |   Initialization: T ← ∅
3  |   for i = 1 : C_I : N do
4  |   |   /* Sample clip */
5  |   |   C ← V[i : i + C_S]
6  |   |
7  |   |   /* Predict detection boxes & scores */
8  |   |   D_clip ← ∅
9  |   |   for frame f_k in C do
10 |   |   |   D_k ← Det(f_k)
11 |   |   |_  D_clip ← D_clip ∪ D_k
12 |   |
13 |   |   /* Intra clip association*/
14 |   |   Initialization: T_intra ← ∅
15 |   |   Associate T_intra and D_clip
16 |   |
17 |   |   /* Inter clip association*/
18 |   |_  Associate T and T_intra
```

---

and get the condensed feature. Finally, this track summary feature is used for the subsequent inter-clip matching.

## 3  Tracking by Associating Clips

We propose a simple yet effective data association method, Tracking by Associating Clips. Unlike the standard tracking-by-detection scheme, which matches object instances frame-by-frame, we instead conduct association at a clip level as shown in Fig. 1. We provide the pseudo-code in Algorithm 1.

The input is a video sequence $V$ and an object detector Det. Also, we set two hyper-parameters, clip size $C_S$ and clip interval $C_I$. The output is the tracks $T$ of the video, and each track contains the bounding box and identity of the object in each frame.

After sampling the clip from the video, we predict the detection boxes and scores using the detector Det for each frame. Then, the first association is performed to link the detection boxes in the clip $D_{clip}$, which results in local clip-level tracks $T_{intra}$. The second association is performed between the local clip-level tracks $T_{intra}$ and the global video-level tracks $T$. The global video-level tracks $T$ keep the history of the tracked objects and use this information to associate with the local clip-level tracks $T_{intra}$. The object tracks are incrementally expanded over time by repeating the intra- and inter-clip associations.

Notably, the proposal degenerates to the standard tracking-by-detection scheme when the clip window size reduces to 1 without overlaps in between.

In this paper, we built our proposal upon the recently presented QDTrack [28], given its strong Re-ID association capability. It is more robust than motion-based trackers [23,47,51,52,55] to target both the low-frame-rate (*e.g.* 1FPS, TAO [11]) and high-frame-rate (*e.g.* 30FPS, MOT17 [27]) video inputs. In the following, we explore effective implementations of intra- and inter-clip association methods.

## 3.1  Intra Clip Association

Given the detection boxes of each frame in the clip, we examine two possible implementations, directional and direction-free matching (see Fig. 2-(a)).

**Directional Matching.** The standard way to associate the clip-level object predictions is to link them sequentially. We see that the matching direction, either left to the right or right to the left, provides similar performance; thus, we only consider the former case. To address object occlusions within the clip, we employ track rebirth [9,46] using a memory mechanism.

**Direction-Free Matching.** Within the clip, the motion patterns and appearances of objects are quite similar due to the inherent redundancy in a video. Given this fact, we can also associate the objects in a direction-free manner.

Specifically, we employ the heap-based hierarchical clustering algorithm [53]. At the beginning, we consider that every detection box in all frames has its own cluster. We calculate their pair-wise appearance distances [28]. We avoid the association of the objects in the same frame by setting their distance to be infinity. Subsequently, every cluster distance will be inserted into a priority queue based on a heap data structure. Afterward, the cluster pair associated with the smallest distance in the priority queue will be popped and will be merged together. For this new cluster, distances to other clusters have to be computed and inserted into the priority queue. To set the distance between the track pairs, we search the minimum distance. The clustering is repeated until there are only distances greater than a threshold left.

For the intra-clip tracking, which is essentially short-term tracking, we observe that the standard directional matching with the lost track management is already competitive. It outperforms the strong heap-based hierarchical clustering algorithm [53] both in accuracy and efficiency.

## 3.2  Inter Clip Association

This section explores how to match and merge the current clip-level predictions into the global video-level tracks. We consider the following two feasible implementations (see Fig. 2(b)).

**IoU-Based Matching.** We adopt IoU-based chaining [31] that associates object tracks based on the IoU in the same frame. However, this method has three

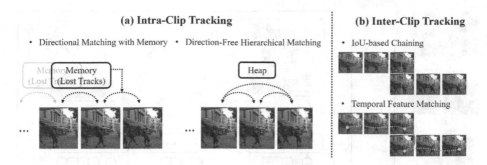

**Fig. 2. Two Basic Operations for Clip-based Tracking.** We define intra- and inter- clip tracking for instantiating the clip-based tracker. For intra-clip tracking, we consider both directional and direction-free matching approaches. The former is a standard frame-by-frame matching with a memory mechanism. The latter is implemented using the heap structure and hierarchically clusters the detection boxes across the frames without considering the frame order [53]. For the inter-clip tracking, we examine IoU-based chaining [31] and temporal average-pooled feature matching.

apparent drawbacks. First, it misses linking all the object tracks not revealed in the overlapping frame, and this phenomenon becomes even more severe as clip window size increases. Second, as the number of overlapping frames increases, the single-frame-based IoU matching does not guarantee optimal matching. Third, the method is basically not applicable when there are no overlapping frames.

**Temporal Feature Matching.** Free from the above limitations, an alternative is based on feature matching. As a simple baseline, we employ temporally average-pooled features for the association.

While simple, temporal feature matching improves over the frame-based tracking baseline and outperforms the IoU-based chaining [31]. However, we found that it is not always the case; For the low frame rate video inputs (*i.e.* TAO), which inherently include severe appearance change across the frame, the simple averaged temporal matching is inferior to the baseline (see Table 3). To improve the clip-level association quality further, we designed a new Transformer-based clip tracker, described in the following section.

### 3.3 Clip Tracker

The most challenging aspect of the inter-clip association is to generate a discriminative *clip-level* embedding for any object tracks. Our key idea for this problem is to use transformer as a track history summarizer (see Fig. 3). By design, the transformer can process and relate set-based elements. Here, we consider the intra-clip results (*i.e.* short object track sequence) as an input for the transformer, and we attempt to temporally-pool their feature information into a condensed feature. During training, the clip tracker learns to produce a good summary of the given object track history, which can link the clip-level predictions over time at test time.

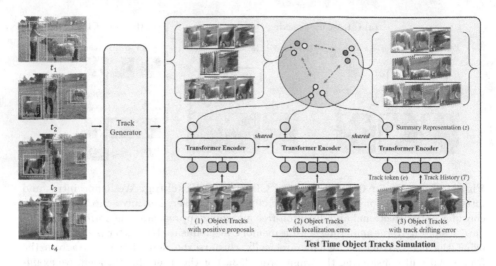

**Fig. 3. The overview of clip tracker.** The solid green line indicates the original ground truth boxes of each instance. The yellow and red dotted lines are positive and negative proposals, respectively. The transformer learns a *weighted temporal pooling* function of track history in a data-driven manner. *Best viewed in color.*

In practice, we design the clip tracker using transformer encoder layers. For object $p$, the clip tracker takes all the feature embeddings in the track $\mathcal{T}^p = \{x_{t_s}^p, \ldots, x_{t_e}^p\} \in R^{L \times C}$ and an extra learnable track token $e \in R^C$ as an input. Here, $t_s$ and $t_e$ denote the track initiation and termination time, respectively. $L$ and $C$ are the track length and the dimension of the feature embeddings, respectively. This input sequence, $[e, \mathcal{T}^p] \in R^{(L+1) \times C}$, is forwarded to the transformer, and we take the output of the track token, $z^p \in R^C$, as a condensed representation of the given object's track history.

This summary representation should be representative enough to match the same object instance over time consistently. Also, it should be discriminative enough to prevent it from being matched to other object instances. This can be achieved with the contrastive learning objective [16], where the positive can be oneself, and set the negatives other object embeddings. However, given that the number of objects appearing in a video is limited in typical, we significantly lack training samples. As a remedy, we introduce three strategies in the following for scaling the training data.

First, we allow using positive proposals[1], and concatenate them over the time axis to generate object tracks. This strategy has two clear advantages: 1) we can significantly increase the number of object tracks compared to only using ground truth boxes. 2) we can enjoy the natural jittering effect of the proposals, allowing the model to be robust to temporal appearance changes (see Fig. 3(1)).

Second, we simulate hard positives and negatives. The first is mislocalization due to some boxes along the track that does not tightly cover the object. The

---

[1] The proposals that have IoU greater than the given threshold with the ground truths.

second is a track drifting due to the incorrect match to other instances in the middle of the track. To make the model robust to these errors, we augment the training samples with the following two new strategies.

1. **Negative Proposals.** For the localization error, we incorporate negative proposals that have loose IoU with the ground truths (in between 0.3 and 0.5). Given both the positive and negative proposals, three different types of object tracks are generated in equal probability during training; positive only, negative only, and hybrid.
2. **Object Track Mixup.** For the track drifting error, we propose to mix two different object tracks [50]. In particular, we switch random portions of the given object track embeddings with randomly selected different object track embeddings. To keep the original identity of the given track, we bound the mixup ratio to 0.3.

With these two new augmentation strategies, we can effectively simulate hard positives and negatives, which can help the model improve embedding quality (see Figs. 3(2) and (3)). The proposal sampling is conducted in an order-free manner, which means the object tracks can be constructed with multiple boxes from the same image.

Finally, we treat the object instances from other videos in the training batch as negatives. This naturally increases the negatives in the contrastive learning context, leading to more discriminative feature embeddings [10,17].

**Objective Function.** Under this setup, we can apply the following contrastive learning formula

$$\mathcal{L} = \log[1 + \sum_{\mathbf{z}^+} \sum_{\mathbf{z}^-} \exp(\mathbf{z} \cdot \mathbf{z}^- - \mathbf{z} \cdot \mathbf{z}^+)]. \tag{1}$$

where $\mathbf{z}$ denotes an anchor, $\mathbf{z}^+$ and $\mathbf{z}^-$ are corresponding positives and negatives. We note the formula allows multiple positives, which is an extension of the standard single-positive formula, and thus can learn more discriminative embeddings [28].

**Track History Management.** At test-time, the clip tracker holds the global video-level object tracks and expands those incrementally by merging the outputs of the intra-clip tracker. In specific, the affinity matrix is computed based on the *summary* feature similarities between clip and global tracks. We associate the tracks with the matching threshold of 0.5. If the match is found, we save all the frame-level predictions of the objects in the memory buffer for the subsequent matching.

**Memory Buffer Size.** In computing the summary embedding of the global tracks, we set a proper memory buffer size. Intuitively, the larger the memory buffer size, the more the model can exploit the temporal context up to its temporal abstraction capacity. In practice, we set to 30 and 10 frames for MOT17 and TAO, respectively.

## 4    Experiments

In this section, we conduct experiments to demonstrate the benefits of our proposals using the TAO [11] and MOT17 [27] benchmarks. We investigate the results focusing mainly on the association aspect. Specifically, we use Track AP for the evaluation on the TAO benchmark. Also, Track $AP_S$, Track $AP_M$, and Track $AP_L$ are adopted which indicates the Track AP of (short $\leq 3$), ($3 \leq$ medium $\leq 10$), and (long $\geq 10$) length object tracks. We use MOTA [5], IDF1 [36], and the recently presented HOTA metrics [25] for the evaluation on the MOT17 benchmark. To see the association quality more thoroughly, we also present AssA performance.

### 4.1    Datasets

**TAO** [11] is the first video benchmark for large vocabulary object tracking. It annotates 482 classes in total, which are the subset of the LVIS [15] dataset. Its training set has 400 videos, covering 216 classes. The validation set consists of 988 videos, spanning 302 classes. The test set has 1419 videos, covering 369 classes. The videos are annotated in 1 FPS.

**MOT17** [27] is the most popular multi-object tracking benchmark, which consists of 7 training and 7 testing videos. While it has only pedestrian annotations, sequences include several challenges such as frequent occlusions and crowd scenes. The video framerate is relatively high, ranging from 14 to 30 FPS. For ablation experiments, we split each training sequence into two halves, and use the first half-frames for training and the second for validation.

Due to the difference in frame rate (1FPS *v.s.* 30FPS) and annotated object categories (482 *v.s.* 1), TAO and MOT17 cover significantly different motion patterns and video contents. We show that our proposal works well on both.

### 4.2    Implementation Details

**Clip Tracker Architecture.** The Clip Tracker model consists of 3 transformer encoder layers, where each layer has 8 heads with embedding dimensions of 256 (for MOT17) and 512 (for TAO). The input of Clip Tracker is the track embedding sequence of each object instance and the trainable track token. We apply a single linear layer to embed the input sequence. Finally, the output of the track token passes through a single MLP layer to produce the summary of the object track history. The positional encodings are not used in this work.

**Hyperparameters.** The proposed clip-based tracking pipeline introduces two new hyperparameters, clip size and clip interval (see Algorithm (1)). The clip size and interval directly affect the video chunking patterns. We observe that overlapping the clip prediction eases the inter-clip association. In practice, we considered the frame rate of the given datasets. For example, for the TAO, which provides low frame rate video inputs, we set clip size and interval value to 6 and 3, respectively. For the MOT, we set clip size and interval to 10 and 5, respectively.

**Table 1.** Tracking Results on TAO *val* and *test*. We use clip size and interval of 6 and 3, respectively.

| Method | TAO val | | | TAO test | | |
|---|---|---|---|---|---|---|
| | TrackAP$_{50}$ | TrackAP$_{75}$ | TrackAP$_{50:95}$ | TrackAP$_{50}$ | TrackAP$_{75}$ | TrackAP$_{50:95}$ |
| SORT [11] | 13.2 | - | - | 10.2 | 4.4 | 4.9 |
| QDTrack [28] | 13.4 | 4.9 | 6.1 | 12.6 | 4.5 | 5.6 |
| Ours | **17.7** | **5.8** | **7.3** | **15.8** | **5.9** | **6.6** |

**Table 2.** Tracking Results on MOT17. We use clip size and interval of 10 and 5, respectively.

| Method | MOT val | | | MOT test | | |
|---|---|---|---|---|---|---|
| | MOTA | IDF1 | HOTA | MOTA | IDF1 | HOTA |
| QDTrack [28] | 68.1 | 69.5 | 57.5 | 71.1 | 70.2 | 57.8 |
| Ours | **68.9** | **72.4** | **59.7** | **71.6** | **72.7** | **59.0** |

**Training.** We use MMdetection and MMTracking frameworks [8]. For the TAO experiments, COCO-style training schedule of 2× and 1× are adopted for LVIS pre-training and TAO fine-tuning, respectively. For the MOT experiments, we pre-trained the model using CrowdHuman dataset [38] for 12 epochs and then fine-tuned on the MOT17 train for 4 epochs. During pre-training, the detection part is learned. A batch size of 16 (2 per GPU) and an initial learning rate of 0.02 are used. We use the backbone ResNet-101 (ResNet-50) for the TAO (MOT17) experiment following the previous studies [11,28]. We train the Clip Tracker by sampling 2 and 6 frames under the frame range of 1 and 30 for TAO and MOT17 experiments, respectively.

**Testing.** Our method processes video frames recursively at clip-level, generating object tracks for the given clip and merging them into the global tracks incrementally. We use standard directional matching for intra- and Clip-Tracker for inter-clip tracking. The overall tracking procedure follows Algorithm (1). While the frame-level association capability within the clip is similar to that of the baseline, video chunking along with the clip-wise association allows tracking performance improvement. We use resized frames of 1080×1080 for testing.

## 4.3  Main Results

Upon the state-of-the-art tracking-by-detection framework, QDTrack [28], we instantiate our proposal, clip-based tracking. The main results on TAO and MOT17 are summarized in Table 1 and Table 2. We observe our proposal pushes the tracking performances on both datasets. The results imply that the clip-based association is generic over various scenarios.

**Table 3. Impact of Clip-Based Tracking.** We use both TAO *val* and MOT *val* to evaluate the impact of the new clip-based tracking approach. We investigate various feasible implementations for both intra and inter clip associations described in Sect. 3.1 and Sect. 3.2. Here, T is an abbreviation of Track AP.

| Method | MOT17 | | | TAO | | | |
|---|---|---|---|---|---|---|---|
| | IDF1 | HOTA | AssA | $T_{50}$ | $T_S$ | $T_M$ | $T_L$ |
| QDtrack [28] | 69.5 | 57.5 | 58.0 | 13.4 | 6.7 | 9.6 | 17.2 |
| Direc-free [53] | 70.3 | 57.9 | 58.9 | 13.1 | 6.1 | 8.9 | 16.8 |
| Direc | 70.3 | 58.6 | 59.4 | 12.3 | 5.1 | 8.3 | 16.5 |

(a) Intra Clip Association Methods

| Method | MOT17 | | | TAO | | | |
|---|---|---|---|---|---|---|---|
| | IDF1 | HOTA | AssA | $T_{50}$ | $T_S$ | $T_M$ | $T_L$ |
| QDtrack [28] | 69.5 | 57.5 | 58.0 | 13.4 | 6.7 | 9.6 | 17.2 |
| IoU-chain [31] | 69.1 | 56.4 | 56.1 | 10.2 | 3.4 | 6.5 | 14.4 |
| Tmp avg. | 70.3 | 58.6 | 59.4 | 12.3 | 5.1 | 8.3 | 16.8 |
| Clip-Tracker | 72.4 | 59.7 | 61.9 | 17.7 | 10.9 | 14.6 | 21.3 |

(b) Inter Clip Association Methods

## 4.4 Ablation Studies

To empirically confirm the effectiveness of our proposals, we conduct ablation studies using the TAO and MOT17 benchmarks. We focus on the association quality; thus, we use the metrics of IDF1, HOTA, and ASSA for MOT, and Track AP for TAO.

**Simple Clip-Based Tracker.** We first analyze how the standard QDTrack framework [28] improves by changing the tracking scheme from frame-based to clip-based. To do so, we design a simple clip-based tracking baseline, which takes the clip as input, performs intra-clip tracking, and links the clip predictions based on the temporal averaged feature matching. The results are shown in Table 3a. We observe that the clip-based tracking scheme improves the association quality in the MOT17 benchmark but not TAO. We see this because the motion change is significant in TAO due to the low frame rate; thus, the simple temporal averaged feature performs poorly, which motivates the design of Clip Tracker.

**Intra-clip Association.** Among the intra-clip variants, we observe that the standard scheme is already competitive and runs in a much faster time. Here, we use directional matching with memory mechanism for the intra-clip tracking.

**Inter-clip Association.** We perform ablations on inter-clip association methods. The results are summarized in Table 3b. We observe that IoU-based chaining performs inferior, even lower than the baseline. This is because the method misses all the object tracks not in the overlapping frame, leading to significant track fragmentation. Finally, the presented Clip Tracker significantly outperforms the simple temporal averaged feature matching. The results show that learning-based temporal pooling is more robust than simple averaging. We use Clip Tracker as our inter-clip association method in the following experiments.

**Parameter Analysis on Clip Size and Interval.** We conducted parameter analysis on the two newly introduced hyperparameters, clip size and interval. These hyperparameters affect the video chunking pattern and, as a result, impact both the intra- and inter-clip association quality. The results are summarized in Table 4a. We observe two tendencies. First, the association improves when the overlapping exists in-between the clips, *i.e.* $C_S > C_I$. Intuitively, the overlapping

**Table 4. Component Analysis on Clip Tracker** using MOT *val*. First, we conduct parameter analysis on two newly introduced hyperparameters: clip size $C_S$ and clip interval $C_I$. Second, We study the impact of two track augmentation strategies, negative proposal sampling (for localization error simulation) and object track mixup (for track drifting simulation), during the Clip Tracker training. Lastly, we investigate three different baseline methods to manage global video-level tracks.

| Method | $[C_S, C_I]$ | IDF1 | HOTA | AssA |
|---|---|---|---|---|
| QDtrack [28] | | 69.5 | 57.5 | 58.0 |
| Clip-Tracker | [5,5] | 71.6 | 59.0 | 60.5 |
| | [10,10] | 71.1 | 58.6 | 59.8 |
| | [10,5] | 72.4 | 59.7 | 61.9 |
| | [20,10] | 71.9 | 59.5 | 61.3 |

(a) Clip Size and Interval

| Loc. Err | Drift. Err | IDF1 | HOTA | AssA |
|---|---|---|---|---|
| | | 70.3 | 58.8 | 60.2 |
| ✓ | | 71.9 | 59.3 | 61.3 |
| ✓ | ✓ | 72.4 | 59.7 | 61.9 |

(b) Track Augmentations

| Method | IDF1 | HOTA | AssA |
|---|---|---|---|
| Two-clip based. | 71.8 | 59.2 | 60.4 |
| Moving avg. | 71.7 | 59.3 | 60.9 |
| Feature bank. (Ours) | 72.4 | 59.7 | 61.9 |

(c) Global Track Management

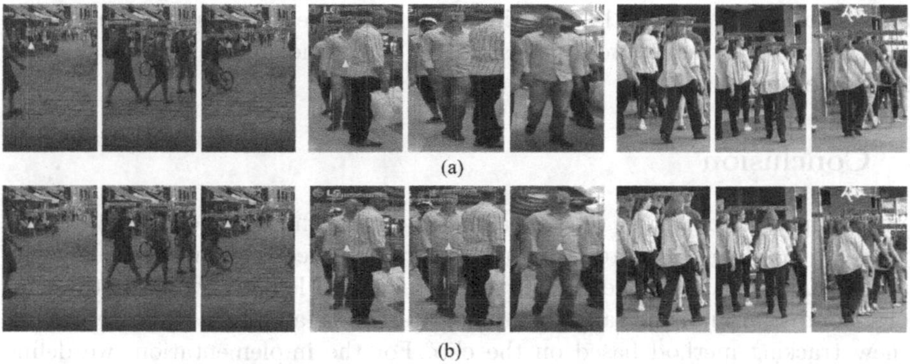

(a)

(b)

**Fig. 4. Qualitative Results.** (a) Tracking by detection. (b) Tracking by associating clips. The colored triangle represents the predicted person id. *Best Viewed in Colors.*

makes the feature embedding sequence quite similar, and thus the Clip Tracker can more easily find the correct match. Second, we see a slight performance drop when the clip size increases, *e.g.* $[5,5] \rightarrow [10,10]$ or $[10,5] \rightarrow [20,10]$. We see this phenomenon is mainly due to the increased false positives with the large clip size, and we mitigate this issue by introducing the overlapping frames, $[10,10] \rightarrow [10,5]$. In practice, proper clip size and interval values should be set, and here we found the clip size of 10 and the interval of 5 strikes a balance.

**Track Augmentations.** In order to improve the robustness of the Clip Tracker, we introduced two new hard training sample generation strategies, negative proposal sampling and object track mixup. We investigate their impacts on the tracking performance in Table 4b. From the baseline of using only the positive proposals, the track performance improves meaningfully with the negative proposal sampling. The object track mixup further improves the score.

**Track Management Strategies.** The inter-clip tracker manages global video-level track over time (see Algorithm (1)). It saves the tracked object's history for matching and merging subsequent clip prediction. Here, we examine three different feasible implementations for this. First is a two-clip-based matching, which only saves the immediately preceding object track features. The second is a moving-average-based matching, which uses smoothed object prototype embeddings. The third is feature bank based matching, which saves all the object track features up to pre-setted buffer size. As can be shown in Table 4c, we observe that the feature bank approach produces the best performance. This is because it has the broadest temporal view and can directly utilize the raw feature sequence rather than the temporally diluted features.

### 4.5  Qualitative Results

The visual comparisons of tracking results between the standard tracking scheme and our proposal are in Fig. 4. We select 3 different difficult sequences from the half validation set of MOT17. This include small objects, occlusion, and crowd scene. We see that our approach consistently tracks the objects without identity changes for long-term.

## 5  Conclusion

In this paper, we point out the fundamental limitations of the current tracking-by-detection scheme. Due to its sequential frame-based matching property, the method suffers from intermediate disturbances in a video and overlooks the temporal context around the target matching frame. As an alternative, we present a new tracking method based on the clip. For the implementation, we define two new tracking operations, intra- and inter-clip tracking. The new formulation views a single long video sequence as multiple short clips. In this way, the intra-clip tracking turns out to be short-term tracking, and we observe that the standard tracking approaches with memory are already competitive in this setup. For the inter-clip tracking, feature-based matching is more stable than IoU-based chaining. We further improve the association quality by designing a novel transformer-based approach, namely Clip Tracker. By connecting together, we show that our proposal achieves new state-of-the-art results on the challenging large vocabulary object tracking benchmark, TAO. We also confirm that our method significantly improves the association quality of the baseline in MOT17. We hope our work opens a new view of the current tracking paradigm.

**Acknowledgement.** This work was supported in part by the National Research Foundation of Korea (NRF-2020M3H8A1115028, FY2021).

## References

1. Andriyenko, A., Schindler, K.: Multi-target tracking by continuous energy minimization. In: CVPR 2011, pp. 1265–1272. IEEE (2011)
2. Andriyenko, A., Schindler, K., Roth, S.: Discrete-continuous optimization for multi-target tracking. In: 2012 IEEE Conference on Computer Vision and Pattern Recognition, pp. 1926–1933. IEEE (2012)

3. Athar, A., Mahadevan, S., Ošep, A., Leal-Taixé, L., Leibe, B.: STEm-Seg: spatio-temporal embeddings for instance segmentation in videos. In: Vedaldi, A., Bischof, H., Brox, T., Frahm, J.-M. (eds.) ECCV 2020. LNCS, vol. 12356, pp. 158–177. Springer, Cham (2020). https://doi.org/10.1007/978-3-030-58621-8_10
4. Bergmann, P., Meinhardt, T., Leal-Taixe, L.: Tracking without bells and whistles. In: Proceedings of the IEEE/CVF International Conference on Computer Vision, pp. 941–951 (2019)
5. Bernardin, K., Stiefelhagen, R.: Evaluating multiple object tracking performance: the clear mot metrics. EURASIP J. Image Video Process. **2008**, 1–10 (2008)
6. Bewley, A., Ge, Z., Ott, L., Ramos, F., Upcroft, B.: Simple online and realtime tracking. In: 2016 IEEE International Conference on Image Processing (ICIP), pp. 3464–3468. IEEE (2016)
7. Carion, N., Massa, F., Synnaeve, G., Usunier, N., Kirillov, A., Zagoruyko, S.: End-to-end object detection with transformers. In: Vedaldi, A., Bischof, H., Brox, T., Frahm, J.-M. (eds.) ECCV 2020. LNCS, vol. 12346, pp. 213–229. Springer, Cham (2020). https://doi.org/10.1007/978-3-030-58452-8_13
8. Chen, K., et al.: MMDetection: open MMLab detection toolbox and benchmark. arXiv preprint arXiv:1906.07155 (2019)
9. Chen, L., Ai, H., Zhuang, Z., Shang, C.: Real-time multiple people tracking with deeply learned candidate selection and person re-identification. In: 2018 IEEE International Conference on Multimedia and Expo (ICME), pp. 1–6. IEEE (2018)
10. Chen, T., Kornblith, S., Norouzi, M., Hinton, G.: A simple framework for contrastive learning of visual representations. In: International Conference on Machine Learning, pp. 1597–1607. PMLR (2020)
11. Dave, A., Khurana, T., Tokmakov, P., Schmid, C., Ramanan, D.: TAO: A Large-scale benchmark for tracking any object. In: Vedaldi, A., Bischof, H., Brox, T., Frahm, J.-M. (eds.) ECCV 2020. LNCS, vol. 12350, pp. 436–454. Springer, Cham (2020). https://doi.org/10.1007/978-3-030-58558-7_26
12. Dosovitskiy, A., et al.: An image is worth 16x16 words: transformers for image recognition at scale. arXiv preprint arXiv:2010.11929 (2020)
13. Feichtenhofer, C., Pinz, A., Zisserman, A.: Detect to track and track to detect. In: Proceedings of the IEEE International Conference on Computer Vision, pp. 3038–3046 (2017)
14. Fortmann, T., Bar-Shalom, Y., Scheffe, M.: Sonar tracking of multiple targets using joint probabilistic data association. IEEE J. Oceanic Eng. **8**(3), 173–184 (1983)
15. Gupta, A., Dollar, P., Girshick, R.: LVIS: a dataset for large vocabulary instance segmentation. In: CVPR, pp. 5356–5364 (2019)
16. Hadsell, R., Chopra, S., LeCun, Y.: Dimensionality reduction by learning an invariant mapping. In: 2006 IEEE Computer Society Conference on Computer Vision and Pattern Recognition (CVPR'06), vol. 2, pp. 1735–1742. IEEE (2006)
17. He, K., Fan, H., Wu, Y., Xie, S., Girshick, R.: Momentum contrast for unsupervised visual representation learning. In: Proceedings of the IEEE/CVF Conference on Computer Vision and Pattern Recognition, pp. 9729–9738 (2020)
18. Hu, H.N., et al.: Joint monocular 3d vehicle detection and tracking. In: Proceedings of the IEEE/CVF International Conference on Computer Vision, pp. 5390–5399 (2019)
19. Hwang, S., Heo, M., Oh, S.W., Kim, S.J.: Video instance segmentation using inter-frame communication transformers. In: Advances in Neural Information Processing Systems, vol. 34 (2021)

20. Janai, J., Güney, F., Ranjan, A., Black, M., Geiger, A.: Unsupervised learning of multi-frame optical flow with occlusions. In: Ferrari, V., Hebert, M., Sminchisescu, C., Weiss, Y. (eds.) ECCV 2018. LNCS, vol. 11220, pp. 713–731. Springer, Cham (2018). https://doi.org/10.1007/978-3-030-01270-0_42

21. Leal-Taixé, L., Canton-Ferrer, C., Schindler, K.: Learning by tracking: Siamese CNN for robust target association. In: Proceedings of the IEEE Conference on Computer Vision and Pattern Recognition Workshops, pp. 33–40 (2016)

22. Leal-Taixé, L., Milan, A., Schindler, K., Cremers, D., Reid, I., Roth, S.: Tracking the trackers: an analysis of the state of the art in multiple object tracking. arXiv:1704.02781 (2017)

23. Liang, C., et al.: Rethinking the competition between detection and ReiD in multi-object tracking. arXiv preprint arXiv:2010.12138 (2020)

24. Liu, Z., et al.: Swin transformer: Hierarchical vision transformer using shifted windows. In: Proceedings of the IEEE/CVF International Conference on Computer Vision, pp. 10012–10022 (2021)

25. Luiten, J., et al.: HOTA: a higher order metric for evaluating multi-object tracking. Int. J. Comput. Vision **129**(2), 548–578 (2021)

26. Meinhardt, T., Kirillov, A., Leal-Taixe, L., Feichtenhofer, C.: Trackformer: Multi-object tracking with transformers. arXiv preprint arXiv:2101.02702 (2021)

27. Milan, A., Leal-Taixé, L., Reid, I., Roth, S., Schindler, K.: MOT16: a benchmark for multi-object tracking. arXiv preprint arXiv:1603.00831 (2016)

28. Pang, J., et al.: Quasi-dense similarity learning for multiple object tracking. In: Proceedings of the IEEE/CVF Conference on Computer Vision and Pattern Recognition, pp. 164–173 (2021)

29. Park, K., Woo, S., Oh, S.W., Kweon, I.S., Lee, J.Y.: Per-clip video object segmentation. In: Proceedings of the IEEE/CVF Conference on Computer Vision and Pattern Recognition, pp. 1352–1361 (2022)

30. Parmar, N., et al.: Image transformer. In: International Conference on Machine Learning, pp. 4055–4064. PMLR (2018)

31. Peng, J., et al.: Chained-tracker: chaining paired attentive regression results for end-to-end joint multiple-object detection and tracking. In: Vedaldi, A., Bischof, H., Brox, T., Frahm, J.-M. (eds.) ECCV 2020. LNCS, vol. 12349, pp. 145–161. Springer, Cham (2020). https://doi.org/10.1007/978-3-030-58548-8_9

32. Ramanan, D., Forsyth, D.A.: Finding and tracking people from the bottom up. In: CVPR, vol. 2, pp. 1–8. IEEE (2003)

33. Redmon, J., Divvala, S., Girshick, R., Farhadi, A.: You only look once: unified, real-time object detection. In: Proceedings of the IEEE Conference on Computer Vision and Pattern Recognition, pp. 779–788 (2016)

34. Ren, S., He, K., Girshick, R., Sun, J.: Faster r-CNN: towards real-time object detection with region proposal networks. In: Advances in Neural Information Processing Systems, vol. 28 (2015)

35. Rezatofighi, S.H., Milan, A., Zhang, Z., Shi, Q., Dick, A., Reid, I.: Joint probabilistic data association revisited. In: Proceedings of the IEEE International Conference on Computer Vision, pp. 3047–3055 (2015)

36. Ristani, E., Solera, F., Zou, R., Cucchiara, R., Tomasi, C.: Performance measures and a data set for multi-target, multi-camera tracking. In: Hua, G., Jégou, H. (eds.) ECCV 2016. LNCS, vol. 9914, pp. 17–35. Springer, Cham (2016). https://doi.org/10.1007/978-3-319-48881-3_2

37. Sadeghian, A., Alahi, A., Savarese, S.: Tracking the untrackable: learning to track multiple cues with long-term dependencies. In: Proceedings of the IEEE International Conference on Computer Vision, pp. 300–311 (2017)

38. Shao, S., et al.: CrowdHuman: a benchmark for detecting human in a crowd. arXiv preprint arXiv:1805.00123 (2018)
39. Streit, R.L., Luginbuhl, T.E.: Maximum likelihood method for probabilistic multihypothesis tracking. In: Signal and Data Processing of Small Targets 1994, vol. 2235, pp. 394–405. International Society for Optics and Photonics (1994)
40. Sun, P., et al.: Transtrack: multiple object tracking with transformer. arXiv preprint arXiv:2012.15460 (2020)
41. Sun, S., Akhtar, N., Song, H., Mian, A., Shah, M.: Deep affinity network for multiple object tracking. IEEE Trans. Pattern Anal. Mach. Intell. **43**(1), 104–119 (2019)
42. Vaswani, A., et al.: Attention is all you need. In: Advances in Neural Information Processing Systems, vol. 30 (2017)
43. Wang, Y., et al.: End-to-end video instance segmentation with transformers. In: Proceedings of the IEEE/CVF Conference on Computer Vision and Pattern Recognition, pp. 8741–8750 (2021)
44. Wang, Z., Zheng, L., Liu, Y., Li, Y., Wang, S.: Towards real-time multi-object tracking. In: Vedaldi, A., Bischof, H., Brox, T., Frahm, J.-M. (eds.) ECCV 2020. LNCS, vol. 12356, pp. 107–122. Springer, Cham (2020). https://doi.org/10.1007/978-3-030-58621-8_7
45. Watson, J., Mac Aodha, O., Prisacariu, V., Brostow, G., Firman, M.: The temporal opportunist: Self-supervised multi-frame monocular depth. In: Proceedings of the IEEE/CVF Conference on Computer Vision and Pattern Recognition, pp. 1164–1174 (2021)
46. Wojke, N., Bewley, A., Paulus, D.: Simple online and realtime tracking with a deep association metric. In: 2017 IEEE International Conference on Image Processing (ICIP), pp. 3645–3649. IEEE (2017)
47. Wu, J., Cao, J., Song, L., Wang, Y., Yang, M., Yuan, J.: Track to detect and segment: an online multi-object tracker. In: Proceedings of the IEEE/CVF Conference on Computer Vision and Pattern Recognition, pp. 12352–12361 (2021)
48. Wu, J., Jiang, Y., Zhang, W., Bai, X., Bai, S.: SeqFormer: a frustratingly simple model for video instance segmentation. arXiv preprint arXiv:2112.08275 (2021)
49. Zeng, F., Dong, B., Wang, T., Zhang, X., Wei, Y.: MOTR: end-to-end multipleobject tracking with transformer. arXiv preprint arXiv:2105.03247 (2021)
50. Zhang, H., Cisse, M., Dauphin, Y.N., Lopez-Paz, D.: mixup: beyond empirical risk minimization. arXiv preprint arXiv:1710.09412 (2017)
51. Zhang, Y., et al.: Bytetrack: multi-object tracking by associating every detection box. arXiv preprint arXiv:2110.06864 (2021)
52. Zhang, Y., Wang, C., Wang, X., Zeng, W., Liu, W.: FairMOT: on the fairness of detection and re-identification in multiple object tracking. Int. J. Comput. Vision **129**(11), 3069–3087 (2021)
53. Zhang, Z., Wu, J., Zhang, X., Zhang, C.: Multi-target, multi-camera tracking by hierarchical clustering: recent progress on dukemtmc project. arXiv preprint arXiv:1712.09531 (2017)
54. Zheng, S., et al.: Rethinking semantic segmentation from a sequence-to-sequence perspective with transformers. In: Proceedings of the IEEE/CVF Conference on Computer Vision and Pattern Recognition, pp. 6881–6890 (2021)
55. Zhou, X., Koltun, V., Krähenbühl, P.: Tracking Objects as points. In: Vedaldi, A., Bischof, H., Brox, T., Frahm, J.-M. (eds.) ECCV 2020. LNCS, vol. 12349, pp. 474–490. Springer, Cham (2020). https://doi.org/10.1007/978-3-030-58548-8_28
56. Zhu, X., Su, W., Lu, L., Li, B., Wang, X., Dai, J.: Deformable DETR: deformable transformers for end-to-end object detection. arXiv preprint arXiv:2010.04159 (2020)

# RealPatch: A Statistical Matching Framework for Model Patching with Real Samples

Sara Romiti[1]([✉])[iD], Christopher Inskip[1][iD], Viktoriia Sharmanska[1,4][iD], and Novi Quadrianto[1,2,3][iD]

[1] Predictive Analytics Lab (PAL),University of Sussex, Brighton, UK
{s.romiti,c.inskip,sharmanska.v,n.quadrianto}@sussex.ac.uk
[2] BCAM Severo Ochoa Strategic Lab on Trustworthy Machine Learning, Bilbao, Spain
[3] Monash University, Cisauk, Indonesia
[4] Imperial College London, London, UK

**Abstract.** Machine learning classifiers are typically trained to minimise the average error across a dataset. Unfortunately, in practice, this process often exploits spurious correlations caused by subgroup imbalance within the training data, resulting in high average performance but highly variable performance across subgroups. Recent work to address this problem proposes *model patching* with CAMEL. This previous approach uses generative adversarial networks to perform intra-class inter-subgroup data augmentations, requiring (a) the training of a number of computationally expensive models and (b) sufficient quality of model's synthetic outputs for the given domain. In this work, we propose RealPatch, a framework for simpler, faster, and more data-efficient data augmentation based on statistical matching. Our framework performs model patching by augmenting a dataset with real samples, mitigating the need to train generative models for the target task. We demonstrate the effectiveness of Real-Patch on three benchmark datasets, CelebA, Waterbirds and a subset of iWildCam, showing improvements in worst-case subgroup performance and in subgroup performance gap in binary classification. Furthermore, we conduct experiments with the imSitu dataset with 211 classes, a setting where generative model-based patching such as CAMEL is impractical. We show that RealPatch can successfully eliminate dataset leakage while reducing model leakage and maintaining high utility. The code for RealPatch can be found at https://github.com/wearepal/RealPatch.

**Keywords:** Classification · Subgroup imbalance · Model patching · Statistical matching · Dataset leakage

**Supplementary Information** The online version contains supplementary material available at https://doi.org/10.1007/978-3-031-19806-9_9.

# 1  Introduction

Machine learning models have fast become powerful yet ferocious pattern matching tools, able to exploit complex relationships and distant correlations present in a dataset. While often improving the average accuracy across a dataset, making use of spurious correlations (i.e. relationships that appear causal but in reality are not) for decision making is often undesirable, hurting generalization in the case that spurious correlations do not hold in the test distribution, and resulting in models that are biased towards certain subgroups or populations.

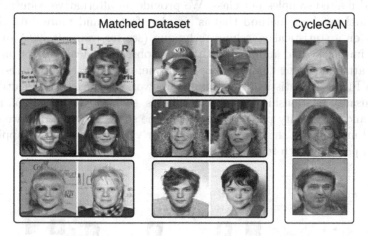

**Fig. 1.** Examples of images and their counterfactuals on the attribute male/female, retrieved using RealPatch (left); both original and matched images are real samples from the CelebA dataset. RealPatch preserves characteristics across matched pairs such as pose, facial expression, and accessories. We also show CycleGAN synthetic counterfactual results (right) on the same attribute.

Recent works in machine learning have studied the close link between invariance to spurious correlations and causation [1,16,24,28,34]. Causal analysis allows us to ask counterfactual questions in the context of machine learning predictions by relying on attribute-labelled data and imagining "what would happen if" some of these attributes were different. For example, "would the prediction of a smile change had this person's cheeks been rosy"? While simple to answer with tabular data, generating counterfactuals for image data is non-trivial.

Recent advances in generative adversarial networks (GAN) aim to build a realistic generative model of images that affords controlled manipulation of specific attributes, in effect generating image counterfactuals. Leveraging research progress in GANs, several works now use counterfactuals for (a) detecting unintended algorithmic bias, e.g. checking whether a classifier's "smile" prediction flips when traversing different attributes such as "heavy makeup" [11], and (b) reducing the gap in subgroup performance, e.g. ensuring a "blonde hair" classifier performs equally well on male and female subgroups [13,33]. The first relies on an *invert then edit* methodology, in which images are first inverted into the latent space of a pre-trained GAN model for generating counterfactuals, while the latter uses an *image-to-image translation* methodology. One of the most recent approaches, CAMEL [13], focuses on the latter usage of counterfactuals to *patch* the classifier's dependence on subgroup-specific features.

GAN-based counterfactual results are encouraging, however, we should note that GAN models have a number of common issues such as mode collapse, failure to converge, and poor generated results in a setting with a large number of class labels and limited samples per class. We provide an alternative counterfactual-based model patching method that is simpler, faster, and more data-efficient. We focus on a statistical matching technique (see for example [29]) such that for every image, we find an image with similar observable features yet having an opposite attribute value than the observed one; our counterfactual results are shown in Fig. 1. A statistical matching framework has been widely utilised to assess causality relationships in numerous fields, such as education [25], medical [4,6,32], and community policies [3,27] to name some. In this work, we explore statistical matching in the context of computer vision, and show its application for model patching with real samples.

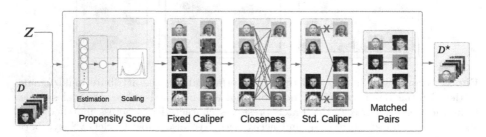

**Fig. 2.** RealPatch: statistical matching pipeline. Given the dataset $D$ and the spurious attribute $Z$, the output is a matched dataset $D^\star$. To produce $D^\star$ we: 1) estimate the propensity score, and adjust it with temperature scaling; 2) restrict $D$ using the fixed caliper to remove *extreme* samples; 3) compute the pair-wise closeness for each sample; 4) use the std-caliper to restrict the possible pairs according to a maximum propensity score distance; 5) for each sample, select the closest sample in the opposite group.

Our paper provides the following contributions:

1. We propose an image-based counterfactual approach for model patching called *RealPatch* that uses real images instead of GAN generated images;
2. We provide an empirical evaluation of different statistical matching strategies for vision datasets. Our results can be used as a *guideline* for future statistical matching applications, for example showing the importance of using calipers;
3. We show applications of RealPatch for improving the worst-case performance across subgroups and reducing the subgroup performance gap in a 2-class

classification setting. We observe that spurious correlation leads to short-cut learning, and show how RealPatch mitigates this by utilising a balanced dataset to regularise the training;

4. We show applications of RealPatch for reducing dataset leakage and model leakage in a multi 211-class classification setting.

**Related Work.** Data augmentation strategies using operations such as translation, rotation, flipping, cutout [12], mixup [39], and cutmix [38] are widely used for increasing the aggregate performance of machine learning models in computer vision applications. To improve performance in a targeted fashion, image transformation techniques that learn to produce semantic changes to an image are used to generate samples for underrepresented subgroups. Sharmanska et al. [33] used a StarGAN model [5] to augment the dataset with respect to a subgroup-specific feature, and subsequently optimized a standard Empirical Risk Minimization (ERM) training objective. Whereas, CAMEL, a framework by Goel et al. [13], used a CycleGAN image transformation approach [42] and minimized a Sub-Group Distributionally Robust Optimization (SGDRO) objective function.

GDRO method [31] aims to minimize the worst-case loss over groups in the training data. CAMEL models [13] minimize the class-conditional worst-case loss over groups. Another approach to reduce the effects of spurious correlation is optimizing a notion of invariance. Invariance serves as a proxy for causality, as features representing "causes" of class labels rather than "effects" will generalize well under intervention. Invariant Risk Minimization (IRM) [1] tries to find a data representation which discards the spurious correlations by enforcing that the classifier acting on that representation is simultaneously optimal in each subgroup. However, more analysis and better algorithms are needed to realize the promise of this framework in practice [13, 24].

Model patching focuses on robustness with respect to the unexpected failure of standard classifiers on subgroups of a class. Subgroups can correspond to environments/domains such as water or land, and can also refer to demographic attributes such as females or males [9]. Our work is therefore also related to many works addressing dataset biases in computer vision, particularly, in which the notion of bias relates to demographic attributes (e.g. [17,18,35,36]). Wang et al. [35] showed that even when datasets are balanced e.g. each class label co-occurs equally with each gender, learned models amplify the association between labels and gender, as much as if data had not been balanced. We refine their conclusions about balanced dataset and show that balancing with a statistical matching framework can successfully eliminate dataset leakage while reducing model leakage and maintaining high utility.

## 2   Our RealPatch Framework

We propose *RealPatch*, a framework that first resamples a dataset such that the *spurious groups* are balanced and equally informative and then utilise such dataset to regularise a classification objective. RealPatch only uses real samples from the original dataset when constructing the augmented dataset, making it faster to perform, and simpler to apply to new tasks, compared to approaches such as CAMEL [13] which require models to generate synthetic samples. Unlike standard data augmentation, our augmentation is in the context of statistical matching; it is a model-based approach for providing joint statistical information based on variables collected through two or more data sources. If we have two sources, e.g. male and female, matching augments the source domain of male images with female images, and the domain of female images with male images. In this section we outline the two stages of RealPatch. In Stage 1, a statistical matching procedure is used to construct a *matched dataset*, a collection of comparable pairs of images that have opposite values of the spurious attribute. In Stage 2, we learn a model to predict the target label by including the representations of instances in the matched dataset.

**Setup.** Given a dataset of $N$ samples $D = \{1, \ldots, N\}$ with target label $Y$ and spurious label $Z$, the dataset is divided into two *spurious groups* $D_T$ and $D_C$ based on the value of $Z$. These partitions define the so-called *treatment* $(Z = 1)$ and *control* $(Z = 0)$ groups of size $N_T$ and $N_C$, respectively. Additionally, we call *target groups* the two partitions created by $Y$ and *subgroups* the four sets caused by both $Y$ and $Z$. We use $X$ to denote feature representations of the input images extracted from a pre-trained model such as ResNet [15], or Big Transfer BiT [20]. In our framework these encoded representations $X$ are the *observed covariates* that are used to compute the distances $M$ between images and identify the matched pairs. Following the work of causal inference, image representations in $X$ are assigned a propensity score, a measure of how likely an image $s$ belongs to the treatment group, $e_s = \hat{P}(Z_s = 1|X_s)$. Propensity scores are used during Stage 1 to help prevent the inclusion of instances that would lead to poor matches.

### 2.1   Stage 1: Statistical Matching

Matching is a sampling method to reduce model dependency and enforce covariate balance in observational studies across a treatment and control group. In this work, we study the nearest-neighbour (NN) matching algorithm, which for each treatment sample selects the closest control sample. Figure 2 depicts our proposed matching pipeline. The pipeline has the following main building blocks: 1) *propensity score estimation*; 2) *closeness measure*; and 3) *calipers* as a threshold mechanism. Before using the matched dataset in Stage 2, the *matching quality* is measured by assessing the achieved balance of the covariates.

**Propensity Score Estimation.** In causal inference, a propensity score $e_s$ is the probability of a sample $s$ being in the *treatment* group $D_T$, given its observed covariates $X_s$. This conditional probability is usually unknown, therefore it has to be estimated. This is typically done using a logistic regression on the observed $X$ to predict the binary variable $Z$ [8]. Logistic regression allows us to reweight samples when optimising the loss function. We explore the use of *spurious reweight-*

*ing*, where samples are weighted inversely proportional to the frequency of their spurious label $Z$; more details are provided in Appendix A.

The shape of the conditional distribution has the potential to impact finding a suitable threshold. In this work we explore the use of *temperature scaling* as a post-processing step to adjust the propensity score distribution before its use for matching. Temperature scaling has become a common approach for re-calibrating models [14], but to the best of our knowledge has not been utilised in the context of statistical matching for causal inference. In binary classification cases such as ours, for each sample $s$ the logits $z_s$ are divided by a (learned or fixed) parameter $t$ before applying the sigmoid function:

$$z_s = \log\left(\frac{e_s}{1 - e_s}\right), \ q_s = \frac{1}{1 + e^{-z_s/t}}.$$

With $t = 1$ we obtain the original probabilities. When $t < 1$ the rescaled probabilities have a sharper distribution reaching a point mass at $t = 0$. When $t > 1$ the rescaled probabilities are smoother, reaching a uniform distribution as $t \to \infty$. As we show in our ablation study, we found rescaling to be beneficial for improving the achieved covariate balance (Table 3).

**Closeness Measure.** There are multiple metrics that can be used to measure the distance $M_{i,j}$ between samples $i \in D_T$ and $j \in D_C$, the most commonly used are *Euclidean* and *propensity score* distances. The *Euclidean distance* is defined as $M_{ij} = (X_i - X_j)^\top (X_i - X_j)$ and the *propensity score distance* as the distance between propensity scores $M_{ij} = |e_i - e_j|$. Both *Euclidean* and *propensity score* distances have the advantage of being able to control how many samples are included via a threshold. While propensity score is the most commonly used matching method, Euclidean distance matching should be preferred [19] as the goal is to produce exact balance of the observed covariates rather than balance them on average.

**Calipers.** Nearest-neighbour matching is forced to find a match for every treatment sample and is therefore at risk of finding poor matched pairs. Caliper matching is a method designed to prevent matching samples with limited covariate overlap. In this work we explore the usage of two different types of caliper, namely *fixed caliper* and *standard deviation (std) based caliper*, both applied to the estimated propensity score. *Fixed caliper* [10] is a selection rule that discards samples that have an estimated propensity score outside of a specific range; i.e. the dataset is restricted to $\{s, \forall s \in D \mid e_s \in [c, 1 - c]\}$. This allows the exclusion of examples with *extreme* propensity scores; a rule-of-thumb used in previous studies [10] considers the interval defined by $c = 0.1$, i.e. $[0.1, 0.9]$. *Standard deviation (std) based caliper* [7] is used to enforce a predetermined maximum discrepancy for each matching pair in terms of propensity score distance. The distance $M_{ij}$ is kept unaltered if $|e_i - e_j| \leq \sigma \cdot \alpha$, and is set to $\infty$ otherwise. The variable $\sigma$ is the standard deviation of the estimated propensity score distribution and $\alpha$ is a parameter controlling the percentage of *bias reduction* of the covariates. Cochran and Rubin [7] showed the smaller the $\alpha$ value the more the bias is reduced, the actual percentage of bias reduction depends on the initial standard deviation $\sigma$. Commonly used $\alpha$ values are $\{0.2, 0.4, 0.6\}$ [7].

In our application we 1) restrict potential matches based on fixed caliper and 2) follow a hybrid approach selecting the closest sample using Euclidean distance matching while defining a maximum propensity score distance between samples. The final outcome of Stage 1 is a *matched dataset* $D^*$.

**Matching Quality.** Matching quality can be assesed through measuring the balance of the covariates across the treatment and control groups. Two commonly used evaluation measures are *standardised mean differences (SMD)* and *variance ratio (VR)* [30]. In the case that high imbalance is identified, Stage 1 should be iterated until an adequate level of balanced is achieved; we provide a guideline of adequacy for each metric below. *Standardised Mean Differences* computes the difference in covariate means between each group, divided by the standard deviation of each covariate. For a single covariate $\mathbf{a}$ from $X$ we have:

$$\text{SMD} = \frac{\bar{\mathbf{a}}_T - \bar{\mathbf{a}}_C}{\sigma}, \text{ where } \sigma = \sqrt{\frac{s_T^2 + s_C^2}{2}}$$

Here, $\bar{\mathbf{a}}_T$ $(\bar{\mathbf{a}}_C)$ and $s_T^2$ $(s_C^2)$ are respectively the sample mean and variance of covariate $\mathbf{a}$ in group $D_T$ $(D_C)$. Intuitively, smaller *SMD* values are better and as a rule of thumb an *SMD* value below 0.1 expresses an adequate balance, a value between 0.1 and 0.2 is considered not balanced but acceptable, and above 0.2 shows a severe imbalance of the covariate [26]. *Variance Ratio* is defined as the ratio of covariate variances between the two groups, with an ideal value close to 1. While in some studies [40] a variance in the interval $(0, 2)$ is defined acceptable, we follow Rubin [30] and use the stricter interval $(4/5, 5/4)$ to indicate the desired proximity to 1. To obtain a single measure for all covariates $X$, we categorise *SMD* into $\leq 0.1$, $(0.1, 0.2)$, and $\geq 0.2$, and *VR* into $\leq 4/5$, $(4/5, 5/4)$, and $\geq 5/4$ and assess the distribution of covariates. We show an assessment of matching quality for one run on each dataset in Sect. 3.1, comparing the covariate balance before and after matching as well the effect of using temperature scaling.

## 2.2   Stage 2: Target Prediction

This stage is concerned with predicting a discrete target label $Y$ from covariates $X$. Inspired by Goel et al. [13] our training process involves the minimization of a loss $\mathcal{L}$ that combines a SGDRO objective function $\mathcal{L}_{SGDRO}$ and a self-consistency regularisation term $\mathcal{L}_{SC}$:

$$\mathcal{L} = \mathcal{L}_{SGDRO} + \lambda \mathcal{L}_{SC}, \tag{1}$$

where $\lambda$ is a hyperparameters controlling the regularisation strength. The SGDRO loss is inspired by GDRO [31], with the difference of considering a non-flat structure between the *target* and *spurious* labels; the hierarchy between target and spurious labels is included by considering the *spurious groups* difference within each *target group*. The SGDRO component of our loss is computed on the entire dataset $D$.

Similarly to [13], our $\mathcal{L}_{SC}$ encourages predictions $f_\theta(\cdot)$ of a matched pair $(x_T, x_C)$ in $D^\star$ to be consistent with each other and is defined as:

$$\mathcal{L}_{SC}(x_T, x_C, \theta) = \frac{1}{2}\left[KL(f_\theta(x_T)\|\tilde{m}) + KL(f_\theta(x_C)\|\tilde{m})\right], \qquad (2)$$

where $\tilde{m}$ is the average output distribution of the matched pair. While the SGDRO objective accounts for the worst-case subgroup performance, the form of the regularisation term induces model's predictions to be subgroup invariant [13].

## 3    Experiments

We conduct two sets of experiments to assess the ability of RealPatch to 1) improve the worst-case subgroup performance and reduce the subgroup performance gap in a binary classification setting, and 2) reduce dataset and model leakage w.r.t. a spurious attribute in a 211-class classification setting. We describe them in turn.

### 3.1    Reducing Subgroup Performance Gap

In this section we study the effect of our RealPatch for increasing the worst-case performance across subgroups and reducing the gap in subgroup performance. We evaluate RealPatch against a variety baselines on three datasets, and perform an ablation analysis on configurations of RealPatch. We compare approaches using **Robust Accuracy**: the lowest accuracy across the four subgroups, **Robust Gap**: the maximum accuracy distance between the subgroups, as well as **Aggregate Accuracy**: a standard measure of accuracy. Our goal is to improve the robust accuracy and gap while retaining the aggregate accuracy performance as much as possible. That is because performance degradation on a subgroup(s) might occur if this improves the worst performing subgroup (e.g. [23]).

**Datasets.** We use three publicly available datasets, CelebA[1] [21], Waterbirds[2] [31] and iWildCam-small[3] [2]. **CelebA** has 200K images of celebrity faces that come with annotations of 40 attributes. We follow the setup in [13], and consider hair colour $Y \in \{\text{blonde, non-blonde}\}$ as target label, and gender $Z \in \{\text{male, female}\}$ as spurious attribute. In this setup, the subgroup $(Y = \text{non-blonde}, Z = \text{female})$ is under-sampled in the training set (from 71,629 to 4,054) as per [13] amplifying a spurious correlation between the target and the demographic attribute. We keep all other subgroups as well as the validation and test sets unchanged. The images are aligned and resized to $128 \times 128$. For stability we repeat our experiments three times using different randomly under-sampled subgroups $(Y = \text{non-blonde}, Z = \text{female})$. **Waterbirds** has 11,788 examples of birds living on land or in water. We follow

---

[1] http://mmlab.ie.cuhk.edu.hk/projects/CelebA.html.
[2] https://github.com/kohpangwei/group_DRO.
[3] https://github.com/visipedia/iwildcam_comp/tree/master/2020.

[31] and predict $Y \in$ {waterbird, landbird}, and use the background attribute $Z \in$ {water, land} as spurious feature. The spurious correlation between target and background is present in the dataset as waterbirds appear more frequently in a water scene, whereas landbirds on land. In order to perform three runs we randomly define the train/validation/test splits while enforcing the original subgroup sizes as per [13]. **iWildCam-small** is a subset of iWildCam dataset [2], whose task is to classify animal species in camera trap images. Here, we consider two species (meleagris ocellata and crax rubra) within two camera trap locations. The dataset contains 3,349 images, specifically 2,005 (train), 640 (val) and 704 (test). These splits have a spurious correlation between animal species and locations. This experiment emphasizes the applicability of RealPatch in a small dataset setting.

**Baselines.** Here we describe the four baseline methods used for comparison. **Empirical Risk Minimization (ERM)** is a standard stochastic gradient descent model trained to minimize the overall classification loss. **Group Distributionally Robust Optimisation (GDRO)** is a stochastic algorithm proposed by [31] with the aim of optimising the worst-case performance across the subgroups. **Sub-Group Distributionally Robust Optimisation (SGDRO)** [13] as described in Sect. 2.2. **CAMEL** is a two stage approach proposed by [13] that uses the synthetic samples to define a subgroup consistency regulariser for model patching. Conceptually this model is most similar to ours, where we use real samples for model patching. The training details are in Appendix A.

**RealPatch Configurations and Hyperparameters.** RealPatch can be instantiated in many different configurations. In these experiments hyperparameters of RealPatch include the choice of *calipers*, *temperature*, and *reweighting strategies* in the propensity score estimation model as well as *self-consistency strength* $\lambda$, *adjustment coefficients* and *learning rates* in the target prediction model. To select hyperparameters for Stage 1 of RealPatch we perform a grid search, selecting the configuration with the best covariates balance in term of *SMD* and *VR*. An ablation study on such hyperparameters is provided in Sect. 3.1. As per the hyperparameters of Stage 2, we perform model selection utilising the robust accuracy on the validation set. Further details of hyperparameters used and best configuration selected are summarised in Appendix A.

**Results on CelebA.** From Table 1, RealPatch is able to significantly improve the worst-case subgroup performance and reduce the subgroup performance gap compared to the other baseline methods such as ERM, GDRO, SGDRO. Our proposed method improves the robust accuracy, robust gaps and aggregate accuracy with respect to the best baseline SGDRO by 1.86%, 1.94% and 0.14% respectively. When compared to CAMEL, RealPatch improves robust accuracy (+3.34%), but slightly worsens the robust gap (+0.1%). Compared with CAMEL, GDRO and SGDRO, RealPatch is very consistent across runs, with a standard deviation of 0.13, 0.85 and 0.9 for aggregate accuracy, robust accuracy and robust gap, in contrast to 5.59, 7.16 and 0.18 (aggregate accuracy), 3.94, 18.99 and 1.39 (robust accuracy) and 0.44, 19.65 and 1.67 (robust

**Table 1.** A comparison between RealPatch and four baselines on two benchmark datasets. The results shown are the average (standard deviation) performances over three runs. RealPatch is able to construct a model that is robust across subgroups with high robust accuracy and small robust gap.

| Dataset | Method | Aggregate Accuracy (%) ↑ | Robust Accuracy (%) ↑ | Robust Gap (%) ↓ |
|---|---|---|---|---|
| CelebA | ERM | 89.21 (0.32) | 55.3 (0.65) | 43.48 (0.68) |
| | GDRO | **90.47** (7.16) | 63.43 (18.99) | 34.77 (19.65) |
| | SGDRO | 88.92 (0.18) | 82.96 (1.39) | 7.13 (1.67) |
| | CAMEL | 84.51 (5.59) | 81.48 (3.94) | **5.09** (0.44) |
| | RealPatch (Ours) | 89.06 (0.13) | **84.82** (0.85) | 5.19 (0.9) |
| Waterbirds | ERM | 86.36 (0.39) | 66.88 (3.76) | 32.57 (3.95) |
| | GDRO | **88.26** (0.55) | 81.03 (1.16) | 14.80 (1.15) |
| | SGDRO | 86.85 (1.71) | 83.11 (3.65) | 6.61 (6.01) |
| | CAMEL | 79.0 (14.24) | 76.82 (18.0) | 7.35 (5.66) |
| | RealPatch (Ours) | 86.89 (1.34) | **84.44** (2.53) | **4.43** (4.48) |

**Table 2.** Experiments with iWildCam-small [2]. The results shown are the average (standard deviation) performances over three runs. CycleGAN-based CAMEL is not applicable for small training data (2K images).

| Method | Aggregate Accuracy (%) ↑ | Robust ↑ Accuracy (%) | Robust Gap (%) ↓ |
|---|---|---|---|
| ERM | **79.97** (1.18) | 75.43 (3.01) | 19.65 (1.96) |
| SGDRO | 78.55 (2.45) | 75.50 (3.58) | 14.28 (4.35) |
| RealPatch (Ours) | 79.36 (2.09) | **76.70** (3.19) | **11.36** (4.87) |

gap) for CAMEL, GDRO and SGDRO respectively. On inspection of matched pairs from the dataset $D^\star$, we observe preservation in pose, facial expression (e.g. smiling in most of the examples), hair style (in many cases the colour as well, but not always), and accessories such as hat and glasses. Figures 1 shows samples of retrieved matched pairs, further examples are in Appendix B. Naturally, due to use of real samples used in matching, RealPatch suffers no issues regarding quality of images in the augmented dataset often observed with generative models. Figure 1 shows CycleGAN generated examples used in the consistency regularizer in the CAMEL's loss.

**Results on Waterbirds.** Our RealPatch model can significantly reduce the gap between subgroup performances and improve the worst-case accuracy compared to all baselines. While GDRO have a better aggregate accuracy up to 1.37%, this model exhibits a higher imbalance over the subgroup performances with a robust gap of 14.80% in comparison to 4.43% of RealPatch and a robust accuracy of 81.03% as opposed to 84.44% of RealPatch. When compared to CAMEL, RealPatch shows improvements across all metrics, with +7.89% aggregate accuracy, +7.62% robust accuracy and −2.92% robust gap. Similar conclusions hold true when comparing RealPatch against the best baseline SGDRO with +1.33% robust accuracy and −2.18% robust gap. The characteristics preserved between matched pairs are less obvious than in CelebA, mainly observing matching across the bird's primary/body colour; examples are shown in Appendix B.

**Results on iWildCam-Small.** We show results comparing RealPatch against ERM and the best baseline SGDRO in Table 2. When compared to the two baseline methods, our RealPatch improves robust accuracy by +1.27% and +1.2% and robust gap by −8.29% and −2.92%. It is worth noticing in this setting CycleGAN-based CAMEL is not applicable due to insufficient data to train CycleGAN. Examples of retrieved matched pairs are in Appendix B.

Please refer to Appendix B for the full results of Table 1 and Table 2 which include the four subgroup performances.

**Ablation Analysis.** We perform ablations on three of the main components of our statistical matching stage, analysing the effect of 1) temperature scaling, 2) fixed caliper and 3) std-based caliper towards matching quality. Since the distribution of propensity scores is altered by temperature scaling, and the propensity score is used by both types of calipers to exclude possible matches, these components are fairly coupled. We compare results obtained using different matching configurations, starting with the best configuration optimised in term of covariates balance achieved and (a) removing temperature scaling (setting $t = 1$), (b) removing the fixed caliper (setting $c = 0$) and (c) removing the std-based caliper (setting $\alpha = \infty$). In Table 3 we report the covariate balance before $(D)$ and after $(D^\star)$ matching for a single run of CelebA and Waterbirds, under all the three settings.

It should be noted that the selected best configuration for all three runs of Waterbirds do not include the usage of std-based caliper, there is therefor no difference between $D^\star$(best) and $D^\star(\alpha = \infty)$ in Table 3. A similar analysis for iWildCam-small is in Appendix B. We evaluate the matching quality through Standardised Mean Difference $(SMD)$ and Variance Ratio $(VR)$ as described in Sect. 2.1. All datasets benefit from matching, resulting in a better covariate balance than the original dataset. In CelebA we are able to produce an adequate balance $(SMD \leq 0.1$ and $4/5 \leq VR \leq 5/4)$ for most of the covariates, 1977 out of 2048 for $SMD$ and 2038 out of 2048 for $VR$. For the Waterbirds dataset, we achieve a slightly less prominent balance, nevertheless, improvements with respect to the original training dataset are achieved. Across all datasets the strongest effect is obtained by removing the influence of the **fixed caliper**. Since the propensity score characterises how likely an image is to belong to a subgroup, preserving all images at the extremes before calculating possible pairs is seen to be highly detrimental. The impact of **temperature scaling** and **std. caliper** is weaker overall, or absent for Waterbids under the setting $\alpha = \infty$, though still worth investigating for the specific application.

While the use of calipers is relatively well known in causal inference, temperature scaling is not commonly explored. We inspect the effect of its usage on the propensity score distribution. For a single run of CelebA, in Fig. 3 we show the estimated propensity score distribution for each of the four subgroups for $D^\star$ (the after matching dataset). Post-matching, the propensity score is approximately bimodal, showing that our procedure is balancing the propensity distribution across the subgroups. We show the distribution of $D^\star$ generated with $t = 1$ (no temperature) and $D^\star$ generated with $t = 0.7$ (selected temperature). Decreas-

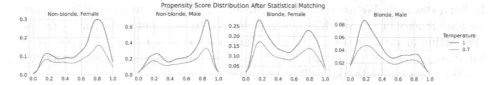

**Fig. 3.** Estimated propensity score distribution on CelebaA dataset after matching, shown for each of the four subgroups. We compare the original distribution (blue, $t = 1$) with its scaled version using the selected temperature (orange, $t = 0.7$). Post-matching, the propensity score is approximately bimodal, showing that our procedure is balancing the propensity distribution across subgroups. Decreasing $t$ makes the two modes have more similar values, resulting in a matched dataset with better covariate balance in terms of *SMD* and *VR* (Table 3).

**Table 3.** Comparison of the covariate balance in 1) the original dataset $D$, 2) the matched dataset $D^*$ 3) the matched dataset $D^*$ with no temperature scaling 4) $D^*$ with no fixed caliper and 5) $D^*$ with no std-based caliper. The results are reported for a single run per dataset. Our matching procedure can successfully improve the covariate balance in both benchmark datasets, with fixed caliper significantly boosting its quality.

| Dataset | | SMD | | | VR | | |
|---|---|---|---|---|---|---|---|
| | | $\leq 0.1$ ↑ | $(0.1, 0.2)$ ↓ | $\geq 0.2$ ↓ | $\leq 4/5$ ↓ | $(4/5, 5/4)$ ↑ | $\geq 5/4$ ↓ |
| CelebA | $D$ | 348 | 344 | 1356 | 309 | 859 | 880 |
| | $D^*$ (best) | **1977** | 71 | 0 | 0 | **2038** | 10 |
| | $D^*$ ($t = 1$) | 1957 | 91 | 0 | 2 | 2032 | 14 |
| | $D^*$ ($c = 0$) | 1522 | 482 | 44 | 13 | 1797 | 238 |
| | $D^*$ ($\alpha = \infty$) | 1909 | 138 | 1 | 11 | 2028 | 9 |
| Waterbirds | $D$ | 376 | 346 | 1326 | 992 | 723 | 333 |
| | $D^*$ (best) | **1436** | 512 | 100 | 18 | **1533** | 497 |
| | $D^*$ ($t = 1$) | 1409 | 526 | 113 | 13 | 1482 | 553 |
| | $D^*$ ($c = 0$) | 852 | 596 | 600 | 50 | 1104 | 894 |
| | $D^*$ ($\alpha = \infty$) | 1436 | 512 | 100 | 18 | 1533 | 497 |

ing $t$ leads to the two modes having more similar values, resulting in matched dataset with better covariate balance in terms of *SMD* and *VR* (Table 3). We observe a similar effect on the Waterbirds dataset, shown in Appendix B.

   dummy

## 3.2 Reducing Dataset and Model Leakage

In this section we study the effect of our RealPatch on dataset and model leakage.

**Leakage.** We use dataset leakage and model leakage [35] to measure dataset bias. Dataset leakage measures how much information the true labels leak about gender, and corresponds to the accuracy of predicting gender from the ground truth annotations. In model leakage, the model is being trained on the dataset, and we measure how much the predicted labels leak about gender.

**imSitu dataset.** We use the imSitu dataset [37] of situation recognition, where we have images of 211 activities being performed by an agent (person). We follow the setting of prior works [35,41] and study the activity bias with respect to a binarised gender of the agent. The dataset contains 24,301 images (training), 7,730 images (validation), 7,669 images (test).

**Matching Results.** We performed matching on the training data, and include all matched pairs as a rebalanced dataset to analyse the leakage. On this dataset, all samples have been matched, and the dataset size after matching has been doubled. This is expected, given the dataset has 211 classes with $44-182$ samples per class, which is significantly less than in CelebA. Doubling the size of the dataset does not mean we include every sample twice. Instead this should be seen as rebalancing/resampling the dataset based on how many times each sample has been matched. For matching we use the features extracted with a pre-trained ResNet101 model. The selected hyperparameters are *spurious reweighting* in propensity score estimation, a temperature of $t = 0.6$, $c = 0$ in the fixed caliper, and $\alpha = 0.2$ in the std-based caliper. This configuration was selected based on the best covariates balanced achieved on the training set: we can reach an adequate balance with an *SMD* value below 0.1 and *VR* close to 1 for most of the 1024 covariates used, 992 and 1010 respectively compared to 327 and 510 of the original dataset. A table with all the covariates balance is in Appendix B.

**Leakage Results.** We follow the same architectures and training procedures as [35] to measure the dataset and model leakage. We compare our results with the rebalancing strategies based on gender-label co-occurrences proposed in [35]. We report our findings in Table 4. The results clearly show that dataset rebalancing via matching helps to achieve the best trade-off between debiasing (the dataset and the model leakage), and performance (F1 and mAP scores). We achieve significant reduction in dataset leakage (nearly no leakage 55.13 versus original 68.35) and model leakage (68.76 versus 76.79), while maintaining the accuracy of the model with mAP and F1 scores comparable to those achieved with the original training data. This is in contrast to rebalancing based on co-occurrences

**Table 4.** Matching-based rebalancing in imSitu achieves the best leakage-accuracy trade-off. It shows nearly no dataset leakage, leading to a reduction in model leakage while maintaining overall accuracy. This is in contrast to the co-occurrence-based rebalancing based on gender-label statistics (e.g. $\alpha = 1$ [35]), where a reduction in dataset leakage does not lead to reduction in model leakage in a meaningful way, and the overall accuracy drops.

| Data | Dataset leakage $\lambda_D \downarrow$ | Model leakage $\lambda_M \downarrow$ | mAP $\uparrow$ | F1 $\uparrow$ |
|---|---|---|---|---|
| original training data | 68.35 (0.16) | 76.79 (0.17) | 41.12 | 39.91 |
| balancing with $\alpha = 3$ [35] | 68.11 (0.55) | 75.79 (0.49) | 39.20 | 37.64 |
| balancing with $\alpha = 2$ [35] | 68.15 (0.32) | 75.46 (0.32) | 37.53 | 36.41 |
| balancing with $\alpha = 1$ [35] | 53.99 (0.69) | 74.83 (0.34) | 34.63 | 33.94 |
| RealPatch (ours) | 55.13 (0.76) | 68.76 (0.69) | 38.74 | 38.13 |

of gender and activity labels [35]. In the case of a rebalanced dataset with $\alpha = 1$ that achieves nearly no dataset leakage (53.99), the model trained on this dataset leaks similarly to the model trained on the original data (74.83 versus 76.79), and has a significant drop in the overall performance. This suggests that statistical matching helps to reduce dataset leakage in a meaningful way as the model trained on the rebalanced dataset can reduce leakage as well.

## 4    Limitations and Intended Use

While *SMD* and *VR* are valuable metrics to indicate the quality of the matched dataset, there is no rule-of-thumb for interpreting whether the covariates have been *sufficiently* balanced. Supplementing *SMD* and *VR* with manual inspection of matched pairs and evaluating on a downstream task is still required.

Additionally, RealPatch currently only handles binary spurious attributes, requiring additional work (such as [22]) to handle matching over multiple treatments. It is worth noticing that also the baselines considered, GDRO, SGDRO and CAMEL, have only been tested on a binary spurious attribute. We intend to explore the usage of RealPatch for non-binary spurious attributes in the future work. A natural extension would be to use a One-vs-Rest approach for matching: for each sample find the closest sample having a different value of the spurious attribute.

## 5    Conclusions

We present RealPatch, a two-stage framework for model patching by utilising a dataset with real samples using statistical matching. We demonstrate the effectiveness of RealPatch on three benchmark datasets, CelebA, Waterbirds and iWildCam-small. We show that RealPatch's Stage 1 is successfully balancing a dataset with respect to a spurious attribute and we effectively improve subgroup performances by including such matched dataset in the training objective of Stage 2. We also highlight the applicability of RealPatch in a small dataset setting experimenting with the so-called iWildCam-small. Compared to CAMEL, a related approach that requires the training of multiple CycleGAN models, we see competitive reductions in the subgroup performance gap without depending on the ability to generate synthetic images. We also show the effectiveness of RealPatch for reducing dataset leakage and model leakage in a 211-class setting, where relying on generative model-based patching such as CAMEL is impractical. RealPatch can successfully eliminate dataset leakage while reducing model leakage and maintaining high utility. Our findings show the importance of selecting calipers to achieve a satisfactory covariates balance and serve as a guideline for future work on statistical matching on visual data. We encourage the use of RealPatch as a competitive baseline for strategic rebalancing and model patching, especially in the case where developing models for image generation is prohibitive or impractical.

**Acknowledgments.** This research was supported by a European Research Council (ERC) Starting Grant for the project "Bayesian Models and Algorithms for Fairness and Transparency", funded under the European Union's Horizon 2020 Framework Programme (grant agreement no. 851538). NQ is also supported by the Basque Government through the BERC 2018-2021 program and by Spanish Ministry of Sciences, Innovation and Universities: BCAM Severo Ochoa accreditation SEV-2017-0718.

# References

1. Arjovsky, M., Bottou, L., Gulrajani, I., Lopez-Paz, D.: Invariant risk minimization. CoRR abs/1907.02893 (2019)
2. Beery, S., Cole, E., Gjoka, A.: The iWildCam 2020 competition dataset. CoRR abs/2004.10340 (2020)
3. Biglan, A., Ary, D., Wagenaar, A.C.: The value of interrupted time-series experiments for community intervention research. Prev. Sci. **1**(1), 31–49 (2000)
4. Chastain, R.L., et al.: Estimated full scale IQ in an adult heroin addict population (1985)
5. Choi, Y., Choi, M., Kim, M., Ha, J.W., Kim, S., Choo, J.: StarGAN: unified generative adversarial networks for multi-domain image-to-image translation. In: Proceedings of the IEEE Conference on Computer Vision and Pattern Recognition (CVPR), June 2018
6. Christian, P., et al.: Prenatal micronutrient supplementation and intellectual and motor function in early school-aged children in Nepal. JAMA **304**(24), 2716–2723 (2010)
7. Cochran, W.G., Rubin, D.B.: Controlling bias in observational studies: a review. Sankhyā Indian J. Stat. Ser. A, 417–446 (1973)
8. Cox, D.R., Snell, E.J.: The Analysis of Binary Data. Chapman and Hall, London (1989)
9. Creager, E., Jacobsen, J., Zemel, R.S.: Environment inference for invariant learning. In: Meila, M., Zhang, T. (eds.) Proceedings of the 38th International Conference on Machine Learning, ICML 2021, 18–24 July 2021, Virtual Event. Proceedings of Machine Learning Research, vol. 139, pp. 2189–2200. PMLR (2021)
10. Crump, R.K., Hotz, V.J., Imbens, G.W., Mitnik, O.A.: Dealing with limited overlap in estimation of average treatment effects. Biometrika **96**(1), 187–199 (2009)
11. Denton, E., Hutchinson, B., Mitchell, M., Gebru, T., Zaldivar, A.: Image counterfactual sensitivity analysis for detecting unintended bias. arXiv preprint arXiv:1906.06439v3 (2020)
12. DeVries, T., Taylor, G.W.: Improved regularization of convolutional neural networks with cutout. arXiv preprint arXiv:1708.04552 (2017)
13. Goel, K., Gu, A., Li, Y., Re, C.: Model patching: closing the subgroup performance gap with data augmentation. In: International Conference on Learning Representations (2020)
14. Guo, C., Pleiss, G., Sun, Y., Weinberger, K.Q.: On calibration of modern neural networks. In: International Conference on Machine Learning, pp. 1321–1330. PMLR (2017)
15. He, K., Zhang, X., Ren, S., Sun, J.: Deep residual learning for image recognition. In: CVPR, pp. 770–778 (2016)
16. Heinze-Deml, C., Meinshausen, N., Peters, J.: Invariant causal prediction for nonlinear models. J. Causal Inference **6**(2) (2018)

17. Kehrenberg, T., Bartlett, M., Sharmanska, V., Quadrianto, N.: Addressing missing sources with adversarial support-matching. arXiv preprint arXiv:2203.13154 (2022)
18. Kehrenberg, T., Bartlett, M., Thomas, O., Quadrianto, N.: Null-sampling for interpretable and fair representations. In: Vedaldi, A., Bischof, H., Brox, T., Frahm, J.-M. (eds.) ECCV 2020, Part XXVI. LNCS, vol. 12371, pp. 565–580. Springer, Cham (2020). https://doi.org/10.1007/978-3-030-58574-7_34
19. King, G., Nielsen, R.: Why propensity scores should not be used for matching. Political Anal. **27**(4), 435–454 (2019)
20. Kolesnikov, A., Beyer, L., Zhai, X., Puigcerver, J., Yung, J., Gelly, S., Houlsby, N.: Big transfer (BiT): general visual representation learning. In: Vedaldi, A., Bischof, H., Brox, T., Frahm, J.-M. (eds.) ECCV 2020. LNCS, vol. 12350, pp. 491–507. Springer, Cham (2020). https://doi.org/10.1007/978-3-030-58558-7_29
21. Liu, Z., Luo, P., Wang, X., Tang, X.: Deep learning face attributes in the wild. In: Proceedings of the IEEE International Conference on Computer Vision, pp. 3730–3738 (2015)
22. Lopez, M.J., Gutman, R.: Estimation of causal effects with multiple treatments: a review and new ideas. Stat. Sci., 432–454 (2017)
23. Martinez, N., Bertran, M., Sapiro, G.: Minimax pareto fairness: a multi objective perspective. In: International Conference on Machine Learning, pp. 6755–6764. PMLR (2020)
24. Mitrovic, J., McWilliams, B., Walker, J.C., Buesing, L.H., Blundell, C.: Representation learning via invariant causal mechanisms. In: International Conference on Learning Representations (2021). https://openreview.net/forum?id=9p2ekP904Rs
25. Morgan, S.L.: Counterfactuals, causal effect heterogeneity, and the catholic school effect on learning. Sociol. Educ., 341–374 (2001)
26. Normand, S.L.T., et al.: Validating recommendations for coronary angiography following acute myocardial infarction in the elderly: a matched analysis using propensity scores. J. Clin. Epidemiol. **54**(4), 387–398 (2001)
27. Perry, C.L., et al.: Project northland: outcomes of a community wide alcohol use prevention program during early adolescence. Am. J. Public Health **86**(7), 956–965 (1996)
28. Peters, J., Bühlmann, P., Meinshausen, N.: Causal inference using invariant prediction: identification and confidence intervals. J. R. Stat. Soc. Ser. B **78**(5) (2016)
29. Rubin, D.B.: Matching to remove bias in observational studies. Biometrics, 159–183 (1973)
30. Rubin, D.B.: Using propensity scores to help design observational studies: application to the tobacco litigation. Health Serv. Outcomes Res. Methodol. **2**(3), 169–188 (2001)
31. Sagawa, S., Koh, P.W., Hashimoto, T.B., Liang, P.: Distributionally robust neural networks for group shifts: On the importance of regularization for worst-case generalization. arXiv preprint arXiv:1911.08731 (2019)
32. Saunders, A.M., et al.: Association of apolipoprotein E allele $\in$4 with late-onset familial and sporadic Alzheimer's disease. Neurology **43**(8), 1467 (1993)
33. Sharmanska, V., Hendricks, L.A., Darrell, T., Quadrianto, N.: Contrastive examples for addressing the tyranny of the majority. arXiv preprint arXiv:2004.06524 (2020)
34. Veitch, V., D'Amour, A., Yadlowsky, S., Eisenstein, J.: Counterfactual invariance to spurious correlations: Why and how to pass stress tests. CoRR abs/2106.00545 (2021). https://arxiv.org/abs/2106.00545

35. Wang, T., Zhao, J., Yatskar, M., Chang, K.W., Ordonez, V.: Balanced datasets are not enough: estimating and mitigating gender bias in deep image representations. In: ICCV (2019)
36. Yang, K., Qinami, K., Fei-Fei, L., Deng, J., Russakovsky, O.: Towards fairer datasets: filtering and balancing the distribution of the people subtree in the ImageNet hierarchy. In: Proceedings of the 2020 Conference on Fairness, Accountability, and Transparency, pp. 547–558. Association for Computing Machinery (2020)
37. Yatskar, M., Zettlemoyer, L., Farhadi, A.: Situation recognition: visual semantic role labeling for image understanding. In: CVPR (2016)
38. Yun, S., Han, D., Oh, S.J., Chun, S., Choe, J., Yoo, Y.: CutMix: regularization strategy to train strong classifiers with localizable features. In: International Conference on Computer Vision (ICCV) (2019)
39. Zhang, H., Cisse, M., Dauphin, Y.N., Lopez-Paz, D.: mixup: Beyond empirical risk minimization. In: International Conference on Learning Representations (2018)
40. Zhang, Z., Kim, H.J., Lonjon, G., Zhu, Y., et al.: Balance diagnostics after propensity score matching. Ann. Transl. Med. 7(1) (2019)
41. Zhao, J., Wang, T., Yatskar, M., Ordonez, V., Chang, K.W.: Men also like shopping: reducing gender bias amplification using corpus-level constraints. In: Conference on Empirical Methods in Natural Language Processing (EMNLP), pp. 2941–2951 (2017)
42. Zhu, J.Y., Park, T., Isola, P., Efros, A.A.: Unpaired image-to-image translation using cycle-consistent adversarial networks. In: Proceedings of the IEEE International Conference on Computer Vision (ICCV), October 2017

# Background-Insensitive Scene Text Recognition with Text Semantic Segmentation

Liang Zhao, Zhenyao Wu, Xinyi Wu, Greg Wilsbacher, and Song Wang[✉]

University of South Carolina, Columbia, SC 29201, USA
{lz4,zhenyao,xinyiw}@email.sc.edu, gregw@mailbox.sc.edu,
songwang@cec.sc.edu

**Abstract.** Scene Text Recognition (STR) has many important applications in computer vision. Complex backgrounds continue to be a big challenge for STR because they interfere with text feature extraction. Many existing methods use attentional regions, bounding boxes or polygons to reduce such interference. However, the text regions located by these methods still contain much undesirable background interference. In this paper, we propose a Background-Insensitive approach BINet by explicitly leveraging the text Semantic Segmentation (SSN) to extract texts more accurately. SSN is trained on a set of existing segmentation data, whose volume is only 0.03% of STR training data. This prevents the large-scale pixel-level annotations of the STR training data. To effectively utilize the segmentation cues, we design new segmentation refinement and embedding blocks for refining text-masks and reinforcing visual features. Additionally, we propose an efficient pipeline that utilizes Synthetic Initialization (SI) for STR models trained only on real data (1.7% of STR training data), instead of on both synthetic and real data from scratch. Experiments show that the proposed method can recognize text from complex backgrounds more effectively, achieving state-of-the-art performance on several public datasets.

**Keywords:** Scene text recognition · Semantic segmentation

## 1 Introduction

Scene Text Recognition (STR) aims at accurately recognizing irregular and incidental texts in complicated scenes and it has wide applications in video information retrieval [63], criminal investigation [1], robotic intelligence [45], and autonomous driving [30]. STR is still a very challenging task in computer vision, due to large variation of the text color, font and size, as well as the possible complex background where the text is located. In real world, the complexity of scene-text background comes from many factors, such as camera motion, scene change, low lighting, etc. In extracting text features for STR, any interference

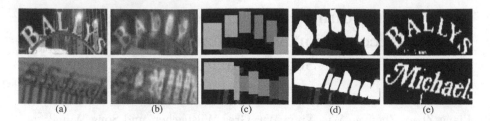

**Fig. 1.** An illustration of strategies focusing on text features for Scene Text Recognition (STR): (a) whole input images, (b) attention map [19,84], (c) bounding box [48], (d) conventional text segmentation [40], and (e) text semantic segmentation (ours).

of background information may negatively affect the recognition performance. In this paper, we study BINet that is less sensitive to the complex background.

To mitigate the background interference for STR, different strategies have been explored to derive only-text-related feature representation. These mainly can be categorized into attention-based [19,49,84,85], bounding-box-based [48], and conventional-segmentation-based [39,40,43] by focusing on different areas around the text, as illustrated in items (b) through (d) of Fig. 1. However, none of these strategies can optimally exclude the background interference. For example, the attention-based strategy could wrongly entangle neighboring characters or miss some distinctive characters, as shown in Fig. 1(b). The bounding box-based and conventional-segmentation-based strategies may still include unrelated background regions as part of the text, as shown in Fig. 1(c–d). Clearly, a strategy that can more accurately separate out text from background may further facilitate accurate text feature extraction and STR.

To achieve this goal, in this paper we propose to conduct *text semantic segmentation* (SSN) for enhancing STR. Following general-purpose image semantic segmentation [52,57], the text semantic segmentation here aims to classify each pixel of text image as either text or background and therefore, partitions the image into two semantic segments, as shown in Fig. 1(e). Note that, text semantic segmentation is different from conventional text segmentation. The latter segments out a compact text region which may still contain part of the background, e.g., the hollow regions in character 'B' in Fig. 1(d). On the contrary, text semantic segmentation fully separates the text and background at pixel level, and they can provide more accurate text features for recognition.

However, the SSN requires accurate pixel-level annotations, which are laborious to obtain. Embedding a pretrained network instead of integrated training for assisting specific tasks has been widely used in many general image segmentation works [6,18,34,66]. However, few studies [17,39] design the text segmentation (usually by generating pseudo mask annotations), let alone any independent text segmentation, and the previous recognition improvements are limited [17]. In this work, we leverage the explicit text semantic segmentation with limited knowledge to our advantage in STR without labeling mask annotations for huge

STR training data. Here, the SSN is trained on existing real data, whose volume is only 0.03% compared to the STR training data.

Furthermore, to address the problems of data deficiencies and domain differences between SSN and STR, and expand SSN's generalization capability in STR task, we further design two blocks of segmentation refinement and embedding that steer the knowledge from SSN to STR. Recent state-of-the-art STR models typically design the pixel-wise fusion [79] or transformer [84] in utilizing the sequential, attentional or positional information. The guiding methods are not sufficiently studied and the transformer is extremely expensive in computing resources. In natural language processing (NLP) community, the large-scale pretrained model [56] is modified for downstream tasks [12] by CNNs or distribution losses [67]. Following this insight, we develop efficient networks to utilize the limited prior knowledge from SSN and facilitate the visual cues in STR.

Typically, the state-of-the-art STR models are required to be end-to-end trained on the synthetic dataset, and further training on real data can boost the performance. However, the whole training process is cumbersome and takes up to 672 GPU hours [19]. Inspired by the wide practice that ResNet based models are initialized by ImageNet weights, we propose to use the backbone weights pretrained on synthetic data for general-purpose STR model initialization denoted as Synthetic Initialization (SI). It can be adopted by any STR models without training on synthetic data. Experiments show that our method, trained after 5 h with 1 GPU card, can achieve the state-of-the-art STR performance on several public evaluation benchmarks.

In summary, our contribution and achievement are described below:

1. We propose a novel and efficient BINet that leverage text semantic segmentation (SSN) for enhancing scene text recognition without large-scale pixel-level annotations. It also gets rid of generating pseudo segmentation labels for self-supervised, semi-supervised, or weakly-supervised training.
2. The text segmentation refinement and embedding modules are specially designed for conditioning background-insensitive features, which efficiently steer the limited knowledge from SSN to STR.
3. We design a new pipeline with Synthetic Initialization (SI) for STR, replacing conventional expensive end-to-end training on synthetic data. The model overcomes great performance degradation when trained only on real data.
4. The proposed method achieves new state-of-the-art performances on various widely-used datasets.

## 2   Related Work

### 2.1   Scene Text Recognition

**Attention-Based Text Recognition.** Initially enlightened by contextual inference in natural language processing (NLP) community, the attention-based STR models are equipped with the RNN [36,81], canonical attention BLSTM [13,42,60,86], bidirectional attention BLSTM [11,61], two-dimension attention

BLSTM [4,38,75,80] and Transformer decoders [3,7,19,55,93], instead of Convolutional Neural Networks (CNN) based classifier [20], in an effort to boost the language expression in STR. The language models utilize one or two dimensional visual features to consider the character relationships from unidirectional or bidirectional way with attention. Later, the attention is expanded to encoders to improve feature representations [19,25,41,55,76,87]. These methods sufficiently explore the linguistic information and feature representations in lack of character details, but the attention maps might easily miss some small characters with arbitrary locations, or entangle with neighbors to generate wrong predictions.

**Box-Based Text Recognition.** Early studies with limited bounding boxes or polygon ground truths mainly adopted segmentation methods for the localization and detection of characters or words. Neumann *et al.* [51] proposed the connected components [24] to binarize the image as coarse segmentation for text recognition. Then a discriminating clustering algorithm [82] and a hybrid HMM Maxout [2] technique were used to capture character substructures from regions. But they fail to separate contiguous characters and integrate broken strokes. The CNN-based supervised methods [29,48,74] usually compute a text saliency map by using the character classifier and then generate character or word bounding boxes. They are usually boosted by strengthened recognizer [10,44,47], or rectification modules [40,42,82,90]. Without well-designed module integration and sufficient pixel-level annotations, the segmentation module is barely learned and evaluated, mainly for text detection, instead of directly for text recognition.

**Conventional Segmentation-Based Text Recognition.** To handle irregular scene text recognition, Jaderberg *et al.* [28] proposed to recognize the characters or words within the detected regions by using at least 9 million images and a 90k word dictionary. The problem is formulated indirectly by embedding text strings into subspace vectors, which could calculate the nearest neighbor prediction results. Following this work, many segmentation-region-based methods [26,36,43,60,64] were proposed for STR. Recently, Liu *et al.* [42] employed a character encoder to rectify the accurate local character region, but it might contain neighboring characters. Liao *et al.* [40] utilized a Fully Convolutional Network (FCN) to estimate character polygons under the supervision of the processed bounding boxes. But such polygons and ground truths still contain background parts. Zhang *et al.* [90] utilized attention to adaptively increase the tightness of the local character regions, and Wan *et al.* [70] further rectified spurious attention by complementing the character regions with position and order attention. These methods applied multiple modules to refine segmentation regions for predicting more accurate recognition probabilities of each class. As mentioned earlier, these conventional text segmentation methods may still mix part of background into text segments. In this paper, we propose to leverage text semantic segmentation into STR by more accurately separating the text and background in the image.

## 2.2   Text Semantic Segmentation

Aiming at predicting all the text pixels, the text semantic segmentation has been studied in several text-related tasks, e.g., text style transfer [33] and scene text removal [22]. These methods directly implement the supervised semantic segmentation and transfer text styles in small datasets of the tasks, in incorporating with generative adversarial networks (GANs). For the Scene Text Recognition (STR), the closest work is from Luo *et al.* [46] that uses the GANs to separate text content from the backgrounds. However, it fails to generate characters on complex backgrounds due to the mode-dropping phenomenon [8] and the lingering gap [92] of GANs trained on the supervised synthesized samples. The power of generators highly depends on the synthesized character style samples and then the capacity of synthesis engines. Several studies [40, 83] purposely generate polygons as pseudo ground truths on self-supervised or weakly-supervised training. To overcome the limitations of synthesized training samples and pseudo ground truths, we independently pretrain text semantic segmentation network (SSN) only on real data, which is only 0.03% of STR training data. The model does not need to generate pseudo ground truths or synthesize reference samples. We also well design text segmentation refinement and embedding modules for steering knowledge from SSN to STR.

## 2.3   Training Strategy

Most state-of-the-art STR models are trained end-to-end from scratch on synthetic data [23, 27]. Some works [38, 39, 41] continually train extra real data to reduce domain drifts. Recently, Beak *et al.* [5] demonstrate that training only on real data (1.7% of synthetic data) causes great performance degradation, while training on synthetic and real data together can definitely boost the recognition. Inspired by NLP works [16, 35] that utilize general pretrained models for diverse downstream tasks, we further propose the Synthetic Initialization (SI) that is a backbone weights solely pretrained on synthetic data. Note that the backbone refers to ResNet (and an encode unit) that is generally used as feature extractor in STR models [19, 55, 84]. Thus, the pretrained backbone weights can be widely used to initialize feature extractor in any STR models. Only the specific design of each method needs to be trained, instead of the whole model trained on synthetic data from scratch. We explore whether it can overcome the performance degradation caused by real data deficiency (1.7% of synthetic data).

## 3   STR with Text Segmentation

### 3.1   Overview

The proposed BINet is shown in Fig. 2. It consists of a text semantic segmentation network (SSN), a feature extractor, a segmentation refinement module, a segmentation embedding module and a transformer-based language decoder.

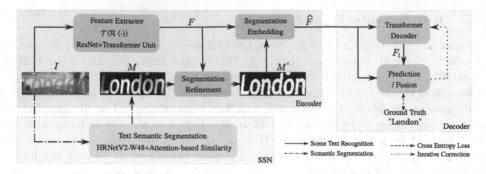

**Fig. 2.** The framework of the proposed BINet. The input image $I$ and text semantic segmentation $M$ from SSN are fed into the network. The extracted feature $F$ is used to refine the segmentation map $M$ and obtain $M'$. Then $M'$ is embedded back to $F$ for visual feature $\hat{F}$. The decoder generates language feature $F_l$ with 3 iterations of correction. The text predictions from the combination of features are supervised by the text ground truths via a cross-entropy recognition loss.

Following recent works [19,55,84], we use the combination of ResNet $\mathcal{R}$ and Transformer units $\mathcal{T}$ as the feature extractor. Given an image $I$, the feature map $F$ is generated by $F = \mathcal{T}(\mathcal{R}(I))$ with the shape of $H \times W \times C$, where $H$ and $W$ are the height and width of the features, and $C$ is the number of channels (we set $C = 512$ in this paper). At the same time, the image $I$ is also fed into the text semantic segmentation network which produces a semantic segmentation $M$. The initial feature $F$ and segmentation map $M$ are fed into the proposed segmentation refinement and the segmentation embedding blocks to obtain the segmentation-embedded feature $\hat{F}$. Later, a language decoder is employed to obtain the final prediction, which is composed of multi-layer transformers [68] with the iterative correction strategy. Specifically, the language decoder is pre-trained on an unlabeled natural language processing dataset following Fang *et al.* [19] to learn the linguistic knowledge $F_l$ and corresponding language vectors $V_d^i$ $(i = 1, 2, 3)$ from $\hat{F}$. Following previous works [84], $\hat{F}$ and $F_l$ are fused recurrently to generate the refined probability distributions as final text prediction.

### 3.2 Semantic Segmentation Network

Text semantic segmentation can indicate accurate characters from background. To achieve background-insensitive text feature representation, we propose to explicitly model the text semantic segmentation network (SSN) on real data. The SSN is firstly pre-trained on two real-world text datasets [14,78] with pixel-level annotations. The total data here is around 4,000 images, accounting for only 0.03% of STR 16 million training data. The SSN is equipped with HRNetV2-W48 [72] as the backbone, and utilizes an attention module [78] as head to generate the final semantic segmentation results. Specifically, the image $I$ is fed into the backbone to get the feature map $x_f$ and initial semantic segmentation

$x_{seg}$. Then taking $x_{seg}$, $x_f$ and $I$ as inputs, the attention module generates the segmentation result $M$, which is a soft map, as shown in Fig. 2.

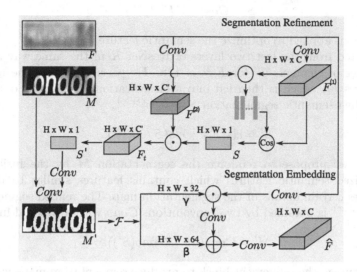

**Fig. 3.** The network of segmentation refinement and embedding blocks in BINet. Different colors of *Conv* represents different series of convolution layers, the *Cos* indicates cosine operation, and the $\odot$ and $+$ mean pixel-wise multiplication and addition, as described in Sects. 3.3 and 3.4.

## 3.3  Segmentation Refinement

Due to limited number of images with pixel-level annotations used for training the SSN and the problem of domain shifts in STR datasets, the quality of text semantic segmentation results produced by the SSN are possibly unsatisfactory for STR. To address these issues, we propose to refine the segmentation $M$ by utilizing the image features from STR training data, which compensate the details of segmentation maps, as shown in Fig. 3. Firstly, the features $F$ is fed into a two-dimensional convolution layer *Conv* to get global features $F^{(1)}$:

$$F^{(1)} = Conv(F) \in \mathbb{R}^{H \times W \times C}, \tag{1}$$

where the number of channels $C$ is 512. Then we extract the representative vector $V_c \in \mathbb{R}^C$ [89] by pixel-wise multiplying $F^{(1)}$ and the segmentation $M$, and then averaging over pixels within $M$,

$$V_c = \frac{\sum_{m=1,n=1}^{W,H} F^{(1)}_{m,n,c} \odot M_{m,n}}{\sum_{m=1,n=1}^{W,H} M_{m,n}}. \tag{2}$$

The vector $V_c$ is related to texts by removing the background interference. To find features similar to the vector $V_c$ and compensate the segmentation map $M$, we use the cosine distance $CosSim$ to calculate the similarity map $S \in \mathbb{R}^{H \times W \times 1}$ between the representative vector $V_c$ and each pixel of the features $F^{(1)}$:

$$S = CosSim(F^{(1)}, V_c). \tag{3}$$

The map is applied to optimize the semantic feature $F^{(2)} \in \mathbb{R}^{H \times W \times C'}$ which is constructed from the last two layers of ResNet $\mathcal{R}$ in the same way as $F^{(1)}$. The number of channels $C'$ for $F^{(2)}$ is 128. $F^{(2)}$ is used to get the accurate text features $F_t$, which is then fed into a classification layer $cls$ to obtain the corresponding semantic segmentation $S' \in \mathbb{R}^{H \times W \times 1}$,

$$S' = cls(F_t) = cls(S \odot F^{(2)}). \tag{4}$$

Finally, we propose to reinforce the segmentation $M$ by the fusion with the optimized semantic features which contains features similar to the text and restores certain details of the segmentation map. The refined segmentation $M' \in \mathbb{R}^{H \times W \times 1}$ is obtained by two convolutions $Conv$ with a residual fusion.

$$M' = Conv(M + Conv(S')). \tag{5}$$

To encourage the refinement block to produce segmentation maps with high confidence, we design a segmentation regularization term $\mathcal{L}_m$ as:

$$\mathcal{L}_m = \frac{1}{H \times W} \sum (\sigma - |M' - \sigma|), \tag{6}$$

where $H \times W$ is the number of pixels in the segmentation map $M'$, and $\sigma$ is a threshold of the convergence.

### 3.4   Segmentation Embedding

The affine transformation could learn to recover high-quality texture based on semantic segmentation maps [77]. Thus, we develop the segmentation embedding module to embed the segmentation $M'$ into image features $F$ to indicate text details for STR. Specifically, the refined segmentation $M'$ is modeled into two transformation parameters $\gamma$ and $\beta$ by a mapping function $\mathcal{F}$ [77]:

$$\gamma, \beta = \mathcal{F}(M'), \tag{7}$$

where $\mathcal{F}$ contains two branches of convolutional layers that are optimized with our BINet. Then, the learned parameters are adopted into the features as:

$$\hat{F} = F \odot \gamma + \beta, \tag{8}$$

where $\odot$ is the element-wise multiplication. With the learned conditions, the feature maps $F$ are guided by the refined text segmentation for text recognition.

## 3.5   Optimization

For the individual training of text recognition in our proposed BINet, the objectives consist of text recognition losses and the segmentation regularization term. The total loss function is defined as:

$$\mathcal{L} = \lambda_e \mathcal{L}_{CE}(V_e, GT) + \frac{\lambda_d}{N} \sum_{i=1}^{N} \mathcal{L}_{CE}(V_d^i, GT) + \frac{\lambda_f}{N} \sum_{i=1}^{N} \mathcal{L}_{CE}(V_f^i, GT) + \lambda_m \mathcal{L}_m,$$

$$(9)$$

where $\mathcal{L}_{CE}$ denotes the cross-entropy recognition losses from the predictions of the encoder vectors $V_e$, decoder vectors $V_d$, and the fusion vectors $V_f$ following Fang et al. [19] with $N = 3$ iterations for the decoder, $GT$ is the ground truth text, and $\mathcal{L}_m$ is our proposed regularization loss. The balanced weights $\lambda_e$, $\lambda_d$, $\lambda_f$ and $\lambda_m$ are set to 1.0, 1.0, 1.0, and 1.0, respectively.

# 4   Experiments

## 4.1   Datasets and Implementation Details

Most STR models are trained on the synthetic text datasets referring to the MJSynth (MJ) [26,27] and SynthText (ST) [23], which totally have more than 16 million images.

Unlike previous works trained on synthetic datasets and real data, we just train the STR model on real data [5] that contains 276K images, which is 1.7% of synthetic data. It contains a group of real datasets. Street View Text (SVT) [73] consists of 257 training and 647 testing street scene text images. IIIT5k-Words dataset (IIIT) [47] is collected from Google images which includes 2,000 training and 3,000 testing images. ICDAR2013 (IC13) is built in the ICDAR 2013 Robust Reading Competition [32] with 848 images for training and 1,015 images for testing. ICDAR2015 (IC15) [31], consisting of 4,468 training and 2,077 testing images, has more irregular texts with perspective and blur attributes. COCO-Text (COCO) [69] includes occluded and low-resolution texts of around 39K images. Further, RCTW [62], Uber-Text (Uber) [91], ArT [15], LSVT [65], MLT19 [50], and ReCTS [88] are also included with 8,186, 92K, 29K, 34K, 46K, and 23K images, respectively. The final real data is accounted to 276K images in total. In addition to the above, for evaluation we also use SVT Perspective (SVTP) [53] which consists of 645 street view perspective-text images, and CUTE [58] which is a dataset of 288 curved texts. The evaluation metric is the widely used word-level recognition accuracy on the benchmark datasets.

The experiment settings are described below. The model is trained on batch size of 64 on one 16G NVIDIA v100 graphic card. The initial learning rate is set to $1e^{-4}$ and then decayed to tenth of it for last four epochs in total 10 epochs, with Adam optimizer. The input images are processed with data augmentation including random rotation, affine transformation, perspective distortion, and color editing [19]. All inputs are resized to $32 \times 128$ for training and testing.

**Table 1.** Accuracy (%) comparison of STR models on different training strategies and six benchmark evaluation datasets. MJ, ST, Real and Real' represent MJSynth, SynthText, and two different unions of real datasets, with 9 million, 7 million, 48K and 276K images, respectively. The "Total" means evaluation on the union of all testing datasets. The top accuracy is in bold for each evaluation dataset on two versions of benchmarks. Most works are evaluated on the original version of IC13 of 1015 images and IC15 of 2,077 images, while recent studies are evaluated on the developed version of IC13 of 857 images and IC15 of 1,811 images, denoted with "*".

| Method | Training Datasets | IIIT | SVT | IC13 | IC15 | SVTP | CUTE | Total |
|---|---|---|---|---|---|---|---|---|
| ESIR [86] | MJ+ST | 93.3 | 90.2 | 91.3 | 76.9 | 79.6 | 83.3 | 86.8 |
| DAN [76] | MJ+ST | 94.3 | 89.2 | 93.9 | 74.5 | 80.0 | 84.4 | 86.9 |
| ASTER [61] | MJ+ST | 93.4 | 89.5 | 91.8 | 76.1 | 78.5 | 79.5 | 86.4 |
| SE-ASTER [55] | MJ+ST | 93.8 | 89.6 | 92.8 | 80.0 | 81.4 | 83.6 | 88.2 |
| ScRN [80] | MJ+ST | 94.4 | 88.9 | 93.9 | 78.7 | 80.8 | 87.5 | 88.2 |
| PlugNet [49] | MJ+ST | 94.4 | 92.3 | 95.0 | 82.2 | 84.3 | 85.0 | 89.8 |
| Bhunia et al. [9] | MJ+ST | 95.2 | 92.2 | 95.5 | 84.0 | 85.7 | 89.7 | 90.9 |
| Li et al. [38] | MJ+ST+Real | 91.5 | 84.5 | 91.0 | 69.2 | 76.4 | 83.3 | 83.2 |
| Hu et al. [25] | MJ+ST+Real | 95.8 | 92.9 | 94.4 | 79.5 | 85.7 | 92.2 | 90.0 |
| TextScanner [70] | MJ+ST+Real | 95.7 | 92.7 | 94.9 | 83.5 | 84.8 | 91.6 | 91.2 |
| RobustScanner [85] | MJ+ST+Real | 95.4 | 89.3 | 94.1 | 79.2 | 82.9 | 92.4 | 89.2 |
| PIMNet [54] | MJ+ST+Real | 96.7 | 94.7 | 95.4 | **85.9** | 88.2 | 92.7 | 92.5 |
| CRNN [59] | MJ+ST | 84.3 | 78.9 | 88.8 | 61.5 | 64.8 | 61.3 | 75.8 |
| CRNN [5] | MJ+ST+Real' | 89.8 | 84.3 | 90.9 | 73.1 | 74.6 | 82.3 | 83.4 |
| TRBA [4] | MJ+ST | 92.1 | 88.9 | 93.1 | 74.7 | 79.5 | 78.2 | 85.7 |
| TRBA [5] | MJ+ST+Real' | 95.2 | 92.0 | 94.7 | 81.2 | 84.6 | 88.7 | 90.0 |
| Ours | SI+Real' | **97.3** | **96.4** | **96.7** | 85.0 | **89.9** | **95.8** | **93.1** |
| SRN [84]* | MJ+ST | 94.8 | 91.5 | 95.5 | 82.7 | 85.1 | 87.8 | 90.4 |
| PREN2D [79]* | MJ+ST | 95.6 | 94.0 | 96.4 | 83.0 | 87.6 | 91.7 | 91.5 |
| PIMNet [54] | MJ+ST+Real | 96.7 | 94.7 | 96.6 | 88.7 | 88.2 | 92.7 | 93.5 |
| ABINet [19]* (original) | SI+MJ+ST | 96.2 | 93.5 | **97.4** | 86.0 | 89.3 | 89.2 | 92.6 |
| ABINet [19]* (reproduce) | SI+Real' | 97.0 | 94.9 | 96.1 | 88.2 | 88.5 | 94.4 | 93.7 |
| Ours* | SI+Real' | **97.3** | **96.4** | 96.8 | **89.2** | **89.9** | **95.8** | **94.4** |

## 4.2 Comparing with State-of-the-Art Methods

We compare our BINet with the state-of-the-art methods in Table 1. Note that it is hard to fairly compare with different methods due to various pre-processing, rectification, training data, training strategies, etc. It is also not possible to reproduce most previous works with the same configuration in this paper due to limited available codes. However, training on synthetic data is a great advantage [5] for existing methods, compared with our data deficiency.

Specifically, there are four training strategies indicated as $MJ + ST + Real$, $MJ + ST + Real'$, $SI + MJ + ST$, and $SI + Real'$, compared with conventional methods on synthetic data $MJ+ST$, as shown in Table 2. The $MJ+ST+Real$ is the STR model trained on two synthetic datasets [23,27] and several real datasets (IIIT5K, SVT, IC03, IC13, IC15, COCO) [25,38,54,70,85]. The $MJ+ST+Real'$ means that the STR model is trained on both synthetic datasets and another version of real data (IIIT5K, SVT, IC13, IC15, COCO, RCTW, Uber-Text,

ArT, MLT19, ReCTS) [5]. The *SI* refers to use synthetic initialization. It is the backbone weights appeared in ABINet [19] and treated as the pre-training of feature extractor on synthetic data. The whole model will be trained on synthetic data, which is denoted as $SI + MJ + ST$. We figure out that the weights from the backbone or feature extractor can be widely used as model initialization for downstream recognition task, instead of training whole STR model on synthetic data from scratch. We remove the positional encoding module designed by the original work and only keep the backbone weights for the feature extractor. To verify this idea, we train our method only on real data denoted as $SI + Real'$.

**Table 2.** Comparison of different training strategies. For different stages, MJ, ST, Real and Real' represent MJSynth, SynthText, and two different unions of real datasets. The SI denotes separated pretraining on synthetic data. The training time is calculated as the sum of "Train" and "Finetune".

| Training strategy | Number of images | Pretrain | Train | Finetune | Training time |
|---|---|---|---|---|---|
| MJ+ST | 16 Million | - | MJ+ST | - | > 1 week |
| MJ+ST+Real | 16 Million + 48K | - | MJ+ST | Real | > 1 week |
| MJ+ST+Real' | 16 Million +276K | - | MJ+ST | Real' | > 1 week |
| SI+MJ+ST | 16 Million | SI | MJ+ST | - | > 1 week |
| SI+Real' | 276K | SI | Real' | - | ~ 5 hours |

Corresponding to the original version of benchmarks (with IC13 of 1015 images and IC15 of 2077 images), most works are trained on synthetic data and real data *Real*. Baek *et al.* [5] constructed another real data *Real'* and reproduced two typical STR models on the synthetic data and *Real'*, i.e., CRNN and TRBA, with additional ROTNet [21] and unlabeled data [37], as shown after corresponding original results. Our method outperforms most previous models with remarkable margins especially on complex and irregular datasets. Specifically, the performance is improved by 2.2%, 4.8%, 2.1%, 4.7%, 6.3%, 8.0% and 3.4% on IIIT, SVT, IC13, IC15, SVTP, CUTE datasets and the total evaluation, respectively, comparing with the latest TRBA [5] trained on the synthetic and real data as well as extra unlabeled datasets. The results are boosted by 0.6%, 1.8%, 1.4%, −1.0%, 1.9%, 3.3% and 0.6% on above datasets and the total evaluation, comparing with the previous SOTA PIMNet [54]. Note that synthetic data of 16 million is extremely large compared to both kinds of real data, which are accounted for 0.3% and 1.7%, respectively. Baek *et al.* [5] demonstrate that training on synthetic data is an advantage for STR models and can beat any models training only on real data. With the novel design of SI, training *only* on real data now can compete the synthetic training of STR models. Besides, it could finish training in several hours that is less than 0.7% of the time for conventional methods training on synthetic datasets.

Several recent works are evaluated on a developed version of IC13 and IC15, which contains 857 and 1,811 images, respectively. Results are shown in the bottom half of the Table 1. For the regular text datasets IIIT, SVT and IC13, there are the 1.1%, 3.1% and −0.7% improvements, respectively, compared to the original ABINet [19]. For the challenging irregular text datasets IC15, SVTP, and CUTE, our model achieves the best results by increasing of 3.7%, 0.7%, and 7.4% performance compared to the same method. The total evaluation result is boosted by around 2.0%. For fair comparison, we reproduce the results of ABINet [19] trained on real data (while other codes are not fully provided for reproducing the results). The reproduced results trained with the same configuration on real data are improved in total evaluation from 92.6% to 93.7%. Training the whole model solely on real data previously causes great performance degradation [5] due to its 1.7% volume of synthetic data. Our results indicate that solely training on real data with SI can beat the end-to-end training on synthetic data in total accuracy. Moreover, BINet shows impressive superiority on the challenging datasets (IC15, SVTP, and CUTE) that contains various kinds of background-interference scene text images (as shown in Fig. 4), which previous works are generally short at confidently recognizing them.

**Fig. 4.** Qualitative challenging examples. Under each image, the left text is the ground truth; the middle one is the prediction from the SOTA work [19] while the red color indicates the wrongly predicted or missed characters; and the right one in green color is the prediction from our model.

The Fig. 4 shows certain qualitative results. For the perspective, curved and blur texts entangled with background shapes in the first row, the attention-based method is vulnerable in missing or wrongly recognizing characters. For the styled texts in the second row, the background interference with unexpected breaks cause the recognition difficulties. When the background is extremely similar to the texts, the interference is much more irregular in STR as shown in the third row of Fig. 4. In the case of complicated background changing in the forth row, the character shapes are much more important in recognizing the characters. Our model handles the challenging cases more robust than the previous method.

## 4.3    Ablation Study

**SSN Strategy and Modules.** To verify the effectiveness of main components in our BINet, we design two different training strategies for the text semantic segmentation (SSN), i.e., conventional jointed training versus pretrained SSN, together with or without the segmentation refinement (SR) and segmentation embedding (SE) blocks described in Sects. 3.3 and 3.4, respectively. Experiments are evaluated on both the original and developed version of benchmarks as described in Sect. 4.2.

**Table 3.** Accuracy (%) comparison on different components of BINet. For the SSN, the "J" represents the jointed training while the "P" represents the pretrained strategy. The developed version of benchmarks is denoted with "*".

| SSN | SR | SE | IIIT | SVT | SVTP | CUTE | IC13 | IC15 | IC13* | IC15* | Total | Total* |
|-----|----|----|------|-----|------|------|------|------|-------|-------|-------|--------|
| J | - | - | 96.2 | 95.1 | 88.5 | 94.4 | 95.3 | 83.9 | 95.8 | 87.9 | 91.9 | 93.2 |
| J | - | ✓ | 96.2 | 94.3 | 87.3 | 92.4 | 94.3 | 82.9 | 96.4 | 89.4 | 91.3 | 93.4 |
| P | - | - | 96.7 | 95.1 | 88.4 | 94.4 | 95.9 | 84.3 | 96.6 | 88.6 | 92.3 | 93.7 |
| P | - | ✓ | 96.9 | 95.2 | 89.0 | 94.4 | 96.2 | 84.6 | 96.7 | 88.6 | 92.6 | 93.8 |
| P | ✓ | ✓ | 97.3 | 96.4 | 89.9 | 95.8 | 96.7 | 85.0 | 96.8 | 89.2 | 93.1 | 94.4 |

As shown in Table 3, the performance of jointed segmentation is inferior to that of explicitly pretrained strategy. More specifically, by using pretrained strategy instead of jointed training, the recognition accuracy increases from 91.9% to 92.3% without SE, and from 91.3% to 92.6% with SE, for the original version of benchmarks. The jointed training might cause insufficient learning of the segmentation and deficient communication with the recognition, but pre-trained SSN could boost the learning of text semantic segmentation and reduce the negative effect for recognition. That is, the text semantic segmentation is not severed as both for improving segmentation and recognition performance at the same time, which reduces the unexpected noises and interruptions from models [6,19]. We equip SR and SE blocks based on the pretrained SSN and the performance further increases 0.5%. Compared with SSN and SE with higher improvements of 0.9% and 1.5% on IC13 and SVTP, SR improves more accuracy of 1.2% and 1.4% on SVT and CUTE, respectively, for the original version of benchmarks. The marked improvements on each of the benchmarks demonstrate the effectiveness of each component in our BINet.

**Segmentation Embedding.** We also try different segmentation embedding strategy to better utilize the semantic segmentation map for STR, including stacking images with masks [71] (Concat), adding feature maps as residual fusion (Add), attention-based multiplying [68] (Multiply), and our proposed segmentation embedding (SE). They are corresponding to each row of Table 4, respectively. The results show that our designed SE block works more effectively than other competitors for STR.

**Segmentation Refinement.** We further explore the effectiveness of segmentation refinement module. Due to the domain gap between the datasets for semantic segmentation and the datasets for STR, directly applying the pretrained model to generate the segmentation map for STR dataset might get inaccurate results. We can see that some initial text segmentation in the middle column of Fig. 5 are not satisfactory. After refinement, the segmentation results are improved as shown in the right column of Fig. 5. It is obvious that some missing strokes and components of segmentation are compensated to exhibit more distinctive features, which is especially important in the recognition of similar characters. For example, the initially segmented first and last characters in the bottom row look like "c" and "i", respectively. After the refinement, it is more easier to identify the characters "F" and "t", respectively.

**Table 4.** Accuracy (%) comparison on different embedding methods. The developed version of benchmarks is denoted with "*".

| Level | Strategy | IIIT | SVT | SVTP | CUTE | IC13 | IC15 | IC13* | IC15* | Total | Total* |
|-------|----------|------|-----|------|------|------|------|-------|-------|-------|--------|
| Image | Concat | 91.2 | 89.2 | 80.6 | 83.3 | 92.2 | 74.6 | 93.1 | 79.4 | 85.5 | 87.0 |
| Feature | Add | 96.6 | 94.7 | 90.2 | 94.8 | 96.0 | 83.7 | 96.6 | 88.0 | 92.3 | 93.6 |
| Feature | Multiply | 96.7 | 95.1 | 88.4 | 94.4 | 95.9 | 84.3 | 96.6 | 88.6 | 92.3 | 93.7 |
| Feature | Ours | 96.9 | 95.2 | 89.0 | 94.4 | 96.2 | 84.6 | 96.7 | 88.6 | 92.6 | 93.8 |

**Fig. 5.** Samples of the initial segmentation map (middle column) and the refined segmentation map (right column).

## 5   Conclusion

In STR models, the background interference always causes ineffective feature representations for recognition. In this paper, we proposed an effective framework BINet that leverages the text semantic segmentation to STR by novel segmentation refinement and segmentation embedding blocks. We also design an efficient pipeline for training the model only on real data with synthetic initialization. It can be widely used for any STR models with ResNet backbone, instead of training the whole model on synthetic datasets from scratch. Experiments showed the superiority of our BINet on standard benchmarks, especially on challenging and irregular scene text recognition.

**Acknowledgment.** The work is supported by XSEDE Program of National Science Foundation, and Aspire-II Research Program in University of South Carolina. This work used GPUs provided by the NSF MRI-2018966.

# References

1. Al-Zaidy, R., Fung, B.C., Youssef, A.M., Fortin, F.: Mining criminal networks from unstructured text documents. Digit. Investig. **8**(3–4), 147–160 (2012)
2. Alsharif, O., Pineau, J.: End-to-end text recognition with hybrid hmm maxout models. arXiv preprint arXiv:1310.1811 (2013)
3. Atienza, R.: Vision transformer for fast and efficient scene text recognition. arXiv preprint arXiv:2105.08582 (2021)
4. Baek, J., et al.: What is wrong with scene text recognition model comparisons? Dataset and model analysis. In: IEEE/CVF International Conference on Computer Vision (ICCV), pp. 4715–4723 (2019)
5. Baek, J., Matsui, Y., Aizawa, K.: What if we only use real datasets for scene text recognition? Toward scene text recognition with fewer labels. In: IEEE/CVF Conference on Computer Vision and Pattern Recognition (CVPR), pp. 3113–3122 (2021)
6. Bao, W., Lai, W.S., Ma, C., Zhang, X., Gao, Z., Yang, M.H.: Depth-aware video frame interpolation. In: IEEE/CVF Conference on Computer Vision and Pattern Recognition (CVPR), pp. 3703–3712 (2019)
7. Bartz, C., Bethge, J., Yang, H., Meinel, C.: Kiss: keeping it simple for scene text recognition. arXiv preprint arXiv:1911.08400 (2019)
8. Bau, D., et al.: Seeing what a GAN cannot generate. In: IEEE/CVF International Conference on Computer Vision (ICCV), pp. 4502–4511 (2019)
9. Bhunia, A.K., Sain, A., Kumar, A., Ghose, S., Chowdhury, P.N., Song, Y.Z.: Joint visual semantic reasoning: multi-stage decoder for text recognition. In: IEEE/CVF International Conference on Computer Vision (ICCV), pp. 14940–14949 (2021)
10. Bissacco, A., Cummins, M., Netzer, Y., Neven, H.: PhotoOCR: reading text in uncontrolled conditions. In: IEEE/CVF International Conference on Computer Vision (ICCV), pp. 785–792 (2013)
11. Chen, X., Wang, T., Zhu, Y., Jin, L., Luo, C.: Adaptive embedding gate for attention-based scene text recognition. Neurocomputing **381**, 261–271 (2020)
12. Chen, Y., Li, V.O., Cho, K., Bowman, S.R.: A stable and effective learning strategy for trainable greedy decoding. arXiv preprint arXiv:1804.07915 (2018)
13. Cheng, Z., Xu, Y., Bai, F., Niu, Y., Pu, S., Zhou, S.: Aon: towards arbitrarily-oriented text recognition. In: IEEE/CVF Conference on Computer Vision and Pattern Recognition (CVPR), pp. 5571–5579 (2018)
14. Ch'ng, C.K., Chan, C.S.: Total-text: a comprehensive dataset for scene text detection and recognition. In: 2017 14th IAPR International Conference on Document Analysis and Recognition (ICDAR), vol. 1, pp. 935–942. IEEE (2017)

15. Chng, C.K., et al.: ICDAR 2019 robust reading challenge on arbitrary-shaped text-RRC-art. In: 2019 International Conference on Document Analysis and Recognition (ICDAR), pp. 1571–1576. IEEE (2019)

16. Devlin, J., Chang, M.W., Lee, K., Toutanova, K.: BERT: pre-training of deep bidirectional transformers for language understanding. arXiv preprint arXiv:1810.04805 (2018)

17. Diaz-Escobar, J., Kober, V.: Natural scene text detection and segmentation using phase-based regions and character retrieval. In: Mathematical Problems in Engineering 2020 (2020)

18. Engelmann, F., Kontogianni, T., Hermans, A., Leibe, B.: Exploring spatial context for 3D semantic segmentation of point clouds. In: IEEE International Conference on Computer Vision workshops, pp. 716–724 (2017)

19. Fang, S., Xie, H., Wang, Y., Mao, Z., Zhang, Y.: Read like humans: autonomous, bidirectional and iterative language modeling for scene text recognition. In: IEEE/CVF Conference on Computer Vision and Pattern Recognition (CVPR), pp. 7098–7107 (2021)

20. Fang, S., Xie, H., Zha, Z.J., Sun, N., Tan, J., Zhang, Y.: Attention and language ensemble for scene text recognition with convolutional sequence modeling. In: ACM International Conference on Multimedia, pp. 248–256 (2018)

21. Gidaris, S., Singh, P., Komodakis, N.: Unsupervised representation learning by predicting image rotations. arXiv preprint arXiv:1803.07728 (2018)

22. Goodfellow, I., et al.: Generative adversarial nets. In: Advances in Neural Information Processing Systems (NeurIPS), vol. 27 (2014)

23. Gupta, A., Vedaldi, A., Zisserman, A.: Synthetic data for text localisation in natural images. In: IEEE/CVF Conference on Computer Vision and Pattern Recognition (CVPR), pp. 2315–2324 (2016)

24. Hong, T., Hull, J.J.: Visual inter-word relations and their use in OCR postprocessing. In: Proceedings of 3rd International Conference on Document Analysis and Recognition (ICDAR), vol. 1, pp. 442–445. IEEE (1995)

25. Hu, W., Cai, X., Hou, J., Yi, S., Lin, Z.: GTC: guided training of CTC towards efficient and accurate scene text recognition. In: Association for the Advancement of Artificial Intelligence (AAAI), vol. 34, pp. 11005–11012 (2020)

26. Jaderberg, M., Simonyan, K., Vedaldi, A., Zisserman, A.: Deep structured output learning for unconstrained text recognition. arXiv preprint arXiv:1412.5903 (2014)

27. Jaderberg, M., Simonyan, K., Vedaldi, A., Zisserman, A.: Synthetic data and artificial neural networks for natural scene text recognition. arXiv preprint arXiv:1406.2227 (2014)

28. Jaderberg, M., Simonyan, K., Vedaldi, A., Zisserman, A.: Reading text in the wild with convolutional neural networks. Int. J. Comput. Vision (IJCV) **116**(1), 1–20 (2016)

29. Jaderberg, M., Vedaldi, A., Zisserman, A.: Deep features for text spotting. In: Fleet, D., Pajdla, T., Schiele, B., Tuytelaars, T. (eds.) ECCV 2014. LNCS, vol. 8692, pp. 512–528. Springer, Cham (2014). https://doi.org/10.1007/978-3-319-10593-2_34

30. Jung, S., Lee, U., Jung, J., Shim, D.H.: Real-time traffic sign recognition system with deep convolutional neural network. In: International Conference on Ubiquitous Robots and Ambient Intelligence (URAI), pp. 31–34. IEEE (2016)

31. Karatzas, D., et al.: ICDAR 2015 competition on robust reading. In: 2015 13th International Conference on Document Analysis and Recognition (ICDAR), pp. 1156–1160. IEEE (2015)

32. Karatzas, D., et al.: ICDAR 2013 robust reading competition. In: 2013 12th International Conference on Document Analysis and Recognition (ICDAR), pp. 1484–1493. IEEE (2013)

33. Krishnan, P., Kovvuri, R., Pang, G., Vassilev, B., Hassner, T.: Textstylebrush: transfer of text aesthetics from a single example. arXiv preprint arXiv:2106.08385 (2021)

34. Kundu, A., Li, Y., Dellaert, F., Li, F., Rehg, J.M.: Joint semantic segmentation and 3D reconstruction from monocular video. In: Fleet, D., Pajdla, T., Schiele, B., Tuytelaars, T. (eds.) ECCV 2014. LNCS, vol. 8694, pp. 703–718. Springer, Cham (2014). https://doi.org/10.1007/978-3-319-10599-4_45

35. Laina, I., Rupprecht, C., Navab, N.: Towards unsupervised image captioning with shared multimodal embeddings. In: IEEE/CVF International Conference on Computer Vision (ICCV), pp. 7414–7424 (2019)

36. Lee, C.Y., Osindero, S.: Recursive recurrent nets with attention modeling for OCR in the wild. In: IEEE/CVF Conference on Computer Vision and Pattern Recognition (CVPR), pp. 2231–2239 (2016)

37. Lee, D.H., et al.: Pseudo-label: the simple and efficient semi-supervised learning method for deep neural networks. In: Workshop on challenges in representation learning, International Conference on Machine Learning (ICML), vol. 3, p. 896 (2013)

38. Li, H., Wang, P., Shen, C., Zhang, G.: Show, attend and read: a simple and strong baseline for irregular text recognition. In: Association for the Advancement of Artificial Intelligence (AAAI), vol. 33, pp. 8610–8617 (2019)

39. Liao, M., Pang, G., Huang, J., Hassner, T., Bai, X.: Mask TextSpotter v3: segmentation proposal network for robust scene text spotting. In: Vedaldi, A., Bischof, H., Brox, T., Frahm, J.-M. (eds.) ECCV 2020. LNCS, vol. 12356, pp. 706–722. Springer, Cham (2020). https://doi.org/10.1007/978-3-030-58621-8_41

40. Liao, M., et al.: Scene text recognition from two-dimensional perspective. In: Association for the Advancement of Artificial Intelligence (AAAI), vol. 33, pp. 8714–8721 (2019)

41. Litman, R., Anschel, O., Tsiper, S., Litman, R., Mazor, S., Manmatha, R.: Scatter: selective context attentional scene text recognizer. In: IEEE/CVF Conference on Computer Vision and Pattern Recognition (CVPR), pp. 11962–11972 (2020)

42. Liu, W., Chen, C., Wong, K.Y.K.: Char-net: A character-aware neural network for distorted scene text recognition. In: Association for the Advancement of Artificial Intelligence (AAAI) (2018)

43. Liu, W., Chen, C., Wong, K.Y.K., Su, Z., Han, J.: Star-net: a spatial attention residue network for scene text recognition. In: British Machine Vision Conference (BMVC), vol. 2, p. 7 (2016)

44. Liu, X., Kawanishi, T., Wu, X., Kashino, K.: Scene text recognition with CNN classifier and WFST-based word labeling. In: 2016 23rd International Conference on Pattern Recognition (ICPR), pp. 3999–4004. IEEE (2016)

45. Looije, R., Neerincx, M.A., Cnossen, F.: Persuasive robotic assistant for health self-management of older adults: design and evaluation of social behaviors. Int. J. Hum.-Comput. Stud. (IJHCS) **68**(6), 386–397 (2010)

46. Luo, C., Lin, Q., Liu, Y., Jin, L., Shen, C.: Separating content from style using adversarial learning for recognizing text in the wild. Int. J. Comput. Vision (IJCV) **129**(4), 960–976 (2021)

47. Mishra, A., Alahari, K., Jawahar, C.: Scene text recognition using higher order language priors. In: British Machine Vision Conference (BMVC). BMVA (2012)

48. Mishra, A., Alahari, K., Jawahar, C.: Enhancing energy minimization framework for scene text recognition with top-down cues. Comput. Vision Image Underst. (CVIU) **145**, 30–42 (2016)

49. Mou, Y., et al.: PlugNet: degradation aware scene text recognition supervised by a pluggable super-resolution unit. In: Vedaldi, A., Bischof, H., Brox, T., Frahm, J.-M. (eds.) ECCV 2020. LNCS, vol. 12360, pp. 158–174. Springer, Cham (2020). https://doi.org/10.1007/978-3-030-58555-6_10

50. Nayef, N., et al.: ICDAR 2019 robust reading challenge on multi-lingual scene text detection and recognition-RRC-MLT-2019. In: 2019 International Conference on Document Analysis and Recognition (ICDAR), pp. 1582–1587. IEEE (2019)

51. Neumann, L., Matas, J.: A method for text localization and recognition in real-world images. In: Kimmel, R., Klette, R., Sugimoto, A. (eds.) ACCV 2010. LNCS, vol. 6494, pp. 770–783. Springer, Heidelberg (2011). https://doi.org/10.1007/978-3-642-19318-7_60

52. Park, T., Liu, M.Y., Wang, T.C., Zhu, J.Y.: Semantic image synthesis with spatially-adaptive normalization. In: IEEE/CVF Conference on Computer Vision and Pattern Recognition (CVPR) (2019)

53. Phan, T.Q., Shivakumara, P., Tian, S., Tan, C.L.: Recognizing text with perspective distortion in natural scenes. In: IEEE/CVF International Conference on Computer Vision (ICCV), pp. 569–576 (2013)

54. Qiao, Z., et al.: PimNet: a parallel, iterative and mimicking network for scene text recognition. In: ACM International Conference on Multimedia, pp. 2046–2055 (2021)

55. Qiao, Z., Zhou, Y., Yang, D., Zhou, Y., Wang, W.: Seed: semantics enhanced encoder-decoder framework for scene text recognition. In: IEEE/CVF Conference on Computer Vision and Pattern Recognition (CVPR), pp. 13528–13537 (2020)

56. Ramesh, A., et al.: Zero-shot text-to-image generation. In: International Conference on Machine Learning (ICML), pp. 8821–8831. PMLR (2021)

57. Ren, W., et al.: Deep video dehazing with semantic segmentation. IEEE Trans. Image Process. (TIP) **28**(4), 1895–1908 (2018)

58. Risnumawan, A., Shivakumara, P., Chan, C.S., Tan, C.L.: A robust arbitrary text detection system for natural scene images. Expert Syst. Appl. **41**(18), 8027–8048 (2014)

59. Shi, B., Bai, X., Yao, C.: An end-to-end trainable neural network for image-based sequence recognition and its application to scene text recognition. IEEE Trans. Pattern Anal. Mach. Intell. (TPAMI) **39**(11), 2298–2304 (2016)

60. Shi, B., Wang, X., Lyu, P., Yao, C., Bai, X.: Robust scene text recognition with automatic rectification. In: IEEE/CVF Conference on Computer Vision and Pattern Recognition (CVPR), pp. 4168–4176 (2016)

61. Shi, B., Yang, M., Wang, X., Lyu, P., Yao, C., Bai, X.: Aster: an attentional scene text recognizer with flexible rectification. IEEE Trans. Pattern Anal. Mach. Intell. (TPAMI) **41**(9), 2035–2048 (2018)

62. Shi, B., et al.: ICDAR 2017 competition on reading Chinese text in the wild (RCTW-17). In: 2017 14th IAPR International Conference on Document Analysis and Recognition (ICDAR), vol. 1, pp. 1429–1434. IEEE (2017)

63. Sivic, J., Zisserman, A.: Video Google: a text retrieval approach to object matching in videos. In: IEEE/CVF International Conference on Computer Vision (ICCV), vol. 3, pp. 1470–1470. IEEE Computer Society (2003)

64. Su, B., Lu, S.: Accurate scene text recognition based on recurrent neural network. In: Cremers, D., Reid, I., Saito, H., Yang, M.-H. (eds.) ACCV 2014. LNCS, vol. 9003, pp. 35–48. Springer, Cham (2015). https://doi.org/10.1007/978-3-319-16865-4_3

65. Sun, Y., et al.: ICDAR 2019 competition on large-scale street view text with partial labeling-RRC-LSVT. In: 2019 International Conference on Document Analysis and Recognition (ICDAR), pp. 1557–1562. IEEE (2019)

66. Tchapmi, L., Choy, C., Armeni, I., Gwak, J., Savarese, S.: SegCloud: semantic segmentation of 3D point clouds. In: 2017 International Conference on 3D Vision (3DV), pp. 537–547. IEEE (2017)

67. Tewel, Y., Shalev, Y., Schwartz, I., Wolf, L.: Zero-shot image-to-text generation for visual-semantic arithmetic. arXiv preprint arXiv:2111.14447 (2021)

68. Vaswani, A., et al.: Attention is all you need. In: Advances in Neural Information Processing Systems (NeurIPS), pp. 5998–6008 (2017)

69. Veit, A., Matera, T., Neumann, L., Matas, J., Belongie, S.: Coco-text: dataset and benchmark for text detection and recognition in natural images. arXiv preprint arXiv:1601.07140 (2016)

70. Wan, Z., He, M., Chen, H., Bai, X., Yao, C.: TextScanner: reading characters in order for robust scene text recognition. In: Association for the Advancement of Artificial Intelligence (AAAI), vol. 34, pp. 12120–12127 (2020)

71. Wang, J., Li, X., Yang, J.: Stacked conditional generative adversarial networks for jointly learning shadow detection and shadow removal. In: IEEE/CVF Conference on Computer Vision and Pattern Recognition (CVPR), pp. 1788–1797 (2018)

72. Wang, J., et al.: Deep high-resolution representation learning for visual recognition. IEEE Trans. Pattern Anal. Mach. Intell. (TPAMI) (2020)

73. Wang, K., Babenko, B., Belongie, S.: End-to-end scene text recognition. In: IEEE/CVF International Conference on Computer Vision (ICCV), pp. 1457–1464. IEEE (2011)

74. Wang, K., Belongie, S.: Word spotting in the wild. In: Daniilidis, K., Maragos, P., Paragios, N. (eds.) ECCV 2010. LNCS, vol. 6311, pp. 591–604. Springer, Heidelberg (2010). https://doi.org/10.1007/978-3-642-15549-9_43

75. Wang, S., Wang, Y., Qin, X., Zhao, Q., Tang, Z.: Scene text recognition via gated cascade attention. In: IEEE International Conference on Multimedia and Expo (ICME), pp. 1018–1023. IEEE (2019)

76. Wang, T., et al.: Decoupled attention network for text recognition. In: Association for the Advancement of Artificial Intelligence (AAAI), vol. 34, pp. 12216–12224 (2020)

77. Wang, X., Yu, K., Dong, C., Loy, C.C.: Recovering realistic texture in image super-resolution by deep spatial feature transform. In: IEEE/CVF Conference on Computer Vision and Pattern Recognition (CVPR), pp. 606–615 (2018)

78. Xu, X., Zhang, Z., Wang, Z., Price, B., Wang, Z., Shi, H.: Rethinking text segmentation: a novel dataset and a text-specific refinement approach. In: IEEE/CVF Conference on Computer Vision and Pattern Recognition (CVPR), pp. 12045–12055 (2021)

79. Yan, R., Peng, L., Xiao, S., Yao, G.: Primitive representation learning for scene text recognition. In: IEEE/CVF Conference on Computer Vision and Pattern Recognition (CVPR), pp. 284–293 (2021)

80. Yang, M., et al.: Symmetry-constrained rectification network for scene text recognition. In: IEEE/CVF International Conference on Computer Vision (ICCV), pp. 9147–9156 (2019)

81. Yang, X., He, D., Zhou, Z., Kifer, D., Giles, C.L.: Learning to read irregular text with attention mechanisms. In: International Joint Conference on Artificial Intelligence (IJCAI), vol. 1, p. 3 (2017)

82. Yao, C., Bai, X., Shi, B., Liu, W.: Strokelets: a learned multi-scale representation for scene text recognition. In: IEEE/CVF Conference on Computer Vision and Pattern Recognition (CVPR), pp. 4042–4049 (2014)

83. Ye, J., Chen, Z., Liu, J., Du, B.: TextFuseNet: scene text detection with richer fused features. In: International Joint Conference on Artificial Intelligence (IJCAI), pp. 516–522 (2020)

84. Yu, D., et al.: Towards accurate scene text recognition with semantic reasoning networks. In: IEEE/CVF Conference on Computer Vision and Pattern Recognition (CVPR), pp. 12113–12122 (2020)

85. Yue, X., Kuang, Z., Lin, C., Sun, H., Zhang, W.: RobustScanner: dynamically enhancing positional clues for robust text recognition. In: Vedaldi, A., Bischof, H., Brox, T., Frahm, J.-M. (eds.) ECCV 2020. LNCS, vol. 12364, pp. 135–151. Springer, Cham (2020). https://doi.org/10.1007/978-3-030-58529-7_9

86. Zhan, F., Lu, S.: ESIR: end-to-end scene text recognition via iterative image rectification. In: IEEE/CVF Conference on Computer Vision and Pattern Recognition (CVPR), pp. 2059–2068 (2019)

87. Zhang, H., Yao, Q., Yang, M., Xu, Y., Bai, X.: AutoSTR: efficient backbone search for scene text recognition. In: Vedaldi, A., Bischof, H., Brox, T., Frahm, J.-M. (eds.) ECCV 2020. LNCS, vol. 12369, pp. 751–767. Springer, Cham (2020). https://doi.org/10.1007/978-3-030-58586-0_44

88. Zhang, R., et al.: ICDAR 2019 robust reading challenge on reading Chinese text on signboard. In: 2019 International Conference on Document Analysis and Recognition (ICDAR), pp. 1577–1581. IEEE (2019)

89. Zhang, X., Wei, Y., Yang, Y., Huang, T.S.: SG-ONE: similarity guidance network for one-shot semantic segmentation. IEEE Trans. Cybern. 50(9), 3855–3865 (2020)

90. Zhang, Y., Nie, S., Liu, W., Xu, X., Zhang, D., Shen, H.T.: Sequence-to-sequence domain adaptation network for robust text image recognition. In: IEEE/CVF Conference on Computer Vision and Pattern Recognition (CVPR), pp. 2740–2749 (2019)

91. Zhang, Y., Gueguen, L., Zharkov, I., Zhang, P., Seifert, K., Kadlec, B.: Uber-text: a large-scale dataset for optical character recognition from street-level imagery. In: IEEE International Conference on Computer Vision workshops, vol. 2017, p. 5 (2017)

92. Zhu, J.Y., Park, T., Isola, P., Efros, A.A.: Unpaired image-to-image translation using cycle-consistent adversarial networks. In: IEEE/CVF International Conference on Computer Vision (ICCV), pp. 2223–2232 (2017)

93. Zhu, Y., Wang, S., Huang, Z., Chen, K.: Text recognition in images based on transformer with hierarchical attention. In: IEEE International Conference on Image Processing (ICIP), pp. 1945–1949. IEEE (2019)

# Semantic Novelty Detection
# via Relational Reasoning

Francesco Cappio Borlino[1,2], Silvia Bucci[1(✉)], and Tatiana Tommasi[1,2]

[1] Politecnico di Torino, Corso Duca degli Abruzzi 24, 10129 Torino, Italy
{francesco.cappio,silvia.bucci,tatiana.tommasi}@polito.it
[2] Italian Institute of Technology, Genova, Italy

**Abstract.** Semantic novelty detection aims at discovering unknown categories in the test data. This task is particularly relevant in safety-critical applications, such as autonomous driving or healthcare, where it is crucial to recognize unknown objects at deployment time and issue a warning to the user accordingly. Despite the impressive advancements of deep learning research, existing models still need a finetuning stage on the known categories in order to recognize the unknown ones. This could be prohibitive when privacy rules limit data access, or in case of strict memory and computational constraints (e.g. edge computing). We claim that a tailored representation learning strategy may be the right solution for effective and efficient semantic novelty detection. Besides extensively testing state-of-the-art approaches for this task, we propose a novel representation learning paradigm based on relational reasoning. It focuses on learning how to measure semantic similarity rather than recognizing known categories. Our experiments show that this knowledge is directly transferable to a wide range of scenarios, and it can be exploited as a plug-and-play module to convert closed-set recognition models into reliable open-set ones.

**Keywords:** Representation learning · Novelty detection · Open set learning · Domain generalization · Relational reasoning

## 1 Introduction

In the last years, deep learning models have brought significant advances in several computer vision tasks. We can identify two main ingredients as the basis of this widespread success. The first one is the pre-training stage: the possibility to rely on a large set of freely available images allows to learn a representation that is generally helpful to initialize the models. The second component is the optimistic assumption that training and test distributions will perfectly match.

F. C. Borlino and S. Bucci—Equal contributions.

**Supplementary Information** The online version contains supplementary material available at https://doi.org/10.1007/978-3-031-19806-9_11.

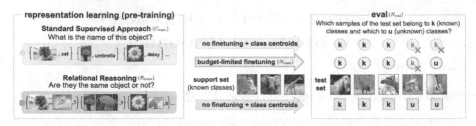

**Fig. 1.** Comparison between standard supervised learning and relational reasoning representation learning. The first aims at recognizing the known object classes, while the second learns a measure of semantic similarity among image pairs. We claim and verify experimentally that relational reasoning is particularly suitable when the final goal is semantic novelty detection. Our pre-trained large-scale relational model can be transferred on semantic novelty detection tasks without the need for a finetuning phase on the known classes of the task at hand.

Indeed, in real-world conditions, it's much more common to encounter differences between the two, for instance, due to a mismatch among their semantic category sets. This condition is particularly dangerous in safety-critical applications like autonomous driving and healthcare, where previously unseen categories should be reliably detected as *unknown*. Several studies have proposed to improve the learning procedure and make it aware of semantic novelties outside of the training distribution. Existing solutions consist in calibrating the softmax output of deep classifiers [29,48,49], or using generative approaches to synthesize outliers [22,51, 53,71,80]. However, a relevant limitation of these techniques is that all of them require to be trained, or at least finetuned, on a reasonably large set of reference data in order to learn what is *known*. In case of limited data access due to privacy concerns, or when dealing with memory and computational constraints (e.g. edge computing), these strategies could be inapplicable.

In this work, we put the spotlight on the pre-training stage. We claim that, rather than considering the usual cross-entropy based classification [28], or self-supervised contrastive learning [10,27], we can exploit ImageNet1k to optimize a relational reasoning objective and obtain a more reliable embedding for novelty detection (see Fig. 1). Specifically, our target is a semantic similarity measure that indicates whether two samples belong to the same class or to different ones. Thus, we focus on learning a representation designed for semantic comparison which does not need further finetuning on the annotated data of the task at hand. It will be enough to compare each test sample with the reference class-prototypes to separate known and unknown categories. Besides being an efficient strategy, our method provides a plug-and-play solution to convert existing closed-set models to open-set ones by including a rejection option for unknown classes.

To summarize, **we focus on Semantic Novelty Detection (SeND) and propose ReSeND, a representation learning approach based on Relational Reasoning that is ready to be used in real-world applications without the need for finetuning.** In particular, our contributions are:

- we conduct a thorough experimental analysis on the ability of several representation learning paradigms to deal with the SeND task, exploring their potentialities and limits;
- we introduce ReSeND and evaluate it on several *intra-* and *cross*-domain scenarios, exploring settings with different ratios of unknown classes in the test data. An extensive benchmark with several competitors confirms the effectiveness and efficiency of our approach;
- we show how ReSeND can be used as a plug-and-play module on closed-set domain generalization approaches converting them into open-set domain generalization strategies that set the new state-of-the-art.

## 2   Related Works

Our work relates to three main research areas: representation learning, relational reasoning, and out-of-distribution detection.

**Representation Learning** makes the difference between classic shallow and modern deep machine learning approaches. The former relies on handcrafted feature representation, while the latter automatically learns to represent the input data through a hierarchy of features during the training process. The literature on this topic is quite extensive [2,26], ranging from the design of neural architectures [25,31,41] to the development of learning paradigms [6,10,19]. The most common approach used to get effective representations from visual data is supervised learning, but recent works have been mainly dedicated to learning representations from unlabeled samples [10,11,23,27,37,46,55,82,84]. They showed how the obtained self-supervised embeddings are able to capture general knowledge of data structure and can be leveraged by a large variety of downstream tasks [20,42,54]. Usually, this happens via a transfer learning procedure that requires finetuning on annotated training data of the final task.

**Relational Reasoning** is a hallmark of human intelligence and it has been formalized by the machine learning community as learning a function to quantify the relationships between a set of objects. This paradigm has attracted particular attention for the combination of language and vision for scene description [38,63, 67]. Other applications are on reinforcement learning [57,66,83], object detection [34], graph networks [1], and few-shot learning [74,85].

*Relational Reasoning and Contrastive Learning.* Recently, it has been shown that relational reasoning can effectively guide self-supervised representation learning [60], with better results than those of popular contrastive learning strategies [10,32]. On the basis of these results, we can identify one important aspect that makes relational reasoning different from contrastive learning. The latter aims at learning a feature space for individual samples, with the similarity between two samples computed a posteriori using a distance metric; the goal of the former is to construct a representation for sample pairs: the position of a point in the final embedding directly represents the similarity between two samples.

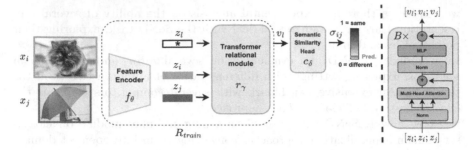

**Fig. 2.** Schematic illustration of the training phase of ReSeND. The features extracted from a pair of images are provided as input to our relational module. It consists of a transformer encoder that elaborates over a tuple composed of the sample pair and of a learnable label token. The output corresponding to this last token is finally provided as input to a semantic similarity head that predicts the sample resemblance.

**Out-Of-Distribution detection (OOD)** studies how to identify whether a given test sample is drawn from the training distribution or not. Both a variation in semantic content and in the visual domain may cause a deviation from the reference distribution. OOD is a wide framework that covers several sub-settings.

*OOD Subsettings.* In *anomaly detection* the training samples belong to a single semantic category and a test sample is considered anomalous both if it contains a novel class and in case it presents the same known class but with perceptual differences from the training (e.g. local defects, global style). When the training data cover more than one class, the setting is usually indicated as *novelty detection*. As in anomaly detection, the cause of novelty can be either a semantic shift, or domain shift or both [30,81]. We use the name *semantic novelty detection* (SeND) to focus on the first case: models that spot unknown categories in the test while being agnostic to domain variations [56]. *Open-set recognition* extends novelty detection by considering not only a binary identification of known and unknown classes in the test, but also a reliable recognition of the known classes. Usually, this setting is well controlled with training and test data sharing the same visual domain. In *open-set domain generalization* the model should be also robust to the domain shift between train and test data [72].

*OOD Strategies in Literature.* From standard classification, we can evaluate whether a test sample is anomalous by applying a threshold on the output score of the top predicted class (maximum-softmax probability, MSP [29]). Improvements over this basic approach have been proposed in [33,48,49]. Instead of the model output, a recent work has shown how the gradients space of neural networks can be used to estimate prediction uncertainty and obtain an OOD scoring function [35]. Generative-based approaches consider the performance of a model trained on reference known classes when reconstructing an input sample. The reconstruction error defines the novelty score [15,40,59]: GAN and flow-based invertible models have been exploited for this purpose [51,71,80]. Some methods synthesize out-of-distribution data [22,44,53] or use external dataset as a source of outlier exposure during training [9,30,58]. A different solution consists in estimating test samples normality by computing their distance from training data using specific embeddings or metrics. [45,68]. A stream of works has also shown the effectiveness of self-supervised representation learning [23,37,46,55,82], and in particular of the contrastive-based strategies for OOD [3,24,70,75,79]. Indeed by removing the focus from the labels, self-supervised models capture analogies and differences among the samples and provide a better way to score similarities. However, training these models needs a non-trivial optimization process with large training batches. Embeddings based on self-attention have been considered as starting point for OOD in [43,73]. Here the powerful transformer architecture ViT [18] pretrained on ImageNet [17] for classification is finetuned on the training data to then score the test samples via MSP. Still, the risks of finetuning a large model on the training data for OOD were discussed in [16], which highlighted how part of the original knowledge gets lost in this process.

Finally, as also noticed by Huang et al. [36], we underline how most of the existing works on OOD consider experimental analysis on datasets containing only digits or low-resolution images. Combined with the limitation of the existing models described above, it becomes clear the need for novel efficient solutions that can be easily deployed in real-world conditions.

## 3   Method

### 3.1   Notation and Background

In the semantic novelty detection task, we have two datasets: a *support set* containing labeled samples $S = \{x^s, y^s\}_{k=1}^K$ drawn from the distribution $p_S$ and a *test set* containing unlabeled samples $T = \{x^t\}_{h=1}^H$ drawn from the distribution $p_T$. The main difference between $p_S$ and $p_T$ is a semantic shift: it holds $y^s \in \mathcal{Y}_s$ and $y^t \in \mathcal{Y}_t$, with $\mathcal{Y}_s \neq \mathcal{Y}_t$. The two sets of classes can be either completely disjoint $\mathcal{Y}_s \cap \mathcal{Y}_t = \emptyset$, or partially overlapping $\mathcal{Y}_s \subset \mathcal{Y}_t$. In the following we will indicate $\mathcal{Y}_s$ as the *known* classes, while we use the term *unknown* to refer to the test classes $\mathcal{Y}_{t\backslash s}$ not appearing in the support set. Domain shift may contribute to the distribution difference among support and test, causing a variation in the appearance of the samples. Still, the class content remains unchanged. A reliable semantic novelty detector should discriminate between known and unknown samples in the test set while being robust to the domain shift.

Given a test sample $x^t$, the detector $D$ should be able to predict a *score* $\in$ [0, 1] that signals whether it is known or unknown with respectively high and low values. Following the traditional strategy, the detector can be formalized as $D : \{C_{train}(\mathcal{I}), N_{train}(S), N_{eval}(x^t)\}$. At first a good representation is learned by training a classification model $C$ on the samples $(x_i, y_i)_{i=1}^I$ of a large-scale dataset $\mathcal{I}$ as ImageNet1k [17]. The representation is then inherited by the model $N$ which is finetuned on the support set to gather the definition of *normality* from the data. When this training is guided by a simple classification objective, the final evaluation of $N$ on the test is usually performed by MSP: $score = \max_{c \in \mathcal{Y}_s} p(y = c | x^t)$. We highlight that the finetuning process has a computational cost that might not be affordable on edge devices. Moreover, in the long term, its catastrophic forgetting effect reduces the original large-scale knowledge, as well as the ability to anticipate potential semantic anomalies [16]. Thus, carefully designing the representation learning approach and choosing how the pre-trained model should be applied for the downstream task is crucial.

We propose to change the learning paradigm for the semantic novelty detector so that it can be written as $D : \{R_{train}(\mathcal{I}), N_{eval}(\mathcal{S}, \boldsymbol{x}^t)\}$. The first component $R$ is a representation learning model based on relational reasoning and trained on ImageNet1k. The learned embedding is directly used by an evaluation system to compare each test sample with the support set to obtain its normality score.

## 3.2   Representation Learning via Relational Reasoning

We consider $R$ composed of a feature extractor $f_\theta$ and a relational module $r_\gamma$. A pair of samples $(\boldsymbol{x}_i, \boldsymbol{x}_j)$ from the reference dataset $\mathcal{I}$ passes first through the feature extractor $(\boldsymbol{z}_i = f_\theta(\boldsymbol{x}_i), \boldsymbol{z}_j = f_\theta(\boldsymbol{x}_j))$, and is then fed to the relational module $r_\gamma$. The output of this module is the input of the semantic similarity head $c_\delta$ which is simply a fully connected (FC) layer. It returns $\sigma_{ij} = c_\delta(r_\gamma(\boldsymbol{z}_i, \boldsymbol{z}_j)) \in [0, 1]$ which represents a semantic similarity measure and can be interpreted as the probability that the two input samples belong to the same category.

The whole representation learning model is trained with a regression objective. Specifically, we assign to each data pair the label $l_{ij} = 0$ if $y_i \neq y_j$ and $l_{ij} = 1$ otherwise, and we minimize the MSE loss:

$$\underset{\theta, \gamma, \delta}{\arg\min} \sum_{m=1}^{M} (\sigma_m - l_m)^2 \, , \tag{1}$$

here the index $m$ specifies the pairs $(\boldsymbol{x}_i, \boldsymbol{x}_j)$ with $i \neq j$ and $x_i, x_j \in \mathcal{I}$. Despite the ground truth supervision being only at the extremes of the prediction interval, we aim at learning a semantic similarity measure in the continuous range $[0, 1]$. For this reason, the regression loss is particularly suited for the task, but the problem could be also casted as binary classification. In the experimental section we compare the two approaches providing empirical evidences about the beneficial effect of our regression choice.

## 3.3   Evaluation Process

Starting from the learned embedding, the component $N_{eval}$ of our approach has the simple role of comparing each test sample with the reference support set, without any further training phase. $N_{eval}$ exploits the relational module and provides to it data pairs composed of the feature of each test sample $\boldsymbol{z}^t = f_\theta(\boldsymbol{x}^t)$, and the set of per-class prototypes $\overline{\boldsymbol{z}}_{y^s}^s \; \forall \; y^s \in \mathcal{Y}_s$ obtained as the average over the samples of each class in the support set. We obtain a vector $\boldsymbol{u}$ of $|\mathcal{Y}_s|$ elements, each corresponding to $c_\delta(r_\gamma(\boldsymbol{z}^t, \overline{\boldsymbol{z}}_{y^s}^s))$ and expressing the similarity of the test sample $\boldsymbol{z}^t$ to one of the known classes. This output is filtered by a softmax function and we apply MSP to get the final normality score: $score = \max(softmax(\boldsymbol{u}))$.

## 3.4  Relational Module

With respect to other standard components of deep neural networks that elaborate on single samples, the peculiarity of the relational module is that it processes pairs of inputs to provide information on their similarity. Of course, the order of appearance of the two samples should not influence the network output as any good similarity measure needs to be symmetric. Considering its natural permutation invariance and its well known capability of comparing multiple inputs, we implement our relational module through a simple transformer encoder. It consists of $B$ identical blocks, each one composed of a Multi-Head Self-Attention (MSA) and a Multi-Layer Perceptron (MLP), both preceded by Layer-Norm (LN) modules and bypassed by residual skip connections as shown in the right part of Fig. 2. The input feature vectors pair, together with a learnable label token, forms the tuple $[z_l, z_i, z_j]$ which is fed as input to the transformer and passes through all its layers, producing the output sequence $[v_l, v_i, v_j]$. Note that, in this architecture each image represents a single input token to the transformer, as done in [12]. We do not include in our encoder the commonly used positional embeddings as we aim at keeping the permutation invariance. In our implementations we use a ResNet18-based backbone as feature extractor $f_\theta$ and select $v_l$ as the output of the relational module $r_\gamma$, which is then passed through the head $c_\delta$ to produce a semantic similarity score $\sigma_{ij}$. In the experimental section we evaluate alternative architectures for our relational module.

# 4  Experimental Setup

With ReSeND we are proposing a novel strategy fully based on representation learning for OOD. We claim that the embedding space learned via relational reasoning is well suited to detect novel classes simply comparing the test samples with the support set which represents the *normal* reference condition. Since this logic substantially differs from that of previous works in OOD, there are several questions that we need to answer with experimental validations.

*Are Existing Representation Learning Approaches Effective for the SeND Task?* (see Sect. 5.1) We focus on the data representation learned via a pre-training stage on ImageNet1k. We consider several state-of-the-art learning methods and for all of them, we keep the same prototype-based evaluation strategy used for ReSeND: every class of the support set is identified by averaging on the feature representation of its samples, and the normality score for each test instance is evaluated by measuring the similarity with the nearest known class centroid.

We choose two families of methods. Among the cross-entropy based classifiers we consider this loss applied to **ResNet** [28] and **ViT** [18] architectures, and the data augmentation-based approach **CutMix** [82]. For the contrastive learning techniques we consider the self-supervised methods **SimCLR** [10] and **CSI** [75], as well as their supervised versions **SupCLR** [39] and **SupCSI** [75]. The relation between each test sample and the class prototypes is measured via the Euclidean similarity (inverse of the Euclidean distance [69]) and the cosine similarity, respective for the cross-entropy and contrastive approaches. We highlight that these methods appeared before in the anomaly and novelty detection literature [43,46,64], but their application always involved a training phase on the support set, while here we run them only on ImageNet1k to get their learned representation. Note also that the different names identify the characteristics of their learning objective, but all of them share the same backbone architecture: ResNet101 [28] with 44M learnable parameters, comparable to the 40M of ReSeND (11M for $f_\theta$, 29M for $r_\gamma + c_\delta$). The only exception is ViT, that we included as an example of Vision Transformer whose usage for OOD was suggested in [43], and for which we use the Vit-Base (86M parameters) implementation from [76].

*Is the Learned Embedding Robust to Domain Variations?* (See Sect. 5.2) ImageNet1k contains pictures of real-world objects and it is important to check if the relations encoded in the learned embedding are still relevant when the final goal is to identify novel classes in completely different contexts as for texture images or among sketches. We consider two levels of difficulty. The first is due to a domain difference between the pre-training and the downstream task: the support and test set are drawn from the same domain which is different from that of ImageNet1k. The second is a domain generalization problem and consider also a domain shift between the support and the test set. The support set can be composed of data from a single or multiple domain sources, while the test is from a target domain. We exploits several datasets to perform a thorough analysis.

**Textures** [13] is a collection of textural images, it consists of 5,640 images organized in 47 categories. We randomly chose 23 categories as known and 24 as unknown. **DomainNet** [61] is a large-scale dataset of common objects from six different domains with 345 object categories. We use this dataset for both intra-domain and cross-domain experiments. For the first case, we used the Natural Language Toolkit [4] to select 50 categories that do not overlap with ImageNet1k classes. We then randomly selected 25 as known and 25 as unknown. **PACS** [47] is composed of four domains and 7 object categories. We follow the known/unknown division proposed in [72] using 6 categories as known and 1 as unknown. **OfficeHome** [77] consists of four domains and 65 categories. We use it in the single-domain generalization experiments by following [5] for the known/unknown category division (25 known and 40 unknown categories). We adopt the same setting of [72] for the multi-source cross-domain experiments. **Multi-Datasets** is a very realistic setting proposed in [72] where the multi-source condition is naturally determined by the use of several datasets as source domains: Office-31 [65], STL-10 [14], Visda2017 [62]. The partial overlap between the source categories, that is simulated for the PACS and OfficeHome benchmarks, in this case is naturally obtained. Here the target domains (Clipart, Real, Painting, Sketch) come from DomainNet.

*How does ReSeND Compare with State-of-the-Art OOD Methods?* (See Sect. 5.3) Considering that ReSeND does not need access to the support set in the training stage but relies on it during the evaluation, we can measure the time and computational resources it uses in this last stage and provide the same to the training procedure of state-of-the-art OOD methods. We consider the following baselines: **MSP** [29] which uses the standard maximum softmax probability, **ODIN** [48] a simple approach based on input perturbation and temperature

**Table 1.** Intra-Domain analysis. Best result in bold and second best underlined.

| Rep. learning | Network | Texture | | Real | | Sketch | | Painting | |
|---|---|---|---|---|---|---|---|---|---|
| | | AUROC ↑ | FPR95 ↓ | AUROC ↑ | FPR95 ↓ | AUROC ↑ | FPR95 ↓ | AUROC ↑ | FPR95 ↓ |
| Cross entropy | ResNet [28] | <u>0.678</u> | <u>0.892</u> | 0.710 | 0.860 | 0.553 | <u>0.936</u> | 0.651 | 0.926 |
| Cross entropy | ViT [18] | 0.562 | 0.919 | 0.696 | <u>0.833</u> | <u>0.554</u> | 0.952 | <u>0.681</u> | <u>0.850</u> |
| CutMix [82] | ResNet | 0.619 | 0.922 | <u>0.721</u> | 0.877 | 0.542 | 0.943 | 0.629 | 0.927 |
| SimCLR [10] | ResNet | 0.529 | 0.942 | 0.481 | 0.944 | 0.502 | 0.956 | 0.510 | 0.956 |
| SupCLR [39] | ResNet | 0.534 | 0.947 | 0.561 | 0.899 | 0.532 | 0.946 | 0.532 | 0.933 |
| CSI [75] | ResNet | 0.651 | 0.906 | 0.663 | 0.887 | 0.514 | 0.955 | 0.621 | 0.910 |
| SupCSI [75] | ResNet | 0.652 | 0.903 | 0.695 | 0.875 | 0.535 | 0.953 | 0.652 | 0.909 |
| ReSeND | | **0.691** | **0.859** | **0.780** | **0.805** | **0.623** | **0.917** | **0.735** | **0.829** |

scaling, **Energy** [49] that uses an energy score for OOD uncertainty estimation, **GradNorm** [35] which relies on test-time extracted gradients to detect the out-of-distribution samples, the ViT-based approach **OODFormer** [43] and two methods based on tailored metric estimation: Mahalanobis [45] and Gram [68].

*Can ReSeND Provide Unknown Detection Abilities to Closed-Set Approaches?* (See Sect. 5.4) ReSeND does not need any training on the support set and it may work as a plug-and-play module to provide close-set approaches the ability to work in open-set conditions. We focus on the challenging open-set domain generalization (DG) setting presented in [72] and show how ReSeND can enhance existing approaches. Besides **DAML** introduced in [72], we consider the state-of-the-art multi-source closed-set DG method **SWAD** [7], which looks for flat minima in the learning objective function, and two single-source closed-set methods: **SagNet** [52] disentangles shape from style in the image features to reduce the style bias, while **Diversify** [78] synthesizes images with unseen styles.

## 5  Experiments

Here we report and discuss the results of our experimental analysis. All the evaluations are done on the basis of two metrics. **AUROC** is the Area Under the Receiver Operating Characteristic curve, obtained by varying the normality decision threshold. **FPR95** corresponds to the false positive rate of out-of-distribution examples when the true positive rate of in-distribution examples is at 95%. For the open-set DG experiments we follow [72] and consider also the overall accuracy on the known samples **Acc** and the harmonic mean between the accuracy on known classes and the unknown detection accuracy **H-score**. Implementation details and more experimental analyses are provided in the supplementary material[1]. All results are averaged over three runs.

### 5.1  Intra-domain Analysis

For the intra-domain analysis, we consider the support and test sets drawn from the same visual distribution but showing significant differences from ImageNet1k.

---

[1] The code is available at https://github.com/FrancescoCappio/ReSeND.

In particular, all the testbeds were explicitly designed to avoid semantic overlaps with ImageNet1k: this means that neither known nor unknown classes appear in its label set. Variation in data type and domain further enlarge the appearance gap. The texture benchmark [13] was already used in [36] and covers a completely different data type with respect to ImageNet1k (objects vs textures). Real, Sketch and Painting benchmarks are obtained from the DomainNet dataset [61] and, differently from Texture, they share the same data type (objects) of ImageNet1k and cover the same (Real) or different (Sketch, Painting) visual domains. In Table 1 we can see that ReSeND obtains the best results showing an excellent knowledge transfer capability. On Texture, the second and third best are respectively Cross Entropy on ResNet and SupCSI, but this ranking is not consistent over all the settings and the performance gap with respect to ReSeND remains evident, especially in the case of Sketch and Painting.

## 5.2   Cross-domain Analysis

In many real-world conditions, it's impossible to avoid the presence of a visual domain shift between training and test data. This usually increases the complexity of the task at hand. A reliable semantic novelty detection method should disregard the domain shift between the support and the test set, focusing only on the semantic content of the data. We compare ReSeND with the same baselines of the previous section, considering two different benchmarks built from the PACS dataset [47]. Here the support set is composed of images of the source domain, while the target domain is used as test set. In the single-source case (Table 2 top), the Photo domain is always used as source, while the three remaining domains are used as target. The multi-source benchmark (Table 2 bottom) is inherited from [72]: each domain is used in turn as target, with the additional difficulty that the support set is composed by multiple sources that have a partial class overlap (see Fig. 3). We notice that SimCLR is particularly effective when the test domain is sketch, but it is outperformed by other approaches in the remaining settings. On the other hand, ReSeND is able to obtain top results in all benchmarks, showing high robustness to the domain shift, despite not including any tailored strategy designed for bridging it.

## 5.3   OOD with Budget-Limited Finetuning

As previously discussed, ReSeND doesn't need finetuning on the support set to be used for semantic novelty detection. Hence it is not trivial to make a fair comparison with existing OOD methods for which instead the learning phase on the support set is essential. Nevertheless, we believe that it's important to contextualize ReSeND in the current literature to provide a clearer overview of its performance. With this objective in mind, we focus on the challenging PACS multi-source setting and compare against a number of standard and state-of-the-art OOD methods by letting them learn (refine the original ImageNet1k pretrained model) on the support set for the same time and using the same computational resources exploited by ReSeND in the prediction phase ($\sim$ 30s

**Table 2.** Cross-domain analysis. Top: single-source results, Bottom: multi-source results. We consider the PACS dataset with all the possible combinations of source/ target as support/test sets. Best result in bold and second best underlined.

| Rep. Learning | Network | PACS Single-Source | | | | | | | |
|---|---|---|---|---|---|---|---|---|---|
| | | ArtPainting | | Sketch | | Cartoon | | Avg | |
| | | AUROC ↑ | FPR95 ↓ | AUROC ↑ | FPR95 ↓ | AUROC ↑ | FPR95 ↓ | AUROC ↑ | FPR95 ↓ |
| Cross Entropy | ResNet [28] | 0.655 | 0.940 | 0.519 | 0.969 | 0.546 | 0.958 | 0.573 | 0.956 |
| Cross Entropy | ViT [18] | 0.593 | 0.895 | 0.595 | 0.881 | 0.500 | 0.953 | 0.562 | 0.910 |
| CutMix [82] | ResNet | 0.663 | 0.949 | 0.372 | 0.981 | 0.419 | 0.980 | 0.485 | 0.970 |
| SimCLR [10] | ResNet | 0.444 | 0.984 | **0.945** | **0.400** | 0.401 | 0.988 | <u>0.597</u> | **0.791** |
| SupCLR [39] | ResNet | 0.500 | 0.909 | 0.176 | 1.000 | 0.469 | 0.919 | 0.381 | 0.942 |
| CSI [75] | ResNet | 0.495 | 0.987 | 0.591 | 0.881 | 0.433 | 0.978 | 0.506 | 0.949 |
| SupCSI [75] | ResNet | 0.546 | 0.976 | <u>0.655</u> | <u>0.819</u> | <u>0.567</u> | <u>0.909</u> | 0.589 | 0.901 |
| **ReSeND** | | **0.828** | **0.668** | 0.576 | 0.981 | **0.651** | **0.891** | **0.685** | <u>0.847</u> |

| Rep. Learning | Network | PACS Multi-Source | | | | | | | | | |
|---|---|---|---|---|---|---|---|---|---|---|---|
| | | ArtPainting | | Sketch | | Cartoon | | Photo | | Avg | |
| | | AUROC ↑ | FPR95 ↓ | AUROC ↑ | FPR95 ↓ | AUROC ↑ | FPR95 ↓ | AUROC ↑ | FPR95 ↓ | AUROC ↑ | FPR95 ↓ |
| Cross Entropy | ResNet [28] | 0.575 | 0.947 | 0.451 | 1.000 | 0.547 | 0.943 | 0.361 | 0.991 | 0.484 | 0.970 |
| Cross Entropy | ViT [18] | <u>0.611</u> | <u>0.837</u> | 0.566 | 0.944 | 0.539 | 0.904 | <u>0.932</u> | <u>0.403</u> | <u>0.662</u> | <u>0.772</u> |
| CutMix [82] | ResNet | 0.604 | 0.895 | 0.411 | 1.000 | 0.407 | 0.975 | 0.655 | 0.942 | 0.519 | 0.953 |
| SimCLR [10] | ResNet | 0.461 | 0.953 | **0.933** | **0.663** | 0.368 | 0.995 | 0.739 | 0.854 | 0.625 | 0.866 |
| SupCLR [39] | ResNet | 0.581 | 0.898 | 0.100 | 1.000 | 0.499 | 0.909 | 0.467 | 0.995 | 0.412 | 0.951 |
| CSI [75] | ResNet | 0.474 | 0.984 | <u>0.702</u> | <u>0.800</u> | <u>0.560</u> | <u>0.977</u> | 0.524 | 0.946 | 0.565 | 0.927 |
| SupCSI [75] | ResNet | 0.417 | 0.984 | 0.660 | 0.869 | 0.323 | 1.000 | 0.601 | 0.946 | 0.500 | 0.950 |
| **ReSeND** | | **0.750** | **0.820** | 0.685 | 0.894 | **0.660** | **0.854** | **0.963** | **0.181** | **0.765** | **0.687** |

**Table 3.** Comparison with finetuning-based state-of-the-art OOD methods. Best result in bold and second best underlined.

| OOD methods | Fine-Tun. | Eval. | PACS Multi-source | | | | | | | | | |
|---|---|---|---|---|---|---|---|---|---|---|---|---|
| | | | ArtPainting | | Sketch | | Cartoon | | Photo | | Avg | |
| | | | AUROC ↑ | FPR95 ↓ | AUROC ↑ | FPR95 ↓ | AUROC ↑ | FPR95 ↓ | AUROC ↑ | FPR95 ↓ | AUROC ↑ | FPR95 ↓ |
| MSP [29] | ✓ | ✓ | 0.617 | 0.973 | 0.412 | 0.998 | <u>0.781</u> | **0.767** | 0.752 | 0.905 | 0.640 | 0.911 |
| ODIN [48] | ✓ | ✓ | 0.602 | 0.977 | 0.425 | 0.998 | **0.785** | <u>0.774</u> | 0.782 | 0.912 | 0.649 | 0.915 |
| Energy [49] | ✓ | ✓ | 0.583 | 0.987 | 0.543 | 0.996 | 0.687 | 0.802 | 0.845 | 0.924 | 0.665 | 0.927 |
| GradNorm [35] | ✓ | ✓ | 0.637 | 0.954 | 0.514 | 1.000 | 0.762 | **0.767** | 0.851 | 0.861 | 0.691 | 0.896 |
| OODformer [43] | ✓ | ✓ | <u>0.703</u> | <u>0.929</u> | 0.610 | 0.973 | 0.776 | 0.802 | 0.732 | 0.773 | <u>0.705</u> | <u>0.869</u> |
| Mahalanobis [45] | ✓ | ✓ | 0.596 | 0.976 | 0.559 | 0.933 | 0.682 | 0.909 | <u>0.861</u> | 0.849 | 0.665 | 0.916 |
| Gram [68] | ✓ | ✓ | 0.448 | 0.962 | **0.885** | **0.713** | 0.536 | 0.946 | 0.838 | <u>0.579</u> | 0.677 | 0.800 |
| Mahalanobis [45] | ✗ | ✓ | 0.596 | 0.976 | 0.466 | 0.981 | 0.593 | 0.926 | 0.808 | 0.935 | 0.616 | 0.954 |
| Gram [68] | ✗ | ✓ | 0.494 | 0.960 | <u>0.840</u> | <u>0.844</u> | 0.494 | 0.954 | 0.797 | 0.981 | 0.656 | 0.935 |
| **ReSeND** | ✗ | ✓ | **0.750** | **0.820** | 0.685 | 0.894 | 0.660 | 0.854 | **0.963** | **0.181** | **0.765** | **0.687** |

on 1 GPU for the considered benchmark). For what concerns Mahalanobis [45] and Gram [68], given that they are metric-based methods, the distance between test samples and the support set can be computed also using a non-finetuned model (although this was not the strategy proposed by the authors). Thus, we tested both the finetuned and not finetuned versions. The results in Table 3 show that ReSeND clearly outperforms all the competitors, which would need a longer training period or more resources in order to converge to a good model. This confirms the role of ReSeND as a powerful tool when semantic novelty detection is performed under restrictive budget constraints.

**Fig. 3.** Open-Set DG setting

**Table 4.** Open-Set DG experiments.

| | Single-Source | | | | | |
| | PACS | | | Office-Home | | |
| | AUROC | Acc | H-Score | AUROC | Acc | H-Score |
|---|---|---|---|---|---|---|
| ReSeND | 0.685 | - | - | 0.685 | - | - |
| SagNet [52] + MSP | 0.643 | 55.85 | 48.64 | 0.699 | 67.58 | 59.92 |
| SagNet+ **ReSeND** | **0.700** | 55.85 | **52.17** | **0.714** | 67.58 | **61.01** |
| Diversify [78] + MSP | 0.643 | 52.06 | 48.12 | 0.696 | 70.49 | 60.03 |
| Diversify+ **ReSeND** | **0.691** | 52.06 | **51.19** | **0.707** | 70.49 | **60.77** |

| | Multi-Source | | | | | | | | |
| | PACS | | | Office-Home | | | Multi-Datasets | | |
| | AUROC | Acc | H-Score | AUROC | Acc | H-Score | AUROC | Acc | H-Score |
|---|---|---|---|---|---|---|---|---|---|
| ReSeND | 0.765 | - | - | 0.674 | - | - | 0.686 | - | - |
| DAML [72] + MSP | 0.657 | 62.85 | 52.99 | 0.651 | 55.28 | 52.37 | 0.695 | 45.90 | 47.88 |
| DAML+**ReSeND** | **0.722** | 62.85 | **57.93** | **0.683** | 55.28 | **54.13** | **0.720** | 45.90 | **49.96** |
| Swad [7] + MSP | 0.570 | 60.52 | 42.85 | 0.661 | 53.49 | 51.06 | 0.661 | 47.90 | 49.10 |
| Swad+**ReSeND** | **0.700** | 60.52 | **57.05** | **0.682** | 53.49 | **52.92** | **0.682** | 47.90 | **50.73** |

**Table 5.** Results obtained by changing the configuration of the relational module. We compare ReSeND with handcrafted feature aggregation strategies for sample pairs.

| | | PACS - Multi-Source | | | | | | | | | |
| | | ArtPainting | | Sketch | | Cartoon | | Photo | | **Avg.** | |
| | | AUROC ↑ | FPR95 ↓ | AUROC ↑ | FPR95 ↓ | AUROC ↑ | FPR95 ↓ | AUROC ↑ | FPR95 ↓ | AUROC ↑ | FPR95 ↓ |
|---|---|---|---|---|---|---|---|---|---|---|---|
| ReSeND | | 0.750 | 0.820 | 0.685 | 0.894 | 0.660 | 0.854 | 0.963 | 0.181 | **0.765** | **0.687** |
| Aggreg. | Max | 0.676 | 0.899 | 0.785 | 0.742 | 0.616 | 0.940 | 0.827 | 0.786 | 0.726 | 0.842 |
| | Sum | 0.583 | 0.976 | 0.446 | 0.988 | 0.514 | 0.996 | 0.575 | 1.000 | 0.530 | 0.990 |
| | Concat | 0.676 | 0.842 | 0.710 | 0.790 | 0.635 | 0.902 | 0.921 | 0.438 | 0.736 | 0.743 |

## 5.4　Open-Set Domain Generalization

The good performance obtained by ReSeND in the analyzed settings suggests that it could be directly and successfully applied in various real-world tasks. We focus on the challenging open-set DG problem that was introduced in [72] (see Fig. 3). Multiple source domains are combined together and their different label sets cause some classes to exist in many more domains than other classes. The target is drawn from a different distribution with a large shift with respect to the source, both in terms of style and semantic content. Indeed, the target contains more classes than the source and they should be identified as unknown at test time. Existing closed-set DG methods are able to learn classification models that generalize to the unseen target domain containing the same categories of the source. One simple way to let them reject samples of novel classes is to add a threshold on MSP, considering unknown the samples with uncertain predictions, as done in DAML. We can apply the same technique on SagNet, Diversify and SWAD. Still, the results can take further advantage from a method better suited to spot semantic novelties across domains, as ReSeND.

We consider the source domains as support set and the target as test, running the evaluation procedure of ReSeND to obtain the normality score for each target sample. The obtained values are combined with the MSP produced by each reference method with a simple score averaging as an ensemble strategy. Since the two normality evaluations originate from different input features we aim at leveraging their complementary nature and maximize the final unknown rejection accuracy. The obtained results are shown in Table 4. In all cases, integrating ReSeND with the other methods provides an improvement both in AUROC and in H-score, with Acc maintaining the exact same values, as ReSeND does not influence predictions on known classes.

# 6  Further Analysis and Discussions

**Learnable Relational Module.** To assess the influence of our design choices for the relational module in ReSeND, we consider alternative strategies to combine the features of sample pairs. Specifically, we evaluate the effect of substituting our transformer-based relational module with hand-designed aggregation functions (*Max/Sum/Concat*), followed by an MLP whose output is fed to the final semantic similarity head. The MLP module is designed to have a similar number of learnable parameters with respect to our transformer-based one. For *Concat* we exploit the feature concatenation as already done in [60]. Note that the *permutation invariance property* of our transformer gets lost by feature concatenation: the order of the images in the pair influences the final predictions.

Table 5 reports the results of this analysis on the PACS multi-source setting. We argue that the superior performance of ReSeND originates from having learned the feature aggregation function rather than relying on a fixed approach imposed a priori. Still, *Max* and *Concat* are able to obtain quite good results (better than what was obtained by the second best in Table 3, OODFormer [43] $Avg_{AUROC}$: 0.705, $Avg_{FPR95}$: 0.869). This is an additional evidence of the effectiveness of the relational reasoning approach for semantic novelty detection.

We remark that an important characteristics of ReSeND is its ability to learn jointly the feature embedding and the semantic similarity metric through an end-to-end training. As highlighted by Sung et al. [74] this is a superior strategy with respect to both methods that learn the feature embeddings but use a fixed similarity measure (e.g. Euclidean) [21], and methods that instead learn a similarity measure on top of a fixed feature representation [8,50].

**Regression vs Classification.** As mentioned in Sec. 3.2, the relational reasoning learning paradigm can be cast as both a binary classification and a regression problem. We believe the latter is more conceptually appropriate as we want to learn a semantic similarity measure with a continuous value. The alternative solution consists in a binary *same* vs *different* task, in which the prediction for the class *same* could be used as semantic similarity measure. In practice, what really differentiates the two approaches is the trend of the loss function.

In Fig. 4 we represent the loss when varying the probability assigned to the correct class for both the classification cross entropy (CE) and the regression MSE. In both cases a high loss is assigned to a low probability and vice-versa. In the very small and rarely populated region of low probability values ($p \approx 0$), CE is higher than MSE. While the MSE gives more importance through higher loss values to hard samples belonging to the intermediate probability region, the CE focuses more on easy samples ($p > 0.75$) pushing their already high

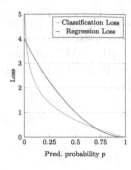
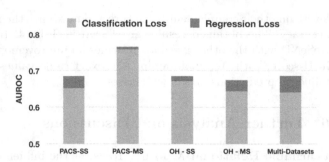

**Fig. 4.** Loss trend for the probability of the correct class.

**Fig. 5.** AUROC comparison with ReSeND trained for classification via Cross Entropy Loss or for Regression via MSE. OH stands for Office-Home. SS and MS indicate respectively the Single- and Multi-Source settings.

probability values to the same even higher output. The final effect of the CE is a minimization of the difference among the samples, which is not ideal when we want to use the confidence as a semantic similarity metric.

We compare the performance obtained by ReSeND with the two different choices for the loss in Fig. 5. We considered all the dataset benchmarks already used for the open-set DG analysis and we show how both the losses provide good results, with the regression outperforming the classification one in all the cases.

## 7 Conclusions

In this paper we analyzed the problem of semantic novelty detection by extensively studying how traditional representation learning methods can be used for this task. Moreover, we introduced ReSeND a representation learning approach that exploits relational reasoning to model semantic similarity among pairs of samples. ReSeND exploits a basic transformer architecture and, once trained on ImageNet1k, it allows to identify whether a test sample belongs to a known or an unknown category by simply comparing it with the reference support set without the need for finetuning. Our thorough experimental analysis has demonstrated the effectiveness of ReSeND in both intra- and cross-domain settings, and its potential as plug-and-play module to transform closed-set domain generalization approaches into reliable open-set methods with state-of-the-art results.

A trustworthy semantic novelty detection method that is able to prevent wrong annotations by identifying unknown categories without any training time latency is a crucial component in many real-world applications. We believe that our work can pave the way for more research in this direction, focusing on novel paradigms or more advanced architectures for relational reasoning.

**Acknowledgements.** Computational resources for this work were provided by IIT (HPC infrastructure). We also acknowledge the CINECA award IsC94 Tr-OSDG under the ISCRA initiative, for the availability of high performance computing resources and support.

# References

1. Battaglia, P., et al.: Relational inductive biases, deep learning, and graph networks. arXiv:1806.01261 (2018)
2. Bengio, Y., Courville, A., Vincent, P.: Representation learning: a review and new perspectives. IEEE TPAMI **35**(8), 1798–1828 (2013)
3. Bergman, L., Hoshen, Y.: Classification-based anomaly detection for general data. In: ICLR (2020)
4. Bird, S., Klein, E., Loper, E.: Natural language processing with Python: analyzing text with the natural language toolkit. O'Reilly Media, Inc. (2009)
5. Bucci, S., Loghmani, M.R., Tommasi, T.: On the effectiveness of image rotation for open set domain adaptation. In: Vedaldi, A., Bischof, H., Brox, T., Frahm, J.-M. (eds.) ECCV 2020. LNCS, vol. 12361, pp. 422–438. Springer, Cham (2020). https://doi.org/10.1007/978-3-030-58517-4_25
6. Caron, M., Misra, I., Mairal, J., Goyal, P., Bojanowski, P., Joulin, A.: Unsupervised learning of visual features by contrasting cluster assignments. In: NeurIPS (2020)
7. Cha, J., et al.: Swad: domain generalization by seeking flat minima. In: NeurIPS (2021)
8. Chen, D., Cao, X., Wang, L., Wen, F., Sun, J.: Bayesian face revisited: a joint formulation. In: Fitzgibbon, A., Lazebnik, S., Perona, P., Sato, Y., Schmid, C. (eds.) ECCV 2012. LNCS, vol. 7574, pp. 566–579. Springer, Heidelberg (2012). https://doi.org/10.1007/978-3-642-33712-3_41
9. Chen, J., Li, Y., Wu, X., Liang, Y., Jha, S.: Atom: robustifying out-of-distribution detection using outlier mining. In: ECML (2021)
10. Chen, T., Kornblith, S., Norouzi, M., Hinton, G.: A simple framework for contrastive learning of visual representations. In: ICML (2020)
11. Chen, X., He, K.: Exploring simple siamese representation learning. In: CVPR (2021)
12. Cheng, Y., Wang, R., Pan, Z., Feng, R., Zhang, Y.: Look, listen, and attend: co-attention network for self-supervised audio-visual representation learning. In: ACM Multimedia (2020)
13. Cimpoi, M., Maji, S., Kokkinos, I., Mohamed, S., Vedaldi, A.: Describing textures in the wild. In: CVPR (2014)
14. Coates, A., Ng, A., Lee, H.: An analysis of single-layer networks in unsupervised feature learning. In: AISTATS (2011)
15. Collin, A.S., De Vleeschouwer, C.: Improved anomaly detection by training an autoencoder with skip connections on images corrupted with stain-shaped noise. In: ICPR (2021)
16. Deecke, L., Ruff, L., Vandermeulen, R.A., Bilen, H.: Transfer-based semantic anomaly detection. In: ICML (2021)
17. Deng, J., Dong, W., Socher, R., Li, L.J., Li, K., Fei-Fei, L.: Imagenet: A large-scale hierarchical image database. In: CVPR (2009)
18. Dosovitskiy, A., et al.: An image is worth $16 \times 16$ words: Transformers for image recognition at scale. In: ICLR (2021)
19. Du, Y., Gan, C., Isola, P.: Curious representation learning for embodied intelligence. In: ICCV (2021)
20. Ericsson, L., Gouk, H., Hospedales, T.M.: How well do self-supervised models transfer? In: CVPR (2021)
21. Fontanel, D., Cermelli, F., Mancini, M., Bulo, S.R., Ricci, E., Caputo, B.: Boosting deep open world recognition by clustering. IEEE RAL **5**(4), 5985–5992 (2020)

22. Ge, Z., Demyanov, S., Chen, Z., Garnavi, R.: Generative openmax for multi-class open set classification. In: BMVC (2017)
23. Gidaris, S., Singh, P., Komodakis, N.: Unsupervised representation learning by predicting image rotations. In: ICLR (2018)
24. Golan, I., El-Yaniv, R.: Deep anomaly detection using geometric transformations. In: NeurIPS (2018)
25. Goodfellow, I., et al.: Generative adversarial nets. In: NeurIPS (2014)
26. Goodfellow, I.J., Bengio, Y., Courville, A.: Deep Learning. MIT Press (2016)
27. He, K., Fan, H., Wu, Y., Xie, S., Girshick, R.: Momentum contrast for unsupervised visual representation learning. In: CVPR (2020)
28. He, K., Zhang, X., Ren, S., Sun, J.: Deep residual learning for image recognition. In: CVPR (2016)
29. Hendrycks, D., Gimpel, K.: A baseline for detecting misclassified and out-of-distribution examples in neural networks. In: ICLR (2017)
30. Hendrycks, D., Mazeika, M., Dietterich, T.: Deep anomaly detection with outlier exposure. In: ICLR (2019)
31. Hinton, G.E., Salakhutdinov, R.R.: Reducing the dimensionality of data with neural networks. Science **313**(5786), 504–507 (2006)
32. Hjelm, R.D., et al.: Learning deep representations by mutual information estimation and maximization. In: ICLR (2019)
33. Hsu, Y.C., Shen, Y., Jin, H., Kira, Z.: Generalized odin: detecting out-of-distribution image without learning from out-of-distribution data. In: CVPR (2020)
34. Hu, H., Gu, J., Zhang, Z., Dai, J., Wei, Y.: Relation networks for object detection. In: CVPR (2018)
35. Huang, R., Geng, A., Li, Y.: On the importance of gradients for detecting distributional shifts in the wild. NeurIPS (2021)
36. Huang, R., Li, Y.: Mos: towards scaling out-of-distribution detection for large semantic space. In: CVPR (2021)
37. Jenni, S., Jin, H., Favaro, P.: Steering self-supervised feature learning beyond local pixel statistics. In: CVPR (2020)
38. Johnson, J., Hariharan, B., van der Maaten, L., Fei-Fei, L., Zitnick, C.L., Girshick, R.B.: CLEVR: a diagnostic dataset for compositional language and elementary visual reasoning. In: CVPR (2017)
39. Khosla, P., et al.: Supervised contrastive learning. In: NeurIPS (2020)
40. Kim, K.H., Shim, S., Lim, Y., Jeon, J., Choi, J., Kim, B., Yoon, A.S.: Rapp: novelty detection with reconstruction along projection pathway. In: ICLR (2020)
41. Kingma, D.P., Welling, M.: Auto-Encoding Variational Bayes. In: ICLR (2014)
42. Kolesnikov, A., Zhai, X., Beyer, L.: Revisiting self-supervised visual representation learning. In: CVPR (2019)
43. Koner, R., Sinhamahapatra, P., Roscher, K., Günnemann, S., Tresp, V.: Oodformer: Out-of-distribution detection transformer. In: BMVC (2021)
44. Lee, K., Lee, H., Lee, K., Shin, J.: Training confidence-calibrated classifiers for detecting out-of-distribution samples. In: ICLR (2018)
45. Lee, K., Lee, K., Lee, H., Shin, J.: A simple unified framework for detecting out-of-distribution samples and adversarial attacks. In: NeurIPS (2018)
46. Li, C.L., Sohn, K., Yoon, J., Pfister, T.: Cutpaste: self-supervised learning for anomaly detection and localization. In: CVPR (2021)
47. Li, D., Yang, Y., Song, Y.Z., Hospedales, T.M.: Deeper, broader and artier domain generalization. In: ICCV (2017)

48. Liang, S., Li, Y., Srikant, R.: Enhancing the reliability of out-of-distribution image detection in neural networks. In: ICLR (2018)

49. Liu, W., Wang, X., Owens, J., Li, Y.: Energy-based out-of-distribution detection. NeurIPS (2020)

50. Mensink, T., Verbeek, J., Perronnin, F., Csurka, G.: Metric learning for large scale image classification: generalizing to new classes at near-zero cost. In: Fitzgibbon, A., Lazebnik, S., Perona, P., Sato, Y., Schmid, C. (eds.) ECCV 2012. LNCS, vol. 7573, pp. 488–501. Springer, Heidelberg (2012). https://doi.org/10.1007/978-3-642-33709-3_35

51. Nalisnick, E., Matsukawa, A., Teh, Y.W., Gorur, D., Lakshminarayanan, B.: Do deep generative models know what they don't know? In: ICLR (2019)

52. Nam, H., Lee, H., Park, J., Yoon, W., Yoo, D.: Reducing domain gap by reducing style bias. In: CVPR (2021)

53. Neal, L., Olson, M., Fern, X., Wong, W.-K., Li, F.: Open set learning with counterfactual images. In: Ferrari, V., Hebert, M., Sminchisescu, C., Weiss, Y. (eds.) ECCV 2018. LNCS, vol. 11210, pp. 620–635. Springer, Cham (2018). https://doi.org/10.1007/978-3-030-01231-1_38

54. Newell, A., Deng, J.: How useful is self-supervised pretraining for visual tasks? In: CVPR (2020)

55. Noroozi, M., Favaro, P.: Unsupervised learning of visual representations by solving jigsaw puzzles. In: Leibe, B., Matas, J., Sebe, N., Welling, M. (eds.) ECCV 2016. LNCS, vol. 9910, pp. 69–84. Springer, Cham (2016). https://doi.org/10.1007/978-3-319-46466-4_5

56. Oza, P., Nguyen, H.V., Patel, V.M.: Multiple class novelty detection under data distribution shift. In: Vedaldi, A., Bischof, H., Brox, T., Frahm, J.-M. (eds.) ECCV 2020. LNCS, vol. 12352, pp. 432–449. Springer, Cham (2020). https://doi.org/10.1007/978-3-030-58571-6_26

57. Pan, J., Chen, S., Shou, M.Z., Liu, Y., Shao, J., Li, H.: Actor-context-actor relation network for spatio-temporal action localization. In: CVPR (2021)

58. Papadopoulos, A.A., Rajati, M.R., Shaikh, N., Wang, J.: Outlier exposure with confidence control for out-of-distribution detection. Neurocomputing 441, 138–150 (2021)

59. Park, H., Noh, J., Ham, B.: Learning memory-guided normality for anomaly detection. In: CVPR (2020)

60. Patacchiola, M., Storkey, A.: Self-supervised relational reasoning for representation learning. In: NeurIPS (2020)

61. Peng, X., Bai, Q., Xia, X., Huang, Z., Saenko, K., Wang, B.: Moment matching for multi-source domain adaptation. In: ICCV (2019)

62. Peng, X., Usman, B., Kaushik, N., Hoffman, J., Wang, D., Saenko, K.: Visda: The visual domain adaptation challenge. arXiv preprint arXiv:1710.06924 (2017)

63. Raposo, D., Santoro, A., Barrett, D.G.T., Pascanu, R., Lillicrap, T., Battaglia, P.W.: Discovering objects and their relations from entangled scene representations. In: ICLR Workshop (2017)

64. Ruff, L., Kauffmann, J.R., Vandermeulen, R.A., Montavon, G., Samek, W., Kloft, M., Dietterich, T.G., Müller, K.R.: A unifying review of deep and shallow anomaly detection. Proc. IEEE 109(5), 756–795 (2021)

65. Saenko, K., Kulis, B., Fritz, M., Darrell, T.: Adapting visual category models to new domains. In: Daniilidis, K., Maragos, P., Paragios, N. (eds.) ECCV 2010. LNCS, vol. 6314, pp. 213–226. Springer, Heidelberg (2010). https://doi.org/10.1007/978-3-642-15561-1_16

66. Santoro, A., et al.: Relational recurrent neural networks. In: NeurIPS (2018)
67. Santoro, A., et al.: A simple neural network module for relational reasoning. In: NeurIPS (2017)
68. Sastry, C.S., Oore, S.: Detecting out-of-distribution examples with Gram matrices. In: ICML (2020)
69. Segaran, T.: Programming Collective Intelligence: Building Smart Web 2.0 Applications. O'Reilly (2007)
70. Sehwag, V., Chiang, M., Mittal, P.: Ssd: A unified framework for self-supervised outlier detection. In: ICLR (2021)
71. Sensoy, M., Kaplan, L.M., Cerutti, F., Saleki, M.: Uncertainty-aware deep classifiers using generative models. In: AAAI (2020)
72. Shu, Y., Cao, Z., Wang, C., Wang, J., Long, M.: Open domain generalization with domain-augmented meta-learning. In: CVPR (2021)
73. Stanislav Fort, J.R., Lakshminarayanan, B.: Exploring the limits of out-of-distribution detection. In: NeurIPS (2021)
74. Sung, F., Yang, Y., Zhang, L., Xiang, T., Torr, P.H., Hospedales, T.M.: Learning to compare: relation network for few-shot learning. In: CVPR (2018)
75. Tack, J., Mo, S., Jeong, J., Shin, J.: Csi: Novelty detection via contrastive learning on distributionally shifted instances. In: NeurIPS (2020)
76. Touvron, H., Cord, M., Douze, M., Massa, F., Sablayrolles, A., Jegou, H.: Training data-efficient image transformers & distillation through attention. In: ICML (2021)
77. Venkateswara, H., Eusebio, J., Chakraborty, S., Panchanathan, S.: Deep hashing network for unsupervised domain adaptation. In: CVPR (2017)
78. Wang, Z., Luo, Y., Qiu, R., Huang, Z., Baktashmotlagh, M.: Learning to diversify for single domain generalization. In: ICCV (2021)
79. Winkens, J., et al.: Contrastive training for improved out-of-distribution detection. arXiv:2007.05566 (2020)
80. Xia, Y., Zhang, Y., Liu, F., Shen, W., Yuille, A.L.: Synthesize then compare: detecting failures and anomalies for semantic segmentation. In: Vedaldi, A., Bischof, H., Brox, T., Frahm, J.-M. (eds.) ECCV 2020. LNCS, vol. 12346, pp. 145–161. Springer, Cham (2020). https://doi.org/10.1007/978-3-030-58452-8_9
81. Yang, J., Wang, H., Feng, L., Yan, X., Zheng, H., Zhang, W., Liu, Z.: Semantically coherent out-of-distribution detection. In: ICCV (2021)
82. Yun, S., Han, D., Oh, S.J., Chun, S., Choe, J., Yoo, Y.: Cutmix: regularization strategy to train strong classifiers with localizable features. In: ICCV (2019)
83. Zambaldi, V., et al.: Deep reinforcement learning with relational inductive biases. In: ICLR (2019)
84. Zbontar, J., Jing, L., Misra, I., LeCun, Y., Deny, S.: Barlow twins: self-supervised learning via redundancy reduction. In: ICML (2021)
85. Zhang, H., Koniusz, P., Jian, S., Li, H., Torr, P.H.S.: Rethinking class relations: absolute-relative supervised and unsupervised few-shot learning. In: CVPR (2021)

# Improving Closed and Open-Vocabulary Attribute Prediction Using Transformers

Khoi Pham[1(✉)], Kushal Kafle[2], Zhe Lin[2], Zhihong Ding[2], Scott Cohen[2], Quan Tran[2], and Abhinav Shrivastava[1]

[1] University of Maryland, College Park, MD, USA
{khoi,abhinav}@cs.umd.edu
[2] Adobe Research, San Jose, CA, USA
{kkafle,zlin,zhding,scohen,qtran}@adobe.com

**Abstract.** We study recognizing attributes for objects in visual scenes. We consider attributes to be any phrases that describe an object's physical and semantic properties, and its relationships with other objects. Existing work studies attribute prediction in a closed setting with a fixed set of attributes, and implements a model that uses limited context. We propose TAP, a new Transformer-based model that can utilize context and predict attributes for multiple objects in a scene in a single forward pass, and a training scheme that allows this model to learn attribute prediction from image-text datasets. Experiments on the large closed attribute benchmark VAW show that TAP outperforms the SOTA by 5.1% mAP. In addition, by utilizing pretrained text embeddings, we extend our model to OpenTAP which can recognize novel attributes not seen during training. In a large-scale setting, we further show that OpenTAP can predict a large number of seen and unseen attributes that outperforms large-scale vision-text model CLIP by a decisive margin. The project page is available at https://vkhoi.github.io/TAP.

**Keywords:** Attribute prediction · Open-vocabulary · Transformer

## 1 Introduction

Accurately describing object attributes plays a key role in a variety of computer vision challenges. Among many others, some uses of attribute prediction include image retrieval from text [25], referring expression and object selection [29,59]. They also form arguably the central part of vision and language problems such as visual question answering (VQA) [2,26,27], and image captioning [4].

While implicitly required and tackled by numerous downstream tasks, research in attribute for objects in the wild is still under-explored. Existing work

---

A portion of this work was done during Khoi Pham's internship at Adobe Research.

---

**Supplementary Information** The online version contains supplementary material available at https://doi.org/10.1007/978-3-031-19806-9_12.

S. Avidan et al. (Eds.): ECCV 2022, LNCS 13685, pp. 201–219, 2022.
https://doi.org/10.1007/978-3-031-19806-9_12

**Fig. 1. Attributes in LSA.** Attributes in LSA cover a wide-range of words/phrases that describe an object, including (a) adjective, (b) verb to describe action, (c) verb-object pairs to describe interaction, and (c) preposition-object to describe location.

is mostly limited to attributes in specific domains such as scenes [69], animals [62], clothing [16,36], and humans [30,33,37]. In recent years, several datasets provide explicit annotations of object attributes, such as [31,46]. However, they are still limited in terms of their coverage of objects and unique attributes, with even the largest datasets only consisting of a few hundreds of attributes.

Additionally, existing work considers attributes to only include adjective properties, and exclude their interactions with other objects in the scene. The latter is often classified as *visual relationship* and is dedicated to an entirely different research topic [38,63,66] which *requires* localization of both subject and object in a subject-predicate-object triplet. We believe this distinction is unnecessarily limiting, *e.g.*, *person wearing hat* conveys information about the property of *person* that is useful even if exact grounding of *hat* is unknown. Hence, we expand the definition of attributes to include adjective- as well as action- and interaction-based properties from the point-of-view of an object.

To this end, we first describe a pipeline to extract object-centric attributes and interactions from large quantities of grounded, weakly grounded, and ungrounded image-text pairs. Then, we propose a novel attribute prediction model called Transformer for Attribute Prediction (TAP). TAP can predict an order of magnitude larger number of unique attributes than previous methods, matching performance of supervised baselines when directly transfer to the VAW benchmark [46]. After finetuning, we outperform prior art by 5.1% mAP and 5.0% mean recall. Furthermore, our model design allows an easy extension to an open-ended attribute prediction branch which we call OpenTAP, by using pretrained text embeddings. OpenTAP can recognize seen attributes, or unseen attributes described by arbitrary text. In our large-scale benchmark, for previously seen attributes, OpenTAP achieves 12.27% mAP higher than CLIP [50], a large-scale image-text matching and zero-shot image classification method, and maintains its superior performance even on attributes that are not seen during training.

In summary, our major contributions are:

– We extend attribute recognition from predicting solely adjectival and action attributes to predicting a larger set that also comprises object interaction. To this end, we propose a new Large-Scale Attribute (LSA) dataset comprising attributes extracted from multiple image-text datasets.

- We propose TAP, a Transformer-based Attribute Prediction model that can effectively utilize the scene context and efficiently make attribute prediction for all objects within an image in a single forward pass, even at the absence of strong grounding information (*i.e.*, object bounding box).
- We propose OpenTAP, a simple extension of TAP to allow open-vocabulary prediction of arbitrary attributes, including those not seen during training.
- We demonstrate state-of-the-art performance on the closed-set attribute prediction dataset (VAW [46]), human-object interaction classification (HICO [6]), as well as a superior performance in our open-vocabulary attribute prediction experiment compared to the recent CLIP model.

## 2   Related Work

Our work is related to a variety of visual attribute prediction works [3,11,12, 16,31,37,44–46,55]. While these often target domain-specific attribute (for constrained set of objects, *e.g. clothing*) or small set of attribute classes, our work differs in three points. First, we extract a large number of attributes from public image-text datasets to be used for training. Second, we propose a training scheme that allows our model to make truly large-scale attribute prediction (orders of magnitude larger than prior works) for unconstrained set of objects. Third, our model can be extended to predict unseen attributes, making it also a zero-shot attribute prediction model. Note that this is different from compositional zero-shot [40–42,49,51] which tackles unseen object-attribute composition.

Our work shares background with vision-language (VL) models [8,28,32, 39,50,56,67] that need to encode object properties and interaction for learning language-grounded visual information. While the goal of these works is to achieve better performance on downstream VL tasks (*e.g.*, VQA, phrase grounding), our goal is solely on accurate large-scale prediction of attributes. In this work, we compare against CLIP, a large scale image-text matching and zero-shot image classifier trained on 400 million images and alt-text from the internet.

Our model architecture is related to the end-to-end object detection Transformer DETR and its language modulated MDETR [5,28]. In DETR, a Transformer encoder is used to contextualize input image features before localizing objects. In the localization step, a Transformer decoder takes in $N$ *object queries*, and decodes them into bounding box and category by cross-attending to the image features from the encoder. Our model also takes after this *object query* approach with a Transformer decoder, but instead of decoding into object category and bounding box, we decode them into attributes.

Open-vocabulary methods have been studied for object recognition and detection using natural language [13–15,22,50,65,68]. Even though attributes can be part of the text query, these works often neglect attributes in their proposal and evaluation, and only focus on object nouns. Earlier works have used object hierarchy from WordNet [68], which is unsuitable for attributes since adjectives/verbs do not have such hierarchy predefined, or search engine to retrieve web text description of object [15] which is costly. Recent works have attempted pretrained text embeddings (e.g., BERT) [22,64] or vision-text embeddings (*e.g.*, CLIP) [13,14] to detect novel objects that are semantically similar to the text in the embedding space. However, their focus is still on objects (nouns) and not their descriptions. [14] attempts to include attributes with their object detector, but it only consists of basic colors. To our knowledge, our work is the first to utilize pretrained text embeddings for large-scale attribute prediction on an unconstrained set of object categories.

## 3    Attribute Data Preparation

**Attribute Extraction:** Our goal is to build an image understanding system that can recognize object-centric attributes as well as its immediate interaction with nearby objects. We refer to these as attribute phrases (or just 'attributes', used interchangeably) as they can be in the form of multiple words (*e.g.*, *wearing hat*). We select the following prominent image-text datasets as our data sources: Visual Genome (VG) [31], GQA [21], COCO-Attributes [45], Flickr30K-Entities [47], MS-COCO [7], and a portion of Localized Narratives (LNar) [48].

VG, GQA, and COCO-Attrs contain object-level attribute labels and bounding boxes, which we directly use. VG-DenseCap, Flickr30K-Entities, MS-COCO, and LNar, on the other hand, contain attributes in their captions. Hence, we rely on language dependency parser [19,53,60] and derive rules to detect attributes, including adjectives, verbs, verb-object and preposition-object pairs. Some of these datasets contain grounding information (bounding box, mouse trace) for each caption that we also extract. We convert LNar mouse trace into bounding box (refer to supplementary). Several examples of these attributes are illustrated in Fig. 1. For the remaining captions, we extract objects without any grounding.

**Large-Scale Object Attribute Dataset (LSA):** We aggregate all images, their parsed objects and attributes into our dataset that we call Large-Scale Attribute (LSA). The overall statistics is in Table 1. From 420k images, we split into 379k images for training, 8k for validation, and 33k for testing. For training, we construct a vocabulary set of attributes that we deem to be common, determined by frequency thresholding for adjective and verb attributes (*e.g.*, adjectives appear $\geq 75$ times), and keeping only those that involve common object categories for interaction and location attributes. More details about this construction and the attribute statistics can be found in the supplementary. Ultimately, this results in a training (or seen) attribute set $\mathcal{C}_s$ with $|\mathcal{C}_s| = 5526$.

## 4    TAP - Transformer for Attribute Prediction

There are two common approaches in attribute prediction in the wild, differing in how multiple objects in an image are processed. First approach, often used with object detector (*e.g.* Faster-RCNN), extracts features for the whole image and pools regions that contain the objects [1,23]. The pooled features are used to predict attributes for each object. These models are normally not used

**Table 1. Statistics** of attributes extracted for LSA. Note that LNar contains 32k and 122k images from Flickr30K and COCO respectively. Among all instances, 7.1M are grounded (bounding box), 1.4M weakly grounded (mouse trace), and 975k ungrounded.

| Datasets | # images | # instances | # attr annotations | Type of grounding |
|---|---|---|---|---|
| VG + GQA | 108k | 6.5M | 10.1M | Box |
| Flickr30K-Entities | 32k | 285k | 503k | Box |
| MS-COCO + COCO-Attrs | 122k | 1.2M | 2.2M | Ungrounded + Box |
| Localized Narratives | 312k | 1.4M | 1.7M | Mouse trace |
| Total | 420k | 9.5M | 14.6M | |

as standalone attribute prediction models but rather as pre-training target for downstream vision-language tasks. Second approach uses crops of each object and processes them separately and independently. While the former encodes more context and is more computationally efficient as it can predict attributes for multiple objects in one forward pass, it suffers from lower accuracy since the feature resolution for each object is lower. Here, we introduce TAP, a new tranformer-based model for attribute prediction that achieves many desirable properties: 1) Use of context information, 2) attribute prediction of multiple objects in a single pass, and 3) easily extendable to unseen attributes.

**Problem setting:** Let $I$ be an input image consisting of $N$ objects with named categories $\{o_i\}_{i=1}^N$ and potentially bounding boxes $\{b_i\}_{i=1}^N$. If an object does not have bounding box, its top-left and bottom-right can be set to the image corners. Let $C_s$ be the set of training attribute classes, then each object has a ground-truth label vector $Y_i = [y_{i,1}, ..., y_{i,C_s}]$, $y_{i,c} \in \{1, 0\}$ denoting whether attribute $c$ is positive or negative. In our work, we treat the unlabeled classes as negatives. Our goal is to train a multi-label classifier to predict these $C_s$ attributes on all $N$ objects. Additionally, we also train a final layer to ensure proximity of the phrase embedding for an attribute, which makes it capable of predicting open-world attributes. We call this extension to our TAP model as **OpenTAP**.

### 4.1 Model Architecture

Figure 2 illustrates the architecture of TAP. TAP takes in two input modalities: (1) a *visual sequence*, and (2) a *query sequence*.

**Visual Sequence:** The first part of our model is a CNN backbone (ResNet-50 in our model) that takes in an input image of size $w \times h$ and returns a grid of features with size $L_v = w/32 \times h/32$. We flatten this feature grid to get a list of feature vectors $\{x_i\}_{i=1}^{L_v} \in \mathbb{R}^{2048}$, which we refer as visual tokens. These visual tokens are then added with a learned 2-D positional encodings similar to [28] so that spatial information can be preserved. Let $r_i$ and $c_i$ be the row and column index of $x_i$ in the feature grid, its final representation $v_i$ is obtained as

$$row_i = \text{RowEmbed}(r_i), \quad col_i = \text{ColumnEmbed}(c_i), \tag{1}$$

$$v_i = x_i + \text{concat}([row_i, col_i]) \tag{2}$$

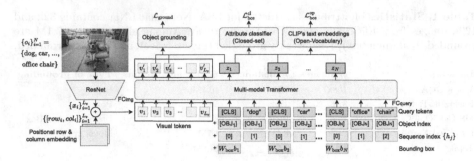

**Fig. 2. Model Architecture.** Sequence of ResNet encodings form the input visual tokens. This is processed jointly with the query token which consists of object query tokens (red), their object index embedding (blue), a sequence index embedding (orange), and a bounding box embedding (green). Contextualized representation $z_i$ of the [CLS] token of all objects are decoded into attributes. In addition, an object grounding loss is used to train object localization (shown here for *dog*). (Color figure online)

**Query Sequence:** Based on the list of $N$ objects, a sequence of *object queries* is created so that our model can decode them into attributes. For every object $i$, we add to our query sequence a [CLS] token, which is the object query that shall be decoded into attributes at the final stage. For every [CLS], we use the following information: (1) the object category name, (2) the image location of the object, (3) the object instance index that the query corresponds to. Specifically, for every object $i$, we tokenize its category $o_i$ using the WordPiece tokenizer [61] into word tokens and append them into the sequence. To provide image location: we encode the object's bounding box [20,39] as a 5-$d$ vector $b_i = \left(\frac{x_0}{W}, \frac{y_0}{H}, \frac{x_1}{W}, \frac{y_1}{H}, \frac{(x_1-x_0)(y_1-y_0)}{H \times W}\right)$ where $(x_0, y_0)$ and $(x_1, y_1)$ are respectively the top-left and bottom-right coordinates of the box, and $H$ and $W$ specify the image size; $b_i$ is then projected via a learned linear layer $W_{\text{box}}$ and added with the [CLS] token. Next, to indicate which object instance a given [CLS] token belongs to, we add to it a cardinal *object index* embedding [OBJ$_i$]. Finally, a cardinal *sequence index* is added for every object category tokens to denote the order of tokens within each object category and account for objects comprising multiple words (*e.g., office chair*). This *sequence index* resets for every new object instance. In summary, given object $i$, its token $w_j$ (at index $j$ w.r.t. object $i$) has its final representation $h_j$ computed as follows:

$$\hat{w}_j = \text{WordEmbed}(w_j), w_{[\text{OBJ}_i]} = \text{WordEmbed}([\text{OBJ}_i]), \tag{3}$$

$$p_j = \text{SequenceIndexEmbed}(j), \tag{4}$$

$$h_j = \hat{w}_j + w_{[\text{OBJ}_i]} + p_j + W_{\text{box}} b_i \mathbb{1}_{w_j = [\text{CLS}]}, \tag{5}$$

where $W_{\text{box}}$ is the learnable linear layer that transform $b_i$ to have the same dimension as the word embeddings.

**Multi-modal Transformer:** Both visual ($\{v_i\}$) and query ($\{h_j\}$) embeddings are mapped to the same embedding space with the help of two fully-connected (FC) layers, $\text{FC}_{\text{img}}$ and $\text{FC}_{\text{query}}$. Both sequences are then concatenated into a single, long sequence and fed to the Transformer. Doing so allows an object's attribute prediction to properly account of its context and surrounding objects, which is crucial for predicting attributes that denote an object property in context of others (*e.g.*, *wearing glasses*). We denote the output visual embeddings to be $\{v'_i\}$ which will be used for the object grounding loss discussed later. For the output query embeddings, we only care about those belong to the [CLS] tokens, which we denote as $z_i$ for the output [CLS] embedding of object $i$.

**Closed-Vocabulary Classifier (TAP):** We apply a linear classifier on every $z_i$ to obtain $\mathcal{C}_s$ logit values for the attribute classes $[r_{i,1}, ..., r_{i,\mathcal{C}_s}]$.

**Open-vocabulary classifier (OpenTAP):** We propose an open-vocabulary classifier head that extends TAP to recognize novel attributes it has not seen during training. As CLIP is a SOTA zero-shot image classifier that has been trained on 400M image-text pairs and potentially seen an enormous amount of attributes, we propose to use pretrained CLIP text embeddings for our open-vocabulary classifier. We train a linear layer on top of $z_i$'s to project them close to the CLIP text embeddings of the ground-truth attributes, while keeping the text embeddings fixed. By fixing the text embeddings, we expect our model to generalize to unseen attributes represented by arbitrary text inputs thanks to the structure in the CLIP embedding space.

Formally, let $q_j$ be the CLIP text embedding of attribute class $j$. To compute similarity between $z_i$ and $q_j$, we use the scaled cosine similarity

$$s_{i,j} = \frac{z_i^T q_j / \tau}{\|z_i\|\|q_j\|}, \tag{6}$$

where $\tau$ is a temperature hyperparameter. Details on how we generate text embeddings of the attributes are presented in Sect. 5. Note that our open-vocabulary classifier head is not limited to CLIP text, but can be used with any pretrained text encoders (*e.g.*, BERT [10]). We select CLIP mainly because it is more representative of the visual world and as determined by empirical results. For example, BERT that is only trained on text corpus is not expected to capture well object appearance characteristics, such as color and texture.

## 4.2    Training and Loss Functions

**Attribute Classification:** We apply a reweighted binary cross entropy loss for our closed-set prediction branch

$$\mathcal{L}_{\text{bce}}^{\text{cl}}(Y, r) = \sum_{i=1}^{N} \sum_{c=1}^{\mathcal{C}_s} - \mathbb{1}_{[y_{i,c}=1]} p_c \log(\sigma(r_{i,c})) - \mathbb{1}_{[y_{i,c}=0]} n_c \log(1 - \sigma(r_{i,c})), \tag{7}$$

where $p_c$ and $n_c$ are the positive and negative weights for attribute $c$ computed in the same way as [46] to handle data imbalance. Similarly, the open-vocabulary branch is also trained with the same BCE loss and we denote it as $\mathcal{L}_{\text{bce}}^{\text{op}}(Y, s)$.

**Object Grounding.** As our training data also contains ungrounded image-text pairs, we employ a grounding loss that trains the model to attend to the correct image regions for objects with known grounding. By providing grounding supervision when available, the model can learn to ground object and transfer that knowledge to softly localize any object of interest when training/testing on ungrounded objects. Specifically, for a query embedding $z_i$ of object $i$, we enforce an alignment between $z_i$ and the output visual embeddings $\{v'_j\}_{j \in O_i^+}$ where $O_i^+$ denotes the indices of those visual tokens that locate inside the bounding box of object $i$ in the image feature grid. Our grounding loss is as follows:

$$\mathcal{L}_{\text{ground}} = \sum_{i=1}^{N} \frac{1}{|O_i^+|} \sum_{j \in O_i^+} - \log \left( \frac{\exp \left( z_i^T v'_j / \tau \right)}{\sum_{k=0}^{L_v-1} \exp \left( z_i^T v'_k / \tau \right)} \right), \tag{8}$$

which is similar to contrastive loss in [28], but instead of using it to strongly supervise a phrase grounding model, we use it to equip TAP with object grounding ability so that it can also learn and predict attributes from ungrounded objects.

Our final loss is the sum of the BCE and the object grounding loss

$$\mathcal{L} = \mathcal{L}_{\text{bce}}^{\text{cl}} + \lambda_{\text{op}} \mathcal{L}_{\text{bce}}^{\text{op}} + \lambda_{\text{ground}} \mathcal{L}_{\text{ground}}. \tag{9}$$

## 5   Experiments

In this section, we describe our main experiments: (1) closed-set attribute prediction on VAW [46], (2) open-vocabulary attribute prediction on LSA, and (3) human-object interaction classification on HICO [6]. Results on VAW and HICO demonstrate our model's understanding of adjective, verb, and interaction classes, while results on LSA shows its ability to predict large number of unique attributes, and even recognize unseen attributes in the open world.

**Architecture:** We use the ImageNet-pretrained ResNet-50 [18] for the image backbone. For word embeddings, we use the pretrained BERT-base [10,58]. Our multi-modal Transformer takes in both visual and query features at once and has 5 self-attention layers with 8 attention heads each. Further implementation details, including hyperparameters, are presented in the supplementary.

**OpenTAP:** As mentioned in Sec. 4.1, we extend TAP to recognize unseen attributes by using CLIP-RN50 to generate text embeddings for the attribute classes. Given an attribute, we extract its embedding using an ensemble of multiple prompts [50], such as 'A photo of something that is <attr>.'. Since object information is already present in the input query (Fig. 2), using object agnostic prompts allows us to pre-compute all attribute embeddings which significantly improves training speed. The supplementary contains all prompts that we use.

## 5.1 Closed-set Attribute Prediction

**Dataset:** We evaluate TAP in a closed setting on VAW [46], a large-scale attribute in the wild dataset that contains positive and negative labels for 620 attributes across multiple types (*e.g.*, *color, material, shape, size*). With explicit negative labels, the VAW dataset allows for reporting better evaluation metrics on this problem, albeit on a much smaller scale than what TAP is capable of.

**Table 2. Results on VAW.** The top box reports results of methods trained only on VAW, while the bottom box shows our newly introduced baseline RN50-Context and TAP on VAW after pre-trained on LSA. LSA-pretrained and VAW-supervised denote whether a model is trained with attribute labels from LSA and VAW respectively

| Methods | LSA pretrained | VAW supervised | mAP | mR@15 | mA | F1@15 |
|---|---|---|---|---|---|---|
| RN50-Baseline [46] | | ✓ | 63.0 | 52.1 | 68.6 | 63.9 |
| ML-GCN [9,46] | | ✓ | 63.0 | 52.8 | 69.5 | 64.1 |
| Sarafianos et al. [46,52] | | ✓ | 64.6 | 51.1 | 68.3 | 64.6 |
| SCoNE [46] | | ✓ | 68.3 | 58.3 | 71.5 | 70.3 |
| TAP [**Ours**] | | ✓ | 65.4 | 54.2 | 67.2 | 66.4 |
| RN50-Context | ✓ | ✓ | 67.3 | 54.1 | 69.3 | 66.1 |
| TAP [**Ours**] | ✓ | | 67.2 | 53.8 | 65.5 | 61.5 |
| TAP [**Ours**] | ✓ | ✓ | **73.4** | **63.3** | **73.5** | **71.1** |

**Setup:** We report 3 versions of TAP: one that is trained only on VAW, one that is trained only on LSA, and one that is first pretrained on LSA and then finetuned on VAW. The 620-attribute set of VAW is also a subset of $C_s$. When pretraining on LSA, we make sure to exclude VAW test images from LSA.

**Baselines:** We compare with ResNet-50 baseline, ML-GCN [9], Sarafianos et al. [52], and the SOTA model SCoNE [46]. These models predict attributes on each cropped object independently, and use ground-truth segmentation mask (provided in VAW) to improve accuracy. Because these models require accurate object box as input for cropping, they cannot be trained on LSA - a dataset with noisy or even no bounding boxes in many cases (refer to Table 1).

Because it can be argued that TAP achieves better results by simply using more context, we introduce another baseline, RN50-Context, which is the RN50-Baseline but takes in the whole image and uses RoIAlign to extract object feature for classification. Because RN50-Context does not perform cropping, we can pretrain it on LSA. More details about this can be found in the supplementary.

**Results:** Following [46], we report mean Average Precision (mAP), mean recall at top-15 (mR@15), mean balanced accuracy (mA), and overall F1 at top-15 (F1@15). The result is presented in Table 2.

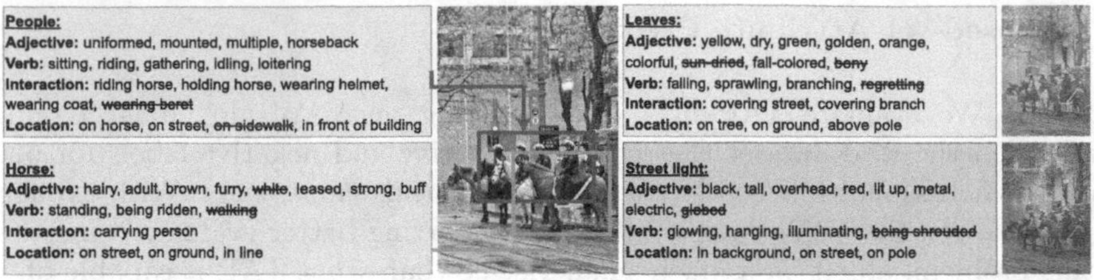

**Fig. 3. Qualitative Results.** Every attribute list is sorted in descending order of the model's confidence. Both **seen attributes** from closed and unseen attributes from open-vocabulary branch are shown. We display the attention mask of TAP for objects without bounding box. Strikethrough represents wrong predictions as judged by us.

- **Without LSA-Pretrained:** After trained only on VAW, TAP achieves better results than RN50-Baseline, ML-GCN [9], and Sarafianos et al. [52]. ML-GCN is not effective since it requires constructing label co-occurrence matrix which is not suited for partially labeled problem such as VAW. Sarafianos et al. has to learn to produce one attention map per attribute, which is costly and redundant because many attributes (*e.g.*, *color*) already share the same attention map that cover the entire object region. However, TAP without LSA-pretrained is lower than SCoNE [46] (-2.9% mAP). Note that SCoNE uses segmentation mask while TAP does not. Transformer is well-known for being data hungry, and VAW consists of 50× less instances than LSA. Hence training only on VAW does not fully utilize TAP's capability that we specifically design it for: large-scale attribute learning from image-text datasets.
- **With LSA-Pretrained:** TAP without finetuning achieves +4.2% mAP than RN50-Baseline, even though it is only trained on sparse attributes parsed from captions and is not trained on VAW densely annotated data. After finetuning, TAP achieves a new SOTA with a substantial improvement of +5.1% mAP and +5.0% mR@15 over SCoNE. RN50-Context, our redesigned RN50-Baseline that uses context, is almost comparable with SCoNE, showing the effectiveness of using context and the LSA data. However, even though TAP and RN50-Context both use context, TAP is clearly better. The impressive performance of TAP is attributed to the effective usage of context, multi-modal Transformer, and our training algorithm that allows to learn attribute from image-caption datasets. In the supplementary, we provide qualitative results and detailed performance breakdown on each attribute type (*e.g.*, TAP achieves much better accuracy on *action* attributes than the baselines).

**More Discussion:** To demonstrate TAP's efficiency that can predict attributes for multiple objects in a scene in a single pass, we report the inference time on VAW: on average, it takes 18.01 ms/img for TAP, while it is 43.71 ms for SCoNE and 40.05 ms for RN50-Baseline. In addition, thanks to object grounding loss, TAP can also work when bounding box is not given. We demonstrate this qualitatively in Fig. 3, and quantitatively by removing all boxes from VAW and re-evaluate TAP, where we obtain 68.9% mAP which is still better than SCoNE.

## 5.2  Open-vocabulary Attribute Prediction

In this section, we evaluate OpenTAP on seen and unseen attributes in LSA. We focus on investigating how a model trained on large number of attributes can generalize to unseen attributes by leveraging fixed text embeddings.

**Setup:** OpenTAP generalizability to unseen attributes can be studied in 2 ways:

1. **LSA Common:** First, we study whether OpenTAP can extrapolate to recognize unseen but common attributes, *e.g.*, can it recognize never-seen *black* from having seen *white* and *gray*? We perform frequency-based sampling to select 605 attributes from set $\mathcal{C}_s$ of 5526 attributes (refer to Sect. 3), and remove them from the training data so that they can be used as unseen attributes. Hence, we have 4921 seen, and 605 unseen attributes. The test set consists of randomly sampled 100k instances from the test images that are labeled with any of these 5526 attributes. By using frequency-based sampling instead of uniform, we ensure the unseen set also contains attributes that are more common (*e.g.*, common colors like *black, orange*).
2. **LSA Common→Rare:** Next, we study whether once trained on common attributes, can OpenTAP generalize to long-tailed unseen attributes. For this, we keep the whole set $\mathcal{C}_s$ of 5526 attributes intact as our seen set. From all attributes in the test images that do not belong in $\mathcal{C}_s$, we construct an unseen set $\mathcal{C}_u$ by selecting those that appear more than 8 times (to filter out noise, typos). We also subsample some types of attributes (*e.g.* location attributes) so that various attribute types are well-balanced in $\mathcal{C}_u$. This results in $|\mathcal{C}_u| = 4012$ classes. We sample 60k instances in LSA test that are labeled with either attributes in $\mathcal{C}_s$ and $\mathcal{C}_u$ for this setup. Since $\mathcal{C}_s$ already contains 5526 most common attributes, the remaining unseen attributes in $\mathcal{C}_u$ are not only unseen, but are also semantically distant from the attributes seen during training because they belong to the long-tail.

For both setups, because we use CLIP for comparison, we make sure all instances in our test set are larger than 25% of the image area in order to not put CLIP at a disadvantage due to small object size.

**Baselines:** We use CLIP as our baseline. As discussed in Sect. 2, CLIP is a SOTA zero-shot image classifier and has used successfully for open-vocabulary object detection [13,14]. However, no existing work have studied CLIP for open-vocabulary attribute recognition. We introduce 3 CLIP baselines based on how the attribute classifiers are constructed from its text encoder:

1. **CLIP (attribute prompt):** Similar to OpenTAP, for every attribute, we create its classifier by ensembling multiple prompts with formats similar to the following 'A photo of something that is <attr>'. This model is agnostic to the object present in the image since the object is not mentioned in the prompts. This is done to establish parity with OpenTAP setup.
2. **CLIP (object-attribute prompt):** We ensemble object-aware prompts with formats similar to the following 'A photo of <obj> <attr>' (*e.g.*, A

*photo of man riding horse*). We observe that this solely object-aware prompt returns drastically low accuracy due to CLIP being unable to detect non-sensical object-attribute pairs, *e.g.*, for an image of a boat with the text *A photo of a boat wearing shirt*, CLIP still returns a high similarity score since CLIP is highly attentive to the object mentioned in the prompt and it is not trained to detect incompatible object-attribute pairs.
3. **CLIP (combined prompt):** To alleviate the above problem, we find that combining the object-aware with the object-agnostic prompts allows CLIP to focus more on the attribute aspect.

All CLIP baselines use ensemble of multiple prompts within each prompt type [50] (refer to supplementary). Furthermore, given an object with its bounding box, we ensemble its CLIP image embeddings from its $1\times, 1.25\times$, and $1.5\times$ crops to incorporate context similar to [14] (this improves $+0.4$ mAP). These are our best-faith effort to augment CLIP model to allow for maximum accuracy.

The baselines from the closed experiment cannot be used in this setup because they do not scale to the large number of classes in LSA. For example, Sarafianos et al. [52] produces one attention map per class, ML-GCN [9] builds a graph of all classes as nodes, SCoNE [46] runs supervised contrastive loss iteratively over every class, all of which is expensive when the number of classes is large.

**Table 3.** Evaluation of **LSA common** and **LSA common→rare**

| Methods | LSA common | | | LSA common → rare | | |
|---|---|---|---|---|---|---|
| | $AP_{seen}$ | $AP_{unseen}$ | $AP_{overall}$ | $AP_{seen}$ | $AP_{unseen}$ | $AP_{overall}$ |
| CLIP (attribute prompt) | 2.53 | 3.37 | 2.64 | 2.62 | 2.52 | 2.58 |
| CLIP (object-attribute prompt) | 0.97 | 1.56 | 1.04 | 1.16 | 0.73 | 0.97 |
| CLIP (combined prompt) | 2.81 | 3.67 | 2.92 | 3.12 | 2.63 | 2.91 |
| OpenTAP | 14.34 | 7.62 | 13.59 | 15.39 | 5.37 | 10.91 |

**Results:** We report in Table 3 the mAP to evaluate the ranklist returned for every attribute by each method. The attributes are categorized into *seen* and *unseen* based on the data OpenTAP is trained on. Unlike OpenTAP, CLIP cannot be entirely zero-shot in these experiments as it presumably has already been trained on these attributes from its 400M image-caption training data [50]. Hence, CLIP shows little difference in performance of seen versus unseen in both experiments. The results show that CLIP ensemble of object-agnostic and object-aware prompt is better than just object-agnostic or just object-aware.

OpenTAP achieves better results than CLIP on both seen/unseen set in both experiments by a clear margin. Despite CLIP having been trained on enormous image-text data and shown to be successful for object recognition [13,14], the results here suggest that CLIP is lacking in terms of attribute understanding. Note that OpenTAP and CLIP still use the same text embeddings as classifiers, and the higher accuracy of OpenTAP is attributed to its architecture and training algorithm to allow OpenTAP to detect better visual cues for attributes.

The results in **LSA common→rare** experiment show that OpenTAP can recognize both seen (common) and unseen (rare) attributes better than CLIP. However, the gap between seen and unseen in this case is not small (10% gap), which suggests there's still room for improvement. When evaluating TAP in **LSA common**, the gap between seen and unseen is less as expected. This result also shows that TAP can extrapolate and recognize unseen but common ones.

excited                    fishing                    salmon-colored

**Fig. 4. Qualitative results.** Top image retrieval results for several unseen classes.

**Qualitative Results:** We show in Fig. 3 example of attribute prediction results. We can see that OpenTAP can predict even attributes that are rare (*loitering, buff, sprawling*). In addition, we present in Fig. 4 top image retrieval results for some unseen attributes. The unseen attributes *excited* and *fishing* from our **LSA common** experiment provide good results, presumably by extrapolating from near seen classes (*e.g.*, *yelling* and *laughing* for *excited*; *holding rod* and *near water* for *fishing*). Similarly, for **LSA common→rare**, *salmon-colored* is rare and unseen but the model is also able to extrapolate based on all common color classes that it has seen during training, such as *orange, pink*.

### 5.3 Ablation Studies

We conduct ablation study on the **LSA common→rare** split to investigate how our choice of attribute embeddings and our constructed dataset LSA is helpful.

**Class Embeddings:** We investigate other text embeddings to be used with OpenTAP: (1) ViCo [17], word embedding learned from object-attributes co-occurrences in Visual Genome, (2) BERT embeddings [10] that has been used for open-vocabulary object detection in [22,65], and (3) PhraseBERT [57]. The results are presented in Table 4, which show that OpenTAP is not dependent solely on CLIP since even BERT embeddings help OpenTAP outperform CLIP baselines on unseen classes. ViCo, even though is trained on object-attributes in VG, results in low mAP. CLIP text embeddings result in the highest mAP.

**Training Data Portion:** Because LSA is an aggregation of multiple datasets with different levels of grounding, we ablate each one to see their contribution to

**Table 4.** Ablation on class embeddings

| Methods | $AP_s$ | $AP_u$ | AP |
|---|---|---|---|
| OpenTAP-ViCo | 11.40 | 3.75 | 7.98 |
| OpenTAP-BERT | 14.00 | 4.81 | 9.90 |
| OpenTAP-Phrase BERT | 14.66 | 4.80 | 10.26 |
| OpenTAP-CLIP | 15.39 | 5.37 | 10.91 |

**Table 5.** Ablation on training portion

| Methods | $AP_s$ | $AP_u$ | AP |
|---|---|---|---|
| VG | 9.59 | 3.88 | 7.04 |
| VG+Flickr | 11.00 | 4.64 | 8.16 |
| VG+Flickr+COCO | 13.27 | 4.98 | 9.56 |
| VG+Flickr+COCO+LNar | 15.39 | 5.37 | 10.91 |

the final performance. We present the results in Table 5, where we can see that all datasets contribute positively, even ungrounded (COCO) and weakly grounded (LNar) one. This shows that with additional ungrounded image-caption (*e.g.*, SBU [43], Conceptual Captions [54]), OpenTAP could achieve even better.

### 5.4   Closed-set Human-Object Interaction Classification

We further show the generalizability of OpenTAP on the human-object interaction dataset HICO [6] which contains image-level interaction labels (*e.g. boarding plane, riding boat*) that are similar to what OpenTAP has learned from LSA.

**Dataset:** HICO [6] contains 600 human-object interaction (HOI) labels of 117 verbs and 80 object categories. Every image in the dataset contains one or more HOI classes that need to be predicted, making this a multi-label prediction problem. HICO training set contains 38,116 images, while the test set comprises 9,658 images. Following prior work, we use 10% of the training images for validation.

**Baselines and Setup:** We compare with PastaNet [35] and HAKE [34] which are SOTA models on HICO that additionally use object detection and human keypoints. We also compare with DEFR [24], a SOTA model that uses ResNet as image backbone and CLIP text embedding as initialization for the classifiers which are later finetuned. For our OpenTAP model, we also finetune the CLIP-initialized classifiers. One difference between DEFR and OpenTAP is the image backbone. While DEFR uses backbone pretrained on CLIP 400M image-text pairs, OpenTAP uses ImageNet- and LSA-pretrained backbone. For fair comparison, we compare with DEFR-RN50 that uses CLIP ResNet-50 as backbone. More implementation details in this experiment are presented in the supplementary.

**Results:** We report results in Table 6, showing that OpenTAP outperforms PastaNet and HAKE without having to use object detector and human keypoints. OpenTAP also surpasses DEFR-RN50 by a clear margin. These are evidence that our proposed architecture and training algorithm for

**Table 6.** Results on HICO image classification

| Methods | Bbox | Pose | CLIP text | mAP |
|---|---|---|---|---|
| PastaNet | ✓ | ✓ | | 46.3 |
| HAKE | ✓ | ✓ | | 47.1 |
| DEFR-RN50 | | | ✓ | 49.7 |
| OpenTAP | | | ✓ | **51.7** |

OpenTAP are effective for learning attributes of objects that can even generalize to HOI classes.

# 6 Conclusions

In this paper, we propose a Transformer-based model for attribute prediction that can predict a large number of unique attributes, and can be extended to learn open-vocabulary attribute by leveraging image-text datasets and pretrained text embeddings. We expand the definition of attributes to include things that a given object interacts with, which we argue to be a part of the object property as well. Our proposed pretrained TAP model not only achieves a new SOTA on a strongly supervised setting after finetuning, but also shows good performance without any finetuning. Our TAP model can be extended to Open-TAP, which is capable of predicting novel attributes unseen during training, with greater accuracy than CLIP.

**Acknowledgements.** This work was partially supported by DARPA SAIL-ON (W911NF2020009) and SemaFor (HR001119S0085) programs, and partially supported by gifts from Adobe.

# References

1. Anderson, P., et al.: Bottom-up and top-down attention for image captioning and visual question answering. In: Proceedings of the IEEE conference on computer vision and pattern recognition, pp. 6077–6086 (2018)
2. Antol, S., et al.: VQA: visual question answering. In: The IEEE International Conference on Computer Vision (ICCV) (2015)
3. Berg, T.L., Berg, A.C., Shih, J.: Automatic attribute discovery and characterization from noisy web data. In: Daniilidis, K., Maragos, P., Paragios, N. (eds.) ECCV 2010. LNCS, vol. 6311, pp. 663–676. Springer, Heidelberg (2010). https://doi.org/10.1007/978-3-642-15549-9_48
4. Bernardi, R., et al.: Automatic description generation from images: a survey of models, datasets, and evaluation measures. J. Artif. Intell. Res. **55**, 409–442 (2016)
5. Carion, N., Massa, F., Synnaeve, G., Usunier, N., Kirillov, A., Zagoruyko, S.: End-to-end object detection with transformers. In: Vedaldi, A., Bischof, H., Brox, T., Frahm, J.-M. (eds.) ECCV 2020. LNCS, vol. 12346, pp. 213–229. Springer, Cham (2020). https://doi.org/10.1007/978-3-030-58452-8_13
6. Chao, Y.W., Wang, Z., He, Y., Wang, J., Deng, J.: HICO: a benchmark for recognizing human-object interactions in images. In: Proceedings of the IEEE International Conference on Computer Vision, pp. 1017–1025 (2015)
7. Chen, X., Fang, H., Lin, T.Y., Vedantam, R., Gupta, S., Dollár, P., Zitnick, C.L.: Microsoft coco captions: Data collection and evaluation server. arXiv preprint arXiv:1504.00325 (2015)
8. Chen, Y.C., et al.: UNITER. learning universal image-text representations (2019)
9. Chen, Z.M., Wei, X.S., Wang, P., Guo, Y.: Multi-label image recognition with graph convolutional networks. In: Proceedings of the IEEE Conference on Computer Vision and Pattern Recognition, pp. 5177–5186 (2019)

10. Devlin, J., Chang, M.W., Lee, K., Toutanova, K.: BERT: pre-training of deep bidirectional transformers for language understanding. arXiv preprint arXiv:1810.04805 (2018)
11. Farhadi, A., Endres, I., Hoiem, D., Forsyth, D.: Describing objects by their attributes. In: 2009 IEEE Conference on Computer Vision and Pattern Recognition, pp. 1778–1785. IEEE (2009)
12. Ferrari, V., Zisserman, A.: Learning visual attributes. In: Advances in neural information processing systems, pp. 433–440 (2008)
13. Gao, M., Xing, C., Niebles, J.C., Li, J., Xu, R., Liu, W., Xiong, C.: Towards open vocabulary object detection without human-provided bounding boxes. arXiv preprint arXiv:2111.09452 (2021)
14. Gu, X., Lin, T.Y., Kuo, W., Cui, Y.: Open-vocabulary object detection via vision and language knowledge distillation. arXiv preprint arXiv:2104.13921 (2021)
15. Guadarrama, S., et al.: Open-vocabulary object retrieval. In: Robotics: science and systems, vol. 2, p. 6 (2014)
16. Guo, S., et al.: The iMaterialist fashion attribute dataset. In: Proceedings of the IEEE International Conference on Computer Vision Workshops (2019)
17. Gupta, T., Schwing, A., Hoiem, D.: VICO: word embeddings from visual co-occurrences. In: Proceedings of the IEEE/CVF International Conference on Computer Vision, pp. 7425–7434 (2019)
18. He, K., Zhang, X., Ren, S., Sun, J.: Deep residual learning for image recognition. In: Proceedings of the IEEE conference on computer vision and pattern recognition, pp. 770–778 (2016)
19. Honnibal, M., Montani, I., Van Landeghem, S., Boyd, A.: SpaCy: industrial-strength Natural Language Processing in Python (2020). https://doi.org/10.5281/zenodo.1212303
20. Huang, H., et al.: Unicoder: a universal language encoder by pre-training with multiple cross-lingual tasks. arXiv preprint arXiv:1909.00964 (2019)
21. Hudson, D.A., Manning, C.D.: GQA: a new dataset for real-world visual reasoning and compositional question answering. In: Proceedings of the IEEE Conference on Computer Vision and Pattern Recognition, pp. 6700–6709 (2019)
22. Huynh, D., Kuen, J., Lin, Z., Gu, J., Elhamifar, E.: Open-vocabulary instance segmentation via robust cross-modal pseudo-labeling. arXiv preprint arXiv:2111.12698 (2021)
23. Jiang, H., Misra, I., Rohrbach, M., Learned-Miller, E., Chen, X.: In defense of grid features for visual question answering. In: Proceedings of the IEEE/CVF Conference on Computer Vision and Pattern Recognition, pp. 10267–10276 (2020)
24. Jin, Y., et al.: Decoupling object detection from human-object interaction recognition. arXiv preprint arXiv:2112.06392 (2021)
25. Johnson, J., et al.: Image retrieval using scene graphs. In: Proceedings of the IEEE conference on computer vision and pattern recognition, pp. 3668–3678 (2015)
26. Kafle, K., Kanan, C.: Visual question answering: Datasets, algorithms, and future challenges. Computer Vision and Image Understanding (2017)
27. Kafle, K., Shrestha, R., Kanan, C.: Challenges and prospects in vision and language research. Front. Artif. Intell. 2, 28 (2019)
28. Kamath, A., Singh, M., LeCun, Y., Synnaeve, G., Misra, I., Carion, N.: MDETR-modulated detection for end-to-end multi-modal understanding. In: Proceedings of the IEEE/CVF International Conference on Computer Vision, pp. 1780–1790 (2021)

29. Kazemzadeh, S., Ordonez, V., Matten, M., Berg, T.: ReferitGame: Referring to objects in photographs of natural scenes. In: Proceedings of the 2014 Conference on Empirical Methods in Natural Language Processing (EMNLP), pp. 787–798 (2014)

30. Kosti, R., Alvarez, J.M., Recasens, A., Lapedriza, A.: Emotion recognition in context. In: Proceedings of the IEEE Conference on Computer Vision and Pattern Recognition, pp. 1667–1675 (2017)

31. Krishna, R., et al.: Visual genome: connecting language and vision using crowdsourced dense image annotations. Int. J. Comput. Vis. **123**(1), 32–73 (2017)

32. Li, X., et al.: OSCAR: object-semantics aligned pre-training for vision-language tasks. In: Vedaldi, A., Bischof, H., Brox, T., Frahm, J.-M. (eds.) ECCV 2020. LNCS, vol. 12375, pp. 121–137. Springer, Cham (2020). https://doi.org/10.1007/978-3-030-58577-8_8

33. Li, Y., Huang, C., Loy, C.C., Tang, X.: Human attribute recognition by deep hierarchical contexts. In: Leibe, B., Matas, J., Sebe, N., Welling, M. (eds.) ECCV 2016. LNCS, vol. 9910, pp. 684–700. Springer, Cham (2016). https://doi.org/10.1007/978-3-319-46466-4_41

34. Li, Y.L., et al.: HAKE: Human activity knowledge engine. arXiv preprint arXiv:1904.06539 (2019)

35. Li, Y.L., et al.: PaStaNet: toward human activity knowledge engine. In: Proceedings of the IEEE/CVF Conference on Computer Vision and Pattern Recognition, pp. 382–391 (2020)

36. Liu, Z., Luo, P., Qiu, S., Wang, X., Tang, X.: DeepFashion: powering robust clothes recognition and retrieval with rich annotations. In: Proceedings of the IEEE Conference on Computer Vision and Pattern Recognition, pp. 1096–1104 (2016)

37. Liu, Z., Luo, P., Wang, X., Tang, X.: Deep learning face attributes in the wild. In: Proceedings of International Conference on Computer Vision (ICCV) (2015)

38. Lu, C., Krishna, R., Bernstein, M., Fei-Fei, L.: Visual relationship detection with language priors. In: Leibe, B., Matas, J., Sebe, N., Welling, M. (eds.) ECCV 2016. LNCS, vol. 9905, pp. 852–869. Springer, Cham (2016). https://doi.org/10.1007/978-3-319-46448-0_51

39. Lu, J., Batra, D., Parikh, D., Lee, S.: VILBERT: pretraining task-agnostic visiolinguistic representations for vision-and-language tasks. arXiv preprint arXiv:1908.02265 (2019)

40. Misra, I., Gupta, A., Hebert, M.: From red wine to red tomato: composition with context. In: Proceedings of the IEEE Conference on Computer Vision and Pattern Recognition, pp. 1792–1801 (2017)

41. Naeem, M.F., Xian, Y., Tombari, F., Akata, Z.: Learning graph embeddings for compositional zero-shot learning. In: Proceedings of the IEEE/CVF Conference on Computer Vision and Pattern Recognition, pp. 953–962 (2021)

42. Nagarajan, T., Grauman, K.: Attributes as operators: factorizing unseen attribute-object compositions. In: Proceedings of the European Conference on Computer Vision (ECCV), pp. 169–185 (2018)

43. Ordonez, V., Kulkarni, G., Berg, T.L.: Im2Text: Describing images using 1 million captioned photographs. In: Neural Information Processing Systems (NIPS) (2011)

44. Parikh, D., Grauman, K.: Relative attributes. In: 2011 International Conference on Computer Vision, pp. 503–510. IEEE (2011)

45. Patterson, G., Hays, J.: COCO attributes: attributes for people, animals, and objects. In: Leibe, B., Matas, J., Sebe, N., Welling, M. (eds.) ECCV 2016. LNCS, vol. 9910, pp. 85–100. Springer, Cham (2016). https://doi.org/10.1007/978-3-319-46466-4_6

46. Pham, K., et al.: Learning to predict visual attributes in the wild. In: Proceedings of the IEEE/CVF Conference on Computer Vision and Pattern Recognition, pp. 13018–13028 (2021)
47. Plummer, B.A., Wang, L., Cervantes, C.M., Caicedo, J.C., Hockenmaier, J., Lazebnik, S.: Flickr30k entities: collecting region-to-phrase correspondences for richer image-to-sentence models. In: Proceedings of the IEEE International Conference on Computer Vision, pp. 2641–2649 (2015)
48. Pont-Tuset, J., Uijlings, J., Changpinyo, S., Soricut, R., Ferrari, V.: Connecting vision and language with localized narratives. In: Vedaldi, A., Bischof, H., Brox, T., Frahm, J.-M. (eds.) ECCV 2020. LNCS, vol. 12350, pp. 647–664. Springer, Cham (2020). https://doi.org/10.1007/978-3-030-58558-7_38
49. Purushwalkam, S., Nickel, M., Gupta, A., Ranzato, M.: Task-driven modular networks for zero-shot compositional learning. In: Proceedings of the IEEE/CVF International Conference on Computer Vision, pp. 3593–3602 (2019)
50. Radford, A., et al.: Learning transferable visual models from natural language supervision. arXiv preprint arXiv:2103.00020 (2021)
51. Saini, N., Pham, K., Shrivastava, A.: Disentangling visual embeddings for attributes and objects. In: Proceedings of the IEEE/CVF Conference on Computer Vision and Pattern Recognition, pp. 13658–13667 (2022)
52. Sarafianos, N., Xu, X., Kakadiaris, I.A.: Deep imbalanced attribute classification using visual attention aggregation. In: Proceedings of the European Conference on Computer Vision (ECCV), pp. 680–697 (2018)
53. Schuster, S., Krishna, R., Chang, A., Fei-Fei, L., Manning, C.D.: Generating semantically precise scene graphs from textual descriptions for improved image retrieval. In: Workshop on Vision and Language (VL15). Association for Computational Linguistics, Lisbon, Portugal (2015)
54. Sharma, P., Ding, N., Goodman, S., Soricut, R.: Conceptual captions: a cleaned, hypernymed, image alt-text dataset for automatic image captioning. In: Proceedings of the 56th Annual Meeting of the Association for Computational Linguistics (Volume 1: Long Papers), pp. 2556–2565. Association for Computational Linguistics, Melbourne, Australia (2018). https://doi.org/10.18653/v1/P18-1238,http://aclanthology.org/P18-1238
55. Siddiquie, B., Feris, R.S., Davis, L.S.: Image ranking and retrieval based on multiattribute queries. In: CVPR 2011, pp. 801–808. IEEE (2011)
56. Tan, H., Bansal, M.: LXMERT: learning cross-modality encoder representations from transformers. arXiv preprint arXiv:1908.07490 (2019)
57. Wang, S., Thompson, L., Iyyer, M.: Phrase-BERT: improved phrase embeddings from bert with an application to corpus exploration. arXiv preprint arXiv:2109.06304 (2021)
58. Wolf, T., et al.: Transformers: state-of-the-art natural language processing. In: Proceedings of the 2020 Conference on Empirical Methods in Natural Language Processing: System Demonstrations, pp. 38–45 (2020)
59. Wu, C., Lin, Z., Cohen, S., Bui, T., Maji, S.: Phrasecut: language-based image segmentation in the wild. In: Proceedings of the IEEE/CVF Conference on Computer Vision and Pattern Recognition, pp. 10216–10225 (2020)
60. Wu, H., et al.: Unified visual-semantic embeddings: bridging vision and language with structured meaning representations. In: Proceedings of the IEEE/CVF Conference on Computer Vision and Pattern Recognition, pp. 6609–6618 (2019)
61. Wu, Y., et al.: Google's neural machine translation system: bridging the gap between human and machine translation. arXiv preprint arXiv:1609.08144 (2016)

62. Xian, Y., Lampert, C.H., Schiele, B., Akata, Z.: Zero-shot learning-a comprehensive evaluation of the good, the bad and the ugly. IEEE Trans. Pattern Anal. Mach. Intell. **41**(9), 2251–2265 (2018)

63. Xu, D., Zhu, Y., Choy, C.B., Fei-Fei, L.: Scene graph generation by iterative message passing. In: Proceedings of the IEEE conference on computer vision and pattern recognition, pp. 5410–5419 (2017)

64. Zareian, A., Karaman, S., Chang, S.-F.: Bridging knowledge graphs to generate scene graphs. In: Vedaldi, A., Bischof, H., Brox, T., Frahm, J.-M. (eds.) ECCV 2020. LNCS, vol. 12368, pp. 606–623. Springer, Cham (2020). https://doi.org/10.1007/978-3-030-58592-1_36

65. Zareian, A., Rosa, K.D., Hu, D.H., Chang, S.F.: Open-vocabulary object detection using captions. In: Proceedings of the IEEE/CVF Conference on Computer Vision and Pattern Recognition, pp. 14393–14402 (2021)

66. Zhang, H., Kyaw, Z., Chang, S.F., Chua, T.S.: Visual translation embedding network for visual relation detection. In: Proceedings of the IEEE conference on computer vision and pattern recognition, pp. 5532–5540 (2017)

67. Zhang, P., et al.: VinVL: Making visual representations matter in vision-language models. arXiv preprint arXiv:2101.00529 (2021)

68. Zhao, H., Puig, X., Zhou, B., Fidler, S., Torralba, A.: Open vocabulary scene parsing. In: Proceedings of the IEEE International Conference on Computer Vision, pp. 2002–2010 (2017)

69. Zhou, B., Lapedriza, A., Khosla, A., Oliva, A., Torralba, A.: Places: a 10 million image database for scene recognition. In: IEEE Transactions on Pattern Analysis and Machine Intelligence (2017)

# Training Vision Transformers
# with only 2040 Images

Yun-Hao Cao(iD), Hao Yu(iD), and Jianxin Wu$^{(\boxtimes)}$(iD)

State Key Laboratory for Novel Software Technology, Nanjing University,
Nanjing, China
{caoyh, yuh}@lamda.nju.edu.cn, wujx2001@gmail.com

**Abstract.** Vision Transformers (ViTs) is emerging as an alternative
to convolutional neural networks (CNNs) for visual recognition. They
achieve competitive results with CNNs but the lack of the typical convolutional inductive bias makes them more data-hungry than common
CNNs. They are often pretrained on JFT-300M or at least ImageNet
and few works study training ViTs with limited data. In this paper, we
investigate how to train ViTs with limited data (e.g., 2040 images). We
give theoretical analyses that our method (based on parametric instance
discrimination) is superior to other methods in that it can capture both
feature alignment and instance similarities. We achieve state-of-the-art
results when training from scratch on 7 small datasets under various
ViT backbones. We also investigate the transferring ability of small
datasets and find that representations learned from small datasets can
even improve large-scale ImageNet training.

**Keywords:** Vision transformers · Small data · Train from scratch

## 1 Introduction

Transformers [32] have recently emerged as an alternative to convolutional neural
networks (CNNs) for visual recognition [13,31,41]. The vision transformer (ViT)
introduced by [13] is an architecture directly inherited from natural language processing [12], but applied to image classification with raw image patches as input.
ViT and variants achieve competitive results with CNNs but require significantly
more training data. For instance, ViT performs worse than ResNets [16] with
similar capacity when trained on ImageNet [29] (1.28 million images). One possible reason may be that ViT lacks certain desirable properties inherently built
into the CNN architecture that make CNNs uniquely suited to solve vision tasks,
e.g., locality, translation invariance and hierarchical structure [38]. As a result,
ViTs need a lot of data for training, usually more data-hungry than CNNs.

---

**Supplementary Information** The online version contains supplementary material
available at https://doi.org/10.1007/978-3-031-19806-9_13.

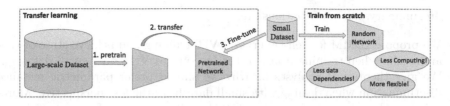

**Fig. 1.** Comparison of transfer learning (left) and training from scratch (right).

In order to alleviate this problem, a lot of works try to introduce convolutions to ViTs [22,36,38,41]. These architectures enjoy the advantages of both paradigms, with attention layers modeling long-range dependencies while convolutions emphasizing the local properties of images. Empirical results show that these ViTs trained on ImageNet outperform ResNets of similar sizes. However, ImageNet is still a large-scale dataset and it is still not clear what is the behavior of these networks when trained on small datasets (e.g., 2040 images). As shown in Fig. 1, we cannot always rely on such large-scale datasets from the perspective of data, computing and flexibility, which will be further analyzed.

In this paper, we investigate how to train ViTs *from scratch* with limited data. We first perform self-supervised pretraining and then supervised fine-tuning on the same target dataset, as done in [3]. We focus on the self-supervised pretraining stage and our method is based on parametric instance discrimination [14]. We theoretically analyze that parametric instance discrimination can not only capture feature alignment between positive pairs but also find potential similarities between instances thanks to the final learnable fully connected layer $W$. Experimental results further verify our analyses and our method achieves better performance than other non-parametric contrastive methods [7–10]. It is known that instance discrimination suffers from high GPU computation, high memory overload and slow convergence for high-dimensional $W$ on large-scale datasets. Since in this paper we focus on small datasets, we do not need complicated strategies for large-scale datasets as in [2,21]. Instead, we adopt small resolution [3], multi-crop [6] and CutMix [42] for the small data setup and we also analyze them from both the theoretical and empirical perspectives.

We call our method **I**nstance **D**iscrimination with **M**ulti-crop and CutMix (IDMM) and achieve state-of-the-art results on 7 small datasets when training from scratch under various ViT backbones. For instance, we achieve 96.7% accuracy when training from scratch on flowers [25] (2040 images), which shows that training ViTs with small data is surprisingly viable. Moreover, we are the first to analyze the transferring ability of small datasets. We find that ViTs also have good transferring ability even when pretrained on small datasets and can even facilitate training on large-scale datasets, e.g., ImageNet. [20] also investigates training ViTs with small-size datasets but they focus on the fine-tuning stage while we focus on the pretraining stage. More importantly, we achieve much better results than [20], where the best reported accuracy on flowers was 56.3%.

In summary, our contributions are:

- We propose IDMM for self-supervised ViT training and achieve state-of-the-art results when training from scratch for various ViTs on 7 small datasets.
- We give theoretical analyses on why we should prefer parametric instance discrimination when dealing with small data from the loss perspective. Moreover, we show how strategies like CutMix alleviate the infrequent updating problem from the gradient perspective.
- We empirically show the projection MLP head is essential for non-parametric contrastive methods (e.g., SimCLR [8]) but not for parametric instance discrimination, thanks to the final learnable $W$ in instance discrimination.
- We analyze the transferring ability of small datasets and find that ViTs also have good transferring ability even when pretrained on small datasets.

## 2    Related Works

**Self-supervised Learning.** Self-supervised learning (SSL) has emerged as a powerful method to learn visual representations without labels. Many recent works follow the contrastive learning paradigm [26], which is also known as non-parametric instance discrimination [39]. For instance, SimCLR [8] and MoCo [15] trained networks to identify a pair of views originating from the same image when contrasted with many views from other images. Unlike the two-branch structure in contrastive methods, some approaches [2,14,21] employed a parametric, one-branch structure for instance discrimination. Exemplar-CNN [14] learned to discriminate between a set of surrogate classes, where each class represents different transformed patches of a single image. [2] and [21] proposed different methods to alleviate the infrequent instance visiting problem or reduce the GPU memory consumption for large-scale datasets, but rely on complicated engineering techniques for CNNs and lack theoretical analyses. In this paper, we not only apply parametric instance discrimination to ViTs, but also focus on small datasets. In addition, we give theoretical analyses of why we should prefer parametric method, at least for small datasets.

Recently, there have also been self-supervised methods designed for ViTs. [10] found that instability is a major issue that impacts self-supervised ViT training and proposed a simple contrastive baseline MoCov3. DINO [7] designed a simple self-supervised approach that can be interpreted as a form of knowledge distillation with no labels. However, they focused on large-scale datasets while we focus on small data. Our method is more stable for various networks and more effective for small data.

**Vision Transformers.** The Vision Transformer (ViT) [13] treated an image as patches/tokens and employed a pure transformer structure. With *sufficient* training data, ViT outperforms CNNs on various image classification benchmarks, and many ViT variants have been proposed since then. [31] introduced a teacher-student distillation token strategy into ViT, namely DeiT. Beyond classification, Transformer has been adopted in diverse vision tasks, including

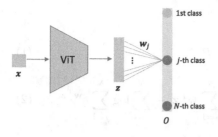

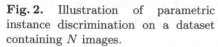

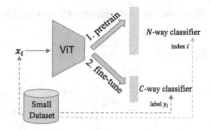

**Fig. 2.** Illustration of parametric instance discrimination on a dataset containing $N$ images.

**Fig. 3.** Pipeline of our methods when training from scratch on a dataset containing $N$ images from $C$ classes

detection [4], segmentation [37], etc. Many ViT variants were proposed in recent months. Swin Transformer [22] applied the shifted window approach to compute self-attention matrix. Wang *et al.* proposed PVT-based model [35,36], which built a progressive shrinking pyramid and a spatial-reduction attention layer to generate multi-resolution feature maps. T2T-ViT [41] introduced a tokens-to-token (T2T) module to aggregate neighboring tokens into one recursively. However, ViTs are known to be data-hungry [20] and how to train ViTs with limited data is an important but not fully investigated question. [20] proposed a self-supervised task for ViTs, which can extract additional information from images and make training much more robust when training data are scarce. In contrast, we focus on the self-supervised pretraining stage while [20] focuses on the supervised fine-tuning stage. Moreover, we achieve much higher accuracy when training from scratch and we investigate the transferring ability when training on small datasets.

## 3 Method

We first explain why we use parametric instance discrimination (Sect. 3.1), then analyze how our strategies help weight updating (Sect. 3.2), and describe the complete method.

### 3.1 Analyses on Instance Discrimination

As shown in Fig. 2, an input image $\boldsymbol{x}_i$ ($i = 1, \cdots, N$) is sent to a network $f(\cdot)$ and get output representation $\mathbf{z}_i = f(\boldsymbol{x}_i) \in \mathbb{R}^d$, where $N$ denotes the total number of instances. Then, a fully connected (fc) layer $W$ is used for classification and the number of classes equals the total number of training images $N$ for parametric instance discrimination. We denote $\mathbf{w}_j \in \mathbb{R}^d$ as the weights for the $j$-th class and $W = [\mathbf{w}_1 | \ldots | \mathbf{w}_N] \in \mathbb{R}^{d \times N}$ contains the weights for all $N$ classes. Hence we have $O^{(i)} = W^T \mathbf{z}_i$, where the output for the $j$-th class $O_j^{(i)} = \mathbf{w}_j^T \mathbf{z}_i$. Finally, $O^{(i)}$ is sent to a softmax layer to get a valid probability distribution $P^{(i)}$.

For instance discrimination, the loss function is:

$$L_{\text{InsDis}} = -\sum_{i=1}^{N}\sum_{c=1}^{N} y_c^{(i)} \log P_c^{(i)} = -\sum_{i=1}^{N} \log P_i^{(i)} \tag{1}$$

$$= -\sum_{i=1}^{N} \log \frac{\exp(\mathbf{w}_i^T \mathbf{z}_i)}{\sum_{j=1}^{N} \exp(\mathbf{w}_j^T \mathbf{z}_i)} = -\sum_{i=1}^{N} \mathbf{w}_i^T \mathbf{z}_i + \sum_{i=1}^{N} \log \sum_{j=1}^{N} e^{\mathbf{w}_j^T \mathbf{z}_i}, \tag{2}$$

where the superscript $i$ sums over instances while the subscript $c$ sums over classes. For instance discrimination, the class label corresponds to the instance ID: $y_c^{(i)} = 1$ iff $c = i$.

Now we move on to the contrastive learning (CL) loss. There are typically 2 views (i.e., positive pairs) for each input $x_i$ and we call them $x_{iA}$, $x_{iB}$ (corresponding representations are $\mathbf{z}_{iA}$, $\mathbf{z}_{iB}$). The contrastive loss can be represented as follows (we omit hyper-parameter $\tau$ for simplicity):

$$L_{CL} = -\sum_{i=1}^{N} \mathbf{z}_{iA}^T \mathbf{z}_{iB} + \sum_{i=1}^{N} \log \left( e^{\mathbf{z}_{iA}^T \mathbf{z}_{iB}} + \sum e^{\mathbf{z}_{iA}^T \mathbf{z}_i^-} \right), \tag{3}$$

where $\mathbf{z}_i^-$ enumerates all negative pairs for $\mathbf{z}_i$, i.e., $\mathbf{z}_{jA}$ and $\mathbf{z}_{jB}$ for all $j \neq i$. Consider the loss term for the $i$-th instance:

$$L_{CL}^{(i)} = \underbrace{-\mathbf{z}_{iA}^T \mathbf{z}_{iB}}_{\text{alignment}} + \underbrace{\log \left( e^{\mathbf{z}_{iA}^T \mathbf{z}_{iB}} + \sum e^{\mathbf{z}_{iA}^T \mathbf{z}_i^-} \right)}_{\text{uniformity}} \tag{4}$$

If we set $\mathbf{w}_i = \mathbf{z}_i$ in instance discrimination, then from Eq. (2) we have (also consider the $i$-th term):

$$L_{\text{InsDis}}^{(i)} = \underbrace{-\mathbf{z}_i^T \mathbf{z}_i}_{\text{alignment}} + \underbrace{\log \left( e^{\mathbf{z}_i^T \mathbf{z}_i} + \sum_{j \neq i} e^{\mathbf{z}_i^T \mathbf{z}_j} \right)}_{\text{uniformity}} \tag{5}$$

Now it is clear that (5) and (4) are almost identical, except that there are two views in Eq. (4) ($\mathbf{z}_{iA}$ and $\mathbf{z}_{iB}$ vs. $\mathbf{z}_i$). Both have two terms: the alignment term encouraging more aligned positive features and the uniformity term encouraging the features to be roughly uniformly distributed on the unit hypersphere, as noted in [34]. Hence, we conclude that instance discrimination is approximately equivalent to the contrastive loss when we set $\mathbf{w}_j = \mathbf{z}_j, \forall j$. Our analyses also give a theoretical interpretation of the contrastive prior used in [21], which initializes $W$ in a contrastive way to accelerate convergence for high-dimensional $W$.

In other words, the contrastive loss is a special case of instance discrimination, with each $\mathbf{w}_i$ set to the representation of $x_i$ in the current batch (i.e., non-parametric instance discrimination). In contrast, the learnable fc $W$ in instance discrimination has at least two advantages:

(i) Separate representation learning from learning specific properties of the loss. As known in many contrastive learning methods (e.g., SimCLR [8]), using an extra projection head (MLPs) after representation is essential to learn good representations. However, we find that this projection head is *not* necessary for instance discrimination, thanks to the learnable weights $W$ of this fc, as will be shown in Sect. 4.4.

(ii) Find potential similarities between instances (classes). Now we consider DeepClustering [5], whose clustering loss can be reformulated as follows using our notation:

$$L_{DC} = -\sum_{i=1}^{N}\sum_{k=1}^{K} y_k^{(i)} \log P_k^{(i)}, \tag{6}$$

where $K$ denotes the number of clusters, $y_k^{(i)}$ indicates whether the $i$-th instance belongs to the $k$-th cluster, and $P_k^{(i)}$ denotes the probability that the $i$-th instance belongs to the $k$-th cluster. Let $C_k$ denotes the index of instances in cluster $k$, then if we set all $\{\mathbf{w}_j | j \in C_k\}$ to the same, i.e., $\mathbf{w}_j = \tilde{\mathbf{w}}_k$ for all $j \in C_k$, we have:

$$L_{InsDis} = -\sum_{i=1}^{N} \log P_i^{(i)} = -\sum_{k=1}^{K}\sum_{j \in C_k} \log P_j^{(j)} \tag{7}$$

$$= -\sum_{k=1}^{K}\sum_{j \in C_K} \log \sigma(\mathbf{w}_j^T \mathbf{z}_j) = -\sum_{k=1}^{K}\sum_{j \in C_K} \log \sigma(\tilde{\mathbf{w}}_k^T \mathbf{z}_j), \tag{8}$$

where $\sigma(\cdot)$ is the softmax function. Similarly, Eq. (6) becomes

$$L_{DC} = -\sum_{k=1}^{K}\sum_{j \in C_k} \log P_k^{(j)} = -\sum_{k=1}^{K}\sum_{j \in C_K} \log \sigma(\tilde{\mathbf{w}}_k^T \mathbf{z}_j). \tag{9}$$

Hence, when the weights $W$ are appropriately set, instance discrimination is equivalent to the deep clustering loss, which can observe potential instance similarities. As can be seen from Fig. 4, instance discrimination learns more distributed representations and captures better intra-class similarities.

Since in this paper we focus on ViTs, there is another important reason why we choose parametric instance discrimination: the simplicity and stability. As noted in [10], instability is a major issue that impacts self-supervised ViT training. Hence, the form of instance discrimination (cross entropy) is more stable and easier to optimize. It will be further demonstrated in Sect. 4.3 and Sect. 4.4 that our method can better adapt to various emerging ViT networks and does not rely on specific designs (e.g., projection MLP head).

## 3.2 Gradient Analysis

Consider the loss term for the $i$-th instance in Eq. (2):

$$L_{InsDis}^{(i)} = -\mathbf{w}_i^T \mathbf{z}_i + \log \sum_{j=1}^{N} e^{\mathbf{w}_j^T \mathbf{z}_i}. \tag{10}$$

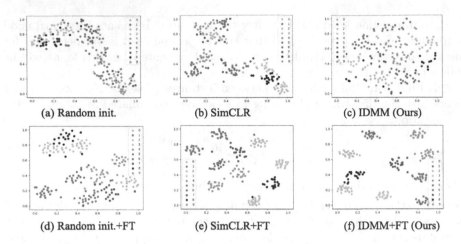

(a) Random init.    (b) SimCLR    (c) IDMM (Ours)

(d) Random init.+FT    (e) SimCLR+FT    (f) IDMM+FT (Ours)

**Fig. 4.** t-SNE [23] visualization of 10 classes selected from flowers using DeiT-Tiny. The first row shows the results before fine-tuning (i.e., without using any class labels) and the second row shows the results after fine-tuning ('FT'). This figure is best viewed in color. (Color figure online)

Then, the gradient w.r.t. $\mathbf{w}_k$ can be calculated as follows:

$$\frac{\partial L}{\partial \mathbf{w}_k} = -\delta_{\{k=i\}}\mathbf{z}_i + \frac{e^{\mathbf{w}_k^T \mathbf{z}_i}}{\sum_{j=1}^N e^{\mathbf{w}_j^T \mathbf{z}_i}}\mathbf{z}_i = (P_k^{(i)} - \delta_{\{k=i\}})\mathbf{z}_i\,, \tag{11}$$

where $\delta$ is an indicator function, equals 1 iff $k = i$.

Notice that for instance discrimination the number of classes $N$ can easily go very large and there exists extremely infrequent visiting of instance samples [2, 21]. Hence for infrequent instances $k \neq i$, we can expect $P_k^{(i)} \approx 0$ and hence $\frac{\partial L}{\partial \mathbf{w}_k} \approx \mathbf{0}$, which means extremely infrequent update of $\mathbf{w}_k$. [2] and [21] introduced different strategies to alleviate the problems for large datasets, such as the high GPU computation and memory overhead. Since in this paper we focus on small datasets, such strategies are not necessary. Instead, we use CutMix [42] and label smoothing [30] to update the weight matrix more frequently by directly modifying the one-hot label, which are also commonly used in supervised training of ViTs. If we use label smoothing, then

$$y_c^{(i)} = \begin{cases} 1 - \epsilon & \text{if } c = i, \\ \frac{\epsilon}{N-1} & \text{otherwise} \end{cases}, \tag{12}$$

where $\epsilon$ is the smoothing factor and we set it to 0.1 throughout this paper. Then the loss becomes:

$$L_{\text{InsDis}}^{(i)} = -(1-\epsilon)\mathbf{w}_i^T\mathbf{z}_i - \frac{\epsilon}{N-1}\sum_{k \neq i}\mathbf{w}_k^T\mathbf{z}_i + \log\sum_{j=1}^N e^{\mathbf{w}_j^T\mathbf{z}_i}\,. \tag{13}$$

If we continue to use CutMix, Eq. (13) becomes:

$$L^{(i)}_{\text{InsDis}} = -C_i \mathbf{w}_i^T \tilde{\mathbf{z}}_{ii'} - C_{i'} \mathbf{w}_{i'}^T \tilde{\mathbf{z}}_{ii'} - C \sum\nolimits_{j \neq i, i'} \mathbf{w}_j^T \tilde{\mathbf{z}}_{ii'} + \log \sum\nolimits_{j=1}^{N} e^{\mathbf{w}_j^T \tilde{\mathbf{z}}_{ii'}}, \quad (14)$$

where $\lambda$ is the mixed coefficient, $i'$ is the index of the other instance in CutMix, $\tilde{\mathbf{z}}_{ii'}$ is the output of the mixed input and

$$\begin{cases} C_i = \lambda(1 - \epsilon) + (1 - \lambda)\frac{\epsilon}{N-1} \\ C_{i'} = (1 - \lambda)(1 - \epsilon) + \lambda\frac{\epsilon}{N-1} \\ C = \lambda\frac{\epsilon}{N-1} \end{cases}. \quad (15)$$

And the gradient w.r.t. $\mathbf{w}_k$ becomes:

$$\frac{\partial L}{\partial \mathbf{w}_k} = \left( P_k^{(ii')} - C_i \delta_{\{k=i\}} - C_{i'} \delta_{\{k=i'\}} - C(1 - \delta_{\{k=i\}} - \delta_{\{k=i'\}}) \right) \tilde{\mathbf{z}}_{ii'}. \quad (16)$$

If we set $\lambda = 0.5$ and $N = 2040$, then $C_i = C_{i'} \approx 0.45$ and $C \approx 2.5e - 5$. Hence, we are able to update $\mathbf{w}_k$ even for instances $k \neq i$ (with relative large gradients for $\mathbf{w}_i$ and $\mathbf{w}_{i'}$ and small gradients for others), which alleviates the infrequent updating problem. Moreover, we can alleviate the overfitting problem by using CutMix as our regularization with limited data, as revealed in [42,43].

In conclusion, we use the following strategies to enhance instance discrimination (InsDis) on small datasets:

(1) Small resolution. It has been shown in [3] that small resolution during pre-training is useful for small datasets.
(2) Multi-crop. As analyzed before, InsDis generalizes the contrastive loss to capture both feature alignment and uniformity when using multiple crops.
(3) CutMix and label smoothing. As analyzed above, it helps us alleviate the overfitting and infrequent accessing problem when applying InsDis.

We call our method **i**nstance **d**iscrimination with **m**ulti-crop and CutMix (IDMM) and we conduct ablation studies on these strategies in Sect. 4.4.

## 4 Experiments

We used 7 small datasets for our experiments, as shown in Table 1. First, we explain the reasons why we need training from scratch in Sect. 4.1 and training from scratch results in Sect. 4.2. Then, we study the transferring ability of ViTs pretrained on small datasets (even facilitate large-scale datasets training) in Sect. 4.3. Finally, we conduct ablation studies on different components in Sect. 4.4. All our experiments were conducted using PyTorch and Titan Xp GPUs.

### 4.1 Why Training from Scratch?

We explain the reasons why do we need training from scratch directly on target datasets from 3 aspects:

- **Data.** Current ViT models are often pretrained on a large-scale dataset (such as ImageNet or even larger ones), and then fine-tuned in various downstream tasks. Moreover, the lack of the typical convolutional inductive bias makes these models more data-hungry than common CNNs. Hence, it is critical to investigate whether we can train ViTs from scratch for a task where the *total* amount of available images is limited (e.g., 100 categories with roughly 20 images per category).
- **Computing.** The combination of a large-scale dataset, a large number of epochs and a complex backbone network means that ViT training is extremely computationally expensive. This phenomenon makes ViT a privilege for researchers at few institutions.
- **Flexibility.** The pretraining followed by downstream fine-tuning paradigm will sometimes become cumbersome. For instance, we may need to train 10 different models for the same task, and deploy them to different hardware platforms [1], but it is impractical to pretrain 10 models on a large-scale dataset.

**Table 1.** Statistics of the 7 small datasets used in the paper.

| Datasets | # Category | # Training | # Testing |
|---|---|---|---|
| Flowers [25] | 102 | 2040 | 6149 |
| Pets [27] | 37 | 3680 | 3669 |
| DTD [11] | 47 | 3760 | 1880 |
| Indoor67 [28] | 67 | 5360 | 1340 |
| CUB200 [33] | 200 | 5994 | 5794 |
| Aircrafts [24] | 100 | 6667 | 3333 |
| Cars [18] | 196 | 8144 | 8041 |

As shown in Fig. 5, it is obvious that ImageNet pretrained models need much more data and computational cost when compared to training from scratch. Moreover, when we need to deploy models of different sizes on terminal devices, training from scratch provides better parameter-accuracy tradeoffs. For instance, the smallest ImageNet pretrained model of PVTv2 (i.e., B0) has 3.4M parameters, which may still be too big for some devices. In contrast, we can train a much smaller model (0.8M) from scratch to adapt to the devices, which reaches 93.8% accuracy using our IDMM.

### 4.2 Training from Scratch Results

In this section, we investigate training ViTs from scratch. Following [3], the full learning process contains two stages: pretraining and fine-tuning. We use the

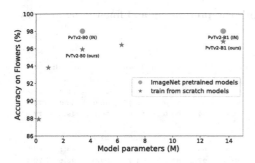 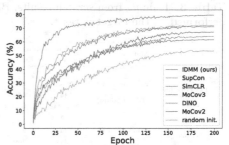

**Fig. 5.** Parameter-Accuracy tradeoff on flowers. The blue circles represent IN pretrained models while the red stars represent models of different sizes training from scratch using our method. (Color figure online)

**Fig. 6.** Comparison of different SSL methods on flowers dataset. All pretrained for 800 epochs and then finetuned for 200 epochs on flowers. (Color figure online)

**Table 2.** Comparison between different pretraining methods.

| Backbone | Pretraining | | Accuracy | | | | | | |
|---|---|---|---|---|---|---|---|---|---|
| | Method | Epochs | Flowers | Pets | Dtd | Indoor67 | CUB | Aircraft | Cars |
| DeiT-Tiny [31] | random init | 0 | 58.1 | 31.8 | 49.4 | 31.0 | 23.8 | 14.6 | 12.3 |
| | SimCLR [8] | | 71.1 | 52.1 | 55.9 | 50.7 | 36.2 | 43.2 | 64.3 |
| | SupCon [17] | | 72.3 | 50.3 | 55.6 | 49.3 | 37.8 | 29.4 | 66.2 |
| | MoCov2 [9] | 800 | 61.8 | 41.5 | 50.6 | 41.1 | 31.6 | 37.7 | 44.0 |
| | MoCov3 [10] | | 67.0 | 52.9 | 52.9 | 49.4 | 20.5 | 32.0 | 53.7 |
| | DINO [7] | | 64.1 | 51.3 | 51.7 | 46.9 | 41.8 | **45.7** | 65.3 |
| | IDMM (ours) | | **79.9** | **56.7** | **61.2** | **53.9** | **43.1** | 43.2 | **66.4** |

pretrained weights obtained by SSL for initialization and then fine-tune networks for classification using the cross entropy loss. As shown in Fig. 3, *SSL pretraining and fine-tuning are both performed* only *on the target dataset*. We focus on the first stage and the fine-tuning stage follows common practices.

For the fine-tuning stage, we follow the setup in DeiT [31] and fine-tune all methods for 200 epochs (except for Table 3). Specifically, we use AdamW with a batch size of 256 and a weight decay of 1e–3. The learning rate (lr) is initialized to 5e–4 and follows the cosine learning rate decay. For the SSL pretraining stage, all methods are pretrained for 800 epochs and our IDMM follows the same training settings as in the fine-tuning stage. We set $\alpha = 0.5$ for CutMix in our IDMM. We follow the settings in the original papers for other methods and more details are included in the appendix. We use $112 \times 112$ resolution during pretraining and $224 \times 224$ during fine-tuning for all methods, as suggested in [3].

First, we compare our method with popular SSL methods for both CNNs and ViTs in Table 2. For fair comparisons, all methods are pretrained for 800 epochs and then fine-tuned for 200 epochs. As can be seen in Table 2 and Fig. 6, SSL pretraining is useful even when training from scratch and all SSL methods perform better than random initialization. Our method achieves the highest

**Table 3.** Training from scratch results. Both the pretraining and fine-tuning are only performed on the target dataset.

| Backbone | Method | Fine-tuning | | Accuracy | | | | | | |
|---|---|---|---|---|---|---|---|---|---|---|
| | | Resolution | Epochs | Flowers | Pets | Dtd | Indoor67 | CUB | Aircraft | Cars |
| DeiT-Tiny [31] | IN super. | 224 | 200 | 97.3 | 88.6 | 73.2 | 75.6 | 76.8 | 78.7 | 90.3 |
| | random init. | 224 | 800 | 67.8 | 44.5 | 54.5 | 40.6 | 24.3 | 33.2 | 38.8 |
| | IDMM (ours) | 224 | 800 | 83.4 | 59.0 | 61.8 | 56.1 | 45.0 | 46.0 | 73.7 |
| | | 224→448 | 800→100 | 85.6 | 64.2 | 64.9 | 59.9 | 50.9 | 48.6 | 77.8 |
| DeiT-Base [31] | IN super. | 224 | 200 | 97.7 | 91.4 | 74.9 | 78.1 | 81.9 | 82.8 | 92.6 |
| | random init. | 224 | 800 | 67.3 | 48.4 | 46.0 | 44.0 | 27.7 | 30.1 | 33.3 |
| | IDMM (ours) | 224 | 800 | 88.1 | 63.2 | 62.3 | 57.4 | 47.8 | 43.1 | 64.5 |
| | | 224→448 | 800→100 | 90.6 | 67.2 | 67.3 | 61.7 | 54.3 | 46.6 | 70.7 |
| PVTv2-B0 [35] | IN super. | 224 | 200 | 98.0 | 90.5 | 75.9 | 76.7 | 81.4 | 88.3 | 92.6 |
| | random init. | 224 | 800 | 90.3 | 80.5 | 57.7 | 66.3 | 66.6 | 74.8 | 87.9 |
| | IDMM (ours) | 224 | 800 | 94.6 | 84.7 | 69.3 | 69.6 | 73.8 | 79.8 | 90.9 |
| | | 224→448 | 800→100 | 95.9 | 88.0 | 73.2 | 73.7 | 77.6 | 83.3 | 92.0 |
| PVTv2-B3 [35] | IN super. | 224 | 200 | 98.7 | 93.6 | 78.1 | 80.8 | 85.5 | 91.7 | 94.4 |
| | random init. | 224 | 800 | 90.5 | 83.4 | 64.5 | 67.5 | 66.2 | 85.0 | 89.9 |
| | Ours | 224 | 800 | 95.9 | 89.8 | 68.9 | 73.2 | 79.0 | 90.5 | 94.0 |
| | | 224→448 | 800→100 | 96.7 | 91.9 | 71.8 | 76.3 | 82.8 | 91.8 | 94.3 |
| T2T-ViT-7 [41] | IN super. | 224 | 200 | 97.7 | 90.5 | 75.2 | 76.6 | 79.0 | 83.8 | 92.8 |
| | random init. | 224 | 800 | 82.1 | 66.2 | 58.5 | 57.7 | 35.7 | 57.2 | 60.3 |
| | IDMM (ours) | 224 | 800 | 90.8 | 75.0 | 64.7 | 66.0 | 59.0 | 71.4 | 89.9 |
| | | 224→448 | 800→100 | 91.7 | 76.9 | 65.7 | 68.9 | 63.2 | 72.9 | 91.2 |

**Table 4.** Training from scratch results on CIFAR-10 ('CF-10') and CIFAR-100 ('CF-100').

| Backbone | Method | Accuracy | |
|---|---|---|---|
| | | CF-10 | CF-100 |
| DeiT-Tiny | random init | 88.9 | 66.3 |
| | MoCov3 | 94.7 | 79.0 |
| | Ours | 95.4 | 79.5 |
| PVTv2-B0 | random init | 93.1 | 77.4 |
| | MoCov3 | 96.1 | 81.5 |
| | Ours | 96.6 | 82.2 |

**Table 5.** Mean and standard deviation of 3 runs for our method. 'PT' and 'FT' represent pretraining and fine-tuning, respectively.

| Backbone | Stage | Flowers | Pets |
|---|---|---|---|
| PVTv2-B0 | PT | 92.5 ± 0.1 | 83.1 ± 0.3 |
| | FT | 92.4 ± 0.2 | 83.5 ± 0.2 |
| T2T-ViT-7 | PT | 89.0 ± 0.3 | 70.9 ± 0.3 |
| | FT | 88.6 ± 0.1 | 70.3 ± 0.2 |

accuracy on all these datasets, except for aircraft. When the number of images is small (e.g., flowers and pets), the advantage of our method is more obvious, which is consistent with our analyses before.

Then, following [3], we fine-tune the models for longer epochs to get better results. Specifically, with the IDMM initialized weights, we first fine-tune for 800 epochs under $224 \times 224$ resolution and then continue fine-tuning for 100 epochs under $448 \times 448$ resolution. As shown in Table 3, we achieve **the state-of-the-art results when training from scratch** on these 7 datasets for all these ViT models, to the best of our knowledge. Moreover, the gap between training from scratch and using ImageNet pretrained models (colored in gray) has been greatly reduced using our method, which indicates that training from scratch is promising even for ViT models. Notice that PVTv2 models achieve better performance than DeiT and T2T by introducing convolutions to ViTs. The introduction of the typical convolutional inductive bias makes it less data-hungry than common ViTs and hence achieving better performance on these small datasets. We also experimented on the popular CIFAR-10 and CIFAR-100 [19] in Table 4 and the results still demonstrate the effectiveness of our method.

Further, we also study the randomness during both the pretraining and fine-tuning stage because the number of training images is small. For the pretraining stage, we pretrain 3 different models (using our method) and fine-tune them separately. For the fine-tuning stage, we run 3 times with one pre-trained model. As shown in Table 5, the standard deviation is small in both stages on the two smallest datasets and hence we only report single run results in Tables 2, 3 and 4.

**Table 6.** Transferring ability when pretrained on small datasets. The element with the highest accuracy in each cell and column is underlined and **bolded**, respectively.

| Backbone | Pretraining | | Transferring accuracy | | | | | | |
|---|---|---|---|---|---|---|---|---|---|
| | Datasets | Method | Flowers | Pets | Dtd | Indoor67 | CUB | Aircraft | Cars |
| PVTv2-B0 | Flowers | IDMM | 92.4 | 83.1 | 64.8 | 66.3 | 69.9 | 77.1 | 87.3 |
| | | SimCLR | 90.1 | 80.7 | 61.6 | 64.3 | 62.3 | 72.8 | 86.6 |
| | | SupCon | 91.2 | 82.4 | 63.1 | 65.3 | 66.3 | 75.0 | 87.0 |
| | Pets | IDMM | 92.8 | 83.2 | 65.3 | 64.9 | 70.1 | 78.1 | 87.3 |
| | | SimCLR | 89.9 | 82.8 | 62.7 | 63.7 | 67.6 | 76.1 | 86.6 |
| | | SupCon | 90.4 | 84.7 | 63.5 | 64.6 | 69.6 | 76.1 | 87.8 |
| | Dtd | IDMM | 92.9 | 82.9 | 66.9 | 67.3 | 70.0 | 78.5 | 86.7 |
| | | SimCLR | 89.1 | 79.4 | 62.3 | 64.0 | 64.4 | 73.9 | 85.4 |
| | | SupCon | 88.9 | 79.7 | 62.3 | 63.6 | 65.1 | 75.8 | 86.2 |
| | Indoor67 | IDMM | 93.2 | 82.7 | 65.4 | 68.5 | 70.4 | **79.7** | 87.7 |
| | | SimCLR | 90.3 | 80.7 | 62.8 | 66.6 | 61.3 | 72.8 | 86.4 |
| | | SupCon | 90.9 | 82.2 | 62.9 | 65.0 | 66.9 | 74.6 | 86.8 |
| | CUB | IDMM | **93.7** | 83.3 | **67.0** | 68.7 | 69.8 | 78.7 | 87.6 |
| | | SimCLR | 91.3 | 82.2 | 63.9 | 64.9 | 68.5 | 76.7 | 87.3 |
| | | SupCon | 90.6 | 83.0 | 63.8 | 66.5 | 68.6 | 77.0 | 87.4 |
| | Aircraft | IDMM | 91.3 | 82.0 | 64.5 | 64.3 | 70.3 | 73.4 | 87.3 |
| | | SimCLR | 87.0 | 78.3 | 60.6 | 62.9 | 65.2 | 74.4 | 86.2 |
| | | SupCon | 87.9 | 79.3 | 62.4 | 61.9 | 66.4 | 76.5 | 86.2 |
| | Cars | IDMM | 93.4 | **85.0** | 66.5 | 69.4 | 72.2 | 79.5 | 87.8 |
| | | SimCLR | 90.9 | 84.5 | 64.3 | 67.4 | 68.8 | 79.1 | 89.3 |
| | | SupCon | 91.1 | 84.6 | 65.1 | 68.3 | 70.4 | 79.3 | **90.6** |
| | N/A | random init. | 76.3 | 65.1 | 55.7 | 58.9 | 55.2 | 41.7 | 76.7 |

**Table 7.** Transferring ability when pretrained on 10,000 images from ImageNet. All elements are obtained by fine-tuning for 200 epochs.

| Backbone | Pretraining | | Transferring Accuracy | | | | | | |
|---|---|---|---|---|---|---|---|---|---|
| | Datasets | Method | Flowers | Pets | Dtd | Indoor67 | CUB | aircraft | Cars |
| PVTv2-B0 | SIN-10k | IDMM | **93.8** | **83.6** | **66.8** | **69.4** | **70.7** | **81.3** | **87.5** |
| | | MoCov3 | 91.0 | 81.4 | 62.3 | 66.3 | 63.7 | 74.5 | 86.2 |
| | | DINO | 92.3 | 82.3 | 65.9 | 68.5 | 65.8 | 76.9 | 86.4 |
| | | Supervised | 92.9 | 81.7 | 66.1 | 65.9 | 66.6 | 78.7 | 86.0 |
| PVTv2-B3 | SIN-10k | IDMM | **95.9** | **88.4** | **70.1** | **73.6** | **76.8** | **87.5** | **92.9** |
| | | MoCov3 | 93.7 | 87.1 | 66.0 | 70.5 | 63.7 | 82.2 | 92.3 |
| | | DINO | 95.0 | 87.8 | 68.3 | 73.4 | 72.4 | 86.1 | 92.5 |
| | | Supervised | 90.9 | 80.9 | 62.9 | 63.3 | 65.6 | 83.8 | 89.7 |
| T2T-ViT-7 | SIN-10k | IDMM | **89.8** | **74.1** | **63.5** | **62.6** | **55.2** | **72.7** | **82.4** |
| | | Supervised | 80.8 | 57.8 | 57.5 | 50.7 | 35.6 | 56.8 | 59.9 |

### 4.3   Transfer Ability of Small Datasets

Having investigated training from scratch on small datasets for various ViT models, we now study the transfer ability of the representations learned on these small datasets. The transfer ability of representations pretrained on large-scale datasets has been well studied, but few works studied the transfer ability of small datasets.

In Table 6 we evaluate the transferring accuracy of models pretrained on different datasets. As in Sect. 4.2, we train 800 epochs for pretraining and fine-tuning 200 epochs. The on-diagonal cells perform pretraining and fine-tuning on the same dataset. The off-diagonal cells evaluate transfer performance across these small datasets. From Table 6 we can conclude:

- ViTs have good transferring ability even when pretrained on small datasets. This means that we can use pretrained models from small datasets to transfer to other datasets in different domains to improve performance.
- Our method also has higher transferring accuracy on all these datasets when compared to SimCLR and SupCon. As analyzed before, we think that it is due to the learnable fully connected layer $W$, which can capture both feature alignment and instance similarity. Also, the learnable fc better protects features from learning specific properties of the loss, as will be shown in Sect. 4.4.
- We can obtain surprisingly good results even if the pretrained dataset and the target dataset are *not* in the same domain. For instance, models pretrained on Indoor67 achieve the highest accuracy when transfer to Aircraft. It is obvious that the number of images in the pretrained dataset matters, because Cars performs best in all. However, we want to argue that it is not the only reason because we can see that Indoor67 and CUB perform better than Cars in some cases despite having fewer training images. We leave it to future work to study what properties matter for pretraining datasets when transferring.

After observing that models pretrained on small datasets have surprisingly good transferring ability, we can further explore the potential of small datasets.

**Table 8.** Top-1 accuracy (%) on ImageNet.

| Backbone | Method | Epochs | Acc. (%) |
|---|---|---|---|
| PVTv2-B0 | random init | 100 | 68.6 |
| | MoCov3 (SIN-10k) | | 68.8 |
| | IDMM (SIN-10k) | | **69.5** |
| | IDMM (SIN-total 10k) | | **69.5** |
| | random init | 300 | 70.0 |
| | IDMM (SIN-10k) | | **70.9** |
| DeiT-Tiny | random init | 100 | 66.8 |
| | IDMM (SIN-10k) | | **67.8** |
| | random init | 300 | 72.2 |
| | IDMM (SIN-10k) | | **72.9** |

We sample the original ImageNet to smaller subsets with 10,000 images (SIN-10k), motivated by [3]. By pretraining models on SIN-10k, we evaluate the performance when transferring to small datasets in Table 7 as well as the large-scale dataset ImageNet in Table 8. In Table 7 we compare our method with various SSL methods as well as the supervised baseline under different backbones. It can be seen that our method has a large edge over these comparison methods and representations learned on SIN-10k can serve as a good initialization when transferring to other datasets. It is worth noting that MoCov3 and DINO fail to converge under T2T-ViT-7 after trying various hyper-parameters so we don't report the results for them in Table 7. It indicates our method can be easily applied to emerging ViTs without the need of special design or tuning.

Furthermore, we investigate whether we can benefit from pretraining on 10,000 images when training on ImageNet. As seen in Table 8, using the representation learned from 10,000 images as initialization can greatly accelerate the training process and finally achieve higher accuracy (about 1 point) on ImageNet. Notice that we sampled a balanced subset before (10 images per class) and we also compare with the setting where we randomly sample 10,000 images without using label information (SIN-total 10k). As seen, whether to use labels when sampling (balanced or not) has no effect on the result, as noted in [40].

### 4.4 Ablation Studies

In this section, we first investigate the effect of different components in our method in Table 9. 'LS', 'SR', 'MC', and 'CM' denote label smoothing, small resolution, multi-crop and CutMix, respectively. Then, we investigate the effect of the projection MLP head in Table 10.

As can be seen in Table 9, all the 4 strategies are useful and combining all these strategies achieves the best results. The experimental results further confirm the analyses in Sect. 3.1 that using multiple views and CutMix is helpful.

**Table 9.** Ablation studies when training from scratch on flowers.

| Method | LS | SR | MC | CM | Acc. (%) |
|--------|----|----|----|----|----------|
| | × | × | × | × | 69.6 |
| | ✓ | × | × | × | 70.4 |
| InsDis | ✓ | ✓ | × | × | 73.1 |
| | ✓ | ✓ | ✓ | × | 76.9 |
| | ✓ | ✓ | ✓ | ✓ | **79.9** |

**Table 10.** Effect of the projection MLP head. All pretrained on SIN-10k with DeiT-Tiny.

| method | proj. head | flowers | pets | dtd | cub |
|--------|-----------|---------|------|-----|-----|
| IDMM | × | **86.6** | **65.3** | **59.1** | 47.6 |
| | ✓ | 85.2 | 65.1 | 57.8 | **48.0** |
| SimCLR | × | 82.2 | 60.2 | 57.8 | 41.7 |
| | ✓ | **83.3** | **62.1** | **58.9** | **45.8** |

In Table 10, all methods are pretrained for 800 epochs on SIN-10k and then fine-tuned for 200 epochs when transferring to target datasets. The projection MLP head is essential for contrastive methods like SimCLR while it is not the case for instance discrimination. It further confirms the analyses in Sect. 3.1 that the learnable fc $W$ protects features from learning specific properties of the loss and hence achieving better transferring ability. In contrast, the $W$ in contrastive loss is not learnable and they need extra projection head.

## 5    Conclusions

In this paper, we proposed a method called IDMM for (pre)training ViTs with small data and the effectiveness of the proposed approach is well validated by both theoretical analyses and experimental studies. We achieved state-of-the-art results on 7 small datasets under various ViT backbones when training from scratch. Moreover, we studied the transferring ability of small datasets and found that ViTs also have good transferring ability even when pre-trained on small datasets. However, there is still room for improvement when training from scratch on these small datasets for architectures like DeiT. Furthermore, it is still unknown what properties matter for pretraining on small datasets when transferring and we leave them to future work.

**Acknowledgments.** This research was partly supported by the National Natural Science Foundation of China under Grant 61921006 and Grant 61772256.

## References

1. Cai, H., Gan, C., Wang, T., Zhang, Z., Han, S.: Once-for-all: train one network and specialize it for efficient deployment. In: The International Conference on Learning Representations, pp. 1–14 (2020)
2. Cao, Y., Xie, Z., Liu, B., Lin, Y., Zhang, Z., Hu, H.: Parametric instance classification for unsupervised visual feature learning. arXiv preprint arXiv:2006.14618 (2020)
3. Cao, Y.H., Wu, J.: Rethinking self-supervised learning: Small is beautiful. arXiv preprint arXiv:2103.13559 (2021)

4. Carion, N., Massa, F., Synnaeve, G., Usunier, N., Kirillov, A., Zagoruyko, S.: End-to-end object detection with transformers. In: Vedaldi, A., Bischof, H., Brox, T., Frahm, J.-M. (eds.) ECCV 2020. LNCS, vol. 12346, pp. 213–229. Springer, Cham (2020). https://doi.org/10.1007/978-3-030-58452-8_13

5. Caron, M., Bojanowski, P., Joulin, A., Douze, M.: Deep Clustering for unsupervised learning of visual features. In: Ferrari, V., Hebert, M., Sminchisescu, C., Weiss, Y. (eds.) Computer Vision – ECCV 2018. LNCS, vol. 11218, pp. 139–156. Springer, Cham (2018). https://doi.org/10.1007/978-3-030-01264-9_9

6. Caron, M., Misra, I., Mairal, J., Goyal, P., Bojanowski, P., Joulin, A.: Unsupervised learning of visual features by contrasting cluster assignments. In: Advances in Neural Information Processing Systems, pp. 9912–9924 (2020)

7. Caron, M., Touvron, H., Misra, I., Jégou, H., Mairal, J., Bojanowski, P., Joulin, A.: Emerging properties in self-supervised vision transformers. In: The IEEE International Conference on Computer Vision, pp. 9650–9660 (2021)

8. Chen, T., Kornblith, S., Norouzi, M., Hinton, G.: A simple framework for contrastive learning of visual representations. In: The International Conference on Machine Learning, pp. 1597–1607 (2020)

9. Chen, X., Fan, H., Girshick, R., He, K.: Improved baselines with momentum contrastive learning. arXiv preprint arXiv:2003.04297 (2020)

10. Chen, X., Xie, S., He, K.: An empirical study of training self-supervised vision transformers. In: The IEEE International Conference on Computer Vision, pp. 9640–9649 (2021)

11. Cimpoi, M., Maji, S., Kokkinos, I., Mohamed, S., Vedaldi, A.: Describing textures in the wild. In: The IEEE Conference on Computer Vision and Pattern Recognition, pp. 3606–3613 (2014)

12. Devlin, J., Chang, M.W., Lee, K., Toutanova, K.: BERT: pre-training of deep bidirectional transformers for language understanding. In: North American Chapter of the Association for Computational Linguistics, pp. 4171–4186 (2019)

13. Dosovitskiy, A., et al.: An Image is Worth 16x16 Words: Transformers for Image Recognition at Scale. In: International Conference on Learning Representations, pp. 1–12 (2021)

14. Dosovitskiy, A., Springenberg, J.T., Riedmiller, M., Brox, T.: Discriminative unsupervised feature learning with convolutional neural networks. In: Advances in Neural Information Processing Systems, pp. 766–774 (2014)

15. He, K., Fan, H., Wu, Y., Xie, S., Girshick, R.: Momentum contrast for unsupervised visual representation learning. In: The IEEE Conference on Computer Vision and Pattern Recognition, pp. 9729–9738 (2020)

16. He, K., Zhang, X., Ren, S., Sun, J.: Deep residual learning for image recognition. In: The IEEE Conference on Computer Vision and Pattern Recognition, pp. 770–778 (2016)

17. Khosla, P., et al.: Supervised contrastive learning. In: Advances in Neural Information Processing Systems, pp. 18661–18673 (2020)

18. Krause, J., Stark, M., Deng, J., Fei-Fei, L.: 3D object representations for fine-grained categorization, In: ICCV Workshop on 3D Representation and Recognition (2013)

19. Krizhevsky, A., Hinton, G.E.: Learning multiple layers of features from tiny images. University of Toronto, Tech. rep. (2009)

20. Liu, Y., Sangineto, E., Bi, W., Sebe, N., Lepri, B., Nadai, M.D.: Efficient training of visual transformers with small-size datasets. In: Advances in Neural Information Processing Systems, pp. 23818–23830 (2021)

21. Liu, Y., Huang, L., Pan, P., Wang, B., Xu, Y., Jin, R.: Train a one-million-way instance classifier for unsupervised visual representation learning. In: Proceedings of the AAAI Conference on Artificial Intelligence, vol. 35,pp. 8706–8714 (2021)

22. Liu, Z., et al.: Swin transformer: hierarchical vision transformer using shifted windows. In: The IEEE International Conference on Computer Vision, pp. 10012–10022 (2021)

23. van der Maaten, L., Hinton, G.: Visualizing data using t-SNE. J. Mach. Learn. Res. **9**(86), 2579–2605 (2008)

24. Maji, S., Rahtu, E., Kannala, J., Blaschko, M., Vedaldi, A.: Fine-grained visual classification of aircraft. arXiv preprint arXiv:1306.5151 (2013)

25. Nilsback, M.E., Zisserman, A.: A visual vocabulary for flower classification. In: The IEEE Conference on Computer Vision and Pattern Recognition, pp. 1447–1454 (2006)

26. van den Oord, A., Li, Y., Vinyals, O.: Representation learning with contrastive predictive coding. arXiv preprint arXiv:1807.03748 (2018)

27. Parkhi, O.M., Vedaldi, A., Zisserman, A., Jawahar, C.V.: Cats and dogs. In: The IEEE Conference on Computer Vision and Pattern Recognition, pp. 3498–3505 (2012)

28. Quattoni, A., Torralba, A.: Recognizing indoor scenes. In: The IEEE Conference on Computer Vision and Pattern Recognition, pp. 413–420 (2009)

29. Russakovsky, Q., et al.: ImageNet large scale visual recognition challenge. Int. J. Comput. Vision **115**(3), 211–252 (2015)

30. Szegedy, C., Vanhoucke, V., Ioffe, S., Shlens, J., Wojna, Z.: Rethinking the inception architecture for computer vision. In: The IEEE Conference on Computer Vision and Pattern Recognition, pp. 2818–2826 (2016)

31. Touvron, H., Cord, M., Douze, M., Massa, F., Sablayrolles, A., Jégou, H.: Training data-efficient image transformers & distillation through attention. In: The International Conference on Machine Learning, pp. 10347–10357 (2021)

32. Vaswani, A., et al.: Attention is All you Need. In: Advances in Neural Information Processing Systems, pp. 5998–6008 (2017)

33. Wah, C., Branson, S., Welinder, P., Perona, P., Belongie, S.: The Caltech-UCSD Birds-200-2011 Dataset. Tech. Rep. CNS-TR-2011-001, California Institute of Technology (2011)

34. Wang, T., Isola, P.: Understanding contrastive representation learning through alignment and uniformity on the hypersphere. In: The International Conference on Machine Learning, pp. 9929–9939 (2020)

35. Wang, W., et al.: PVTv 2: improved baselines with pyramid vision transformer. arXiv preprint arXiv:2106.13797 (2021)

36. Wang, W., et al.: Pyramid vision transformer: a versatile backbone for dense prediction without convolutions. In: The IEEE International Conference on Computer Vision, pp. 568–578 (2021)

37. Wang, Y., et al.: End-to-end video instance segmentation with transformers. In: The IEEE Conference on Computer Vision and Pattern Recognition, pp. 8741–8750 (2021)

38. Wu, H., et al.: CvT: introducing convolutions to vision transformers. In: The IEEE International Conference on Computer Vision, pp. 22–31 (2021)

39. Wu, Z., Xiong, Y., Yu, S.X., Lin, D.: Unsupervised feature learning via nonparametric instance discrimination. In: The IEEE Conference on Computer Vision and Pattern Recognition, pp. 3733–3742 (2018)

40. Yang, Y., Xu, Z.: Rethinking the value of labels for improving class-imbalanced learning. In: Advances in Neural Information Processing Systems, pp. 19290–19301 (2020)
41. Yuan, L., et al.: Tokens-to-token ViT: training vision transformers from scratch on imagenet. arXiv preprint arXiv:2101.11986 (2021)
42. Yun, S., Han, D., Oh, S.J., Chun, S., Choe, J., Yoo, Y.: CutMix: regularization strategy to train strong classifiers with localizable features. In: The IEEE International Conference on Computer Vision, pp. 6023–6032 (2019)
43. Zhang, H., Cisse, M., Dauphin, Y.N., Lopez-Paz, D.: Mixup: beyond empirical risk minimization. In: The International Conference on Learning Representations, pp. 1–13 (2018)

# Bridging Images and Videos: A Simple Learning Framework for Large Vocabulary Video Object Detection

Sanghyun Woo[1], Kwanyong Park[1], Seoung Wug Oh[2], In So Kweon[1], and Joon-Young Lee[2(✉)]

[1] KAIST, Daejeon, South Korea
[2] Adobe Research, San Jose, USA
jolee@adobe.com

**Abstract.** Scaling object taxonomies is one of the important steps toward a robust real-world deployment of recognition systems. We have faced remarkable progress in images since the introduction of the LVIS benchmark. To continue this success in videos, a new video benchmark, TAO, was recently presented. Given the recent encouraging results from both detection and tracking communities, we are interested in marrying those two advances and building a strong large vocabulary video tracker. However, supervisions in LVIS and TAO are inherently sparse or even missing, posing two new challenges for training the large vocabulary trackers. First, no tracking supervisions are in LVIS, which leads to inconsistent learning of detection (with LVIS and TAO) and tracking (only with TAO). Second, the detection supervisions in TAO are partial, which results in catastrophic forgetting of absent LVIS categories during video fine-tuning. To resolve these challenges, we present a simple but effective learning framework that takes full advantage of all available training data to learn detection and tracking while not losing any LVIS categories to recognize. With this new learning scheme, we show that consistent improvements of various large vocabulary trackers are capable, setting strong baseline results on the challenging TAO benchmarks.

**Keywords:** Large vocabulary · Video object detection and tracking

## 1 Introduction

A central goal of computer vision is to produce a general-purpose perception system that robustly works in the wild. Towards this ambitious goal, extending the current short category regime is one of the essential key milestones. As an

S. Woo and K. Park—This work was done during an internship at Adobe Research.

**Supplementary Information** The online version contains supplementary material available at https://doi.org/10.1007/978-3-031-19806-9_14.

initial effort in this direction, the large-scale image benchmark, LVIS [16], was introduced and fostered significant progress in developing solid image domain solutions [24,58,70,71,76,104]. Recently, a video benchmark, TAO [12], calls for a shift from image to video, opening the new task of detecting and tracking large vocabulary objects.

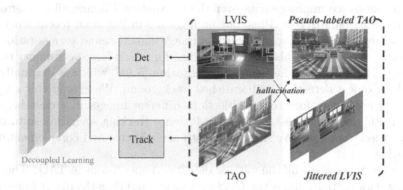

**Fig. 1. The Proposed Learning Framework for Large Vocabulary Tracker Training.** While the current learning paradigm learns detection and tracking separately from LVIS and TAO (decoupled), our proposal takes all training data to learn detection and tracking jointly (**unified**). This is achieved through missing supervision hallucination.

With these new datasets of images and videos, LVIS and TAO, we are interested in building a strong large vocabulary video tracker. However, as the annotation difficulty between images and videos is even more severe in large vocabulary datasets, the significant gap in dataset scale and label vocabularies naturally exists. Therefore, pre-training the model on images for learning large vocabularies and then fine-tuning on video for seamless video domain adaptation is a standard learning protocol. Given this context, can the current advances of large-vocabulary detection and multi-object tracking be successfully unified and tied into a single model? In particular, we see there are two main challenges for the successful marriage of two streams: **First, no tracking supervisions are in LVIS.** This essentially leads to inconsistent learning of detection (with LVIS and TAO) and tracking (only with TAO), resulting in sub-optimal video feature representations. **Second, detection supervisions in TAO are partial[1].** Thus, catastrophic forgetting [45] is inevitable if one naively fine-tunes the LVIS tracker directly on the TAO.

In this work, we present simple, effective, and generic methods for hallucinating missing supervisions in each dataset. Below, we describe the challenges and our solutions in turn.

---

[1] TAO dataset annotates 482 classes in total, which are the subset of LVIS dataset [16], and only 216 classes are in the training set.

First, how can we simulate the tracking supervisions only with images in LVIS? Given an image, our idea is to apply spatial jittering artifacts to mimic temporal changes in video and form a natural pair for tracking. Here, we present two new spatial jittering methods. The first is strong zoom-in/out augmentation, which has a large scale-jittering effect that can effectively simulate the low sampling rate test-time inputs in large vocabulary tracking. It yields significant performance improvements over the conventional image affine augmentation [20,48,52,66,102,105]. Plus, our findings are in line with recent work that shows a large scale jittering is effective in image detection and segmentation [15], and here we examine this observation on video for robust large vocabulary tracker training. The second is mosaicing augmentation [5,94], which is originally presented for object detection with enriched background. We extend this augmentation for combining foreground objects in different images in a class-balanced manner [16] and simulate test-time hard, dense tracking scenarios suitable for "many object" trackers. We show that both are effective and complementary to each other.

Second, how can we fill the missing detection supervisions in TAO? The TAO training data partially spans the LVIS categories, and thus the direct fine-tuning of LVIS tracker on TAO causes catastrophic forgetting of absent categories. A straightforward way to avoid this issue is to learn only the tracking part of the model with TAO [51]. However, this hinders full model training and abandons all the TAO detection labels, limiting the overall performance. We instead approach this problem by combining the self-training [60,61,63] with a teacher-student framework [21,89]. In practice, the teacher and student are identical copies of the LVIS pre-trained model, and we freeze the weights of the teacher during training. The overall learning pipeline consists of two steps: First, given an input, we predict pseudo labels using the teacher model. The idea behind the pseudo labeling is to leverage the past knowledge acquired from LVIS and fill in the missing annotations in TAO. Second, using the augmented labels, we train the student model with both distillation loss and ordinal detection loss. Unlike the typical teacher-student schemes used in semi-supervised object detection studies [67,91,92], we introduce two new adaptations suitable for large vocabulary learning setup. The first is using *soft* pseudo labels, i.e., distilling class logits directly, to fire all the student's classifier weights, rather than using common one-hot (hard) pseudo labels. This is crucial as standard hard pseudo labels tend to bias distillation only toward the frequent class objects due to inherent classifier calibration issue [11,50]. The second is to use *MSE* loss in order to equally impact all the classifier weights [28,72], rather than using picky KL-divergence loss [21]. We found the type of the loss function is also very important for the successful large vocabulary classifier distillation. Despite the simplicity, we empirically show that the distillation results are greatly improved with these adaptations. We also show that our proposal works well on the common vocabulary setup, e.g., COCO, and can be easily extended to new class learning scenarios, COCO → YTVIS.

Combining all these proposals together, unified learning of detection and tracking with both LVIS images and TAO videos becomes possible without forgetting any LVIS categories (see Fig. 1). Furthermore, we also introduce a new regularization objective, semantic consistency loss. It aims to prevent the common tracking failure in large vocabulary tracking due to semantic flicker between similar classes. We study the efficacy of our final framework on the TAO benchmark and achieve new state-of-the-art results. Our extensive ablation studies confirm that the proposals are generic and effective.

## 2   Related Work

**Large Vocabulary Recognition.** The object categories in natural images follow the Zipfian distribution [44], and thus, the large vocabulary recognition is naturally tied with the long-tailed recognition [17,42,86]. Based on this connection, lots of solid approaches are introduced. The existing methods can be roughly categorized into *data re-sampling* or *loss re-weighting*. The data re-sampling methods more often sample data from rare classes to balance the long-tailed training distribution [8,16]. The loss re-weighting aims at adjusting the loss of each data instance based on their labels or train-time accumulated statistics [22,70,71,76]. Some approaches perform multi-staged training upon these methods, which first pre-train the model in a standard way and then fine-tune using either data re-sampling or loss re-weighting [23,24,39,58,78,79,82,98]. Also, there are new approaches based on data augmentations [15,95,97] or test time calibration [50].

Apart from all these previous efforts on the image, we study a new video extension of the task [12]. We show that our proposal is generic and not sensitive to a specific method, data re-sampling or loss re-weighting, in successfully converting the current large vocabulary detectors to large vocabulary trackers.

**Multi-object Tracking.** Most modern multi object trackers [35] follow the tracking-by-detection paradigm [56]. An off-the-shelf object detector is first employed to localize all objects in each frame, and then track association is performed between adjacent frames. The main difference among existing methods is in how they estimate the similarity between detected objects and previous tracks for the association. To name a few, Kalman Filter [4,84], optical flow [88], displacement regression [53,105], and appearance similarities [3,25,34,35,43,47,51,62,68,83,93,99,100] are the representatives. On the other side, there are also efforts on joining detection and tracking [13,85,101], and recently by transformer-based architectures [46,69,96]. We note that all these methods only focus on a few object categories such as people or vehicles, ignoring the vast majority of objects in the world.

Our work is an early attempt for extending the current short category regime of modern trackers [12,41,80,107]. In this paper, we build our proposal upon the tracking-by-detection paradigm. We choose the state-of-the-art method, QDTrack [51], which adopts Faster R-CNN [59] and lightweight embedding head for detection and tracking, respectively. The tracking is learned through a dense matching between quasi-dense samples on the pair of images and optimized with multiple positive contrastive learning. Given the state-of-the-art large vocabulary detection [16,70,76] and multi-object tracking [51] methods, we primarily investigate the new challenges in developing a strong large vocabulary tracker.

**Tracking Without Video Annotations.** There is a line of recent research on self-supervised learning for tracking, either using unlabeled videos [32,33,38,55, 73,77,81,90] or images [14,20,48,52,66,102,105]. Our work belongs to the latter category. Applying random affine augmentation to the original image provides a spatially jittered version, which mimics the temporal changes in the video. By letting the model find the correspondence between those two images, meaningful tracking supervision can be provided [17,48,105]. Sio *et al.* [66] present that an image and any cropped region of it can generate a similar effect. Zheng *et al.* [102] extend this idea to incorporate only the foreground objects in cropped regions for stable training.

In this work, we explore this general idea under a more specific large vocabulary tracking setting. First, we focus on the fact that conventional motion cues are not applicable for large-vocabulary trackers as the input are temporally distant (1FPS) due to the annotation difficulties and there are severe camera movements in natural videos. This motivate us to train the tracker's vision feature matching more discriminative. To this end, we present a strong zoom-in/out augmentation that can not only simulate low sampling rate input but also includes large scale-jittering effect [15] which is known to be effective in the image domain vision tasks. Second, we recast the image mosaicing augmentation [5], which was initially proposed for robust object detection with enriched backgrounds [94], to simulate test-time dense tracking in the large vocabulary setting. We show that both are complementary in providing discriminative tracking supervisions for this task.

**Catastrophic Forgetting.** The phenomenon wherein neural networks forget how to solve past tasks because of the exposure to new tasks is known as catastrophic forgetting [45]. It occurs because the model weights that contain important information for the old task are over-written by information relevant to the new one. While the catastrophic forgetting can occur in various scenarios, many existing efforts are focused on the class incremental learning setup, where it incrementally adds new object categories phase-by-phase, in image classification [1,9,29,36,54,57,64,87]. Also, there are some few approaches tackling incremental object detection [30,65,75,103].

We target a different setup, transfer learning from image to video without forgetting. Specifically, we aim to train the model on images covering the entire evaluation categories and then fine-tune it on videos, which partially covers the evaluation categories, without forgetting. While lots of current video models [27, 49,93] are trained in this way for generic feature learning, the label difference issue between images and videos has been rarely studied and explored. We study this issue, as this is a practical setup for training large vocabulary trackers using both images and videos.

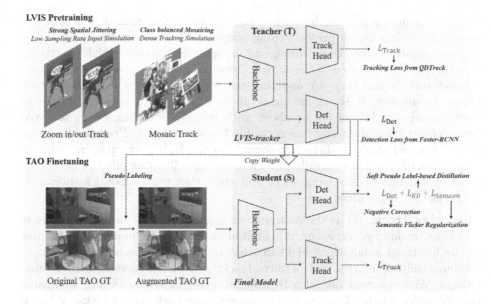

**Fig. 2. Overview of the proposed learning framework.** The red colored objective functions are generated supervisions with our proposals. (Color figure online)

## 3 Proposed Method

We introduce a general learning framework that allows joint learning of detection and tracking from all training data, LVIS and TAO, for robust large vocabulary tracking. The overview of our pipeline is shown in Fig. 2. We first present how we can learn tracking from images through zoom-in/out and mosaicing augmentations in Sect. 3.1. We then describe how we avoid catastrophic forgetting when the videos for fine-tuning have fewer label vocabularies than pre-trained images in Sect. 3.2. Finally, we present a new regularization loss term, namely semantic consistency loss, for preventing semantic flicker in Sect. 3.3.

### 3.1 Learn to Track in LVIS

Our approach is straightforward. An original image and a transformed image with the spatial jittering artifacts can form a natural input pair for tracking. For the jittering artifacts, we present two new augmentations, zoom-in/out and mosaicing (see Fig. 2). Note that tracking annotations come for free as we know the exact transformation relationship between the images. We assign the same unique track-id to the same object in the transformed image.

**Strong Zoom-in/Out Track.** Due to the annotation difficulty of the large-vocabulary tracking dataset, the train and test time inputs are temporally sparse, i.e., low sampling rate, which naturally results in conventional motion cues not applicable and rather rely on pure vision feature matching. To make the vision feature matching more discriminative, and to effectively simulate test-time low sampling rate inputs, we present strong zoom-in/out augmentation.

It is mainly composed of scaling and cropping operations, which essentially vary the scale and position of the objects. Specifically, for an image I, we generate a input pair, $I_t$ and $I_{t+\tau}$, by applying the scale_and_crop($\cdot$) function to each image. In practice, it scales an image up to 2 times and crops the image to have a minimum IoU of 0.4 or above with original bounding boxes to avoid heavy object truncation and ensure stable tracker training. Prior works either adopt standard random affine transformation [17,48,105] or cropping without scaling [66,102], which generally provide *weak* scale-jittering effect. Instead, we focus on enlarging the scaling effect and show that our proposal significantly outperforms the baselines.

**Mosaicing Track.** While the zoom-in/out augmentation is already effective in providing tracking supervisions, it is limited in the tracking of a few objects due to the federated annotations of LVIS [16]. To resolve the issue, we present to combine multiple images and perform tracking with the increased foreground objects. We implement our idea by extending the image mosaicing augmentation [5], which stitches four random training images with certain ratios. While it was originally presented for object detection with enriched background [94], we recast it to simulate hard, dense tracking scenarios in large vocabulary tracking. In practice, four random images, $\{I_a, I_b, I_c, I_d\}$, are sampled from RFS (Repeat Factor Sampling)-based dataset [16] to maintain the class-balance. Then, image stitching followed by random affine (with large scale jittering within a range of 0.1 to 2) and crop is applied. We summarize these procedure as mosaic($\cdot$). The tracking pair then can be obtained by applying the mosaic($\cdot$) function to the sampled images twice. However, we see that unnatural layout pair results in train and test time inconsistency. To this end, we propose to sample tracking input pairs in a mixed way from two different augmentations, zoom-in/out and mosaicing, with equal probability during training. We empirically confirm that this works well in practice.

With our proposal, the model can receive tracking supervisions from all LVIS object categories. The tracking objective function is adopted from the QDtrack [51] (see Fig. 2-top), and we call this model LVIS-Tracker. While the model is only trained on LVIS dataset, it already outperforms the previous state-of-the-art tracker (trained with the standard decoupled learning scheme) significantly (see Table 2a).

### 3.2 Learn to Unforget in TAO

Due to the fundamental annotation difficulties in videos, the images are in general bigger in dataset scale and larger in taxonomies. Therefore, pre-training the model on images to acquire generic features and fine-tuning on videos for target domain adaptation has become a common protocol for obtaining satisfactory performance in various video tasks [27,49,93]. This also applies to training the large vocabulary video trackers, where we first learn a large number of vocabulary from LVIS images and then adapt to the evaluation domain with TAO videos. However, as TAO partially spans the full LVIS vocabularies, a naive transfer learning scheme results in catastrophic forgetting.

Here, our goal is to keep the ability to detect the previously seen object categories while also adapting to learn from new video labels. We mainly focus on the catastrophic forgetting in the detector, as the tracking head is learned in a category-agnostic manner. We detail the proposal using the standard two-staged Faster-RCNN detector (FPN backbone) [40,59]. Without loss of generality, the proposals can be extended to multi-staged architectures [6,7,10,74], where we apply the proposal for each RCNN head and average them. In fact, the main issue is missing annotations for the seen, known object categories during the image to video transfer learning. Since they are not annotated, we can neither provide detection supervision nor prevent them from being treated as background. This basically perturbs the pre-trained classifier boundaries of both RPN and RCNN, leading to catastrophic forgetting. We remedy this issue by presenting a pseudo-label guided teacher-student framework.

Our key idea is intuitive. The pre-trained model already has sufficient knowledge to detect the seen, known categories. Based on this fact, we first fill in the missing annotations by pseudo-labeling the input. We adopt the basic pseudo-labeling scheme with a threshold of 0.3. The redundant pseudo labels that highly overlap with the current labels are filtered out with NMS. With these augmented labels, we 1) design a teacher-student network to provide (soft) supervisions, i.e., class logit, for preserving the past knowledge, and 2) update the incorrect background samples, i.e., negatives, in RPN and RCNN to prevent seen objects from being background (see Fig. 2-bottom). Using soft class logit is important for the large vocabulary classifier distillation, as the hard pseudo labels bias the operation towards the frequent class objects. Moreover, we use MSE loss instead of Kullback-Leibler (KL) divergence loss [21] for the logit matching. This is because the MSE loss treats all classes equally and thus it allows the rare classes with low probability also to be updated properly [72]. This two new adaptation leads to the successful distillation of the previous knowledge of the large vocabulary classifier (see Table 2b).

**Teacher-Student Framework Setup.** To effectively retain the previous knowledge, we design a teacher-student framework. We first make identical copies of the image pre-trained model, teacher (T) and student (S). The teacher model (T) is frozen to keep the previous knowledge and guide the student. The student model (S) adapts to the new domain with incoming video labels (via detection loss) and also mimics the teacher model to preserve the past information (via distillation loss). We detail the components in the following.

**RPN Knowledge Distillation Loss.** The RPN takes multi-level features from the ResNet feature pyramid [40]. In particular, each feature map is embedded through the convolution layer, followed by two separate layers, one for objectness classification and the other for proposal regression. We collect the outputs of both heads from the teacher and student to compute RPN distillation loss, which is defined as $L_{\text{KD}}^{\text{RPN}} = \frac{1}{N_{cls}}\sum_{i=1} L_{cls}(u_i, u_i^*) + \frac{1}{N_{reg}}\sum_{i=1} L_{reg}(v_i, v_i^*)$. Here, $i$ is the index of an anchor. $u_i$ and $u_i^*$ are the mean subtracted objectness logits obtained from the student and the teacher, respectively. $v_i$ and $v_i^*$ are four parameterized coordinates for the anchor refinement obtained from the student and teacher, respectively. $L_{cls}$ and $L_{reg}$ are MSE loss and smooth L1 loss, respectively. Here, we note that $L_{reg}$ is only computed for the positive anchors that have an IoU larger than 0.7 *with the augmented ground-truth boxes*. $N_{cls}(= 256)$ and $N_{reg}$ are the effective number of anchors for the normalization.

**RCNN Knowledge Distillation Loss.** We perform RoIAlign [18] on top-scoring proposals from RPN, extracting the region features from each feature pyramid level. Each region feature is embedded through two FC layers, one for classification and the other for bounding box regression. We collect the outputs of both heads from the teacher and student to compute RCNN distillation loss, which is defined as $L_{KD}^{RCNN} = \frac{1}{M_{cls}}\sum_{j=1} L_{cls}(p_j, p_j^*) + \frac{1}{M_{reg}}\sum_{j=1} L_{reg}(t_j, t_j^*)$. Here, $j$ is the index of a proposal. $p_j$ and $p_j^*$ are the mean subtracted classification logits obtained from the student and the teacher, respectively. $t_j$ and $t_j^*$ are four parameterized coordinates for the proposal refinement obtained from the student and teacher, respectively. $L_{cls}$ and $L_{reg}$ are MSE loss and smooth L1 loss, respectively. We only impose $L_{reg}$ for the positive proposals that have an IoU larger than 0.5 *with the augmented ground-truth boxes*. $M_{cls}(= 512)$ and $M_{reg}$ are the effective number of proposals for the normalization.

**Correcting Negatives in Computing the Detection Loss.** We avoid sampling the anchors or proposals that have significant IoU overlaps *with the augmented ground-truth boxes* as a background (>0.7 for RPN and >0.5 for RCNN). We note that positives are only sampled based on the provided original ground truth labels. This is because the detectors, especially the large vocabulary detectors, suffer from predicting the precise labels [11,50] while they are good at recalling the objects. We empirically verify this in the experiment.

**Extension to Other Transfer Learning Setup.** COCO to YTVIS is another important transfer learning setup (see Fig. 3-(a)). This is more challenging than LVIS to TAO, as the superset-subset relationship does not hold, and new object categories to learn are added. To deal with this new pattern, we take a two-step approach (see Fig. 3-(b)). First, we adapt the RCNN classifier of the pre-trained model, increasing the number of output channels to accommodate newly added classes, and train on the videos, YTVIS − COCO, that contain new object categories. In practice, we freeze the original detector, and thus the past information is intact, and only the newly added weight matrices are updated accordingly. The key idea here is to use the original pretrained weight as an anchor and update the newly added weight to be compatible. Second, after sufficient training of the new weights, we now unlock the original detector and update the whole weights with the remaining videos, YTVIS∩COCO, using the presented teacher-student scheme.

### 3.3   Regularizing Semantic Flickering

One of the common tracking failures in large vocabulary tracking is due to semantic flicker between similar object categories [12]. To cope with this issue,

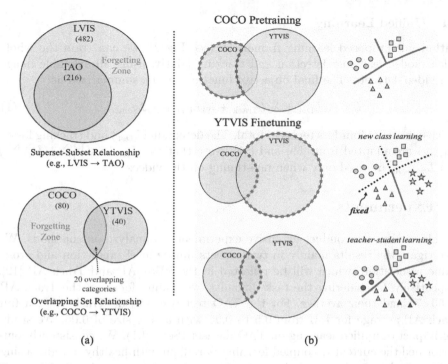

(a)                                    (b)

**Fig. 3. (a) Two standard image to video transfer learning setups.** In typical, a naive transfer learning from images to videos leads to catastrophic forgetting due to the missing annotations in the video. We present a generic teacher-student scheme that works on both scenarios. **(b) Two-step approach for COCO → YTVIS transfer learning setup.** We first learn new object classifier weights with the pretrained classifier as a fixed anchor and then fine-tune the whole classifier through the proposed teacher-student scheme. The red-dotted line along the circle in the set relationship figure indicates the training data used in each stage. The shape figures (e.g., square, triangle) and the separating line denote class instances and the associated classifier. (Color figure online)

we attempt to regularize the model during training with a new objective function, namely semantic consistency loss. The proposal is motivated by the temporal consistency loss [2,26,31,37], which enforces the outputs of the model for corresponding pixels (or patches) in video frames to be consistent. It is often used in video processing tasks to ensure the output temporal smoothness at a pixel level. The proposal extends this idea from pixels to instances; We enforce the class predictions of the same instances in two different frames to be equivalent. In practice, we forward the ground truth bounding boxes of the same instance in two different frames to the RCNN head. The mean subtracted classification logits, $p$, are used for the consistency regularization as, $L_{\text{Semcon}} = |p^t - p^{t+\tau}|_2$. ere, $p^t$ and $p^{t+\tau}$ denote the logits of the same instance in two different frames, $I_t$ and $I_{t+\tau}$.

### 3.4  Unified Learning

Within our proposed learning framework (see Fig. 2), we can train the whole video model, learning detection and tracking jointly, using all available image and video datasets. The final objective function can be summarized as

$$L = \lambda_1 L_{\text{Det}} + \lambda_2 L_{\text{Track}} + \lambda_3 L_{\text{KD}} + \lambda_4 L_{\text{Semcon}}, \tag{1}$$

which consists of four loss terms in total. The detection ($L_{\text{Det}}$) and tracking losses ($L_{\text{Track}}$) are adopted from [59] and [51]. Note that the $L_{\text{KD}} (= L_{\text{KD}}^{\text{RPN}} + L_{\text{KD}}^{\text{RCNN}})$ and $L_{\text{Semcon}}$ are used only when fine-tuning on the videos.

## 4  Experiments

In this section, we conduct extensive experiments to analyze our methods. We investigate the results mainly in two aspects: image-level prediction and cross-frame association, which will be reflected in the BBox AP and Track AP [12], respectively. Considering the task difficulty, we mainly focus on the Track AP of 50, 75 and their average. For the TAO test, we provide Track AP*, a full Track AP average for IoU from 0.5 to 0.95 with a step size of 0.05. We study the impact of unified learning on TAO dataset (Sect. 4.1). We consistently outperformed the current decoupled learning paradigm with healthy margins using various models, and pushed the state-of-the-art performance significantly. Second, to investigate the importance of the major components in our proposals, we provide ablation studies on TAO validation set (Sect. 4.2). Lastly, we evaluate our teacher-student scheme on two representative image-video transfer learning scenarios, LVIS → TAO and COCO → YTVIS[2](Sect. 4.3). In the following, we provide experiment setups, evaluation protocol and results for each section. More details are in supplementary materials.

### 4.1  Main Results

Upon the state-of-the-art tracking-by-detection framework [51], we instantiate various large vocabulary trackers. In specific, we consider two important detection architecture, two-staged (Faster-RCNN [59]) and multi-staged (CenterNet2 [106]), and three different long-tailed learning methods, Repeat Factor Sampling (RFS) [16], Equalization Loss V2 (EQLv2) [70], and Seesaw Loss [76]. All the models use the same ResNet-101 [19] with feature pyramid [40] backbone following the previous works [12,51]. Based on these baseline models, we compare our learning framework with the current standard learning protocol, decoupled learning. The comparison is in Table 1. We observe that our unified learning scheme consistently outperforms the current decoupled learning paradigm on various models, showing the strong generalizabilty of the proposal. With our method, we push the state-of-the-art performance significantly, achieving 21.6 and 20.1 Track AP50 on TAO-*val* and TAO-*test*, respectively.

---

[2] For the experiment, we contact the authors for the YTVIS-*val* annotations.

A Simple Learning Framework for Large Vocabulary Video Trackers    249

**Table 1.** Our learning framework couples well with different model architectures and learning methods. All the baseline scores are obtained after the decoupled training, i.e., training the detector and tracker on LVIS and TAO, respectively. FasterRCNN-RFS* is a re-implementation of [51] baseline.

| Method | Track $AP_{50}$ | Track $AP_{75}$ | Track $AP_{avg}$ |
|---|---|---|---|
| SORT_TAO [12] | 13.2 | - | - |
| FasterRCNN-RFS [51] | 16.1 | 5.0 | 10.6 |
| FasterRCNN-RFS* | 13.4 | 4.9 | 9.2 |
| w/ SimLearn | **19.6** | **7.3** | (+4.4) **13.6** |
| FasterRCNN-EQLv2 | 14.2 | 5.5 | 10.1 |
| w/ SimLearn | **19.8** | **8.8** | (+4.1) **14.2** |
| FasterRCNN-Seesaw | 15.4 | 5.7 | 10.5 |
| w/ SimLearn | **20.2** | **9.4** | (+4.3) **14.8** |
| CenterNet2-RFS | 18.9 | 9.1 | 14.0 |
| w/ SimLearn | **21.6** | **10.4** | (+2.1) **16.1** |

(a) **State-of-the-art results** in TAO-*val*.

| Method | Track $AP_{50}$ | Track $AP_{75}$ | Track $AP_{50:95}$ |
|---|---|---|---|
| SORT_TAO [12] | 10.2 | 4.4 | 4.9 |
| FasterRCNN-RFS [51] | 12.4 | 4.5 | 5.2 |
| FasterRCNN-RFS* + SimLearn. | 17.1 | 6.9 | 7.8 |
| FasterRCNN-EQLv2 + SimLearn. | 16.8 | 7.2 | 8.0 |
| FasterRCNN-Seesaw + SimLearn. | 17.6 | 8.0 | 8.5 |
| CenterNet2-RFS + SimLearn. | 20.1 | 9.6 | **10.3** |

(b) **State-of-the-art results** in TAO-*test*.

## 4.2    Ablation Studies

**Impact of Image Spatial Jitterings.** The results are presented in Table 2b. Compared to the standard affine transformation [17,48,105] or simple cropping without scaling [66,102], the presented strong zoom-in/out and mosaicing provides a large Track AP improvement. This indicates both the low sampling rate input simulation (with large-scale jittering) and dense tracking simulation (with mosaicing) enables more accurate large vocabulary object associations at test-time. To concretely investigate the scaling effects of zoom-in/out, we also provide its variant with small scale-jittering, Z-in/out*, and confirm that the large scale-jittering [15] is indeed important for the performance. We notice that mosaicing augmentation drops the Box AP. We conjecture this happens due to the train and test time inconsistency of input pairs. To this end, we present to form a tracking pair from two different augmentations in equal probability. We found that this mixed sampling strategy provides the best Track AP.

**Impact of Teacher-Student Framework.** In Table 2b, we study the impact of the key proposals in teacher-student framework. For the baselines, we provide the Naive-ft and Vanilla Teacher-Student schemes. Naive-ft indicates fine-tuning on TAO videos without any proper regulation for forgetting, which results in a significant performance drop. Vanilla Teacher-Student scheme samples the distillation targets only from the original ground truth labels, and no negative correction is performed. While it shows the past knowledge preservation effect to some extent, the performance is still worse than the LVIS-tracker. The vanilla scheme starts to improve over the LVIS-tracker when our proposal is added. This implies that pseudo labeling is essential, and 1) keeping the past knowledge of seen objects (by sampling distillation targets from the augmented labels) and 2) preventing the seen objects from being background (by correcting negatives using the augmented labels) are the key to avoid catastrophic forgetting.

One may wonder if the standard (hard) pseudo-labeling approach can directly preserve the previous knowledge as typical teacher-student scheme do [67,91,92]. However, as can be shown in the results, we instead observe inferior results than the baseline. The large vocabulary classifier fundamentally suffers from the confidence calibration issue [11,50] as it is trained on the long-tailed class-imbalanced data. It results in the classifier bias; predictions are made mainly toward the frequent object categories, missing rare objects in one-hot hard pseudo labels. In contrast, the (soft) pseudo labels essentially affect all classes. Furthermore, we suggest to employ MSE loss rather than standard KL-loss [21] as objective function in distillation. As MSE loss treats all classes equally the impact of the gradient is not attenuated for the rare classes. Recent study also reveals that MSE loss offers better generalization capability due to the direct matching of logits compared to the KL loss [28].

**Impact of Semantic Consistency Loss.** Finally, we study the impact of semantic consistency loss. It regularizes the model's class logits of the same instance in different frames to be the equivalent. In Table 2b, we observed mean-

**Table 2.** (a) Zoom-in/out* and Zoom-in/out denote zoom-in/out augmentation with scaling range of [0.8, 1.25] and [0.1, 2.0], respectively. (b) Pseudo Labeled Training denotes the standard (hard) pseudo label-based training.

(a)

| Method | Box AP | Track $AP_{50}$ | Track $AP_{75}$ |
|---|---|---|---|
| Decoupled TAO-tracker [51] | 18.1 | 16.1 | 5.0 |
| Random Affine [20,48,105] | 17.4 | 13.6 | 5.0 |
| Random Crop [66,102] | 15.9 | 11.5 | 1.5 |
| Zoom in/out* | 18.1 | 13.2 | 4.4 |
| Zoom in/out | **19.0** | 14.4 | **6.0** |
| Mosaic | 16.2 | 16.5 | 4.7 |
| Both (LVIS-tracker) | 18.5 | **17.8** | 5.7 |

(a) **Effect of image spatial jitterings in LVIS pre-train.**

(b)

| Method | Box AP | Track $AP_{50}$ | Track $AP_{75}$ |
|---|---|---|---|
| LVIS-tracker | 18.5 | 17.8 | 5.7 |
| Naive-ft | 11.7 | 11.4 | 2.7 |
| Vanilla Teacher-Student | 18.0 | 15.9 | 6.7 |
| + Pseudo-distill target | 18.6 | 17.8 | 7.2 |
| + Pseudo-neg sample | 18.8 | 17.9 | 7.3 |
| Both (Ours) | 19.5 | 18.5 | **7.5** |
| w. Hard Pseudo label [67,91,92] | 17.1 | 15.9 | 5.3 |
| w. KL-based distill [21] | 17.7 | 16.8 | 6.0 |
| w. Semcon. (Final Tracker) | **19.6** | **19.5** | 7.3 |

(b) **Effect of Teacher-Student framework in TAO fine-tune.**

ingful improvement in Track AP. This implies that semantic flicker regularization is indeed effective for the large vocabulary object tracking.

### 4.3   Image to Video Transfer Learning

Here, we evaluate our teacher-student scheme on two representative image to video transfer learning setups (see Fig. 3). In LVIS → TAO setup, we pre-train FasterRCNN-RFS tracker on LVIS (with 482 categories) and fine-tune on TAO (with 216 categories). We evaluate the model on TAO-*val* with Track AP metric. In COCO → YTVIS setup, we pre-train Mask-RCNN [18] on COCO, transfer the weights to MaskTrack RCNN [93], add new randomly initialized classifier weights to accommodate newly added classes, and fine-tune on YTVIS. More details of the setup are in supplementary materials. We evaluate the model on YTVIS-*val* with Mask AP [93] metric. To quantitatively analyze whether the proposal properly preserves the past knowledge and benefits from the new video labels, we provide the scores of OLD and NEW. Here, OLD indicates the classes that only reveal in the image pre-training stage. NEW denotes the classes that appears in the video fine-tuning stage. For each setup, we provide a baseline of naive fine-tuning, which results in a severe catastrophic forgetting. The results are summarized in Table 3 and Table 4.

**Table 3.** Teacher-student framework in **LVIS → TAO** transfer learning setup. Evaluated on TAO-*val*.

| Method | OLD (LVIS − TAO) | | | NEW (TAO) | | | ALL | | |
|---|---|---|---|---|---|---|---|---|---|
| | Box AP | Track $AP_{50}$ | $Track_{75}$ | Box AP | Track $AP_{50}$ | $Track_{75}$ | Box AP | Track $AP_{50}$ | $Track_{75}$ |
| LVIS-tracker | 15.7 | 16.1 | 5.7 | 21.1 | 17.2 | 9.0 | 18.5 | 17.8 | 5.8 |
| Naive-ft | 7.1 | 7.7 | 1.3 | 16.2 | 14.9 | 3.7 | 11.7 | 11.4 | 2.6 |
| Track-only | 15.7 | 15.3 | 5.5 | 21.1 | 16.9 | 7.1 | 18.5 | 16.1 | 6.3 |
| Teacher-Student | **15.7** | **16.3** | **6.5** | **23.1** | **20.6** | **9.0** | **19.5** | **18.5** | **7.5** |

**Table 4.** Teacher-Student framework in **COCO → YTVIS** transfer learning setup. Evaluated on YTVIS-*val*.

| Method | OLD (COCO − YTVIS) | | | NEW (YTVIS) | | | ALL | | |
|---|---|---|---|---|---|---|---|---|---|
| | $AP_{50}$ | $AP_{75}$ | AP | $AP_{50}$ | $AP_{75}$ | AP | $AP_{50}$ | $AP_{75}$ | AP |
| Naive-ft | 5.2 | 2.6 | 2.7 | 38.2 | 21.0 | 20.6 | 30.0 | 16.4 | 16.1 |
| Teacher-Student (1-step) | 38.9 | 31.2 | 26.2 | 36.2 | 19.4 | 20.1 | 36.9 | 22.4 | 21.6 |
| Teacher-Student (2-step) | 51.0 | 44.3 | 36.1 | **43.3** | 23.8 | **23.8** | **45.2** | 28.9 | 26.9 |
| Full-ft (Oracle) | **54.9** | **46.9** | **38.9** | 40.7 | **25.1** | 23.3 | 44.3 | **30.6** | **27.2** |

**LVIS → TAO Transfer Learning.** Especially in this setup, all necessary vocabularies are already learned at the image pre-training stage. Therefore, we can avoid catastrophic forgetting by fine-tuning only the tracking part. However, as it only updates the video model partially, it leads to inconsistent video representations, and thus performance rather slightly drops from the baseline LVIS-tracker. Instead, our method preserves the performance of OLD classes (preventing catastrophic forgetting) and significantly improves the NEW class performance (benefiting from labeled learning).

**COCO → YTVIS Transfer Learning.** This setup is more challenging as the model is required to achieve two goals, new class learning and old class preserving simultaneously. We decompose these goals and approach this setup in two-step as described in Sect. 3.2. As can be shown in the results, the proposed two-step approach performs better than the direct application of teacher student scheme. The final performance is comparable with, and in NEW classes outperforms, the oracle setup that use all the YTVIS training videos. This shows that our proposal is generic and effective for standard image to video transfer learning setups.

## 5 Conclusion

In this paper, we tackle the challenging problem of learning a large vocabulary video tracker. We present a simple learning framework that uses all LVIS images and TAO videos to jointly learn the detection and tracking. In specific, first, two spatial jittering methods, strong zoom-in/out and mosaicing, which effectively simulate the test-time large vocabulary object tracking are presented to enable tracker training with LVIS. Second, a generic teacher-student scheme is proposed to prevent catastrophic forgetting while fine-tuning the image pre-trained models on videos. We show that two new adaptation of using soft labels with MSE loss is crucial for the large vocabulary classifier distillation. We hope our new learning framework settles as a baseline learning scheme for many follow-up large-vocabulary trackers in the future.

**Acknowledgement.** This work was supported in part supported by Samsung Electronics Co., Ltd (G01200447).

## References

1. Aljundi, R., Lin, M., Goujaud, B., Bengio, Y.: Gradient based sample selection for online continual learning. arXiv:1903.08671 (2019)
2. Barnes, C., Shechtman, E., Finkelstein, A., Goldman, D.B.: PatchMatch: a randomized correspondence algorithm for structural image editing. ACM Trans. Graph. **28**(3), 24 (2009)
3. Bergmann, P., Meinhardt, T., Leal-Taixe, L.: Tracking without bells and whistles. In: ICCV, pp. 941–951 (2019)
4. Bewley, A., Ge, Z., Ott, L., Ramos, F., Upcroft, D.: Simple online and realtime tracking. In: ICIP, pp. 3464–3468 (2016)
5. Bochkovskiy, A., Wang, C.Y., Liao, H.Y.M.: Yolov4: optimal speed and accuracy of object detection. arXiv:2004.10934 (2020)

6. Cai, Z., Vasconcelos, N.: Cascade R-CNN: delving into high quality object detection. In: CVPR, pp. 6154–6162 (2018)
7. Cai, Z., Vasconcelos, N.: Cascade R-CNN: high quality object detection and instance segmentation. PAMI **43**, 1483–1498 (2019)
8. Chang, N., Yu, Z., Wang, Y.X., Anandkumar, A., Fidler, S., Alvarez, J.M.: Image-level or object-level? A tale of two resampling strategies for long-tailed detection. arXiv:2104.05702 (2021)
9. Chaudhry, A., Dokania, P.K., Ajanthan, T., Torr, P.H.S.: Riemannian walk for incremental learning: understanding forgetting and intransigence. In: Ferrari, V., Hebert, M., Sminchisescu, C., Weiss, Y. (eds.) ECCV 2018. LNCS, vol. 11215, pp. 556–572. Springer, Cham (2018). https://doi.org/10.1007/978-3-030-01252-6_33
10. Chen, K., et al.: Hybrid task cascade for instance segmentation. In: CVPR, pp. 4974–4983 (2019)
11. Dave, A., Dollár, P., Ramanan, D., Kirillov, A., Girshick, R.: Evaluating large-vocabulary object detectors: The devil is in the details. arXiv:2102.01066 (2021)
12. Dave, A., Khurana, T., Tokmakov, P., Schmid, C., Ramanan, D.: TAO: a large-scale benchmark for tracking any object. In: Vedaldi, A., Bischof, H., Brox, T., Frahm, J.-M. (eds.) ECCV 2020. LNCS, vol. 12350, pp. 436–454. Springer, Cham (2020). https://doi.org/10.1007/978-3-030-58558-7_26
13. Feichtenhofer, C., Pinz, A., Zisserman, A.: Detect to track and track to detect. In: ICCV, pp. 3038–3046 (2017)
14. Fu, Y., Liu, S., Iqbal, U., De Mello, S., Shi, H., Kautz, J.: Learning to track instances without video annotations. In: CVPR, pp. 8680–8689 (2021)
15. Ghiasi, G., et al.: Simple copy-paste is a strong data augmentation method for instance segmentation. In: CVPR, pp. 2918–2928 (2021)
16. Gupta, A., Dollar, P., Girshick, R.: LVIS: a dataset for large vocabulary instance segmentation. In: CVPR, pp. 5356–5364 (2019)
17. He, H., Garcia, E.A.: Learning from imbalanced data. IEEE Trans. Knowl. Data Eng. **21**(9), 1263–1284 (2009)
18. He, K., Gkioxari, G., Dollár, P., Girshick, R.: Mask R-CNN. In: ICCV, pp. 2961–2969 (2017)
19. He, K., Zhang, X., Ren, S., Sun, J.: Deep residual learning for image recognition. In: CVPR, pp. 770–778 (2016)
20. Held, D., Thrun, S., Savarese, S.: Learning to track at 100 FPS with deep regression networks. In: Leibe, B., Matas, J., Sebe, N., Welling, M. (eds.) ECCV 2016. LNCS, vol. 9905, pp. 749–765. Springer, Cham (2016). https://doi.org/10.1007/978-3-319-46448-0_45
21. Hinton, G., Vinyals, O., Dean, J.: Distilling the knowledge in a neural network. arXiv:1503.02531 (2015)
22. Hsieh, T.I., Robb, E., Chen, H.T., Huang, J.B.: Droploss for long-tail instance segmentation. arXiv:2104.06402 (2021)
23. Hu, X., Jiang, Y., Tang, K., Chen, J., Miao, C., Zhang, H.: Learning to segment the tail. In: CVPR, pp. 14045–14054 (2020)
24. Kang, B., et al.: Decoupling representation and classifier for long-tailed recognition. arXiv:1910.09217 (2019)
25. Kim, C., Li, F., Ciptadi, A., Rehg, J.M.: Multiple hypothesis tracking revisited. In: ICCV, pp. 4696–4704 (2015)
26. Kim, D., Woo, S., Lee, J.Y., Kweon, I.S.: Deep video inpainting. In: CVPR, pp. 5792–5801 (2019)
27. Kim, D., Woo, S., Lee, J.Y., Kweon, I.S.: Video panoptic segmentation. In: CVPR, pp. 9859–9868 (2020)

28. Kim, T., Oh, J., Kim, N., Cho, S., Yun, S.Y.: Comparing Kullback-Leibler divergence and mean squared error loss in knowledge distillation. arXiv:2105.08919 (2021)

29. Kirkpatrick, J., et al.: Overcoming catastrophic forgetting in neural networks. Proc. Natl. Acad. Sci. **114**(13), 3521–3526 (2017)

30. Kuznetsova, A., Ju Hwang, S., Rosenhahn, B., Sigal, L.: Expanding object detector's horizon: Incremental learning framework for object detection in videos. In: CVPR, pp. 28–36 (2015)

31. Lai, W.-S., Huang, J.-B., Wang, O., Shechtman, E., Yumer, E., Yang, M.-H.: Learning blind video temporal consistency. In: Ferrari, V., Hebert, M., Sminchisescu, C., Weiss, Y. (eds.) ECCV 2018. LNCS, vol. 11219, pp. 179–195. Springer, Cham (2018). https://doi.org/10.1007/978-3-030-01267-0_11

32. Lai, Z., Lu, E., Xie, W.: MAST: a memory-augmented self-supervised tracker. In: CVPR, pp. 6479–6488 (2020)

33. Lai, Z., Xie, W.: Self-supervised learning for video correspondence flow. arXiv:1905.00875 (2019)

34. Leal-Taixé, L., Canton-Ferrer, C., Schindler, K.: Learning by tracking: siamese CNN for robust target association. In: CVPR Workshops, pp. 33–40 (2016)

35. Leal-Taixé, L., Milan, A., Schindler, K., Cremers, D., Reid, I., Roth, S.: Tracking the trackers: an analysis of the state of the art in multiple object tracking. arXiv:1704.02781 (2017)

36. Lee, S.W., Kim, J.H., Jun, J., Ha, J.W., Zhang, B.T.: Overcoming catastrophic forgetting by incremental moment matching. arXiv:1703.08475 (2017)

37. Lei, C., Xing, Y., Chen, Q.: Blind video temporal consistency via deep video prior. In: Advances in Neural Information Processing Systems 33 (2020)

38. Li, X., Liu, S., De Mello, S., Wang, X., Kautz, J., Yang, M.H.: Joint-task self-supervised learning for temporal correspondence. arXiv:1909.11895 (2019)

39. Li, Y., Wang, T., Kang, B., Tang, S., Wang, C., Li, J., Feng, J.: Overcoming classifier imbalance for long-tail object detection with balanced group softmax. In: CVPR, pp. 10991–11000 (2020)

40. Lin, T.Y., Dollár, P., Girshick, R., He, K., Hariharan, B., Belongie, S.: Feature pyramid networks for object detection. In: CVPR, pp. 2117–2125 (2017)

41. Liu, Y., Zulfikar, I.E., et al.: Opening up open-world tracking. arXiv:2104.11221 (2021)

42. Liu, Z., Miao, Z., Zhan, X., Wang, J., Gong, B., Yu, S.X.: Large-scale long-tailed recognition in an open world. In: CVPR, pp. 2537–2546 (2019)

43. Lu, Z., Rathod, V., Votel, R., Huang, J.: RetinaTrack: online single stage joint detection and tracking. In: CVPR, pp. 14668–14678 (2020)

44. Manning, C., Schutze, H.: Foundations of Statistical Natural Language Processing. MIT Press, Cambridge (1999)

45. McCloskey, M., Cohen, N.J.: Catastrophic interference in connectionist networks: the sequential learning problem. Psychol. Learn. Motiv. **24**, 109–165 (1989)

46. Meinhardt, T., Kirillov, A., Leal-Taixe, L., Feichtenhofer, C.: TrackFormer: multi-object tracking with transformers. arXiv:2101.02702 (2021)

47. Milan, A., Rezatofighi, S.H., Dick, A., Reid, I., Schindler, K.: Online multi-target tracking using recurrent neural networks. In: Thirty-First AAAI Conference on Artificial Intelligence (2017)

48. Oh, S.W., Lee, J.Y., Sunkavalli, K., Kim, S.J.: Fast video object segmentation by reference-guided mask propagation. In: CVPR, pp. 7376–7385 (2018)

49. Oh, S.W., Lee, J.Y., Xu, N., Kim, S.J.: Video object segmentation using space-time memory networks. In: ICCV, pp. 9226–9235 (2019)

50. Pan, T.Y., et al.: On model calibration for long-tailed object detection and instance segmentation. arXiv:2107.02170 (2021)
51. Pang, J., et al.: Quasi-dense similarity learning for multiple object tracking. In: CVPR, pp. 164–173 (2021)
52. Park, K., Woo, S., Oh, S.W., Kweon, I.S., Lee, J.Y.: Per-clip video object segmentation. In: Proceedings of the IEEE/CVF Conference on Computer Vision and Pattern Recognition, pp. 1352–1361 (2022)
53. Peng, J., et al.: Chained-tracker: chaining paired attentive regression results for end-to-end joint multiple-object detection and tracking. In: Vedaldi, A., Bischof, H., Brox, T., Frahm, J.-M. (eds.) ECCV 2020. LNCS, vol. 12349, pp. 145–161. Springer, Cham (2020). https://doi.org/10.1007/978-3-030-58548-8_9
54. Prabhu, A., Torr, P.H.S., Dokania, P.K.: GDumb: a simple approach that questions our progress in continual learning. In: Vedaldi, A., Bischof, H., Brox, T., Frahm, J.-M. (eds.) ECCV 2020. LNCS, vol. 12347, pp. 524–540. Springer, Cham (2020). https://doi.org/10.1007/978-3-030-58536-5_31
55. Purushwalkam, S., Ye, T., Gupta, S., Gupta, A.: Aligning videos in space and time. In: Vedaldi, A., Bischof, H., Brox, T., Frahm, J.-M. (eds.) ECCV 2020. LNCS, vol. 12371, pp. 262–278. Springer, Cham (2020). https://doi.org/10.1007/978-3-030-58574-7_16
56. Ramanan, D., Forsyth, D.A.: Finding and tracking people from the bottom up. In: CVPR, vol. 2, pp. II–II. IEEE (2003)
57. Rebuffi, S.A., Kolesnikov, A., Sperl, G., Lampert, C.H.: iCaRL: incremental classifier and representation learning. In: CVPR, pp. 2001–2010 (2017)
58. Ren, J., et al.: Balanced meta-softmax for long-tailed visual recognition. arXiv:2007.10740 (2020)
59. Ren, S., He, K., Girshick, R., Sun, J.: Faster R-CNN: towards real-time object detection with region proposal networks. In: NIPS, vol. 28, pp. 91–99 (2015)
60. Riloff, E.: Automatically generating extraction patterns from untagged text. In: Proceedings of the National Conference on Artificial Intelligence, pp. 1044–1049 (1996)
61. Riloff, E., Wiebe, J.: Learning extraction patterns for subjective expressions. In: Proceedings of the 2003 Conference on Empirical Methods in Natural Language Processing, pp. 105–112 (2003)
62. Sadeghian, A., Alahi, A., Savarese, S.: Tracking the untrackable: learning to track multiple cues with long-term dependencies. In: ICCV, pp. 300–311 (2017)
63. Scudder, H.: Probability of error of some adaptive pattern-recognition machines. IEEE Trans. Inf. Theory 11(3), 363–371 (1965)
64. Shin, H., Lee, J.K., Kim, J., Kim, J.: Continual learning with deep generative replay. arXiv:1705.08690 (2017)
65. Shmelkov, K., Schmid, C., Alahari, K.: Incremental learning of object detectors without catastrophic forgetting. In: ICCV, pp. 3400–3409 (2017)
66. Sio, C.H., Ma, Y.J., Shuai, H.H., Chen, J.C., Cheng, W.H.: S2SiamFC: self-supervised fully convolutional siamese network for visual tracking. In: Proceedings of ACM International Conference on Multimedia, pp. 1948–1957 (2020)
67. Sohn, K., Zhang, Z., Li, C.L., Zhang, H., Lee, C.Y., Pfister, T.: A simple semi-supervised learning framework for object detection. arXiv preprint arXiv:2005.04757 (2020)
68. Son, J., Baek, M., Cho, M., Han, B.: Multi-object tracking with quadruplet convolutional neural networks. In: CVPR, pp. 5620–5629 (2017)
69. Sun, P., et al.: Transtrack: multiple-object tracking with transformer. arXiv:2012.15460 (2020)

70. Tan, J., Lu, X., Zhang, G., Yin, C., Li, Q.: Equalization loss V2: a new gradient balance approach for long-tailed object detection. In: CVPR, pp. 1685–1694 (2021)
71. Tan, J., et al.: Equalization loss for long-tailed object recognition. In: CVPR, pp. 11662–11671 (2020)
72. Tang, Y., Chen, W., Luo, Y., Zhang, Y.: Humble teachers teach better students for semi-supervised object detection. In: Proceedings of the IEEE/CVF Conference on Computer Vision and Pattern Recognition, pp. 3132–3141 (2021)
73. Vondrick, C., Shrivastava, A., Fathi, A., Guadarrama, S., Murphy, K.: Tracking emerges by colorizing videos. In: Ferrari, V., Hebert, M., Sminchisescu, C., Weiss, Y. (eds.) ECCV 2018. LNCS, vol. 11217, pp. 402–419. Springer, Cham (2018). https://doi.org/10.1007/978-3-030-01261-8_24
74. Vu, T., Jang, H., Pham, T.X., Yoo, C.D.: Cascade RPN: delving into high-quality region proposal network with adaptive convolution. arXiv:1909.06720 (2019)
75. Wang, J., Wang, X., Shang-Guan, Y., Gupta, A.: Wanderlust: online continual object detection in the real world. In: ICCV, pp. 10829–10838 (2021)
76. Wang, J., et al.: Seesaw loss for long-tailed instance segmentation. In: CVPR, pp. 9695–9704 (2021)
77. Wang, N., Song, Y., Ma, C., Zhou, W., Liu, W., Li, H.: Unsupervised deep tracking. In: CVPR, pp. 1308–1317 (2019)
78. Wang, T., et al.: The devil is in classification: a simple framework for long-tail instance segmentation. In: Vedaldi, A., Bischof, H., Brox, T., Frahm, J.-M. (eds.) ECCV 2020. LNCS, vol. 12359, pp. 728–744. Springer, Cham (2020). https://doi.org/10.1007/978-3-030-58568-6_43
79. Wang, T., Zhu, Y., Zhao, C., Zeng, W., Wang, J., Tang, M.: Adaptive class suppression loss for long-tail object detection. In: CVPR, pp. 3103–3112 (2021)
80. Wang, W., Feiszli, M., Wang, H., Tran, D.: Unidentified video objects: a benchmark for dense, open-world segmentation. arXiv:2104.04691 (2021)
81. Wang, X., Jabri, A., Efros, A.A.: Learning correspondence from the cycle-consistency of time. In: CVPR, pp. 2566–2576 (2019)
82. Wang, X., Huang, T.E., Darrell, T., Gonzalez, J.E., Yu, F.: Frustratingly simple few-shot object detection. arXiv:2003.06957 (2020)
83. Wang, Z., Zheng, L., Liu, Y., Li, Y., Wang, S.: Towards real-time multi-object tracking. In: Vedaldi, A., Bischof, H., Brox, T., Frahm, J.-M. (eds.) ECCV 2020. LNCS, vol. 12356, pp. 107–122. Springer, Cham (2020). https://doi.org/10.1007/978-3-030-58621-8_7
84. Wojke, N., Bewley, A., Paulus, D.: Simple online and realtime tracking with a deep association metric. In: ICIP, pp. 3645–3649. IEEE (2017)
85. Wu, J., Cao, J., Song, L., Wang, Y., Yang, M., Yuan, J.: Track to detect and segment: an online multi-object tracker. In: CVPR, pp. 12352–12361 (2021)
86. Wu, T., Huang, Q., Liu, Z., Wang, Yu., Lin, D.: Distribution-balanced loss for multi-label classification in long-tailed datasets. In: Vedaldi, A., Bischof, H., Brox, T., Frahm, J.-M. (eds.) ECCV 2020. LNCS, vol. 12349, pp. 162–178. Springer, Cham (2020). https://doi.org/10.1007/978-3-030-58548-8_10
87. Wu, Y., et al.: Large scale incremental learning. In: CVPR, pp. 374–382 (2019)
88. Xiao, B., Wu, H., Wei, Y.: Simple baselines for human pose estimation and tracking. In: Ferrari, V., Hebert, M., Sminchisescu, C., Weiss, Y. (eds.) ECCV 2018. LNCS, vol. 11210, pp. 472–487. Springer, Cham (2018). https://doi.org/10.1007/978-3-030-01231-1_29
89. Xie, Q., Luong, M.T., Hovy, E., Le, Q.V.: Self-training with noisy student improves ImageNet classification. In: CVPR, pp. 10687–10698 (2020)

90. Xu, J., Wang, X.: Rethinking self-supervised correspondence learning: a video frame-level similarity perspective. arXiv:2103.17263 (2021)
91. Xu, M., et al.: End-to-end semi-supervised object detection with soft teacher. In: ICCV, pp. 3060–3069 (2021)
92. Xu, M., et al.: Bootstrap your object detector via mixed training 34 (2021)
93. Yang, L., Fan, Y., Xu, N.: Video instance segmentation. In: ICCV, pp. 5188–5197 (2019)
94. Yun, S., Han, D., Oh, S.J., Chun, S., Choe, J., Yoo, Y.: CutMix: regularization strategy to train strong classifiers with localizable features. In: ICCV, pp. 6023–6032 (2019)
95. Zang, Y., Huang, C., Loy, C.C.: FASA: feature augmentation and sampling adaptation for long-tailed instance segmentation. arXiv:2102.12867 (2021)
96. Zeng, F., Dong, B., Wang, T., Zhang, X., Wei, Y.: MOTR: end-to-end multiple-object tracking with transformer. arXiv:2105.03247 (2021)
97. Zhang, C., et al.: Mosaicos: A simple and effective use of object-centric images for long-tailed object detection. arXiv:2102.08884 (2021)
98. Zhang, S., Li, Z., Yan, S., He, X., Sun, J.: Distribution alignment: a unified framework for long-tail visual recognition. In: CVPR, pp. 2361–2370 (2021)
99. Zhang, Y., et al.: ByteTrack: multi-object tracking by associating every detection box. arXiv:2110.06864 (2021)
100. Zhang, Y., Wang, C., Wang, X., Zeng, W., Liu, W.: FairMOT: on the fairness of detection and re-identification in multiple object tracking. Int. J. Comput. Vis., 1–19 (2021)
101. Zhang, Z., Cheng, D., Zhu, X., Lin, S., Dai, J.: Integrated object detection and tracking with tracklet-conditioned detection. arXiv:1811.11167 (2018)
102. Zheng, J., Ma, C., Peng, H., Yang, X.: Learning to track objects from unlabeled videos. In: ICCV, pp. 13546–13555 (2021)
103. Zhou, W., Chang, S., Sosa, N., Hamann, H., Cox, D.: Lifelong object detection. arXiv:2009.01129 (2020)
104. Zhou, X., Girdhar, R., Joulin, A., Krähenbühl, P., Misra, I.: Detecting twenty-thousand classes using image-level supervision. arXiv preprint arXiv:2201.02605 (2022)
105. Zhou, X., Koltun, V., Krähenbühl, P.: Tracking objects as points. In: Vedaldi, A., Bischof, H., Brox, T., Frahm, J.-M. (eds.) ECCV 2020. LNCS, vol. 12349, pp. 474–490. Springer, Cham (2020). https://doi.org/10.1007/978-3-030-58548-8_28
106. Zhou, X., Koltun, V., Krähenbühl, P.: Probabilistic two-stage detection. arXiv:2103.07461 (2021)
107. Zhou, X., Yin, T., Koltun, V., Krähenbühl, P.: Global tracking transformers. In: Proceedings of the IEEE/CVF Conference on Computer Vision and Pattern Recognition, pp. 8771–8780 (2022)

# TDAM: Top-Down Attention Module for Contextually Guided Feature Selection in CNNs

Shantanu Jaiswal[1]([✉]), Basura Fernando[1,3], and Cheston Tan[1,2,3]

[1] Institute of High Performance Computing, A*STAR, Singapore, Singapore
`jaiswals@ihpc.a-star.edu.sg`
[2] Institute for Infocomm Research, A*STAR, Singapore, Singapore
[3] Centre for Frontier AI Research, A*STAR, Singapore, Singapore

**Abstract.** Attention modules for Convolutional Neural Networks (CNNs) are an effective method to enhance performance on multiple computer-vision tasks. While existing methods appropriately model channel-, spatial- and self-attention, they primarily operate in a feed-forward bottom-up manner. Consequently, the attention mechanism strongly depends on the local information of a single input feature map and does not incorporate relatively semantically-richer contextual information available at higher layers that can specify "what and where to look" in lower-level feature maps through top-down information flow.

Accordingly, in this work, we propose a lightweight top-down attention module (TDAM) that iteratively generates a "visual searchlight" to perform channel and spatial modulation of its inputs and outputs more contextually-relevant feature maps at each computation step. Our experiments indicate that TDAM enhances the performance of CNNs across multiple object-recognition benchmarks and outperforms prominent attention modules while being more parameter and memory efficient. Further, TDAM-based models learn to "shift attention" by localizing individual objects or features at each computation step without any explicit supervision resulting in a 5% improvement for ResNet50 on weakly-supervised object localization. Source code and models are publicly available at: https://github.com/shantanuj/TDAM_Top_down_attention_module.

**Keywords:** Object recognition · Visual attention mechanisms · Top-down feedback

## 1 Introduction

The design and incorporation of attention modules in deep CNNs has gained considerable recognition in computer vision due to their ability to enhance the

**Supplementary Information** The online version contains supplementary material available at https://doi.org/10.1007/978-3-031-19806-9_15.

**Fig. 1.** Illustration of how iterative top-down feedback computation can help increase feature selectivity and thereby process individual salient features (left) or objects (right) at each computation step. Green arrows indicate feedforwarded inputs to TD blocks and red dotted arrows indicate top-down computation within TD block. (Color figure online)

representation power and performance of these networks in a task-agnostic manner. These modules typically formulate attention as a mechanism of feature modulation in outputs of traditional convolutional blocks by learning to intensify activations for deemed salient features and suppress activations for irrelevant ones. As a prominent method, Squeeze & Excitation (SE) [18] introduces channel attention modelling of global-average-pooled (GAP) feature representations, which is then enhanced by CBAM [47] through additional incorporation of spatial attention and utilization of both global-max-pooled (GMP) and GAP representations. Further, recent works [13,34,44] identify how channel attention can be made more efficient and effective, while a different direction of work augments convolutional operations with self-attention and calibration methods [3,27] to learn more effective feature representations.

However, conventional attention modules predominantly operate in a feedforward manner, i.e. they only utilize the output feature map of a convolutional block to both determine attention weights and perform attention modulation. As a result, the attentional mechanism is constrained to the representational capacity and local information of a single feature map input to the module. It does not incorporate relatively semantically-richer or task-specific contextual information available at higher layers while performing feature attention that can complement the initial bottom-up processing. This can be effectively facilitated by introducing top-down information flow between higher-level and lower-level feature representations within a convolutional block. Such feedback connections are also prevalent in the primate visual cortex [23] and recognized by neuroscientists as a key component in primate visual attention [15,24]. Hence, in this work, we explore how top-down feedback computation can be effectively modelled to enable more contextually-guided feature activations across the CNN hierarchy.

**Top-Down Guided Feature Attention.** A foundational formulation of top-down computation during visual processing was introduced by Crick in his "searchlight hypothesis" [9], where he postulated the presence of an internal "attentional searchlight" in the brain that operates by iteratively selecting lower-level neurons to "co-fire" with semantically richer higher-level neurons, such that at any given instance, a sparse and strongly correlated set of selected lower and higher-level neurons fired together.

Taking inspiration from his hypothesis, we illustrate how top-down feedback can guide feature attention in CNNs by taking an example of fine-grained bird classification. As shown in the first image input of Fig. 1, the initial feedforward computation provides a coarse feature activation which is sufficient to indicate that a "bird-like" object is present, but is not precise to determine which exact "bird". To guide feature attention, this top-level representation, which carries higher-level semantic information [52], can be used to obtain an "attentional searchlight" [9,41] that indicates which lower-level channels should be searched (in this case the particular beak type) and consequently does feedback computation to increase activation of the feature maps and spatial locations corresponding to selected lower-level channels. This results in a more precise lower-level representation which when consequently feedforwarded lends a more task-relevant top-level feature activation. The same mechanism for top-down guided feature attention can also enable the model to localize and process individual objects at each computation step as shown in second input of Fig. 1.

While discussed for a single feedback step in the penultimate layer, the same operation can be done iteratively for multiple computation steps and at lower levels of the hierarchy. Note, in our discussion, we treat channel activation of intermediate feature maps to indicate presence of an individual feature and the corresponding 2D feature map of a channel to indicate the spatial location of a feature based on the findings in [52].

**Designing a Top-Down Attention Module with Visual Searchlights for Feature Attention.** Based on the above insights, we propose a novel top-down (TD) attention module that jointly models constituent higher-level and lower-level features to obtain a "visual searchlight" that carries information on which lower-level features are of interest for subsequent computation. This searchlight then does attentional modulation of lower-level features by first performing channel attention through conventional channel scaling ("highlighting features of interest") and then performing spatial scaling ("intensifying spatial locations of highlighted features") by applying a spatial map obtained through its utilization in a single pointwise convolution.

**Our proposed module is lightweight (in terms of parameters) and can be conveniently integrated** at multiple levels of the CNN hierarchy as a standard plug-in attention module and trained end-to-end with standard backpropagation. We discuss more details of our approach in Sect. 3, and here briefly indicate two distinct advantages of the described operation of the visual searchlight – (i) it enables task-specific and more informative activation of features at each computation step by localizing and processing individual features at each step (ii) it is more robust in performing spatial attention at changing input resolutions [40] in comparison to static convolutional kernel-based attention methods [37,47].

**Contributions:** (i) We introduce a novel lightweight top-down attention module for CNNs by incorporating appropriate computational and neuroscience motivations in its design. (ii) We show the effectiveness of our module in enhancing performance of mainstream CNN models (ResNet, MobileNetV3 and ConvNeXt), outperforming state-of-the-art attention modules across multiple object recognition benchmarks, besides performing extensive ablation analysis to highlight key factors influencing the module's performance. (iii) We demonstrate how our proposed module makes CNNs more robust to input resolution changes during inference and enables the emergent property of "attention-shifting" through appropriate qualitative and quantitative analyses.

## 2    Related Work

### 2.1    Attention Modules for CNNs and Feedforward Attention Mechanisms

Initial work in the design of attention modules for CNNs includes the proposal of stacked attention modules for residual networks [43] and squeeze-and-excitation (SE) network's [18] channel attention formulation for feature aggregation and recalibration of GAP representations through fully connected layers. As extensions to SE, many works have focused on how to enhance the feature aggregation process by incorporating spatial and graph operations and more effective methods to estimate channel interactions than GAP. GE [17] introduces a spatial gather-excite operator to augment channel attention, GSoP proposes second-order global pooling methods [13], C3 [49] incorporates graph convolutional networks for channel interactions and $A^2$-Nets [8] incorporate second-order attentional pooling for long-range dependencies in image/video recognition. Notably, CBAM [47] along with [31,37] demonstrate the advantage of incorporating spatial attention in conjunction to channel attention, while CBAM also indicates effectiveness of using GMP and GAP for feature aggregation. Further, AANets [3] and SCNet [27] demonstrate how self-attention and self-calibration operations can augment standard convolutions, while GCNet [6] extends non-local neural networks to augment SE operations. More recently, prominent modules include ECA [44] which proposes one-dimensional convolutions to efficiently capture inter-channel interactions for channel attention and FCA [34] which proposes utilization of discrete cosine transform based frequency compression methods to effectively perform feature aggregation in SE in place of GAP. Additionally, modules such as DIANet [21] and RLA [54] propose to apply attention across layers, with the former applying a shared module across layers while the latter performs recurrent aggregation of features over layers.

In contrast to modelling attention for CNN architectures, recent works have studied how purely self-attention based Transformers [42] can be effectively applied in computer vision tasks. Starting from the first Vision Transformer [11], refinements in both model design [28,45] and training strategies [39] have made Vision Transformers emerge as a strong class of vision backbones that utilize feedforward attention mechanisms for computer-vision tasks.

### 2.2    Top-down Feedback Computation in CNNs

Integrating top-down feedback computation in CNNs has in general been shown to improve performance on a variety of computer vision tasks. For instance, in neural image captioning and visual question answering, multiple methods employ variants of recurrent neural networks (RNNs) along with visual features from a CNN in an encoder-decoder setup [1,7,48,50]. Similarly, RNNs have also been proposed to model visual attention for context-driven sequential computation in scene labelling [4,33], object recognition [51,53] and "glimpse" based processing [2,30] for multi-object classification. Finally, approaches also model top-down feedback to iteratively localize salient features [12], keypoints [19] or objects [5] and improve performance for fine-grained classification and object classification with cluttered inputs. While these approaches propose novel top-down feedback formulations, they are specifically formulated for target tasks and applied on existing ImageNet-1k pretrained backbone CNN models. In contrast, our top-down formulation serves a more general function of contextually-informed feature modulation of intermediate features across the CNN hierarchy and is integrated internally as a standard plug-in attention module trained with standard back-propagation. Consequently, we provide all together new ImageNet-1k pretrained backbones that we show to be effective on multiple object-recognition tasks.

## 3 Top-down (TD) Attention Module

We are given a convolutional block $\mathbf{B}$ comprising of $N$ convolutional layers, each denoted by $\mathbf{L_n}$ where $n \in \{1..N\}$, that maps an input feature map $\mathbf{X^0} \in \mathbb{R}^{C_0 \times H_0 \times W_0}$ to an output feature map $\mathbf{X^N} \in \mathbb{R}^{C_N \times H_N \times W_N}$ through feedforward operation denoted by $\mathbf{L_N}(\mathbf{L_{N-1}}..(\mathbf{L_1}(\mathbf{X^0})))$. We denote the output of the top-down feedback operation in the block $\mathbf{B}$ for a given $t$ number of computational steps by $\mathbf{X_t^N}$ where $t \in \{1..T\}$. Similarly, $\mathbf{X_t^0}$ is the input at computational step $t$. We infer a 1D attentional searchlight $\mathcal{S}_t \in \mathbb{R}^{C_0 \times 1 \times 1}$ that is used to sequentially perform channel and spatial attention of $\mathbf{X_t^0}$ to obtain the next computational step input $\mathbf{X_{t+1}^0}$, which is subsequently feedforwarded to obtain $\mathbf{X_{t+1}^N}$ as illustrated in Fig. 2. The operations for each computational step $t$ can be summarized as follows:

$$\mathbf{X_t^N} = \mathbf{L_N}(\mathbf{L_{N-1}}..(\mathbf{L_1}(\mathbf{X_t^0}))) \tag{1}$$

$$\mathcal{S}_t = \begin{cases} \mathbf{g}(\mathbf{X_t^N}, \mathbf{X_t^0}) & \text{if joint attention} \\ \mathbf{g}(\mathbf{X_t^N}) & \text{if top attention} \end{cases} \tag{2}$$

$$\mathbf{X_{t+1}^0} = \mathbf{att}(\mathbf{X_t^0}; \mathcal{S}_t) \tag{3}$$

where $\mathbf{g}(.)$ is a learnable transformation and $\mathbf{att}(.)$ denotes channel and spatial attention. We provide more details for both below. The computation is repeated for $T$ computational steps and the final output of the block is $\mathbf{X_T^N}$.

**Obtaining the Attentional Searchlight.** In our proposed module, the attentional searchlight $\mathcal{S}_t$ aims to specify which channels and spatial locations in a lower-level feature map should be emphasized for the next computational step and is derived from joint modelling of a higher-level feature map that captures

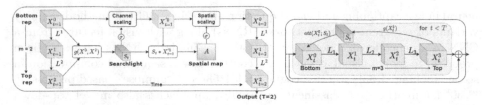

**Fig. 2. Left: Overview of our proposed top-down attention module** with "joint" bottom and top attention (Eq. 4). Given an input bottom feature map and feedforwarded top feature map, an "attentional searchlight" $\mathcal{S}_t$ is inferred to perform channel and spatial attention of the existing input to obtain its next computational step representation, which is subsequently feedforwarded. This is repeated for T computational steps to obtain the final output $\mathbf{X}_{t=T}^{N}$ (N and T=2 in figure). 'm' denotes the feedback distance between top and bottom representations. **Right: Integration of top-down (TD) module using "top" attention (Eq. 5) in a ResNet** [14] **bottleneck block.** As shown, TD operates before the residual connection for preset computational steps T and its output is added to the ResNet block input.

a higher degree of semantic information [52] and lower-level feature map that contains local feature information. Hence, we model the generation of $\mathcal{S}_t$ as a joint learnable transformation of the higher-level feature map $\mathbf{X}_t^N$ and lower-level feature map $\mathbf{X}_t^0$. To perform the transformation, we first individually estimate channel activations by squeezing [18] the spatial dimensions of respective feature maps with an unparameterized pooling operation for both feature maps resulting in corresponding 1D channel vectors, for higher-level $\in \mathbb{R}^{C_N}$ and for lower-level $\in \mathbb{R}^{C_0}$. These vectors are then individually passed through distinct single hidden layer multi-layer perceptrons (MLP) and subsequently concatenated and passed through another single layer MLP to obtain a target 1D vector which we coin as *Attention Searchlight* (i.e. $\mathcal{S}_t$ given by Eq. 2). This computation is shown to be effective and efficient and also allows us to perform top-down feedback independent of the channel and spatial dimensions of top and bottom feature maps (i.e. $\mathbf{X}_t^N$ and $\mathbf{X}_t^0$ can be of different dimensions). The specific computation to obtain *Attention Searchlight* is summarized as follows:

$$\mathcal{S}_t = \mathbf{g}(\mathbf{X}_t^N, \mathbf{X}_t^0) = \mathbf{W}_s(\text{ReLU}[\mathbf{W}_t(\mathbf{X}_{t,p}^N); \mathbf{W}_b(\mathbf{X}_{t,p}^0)] \tag{4}$$

where $\mathbf{W}_t \in \mathbb{R}^{C_N/r \times C_N}$, $\mathbf{W}_b \in \mathbb{R}^{C_0/r \times C_0}$ and $\mathbf{W}_s \in \mathbb{R}^{C_0 \times (C_N + C_0)/r}$ are weights of the MLP with ReLU activation applied after $\mathbf{W}_t$ and $\mathbf{W}_b$, $r$ is a reduction ratio to reduce parameter complexity (we use 16), $\sigma$ is the sigmoid activation function and pooled representations are indicated by subscript $\mathbf{p}$, i.e., $\mathbf{X}_{t,p}^N = Pool(\mathbf{X}_t^N)$ and we utilize spatial average-pooling for the $Pool()$ operator. Accordingly, we term the formulation in Eq. 4 as **joint attention** as it depends on both top and bottom feature-maps.

For cases where more parameter efficiency is desired (e.g. relatively large number of bottom channels), we model the generation of $\mathcal{S}_t$ based on the hidden layer MLP representation of only the top feature map $\mathbf{X}_t^N$. We coin the below formulation as **top attention**:

$$S_t = g(\mathbf{X}_t^N) = \mathbf{W}_s[\text{ReLU}(\mathbf{W}_t (\mathbf{X}_{t,p}^N)])] \tag{5}$$

where $\mathbf{W}_t \in \mathbb{R}^{C_N/r \times C_N}$ and $\mathbf{W}_s \in \mathbb{R}^{C_0 \times C_N/r}$ are weights of the MLP with ReLU activation applied after $\mathbf{W}_t$, and $\sigma$ is the sigmoid activation function.

**Performing Channel and Spatial Attention.** We interpret the obtained attentional searchlight $S_t$ to first be a channel attention vector signifying which channels of $\mathbf{X}_t^0$ should be "highlighted" for the next computation step. Consequently, as a first step, we scale the existing representation $\mathbf{X}_t^0$ through element-wise multiplication with $S_t$ (broadcasted spatially to match dimensions) to obtain its channel-scaled representation $\mathbf{X}_t^{\prime 0}$. We then perform pointwise convolution of $S_t$ and $\mathbf{X}_t^{\prime 0}$ with $S_t$ treated as a single $1 \times 1$ filter $\in \mathbb{R}^{1 \times 1 \times C_0}$ to obtain a 2D spatial map $\mathcal{A} \in \mathbb{R}^{H_0 \times W_0}$ that specifies salient spatial locations in the scaled feature map $\mathbf{X}_t^{\prime 0}$. Then, $\mathbf{X}_t^{\prime 0}$ is scaled spatially through element-wise multiplication with the sigmoidal activation of $\mathcal{A}$ (broadcasted channel-wise to match dimensions) to obtain the next computational-step input representation $\mathbf{X}_{t+1}^0$. We denote these set of operations as $\text{att}(\mathbf{X}_t^0; S_t)$ and summarize it as:

$$\mathbf{X}_t^{\prime 0} = \mathbf{X}_t^0 \otimes \sigma(S_t) \tag{6}$$

$$\mathcal{A} = S_t * \mathbf{X}_t^{\prime 0} \tag{7}$$

$$\mathbf{X}_{t+1}^0 = \mathbf{X}_t^{\prime 0} \otimes \sigma(\mathcal{A}) \tag{8}$$

where $\otimes$ denotes element-wise product and $*$ denotes pointwise convolution.

The intuition to perform pointwise convolution to obtain $\mathcal{A}$ is that the channel weights in $S_t$ and increased activations for selected channels in $\mathbf{X}_t^{\prime 0}$ ensure that only those spatial locations that correspond to selected channels are activated with convolution behaving as a spatial "search" operation of selected lower-level features. A benefit of this formulation is that it can enable the model to be more robust to changes in input resolution that may occur during model inference and that can impact activation statistics of pooling layers [40] and spatial attention techniques that utilize fixed convolutional kernels [37,47].

**Integration in Existing CNN Models.** As mentioned previously, our proposed module does not require the bottom input $\mathbf{X}_t^0$ to be of the same dimensions as the top output $\mathbf{X}_t^N$. Hence, it can be integrated into many CNN models as a standard attention module at multiple levels of the processing hierarchy and be trained end-to-end with standard backpropagation. Further, the formulation can be generalized to be a single block spanning the entire CNN model with the bottom input $\mathbf{X}_t^0 = $ image input and $\mathbf{X}_t^N = $ pre-classifier feature map. However, we empirically find that having a large feedback-distance (number of feedforward convolutional layers) denoted by 'm' between bottom representation $\mathbf{X}_t^0$ and the top representation $\mathbf{X}_t^N$ leads to unstable training and significantly worsen the performance. This is possibly due to a radical shift in input distributions over computational-steps for intermediate convolutional layers (i.e. the layer receives two radically different inputs over computational-steps) due to changes accumulated over previous layer outputs that amplify with higher number of previous

**Table 1.** Top1 & Top5 single-crop classification accuracy (%) of ResNet50 and ResNet101 integrated with our TD module in comparison to baselines on original ImageNet-V1 [10] and recent ImageNet-V2 [35] validation sets. All models are reproduced and trained with same experimental setup and selected on best ImageNet-V1 performance. Further backbones and baselines in supplemental for better readability.

| Method | BB. | Param. | FLOPs | Mem.(Gb) | | FPS/gpu | | ImageNet-V2 | | ImageNet-V1 | |
|---|---|---|---|---|---|---|---|---|---|---|---|
| - | - | - | - | Trn | Val | Trn | Val | Top1 | Top5 | Top1 | Top5 |
| ResNet [14] | Resnet50 | 25.56 M | 4.12 G | 29.5 | 16.1 | 704 | 2143 | 66.39 | 86.59 | 77.51 | 93.64 |
| SE [18] | | 28.07 M | 4.13 G | 32.4 | 16.0 | 615 | 1911 | 66.92 | 86.88 | 78.03 | 93.88 |
| CBAM [47] | | 28.07 M | 4.14 G | 37.6 | 20.7 | 420 | 1442 | 67.28 | 87.04 | 78.59 | 93.95 |
| ECA [44] | | 25.56 M | 4.13 G | 31.5 | 16.1 | 652 | 1989 | 66.72 | 86.95 | 78.11 | 93.85 |
| FCA-TS [34] | | 28.07 M | 4.13 G | 32.4 | 16.3 | 590 | 1876 | 67.19 | 87.02 | 78.70 | 94.01 |
| TDjoint (t=2, m=1) | | 27.65 M | 4.59 G | 31.9 | 16.2 | 601 | 1890 | 67.66 | 87.02 | **78.96** | 94.19 |
| TDtop (t=2, m=1) | | 27.06 M | 4.59 G | 31.8 | 16.0 | 612 | 1905 | 67.21 | 86.98 | 78.82 | 93.98 |
| TDtop (t=2, m=3) | | 27.66 M | 5.98 G | 35.3 | 16.3 | 498 | 1539 | **67.70** | **87.08** | 78.90 | **94.23** |
| ResNet [14] | Resnet101 | 44.55 M | 7.85 G | 39.2 | 16.6 | 460 | 1376 | 69.64 | 89.09 | 80.36 | 95.31 |
| SE [18] | | 49.29 M | 7.86 G | 45.5 | 16.9 | 368 | 1201 | 69.88 | 89.17 | 80.84 | 95.42 |
| CBAM [47] | | 49.29 M | 7.88 G | 53.3 | 21.4 | 269 | 862 | 70.03 | 89.35 | 81.20 | 95.64 |
| FCA-TS [34] | | 49.29 M | 7.86 G | 47.0 | 17.1 | 312 | 1164 | 70.12 | 89.42 | 81.15 | 95.59 |
| TDjoint (t=2, m=1) | | 46.75 M | 8.37 G | 41.0 | 16.8 | 396 | 1237 | **70.56** | **89.44** | **81.62** | **95.76** |
| TDjoint (t=2, m=1, L4) | | 45.94 M | 8.01 G | 40.3 | 16.8 | 413 | 1258 | 70.28 | 89.39 | 81.12 | 95.49 |

layers. Hence, for our experiments, we study 'm' between 1 to 3 within a standard convolutional block, and specifically apply multiple instantiations of the module at deeper semantically-richer [52] levels of a CNN model. Further, we use unique batch normalization layers for each computation step to stabilize training as suggested in findings of [25]. We denote our proposed top-down module which operates for **T** computational steps and over feedback-distance **M** with **TD (t = T, m = M)** where TD is further specified as top attention (Eq. 5) or joint attention (Eq. 4).

An example integration of the module in a ResNet [14] block is shown in Fig. 2(right).

## 4   Experimental Results and Discussion

We evaluate our proposed top-down (TD) attention module on the standard benchmarks: ImageNet-1k [10] for large-scale object classification and localization, CUB-200 [46] and Stanford Dogs [22] for fine-grained classification and MS-COCO [26] for multi-label image classification.

We perform experiments with three mainstream CNN model types – ResNet [14], MobilenetV3 [16] and the recent ConvNeXt [29]. We compare performance with the original models and prominent attention modules including Squeeze & Excitation networks (SE) [18], CBAM [47], ECA [44] and FCA [34]. To our knowledge, FCA is the most recent attention module shown to effectively enhance performance of multiple CNN variants. For ResNet models, we apply our module at all blocks of layers 3 and 4 (with exception of ResNet101 wherein we either simply apply only at layer 4 or at layer 4 and 10 alternating blocks in

**Table 2.** Performance of models with ResNet50 backbone on ImageNet-V1 single crop object classification at different testing resolutions (all models were trained on $224^2$ resolution). Most models obtain best accuracy at $280^2$ resolution as shown in Fig. 3.

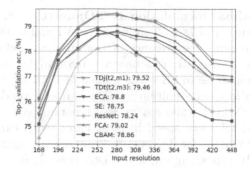

**Fig. 3.** Performance of models (ResNet50 backbone) on ImageNet-V1 (ILSVRC-12 [10]) at different test resolutions with best accuracy reported in plot legend and Table 2. TD models obtain better results at higher resolutions in comparison to baselines.

| Model (RNet50) | ImageNet-V1 Top1 Acc. | | | |
|---|---|---|---|---|
| - | Best | $224^2$ | $168^2$ | $448^2$ |
| ResNet [14] | 78.24 | 77.51 | 74.53 | 75.64 |
| SE [18] | 78.75 | 78.03 | 75.52 | 76.78 |
| CBAM [47] | 78.86 | 78.59 | 75.10 | 75.21 |
| ECA [44] | 78.80 | 78.11 | 75.46 | 76.85 |
| FCA-TS [34] | 79.02 | 78.70 | 75.74 | 76.99 |
| TDjoint(t2,m1) | **79.52** | **78.96** | 76.03 | 77.41 |
| TDtop(t2,m3) | 79.46 | 78.90 | **76.12** | **77.57** |

layer 3 to preserve computational complexity in comparison to baselines). Similarly, for ConvNeXt, we apply at blocks of stages 3 and 4. For MobileNetV3 large, we apply our module at the final three layers, replacing the existing SE blocks in those layers. We choose penultimate model layers as they generally constitute semantically-richer activations [52] where our described top-down attention mechanism can be most beneficial with marginal parameter overhead. For fair comparison, we reproduce all experiments in PyTorch [32] with the same training strategy used for all models. Training details and hyperparameter configurations for all experiments are provided in supplemental.

## 4.1 Large-scale Object Classification (ImageNet-1k)

We first perform experiments on large-scale object classification with the ImageNet-1k dataset and evaluate our module on ResNet variants (ResNet18, ResNet34, ResNet50 and ResNet101) and ConvNext-Tiny. For comprehensive evaluation, we consider two distinct validation sets – the original ILSVRC-12 set comprising 50,000 images [10] and the recent more challenging ImageNet V2 [35] "Matched-Frequency" set with 10,000 new images. We hereafter refer them as ImageNet-V1 and ImageNet-V2 respectively. We assess models based on their top1 and top5 single crop validation accuracy. Additionally, for models with our TD module, which output localized object predictions at each computation step (as shown in Fig. 4), we only consider the most confident prediction during both training and evaluation with exception of a minority of images that comprise multiple objects, for which we consider only predictions with unique localization maps (having an IOU < 0.5).

We summarize our experimental results for ResNet50 and ResNet101 in Table 1, and compare the top configurations of our TD module with aforementioned baselines. We report results for other backbones in supplemental to not overload the reader and discuss ablations of our module in Sect. 4.4. We find that **our**

**optimal formulation is TDjoint(t = 2, m = 1)**, which achieves a top1 accuracy of 78.96% on ImageNet-V1 and 67.66% on ImageNet-V2 for ResNet50, improving performance of the original model by 1.5% and 1.3% respectively. For ResNet101, it achieves a 0.8% higher top1 accuracy on ImageNet-V1 in comparison to SE when applied at both layers 3 and 4. Further, it outperforms feedforward attention modules on both validation sets for both ResNet50 and ResNet101 while having lesser parameters and comparable or higher training and inference speed in most cases (with exception of ECA). We find similar increments for TDtop(t = 2, m = 1), a lighter variant of our module utilizing only top attention, and TDtop(t = 2, m = 3), a computationally expensive variant with larger feedback distance.

Overall, our method outperforms all prior state-of-the-art attention modules including the recent FCA-TS [34], suggesting the effectiveness of the top-down attention mechanism of our module, which becomes more prominent for challenging tasks such as weakly supervised localization as shown later.

**Computation Cost Comparison:** Since our modules perform iterative top-down computation, they have a higher associated number of FLOPs than existing feedforward modules. Further, the number of FLOPs grows as the feedback distance ('m') increases – growing by 20% in case of ResNet50 from m = 1 to m = 3. However, we find that this limitation can be managed in practice during both training and inference in comparison to baseline modules since our models (specifically with m = 1) require lesser parameters and memory operations, and hence have comparable or higher FPS (speed). As shown in Table 1, TD models with m = 1 have higher FPS than both CBAM and FCA for ResNet50, and higher FPS than SE as well for ResNet101.

**Evaluation of Models at Different Input Resolutions.** The activation statistics of the global pooling in CNNs have been shown to be strongly impacted by changes in input resolutions [40], thereby making performance of CNNs susceptible to variations in input resolution. Hence, in this experiment, we study whether attention modules including TD can enhance robustness of CNNs by evaluating ResNet50 models at different resolutions for ImageNet-V1. We plot results for all models in Fig. 3 for testing resolutions from 168 × 168 to 448 × 448 with increments of 28 (further lower resolutions provided in supplemental). Additionally, in Table 2, we indicate each model's performance at lowest resolution of 168 × 168 (denoted by $168^2$), performance at highest resolution of 448 × 448, best testing performance and original 224 × 224 performance.

We find that: (i) TD-models largely prevent performance from dropping drastically at higher resolutions, particularly obtaining a 2% better performance than the original ResNet model at 448 × 448. (ii) CBAM, which utilizes a fixed convolutional kernel to model spatial attention, has a significant drop in performance at higher resolutions. (iii) Other attention modules have appreciable robustness in comparison to original ResNet, but have lesser benefits at higher resolutions in comparison to TD-models, with the best performing module (FCA) having a 0.5% lesser performance than TD-models at best resolution setting.

## 4.2 Attention Visualization and Weakly-Supervised Object Localization

To better understand the workings of our proposed TD module, we utilize Grad-CAM maps [38] to visualize the model's attention at each computation step for images drawn from the aforementioned validation sets. As shown in Fig. 4, we find that the model implicitly learns to shift its attention over computation steps. We conjecture that this imparts the model two important capabilities – one, choosing which object to "focus" on at each computational step when multiple objects (known to the model) are present and two, which feature to "focus" on at a given computational step when a more ambiguous or "difficult" object is present as the input. As an example of the first case, consider the second image input in Fig. 4, wherein the model at its first computational step accurately locates a 'vine snake' to be present in the scene (which the original model gets incorrect) and then shifts its attention to the radiator. In contrast, in input five (of same Fig. 4), the model iteratively attends to different features to make a more informed prediction. At its first computational step, it identifies water as a primary feature and has an initial prediction of a 'water-ouzel', but in the second computational step, it shifts its attention to the head of the bird and consequently predicts the correct category – 'goldfinch'. In comparison, the original Resnet50's prediction ('water-ouzel') is based on a less selective and conjoined feature map of the bird and water.

To quantitatively assess the model's attention capability and resulting enhancement in feature selectivity, we evaluate it on weakly supervised ImageNet-1k localization challenge [10], which requires models to provide bounding boxes in addition to classification labels. For all models, we follow the same strategy as [38] to generate bounding boxes for output predicted classes, and report top-1 and top-5 localization accuracy on ImageNet-V1 in Table 3. We find that both top performing TD configurations for object classification improve performance of ResNet50, with TDtop(t = 2, m = 3) notably increasing accuracy by 5%, and being 3% over the best baseline model – CBAM. Interestingly, channel attention methods of SE, ECA and FCA obtain worse performance than original ResNet50, suggesting strong importance of spatial attention in localization tasks. The resulting improvement also highlights the importance of the top-down searchlight-driven feedback mechanism introduced in this paper for obtaining a better attention module.

## 4.3 Fine-grained and Multi-label Classification

To demonstrate the general applicability of our TD module across different tasks and assess its capability as a robust feature extractor, we evaluate its performance as a backbone for existing state-of-the-art methods for fine-grained classification and multi-label object classification. We use the "Weakly Supervised Data Augmentation" method [20] for fine-grained classification and "Asymmetric loss" method [36] for multi-label classification, and simply replace the model

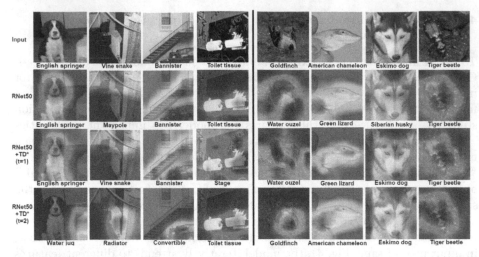

**Fig. 4. Representative examples of "attention shifting" over computational steps of our model based on Grad-CAM analysis.** In the first 4 examples, the TD model iteratively attends to distinct objects and has a more selective and complete feature activation at each computation step compared to original ResNet50. In the next 4 examples, it iteratively attends to relevant features for better discrimination of finer classes. See supplemental for more types and code to generate arbitrary examples.

**Table 3.** Weakly supervised object localization accuracy (%) on ImageNet (V1). TD models and CBAM that incorporate spatial attention increase performance of ResNet50 while purely channel attention methods reduce performance.

| Model | ImageNet(V1) | |
|---|---|---|
| - | Top1 | Top5 |
| RNet50 | 57.04 | 68.67 |
| RNet101 | 58.54 | 69.86 |
| RNet50 + SE | 56.62 | 67.88 |
| RNet50 + CBAM | 58.91 | 70.54 |
| RNet50 + ECA | 56.94 | 68.38 |
| RNet50 + FCA-TS | 56.88 | 67.86 |
| RNet50 + TDjoint(t=2,m=1) | 61.55 | 72.10 |
| RNet50 + TDtop(t=2,m=3) | **61.97** | **72.37** |

**Table 4.** Performance of models as backbones for fine-classification (val. acc. % for CUB and Stanford Dogs) and multi-label classification (val. mAP and overall F1 for MS-COCO). TD-based ResNet50 backbones outperform baselines in both tasks.

| Model (ResNet50) | CUB | Dogs | MS-COCO | |
|---|---|---|---|---|
| - | Top1 | Top1 | mAP | F1-O |
| ResNet | 88.26 | 85.97 | 77.58 | 75.45 |
| SE | 88.89 | 86.55 | 78.21 | 76.37 |
| CBAM | 89.37 | 86.98 | 79.17 | 77.15 |
| FCA-TS | 88.94 | 86.76 | 79.05 | 77.08 |
| TDjoint(t=2,m=1) | 89.61 | 87.08 | **79.61** | **77.71** |
| TDtop(t=2,m=3) | **89.75** | **87.30** | 79.56 | 77.62 |

backbone in both methods with our pretrained ImageNet-1k models. For fine-grained classification, we consider the Caltech-birds (CUB) and Stanford Dogs (Dogs) datasets and assess models on top-1 validation accuracy. For multi-label classification, we use MS-COCO and assess models on mAP and overall F1.

As shown in Table 4, using TD models (denoted as TDj for TDjoint and TDt for TDtop) as a backbone leads to a notable improvement in all three tasks compared to a baseline ResNet50, specifically achieving 1.5% increment on CUB-200 and 2 points better mAP on MS-COCO. The relative improvement over CBAM, which performs purely feedforward channel and spatial attention, suggests the benefits of feedback-driven channel and spatial attention in enabling iterative task-specific refinement of constituent feature-maps within the backbone.

### 4.4    Ablative Analysis of Feedback Computation

As indicated in Sect. 3, our proposed TD module has four primary factors – (i) choice of attention "TDjoint" or "TDtop" (ii) feedback distance 'm', (iii) feedback channel and spatial attention technique, and (iv) feedback steps 't'. Accordingly, we assess the impact of each factor by evaluating resulting module configurations on ImageNet classification. To evaluate factors (i), (ii) and (iii), we utilize ResNet50. For factor (iv), we utilize relatively shallower models of MobileNetV3-large and ResNet18 and evaluate on a hierarchically reduced subset of ImageNet with 200 classes due to the high computation cost and training time associated with models with more than 3 feedback steps.

**Impact of Feedback Distance 'm' and "Joint" vs "Top" Attention.** In the left plot of Fig.5, we see that having a feedback distance of at least 1 improves the performance of the module, i.e. the module requires distinct top and bottom feature maps, and applying top-down attention on the same single feature map as done in existing attention modules provides negligible performance benefit over the baseline ResNet50 while introducing high number of parameters. Next, the performance is most improved at m = 1 and m = 3 for both TDjoint and TDtop. However, note this does not indicate that m = 2 is an inferior option in general, as in the case of ResNet50, the bottom representation at m = 2 is the bottleneck block input, which may not sufficiently benefit from attentional modulation. Finally, TDjoint(m = 3) and TDjoint(m = 1) are the top-2 performing modules configurations indicating the enhanced representation capacity offered in joint modelling of top and bottom feature maps. However, while TDjoint(m = 3) has the highest performance, it has 8% higher parameters than TDjoint(m = 1) and TDtop(m = 3). Hence, other variants are more preferable, and in particular, **we recognize TDjoint (t = 2, m = 1) as our primary TD attention module.**

**Impact of Feedback Steps 't'.** As shown in center plot of Fig. 5, the performance peaks at 2 feedback steps, and thereafter declines, but still retains higher performance than both a purely feedforward (t = 1) model and single feedback (t = 2) model. We conjecture that this decline at higher computation steps may be a result of possibly reduced value of gradients while training of the model (akin to "vanishing gradients"), leading to a less effective attentional searchlight at each feedback step. Note that in case of MobileNet, models with TD exhibit higher performance than the original model while having 15% lesser parameters and smaller model size, suggesting TD attention is useful for low-end devices.

**Impact of Feedback Attention Technique.** To study the individual contributions of channel and spatial attention, as well as the applied order of attention operations, we consider six variants of the feedback operation in our TD module – (i) channel then spatial attention (as described in Sect. 3), (ii) spatial then channel attention, (iii) channel and spatial attention performed independently and parallely, (iv) only channel attention, (v) only spatial attention, and (vi) use of a recurrently-applied convolutional layer to map output feature maps to next computation step input feature maps (instead of explicitly performing attention). As shown in the right plot of Fig. 5, we find that performing channel and spatial attention independently has lesser performance than our searchlight's intended operation of first performing channel attention and then spatial attention. Additionally, only doing channel attention led to a noticeable drop in performance indicating the contribution of spatial attention in the searchlight's operation. Similarly, iteratively applying a convolutional layer on the output feature map to obtain next computation step inputs had lesser performance indicating the benefit of the iterative top-down attention method utilized in our work. For only spatial attention and spatial followed by channel attention, we found the network did not converge while training and had significantly worse performance. Apart from the above-mentioned primary factors of our module, we also quantitatively study how our module impacts selectivity of channels in its output feature maps, and report other ablations in the supplemental.

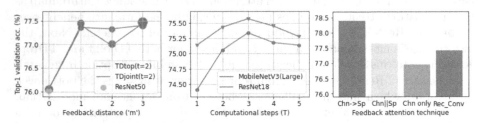

**Fig. 5. Ablative analysis of our TD module. Left**: choice of attention operation (TDjoint or TDtop) and feedback distance 'm' (with ResNet50 on ImageNet-1k). **Center**: number of feedback steps 't' (for MobileNetV3 large and ResNet18 on a hierarchically reduced subset of ImageNet with 200 classes). **Right**: Impact of feedback attention technique (with ResNet50) where Chn→ Sp denotes spatial attention performed after channel, Chn||Sp denotes independent parallel channel and spatial attention, and Conv_Map denotes a feedback convolution. Numerical reports in supplemental.

## 5    Conclusions

We introduced a lightweight module for CNNs that iteratively generates a "visual searchlight" to perform top-down channel and spatial attention of its constituent representations and outputs more selective feature activations. We performed extensive experiments with mainstream CNNs and showed that integrating our module outperforms baseline attention modules on large-scale object classification, fine-grained and multi-label classification. Further, we demonstrated the effectiveness of TD-models in increasing robustness to changes in image resolutions during inference and also illustrated the emergent "attention shifting" behaviour and quantitatively assessed it on weakly supervised object localization, finding that it outputs significantly more precise localization maps. This can be especially beneficial for applications with varying input resolutions or requiring fine-resolution processing such as ego-centric action anticipation.

**Acknowledgment.** This research/project is supported in part by the National Research Foundation, Singapore under its AI Singapore Program (Award Number: AISG-RP-2019-010). This research is also supported by funding allocation to C.T. and B.F. by the Agency for Science, Technology and Research (A*STAR) under its SERC Central Research Fund (CRF), as well as its Centre for Frontier AI Research (CFAR).

# References

1. Anderson, P., et al.: Bottom-up and top-down attention for image captioning and visual question answering. In: Proceedings of the IEEE Conference on Computer Vision and Pattern Recognition, pp. 6077–6086 (2018)
2. Ba, J., Mnih, V., Kavukcuoglu, K.: Multiple object recognition with visual attention. In: ICLR (Poster) (2015). http://arxiv.org/abs/1412.7755
3. Bello, I., Zoph, B., Vaswani, A., Shlens, J., Le, Q.V.: Attention augmented convolutional networks. In: Proceedings of the IEEE/CVF International Conference on Computer Vision (ICCV), October 2019
4. Byeon, W., Breuel, T.M., Raue, F., Liwicki, M.: Scene labeling with lstm recurrent neural networks. In: Proceedings of the IEEE Conference on Computer Vision and Pattern Recognition, pp. 3547–3555 (2015)
5. Cao, C., et al.: Look and think twice: capturing top-down visual attention with feedback convolutional neural networks. In: Proceedings of the IEEE International Conference on Computer Vision, pp. 2956–2964 (2015)
6. Cao, Y., Xu, J., Lin, S., Wei, F., Hu, H.: Gcnet: non-local networks meet squeeze-excitation networks and beyond. In: Proceedings of the IEEE/CVF International Conference on Computer Vision Workshops (2019)
7. Chen, L., et al.: Sca-cnn: spatial and channel-wise attention in convolutional networks for image captioning. In: Proceedings of the IEEE Conference on Computer Vision and Pattern Recognition, pp. 5659–5667 (2017)
8. Chen, Y., Kalantidis, Y., Li, J., Yan, S., Feng, J.: A^2-nets: double attention networks. In: Bengio, S., Wallach, H., Larochelle, H., Grauman, K., Cesa-Bianchi, N., Garnett, R. (eds.) Advances in Neural Information Processing Systems, vol. 31. Curran Associates, Inc. (2018). https://proceedings.neurips.cc/paper/2018/file/e165421110ba03099a1c0393373c5b43-Paper.pdf
9. Crick, F.: Function of the thalamic reticular complex: the searchlight hypothesis. Proc. Nat. Acad. Sci. **81**(14), 4586–4590 (1984)
10. Deng, J., Dong, W., Socher, R., Li, L.J., Li, K., Fei-Fei, L.: Imagenet: a large-scale hierarchical image database. In: 2009 IEEE Conference on Computer Vision and Pattern Recognition, pp. 248–255. IEEE (2009)
11. Dosovitskiy, A., et al.: An image is worth 16x16 words: transformers for image recognition at scale. arXiv preprint arXiv:2010.11929 (2020)

12. Fu, J., Zheng, H., Mei, T.: Look closer to see better: recurrent attention convolutional neural network for fine-grained image recognition. In: Proceedings of the IEEE Conference on Computer Vision and Pattern Recognition, pp. 4438–4446 (2017)

13. Gao, Z., Xie, J., Wang, Q., Li, P.: Global second-order pooling convolutional networks. In: Proceedings of the IEEE/CVF Conference on Computer Vision and Pattern Recognition, pp. 3024–3033 (2019)

14. He, K., Zhang, X., Ren, S., Sun, J.: Deep residual learning for image recognition. In: Proceedings of the IEEE Conference on Computer Vision and Pattern Recognition, pp. 770–778 (2016)

15. Hochstein, S., Ahissar, M.: View from the top: hierarchies and reverse hierarchies in the visual system. Neuron **36**(5), 791–804 (2002)

16. Howard, A., et al.: Searching for mobilenetv3. In: Proceedings of the IEEE/CVF International Conference on Computer Vision, pp. 1314–1324 (2019)

17. Hu, J., Shen, L., Albanie, S., Sun, G., Vedaldi, A.: Gather-excite: exploiting feature context in convolutional neural networks. In: Bengio, S., Wallach, H., Larochelle, H., Grauman, K., Cesa-Bianchi, N., Garnett, R. (eds.) Advances in Neural Information Processing Systems, vol. 31. Curran Associates, Inc. (2018). https://proceedings.neurips.cc/paper/2018/file/dc363817786ff182b7bc59565d864523-Paper.pdf

18. Hu, J., Shen, L., Sun, G.: Squeeze-and-excitation networks. In: Proceedings of the IEEE Conference on Computer Vision and Pattern Recognition, pp. 7132–7141 (2018)

19. Hu, P., Ramanan, D.: Bottom-up and top-down reasoning with hierarchical rectified gaussians. In: Proceedings of the IEEE Conference on Computer Vision and Pattern Recognition, pp. 5600–5609 (2016)

20. Hu, T., Qi, H., Huang, Q., Lu, Y.: See better before looking closer: weakly supervised data augmentation network for fine-grained visual classification. arXiv preprint arXiv:1901.09891 (2019)

21. Huang, Z., Liang, S., Liang, M., Yang, H.: Dianet: dense-and-implicit attention network. In: Proceedings of the AAAI Conference on Artificial Intelligence, vol. 34, pp. 4206–4214 (2020)

22. Khosla, A., Jayadevaprakash, N., Yao, B., Fei-Fei, L.: Novel dataset for fine-grained image categorization. In: First Workshop on Fine-Grained Visual Categorization, IEEE Conference on Computer Vision and Pattern Recognition, Colorado Springs, CO, June 2011

23. Kok, P., Bains, L.J., van Mourik, T., Norris, D.G., de Lange, F.P.: Selective activation of the deep layers of the human primary visual cortex by top-down feedback. Curr. Biol. **26**(3), 371–376 (2016)

24. Kreiman, G., Serre, T.: Beyond the feedforward sweep: feedback computations in the visual cortex. Ann. N. Y. Acad. Sci. **1464**(1), 222–241 (2020)

25. Liao, Q., Poggio, T.: Bridging the gaps between residual learning, recurrent neural networks and visual cortex. arXiv preprint arXiv:1604.03640 (2016)

26. Lin, T.-Y., et al.: Microsoft COCO: common objects in context. In: Fleet, D., Pajdla, T., Schiele, B., Tuytelaars, T. (eds.) ECCV 2014. LNCS, vol. 8693, pp. 740–755. Springer, Cham (2014). https://doi.org/10.1007/978-3-319-10602-1_48

27. Liu, J.J., Hou, Q., Cheng, M.M., Wang, C., Feng, J.: Improving convolutional networks with self-calibrated convolutions. In: Proceedings of the IEEE/CVF Conference on Computer Vision and Pattern Recognition, pp. 10096–10105 (2020)

28. Liu, Z., et al.: Swin transformer: hierarchical vision transformer using shifted windows. In: Proceedings of the IEEE/CVF International Conference on Computer Vision. pp. 10012–10022 (2021)

29. Liu, Z., Mao, H., Wu, C.Y., Feichtenhofer, C., Darrell, T., Xie, S.: A convnet for the 2020s. arXiv preprint arXiv:2201.03545 (2022)

30. Mnih, V., Heess, N., Graves, A., kavukcuoglu, K.: Recurrent models of visual attention. In: Ghahramani, Z., Welling, M., Cortes, C., Lawrence, N., Weinberger, K.Q. (eds.) Advances in Neural Information Processing Systems, vol. 27. Curran Associates, Inc. (2014). https://proceedings.neurips.cc/paper/2014/file/09c6c3783b4a70054da74f2538ed47c6-Paper.pdf

31. Park, J., Woo, S., Lee, J., Kweon, I.S.: BAM: bottleneck attention module. In: British Machine Vision Conference 2018, BMVC 2018, Newcastle, UK, 3–6 September 2018, p. 147. BMVA Press (2018). http://bmvc2018.org/contents/papers/0092.pdf

32. Paszke, A., et al.: Pytorch: an imperative style, high-performance deep learning library. In: Wallach, H., Larochelle, H., Beygelzimer, A., d'Alché-Buc, F., Fox, E., Garnett, R. (eds.) Advances in Neural Information Processing Systems, vol. 32. Curran Associates, Inc. (2019). https://proceedings.neurips.cc/paper/2019/file/bdbca288fee7f92f2bfa9f7012727740-Paper.pdf

33. Pinheiro, P., Collobert, R.: Recurrent convolutional neural networks for scene labeling. In: International Conference on Machine Learning, pp. 82–90. PMLR (2014)

34. Qin, Z., Zhang, P., Wu, F., Li, X.: Fcanet: frequency channel attention networks. In: Proceedings of the IEEE/CVF International Conference on Computer Vision, pp. 783–792 (2021)

35. Recht, B., Roelofs, R., Schmidt, L., Shankar, V.: Do imagenet classifiers generalize to imagenet? In: International Conference on Machine Learning, pp. 5389–5400. PMLR (2019)

36. Ridnik, T., et al.: Asymmetric loss for multi-label classification. In: Proceedings of the IEEE/CVF International Conference on Computer Vision, pp. 82–91 (2021)

37. Roy, A.G., Navab, N., Wachinger, C.: Recalibrating fully convolutional networks with spatial and channel "squeeze and excitation" blocks. IEEE Trans. Med. Imaging 38(2), 540–549 (2018)

38. Selvaraju, R.R., Cogswell, M., Das, A., Vedantam, R., Parikh, D., Batra, D.: Gradcam: visual explanations from deep networks via gradient-based localization. In: Proceedings of the IEEE International Conference on Computer Vision, pp. 618–626 (2017)

39. Touvron, H., Cord, M., Douze, M., Massa, F., Sablayrolles, A., Jégou, H.: Training data-efficient image transformers & distillation through attention. In: International Conference on Machine Learning, pp. 10347–10357. PMLR (2021)

40. Touvron, H., Vedaldi, A., Douze, M., Jegou, H.: Fixing the train-test resolution discrepancy. In: Wallach, H., Larochelle, H., Beygelzimer, A., d'Alché-Buc, F., Fox, E., Garnett, R. (eds.) Advances in Neural Information Processing Systems, vol. 32. Curran Associates, Inc. (2019). https://proceedings.neurips.cc/paper/2019/file/d03a857a23b5285736c4d55e0bb067c8-Paper.pdf

41. Treisman, A.M., Gelade, G.: A feature-integration theory of attention. Cogn. Psychol. 12(1), 97–136 (1980)

42. Vaswani, A., et al.: Attention is all you need. Adv. Neural Inf. Process. Syst. 30 (2017)

43. Wang, F., et al.: Residual attention network for image classification. In: Proceedings of the IEEE Conference on Computer Vision and Pattern Recognition, pp. 3156–3164 (2017)

44. Wang, Q., Wu, B., Zhu, P., Li, P., Zuo, W., Hu, Q.: Eca-net: efficient channel attention for deep convolutional neural networks, 2020 IEEE. In: CVF Conference on Computer Vision and Pattern Recognition (CVPR), IEEE (2020)

45. Wang, Y., Huang, R., Song, S., Huang, Z., Huang, G.: Not all images are worth 16 x 16 words: dynamic transformers for efficient image recognition. Adv. Neural Inf. Process. Syst. **34** (2021)

46. Welinder, P., et al.: Caltech-UCSD Birds 200. Technical Report, CNS-TR-2010-001, California Institute of Technology (2010)

47. Woo, S., Park, J., Lee, J.Y., Kweon, I.S.: Cbam: convolutional block attention module. In: Proceedings of the European Conference on Computer Vision (ECCV), pp. 3–19 (2018)

48. Xu, K., et al.: Show, attend and tell: neural image caption generation with visual attention. In: International Conference on Machine Learning, pp. 2048–2057. PMLR (2015)

49. Yang, J., Ren, Z., Gan, C., Zhu, H., Lin, J., Parikh, D.: Cross-channel communication networks (2019)

50. Yang, Z., He, X., Gao, J., Deng, L., Smola, A.: Stacked attention networks for image question answering. In: Proceedings of the IEEE Conference on Computer Vision and Pattern Recognition, pp. 21–29 (2016)

51. Zamir, A.R., et al.: Feedback networks. In: Proceedings of the IEEE Conference on Computer Vision and Pattern Recognition, pp. 1308–1317 (2017)

52. Zeiler, M.D., Fergus, R.: Visualizing and understanding convolutional networks. In: Fleet, D., Pajdla, T., Schiele, B., Tuytelaars, T. (eds.) ECCV 2014. LNCS, vol. 8689, pp. 818–833. Springer, Cham (2014). https://doi.org/10.1007/978-3-319-10590-1_53

53. Zhang, M., Tseng, C., Kreiman, G.: Putting visual object recognition in context. In: Proceedings of the IEEE/CVF Conference on Computer Vision and Pattern Recognition, pp. 12985–12994 (2020)

54. Zhao, J., Fang, Y., Li, G.: Recurrence along depth: deep convolutional neural networks with recurrent layer aggregation. Adv. Neural Inf. Process. Syst. **34**, 10627–10640 (2021)

# Automatic Check-Out
# via Prototype-Based Classifier Learning
# from Single-Product Exemplars

Hao Chen[1,2], Xiu-Shen Wei[1,2,3](✉), Faen Zhang[4], Yang Shen[1], Hui Xu[4],
and Liang Xiao[1](✉)

[1] School of Computer Science and Engineering, Nanjing University of Science
and Technology, Nanjing, China
weixs@njust.edu.cn, xiaoliang@mail.njust.edu.cn
[2] State Key Laboratory of Integrated Services Networks, Xidian University,
Xi'an, China
[3] State Key Laboratory for Novel Software Technology, Nanjing University,
Nanjing, China
[4] Qingdao AInnovation Technology Group Co., Ltd, Qingdao, China

**Abstract.** Automatic Check-Out (ACO) aims to accurately predict the
presence and count of each category of products in check-out images,
where a major challenge is the significant domain gap between training data (single-product exemplars) and test data (check-out images).
To mitigate the gap, we propose a method, termed as PSP, to perform
Prototype-based classifier learning from Single-Product exemplars. In
PSP, by revealing the advantages of representing category semantics, the
prototype representation of each product category is firstly obtained from
single-product exemplars. Based on the prototypes, it then generates categorical classifiers with a background classifier to not only recognize fine-
grained product categories but also distinguish background upon product
proposals derived from check-out images. To further improve the ACO
accuracy, we develop discriminative re-ranking to both adjust the predicted scores of product proposals for bringing more discriminative ability in classifier learning and provide a reasonable sorting possibility by

X.-S. Wei and Y. Shen are also with Key Lab of Intelligent Perception and Systems
for High-Dimensional Information of Ministry of Education, and Jiangsu Key Lab of
Image and Video Understanding for Social Security, Nanjing University of Science and
Technology, China. This work is supported by National Key R&D Program of China
(2021YFA1001100), Natural Science Foundation of China under Grant (61871226),
Natural Science Foundation of Jiangsu Province of China under Grant (BK20210340),
the Fundamental Research Funds for the Central Universities (No. 30920041111, No.
NJ2022028), CAAI-Huawei MindSpore Open Fund, Beijing Academy of Artificial Intel-
ligence (BAAI), and Postgraduate Research & Practice Innovation Program of Jiangsu
Province (KYCX22_0464).

**Supplementary Information** The online version contains supplementary material
available at https://doi.org/10.1007/978-3-031-19806-9_16.

considering the fine-grained nature. Moreover, a multi-label recognition loss is also equipped for modeling co-occurrence of products in check-out images. Experiments are conducted on the large-scale RPC dataset for evaluations. Our ACO result achieves 86.69%, by 6.18% improvements over state-of-the-arts, which demonstrates the superiority of PSP. Our codes are available at https://github.com/Hao-Chen-NJUST/PSP.

**Keywords:** Automatic check-out · Prototype · Classifier learning

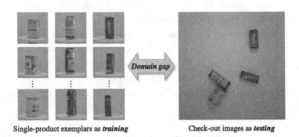

(a)  Domain gap between training and testing in ACO

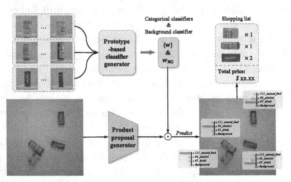

(b)  Basic idea of our PSP method

**Fig. 1.** (a) shows the significant domain gap between single-product exemplars (as training) and check-out images (as testing) in Automatic Check-Out (ACO). (b) illustrates the basic idea of our Prototype-based classifier learning with Single-Product exemplars (PSP) method. To mitigate this gap, we hereby develop a prototype-based classifier generator to learn both product categorical classifiers and a background classifier based product prototypes to recognize product proposals derived from the input check-out image, and finally return a shopping list.

## 1   Introduction

As a crucial field of intelligent retail [7,8,17,29,35,50], Automatic Check-Out (ACO) [26,39,41,46] has been evolving and promoting in recent years. The basic design requirement for an automatic check-out system is to automatically identify and count the products purchased by customers. Thus, how to accurately count the fine-grained subordinate categories and quantities of products in check-out images becomes a key task in ACO [21,41,46].

There exist three main challenges in ACO [41], *i.e.*, the large-scale data of products images, the domain gap between training and test (cf. Fig. 1 (a)), and the fine-grained [42,43] characteristics of product categories. To deal with these issues, Wei *et al.* [41] proposed a baseline approach based on object detection to achieve domain adaptation by synthesizing and rendering check-out images. This baseline approach provides a way for dealing with the domain gap in ACO. Then, two latter works [21,46] modified the synthesized-and-rendered strategy of [41] for achieving better domain adaptation ability, and thus improved ACO accuracy. Different from these methods [21,41,46], in this paper, we attempt to mitigate the significant domain gap between single-product exemplars (as training) and check-out images (as test) *by learning corresponding categorical classifiers directly from the categorical prototype of each product*, cf. Fig. 1.

More specifically, the so-called prototype refers to a vector representation that can accurately represents the semantics of the category (*i.e.*, genuine class representation) in the visual space, which is usually realized by the feature center of a specific class [38]. For ACO, beyond the potential of handling domain gap, another advantage of using product prototypes is to avoid the multi-view issue of single-product exemplars. Thanks to the generalization and robustness, compared with using single view or several views from exemplar images, categorical prototypes can more accurately represent category semantics of products. As shown in Fig. 2, we first feed the single-product exemplars $\{I_s^{k,i}\}$ into the proposed prototype-based classifier generator to obtain the categorical classifier $w_k$ corresponding to product category $k$. Meanwhile, a background classifier is also generated based on all categorical prototypes to learn general patterns and thus distinguish product proposals containing background or incomplete products in check-out images. After that, the learned categorical classifiers and the background classifier can be employed for recognizing product proposals returned by a traditional proposal generation process, *e.g.*, RPN [34].

To further improve the discriminative ability of these learned classifiers, we develop a discriminative re-ranking approach by adjusting the predicted scores of these product proposals, cf. Fig. 2. In concretely, we rank the predicted score of the ground truth category as the highest to improve the prediction confidence, and meanwhile re-rank the score of background as the second highest due to the characteristics of the background classifier (cf. Sect. 3.3). Moreover, by further considering the fine-grained nature of products, we introduce a slack variable as a soft re-ranking strategy to provide a reasonable sorting possibility w.r.t. the predicted scores of fine-grained products. Additionally, we also equip a multi-label recognition loss with PSP for modeling co-occurrence of products in check-out images, which could further bring improvements of the ACO accuracy.

For empirical comparisons, we conduct experiments on the large-scale benchmark dataset in ACO, *i.e.*, RPC [41], by comparing with competing methods [21,41,46] in the literature. In experiments, we evaluate our PSP method on two detection backbones, *i.e.*, Faster RCNN [34] and Cascade RCNN [2] with Feature Pyramid Network (FPN) [24] for justifying its generalization ability. Our check-out accuracy of Faster RCNN and Cascade RCNN are 86.69% and 92.05%, which are improved by 6.18% and 11.54% over state-of-the-arts. The results of ablation studies are also reported for validating the effectiveness of the main components of PSP.

The main contributions of our work are three-fold. (1) We propose a novel method, *i.e.*, prototype-based classifier learning from single-product exemplars, for dealing with the ACO task, especially for the domain gap. (2) We design a discriminative re-ranking approach to enhance the discriminative ability of these prototype-based classifiers. (3) Experimental results on the benchmark RPC dataset show that our PSP achieves significant improvements over competing methods.

## 2  Related Work

### 2.1  Automatic Check-Out

Automatic check-out [41] is a branch of intelligent retail that aims to automatically and accurately detect the products selected by customers and complete the check-out. The popular used ACO datasets in the related works include SOIL-47 [18], Grozi-120 [28], Grocery Products Dataset [9], Freiburg Groceries Dataset [17], MVTec D2S [7] and RPC [41]. To drive the development of ACO, RPC [41] also proposed an object detection baseline. This baseline approach enabled domain adaptation at the data level by segmenting single-product exemplar images to synthesize and render check-out images. Afterwards, Li *et al.* [21] improved the aforementioned baseline method, which restricted the pose of single-product images to create synthesized check-out images. Moreover, Li *et al.* [21] proposed DPNet to accurately detect single-product from the check-out image by collaborating detection and counting. Then, based on DPNet [21] as a pipeline, Yang *et al.* [46] proposed IncreACO with photorealistic exemplar augmentation (PEA). PEA was developed to generate physically reliable and photorealistic check-out images from typical samples scanned for each product, with an incremental learning strategy to match the updated nature of the ACO system and reduce the training effort. Different from the existing ACO methods, our PSP applies prototype-based classifiers derived from single-product exemplars to directly mitigate the domain gap between training and test in ACO. These prototype-based classifiers are able to both recognize fine-grained products in check-out scenario and distinguish background bounding box proposals, without requiring synthesized-rendered process or complicated data augmentation.

### 2.2  Object Detection

Object detection is one of the basic tasks of computer vision, which includes two sub-tasks of object localization [12] and recognition [27]. The current mainstream object detection methods include both single-stage [1,3,5,25,27,31–33,49] and two-stage [2,11,12,14,22,24,34,36,45] detection paradigms. Faster RCNN [34] introduced Region Proposal Network (RPN) to generate proposals. FPN [24] built a top-down architecture with lateral connections to extract features across multiple layers. Cascade RCNN [2] constructed a sequence of detection heads trained with increasing Intersection of Union (IoU) thresholds. Double-Head RCNN [45] rethought classification and localization for object detection and proposed the double-head network with a fully-connected head for classification and a convolution head for bounding box regression. I$^3$Net [3] aimed at learning instance-level features with invariance from different layers for one-stage cross-domain detection. Different from these previous object detection methods, we improve the product proposal classifier for the object detection. Particularly, We develop a prototype-based classifier generator to handle the multi-view issue of single-product exemplars and the domain adaptation issue between exemplars with check-out images.

### 2.3 Classifier Boundary Transformation

Classifier boundary transformation is a kind of strategies for learning discriminative classifier boundaries, which is always conducted within the meta learning framework. Several related work [19,40,44] involved the boundary transformation where a mapping from a decision boundary (or a sample) to another decision boundary is learned. Specifically, in early years, Wang and Hebert [40] proposed a model regression network which learns how to transform from a classifier trained with large-scale data to another one trained with easy small samples. Wei *et al.* [44] utilized the meta learning method to create piecewise classifiers for few-shot fine-grained classification. In CLEAR [19], the authors proposed a cumulative learning approach by meta learning for the one-shot one-class classification task. Different from these previous work, our PSP method is able to directly generate both categorical classifiers and the background classifier, rather than requiring the meta learning process, which shows its efficiency and practicality.

## 3 Methodology

### 3.1 Overall Framework and Notations

As shown in Fig. 2, our proposed PSP method consists of two crucial components, *i.e.*, prototype-based classifier generator and discriminative re-ranking. More specifically, the prototype-based classifier generator is developed to map product prototypes derived from single-product exemplars towards both categorical classifiers and a background classifier. Such a mapping is designed to handle not only the multi-views issue of exemplar images but also the domain change issue between training and test of ACO, cf. Fig. 1 (a). The discriminative re-ranking component could adjust the predicted scores of the corresponding

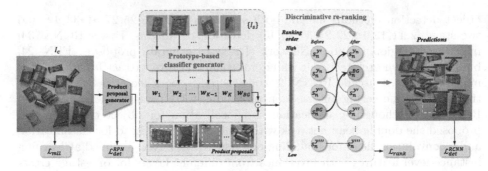

**Fig. 2.** Overall framework of our PSP method. Regarding the check-out image $I_c$, after product proposal generation, a set of product proposals is obtained, which involves both effective proposals and non-effective proposals (*i.e.*, background or incomplete products). By performing the proposed prototype-based classifier generator based on the prototype of single-product exemplars $\{I_s^{k,i}\}$, we have categorical classifiers (*i.e.*, $\boldsymbol{w}_k$, $k \in \{1, \dots, K\}$) for recognizing these fine-grained products of $K$ classes in $I_c$, as well as a background classifier (*i.e.*, $\boldsymbol{w}_{BG}$) for distinguishing background proposals containing no products. Based on these learned classifiers, for the $n$-th proposal, a series of corresponding predicted scores is returned as $s_n$. To further improve the discriminative ability of $\{\boldsymbol{w}\}$, we develop discriminative re-ranking to push the score $s_n^{y_n}$ highest and the score $s_n^{BG}$ the second highest (cf. Sect. 3.3). Particularly, $s_n^{y_n}$ is the predicted score of its ground truth label $y_n$, and $s_n^{BG}$ represents the probability as predicted as background. (Best viewed in colors.) (Color figure online)

proposals, which further improves the discriminative ability of the learned classifiers.

In the following subsections, we present these components in details, and introduce the notations as follows.

Let $\mathcal{S} = \{I_s^{k,i}\}$ ($k \in \{1, \dots, K\}, i \in \{1, \dots, N_s^k\}$) denote the set of the single-product exemplar images, where $I_s^{k,i}$ indicates the $i$-th single-product exemplar of the $k$-th product category. $K$ is the number of product categories and $N_s^k$ is the number of exemplar images belonging to category $k$. Also, we notate the check-out image set as $\mathcal{C} = \{(I_c, Y_c)\}$, where $Y_c$ includes the category label and the bounding box coordinate parameters of each product. Let $\bar{\boldsymbol{x}}_k$ denote the product prototype representation of the $k$-th category, and $\bar{\boldsymbol{x}}_{BG}$ represents the prototype feature of the background. Regarding the learned classifiers, let $\boldsymbol{w}_k$ denote the classifier weights of the $k$-th categorical prototype-based classifier, and $\boldsymbol{w}_{BG}$ is the classifier corresponding to the background. In addition, $\boldsymbol{m}_n$ indicates the feature of the $n$-th product proposal from an check-out image $I_c$.

## 3.2 Prototype-Based Classifier Generation

As illustrated in Fig. 2, given an input check-out image $I_c$, a product proposal generator firstly returns product proposals $\boldsymbol{m}_n$ from $I_c$. These product proposals (including proposals containing background or incomplete products) are then categorized by the generated prototype-based classifiers $\{w\}$. Regarding $\{w\}$, in concretely, we first obtain the categorical prototypes $\bar{x}_k$ of category $k$ based on single-product exemplars $\{I_s^{k,i}\}$ of each product category as training, which is formulated as

$$\bar{x}_k = \frac{1}{N_s^k} \sum_{i=1}^{N_s^k} \left[ f_{GMP}(f_{CNN}(I_s^{k,i}; \Theta)] \right], \tag{1}$$

where $f_{CNN}(\cdot; \Theta)$ represents the backbone CNN model (a pre-trained ResNet-50 [15] by feeding with merely $N_s^k$ product exemplars for category $k$) for extracting features of $\{I_s^{k,i}\}$, $f_{GMP}(\cdot)$ is the global max-pooling function to aggregate and obtain the categorical prototypes, and $\Theta$ indicates the model parameters. These prototypes are used for both training and testing processes. Then, we can generate categorical classifiers $w_k$ based on $\bar{x}_k$.

Beyond $w_k$ for recognizing fine-grained products, it is also desirable to learn a classifier for distinguishing non-effective proposals, i.e., bounding box proposals containing no or incomplete products (aka "background proposals"). However, there is no exemplar of "background proposals" in the training data $\{I_s^{k,i}\}$ to learn such a classifier. Therefore, we average the category prototypes of all product categories as the "background prototype", since the background prototype should correspond to a meta concept with general patterns, rather than specific product concepts with discriminative patterns. The background prototype $\bar{x}_{BG}$ can be represented by

$$\bar{x}_{BG} = \frac{1}{K} \sum_{k=1}^{K} \bar{x}_k. \tag{2}$$

After obtaining both $\bar{x}_k$ and $\bar{x}_{BG}$, they are fed into the prototype-based classifier generator $f_{generator}(\cdot; \theta)$ to learn the corresponding categorical classifiers $w_k$ and the background classifier $w_{BG}$ as outputs:

$$w_k = f_{generator}(\bar{x}_k; \theta), \tag{3}$$

$$w_{BG} = f_{generator}(\bar{x}_{BG}; \theta), \tag{4}$$

where $\theta$ is the parameter of the generator and it is realized as a multi-layer perceptron with two fully connected layers plus ReLU as the activation function.

Finally, the weight matrix $W = [w_1; w_2; \ldots; w_K; w_{BG}]$ is obtained and employed for recognizing the proposals $m_n$ as fine-grained product categories or background by

$$s_n = W \cdot m_n \in \mathbb{R}^{K+1}, \tag{5}$$

where the elements in $s_n$ are the predicted scores belonging to the product categories or as background.

### 3.3  Discriminative Re-Ranking

Based on the predicted scores $s_n$, the predictions of these proposals can be obtained by ranking $s_n$, where the corresponding category with the highest score indicates the predicted category.

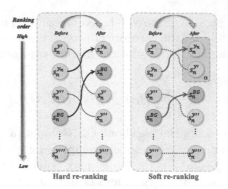

**Fig. 3.** Proposed discriminative re-ranking. The original ranking order of predicted scores is directly obtained by Eq. (5). Compared with hard re-ranking, our soft re-ranking not only re-ranks the predicted scores for bringing more discriminative ability in classifier learning, but also provides a more reasonable sorting possibility for the predicted scores of fine-grained products.

In order to further achieve a better discriminative ability during training, we propose to adjust the score of the ground truth category (*i.e.*, $s_n^{y_n}$) as the highest and the score of background (*i.e.*, $s_n^{BG}$) as the second highest, while other scores of the rest categories are smaller than $s_n^{y_n}$ and $s_n^{BG}$. The process can be formulated by

$$
\begin{aligned}
s_n^{y_n} > s_n^k, & \quad \forall k \in \Omega - \{y_n\}, \\
s_n^{BG} > s_n^j, & \quad \forall j \in \Omega - \{y_n, BG\},
\end{aligned}
\tag{6}
$$

where $y_n$ is the ground truth category of the $n$-th product proposal, and $\Omega = \{1, 2, \ldots, K-1, K, BG\}$.

In particular, it is straightforward to rank $s_n^{y_n}$ as the highest. The reason why we set up the constraint of ranking $s_n^{BG}$ as the second highest is that: the background classifier $\boldsymbol{w}_{BG}$ is derived from the *meta* prototype $\bar{\boldsymbol{x}}_{BG}$ (containing information of all categories). Thus, regarding a proposal $\boldsymbol{m}_n$, its value of dot product upon $\boldsymbol{w}_{BG}$ is natural expected to be larger than the values upon other categorical classifiers, since the ability of discriminative classifiers is to clearly distinguish different product categories, even similar categories.

Another advantage of Eq. (6) is that: for the background proposal, its highest predicted score is $s^{BG}$. Therefore, we can use it as a clue to filter out the false positive bounding box predictions in check-out images during testing.

However, in ACO, products are always belonging to subordinate categories, aka *fine-grained* categories. That is to say that, there exist product categories from one meta-category are extremely visually similar, cf. Fig. (2) in the supplementary materials. For these sub-categories, the re-ranking constraint in Eq. (6) might be not strictly obeyed. Thus, in order to not only deal with the fine-grained nature of products, but also remain the discriminative ability of re-ranking, we modify Eq. (6) into a **soft re-ranking** by introducing a slack variable $\epsilon$, which is as follows:

$$s_n^{y_n} > s_n^k, \quad \forall k \in \Omega - \{y_n\},$$
$$s_n^{j'} > s_n^{BG} - \epsilon, \quad \forall j' \in \Omega', \qquad (7)$$
$$s_n^{BG} > s_n^{j''}, \quad \forall j'' \in \Omega - \{y_n, BG\} - \Omega',$$

where $\Omega' = \{j'|s_n^{j'} > \alpha \cdot \max s_n^j, \forall j\}$ and $\alpha$ is a hyper-parameter in the range of $(0, 1)$. For more clearly presentations, we show the proposed discriminative re-ranking approach in Fig. 3. Specifically, compared with our soft re-ranking, the re-ranking constraint in Eq. (6) can be termed as **hard re-ranking**.

Collaborated with Eq. (7), the discriminative re-ranking process can be written as a loss function by

$$\mathcal{L}_{rank} = \sum_{n=1}^{N} \sum_{k=1}^{K+1} y_{cls}^{k,n} s_n^k + (1 - y_{cls}^{k,n}) \left[ s_n^{BG} - s_n^k \right]_+ + C\epsilon, \qquad (8)$$

where $y_{cls}^{k,n} \in \{0, 1\}$ is the $k$-th category ground truth label of the $n$-th proposal, $[\cdot]$ indicates the hinge function $\max(0, \cdot)$, and $C$ is the penalty factor on the slack variable. In addition, except for the re-ranking loss function, the whole model of PSP is further driven by the traditional regression/classification loss in detection, as well as a multi-label learning loss for modeling the correlation of purchased products (*i.e.*, the co-occurrence), cf. Sect. 3.4.

## 3.4   Loss Functions

**Detection Loss.** According to the general two-stage object detection framework [13,34], the detection loss $\mathcal{L}_{det}$ in our PSP consists of two parts as well, i.e., the region proposal network (RPN) [34] detection loss $\mathcal{L}_{det}^{RPN}$ in the first stage and the RCNN detection loss $\mathcal{L}_{det}^{RCNN}$ in the second stage. In particular, the detection loss of each stage contains both losses of classification and regression for proposals. For more details of the detection loss, please refer to [13,34] for detailed techniques.

**Multi-label Loss.** Multi-label recognition is a fundamental computer vision topic in the literature [20,47], which aims to model the label dependencies among multiple labels associated with images to improve the recognition performance. Recently, multi-label recognition shows its advantages in object detection tasks, *e.g.*, [6]. We hereby introduce the multi-label loss upon the check-out images $I_c$ to model the correlation of co-occurrence products in the check-out scenario. More specifically, we denote $F$ as the feature map of the last layer from $I_c$, and utilize a fully connected layer $f_{FC}(\cdot; \phi)$ with its parameter $\phi$ to conduct multi-label recognition, which can be presented by

$$\hat{y}_{mll} = f_{FC}(f_{GAP}(F) + f_{GMP}(F); \phi), \qquad (9)$$

where $f_{GAP}(\cdot)$ and $f_{GMP}(\cdot)$ are global average- and max-pooling for aggregating $F$ into a single vector. In general, GAP captures common information while

GMP captures the most salient information. In Eq. (9), the sum of GAP and GMP can jointly exploit these two complementary information. $\hat{\boldsymbol{y}}_{mll}$ is the multi-label predictions and its each element is a confidence score. We assume that the ground truth label of an image is $\boldsymbol{y}_{mll}$, where $y_{mll}^k = \{0,1\}$ denotes whether product of category $k$ appears in the image or not. Thus, the multi-label loss $\mathcal{L}_{mll}$ can be formulated as

$$\mathcal{L}_{mll} = \sum_{k=1}^{K} y_{mll}^k \log(\sigma(\hat{y}_{mll}^k)) + (1 - y_{mll}^k) \log(1 - \sigma(\hat{y}_{mll}^k)), \tag{10}$$

where $\sigma(\cdot)$ is the sigmoid function.

Finally, the whole network of our PSP is driven by

$$\mathcal{L} = \mathcal{L}_{det} + \mathcal{L}_{rank} + \mathcal{L}_{mll}, \tag{11}$$

where the weight of each loss is the same because they are equally important and be set as the default setting. Additionally, for performing post-processing, we apply a class-agnostic NMS [37] to keep the bounding boxes with the top confidence score for similar locations, and filter out the false positives.

## 4    Experiments

### 4.1    Dataset

We adopt the large-scale Retail Product Check-out (RPC) dataset [41] as benchmarks to evaluate our method. It includes 200 categories and 83,739 images, where these 200 fine-grained categories belong to 17 meta-categories. It means that the RPC dataset is currently the largest dataset in ACO tasks, which is practical and challenging. The training data of RPC contains 53,739 single-product images in total, where each image has a particular instance of a product category. The RPC test data contains three sub-sets with different clutter modes, each containing 10,000 images. Notably, according to the number of items in an image, the three clutter modes in the RPC dataset consist of **easy** (3~5 categories and 3~10 instances), **medium** (5~8 categories and 10~15 instances), and **hard** (8~10 categories and 15~20 instances). In our experiments, the single-product image set is applied to obtain the prototype-based classifiers, and 6,000 (RPC valid set) and 24,000 (RPC test set) check-out images are used for training and test, respectively. Meanwhile, we apply the four evaluation metrics [41] to measure the advantages and disadvantages between our method and the comparison methods, including check-out accuracy (cAcc), average counting distance (ACD), mean category counting distance (mCCD), mean category intersection of union (mCIoU). The specific formulas are given in the supplementary materials. In addition, other related datasets such as Products-6K [10] and Product1M [48] lack the necessary conditions to satisfy the ACO task or our PSP design, *e.g.*, check-out images or bounding box annotations.

## 4.2 Baseline Methods and Implementation Details

**Baseline Methods.** Specifically, we adopt the method of [41], DPNet [21] and IncreACO [46] as the baselines. [41] first proposed an object detection based ACO pipeline to locate and count products by detecting them in check-out images. Specifically, the backbone of object detection is Faster RCNN [34] with Feature Pyramid Networks (FPN) [24]. To reduce the gap where the check-out image has multiple objects and the training exemplar has only one, [41] proposed a *copy and paste* method to synthesize the image, denoted as *Syn*. In addition, *Render* was used to represent rendered synthesized images using Cycle-GAN [51] for more realistic lighting and shading effects. Then, DPNet [21] modified and improved this baseline. DPNet [21] was an improved FPN [24] and Mask RCNN [13] detector with both detection and counting heads, which is optimized by collaborative detection and counting learning. In particular, DPNet designed a pose pruning step when synthesizing the images to remove exemplars with too small relative areas. IncreACO [46] improved the DPNet by incremental learning LwF [23] and knowledge distillation [16], where the output of the teacher provides the student with the soft label of the old categories. All three approaches utilize a large amount of synthesized and rendered data to train the detection network to achieve domain adaptation at the data level.

**Implementation Details.** Our proposed method is implemented by PyTorch [30] and MMDetection [4]. The relevant parameters in experiments basically follow the default settings in [4] and the backbone network we use is ResNet-50 [15]. In concretely, we set the size of input images to 800×800. The number of $N_s^k$ is all set to 8. The total number of training epochs is 36. While, different from existing methods [21,41,46], our method only requires a smaller iteration time until convergence. The learning rate, momentum and weight decay of the stochastic gradient descent optimizer are initialized to 0.0025, 0.9 and $10^{-4}$, respectively. $\alpha$, $C$ and $\epsilon$ are set in 0.97, 5 and $10^{-6}$ in Eq. (8), respectively. Our training strategy is to decrease the learning rate as 0.1 time of the previous one at the 24-th and 33-th epoch. All experiments are conducted with a GeForce RTX 2080 Ti GPU card (11G memory).

## 4.3 Main Results

Table 1 presents the four evaluation metrics of our method and the existing methods. All the three existing methods have the *Syn+Render* training setting. Specifically, the *Syn+Render* training setting trains the detector with 100,000 synthesized images and 100,000 rendered images simultaneously. Meanwhile, "*Faster RCNN + FPN*" and "*Cascade RCNN + FPN*" represent the Faster RCNN [34] and Cascade RCNN [2] frameworks with the addition of the FPN module, respectively. We apply our proposed method on basis of these two object detection frameworks. In addition, the structure of "*Faster RCNN + FPN*" is the closest to that of existing methods. For fair comparisons, we report the results of different clutter modes. As shown in this table, our method achieves the best experimental results in all clutter modes and evaluation metrics. For example, in the average clutter mode, the cAcc measure of our PSP method is 86.69%, which is an improvement of 6.18% compared to the previous optimal result. The cAcc results of *"Faster RCNN + FPN"* in easy, medium, and hard modes are improved by 1.80%, 6.60%, and 9.91%, over the results of the previous state-of-the-art methods when analyzed for each of the three clutter modes. The amount of improvement, especially in the hard and medium modes, is very significant. In addition, we use our method on a more powerful object detection framework, *i.e.*, *"Cascade RCNN + FPN"*, with a cAcc result of 92.05%, which is 5.36% higher than the result of *"Faster RCNN + FPN"*.

## 4.4   Ablation Studies

**Table 1.** Experimental results on the RPC dataset. "↑" indicates that the larger the value, the better, and "↓" indicates that the smaller the value, the better. The best results are marked in red and the second best results are in **blue**.

| Clutter mode | Methods | cAcc↑ | ACD↓ | mCCD↓ | mCIoU↑ |
|---|---|---|---|---|---|
| Easy | Wei *et al.* [41] (Syn+Render) | 73.17% | 0.49 | 0.07 | 93.66% |
| | IncreACO [46] (Syn+Render) | 88.06% | 0.21 | 0.03 | 96.95% |
| | DPNet [21] (Syn+Render) | 90.32% | **0.10** | **0.02** | 97.87% |
| | PSP (Faster RCNN + FPN) | **92.12%** | 0.11 | **0.02** | **98.40%** |
| | PSP (Cascade RCNN + FPN) | 94.90% | 0.08 | 0.01 | 98.88% |
| Medium | Wei *et al.* [41] (Syn+Render) | 54.69% | 0.90 | 0.08 | 92.95% |
| | IncreACO [46] (Syn+Render) | 77.31% | 0.40 | 0.03 | 96.82% |
| | DPNet [21] (Syn+Render) | 80.68% | 0.32 | 0.03 | 97.38% |
| | PSP (Faster RCNN + FPN) | **87.28%** | **0.18** | **0.01** | **98.59%** |
| | PSP (Cascade RCNN + FPN) | 92.94% | 0.11 | 0.01 | 99.12% |
| Hard | Wei *et al.* [41] (Syn+Render) | 42.48% | 1.28 | 0.07 | 93.06% |
| | IncreACO [46] (Syn+Render) | 66.14% | 0.64 | 0.04 | 96.35% |
| | DPNet [21] (Syn+Render) | 70.76% | 0.53 | 0.03 | 97.04% |
| | PSP (Faster RCNN + FPN) | **80.67%** | **0.29** | **0.02** | **98.29%** |
| | PSP (Cascade RCNN + FPN) | 88.33% | 0.19 | 0.01 | 98.88% |
| Averaged | Wei *et al.* [41] (Syn+Render) | 56.68% | 0.89 | 0.07 | 93.19% |
| | IncreACO [46] (Syn+Render) | 77.15% | 0.41 | 0.03 | 96.72% |
| | DPNet [21] (Syn+Render) | 80.51% | 0.34 | 0.03 | 97.33% |
| | PSP (Faster RCNN + FPN) | **86.69%** | **0.19** | **0.02** | **98.44%** |
| | PSP (Cascade RCNN + FPN) | 92.05% | 0.13 | 0.01 | 98.98% |

**Effectiveness of Our Proposed PSP.** Beyond the main results, we also perform ablation studies to determine the effectiveness of main components of PSP with *"Faster RCNN + FPN"*. Table 2 reports the results in the averaged clutter mode. Specifically, "Prototype" indicates that the inputs of our proposed prototype-based classifier learning are either single-product "Exemplars" or ground truth product instances in "Check-out" images. Comparisons on "Exemplars" and "Check-out" can reveal the ability of our PSP on handling the domain gap challenge. Besides, "Re-ranking" in Table 2 denotes our discriminative re-ranking strategy, including hard re-ranking or soft re-ranking, cf.

**Table 2.** Experimental results of ablation studies. "↑" indicates that the larger the value, the better, and "↓" indicates that the smaller the value, the better. "Exemplars" denotes that a prototype-based classifier is generated from single-product exemplars, while "Check-out" denotes a prototype-based classifier generated from ground truth product instances in check-out images. Best results are marked in **bold**.

| Methods | | | | cAcc↑ | ACD↓ | mCCD↓ | mCIoU↑ |
|---|---|---|---|---|---|---|---|
| | Prototype | Re-ranking | Multi-label loss | | | | |
| FC | – | – | – | 82.87% | 0.31 | 0.02 | 98.04% |
| # 1 | Check-out | – | – | 85.31% | 0.22 | 0.02 | 98.26% |
| # 2 | Exemplars | – | – | 85.12% | 0.22 | 0.02 | 98.28% |
| # 3 | Check-out | Hard | – | 85.60% | 0.21 | 0.02 | 98.34% |
| # 4 | Check-out | Soft | – | 85.56% | 0.21 | 0.02 | 98.30% |
| # 5 | Exemplars | Hard | – | 85.75% | 0.21 | 0.02 | 98.34% |
| # 6 | Exemplars | Soft | – | 85.93% | 0.20 | 0.02 | 98.37% |
| # 7 | Check-out | Hard | ✓ | 85.90% | 0.20 | 0.02 | 98.39% |
| # 8 | Check-out | Soft | ✓ | 85.65% | 0.21 | 0.02 | 98.31% |
| # 9 | Exemplars | Hard | ✓ | 85.90% | 0.20 | 0.02 | 98.40% |
| # 10 | Exemplars | Soft | ✓ | **86.69%** | **0.19** | 0.02 | **98.44%** |

Sect. 3.3. In addition, "Multi-label loss" represents whether using the multi-label loss for capturing the co-occurrence of products in check-out images. Meanwhile, the "FC" row is the baseline with a fully-connected layer as the bounding box classifier.

As the results shown in that table, comparing the results of "FC" and row #2, the effectiveness of our prototype-based classifier learning is validated, *i.e.*, cAcc is improved by 2.25%. Similarly, we can justify the effect of "Re-ranking" and "Multi-label loss" by comparing the results of row #2, #6 and #10, which can improve the cAcc results by 0.81% and 0.76%, respectively. Such improvements of cAcc are significant. In addition, comparing the results in row #9 and #10, it can be found that soft re-ranking performs 0.79% higher than hard re-ranking, which shows the effectiveness and rationality of considering the fine-grained nature by introducing the slack variable. Moreover, comparing #8 with #10, the classifiers generated from the single-product exemplars have 1.04% improvement with these from the check-out instances.

Overall, our PSP improves the cAcc results by 3.82% over the baseline methods in Table 2. Furthermore, we also verify the effectiveness of PSP for mitigating the domain gap challenge. In particular, we generate another prototype-based classifier by feeding the ground truth product instances from the check-out images. Comparing these cAcc results from row #3 to #10, it can be observed the learned classifiers based on "Exemplar" perform equally or even slightly better than the classifiers based on "Check-out" in different empirical settings. The phenomenons demonstrate that our PSP can effectively mitigate the domain gap between the source and target domains. In addition, we discuss the domain adaptation mechanism of PSP in the supplementary materials.

**Sensitivity to Hyper Parameters $N_s^k$, $C$ and $\epsilon$.** It is also noteworthy to know that how the exemplars and their number are collected will affect the per-

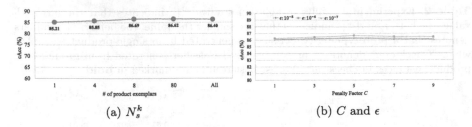

(a) $N_s^k$                                  (b) $C$ and $\epsilon$

**Fig. 4.** The analysis results of these three hyper parameters $N_s^k$, $C$ and $\epsilon$. (a) is the cAcc results of different numbers of exemplars $N_s^k$ and (b) is the cAcc results of different settings of the penalty factor $C$ and the slack variable $\epsilon$.

formance of the prototype-based classifiers. Thus, we compare the cAcc results of different numbers of exemplars $N_s^k$ (*i.e.*, 1, 4, 8, 80 and all exemplars) collected by certain rules, which is reported in Fig. 4 (a). The specific sampling rules for these five cases are as follows. (1) $N_s^k = 1$: Only one exemplar is randomly selected to form the $k$ category prototype. (2) $N_s^k = 4$: Four exemplars at a certain angle are selected based on the front and back of the product and two of the camera viewpoints. (3) $N_s^k = 8$: All the four camera viewpoints at the same angle are considered to sample 8 exemplars compared to $N_s^k = 4$. (4) $N_s^k = 80$: Based on the rule of $N_s^k = 8$, a total of 80 exemplars with 10 randomly selected angles are used to obtain the $k$-th category prototype. (5) $N_s^k = All$: All exemplars of the $k$-th category are utilized to generate the prototype. It is apparent from Fig. 4 (a) that the prototype-based classifiers perform best when $N_s^k$ is set to 8. As analyzed, the lack of exemplar features (*i.e.*, $N_s^k \leq 8$) may result in that the prototypes are under-represented for distinguishing subtle visual differences, while redundant multi-angle exemplar features (*i.e.*, $N_s^k > 8$) might caused redundancies in exemplar feature representation, leading to a reduction in classifier performance. Those might be the reasons why $N_s^k$ is too small or large will cause slightly cAcc drops. Moreover, the cAcc results of different $N_s^k$ values show that our PSP is not sensitive to $N_s^k$. Except for using only 1 exemplar, there is no significant difference between 4, 8, 80 and all exemplars (the precise cAcc gap is less than 0.8%). Meanwhile, even using 1 exemplar, the cAcc score (85.21%) is greatly larger than state-of-the-art results (*e.g.*, 80.51% of DPNet).

Subsequently, we similarly analyze the sensitivity of the penalty factor $C$ and the slack variable $\epsilon$ in Eq. (8). As shown in Fig. 4 (b), the values of $C$ and $\epsilon$ are $1, 3, 5, 7, 9$ and $10^{-5}, 10^{-6}, 10^{-7}$, respectively. We can see that our soft re-ranking is not sensitive to the values of $C$ and $\epsilon$, and the difference between the best and worst cAcc should not exceed 0.7%. Moreover, we show some other qualitative results and the analyses of working mechanism in the supplementary materials.

## 5   Conclusion

In this paper, we proposed a prototype-based classifier learning from single-product exemplars with a discriminative re-ranking for Automatic Check-Out.

The prototype-based classifier learning was developed to mitigate the domain gap between exemplars as training and check-out images as test. Furthermore, we designed a discriminative re-ranking to improve ACO accuracy by bringing more discriminative ability in classifier learning. Also, the multi-label loss was applied to model the co-occurrence of products in check-out images. On the large-scale benchmark RPC dataset, our PSP achieved 86.69% ACO accuracy, which outperformed previous competing methods by 6.18%. In the future, we will investigate PSP for class incremental learning to meet the practical and realistic requirement in ACO.

**Acknowledgments.** The authors would like to thank the anonymous reviewers for their critical and constructive comments and suggestions. We gratefully acknowledge the support of MindSpore, CANN (Compute Architecture for Neural Networks) and Ascend AI Processor used for this research.

# References

1. Bochkovskiy, A., Wang, C.Y., Liao, H.Y.M.: YOLOv4: optimal speed and accuracy of object detection. arXiv preprint arXiv:2004.10934 (2020)
2. Cai, Z., Vasconcelos, N.: Cascade R-CNN: delving into high quality object detection. In: CVPR, pp. 6154–6162 (2018)
3. Chen, C., Zheng, Z., Huang, Y., Ding, X., Yu, Y.: I3Net: implicit instance-invariant network for adapting one-stage object detectors. In: CVPR, pp. 12576–12585 (2021)
4. Chen, K., et al.: MMDetection: open MMLab detection toolbox and benchmark. arXiv preprint arXiv:1906.07155 (2019)
5. Chen, Q., Wang, Y., Yang, T., Zhang, X., Cheng, J., Sun, J.: You only look one-level feature. In: CVPR, pp. 13039–13048 (2021)
6. Chen, Z.M., Jin, X., Zhao, B., Wei, X.S., Guo, Y.: Hierarchical context embedding for region-based object detection. In: ECCV, pp. 633–648 (2020)
7. Follmann, P., Bottger, T., Hartinger, P., Konig, R., Ulrich, M.: MVTec D2S: densely segmented supermarket dataset. In: ECCV, pp. 569–585 (2018)
8. Frontoni, E., Raspa, P., Mancini, A., Zingaretti, P., Placidi, V.: Customers' activity recognition in intelligent retail environments. In: ICIAP, pp. 509–516 (2013)
9. George, M., Floerkemeier, C.: Recognizing products: a per-exemplar multi-label image classification approach. In: ECCV, pp. 440–455 (2014)
10. Georgiadis, K., et al.: Products-6K: a large-scale groceries product recognition dataset. In: PETRA, pp. 1–7 (2021)
11. Girshick, R.: Fast R-CNN. In: CVPR, pp. 1440–1448 (2015)
12. Girshick, R., Donahue, J., Darrell, T., Malik, J.: Rich feature hierarchies for accurate object detection and semantic segmentation. In: CVPR, pp. 580–587 (2014)
13. He, K., Gkioxari, G., Dollar, P., Girshick, R.: Mask R-CNN. In: ICCV, pp. 2961–2969 (2017)
14. He, K., Zhang, X., Ren, S., Sun, J.: Spatial pyramid pooling in deep convolutional networks for visual recognition. IEEE TPAMI **37**(9), 1904–1916 (2015)
15. He, K., Zhang, X., Ren, S., Sun, J.: Deep residual learning for image recognition. In: CVPR, pp. 770–778 (2016)
16. Hinton, G., Vinyals, O., Dean, J.: Distilling the knowledge in a neural network. CoRR abs/1503.02531 (2015)

17. Jund, P., Abdo, N., Eitel, A., Burgard, W.: The freiburg groceries dataset. CoRR abs/1611.05799 (2016)
18. Koubaroulis, D., Matas, J., Kittler, J.: Evaluating colour-based object recognition algorithms using the SOIL-47 database. In: ACCV, pp. 840–845 (2002)
19. Kozerawski, J., Turk, M.: CLEAR: cumulative learning for one-shot one-class image recognition. In: CVPR, pp. 3446–3455 (2018)
20. Lapin, M., Hein, M., Schiele, B.: Analysis and optimization of loss functions for multiclass, top-k, and multilabel classification. IEEE TPAMI 40(7), 1533–1554 (2018)
21. Li, C., Du, D., Zhang, L., Luo, T., Wu, Y., Tian, Q., Wen, L., Lyu, S.: Data priming network for automatic check-out. In: ACM MM, pp. 2152–2160 (2019)
22. Li, Z., Peng, C., Yu, G., Zhang, X., Deng, Y., Sun, J.: Light-head R-CNN: in defense of two-stage object detector. arXiv preprint arXiv:1711.07264 (2017)
23. Li, Z., Hoiem, D.: Learning without forgetting. IEEE TPAMI 40(12), 2935–2947 (2018)
24. Lin, T.Y., Dollár, P., Girshick, R., He, K., Hariharan, B., Belongie, S.: Feature pyramid networks for object detection. In: CVPR, pp. 936–944 (2017)
25. Lin, T.Y., Goyal, P., Girshick, R., He, K., Dollar, P.: Focal loss for dense object detection. In: ICCV, pp. 2980–2988 (2017)
26. Liu, A., Wang, J., Liu, X., Cao, B., Zhang, C., Yu, H.: Bias-based universal adversarial patch attack for automatic check-out. In: ECCV, pp. 395–410 (2020)
27. Liu, W., et al.: SSD: single shot multibox detector. In: ECCV, pp. 21–37 (2016)
28. Merler, M., Galleguillos, C., Belongie, S.: Recognizing groceries in situ using in vitro training data. In: CVPR, pp. 1–8 (2007)
29. Paolanti, M., Liciotti, D., Pietrini, R., Mancini, A., Frontoni, E.: Modelling and forecasting customer navigation in intelligent retail environments. JINT 91(2), 165–180 (2018)
30. Paszke, A., et al.: PyTorch: an imperative style, high-performance deep learning library. In: NeurIPS, pp. 8026–8037 (2019)
31. Redmon, J., Divvala, S., Girshick, R., Farhadi, A.: You Only look once: unified, real-time object detection. In: CVPR, pp. 779–788 (2016)
32. Redmon, J., Farhadi, A.: YOLO9000: better, faster, stronger. In: CVPR, pp. 7263–7271 (2017)
33. Redmon, J., Farhadi, A.: YOLOv3: an incremental improvement. arXiv preprint arXiv:1804.02767 (2018)
34. Ren, S., He, K., Girshick, R., Sun, J.: Faster R-CNN: towards real-time object detection with region proposal networks. In: NeurIPS, pp. 91–99 (2015)
35. Sciucca, L.D., Manco, D., Contigiani, M., Pietrini, R., Bello, L.D., Placidi, V.: Shoppers detection analysis in an intelligent retail environment. In: ICPR, pp. 534–546 (2021)
36. Tan, Z., Nie, X., Qian, Q., Li, N., Li, H.: Learning to rank proposals for object detection. In: ICCV, pp. 8273–8281 (2019)
37. Tychsen-Smith, L., Petersson, L.: Improving object localization with fitness NMS and bounded iou loss. In: CVPR, pp. 6877–6885 (2018)
38. Vieville, T., Crahay, S.: Using an hebbian learning rule for multi-class SVM classifiers. J. Comput. Neurosci. 17(3), 271–287 (2004)
39. Wang, Q., Liu, X., Liu, W., Liu, A.A., Liu, W., Mei, T.: MetaSearch: incremental product search via deep meta-learning. IEEE TIP 29, 7549–7564 (2020)
40. Wang, Y.X., Hebert, M.: Learning to learn: model regression networks for easy small sample learning. In: ECCV, pp. 616–634 (2016)

41. Wei, X.S., Cui, Q., Yang, L., Wang, P., Liu, L., Yang, J.: RPC: a large-scale and fine-grained retail product checkout dataset. Sci. China Inf. Sci. (2022). https://doi.org/10.1007/s11432-022-F3513-y

42. Wei, X.S., Shen, Y., Sun, X., Ye, H.J., Yang, J.: $A^2$-Net: Learning attribute-aware hash codes for large-scale fine-grained image retrieval. In: NeurIPS, pp. 5720–5730 (2021)

43. Wei, X.S., et al.: Fine-grained image analysis with deep learning: a survey. IEEE TPAMI (2021). https://doi.org/10.1109/TPAMI.2021.3126648

44. Wei, X.S., Wang, P., Liu, L., Shen, C., Wu, J.: Piecewise classifier mappings: Learning fine-grained learners for novel categories with few examples. IEEE TIP **28**(12), 6116–6125 (2019)

45. Wu, Y., et al.: Rethinking classification and localization for object detection. In: CVPR, pp. 10186–10195 (2020)

46. Yang, Y., Sheng, L., Jiang, X., Wang, H., Xu, D., Cao, X.B.: IncreACO: incrementally learned automatic check-out with photorealistic exemplar augmentation. In: WACV, pp. 626–634 (2021)

47. Yeh, M.C., Li, Y.N.: Multilabel deep visual-semantic embedding. IEEE TPAMI **42**(6), 1530–1536 (2020)

48. Zhan, X., et al.: Product1M: towards weakly supervised instance-level product retrieval via cross-modal pretraining. In: ICCV, pp. 11782–11791 (2021)

49. Zhang, X., Wan, F., Liu, C., Ji, R., Ye, Q.: FreeAnchor: learning to match anchors for visual object detection. In: NeurIPS, pp. 147–155 (2019)

50. Zhao, L., Yao, J., Du, H., Zhao, J., Zhang, R.: A unified object detection framework for intelligent retail container commodities. In: ICIP, pp. 3891–3895 (2019)

51. Zhu, J.Y., Park, T., Isola, P., Efros, A.A.: Unpaired image-to-image translation using cycle-consistent adversarial networks. In: ICCV, pp. 2223–2232 (2017)

# Overcoming Shortcut Learning in a Target Domain by Generalizing Basic Visual Factors from a Source Domain

Piyapat Saranrittichai[1,2]([✉]) [iD], Chaithanya Kumar Mummadi[2,3] [iD],
Claudia Blaiotta[1] [iD], Mauricio Munoz[1] [iD], and Volker Fischer[1] [iD]

[1] Bosch Center for Artificial Intelligence, Renningen, Germany
`piyapat.saranrittichai@de.bosch.com`
[2] University of Freiburg, Freiburg im Breisgau, Germany
[3] Bosch Center for Artificial Intelligence, Pittsburgh, USA

**Abstract.** Shortcut learning occurs when a deep neural network overly relies on spurious correlations in the training dataset in order to solve downstream tasks. Prior works have shown how this impairs the compositional generalization capability of deep learning models. To address this problem, we propose a novel approach to mitigate shortcut learning in uncontrolled target domains. Our approach extends the training set with an additional dataset (the source domain), which is specifically designed to facilitate learning independent representations of basic visual factors. We benchmark our idea on synthetic target domains where we explicitly control shortcut opportunities as well as real-world target domains. Furthermore, we analyze the effect of different specifications of the source domain and the network architecture on compositional generalization. Our main finding is that leveraging data from a source domain is an effective way to mitigate shortcut learning. By promoting independence across different factors of variation in the learned representations, networks can learn to consider only predictive factors and ignore potential shortcut factors during inference.

## 1 Introduction

Humans seamlessly categorize objects in the real world by their basic visual factors (e.g., shape, texture, color). For example, we perceive a red fire truck as a object with *red* color and the shape of a *fire truck*. We are able to do this because we have learned abstract concepts of shape and color, which easily generalize to common objects including unseen, out-of-distribution (OOD) data [28]. Unlike humans, modern deep neural networks (DNNs) do not possess a generalized notion of basic visual factors and therefore tend to perform poorly on OOD data. This is especially true when networks exploit shortcuts inherent in the data, i.e., when they excessively rely on visual factors that are easy to learn and predictive on in-distribution data but fail to generalize on OOD samples [8,27]. For example, DNNs trained on

**Supplementary Information** The online version contains supplementary material available at https://doi.org/10.1007/978-3-031-19806-9_17.

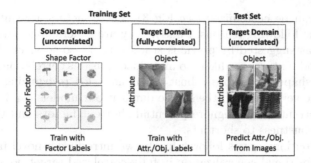

**Fig. 1.** Our task is to predict attribute/object labels in the target domain whose correlated training labels induce high shortcut opportunities. To improve generalization, we propose to augment the training set with a cheap source domain to learn representations of visual factors. In this given example, attribute and object in the target domain associate to color and shape factors respectively.

a dataset in which all fire trucks are red might use color as a shortcut to recognize fire trucks while ignoring the more semantically meaningful attribute of shape. As a result, such a network may misclassify a yellow fire truck as a school bus.

In this work, we study the ability of DNNs to recognize OOD samples in the context of compositional generalization, i.e., the ability to understand unseen combinations of known elements. While a few approaches have already been proposed to improve generalization in compositional zero-shot recognition tasks [2,22,23], the performance of all these methods heavily depends on the number of combinations observed during training. This is due to the fact that a low number of seen combinations generates more shortcut opportunities [8]. A naïve remedy to shortcut learning is to collect missing combinations but this could be costly as some combinations can be rare in practice. In this work, we aim to investigate the underpinning of compositional generalization in DNNs and hence focus on the challenging and unexplored regime in which different visual attributes are fully-correlated in the training data (e.g. where one attribute such as color is a deterministic function of another one, such as shape). In the rest of this paper, we will refer to the domain in which we aim to achieve compositional generalization as the *target domain*.

We propose a novel approach to mitigate shortcut learning in such a target domain by introducing a well-controlled *source domain* in the form of an additional training dataset, which can be cheaply generated. This source dataset is specifically designed to facilitate learning of basic visual factors by constraining them to be uncorrelated (all factor combinations appear uniformly during training). With this source dataset, we aim to learn independent representations of generic visual factors in order to improve OOD generalization in the target domain. Overview of our setup is shown in Fig. 1. We show practical benefits of such a simple and easy-to-generate source domain for improving the performance across multiple, more complex, target domains. Our approach provides a low-cost and effective strategy to improve compositional generalization.

Considering our source dataset, we employ DiagVib [6], a framework to generate datasets whose visual factors (i.e., shape, color, texture, lightness and background) can be customized (see Fig. 3). These factors are suitable for our purpose for the following reasons. Firstly, they are generic for common objects. Additionally, as suggested by previous studies [9,27], some visual factors (e.g., background and texture) are likely to introduce spurious correlations while other factors (e.g., shape) are more robust when used for recognizing objects. By including these key factors in the source dataset, our models can learn to focus more on important factors, ignore potential shortcut factors and thus improve the models' robustness to shortcuts.

Our contributions are as follows: firstly, we introduce a novel framework to improve compositional generalization in fully-correlated target domains. This is achieved by leveraging a source domain in order to alleviate shortcut learning. Secondly, we propose a simple network architecture exploiting the source domain to learn independent representations of visual factors. We also show that, if the target domain is not strictly fully-correlated, we can require less *a priori* knowledge for our approach. Lastly, we perform ablation studies to investigate effects of different source dataset configurations. Our main finding is that the source domain can act as a regularizer that encourages the internal representations of basic visual factors in DNNs to be less entangled. We show that this consistently improves compositional generalization across different target domains.

## 2    Related Works

*Compositional Generalization (CG).* We study CG in the context of compositional zero-shot learning, where the goal is to recognize images of unseen attribute-object combinations, given only some combinations seen during training. A simple baseline VisProd [19,22] uses multiple classifiers to predict attribute and object labels. More recently, [2,14,17,21–23] learn to map images and labels (i.e., attribute-object combinations) to their joint feature space. It is commonly assumed that the same object can be seen in combination with certain number of attribute values during training. In our work, we study the corner case where the number of seen combinations is minimal, e.g., a fully-correlated attribute-object combinations setting, which introduces severe shortcut opportunities. A recent work [2] shows dramatic performance degradation of DNNs when reducing the number of seen combinations. The objective of this work is to mitigate this effect by incorporating a suitable source domain. We remark that, in most CG approaches, the label space has only two dimensions (i.e., attribute and object types). Instead, in our work the label space of the source domain is not restricted to two dimensions but can be as high-dimensional as the number of annotated factors. In particular, we consider basic visual factors as considered in [6], which are more likely to generalize across different tasks.

*Domain Generalization.* The aim of domain generalization is to learn models that generalize to unseen domains at test time. The problem we address in this work is therefore related to this line of research. More specifically, our problem setting loosely resembles *Heterogeneous Domain Generalization* (HeDG) [12,13,

26, 30, 31], because we assume that the label distributions in the source and target domains have different, possibly disjoint, support (e.g., the labels represent objects in the source domain and animals in the target domain). Nevertheless, it should be noted that our work stems from a different motivation compared to the domain generalization literature. Unlike domain generalization, we do not assume the target data distribution to be unavailable during training. Instead, we assume to have access to a heavily biased sample from the target domain. From this perspective, our setup is also related to domain adaptation [5,7], where training is performed on both the source and target domains together.

*Learning Independent Representations.* The topic of compositional generalization is also linked to the notion of disentanglement in generative modeling. The goal of disentangled representation learning is to construct a compact and interpretable latent representation, by discovering independent factors of variation (FoVs) in the data [4, 11, 24]. Most methods proposed in the disentanglement literature assume statistical independence between the factors of variation and perform learning without supervision. Thus, they are predominantly trained and evaluated on synthetic data where the ground truth FoVs are perfectly uncorrelated [16]. This is an idealized setting, which is almost never encountered in the real world. Therefore, the usefulness and generalization ability of these methods when the training data is biased remains unclear. For instance, a recent large-scale empirical study found that several state-of-the-art methods from the disentanglement literature fail to disentangle pairs of correlated factors [25]. Our work is also concerned with learning independent representations of basic visual factors, but, as opposed to prior works, we specifically focus on the problem of mitigating shortcut learning. It should be noted that, in contrast to unsupervised representation learning, we train representations of visual factors with factor annotations. However, we will discuss a scenario in which unsupervised representation learning can be integrated into our framework in Sect. 4.3.

# 3   Methodology

## 3.1   Problem Formulation

Our task measures generalization performance in the presence of shortcuts from the perspective of compositional generalization. Specifically, let us consider a *target domain/dataset t*, where each sample consists of an image $x_t \in \mathcal{X}_t \subset \mathcal{I}$ containing a single object. Such object is associated with one attribute: $y_t = (a, o) \in \mathcal{Y}_t = \mathcal{A}_t \times \mathcal{O}_t$, where $\mathcal{A}_t = \{a_1, a_2, \ldots\}$ and $\mathcal{O}_t = \{o_1, o_2, \ldots\}$ are sets of attribute and object type values respectively. In our task, not all attribute-object combinations are seen during training. The goal is to learn a model for the joint probability distribution $p(a, o \mid x_t)$ which yields good predictive performance on images of both seen and unseen attribute-object combinations.

The target dataset may be heavily biased, and thus naively training a classifier to predict object and attribute types can lead to shortcut learning resulting in poor OOD generalization. We define a dataset in a target domain,

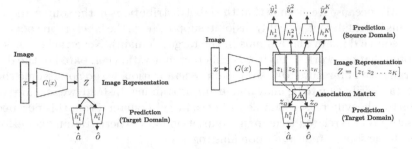

(a) Global Image Representation    (b) Factor Image Representation

**Fig. 2.** Architectures with different image representations. a) Global: a single vector contains all visual clues. b) Factor: multiple factor representations encode different visual factors provided in source domain.

to be *fully-correlated* when each annotated attribute label appears together with only one annotated object label or vice versa. We aim to investigate whether introducing an additional, specifically designed, dataset from a different *source domain s* can discourage DNNs from exploiting shortcuts when trained for attribute and object prediction in the target domain. For this purpose, each image $x_s \in \mathcal{X}_s \subset \mathcal{I}$ in the source domain $s$ is assumed to be labeled with a tuple $y_s = (f_1, f_2, \ldots, f_K) \in \mathcal{F}_s^1 \times \mathcal{F}_s^2 \times \ldots \times \mathcal{F}_s^K$, where $K$ is the number of factors and each $\mathcal{F}_s^k$ denotes the set possible values for an individual basic visual factor capturing generic image properties such as shape, color, texture, etc.

To utilize source factor information in the target domain, we build an association matrix that models the connection between different source factor representations to target attribute or object. For fully-correlated target domains, we assume that the association is given as *a priori* knowledge regarding the possible source factor(s) the model is expected to rely to avoid shortcuts. For example, in the Color-Fruit dataset (Fig. 4c/4d), attribute and object can be manually associated to color and shape factors respectively. This *a priori* knowledge requirement can be relaxed in semi-correlated setting as presented in Sect. 3.4.

### 3.2 Network Architecture

***Architecture.*** We study a simple baseline model (similar to VisProdNN [22]), which naturally lends itself to exploiting the availability of a source dataset. The baseline model (Fig. 2a) consists of an encoder backbone $G$ and multiple prediction heads. It maps an input image to a global latent representation, which is then used to predict both the attribute and object labels. A crucial limitation of this model is that, without additional inductive biases, its latent representation will encode all predictive image factors. This makes the model more vulnerable to learning shortcuts, since it will be free to rely on easy to learn, predictive signals irrespective of their (in)ability to generalize to novel combinations [10].

We extend the model of Fig. 2a by splitting the latent representation into multiple factor representations, as in Fig. 2b. As opposed to Fig. 2a, the encoder $G$ produces $K$ non-overlapping factor representations. Each representation is intended to contain only information related to its corresponding basic factor (e.g., shape, color, texture). The encoder's output can then be written as $G(x) = Z = [z_1\ z_2 \dots z_K] \in \mathbb{R}^{D \times K}$ ($D$ is the size of a factor representation).

The prediction heads are divided in two subsets for predicting labels in source and target domains respectively. While in principle we could feed $Z$ as an input to all the prediction heads, as discussed above, this approach leads to poor compositional generalization. Instead, we introduce an additional inductive bias, namely that each source prediction logit should only depend on a single factor representation. Therefore, predictions for the source data $H_s$ are:

$$\hat{y}_s = H_s(Z) = \left[ h_s^1(z_1)\ h_s^2(z_2) \dots h_s^K(z_K) \right] , \tag{1}$$

where $\hat{y}_s = \left[ \hat{y}_s^1\ \hat{y}_s^2 \dots \hat{y}_s^K \right]$ contains the predicted factor values for a sample from the source domain. Ideally, each $\hat{y}_s^k$ should only depend on $z_k$ to discourage the latent representation from encoding information irrelevant to predict the $k$-th factor. Due to biases in the target domain, and in the absence of additional constraints, the architecture introduced above does not ensure invariance of every representation to the other factors. We explore different strategies to promote independence of the learned representations in Sect. 3.3.

In fully-correlated scenario, the association matrix can manually be defined as a binary matrix $A \in \{0,1\}^{K \times 2}$ where $A_{k1}$ and $A_{k2}$ are set to 1 only if the $k$-th factor informs the attribute and object prediction respectively. The representations of attribute ($z_a$) and object ($z_o$) can be obtained by $[z_a\ z_o] = ZA$. The prediction on target data can then be computed as follows:

$$\hat{y}_t = H_t(ZA) = \left[ h_t^a(z_a)\ h_t^o(z_o) \right] , \tag{2}$$

where $\hat{y}_t = (\hat{a}, \hat{o})$ is a tuple of the predicted attribute and object labels.

**Loss.** To train the encoder and the predictors, we use a linear combination of the two loss terms $\mathcal{L}_{source} = \frac{1}{K} \sum_{\forall k} CE(\hat{y}_s^k, y_s^k)$ and $\mathcal{L}_{target} = \frac{1}{2} \sum_{l \in \{a,o\}} CE(\hat{y}_t^l, y_t^l)$, where $CE$ denotes the cross-entropy loss. $\lambda \geq 0$ is a hyperparameter weighting the importance of the regularizing loss term $\mathcal{L}_{source}$, which encourages a factor representation via the source samples.

**Training.** An equal number of samples from the source and target domains are sampled for every minibatch and fed to the network in order to compute $\mathcal{L}_{source}$ and $\mathcal{L}_{target}$ separately. The network is optimized via gradient-based minimization of the total loss. In this regard, all source samples will affect $G$ and $H_s$ and all target samples will affect $G$ and $H_t$.

### 3.3   Additional Constraints

The factor representations $\{z_k\}_{k=1}^K$ may still be correlated when using the loss and model architecture described above. Consequently, in the target domain,

$z_a$ (attribute representation) may be predictive of the object label, and $z_o$ (object representation) may be predictive of the attribute label. These are unintended shortcuts that lead to poor compositional generalization. We explore two additional constraints to further encourage independence among factor representations: the *Isolated Latent Constraint* and the *Cross Independence Constraint*.

**Isolated Latent (IL) Constraint** completely prevents factor representations from being influenced by the target domain. While this suppresses the effect of biases in the target dataset, it may harm discriminative performance in the target domain. This constraint is implemented by stopping gradients from $\mathcal{L}_{target}$ to the encoder $G$.

**Cross-Factor Independence (CI) Constraint** promotes independence of factor representations, by adding a set of small auxiliary networks $\left\{ H'_{k_1 k_2} \right\}_{k_1 \neq k_2}$ for cross-factor predictions. While each $H'_{k_1 k_2}$ is trained to predict $y_s^{k_2}$ from $z_{k_1}$, $G$ is trained to produce $Z$ such that all $H'$ are poor predictors. More details are presented in the Appendix A.8. Although the CI constraint only encourages independence with respect to the source domain, we investigate if this property can be transferred to target domains in Sect. 4.2.

### 3.4   Learning Factor Association Matrix $A$

In non-fully-correlated target domains (e.g., semi-correlated setting mentioned in Sect. 4.3), we can relax the requirement that the association matrix $A$ must be manually given *a priori* and, instead, learn it in an end-to-end fashion together with the network parameters. To this end, we apply a continuous relaxation of the binary matrix $A$, and allow it to contain real numbers within $[0, 1]$ such that each column sums to 1 (i.e. overall weightage across source factors) to maintain scales of the attribute/object representations using the softmax function.

We found that naïvely learning $A$ without any additional constraints can lead to poor properties of the association matrix. Ideally, the association matrix should match the target attribute or object type to only one (or a few) robust source factor(s), and ignore factors vulnerable to shortcuts. For this reason, we propose to add an additional regularization $\mathcal{L}_{Reg} = \alpha \mathcal{L}_{Entropy} + \beta \mathcal{L}_{Suppress}$.

$\mathcal{L}_{Entropy}$ is the sum of the entropy values of both columns of $A$. Minimizing this entropy loss will reduce the number of source factors used to predict target properties, encouraging only robust factors to be considered when minimizing together with cross-entropy losses. On the other hand, $\mathcal{L}_{Suppress}$ applies a regularization along the rows of $A$ to make sure no same source factor is predictive of both target predictions. In particular, for each row $i$, if its maximum value $A_{ij^{max}}$ is higher than a threshold $\tau$, all other entries will be suppressed by adding $\left( \sum_{j \neq j^{max}} A_{ij} \right) * (\text{sg}(A_{ij^{max}}) - \tau)$ to the loss term. The symbol $\text{sg}(A_{ij^{max}})$ indicates the stop gradient operation, such that minimizing $\mathcal{L}_{Suppress}$ only affects the cell whose values are not maximum in each row. Detailed experiments on the automatic learning of the association matrix are presented in Sect. 4.3.

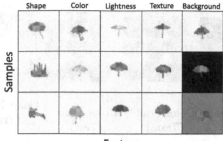

**Fig. 3.** Illustration of DiagVib-Caltech (main source dataset) showing its multiple independent factors. More details of each factor is presented in the Appendix A.1. (Color figure online)

## 4    Experiments

We conduct several experiments to understand how incorporating the source domain affects compositional generalization in scenarios which are vulnerable to shortcut learning. We start by describing our experiment setup below.

***Datasets.*** We use the following datasets in our experiments:
*DiagVib.* [6] We extend the original framework to use shapes other than MNIST to increase variances. Our main configurations based on this framework are *a) DiagVib-Caltech*: With 50 non-animal shapes from Caltech101 [18] in 12 colors. 5 basic visual factors are available as shown in Fig. 3. This dataset is our main source dataset. We will later show that compositional generalization can be improved by this low-cost dataset even in more complex target domains. *b) DiagVib-Animal*: With 10 animal shapes from [3] in 10 colors on 3 backgrounds and scales (see Fig. 4a/4b).

***Color-Fruit.*** This dataset is comprised of real fruit images (of 5 types) from the Fruit-360 dataset [20]. Additionally, we control colors of the fruits using the recolorization approach from [29] (see Fig. 4c/4d). More details on this dataset generation are described in the appendix A.10.

***AO-CLEVR.*** This dataset is proposed in [2] to benchmark compositional generalization. It contains 3 basic shapes in 7 different colors. We will use this dataset as an additional target domain. We simulate correlation between attributes and objects by limiting one color to appear with only one shape during training.

***Color-Fashion.*** This dataset is originally proposed in [15] in which each image sample depicts a person dressed with cloth combinations. For each sample, cloth type and color segmentations are provided. In this paper, original images are cropped so that only one cloth type is appeared in individual images (see Fig. 4e/4f). 5 cloth types (T-shirt, skirt, jeans, shoes and dress) and 5 colors (Black, White, Yellow, Green and Blue) are selected from the original dataset.

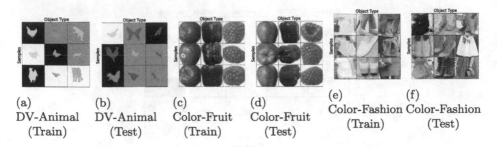

| (a) | (b) | (c) | (d) | (e) | (f) |
|---|---|---|---|---|---|
| DV-Animal (Train) | DV-Animal (Test) | Color-Fruit (Train) | Color-Fruit (Test) | Color-Fashion (Train) | Color-Fashion (Test) |

**Fig. 4.** Samples from target domains. A column of each grid corresponds to an object type. Notice that each object (shape) corresponds to a single attribute (color) during training (see a, c and e) but not during testing (see b, d and f). (Color figure online)

For all target domains in our work, if a manual factor association matrix $A$ is required for any algorithms, attribute and object types (i.e., shapes, fruit types, cloth types) are associated to color and shape factors respectively. This is intuitive since shape can robustly predict object types in general. Poorly assigned association can lead to poor performance as detailed in the Appendix A.4.

*Evaluation.* We evaluate compositional generalization in the open world setting as in [23] by computing predictive accuracies on seen and unseen attribute-object combinations as well as their harmonic mean (HM). One difference to [23] is that, for fair comparison, we do not use an additional hyperparameter (i.e. bias term) to calibrate the likelihood of predicting unseen attribute-object combinations (More details regarding the bias term are described in the Appendix A.6). During testing, any attribute-object combinations in the target domain can appear. All quantitative results are averaged across 6 different random training seeds.

*Network Configurations.* We follow the same convention as in [2,22,23] by using ImageNet pretrained features from ResNet-50 as network inputs. $G$, $H_s$ and $H_t$ are modeled as fully-connected networks. Factor-0 and FactorSRC refers to our architecture when a source domain is ignored and used, respectively. IL and CI constraints are appended as suffixes if the constraints are applied. Also, we benchmark the architecture with the global image representation (Fig. 2a). Similarly, Global-0 and GlobalSRC denote its configurations where a source domain is not incorporated and incorporated respectively. More implementation details can be found in the Appendix A.5. The code for our implementation is publicly available at https://github.com/boschresearch/sourcegen.

*Baselines.* We compare our approach against the following baselines (1) **LabelEmbed+** [22]: a vanilla baseline, which performs recognition with a joint feature space for images and labels. (2) **TMN** [23], which employs automatic network rewiring conditioned on attribute-object pair hypotheses. (3) **CGE** [21], which exploits graph structure to regularize the joint feature space.

## 4.1 Compositional Generalization in Fully-Correlated Scenario

We investigate the impact of using an uncorrelated source domain (all factor combinations can appear uniformly) across different target domains whose labels are fully-correlated. We compare several variants of our approach against baselines that do not use a source domain. The results are shown in Table 1.

We begin by noting that, without a source domain (first five rows), baselines generally perform well only on the seen combinations but not on the unseen ones. E.g., Factor-0 on the Color-Fruit dataset has seen accuracy of 100% compared to only 2.9% on unseen combinations (Low seen accuracies of some baselines are discussed in the Appendix A.6). This occurs as these networks are trained only on the target datasets with correlated combinations so that they learn to excessively exploit the easiest predictive visual factors present in the datasets. On the unseen combinations, these predictive factors do not necessarily generalize to the intended labels. This degrades the generalization of the networks.

In contrast, using a source domain (see FactorSRC variations) consistently improves the HM accuracy by increasing accuracy on unseen combinations, at the expense of a partial loss of performance on seen combinations. For example, the FactorSRC-IL baseline on the Color-Fruit dataset has a seen accuracy of 95.5%, which is lower compared to baselines that do not use the source domain, but in turn exhibits the highest unseen accuracy (40.7%). This shows a reduction of shortcut learning. The same trend holds for all other datasets we consider, with different seen/unseen accuracy trade-offs across datasets.

Compared to previous works, our results show that a *single* and *simple* source domain improves generalization performance on unseen combinations across different target domains. An alternative *naïve* solution would be to collect data corresponding to unseen combinations directly in the target domain and include them in the training set. However, this is in practice not a viable solution: not only is collecting data in a real-world target domain expensive but, perhaps more importantly, the biases that affect the training set are often unknown, which makes collecting an uncorrelated dataset difficult in practice. Rather, generalization improvement on those target domains can be achieved without much additional costs if we have a *universal* (a source domain can be used for multiple target domains) source domain at hand that can be *generated cheaply*. One open problem is the trade-off between generalization and in-distribution accuracy, which in some cases is still sub-optimal, especially when the target domain has a large domain shift from the source domain (see the drop of seen accuracy of the FactorSRC-IL on the Color-Fashion dataset). Improving this trade-off is an open research question leaving a scope for improvement in future works.

***Global vs Factor Image Representations.*** Our results suggest that a factor representation is essential to exploit the source domain for compositional generalization. In fact, all GlobalSRC variations, in spite of incorporating the source domain during training, exhibit significantly lower unseen accuracy compared to the FactorSRC variants. This is due to the fact that the global representation contains information about all visual factors that are relevant for the

**Table 1.** Accuracies on DiagVib-Animal, Color-Fruit, AO-CLEVR (each has random chance accuracy of 1%, 4% and 4.7% respectively) and Color-Fashion target domains. DiagVib-Caltech is used as the source domain.

| Approach | Use source? | DiagVib-Animal | | | Color-Fruit | | | AO-CLEVR | | | Color-Fashion | | |
|---|---|---|---|---|---|---|---|---|---|---|---|---|---|
| | | Seen | Unseen | HM | Seen | Unseen | HM | Seen | Unseen | HM | Seen | Unseen | HM |
| LabelEmbed+ | ✗ | 69.6 | 7.3 | 13.2 | 100 | 6.8 | 12.5 | 100 | 0.7 | 1.5 | 37.0 | 7.1 | 11.9 |
| TMN | ✗ | 95.5 | 0.1 | 0.3 | 100 | 0.0 | 0.0 | 100 | 0.0 | 0.0 | 86.5 | 0.7 | 1.4 |
| CGE | ✗ | 43.8 | 9.1 | 15.0 | 84.4 | 7.8 | 14.3 | 94.0 | 9.3 | 16.9 | 21.6 | **20.5** | 21.0 |
| Global-0 | ✗ | **96.1** | 0.0 | 0.1 | 100 | 1.5 | 3.0 | 100 | 0.3 | 0.5 | **93.6** | 0.0 | 0.0 |
| Factor-0 | ✗ | 95.2 | 0.8 | 1.5 | 100 | 2.9 | 5.5 | 100 | 2.2 | 4.3 | 92.7 | 1.8 | 3.6 |
| GlobalSRC | ✓ | 94.2 | 0.3 | 0.5 | 100 | 1.1 | 2.2 | 100 | 0.3 | 0.7 | 85.5 | 0.2 | 0.4 |
| GlobalSRC-IL | ✓ | 92.4 | 0.3 | 0.7 | 100 | 0.7 | 1.4 | 98.9 | 0.8 | 1.6 | 61.8 | 2.2 | 4.2 |
| FactorSRC | ✓ | 90.0 | 7.0 | 13.0 | 99.7 | 27.3 | 42.4 | 99.9 | 3.2 | 6.3 | 76.4 | 8.3 | 15.0 |
| FactorSRC-CI | ✓ | 91.2 | 7.9 | 14.5 | 100 | 10.9 | 19.6 | 100 | 2.3 | 4.5 | 87.3 | 8.2 | 14.8 |
| FactorSRC-IL | ✓ | 56.3 | **32.6** | **41.3** | 95.5 | **40.7** | **57.0** | 89.5 | **19.6** | **32.1** | 32.7 | 17.0 | **22.3** |

**Table 2.** Cross prediction accuracies on DiagVib-Animal. These are obtained by using each associated factor representation ($z_a$ or $z_o$) to predict each target label (attribute or object) with a linear model. Ideal independence representations will have high direct prediction accuracies (predict their own labels well) but low cross prediction accuracies (predict others' labels poorly).

| Approach | Direct-Prediction ↑ | | Cross-Prediction ↓ | |
|---|---|---|---|---|
| | $z_a \to \hat{a}$ | $z_o \to \hat{o}$ | $z_a \to \hat{o}$ | $z_o \to \hat{a}$ |
| FactorSRC | **62** | **86** | 77 | 44 |
| FactorSRC-CI | 54 | 83 | 73 | 35 |
| FactorSRC-IL | 58 | 85 | **46** | **23** |

object-attribute prediction task, thus offering easy-to-learn shortcuts that harm generalization performance. In contrast, by using factor representations, we promote factor disentanglement such that shortcuts are harder to learn.

## 4.2   Impact of Additional Constraints

We investigate the role of IL and CI constraints. We begin by noting that FactorSRC-IL gives the best HM accuracies across all target domains. Our hypothesis is that this result can be explained by a larger cross-factor information flow into the learned factor representations when adding the CI constraint compared to IL. To quantitatively measure the magnitude of cross-factor leakage, we extract $z_k$ from all test samples and use them to predict all labels ($y_s^1, y_s^2, \ldots y_s^K$ for a source domain or $\hat{a}, \hat{o}$ for a target domain) with linear models. Ideally, $z_k$ should predict its associated label (direct prediction) well but should fail to predict other labels (cross-prediction). We present these results in Table 2.

First, we are interested whether the CI constraint can encourage independence, not only in the source domain, but more importantly in the target domain.

**Table 3.** Accuracies on various target domains in semi-correlated scenarios.

| Approach | DiagVib-Animal | | | Color-Fruit | | | Color-Fashion | | |
|---|---|---|---|---|---|---|---|---|---|
| | Seen | Unseen | HM | Seen | Unseen | HM | Seen | Unseen | HM |
| TMN | **83.4** | 3.2 | 6.2 | **99.9** | 3.1 | 6.0 | **68.6** | 3.7 | 6.9 |
| CGE | 51.8 | 1.9 | 3.6 | 72.0 | 8.4 | 15.0 | 42.5 | 13.0 | 19.9 |
| FactorSRC-IL | 52.8 | **35.0** | **42.1** | 93.7 | **36.3** | **52.3** | 32.5 | **15.0** | **20.5** |
| FactorSRC-IL-LA | 72.7 | 3.7 | 7.1 | 99.0 | 17.5 | 29.6 | 53.1 | 8.0 | 13.9 |
| FactorSRC-IL-LA$^{\text{R}}$ | 60.9 | 24.2 | 34.7 | 96.0 | 32.7 | 48.6 | 35.2 | 14.3 | 20.2 |

We observe that, while independence is promoted by FactorSRC-CI in the source domain well (see the Appendix A.3), in the target domain, cross-prediction accuracies decrease only slightly compared to FactorSRC. Thereby, we can infer that the independence enforced by $\mathcal{L}_{H'}$ in the source domain is not necessarily transferable to the target domain. One possible reason is that factor representations are still affected by the dataset biases in the target domain via $\mathcal{L}_{target}$.

On the other hand, dataset bias in the target domain cannot affect the factor representations with the IL constraint. In Table 2, although an explicit independent constraint is not introduced, the factor representations are less entangled in the target domain, which is indicated by lower cross-prediction accuracies (while high direct-prediction accuracies are preserved). The independence which is indirectly encouraged only by $\mathcal{L}_{source}$ enables shortcut-robust factor representations resulting in better HM accuracies in Table 1.

### 4.3   Learning Association Matrix for Semi-correlated Scenario

The association matrix $A$ must be known *a priori* for fully-correlated target domains because the target data alone does not contain enough information to distinguish object types from their attributes. For a *semi-correlated* target domain, a more general solution is viable, in which the association matrix is learned. In this case, each object type is observed in combination with at least two attribute values. The additional combinations make it possible to distinguish attribute from object type. In order to learn the association matrix $A$, we adopt the algorithm introduced in Sect. 3.4.

Table 3 reports performance of different algorithms. FactorSRC-IL-LA and FactorSRC-IL-LA$^{\text{R}}$ indicate algorithms that learn the association matrix without and with association regularization respectively. Results suggest that naïvely backpropagating through the matrix $A$ is not an effective strategy as indicated by the large gap between HM accuracy of FactorSRC-IL and FactorSRC-IL-LA. This is due to an undesired property of the association matrix which we will later investigate. Fortunately, this undesired property can be alleviated by incorporating our proposed regularization constraints during training, as indicate by the comparable performance of FactorSRC-IL and FactorSRC-IL-LA$^{\text{R}}$.

To qualitatively assess the correctness of learned associations, we visualize $A$ as heatmaps in Fig. 5a. In addition, we compare the association matrix that

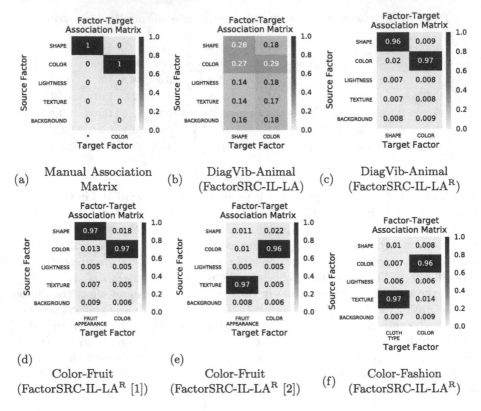

**Fig. 5.** Factor association matrices learned from different target datasets with various approaches resulted from representative runs. Manual Association Matrix in Figure a is only used for our manual association (not the groundtruth).

we manually assigned in FactorSRC* (Fig. 5a) and the learned ones. First we consider the simplest target dataset, DiagVib-Animal. In this case, FactorSRC-IL-LA, which does not apply any regularization, fails to retrieve the association matrix (Fig. 5b). Even if the association matrix has the high weights that associate shape factor to shape target and color factor to color target correctly, the matrix is still far from sparse, making the model vulnerable to shortcuts (see results in Table 3). On the other hand, when regularization constraints are introduced in FactorSRC-IL-LA$^R$, the learned matrix is more sparse and closer to the manually assigned matrix (see Fig. 5c), which results in lower shortcut vulnerability of the model and higher compositional generalization performance.

In the more realistic case of the Color-Fruit dataset, we find that with multiple random seeds, FactorSRC-IL-LA$^R$ can converge to two possible configurations for the estimated matrix $A$. The first configuration (Fig. 5d) is close to our manual association as it matches the fruit type to the shape factor. Another configuration, on the other hand, associates the fruit type to the texture factor

(Fig. 5e). This is not surprising, since in the color-fruit dataset, both shape and texture factors are predictive of fruit type. The same observation has already been made in the context of conventional image classification [9] especially with complex object shapes. We observed the same behaviour in the case of the Color-Fashion dataset where the learned matrix associates garment type to the texture factor (Fig. 5f). Another advantage of our approach indicated by this observation is that it yields higher model interpretability, as we can understand which visual factors are important for network predictions.

The fact that learning of the association is possible when target datasets are not fully-correlated makes our approach well suited to practical applications. As the association is determined automatically, minimal *a priori* knowledge is required. In other words, factor representations can also be learned from images by any approaches including unsupervised representation learning that disentangle image representations into multiple independent factor representations [11].

### 4.4  Properties of the Source Domains

We also investigate the properties of source domains which encourage generalization. Our main findings can be summarized as follows: first, basic visual factors represented in the source domain should be sufficiently diverse and aligned with visual properties of the target data. Second, the fact that all factor combinations are available in the source domain during training is crucial. This allows deep networks to learn meaningful representation for each factor. Lastly, large intra-class variation of factors is also important to encourage better generalization. More details of our ablation studies can be found in the Appendix A.2.

## 5  Conclusion

We study vulnerability of DNNs to shortcuts by evaluating their compositional generalization on target domains with correlated attribute-object combinations. We provide empirical evidence that incorporating an additional source domain can improve generalization on unseen combinations on target domains. The source domain enables certain networks to represent inputs in terms of multiple independent visual factors. From our findings, the impact of the source domain on compositional generalization relies on two major conditions: (1) Choice of network model: networks should have internal representations in which visual factors are disentangled and independent with respect to target domains (2) Choice of source domain: the source domain should be uncorrelated and cover main basic factors. The fact that our source domain is simple also shows a practical benefit that performance on certain target tasks can efficiently improve using an easy-to-generate source domain. This is relatively cheaper compared to acquiring samples from complex target domains. If target domains are not fully-correlated, some requirements of manual labels/annotations can be relaxed, leading to more practical applications of this work. We hope this work will serve as an inspiration to integrate inductive biases in the forms of datasets and network design.

# References

1. Ahmed, F., Bengio, Y., van Seijen, H., Courville, A.: Systematic generalisation with group invariant predictions. In: International Conference on Learning Representations (2020)
2. Atzmon, Y., Kreuk, F., Shalit, U., Chechik, G.: A causal view of compositional zero-shot recognition. In: Larochelle, H., Ranzato, M., Hadsell, R., Balcan, M.F., Lin, H. (eds.) Advances in Neural Information Processing Systems, vol. 33, pp. 1462–1473. Curran Associates, Inc. (2020)
3. Bai, X., Liu, W., Tu, Z.: Integrating contour and skeleton for shape classification. In: 2009 IEEE 12th International Conference on Computer Vision Workshops, ICCV Workshops, pp. 360–367. IEEE (2009)
4. Bengio, Y., Courville, A., Vincent, P.: Representation learning: A review and new perspectives. IEEE Trans. Pattern Anal. Mach. Intell. **35**(8), 1798–1828 (2013)
5. Chang, W.G., You, T., Seo, S., Kwak, S., Han, B.: Domain-specific batch normalization for unsupervised domain adaptation. In: Proceedings of the IEEE/CVF Conference on Computer Vision and Pattern Recognition, pp. 7354–7362 (2019)
6. Eulig, E., et al.: DiagViB-6: a diagnostic benchmark suite for vision models in the presence of shortcut and generalization opportunities. arXiv preprint arXiv:2108.05779 (2021)
7. Ganin, Y., Lempitsky, V.: Unsupervised domain adaptation by backpropagation. In: International Conference on Machine Learning, pp. 1180–1189. PMLR (2015)
8. Geirhos, R., et al.: Shortcut learning in deep neural networks. Nat. Mach. Intell. **2**(11), 665–673 (2020)
9. Geirhos, R., ImageNet-trained CNNs are biased towards texture; increasing shape bias improves accuracy and robustness. arXiv preprint arXiv:1811.12231 (2018)
10. Hermann, K., Lampinen, A.: What shapes feature representations? Exploring datasets, architectures, and training. In: Larochelle, H., Ranzato, M., Hadsell, R., Balcan, M.F., Lin, H. (eds.) Advances in Neural Information Processing Systems, vol. 33, pp. 9995–10006. Curran Associates, Inc. (2020)
11. Higgins, I., et al.: beta-VAE: learning basic visual concepts with a constrained variational framework. International Conference on Learning Representations (2016)
12. Huang, B., Chen, S., Zhou, F., Zhang, C., Zhang, F.: Episodic training for domain generalization using latent domains. In: Sun, F., Liu, H., Fang, B. (eds.) ICCSIP 2020. CCIS, vol. 1397, pp. 85–93. Springer, Singapore (2021). https://doi.org/10.1007/978-981-16-2336-3_7
13. Li, Y., Yang, Y., Zhou, W., Hospedales, T.: Feature-critic networks for heterogeneous domain generalization. In: Chaudhuri, K., Salakhutdinov, R. (eds.) Proceedings of the 36th International Conference on Machine Learning. Proceedings of Machine Learning Research, vol. 97, pp. 3915–3924. PMLR, 09–15 June 2019
14. Li, Y.L., Xu, Y., Xu, X., Mao, X., Lu, C.: Learning single/multi-attribute of object with symmetry and group. In: IEEE Transactions on Pattern Analysis and Machine Intelligence (2021)
15. Lin, S., et al.: Fashion parsing with weak color-category labels. IEEE Trans. Multim. **16**(1), 253–265 (2013)
16. Locatello, F., et al.: Challenging common assumptions in the unsupervised learning of disentangled representations. In: International Conference on Machine Learning, pp. 4114–4124. PMLR (2019)
17. Mancini, M., Naeem, M.F., Xian, Y., Akata, Z.: Open world compositional zero-shot learning. In: Proceedings of the IEEE/CVF Conference on Computer Vision and Pattern Recognition, pp. 5222–5230 (2021)

18. Marlin, B., Swersky, K., Chen, B., Freitas, N.: Inductive principles for restricted Boltzmann machine learning. In: Proceedings of the thirteenth International Conference on Artificial Intelligence and Statistics, pp. 509–516. JMLR Workshop and Conference Proceedings (2010)

19. Misra, I., Gupta, A., Hebert, M.: From red wine to red tomato: composition with context. In: Proceedings of the IEEE Conference on Computer Vision and Pattern Recognition, pp. 1792–1801 (2017)

20. Mureşan, H., Oltean, M.: Fruit recognition from images using deep learning. arXiv preprint arXiv:1712.00580 (2017)

21. Naeem, M.F., Xian, Y., Tombari, F., Akata, Z.: Learning graph embeddings for compositional zero-shot learning. In: Proceedings of the IEEE/CVF Conference on Computer Vision and Pattern Recognition, pp. 953–962 (2021)

22. Nagarajan, T., Grauman, K.: Attributes as operators: factorizing unseen attribute-object compositions. In: Proceedings of the European Conference on Computer Vision (ECCV), pp. 169–185 (2018)

23. Purushwalkam, S., Nickel, M., Gupta, A., Ranzato, M.: Task-driven modular networks for zero-shot compositional learning. In: Proceedings of the IEEE/CVF International Conference on Computer Vision, pp. 3593–3602 (2019)

24. Sauer, A., Geiger, A.: Counterfactual generative networks. In: ICLR (2021)

25. Träuble, F., et al.: On disentangled representations learned from correlated data. In: Proceedings of the38th International Conference on Machine Learning, PMLR (2021)

26. Wang, Y., Li, H., Kot, A.C.: Heterogeneous domain generalization via domain mixup. In: ICASSP 2020–2020 IEEE International Conference on Acoustics, Speech and Signal Processing (ICASSP), pp. 3622–3626. IEEE (2020)

27. Xiao, K., Engstrom, L., Ilyas, A., Madry, A.: Noise or signal: The role of image backgrounds in object recognition. arXiv preprint arXiv:2006.09994 (2020)

28. Zeithamova, D., Bowman, C.R.: Generalization and the hippocampus: more than one story? Neurobiol. Learn. Memory **175**, 107317 (2020)

29. Zhang, R., et al.: Real-time user-guided image colorization with learned deep priors. ACM Trans. Graph.9(4) (2017)

30. Zhou, K., Yang, Y., Hospedales, T., Xiang, T.: Deep domain-adversarial image generation for domain generalization. In: Proceedings of the AAAI Conference on Artificial Intelligence, vol. 34, pp. 13025–13032 (2020)

31. Zhou, K., Yang, Y., Hospedales, T., Xiang, T.: Learning to generate novel domains for domain generalization. In: Vedaldi, A., Bischof, H., Brox, T., Frahm, J.-M. (eds.) ECCV 2020. LNCS, vol. 12361, pp. 561–578. Springer, Cham (2020). https://doi.org/10.1007/978-3-030-58517-4_33

# Photo-realistic Neural Domain Randomization

Sergey Zakharov[1(✉)], Rareş Ambruş[1(✉)], Vitor Guizilini[1], Wadim Kehl[2], and Adrien Gaidon[1]

[1] Toyota Research Institute, Los Altos, CA, USA
sergey.zakharov@tri.global
[2] Woven Planet, Tokyo, Japan

**Abstract.** Synthetic data is a scalable alternative to manual supervision, but it requires overcoming the sim-to-real domain gap. This discrepancy between virtual and real worlds is addressed by two seemingly opposed approaches: improving the realism of simulation or foregoing realism entirely via domain randomization. In this paper, we show that the recent progress in neural rendering enables a new unified approach we call Photo-realistic Neural Domain Randomization (PNDR). We propose to learn a composition of neural networks that acts as a physics-based ray tracer generating high-quality renderings from scene geometry alone. Our approach is modular, composed of different neural networks for materials, lighting, and rendering, thus enabling randomization of different key image generation components in a differentiable pipeline. Once trained, our method can be combined with other methods and used to generate photo-realistic image augmentations online and significantly more efficiently than via traditional ray-tracing. We demonstrate the usefulness of PNDR through two downstream tasks: 6D object detection and monocular depth estimation. Our experiments show that training with PNDR enables generalization to novel scenes and significantly outperforms the state of the art in terms of real-world transfer.

## 1 Introduction

Collecting labelled data for various machine learning tasks is an expensive, error-prone process that does not scale. Instead, simulators hold the promise of unlimited, perfectly annotated data without any human intervention but often introduce a domain gap that affects real-world performance. Effectively using simulated data requires overcoming the *sim-to-real* domain gap which arises due to differences in content or appearance. *Domain adaptation* methods rely on target data (i.e., real-world data) to bridge that gap [16,33,40,53,56,62,64,67]. A separate paradigm that requires no target data is that of *Domain Randomization* [51,52], which forgoes expensive, photo-realistic rendering in favor of random scene augmentations. In the context of object detection, CAD models are typically assumed known [18,42,60] and a subset of lighting, textures, materials, and object poses

**Supplementary Information** The online version contains supplementary material available at https://doi.org/10.1007/978-3-031-19806-9_18.

are randomized. Although typically inefficient, sample efficiency can be improved via differentiable guided augmentations [59], while content [10,25] and appearance [35,44] gaps can also be addressed by leveraging real data. However, a significant gap remains in terms of the photo-realism of the images generated. As an alternative, recent work [1,16] has shown that downstream task performance can be improved by increasing the quality of synthetic data. However, generating high-quality photo-realistic synthetic data is an expensive process that requires access to detailed assets and environments, as well as modeling light sources and materials inside complex graphics pipelines which are typically not differentiable.

We propose a novel method that brings together these two separate paradigms by generating high-quality synthetic data in a domain randomization framework. We combine intermediate geometry buffers ( *"G-buffers"*) generated by modern simulators and game engines together with recent advances in neural rendering [2,36,45], and build a neural physics-based ray tracer that models scene materials and light positions for photo-realistic rendering. Our Photo-realistic Neural Domain Randomization (PNDR) pipeline learns to map scene geometry to high quality renderings and is trained on a small amount of high-quality photo-realistic synthetic data generated by a traditional ray-tracing simulator. Thanks to its geometric input, PNDR generalizes to novel scenes and novel object configurations. Once trained, PNDR can be integrated in various downstream task training pipelines and used online to generate photo-realistic augmentations. This alleviates the need to resort to expensive simulators to generate additional high-quality image data when training the downstream task. Our method is more efficient in terms of time (PNDR renderings are generated 3 orders of magnitude faster than traditional simulators), space (PNDR renderings are generated on-the-fly during training and therefore do not need storage space) and leads to better generalization. Although our proposed pipeline is generic in nature, we quantify the usefulness of our synthetic training for the specific tasks of 6D object detection and monocular depth estimation in a zero-shot setting (i.e., without using any real-world data), and demonstrate that our method presents a distinct improvement over current SoTA approaches.

In summary, our contributions are:

- We unify photo-realistic rendering and domain randomization for synthetic data generation using neural rendering;
- Our learned deferred renderer, *RenderNet*, allows flexible randomization of physical parameters while being $1,600\times$ faster than comparable ray-tracers;
- Our *Photo-realistic Neural Domain Randomization (PNDR)* approach yields state-of-the-art zero-shot sim-to-real transfer for 6D object detection and monocular depth estimation, almost closing the domain gap;
- We show that realistic physics-based randomization, especially for lighting, is key for out-of-domain generalization.

## 2   Related Work

**Domain Adaptation.** Due to the domain gap, models trained on synthetic data suffer performance drops when applied on statistically different unlabelled target

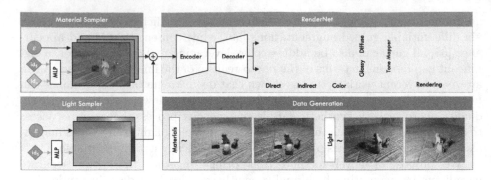

**Fig. 1. PNDR Architecture**. The main component of our domain randomization method is the ray tracer approximator (RenderNet). It takes a G-buffer as well as random material maps and light maps produced by corresponding samplers and generates intermediate light outputs. These outputs are then combined using a tone mapper to generate a final rendering. The lower-right row shows different material and light samples (e.g., roughness, specularity, light position).

datasets. Domain Adaptation is an active area of research [7] with the aim of minimizing the *sim-to-real* gap. Common approaches rely on adversarial learning for feature or pixel adaptation [6,13,53], paired [56] or unpaired [30,40,66] image translation, style transfer [62], refining pseudo-labels [33,64,67], or unsupervised geometric guidance [16].

**Domain Randomization.** A different approach to closing the sim-to-real gap relies on generating augmentations of the input data through random perturbations of the environment (e.g., lights, materials, background) [18,51,52]. The aim is to learn more discriminative features that generalize to other domains. While simple and inexpensive, this method is sample inefficient because the randomization is essentially unguided with many superfluous (or even harmful) augmentations, and it rarely captures the complexity and distribution of real scenes. Differently, procedurally generating synthetic scenes [43] can preserve the context of real scenes while minimizing the gaps in content [10,20,25] and appearance [42,44,60]. While some of these methods require expensive, bespoke simulators [10,25], pixel-based augmentations can be generated differentiably and combined with the task network to generate adversarial augmentations [59]. Similarly to [59] our pipeline is also differentiable, however while [59] is limited to handcrafted image augmentations where respective parameters are sampled from artificial distributions, our method approximates a material-based ray tracer simulating the physical process of light scattering and global illumination, enabling effects such as shadows and diffuse interreflection. Our augmentations are solely based on light and material changes, thus reducing the randomization set to physically plausible augmentations. Moreover, as opposed to [59], we assume no color information of the objects of interest, making our method more practical for real-world applications.

**Photo-Realistic Data Generation.** Although expensive to generate, high-quality synthetic data (i.e., photo-realistic) can increase model generalization capabilities [1,16]. The task of view synthesis allows the rendering of novel data given a set of input images [49]. Neural Radiance Fields [34] overfit to specific scenes and can generate novel data with very high levels of fidelity, while also accounting for materials and lights [4,5,48]. Alternative methods use point-based differentiable rendering [3,46] and can optimize over scene geometry, camera model, and various image formation properties. While these methods overfit to specific scenes, recent self-supervised approaches learn generative models of specific objects [35] and can render novel and controllable complex scenes by exploiting compositionality [37]. While neural volume rendering and point based techniques can yield impressive results, other methods aim to explicitly model various parts of traditional graphics pipelines [2,24,36,45,50]. Our work is similar to [45] in that we also use intermediate simulation buffers to generate photo-realistic scenes. However, while [45] relies on real data and minimizes a perceptual loss in an adversarial framework, we focus on the task of 6D object detection in a zero-shot setting using only object CAD model information and no real images.

**6D Object Detection.** *Correspondence-based* methods [19,23,32,39,41,61] tend to show superior generalization performance in terms of adapting to different pose distributions. However, they use PnP and RANSAC to estimate poses from correspondences, which makes them non-differentiable. Additionally, they are very reliant on the quality of these correspondences, and errors can result in unreasonable estimates (e.g., behind the camera, or very far away). Conversely, *regression-based* methods [12,28,65] show superior performance for in-domain pose estimation. However they do not generalize very well to out-of-domain settings. To validate our method we implement a correspondence-based object detector, which allows us to also evaluate instance segmentation and object correspondences in addition to the object pose regressed.

## 3 Photo-Realistic Neural Domain Randomization

Our photo-realistic neural domain randomization (*PNDR*) approach consists of two main components: a neural ray tracer approximator (RenderNet), and sampling blocks for material and light. To increase perceptual quality and realism, the network outputs are passed through a non-linear tone-mapping function which yields the final rendering. We now describe the main two components of PNDR. All other implementation and training details are provided in the supplementary.

### 3.1 Geometric Scene Representation

As a first step, we define a geometric room representation outlining our synthetic environment. We place 3D objects inside an empty room ensuring no collisions. Next, we assign random materials to both objects and room walls and position a point light source to illuminate the scene (see Fig 2). Resulting output buffers, consisting of G-Buffer (scene coordinates in camera space $X$, surface normals

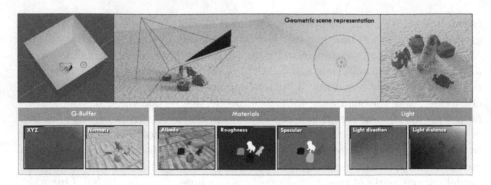

**Fig. 2. Geometric scene representation.** Visualization of RenderNet's input consisting of G-Buffer (scene coordinates in camera space $X$, surface normals map $N$), material properties (albedo $A$, roughness $R$, specularity $S$), and lighting (light direction map $L_{dir}$, and light distance map $L_{dist}$).

map $N$), material properties (albedo $A$, roughness $R$, specularity $S$), and lighting (light direction map $L_{dir}$, and light distance map $L_{dist}$), are used by our neural ray tracer approximator to generate high fidelity renderings in real time (~2.5 ms per image), as opposed to ~4s per image with a conventional ray tracer.

### 3.2 Neural Ray Tracer Approximator

Our neural ray tracer RenderNet $f_R$ is an encoder-decoder CNN taking G-buffer, material properties, and lighting as input, and generating a final high-fidelity rendering (see Fig. 1). This is akin to *deferred rendering*, a common practice in computer graphics [8]. Instead of outputting a final rendering directly, we split the output into direct and indirect light outputs and colors which can be easily combined to form a final, shaded image. This allows not only for a much more explainable representation, but also for better control over the complexity of the rendering. As a result, our RenderNet $f_R$ is capable of generating photo-realistic images, generalizes well to novel material and light distributions, and even novel scenes, objects, and poses.

**Light Modelling.** Lighting in ray tracers can often be decomposed into (1) direct lighting as coming from lamps, emitting surfaces, the background, or ambient occlusion after a single reflection or transmission from a surface; and (2) indirect lighting that comes from lamps, emitting surfaces or the background after more than one reflection or transmission. Simulating indirect lighting approximates realistic energy transfer much closer and produces better images, but comes at much higher computational cost. To be computationally reasonable, we render all scenes with a single point light source.

**Light Sampler.** Our light sampler is a uniform random 3D coordinate generator. We limit the light pose space to the upper hemisphere and normalize the position to be at a distance of 1.5m from the scene center as defined in our training data. The resulting light source position in scene coordinates is then brought into the camera space given a fixed transform. Next, we parametrize the scene lighting by composing two light maps: $L_{dir}$ defines the direction to the light source from each visible coordinate and $L_{dist}$ defines the metric distance to the light source. Since RenderNet $f_R$ is fully differentiable, we can also use it to recover scene parameters in terms of lighting, particularly when combined with a correspondence-based object detector (see Sec. 4 with qualitative results in 6.6). In this case we define the light sampling network $f_L$ as a SIREN-based MLP [47] conditioned on the scene ID, which allows us to optimize for the light position given an input image.

**Material Modelling.** For both direct and indirect lighting our RenderNet $f_R$ outputs two separate images representing diffuse and glossy bidirectional scattering distribution functions (BSDF). The diffuse BSDF is used to add Lambertian [29] and Oren-Nayar [38] diffuse reflection, whereas the glossy BSDF adds a GGX microfacet distribution [54] that models metallic and mirror-like materials.

**Material Sampler.** Similarly to the light sampler, the material sampler is a uniform random value generator. It samples five values per object: RGB values for albedo $A$, roughness $R$ and specularity $S$ values. We query the material sampler for all objects in the scene including the background and, given ground truth instance masks, compose final 2D maps for each output property. The RGB albedo values are then multiplied by the GT decolorized albedo to form the final coloring map. Roughness and specular values are assigned to corresponding object masks to form full 2D maps.

Following a similar architecture to LightNet, we introduce an object material sampling network $f_M$, outputting material properties for each of the objects present in the dataset as well as the background environment. As shown in Fig. 1, it takes an object ID and scene ID values as input, and as before, produces the same object-specific material properties, i.e., albedo $A$, roughness $R$, and specularity $S$. Similarly to the uniform sampler, we query MaterialNet for all scene objects and compose final 2D maps for each output property.

**Image Compositing and Tone Mapping.** Supplied with the G-buffer that provides us with scene coordinates in camera space $X$ and surface normals map $N$, we can form the final input to the RenderNet $f_R$ by concatenating all intermediate results and passing them through the encoder-decoder structure:

$$f_R(X, N, A, S, R, L_{dir}, L_{dist}) = [D_{dir}, D_{ind}, G_{dir}, G_{ind}]. \tag{1}$$

Here, $A, S, R, L_{dir}, L_{dist}$ are the outputs of the material and light submodules, as previously explained, whereas $D_{dir}, D_{ind}$ and $G_{dir}, G_{ind}$ are the diffuse and glossy BRDF outputs for direct and indirect lighting, respectively. During training we supervise the 4 outputs of RenderNet using corresponding ground truth quantities through an L1 loss. As outlined in Fig. 1, the final HDR image is a combination of the light and BSDF outputs. In particular:

$$I_{HDR} = (D_{dir} + D_{ind}) * D_{col} + (G_{dir} + G_{ind}) * G_{col}, \tag{2}$$

where $D_{col}$ represents object albedo and $G_{col}$ represents the probability that light is reflected for each wavelength. All compositing computations are performed in linear color space, which corresponds closer to nature and results in a more physically accurate output, i.e., there is a linear relationship between color intensity and the number of incident photons. However, these values do not directly correspond to human color perception and display devices.

To address the limited color spectrum and brightness of displays, we apply a non-linear tone mapping to fit the device gamut. Although there are many families of mappings to choose from, we picked the commonly-used operator proposed by Jim Hejl and Richard Burgess-Dawson [21]. At its core, it is a rational function that mimics the response curve of a Kodak film commonly used in cinematography:

$$I_{final} = \frac{I_s * (6.2 * I_s + .5)}{I_s * (6.2 * I_s + 1.7) + 0.06},$$ (3)

where $I_s = max(0, I_{HDR} - 0.004)$.

## 4    Downstream Tasks

We combine PNDR with two downstream task methods. At each training step, PNDR is used to generate photo-realistic augmentations on the fly, which are fed to the downstream task network.

**Correspondence-Based 6D Object Detection.** Following related work [19, 23,32,39,61], our *Correspondence-Based 6D Object Detector (CBOD)* operates on RGB images and outputs the probability of each pixel belonging to a certain local object coordinate. Estimated 2D-3D correspondences are then fed into a PnP+RANSAC solver together with camera parameters to estimate final poses. We use non-uniform *Normalized Object Coordinates Space (NOCS)* [55,58] maps that maximize the volume inside a unit cube, and we train using a cross-entropy loss. To disambiguate objects, our detector also outputs an instance segmentation mask. We then define object regions relying on instance mask probabilities and use respective correspondences to compute final poses. In addition to achieving competitive results, this simple yet effective architecture allows us to analyze the benefit of *PNDR* not just for a single task of 6D pose estimation, but also for instance mask estimation and geometric correspondence accuracy, which are

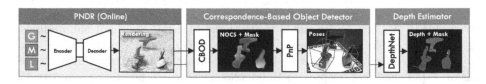

**Fig. 3. Downstream Tasks Coupled with PNDR.** During training, both downstream tasks (detection and depth estimation) take PNDR renderings generated online, providing new realistic augmentations at each iteration.

crucial components of general scene understanding. The structure of our detector is shown in Fig. 3, while the network architecture details are provided in the supplementary material.

**Monocular Depth Estimation.** We aim to learn a function $f_D : I \to D$ that recovers the depth $\hat{D} = f_D(I(p))$ for every pixel $p \in I$. We operate in the supervised setting where we have access to the ground truth depth map, and we train the monocular depth network using the SILog loss [11,31] defined between the predicted and the ground truth depth maps. We evaluate the effect of PNDR using two network architectures: *monodepth2* [14] and *packnet-sfm* [15].

## 5   Experiments

We designed a number of experiments aimed at exploring how PNDR-generated data compares to real data as well as expensive, ray-tracer based simulation data in terms of downstream task performance.

### 5.1   Evaluation Metrics

**6D Object Detection.** Following related work [27,61], we use ADD [17] as the metric to evaluate object detection. ADD is defined as the average Euclidean distance between the model vertices transformed with ground truth and predicted poses:

$$m = \underset{\mathbf{x} \in \mathcal{M}}{\mathrm{avg}} \left\| (\mathbf{R}\mathbf{x} + \mathbf{t}) - (\hat{\mathbf{R}}\mathbf{x} + \hat{\mathbf{t}}) \right\|_2, \tag{4}$$

where $\mathcal{M}$ is a set of vertices of a 3D model, $(\mathbf{R}, \mathbf{t})$ and $(\hat{\mathbf{R}}, \hat{\mathbf{t}})$ are ground truth and predicted rotation and translation, respectively. Most commonly, a predicted pose is considered to be correct if ADD calculated with this pose is less than 10% of a model diameter. However, this is a very strict metric especially for objects with a small diameter since it can completely disregard good pose estimates and estimates that could be refined. To be able to better analyze pose quality, we instead compute ADD under multiple thresholds (from 5 to 50 with a step of 5) and then estimate the area under the curve (AUC).

**Instance Segmentation.** To evaluate the quality of the instance segmentation we use a standard Intersection over Union (IoU) metric, which quantifies the percent overlap between the target mask and our prediction output.

**Object Correspondences.** To evaluate the quality of estimated object correspondences, we compare per-point metric distances in object's coordinate space between the GT partial shape and the predicted one. To do that we first use GT masks to recover partial object shapes and compute their absolute scale given provided model information. Then, we measure one-to-one distances between the GT shape and predicted shape in millimeters.

**Depth Estimation.** We evaluate the performance of our depth networks using the standard metrics found in the literature: *AbsRel*, *RMSE* and $\delta_1$, which are defined in detail in the supplementary.

**Table 1. HB Dynamic Lighting Benchmark**: All methods are trained on the training set of $HB_5$ and evaluated on the $HB_5$ test set and on $HB_{10}$. † indicates that [22,56] are trained with synthetic and real image pairs, while ‡ indicates unpaired synthetic and real images for [40,66]. Training on photo-realistic synthetic data is competitive with real data training and generalizes better to new domains. By training on $PNDR$ images we further close the gap to training on real data in $HB_5$ and increase generalization performance to the novel lighting setting of $HB_{10}$.

| Train | Method | HB Scene 5 | | | | | | HB Scene 10 (Lighting) | | | | | |
|---|---|---|---|---|---|---|---|---|---|---|---|---|---|
| | | Car | P12 | P15 | Pumba | Dog | Mean | Car | P12 | P15 | Pumba | Dog | Mean |
| Real | | 91.76 | 94.12 | 79.34 | 94.41 | 95.00 | 90.93 | 26.69 | 35.88 | 8.75 | 25.22 | 14.63 | 22.24 |
| Real + CAD† | Pix2Pix [22] | 81.84 | 76.47 | 38.53 | 76.76 | 94.12 | 73.54 | 37.13 | 35.59 | 13.75 | 24.78 | 33.82 | 29.01 |
| | Pix2PixHD [56] | 90.96 | 92.21 | 73.09 | 91.91 | 95.00 | 89.59 | 37.21 | 40.96 | 21.25 | 29.26 | 15.59 | 32.33 |
| Real + CAD‡ | CycleGAN [66] | 49.41 | 31.10 | 24.12 | 40.88 | 73.24 | 43.75 | 27.72 | 2.28 | 6.91 | 7.06 | 11.47 | 11.09 |
| | CUT [40] | 56.10 | 28.97 | 29.34 | 41.47 | 85.29 | 66.49 | 27.35 | 4.63 | 7.35 | 8.90 | 12.13 | 25.36 |
| CAD | RayTraced - 1088 | 85.59 | 86.76 | 61.18 | 89.71 | 94.85 | 83.62 | 47.28 | 36.84 | 9.12 | 36.25 | 23.38 | 30.57 |
| | RayTraced - 2176 | 86.99 | 90.00 | 63.01 | 91.47 | 95.00 | 85.29 | 50.88 | 38.82 | 10.00 | 35.29 | 30.96 | 33.19 |
| | RayTraced - 4352 | 89.71 | 88.97 | 66.91 | 92.35 | 95.00 | 86.59 | 52.43 | 38.75 | 10.29 | 41.47 | 43.82 | 37.35 |
| | Ours - 1088 | 89.93 | 91.62 | 71.99 | 92.35 | 95.00 | 88.18 | 58.01 | 42.50 | 10.59 | 46.18 | 44.93 | 40.44 |

**Perceptual Quality.** To evaluate generated RenderNet images, we use the standard image quality metrics PSNR and SSIM [57] for all evaluations. Moreover, we include LPIPS [63], more accurately reflecting human perception.

# 6    Results

## 6.1    HB Dynamic Lighting Benchmark

In this first experiment we aim to isolate the effects of training and testing under significantly different illumination while keeping the scene contents constant. We use scenes 5 and 10 of the *HomeBrewedDB* (HB) dataset [26] ($HB_5$ and $HB_{10}$ for short), as shown in Fig. 4. Both scenes contain the same objects in the same environment and consist of 340 images with associated depth maps and object annotations (CAD models and poses). $HB_5$ and $HB_{10}$ are captured with drastically different lighting conditions, allowing us to isolate the effect

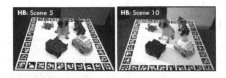

**Fig. 4. HB Dynamic Lighting Benchmark:** two scenes containing same the objects under significantly different lighting conditions.

**Fig. 5. HB-LM Cross-Domain Adaptation Benchmark:** four scenes containing the same objects in different environments and recorded with different cameras.

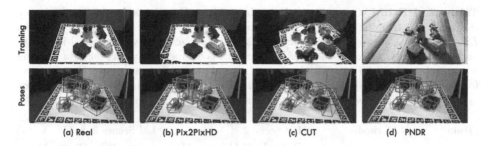

**Fig. 6. 6D Object detection qualitative results.** We compare object detection results when trained on *PNDR* renderings with our image-to-image translation GAN baselines and with the baseline trained on real data. All methods are evaluated on an $HB_5$ test image.

simulated data has on overcoming this perceptual domain gap. We split $HB_5$ into a training and in-domain testing subsets consisting of 272 and 68 frames respectively; $HB_{10}$ is used entirely for testing.

We present the benchmark results in Table 1 (qualitative results are shown in Fig. 6). Our first baseline consists of training CBOD directly on the $HB_5$ real images, and we record good in-domain performance (90.93) and poor transfer to different light configurations (22.24). Our second baseline uses entirely synthetic photo-realistic images of increasing sizes. Using the object CAD models and associated poses corresponding to the different training frames (i.e. we have a total of 272 different object configurations), we generate Domain Randomized synthetic photo-realistic images with *BlenderProc* [9]. Specifically, for each training configuration we vary object materials and light positions. For backgrounds we randomly select from 5 different asset classes (*Bricks, Wood, Carpet, Tile, Marble*[1]) and also randomize their materials. For each training configuration we generate an increasing number of augmentations using this technique, leading to larger synthetic datasets with very high perceptual quality at the expense of rendering time and storage space. We train CBOD on the synthetic images, and, as expected, downstream task performance improves as more high-quality synthetic data is available (i.e., with 4352 synthetic images we achieve 37.35 generalization performance). We compare this with the proposed PNDR method as follows: using the high-quality synthetic data along with the corresponding G-buffer information, we train PNDR, and use it in the training pipeline of CBOD to generate new, high-quality augmentations on the fly, saving rendering time and storage space. As shown in our experiments, 1088 synthetic images are enough to train PNDR, and we almost match the performance of training on real data and increase generalization to scenes with significant light variation by 82% (40.44 vs 22.24). We note that as CBOD is trained over 400 epochs, it would require ~30h and 600GB storage space to generate as many images with the raytracer as were generated by PNDR.

---

[1] https://ambientcg.com.

**Table 2. HB-LM Cross-Domain Adaptation Benchmark**: All methods are trained on the training set of $HB_2$ and evaluated on $HB_2$ test set as well as on the $LM_2$, $LM_8$ and $LM_{15}$ scenes. Training on real data generalizes poorly to novel object categories. Training on photo-realistic synthetic data is competitive with real data training when evaluated on the same object categories, and greatly increases generalization performance for novel object categories. † indicates that [22,56] are trained with paired synthetic and real image pairs, while ‡ indicates unpaired images for [40,66].

| Train | Method | HB Scene 2 | | | | LM Scenes 2, 8, 15 | | | |
|---|---|---|---|---|---|---|---|---|---|
| | | Bvise | Drill | Phone | Mean | Bvise | Drill | Phone | Mean |
| Real | | 94.71 | 95.00 | 94.41 | 94.71 | 4.43 | 0.30 | 0.35 | 1.69 |
| Real + CAD† | Pix2Pix [22] | 75.66 | 77.94 | 67.65 | 73.75 | 4.97 | 1.38 | 0.28 | 2.21 |
| | Pix2PixHD [56] | 92.57 | 94.41 | 91.76 | 92.92 | 4.65 | 1.62 | 0.47 | 2.25 |
| Real + CAD‡ | CycleGAN [66] | 35.37 | 26.76 | 45.22 | 35.78 | 5.68 | 5.40 | 3.23 | 4.77 |
| | CUT [40] | 78.53 | 61.25 | 65.44 | 68.41 | 21.70 | 10.05 | 6.33 | 12.69 |
| CAD | RayTraced - 1088 | 84.49 | 72.43 | 80.81 | 79.24 | 33.67 | 9.55 | 15.90 | 19.71 |
| | Ours - 1088 | 85.88 | 81.54 | 83.09 | 83.50 | 35.50 | 28.02 | 18.48 | 27.33 |

Additionally we train state-of-the-art image-translation methods on the same images we train $PNDR$ on, and we use the corresponding real images as translation targets. Specifically, we compare against (i) pix2pix [22] and pix2pixHD [56] using BlenderProc and real image pairs; and (ii) cycleGAN [66] and CUT [40] using unpaired BlenderProc and real images. Although our method does not require any real images, adversarial image translation methods are representative of the state-of-the-art in domain adaptation and serve as good baselines. The training details of all the baselines are provided in the supplementary. The paired GAN baselines [22,56] increase generalization performance, although we note that having access to synthetic and image pairs is an unrealistic scenario in practice and this serves as an upper-bound, at least for in-domain evaluation. The more realistic case of unpaired translation [40,66] performs much worse, as expected. This is easily explained by the rather large domain shift induced from the different scene setups and cameras.

## 6.2 HB-LM Cross-Domain Adaptation Benchmark

Our HB-LM cross-domain benchmark (see Fig. 5) is represented by $HB_2$ covering three objects of the LineMOD (LM) [17] dataset (*benchvise*, *driller*, and *phone*). Additionally, we use scenes 2, 8 and 15 from the LM dataset for testing: these scenes contain the same objects as $HB_2$ but with significantly different poses and in a different setting. This setting allows us to evaluate the generalization performance of $PNDR$ to new scenes and new object poses. As before, we partition the $HB_2$ into a training and test split consisting of 272 and 68 images, respectively, and we use *BlenderProc* [9] to generate the same synthetic photo-realistic renderings and G-buffer information. In addition to the $HB_2$ data, we also generate 1000 photo-realistic images using *BlenderProc* while randomizing both the camera and the poses of the 3 objects from $HB_2$. As we show in the experiments, using this extra simulated data allows us to generalize much better to the $LM$ scenes where the object pose distribution is significantly different. We train $PNDR$ as before and use its output to train $CBOD$, which is evaluated both in domain, i.e., on the test split of $HB_2$ as well as out of domain on $LM_2$, $LM_8$ and $LM_{15}$.

We analyze how well we generalize to completely different scenes with different lighting conditions, environment, camera setup and object poses; our results are summarized in Table 2. As before, we report the best in-domain results when training on real data, with a slight performance drop when training directly on the photo-realistic synthetic BlenderProc data. We note that by using $PNDR$ we significantly increase performance. As before, the paired translation GAN baselines compare quite well, and we record a similar performance drop when doing unpaired image translation. Both the GAN and the baseline trained on real data generalize poorly to the LM scenes, reflecting the challenging nature of this benchmark. Interestingly, the unpaired image translation baselines generalize better in this setting - we provide qualitative examples in the supplementary. By training on the synthetic data which contains additional renderings with randomized object poses we significantly improve performance. As before, using $PNDR$ as part of the training pipeline further improves performance, achieving 27.33 on the LM scenes.

### 6.3 HB Generalization Benchmark

Here we aim to evaluate how well $PNDR$ can generate novel photo-realistic images in and out of domain. We train $PNDR$ on $HB_2$ and evaluate on the test set of $HB_2$ as well as $HB_5$. Note that these two scenes contain different objects, allowing us to investigate if our learned ray-tracing network generalizes to novel scene geometries. For completeness, we also perform the same experiment by training on $HB_5$ and evaluating on $HB_2$.

We quantify the generalization capabilities of $PNDR$ when applied to novel scenes, object arrangements, material properties and lighting. We train $PNDR$ on

 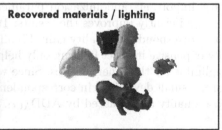

**Fig. 7. Recovering scene properties via our RenderNet.** Given the recovered G-Buffer we optimize over *MaterialNet* and *LightNet* to find the best fit explaining the input image.

**Table 3. PNDR Generalization:** We achieve strong performance not only when applied to a test image of the same scene containing the same objects with different material properties and different poses, but also when applied on a completely different scene.

| Train | Test | PSNR↑ | SSIM↑ | LPIPS↓ |
|-------|------|-------|-------|--------|
| $HB_2$ - Train | $HB_2$ - Train | 30.36 | 0.96 | 0.03 |
| | $HB_2$ - Test | 26.14 | 0.94 | 0.05 |
| | $HB_5$ - Test | 24.14 | 0.92 | 0.06 |
| $HB_5$ - Train | $HB_5$ - Train | 30.39 | 0.96 | 0.03 |
| | $HB_5$ - Test | 26.40 | 0.94 | 0.06 |
| | $HB_2$ - Test | 23.72 | 0.92 | 0.07 |

**Table 4. Ablation:** We analyze the effect of different augmentations on downstream task performance. All methods are trained on the $HB_5$ train set and evaluated on the $HB_5$ test set.

| | Modes | ADD$_{AUC}$ ↑ | IoU ↑ | Corr (mm) ↓ |
|---|-------|---------------|-------|-------------|
| Material | $A$ | 85.43 | 83.29 | 38.56 |
| | $+S+R$ | 3% | 3% | 11% |
| Light | Fixed | 73.04 | 72.24 | 76.94 |
| | Dynamic | 21% | 19% | 55% |
| Rendering | $D_{dir}, G_{dir}$ | 87.09 | 85.55 | 38.42 |
| | $+ D_{ind}, G_{ind}$ | 1% | 0% | 11% |
| Full | | 88.18 | 85.97 | 34.32 |

the training split of $HB_2$ and evaluate how it performs when applied to: (1) the training split, (2) the test split, (3) the test split of a different scene (i.e., $HB_5$). For completeness, we also perform the reverse experiment (i.e., train on $HB_5$ and evaluate on $HB_2$). The results in Table 3 suggest a high level of visual quality when assessed with PSNR, SSIM, and LPIPS (please refer to the supplementary for details on these metrics). *PNDR* not only shows strong results on the test set containing the same objects under different poses and with different material properties, but also generalizes well to a scene with completely different objects.

### 6.4   Ablation Study

We analyze how different physically-based augmentations affect the downstream task performance, and consider: material randomization, light randomization, and rendering complexity. *PNDR* is conditioned on material properties of the objects, i.e., albedo $A$, specularity $S$, and roughness $R$, with $A$ being the most important property. In Table 4 we see that training with just albedo randomization results in very good performance already. Additionally simulating $S$ and $R$ brings a relative gain of 2% with respect to ADD$_{AUC}$, 3% to mIoU, and 11% to correspondence quality. Furthermore, we note that lighting is by far the most important randomization parameter. Going from fixed to dynamic lighting significantly improves the results: 19% ADD$_{AUC}$ gain, 19% mIoU gain, and 55% correspondence quality gain. Finally, we note that simulating computationally expensive indirect lighting only helps improve correspondence quality but is negligible for the other metrics. Since we use an outlier-robust $PnP$+RANSAC solver, small deviations in correspondence quality do not significantly affect the pose quality as evaluated by ADD$_{AUC}$.

### 6.5   Monocular Depth Estimation

We quantify the impact of PNDR when applied for the task of monocular depth estimation. We use the same data as for the Dynamic Lighting Benchmark

Table 5. PNDR vs Raytraced - monocular depth results.

| Method | Training | HB5 | | | HB10 | | |
|---|---|---|---|---|---|---|---|
| | | AbsRel↓ | RMSE↓ | a1↑ | AbsRel↓ | RMSE↓ | a1↑ |
| Monodepth2 | Raytraced | 0.082 | 0.09 | 0.951 | 0.162 | 0.148 | 0.805 |
| | PNDR | **0.075** | **0.083** | **0.966** | **0.154** | **0.14** | **0.83** |
| PackNet-SfM | Raytraced | 0.11 | 0.111 | 0.884 | 0.141 | 0.136 | 0.833 |
| | PNDR | **0.082** | **0.087** | **0.977** | **0.135** | **0.131** | **0.852** |

(see 6.1). For both *monodepth2* and *packnet-sfm* we compare performance when training directly on the 1088 raytraced images with performance when PNDR is integrated in the training pipeline and generates novel augmentations on the fly. As before, we note that when training with PNDR we achieve better in-domain and better generalization performance (see Table 5).

### 6.6   Object Material and Light Recovery

The fact that *RenderNet* is fully differentiable allows us to optimize over scene parameters. In particular, given an initial scene prediction provided by *CBOD* we can recover material properties of the objects and scene light (see Fig. 7). First, we construct a G-buffer by estimating a depth map using estimated poses and object models, which is in turn used to estimate scene coordinates $X$ and surface normals $N$. LightNet $f_L$ and MaterialNet $f_M$ conditioned on the scene and object IDs output the remaining maps $A$, $R$, $S$, $L_{dir}$, and $L_{dist}$ required for the RenderNet. Finally we generate a rendering that is then compared to the GT RGB image to find the best fit. Estimated scene parameters can be used to learn a distribution of material and light configurations across the entire dataset. This information might not only be useful for analysis, but also for domain-specific data generation using our RenderNet, especially where the same object instances exist in multiple material variations.

## 7   Conclusion

We have presented a novel approach towards sim-to-real adaptation by means of a neural ray tracer approximator with randomizable material and light modules that we named *PNDR*. We have demonstrated that applying our photo-realistic randomized output to the problem of zero-shot 6D object detection significantly outperforms other established DA approaches, and even comes close to training on real data. We have identified lighting as the most crucial component, but it remains an open question what kind of additional randomization could further benefit the domain transfer. One possible future research avenue would be randomized sampling of low-level camera sensor artifacts, or the coupling of randomization and downstream task optimization in a common framework.

# References

1. Alghonaim, R., Johns, E.: Benchmarking domain randomisation for visual sim-to-real transfer. In: 2021 IEEE International Conference on Robotics and Automation (ICRA), pp. 12802–12808. IEEE (2021)
2. Abu Alhaija, H., Mustikovela, S.K., Geiger, A., Rother, C.: Geometric image synthesis. In: Jawahar, C.V., Li, H., Mori, G., Schindler, K. (eds.) ACCV 2018. LNCS, vol. 11366, pp. 85–100. Springer, Cham (2019). https://doi.org/10.1007/978-3-030-20876-9_6
3. Aliev, K.-A., Sevastopolsky, A., Kolos, M., Ulyanov, D., Lempitsky, V.: Neural point-based graphics. In: Vedaldi, A., Bischof, H., Brox, T., Frahm, J.-M. (eds.) ECCV 2020. LNCS, vol. 12367, pp. 696–712. Springer, Cham (2020). https://doi.org/10.1007/978-3-030-58542-6_42
4. Boss, M., Braun, R., Jampani, V., Barron, J.T., Liu, C., Lensch, H.: Nerd: neural reflectance decomposition from image collections. In: Proceedings of the IEEE/CVF International Conference on Computer Vision, pp. 12684–12694 (2021)
5. Boss, M., Jampani, V., Braun, R., Liu, C., Barron, J.T., Lensch, H.: Neural-pil: neural pre-integrated lighting for reflectance decomposition. arXiv preprint arXiv:2110.14373 (2021)
6. Bousmalis, K., Silberman, N., Dohan, D., Erhan, D., Krishnan, D.: Unsupervised pixel-level domain adaptation with generative adversarial networks. In: Proceedings of the IEEE Conference on Computer Vision and Pattern Recognition, pp. 3722–3731 (2017)
7. Csurka, G.: Domain adaptation for visual applications: a comprehensive survey. arXiv preprint arXiv:1702.05374 (2017)
8. Deering, M., Winner, S., Schediwy, B., Duffy, C., Hunt, N.: The triangle processor and normal vector shader: a vlsi system for high performance graphics. Acm siggraph Comput. Graph. **22**(4), 21–30 (1988)
9. Denninger, M., et al.: Blenderproc. arXiv preprint arXiv:1911.01911 (2019)
10. Devaranjan, J., Kar, A., Fidler, S.: Meta-Sim2: unsupervised learning of scene structure for synthetic data generation. In: Vedaldi, A., Bischof, H., Brox, T., Frahm, J.-M. (eds.) ECCV 2020. LNCS, vol. 12362, pp. 715–733. Springer, Cham (2020). https://doi.org/10.1007/978-3-030-58520-4_42
11. Eigen, D., Puhrsch, C., Fergus, R.: Depth map prediction from a single image using a multi-scale deep network. In: NIPS (2014)
12. Engelmann, F., Rematas, K., Leibe, B., Ferrari, V.: From points to multi-object 3d reconstruction. In: CVPR, pp. 4588–4597 (2021)
13. Ganin, Y., et al.: Domain-adversarial training of neural networks. In: JMLR (2016)
14. Godard, C., Mac Aodha, O., Firman, M., Brostow, G.J.: Digging into self-supervised monocular depth estimation. In: Proceedings of the IEEE/CVF International Conference on Computer Vision, pp. 3828–3838 (2019)
15. Guizilini, V., Ambrus, R., Pillai, S., Raventos, A., Gaidon, A.: 3d packing for self-supervised monocular depth estimation. In: Proceedings of the IEEE/CVF Conference on Computer Vision and Pattern Recognition, pp. 2485–2494 (2020)
16. Guizilini, V., Li, J., Ambrus, R., Gaidon, A.: Geometric unsupervised domain adaptation for semantic segmentation. arXiv preprint arXiv:2103.16694 (2021)
17. Hinterstoisser, S., et al.: Model based training, detection and pose estimation of texture-less 3d objects in heavily cluttered scenes. In: ACCV (2012)
18. Hinterstoisser, S., Pauly, O., Heibel, H., Martina, M., Bokeloh, M.: An annotation saved is an annotation earned: using fully synthetic training for object detection.

In: Proceedings of the IEEE/CVF International Conference on Computer Vision Workshops (2019)

19. Hodan, T., Barath, D., Matas, J.: Epos: estimating 6d pose of objects with symmetries. In: CVPR, pp. 11703–11712 (2020)

20. Hodaň, T., et al.: Photorealistic image synthesis for object instance detection. In: 2019 IEEE International Conference on Image Processing (ICIP), pp. 66–70. IEEE (2019)

21. Hoffman, N.: Crafting physically motivated shading models for game development. part of "Physically Based Shading Models in Film and Game Production". In: SIGGRAPH (2010)

22. Isola, P., Zhu, J.Y., Zhou, T., Efros, A.A.: Image-to-image translation with conditional adversarial networks. In: Proceedings of the IEEE Conference on Computer Vision and Pattern Recognition, pp. 1125–1134 (2017)

23. Hosseini Jafari, O., Mustikovela, S.K., Pertsch, K., Brachmann, E., Rother, C.: iPose: instance-aware 6d pose estimation of partly occluded objects. In: Jawahar, C.V., Li, H., Mori, G., Schindler, K. (eds.) ACCV 2018. LNCS, vol. 11363, pp. 477–492. Springer, Cham (2019). https://doi.org/10.1007/978-3-030-20893-6_30

24. Janner, M., Wu, J., Kulkarni, T.D., Yildirim, I., Tenenbaum, J.B.: Self-supervised intrinsic image decomposition. arXiv preprint arXiv:1711.03678 (2017)

25. Kar, A., et al.: Meta-sim: Learning to generate synthetic datasets. In: Proceedings of the IEEE/CVF International Conference on Computer Vision, pp. 4551–4560 (2019)

26. Kaskman, R., Zakharov, S., Shugurov, I., Ilic, S.: Homebreweddb: Rgb-d dataset for 6d pose estimation of 3d objects. In: Proceedings of the IEEE/CVF International Conference on Computer Vision Workshops (2019)

27. Kehl, W., Manhardt, F., Tombari, F., Ilic, S., Navab, N.: Ssd-6d: making rgb-based 3d detection and 6d pose estimation great again. In: Proceedings of the IEEE International Conference on Computer Vision, pp. 1521–1529 (2017)

28. Labbé, Y., Carpentier, J., Aubry, M., Sivic, J.: CosyPose: consistent multi-view multi-object 6d pose estimation. In: Vedaldi, A., Bischof, H., Brox, T., Frahm, J.-M. (eds.) ECCV 2020. LNCS, vol. 12362, pp. 574–591. Springer, Cham (2020). https://doi.org/10.1007/978-3-030-58520-4_34

29. Lambert, J.H.: Photometria sive de mensura et gradibus luminis, colorum et umbrae. sumptibus vidvae E. Klett, typis CP Detleffsen (1760)

30. Lee, H.Y., Tseng, H.Y., Huang, J.B., Singh, M., Yang, M.H.: Diverse image-to-image translation via disentangled representations. In: ECCV (2018)

31. Lee, J.H., Han, M.K., Ko, D.W., Suh, I.H.: From big to small: multi-scale local planar guidance for monocular depth estimation (2019)

32. Li, Z., Wang, G., Ji, X.: Cdpn: coordinates-based disentangled pose network for real-time RGB-based 6-dof object pose estimation. In: ICCV, pp. 7678–7687 (2019)

33. Liu, X., et al.: Adversarial unsupervised domain adaptation with conditional and label shift: Infer, align and iterate. In: Proceedings of the IEEE/CVF International Conference on Computer Vision, pp. 10367–10376 (2021)

34. Mildenhall, B., Srinivasan, P.P., Tancik, M., Barron, J.T., Ramamoorthi, R., Ng, R.: NeRF: representing scenes as neural radiance fields for view synthesis. In: Vedaldi, A., Bischof, H., Brox, T., Frahm, J.-M. (eds.) ECCV 2020. LNCS, vol. 12346, pp. 405–421. Springer, Cham (2020). https://doi.org/10.1007/978-3-030-58452-8_24

35. Mustikovela, S.K., et al.: Self-supervised object detection via generative image synthesis. In: Proceedings of the IEEE/CVF International Conference on Computer Vision, pp. 8609–8618 (2021)

36. Nalbach, O., Arabadzhiyska, E., Mehta, D., Seidel, H.P., Ritschel, T.: Deep shading: convolutional neural networks for screen space shading. In: Computer Graphics Forum, vol. 36, pp. 65–78. Wiley Online Library (2017)
37. Niemeyer, M., Geiger, A.: Giraffe: representing scenes as compositional generative neural feature fields. In: Proceedings of the IEEE/CVF Conference on Computer Vision and Pattern Recognition, pp. 11453–11464 (2021)
38. Oren, M., Nayar, S.K.: Generalization of lambert's reflectance model. In: Proceedings of the 21st Annual Conference on Computer Graphics and Interactive Techniques, pp. 239–246 (1994)
39. Park, K., Patten, T., Vincze, M.: Pix2pose: pixel-wise coordinate regression of objects for 6d pose estimation. In: ICCV, pp. 7668–7677 (2019)
40. Park, T., Efros, A.A., Zhang, R., Zhu, J.-Y.: Contrastive learning for unpaired image-to-image translation. In: Vedaldi, A., Bischof, H., Brox, T., Frahm, J.-M. (eds.) ECCV 2020. LNCS, vol. 12354, pp. 319–345. Springer, Cham (2020). https://doi.org/10.1007/978-3-030-58545-7_19
41. Peng, S., Liu, Y., Huang, Q., Zhou, X., Bao, H.: Pvnet: pixel-wise voting network for 6dof pose estimation. In: CVPR, pp. 4561–4570 (2019)
42. Planche, B., Zakharov, S., Wu, Z., Hutter, A., Kosch, H., Ilic, S.: Seeing beyond appearance-mapping real images into geometrical domains for unsupervised cad-based recognition. In: 2019 IEEE/RSJ International Conference on Intelligent Robots and Systems (IROS), pp. 2579–2586. IEEE (2019)
43. Prakash, A., et al.: Structured domain randomization: bridging the reality gap by context-aware synthetic data. In: 2019 International Conference on Robotics and Automation (ICRA), pp. 7249–7255. IEEE (2019)
44. Prakash, A., Debnath, S., Lafleche, J.F., Cameracci, E., Birchfield, S., Law, M.T., et al.: Self-supervised real-to-sim scene generation. In: Proceedings of the IEEE/CVF International Conference on Computer Vision, pp. 16044–16054 (2021)
45. Richter, S.R., AlHaija, H.A., Koltun, V.: Enhancing photorealism enhancement. arXiv preprint arXiv:2105.04619 (2021)
46. Rückert, D., Franke, L., Stamminger, M.: Adop: approximate differentiable one-pixel point rendering. arXiv preprint arXiv:2110.06635 (2021)
47. Sitzmann, V., Martel, J., Bergman, A., Lindell, D., Wetzstein, G.: Implicit neural representations with periodic activation functions. In: NeurIPS (2020)
48. Srinivasan, P.P., Deng, B., Zhang, X., Tancik, M., Mildenhall, B., Barron, J.T.: Nerv: neural reflectance and visibility fields for relighting and view synthesis. In: Proceedings of the IEEE/CVF Conference on Computer Vision and Pattern Recognition, pp. 7495–7504 (2021)
49. Tewari, A., et al.: Advances in neural rendering. arXiv preprint arXiv:2111.05849 (2021)
50. Thies, J., Zollhöfer, M., Nießner, M.: Deferred neural rendering: Image synthesis using neural textures. ACM Trans. Graph. (TOG) 38(4), 1–12 (2019)
51. Tobin, J., Fong, R., Ray, A., Schneider, J., Zaremba, W., Abbeel, P.: Domain randomization for transferring deep neural networks from simulation to the real world. In: IROS (2017)
52. Tremblay, J., et al.: Training deep networks with synthetic data: bridging the reality gap by domain randomization. In: Proceedings of the IEEE Conference on Computer Vision and Pattern Recognition Workshops, pp. 969–977 (2018)
53. Volpi, R., Morerio, P., Savarese, S., Murino, V.: Adversarial feature augmentation for unsupervised domain adaptation. In: Proceedings of the IEEE Conference on Computer Vision and Pattern Recognition, pp. 5495–5504 (2018)

54. Walter, B., Marschner, S.R., Li, H., Torrance, K.E.: Microfacet models for refraction through rough surfaces. Rendering Tech. **2007**, 18th (2007)
55. Wang, H., Sridhar, S., Huang, J., Valentin, J., Song, S., Guibas, L.J.: Normalized object coordinate space for category-level 6d object pose and size estimation. In: Proceedings of the IEEE/CVF Conference on Computer Vision and Pattern Recognition, pp. 2642–2651 (2019)
56. Wang, T.C., Liu, M.Y., Zhu, J.Y., Tao, A., Kautz, J., Catanzaro, B.: High-resolution image synthesis and semantic manipulation with conditional GANs. In: Proceedings of the IEEE Conference on Computer Vision and Pattern Recognition, pp. 8798–8807 (2018)
57. Wang, Z., Bovik, A.C., Sheikh, H.R., Simoncelli, E.P.: Image quality assessment: from error visibility to structural similarity. IEEE Trans. Image Process. **13**(4), 600–612 (2004)
58. Zakharov, S., et al.: Single-shot scene reconstruction. In: 5th Annual Conference on Robot Learning (2021)
59. Zakharov, S., Kehl, W., Ilic, S.: Deceptionnet: network-driven domain randomization. In: Proceedings of the IEEE/CVF International Conference on Computer Vision, pp. 532–541 (2019)
60. Zakharov, S., Planche, B., Wu, Z., Hutter, A., Kosch, H., Ilic, S.: Keep it unreal: bridging the realism gap for 2.5d recognition with geometry priors only. In: 3DV (2018)
61. Zakharov, S., Shugurov, I., Ilic, S.: Dpod: 6d pose object detector and refiner. In: ICCV (2019)
62. Zhang, H., Dana, K.: Multi-style generative network for real-time transfer. In: Proceedings of the European Conference on Computer Vision (ECCV) Workshops (2018)
63. Zhang, R., Isola, P., Efros, A.A., Shechtman, E., Wang, O.: The unreasonable effectiveness of deep features as a perceptual metric. In: Proceedings of the IEEE Conference on Computer Vision and Pattern Recognition, pp. 586–595 (2018)
64. Zheng, Z., Yang, Y.: Rectifying pseudo label learning via uncertainty estimation for domain adaptive semantic segmentation. Int. J. Comput. Vision **129**(4), 1106–1120 (2021)
65. Zhou, X., Wang, D., Krähenbühl, P.: Objects as points. arXiv preprint arXiv:1904.07850 (2019)
66. Zhu, J.Y., Park, T., Isola, P., Efros, A.A.: Unpaired image-to-image translation using cycle-consistent adversarial networks. In: ICCV (2017)
67. Zou, Y., Yu, Z., Liu, X., Kumar, B., Wang, J.: Confidence regularized self-training. In: Proceedings of the IEEE/CVF International Conference on Computer Vision, pp. 5982–5991 (2019)

# Wave-ViT: Unifying Wavelet and Transformers for Visual Representation Learning

Ting Yao[1] , Yingwei Pan[1(✉)] , Yehao Li[1], Chong-Wah Ngo[2] ,
and Tao Mei[1]

[1] JD Explore Academy, Beijing, China
tingyao.ustc@gmail.com, panyw.ustc@gmail.com, yehaoli.sysu@gmail.com,
tmei@jd.com
[2] Singapore Management University, Singapore, Singapore
cwngo@smu.edu.sg

**Abstract.** Multi-scale Vision Transformer (ViT) has emerged as a powerful backbone for computer vision tasks, while the self-attention computation in Transformer scales quadratically w.r.t. the input patch number. Thus, existing solutions commonly employ down-sampling operations (*e.g.*, average pooling) over keys/values to dramatically reduce the computational cost. In this work, we argue that such over-aggressive down-sampling design is not invertible and inevitably causes information dropping especially for high-frequency components in objects (*e.g.*, texture details). Motivated by the wavelet theory, we construct a new Wavelet Vision Transformer (**Wave-ViT**) that formulates the invertible down-sampling with wavelet transforms and self-attention learning in a unified way. This proposal enables self-attention learning with lossless down-sampling over keys/values, facilitating the pursuing of a better efficiency-vs-accuracy trade-off. Furthermore, inverse wavelet transforms are leveraged to strengthen self-attention outputs by aggregating local contexts with enlarged receptive field. We validate the superiority of Wave-ViT through extensive experiments over multiple vision tasks (*e.g.*, image recognition, object detection and instance segmentation). Its performances surpass state-of-the-art ViT backbones with comparable FLOPs. Source code is available at https://github.com/YehLi/ImageNetModel.

**Keywords:** Vision transformer · Wavelet transform · Self-attention learning · Image recognition

## 1 Introduction

Recently, leveraging Transformer architecture [53] for visual representation learning has achieved widespread dominance in computer vision field. Transformer architecture has brought forward milestone improvement for a series of downstream vision tasks [4,9,13,29,35–37,42,43,45,48,56,58,59,67,71,74], including

© The Author(s), under exclusive license to Springer Nature Switzerland AG 2022
S. Avidan et al. (Eds.): ECCV 2022, LNCS 13685, pp. 328–345, 2022.
https://doi.org/10.1007/978-3-031-19806-9_19

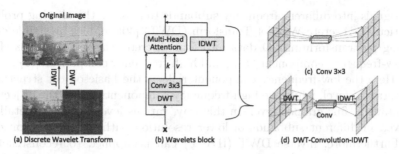

**Fig. 1.** An illustration of (a) Discrete Wavelet Transform (DWT) and Inverse DWT (IDWT) over an image, (b) our Wavelets block, and the comparison between (c) a single 3 × 3 convolution and (d) DWT-Convolution-IDWT process in our Wavelets block.

both image recognition and dense prediction tasks (*e.g.*, object detection and semantic segmentation). At its heart is a basic self-attention block that triggers long-range interaction among visual tokens. The Vision Transformer (ViT) [13] is one of the early attempts that directly employs a pure Transformer over image patches, and manages to attain competitive image recognition performance against CNN counterparts. However, applying the primary ViT architecture using its outputs of single-scale and low-resolution feature map for the pixel-level dense prediction tasks (*e.g.*, instance/semantic segmentation) is not trivial. Therefore, considering that visual patterns commonly occur at multiple scales in natural scenery, there has been research efforts pushing the limits of ViT backbones by aggregating contexts from multiple scales (*e.g.*, "pyramid" strategy). For example, Pyramid Vision Transformer (PVT) [59,60] integrates pyramid structure into Transformer framework, yielding multi-scale feature maps for dense prediction tasks. Multiscale Vision Transformers (MViT) [14] learns multi-scale feature hierarchies in Transformer architecture by hierarchically expanding the channel capacity while reducing the spatial resolution.

One primary challenge of applying self-attention over multi-scale feature maps is the quadratical computational cost that scales w.r.t the number of input patches (*i.e.*, spatial resolution). Thus, typical multi-scale ViT approaches usually perform down-sampling operations (*e.g.*, average pooling in [59] or pooling kernels in [14]) over keys/values to reduce computational cost. Nevertheless, these pooling based operations inevitably result in information dropping (*e.g.*, the high-frequency components of object texture details), and thus adversely affect the performances especially for dense prediction tasks. Furthermore, the recent studies (*e.g.*, [72]) also have shown that applying pooling operations in CNNs would hurt the shift-equivariance of deep networks.

In this paper, we propose **Wavelets block** to perform invertible down-sampling through wavelet transforms, aiming to preserve the original image details for self-attention learning while reducing computational cost. Wavelet transform is a fundamental time-frequency analysis method that decomposes input signals into different frequency subbands to address the aliasing problem. In particular, Discrete Wavelet Transform (DWT) [40] enables invertible down-sampling by transforming 2D data into four discrete wavelet subbands (Fig. 1 (a)): low-frequency component ($I_{LL}$) and high-frequency components ($I_{LH}$, $I_{HL}$, $I_{HH}$). Here the low-frequency component reflects the basic object structure at coarse-grained level, while the high-frequency components retain the object texture details at fine-grained level. In this way, various levels of image details are preserved in different subbands of lower resolution without information dropping. Furthermore, inverse DWT (IDWT) can be applied to reconstruct the original image. The information preserving transformation motivates the design of an efficient Transformer block with lossless and invertible down-sampling for self-attention learning over multi-scale feature maps.

Technically, as shown in Fig. 1 (b), Wavelets block first employs DWT to transform each input key/value to four subbands of lower resolution. After stacking the four subbands into a down-sampled feature map, a $3 \times 3$ convolution is performed to further impose spatial locality over the frequency subbands. This leads to locally contextualized down-sampled keys/values. The multi-head self-attention learning is conducted on the down-sampled keys/values and input query. Meanwhile, IDWT can be applied over the down-sampled keys/values to reconstruct high-resolution feature map that preserves image details. Compared to the single $3 \times 3$ convolution (Fig. 1 (c)), the process of DWT-Convolution-IDWT (Fig. 1 (d)) enables a stronger local contextualization via enlarged receptive field, with negligible increase in computation and memory. Finally, we combine the attended feature map via self-attention learning and the reconstructed feature map with local contextualization as the outputs of Wavelets block.

By operating Wavelets block over multi-scale features in the multi-stage Transformer framework, we present a new Wavelet Vision Transformer (**Wave-ViT**) for visual representation learning. Wave-ViT has been properly analyzed and verified through extensive experiments over different vision tasks, which demonstrate its superiority against state-of-the-art ViTs. More remarkably, under a comparable number of parameters, Wave-ViT achieves 85.5% top-1 accuracy on ImageNet for image recognition, which absolutely improves PVT (83.8%) with 1.7%. For object detection and instance segmentation on COCO, Wave-ViT absolutely surpasses PVT with 1.3% and 0.5% mAP, with 25.9% less parameters.

## 2    Related Work

**Visual Representation Learning.** Early studies predominantly focused on exploring CNN for visual representation learning, leading to a series of CNN backbones, *e.g.*, [21,26,27,46,50]. Most of them stack low-to-high convolutions by going deeper, targeting for producing low-resolution and high-level representations tailored for image recognition. However, dense prediction tasks like semantic segmentation require high-resolution and even pixel-level representations. To tackle this, several multi-scale CNNs are established. For example,

Res2Net [16] presents a multi-scale building block that contains hierarchical residual-like connections. HRNet [55] connects high-to-low resolution convolution streams in parallel and meanwhile exchanges the information across resolutions repeatedly.

Recently, due to the powerful long-range interaction modeling in Transformer [53], Transformer has advanced natural language understanding. Inspired by this, numerous Transformer-based architectures for vision understanding have started. A few attempts augment convolutional operators with the global self-attention [2] or local self-attention [22,44,47,75], yielding a hybrid backbone of CNN and Transformer. On a parallel note, Vision Transformer (ViT) [13] first employs a pure Transformer over the sequence of image patches for image recognition. DETR [4] also leverages a pure Transformer to construct an end-to-end detector for object detection. Different from ViT that solely divides input image into patches, TNT [19] further decomposes patches into sub-patches as "visual words". A sub-transformer is additionally integrated into Transformer to perform self-attention over smaller "visual words". Subsequently, to facilitate dense prediction tasks, multi-scale paradigm is introduced into Transformer structure, leading to multi-scale Vision Transformer backbones [14,35,59,60]. In particular, Swin Transformer [35] upgrades ViT by constructing hierarchical feature maps via merging image patches in deeper layers. Pyramid Vision Transformer (PVT) [60] designs a pyramid structure Transformer that produces multi-scale feature maps in a four-stage architecture. PVTv2 [59] further improves PVT by using average pooling to reduce spatial dimension of keys/values, rather than convolutions in PVT. Multiscale Vision Transformers (MViT) [14] integrates Transformer architecture with multi-scale feature hierarchies, and pooling kernels is employed over query/keys/values for spatial reduction.

Our Wave-ViT is also a type of multi-scale ViT. Existing multi-scale ViTs (e.g., [14,59,60]) commonly adopt irreversible down-sampling operations like average pooling or pooling kernels for spatial reduction. In contrast, Wave-ViT capitalizes on wavelet transforms to reduce spatial dimension of keys/values via invertible down-sampling for self-attention learning over multi-scale features, leading to a better trade-off between computation cost and performance.

**Wavelet Transform in Computer Vision.** Wavelet Transform is effective for time-frequency analysis. Considering that Wavelet Transform is invertible and capable of preserving all information, Wavelet Transform has been exploited in CNN architectures for performance boosting in various vision tasks. For example, in [1], Bae et al. validate that learning CNN representations over wavelet subbands can benefit the task of image restoration. DWSR [18] takes low-resolution wavelet subbands as inputs to recover the missing details for image super-resolution task. Multi-level wavelet transform [34] is utilized to enlarge receptive field without information dropping for image restoration. Williams et al. [61] utilize Wavelet Transform to decompose input features into a second level decomposition, and discard first-level subbands to reduce feature dimensions for image recognition. Haar wavelet CNNs is integrated with multi-resolution analysis in [15] for texture classification and image annotation. In [41], ResNet is remoulded by combining the first layer with a wavelet scattering network, which achieves comparable performances on image recognition with less parameters.

Although wavelet transform has been exploited as down-sampling/up-sampling operations in CNNs, it is never explored for Transformer architecture. In this work, our Wave-ViT goes beyond existing CNNs that operate wavelet transform over feature maps across different stages, and leverages wavelet transform to down-sample keys/values within Transformer block, making the impact more thorough for feature learning.

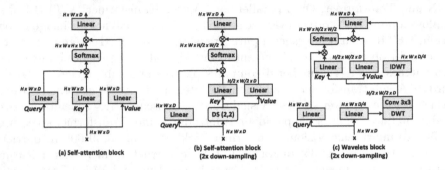

**Fig. 2.** The detailed architectures of (a) basic self-attention block in ViT Backbones, (b) self-attention block with down-sampling operation (*i.e.*, DS(2, 2)) that reduces the spatial scale of both height and width by half, and (c) our Wavelets block that capitalizes on wavelet transforms to enable lossless down-sampling.

## 3    Our Approach: Wavelet Vision Transformer

This section starts by briefly reviewing the most typical multi-head self-attention block in ViTs, particularly on how the self-attention block is scaled down for reducing computational cost in the existing multi-scale ViTs. After that, a novel principled Transformer building block, named Wavelets block, is designed to integrate self-attention learning with wavelet transforms in a unified fashion. Such design upgrades typical self-attention block by exploiting wavelet transforms to perform invertible down-sampling, which elegantly reduces spatial dimension of keys/values without information dropping. Furthermore, this block applies inverse wavelet transforms over down-sampled keys/values to enhance outputs with enlarged receptive field. Finally, after applying Wavelets block over multi-scale features in the multi-stage Transformer architecture, we elaborate a new multi-scale ViT backbone, *i.e.*, Wavelet Vision Transformer.

### 3.1    Preliminaries

**Multi-head Self-attention in ViT Backbones.** Mainstream Transformer architectures, especially Vision Transformer backbones [13], often rely on the typical multi-head self-attention that captures long-range dependencies among inputs in a scalable fashion. Here we present a general formulation of multi-head self-attention as illustrated in Fig. 2 (a). Technically, let $X \in \mathbb{R}^{H \times W \times D}$ be the input 2D feature map, where $H/W/D$ denote the height/width/channel number, respectively. Here $X$ can be reshaped as a patch sequence, consisting of $n = H \times W$ image patches and the dimension of each patch is $D$. We linearly transform the input patch sequence $X$ into three groups in parallel: queries $Q \in \mathbb{R}^{n \times D}$, keys $K \in \mathbb{R}^{n \times D}$, and values $V \in \mathbb{R}^{n \times D}$. After that, the multi-head self-attention (**MultiHead**) module [53] decomposes each query/key/value into $N_h$ parts along channel dimension, leading to queries $Q_j \in \mathbb{R}^{n \times D_h}$, keys $K_j \in \mathbb{R}^{n \times D_h}$, and values $V_j \in \mathbb{R}^{n \times D_h}$ for the $j$-th head. Note that $N_h$ is head number and $D_h$ denotes the dimension of each head. Then, we perform self-attention learning (**Attention**) over queries, keys and values for each head, and the outputs of each head are concatenated, followed by a linear transformation to compose the final outputs:

$$
\begin{aligned}
\textbf{MultiHead}(Q, K, V) &= \textbf{Concat}(head_0, head_1, ..., head_{N_h})W^O, \\
head_j &= \textbf{Attention}(Q_j, K_j, V_j), \\
\textbf{Attention}(Q_j, K_j, V_j) &= \textbf{Softmax}(\frac{Q_j K_j^T}{\sqrt{D_h}})V_j,
\end{aligned}
\tag{1}
$$

where $\textbf{Concat}(\cdot)$ denotes concatenation and $W^O$ is the transformation matrix. According to the general formulation in Eq.(1), the computational cost of multi-head self-attention for the input feature map $X \in \mathbb{R}^{H \times W \times D}$ is $\mathcal{O}(H^2 W^2 D)$, which scales quadratically w.r.t. the input patch number. Such design inevitably leads to a sharp rise in computational cost especially for high-resolution inputs.

**Self-attention with Down-sampling in Multi-scale ViT Backbones.** To alleviate the heavy self-attention computation overhead for high-resolution inputs, the existing multi-scale ViT backbones commonly adopt the down-sampling operations (*e.g.*, average pooling in [59] or pooling kernels in [14]) over keys/values for spatial reduction. Taking the self-attention block with 2 × down-sampling in Fig. 2 (b) as an example, the input 2D feature map $X$ is first down-sampled by a factor $r$ ($r = 2$ in this case). Here the down-sampling operator is denoted as $DS(2, 2)$, that reduces the spatial scale of both height and width by half. Next, the down-sampled feature map is linearly transformed into keys $K^d \in \mathbb{R}^{\frac{n}{r^2} \times D}$ and values $V^d \in \mathbb{R}^{\frac{n}{r^2} \times D}$ to trigger multi-head self-attention learning. As such, the overall computational cost of multi-head self-attention is dramatically reduced by a factor of $r^2$ (*i.e.*, $\mathcal{O}(\frac{H^2 W^2 D}{r^2})$).

### 3.2   Wavelets Block

Although the aforementioned multi-scale ViT backbones reduce self-attention computation via down-sampling, the commonly adopted down-sampling operations like average pooling are irreversible, and inevitably result in information dropping. To mitigate this issue, we design a principled self-attention block, named **Wavelets block**, that novelly capitalizes on wavelet transforms to enable invertible down-sampling for self-attention learning. Such invertible down-sampling is seamlessly incorporated into the typical self-attention block, pursuing efficient multi-head self-attention learning with lossless down-sampling. Figure 2 (c) details the architecture of our Wavelets block.

Formally, given the input 2D feature map $X \in \mathbb{R}^{H \times W \times D}$, we first linearly transform it into $\widetilde{X} = XW_d$ with reduced channel dimension via embedding matrix $W_d \in \mathbb{R}^{D \times \frac{D}{4}}$. Next, we employ Discrete Wavelet Transform (DWT) to down-sample the input $\widetilde{X} \in \mathbb{R}^{H \times W \times \frac{D}{4}}$ by decomposing it into four wavelet subbands. Note that here we choose the classical Haar wavelet for DWT as in [33] for simplicity. Concretely, DWT applies the low-pass filter $f_L = (1/\sqrt{2}, 1/\sqrt{2})$ and high-pass filter $f_H = (1/\sqrt{2}, -1/\sqrt{2})$ along the rows to encode $\widetilde{X}$ into two subbands $X_L$ and $X_H$. Next, the same low-pass filter $f_L$ and high-pass filter $f_H$ are employed along the columns of the learnt subbands $X_L$ and $X_H$, leading to all the four wavelet subbands: $X_{LL} \in \mathbb{R}^{\frac{H}{2} \times \frac{W}{2} \times \frac{D}{4}}$, $X_{LH} \in \mathbb{R}^{\frac{H}{2} \times \frac{W}{2} \times \frac{D}{4}}$, $X_{HL} \in \mathbb{R}^{\frac{H}{2} \times \frac{W}{2} \times \frac{D}{4}}$, and $X_{HH} \in \mathbb{R}^{\frac{H}{2} \times \frac{W}{2} \times \frac{D}{4}}$. $X_{LL}$ refers to the low-frequency component that reflects the basic object structure at coarse-grained level. $X_{LH}$, $X_{HL}$, and $X_{HH}$ represent the high-frequency components that retain the object texture details at fine-grained level. In this way, each wavelet subband can be regarded as the down-sampled version of $\widetilde{X}$, and all of them cover every detail of inputs without any information dropping.

We concatenate the four wavelet subbands along the channel dimension to form $\hat{X} = [X_{LL}, X_{LH}, X_{HL}, X_{HH}] \in \mathbb{R}^{\frac{H}{2} \times \frac{W}{2} \times D}$. A $3 \times 3$ convolution is further applied to impose spatial locality over $\hat{X}$, yielding the locally contextualized down-sampled feature map $X^c$. Next, this down-sampled feature map $X^c$ is linearly transformed into down-sampled keys $K^w \in {}^{m \times D}$ and values $V^w \in {}^{m \times D}$, where $m = \frac{H}{2} \times \frac{W}{2}$ is the number of patches. Similarly, the wavelet-based multi-head self-attention learning **Attention$^w$** is thus performed over the queries and the corresponding down-sampled keys/values for each head:

$$head_j = \textbf{Attention}^{\textbf{w}}(Q_j, K_j^w, V_j^w) = \textbf{Softmax}(\frac{Q_j K_j^{wT}}{\sqrt{D_h}})V_j^w, \qquad (2)$$

where $K_j^w / V_j^w$ denotes the down-sampled keys/values for the $j$-th head, respectively. Here the aggregated output of self-attention learning for each head ($head_j$) can be interpreted as the long-range contextualized information of inputs.

As a beneficial by-product, we additionally apply inverse DWT (IDWT) over the locally contextualized down-sampled feature $X^c$. According to the wavelet theory, the reconstructed feature map $X^r$ is able to retain every detail of primary input $\widetilde{X}$. It is worthy to note that compared to a single $3 \times 3$ convolution, such process of DWT-Convolution-IDWT in Wavelets block triggers a stronger local contextualization with enlarged receptive field, with negligible increase in computational cost/memory.

Finally, we concatenate all the long-range contextualized information of each head plus the reconstructed locally contextualized information $X^r$, followed by a linear transformation to compose the outputs of our Wavelets block:

$$\textbf{WaveletsBlock}(X) = \textbf{MultiHead}^{\textbf{w}}(XW^q, X^c W^k, X^c W^v, X^r),$$
$$\textbf{MultiHead}^{\textbf{w}}(Q, K, V, X^r) = \textbf{Concat}(head_0, head_1, ..., head_{N_h}, X^r)\widetilde{W}^O, \tag{3}$$

where $\widetilde{W}^O$ is the transformation matrix.

### 3.3   Wavelet Vision Transformer

Recall that our Wavelets block is a principled unified self-attention block, it is feasible to construct multi-scale ViT backbones with Wavelets blocks. Following the basic configuration of existing multi-scale ViTs [35,60], we present three variants of our Wavelet Vision Transformer (Wave-ViT) with different model sizes, *i.e.*, Wave-ViT-S (small size), Wave-ViT-B (base size), and Wave-ViT-L (large size). Note that Wave-ViT-S/B/L shares similar model size and computational complexity with Swin-T/S/B [35]. Specifically, given the input image (size: 224 × 224), the entire architecture of Wave-ViT consists of four stages, and each stage is comprised of a patch embedding layer, and a stack of Wavelets blocks followed by feed-forward layers. We follow the design principle of ResNet [21] by progressively increasing the channel dimensions of all the four stages and meanwhile shrinking the spatial resolutions. Table 1 details the architectures of all the three variants of Wave-ViT, where $E_i$, $Head_i$, and $C_i$ is the expansion ratio of feed-forward layer, head number, and the channel dimension in stage $i$.

**Table 1.** Detailed architecture specifications for three variants of our Wave-ViT with different model sizes, *i.e.*, Wave-ViT-S (small size), Wave-ViT-B (base size), and Wave-ViT-L (large size). $E_i$, $Head_i$, and $C_i$ represents the expansion ratio of feed-forward layer, the head number, and the channel dimension in each stage $i$, respectively.

| | Output Size | Wave-ViT-S | Wave-ViT-B | Wave-ViT-L |
|---|---|---|---|---|
| Stage 1 | $\frac{H}{4} \times \frac{W}{4}$ | $\begin{bmatrix} E_1 = 8 \\ Head_1 = 2 \\ C_1 = 64 \end{bmatrix} \times 3$ | $\begin{bmatrix} E_1 = 8 \\ Head_1 = 2 \\ C_1 = 64 \end{bmatrix} \times 3$ | $\begin{bmatrix} E_1 = 8 \\ Head_1 = 3 \\ C_1 = 96 \end{bmatrix} \times 3$ |
| Stage 2 | $\frac{H}{8} \times \frac{W}{8}$ | $\begin{bmatrix} E_2 = 8 \\ Head_2 = 4 \\ C_2 = 128 \end{bmatrix} \times 4$ | $\begin{bmatrix} E_2 = 8 \\ Head_2 = 4 \\ C_2 = 128 \end{bmatrix} \times 4$ | $\begin{bmatrix} E_2 = 8 \\ Head_2 = 6 \\ C_2 = 192 \end{bmatrix} \times 6$ |
| Stage 3 | $\frac{H}{16} \times \frac{W}{16}$ | $\begin{bmatrix} E_3 = 4 \\ Head_3 = 10 \\ C_3 = 320 \end{bmatrix} \times 6$ | $\begin{bmatrix} E_3 = 4 \\ Head_3 = 10 \\ C_3 = 320 \end{bmatrix} \times 12$ | $\begin{bmatrix} E_3 = 4 \\ Head_3 = 12 \\ C_3 = 384 \end{bmatrix} \times 18$ |
| Stage 4 | $\frac{H}{32} \times \frac{W}{32}$ | $\begin{bmatrix} E_4 = 4 \\ Head_4 = 14 \\ C_4 = 448 \end{bmatrix} \times 3$ | $\begin{bmatrix} E_4 = 4 \\ Head_4 = 16 \\ C_4 = 512 \end{bmatrix} \times 3$ | $\begin{bmatrix} E_4 = 4 \\ Head_4 = 16 \\ C_4 = 512 \end{bmatrix} \times 3$ |

# 4    Experiments

We evaluate the effectiveness of Wave-ViT via various empirical evidence on several mainstream CV tasks. Concretely, we consider the following evaluations to compare the quality of learnt features obtained from various vision backbones: (a) Training from scratch for image recognition task on ImageNet1K [12]; (b) Fine-tuning the backbones (pre-trained on ImageNet1K) for downstream tasks, *i.e.*, object detection and instance segmentation on COCO [32], and semantic segmentation on ADE20K [77]; (c) Ablation studies that support each design in our Wavelets block; (d) Visualization of learnt representation by Wave-ViT.

## 4.1    Image Recognition on ImageNet1K

**Dataset and Optimization Setups.** In the task of image recognition, we adopt the ImageNet1K benchmark, which comprises 1.28 million training images and 50K validation images from 1,000 classes. All vision backbones are trained

**Table 2.** The performances of various vision backbones on ImageNet1K for image recognition. ⋆ indicates that the backbone is additionally trained with Token Labeling objective with MixToken [24] and convolutional stem [57] for patch encoding. We group all runs into three categories, and all backbones within each category shares similar GFLOPs: Small (GFLOPs < 6), Base (6 ≤ GFLOPs < 10), Large (10 ≤ GFLOPs < 22).

| Method | Params | GFLOPs | Top-1 | Top-5 | Method | Params | GFLOPs | Top-1 | Top-5 |
|---|---|---|---|---|---|---|---|---|---|
| Small | | | | | Large | | | | |
| ResNet-50 [21] | 25.5M | 4.1 | 78.3 | 94.3 | ResNet-152 [21] | 60.2M | 11.6 | 81.3 | 95.5 |
| BoTNet-S1-50 [47] | 20.8M | 4.3 | 80.4 | 95.0 | ResNeXt101 [64] | 83.5M | 15.6 | 81.5 | – |
| Swin-T [35] | 29.0M | 4.5 | 81.2 | 95.5 | DeiT-B [51] | 86.6M | 17.6 | 81.8 | 95.6 |
| ConViT-S [11] | 27.8M | 5.4 | 81.3 | 95.7 | SE-ResNet-152 [23] | 66.8M | 11.6 | 82.2 | 95.9 |
| T2T-ViT-14 [68] | 21.5M | 4.8 | 81.5 | 95.7 | ResNeSt-101 [70] | 48.3M | 10.2 | 82.3 | – |
| RegionViT-Ti+ [6] | 14.3M | 2.7 | 81.5 | – | ConViT-B [11] | 86.5M | 16.8 | 82.4 | 95.9 |
| SE-CoTNetD-50 [30] | 23.1M | 4.1 | 81.6 | 95.8 | T2T-ViTt-24 [68] | 64.1M | 15.0 | 82.6 | 95.9 |
| Twins-SVT-S [9] | 24.1M | 2.9 | 81.7 | 95.6 | TNT-B [19] | 65.6M | 14.1 | 82.9 | 96.3 |
| CoaT-Lite Small [65] | 20.0M | 4.0 | 81.9 | 95.5 | DeepViT-L [78] | 58.9M | 12.8 | 83.1 | – |
| PVTv2-B2 [59] | 25.4M | 4.0 | 82.0 | 96.0 | RegionViT-B [6] | 72.7M | 13.0 | 83.2 | 96.1 |
| Wave-ViT-S | 19.8M | 4.3 | 82.7 | 96.2 | CaiT-S36 [52] | 68.4M | 13.9 | 83.3 | – |
| Wave-ViT-S⋆ | 22.7M | 4.7 | **83.9** | **96.6** | CrossViT-15-384 [5] | 28.5M | 21.4 | 83.5 | – |
| Base | | | | | BoTNet-S1-128 [47] | 75.1M | 19.3 | 83.5 | 96.5 |
| ResNet-101 [21] | 44.6M | 7.9 | 80.0 | 95.0 | Swin-B [35] | 88.0M | 15.4 | 83.5 | 96.5 |
| BoTNet-S1-59 [47] | 33.5M | 7.3 | 81.7 | 95.8 | PVTv2-B4 [59] | 62.6M | 10.1 | 83.6 | 96.7 |
| T2T-ViT-19 [68] | 39.2M | 8.5 | 81.9 | 95.7 | Twins-SVT-L [9] | 99.3M | 15.1 | 83.7 | 96.5 |
| CvT-21 [62] | 32.0M | 7.1 | 82.5 | – | RegionViT-B+ [6] | 73.8M | 13.6 | 83.8 | – |
| Swin-S [35] | 50.0M | 8.7 | 83.2 | 96.2 | Focal-Base [66] | 89.8M | 16.0 | 83.8 | 96.5 |
| Twins-SVT-B [9] | 56.1M | 8.6 | 83.2 | 96.3 | PVTv2-B5 [59] | 82.0M | 11.8 | 83.8 | 96.6 |
| SE-CoTNetD-101 [30] | 40.9M | 8.5 | 83.2 | 96.5 | SE-CoTNetD-152 [30] | 55.8M | 17.0 | 84.0 | 97.0 |
| PVTv2-B3 [59] | 45.2M | 6.9 | 83.2 | 96.5 | LV-ViT-M⋆ [24] | 55.8M | 16.0 | 84.1 | 96.7 |
| RegionViT-M+ [6] | 42.0M | 7.9 | 83.4 | – | VOLO-D2⋆ [69] | 58.7M | 14.1 | 85.2 | – |
| VOLO-D1⋆ [69] | 26.6M | 6.8 | 84.2 | – | VOLO-D3⋆ [69] | 86.3M | 20.6 | 85.4 | – |
| Wave-ViT-B⋆ | 33.5M | 7.2 | **84.8** | **97.1** | Wave-ViT-L⋆ | 57.5M | 14.8 | **85.5** | **97.3** |

from scratch on the training set, and both top-1 and top-5 accuracies metrics are used to evaluate the trained backbones on the validation set. During training, we follow the setups in [69] by applying RandAug [10], CutOut [76], and Token Labeling objective with MixToken [24] for data augmentation. We adopt the AdamW optimizer [39] with a momentum of 0.9. In particular, the optimization process includes 10 epochs of linear warm-up and 300 epochs with cosine decay learning rate scheduler [38]. The batch size is set as 1,024, which is distributed on 8 V100 GPUs. We fix the learning rate and weight decay as 0.001 and 0.05.

**Performance Comparison.** Table 2 summarizes the performance comparisons between the state-of-the-art vision backbones and our Wave-ViT variants. Note that the most competitive ViT backbones VOLO variants (*i.e.*, VOLO-D1*, VOLO-D2*, and VOLO-D3*) are trained with additional Token Labeling objective with MixToken [24] and convolutional stem (conv-stem) [57] for better patch encoding. We also adopt the same upgraded strategies to train our Wave-ViT, yielding the variants in each size (*i.e.*, Wave-ViT-S*, Wave-ViT-B*, Wave-ViT-L*). Moreover, for fair comparison with other vision backbones without these strategies, we also implement a degraded version of Wave-ViT in Small size without Token Labeling objective and conv-stem (*i.e.*, Wave-ViT-S). As shown in this table, under the similar GFLOPs for each group, our Wave-ViT variants consistently achieve better performances against the existing vision backbones, including both CNN backbones (*e.g.*, ResNet and SE-ResNet), single-scale ViTs (*e.g.*, TNT, CaiT, and CrossViT), and multi-scale ViTs (*e.g.*, Swin, Twins-SVT, PVTv2, VOLO). In particular, under the Base size, the Top-1 accuracy score of Wave-ViT-B* can reach 84.8%, which leads to the absolute improvement of 0.6% against the best competitive VOLO-D1* (Top-1 accuracy: 84.2%). Moreover, when removing the upgraded strategies as in VOLO for training, our Wave-ViT-S still manages to outperform the best multi-scale ViT in Small size (PVTv2-B2). These results generally demonstrate the key advantage of unifying self-attention learning and invertible down-sampling with wavelet transforms to facilitate visual representation learning. Most specifically, under the same Large size, compared to ResNet-152 and SE-ResNet-152 that solely capitalize on CNN architectures, the single-scale ViTs (*e.g.*, TNT-B, CaiT-S36, and CrossViT-15-384) outperform them by capturing long-range dependency via Transformer structure. However, the performances of CaiT-S36 and CrossViT-15-384 are still lower than most multi-scale ViTs (PVTv2-B5 and VOLO-D3*) that aggregates multi-scale contexts for image recognition. Furthermore, instead of using irreversible down-sampling for self-attention learning in PVTv2-B5, our Wave-ViT-L* enables invertible down-sampling with wavelet transforms, and thus achieves better efficiency-vs-accuracy trade-off. It is worthy to note that VOLO-D3* does not employ down-sampling operations to reduce computational cost for high-resolution inputs, but instead directly reduces the input resolution $(28 \times 28)$ at initial stage. In contrast, Wave-ViT-L* keeps the high-resolution inputs $(56 \times 56)$, and exploits wavelet transforms to trigger lossless down-sampling for multi-scale self-attention learning, leading to performance boosts.

## 4.2   Object Detection and Instance Segmentation on COCO

**Dataset and Optimization Setups.** Here we examine the pre-trained Wave-ViT's behavior on COCO for two tasks that localize objects ranging from bounding-box level to pixel level, *i.e.*, object detection and instance segmentation. Two mainstream detectors, *i.e.*, RetinaNet [31] and Mask R-CNN [20], are employed for each downstream task, and we replace the CNN backbones in each detector with our Wave-ViT for evaluation. Specifically, each vision backbone is first pre-trained over ImageNet1K, and the newly added layers are initialized with Xavier [17]. Next, we follow the standard setups in [35] to train all models on the COCO train2017 (~118K images). Here the batch size is set as 16, and AdamW [39] is utilized for optimization (weight decay: 0.05, initial learning rate: 0.0001). All models are finally evaluated on the COCO val2017 (5K images). For the downstream task of object detection, we report the Average Precision($AP$) at different IoU thresholds and for three different object sizes (*i.e.*, small, medium, large (S/M/L)). For the downstream task of instance segmentation, both bounding box and mask Average Precision (*i.e.*, $AP^b$, $AP^m$) are reported. During training, we resize each input training image by fixing the shorter side as 800 pixels and meanwhile making the longer side not exceeding 1,333 pixels. Note that for RetinaNet and Mask R-CNN, 1 × training schedule

**Table 3.** The performances of various vision backbones on COCO val2017 for object detection and instance segmentation tasks. For object detection, we employ RetinaNet as the object detector, and the Average Precision($AP$) at different IoU thresholds or three different object sizes (*i.e.*, small, medium, large (S/M/L)) are reported for evaluation. For instance segmentation, we adopt Mask R-CNN as the base model, and the bounding box and mask Average Precision (*i.e.*, $AP^b$ and $AP^m$) are reported for evaluation. We group all vision backbones into two categories: Small size and Base size.

| Backbone | RetinaNet 1x [31] | | | | | | Mask R-CNN 1x [20] | | | | | |
|---|---|---|---|---|---|---|---|---|---|---|---|---|
| | $AP$ | $AP_{50}$ | $AP_{75}$ | $AP_S$ | $AP_M$ | $AP_L$ | $AP^b$ | $AP^b_{50}$ | $AP^b_{75}$ | $AP^m$ | $AP^m_{50}$ | $AP^m_{75}$ |
| ResNet50 [21] | 36.3 | 55.3 | 38.6 | 19.3 | 40.0 | 48.8 | 38.0 | 58.6 | 41.4 | 34.4 | 55.1 | 36.7 |
| Swin-T [35] | 41.5 | 62.1 | 44.2 | 25.1 | 44.9 | 55.5 | 42.2 | 64.6 | 46.2 | 39.1 | 61.6 | 42.0 |
| Twins-SVT-S [9] | 43.0 | 64.2 | 46.3 | 28.0 | 46.4 | 57.5 | 43.4 | 66.0 | 47.3 | 40.3 | 63.2 | 43.4 |
| RegionViT-S [6] | 43.9 | – | – | – | – | – | 44.2 | – | – | 40.8 | – | – |
| PVTv2-B2 [59] | 44.6 | 65.6 | 47.6 | 27.4 | 48.8 | 58.6 | 45.3 | 67.1 | 49.6 | 41.2 | 64.2 | 44.4 |
| Wave-ViT-S | **45.8** | **67.0** | **49.4** | **29.2** | **50.0** | **60.8** | **46.6** | **68.7** | **51.2** | **42.4** | **65.5** | **45.8** |
| ResNet101 [21] | 38.5 | 57.8 | 41.2 | 21.4 | 42.6 | 51.1 | 40.4 | 61.1 | 44.2 | 40.4 | 61.1 | 44.2 |
| ResNeXt101-32x4d [64] | 39.9 | 59.6 | 42.7 | 22.3 | 44.2 | 52.5 | 41.9 | 62.5 | 45.9 | 37.5 | 59.4 | 40.2 |
| Swin-S [35] | 44.5 | 65.7 | 47.5 | 27.4 | 48.0 | 59.9 | 44.8 | 66.6 | 48.9 | 40.9 | 63.4 | 44.2 |
| Twins-SVT-B [9] | 45.3 | 66.7 | 48.1 | 28.5 | 48.9 | 60.6 | 45.2 | 67.6 | 49.3 | 41.5 | 64.5 | 44.8 |
| RegionViT-B [6] | 44.6 | – | – | – | – | – | 45.4 | – | – | 41.6 | – | – |
| PVTv2-B3 [59] | 45.9 | 66.8 | 49.3 | 28.6 | 49.8 | 61.4 | 47.0 | 68.1 | 51.7 | 42.5 | 65.7 | 45.7 |
| Wave-ViT-B | **47.2** | **68.2** | **50.9** | **29.7** | **51.4** | **62.3** | **47.6** | **69.1** | **52.4** | **43.0** | **66.4** | **46.0** |

**Table 4.** The performances of various vision backbones on COCO val2017 for object detection. Four kinds of object detectors, *i.e.*, GFL [28], Sparse RCNN [49], Cascade Mask R-CNN [3], and ATSS [73] in mmdetection [7], are adopted for evaluation. We report the bounding box Average Precision ($AP^b$) in different IoU thresholds.

| Backbone | Method | $AP^b$ | $AP^b_{50}$ | $AP^b_{75}$ | Backbone | Method | $AP^b$ | $AP^b_{50}$ | $AP^b_{75}$ |
|---|---|---|---|---|---|---|---|---|---|
| ResNet50 [21] | GFL [28] | 44.5 | 63.0 | 48.3 | ResNet50 [21] | Sparse R-CNN [49] | 44.5 | 63.4 | 48.2 |
| Swin-T [35] | | 47.6 | 66.8 | 51.7 | Swin-T [35] | | 47.9 | 67.3 | 52.3 |
| PVTv2-B2 [59] | | 50.2 | 69.4 | 54.7 | PVTv2-B2 [59] | | 50.1 | 69.5 | 54.9 |
| Wave-ViT-S | | **50.9** | **70.2** | **55.4** | Wave-ViT-S | | **50.7** | **70.4** | **55.5** |
| ResNet50 [21] | Cascade Mask R-CNN [3] | 46.3 | 64.3 | 50.5 | ResNet50 [21] | ATSS [73] | 43.5 | 61.9 | 47.0 |
| Swin-T [35] | | 50.5 | 69.3 | 54.9 | Swin-T [35] | | 47.2 | 66.5 | 51.3 |
| PVTv2-B2 [59] | | 51.1 | 69.8 | 55.3 | PVTv2-B2 [59] | | 49.9 | 69.1 | 54.1 |
| Wave-ViT-S | | **52.1** | **70.7** | **56.6** | Wave-ViT-S | | **50.7** | **69.8** | **55.5** |

(*i.e.*, 12 epochs) is adopted to train the two mainstream detectors. In addition to RetinaNet, we also include four state-of-the-arts detectors (GFL [28], Sparse RCNN [49], Cascade Mask R-CNN [3], and ATSS [73]) for object detection task. Following [35,59], we utilize 3 × schedule (*i.e.*, 36 epochs) with multi-scale strategy for training, and the shorter side of each input image is randomly resized within the range of [480, 800] while the longer side is forced to be less than 1,333 pixels.

**Performance Comparison.** Table 3 lists the performance comparisons across different pre-trained vision backbones under the base detector of RetinaNet and Mask R-CNN for object detection and instance segmentation, respectively. Note that we follow the evaluation for image recognition by grouping all the pre-trained backbones into two categories (*i.e.*, Small size and Base size). As shown in this table, the performance trends in each downstream task are similar to those in image recognition task. Concretely, under the similar model size for each group, the multi-scale ViT backbones (*e.g.*, Swin-T/S and PVTv2-B2/B3) consistently exhibit better performances than CNN backbones (*e.g.*, ResNet50/101) across all evaluation metrics. Furthermore, by capitalizing on wavelet transforms to enable lossless down-sampling in multi-scale self-attention learning, Wave-ViT variants outperform PVTv2-B2/B3 that explore sub-optimal down-sampling with pooling kernels. The results confirm that unifying self-attention learning and lossless down-sampling with wavelet transforms can improve the transfer capability of pre-trained multi-scale representations on dense prediction tasks.

To further verify the generalizability of the pre-trained multi-scale features via Wave-ViT for object detection, we evaluate various pre-trained vision backbones on four state-of-the-arts detectors (GFL, Sparse RCNN, Cascade Mask R-CNN, and ATSS). Table 4 shows the detailed performances of four object detectors with different pre-trained vision backbones under Small size. Similar to the observations in the base detector of RetinaNet, our Wave-ViT-S achieves consistent performance gains against both CNN backbone (ResNet50) and multi-scale ViT backbones (Swin-T and PVTv2-B2) across all the four state-of-the-

**Table 5.** The performances of various vision backbones on ADE20K validation dataset for semantic segmentation. We employ the commonly adopted base model (UPerNet) and report the mean IoU (mIoU) averaged over all classes for evaluation. We group all vision backbones into two categories: Small size and Base size.

| Small | | | Base | | |
|---|---|---|---|---|---|
| Method | Backbone | mIoU | Method | Backbone | mIoU |
| UPerNet [63] | ResNet-50 [21] | 42.8 | UPerNet [63] | ResNet-101 [21] | 44.9 |
| UPerNet [63] | DeiT-S [51] | 43.8 | UPerNet [63] | DeiT-B [51] | 47.2 |
| DeeplabV3 [8] | ResNeSt-50 [70] | 45.1 | DeeplabV3 [8] | ResNeSt-101 [70] | 46.9 |
| Semantic FPN [25] | PVTv2-B2 [59] | 45.2 | Semantic FPN [25] | PVTv2-B3 [59] | 47.3 |
| UPerNet [63] | RegionViT-S [6] | 45.3 | UPerNet [63] | RegionViT-B [6] | 47.5 |
| UPerNet [63] | Swin-T [35] | 45.8 | UPerNet [63] | Twins-SVT-B [9] | 48.9 |
| UPerNet [63] | Twins-SVT-S [9] | 47.1 | UPerNet [63] | Swin-S [35] | 49.5 |
| UPerNet [63] | Wave-ViT-S | **49.6** | UPerNet [63] | Wave-ViT-B | **51.5** |

arts detectors. This again validates the advantage of integrating multi-scale self-attention with invertible down-sampling in our Wave-ViT for object detection.

### 4.3   Semantic Segmentation on ADE20K

**Dataset and Optimization Setups.** We next evaluate our pre-trained Wave-ViT in the downstream task of semantic segmentation on ADE20K dataset. This dataset is the most typical benchmark for evaluating semantic segmentation techniques, which consists of 25K images (20K training images, 2K validation images, and 3K testing images) derived from 150 semantic categories. Here we choose the commonly adopted UPerNet [63] as the base model for this task and the CNN backbone in primary UPerNet is replaced with our Wave-ViT. During training, we train the models on 8 GPUs for 160K iterations via AdamW [39] optimizer (batch size: 16, initial learning rate: 0.00006, weight decay: 0.01). Both linear learning rate decay scheduler and a linear warmup of 1,500 iterations are utilized for optimization. The scale of input images is fixed as $512 \times 512$. We perform the random horizontal flipping, random photometric distortion, and random re-scaling within the ratio range [0.5, 2.0] as data augmentations. We report the metric of mean IoU (mIoU) averaged over all classes for evaluation. For fair comparison with other vision backbones for semantic segmentation downstream task, we set all the hyperparameters and detection heads as in Swin [35].

**Performance Comparison.** Table 5 shows the mIoU scores of different pre-trained vision backbones under the base models (*e.g.*, UPerNet, DeeplabV3, Semantic FPN) for semantic segmentation. As in the evaluation for image recognition, object detection, and instance segmentation tasks, we group all the pre-trained backbones into two categories (*i.e.*, Small size and Base size). Similarly, by upgrading multi-scale self-attention learning with Wavelet based invertible down-sampling, our Wave-ViT variants yield consistent gains against both CNN

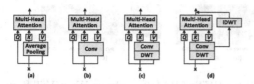

| | Params | GFLOPs | Top-1 | Top-5 |
|---|---|---|---|---|
| a | 18.7M | 3.9 | 82.0 | 96.0 |
| b | 20.4M | 4.0 | 82.0 | 96.0 |
| c | 19.8M | 4.3 | 82.5 | 96.1 |
| d | 19.8M | 4.3 | **82.7** | **96.2** |

**Fig. 3.** Performance comparisons across different ways on designing self-attention blocks with down-sampling in multi-scale ViT backbones (under Small size): (a) self-attention block with irreversible down-sampling operation of average pooling, (b) self-attention block with irreversible down-sampling operation of pooling kernels, (c) a degraded version of Wavelets block that solely equips self-attention block with invertible down-sampling via wavelet transforms (DWT), and (d) the full version of our Wavelets block with inverse wavelet transforms (IDWT).

backbones (*e.g.*, ResNet-50/101 and ResNeSt-50/101) and existing multi-scale ViT backbones (*e.g.*, Swin-T/S and Twins-SVT-S/B). Concretely, under a comparable model size within each group, Wave-ViT-S/B achieves 49.6%/51.5% mIoU on ADE20K validation dataset, which absolutely improves the best competitor Twins-SVT-S/Swin-S (47.1%/49.5%) with 2.5%/2.0%. The results basically demonstrates the superiority of Wave-ViT for semantic segmentation task.

### 4.4  Ablation Study

We investigate how each design in Wavelets block influences the overall performance on ImageNet1K for image recognition, as summarized in Fig. 3. All the variants here are constructed under Small size for fair comparison.

**Block (a)** is a typical self-attention block with irreversible down-sampling. By directly operating average pooling over the input keys/values, (a) significantly reduces the computational cost for self-attention learning and the Top-1 score achieves 82.0%. **Block (b)** is another typical self-attention block with irreversible down-sampling via pooling kernels (convolution), rather than average pooling in (a). (b) reduces the spatial dimension of keys/values through pooling kernels, leading to the same performances as in (a). However, the number of parameters is inevitably increased. **Block (c)** can be regarded as a degraded version of our Wavelets block, that solely equips self-attention block with invertible down-sampling based on wavelet transforms (DWT). Compared to the most efficient (a) with irreversible down-sampling, the Top-1 score of (c) increases from 82.0% to 82.5%. This validates the effectiveness of unifying self-attention block and invertible down-sampling without information dropping. **Block (d)** (*i.e.*, the full version of Wavelets block) further upgrades (c) by additionally exploiting inverse wavelet transforms (IDWT) to strengthen outputs with enlarged receptive field. Such design leads to performance boosts in Top-1 and Top-5 scores, with negligible increase in computational cost/memory.

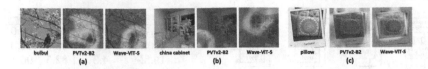

**Fig. 4.** Visualization of Score-CAM [54] for PVTv2-B2 [59] and our Wave-ViT-S on six images in ImageNet1K dataset.

### 4.5  Visualization of Learnt Visual Representation

In order to further explain the visual representations learnt by our Wave-ViT, we produce the saliency map through Score-CAM [54] to identify the importance of each pixel in presenting the class discrimination of the input image. Figure 4 visualizes the saliency map derived from the visual representations learnt by two backbones with similar model size (PVTv2-B2 and our Wave-ViT-S). As illustrated in the figure, Wave-ViT-S consistently shows higher concentration at the semantically relevant object than PVTv2-B2, which validates that the representations learnt by Wave-ViT-S are more robust.

## 5  Conclusions

In this paper, we delve into the idea of unifying typical Transformer module and invertible down-sampling, thereby pursuing efficient multi-scale self-attention learning with lossless down-sampling. To verify our claim, we present a new principled Transformer module, *i.e.*, Wavelets block, that capitalizes on Discrete Wavelet Transform (DWT) to perform invertible down-sampling over keys/values in self-attention learning. In addition, we adopt inverse DWT (IDWT) to reconstruct the down-sampled DWT outputs, which are utilized to strengthen the outputs of Wavelets block by aggregating local contexts with enlarged receptive field. Our Wavelets block is appealing in view that it is feasible to construct multi-scale ViT backbone with Wavelets blocks, with light computational cost/memory budget. In particular, by operating stacked Wavelets blocks over multi-scale features in four-stage architecture, a series of Wavelet Vision Transformer (Wave-ViT) are designed with different model sizes. We empirically validate the superiority of Wave-ViT over the state-of-the-art multi-scale ViTs for several mainstream CV tasks, under comparable numbers of parameters.

## References

1. Bae, W., Yoo, J., Chul Ye, J.: Beyond deep residual learning for image restoration: persistent homology-guided manifold simplification. In: CVPR Workshops (2017)
2. Bello, I., Zoph, B., Vaswani, A., Shlens, J., Le, Q.V.: Attention augmented convolutional networks. In: ICCV (2019)
3. Cai, Z., Vasconcelos, N.: Cascade r-cnn: delving into high quality object detection. In: CVPR (2018)

4. Carion, N., Massa, F., Synnaeve, G., Usunier, N., Kirillov, A., Zagoruyko, S.: End-to-end object detection with transformers. In: ECCV (2020)
5. Chen, C.F., Fan, Q., Panda, R.: Crossvit: cross-attention multi-scale vision transformer for image classification. In: ICCV (2021)
6. Chen, C.F., Panda, R., Fan, Q.: Regionvit: regional-to-local attention for vision transformers. In: ICLR (2022)
7. Chen, K., et al.: Mmdetection: open mmlab detection toolbox and benchmark. arXiv preprint arXiv:1906.07155 (2019)
8. Chen, L.C., Zhu, Y., Papandreou, G., Schroff, F., Adam, H.: Encoder-decoder with atrous separable convolution for semantic image segmentation. In: ECCV (2018)
9. Chu, X., et al.: Twins: revisiting the design of spatial attention in vision transformers. In: NeurIPS (2021)
10. Cubuk, E.D., Zoph, B., Shlens, J., Le, Q.V.: Randaugment: practical automated data augmentation with a reduced search space. In: CVPR Workshops (2020)
11. dAscoli, S., Touvron, H., Leavitt, M.L., Morcos, A.S., Biroli, G., Sagun, L.: Convit: improving vision transformers with soft convolutional inductive biases. In: ICML (2021)
12. Deng, J., Dong, W., Socher, R., Li, L.J., Li, K., Fei-Fei, L.: Imagenet: a large-scale hierarchical image database. In: CVPR (2009)
13. Dosovitskiy, A., et al.: An image is worth 16 x 16 words: transformers for image recognition at scale. In: ICLR (2020)
14. Fan, H., et al.: Multiscale vision transformers. In: ICCV (2021)
15. Fujieda, S., Takayama, K., Hachisuka, T.: Wavelet convolutional neural networks. arXiv preprint arXiv:1805.08620 (2018)
16. Gao, S.H., Cheng, M.M., Zhao, K., Zhang, X.Y., Yang, M.H., Torr, P.: Res2net: a new multi-scale backbone architecture. In: IEEE TPMAI (2021)
17. Glorot, X., Bengio, Y.: Understanding the difficulty of training deep feedforward neural networks. In: AISTATS (2010)
18. Guo, T., Seyed Mousavi, H., Huu Vu, T., Monga, V.: Deep wavelet prediction for image super-resolution. In: CVPR Workshops (2017)
19. Han, K., Xiao, A., Wu, E., Guo, J., Xu, C., Wang, Y.: Transformer in transformer. In: NeurIPS (2021)
20. He, K., Gkioxari, G., Dollár, P., Girshick, R.: Mask r-cnn. In: ICCV (2017)
21. He, K., Zhang, X., Ren, S., Sun, J.: Deep residual learning for image recognition. In: CVPR (2016)
22. Hu, H., Zhang, Z., Xie, Z., Lin, S.: Local relation networks for image recognition. In: ICCV (2019)
23. Hu, J., Shen, L., Sun, G.: Squeeze-and-excitation networks. In: CVPR (2018)
24. Jiang, Z.H., et al.: All tokens matter: token labeling for training better vision transformers. In: NeurIPS (2021)
25. Kirillov, A., Girshick, R., He, K., Dollár, P.: Panoptic feature pyramid networks. In: CVPR (2019)
26. Krizhevsky, A., Sutskever, I., Hinton, G.E.: Imagenet classification with deep convolutional neural networks. In: NeurIPS (2012)
27. LeCun, Y., Bottou, L., Bengio, Y., Haffner, P.: Gradient-based learning applied to document recognition. In: Proceedings of the IEEE (1998)
28. Li, X., et al.: Generalized focal loss: Learning qualified and distributed bounding boxes for dense object detection. In: NeurIPS (2020)
29. Li, Y., Pan, Y., Yao, T., Mei, T.: Comprehending and ordering semantics for image captioning. In: CVPR (2022)

30. Li, Y., Yao, T., Pan, Y., Mei, T.: Contextual transformer networks for visual recognition. In: IEEE TPAMI (2022)
31. Lin, T.Y., Goyal, P., Girshick, R., He, K., Dollár, P.: Focal loss for dense object detection. In: ICCV (2017)
32. Lin, T.Y., et al.: Microsoft coco: common objects in context. In: ECCV (2014)
33. Liu, L., et al.: Wavelet-based dual-branch network for image demoiréing. In: ECCV (2020)
34. Liu, P., Zhang, H., Zhang, K., Lin, L., Zuo, W.: Multi-level wavelet-cnn for image restoration. In: CVPR Workshops (2018)
35. Liu, Z., et al.: Swin transformer: hierarchical vision transformer using shifted windows. In: ICCV (2021)
36. Long, F., Qiu, Z., Pan, Y., Yao, T., Luo, J., Mei, T.: Stand-alone inter-frame attention in video models. In: CVPR (2022)
37. Long, F., Qiu, Z., Pan, Y., Yao, T., Ngo, C.W., Mei, T.: Dynamic temporal filtering in video models. In: ECCV (2022)
38. Loshchilov, I., Hutter, F.: Sgdr: stochastic gradient descent with warm restarts. arXiv preprint arXiv:1608.03983 (2016)
39. Loshchilov, I., Hutter, F.: Decoupled weight decay regularization. arXiv preprint arXiv:1711.05101 (2017)
40. Mallat, S.G.: A theory for multiresolution signal decomposition: the wavelet representation. In: IEEE TPAMI (1989)
41. Oyallon, E., Belilovsky, E., Zagoruyko, S.: Scaling the scattering transform: deep hybrid networks. In: ICCV (2017)
42. Pan, Y., et al.: Smart director: an event-driven directing system for live broadcasting. In: ACM TOMM (2021)
43. Pan, Y., Yao, T., Li, Y., Mei, T.: X-linear attention networks for image captioning. In: CVPR (2020)
44. Ramachandran, P., Parmar, N., Vaswani, A., Bello, I., Levskaya, A., Shlens, J.: Stand-alone self-attention in vision models. In: NeurIPS (2019)
45. Ruan, B.K., Shuai, H.H., Cheng, W.H.: Vision transformers: state of the art and research challenges. arXiv preprint arXiv:2207.03041 (2022)
46. Simonyan, K., Zisserman, A.: Very deep convolutional networks for large-scale image recognition. In: ICLR (2015)
47. Srinivas, A., Lin, T.Y., Parmar, N., Shlens, J., Abbeel, P., Vaswani, A.: Bottleneck transformers for visual recognition. In: CVPR (2021)
48. Su, Z., Zhang, H., Chen, J., Pang, L., Ngo, C.W., Jiang, Y.G.: Adaptive split-fusion transformer. arXiv preprint arXiv:2204.12196 (2022)
49. Sun, P., et al.: Sparse r-cnn: end-to-end object detection with learnable proposals. In: CVPR (2021)
50. Szegedy, C., et al.: Going deeper with convolutions. In: CVPR (2015)
51. Touvron, H., Cord, M., Douze, M., Massa, F., Sablayrolles, A., Jégou, H.: Training data-efficient image transformers & distillation through attention. In: ICML (2021)
52. Touvron, H., Cord, M., Sablayrolles, A., Synnaeve, G., Jégou, H.: Going deeper with image transformers. In: ICCV (2021)
53. Vaswani, A., et al.: Attention is all you need. In: NeurIPS (2017)
54. Wang, H., et al.: Score-cam: score-weighted visual explanations for convolutional neural networks. In: CVPR workshops (2020)
55. Wang, J., et al.: Deep high-resolution representation learning for visual recognition. In: IEEE TPAMI (2020)
56. Wang, J., et al.: Objectformer for image manipulation detection and localization. In: CVPR (2022)

57. Wang, P., et al.: Scaled relu matters for training vision transformers. arXiv preprint arXiv:2109.03810 (2021)
58. Wang, R., et al.: Bevt: bert pretraining of video transformers. In: CVPR (2022)
59. Wang, W., et al.: Pvtv 2: improved baselines with pyramid vision transformer. arXiv preprint arXiv:2106.13797 (2021)
60. Wang, W., et al.: Pyramid vision transformer: a versatile backbone for dense prediction without convolutions. In: ICCV (2021)
61. Williams, T., Li, R.: Wavelet pooling for convolutional neural networks. In: ICLR (2018)
62. Wu, H., Xiao, B., Codella, N., Liu, M., Dai, X., Yuan, L., Zhang, L.: Cvt: introducing convolutions to vision transformers. In: ICCV (2021)
63. Xiao, T., Liu, Y., Zhou, B., Jiang, Y., Sun, J.: Unified perceptual parsing for scene understanding. In: ECCV (2018)
64. Xie, S., Girshick, R., Dollár, P., Tu, Z., He, K.: Aggregated residual transformations for deep neural networks. In: CVPR (2017)
65. Xu, W., Xu, Y., Chang, T., Tu, Z.: Co-scale conv-attentional image transformers. In: ICCV (2021)
66. Yang, J., et al.: Focal self-attention for local-global interactions in vision transformers. arXiv preprint arXiv:2107.00641 (2021)
67. Yao, T., Li, Y., Pan, Y., Wang, Y., Zhang, X.P., Mei, T.: Dual vision transformer. arXiv preprint arXiv:2207.04976 (2022)
68. Yuan, L., et al.: Tokens-to-token vit: training vision transformers from scratch on imagenet. In: ICCV (2021)
69. Yuan, L., Hou, Q., Jiang, Z., Feng, J., Yan, S.: Volo: vision outlooker for visual recognition. arXiv preprint arXiv:2106.13112 (2021)
70. Zhang, H., et al.: Resnest: split-attention networks. arXiv preprint arXiv:2004.08955 (2020)
71. Zhang, H., Hao, Y., Ngo, C.W.: Token shift transformer for video classification. In: ACM Multimedia (2021)
72. Zhang, R.: Making convolutional networks shift-invariant again. In: ICML (2019)
73. Zhang, S., Chi, C., Yao, Y., Lei, Z., Li, S.Z.: Bridging the gap between anchor-based and anchor-free detection via adaptive training sample selection. In: CVPR (2020)
74. Zhang, Y., Pan, Y., Yao, T., Huang, R., Mei, T., Chen, C.W.: Exploring structure-aware transformer over interaction proposals for human-object interaction detection. In: CVPR (2022)
75. Zhao, H., Jia, J., Koltun, V.: Exploring self-attention for image recognition. In: CVPR (2020)
76. Zhong, Z., Zheng, L., Kang, G., Li, S., Yang, Y.: Random erasing data augmentation. In: AAAI (2020)
77. Zhou, B., et al.: Semantic understanding of scenes through the ade20k dataset. In: IJCV (2019)
78. Zhou, D., et al.: Deepvit: towards deeper vision transformer. arXiv preprint arXiv:2103.11886 (2021)

# Tailoring Self-Supervision for Supervised Learning

WonJun Moon, Ji-Hwan Kim, and Jae-Pil Heo[✉]

Sungkyunkwan University, Suwon, South Korea
{wjun0830,damien,jaepilheo}@skku.edu

**Abstract.** Recently, it is shown that deploying a proper self-supervision is a prospective way to enhance the performance of supervised learning. Yet, the benefits of self-supervision are not fully exploited as previous pretext tasks are specialized for unsupervised representation learning. To this end, we begin by presenting three desirable properties for such auxiliary tasks to assist the supervised objective. First, the tasks need to guide the model to learn rich features. Second, the transformations involved in the self-supervision should not significantly alter the training distribution. Third, the tasks are preferred to be light and generic for high applicability to prior arts. Subsequently, to show how existing pretext tasks can fulfill these and be tailored for supervised learning, we propose a simple auxiliary self-supervision task, predicting localizable rotation (**LoRot**). Our exhaustive experiments validate the merits of LoRot as a pretext task tailored for supervised learning in terms of robustness and generalization capability. Our code is available at https://github.com/wjun0830/Localizable-Rotation.

**Keywords:** Pretext task · Auxiliary self-supervision · Supervised learning

## 1 Introduction

Beyond the success in visual recognition without human supervision [5,8,19,56, 57,61], there have been attempts to adopt self-supervision to supervised learning. Pioneering methods demonstrated that self-supervision indeed improves robustness along with human guidance [4,29,50]. They utilized self-supervision as an auxiliary task to support the feature learning. However, as these methods utilize the existing self-supervisions specialized for unsupervised representation learning, the benefits of self-supervision are restrained. Specifically, self-supervision is generally designed for representation learning which is performed better by the primary objective of supervised learning. Furthermore, employed transformations for pretext tasks often trigger significant data distribution shifts. For instance, rotation task, the most popular self-supervision in supervised domain,

**Supplementary Information** The online version contains supplementary material available at https://doi.org/10.1007/978-3-031-19806-9_20.

is not an exception since learning rotation-invariant features barely help the primary task [22,35]. In fact, rotation task only achieves insignificant gains or sometimes even degrades the performance when applied in the form of multi-task learning or as an augmentation technique [10,35]. This motivates us to develop a complementary pretext task to supervised objectives.

Therefore, in this paper, we first introduce three desirable properties of auxiliary self-supervision to maximize the benefits in supervised learning: 1) learning rich representations, 2) maintaining data distribution, 3) providing high applicability. First, the pretext task should guide the model to learn complementary features with the original ones from supervised learning. Models trained only with a primary task such as the classification often focuses on most discriminative parts of objects where such features provide shortcuts to solve the problem [20,46]. Thus, the primary goal of an auxiliary task is to help the model to capture additional detailed features, which are known to improve the robustness of the model such as detecting out-of-distribution samples as well as its accuracy [29]. Second, the transformation itself should not bring significant data distribution shifts. Although an ideal convolutional neural network (CNN) should be invariant to the transformations such as translation or rotation [42], in realistic circumstances, the shift of global views of images is often known to be harmful to classification tasks [10,53]. Third, the pretext task is preferred to be highly applicable to existing model architectures and strategies of supervised learning in terms of the computational overhead and the amount of modification.

To validate the importance of these properties, we propose an auxiliary self-supervision task tailored for supervised learning, Localizable Rotation (LoRot), which forms the localization quizzes by rotating only a part of an image. Note that we choose rotation task to be modified into a tailored version for supervised domain on behalf of other pretext tasks due to its effectiveness of localizing the salient objects following previous works [29,35]. LoRot provides complementary benefits to supervised learning since the model should first localize the patch to solve the rotation task. Specifically, it encourages the model to learn rich features for rotational clues within a part of the image even if they are less discriminative for the supervised objectives. Furthermore, we found that rotating a small patch does not incur a significant data distribution shifts. Finally, the LoRot requires small extra computational costs and implementation efforts, since it is designed for multi-task learning that only requires one additional classifier. In our extensive experiments, we validate that LoRot is effective at boosting the robustness and generalization capability of supervised models and even provides state-of-the-art results. Specifically, we evaluate LoRot on various tasks including out-of-distribution (OOD) detection, imbalanced classification, adversarial attack, image classification, localization, and transfer learning in Sect. 4.

## 2 Related Work

**Self-supervised Learning.** Self-supervised learning has received considerable attention in past years. Its typical objective is to learn general features through solving pretext tasks. According to the number of instances to define pretext tasks, we can categorize the self-supervision into two groups, relation- and transformation-based ones. Relation-based approaches learn features to increase the similarity among a sample [6,10,11,25,54] and its transformed positive instances while some also treat other training samples as negative instances. The memory bank [25,43] and in-batch [10,59] samplings are notable negative instance selection techniques. In contrast, there have been approaches to only use the positive pairs with siamese networks [6,24] or adding a relation module [49]. Moreover, transform-based self-supervision is another main stream of representation learning that substantial efforts are made. Remarkable methods are generating surrogate classes with data augmentation [18], predicting the relative position of patches [16], solving jigsaw puzzle [9,32,44,47,48], and predicting the degree of rotation [22]. LoRot also belongs to transform-based self-supervision but is devised for a different objective: to assist supervised learning.

Meanwhile, there have been new attempts to transfer the benefits of self-supervisions to supervised learning. SupCLR [31] modified the relation-based self-supervision framework to directly take advantage of labeled data since the class labels clearly define both positive and negative instances. Moreover, self-label augmentation (SLA) augmented the label space based on the Cartesian product of the supervised class label set and the data transformations label set because learning auxiliary pretext task degrades the performance [35]. In contrast, LoRot is an adequate self-supervision for supervised learning that can be directly applied to existing methods. Further discussion is in Sect. 3.1.

**Regional Data Transformation.** Data augmentation is one of the most popular ways to improve classification accuracy [12,37,63]. Among them, we introduce methods that modify local regions of an image. Cutout [15] and random erasing [65] randomly mask out square regions of input, while Cutmix [60] cuts and pastes rectangular regions from other samples. LoRot shares the property of editing the local patch with them, however, the main difference is that our transformation retains all information within the image and is a solvable task.

## 3    Methodology

We first discuss three desired properties for the auxiliary self-supervision for supervised learning in Sect. 3.1. Based on those, we introduce and discuss two forms of LoRot (Localizable Rotation): having explicit and implicit localization tasks, both tailored for supervised learning in Sect. 3.2.

### 3.1    Desired Properties in Supervised Learning

In this section, we discuss three preferred properties of auxiliary self-supervision for supervised learning: (i) extracting rich representation, (ii) maintaining distribution, and (iii) high applicability, and point out the limitations of previous self-supervised methods in the manner of supervised learning.

In typical training of CNN for the classification task, the model tends to focus on identifying class-specific highly discriminative features to reach a high training accuracy. However, these features usually cover a limited portion of the

**Table 1.** CIFAR10 classification accuracy (%) with rotation using different strategies.

|            | Accuracy |
|------------|----------|
| Baseline   | 95.01    |
| +Rot (DA)  | 92.76    |
| +Rot (MT)  | 93.38    |

**Table 2.** Distribution shift measured by affinity score (%). Lower the score, the transformation function triggers a larger distribution shift.

|              | Affinity |
|--------------|----------|
| Rotation [22]| 58.06    |
| LoRot-I      | 93.78    |
| LoRot-E      | 90.15    |

objects since other parts can be unnecessary to achieve high training accuracy. This phenomenon is often called shortcut learning [20]. It can be problematic when the model faces samples that do not belong to known classes but have the learned discriminative features [46]. In such cases, discovering rich features including detailed parts of objects can enhance the robustness of the model [50]. Auxiliary tasks for supervised learning can encourage the model to learn such less discriminative features with the complementary objectives [2,51]. For instance, the popular rotation prediction task [22] can spread the attention of the model toward object parts for predicting the degree of rotation. However, discriminative clues for predicting rotation degrees also exist, e.g., location and orientation. Indeed, the rotation prediction task requires the model to focus on high-level object parts, which are roughly the same image regions as the supervised classification task [22]. So thus, the supervised learning with the auxiliary rotation task is still limited to identifying the most discriminative parts for both tasks.

Multi-task learning is an efficient and effective strategy when there exist multi objectives. It only employs a single shared feature extractor and improves generalization by utilizing the domain-specific information contained in the training signals of related tasks [7,51]. To employ such a strategy, the transformation function should not incur the degree of the data distribution shift or should smooth the target label as the modified data distribution can impede the primary objective [60,63]. However, previous self-supervision [22,47] and following works in supervised domains [4,21,29,50] do not satisfy above which leads them to use inefficient ways to adopt in supervised domains (Discussed in next paragraph). Particularly, in Table 1, we conduct a simple experiment with the rotation task [22] to show how the classification result is affected when the transformed input is utilized to learn the primary task. In the table, using the global rotation [22] only as an data augmentation technique (DA) shows the degraded performance. Moreover, sharing the input features for multi-classifiers as the multi-task learning (MT) also provides worse performance than the supervised learning (Baseline). To support our claims, we measure the distribution shift. To quantitatively measure the distribution shift, we use the affinity score [23] on CIFAR-10 in Table 2. Affinity score is a metric to evaluate the distribution shift measured as follows:

$$\text{Affinity} = \frac{A(m, D'_{val})}{A(m, D_{val})}, \tag{1}$$

where $m$ is a model trained on training set, and $A(m, D)$ is the accuracy of $m$ on a dataset $D$. $D_{val}$ and $D'_{val}$ are the original and augmented validation

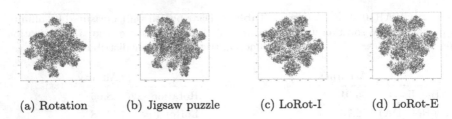

| (a) Rotation | (b) Jigsaw puzzle | (c) LoRot-I | (d) LoRot-E |

**Fig. 1.** t-SNE [40] visualization of feature distributions of original (Red) and transformed (Blue) test samples to see the data distribution shifts induced by each data transformation deployed in different self-supervision tasks. Embedding features are extracted from the last convolution layer by forwarding original and transformed test samples to ResNet18 [26] trained on the original train images of CIFAR-10.

sets, respectively. Furthermore, we also qualitatively show in Fig. 1 (a) and (b) that transformations from previous self-supervision lead distribution gap from its original one. Therefore, we can derive that the data distribution shift triggers unstable training and a new transformation that maintains the semantics of the image is needed to employ multi-task learning.

Applicability is an another important aspect of an auxiliary task in practical view. Devising lightweight architectures and methods is one of the current research trend [30]. However, since current self-supervised methods are not studied thoroughly in supervised learning, they often trigger high extra cost. Specifically, previous works [4,29,50] adopted self-supervision into the supervised domains in rather inefficient ways: parallel-task learning strategy or label augmentation strategy. We define parallel-task learning as each separate input sets being forwarded to handle each tasks in contrast to multi-task learning. For more details, See Fig. 3 (c). We further note that label augmentation requires all possible transformations to be applied per sample at both the training and inference times. At this point, when the usage of pretext tasks in the supervised domain is increasing on the sacrifice of expensive costs, applicability is the next mission for self-supervision to be more widely applied in supervised domains.

### 3.2   Localizable Rotation (LoRot)

Localizable rotation is designed to rotate a local region. To solve the localizable rotation task, the model should first localize the patch and then identify the high-level clues to predict the rotation degree, e.g., object parts such as eyes, tails, and heads within the patch [22]. Therefore, an explicit localization task to predict the position of the patch may not be necessary to guide the model to learn the localization capability. In this context, we introduce two versions of LoRot with explicit and implicit localization tasks as shown in Fig. 2. For the rest of this paper, we define LoRot-E and LoRot-I as each LoRot having the localization task explicitly and implicitly.

Let $X \in \mathbb{R}^{H \times W \times C}$ be a training image with the width $W$, height $H$, and channels $C$, and $y$ be its class label of supervised learning. Unless mentioned,

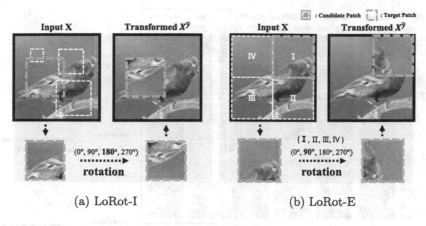

(a) LoRot-I                                    (b) LoRot-E

**Fig. 2.** Illustration of LoRot-I and LoRot-E. (a) LoRot-I draws and rotates a random patch from the image, while (b) LoRot-E chooses and rotates a cell from the predefined grid layout. For both methods, the degree of rotation is randomly chosen from $\{0°, 90°, 180°, 270°\}$. Note that, white and green boxes indicate possible and selected patches in this example, respectively.

LoRot is used in the form of multi-task learning with two classifiers each for the primary task and localizable rotation. Let also the feature extractor and two softmax classifiers be $F_\theta, \sigma_u$, and $\sigma_v$ parameterized by $\theta$, $u$ and $v$, respectively. We also define the transformation function $T$ and the pretext label $\hat{y}$ in which $T$ generates the transformed sample $X^{\hat{y}}$ as follows:

$$X^{\hat{y}} = T(X|\hat{y}, S), \tag{2}$$

where $S$ stands for patch selection strategy. We define possible rotation degrees to $(0, 90, 180, 270°)$ following the rotation task [22]. Then, as shown in Fig. 2, the number of classes for LoRot-I would be 4 and 16 for LoRot-E with the position in the 2x2 grid layout. Note that, for LoRot-E, we keep redundant cases with 0° at every cell as we pursue to place more weights on the original image.

Moreover, we define $P_u(X^{\hat{y}}) = \sigma_u(F_\theta(X^{\hat{y}}))$ and $P_v(X^{\hat{y}}) = \sigma_v(F_\theta(X^{\hat{y}}))$ as the probability distributions over the labels of the primary and pretext tasks, respectively. When $P^j(.)$ is the probability of the j-th class with a batch of $N$ training images $\{X_i\}_{i=1}^N$, the overall objective is:

$$\min_\theta -\frac{1}{N} \sum_{i=1}^N (\log(P_u^y(X_i^{\hat{y}})) + \lambda \log(P_v^{\hat{y}}(X_i^{\hat{y}}))), \tag{3}$$

where $\lambda$ is a hyperparameter to control the weight of learning LoRot.

**Patch Selection.** We use different strategies to generate patches for LoRot-E and LoRot-I. Simply put, we pre-define the 2x2 grid layout for LoRot-E to easily design the localization task. Then, the sampling method S does not need any parameters. Specifically, we divide each image into a $K \times K$ uniform grid and

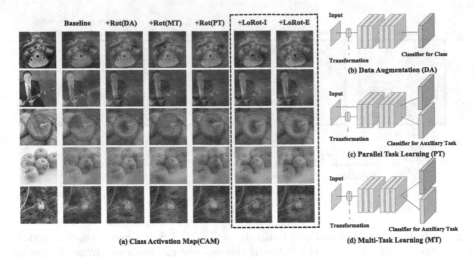

**Fig. 3.** (a) Comparison of class activation maps (CAMs) [66] of differently learned models. Rot indicates the global rotation task. DA, PT and MT stand for each strategy of utilizing the rotation task: Data Augmentation, Parallel-Task learning, and Multi-Task learning, as illustrated in (b), (c) and (d). DA and MT take augmented input to predict single- or multi-tasks. On the other hand, PT requires separate input batches to predict primary and auxiliary tasks, respectively. LoRot-I and LoRot-E are applied to the baseline by MT as designed. The CAMs show that our LoRot provide the activation of higher coverage to the object compared to global rotations. In other words, LoRot auxiliary task encourages the model to learn rich features. Best viewed in color.

rotate a single cell of the grid with the dimension of $\mathbb{R}^{\frac{H}{K} \times \frac{W}{K} \times C}$. In this paper, we set $K$ to 2 which each quadrant of an image can be the target.

Meanwhile, we choose random sampling method for LoRot-I. We randomly sample a length $l$ and the position of the top-left corner $(p_x, p_y)$ from the uniform distribution U to form sampling strategy $S$ as follows:

$$S(l, p_x, p_y) \begin{cases} l \sim \mathrm{U}(2, \min(\lfloor W/2 \rfloor, \lfloor H/2 \rfloor)), \\ p_x \sim \mathrm{U}(0, W - l), \\ p_y \sim \mathrm{U}(0, H - l) \end{cases} \tag{4}$$

Note that only a square-shaped patch is used in our work for simplicity. Also, we limit the length of the patch up to half of $\min(H, W)$ to prevent rotating an overly large region. Next, we detail how LoRot satisfies the desired properties.

**Rich Representations.** LoRot encourages the model to consider even the less-discriminative features by setting rotation prediction quizzes on different locations within an image. Particularly, the model should learn rich features to solve rotation tasks for patches of various sizes at different locations. One may ask that the LoRot can produce many useless features. For instance, the rotation problem with patches totally outside object regions can disturb learning good representations. However, this is alleviated by joint optimization with the supervised objective. Since the primary loss is rather dominant compared to LoRot's, such certainly unnecessary features are dropped throughout the training iterations. To support our argument, we investigate the class activation maps [66] of various models trained with only the primary task (Baseline), and the primary task with auxiliary tasks of global rotation (Rot(*)), and LoRot.

As shown in Fig. 3 (a), LoRot provides larger coverage of activations on the object compared to others. We also quantitatively validate the aforementioned in terms of model robustness and localization performance in Sect. 4. As discussed, LoRot discovers features and asks their necessity to the primary task. In Fig. 4, we show how LoRot discovers sub-discriminative features. Whenever the position of the patch moves, the model adjusts its focus to the other parts of the image to solve the auxiliary task. This also promotes the model to neglect unnecessary parts to solve specific LoRot tasks since the salient clues for predicting LoRot is random.

**Maintaining Data Distribution.** Unlike the existing transformations of pretext tasks, LoRot is less likely to incur data distribution shift since it only carries out geometric transformations locally. Specifically, most parts are kept intact in LoRot so that data distribution shift is restrained. Not just the smaller number of the transformed pixels but also the preserved high-level semantics contribute to keep the distribution close to the original one. In Fig. 1 (c) and (d), we observe that LoRot maintains the data distribution as the blue obscures the red in the embedding space. Affinity score also validates it as shown in Table 2.

**Fig. 4.** Class activation mapping visualizations for predicting LoRot. From top to bottom, we show that the model focuses on the high-level clues in the rotated patch at each quadrant, i.e., in the first column, the model spotlights the head, leg, wheel, and hand.

**Applicability.** To apply self-supervision of LoRot, we adopt multi-task learning so that a single transformed input is shared by both the primary and pretext tasks as shown in Fig. 3 (d). This provides the advantages in the computational cost and easy deployment to existing models since LoRot only requires one extra classifier without requiring multi-batches. In fact, previous pretext tasks usually require several times more samples to be forwarded and backpropagated to achieve their performances as they apply all possible transformations per sample [29,35]. Throughout Sect. 4, we validate LoRot's high applicability, a lightweight task boosting baselines' performances. Particularly, we observe that LoRot is not only complementary to standard baselines, but also to contrastive approaches in Table 3 and Table 8. This spotlights LoRot as an easily attachable self-supervised module for many supervised methods.

**Table 3.** AUROC scores for distinguishing in- and out-distribution data for image classification. The model is trained with CIFAR-10 dataset and evaluated on both CIFAR-10 and each OOD dataset. '*' indicates our reproduced version based on official implementations to unify the backbone network and training protocols. All experiments are averaged over five runs and '±' denotes the standard deviation. 'FS' and 'IN' stand for the number of forwarded samples to train each model and ImageNet, respectively.

| Method | SVHN | LSUN | IN | LSUN (FIX) | IN (FIX) | CIFAR-100 | FS |
|---|---|---|---|---|---|---|---|
| Cross Entropy* | $84.6_{\pm5.2}$ | $90.9_{\pm0.7}$ | $87.8_{\pm1.4}$ | $84.3_{\pm1.0}$ | $85.3_{\pm0.6}$ | $83.5_{\pm0.5}$ | 5M |
| Cutmix [60]* | $75.5_{\pm9.5}$ | $92.5_{\pm3.3}$ | $92.1_{\pm2.0}$ | $86.2_{\pm1.0}$ | $84.3_{\pm1.0}$ | $80.9_{\pm1.1}$ | 5M |
| SLA+SD [35]* | $89.1_{\pm4.4}$ | $90.7_{\pm1.3}$ | $89.8_{\pm0.8}$ | $82.9_{\pm1.6}$ | $86.0_{\pm0.7}$ | $83.6_{\pm0.4}$ | 20M |
| Rotations [29]* | $96.1_{\pm1.8}$ | $97.3_{\pm0.5}$ | $96.9_{\pm0.9}$ | $91.0_{\pm0.4}$ | $91.8_{\pm0.2}$ | $89.1_{\pm0.4}$ | 25M |
| SupCLR [31] | $97.3_{\pm0.1}$ | $92.8_{\pm0.5}$ | $91.4_{\pm1.2}$ | $91.6_{\pm1.5}$ | $90.5_{\pm0.5}$ | $88.6_{\pm0.2}$ | 70M |
| CSI [53] | $96.5_{\pm0.2}$ | $96.3_{\pm0.5}$ | $96.2_{\pm0.4}$ | $92.1_{\pm0.5}$ | $92.4_{\pm0.0}$ | $90.5_{\pm0.1}$ | 280M |
| LoRot-I | $92.6_{\pm2.1}$ | $\underline{98.6}_{\pm0.7}$ | $\underline{98.0}_{\pm0.8}$ | $94.4_{\pm0.9}$ | $93.6_{\pm1.0}$ | $90.1_{\pm0.7}$ | 5M |
| LoRot-E | $94.4_{\pm0.9}$ | $\mathbf{98.7}_{\pm0.6}$ | $\mathbf{98.1}_{\pm0.5}$ | $94.1_{\pm0.3}$ | $93.1_{\pm0.4}$ | $\underline{90.6}_{\pm0.3}$ | 5M |
| CSI+LoRot-I | $\mathbf{97.7}_{\pm0.6}$ | $98.3_{\pm0.1}$ | $\underline{98.0}_{\pm0.3}$ | $\mathbf{95.7}_{\pm0.1}$ | $\mathbf{95.6}_{\pm0.1}$ | $\mathbf{93.8}_{\pm0.0}$ | 280M |
| CSI+LoRot-E | $\underline{97.5}_{\pm0.4}$ | $98.0_{\pm0.2}$ | $97.8_{\pm0.1}$ | $\underline{95.5}_{\pm0.2}$ | $\underline{95.4}_{\pm0.2}$ | $\mathbf{93.8}_{\pm0.1}$ | 280M |

# 4  Experiments

We first examine the robustness of LoRot in Sect. 4.1 and validate the generalization capability in Sect. 4.2. Unless otherwise mentioned, LoRot is applied to supervised baseline with cross-entropy loss. For baselines, we compare rotation [22], the most popular pretext task in supervise domain, and previous works that adopted self-supervision in supervised domains (Rotations [29], SLA+SD [35], and SSP [58]). We also compare SOTA methods between benchmarks and show that contrastive learning is a complementary method, not our baseline. For other pretext tasks, we claim these are neither our baseline nor better than our baselines since our baselines are modified versions for supervised domain on top of existing pretext tasks. Throughout this section, we use bolds and underlines to represent the best and the second best scores. Furthermore, as LoRot is robust to $\lambda$, we set $\lambda$ to 0.1 for all experiments and further explore the effects of $\lambda$ in the supplementary.

## 4.1  Robustness

**Out-of-Distribution Detection** is to assess the model's uncertainty against unknown data. It is essential when deploying the model in real-world systems since DNNs are vulnerable to shortcut learning [20,27,46]. For the experiment, we train the model with CIFAR-10 [34] which we call it in-distribution dataset. Then, we use SVHN [45], resized ImageNet and LSUN [36], fixed versions of ImageNet and LSUN [53], and CIFAR-100 [34] as out-of-distribution datasets. We compare our method against the previous SOTA works on OOD detection [29,53] as well as approaches that utilize a rotation technique [35] and regional modification [60] to enhance the robustness. Unlike the previous SOTA works that require huge costs either at the training [53] or inference time [29] to yield their best performance, LoRot does not require huge costs neither at the training nor inference time. Indeed, we only take 3.6% of training time compared to [53] and 50% of inference time compared to [29] (Measured with 2 Quadro RTX 8000). Still, we acquired significant gains on detecting OOD samples. For fair comparison, we use the ResNet18 [26] following the previous SOTA work [53] to unify the benchmarks.

**Table 4.** Imbalanced classification accuracy (%) on CIFAR-10/100. We add LoRot and other self-supervised approaches on LDAM-DRW and compare the gains.

| Imbalance ratio | 0.01 | 0.02 | 0.05 | 0.01 | 0.02 | 0.05 |
|---|---|---|---|---|---|---|
| LDAM-DRW [3] | 77.03 | 80.94 | 85.46 | 42.04 | 46.15 | 53.25 |
| +Rot (DA) | 71.91 | 74.50 | 77.94 | 40.32 | 43.70 | 46.97 |
| +Rot (MT) | 71.63 | 74.26 | 78.02 | 39.22 | 43.43 | 46.76 |
| +Rot (PT) | 75.86 | 81.13 | 84.90 | 43.08 | 47.67 | 52.81 |
| +SSP [58] | 77.83 | 82.13 | – | 43.43 | 47.11 | – |
| +SLA+SD [35] | 80.24 | – | – | 45.53 | – | – |
| +LoRot-I | 81.13 | 83.69 | 86.52 | 45.82 | 49.33 | **54.69** |
| +LoRot-E | **81.82** | **84.41** | **86.67** | **46.48** | **50.05** | 54.66 |

As we can see in Table 3, our proposed LoRot outperforms the state-of-the-art methods on five benchmarks. To measure the performance of LoRot, we utilize the KL-divergence between the softmax predictions and the uniform distribution as in [28,29]. However, we use the softmax predictions for SLA+SD [35] and CutMix [60] as the softmax results fit better with their methods. The results for SupCLR [31] and CSI [53] are from its paper and we further report the performances of LoRot when applied to contrastive approach, CSI. Interestingly, we observe that the AUROC score of CutMix [60] degrades on harder benchmarks in OOD detection. We conjecture that the label smoothing effect of CutMix could degrade their robustness to unseen samples in harder benchmarks. In contrast, LoRot consistently improves the baselines by large margin (including 11%p and 4%p improvement on LSUN(FIX) dataset to cross-entropy and CSI, respectively). For the slightly low performance on SVHN, we think that it is because there is no difference when a small patch is rotated against a plain background of the SVHN dataset. Thus, we believe LoRot-E is better when images are composed of a simple background and, otherwise both approaches would work fine.

**Table 5.** Classification accuracy (%) against the adversarial attack on CIFAR10. The results show that our model outperforms the baselines in 20-step PGD and 100-step PGD with less degradation of the accuracy for the clean dataset.

| Method | Clean | 20-step | 100-step |
|---|---|---|---|
| Baseline | 95.3 | 0.0 | 0.0 |
| Adv. Training | 83.4 | 46.5 | 46.5 |
| +Rotations [29] | 82.8 | 49.3 | 49.2 |
| +LoRot-I (**Ours**) | 82.1 | <u>52.7</u> | <u>52.6</u> |
| +LoRot-E (**Ours**) | 82.6 | **52.8** | **52.8** |

**Imbalanced Classification.** Following [3], we use CIFAR to design imbalanced scenarios. To make imbalanced set, $v \in (\mu, 1)^K$ is multiplied to define the sample numbers for each class as $n_i = n_i v_i$ where $i$ and $n$ are the class index and the number of the original train set. $\mu$ and $K$ denote imbalance ratio and number of classes, respectively. Then, we measure the accuracy using the original test set. As the baseline, we deploy LDAM-DRW [3] and follow experimental configurations from them. Meanwhile, to compare ours with other self-supervision techniques, we also report the results of Rotation [22], SLA+SD [35], and SSP [58]. To be specific, we apply rotation in the form of DA, MT, and PT as described in Fig. 3. SSP [58] is the method of pre-training the network with self-supervised learning.

In Table 4, we show LoRot has clear complementary effects and consistently improves the SOTA model by a large gain of up to +4.44%p (10.56%) in the highly imbalanced scenario in CIFAR100. As an analysis, the classifier might not learn the discriminative parts for specific classes only with a few examples in an imbalanced setting since the classifier has a bias towards a small number of samples for such categories. However, LoRot alleviates this issue since LoRot complements the classifier by discovering sub-discriminative features. More results with the fully supervised baseline are in the supplementary report.

**Adversarial Perturbations.** Substantial efforts were put into improving DNN's robustness [1,17,41] to compensate for the vulnerability against adversarial noise [52]. For the evaluation, we adopt the PGD training [41] as the baseline following the settings from Rotations [29]. We conduct experiments on CIFAR10 against $\ell_\infty$ perturbations with $\epsilon$ set to 8/255. We adversarially train the network with 10-step adversaries and use 20-step and 100-step adversaries. We set the $\alpha$ to 2/255 for 10, 20-step and 0.3/255 for 100-step as in [29,41]. Table 5 shows the results of LoRot along with the rotation task under the same codebase. Using LoRot led the network to be robust with the increase in PGD attacks by large improvement compared to the baselines. Note that the tradeoff between accuracy and robustness against adversarial noise is very natural [62].

## 4.2   Generalization Capability

**Image Classification.** To validate LoRot's benefits in terms of the generalization capability, we evaluate on ImageNet [14] and CIFAR datasets. We compare ours with rotation [22] in multiple forms, SLA+SD [35], and patch-based augmentations [15,60]. SLA+SD augments the class label by applying rotation and utilizes self-distillation to yield a similar output to ensemble results at inference time. Table 6 shows that LoRot clearly achieves the best performance among the methods utilizing rotation. Furthermore, we newly spotlight the potential of self-supervision in the perspective of generalization capability in that the gap between LoRot and popular patch-based augmentation, CutMix, is less than 1% on ImageNet while achieving robustness multifariously.

**Table 6.** Top-1 and Top-5 Classification accuracy (%) on ImageNet. Numbers in the parenthesis are the baseline accuracy.

| Method | Backbone | Top-1 | Top-5 |
|---|---|---|---|
| Baseline | ResNet50 | 76.32 | 92.95 |
| + Rot(DA) | ResNet50 | 76.42 | 93.06 |
| + Rot(MT) | ResNet50 | 76.68 | 93.10 |
| + Rot(SS) | ResNet50 | 76.79 | 93.16 |
| SLA+SD [35] | ResNet50 | $76.17_{(75.17)}$ | – |
| LoRot-I (**Ours**) | ResNet50 | 77.71 | 93.60 |
| LoRot-E (**Ours**) | ResNet50 | <u>77.72</u> | <u>93.65</u> |
| Cutout [15] | ResNet50 | 77.07 | 93.34 |
| CutMix [60] | ResNet50 | **78.60** | **94.08** |

**Table 7.** Additive benefits of LoRot with augmentation methods on ImageNet classification (%). LoRot shows a consistent trend of performance gains.

| Method | Backbone | Baseline | | +LoRot-I | | +LoRot-E | |
|---|---|---|---|---|---|---|---|
| | | Top-1 | Top-5 | Top-1 | Top-5 | Top-1 | Top-5 |
| Mixup [63] | ResNet50 | 77.58 | 93.60 | **78.36** | **94.15** | <u>78.18</u> | <u>94.05</u> |
| AutoAug [12] | ResNet50 | 77.60 | 93.80 | <u>78.09</u> | <u>93.76</u> | **78.22** | **93.86** |
| RandAug [13] | ResNet50 | 77.52 | 93.47 | <u>78.12</u> | <u>93.84</u> | **78.24** | **93.95** |

We further apply our LoRot with data augmentation techniques and contrastive learning. Particularly, we test with AutoAugment [12], RandAugment [13], and Mixup [63] on ImageNet [14] and SupCLR [31] of contrastive learning on CIFAR datasets. The results in Table 7 show the consistent trend of the performance gain with three data-augmentation methods without a large number of additional parameters (+0.12%) and extra training time (+6%). Interestingly, we notice that Mixup [63] better fits to LoRot-I while Auto- and

**Table 8.** Additive benefits of LoRot with contrastive learning on CIFAR-10/100 classification and OOD detection. '†' indicates the number taken from the paper [31] using batch size of 1024. The rest of the results were reproduced with batch size of 512 due to lack of GPU memory. OOD scores are measured with the trained model on CIFAR-10 and averaged over the datasets in Table. 3. All results are averaged on three trials.

| Method | CIFAR10 | CIFAR100 | OOD |
|---|---|---|---|
| SupCLR [31]† | 96.0 | 76.5 | N/A |
| SupCLR [31] | 95.75 | 76.52 | 96.98 |
| + Rotation (MT) | 94.24 | 71.80 | 96.28 |
| + Rotation (PT) | 96.07 | 76.73 | 96.90 |
| + LoRot-I | **96.79** | **78.78** | **97.95** |
| + LoRot-E | 96.73 | 78.77 | 97.92 |

Rand-Augment are better with LoRot-E. In the viewpoint of LoRot-E, we speculate that this is because Auto- and Rand-Augment provide the randomness to the grid layout which results in more diverse inputs while Mixup causes a large modification to the image when used with LoRot-E. Note that LoRot's limitation is that it does not bring surplus benefits to CutMix [60] (±0%) since LoRot and patch-based augmentations may modify overlapped region and interrupt each other.

Contrastive Learning has achieved promising results for both unsupervised [6,10] and supervised learning [31]. As it is shown that relation-based and transform-based methods are complementary in PIRL [43], we also examine it in terms of supervised domain. We report the performance of SupCLR [31] both from its paper and our reproduced version in Table 8. We first applied rotation [22] with two different strategies: MT and PT. However, applying rotation with MT provoked the decline in the performance as mentioned in contrastive learning [8] that rotation as augmentation degrades the discriminative performance. As is, using rotation only for self-supervised loss (PT) was not very efficient either, in that it requires twice more computational cost to yield insignificant increase. On the contrary, LoRot benefits additive effects to contrastive learning by enriching the representation vectors that are to be pushed or pulled between other samples.

**Localization and Transfer Learning** are important criteria to evaluate the model's localization capability. For these experiments, we used our pretrained model yielded from Table 6. Briefly, for weakly supervised object localization, the model needs to localize the object when only given with class labels. Thus, the model is required to not only find the class-descriptive clues but also understand the image. Table 9 demonstrates that LoRot better guides the model to focus on salient regions. Particularly, we observe that LoRot-E, explicitly having the localization task, leads to better localization capability. For evaluation, we use CAM [66] following ACOL [64] and Co-mixup [33]. As ACOL searched for threshold for CAM results between 0.5 to 0.9, we report all these results.

**Table 9.** Weakly Supervised Object Localization accuracy (%) on ImageNet.

| Threshold | 0.5 | 0.6 | 0.7 | 0.8 | 0.9 |
|---|---|---|---|---|---|
| Baseline | 46.72 | 31.55 | 14.49 | 4.22 | 1.91 |
| CutMix | 47.39 | 30.24 | 13.86 | 4.57 | 2.03 |
| LoRot-I | 49.73 | 35.49 | 17.21 | 5.08 | 2.03 |
| LoRot-E | **50.24** | **36.07** | **17.81** | **5.49** | **2.12** |

**Table 10.** AP (%) of object detection and instance segmentation models initialized with each pretrained method.

| Pretrained | RetinaNet | SOLOv2 |
|---|---|---|
| Baseline | 33.8 | 33.7 |
| LoRot-I | **35.3** | **34.5** |
| LoRot-E | 35.2 | 34.4 |

Object detection and instance segmentation are another tasks that require precise localization capability of the model. Indeed, backbones are commonly initialized with ImageNet pretrained weights to deal with the lack of labeled train data. Thus, we examine whether pretrained models trained with LoRot yield any benefits. For evaluation, we employ Retinanet [38] and SOLOv2 [55] for each task and use COCO 2017 dataset [39] for experiments. Table 10 shows our findings: pretrained models with LoRot consistently outperform standard models.

### 4.3 Further Study

To understand why LoRot is effective in enhancing robustness, we conducted an in-depth analysis of OOD detection shown in Table 3. In Fig. 5, we compare the class-wise average confidence scores for OOD (SVHN) dataset between the baseline and the LoRot. We observe a clear tendency that both the LoRot-I and LoRot-E effectively lower all the confidence scores for OOD classes while retaining high confidence for in-distribution dataset. Therefore, LoRot can achieve higher AUROC scores.

Furthermore, we visualized the final embedding space with t-SNE to explore underneath reason for why a better separation has been achieved by the proposed method. In Fig. 6, ten red clusters and blue dots can be found for three methods. Red clusters represent classes in in-distribution dataset, CIFAR10, and blue dots are embeddings of OOD dataset, SVHN. Yet, we can observe that the red and blue dots are significantly mixed in the baseline's embedding space. Meanwhile, two colors overlie less on top of the other in LoRot's feature space and tighter boundaries are formed for red clusters. As discussed, this observation is because the model obtains rich features through learning LoRot which enables the model to understand the input even when the most discriminative hint for each class is not available. In other words, the model is less vulnerable to mispredicting OOD samples with learned features of some classes because it considers a broader spectrum of class-descriptive features.

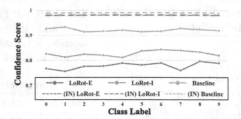

**Fig. 5.** Average confidence scores for in- and out-of-distribution data (CIFAR10 and SVHN) of the baseline and LoRot. Dotted lines are the averaged confidence scores of in-distribution (IN-) dataset for each method. Solid lines represent the confidence scores (y-axis) for each class in out-distribution dataset (x-axis). These results demonstrate that LoRot improves the capability of the models to detect unknown samples.

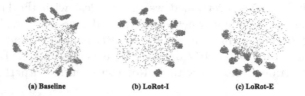

**Fig. 6.** From left to right, t-SNE visualization for the baseline, LoRot-I, and LoRot-E, respectively. We plot the feature distributions of in-distribution instances (Red) and out-distribution instances (Blue). Unlike the baseline where many red dots are scattered with the blue dots, it is evident that clusters appearing under LoRot is more compact. (Color figure online)

## 5    Conclusion

Although self-supervision has been proved to be powerful in supervised domain, its potential is still an untapped question since existing works are designed for unsupervised condition. Thus, we presented three desirable properties of self-supervision to be tailored for supervised learning: enriching representations, maintaining data distribution, and high applicability. To comply with them, we introduced LoRot, a self-supervised localization task that assists supervised learning to further improve robustness and generalization capability. Our extensive experiments demonstrated the merits of LoRot as well as the complementary benefits to prior arts. Furthermore, as we revisited the potential of self-supervision in a simple applicable way in supervised settings, we believe this line is worth further study to be a standard technique in supervised learning.

**Acknowledgements.** This work was supported in part by MSIT/IITP (No. 2022-0-00680, 2020-0-00973, 2020-0-01821, and 2019-0-00421), MCST/KOCCA (No. R2020070002), and MSIT&KNPA/KIPoT (Police Lab 2.0, No. 210121M06).

# References

1. Athalye, A., Carlini, N., Wagner, D.: Obfuscated gradients give a false sense of security: Circumventing defenses to adversarial examples. In: International Conference on Machine Learning, PMLR (2018)
2. Baxter, J.: A bayesian/information theoretic model of learning to learn via multiple task sampling. Mach. Learn. **28**, 7–39 (1997). https://doi.org/10.1023/A:1007327622663
3. Cao, K., Wei, C., Gaidon, A., Arechiga, N., Ma, T.: Learning imbalanced datasets with label-distribution-aware margin loss. In: Advances in Neural Information Processing Systems (2019)
4. Carlucci, F.M., D'Innocente, A., Bucci, S., Caputo, B., Tommasi, T.: Domain generalization by solving jigsaw puzzles. In: Proceedings of the IEEE/CVF Conference on Computer Vision and Pattern Recognition (2019)
5. Caron, M., Bojanowski, P., Joulin, A., Douze, M.: Deep clustering for unsupervised learning of visual features. In: Proceedings of the European Conference on Computer Vision (ECCV) (2018)
6. Caron, M., Misra, I., Mairal, J., Goyal, P., Bojanowski, P., Joulin, A.: Unsupervised learning of visual features by contrasting cluster assignments. In: Proceedings of Advances in Neural Information Processing Systems (NeurIPS) (2020)
7. Caruana, R.: Multitask learning. Mach. Learn. **28**, 41–75 (1997). https://doi.org/10.1023/A:1007379606734
8. Chen, G., et al.: Learning open set network with discriminative reciprocal points (2020)
9. Chen, P., Liu, S., Jia, J.: Jigsaw clustering for unsupervised visual representation learning. In: Proceedings of the IEEE/CVF Conference on Computer Vision and Pattern Recognition (2021)
10. Chen, T., Kornblith, S., Norouzi, M., Hinton, G.: A simple framework for contrastive learning of visual representations. In: International Conference on Machine Learning, PMLR (2020)
11. Chen, X., He, K.: Exploring simple siamese representation learning. In: Proceedings of the IEEE/CVF Conference on Computer Vision and Pattern Recognition (2021)
12. Cubuk, E.D., Zoph, B., Mane, D., Vasudevan, V., Le, Q.V.: Autoaugment: learning augmentation strategies from data. In: Proceedings of the IEEE/CVF Conference on Computer Vision and Pattern Recognition (2019)
13. Cubuk, E.D., Zoph, B., Shlens, J., Le, Q.V.: Randaugment: practical automated data augmentation with a reduced search space. In: Proceedings of the IEEE/CVF Conference on Computer Vision and Pattern Recognition Workshops (2020)
14. Deng, J., Dong, W., Socher, R., Li, L.J., Li, K., Fei-Fei, L.: Imagenet: a large-scale hierarchical image database. In: 2009 IEEE Conference on Computer Vision and Pattern Recognition, IEEE (2009)
15. DeVries, T., Taylor, G.W.: Improved regularization of convolutional neural networks with cutout. arXiv preprint arXiv:1708.04552 (2017)
16. Doersch, C., Gupta, A., Efros, A.A.: Unsupervised visual representation learning by context prediction. In: Proceedings of the IEEE International Conference on Computer Vision (2015)
17. Dong, Y., et al.: Benchmarking adversarial robustness on image classification. In: Proceedings of the IEEE/CVF Conference on Computer Vision and Pattern Recognition (2020)

18. Dosovitskiy, A., Springenberg, J.T., Riedmiller, M., Brox, T.: Discriminative unsupervised feature learning with convolutional neural networks. In: Advances in Neural Information Processing Systems, Citeseer (2014)
19. Feng, Z., Xu, C., Tao, D.: Self-supervised representation learning by rotation feature decoupling. In: Proceedings of the IEEE/CVF Conference on Computer Vision and Pattern Recognition (2019)
20. Geirhos, R., et al.: Shortcut learning in deep neural networks. Nat. Mach. Intell. **2**(11), 665–673 (2020)
21. Gidaris, S., Bursuc, A., Komodakis, N., Pérez, P., Cord, M.: Boosting few-shot visual learning with self-supervision. In: Proceedings of the IEEE/CVF International Conference on Computer Vision, pp. 8059–8068 (2019)
22. Gidaris, S., Singh, P., Komodakis, N.: Unsupervised representation learning by predicting image rotations. In: International Conference on Learning Representations (2018)
23. Gontijo-Lopes, R., Smullin, S., Cubuk, E.D., Dyer, E.: Tradeoffs in data augmentation: an empirical study. In: International Conference on Learning Representations (2020)
24. Grill, J.B., et al.: Bootstrap your own latent: a new approach to self-supervised learning. In: Proceedings of Advances in Neural Information Processing Systems (NeurIPS) (2020)
25. He, K., Fan, H., Wu, Y., Xie, S., Girshick, R.: Momentum contrast for unsupervised visual representation learning. In: Proceedings of the IEEE/CVF Conference on Computer Vision and Pattern Recognition (2020)
26. He, K., Zhang, X., Ren, S., Sun, J.: Deep residual learning for image recognition. In: Proceedings of the IEEE Conference on Computer Vision and Pattern Recognition (2016)
27. Hendrycks, D., Gimpel, K.: A baseline for detecting misclassified and out-of-distribution examples in neural networks. In: International Conference on Learning Representations, ICLR 2017 (2016)
28. Hendrycks, D., Mazeika, M., Dietterich, T.: Deep anomaly detection with outlier exposure. In: International Conference on Learning Representations (2019)
29. Hendrycks, D., Mazeika, M., Kadavath, S., Song, D.: Using self-supervised learning can improve model robustness and uncertainty. In: Advances in Neural Information Processing Systems (NeurIPS) (2019)
30. Khan, A., Sohail, A., Zahoora, U., Qureshi, A.S.: A survey of the recent architectures of deep convolutional neural networks. Artif. Intell. Rev. **53**(8), 5455–5516 (2020). https://doi.org/10.1007/s10462-020-09825-6
31. Khosla, P., et al.: Supervised contrastive learning (2020)
32. Kim, D., Cho, D., Yoo, D., Kweon, I.S.: Learning image representations by completing damaged jigsaw puzzles. In: 2018 IEEE Winter Conference on Applications of Computer Vision (WACV), IEEE (2018)
33. Kim, J.H., Choo, W., Jeong, H., Song, H.O.: Co-mixup: saliency guided joint mixup with supermodular diversity. In: International Conference on Learning Representations, ICLR 2021 (2021)
34. Krizhevsky, A., Hinton, G., et al.: Learning multiple layers of features from tiny images (2009)
35. Lee, H., Hwang, S.J., Shin, J.: Self-supervised label augmentation via input transformations. In: International Conference on Machine Learning, PMLR (2020)
36. Liang, S., Li, Y., Srikant, R.: Enhancing the reliability of out-of-distribution image detection in neural networks. In: International Conference on Learning Representations, ICLR 2018 (2017)

37. Lim, S., Kim, I., Kim, T., Kim, C., Kim, S.: Fast autoaugment. In: Advances in Neural Information Processing Systems (NeurIPS) (2019)
38. Lin, T.Y., Goyal, P., Girshick, R., He, K., Dollár, P.: Focal loss for dense object detection. In: Proceedings of the IEEE International Conference on Computer Vision (2017)
39. Lin, T.-Y., et al.: Microsoft coco: common objects in context. In: Fleet, D., Pajdla, T., Schiele, B., Tuytelaars, T. (eds.) ECCV 2014. LNCS, vol. 8693, pp. 740–755. Springer, Cham (2014). https://doi.org/10.1007/978-3-319-10602-1_48
40. Van der Maaten, L., Hinton, G.: Visualizing data using t-SNE. J. Mach. Learn. Res. 9, 2579–2605 (2008)
41. Madry, A., Makelov, A., Schmidt, L., Tsipras, D., Vladu, A.: Towards deep learning models resistant to adversarial attacks. In: International Conference on Learning Representations, ICLR 2018 (2017)
42. Mallat, S.: Understanding deep convolutional networks. Philosophical Transactions of the Royal Society A, Mathematical, Physical and Engineering Sciences (2016)
43. Misra, I., Maaten, L.V.D.: Self-supervised learning of pretext-invariant representations. In: Proceedings of the IEEE/CVF Conference on Computer Vision and Pattern Recognition (2020)
44. Mundhenk, T.N., Ho, D., Chen, B.Y.: Improvements to context based self-supervised learning. In: Proceedings of the IEEE Conference on Computer Vision and Pattern Recognition (2018)
45. Netzer, Y., Wang, T., Coates, A., Bissacco, A., Wu, B., Ng, A.Y.: Reading digits in natural images with unsupervised feature learning. In: NIPS Workshop on Deep Learning and Unsupervised Feature Learning 2011 (2011)
46. Nguyen, A., Yosinski, J., Clune, J.: Deep neural networks are easily fooled: high confidence predictions for unrecognizable images. In: Proceedings of the IEEE Conference on Computer Vision and Pattern Recognition (2015)
47. Noroozi, M., Favaro, P.: Unsupervised learning of visual representations by solving jigsaw puzzles. In: Leibe, B., Matas, J., Sebe, N., Welling, M. (eds.) ECCV 2016. LNCS, vol. 9910, pp. 69–84. Springer, Cham (2016). https://doi.org/10.1007/978-3-319-46466-4_5
48. Noroozi, M., Vinjimoor, A., Favaro, P., Pirsiavash, H.: Boosting self-supervised learning via knowledge transfer. In: Proceedings of the IEEE Conference on Computer Vision and Pattern Recognition (2018)
49. Patacchiola, M., Storkey, A.: Self-supervised relational reasoning for representation learning (2020)
50. Perera, P., et al.: Generative-discriminative feature representations for open-set recognition. In: Proceedings of the IEEE/CVF Conference on Computer Vision and Pattern Recognition (2020)
51. Ruder, S.: An overview of multi-task learning in deep neural networks. arXiv preprint arXiv:1706.05098 (2017)
52. Szegedy, C., et al.: Intriguing properties of neural networks. International Conference on Learning Representations. In: ICLR 2014 (2013)
53. Tack, J., Mo, S., Jeong, J., Shin, J.: Csi: novelty detection via contrastive learning on distributionally shifted instances. In: Advances in Neural Information Processing Systems (2020)
54. Tian, Y., Chen, X., Ganguli, S.: Understanding self-supervised learning dynamics without contrastive pairs. In: Proceedings of the International Conference on Machine Learning, (ICML) (2021)

55. Wang, X., Zhang, R., Kong, T., Li, L., Shen, C.: Solov2: dynamic and fast instance segmentation. In: Advances in Neural Information Processing Systems (NeurIPS) (2020)
56. Wu, Z., Xiong, Y., Yu, S.X., Lin, D.: Unsupervised feature learning via non-parametric instance discrimination. In: Proceedings of the IEEE Conference on Computer Vision and Pattern Recognition (2018)
57. Yang, J., Parikh, D., Batra, D.: Joint unsupervised learning of deep representations and image clusters. In: Proceedings of the IEEE Conference on Computer Vision and Pattern Recognition (2016)
58. Yang, Y., Xu, Z.: Rethinking the value of labels for improving class-imbalanced learning. In: Conference on Neural Information Processing Systems (NeurIPS) (2020)
59. Ye, M., Zhang, X., Yuen, P.C., Chang, S.F.: Unsupervised embedding learning via invariant and spreading instance feature. In: Proceedings of the IEEE/CVF Conference on Computer Vision and Pattern Recognition (2019)
60. Yun, S., Han, D., Oh, S.J., Chun, S., Choe, J., Yoo, Y.: Cutmix: regularization strategy to train strong classifiers with localizable features. In: Proceedings of the IEEE/CVF International Conference on Computer Vision (2019)
61. Zhai, X., et al.: A large-scale study of representation learning with the visual task adaptation benchmark. arXiv preprint arXiv:1910.04867 (2019)
62. Zhang, H., Yu, Y., Jiao, J., Xing, E., El Ghaoui, L., Jordan, M.: Theoretically principled trade-off between robustness and accuracy. In: International Conference on Machine Learning, PMLR (2019)
63. Zhang, H., Cisse, M., Dauphin, Y.N., Lopez-Paz, D.: mixup: beyond empirical risk minimization. In: International Conference on Learning Representations (2018)
64. Zhang, X., Wei, Y., Feng, J., Yang, Y., Huang, T.S.: Adversarial complementary learning for weakly supervised object localization. In: Proceedings of the IEEE Conference on Computer Vision and Pattern Recognition (2018)
65. Zhong, Z., Zheng, L., Kang, G., Li, S., Yang, Y.: Random erasing data augmentation. In: Proceedings of the AAAI Conference on Artificial Intelligence (2020)
66. Zhou, B., Khosla, A., Lapedriza, A., Oliva, A., Torralba, A.: Learning deep features for discriminative localization. In: Proceedings of the IEEE Conference on Computer Vision and Pattern Recognition (2016)

# Difficulty-Aware Simulator for Open Set Recognition

WonJun Moon, Junho Park, Hyun Seok Seong, Cheol-Ho Cho,
and Jae-Pil Heo(✉)

Sungkyunkwan University, Suwon, South Korea
{wjun0830,pjh4993,gustjrdl95,gersys,jaepilheo}@skku.edu

**Abstract.** Open set recognition (OSR) assumes unknown instances appear out of the blue at the inference time. The main challenge of OSR is that the response of models for unknowns is totally unpredictable. Furthermore, the diversity of open set makes it harder since instances have different difficulty levels. Therefore, we present a novel framework, DIfficulty-Aware Simulator (DIAS), that generates fakes with diverse difficulty levels to simulate the real world. We first investigate fakes from generative adversarial network (GAN) in the classifier's viewpoint and observe that these are not severely challenging. This leads us to define the criteria for difficulty by regarding samples generated with GANs having moderate-difficulty. To produce hard-difficulty examples, we introduce Copycat, imitating the behavior of the classifier. Furthermore, moderate- and easy-difficulty samples are also yielded by our modified GAN and Copycat, respectively. As a result, DIAS outperforms state-of-the-art methods with both metrics of AUROC and F-score. Our code is available at https://github.com/wjun0830/Difficulty-Aware-Simulator.

**Keywords:** Open set recognition · Unknown detection

## 1 Introduction

Thanks to the advance of convolutional neural network (CNN), downstream tasks of computer vision have been through several breakthroughs [14,24]. Although the performance of deep learning is now comparable to that of humans, distilling knowledge learned from known classes to detect unseen categories lags behind [10,13]. Hence, unseen categories are often misclassified into one of the known classes. In this context, open set recognition was proposed to learn for the capability of detecting unknowns [2,3,36].

Generally, CNN are often highly biased to yield high confidence scores [32]. However, calibrating the confidence to distinguish open set data is infeasible due to the inaccessibility of those unseen data in the training phase [12]. Furthermore, it is known that the learned CNN classifiers tend to highly rely on the

---

**Supplementary Information** The online version contains supplementary material available at https://doi.org/10.1007/978-3-031-19806-9_21.

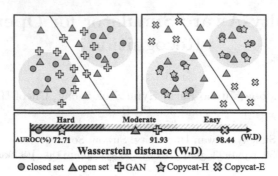

**Fig. 1.** Given a set of closed and open classes, we intuitively describe how the classifier recognizes fake examples from the image-generator and the Copycat. Green circles indicate the confident class boundaries. (Left) Both open set and generated instances by GAN usually project nearby the class boundaries or sometimes inside. (Right) Hard-fake instances produced by the Copycat embed deep inside the class boundaries, while easy ones usually embed far. (Bottom) Each set of fakes are represented on a line based on normalized Wasserstein distances (W.D) to closed set with the corresponding AUROC score. To measure W.D and AUROC scores, we conduct a primary experiment on CIFAR10 with the classifier trained only on closed set. In this paper, we define the difficulty levels according to two measures from the perspective of the classifier.

discriminative features to distinguish classes but ignore the other details [33]. Therefore, open set instances that share such discriminative features with closed set can be easily confused. In other words, open set may have a level of difficulty, which is determined according to the degrees of feature sharing with the closed set. In this regard, it is challenging to cope with all open set with various difficulty levels which can be encountered in the real world.

Due to the inaccessibility to open set during training, substantial efforts were put to simulate virtual open set [4,5,8,28,47]. RPL [5] applied 1-vs-rest training scheme and exploited features from other classes to form open set space, and PROSER [47] mixed features to simulate open set. Furthermore, GAN [11] is actively used to synthesize unknown samples [4,8,28]. However, diverse difficulty levels of open set are not taken into account. Specifically, feature simulation methods only utilize the features outside the class boundaries which are easy to be distinguished [5,47]. Besides, image generation-based methods mostly produce samples being predicted as unknown class by the classifier to represent open set [4,8,27,28]. These samples hardly have high difficulty, so the classifiers learned with them can be still vulnerable to difficult open set that contains semantically meaningful features of one of the known classes [9,30].

In this context, we propose a novel framework, DIfficulty-Aware Simulator (DIAS), that exposes diverse samples to the classifier with various difficulty levels from the classifier's perspective. As shown in Fig. 1, we found that a set of generated images with GAN is not very challenging for the classifier. Therefore, with the GAN as a criterion, we define the difficulty levels and introduce the Copycat, a feature generator producing hard fake instances. As the training iteration proceeds, the Copycat mimics the behavior of the classifier and generates real-like fake features that the classifier will likely yield a high probability. In other words, the classifier faces unknown features within its decision boundaries at every iteration. In this way, the classifier is repeatedly exposed to confusing instances and learns to calibrate even within the class boundaries. Moreover, we further ask the Copycat to create easy fake samples and also modify the image-level generator to take the classifier's perspective into account. These fake instances are additionally utilized to simulate the real world in which unseen examples with various difficulties may exist. Besides, DIAS is inherently equipped with a decent threshold to distinguish open set. It enables to avoid expensive process to search an appropriate confidence threshold of the classifier for OSR.

In summary, our contributions are: (i) We propose a novel framework, DIAS, for difficulty-aware open set simulation from the classifier's perspective. To the best of our knowledge, this is the first attempt to consider the difficulty level in OSR. (ii) We present Copycat, the difficult fake feature generator, by imitating the classifier's behavior with the distilled knowledge. (iii) We prove effectiveness with competitive results and demonstrate feasibility with an inherent threshold to identify open set samples.

## 2    Background and Related Works

**Open Set Recognition.** To apply the classification models to real world with high robustness, OSR was first formalized as a constrained minimization problem [36]. Following them, earlier works used traditional approaches: support vector machines, Extreme Value Theory (EVT), nearest class mean classifier, and nearest neightbor [2,20,21,35,45]. Then, along with the development in CNN, deep learning algorithms have been widely adopted. In the beginning, softmax was tackled for its closed nature. To replace this, Openmax [3] tried to extend the classifier and K-sigmoid [37] conducted score analysis to search for threshold.

A recently popular stream for OSR is employing generative models to learn a representation that only preserves known samples. Conditional Variational AutoEncoder (VAE) was utilized in C2AE [31] to model the reconstruction error based on the EVT. CGDL [38] improved the VAE's weakness in closed set classification with conditional gaussian distribution learning. Moreover, flow-based model was employed for density estimation [46] and capsule network was adopted to support representation learning with conditional VAE [13]. Other approaches exploited the generative model's representation as an additional feature. GFROSR [32] employed reconstructed image from an autoencoder to augment the image while CROSR [42] adopted ladder network to utilize both the prediction and the latent features for unknown detection.

Other methods mostly fall into the category of simulating unknown examples, a more intuitive way for OSR. RPL [5] tried to conduct simulation with prototype learning. With prototypes, they designed an embedding space for open set at the center where the samples will yield low confidence scores. Then, based on manifold mixup [40], PROSER [47] set up the open space between class boundaries to keep each boundary far from others. GAN was also employed to simulate open set. G-openmax [8] improved openmax [3] via generating extra images to represent the unknown class and OSRCI [28] developed encoder-decoder GAN architecture to generate counterfactual examples. Additionally, ARPL [4] enhanced prototype learning with generated fake samples and GAN was further extended to feature space [22]. DIAS shares similarity with these methods in that we simulate open set. However, the main difference comes from the consideration of difficulty gaps between open set instances from the classifier's perspective.

**Multi-level Knowledge distillation.** Knowledge Distillation (KD) was introduced in [17] where the student learns from the ground-truth labels and the soft-labels from the teacher. AT [44] exploited attention maps in every layer to transfer the knowledge and FSP [41] utilized the FSP matrix that contains the distilled knowledge from the teacher. Moreover, cross-stage connection paths were also introduced to overcome information mismatch arising from differences in model size [6]. Copycat share similar concept with multi-stage KD methods that it imitates encoding behavior of the classifier. Up to we know, developing a fake generator with KD is a novel strategy in the literature of OSR.

## 3   Methodology

### 3.1   Problem Formulation and Motivation

The configuration of OSR is different from classification since models can face unseen objects at the inference time. Suppose that a model trained with $\mathcal{D}_{tr} = (X, Y)$ over a set of classes $K$. $X$ is a set of input data $\mathbf{x}$ and $Y$ is a set of one-hot labels which each sample $\mathbf{y} \in \{0, 1\}^K$, where its value is 1 for the ground-truth class and 0 for the others. A typical classification evaluates the trained model on $\mathcal{D}_{te} = (T, Y)$ where $X$ and $T$ are sampled from the same set of classes.

On the contrary, $\hat{\mathcal{D}}_{te} = (\hat{T})$ of OSR contains instances over a novel category set $\hat{K}$. Since the conventional classifier assumes $K$ categories, common approach is to distinguish open set based on confidence thresholding [16]. However, challenges in OSR come from the similarity between $\mathcal{D}_{te}$ and $\hat{\mathcal{D}}_{te}$ which often leads to high confidence scores for both. Furthermore, the diverse relationships between $\mathcal{D}_{te}$ and $\hat{\mathcal{D}}_{te}$ affect the threshold to be vulnerable to different datasets. To this end, the classifier is preferred to be calibrated to yield low score on unknown classes.

Intuitive approach to calibrate the classifier is to simulate the $\hat{\mathcal{D}}_{te}$ with fake set $\bar{X}$. Then, while the classifier is trained on $\mathcal{D}_{tr}$, it is also enforced to suppress the output logit of the fake sample $\bar{\mathbf{x}}$ to a uniform probability distribution:

$$\mathcal{L} = \mathcal{L}_{ce}(\mathbf{x}, \mathbf{y}) + \lambda \cdot \mathcal{L}_{ce}(\bar{\mathbf{x}}, 1/K \cdot \mathbf{u}), \tag{1}$$

where $\mathcal{L}_{ce}$, $\lambda$, and $\mathbf{u}$ each denotes cross-entropy loss, scale parameter for fake sample calibration, and the all-one vector.

Nevertheless, due to the nature of the real world where unknown classes are rampant, a single set of fakes cannot represent all unknowns [18]. This is because the difficulty levels of data in the perspective of the classifier can be significantly varying [34,39]. This motivates us to develop a simulator to rehearse with fake

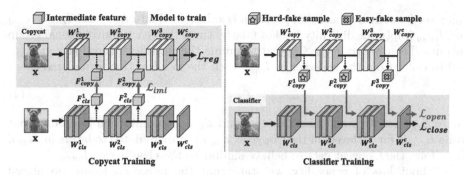

**Fig. 2.** Illustration of the joint training scheme between the Copycat and the classifier. (Left) Knowledge is distilled from the classifier to the Copycat while its parameters are also updated by the regularization loss. (Right) The classifier is exposed to fakes generated by the Copycat. Depending on the existence of the imitation loss $\mathcal{L}_{imi}$ in its group $(W^1, W^2, W^3)$, each convolutional group of the Copycat outputs hard- or easy-fake instances. $\mathcal{L}_{open}$ is a general term for the loss computed from fake examples.

examples in diverse difficulty levels. To overcome the new challenge in generating the hard-fake instances, we first introduce Copycat learning which generates hard fakes in Sect. 3.2 and describe the DIAS in Sect. 3.3. Finally, we explain the inherent threshold of DIAS which benefits inference procedure in Sect. 3.4

### 3.2 Copycat: Hard-fake Feature Generator

In Fig. 2, we illustrate how the Copycat interacts with the classifier to introduce fake examples. Note that, throughout the paper, the terms regarding the difficulty level (e.g. Hard, Moderate, and Easy) are the data difficulty from the perspective of the classifier, as in Fig. 1. Given an input image $\mathbf{x}$ and network $W$, we let $\mathbf{p} = W(\mathbf{x})$ stand for the output probability. $W$ can be separted into different parts $(W^1, \cdots, W^n, W^c)$, where $W^c$ is the fully-connected layer with the softmax activation and $W^1, \cdots, W^n$ are different groups of layers separated by predefined criteria. Then, predicting $\mathbf{p}$ with network $W$ can be expressed as

$$\mathbf{p} = W^c \circ W^n \circ \cdots \circ W^1(\mathbf{x}). \tag{2}$$

We refer to "$\circ$" as nesting of functions where $g \circ f(x) = g(f(x))$ . Note that the overall architecture for the Copycat and the classifier is equivalent and layers are grouped with the same criteria. For simplicity, we split the Copycat and the classifier into three groups of layers. This can be easily applied to other models [15,19] as the number of groups can be adjusted. We also let intermediate features to be denoted as $(F^1, \cdots, F^n)$. For instance, $i$th feature is calculated as:

$$F^i = W^i \circ W^{i-1} \circ \cdots \circ W^1(\mathbf{x}). \tag{3}$$

The key objective of the Copycat is to create virtual features of hard- and easy-difficulty levels. To introduce the training procedure, we first define $I$ as an index set for convolutional groups which is subdivided into $I_{hard}$ and $I_{easy}$. $I_{hard}$ and $I_{easy}$ imply the difficulty level of fake features that each convolutional group outputs. Then, we train the Copycat to mimic the classifier's knowledge at $I_{hard}$ and to differ from the classifier at $I_{easy}$ with the loss function formulated as:

$$\mathcal{L}_{copy} = \mathcal{L}_{reg} + \mathcal{L}_{imi}, \tag{4}$$

where $\mathcal{L}_{reg}$ denote a regularization loss and $\mathcal{L}_{imi}$ is an imitation loss. Note that while $\mathcal{L}_{reg}$ is for all layers in the Copycat, $\mathcal{L}_{imi}$ is only updated to layers in $I_{hard}$. Therefore, the Copycat gets to behave similar to the classifier at $I_{hard}$.

Without loss of generality, we state that the imitation losses are placed between the features of the Copycat and the classifier where they are of the same convolutional group index. We define the imitation loss as:

$$\mathcal{L}_{imi} = \sum_{j \in I_{hard}} \|F_{copy}^j - F_{cls}^j\|_1, \tag{5}$$

where $F_{copy}^j$ and $F_{cls}^j$ are the feature vectors from $j$-th convolutional group of the Copycat $W_{copy}^j$ and the classifier $W_{cls}^j$. Then, with $\mathcal{L}_{imi}$, forcing the convolutional groups at $I_{hard}$ of the Copycat to behave similarly to classifier's, hard layers in the Copycat become to produce difficult fake features from the classifier's perspective. However, if $I_{easy}$ is defined in front of $I_{hard}$, corrupted features from $I_{easy}$ can lead to unstable $\mathcal{L}_{imi}$ because $I_{easy}$ is to yield abnormal features that are different from the ones of the classifier. Thus, as the quality of hard fakes is crucial in the Copycat, we define $I_{easy}$ at the last.

Regularization loss has two purposes: hindering the replication procedure to prevent Copycat from being exactly the same as the classifier and diversifying easy fakes. Since the groups at $I_{easy}$ of the Copycat do not have any connectivity to the classifier and are updated only with $\mathcal{L}_{reg}$, features from $I_{easy}$ of the Copycat would be abnormal which are easy to be identified by the classifier. Moreover, as $\mathcal{L}_{reg}$ is iteratively applied, diverse easy fakes are produced. For $\mathcal{L}_{reg}$, we simply use $\mathcal{L}_{ce}$ with real labels since the classification loss plays two roles well.

### 3.3    Difficulty-Aware Simulator

The key idea of DIAS is to expose the classifier with open set of various difficulty levels. To consider the classifier's perspective in real-time, we apply joint scheme of the training phase between each generative model and the classifier.

**Stage I: Generator Training.** To come up with virtual open set for simulation, we employ a Copycat and an image-generator. As we discussed in Sect. 3.2, the Copycat is to prepare hard- and easy-fake features for robust training of the classifier. Moreover, inspired by Fig. 1, we employ GAN to generate moderate-level fake images but with a little modification to consider the classifier's viewpoint.

To synthesize fake images of the moderate difficulty, the generator is adversarially trained with the discriminator. Let $D$ and $G$ be the discriminator and the generator, respectively. The generator receives the noise vector $\mathbf{z}$ sampled

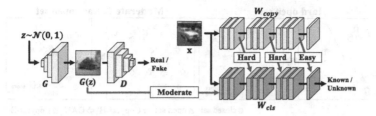

**Fig. 3.** Illustration of the proposed DIAS. Our GAN and Copycat each receives the noise vector $z$ and input image $x$ to produce fake instances with various difficulties. These instances are provided to the classifier to have a rehearsal for OSR.

from normal distribution $\mathcal{N}$ and generates the output as $G(\mathbf{z})$. Then, the discriminator encodes both the image $\mathbf{x}$ and fake images $G(\mathbf{z})$ to the probability $[0, 1]$ whether to predict the input is from a real distribution or not.

Furthermore, our focus of generating fake images is to prepare the classifier for open set. Thus, optimization process for the generator should consider the classifier's prediction. However, arranging the process should be carefully designed to avoid two situations. On the one hand, when the perfect generator is trained, the classifier would not be capable of discriminating open set due to the equilibrium in the mini-max game [1,22]. On the other hand, when the generator only outputs images that the classifier predicts with the uniform distribution, generated samples would not be representative for simulating moderate-difficulty open set. Therefore, we encourage the generator to output closed set-like images, but very cautiously, with the classifier's predictions. Specifically, we use the negative cross-entropy loss to a uniform target vector. Accordingly, the generator is trained to produce fake images that are neither the known nor the outlier from the classifier's perspective. Formally, the overall optimization process of our GAN is conducted by:

$$\max_D \min_G \ \mathcal{L}_{gan} = \mathbb{E}_{\mathbf{x} \sim \mathcal{D}_{tr}} \big[ \log D(\mathbf{x}) \big]$$
$$+ \mathbb{E}_{\mathbf{z} \sim \mathcal{N}} \big[ \log \big( 1 - D(G(\mathbf{z})) \big) - \beta/K \sum_{k=1}^{K} \log C_k \big( G(\mathbf{z}) \big) \big] \tag{6}$$

where $\beta$ is the scale parameter for negative cross-entropy and $C_k(\cdot)$ outputs probability of class $k$ for given input.

**Stage II: Classifier Training.** Facing all kinds of difficulty through virtual open set at training time, we pursue to drive the classifier to be prepared for handling unseen classes. Thus, we formulate the loss for the classifier as:

$$\mathcal{L}_{cls} = \mathcal{L}_{close} + \lambda \cdot \mathcal{L}_{open}, \tag{7}$$

where $\mathcal{L}_{close}$ and $\mathcal{L}_{open}$ are to discriminate within known and between known and unknown classes, respectively. To consider the difficulty levels in the classifier's behavior, we need to differentiate the objectives with their difficulties. Therefore, we employ the $\mathcal{L}_{ce}$ for both but with the smoothed label for calculating the $\mathcal{L}_{open}$. The smoothed label $\tilde{\mathbf{y}}$ is formed with smoothing ratio $\alpha$ as below:

$$\tilde{\mathbf{y}} = (1 - \alpha) \cdot \mathbf{y} + \alpha/K \cdot \mathbf{u}. \tag{8}$$

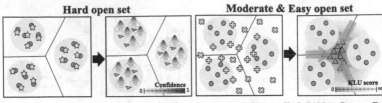

⊙ closed set  △ open set  ☆ Copycat-H  ⊕ GAN  ⊗ Copycat-E

**Fig. 4.** Illustration about the changes in the classifier's perspective by facing fake open set. Confidence bar represents **p** and KLU score bar stands for the KL-divergence to the uniform distribution. (Left) Hard-difficulty open set samples are mostly located within the decision boundary of the classifier. They lead the classifier to calibrate its find-grained confidence distribution to distinguish such hard-difficulty samples. (Right) Moderate- and easy-difficulty samples are likely located near the boundary or free space. The classifier tries to gather them to the region with the uniform probability.

Generated fakes are encoded by the classifier to make a prediction as illustrated in Fig. 3. Specifically, intermediate features from the Copycat and fake images from GAN are passed on to the classifier to predict $\mathbf{p}_{copy}^i$ and $\mathbf{p}_{gan}$ as:

$$\mathbf{p}_{copy}^i = W_{cls}^c \circ W_{cls}^n \circ \cdots \circ W_{cls}^{i+1}(F_{copy}^i) \tag{9}$$

$$\mathbf{p}_{gan} = W_{cls}^c \circ W_{cls}^n \circ \cdots \circ W_{cls}^1(G(z)) \tag{10}$$

Then, open loss is calculated alternately depending on the training phase:

$$\mathcal{L}_{open} = \begin{cases} \sum_{i \in I} \mathcal{L}_{ce}(\tilde{\mathbf{y}}, \mathbf{p}_{copy}^i) \\ \sum_{z \sim \mathcal{N}} \mathcal{L}_{ce}(\frac{1}{K} \cdot \mathbf{u}, \mathbf{p}_{gan}) \end{cases} \tag{11}$$

To define $\tilde{\mathbf{y}}$ for each difficulty group, we grant a smaller value to $\alpha$ when the input has a high probability of belonging to one of the known categories. To be specific, we divide $\alpha$ into $\alpha_{hard}$ and $\alpha_{easy}$. Note that motivated by ARPL [4], we set the target label for the fake image of the GAN to a uniform distribution since it works better to regard them as unknown. Likewise, we also set $\alpha_{easy}$ to 1 to further regard easy fakes as unknown. On the other hand, since identifying hard fake instances as open set might contradict the training procedure, $\alpha_{hard}$ is set to 0.5.

**Algorithm 1.** Training DIAS

**Require:** Parameters of Classifier, Copycat, Generator and Discriminator $(\theta, \phi, \psi, \omega)$, Learning rate $\eta$
$\quad$ **for** $i \in \{1, ..., epoch\}$ **do**
$\quad\quad$ ▷ Phase I: Training with Copycat
$\quad\quad$ $\mathcal{L}_{copy} = \mathcal{L}_{imi} + \mathcal{L}_{reg}$
$\quad\quad$ $\phi \leftarrow \phi - \eta \nabla_\phi \mathcal{L}_{copy}$
$\quad\quad$ $\mathcal{L}_{cls} = \mathcal{L}_{close} + \lambda \cdot \mathcal{L}_{open}$
$\quad\quad$ $\theta \leftarrow \theta - \eta \nabla_\theta \mathcal{L}_{cls}$
$\quad\quad$ ▷ Phase II: Training with GAN
$\quad\quad$ $\psi \leftarrow \psi - \eta \nabla_\psi \mathcal{L}_{gan}$
$\quad\quad$ $\omega \leftarrow \omega - \eta \nabla_\omega \mathcal{L}_{gan}$
$\quad\quad$ $\mathcal{L}_{cls} = \mathcal{L}_{close} + \lambda \cdot \mathcal{L}_{open}$
$\quad\quad$ $\theta \leftarrow \theta - \eta \nabla_\theta \mathcal{L}_{cls}$
$\quad$ **end for**

Therefore, the easy and moderate fake examples are forced to reside outside the class boundaries, while a difficult set of fakes are implemented to be calibrated within the class boundaries.

In Fig. 4, we describe how diverse levels of difficulty assist the classifier to build robust decision boundaries. As can be seen, while easy and moderate fake sets play a role of gathering open set to the parts where they can retain uniform distribution, hard fakes force the classifier to calibrate its decision boundaries with the smoothed label. Our training procedure is outlined in Algorithm 1.

### 3.4 Inherent Threshold of DIAS

DIAS has its benefits at the inference for threshold selection. In general, cross-validation is a widely adopted strategy to specify threshold when identifying the open set, although it is time-consuming work to find an appropriate threshold. On top of this, the value of threshold is very sensitive that it must be explored for every pair of known and unknown dataset [28]. In contrast, our proposed DIAS is inherently equipped with a criterion to detect unknowns. To be precise, we observe that $\max_{k} \tilde{\mathbf{y}}$ computed with $\alpha_{hard}$ works out to be the decent threshold. This is because we enforce the confidence scores for virtual open set to be equal or lower than the target confidence for difficult fake samples $\max_{k} \tilde{\mathbf{y}}$. Formally, given an image $\mathbf{x}$, we extend the closed set classifier by predicting label $\hat{y}$ as:

$$\hat{y} = \begin{cases} K + 1 & \text{if } \max\{W(\mathbf{x})\} < \tau + \epsilon \\ \arg\max_{k=1,\cdots,K} \{W(\mathbf{x})\} & \text{otherwise} \end{cases} \quad (12)$$

where $K + 1$ is a class for unknown and $\tau = (1 - \alpha_{hard}) + \alpha_{hard}/K$. Note that $\tau$ is same as simply calculating the maximum value in Eq. 8 with $\alpha_{hard}$. Therefore, we do not need any extra algorithm to compute the threshold.

## 4 Experiments

### 4.1 Evaluation Protocols, Metrics, and Datasets

**Evaluation Protocols.** With a $c$-class dataset, OSR scenario is generally designed by randomly selecting $K$ classes as known where $(c \gg K)$. Then, the remaining $c - K$ classes are considered as open set classes. Then, five-randomized scenarios are simulated to measure the Area Under the Receiver Operating Characteristic (AUROC) curve or F-score. Note that the split information can be different over methods since they conduct experiments on randomized trials [5, 28, 31, 43]. However, as different split often leads to unfair comparison, recent methods pre-define split information on each AUROC [13, 28, 42] and F1-score benchmark [43]. Following them, we conduct experiments on two standardized split information for a fair comparison. Split information is in the supplementary.

**Metrics.** We use two metrics: F1-score and AUROC score. F1 is a more practical measure, representing the classification accuracy. It is calculated as a weighted average of precision and recall. For OSR, F1-score is commonly obtained by adding an extra class for open set and searching for proper threshold. On the other hand, AUROC is a metric that does not require any calibration process. It considers the trade-off between true positive rate and false positive rate across different decision thresholds.

**Table 1.** AUROC score for detecting known and unknown samples. † indicates the reproduced result to unify the split information. The best results are indicated in bolds.

| Method | MNIST | SVHN | CIFAR10 | CIFAR+10 | CIFAR+50 | Tiny-IN |
|---|---|---|---|---|---|---|
| Softmax | 0.978 | 0.886 | 0.677 | 0.816 | 0.805 | 0.577 |
| OpenMax | 0.981 | 0.894 | 0.695 | 0.817 | 0.796 | 0.576 |
| G-OpenMax [8] | 0.984 | 0.896 | 0.675 | 0.827 | 0.819 | 0.580 |
| OSRCI [28] | $0.988_{\pm 0.004}$ | $0.91_{\pm 0.01}$ | $0.699_{\pm 0.038}$ | 0.838 | 0.827 | 0.586 |
| CROSR [42] | $0.991_{\pm 0.004}$ | $0.899_{\pm 0.018}$ | - | - | - | 0.589 |
| C2AE [31] | - | $0.892_{\pm 0.013}$ | $0.711_{\pm 0.008}$ | $0.810_{\pm 0.005}$ | $0.803_{\pm 0.000}$ | $0.581_{\pm 0.019}$ |
| GFROSR [32] | - | $0.955_{\pm 0.018}$ | $0.831_{\pm 0.039}$ | - | - | $0.657_{\pm 0.012}$ |
| CGDL [38] | $0.977_{\pm 0.008}$ | $0.896_{\pm 0.023}$ | $0.681_{\pm 0.029}$ | $0.794_{\pm 0.013}$ | $0.794_{\pm 0.003}$ | $0.653_{\pm 0.002}$ |
| RPL [5] | $0.917_{\pm 0.006}$ | $0.931_{\pm 0.014}$ | $0.784_{\pm 0.025}$ | $0.885_{\pm 0.019}$ | $0.881_{\pm 0.014}$ | $0.711_{\pm 0.026}$ |
| PROSER [47]† | $0.964_{\pm 0.019}$ | $0.930_{\pm 0.005}$ | $0.801_{\pm 0.031}$ | $0.898_{\pm 0.015}$ | $0.881_{\pm 0.003}$ | $0.684_{\pm 0.029}$ |
| ARPL+cs [4]† | $0.991_{\pm 0.004}$ | $0.946_{\pm 0.005}$ | $0.819_{\pm 0.029}$ | $0.904_{\pm 0.002}$ | $0.901_{\pm 0.002}$ | $0.710_{\pm 0.002}$ |
| CVAECap [13] | $\mathbf{0.992}_{\pm 0.004}$ | $\mathbf{0.956}_{\pm 0.012}$ | $0.835_{\pm 0.023}$ | $0.888_{\pm 0.019}$ | $0.889_{\pm 0.017}$ | $0.715_{\pm 0.018}$ |
| DIAS (Ours) | $\mathbf{0.992}_{\pm 0.004}$ | $0.943_{\pm 0.008}$ | $\mathbf{0.850}_{\pm 0.022}$ | $\mathbf{0.920}_{\pm 0.011}$ | $\mathbf{0.916}_{\pm 0.007}$ | $\mathbf{0.731}_{\pm 0.015}$ |

**Table 2.** Comparison of accuracy for closed set classes between baseline and DIAS.

| Method | MNIST | SVHN | CIFAR10 | CIFAR+ | Tiny-IN |
|---|---|---|---|---|---|
| Softmax | **0.997** | 0.966 | 0.934 | 0.960 | 0.653 |
| DIAS (Ours) | **0.997** | **0.970** | **0.947** | **0.964** | **0.700** |

**Datasets.** Prior to dataset explanation, we describe the term, openness, which indicates the ratio between the known and the unknown:

$$Openness = 1 - \sqrt{K/(K + \hat{K})} \tag{13}$$

where $K$ and $\hat{K}$ stand for the number of classes for known and unknown, respectively. With openness, we discuss several benchmarking datasets: **MNIST, SVHN, CIFAR10** [23,26,29] contain 10 classes. Six classes are chosen to be known and four classes are to be unknown classes. Openness is 22.54%. **CIFAR+10, CIFAR+50** are artificially synthesized with four non-animal classes from CIFAR10 and N non-overlapping classes from CIFAR100 [38,43]. As more classes are considered as open set, openness is higher. Openness for each are 46.54% and 72.78%. **Tiny-ImageNet** [7] Tiny-IN is a subset of ImageNet which has 200 classes. We follow the common protocol [13,28] to resize it to 32 × 32. Afterwards, 20 classes are sampled to be used as closed set and the remaining classes as open set classes. Openness is 68.38%.

### 4.2 Experimental Results

OSR performances are in Tables 1 and 3. Most of the baseline results in Table 1 are taken from the [13] where they reproduced papers' performances with the same configuration for a fair comparison. The scores of DIAS, PROSER [47], and ARPL+cs [4] are evaluated based on the same protocol with [13] on the split publicized by [13,28]. We use their hyperparameters except the model architecture

**Table 3.** Average of macro-averaged F1-scores in five splits. We adopt the protocol from GCM-CF [43]. † indicates the reproduced performance with official code.

| Method | MNIST | SVHN | CIFAR10 | CIFAR+10 | CIFAR+50 |
|---|---|---|---|---|---|
| Softmax | 0.767 | 0.762 | 0.704 | 0.778 | 0.660 |
| Openmax | 0.859 | 0.780 | 0.714 | 0.787 | 0.677 |
| CGDL [38] | 0.890 | 0.763 | 0.710 | 0.779 | 0.710 |
| GCM-CF [43] | 0.914 | 0.793 | 0.726 | 0.794 | 0.746 |
| ARPL+cs [4] † | $0.951_{\pm0.009}$ | $0.857_{\pm0.008}$ | $0.753_{\pm0.033}$ | $0.827_{\pm0.010}$ | $0.753_{\pm0.001}$ |
| DIAS (Ours) | $\mathbf{0.953}_{\pm0.015}$ | $\mathbf{0.880}_{\pm0.010}$ | $\mathbf{0.809}_{\pm0.026}$ | $\mathbf{0.859}_{\pm0.010}$ | $\mathbf{0.829}_{\pm0.006}$ |

**Table 4.** Macro-averaged F1-scores on the MNIST with three other datasets as unknown.

| Method | Omniglot | MNIST-noise | Noise |
|---|---|---|---|
| Softmax | 0.595 | 0.801 | 0.829 |
| Openmax [3] | 0.780 | 0.816 | 0.826 |
| CROSR [42] | 0.793 | 0.827 | 0.826 |
| CGDL [38] | 0.850 | 0.887 | 0.859 |
| PROSER [47] | 0.862 | 0.874 | 0.882 |
| CVAECapOSR [13] | 0.971 | **0.982** | 0.982 |
| DIAS (Ours) | **0.989** | **0.982** | **0.989** |

in PROSER to unify the backbone. Note that some papers cannot be compared under the same codebase due to non-reproducible results (split information nor the codes are not publicized) [46] and the contrasting assumption in the existence of open set data [22]. As shown, our method achieves significant improvements over the state-of-the-art techniques in CIFAR10, CIFAR+10, CIFAR+50, and tiny-ImageNet datasets, and shows comparable results in digit datasets where the performances are almost saturated. Also, Table 2 shows that DIAS improves the accuracy of the closed set along with its capability of detecting unknowns.

We discussed that DIAS establishes a standard to determine a proper threshold for unknowns in Sect. 3.4. In Table 3, we validate such claim that DIAS does not require expensive and complex tuning for the threshold search so thus it is much more practical than previous works. For a fair comparison, baseline results are from [43], and ARPL+cs and ours are tested on the same split. The results show that DIAS consistently outperforms the baselines with noticeable margins. For the threshold, we find $\epsilon$ in Eq. 12 works well when set to -0.05 for all experiments.

As previously did in [13,38,47], we conduct an additional open set detection experiment. Briefly, we train the classifier on MNIST and evaluate on Omniglot [25], MNIST-Noise, and Noise. Omniglot is an alphabet dataset of 1623 handwritten characters from 50 writing systems, and Noise is a synthesized dataset where each pixel is sampled from a gaussian distribution. MNIST-Noise is noise-embedded MNIST dataset. We sample 10000 examples from each dataset since MNIST contains 10000 instances. The macro F-score between ten digit classes and open set classes are measured to compare performances. The experimental results are reported in Table 4. Although the performances on all three datasets are almost saturated, DIAS provides competitive results with state-of-the-art methods.

**Table 5.** Ablation study on varying difficulties of fake examples. We report the AUROC scores on CIFAR100 dataset against varying openness.

| Copycat Hard | GAN Moderate | Copycat Easy | Openness (%) 22.54 | 29.29 | 55.28 | 68.38 |
|---|---|---|---|---|---|---|
| – | – | – | 72.28 | 71.72 | 78.85 | 77.34 |
| – | – | ✓ | 72.45 | 72.51 | 78.67 | 78.36 |
| – | ✓ | – | 73.69 | 72.46 | 79.20 | 81.13 |
| ✓ | – | – | 76.59 | 74.82 | 81.05 | 80.91 |
| ✓ | – | ✓ | 76.79 | 74.92 | 81.06 | 81.56 |
| ✓ | ✓ | ✓ | **76.92** | **75.55** | **81.59** | **83.95** |

**Table 6.** Ablation study on each generator in DIAS with F1-score.

| Copycat | GAN | MNIST | SVHN | C10 | C+10 | C+50 |
|---|---|---|---|---|---|---|
| – | – | 0.767 | 0.762 | 0.704 | 0.778 | 0.660 |
| – | ✓ | 0.926 | 0.840 | 0.777 | 0.850 | 0.775 |
| ✓ | - | 0.948 | 0.860 | 0.788 | 0.846 | 0.816 |
| ✓ | ✓ | **0.953** | **0.880** | **0.809** | **0.859** | **0.829** |

### 4.3   Ablation Study and Further Analysis

**Effect of Varying Difficulty Levels.** In Table 5, we summarize the ablation analysis on varying difficulties of fake samples. As reported, our hard-difficulty fakes have highest contribution to improve the OSR performance. It validates that the detailed calibration of decision boundaries by facing with hard-difficulty fake examples is significantly helpful to enhance the model robustness toward unseen samples. For the relatively small improvement brought by the easy-difficulty examples, we think that the supervised models are already quite robust against such easy cases. More importantly, by utilizing all the difficulty-level samples for the simulation, DIAS boosts the AUROC at various openness configurations. On top of this, we also evaluate each generator in Table 6 with F1-score to show their relative importance. Note that, we search for the best threshold by Eq. 12 to distinguish open set with F1-score for approaches without the Copycat, while it occurs by itself for DIAS when processing the hard fakes of Copycat. Results demonstrate that both our generators are suitable for simulating open set instances and also validate the unique advantages of Copycat; significantly improving the performance with its inherent threshold for identifying unknowns.

**Effect of Smoothing Ratio.** Since $\alpha_{hard}$ is an important parameter, we study its impact in Fig. 5 (a). Intuitively, the target label for the fake samples become uniform distribution when $\alpha_{hard}$ is 1, while it becomes one-hot label with $\alpha_{hard}$ of 0. The tendency observed from the gray bar with $\alpha_{hard} = 1$, forcing the hard-difficulty samples to have uniformly distributed class probability drastically degrades the performance. On the other hand, the performance is also dropped if we treat the fake samples as known classes with $\alpha_{hard} = 0$, since in such case the hard-difficulty samples are no longer utilized to calibrate within the class decision boundaries. Excepting those extreme cases, we observe that DIAS has low sensitivity to the choice of the hyperparameter $\alpha_{hard}$. Note that, all the results reported in Table 3 is produced with $\alpha_{hard}$ of 0.5.

**Table 7.** Validity of the inherent threshold in DIAS. For DIAS (*), we searched the best threshold for identifying unknowns in DIAS.

| Method | MNIST | SVHN | CIFAR10 | CIFAR+10 | CIFAR+50 |
|---|---|---|---|---|---|
| DIAS | $0.953_{\pm0.015}$ | $0.880_{\pm0.010}$ | $0.809_{\pm0.026}$ | $0.859_{\pm0.010}$ | $0.829_{\pm0.006}$ |
| DIAS (*) | $0.970_{\pm0.004}$ | $0.883_{\pm0.009}$ | $0.809_{\pm0.026}$ | $0.861_{\pm0.009}$ | $0.833_{\pm0.005}$ |

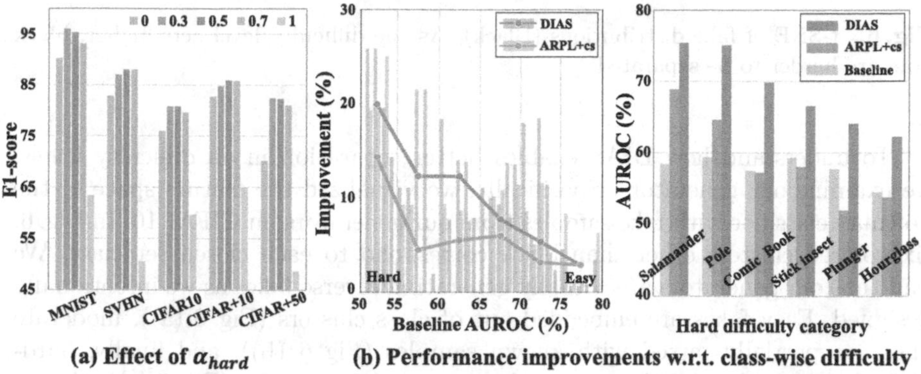

(a) Effect of $\alpha_{hard}$     (b) Performance improvements w.r.t. class-wise difficulty

**Fig. 5.** (a) Effect of $\alpha_{hard}$. Results demonstrate that hard fake samples significantly contribute to calibrate the decision boundary. Regarding these as either known (green) or unknown (gray) decreases the performances. (b) Performance improvements over the baseline Softmax classifier w.r.t. the class-wise difficulty. (b-Left) The difficulty of open classes are determined by the AUROC scores of the Softmax classifier (x-axis). Thus, the lower AUROC scores, the harder the classes are, and placed on the left side. The bars in the graph show the class-wise improvements from the baseline Softmax classifier in order of the difficulty level, while the curves represent the average improvements over classes within 5% intervals on the AUROC scores of the Softmax classifier. As shown, DIAS is more effective in distinguishing harder open classes. (b-Right) Comparison of class-specific AUROC scores on harder open classes. Such results validate the effectiveness of DIAS for identifying open set classes which our baseline classifiers find difficult.

**Validity of the inherent threshold** is confirmed in Table 7. Although the optimal threshold may differ between datasets, only small gaps between the best and inherent thresholds verify that smoothed probability for hard fake examples is suitable to be an adequate threshold because there is no searching cost.

**Further Analysis.** We conducted an in-depth analysis on Tiny-ImageNet to explore why the proposed method is effective in detecting unknowns and how effective it is on each class and each difficulty group. For this study, we assume that difficulty levels are only varying across classes. In other words, we do not consider the instance-wise difficulty in this experiment. Specifically, we utilize class-wise AUROC score of the Softmax classifier to determine the difficulty. The class-wise improvements of the OSR is reported in Fig. 5 (b) with comparison against the most recent simulation method [4]. Those results validate the merits of proposed DIAS especially in distinguishing confusing known and unknown instances, while it provides improvements across all levels of difficulties.

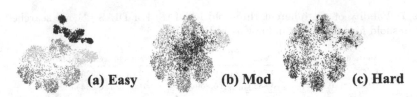

**(a) Easy**        **(b) Mod**        **(c) Hard**

**Fig. 6.** t-SNE of fake distributions (Black). As the difficulty level gets higher, black dots are harder to be separated.

To understand how DIAS enables better separation in all difficulty levels, we examine our generators. Specifically, we visualized the feature space of the Softmax classifier with fake samples from our generators on CIFAR10. In Fig. 6, six colored clusters other than black correspond to each closed set class. We find that our generators are actually generating diverse fakes as we intentionally designed. Easy fakes are embedded out of class clusters (Fig. 6 (a)), moderate ones are partially mixed with known samples (Fig. 6 (b)), and finally, hard-difficulty examples significantly overlie on top of the knowns (Fig. 6 (c)). Hence, as our virtual open set covers broader range of difficulty levels in open set, DIAS produced better results across all difficulty levels.

In addition, one may ask how the Copycat is able to generate more confusing fakes than GAN. This is because the generator in GAN learn to generate fakes that share features with knowns in the viewpoint of the discriminator, while the difficulty levels depend on the viewpoint of the classifier. As the Copycat learns the classifier's perspective iteratively, the Copycat is equipped with the strength to generate confusing fake instances from the classifier's viewpoint. AUROC and W.D from Fig. 1 and visualized feature maps in Fig. 6 further support the choice of setting the Copycat as the most difficult-fake instance generator.

### 4.4    Implementation Details

DIAS is an end-to-end framework that all components are learned from the scratch. For the Copycat and the classifier, we use vanilla CNN [28], which is composed of 9 convolution layers. For the subgroups of convolutional layers, each group contains three $3 \times 3$ convolution layers. Additionally, the backbone network for the generator and the discriminator each contains 4 convolutional layers. Moreover, we adopt multi-batch normalization layers to process generated images from GAN separately, as we hope to prevent the problem from distribution mismatch, following [4]. Note that features from the Copycat do not need to be processed separately. For scaling parameters, we fix both $\lambda$, and $\beta$ to 0.1.

## 5    Conclusion

OSR assumes numerous objects are present that do not belong to learned classes. When classifiers are facing with these, they misclassify them into one of the known categories, often with high confidence. To prepare the classifier for handling unknowns, there have been works to simulate virtual open instances. However, these works only considered unknowns as one set. We claim that considering various levels of difficulty in OSR is an untapped question to be studied. To this end, we proposed the Difficulty-Aware Simulator to simulate open set with fakes at various difficulty levels. Also, we introduced the Copycat and the GAN-based generator in the classifier's perspective for preparing adequate fake samples for classifier tuning. Extensive experiments demonstrate that our proposed DIAS significantly improves the robustness of the classifier toward open set instances.

**Acknowledgements.** This work was supported in part by MSIT/IITP (No. 2022-0-00680, 2020-0-00973, 2020-0-01821, and 2019-0-00421), MCST/KOCCA (No. R20200 70002), and MSIT&KNPA/KIPoT (Police Lab 2.0, No. 210121M06).

# References

1. Arora, S., Ge, R., Liang, Y., Ma, T., Zhang, Y.: Generalization and equilibrium in generative adversarial nets (GANs). In: International Conference on Machine Learning. PMLR (2017)
2. Bendale, A., Boult, T.: Towards open world recognition. In: Proceedings of the IEEE Conference on Computer Vision and Pattern Recognition (2015)
3. Bendale, A., Boult, T.E.: Towards open set deep networks. In: Proceedings of the IEEE Conference on Computer Vision and Pattern Recognition (2016)
4. Chen, G., Peng, P., Wang, X., Tian, Y.: Adversarial reciprocal points learning for open set recognition. IEEE Trans. Pattern Anal. Mach. Intell. (TPAMI) (2021). https://doi.org/10.1109/TPAMI.2021.3106743
5. Chen, G., et al.: Learning open set network with discriminative reciprocal points. In: Vedaldi, A., Bischof, H., Brox, T., Frahm, J.-M. (eds.) ECCV 2020. LNCS, vol. 12348, pp. 507–522. Springer, Cham (2020). https://doi.org/10.1007/978-3-030-58580-8_30
6. Chen, P., Liu, S., Zhao, H., Jia, J.: Distilling knowledge via knowledge review. In: Proceedings of the IEEE/CVF Conference on Computer Vision and Pattern Recognition (2021)
7. Deng, J., Dong, W., Socher, R., Li, L.J., Li, K., Fei-Fei, L.: ImageNet: a large-scale hierarchical image database. In: 2009 IEEE Conference on Computer Vision and Pattern Recognition. IEEE (2009)
8. Ge, Z., Demyanov, S., Chen, Z., Garnavi, R.: Generative openmax for multi-class open set classification. In: Proceedings of the British Machine Vision Conference (BMVC) (2017)
9. Geirhos, R., et al.: Shortcut learning in deep neural networks. Nature Machine Intelligence (2020)
10. Girish, S., Suri, S., Rambhatla, S.S., Shrivastava, A.: Towards discovery and attribution of open-world GAN generated images. In: Proceedings of the IEEE/CVF International Conference on Computer Vision, pp. 14094–14103 (2021)
11. Goodfellow, I., et al.: Generative adversarial nets. Advances in neural information processing systems (2014)
12. Guo, C., Pleiss, G., Sun, Y., Weinberger, K.Q.: On calibration of modern neural networks. In: International Conference on Machine Learning. PMLR (2017)

13. Guo, Y., Camporese, G., Yang, W., Sperduti, A., Ballan, L.: Conditional variational capsule network for open set recognition. In: Proceedings of the IEEE International Conference on Computer Vision (ICCV) (2021)
14. He, K., Zhang, X., Ren, S., Sun, J.: Deep residual learning for image recognition. In: Proceedings of the IEEE Conference on Computer Vision and Pattern Recognition (2016)
15. He, K., Zhang, X., Ren, S., Sun, J.: Deep residual learning for image recognition. In: Proceedings of the IEEE Conference on Computer Vision and Pattern Recognition (2016)
16. Hendrycks, D., Gimpel, K.: A baseline for detecting misclassified and out-of-distribution examples in neural networks. In: International Conference on Learning Representations (ICLR) (2017)
17. Hinton, G., Vinyals, O., Dean, J.: Distilling the knowledge in a neural network. In: NIPS Workshop on Deep Learning and Representation Learning Workshop (2015)
18. Hsu, Y.C., Shen, Y., Jin, H., Kira, Z.: Generalized ODIN: detecting out-of-distribution image without learning from out-of-distribution data. In: Proceedings of the IEEE/CVF Conference on Computer Vision and Pattern Recognition (2020)
19. Huang, G., Liu, Z., Van Der Maaten, L., Weinberger, K.Q.: Densely connected convolutional networks. In: Proceedings of the IEEE Conference on Computer Vision and Pattern Recognition (2017)
20. Jain, L.P., Scheirer, W.J., Boult, T.E.: Multi-class open set recognition using probability of inclusion. In: Fleet, D., Pajdla, T., Schiele, B., Tuytelaars, T. (eds.) ECCV 2014. LNCS, vol. 8691, pp. 393–409. Springer, Cham (2014). https://doi.org/10.1007/978-3-319-10578-9_26
21. Júnior, P.R.M., et al.: Nearest neighbors distance ratio open-set classifier. Machine Learning (2017)
22. Kong, S., Ramanan, D.: OpenGAN: Open-set recognition via open data generation. In: ICCV (2021)
23. Krizhevsky, A., Hinton, G., et al.: Learning multiple layers of features from tiny images (2009)
24. Krizhevsky, A., Sutskever, I., Hinton, G.E.: ImageNet classification with deep convolutional neural networks. In: Advances in Neural Information Processing Systems (2012)
25. Lake, B.M., Salakhutdinov, R., Tenenbaum, J.B.: Human-level concept learning through probabilistic program induction. Science **350**, 1332–1338 (2015)
26. LeCun, Y., Bottou, L., Bengio, Y., Haffner, P.: Gradient-based learning applied to document recognition. In: Proceedings of the IEEE (1998)
27. Lee, K., Lee, H., Lee, K., Shin, J.: Training confidence-calibrated classifiers for detecting out-of-distribution samples. In: International Conference on Learning Representations (ICLR) (2018)
28. Neal, L., Olson, M., Fern, X., Wong, W.K., Li, F.: Open set learning with counterfactual images. In: Proceedings of the European Conference on Computer Vision (ECCV) (2018)
29. Netzer, Y., Wang, T., Coates, A., Bissacco, A., Wu, B., Ng, A.Y.: Reading digits in natural images with unsupervised feature learning. In: NIPS Workshop on Deep Learning and Unsupervised Feature Learning (2011)
30. Nguyen, A., Yosinski, J., Clune, J.: Deep neural networks are easily fooled: High confidence predictions for unrecognizable images. In: Proceedings of the IEEE Conference on Computer Vision and Pattern Recognition (2015)

31. Oza, P., Patel, V.M.: C2ae: Class conditioned auto-encoder for open-set recognition. In: Proceedings of the IEEE/CVF Conference on Computer Vision and Pattern Recognition (2019)
32. Perera, P., et al.: Generative-discriminative feature representations for open-set recognition. In: Proceedings of the IEEE/CVF Conference on Computer Vision and Pattern Recognition (2020)
33. Roady, R., Hayes, T.L., Kemker, R., Gonzales, A., Kanan, C.: Are open set classification methods effective on large-scale datasets? PLOS one (2020)
34. Russakovsky, O., et al.: ImageNet large scale visual recognition challenge. Int. J. Comput. Vis. (2015)
35. Scheirer, W.J., Jain, L.P., Boult, T.E.: Probability models for open set recognition. In: IEEE Transactions on Pattern Analysis and Machine Intelligence (2014)
36. Scheirer, W.J., de Rezende Rocha, A., Sapkota, A., Boult, T.E.: Toward open set recognition. In: IEEE Transactions on Pattern Analysis and Machine Intelligence (2012)
37. Shu, L., Xu, H., Liu, B.: Doc: Deep open classification of text documents. In: Proceedings of the 2017 Conference on Empirical Methods in Natural Language Processing, (EMNLP) (2017)
38. Sun, X., Yang, Z., Zhang, C., Ling, K.V., Peng, G.: Conditional gaussian distribution learning for open set recognition. In: Proceedings of the IEEE/CVF Conference on Computer Vision and Pattern Recognition (CVPR) (2020)
39. Tudor Ionescu, R., Alexe, B., Leordeanu, M., Popescu, M., Papadopoulos, D.P., Ferrari, V.: How hard can it be? estimating the difficulty of visual search in an image. In: Proceedings of the IEEE Conference on Computer Vision and Pattern Recognition (2016)
40. Verma, V., et al.: Manifold mixup: better representations by interpolating hidden states. In: International Conference on Machine Learning. PMLR (2019)
41. Yim, J., Joo, D., Bae, J., Kim, J.: A gift from knowledge distillation: Fast optimization, network minimization and transfer learning. In: Proceedings of the IEEE Conference on Computer Vision and Pattern Recognition (2017)
42. Yoshihashi, R., Shao, W., Kawakami, R., You, S., Iida, M., Naemura, T.: Classification-reconstruction learning for open-set recognition. In: Proceedings of the IEEE/CVF Conference on Computer Vision and Pattern Recognition (2019)
43. Yue, Z., Wang, T., Sun, Q., Hua, X.S., Zhang, H.: Counterfactual zero-shot and open-set visual recognition. In: Proceedings of the IEEE/CVF Conference on Computer Vision and Pattern Recognition (CVPR) (2021)
44. Zagoruyko, S., Komodakis, N.: Paying more attention to attention: Improving the performance of convolutional neural networks via attention transfer. In: International Conference on Learning Representations (ICLR) (2017)
45. Zhang, H., Patel, V.M.: Sparse representation-based open set recognition. IEEE Trans. Pattern Anal. Mach. Intell. **39**, 1690–1696 (2016)
46. Zhang, H., Li, A., Guo, J., Guo, Y.: Hybrid models for open set recognition. In: Vedaldi, A., Bischof, H., Brox, T., Frahm, J.-M. (eds.) ECCV 2020. LNCS, vol. 12348, pp. 102–117. Springer, Cham (2020). https://doi.org/10.1007/978-3-030-58580-8_7
47. Zhou, D.W., Ye, H.J., Zhan, D.C.: Learning placeholders for open-set recognition. In: Proceedings of the IEEE/CVF Conference on Computer Vision and Pattern Recognition (2021)

# Few-Shot Class-Incremental Learning from an Open-Set Perspective

Can Peng[1]($\boxtimes$) (iD), Kun Zhao[2], Tianren Wang[1], Meng Li[1], and Brian C. Lovell[1]

[1] The University of Queensland, Brisbane, QLD, Australia
{can.peng,tianren.wang,meng.li6}@uq.net.au, lovell@itee.uq.edu.au
[2] Sullivan Nicolaides Pathology, Brisbane, Australia
kun_zhao@snp.com.au

**Abstract.** The continual appearance of new objects in the visual world poses considerable challenges for current deep learning methods in real-world deployments. The challenge of new task learning is often exacerbated by the scarcity of data for the new categories due to rarity or cost. Here we explore the important task of Few-Shot Class-Incremental Learning (FSCIL) and its extreme data scarcity condition of one-shot. An ideal FSCIL model needs to perform well on all classes, regardless of their presentation order or paucity of data. It also needs to be robust to open-set real-world conditions and be easily adapted to the new tasks that always arise in the field. In this paper, we first reevaluate the current task setting and propose a more comprehensive and practical setting for the FSCIL task. Then, inspired by the similarity of the goals for FSCIL and modern face recognition systems, we propose our method—Augmented Angular Loss Incremental Classification or ALICE. In ALICE, instead of the commonly used cross-entropy loss, we propose to use the angular penalty loss to obtain well-clustered features. As the obtained features not only need to be compactly clustered but also diverse enough to maintain generalization for future incremental classes, we further discuss how class augmentation, data augmentation, and data balancing affect classification performance. Experiments on benchmark datasets, including CIFAR100, miniImageNet, and CUB200, demonstrate the improved performance of ALICE over the state-of-the-art FSCIL methods. Code is available at https://github.com/CanPeng123/FSCIL_ALICE.

**Keywords:** Few shot · One shot · Incremental learning · Classification

## 1 Introduction

In recent years, the computer vision community has witnessed astonishing performance breakthroughs in many traditional vision tasks. These breakthroughs

**Supplementary Information** The online version contains supplementary material available at https://doi.org/10.1007/978-3-031-19806-9_22.

are mainly due to the emergence of deep learning models and algorithms, publicly available large data sets for training, and powerful GPU computing devices. Despite their popularity, current deep learning techniques mostly rely on large-scale supervised data to train accurate models. A deep neural network (DNN) with tens of thousands of parameters cannot be easily adapted to a new task by training on just a few examples. In addition, conventional deep learning models lack the capability of preserving previous knowledge while adapting to new tasks. When a neural network is fine-tuned to learn a new task, its performance on previously trained tasks will significantly deteriorate, a problem known as catastrophic forgetting [8,16]. Exploring the fast learning and memorizing capability of deep learning models is an important step toward improving their practical application ability.

In this paper, we tackle this significant research direction—Few-Shot Class-Incremental Learning (FSCIL). FSCIL requires the trained model to not only quickly adapt to continually arriving new tasks, but also to retain the old knowledge about previously learned tasks. Considering real-life application, an ideal FSCIL model needs to have the following characteristics: 1) The model needs to perform well on all classes equally, no matter what the training presentation sequence is; and 2) the model needs to be robust to extreme data scarcity, such as the one-shot scenario. However, current SOTA methods mainly use sole class-wise average accuracy to evaluate the model performance which cannot assess whether there is a prediction bias due to class imbalance and data imbalance. As there are normally more base classes than incremental classes and only limited data is provided for each incremental class, prediction bias towards base classes can easily happen. In addition, current SOTA methods rarely consider the extreme one-shot setting which can happen in the real world due to incremental data collection and rare data types. A well-established task setup is a cornerstone for the development of this task since an improper task setup will misguide the method design and lead to methods with limited application. Thus, before designing our method, we reformulate the setup for the FSCIL task.

Considering the paucity of incremental session data and the absence of old session data, we think the feature extractor trained on the base session should not be limited to extracting discriminative features for the base categories. The ability of representing new unseen samples from future novel classes is also critical. On the one hand, we are motivated by the similarity between FSCIL and face recognition tasks. The face recognition system learns to distinguish and recognize new faces quickly via its deep metric learning framework. The capability of handling new identities without the need for retraining is a major achievement of modern face recognition methods and is also what the FSCIL task desires. On the other hand, we are motivated by the intuitive connection between FSCIL and data augmentation. Data augmentation focuses on improving the generalization of a DNN. The capability of extracting diverse features that is transferable across base and incremental classes is important for the FSCIL task. Hence in this work, we adopt some ideas from both modern face recognition and data augmentation to design our method.

**The contributions** of this paper are: (**1**) We reevaluate the current benchmark task settings of FSCIL and propose additional experimental settings and evaluation metrics to more comprehensively assess the capability of FSCIL methods. (**2**) We solve the FSCIL task from a new perspective of the open-set problem. We analyze the angular penalty loss from face recognition and adapt it to FSCIL to improve the discrimination of the model. (**3**) We further analyze how data processing, such as class augmentation, data augmentation, and balanced data embedding affect FSCIL performance and aim to improve the generalization of the model. (**4**) Significant improvements on three benchmark datasets, CIFAR100, miniImageNet, and CUB200, demonstrate the effectiveness of our method against SOTA methods.

## 2    Related Work

**Few-shot Class-incremental Learning.** The FSCIL task is a newly emerged challenge evolved from class-incremental learning [1,11,17]. Once established, the research community has spent much effort developing algorithms for this important FSCIL task. For SOTA FSCIL methods, after base session training, some update the backbone [4,7,19,25] and some freeze the backbone [5,23,27]. Backbone updating methods commonly use the knowledge distillation [10] technique to preserve the old knowledge. Knowledge distillation relies on having sufficient data to simulate the input-output function of the old model. To adapt knowledge distillation to FSCIL, these methods store old exemplars, require a complex updating scheme for each incremental task, or are incapable of extreme data scarcity conditions such as 1-shot. However, high performance and flexible operation are both important for real-world applications. Also, storing old exemplars is undesirable due to memory restrictions. In addition, the backbone network has a large number of parameters despite there being extremely limited new task data. The large imbalance between parameters and data causes the backbone updating methods to normally show lower performance than backbone freezing methods under the same experimental setup.

On the contrary, freezing the backbone network is a good choice to well balance not only the real-life application requirements but also the stability and plasticity trade-off. This backbone freezing strategy decouples the learning of representations and classifiers to avoid overfitting and catastrophic forgetting in the representations. Also, the fundamental feature characteristics are similar for many objects, so features learned from the base session can be readopted for recognizing new classes. Our method belongs to the backbone freezing type of methods. Although this decoupling strategy has been explored by Zhang *et al.* [23], their method focuses on designing a discriminative classifier. On the contrary, we focus on feature distribution, since this is a cornerstone of robust classification performance. Last but not the least, a good FSCIL method needs to perform equally well on all the classes no matter whether they are base or incremental classes. This is a problem for the current backbone freezing type of methods that their good overall accuracy is mainly derived from the base session.

In this paper, we target on proposing an FSCIL method that takes advantage of decoupling representation and classification via backbone freezing, and at the same time, solves the side effect of prediction bias.

**Deep Metric Learning.** Deep metric learning is commonly used for face recognition tasks. Inspired by the relation between normalized weights on the last fully connected layer and class centers, Liu *et al.* proposed SphereFace [14] which uses an angular margin penalty to enforce extra intra-class compactness and inter-class discrepancy. Following SphereFace, CosFace [21] and ArcFace [6] were proposed to reduce the complex loss calculation and make the training procedure more stable. There are many similarities between face recognition and FSCIL tasks: 1) both tasks are open-set object recognition tasks that need to classify a large amount of continually arriving new objects (classes/face identities); 2) both tasks are provided with unbalanced data; and 3) both tasks require fast adaptation on new objects as well as maintaining performance on old objects. Inspired by these similarities, in this paper, we try to solve the FSCIL task from a new perspective of the open-set problem. We adopt the idea of angular penalty loss from face recognition to the more general problem of object recognition.

As real-world classification problems typically exhibit class imbalance or long-tailed data distribution, some methods have explored deep metric learning for incremental and long-tail tasks [12,15,22]. However, these methods normally assume sufficient data is available which is a different setting from FSCIL. Most FSCIL methods solve this problem from the perspective of either incremental learning (advanced knowledge distillation) [4,7,25] or few-shot learning (freezing backbone and evolving prototypes) [5,23,27]. We follow the proposal of freezing the backbone network to decouple the learning of representations and classifiers. However, different from current backbone freezing type of methods that maintain the incremental learning ability by evolving classification prototypes, we focus on improving the transfer capability of the feature extractor.

## 3 Problem Formulation

FSCIL task comprises a base task with sufficient training data and multiple incremental tasks with limited training data. During the learning of each new task, only the data for the current task is available and the model is required to learn this new task information whilst retaining old task knowledge.

To be specific, assume an $M$-step FSCIL task. Let $\{D^0_{train}, D^1_{train}, ..., D^m_{train}\}$ and $\{D^0_{test}, D^1_{test}, ..., D^m_{test}\}$ denotes the training and testing data for sessions $\{0, 1, ..., m\}$, respectively. For session $i$, it has training data $D^i_{train}$ with the corresponding label space of $C^i$. Training data from different sessions have no overlapped classes, so when $i \neq j$, $C^i \cap C^j = \varnothing$. During testing, the model will be evaluated on all seen classes so far, so for session $i$, its testing data $D^i_{test}$ has the corresponding label space of $C^0 \cup C^1 ... \cup C^i$. In addition, for the base session ($i = 0$), a sufficient amount of training data is provided and for the following incremental sessions ($i > 0$), only a limited amount of data is provided.

Most papers about FSCIL [4,5,7,23,25,27] follow the task setting proposed by Tao *et al.* [19]. As FSCIL focuses on mimicking real-life situations, we think

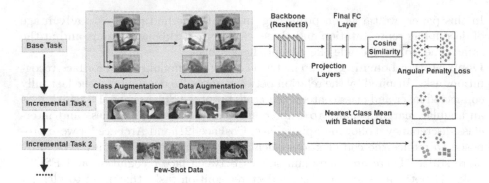

**Fig. 1.** The framework of our proposed method. On the one hand, with sufficient base task data available, angular penalty loss, class augmentation, and data augmentation are utilized to obtain a general open-set feature extractor. On the other hand, as only limited incremental task data is available, the few-shot new class data and the carefully chosen same number of base class data are utilized to generate the balanced class-wise prototypes. Nearest class mean and cosine similarity are adopted to do the final classification.

some aspects of the current benchmark experimental protocol are not sufficient to evaluate the efficiency of an FSCIL method. Thus, before proposing our method, we propose a more comprehensive and practical setup for the FSCIL task.

**Number of Few-Shot Data.** Current benchmark experiments are performed with 5-shot, 10-shot, or more data being available for each incremental step. The extreme data scarcity condition of 1-shot which can easily happen in the real world due to extremely scarce data type is rarely considered.

**Evaluation Metric.** Current benchmark evaluation metrics mainly use class-wise average accuracy to evaluate the performance of an FSCIL model. As there are normally more base classes than incremental new classes, using average accuracy cannot indicate if there is a prediction bias between base and incremental classes. A method cannot be regarded as a good FSCIL method if its good performance is mainly determined by the base class performance.

**Dataset.** The similarity between base classes and new classes will strongly affect model performance since the high re-usability of base features such as fine-grained datasets will naturally reduce the challenge of catastrophic forgetting. An optimal FSCIL model needs to not only perform well on high-distributional-match fine-grained datasets but also on low-distributional-match datasets.

To sum up, to comprehensively simulate the real-world FSCIL condition and evaluate the robustness of an FSCIL method, we consider both benchmark 5-shot and 1-shot settings. Also, for the evaluation metric, we propose to use both average accuracy and harmonic accuracy to evaluate not only the overall performance but also the performance balance between base and incremental classes. In addition, we perform experiments on both general (CIFAR100 and mini-ImageNet) and fine-grained (CUB200) datasets to remove the possible performance benefit due to high similarity between base and incremental classes.

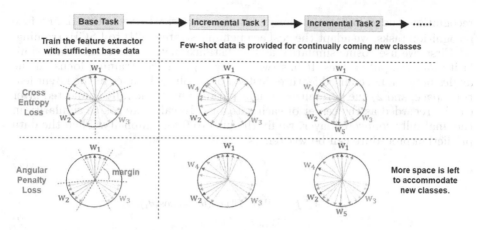

**Fig. 2.** An illustration of feature distributions of a cross-entropy loss trained model and an angular penalty loss trained model. The light color arrows represent examples of different class features on the latent feature space. The dark color arrows represent the average feature prototype of corresponding classes. Angular penalty loss provides more compact intra-class clustering and wider inter-class separation than cross-entropy loss. Compact clustering leaves more room on the latent feature space to accommodate the new classes.

## 4  Methodology

In this section, we propose the FSCIL method ALICE using angular penalty, class and data augmentation, and data balancing. First, for the base session, we apply the angular penalty loss to train the feature extractor to obtain compact intra-class clustering and wide inter-class separation. Class augmentation and data augmentation are also adopted to improve the generalization of the feature extractor. Then, for the incremental sessions, specifically chosen balanced data are utilized to generate prototypes for each class. Nearest class mean and cosine similarity are combined to perform the classification. Figure 1 demonstrates the framework of our method.

### 4.1  Angular Penalty

Under the FSCIL setting, we want to obtain a feature extractor which can rapidly adapt to continually coming new tasks, as well as be stable to overcome catastrophic forgetting for the previously learned tasks. Thus, we want to use a loss function that: 1) minimizes the distance between intra-class feature vectors, and 2) maximizes the distance between inter-class feature vectors. The compact intra-class clustering and wide inter-class separation will leave more room in the latent feature space for the incrementally arriving new classes and hence lead to better open-set classification. Figure 2 illustrates an example. As many innovative angular penalty losses have been explored and proposed for face recognition studies [6,21] and considering the similarity between FSCIL and face recognition tasks, we adapt the cosFace penalty strategy [21] to FSCIL training.

First, we use cosine similarity as the distance metric to measure data similarity and compute scores. It has two effects: 1) it makes training focus on the angles between normalized features instead of absolute distance in the latent feature space, and 2) the normalized weight parameters of the fully connected layer can be regarded as the center of each category. To calculate cosine similarity in the final fully connected layer, we fix the bias to 0 for simplicity. Then the data prediction procedure can be written as:

$$f = \mathcal{F}(x) \tag{1}$$

$$y_i = W_i^T f = \|W_i\| \|f\| \cos(\theta_i) = \cos(\theta_i),$$
$$\|W_i\| = \|f\| = 1 \tag{2}$$

where $f$ is the feature obtained from the input image $x$ through the feature extractor $\mathcal{F}$. The feature $f$ and the weight parameter $W_i$ are normalized by $\ell 2$ normalization, so the magnitude is 1. The quantity $y_i$ is the calculated cosine similarity between the feature $f$ and the weight parameter $W_i$ for class $i$. It measures the angular similarity of image $x$ towards class $i$ which indicates the likelihood that image $x$ belongs to class $i$.

Normally, the cosine similarity prediction is used with cross-entropy loss to separate features from different classes by maximizing the probability of the ground-truth class. The loss function is:

$$
\begin{aligned}
L &= -\frac{1}{N} \sum_{j=1}^{N} \log(p_j) = -\frac{1}{N} \sum_{j=1}^{N} \log(\frac{e^{y_j}}{\sum_{i=1}^{C} e^{y_i}}), \\
&= -\frac{1}{N} \sum_{j=1}^{N} \log(\frac{e^{\|W_j\| \|f\| \cos(\theta_j)}}{\sum_{i=1}^{C} e^{\|W_i\| \|f\| \cos(\theta_i)}}), \\
&= -\frac{1}{N} \sum_{j=1}^{N} \log(\frac{e^{\cos(\theta_j)}}{\sum_{i=1}^{C} e^{\cos(\theta_i)}})
\end{aligned}
\tag{3}
$$

where $N$ is the number of training images and $C$ is the number of classes. The quantity $p_j$ describes the softmax probability for image $j$. The quantity $y_j$ describes the cosine similarity towards its ground truth class for image $j$.

To make features better clustered, inspired by cosFace [21], a cosine margin $m$ is introduced to the classification boundary. With the help of the extra margin, the intra-class features become more compactly clustered and the inter-class features become more widely separated. Following cosFace, we also re-scale the normalized feature by a preset scale factor $s$. The loss function is:

$$L_{AP} = -\frac{1}{N} \sum_{j=1}^{N} \log(\frac{e^{s(\cos(\theta_j)-m)}}{e^{s(\cos(\theta_j)-m)} + \sum_{i \neq j} e^{s \cos(\theta_i)}}) \tag{4}$$

The scale factor $s$ is set to 30 and the cosine margin $m$ is set to 0.4 for all experiments.

## 4.2  Augmented Training

Diverse and transferable representation is the key for open-set problems. Exposure to a large number of classes is one way to obtain such kind of feature extractors. To this end, a simple and effective method is to introduce auxiliary classes.

Inspired by Mixup [24] and IL2A [26], we randomly combine pairs of different class examples from the base session data to synthesize auxiliary new class data. The new class data generating function is:

$$x_k = \lambda x_i + (1 - \lambda)x_j \qquad (5)$$

where $x_i$ and $x_j$ are two training samples from two different classes $i$ and $j$ randomly picked from the $C$ base session classes. $\lambda$ is the interpolation coefficient. $x_k$ is the generated new class data. Figure 3 shows an example. In our experiments, following IL2A [26], we restrict $\lambda$ to be a randomly chosen value between

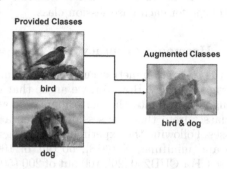

Fig. 3. An example of class augmentation. Auxiliary new class data is generated by interpolating two different class samples from base session data.

$[0.4, 0.6]$ to reduce the overlap between the augmented and original classes. For a $C$-class classification task, by pair combination, we will generate $(C \times (C-1)/2)$ new classes, so the original $C$-class classification task now becomes a $(C + C \times (C-1)/2)$-class classification task.

Exposure to various image conditions during training is also a good method to obtain a general feature extractor. Inspired by self-supervised learning [2,3], we use two augmentations of each image to enhance training data diversity. Figure 1 shows the augmentation procedure. During training, for each input image, we randomly generate two augmentations from a set of preset transformation strategies. For the utilized transformation methods, we randomly apply resized crop, horizontal flip, color jitter, and grayscale. Then both transformed data are sent to the backbone network. The losses from two sets of augmentation are averaged and back-propagated to update model parameters. In addition, to avoid the feature extractor over-specialize to base session data, following SimCLR [2], we utilize extra projection layers before the final fully connected layer. By leveraging the nonlinear projection head, more information can be formed and maintained in the feature extractor.

## 4.3  Balanced Testing

After base session training, the projection head and the augmented classification head are discarded. Only the feature extractor is left and it is frozen to avoid both overfitting and catastrophic forgetting. During testing, nearest class mean and cosine similarity are utilized to do the classification. As there is only limited data provided for each incremental session, to alleviate the possible prediction bias due to data imbalance, we use the same amount of few-shot data as the following incremental steps to generate the base class prototypes. To select suitable examples, we first use all base session data to calculate the class-wise mean for each base class. Then the required few-shot amount of data which has the smallest cosine distance with the calculated mean is used to generate the final prototype for each base session class.

### 4.4  Harmonic Accuracy

For the evaluation metric, current SOTA methods generally report the class-wise average accuracy. However, we argue that the class-wise average accuracy is not enough to evaluate the performance of an FSCIL method, since the number of classes from the base session is often a large fraction of the total number of classes. Following the experimental settings on benchmark papers, for CIFAR100 [13] and miniImageNet [18], 60 out of 100 (60%) categories are used as base classes. For CUB200 [20], 100 out of 200 (50%) categories are used as base classes. A model with good performance on the base session and poor performance on the following incremental sessions can still have a good average accuracy due to the high ratio of base classes to the overall classes. For example, with 60 base classes, on one step of incremental learning 5 classes, an algorithm that shows 100% accuracy on base classes with 0% on incremental classes would be rated 92.3% using average accuracy, yet it would have demonstrated no learning on the new task. To compensate for this deficiency of average accuracy, we adapt the harmonic accuracy metric that requires well-balanced performance across both base and incremental classes. The formula for harmonic accuracy ($A_h$) is:

$$A_h = \frac{2 \times A_b \times A_i}{A_b + A_i} \tag{6}$$

where $A_b$ is the average accuracy for base session classes and $A_i$ is the average accuracy for the following incremental session classes. In the simple example above, the harmonic accuracy would be 0% which is much more appropriate as the network has indeed learned nothing at all. An ideal balanced FSCIL classifier will have equally high performance on both average accuracy and harmonic accuracy. If a model has good average accuracy but poor harmonic accuracy, this means that its good performance is mainly due to performance on the base session classes and the model has poor incremental learning capability overall.

## 5  Experiments

### 5.1  Dataset and Evaluation Metric

We use three benchmark datasets CIFAR100 [13], miniImageNet [18] and Caltech-UCSD Birds-200-2011 (CUB200) [20] for our experiments. CIFAR100 contains 100 classes with 600 images per class, 500 for training and 100 for testing. Each image has a size of $32 \times 32$ pixels. MiniImageNet also contains 100 classes with 600 images per class, 500 for training and 100 for testing. Each image has a size of 84 × 84 pixels. CUB200 is a fine-grained image classification dataset. It contains 200 classes of different species of birds with 5994 training images and 5794 testing images. Each image has a size of 224 × 224 pixels.

As mentioned in Sect. 3, to comprehensively evaluate an FSCIL method, we follow the benchmark 5-shot setting and also perform an additional 1-shot setting. For experiments on CIFAR100 and miniImageNet, the 8-step 5-way 5-shot and 8-step 5-way 1-shot incremental settings are used. In this protocol, 60 classes are used as base classes with all training data provided; then 40 classes are used as incremental classes with 5-shot or 1-shot training data provided in a 5-way manner in 8 steps. For experiments on CUB200, 10-step 10-way 5-shot and 10-step 10-way 1-shot settings are used. 100 classes are used as base classes and the remaining 100 classes are used as incremental classes with 5-shot or 1-shot training data provided in a 10-way manner in 10 steps. To make the evaluation comprehensive and fair, we report both average accuracy and harmonic accuracy.

## 5.2    Implementation Details

For our experiments, we use ResNet18 [9] as the backbone network. We implement the projection head as a two-layer MLP with a hidden feature size of 2048 and ReLU as the activation function. Our method is built with PyTorch library and SGD with momentum is used for optimization. The initial learning rate is set to 0.01 for CIFAR100 and miniImageNet dataset training, and 0.001 for CUB200 dataset training. Following the settings on [19,23], models for CIFAR100 and miniImageNet are trained from scratch, and models for CUB200 are initialized by an ImageNet pretrained model. When class augmentation is not applied, a batch size of 512 is used for training. When class augmentation is used, we use a batch size of 128 for CIFAR100 and a batch size of 64 for miniImageNet. The experimental results for CEC [23] are reproduced by their publicly available source code.

## 5.3    Comparison with the State-of-the-art Methods

We compare our method with the SOTA methods [1,4,5,11,17,19,23] on three datasets. According to Fig. 4, for experiments on CIFAR100 and miniImageNet dataset, under both 8-step 5-way 5-shot and 1-shot settings, our method achieves the highest class-wise accuracy over all the sessions. Also, on both datasets, our ALICE method shows much higher harmonic accuracy on all sessions compared to the SOTA CEC [23] method. The high harmonic accuracy proves that our method can largely alleviate the prediction bias problem. To be more specific, in CIFAR100, for the 5-shot (1-shot) setting, in the last session, we get 54.1% (47.5%) average accuracy and 50.6% (26.5%) harmonic accuracy which is 6.0% (2.7%) and 19.3% (13.5%) higher than the CEC method, respectively. In miniImageNet, for the 5-shot (1-shot) setting, in the last session, we get 55.7% (48.6%) average accuracy and 50.9% (27.1%) harmonic accuracy which is 8.5% (4.9%) and 22.8% (19.3%) higher than the CEC method, respectively.

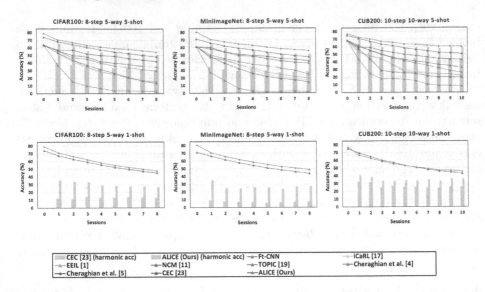

**Fig. 4.** Comparison with SOTA methods under both 5-shot and 1-shot incremental settings on CIFAR100, miniImageNet, and CUB200 dataset. The line chart represents average accuracy and the histogram represents harmonic accuracy. Our method outperforms SOTA works with significant performance advantages.

For experiments on the CUB200 dataset, we find that applying class augmentation will deteriorate the model performance. As CUB200 is a fine-grained dataset, the feature extractor needs to focus on learning tiny differences between categories. However, class augmentation targets obscuring the class difference and forcing the feature extractor to focus on general features. It is a good augmentation strategy to extract transferable features for general FSCIL tasks but will adversely obscure the class boundaries for fine-grained FSCIL tasks. Thus, for experiments on CUB200, we do not use class augmentation and train the feature extractor only by angular penalty and data augmentation. According to Fig. 4, our method outperforms all SOTA methods by a large margin on the 5-shot setting. This proves that for fine-grained classification where the re-usability of features is high, angular penalty and data augmentation is enough to obtain a robust open-set feature extractor. Under the 1-shot setting, we get similar average accuracy as CEC, since both of us freeze the backbone network after base session training to avoid catastrophic forgetting. When considering incremental class performance, our method can better adapt to new classes and obtain much higher harmonic accuracy than the CEC method.

Besides, we also compare the confusion matrices produced by CEC and our method after the last incremental session. The results are shown in Fig. 5. Compared with CEC, our method produces a more balanced base and incremental class performance, especially under 5-shot settings. When under 1-shot settings, although our method can outperform the CEC method, the prediction bias towards base classes still exists. This is because the 1-shot setting is the most extreme FSCIL setting due to maximal data scarcity and data imbalance. We will focus on solving this problem in future work.

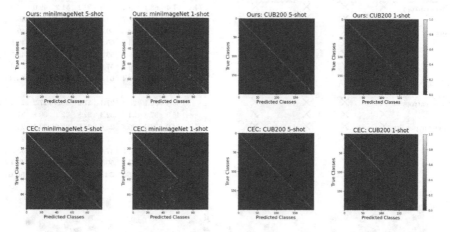

**Fig. 5.** Comparison of the confusion matrices produced by CEC and our method on the last incremental session for 5-shot and 1-shot incremental experiments on miniImageNet and CUB200 dataset.

### 5.4 Ablation Study

To validate the effectiveness of each part of our method, we perform an ablation study on the CIFAR100 dataset under the 8-step 5-way 5-shot setting. Table 1 shows the experimental results for the ablation study. When balanced data are used for prototype generation, compared with the cross-entropy loss trained model, in the last incremental step, the angular penalty loss trained model provides 3.3% average accuracy improvement. But the harmonic accuracy is 6.2% lower. This means that solely using angular penalty loss will make the feature extractor over-specialize to the base session data and lose its generalization performance. The high average accuracy produced by the angular penalty loss trained model with all data used for prototype generation also shows the over-specialization. Their good average performance is mainly due to the base classes since at the first several sessions, the ratio of base classes among all classes is high. To compensate for the loss of generalization, projection layers are utilized to help the feature extractor maintain more information. With the help of the projection layers, in the last incremental session, the average accuracy remains unchanged but the harmonic accuracy is increased from 25.2% to 43.8% which is 12.4% higher than the cross-entropy loss trained model. Then, when two transformations of each input image are utilized for loss calculation, the average accuracy (harmonic accuracy) is 1.8% (3.6%) increased in the last step. After that, when class augmentation is applied, the average accuracy (harmonic accuracy) is increased by 2.8% (3.2%) in the last step. In addition, when

**Table 1.** Ablation study on CIFAR100 under the 8-step 5-way 5-shot setting.

| loss type | Class aug | Data aug | Project layer | Balanced data | 0 | 1 | 2 | 3 | 4 | 5 | 6 | 7 | 8 |
|---|---|---|---|---|---|---|---|---|---|---|---|---|---|
| | | | | | Class-wise average accuracy | | | | | | | | |
| Cross entropy | ✗ | ✗ | ✗ | ✗ | 74.2 | 67.4 | 63.4 | 59.4 | 55.9 | 53.2 | 51.2 | 49.0 | 46.9 |
| | ✗ | ✗ | ✗ | ✓ | 74.2 | 65.4 | 61.6 | 57.7 | 54.5 | 52.1 | 49.9 | 47.9 | 46.2 |
| Angular penalty | ✗ | ✗ | ✗ | ✗ | 76.9 | **72.9** | **68.2** | **64.1** | 60.3 | 57.0 | 54.3 | 51.9 | 49.7 |
| | ✗ | ✗ | ✗ | ✓ | 76.9 | 72.8 | 68.0 | 63.8 | 60.2 | 56.8 | 54.1 | 51.8 | 49.5 |
| | ✗ | ✗ | ✓ | ✓ | 74.2 | 67.1 | 63.7 | 59.9 | 56.8 | 54.1 | 52.8 | 51.1 | 49.5 |
| | ✗ | ✓ | ✓ | ✓ | 75.6 | 68.2 | 64.2 | 60.3 | 57.9 | 55.6 | 54.7 | 53.1 | 51.3 |
| | ✓ | ✓ | ✓ | ✓ | **79.0** | 70.5 | 67.1 | 63.4 | **61.2** | **59.2** | **58.1** | **56.3** | **54.1** |
| | | | | | Harmonic accuracy | | | | | | | | |
| Cross entropy | ✗ | ✗ | ✗ | ✗ | – | 36.5 | 32.1 | 29.4 | 27.1 | 27.2 | 28.3 | 27.2 | 27.4 |
| | ✗ | ✗ | ✗ | ✓ | – | 45.5 | 37.8 | 34.7 | 32.4 | 32.8 | 32.1 | 30.8 | 31.4 |
| angular penalty | ✗ | ✗ | ✗ | ✗ | – | 34.0 | 28.2 | 26.4 | 23.6 | 23.3 | 22.6 | 22.1 | 22.3 |
| | ✗ | ✗ | ✗ | ✓ | – | 40.4 | 32.8 | 29.7 | 27.5 | 26.2 | 25.4 | 24.6 | 25.2 |
| | ✗ | ✗ | ✓ | ✓ | – | 58.9 | 57.2 | 50.5 | 47.9 | 46.4 | 46.4 | 45.0 | 43.8 |
| | ✗ | ✓ | ✓ | ✓ | – | 65.0 | 60.0 | 52.2 | 50.9 | 49.6 | 50.1 | 48.6 | 47.4 |
| | ✓ | ✓ | ✓ | ✓ | – | **65.3** | **62.3** | **55.7** | **54.5** | **54.0** | **53.9** | **52.1** | **50.6** |

(a) Feature distribution trained by cross-entropy loss.

(b) Feature distribution trained by angular penalty loss.

(c) Trained by angular penalty loss with projection layers. Class and data augmentation are applied.

**Fig. 6.** t-SNE visualization of the feature embeddings for the 60 base classes on CIFAR100. Each small colored number represents one feature instance for that class. The bold black number represents the average prototype for the class.

balanced data is used for prototype generation, the harmonic accuracy for both cross-entropy and angular penalty loss trained model is increased. This shows that simply utilizing the same amount of data from the base and incremental sessions to generate class prototypes can effectively alleviate the prediction bias due to data imbalance.

Figure 6 shows the t-SNE visualization of the training data feature generated by different training strategies. The model trained via angular penalty loss makes the training data cluster better in the latent feature space than the model trained via cross-entropy loss. Then with the further help of projection layers, class and data augmentation, diverse and transferable features are obtained while different class features are still well separated.

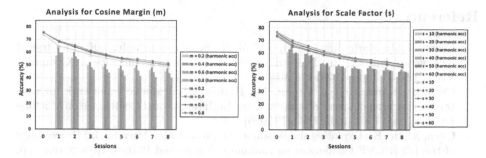

**Fig. 7.** Hyper-parameter studies for cosine margin $(m)$ and scale factor $(s)$ on CIFAR100 under the 8-step 5-way 5-shot setting.

## 5.5 Hyper-parameter Analysis

For the angular penalty loss calculation, there are two hyper-parameters—the cosine margin $(m)$ and the scale factor $(s)$. To find the most suitable hyper-parameter value, we perform the hyper-parameter grid analysis on the CIFAR100 dataset under the 8-step 5-way 5-shot protocol. All the experiments for hyper-parameter analysis are trained using angular penalty loss with data augmentation. Figure 7 shows the experimental results. First, we set the scale factor to 30 and vary the value for the cosine margin. According to Fig. 7, we find that when the cosine margin is set to 0.4, in most sessions, the best average and harmonic accuracy are acquired. Then, we set the cosine margin to 0.4 and vary the value for the scale factor. We find that when the scale factor is set to 20 or 30, a good performance is usually acquired in most sessions. Thus, for all our experiments, we set the cosine margin to 0.4 and the scale factor to 30.

## 6  Conclusion

In this paper, we first reformulate the FSCIL task and propose a more practical and comprehensive setup. After that, inspired by techniques from modern face recognition and data augmentation, we proposed our ALICE method. We link the relationship between FSCIL and open-set tasks and emphasize the importance of using base session training to obtain generalizable features for the FSCIL task. We show that with only balanced nearest class mean and no further action in prototype evolution, our method outperforms the SOTA methods by substantial improvements in all benchmark datasets.

**Acknowledgments.** We thank Dr. Yadan Luo and Kaiyu Guo for their help, discussion, and support. This research was funded by the Australian Government through the Australian Research Council and Sullivan Nicolaides Pathology under Linkage Project LP160101797.

# References

1. Castro, F.M., Marín-Jiménez, M.J., Guil, N., Schmid, C., Alahari, K.: End-to-end incremental learning. In: Proceedings of the European Conference on Computer Vision (ECCV), pp. 233–248 (2018)
2. Chen, T., Kornblith, S., Norouzi, M., Hinton, G.: A simple framework for contrastive learning of visual representations. In: International Conference on Machine Learning, pp. 1597–1607. PMLR (2020)
3. Chen, X., He, K.: Exploring simple siamese representation learning. In: Proceedings of the IEEE/CVF Conference on Computer Vision and Pattern Recognition, pp. 15750–15758 (2021)
4. Cheraghian, A., Rahman, S., Fang, P., Roy, S.K., Petersson, L., Harandi, M.: Semantic-aware knowledge distillation for few-shot class-incremental learning. In: Proceedings of the IEEE/CVF Conference on Computer Vision and Pattern Recognition, pp. 2534–2543 (2021)
5. Cheraghian, A., et al.: Synthesized feature based few-shot class-incremental learning on a mixture of subspaces. In: Proceedings of the IEEE/CVF International Conference on Computer Vision, pp. 8661–8670 (2021)
6. Deng, J., Guo, J., Xue, N., Zafeiriou, S.: Arcface: additive angular margin loss for deep face recognition. In: Proceedings of the IEEE/CVF Conference on Computer Vision and Pattern Recognition, pp. 4690–4699 (2019)
7. Dong, S., Hong, X., Tao, X., Chang, X., Wei, X., Gong, Y.: Few-shot class-incremental learning via relation knowledge distillation. In: Proceedings of the AAAI Conference on Artificial Intelligence, vol. 35, pp. 1255–1263 (2021)
8. Goodfellow, I.J., Mirza, M., Xiao, D., Courville, A., Bengio, Y.: An empirical investigation of catastrophic forgetting in gradient-based neural networks. In: Proceedings of International Conference on Learning Representations (2014)
9. He, K., Zhang, X., Ren, S., Sun, J.: Deep residual learning for image recognition. In: Proceedings of the IEEE Conference on Computer Vision and Pattern Recognition, pp. 770–778 (2016)
10. Hinton, G., Vinyals, O., Dean, J.: Distilling the knowledge in a neural network. In: NIPS Deep Learning and Representation Learning Workshop (2015)
11. Hou, S., Pan, X., Loy, C.C., Wang, Z., Lin, D.: Learning a unified classifier incrementally via rebalancing. In: Proceedings of the IEEE Conference on Computer Vision and Pattern Recognition, pp. 831–839 (2019)
12. Kang, B., Xie, S., Rohrbach, M., Yan, Z., Gordo, A., Feng, J., Kalantidis, Y.: Decoupling representation and classifier for long-tailed recognition. arXiv preprint arXiv:1910.09217 (2019)
13. Krizhevsky, A., Hinton, G., et al.: Learning multiple layers of features from tiny images (2009)
14. Liu, W., Wen, Y., Yu, Z., Li, M., Raj, B., Song, L.: Sphereface: deep hypersphere embedding for face recognition. In: Proceedings of the IEEE Conference on Computer Vision and Pattern Recognition, pp. 212–220 (2017)
15. Mai, Z., Li, R., Kim, H., Sanner, S.: Supervised contrastive replay: revisiting the nearest class mean classifier in online class-incremental continual learning. In: Proceedings of the IEEE/CVF Conference on Computer Vision and Pattern Recognition, pp. 3589–3599 (2021)
16. McCloskey, M., Cohen, N.J.: Catastrophic interference in connectionist networks: the sequential learning problem. In: Psychology of Learning and Motivation, vol. 24, pp. 109–165. Elsevier (1989)

17. Rebuffi, S.A., Kolesnikov, A., Sperl, G., Lampert, C.H.: icarl: incremental classifier and representation learning. In: Proceedings of the IEEE Conference on Computer Vision and Pattern Recognition, pp. 2001–2010 (2017)
18. Russakovsky, O., et al.: Imagenet large scale visual recognition challenge. Int. J. Comput. Vis. **115**(3), 211–252 (2015)
19. Tao, X., Hong, X., Chang, X., Dong, S., Wei, X., Gong, Y.: Few-shot class-incremental learning. In: Proceedings of the IEEE/CVF Conference on Computer Vision and Pattern Recognition, pp. 12183–12192 (2020)
20. Wah, C., Branson, S., Welinder, P., Perona, P., Belongie, S.: The caltech-ucsd birds-200-2011 dataset (2011)
21. Wang, H., et al.: Cosface: large margin cosine loss for deep face recognition. In: Proceedings of the IEEE Conference on Computer Vision and Pattern Recognition, pp. 5265–5274 (2018)
22. Yu, L., et al.: Semantic drift compensation for class-incremental learning. In: Proceedings of the IEEE/CVF Conference on Computer Vision and Pattern Recognition, pp. 6982–6991 (2020)
23. Zhang, C., Song, N., Lin, G., Zheng, Y., Pan, P., Xu, Y.: Few-shot incremental learning with continually evolved classifiers. In: Proceedings of the IEEE/CVF Conference on Computer Vision and Pattern Recognition, pp. 12455–12464 (2021)
24. Zhang, H., Cisse, M., Dauphin, Y.N., Lopez-Paz, D.: mixup: Beyond empirical risk minimization. arXiv preprint arXiv:1710.09412 (2017)
25. Zhao, H., Fu, Y., Kang, M., Tian, Q., Wu, F., Li, X.: Mgsvf: Multi-grained slow vs. fast framework for few-shot class-incremental learning. arXiv preprint arXiv:2006.15524 (2020)
26. Zhu, F., Cheng, Z., Zhang, X.Y., Liu, C.l.: Class-incremental learning via dual augmentation. Adv. Neural Inf. Process. Syst. **34**, 14306–14318 (2021)
27. Zhu, K., Cao, Y., Zhai, W., Cheng, J., Zha, Z.J.: Self-promoted prototype refinement for few-shot class-incremental learning. In: Proceedings of the IEEE/CVF Conference on Computer Vision and Pattern Recognition, pp. 6801–6810 (2021)

# FOSTER: Feature Boosting and Compression for Class-Incremental Learning

Fu-Yun Wang(ID), Da-Wei Zhou(ID), Han-Jia Ye$^{(\boxtimes)}$(ID), and De-Chuan Zhan(ID)

State Key Laboratory for Novel Software Technology, Nanjing University, Nanjing, China
wangfuyun@smail.nju.edu.cn, {zhoudw,yehj,zhandc}@lamda.nju.edu.cn

**Abstract.** The ability to learn new concepts continually is necessary in this ever-changing world. However, deep neural networks suffer from catastrophic forgetting when learning new categories. Many works have been proposed to alleviate this phenomenon, whereas most of them either fall into the stability-plasticity dilemma or take too much computation or storage overhead. Inspired by the gradient boosting algorithm to gradually fit the residuals between the target model and the previous ensemble model, we propose a novel two-stage learning paradigm FOSTER, empowering the model to learn new categories adaptively. Specifically, we first dynamically expand new modules to fit the residuals between the target and the output of the original model. Next, we remove redundant parameters and feature dimensions through an effective distillation strategy to maintain the single backbone model. We validate our method FOSTER on CIFAR-100 and ImageNet-100/1000 under different settings. Experimental results show that our method achieves state-of-the-art performance. Code is available at https://github.com/G-U-N/ECCV22-FOSTER.

**Keywords:** Class-incremental learning · Gradient boosting

## 1 Introduction

The real world is constantly changing, with new concepts and categories continuously springing up [14,35,46,48]. Retraining a model every time new classes emerge is impractical due to data privacy [5] and expensive training costs. Therefore, it is necessary to enable the model to continuously learn new categories, namely class-incremental learning [34,44,49]. However, directly fine-tuning the original neural networks on new data causes a severe problem known as catastrophic forgetting [11] that the model entirely and abruptly forgets previously learned information. Inspired by this, class-incremental learning aims to design a learning paradigm that enables the model to continuously learn novel categories in multiple stages while maintaining the discrimination ability for old classes.

**Supplementary Information** The online version contains supplementary material available at https://doi.org/10.1007/978-3-031-19806-9_23.

In recent years, many approaches have been proposed from different aspects. So far, the most widely recognized and utilized class-incremental learning strategy is based on knowledge distillation [19]. Methods [1,27,32,38,43,47] retain an old model additionally and use knowledge distillation to constrain output for original tasks of the new model to be similar to that of the old one [27]. However, these methods with a single backbone may not have enough plasticity [17] to cope with the coming new categories. Besides, even with restrictions of KD, the model still suffer from feature degradation [40] of old concepts due to limited access [5] to old data. Recently, methods [9,28,40] based on dynamic architectures achieve state-of-the-art performance in class-incremental learning. Typically, they preserve some modules with their parameters frozen to maintain important sections for old categories and expand new trainable modules to strengthen plasticity for learning new categories. Nevertheless, they have two inevitable defects: First, constantly expanding new modules for coming tasks will lead to a drastic increase in the number of parameters, resulting in severe storage and computation overhead, which makes these methods not suitable for long-term incremental learning. Second, since old modules have never seen new concepts, directly retaining them may harm performance in new categories. The more old modules kept, the more remarkable the negative impact.

In this paper, we propose a novel perspective from gradient boosting to analyze and achieve the goal of class-incremental learning. Gradient boosting methods use the additive model to gradually converge the ground-truth target model where the subsequent one fits the residuals between the target and the prior one. In class-incremental learning, since distributions of new categories are constantly coming, the distribution drift will also lead to the residuals between the target label and model output. Therefore, we propose a similar boosting framework to solve the problem of class-incremental learning by applying an additive model, gradually fitting residuals, where different models mainly handle their special tasks (with nonoverlapping sets of classes). And as we discuss later, our boosting framework is a more generalized framework for dynamic structure methods (e.g., DER [40]). It has positive significance in two aspects: On the one hand, the new model enhances the plasticity and thus helps the model learn to distinguish between new classes. On the other hand, training the new model to classify all categories might contribute to discovering some critical elements ignored by the original model. As shown in Fig. 1, when the model learns old categories, including tigers, cats, and monkeys, it may think that stripes are essential information but mistakenly regard auricles as meaningless features. When learning new categories, because the fish and birds do not have auricles, the new model will discover this mistake and correct it.

However, as we discussed above, creating new models not only leads to an increase in the number of parameters but also might cause inconsistency between the old and the new model at the feature level. To this end, we compress the boosting model to remove unnecessary parameters and inconsistent features, thus avoiding the above-mentioned drawbacks of dynamic structure-based methods, preserving crucial information, and enhancing the robustness of the model.

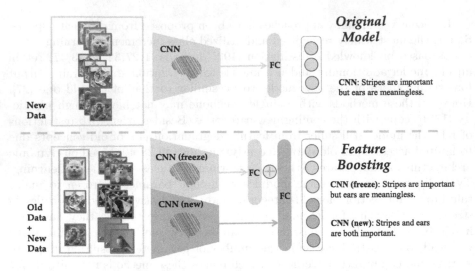

**Fig. 1. Feature Boosting.** Illustration of feature boosting. When the task comes, we freeze the old model and create a new module to fit the residuals between the target and the output. The new module helps the model learn both new and old classes better.

In conclusion, our paradigm can be decoupled into two steps: boosting and compression. The first step can be seen as boosting to alleviate the performance decline due to the arrival of new classes. Specifically, we retain the old model with all its parameters frozen. Then we expand a trainable new feature extractor and concatenate it with the extractor of the old model and initialize a constrained, fully-connected layer to transform the super feature into logits, which we will demonstrate later in detail. In the second step, we aim to eliminate redundant parameters and meaningless dimensions caused by feature boosting. Specifically, we propose an effective distillation strategy that can transfer knowledge from the boosting model to a single model with negligible performance loss, even if the data is limited when learning new tasks. Extensive experiments on three benchmarks, including CIFAR-100, ImageNet-100/1000 show that our method **F**eature Bo**OST**ing and Compr**E**ssion for class-inc**R**emental learning (**FOSTER**) obtains the state-of-the-art performance.

## 2   Related Work

Many works have been done to analyze the reasons for performance degradation in class-incremental learning and alleviate this phenomenon. In this section, we will give a brief discussion of these methods and boosting algorithms.

**Knowledge Distillation.** Knowledge distillation [19] aims to transfer dark knowledge [24] from the teacher to the student by encouraging the outputs of the student model to approximate the outputs of the teacher model [27]. LwF [27] retains an old model additionally and applies a modified cross-entropy loss to constrain the outputs for old categories of the new model to preserve the capability for the old one. Bic [38], WA [43] propose effective strategies to alleviate the bias of the classifier caused by imbalanced training data after distillation.

**Rehearsal.** The rehearsal strategy enables the model to have partial access to old data. [32,36,38,43] allocate a memory to store exemplars of previous tasks for replay when learning tasks. [21] preserves low dimensional features instead of raw instances to reduce the storage overhead. In [39], instances are synthesized by a generative model [16] for rehearsal [30] test various exemplar selection strategies, showing that different ways of exemplar selection have a significant impact on performance and herding surpass other strategies in most settings.

**Dynamic Architectures.** Many works [10,15,20,33,37] create new modules to handle the growing training distribution [26,41] dynamically. However, an accurate task id, which is usually unavailable in real-life, is needed for most of these approaches to help them choose the corresponding id-specific module. Recently, methods [9,28,40] successfully apply the dynamic architectures into class incremental learning where the task id is unavailable, showing their advantages over the single backbone methods. However, as we illustrate in Sect. 1, they have two unavoidable shortcomings: (i) Continually adding new modules causes unaffordable overhead. (ii) Directly retaining old modules leads to noise in the representations of new categories, harming the performance in new classes.

**Boosting.** Boosting represents a family of machine learning algorithms that convert weak learners to strong ones [50]. AdaBoost [12] is one of the most famous boosting algorithms, aiming to minimize the exponential loss of the additive model. The crucial idea of AdaBoost is to adjust the weights of training samples to make the new base learner pay more attention to samples that the former ensemble model cannot recognize correctly. In recent years, gradient boosting [13] based algorithms [2,7,23] achieve excellent performance on various tasks.

## 3   Preliminary

In this section, we first briefly discuss the basic process of gradient boosting in Sect. 3.1. Then, we describe the setting of class-incremental learning in Sect. 3.2. In Sect. 4, we will give an explicit demonstration of how we apply the idea of gradient boosting to the scenario of class-incremental learning.

### 3.1   Gradient Boosting

Given a training set $\mathcal{D}_{train} = \{(x_i, y_i)\}_{i=1}^{n}$, where $x_i \in \mathcal{X}$ is the instance and $y_i \in \mathcal{Y}$ is the corresponding label, the gradient boosting methods seek a hypothesis $F : \mathcal{X} \to \mathcal{Y}$ to minimize the empirical risk (with loss function $\ell(\cdot, \cdot)$)

$$F^* = \arg\min_{F} \mathbb{E}_{(x,y)\in\mathcal{D}_{train}} \left[ \ell\left(y, F(x)\right) \right], \tag{1}$$

by iteratively adding a new weighted weak function $h_i(\cdot)$ chosen from a specific function space $\mathcal{H}_i$ (*e.g.*, the set of all possible decision trees) to gradually fit residuals. After $m$ iterations, the hypothesis F can be represented as

$$F(x) = F_m(x) = \sum_{i=1}^{m} \alpha_i h_i(x) \,, \tag{2}$$

where $\alpha_i$ is the coefficient of $h_i(\cdot)$. Then we are supposed to find $F_{m+1}$ for further optimization of the objective

$$F_{m+1}(x) = F_m(x) + \underset{h_{m+1} \in \mathcal{H}_{m+1}}{\arg\min} \; \mathbb{E}_{(x,y) \in \mathcal{D}_{train}} \left[ \ell \left( y, F_m(x) + h_{m+1}(x) \right) \right] \,. \tag{3}$$

However, directly optimizing the above function to find the best $h_{m+1}$ is typically infeasible. Therefore, we use the steepest descent step for iterative optimization:

$$F_{m+1}(x) = F_m(x) - \alpha_m \nabla_{F_m} \mathbb{E}_{(x,y) \in \mathcal{D}_{train}} \left[ \ell \left( y, F_m(x) \right) \right] \,, \tag{4}$$

where $-\nabla_{F_m} \mathbb{E}_{(x,y) \in \mathcal{D}_{train}} \left[ \ell \left( y, F_m(x) \right) \right]$ is the objective for $h_{m+1}(x)$ to approximate. Specifically, if $\ell(\cdot, \cdot)$ is the mean-squared error (MSE), it transforms into

$$- \nabla_{F_m} \mathbb{E}_{(x,y) \in \mathcal{D}_{train}} \left[ \left( y - F_m(x) \right)^2 \right] = 2 \times \mathbb{E}_{(x,y) \in \mathcal{D}_{train}} \left[ y - F_m(x) \right] \,. \tag{5}$$

Ideally, let $\alpha_m = 1/2$, if $h_{m+1}(x)$ can fit $2\alpha_m(y - F_m(x)) = (y - F_m(x))$ for each $(x, y) \in \mathcal{D}_{train}$, $F_{m+1}$ is the optimal function, minimizing the empirical error.

## 3.2   Class-Incremental Learning Setup

Unlike the traditional case where the model is trained on all classes with all training data available, in class-incremental learning, the model receives a batch of new training data $\mathcal{D}_t = \{(x_i^t, y_i^t)\}_{i=1}^n$ in the $t^{\text{th}}$ stage. Specifically, $n$ is the number of training samples, $x_i^t \in \mathcal{X}_t$ is the input image, and $y_i^t \in \mathcal{Y}_t$ is the corresponding label for $x_i^t$. Label space of all seen categories is denoted as $\hat{\mathcal{Y}}_t = \cup_{i=0}^t \mathcal{Y}_i$, where $\mathcal{Y}_t \cap \mathcal{Y}_{t'} = \emptyset$ for $t \neq t'$. In the $t^{\text{th}}$ stage, rehearsal-based methods also save a part of old data as $\mathcal{V}_t$, a limited subset of $\cup_{i=0}^{t-1} \mathcal{D}_i$. Our model is trained on $\hat{\mathcal{D}}_t = \mathcal{D}_t \cup \mathcal{V}_t$ and is required to perform well on all seen categories.

## 4   Method

In this section, we give a description of FOSTER and how it works to prompt the model to simultaneously learn all classes well. Below, we first give a full demonstration of how the idea of the gradient boosting algorithm is applied to class-incremental learning in Sect. 4.1. Then we propose novel strategies to further enhance and balance the learning, which greatly improves the performance in Sect. 4.2. Finally, in order to avoid the explosive growth of parameters and remove redundant parameters and feature dimensions, we utilize a straightforward and effective compression method based on knowledge distillation in Sect. 4.3.

## 4.1   From Gradient Boosting to Class-Incremental Learning

Assuming in the $t^{\text{th}}$ stage, we have saved the model $F_{t-1}$ from the last stage. $F_{t-1}$ can be further decomposed into feature embedding and linear classifier: $F_{t-1}(\boldsymbol{x}) = (\mathbf{W}_{t-1})^{\top} \Phi_{t-1}(\boldsymbol{x})$, where $\Phi_{t-1}(\cdot) : \mathbb{R}^{D} \rightarrow \mathbb{R}^{d}$ and $\mathbf{W}_{t-1} \in \mathbb{R}^{d \times |\hat{\mathcal{Y}}_{t-1}|}$. When a new data stream comes, directly fine-tuning $F_{t-1}$ on the new data will impair its capacity for old classes, which is inadvisable. On the other hand, simply freezing $F_{t-1}$ causes it to lose plasticity for new classes, making the residuals between target $y$ and $F_{t-1}(\boldsymbol{x})$ large for $(\boldsymbol{x}, y) \in \mathcal{D}_t$. Inspired by gradient boosting, we train a new model to fit the residuals. Specifically, the new model $\mathcal{F}_t$ consists of a feature extractor $\phi_t(\cdot) : \mathbb{R}^{D} \rightarrow \mathbb{R}^{d}$ and a linear classifier $\mathcal{W}_t \in \mathbb{R}^{d \times |\mathcal{Y}_t|}$. $\mathcal{W}_t$ can be further decomposed into $\left[ \mathcal{W}_t^{(o)}, \mathcal{W}_t^{(n)} \right]$, where $\mathcal{W}_t^{(o)} \in \mathbb{R}^{d \times |\hat{\mathcal{Y}}_{t-1}|}$ and $\mathcal{W}_t^{(n)} \in \mathbb{R}^{d \times |\mathcal{Y}_t|}$ . Accordingly, the training process can be represented as

$$F_t(\boldsymbol{x}) = F_{t-1}(\boldsymbol{x}) + \arg\min_{\mathcal{F}_t} \mathbb{E}_{(\boldsymbol{x},y) \in \hat{\mathcal{D}}_t} \left[ \ell \left( y, F_{t-1}(\boldsymbol{x}) + \mathcal{F}_t(\boldsymbol{x}) \right) \right] . \quad (6)$$

Similar to Sect. 3.1, let $\ell(\cdot, \cdot)$ be the mean-squared error function, considering the strong feature representation learning ability of neural networks, we expect $\mathcal{F}_t(\boldsymbol{x})$ can fit residuals of $y$ and $F_{t-1}(\boldsymbol{x})$ for every $(\boldsymbol{x}, y) \in \hat{\mathcal{D}}_t$. Ideally, we have

$$\boldsymbol{y} = F_{t-1}(\boldsymbol{x}) + \mathcal{F}_t(\boldsymbol{x}) = \mathcal{S}\left( \begin{bmatrix} \mathbf{W}_{t-1}^{\top} \\ \mathbf{O} \end{bmatrix} \Phi_{t-1}(\boldsymbol{x}) \right) + \mathcal{S}\left( \begin{bmatrix} (\mathcal{W}_t^{(o)})^{\top} \\ (\mathcal{W}_t^{(n)})^{\top} \end{bmatrix} \phi_t(\boldsymbol{x}) \right) , \quad (7)$$

where $\mathcal{S}(\cdot)$ is the softmax operation, $\mathbf{O} \in \mathbb{R}^{d \times |\mathcal{Y}_t|}$ is set to zero matrix or finetuned on $\hat{\mathcal{D}}_t$ with $\Phi_{t-1}$ frozen, and $\boldsymbol{y}$ is the corresponding one-hot vector of $y$. We set $\mathbf{O}$ to zero matrix as default in our discussion.

Denote the parameters of $\mathcal{F}_t$ as $\theta_t$ and $\text{Dis}(\cdot, \cdot)$ as a distance metric (*e.g.*, euclidean metric), this process can be represented as the following optimization problem:

$$\theta_t^* = \arg\min_{\theta_t} \text{Dis}\left( \boldsymbol{y}, \mathcal{S}\left( \begin{bmatrix} \mathbf{W}_{t-1}^{\top} \\ \mathbf{O} \end{bmatrix} \Phi_{t-1}(\boldsymbol{x}) \right) + \mathcal{S}\left( \begin{bmatrix} (\mathcal{W}_t^{(o)})^{\top} \\ (\mathcal{W}_t^{(n)})^{\top} \end{bmatrix} \phi_t(\boldsymbol{x}) \right) \right) . \quad (8)$$

We replace the $\mathcal{S}(\cdot) + \mathcal{S}(\cdot)$ with $\mathcal{S}(\cdot + \cdot)$ and substitute the $\text{Dis}(\cdot, \cdot)$ for the Kullback-Leibler divergence (KLD), then the objective function changes into:

$$\theta_t^* = \arg\min_{\theta_t} \text{KL}\left( y \,\middle\|\, \mathcal{S}\left( \begin{bmatrix} \mathbf{W}_{t-1}^{\top} & (\mathcal{W}_t^{(o)})^{\top} \\ \mathbf{O} & (\mathcal{W}_t^{(n)})^{\top} \end{bmatrix} \begin{bmatrix} \Phi_{t-1}(\boldsymbol{x}) \\ \phi_t(\boldsymbol{x}) \end{bmatrix} \right) \right) . \quad (9)$$

We provide an illustration about the reasons for this substitution in the supplementary material. Therefore, $F_t$ can be further decomposed as an expanded linear classifier $\mathbf{W}_t$ and a concatenated super feature extractor $\Phi_t(\cdot)$, where

$$\mathbf{W}_t^{\top} = \begin{bmatrix} \mathbf{W}_{t-1}^{\top} & (\mathcal{W}_t^{(o)})^{\top} \\ \mathbf{O} & (\mathcal{W}_t^{(n)})^{\top} \end{bmatrix} , \qquad \Phi_t(\boldsymbol{x}) = \begin{bmatrix} \Phi_{t-1}(\boldsymbol{x}) \\ \phi_t(\boldsymbol{x}) \end{bmatrix} . \quad (10)$$

Note that $\mathbf{W}_{t-1}^{\top}$, $\mathbf{O}$, and $\Phi_{t-1}$ are all frozen, the trainable modules are the $\phi_t, \mathcal{W}_t^{(o)}, \mathcal{W}_t^{(n)}$. Here we explain their roles. Eventually, logits of $F_t$ is

$$\mathbf{W}_t^{\top}\Phi_t(\boldsymbol{x}) = \begin{bmatrix} \mathbf{W}_{t-1}^{\top}\Phi_{t-1}(\boldsymbol{x}) + (\mathcal{W}_t^{(o)})^{\top}\phi_t(\boldsymbol{x}) \\ (\mathcal{W}_t^{(n)})^{\top}\phi_t(\boldsymbol{x}) \end{bmatrix}. \tag{11}$$

The lower part is the logits of new classes, and the upper part is that of old ones. As we claimed in Sect. 1, the lower part requires the new module $\mathcal{F}_t$ to learn how to correctly classify new classes, thus enhancing the model's plasticity to redeem the performance on new classes. The upper part encourages the new module to fit the residuals between $y$ and $F_{t-1}$, thus encouraging $\mathcal{F}_t$ to exploit more pivotal patterns for classification.

### 4.2   Calibration for Old and New

When training on new tasks, we only have an imbalanced training set $\hat{\mathcal{D}}_t = \mathcal{D}_t \cup \mathcal{V}_t$. The imbalance on categories of $\mathcal{D}_t$ will result in a strong classification bias in the model [1,22,38,43]. Besides, the boosting model tends to ignore the residuals of minor classes due to insufficient supervision. To alleviate the classification bias and encourage the model to equally learn old and new classes, we propose Logits Alignment and Feature Enhancement strategies in the following sections.

**Logits Alignment.** To strengthen the learning of old instances and mitigate the classification bias, we add a scale factor to the logits of the old and new classes in Eq. 11 respectively during training. Thus, the logits during training are:

$$\gamma\mathbf{W}_t^{\top}\Phi_t(\boldsymbol{x}) = \begin{bmatrix} \gamma_1\left(\mathbf{W}_{t-1}^{\top}\Phi_{t-1}(\boldsymbol{x}) + (\mathcal{W}_t^{(o)})^{\top}\phi_t(\boldsymbol{x})\right) \\ \gamma_2(\mathcal{W}_t^{(n)})^{\top}\phi_t(\boldsymbol{x}) \end{bmatrix}, \tag{12}$$

where $0 < \gamma_1 < 1$, $\gamma_2 > 1$, and $\gamma$ is a diagonal matrix composed of $\gamma_1$ and $\gamma_2$. Through this scaling strategy, the absolute value of logits for old categories is reduced, and the absolute value of logits for new ones is enlarged, thus forcing the model $F_t$ to produce larger logits for old categories and smaller logits for new categories.

We get the scale factors $\gamma_1, \gamma_2$ trough the normalized effective number $E_n$ [4] of each class, which can be seen as the summation of proportional series, where $n$ equal to the number of instances and $\beta$ is an adjustable hyperparameter

$$E_n = \begin{cases} \frac{1-\beta^n}{1-\beta}, & \beta \in [0,1) \\ n, & \beta = 1 \end{cases}, \tag{13}$$

concretely, $(\gamma_1, \gamma_2) = \left(\frac{E_{n_{\text{old}}}}{E_{n_{\text{old}}}+E_{n_{\text{new}}}}, \frac{E_{n_{\text{new}}}}{E_{n_{\text{old}}}+E_{n_{\text{new}}}}\right)$. Hence the objective is formulated as:

$$\mathcal{L}_{LA} = \text{KL}\big(y \parallel \mathcal{S}\left(\gamma\mathbf{W}_t^{\top}\Phi_t(\boldsymbol{x})\right)\big). \tag{14}$$

**Feature Enhancement.** We argue that simply letting a new module $\mathcal{F}_t(\boldsymbol{x})$ fit the residuals of $F_{t-1}(\boldsymbol{x})$ and label $y$ is sometimes insufficient. At the extreme,, for instance, the residuals of $F_{t-1}(x)$ and $y$ is zero. In that case, the new module $\mathcal{F}_t$ can not learn anything about old categories, and thus it will damage the performance of our model for old classes. Hence, we should prompt the new module $\mathcal{F}_t$ to learn old categories further.

Our Feature Enhancement consists of two parts. First, we initialize a new linear classifier $\mathbf{W}_t^{(a)} \in \mathbb{R}^{d \times |\hat{\mathcal{Y}}_t|}$ to transform the new feature $\phi_t(x)$ into logits of all seen categories and require the new feature itself to correctly classify all of them:

$$\mathcal{L}_{FE} = \mathrm{KL}\left(y \,\middle\|\, \mathcal{S}\left((\mathbf{W}_t^{(a)})^\top \phi_t(x)\right)\right). \tag{15}$$

Hence, even if the residuals of $F_{t-1}(x)$ and $y$ is zero, the new feature extractor $\phi_t$ can still learn how to classify the old categories. Besides, it should be noted that simply using one-hot targets to train the new feature extractor in an imbalanced dataset might lead to overfitting to small classes, failing to learn a feature representation with good generalization ability for old categories. To alleviate this phenomenon and provide more supervision for old classes, we utilize knowledge distillation to encourage $F_t(x)$ to have similar output distribution as $F_{t-1}$ on old categories,

$$\mathcal{L}_{KD} = \mathrm{KL}\left(\mathcal{S}\left(F_{t-1}(x)\right) \,\middle\|\, \mathcal{S}\left(F_{t-1}(x) + (\mathcal{W}_t^{(o)})^\top \phi_t(x)\right)\right). \tag{16}$$

Note that this process requires only one more time matrix multiplication computation because the forward process of the original model $F_{t-1}$ and the expanded model $F_t$ are shared, except for the final linear classifier.

**Summary of Feature Boosting.** To conclude, feature-boosting consists of three components. First, we create a new module to fit the residuals between targets and the output of the original model, following the principle of gradient boosting. With reasonable simplification and deduction, the optimization objective is transformed into the minimization of KL divergence of the target and the output of the concatenated model. To alleviate the classification bias caused by imbalanced training, we proposed logits alignment (LA) to balance the training of old and new classes. Moreover, we argued that simply letting the new module fit the residuals is sometimes insufficient. To further encourage the new module to learn old instances, we proposed feature enhancement, where $\mathcal{L}_{FE}$ aims to make the new module learn the difference among all categories by optimizing the cross-entropy loss of target and the output of the new module, and $\mathcal{L}_{KD}$ utilize the original output to instruct the expanded model through knowledge distillation. The final FOSTER loss for boosting combines the above three components:

$$\mathcal{L}_{Boosting} = \mathcal{L}_{LA} + \mathcal{L}_{FE} + \mathcal{L}_{KD}. \tag{17}$$

### 4.3   Feature Compression

Our method FOSTER achieves excellent performance through gradient boosting. However, gradually adding a new module $\mathcal{F}$ to our model $F_t$ will lead to the

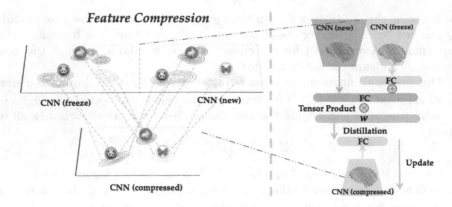

**Fig. 2. Feature Compression.** Left: the process of feature compression. We remove insignificant dimensions and parameters to make the distribution of the same categories more compact. Right: the implementation of feature compression. Outputs of the dual branch model are used to instruct the representation learning of the compressed model. Different weights are assigned to old and new classes to alleviate the classification bias.

growing number of parameters and feature dimensions of our model $F_t$, making it unable to be applied in long-term incremental learning tasks. Do we really require so many parameters and feature dimensions? For example, we create the same module $\mathcal{F}$ to learn tasks with 2 classes and 50 classes and achieve similar effects. Thus, there must be redundant parameters and meaningless feature dimensions in the task with 2 classes. Are we able to compress the expanded feature space of $F_t$ to a smaller one with almost no performance degradation?

Knowledge distillation [19] is a simple yet effective way to achieve this goal. Since our model $F_t$ can handle all seen categories with excellent performance, it can give any input a soft target, namely the output distribution on all known categories. Therefore, except for the current training set $\hat{\mathcal{D}}_t$, we can sample other unlabeled data from a similar domain for further distillation. Note that these unlabeled data can be obtained from the Internet during distillation and discarded after that, so it does not occupy additional memory.

Here, we do not expect any additional auxiliary data to be available and achieve remarkable performance with only the imbalanced dataset $\hat{\mathcal{D}}_t$.

**Balanced Distillation.** Suppose there is a single backbone student model $F_t^{(s)}$ to be distilled. To mitigate the classification bias caused by imbalanced training datasets $\hat{\mathcal{D}}_t$, we should consider the class priors and adjust the weights of distilled information for different classes [42]. Therefore, the Balanced Distillation loss is formulated as:

$$\mathcal{L}_{\text{BKD}} = \text{KL}\left(\boldsymbol{w} \otimes \mathcal{S}\left(F_t(\boldsymbol{x})\right) \,\middle\|\, \mathcal{S}(F_t^{(s)}(\boldsymbol{x}))\right), \tag{18}$$

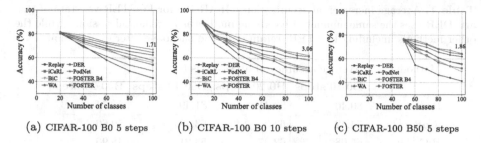

(a) CIFAR-100 B0 5 steps     (b) CIFAR-100 B0 10 steps     (c) CIFAR-100 B50 5 steps

**Fig. 3. Incremental Accuracy on CIFAR-100.** Replay is the baseline with naive rehearsal strategy. FOSTER B4 records the accuracy of the dual branch model after feature boosting. FOSTER records the accuracy of the single backbone model after feature compression. The performance gap is annotated at the end of each curve.

where $\otimes$ means the tensor product (*i.e.*, automatically broadcasting to different batchsizes.) and $w$ is the weighted vector obtained from Eq. 13 to make classes with fewer instances have larger weights.

## 5  Experiments

In this section, we compare our FOSTER with other SOTA methods on benchmark incremental learning datasets. We also perform ablations to validate the effectiveness of FOSTER components and their robustness to hyperparameters.

### 5.1  Experimental Settings

**Datasets.** We validate our methods on widely used benchmark of class-incremental learning CIFAR-100 [25] and ImageNet100/1000 [6]. **CIFAR-100**: CIFAR-100 consists of 50,000 training images with 500 images per class, and 10,000 testing images with 100 images per class. **ImageNet-1000**: ImageNet-1000 is a large scale dataset composed of about 1.28 million images for training and 50,000 for validation with 500 images per class. **ImageNet-100**: ImageNet-100 is composed of 100 classes randomly chosen from the original ImageNet-1000.
**Protocol.** For both the CIFAR-100 and ImageNet-100, we validate our method on two widely used protocols: (i) **CIFAR-100/ImageNet-100 B0 (base 0)**: In the first protocols, we train all 100 classes gradually with 5, 10, 20 classes per step with the fixed memory size of 2,000 exemplars. (ii) **CIFAR-100/ImageNet-100 B50 (base 50)**: We also start by training the models on half the classes. Then we train the rest 50 classes with 2, 5, 10 classes per step with 20 exemplars per class. For ImageNet-1000, we train all 1000 classes with 100 classes per step (10 steps in total) with a fixed memory size of 20,000 exemplars.
**Implementation Details.** Our method and all compared methods are implemented with Pytorch [31] and PyCIL [45]. For ImageNet, we adopt the standard ResNet-18 [18] as our feature extractor and set the batch size to 256. The learning rate starts from 0.1 and gradually decays to zero with a cosine annealing

**Table 1.** Average incremental accuracy on CIFAR-100 for FOSTER vs. state-of-the-art. DER uses the same number of backbone models as incremental sessions, while the other methods, including FOSTER, retain only one backbone after each session.

| Methods | Average accuracy of all sessions (%) | | | |
|---|---|---|---|---|
| | B0 10 steps | B0 20 steps | B50 10 steps | B50 25 steps |
| Bound | 80.40 | 80.41 | 81.49 | 81.74 |
| iCaRL [32] | 64.42 | 63.5 | 53.78 | 50.60 |
| BiC [38] | 65.08 | 62.37 | 53.21 | 48.96 |
| WA [43] | 67.08 | 64.64 | 57.57 | 54.10 |
| COIL[47] | 65.48 | 62.98 | 59.96 | – |
| PODNet [8] | 55.22 | 47.87 | 63.19 | 60.72 |
| DER [40] | 69.74 | 67.98 | 66.36 | – |
| Ours | **72.90** | **70.65** | **67.95** | **63.83** |
| Improvement | (+3.06) | (+2.67) | (+1.59) | (+3.11) |

scheduler [29] (170 epochs in total). For CIFAR-100, we use a modified ResNet-32 [32] as the most previous works as our feature extractor and set the batch size to 128. The learning rate also starts from 0.1 and gradually decays to zero with a cosine annealing scheduler (170 epochs in total). For both ImageNet and CIFAR-100, we use SGD with the momentum of 0.9 and the weight decay of 5e–4 in the boosting stage. In the compression stage, we use SGD with the momentum of 0.9 and set the weight decay to 0. We set the temperature scalar $T$ to 2. For data augmentation, AutoAugment [3], random cropping, horizontal flip, and normalization are employed to augment training images. The hyperparameter $\beta$ in Eq. 18 is set to 0.97 in most settings, while the $\beta$ in Eq. 14 on CIFAR-100 and ImageNet-100/1000 is set to 0.95 and 0.97, respectively.

## 5.2   Quantitative Results

**CIFAR-100.** Table 1 and Fig. 3 summarize the results of CIFAR-100 benchmark. We use replay as the baseline method, which only uses rehearsal strategy to alleviate forgetting. Experimental results show that our method outperforms the other state-of-the-art strategies in all six settings on CIFAR-100. Our method achieves excellent performance on both long-term incremental learning tasks and large-step incremental learning tasks. Particularly, we achieve 3.11% and 2.67% improvement under the long-term incremental setting of base 50 with 25 steps and base 0 with 20 steps, respectively. We also surpass the state-of-the-art method by 1.71% and 3.06% under the large step incremental learning setting of 20 classes per step and 10 classes per step. It should also be noted that although our method FOSTER expands a new module every time, we compress it to a single backbone every time. Therefore, the parameters and feature dimensions of our model do not increase with the number of tasks, which is our advantage over methods [9,28,40] based on dynamic architecture. From Fig. 3, we can see that

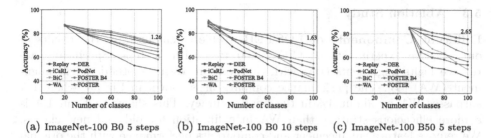

(a) ImageNet-100 B0 5 steps    (b) ImageNet-100 B0 10 steps    (c) ImageNet-100 B50 5 steps

**Fig. 4. Incremental Accuracy on ImageNet-100.** Replay is the baseline with naive rehearsal strategy. FOSTER B4 records the accuracy of the dual branch model after feature boosting. FOSTER records the accuracy of the single backbone model after feature compression. The performance gap is annotated at the end of each curve.

**Table 2.** Average incremental accuracy on ImageNet for FOSTER vs. state-of-the-art. DER uses the same number of backbone models as incremental sessions, while the other methods, including FOSTER, retain only one backbone after each session. The left three columns are experimental results on ImageNet-100. The rightmost column is the results of ImageNet-1000 with 100 classes per step (10 steps in total).

| Methods | Average accuracy of all sessions (%) | | | |
|---|---|---|---|---|
| | B0 20 steps | B50 10 steps | B50 25 steps | ImageNet-1000 |
| Bound | 81.20 | 81.20 | 81.20 | 89.27 |
| iCaRL [32] | 62.36 | 59.53 | 54.56 | 38.4 |
| BiC [38] | 58.93 | 65.14 | 59.65 | – |
| WA [43] | 63.2 | 63.71 | 58.34 | 54.10 |
| PODNet [8] | 53.69 | 74.33 | 67.28 | - |
| DER [40] | 73.79 | 77.73 | – | 66.73 |
| Ours | **74.49** | **77.54** | **69.34** | **68.34** |
| Improvement | (+0.7) | ( 0.19) | (+2.06) | (+1.61) |

the compressed single backbone model FOSTER has a tiny gap with FOSTER B4 in each step, which verifies the effectiveness of our distillation method.

**ImageNet.** Table 2 and Fig. 4 summarize the experimental results for ImageNet-100 and ImageNet-1000 benchmarks. Our method, FOSTER, still outperforms the other method in most settings. In the setting of ImageNet-100 B0, we surpass the state-of-the-art method by 1.26, 1.63, and 0.7 percent points for, respectively, 5, 10, and 20 steps. The results shown in Fig. 4 again verify the effectiveness of our distillation strategy, where the performance degradation after compression is negligible. The results on ImageNet-1000 benchmark is shown in the rightmost column in Table 2. Our method improves the average top-1 accuracy on ImageNet-1000 with 10 steps from 66.73% to 68.34% (+1.61%), showing that our method is also efficacious in large-scale incremental learning.

## 5.3   Ablation Study

**Different Components of FOSTER.** Table 5 demonstrates the results of our ablative experiments on CIFAR-100 B50 with 5 steps. Specifically, we replace logits alignments (LA) with the post-processing method weight alignment (WA) [43]. The performance comparison is shown in Fig. 5a, where LA surpasses WA by about 4% in the final accuracy. This shows that our LA is a more efficacious strategy than WA in calibration for old and new classes. We remove feature enhancement and compare its performance with the original result in Fig. 5b, the model suffers from more than 3% performance decline in the last stage. We find that, in the last step, there is almost no difference in the accuracy of new classes between the model with feature enhancement and the model without that. Nevertheless, the model with feature enhancement outperforms the model without that by more than 4 % on old categories, showing that feature enhancement encourages the model to learn more about old categories. We compare the performance of balanced knowledge distillation (BKD) with that of normal knowledge distillation (KD) in Fig. 5c. BKD surpasses KD in all stages, showing that BKD is more effective when training on imbalanced datasets.

**Sensitive Study of Hyper-parameters.** To verify the robustness of FOSTER, we conduct experiments on CIFAR-100 B50 5 steps with different hyperparameters $\beta \in (0, 1)$. Typically, $\beta$ is set to more than 0.9. We test $\beta = 0.93, 0.95, 0.97, 0.99, 0.995, 0.999$ respectively. The experimental results are shown in Fig. 6a. We can see that the performance changes are minimal under different $\beta$s.

**Effect of Number of Exemplars.** In Fig. 6b, We gradually increase the number of exemplars from 5 to 200 and record the performance of the model on CIFAR-100 B50 with 5 steps. The accuracy in the last step increases from 53.53% to 71.4% as the number of exemplars for every class changes from 5 to 200. From the results, we can see that with the increase in the number of exemplars, the accuracy of the last stage of the model gradually improves, indicating that our model can make full use of more exemplars to improve performance. In addition,

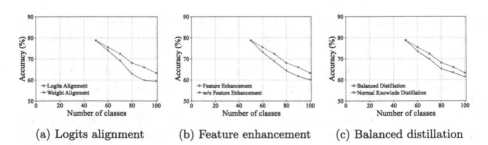

(a) Logits alignment     (b) Feature enhancement     (c) Balanced distillation

**Fig. 5. Ablations** of the different key components of FOSTER. (a): Performance comparison between logits alignment and weight alignment [43]. (b): Performance comparison with or without Feature Enhancement. (c): Performance comparison between balanced distillation and normal knowledge distillation [19].

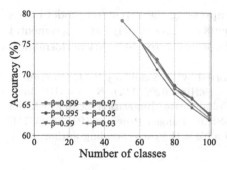 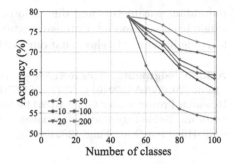

(a) Sensitive study of hyper-parameters    (b) Influence of number of exemplars

**Fig. 6. Robustness Testing.** Left: Performance under different hyperparameter $\beta$s. Right: Performance with different numbers of exemplars. Both of them are evaluated on CIFAR-100 B50 with 5 steps.

*Input    freeze CNN  new CNN    Input    freeze CNN  new CNN    Input    freeze CNN  new CNN*

**Fig. 7. Grad-CAM before and after feature boosting.** The freeze CNN only focuses on some areas of an object and is not accurate enough, but the new CNN can discover those important but ignored patterns and correct the original output.

notice that our model achieves more than 60% accuracy in the last round, even when there are only 10 exemplars for each class, surpassing most state-of-the-art methods using 20 exemplars shown in Fig. 3c. This indicates that FOSTER is more effective and robust; it can overcome forgetting even with fewer exemplars. **Visualization of Grad-CAM.** We visualize the grad-CAM before and after feature boosting. As shown in Fig. 7 (left), the freeze CNN only focuses on the head of the birds, ignoring the rest of their bodies, while the new CNN learns that the whole body is important for classification, which is consistent with our claim in Sect. 1. Similarly, the middle and right figures show that the new CNN also discovers some essential but ignored patterns of the mailbox and the dog.

## 6    Conclusions

In this work, we apply the concept of gradient boosting to the scenario of class-incremental learning and propose a novel learning paradigm FOSTER based on that, empowering the model to learn new categories adaptively. At each step, we create a new module to learn residuals between the target and the original model. We also introduce logits alignment to alleviate classification bias and feature enhancement to balance the representation learning of the old and new classes. Furthermore, we propose a simple yet effective distillation strategy to remove redundant parameters and dimensions, compressing the expanded model into a single backbone model. Extensive experiments on three widely used incremental learning benchmarks show that our method obtains state-of-the-art performance.

**Acknowledgments.** This research was supported by National Key R&D Program of China (2020AAA0109401), NSFC (61773198, 61921006,62006112), NSFC-NRF Joint Research Project under Grant 61861146001, Collaborative Innovation Center of Novel Software Technology and Industrialization, NSF of Jiangsu Province (BK20200313), CCF-Hikvision Open Fund (20210005). Han-Jia Ye is the corresponding author.

# References

1. Castro, F.M., Marín-Jiménez, M.J., Guil, N., Schmid, C., Alahari, K.: End-to-end incremental learning. In: Proceedings of the European conference on computer vision (ECCV), pp. 233–248 (2018)
2. Chen, T., Guestrin, C.: Xgboost: a scalable tree boosting system. In: KDD, pp. 785–794 (2016)
3. Cubuk, E.D., Zoph, B., Mane, D., Vasudevan, V., Le, Q.V.: Autoaugment: learning augmentation strategies from data. In: CVPR, pp. 113–123 (2019)
4. Cui, Y., Jia, M., Lin, T.Y., Song, Y., Belongie, S.: Class-balanced loss based on effective number of samples. In: CVPR, pp. 9268–9277 (2019)
5. Delange, M., et al.: A continual learning survey: defying forgetting in classification tasks. IEEE Trans. Pattern Anal. Mach. Intell. **44**(7), 3366–3385 (2021)
6. Deng, J., Dong, W., Socher, R., Li, L.J., Li, K., Fei-Fei, L.: Imagenet: a large-scale hierarchical image database. In: CVPR, pp. 248–255. IEEE (2009)
7. Dorogush, A.V., Ershov, V., Gulin, A.: Catboost: gradient boosting with categorical features support. arXiv preprint arXiv:1810.11363 (2018)
8. Douillard, A., Cord, M., Ollion, C., Robert, T., Valle, E.: PODNet: pooled outputs distillation for small-tasks incremental learning. In: Vedaldi, A., Bischof, H., Brox, T., Frahm, J.-M. (eds.) ECCV 2020. LNCS, vol. 12365, pp. 86–102. Springer, Cham (2020). https://doi.org/10.1007/978-3-030-58565-5_6
9. Douillard, A., Ramé, A., Couairon, G., Cord, M.: Dytox: Transformers for continual learning with dynamic token expansion. arXiv preprint arXiv:2111.11326 (2021)
10. Fernando, C., et al.: Pathnet: Evolution channels gradient descent in super neural networks. arXiv preprint arXiv:1701.08734 (2017)
11. French, R.M.: Catastrophic forgetting in connectionist networks. Trends Cogn. Sci. **3**(4), 128–135 (1999)
12. Friedman, J., Hastie, T., Tibshirani, R.: Additive logistic regression: a statistical view of boosting (with discussion and a rejoinder by the authors). Ann. Stat. **28**(2), 337–407 (2000)
13. Friedman, J.H.: Greedy function approximation: a gradient boosting machine. Ann. Stat. 1189–1232 (2001)
14. Golab, L., Özsu, M.T.: Issues in data stream management. ACM Sigmod Rec. **32**(2), 5–14 (2003)
15. Golkar, S., Kagan, M., Cho, K.: Continual learning via neural pruning. arXiv preprint arXiv:1903.04476 (2019)
16. Goodfellow, I., et al.: Generative adversarial nets. Adv. Neural Inf. Process. Syst. **27** (2014)

17. Grossberg, S.: Adaptive resonance theory: how a brain learns to consciously attend, learn, and recognize a changing world. Neural Netw. **37**, 1–47 (2013)
18. He, K., Zhang, X., Ren, S., Sun, J.: Deep residual learning for image recognition. In: CVPR, pp. 770–778 (2016)
19. Hinton, G., Vinyals, O., Dean, J., et al.: Distilling the knowledge in a neural network. arXiv preprint arXiv:1503.02531 2(7) (2015)
20. Hung, C.Y., Tu, C.H., Wu, C.E., Chen, C.H., Chan, Y.M., Chen, C.S.: Compacting, picking and growing for unforgetting continual learning. Adv. Neural Inf. Process. Syst. **32** (2019)
21. Iscen, A., Zhang, J., Lazebnik, S., Schmid, C.: Memory-efficient incremental learning through feature adaptation. In: Vedaldi, A., Bischof, H., Brox, T., Frahm, J.-M. (eds.) ECCV 2020. LNCS, vol. 12361, pp. 699–715. Springer, Cham (2020). https://doi.org/10.1007/978-3-030-58517-4_41
22. Kang, B., Xie, S., Rohrbach, M., Yan, Z., Gordo, A., Feng, J., Kalantidis, Y.: Decoupling representation and classifier for long-tailed recognition. arXiv preprint arXiv:1910.09217 (2019)
23. Ke, G., et al.: Lightgbm: a highly efficient gradient boosting decision tree. Adv. Neural Inf. Process. Syst. **30** (2017)
24. Korattikara Balan, A., Rathod, V., Murphy, K.P., Welling, M.: Bayesian dark knowledge. Adv. Neural Inf. Process. Syst. **28** (2015)
25. Krizhevsky, A., Hinton, G., et al.: Learning multiple layers of features from tiny images (2009)
26. Lesort, T., Caselles-Dupré, H., Garcia-Ortiz, M., Stoian, A., Filliat, D.: Generative models from the perspective of continual learning. In: IJCNN, pp. 1–8. IEEE (2019)
27. Li, Z., Hoiem, D.: Learning without forgetting. IEEE Trans. Pattern Anal. Mach. Intell. **40**(12), 2935–2947 (2017)
28. Li, Z., Zhong, C., Liu, S., Wang, R., Zheng, W.S.: Preserving earlier knowledge in continual learning with the help of all previous feature extractors. arXiv preprint arXiv:2104.13614 (2021)
29. Loshchilov, I., Hutter, F.: Sgdr: Stochastic gradient descent with warm restarts. arXiv preprint arXiv:1608.03983 (2016)
30. Masana, M., Liu, X., Twardowski, B., Menta, M., Bagdanov, A.D., van de Weijer, J.: Class-incremental learning: survey and performance evaluation on image classification. arXiv preprint arXiv:2010.15277 (2020)
31. Paszke, A., et al.: Automatic differentiation in pytorch (2017)
32. Rebuffi, S.A., Kolesnikov, A., Sperl, G., Lampert, C.H.: icarl: Incremental classifier and representation learning. In: CVPR, pp. 2001–2010 (2017)
33. Rusu, A.A., et al.: Progressive neural networks. arXiv preprint arXiv:1606.04671 (2016)
34. Wang, L., Yang, K., Li, C., Hong, L., Li, Z., Zhu, J.: Ordisco: effective and efficient usage of incremental unlabeled data for semi-supervised continual learning. In: CVPR, pp. 5383–5392 (2021)
35. Wang, L., Zhang, M., Jia, Z., Li, Q., Bao, C., Ma, K., Zhu, J., Zhong, Y.: Afec: active forgetting of negative transfer in continual learning. NeurIPS **34**, 22379–22391 (2021)
36. Wang, L., et al.: Memory replay with data compression for continual learning. In: ICLR (2022)
37. Wen, Y., Tran, D., Ba, J.: Batchensemble: an alternative approach to efficient ensemble and lifelong learning. arXiv preprint arXiv:2002.06715 (2020)
38. Wu, Y., et al.: Large scale incremental learning. In: CVPR, pp. 374–382 (2019)

39. Wu, Z., Baek, C., You, C., Ma, Y.: Incremental learning via rate reduction. In: CVPR, pp. 1125–1133 (2021)
40. Yan, S., Xie, J., He, X.: Der: dynamically expandable representation for class incremental learning. In: CVPR, pp. 3014–3023 (2021)
41. Yoon, J., Yang, E., Lee, J., Hwang, S.J.: Lifelong learning with dynamically expandable networks. arXiv preprint arXiv:1708.01547 (2017)
42. Zhang, S., Chen, C., Hu, X., Peng, S.: Balanced knowledge distillation for long-tailed learning. arXiv preprint arXiv:2104.10510 (2021)
43. Zhao, B., Xiao, X., Gan, G., Zhang, B., Xia, S.T.: Maintaining discrimination and fairness in class incremental learning. In: CVPR, pp. 13208–13217 (2020)
44. Zhou, D.W., Wang, F.Y., Ye, H.J., Ma, L., Pu, S., Zhan, D.C.: Forward compatible few-shot class-incremental learning. In: CVPR, pp. 9046–9056 (2022)
45. Zhou, D.W., Wang, F.Y., Ye, H.J., Zhan, D.C.: Pycil: a python toolbox for class-incremental learning. arXiv preprint arXiv:2112.12533 (2021)
46. Zhou, D.W., Yang, Y., Zhan, D.C.: Learning to classify with incremental new class. IEEE Trans. Neural Netw. Learn. Syst. (2021)
47. Zhou, D.W., Ye, H.J., Zhan, D.C.: Co-transport for class-incremental learning. In: ACM MM, pp. 1645–1654 (2021)
48. Zhou, D.W., Ye, H.J., Zhan, D.C.: Learning placeholders for open-set recognition. In: CVPR, pp. 4401–4410 (2021)
49. Zhou, D.W., Ye, H.J., Zhan, D.C.: Few-shot class-incremental learning by sampling multi-phase tasks. arXiv preprint arXiv:2203.17030 (2022)
50. Zhou, Z.H.: Ensemble Methods: Foundations and Algorithms. CRC Press (2012)

# Visual Knowledge Tracing

Neehar Kondapaneni[1]([✉]), Pietro Perona[1], and Oisin Mac Aodha[2]

[1] Caltech, Pasadena, USA
nkondapa@caltech.edu
[2] University of Edinburgh, Edinburgh, UK

**Abstract.** Each year, thousands of people learn new visual categorization tasks – radiologists learn to recognize tumors, birdwatchers learn
to distinguish similar species, and crowd workers learn how to annotate
valuable data for applications like autonomous driving. As humans learn,
their brain updates the visual features it extracts and attend to, which
ultimately informs their final classification decisions. In this work, we
propose a novel task of tracing the evolving classification behavior of
human learners as they engage in challenging visual classification tasks.
We propose models that jointly extract the visual features used by learners as well as predicting the classification functions they utilize. We collect three challenging new datasets from real human learners in order to
evaluate the performance of different visual knowledge tracing methods.
Our results show that our recurrent models are able to predict the classification behavior of human learners on three challenging medical image
and species identification tasks.

**Keywords:** Visual classification · Knowledge tracing · Human learning

## 1 Introduction

Humans excel at learning new concepts even when they have only received limited explicit supervision [28,55]. Key to our success is our ability to extract
informative and generalizable representations from the world around us and our
ability to update these representations given relatively sparse feedback. This
capacity, in turn, enables us to perform complex tasks such as spatial navigation
and visual categorization with apparent ease.

Despite recent progress that has been made in computer vision in learning
visual representations through self-supervision alone [9,14,54], large amounts
of supervision are still required to make best use of the resulting features [12].
In light of this, it is important for us to better understand: (i) what are the
properties that make representations learned by *humans* so effective, (ii) how are
these representations learned, and (iii) can we predict the classification behavior

**Supplementary Information** The online version contains supplementary material
available at https://doi.org/10.1007/978-3-031-19806-9_24.

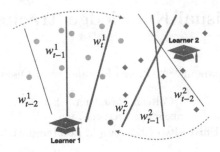

**Fig. 1.** We model a learner as an evolving classifier in a learned feature space. We assume the feature space is static and, as the learner is presented with images and class labels over time, their internal classification function self-updates. Here, we illustrate this for three time-steps, for two learners, learning a binary classification task (orange versus blue). (Color figure online)

of humans during learning? Our ultimate goal is to obtain better insight into how humans are such effective learners, which can then potentially inform new learning mechanisms for future artificial systems.

In order to attempt to address some of these questions, in this work we explore the problem of visual knowledge tracing. In the educational data mining community, knowledge tracing is the problem of monitoring and predicting the evolving knowledge state of a learner engaged in a learning task [26]. Recent work has applied advances in deep learning to knowledge tracing for question and answer-style text datasets and has investigated applications in domains such as mathematics education [33–35]. However, tracing the behavior of humans that are engaged in learning and performing challenging visual categorization tasks is underexplored. Most closely related is the work on deep metric learning that attempts to learn human aligned visual representations from sparse human annotations [19]. However, these works typically make simplifying assumptions, e.g. assuming the learners are not changing over time (i.e. they are 'static') or that the visual criteria used by the learners is the same across all learners. Instead, we explore a more challenging visual knowledge tracing setting where the learners are assumed to be non-stationary during learning, i.e. the visual features they use to perform the classification task at hand can, and likely do, change over time (see Fig. 1).

We present a recurrent neural network-based approach for visual knowledge tracing. Once trained, our models are capable of predicting the classification behavior of human learners that were not observed during training. The proposed models make use of the history of previous learner responses, images, and ground truth class labels in order to predict their future responses. Through experiments on three challenging image classification datasets we show that our models are superior to baseline approaches. Our models are capable of tracing the learning dynamics more accurately than non-recurrent baselines.

We make the following three contributions: (i) A new model for visual knowledge tracing that jointly estimates the visual features and per-time-step classification function used by non-stationary human learners. (ii) A new set of annotations for three benchmark evaluation datasets collected from humans engaged in learning challenging visual classification tasks. (iii) A detailed comparison of several visual knowledge tracing methods on these datasets.

## 2    Related Work

### 2.1    Metric Learning

The goal of metric learning is to learn perceptual embeddings such that distance in the lower dimensional embedding space encodes information related to semantic similarity. Pre-deep learning approaches to metric learning were primarily concerned with learning embeddings directly for each item in an input set. In the case of learning from human supervision, approaches that use relative similarity judgements have been shown to be effective [23,37,45,53]. These methods have also been extended to the adaptive setting where the model can decide which items to request annotations for in order to speed up training [43].

More recently, end-to-end metric learning methods have attempted to parameterize an embedding function (e.g. a convolutional neural network) directly [29,38]. As a result, they are able to embed any new item into the embedding space, even those not seen at training time. Representative earlier applications of this line of work include image ranking [49] and face recognition [40]. The standard assumption made by the majority of these methods is that only *one* similarity criterion is being used. However, when collecting data from human annotators, different individuals may be using different visual criteria when making classification and similarity judgements, e.g. one individual could be using shape, while the other is using color. Furthermore, the same individual may change the criteria they use conditioned on the specific items they are shown, and could change to another criteria when shown another set of items at a different point in time.

There has been some work that attempts to deal with the fact that *different* similarity criteria may be being used. These range from fully supervised, where the similarity criteria is known at training time [48], through to unsupervised methods that attempt to estimate the criteria [21,30,44,52]. Attempts have also been made to probabilistically estimate item embeddings along with annotator-specific parameters representing the individual criteria they are using [52].

One common assumption made by the above methods is that the learner is stationary, i.e. they are used a predefined and fixed similarity criteria, or small set of criteria, which do not evolve or change over time. This is a reasonable assumption to make when dealing with common everyday object categories where the annotators will likely be familiar with the objects depicted and have an a priori understanding of how the visual features of the objects may vary. However, this assumption is violated in cases where the annotator is in the process of *learning* the visual concepts of interest. In this work, we address this non-stationary setting and show that by doing this, we can more accurately predict the visual classification behavior of real human learners.

## 2.2  Human Category Representation

Existing models of human category representation and learning can be clustered into five major groups: rule-based, prototype-based, exemplar-based, knowledge/theory-based, and decision boundary-based approaches [4,56]. The current consensus is that humans likely use multiple different category-learning systems depending on the specific nature of the task at hand [3,5]. For example, in rule-based tasks, the optimal policy may be easy to verbalize and thus efficiently encoded via a set of rules. In practice however, perceptual tasks such as fine-grained visual categorization can be much harder to represent in this way [8]. Several works have attempted to extract perceptual embeddings that align with human similarity judgements from coarse [15,36] and more fine-grained [32] image collections. [6] showed that with simple linear transformations, pre-trained deep image classifiers can be predictive of human similarity judgements. Relevant to our work, [7] investigated whether human learning dynamics mimic gradient descent in Artificial Neural Networks when learning visual categories. However, they assumed they had access to the feature space used by the human, whereas we instead attempt to learn this. In this work, we also aim to extract human-aligned representations, but in the more challenging setting whereby our learners are not static, but instead are in the process of learning the categorization task.

## 2.3  Knowledge Tracing

The problem of modelling the hidden state of dynamic learners as they interact with a learning task has also been tackled in the knowledge tracing literature. Bayesian Knowledge Tracing-based methods model a learner's knowledge state by assuming that the learner can be represented as a Markov process which updates online during learning [13]. Building on this line of work, Deep Knowledge Tracing (DKT) instead uses a recurrent neural network as the underlying tracing model [34], and fully self-attention-based methods have also been proposed [33,35]. It is important to note that conventional knowledge tracing attempts to model knowledge acquisition as a binary variable at the 'skill' level (i.e. the visual class) as opposed to the 'instance' level (i.e. a specific image). In contrast, our approach jointly learns an image embedding function in addition to being able to capture and predict the individual learning trajectories of multiple different learners. A detailed comparison of the original DKT model and our model is provided in the supplementary material (see Sect. A.2).

## 2.4  Machine Teaching

Estimating the representations used by humans is an important component for developing automated teaching algorithms and systems. Machine teaching algorithms address the teaching problem by generating sequences of instructional examples to show to novice learners in order to improve their ability on a given task [57]. Machine teaching has applications in crowdsourcing where the aim is to efficiently train crowdworkers, in addition to education where the goal is to train new experts, e.g. in medical image analysis [2,10].

There is a growing body of work in computer vision that attempts to teach visual concepts to human learners, e.g. [18,27,42,50,51]. However, many of these works assume a fixed feature space that is generated before teaching begins [18,27,42]. In one experiment, [27] showed that representations that are better aligned with human perception result in improved learner performance on the downstream teaching task. While we do not explicitly investigate teaching algorithms in this work, we instead explore a setting where data is collected from humans engaged in learning a visual categorization task with instructional images selected by a 'random' teacher. Importantly, the representations and learner parameterizations extracted by our model can be used directly with computer assisted teaching methods.

## 3   Method

Our goal is to estimate the image classification function used by a human learner that has been provided with a sequence of images and corresponding ground truth class labels as training data. We begin by outlining the problem, and then present our approach to human visual knowledge tracing.

### 3.1   Problem Setup

Given an image $\mathbf{x}$ as input, we model a human learner as a classification function that returns a response, $r^k = \text{argmax}_c P(c|\mathbf{x}, \theta^k)$. Here, $r$ is a discrete class label representing the class response for learner $k$, i.e. $r \in \{1, ..., C\}$, where $C$ is the number of possible classes, and $\theta^k$ are unobserved parameters representing the state of the learner. Our learners are not stationary as their internal 'knowledge state' changes depending on the information they have previously been exposed to that is relevant to the task. As a result, for a given learner $k$ we model their classification function at time $t$ as $r_{t+1}^k = \text{argmax}_c P(c|\mathbf{x}, \theta_t^k, \mathbf{x}_{1:t}^k, y_{1:t}^k, r_{1:t}^k)$. Here, $(\mathbf{x}_{1:t}^k, y_{1:t}^k, r_{1:t}^k)$ is the history of images, ground truth class labels, and responses that a learner $k$ has seen, and provided, up to and including time $t$.

Specifically, at each training time-step, a learner $k$ is presented with an image $\mathbf{x}$, they provide their response $r$, and are given feedback in the form of the correct class label $y$ (Fig. 2B). However, fitting a model for an individual learner with a single response per time-step is difficult. Alternatively, requesting more responses per time-step would reduce the number of teaching examples presented to the learner in the same amount of time. Instead, to overcome this limited information setting, we train a model $\phi$ across many learners, allowing the model to discover knowledge states and learning rules shared across all learners. Once trained, our model can make predictions for how a learner, who was not observed during training, will classify an image based on their prior classification behavior.

## 3.2    Tracing Human Learners

Our tracing model $\phi$ can be decomposed into a feature extractor $f$, a classification function $\psi$, and a non-learned and non-linear transformation $\sigma$ (softmax). We explore how to represent the feature extractor and classification function.

A natural choice for the feature extractor $f$ is a Convolutional Neural Network (CNN). Given an image $\mathbf{x}$ as input, the feature extractor outputs a $D$ dimensional vector $\mathbf{z} = f(\mathbf{x})$. We will assume that all learners use the same underlying feature extractor which remains constant over time i.e. $f = f_t^k$, and that they simply differ in the relative importance they place on different visual features. While these are both big assumptions to make, they are not overly restrictive. For example, a novice and an expert might engaged in the same visual classification task but differ in the set of visual features they select in order to make their decision. Furthermore, while we assume that the feature extractor remains constant over the time interval of our experiments, we do not assume that the classification function $\psi$ used by a learner remains static. In the next sections we will explore different choices for this classification function, comparing simple static classifiers with more expressive recurrent models.

**Static Tracing Model.** The first model we explore is the simplest. Here we assume that all learners use the same classifier which does not vary over time. In this setting, $\psi$ is a multi-class linear classifier with a weight matrix $\mathbf{w}$ and per-class biases $\mathbf{b}$,

$$\phi_{static}(\mathbf{x}) = \sigma(\psi(f(\mathbf{x}))) = \sigma(\mathbf{w}^\mathsf{T} f(\mathbf{x}) + \mathbf{b}). \tag{1}$$

This model is similar to conventional metric learning approaches which do not attempt to capture any annotator specific differences related to individual biases or temporal changes. At training time we simply estimate one set of parameters for all learners. This model does not take the response history into account.

**Time-Sensitive Tracing Model.** One obvious limitation of the static tracing model is that it does not take into account the fact that a learner will likely change over time, i.e. they may be much worse at a new classification task early on, but may improve over time as they are shown sequences of example images along with their associated ground truth class labels. A more advanced model, that captures this temporal evolution, is one that has a different classifier for each time-step,

$$\phi_{static\_time}(\mathbf{x}) = \sigma(\mathbf{w}_t^\mathsf{T} f(\mathbf{x}) + \mathbf{b}_t). \tag{2}$$

Again, the same classifiers are shared across all learners, but in this case the weights and biases are different at each time-step, i.e. $\mathbf{w}_t \neq \mathbf{w}_{t-1}$.

## 3.3    Recurrent Tracing Models

The previous tracing models do not account for the fact that individual learners may start with different levels of ability and update their internal knowledge state in different ways depending on the information that they are provided with. [34] showed that recurrent networks could be used to track the skill acquisition of human learners engaged in learning math quiz questions. Direct application of their model to our visual categorization setting is not possible as they assume one hot encodings of the query and learner responses as input. Their approach also uses large training sets – on the order of thousands of learners and tens of thousands of interactions. Furthermore, they model knowledge acquisition at the 'concept' (i.e. visual category) and not 'instance' (i.e. a specific image) level, and thus their approach is not capable of making predictions for items not seen during training. We build on [34] and adapt it to our visual category learning setting by presenting two different recurrent-based models for human visual knowledge tracing.

**Direct Response Model.** Our first model uses a recurrent network to directly predict the responses of a learner given their previous response history,

$$\phi_{direct}(\mathbf{x}) = \sigma(\psi_{rnn}(\mathbf{z}_{1:t}^k, y_{1:t}^k, r_{1:t}^k, \mathbf{z}, y)). \tag{3}$$

Here, $\psi_{rnn}$ is a recurrent network (in practice we represent this using an LSTM [16]) and $\mathbf{z}_t = f(\mathbf{x}_t)$ are visual features extracted from our CNN.

This model assumes that a learner's knowledge state at time $t$ is defined by the images they have previously seen and their past classification responses. Recurrent models can produce unique transformations for individual learners by conditioning on their hidden states. In this case, after the shared feature extractor transforms an image into a feature vector, the model modifies the feature vector with a series of non-linear transformations conditioned on the learner's hidden state. The final linear layer transforms the feature vector into a predicted response. Note that this model is also conditioned on the current query image $\mathbf{z} = f(\mathbf{x})$ and the corresponding ground truth class label $y$.

**Classifier Prediction Model.** Our second recurrent model attempts to provide a more interpretable approximation of human classification. In this case, instead of letting the recurrent model directly predict the probability for each response, it instead attempts to approximate the weights of a linear classifier used internally by the learner. Importantly, the values this classifier takes will depend on the response history of a given learner and will differ at each time-step,

$$\mathbf{w}_t^k, \mathbf{b}_t^k = \psi_{rnn}(\mathbf{z}_{1:t}^k, y_{1:t}^k, r_{1:t}^k, y), \tag{4}$$

$$\phi_{cls\_pred}(\mathbf{x}) = \sigma(\mathbf{w}_t^\mathsf{T} \mathbf{z} + \mathbf{b}_t). \tag{5}$$

Unlike the previous direct prediction recurrent model, we now explicitly represent the classification function used by an individual learner. Also, here the features $\mathbf{z}$ for the query image are not processed by the recurrent network in Eqn. 4.

Instead they are evaluated using the much simpler predicted classifier weights in Eq. 5. This decoupling is advantageous in applications like machine teaching where we have to query the tracing model multiple times at each time-step in order to determine the next image to show learners. Reducing the computation required to perform these queries will result in faster teacher algorithms.

## 3.4    Training Tracing Models

We jointly estimate the parameters of the feature extractor $f$ and classification functions $\phi$ for each of the above models using a standard cross entropy loss,

$$\mathcal{L} = -\frac{1}{KT} \sum_{k=1}^{K} \sum_{t=1}^{T} \log(\phi(\mathbf{x}_t^k)_r). \tag{6}$$

Here, $\phi(\mathbf{x}_t^k)_r$ indicates the predicted probability from a model $\phi$ choosing class $r$, for learner $k$, at time-step $t$. The training objective aims to minimize the difference between the learner responses from our training set and the tracing model outputs.

# 4    Experiments

In this section we evaluate the different proposed models for visual knowledge tracing on data we collected from real human participants[1].

## 4.1    Datasets

Traditional image classification datasets mostly contain labels produced by annotators familiar with the subject material, e.g. [24,25,46], or they have at least received detailed instructions and examples on how to annotate them, e.g. [39]. As a result, these datasets do not contain annotations from learners engaged in learning a task and are thus not suitable for evaluating visual knowledge tracing. While some work has focused on teaching crowd learners (e.g. [27,42,50]), they often use teaching image sequences that are determined offline and fixed. For our tracing experiments, we require unbiased sequences of images that are randomly selected for each learner. Some of these existing works compare their approaches to a random image selection baseline, but the size of these random teaching subsets is insufficient for thorough evaluation of our different tracing approaches, e.g. [27] have random selection data from only ~40 participants. Due to these limitations, we collected annotations from human learners for three challenging fine-grained visual classification datasets.

---

[1] Code and dataset - https://github.com/nkondapa/VisualKnowledgeTracing.

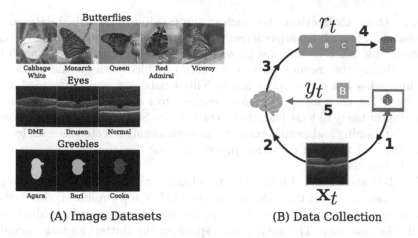

**(A) Image Datasets**                    **(B) Data Collection**

**Fig. 2. (A)** Example images from the three different datasets from our experiments. 'Butterflies' contains images of five different species and was originally presented in [27]. 'Eyes' contains optical coherence tomography images of the human retina from [20], and features two diseased classes and one normal one. 'Greebles' is a synthetic dataset we created where the three object classes vary in terms of shape and color. **(B)** Data collection pipeline. A random image is selected (1), shown to the learner (2), and the learner provides a response (3). Their response is stored (4) and the correct class label is provided to them (5).

**Image Data.** We selected three different image datasets that cover three distinct domains: artificial data where we have full knowledge of the underlying distribution, medical image data, and images of different wildlife species. The first two datasets in particular are representative of the types of visual identification tasks that many humans are interested in learning.

Our first dataset, 'Butterflies', contains images from five different common species of North American butterflies. The 'Cabbage White' class is immediately recognizable, 'Red Admiral' can be learned relatively easily, and the remaining three are difficult to discriminate. This dataset was originally used in [27] and contains between 386 and 481 images per class, for a total of 2,224 images. Our second dataset, 'Eyes', is a three-class subset of a large collection of publicly available images of the human retina from [20]. It contains two diseased classes, 'Diabetic Macular Edema' (DME) and 'Drusen', and one 'Normal' class. We manually selected 200 images from each class. The third dataset is a challenging synthetic one we created called 'Greebles'. It contains three classes, where the underlying feature space used to generate the images is known by design. The relevant features are the body length and color, but the images also includes some irrelevant variation in the form of the head size and body width. The distinctions between the classes can be subtle, making the task challenging. It contains 1,200 images in total, with an even number per class. Visual examples for each of the datasets are presented in Fig. 2A. Note that the single examples in Fig. 2A do not covey the visual diversity of the datasets.

**Human Data Collection.** For each of the previously described datasets, we collected data from human participants that were engaged in learning the classification task. Each learner was presented with 30 training images and 15 test images. During the training phase they were provided with ground truth feedback indicating the correct class labels. This feedback was not provided in the test phase. For each image, we asked learners to rank the top three classes in order of most likely to least likely to be correct (see Sect. F.1 for further information). The training and testing examples were randomly selected for each learner. An overview of the data collection process for one iteration, for one learner, is shown in Fig. 2B.

The data was collected using a custom built a web application and the participants were recruited through the crowd sourcing app Prolific [1]. In total, we collected data from 150 learners for each dataset, where each individual could only do the task once. The median time spent on the Butterflies task, including training and testing, was –11.7 min with a median of 11 correct on the test phase. The corresponding statistics for the Eyes dataset was –12.1 min with a median of 13 correct, and for the Greebles dataset is was –8.8 min with a median of 9 correct.

Our human learners demonstrated learning across all three datasets. In Fig. 3 we plot two histograms for each dataset, the first histogram displays the number of correct responses during the training (i.e. teaching) phase and the second reports the same for the test phase. For all of the datasets, we see a right skew in the histogram of correct responses in the testing phase, indicating that most learners are providing correct answers after training. The skewness for each dataset is –0.45 for Butterflies, –0.81 for Eyes, and –0.37 for Greebles. The skewness is correlated to the amount of improvement learners showed on a given dataset. The numbers imply that the Greebles task is the most difficult and the learners demonstrate the least improvement. The Eyes dataset, on the other hand, is clearly the easiest. We provide additional analysis in the supplementary material (Sect. C).

## 4.2   Implementation Details

All models we are considering primarily consist of a feature extractor and a classification function. The feature extractor is implemented as a CNN with eight layers (two convolutional, two max-pool, four linear), and is the same across all models (Sect. B). The feature extractor produces a 16 dimensional embedding for an input image which is then processed by the respective classification function. We evaluated one of our models on higher dimensional feature spaces, but found no impact on performance (Sect. A.7). For the two recurrent models, $\phi_{direct}$ and $\phi_{cls\_pred}$, we use a three layer LSTM-based [16] fully connected network with a hidden dimension of size 128. The output of the LSTM is passed to a small two-layer network that transforms the output into the desired representation (either a response or a classifier (see Sect. 3.3)). We provide a detailed description of the architectures and inputs in the supplementary material (Sect. F.2).

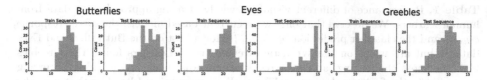

**Fig. 3.** Human learner performance on our three datasets. For each dataset we provide histograms of learner performance on the respective training and testing sequences. The training results are always worse as it include responses from all time-steps, including when the learner has just started the task and is unfamiliar with the classes. For 'Greebles', the worse performance on the test set compared to the other datasets indicates that learners find this task more challenging.

All models are trained using mini-batch stochastic gradient descent with a batch size of 16 using the Adam optimizer [22]. For the feature extractor, we use a learning rate of 1e-5, and we use a learning rate of 1e-3 for each of the different classification functions. We train using a cross entropy loss. Models are trained with early stopping. Training ends when the best validation loss does not improve for 35 epochs. The upper limit on the number of training epochs is 400. Data is split into train (70%), validation (13.3%), and test (16.7%) splits at the learner level, i.e. sequences from the same individual learner cannot be in more than one split. To ensure more robust results, we validate models by re-shuffling the data five times and report the averages across the splits using micro and macro average precision.

### 4.3   Results

**Tracing Human Learners.** We compute the precision and recall curves for each of the visual knowledge tracing models on the held-out learners and report the average precision for each. We also include one additional model for completeness, the ground truth baseline model (GT Label). This baseline does not fit any parameters and simply predicts the corresponding ground truth label of the image for all learners at all time-steps (instead of predicting the learner's response). Results are summarized in Table 1. Standard deviations are between 0.01 and 0.03 for all models, and do not change the interpretation of the results.

We observe that the recurrent models, $\phi_{direct}$ and $\phi_{cls\_pred}$, out-perform the baselines in tracing the learner on the Butterflies –8% and Eyes datasets –6%. However, on the Greebles dataset, the static tracing model, $\phi_{static}$, outperforms the recurrent models by –3%. Both recurrent models are comparable in terms of performance, indicating the reduction in computation described in Sect. 3.3 does not come with a reduction in performance. The time-sensitive tracing model, $\phi_{static\_time}$, is clearly the worst at tracing learners, likely owing to the unrealistic assumptions it makes about them.

Finally we explore the differences between how different models trace human learners. Fig. 4 shows the average probability of predicting an image correctly

**Table 1.** Performance of different visual knowledge tracing approaches on data from human learners. We observe that our two recurrent based models, the direct response $\phi_{direct}$ and the classifier prediction $\phi_{cls\_pred}$, perform best on the Butterflies and Eyes dataset but are worse on the synthetic Greebles task. Learners found the Greebles task the most challenging, and as a result, there was much less learning occurring compared to the first two datasets. 'GT Label' is an additional baseline that uses the corresponding ground truth class label $y$ as the prediction of the learner's response $r$.

| | Greebles | | | | Eyes | | | | Butterflies | | | |
|---|---|---|---|---|---|---|---|---|---|---|---|---|
| | Train | | Test | | Train | | Test | | Train | | Test | |
| | Micro | Macro | Micro | Macro | Micro | Macro | Micro | Macro | Micro | Macro | Micro | Macro |
| GT Label | 0.48 | 0.51 | 0.58 | 0.61 | 0.56 | 0.56 | 0.69 | 0.69 | 0.45 | 0.44 | 0.50 | 0.49 |
| $\phi_{static}$ | 0.63 | 0.52 | 0.67 | 0.58 | 0.60 | 0.59 | 0.67 | 0.68 | **0.55** | **0.53** | **0.64** | **0.61** |
| $\phi_{static\_time}$ | 0.52 | 0.44 | 0.49 | 0.40 | 0.34 | 0.34 | 0.33 | 0.34 | 0.54 | 0.52 | 0.61 | 0.59 |
| $\phi_{direct}$ | 0.70 | 0.59 | **0.77** | 0.64 | **0.66** | **0.65** | **0.75** | **0.74** | **0.55** | **0.53** | 0.60 | 0.57 |
| $\phi_{cls\_pred}$ | **0.71** | **0.62** | **0.77** | **0.65** | 0.65 | **0.65** | 0.74 | **0.74** | 0.54 | 0.52 | 0.60 | 0.57 |

for each time-step conditioned on each class for the Butterflies dataset. In the top row, we present the training and test-split average accuracy on each of the fives classes over time for the human learners. As previously noted, the training sequences contains 30 randomly selected images and the test sequence contains 15 images. We can see that on average, some classes are much easier than others. In the bottom row, we average model-predicted probabilities for –50 images in each class. To produce the probabilities for the recurrent $\phi_{cls\_pred}$ model, we processes the sequential data of the same set of learners in the top panel. The static tracing model, $\phi_{static}$, estimates a hyperplane for each class that roughly tracks the average probability of being correct per class. As expected, this model is not capable of capturing any learning behavior. In contrast, $\phi_{cls\_pred}$ more faithfully traces how the average probability evolves over time. Note, that we process each of the test images independently for $\phi_{cls\_pred}$.

## 4.4   Discussion

**Comparing Models.** We observe that our recurrent models are quite effective at tracing human learner knowledge on visual categorization tasks for datasets where there is a clear learning signal. On the Greebles dataset, which is the most challenging and displays the least amount of learning, we see that the simple static tracing model $\phi_{static}$ is less prone to over-fitting and is thus marginally better. The time-sensitive tracing model $\phi_{static\_time}$ performs the worst overall. Unlike the recurrent methods, it is unable to share information between time-steps, forcing it to fit a classifier at each time-step with only –90 training points (the number of learners in the training set after we split out the validation and test sets). This makes it extremely prone to over-fitting on the limited training data that is available.

The direct response model $\phi_{direct}$ and the classifier prediction model $\phi_{cls\_pred}$ differ in their outputs and their inputs. $\phi_{direct}$ includes $\mathbf{z}$, the representation of

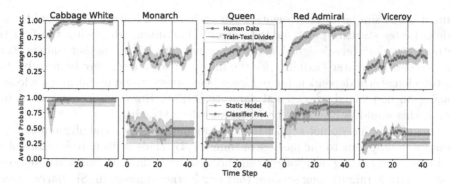

**Fig. 4. (Top)** The smoothed average human learner accuracy for class over time from the Butterflies dataset. The shadowed regions indicate confidence intervals as the number of samples in each time and class bin are not guaranteed to be the same. **(Bottom)** The average probability of having a class correctly predicted by the static $\phi_{static}$ model (orange) and the recurrent $\phi_{cls\_pred}$ model (green). At each time-step, for each learner in the test set, the models predict class probabilities for ~50 images per class. The probabilities are averaged (solid line) and the shadows indicate one standard deviation. In both rows, the red line indicates the point at which the learners switch from training to testing. After that, the models will continue to produce the same probabilities on the test images for the remaining time-steps as the sampled images do not change.

the query image $\mathbf{x}$ to be classified by the learner, as input to the LSTM. $\phi_{cls\_pred}$ outputs weights of a multi-class linear classifier that is used to classify the representation $\mathbf{z}$. Unlike $\phi_{direct}$, $\mathbf{z}$ is not an input to the LSTM for $\phi_{cls\_pred}$. However, both models incorporate the ground truth label $y$ for $\mathbf{x}$ as input. These structural differences between the models make little difference to the tracing performance, but the $\phi_{cls\_pred}$ model is more efficient if it needs perform evaluation multiple times for new query items. In supplementary experiments (A.1), we explore the impact of removing the ground truth class label $y$ for the query image from the input. We observe that this results in a large decrease in performance for both models, suggesting that this class information is valuable to the model when making future predictions. Also in the supplement, we compare two cognitive models (prototype and exemplar [31]) (A.3), a Transformer model [11] (A.4), a pre-trained ResNet feature extractor (A.5), and input meta-information to the tracing models (A.6). We find that the cognitive, Transformer, and ResNet models do not out-perform the recurrent architectures, but are worth further exploration. Additionally, including meta-information in the input vectors results in a performance increase across all models we tested, suggesting this a promising direction for future work. Finally, we explore the representations learned by the recurrent models (Sects. D, E).

**Limitations and Future Work.** Currently, we train our feature encoder $f$ from scratch for each task on relatively small amounts of image data. One source of improvement would be to pre-train the feature space so that it better reflects human visual similarity judgements. Such an improved feature space would provide a better starting point for task specific finetuning. Replacing the LSTM with an appropriately designed Transformer network [47] is another change that could result in greater flexibility for the model. Transformers are better able to capture long-term dependencies and have been shown to be useful in knowledge tracing on non-visual educational datasets [11,33]. However, it remains to be seen if this would be valuable for visual knowledge tracing.

Our approaches do not explicitly model memory decay – the phenomenon of memory 'fading' due to the passage of time [17,41]. This is likely to be more of a problem when tracing over longer time horizons, e.g. days or weeks, as opposed to the multiple minute long sessions that our learners engage in. Similarly, given the short time durations of our teaching sessions, we assume that no significant 'feature learning' is happening for individual learners. Instead we model learners as attending to a subset of the different visual features that are captured in our joint embedding space. In future work, it would be interesting to further explore if these two assumptions are valid.

**Applications.** Successful tracing of human learners has implications for crowd-sourcing annotations, metric learning, and machine teaching. Early detection of poor annotators in crowd sourcing would reduce monetary and time costs in labelling datasets. Additionally, identifying annotators with 'specialist' knowledge could allow for targeted crowd sourcing, tailoring to the abilities of each individual annotator. A successful tracing algorithm should be able to predict future performance with increasing confidence as the learners are being trained on the annotation task.

The most impactful domain for a successful tracing algorithm is automated teaching, e.g. teaching medical image interpretation skills [2,10]. Teaching humans is challenging because their knowledge state is unobserved, it changes over time, and the information they provide using current interfaces can be limited. In this work, we show that with a reasonable amount of training data (i.e. data from ~150 learners), and only a single response at each time-step, we are able to capture information about the learner's current knowledge for visual classification tasks. The types of visual knowledge tracing approaches presented could be used in conjunction with machine teaching methods. The more a teaching algorithm knows about the learner, the more effective it can be when selecting examples to present to them.

## 5    Conclusion

More accurate models of human visual classification will lead to improved methods for crowd annotation collection, better techniques for automatically teaching visual knowledge to human learners, and perhaps provide us with insight into how we can build future artificial systems that are more data efficient. To this end, in this work we explored the problem of visual knowledge tracing – the task of predicting the internal, potentially time varying, image classification function used by human learners. To do this, we presented a series of models that range in complexity from basic static linear classifiers all the way to recurrent models that take a learner's prior response history into account when making predictions about their future behavior. We collected new annotations for three challenging visual classification tasks from humans engaged in a visual learning task in order to benchmark the performance of these different models. Our results show that our recurrent neural network-based models resulted in the most faithful reproductions of unobserved learner predictions on real image datasets. Finally, we outlined limitations of our work and pointed to open questions that require further investigation.

**Acknowledgements.** Thanks to the anonymous reviews for their valuable feedback. This work was in part supported by the Turing 2.0 'Enabling Advanced Autonomy' project funded by the EPSRC and the Alan Turing Institute and also by the Simons Collaboration on the Global Brain.

# References

1. Prolific. https://www.prolific.co. Accessed Mar 7 2022
2. Amiri, E., Sha, P., Palmer, E.M.: Training novices to discriminate retinal diseases using perceptual learning. In: Proceedings of the Human Factors and Ergonomics Society Annual Meeting, pp. 1456–1460 (2020)
3. Ashby, F.G., Maddox, W.T.: Human category learning. Annu. Rev. Psychol. **56**, 149–178 (2005)
4. Ashby, F.G., Maddox, W.T.: Human category learning 2.0. Ann. N. Y. Acad. Sci. **1224** (1), 147–161 (2011)
5. Ashby, F.G., O'Brien, J.B.: Category learning and multiple memory systems. Trends Cogn. Sci. **9**(2), 83–89 (2005)
6. Attarian, M., Roads, B.D., Mozer, M.C.: Transforming neural network visual representations to predict human judgments of similarity. arXiv:2010.06512 (2020)
7. Barry, D.N., Love, B.C.: Human learning follows the dynamics of gradient descent. PsyArXiv (2021)
8. Biederman, I., Shiffrar, M.M.: Sexing day-old chicks: a case study and expert systems analysis of a difficult perceptual-learning task. J. Exper. Psychol. Learn. Mem. Cogn. **13**(4), 640 (1987)
9. Chen, T., Kornblith, S., Norouzi, M., Hinton, G.: A simple framework for contrastive learning of visual representations. In: ICML, pp. 1597–1607 (2020)
10. Cheng, C.T., Chen, C.C., Fu, C.Y., Chaou, C.H., Wu, Y.T., Hsu, C.P., Chang, C.C., Chung, I., Hsieh, C.H., Hsieh, M.J., et al.: Artificial intelligence-based education assists medical students' interpretation of hip fracture. Insights into Imaging **11**(1), 1–8 (2020)
11. Choi, Y., et al.: Towards an appropriate query, key, and value computation for knowledge tracing. In: Proceedings of the Seventh ACM Conference on Learning@ Scale, pp. 341–344 (2020)
12. Cole, E., Yang, X., Wilber, K., Mac Aodha, O., Belongie, S.: When does contrastive visual representation learning work? In: CVPR, 14755–14764 (2022)
13. Corbett, A.T., Anderson, J.R.: Knowledge tracing: Modeling the acquisition of procedural knowledge. User Model. User-Adapt. Interact. **4**(4), 253–278 (1994)

14. He, K., Fan, H., Wu, Y., Xie, S., Girshick, R.: Momentum contrast for unsupervised visual representation learning. In: CVPR, pp. 9729–9738 (2020)

15. Hebart, M.N., Zheng, C.Y., Pereira, F., Baker, C.I.: Revealing the multidimensional mental representations of natural objects underlying human similarity judgements. Nat. Hum. Behav. 4(11), 1173–1185 (2020)

16. Hochreiter, S., Schmidhuber, J.: Long short-term memory. Neural Comput. 9(8), 1735–1780 (1997)

17. Hunziker, A., et al.: Teaching multiple concepts to a forgetful learner. NeurIPS (2019)

18. Johns, E., Mac Aodha, O., Brostow, G.J.: Becoming the expert-interactive multiclass machine teaching. In: CVPR, pp. 2616–2624 (2015)

19. Kaya, M., Bilge, H.Ş.: Deep metric learning: a survey. Symmetry 11(9), 1066(2019)

20. Kermany, D.S., Goldbaum, M., Cai, W., Valentim, C.C., Liang, H., Baxter, S.L., McKeown, A., Yang, G., Wu, X., Yan, F., et al.: Identifying medical diagnoses and treatable diseases by image-based deep learning. Cell 172(5), 1122–1131 (2018)

21. Kim, K.H., Mac Aodha, O., Perona, P.: Context embedding networks. In: CVPR, pp. 8679–8687 (2018)

22. Kingma, D.P., Ba, J.: Adam: a method for stochastic optimization. arXiv:1412.6980 (2014)

23. Kruskal, J.B., Wish, M.: Multidimensional scaling. no. 11, Sage (1978)

24. Kuznetsova, A., et al.: The open images dataset V4. Int. J. Comput. Vis. 128(7), 1956–1981 (2020). https://doi.org/10.1007/s11263-020-01316-z

25. Lin, T.Y., et al.: Microsoft COCO: common objects in context. In: Fleet, D., Pajdla, T., Schiele, B., Tuytelaars, T. (eds.) ECCV 2014. LNCS, vol. 8693, pp. 740–755. Springer, Cham (2014). https://doi.org/10.1007/978-3-319-10602-1_48

26. Liu, Q., Shen, S., Huang, Z., Chen, E., Zheng, Y.: A survey of knowledge tracing. arXiv:2105.15106 (2021)

27. Mac Aodha, O., Su, S., Chen, Y., Perona, P., Yue, Y.: Teaching categories to human learners with visual explanations. In: CVPR, pp. 3820–3828 (2018)

28. Markman, E.M.: Categorization and Naming in Children: Problems of Induction. MIT Press (1989)

29. Musgrave, K., Belongie, S., Lim, S.-N.: A metric learning reality check. In: Vedaldi, A., Bischof, H., Brox, T., Frahm, J.-M. (eds.) ECCV 2020. LNCS, vol. 12370, pp. 681–699. Springer, Cham (2020). https://doi.org/10.1007/978-3-030-58595-2_41

30. Nigam, I., Tokmakov, P., Ramanan, D.: Towards latent attribute discovery from triplet similarities. In: ICCV, pp. 402–410 (2019)

31. Nosofsky, R.M., Meagher, B., Kumar, P.: Contrasting exemplar and prototype models in a natural-science category domain. In: CogSci (2020)

32. Nosofsky, R.M., Sanders, C.A., Meagher, B.J., Douglas, B.J.: Toward the development of a feature-space representation for a complex natural category domain. Behav. Res. Meth. 50(2), 530–556 (2017). https://doi.org/10.3758/s13428-017-0884-8

33. Pandey, S., Karypis, G.: A self-attentive model for knowledge tracing. arXiv:1907.06837 (2019)

34. Piech, C., Spencer, J., Huang, J., Ganguli, S., Sahami, M., Guibas, L., Sohl-Dickstein, J.: Deep knowledge tracing. NeurIPS (2015)

35. Pu, S., Yudelson, M., Ou, L., Huang, Y.: Deep knowledge tracing with transformers. In: Bittencourt, I.I., Cukurova, M., Muldner, K., Luckin, R., Millán, E. (eds.) AIED 2020. LNCS (LNAI), vol. 12164, pp. 252–256. Springer, Cham (2020). https://doi.org/10.1007/978-3-030-52240-7_46

36. Roads, B.D., Love, B.C.: Enriching imagenet with human similarity judgments and psychological embeddings. In: CVPR, pp. 3547–3557 (2021)
37. Roads, B.D., Mozer, M.C.: Predicting the ease of human category learning using radial basis function networks. Neural Comput. **33**(2), 376–397 (2021)
38. Roth, K., Milbich, T., Sinha, S., Gupta, P., Ommer, B., Cohen, J.P.: Revisiting training strategies and generalization performance in deep metric learning. In: ICML, pp. 8242–8252 (2020)
39. Russakovsky, O., et al.: ImageNet large scale visual recognition challenge. Int. J. Comput. Vis. **115**(3), 211–252 (2015). https://doi.org/10.1007/s11263-015-0816-y
40. Schroff, F., Kalenichenko, D., Philbin, J.: Facenet: a unified embedding for face recognition and clustering. In: CVPR, pp. 815–823 (2015)
41. Settles, B., Meeder, B.: A trainable spaced repetition model for language learning. In: ACL, pp. 1848–1858 (2016)
42. Singla, A., Bogunovic, I., Bartók, G., Karbasi, A., Krause, A.: Near-optimally teaching the crowd to classify. In: ICML, pp. 154–162 (2014)
43. Tamuz, O., Liu, C., Belongie, S.J., Shamir, O., Kalai, A.: Adaptively learning the crowd kernel. In: ICML (2011)
44. Tan, R., Vasileva, M.I., Saenko, K., Plummer, B.A.: Learning similarity conditions without explicit supervision. In: ICCV, pp. 10373–10382 (2019)
45. Van Der Maaten, L., Weinberger, K.: Stochastic triplet embedding. In: International Workshop on Machine Learning for Signal Processing, pp. 1–6 (2012)
46. Van Horn, G., et al.: Building a bird recognition app and large scale dataset with citizen scientists: the fine print in fine-grained dataset collection. In: CVPR, pp. 595–604 (2015)
47. Vaswani, A., et al.: Attention is all you need. NeurIPS **40** (2017)
48. Veit, A., Belongie, S., Karaletsos, T.: Conditional similarity networks. In: CVPR, pp. 830–838 (2017)
49. Wang, J., et al.: Learning fine-grained image similarity with deep ranking. In: CVPR, pp. 1386–1393 (2014)
50. Wang, P., Nagrecha, K., Vasconcelos, N.: Gradient-based algorithms for machine teaching. In: CVPR, pp. 1387–1396 (2021)
51. Wang, P., Vasconcelos, N.: A machine teaching framework for scalable recognition. In: ICCV, pp. 4945–4954 (2021)
52. Welinder, P., Branson, S., Perona, P., Belongie, S.: The multidimensional wisdom of crowds. Adv. Neural Inf. Process. Syst. **23** (2010)
53. Wilber, M., Kwak, I., Belongie, S.: Cost-effective hits for relative similarity comparisons. In: Proceedings of the AAAI Conference on Human Computation and Crowdsourcing, vol. 2, pp. 227–233 (2014)
54. Wu, Z., Xiong, Y., Yu, S.X., Lin, D.: Unsupervised feature learning via nonparametric instance discrimination. In: CVPR, pp. 3733–3742 (2018)
55. Xu, F., Tenenbaum, J.B.: Word learning as Bayesian inference. Psychol. Rev. **1114**(2), 245 (2007)
56. Zeithamova, D.: Category Learning Systems. The University of Texas at Austin (2008)
57. Zhu, X., Singla, A., Zilles, S., Rafferty, A.N.: An overview of machine teaching. arXiv:1801.05927 (2018)

# S3C: Self-Supervised Stochastic Classifiers for Few-Shot Class-Incremental Learning

Jayateja Kalla[✉] and Soma Biswas

Department of Electrical Engineering, Indian Institute of Science, Bangalore, India
{jayatejak,somabiswas}@iisc.ac.in

**Abstract.** Few-shot class-incremental learning (FSCIL) aims to learn progressively about new classes with very few labeled samples, without forgetting the knowledge of already learnt classes. FSCIL suffers from two major challenges: (i) *over-fitting* on the new classes due to limited amount of data, (ii) *catastrophically forgetting* about the old classes due to unavailability of data from these classes in the incremental stages. In this work, we propose a self-supervised stochastic classifier (S3C) (code: https://github.com/JAYATEJAK/S3C) to counter both these challenges in FSCIL. The stochasticity of the classifier weights (or class prototypes) not only mitigates the adverse effect of absence of large number of samples of the new classes, but also the absence of samples from previously learnt classes during the incremental steps. This is complemented by the self-supervision component, which helps to learn features from the base classes which generalize well to unseen classes that are encountered in future, thus reducing catastrophic forgetting. Extensive evaluation on three benchmark datasets using multiple evaluation metrics show the effectiveness of the proposed framework. We also experiment on two additional realistic scenarios of FSCIL, namely where the number of annotated data available for each of the new classes can be different, and also where the number of base classes is much lesser, and show that the proposed S3C performs significantly better than the state-of-the-art for all these challenging scenarios.

**Keywords:** Few-shot class-incremental learning · Stochastic classifiers · Self-supervised learning

## 1 Introduction

In recent years, Deep Neural Networks (DNN) have shown significant performance improvement on various computer vision applications [19,27,29]. Usually, the DNN models require enormous amount of annotated data from all the classes of interest to be available for training. In real-world, since data from different classes may become available at different instants of time, we want the model to learn about the new classes incrementally without forgetting about the old classes, which is precisely the task addressed in Class-Incremental Learning

© The Author(s), under exclusive license to Springer Nature Switzerland AG 2022
S. Avidan et al. (Eds.): ECCV 2022, LNCS 13685, pp. 432–448, 2022.
https://doi.org/10.1007/978-3-031-19806-9_25

(CIL). CIL approaches are very useful and practical, not only because it is computationally expensive and time-consuming to retrain the model from scratch, but also because data from the previous classes may not be available due to storage and privacy issues.

Since collecting large number of annotated data from all the new classes is also very difficult, recently, the more challenging but realistic few-shot class-incremental learning (FSCIL) is gaining increasing attention, where the new classes have few labeled samples per class [35]. In FSCIL, a model is first learnt using a set of base classes with large number of labeled examples per class. At each incremental step (task), the model has access to a few labeled samples of the new classes and a single prototype for each of the previously learnt classes. The goal is to learn a unified classifier to recognize the old as well as the new classes, without having access to any task labels. This helps the model to quickly learn about the new classes without requiring to collect and annotate large amounts of data for the new classes. FSCIL faces two major challenges, namely overfitting due to limited samples for the new classes, and catastrophic forgetting of the already learnt classes due to absence of old classes data at the incremental steps.

In this work, we propose a novel framework, S3C (**S**elf-**S**upervised **S**tochastic **C**lassifier) to simultaneously address both these challenges in the FSCIL setting. Unlike the standard classifiers, stochastic classifiers (SC) are represented by weight distributions, i.e. a mean and variance vector [24]. Thus, each classifier weight sampled from this distribution is expected to correctly classify the input samples. We show for the first time, that SC learnt for both the base and new classes can significantly reduce the over-fitting problem on the new classes for FSCIL task. It can also arrest the catastrophic forgetting of the previously learnt classes to a certain extent. As is common in most FSCIL approaches [25,44], we propose to freeze the feature extractor and learn only the SC at each incremental step. In order to compute features from the base classes which generalize to unseen classes, inspired by recent works [22,47], we use self-supervision along with SC giving our final S3C framework. As expected, this helps to significantly mitigate the effect of catastrophic forgetting, while at the same time retaining the advantage on the new classes. To this end, our contributions are as follows:

1. We propose a novel framework, termed S3C (Self-Supervised Stochastic Classifier) to address the FSCIL task.
2. We show that stochastic classifiers can help to significantly reduce over-fitting on the new classes with limited amount of data for FSCIL.
3. We also show that self-supervision with stochastic classifier can be used to better retain the information of the base classes, without hindering the enhanced performance of the stochastic classifiers for the new classes.
4. We set the new state-of-the-art for three benchmark datasets, namely CIFAR100 [18], CUB200 [37] and miniImageNet [44].
5. We also propose and evaluate on two additional, realistic FSCIL settings, namely FSCIL-im (FSCIL-imbalanced) - where the new classes may have different number of samples/class and (ii) FSCIL-lb (FSCIL-less base) - where there are less number of base classes, which further justifies the effectiveness of the proposed S3C framework.

## 2    Related Works

Here, we provide some pointers to the related work in literature.

**Class-Incremental Learning (CIL):** The goal of CIL is to learn new classes progressively without any task information. Due to plenty of annotated new class data, mitigating catastrophic forgetting is a challenging problem. LwF [23] proposed to use knowledge distillation [15] to alleviate catastrophic forgetting. iCaRL [31] showed that nearest classifier mean (NCM) using old class exemplars can generate robust classifiers for CIL. EEIL [7] used knowledge distillation to remember old classes and cross-entropy to learn new classes in an end-to-end training. UCIR [16] proposed cosine-based classifiers and used feature-space distillation and inter-class separation margin loss to mitigate catastrophic forgetting. Several state-of-art-works [2,3,12,38,45] proposed different techniques to address the class imbalance problem in CIL like rescaling scores or balanced finetuning of classifiers, etc. Some of the recent works [41,46,47] have focused on non-exemplar based methods, with no access to exemplars from the old classes.

**Few-Shot Class-Incremental Learning (FSCIL):** Recently, there has been a significant focus on the more realistic and challenging FSCIL task, where very few samples per class are available for training at each incremental task. Tao et al. [35] proposed this protocol and used neural network gas architecture to preserve the feature topologies of the base and new classes. Mazumder et al. [25] proposed to identify unimportant parameters in the model based on their magnitudes and learn only these parameters during the incremental tasks. The works proposed in [1,8–10,21,32,48] focus on learning robust manifolds by regularizing feature space representations. The works in [11,34,44] used graph-based networks for old classes' knowledge retention. Recently, CEC [44] proposed a meta-learning strategy and achieved state-of-art results for the FSCIL setting.

**Self-Supervised Learning (SSL):** SSL uses predefined pretext tasks to learn features from unlabeled data. Different pretext tasks have been proposed like image rotations [17], image colourization [20], clustering [6], and solving jigsaw puzzles from image patch permutations [28]. These features can notably improve the performance of downstream tasks like few-shot learning [13], semi-supervised learning [43], to improve the model robustness [14], class imbalance [40], etc. Recently, Lee et al. [22] used SSL to improve the performance for supervised classification, by augmenting the original labels using the input transformations. In this work, we show that SSL [22] can be used very effectively for the FSCIL task.

**Stochastic Neural Networks:** Traditional neural networks cannot model uncertainty well due to their deterministic nature [5]. Stochastic neural networks [26] give robust representations in the form of distributions. Subedar et al. [33] proposed uncertainty aware variational layers for activity recognition. Recently, it has been used for person re-identification [42] and unsupervised domain adaptation [24] tasks.

# 3  Problem Definition and Notations

Here, we explain the FSCIL task, which consists of a base task and several incremental stages, and also the notations used in the rest of the paper. In the base task, the goal is to learn a classifier using large number of labeled samples from several base classes. At each incremental step, using a few labeled samples per new class and a single class prototype of the old (previously learnt) classes, the model needs to be updated such that it can classify both the old and the new classes. Let $\mathcal{D}^{(0)}$ denote the base task which contains large number of annotated data from classes $\mathcal{C}^{(0)}$. Let the incremental task data be denoted as $\{\mathcal{D}^{(1)}, .., \mathcal{D}^{(t)}, .., \mathcal{D}^{(\mathcal{T})}\}$, and the corresponding label spaces be denoted as $\mathcal{C}^{(t)}$, where $t = 1, \ldots, \mathcal{T}$. Thus, the model will learn a total of $\mathcal{T}$ tasks incrementally and there is no overlap in the label space between the different tasks, i.e. $C^{(t)} \cap C^{(s)} = \phi$; $(t \neq s)$. Once the model has learned on the data $\mathcal{D}^{(t)}$, it has to perform well on all the classes seen so far i.e $\{C^{(0)} \cup C^{(1)} \cup \cdots \cup C^{(t)}\}$.

# 4  Proposed Method

Here, we describe the proposed S3C framework for the FSCIL task. In many of the initial FSCIL approaches [8,25,35], the main focus was to develop novel techniques for the incremental step to prevent catastrophic forgetting and over-fitting. Recently, CEC [44] showed that the base network training has a profound effect on the performance of the incremental tasks. Using appropriate modifications while learning the base classifier can significantly enhance not only the base class accuracies, but also the performance for the incrementally added classes. Even without any fine-tuning during the incremental steps, CEC reports the state-of-the-art results for FSCIL. In the proposed S3C framework, we combine the advantages of both these techniques and propose to not only improve the base classifier training, but also update all the classifiers during the incremental steps. First, we describe the two main modules of S3C, namely Stochastic Classifier and Self-Supervision and then discuss how to integrate them.

**Stochastic Classifier:** One of the major challenges in FSCIL is the few number of annotated samples that is available per class at each incremental step. This may result in overfitting on the few examples and learning classification boundaries which do not generalize well on the test data. Now, we discuss how stochastic classifiers can be used to mitigate this problem.

In this work, we use cosine similarity between the features and the classifier weights to compute the class score for that particular feature. For a given input image $\mathbf{x}$ from class $C_i$, let us denote its feature vector as $f_\theta(\mathbf{x})$, where the parameters of the feature extractor $f$ is denoted by $\theta$. Let the classifier weights corresponding to class $C_i$ be denoted as $\phi_i$. Then the cosine similarity of the feature with this classifier weight can be computed as $\langle \overline{\phi_i}, \overline{f_\theta(\mathbf{x})} \rangle$, where $\overline{u} = u/||u||_2$ denotes the $l_2$ normalized vector. Figure 1(a) shows the normalized feature extractor, and classifier weights for two classes, $C_i$ and $C_j$. The green shaded area denotes the region where $f_\theta(\mathbf{x})$ will be correctly classified to class $C_i$, and $m_{ij}$ is the classification boundary between the two classifiers (considering only the upper sector between $\phi_i$ and $\phi_j$).

Now, instead of a single classifier, let us learn two different classifiers for each class (eg. $\phi_i^1$ and $\phi_i^2$ for class $C_i$). In Fig. 1 (b), $\{m_{ij}^{11}, m_{ij}^{12}, m_{ij}^{21}, m_{ij}^{22}\}$ are the four classification boundaries for four combination of classifiers. To ensure that the input data is correctly classified using all the classifiers, the feature embedding $f_\theta(\mathbf{x})$ has to move closer to the classifier of its correct class, thus making the samples of a class better clustered and further from samples of other classes. But it is difficult to choose (and compute) how many classifiers should be used. By using a stochastic classifier (Fig. 1 (c)), we can ensure that we have infinite such classifiers around the mean classifier.

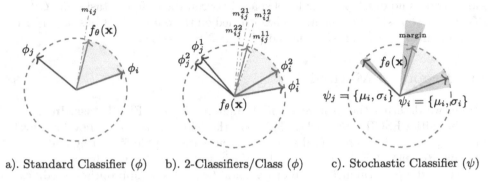

a). Standard Classifier ($\phi$)     b). 2-Classifiers/Class ($\phi$)     c). Stochastic Classifier ($\psi$)

**Fig. 1.** Figure shows the classification boundary between two classes in (a) standard classifier, (b) two-classifiers per class and (c) stochastic classifier. The margin in (c) results in more discriminative classification boundaries. (Color figure online)

Using a stochastic classifier $\psi = \{\mu, \sigma\}$ at the classification head resembles the use of multiple classifiers, where $\mu$ and $\sigma$ denotes the mean and variance of the classifier $\psi$. For a given input image $\mathbf{x}$, the output score of the stochastic classifiers is proportional to $\langle \bar{\hat{\mu}}, \overline{f_\theta(\mathbf{x})} \rangle$ ($\hat{\mu} = \mu + \mathcal{N}(0,1) \odot \sigma$), where the classifier is sampled from the distribution. This has similarity with feature augmentations which are also commonly used [47]. There are two main advantages of using a stochastic classifier instead of feature augmentations: (1) Instead of using a fixed variance for the features (which has to be manually calculated), the means and variances used in the proposed framework are automatically learnt in an end-to-end manner. (2) The means and variances learnt using the base classes also help to initialize the corresponding parameters for the new classes in a semantically meaningful manner as explained later.

**Self-supervision:** At the incremental stages, due to presence of few examples from the new classes, in general, most of the FSCIL approaches either fix the feature extractor after learning the base classes [9,44] or fine-tune it with a very small learning rate [8,25,35], so that it does not change significantly. This reduces catastrophic forgetting as well as overfitting. In our work, we fix the feature extractor after learning the base classes and only fine-tune the classifiers. To make the base feature extractor generalize well to unseen data, we propose to use self-supervision for the base classifier training as well as during the incremental learning stages. Since self-supervised training does not use class labels, more generic features can be learnt, which can generalize well to unseen classes. SSL has been used successfully for several tasks [13,14,40,43,47], including the standard class-incremental setting [47]. Here, we use the recently proposed SSL approach [22], where image augmentations are used to generate artificial labels, which are used to train the classification layer. For a given input image $\mathbf{x}$, let the augmented versions be denoted as $\tilde{\mathbf{x}}_r = t_r(\mathbf{x})$, where $\{t_r\}_{r=1}^{M}$ denotes pre-defined transformations. In this work, we use images rotated by $\{0°, 90°, 180°, 270°\}$, i.e. (M=4) as the augmented images. We show that the feature extractor learnt using self-supervision performs very well in the incremental stages. First, we describe the integrated S3C loss which is used in the training process.

**Construction of S3C Loss:** At task $t$, $C_i^{(s)}$ denotes the $i^{th}$ class in task $s \in \{0, 1, .., t\}$. Then its corresponding stochastic classifier is denoted as $\psi_i^{(s)}$ with mean $\mu_i^{(s)}$ and variance $\sigma_i^{(s)}$. To integrate the stochastic classifiers with self-supervision, for each class, we create four classifier heads corresponding to each of the four rotations as in [22]. In this work, we want to jointly predict the class and its rotation $r = \{0°, 90°, 180°, 270°\}$, thus we denote the final classifiers as $\psi_{i,r}^{(s)}$, with individual means $(\mu_{i,r}^{(s)})$, but with the same class-wise variance $(\sigma_i^{(s)})$. Since the same data is present in different rotations, we enforce that the classifiers for the same class share the same variances, which reduces the number of parameters to be computed. Thus, the joint softmax output of a given sample $\mathbf{x}$ for $C_i^{(s)}$ class at $r^{th}$ rotation is given by

$$\rho_{ir}^{(s)}(\mathbf{x}; \theta, \psi^{(0:t)}) = \frac{exp(\eta \langle \overline{\hat{\mu}_{ir}^{(s)}, f_\theta(\mathbf{x})} \rangle)}{\sum_{j=0}^{t} \sum_{k=0}^{|C^{(t)}|} \sum_{l=0}^{M} exp(\eta \langle \overline{\hat{\mu}_{kl}^{(j)}, f_\theta(\mathbf{x})} \rangle)} \tag{1}$$

where $\hat{\mu}_{ir}^{(j)} = \mu_{ir}^{(j)} + \mathcal{N}(0,1) \odot \sigma_i^{(j)}$ represents the sampled weight from the stochastic classifier $\psi_{ir}^{(j)}$, $\eta$ is a scaling factor used to control peakiness of the softmax distribution. Finally, the S3C training objective for a training sample $\mathbf{x}$ with label $y$ from task $s$ can be written as

$$\mathcal{L}_{S3C}(\mathbf{x}, y; \theta, \psi^{(0:t)}) = -\frac{1}{M} \sum_{r=1}^{M} \log(\rho_{yr}^{(s)}(\tilde{\mathbf{x}}_r; \theta, \psi^{(0:t)})) \tag{2}$$

This implies that the input image is transformed using the chosen image transformations (4 rotations in this work) and the loss is combined for that input. Note that the first transformation corresponding to $0°$ is the identity transformation (i.e. the original data itself). We now describe the base and incremental stage training of the S3C framework (Fig. 2).

## 4.1    Base Network Training of S3C

In FSCIL setting, we assume that we have access to several base classes with sufficient number of annotated data for base training. Given the data from the base classes $C^{(0)}$, we use a base network (ResNet20 for CIFAR100 and ResNet18 for CUB200 and miniImageNet) along with a Graph Attention Network inspired by [36,44]. We train the base network, i.e. the feature extractor with parameters $\theta$ and the stochastic classifiers corresponding to the base classes $(\psi^{(0)})$ with S3C objective $\mathcal{L}_{base} = \mathcal{L}_{S3C}(\mathbf{x}, y; \theta, \psi^{(0)})$, with the base training data given by $\{\mathbf{x}, y\} \in \mathcal{D}^{(0)}$. The proposed objective improves the performance of the base classes, in addition to that of the new classes that will be encountered in the incremental stages as we will observe in the experimental evaluation.

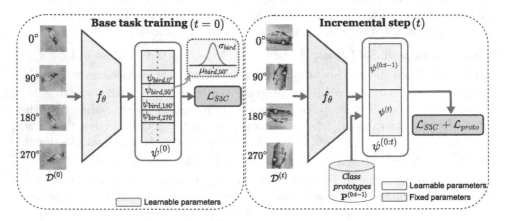

**Fig. 2.** Illustration of the proposed S3C framework: Left: Base network training, Right: Training at each incremental step.

## 4.2    Preparing for the Incremental Step

After the base classifier training, the training data of the base classes may not be available any longer. This may be due to limited storage capacity, privacy issues, etc. After the first incremental step, we want the unified classifier to perform well on the base as well as on the new classes. For this, to mitigate catastrophic forgetting of the base classes, their class prototypes are stored as is the common practice [35,44]. These stored class prototypes can be treated as class representatives of the base classes and thus can be used for updating the network at the incremental step. The class prototypes are computed by averaging the training features given by the feature extractor $(f_\theta(\cdot))$ for each class. This is done not only at the end of the base training, but after each incremental step as well, i.e. after incremental step $t$, we store the class prototypes of all the classes that the model has encountered till step $t$. The class prototype set $\mathbf{P}^{(t)}$ contains the classes prototypes encountered in task $t$. The class prototype $P_i^{(t)}$ after task $t$ for $i^{th}$ class is calculated as

$$P_i^{(t)} = \frac{1}{N_i^{(t)}} \sum_{n=1}^{N^{(t)}} \mathbb{I}_{(y_n=i)} \, f_\theta(\mathbf{x}_n) \tag{3}$$

where $N^{(t)}$ is the number of samples in the dataset $\mathcal{D}^{(t)}$, $N_i^{(t)}$ is number of samples in $i^{th}$ class of task $t$, and $\{\mathbf{x}_n, y_n\}_{n=1}^{N^{(t)}} \in \mathcal{D}^{(t)}$. The indicator variable $\mathbb{I}_{(y_n=i)}$ will be 1 if the sample belongs to the $i^{th}$ class (i.e. $y_n = i$). Thus, the class prototype set is updated at the end of each task.

### 4.3   Incremental Step

Here, we will discuss the training process involved in each incremental step. As in [9,44], we propose to freeze the already learnt feature extractor, since the self-supervision has ensured that it will generalize well to previously unseen classes. This also helps in mitigating the catastrophic forgetting and over-fitting problems. In our work, we propose to update the classifiers of the previous as well as the new classes with the stored class-prototypes and the few examples of the new classes. This will help the model better adapt to the new set of classes. Now, we discuss how to initialize the stochastic classifiers for the new classes.

*Initialization of the Stochastic Classifiers of the New Classes:* For the new classes, we need to initialize the stochastic classifiers before fine-tuning. The means are initialized with the centroid of the features for that class (calculated using the previous model). We initialize the variances of the new classes using that of the most semantically similar class from the base set. Semantic similarity is computed using GloVE embeddings [30] of the base and new class names.

*Fine-Tuning the Classifiers:* With this initialization, we fine-tune the classifiers of the new as well as the previous classes using the few labeled examples of the new classes and the stored class-prototypes of the previous classes. Let $q \in \mathbf{P}^{(0:t-1)}$ be a prototype from any old class, then the joint softmax output of the stochastic classifier for $i^{th}$ class and $r^{th}$ rotation (task $s$) is

$$\zeta_{ir}^{(s)}(q; \psi^{(0:t)}) = \frac{exp(\eta \, \langle \, \overline{\hat{\mu}_{ir}^{(s)}}, \overline{q} \, \rangle)}{\sum\limits_{j=0}^{t} \sum\limits_{k=0}^{|C^{(t)}|} \sum\limits_{l=0}^{M} exp(\eta \, \langle \, \overline{\hat{\mu}_{kl}^{(j)}}, \overline{q} \, \rangle)} \tag{4}$$

For fair comparison with the state-of-the-art approaches, we only store a single class-prototype per class corresponding to the original images (i.e. 0° rotation). Thus for the previous classes, only the parameters of the stochastic classifier corresponding to the 0° rotation are updated. To mitigate catastrophic forgetting, we use cross entropy loss based on the class prototypes as

$$\mathcal{L}_{proto}(q, \breve{y}, \psi^{(0:t)}) = -\log(\zeta_{\breve{y}r}^{(s)}(q; \psi^{(0:t)})) \tag{5}$$

where $\tilde{y}$ is the class label of the prototype in task $s$.

For the new classes, very few labeled samples per class is available. Since the few examples cannot cover the entire distribution, generalization to new classes is quite challenging. As discussed before, we propose to use stochastic classifiers which mitigates the problem of overfitting and generalizes well to the new classes even with few examples. To this end, we calculate a loss as in Eq. (2) on the new task data using stochastic classifiers. Finally, the total loss at each incremental task is given by

$$\mathcal{L}_{inc}^{(t)} = \lambda_1 \cdot \mathcal{L}_{proto}(q, \tilde{y}, \psi^{(0:t)}) + \lambda_2 \cdot \mathcal{L}_{S3C}(\mathbf{x}, y; \theta, \psi^{(0:t)}) \qquad (6)$$

where $\{\mathbf{x}, y\} \in \mathcal{D}^{(t)}$ and $t > 0$. $\lambda_1, \lambda_2$ are hyper-parameters to balance the performance between old and new classes. At the end of task $t$, we have the learnt classifiers for all the classes seen so far, namely $\psi^{(0)}, \ldots, \psi^{(t)}$.

## 5   Testing Phase

At inference time, the test image $\mathbf{x}$ can belong to any of the classes seen so far. To utilize the learnt classifiers effectively, we generate transformed versions of $\mathbf{x}$ and aggregate all the corresponding scores. Thus, the aggregate score for the $i^{th}$ class in task $s$ is computed as $z_i^{(s)} = \frac{1}{M} \sum_{r=1}^{M} \eta \langle \mu_{ir}^{(s)}, \overline{f_\theta(\tilde{\mathbf{x}}_r)} \rangle$. Then the aggregated probability used for predicting the class is given by

$$P_{agg}(i, s/\mathbf{x}, \theta, \psi^{(0:t)}) = \frac{\exp\left(z_i^{(s)}\right)}{\sum\limits_{j=0}^{t} \sum\limits_{k=1}^{|C^{(j)}|} \exp\left(z_k^{(j)}\right)} \qquad (7)$$

Thus, the final prediction for the test sample $\mathbf{x}$ is

$$\hat{i}, \hat{s} = \arg\max_{i,s} P_{agg}(i, s/\mathbf{x}) \qquad (8)$$

which implies that the input $\mathbf{x}$ belongs to $\hat{i}^{th}$ class of task $\hat{s}$. This aggregation scheme improves the model performance significantly.

## 6   Experimental Evaluation

Here, we describe the extensive experiments performed to evaluate the effectiveness of the proposed S3C framework. Starting with a brief introduction of the datasets, we will discuss the performance of the proposed framework on three standard benchmark datasets. In addition, we also discuss its effectiveness on two real and challenging scenarios, where (i) the data may be imbalanced at each incremental step and (ii) fewer classes may be available during base training. We also describe the ablation study to understand the usefulness of each module.

**Datasets Used:** To evaluate the effectiveness of the proposed S3C framework, we perform experiments on three benchmark datasets, namely CIFAR100 [18], miniImageNet [19] and CUB200 [37].

**CIFAR100** [18] contains $32 \times 32$ RGB images from 100 classes, where each class contains 500 training and 100 testing images. We follow the same FSCIL dataset splits as in [44], where the base task is trained with 60 classes and the remaining 40 classes is trained in eight incremental tasks in a 5-*way* 5-*shot* setting. Thus, there are a total of 9 training sessions (i.e., base + 8 incremental).

**MiniImageNet** [19] is a subset of the ImageNet dataset and contains 100 classes with images of size $84 \times 84$. Each class has 600 images, 500 for training and 100 for testing. We follow the same task splits as in [44], where 60 classes are used for base task training and the remaining 40 classes are learned incrementally in 8 tasks. Each task contains 5 classes with 5 images per class.

**CUB200** [37] is a fine-grained birds dataset with 200 classes. It contains a total of 6000 images for training and 6000 images for testing. All the images are resized to $256 \times 256$ and then cropped to $224 \times 224$ for training. We used the same data splits proposed in [44], where there are 100 classes in the base task, and each of the 10 incremental tasks are learned in a 10-*way* 5-*shot* manner.

**Implementation Details:** For fair comparison, we use the same backbone architecture as the previous FSCIL methods [44]. We use ResNet20 for CIFAR100 and ResNet18 for miniImageNet and CUB200 as in [44]. Inspired by CEC [44], we used the same GAT layer at the feature extractor output for better feature representations. We trained the base network for 200 epochs with a learning rate of 0.1 and reduced it to 0.01 and 0.001 after 120 and 160 epochs for CIFAR100 and miniImageNet datasets. For CUB200, the initial learning rate was 0.03 and was decreased to 0.003, 0.0003 after 40 and 60 epochs. We freeze the backbone network and fine-tune the stochastic classifiers for 100 epochs with a learning rate of 0.01 for CIFAR100 and miniImageNet and 0.003 for CUB200 at each incremental step. The base network was trained with a batch size of 128, and for the newer tasks, we used all the few-shot samples in a mini-batch for incremental learning. All the experiments are run on a single NVIDIA RTX A5000 GPU using PyTorch. We set $\eta = 16$, $\lambda_1 = 5$ and $\lambda_2 = 1$ for all our experiments.

**Evaluation Protocol:** We evaluate the proposed framework using the following three evaluation metrics as followed in the FSCIL literature: (1) First, at the end of each task, we report the **Top1 accuracy** [8,25,35,44] of all the classes seen so far, which is the most commonly used metric; (2) To be practically useful, the model needs to perform well on all the tasks seen so far (i.e. have a good performance balance between the previous and new tasks). To better capture this performance balance, inspired from [39], recent FSCIL works [4,9] propose to use the **Harmonic Mean** (HM) of the performance of the previous and new classes at the end of each incremental task. If $t$ denotes the task id, $t \in [0, 1, ..., T]$, let $Acc_n^t$ denote the model accuracy on test data of task $n$ after learning task $t$, where $n \in \{0, 1, 2, ..., t\}$. Then at the end of task $t$, to analyze the contribution of base and novel classes in the final accuracy, harmonic mean is calculated between $Acc_0^t$ and $Acc_{1:t}^t$. Inspired by CEC, we also report **performance dropping rate** $(PD = Acc_0^0 - Acc_{0:T}^T)$ that measures the absolute difference between initial model accuracy after task 0 and model accuracy at the end of all tasks $\mathcal{T}$. Here, we report the performance of S3C framework for the standard FSCIL setting on all the three benchmark datasets. Note that all the compared approaches have used the same backbone architecture, i.e. ResNet20 for CIFAR100 and ResNet18 for miniImageNet and CUB200 datasets. As mentioned earlier, most of the FSCIL approaches like TOPIC [35], Ft-CNN [35], EEIL [7], iCaRL [31], UCIR [16], adopted this classifier as it is and proposed different techniques in the incremental stage. Thus they have the same base task accuracy as can be observed from the results. The current state-of-the-art in FSCIL, CEC [44] showed that using the same backbone along with appropriate modifications for learning the base classifier can significantly enhance not only the base class accuracies, but also the performance on the incrementally added classes. We combine the advantages of both these techniques, i.e. making the base classifier better (using the same backbone), and at the same time, effectively fine-tuning the stochastic-classifiers in S3C. Thus the base accuracy of CEC and the proposed S3C is better than the other approaches.

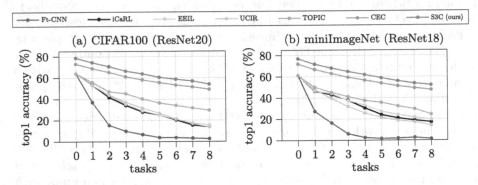

**Fig. 3.** Comparison of S3C with the state-of-art approaches on CIFAR100 and mini-ImageNet datasets using the backbone given in the caption.

**Table 1.** Comparison of S3C with the state-of-the-art CEC in terms of Harmonic Mean on CIFAR100 and miniImageNet datasets. On both datasets S3C outperforms CEC by a considerable margin.

| Dataset | Method | Harmonic Mean (%) ↑ | | | | | | | |
|---------|--------|------|------|------|------|------|------|------|------|
| | | 1 | 2 | 3 | 4 | 5 | 6 | 7 | 8 |
| CIFAR100 | CEC [44] | 41.57 | 38.75 | 32.36 | 31.53 | 32.55 | 32.40 | 32.25 | 31.27 |
| | **S3C (Ours)** | **61.60** | **54.57** | **48.94** | **47.60** | **47.00** | **46.75** | **45.96** | **45.22** |
| miniImageNet | CEC [44] | 31.68 | 30.86 | 29.52 | 29.01 | 26.75 | 24.46 | 26.14 | 26.24 |
| | **S3C (Ours)** | **35.30** | **38.18** | **40.62** | **38.86** | **35.02** | **34.49** | **36.06** | **36.20** |

CEC                                          S3C

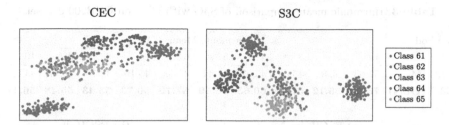

**Fig. 4.** Figure shows t-SNE plot (of test samples) from 5 new classes after task 1 for CIFAR100 dataset.

## 6.1   Results on Standard FS-CIL Propocol

Here, we report the results on the three benchmark datasets. Figure 3 compares the proposed SC3 framework with the state-of-the-art approaches in terms of top1 accuracy on CIFAR100. We observe that the modifications while learning the base classifier improves the performance for both CEC and S3C significantly. At the end of all tasks, S3C achieves a top1 accuracy of 53.96% compared to 49.14% obtained by the state-of-art CEC (relative improvement is 4.82%). The performance of all the compared approaches are directly taken from [44]. Table 1 shows the HM of S3C at the end of each incremental task. We observe that S3C obtains a relative improvement of 13.95% compared to CEC in terms of HM. This shows the effectiveness of S3C in achieving a better balance between the base and new class performance. Figure 4 shows the t-SNE plot for new classes after task 1, where we observe that the new classes in S3C are relatively well clustered compared to CEC. In terms of PD, S3C is close to CEC (higher by 0.7%), but it outperforms CEC in terms of the other two metrics, namely top1 accuracy and HM.

From Fig. 3 (right), we observe that S3C achieves 52.14% top1 accuracy on miniImageNet, with a relative improvement of 4.51% over the second best of 47.63% obtained by CEC. In terms of HM (Table 1) S3C achieves 9.96% relative improvement over CEC. Performance dropping rate (PD) of CEC is slightly lower (0.35%) than S3C.

**Table 2.** Comparison of S3C with other approaches on CUB200 dataset. All the compared results are directly taken from [44].

| Method | Accuracy in each session (%) ↑ | | | | | | | | | | | PD ↓ | Our relative improvement |
|---|---|---|---|---|---|---|---|---|---|---|---|---|---|
| | 0 | 1 | 2 | 3 | 4 | 5 | 6 | 7 | 8 | 9 | 10 | | |
| Ft-CNN [35] | 68.68 | 43.7 | 25.05 | 17.72 | 18.08 | 16.95 | 15.1 | 10.6 | 8.93 | 8.93 | 8.47 | 60.21 | +39.83 |
| iCaRL [31] | 68.68 | 52.65 | 48.61 | 44.16 | 36.62 | 29.52 | 27.83 | 26.26 | 24.01 | 23.89 | 21.16 | 47.52 | +26.69 |
| EEIL [7] | 68.68 | 53.63 | 47.91 | 44.2 | 36.3 | 27.46 | 25.93 | 24.7 | 23.95 | 24.13 | 22.11 | 46.57 | +25.74 |
| UCIR [16] | 68.68 | 57.12 | 44.21 | 28.78 | 26.71 | 25.66 | 24.62 | 21.52 | 20.12 | 20.06 | 19.87 | 48.81 | +27.08 |
| TOPIC [35] | 68.68 | 62.79 | 54.81 | 49.99 | 45.25 | 41.4 | 38.35 | 35.36 | 32.22 | 28.31 | 26.28 | 42.40 | +21.97 |
| CEC [44] | 75.85 | 71.94 | 68.50 | 63.50 | 62.43 | 58.27 | 57.73 | 55.81 | 54.83 | 53.52 | 52.28 | 23.57 | +2.74 |
| **S3C (Ours)** | **80.62** | **77.55** | **73.19** | **68.54** | **68.05** | **64.33** | **63.58** | **62.07** | **60.61** | **59.79** | **58.95** | **20.83** | |

**Table 3.** Harmonic mean comparison of S3C with CEC on CUB200 dataset.

| Method | Harmonic Mean (%) ↑ | | | | | | | | | |
|--------|-------|-------|-------|-------|-------|-------|-------|-------|-------|-------|
| | 1 | 2 | 3 | 4 | 5 | 6 | 7 | 8 | 9 | 10 |
| CEC [44] | 57.63 | 52.83 | 45.08 | 45.97 | 44.44 | 45.63 | 45.10 | 43.76 | 45.77 | 44.69 |
| S3C (Ours) | **76.29** | **65.12** | **57.30** | **60.63** | **56.59** | **57.79** | **56.73** | **55.43** | **55.48** | **56.41** |

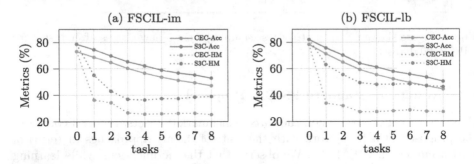

**Fig. 5.** Comparison of S3C and CEC in terms of top1 accuracy and harmonic mean for two challenging scenarios, namely (a) FSCIL-im and (b) FSCIL-lb.

We observe from Table 2 and Table 3 that S3C outperforms CEC by 6.67% and 11.72% respectively in terms of top1 accuracy and HM for CUB200 dataset. For this dataset, the proposed S3C has the least performance dropping (PD) rate compared to all the other approaches.

## 6.2   Analysis and Ablation

Here, we perform additional experiments and ablation studies on the CIFAR100 dataset to evaluate the effectiveness of the proposed S3C framework.

**Experiments on More Realistic and Challenging Scenarios:** First, we show the effectiveness of S3C for two realistic scenarios, (i) where there is class imbalance at each incremental task; (ii) where the number of base classes is less.

*1. FSCIL-im (Imbalance in New Classes):* The standard FSCIL setting assumes that equal number of images per new class are available at each incremental task. For example, 5 images for each of the 5 new classes are available at each incremental task in a 5-way 5-shot setting, In real-world, number of samples per class can vary, since for some classes, it is easier to collect data compared to others. Obviously, one can collect more samples from the minority classes, or select a sub-set from the majority classes. But it is more practical if the algorithm can satisfactorily work without this constraint.

To create the data imbalance, at each incremental step, we consider the number of training samples for the 5 new classes as $\{5, 4, 3, 2, 1\}$. Few samples along with the imbalance makes this setting very challenging. Figure 5 (left) shows the top 1 accuracy and HM of S3C and CEC for this scenario without any modification of the algorithms. We observe that S3C performs very well for both the metrics, thus showing its effectiveness in handling imbalanced new class data.

**Table 4.** Ablation Study: We observe that both self-supervision and stochastic classifiers help to improve the performance significantly.

| Self-supervision | Classifier | After task 0 base task accuracy | After task $T$ top1 accuracy | After task $T$ harmonic mean |
|---|---|---|---|---|
| ✗ | Linear | 74.70 | 48.98 | 26.76 |
| ✓ | Linear | 76.14 | 53.55 | 41.80 |
| ✓ | Stochastic | 78.03 | 53.96 | 45.22 |

*2. FSCIL-lb (Fewer Base Classes):* The standard FSCIL setting assumes that the number of base classes is quite high, with many annotated samples per class. Here, we analyze the performance of S3C when the number of base classes is lower. A similar setting has been explored in [31] for CIL. The advantage of having lesser number of base classes is that the base learner becomes ready for incremental learning quickly (with fewer classes requiring many annotated samples) and the remaining classes can be learnt incrementally with fewer number of labeled samples per class. For the CIFAR100 experiments conducted so far, there were 60 base and 40 new classes. For this experiment, we use only 40 base classes, and keep the incremental tasks unchanged. From Fig. 5 (right), we observe that S3C obtains a relative improvement of 5.29% in top1 accuracy (18.83% in HM) over CEC. This shows that S3C can start learning incrementally at an early stage of data collection, which makes it more suited for real-world scenarios.

**Ablation Studies:** Table 4 shows the effect of self-supervision and type of classifier on CIFAR100 base task accuracy. The top 1 accuracy and HM after all the incremental stages are also reported. We observe that both the modules help in improving the performance of the base and incremental classes. Though the top 1 accuracy of both linear and stochastic classifiers are close after the incremental stages, there is significant improvement in HM with the stochastic classifier. This implies that both the modules help in achieving very good performance on the new classes, in addition to retaining the performance on the base, thus achieving a great performance balance between the two.

## 7    Conclusions

In this paper, we proposed a novel S3C framework, which integrates self-supervision with stochastic classifiers seamlessly for the FSCIL task. We show that this framework not only reduces overfitting on the few labeled samples of the new classes, but also mitigates catastrophic forgetting of the previously learnt classes. Extensive experiments on three benchmark datasets, namely CIFAR100, CUB200 and miniImageNet and additional analysis show that the proposed S3C significantly outperforms the state-of-art approaches.

**Acknowledgements.** This work is partly supported through a research grant from SERB, Department of Science and Technology, Govt. of India and Google Research, India.

# References

1. Akyürek, A.F., Akyürek, E., Wijaya, D., Andreas, J.: Subspace regularizers for few-shot class incremental learning. ICLR (2022)
2. Belouadah, E., Popescu, A.: IL2M: class incremental learning with dual memory. In: ICCV, pp. 583–592 (2019)
3. Belouadah, E., Popescu, A.: ScaIL: classifier weights scaling for class incremental learning. In: WACV, pp. 1266–1275 (2020)
4. Bhat, S.D., Banerjee, B., Chaudhuri, S.: SemGIF: a semantics guided incremental few-shot learning framework with generative replay. In: BMVC (2021)
5. Blundell, C., Cornebise, J., Kavukcuoglu, K., Wierstra, D.: Weight uncertainty in neural network. In: ICML, pp. 1613–1622 (2015)
6. Caron, M., Bojanowski, P., Joulin, A., Douze, M.: Deep clustering for unsupervised learning of visual features. In: Ferrari, V., Hebert, M., Sminchisescu, C., Weiss, Y. (eds.) Computer Vision – ECCV 2018. LNCS, vol. 11218, pp. 139–156. Springer, Cham (2018). https://doi.org/10.1007/978-3-030-01264-9_9
7. Castro, F.M., Marín-Jiménez, M.J., Guil, N., Schmid, C., Alahari, K.: End-to-end incremental learning. In: Ferrari, V., Hebert, M., Sminchisescu, C., Weiss, Y. (eds.) ECCV 2018. LNCS, vol. 11216, pp. 241–257. Springer, Cham (2018). https://doi.org/10.1007/978-3-030-01258-8_15
8. Chen, K., Lee, C.G.: Incremental few-shot learning via vector quantization in deep embedded space. In: ICLR (2020)
9. Cheraghian, A., Rahman, S., Fang, P., Roy, S.K., Petersson, L., Harandi, M.: Semantic-aware knowledge distillation for few-shot class-incremental learning. In: CVPR, pp. 2534–2543 (2021)
10. Cheraghian, A., et al.: Synthesized feature based few-shot class-incremental learning on a mixture of subspaces. In: ICCV, pp. 8661–8670 (2021)
11. Dong, S., Hong, X., Tao, X., Chang, X., Wei, X., Gong, Y.: Few-shot class-incremental learning via relation knowledge distillation. In: AAAI, pp. 1255–1263 (2021)
12. Douillard, A., Cord, M., Ollion, C., Robert, T., Valle, E.: PODNet: pooled outputs distillation for small-tasks incremental learning. In: Vedaldi, A., Bischof, H., Brox, T., Frahm, J.-M. (eds.) ECCV 2020. LNCS, vol. 12365, pp. 86–102. Springer, Cham (2020). https://doi.org/10.1007/978-3-030-58565-5_6
13. Gidaris, S., Bursuc, A., Komodakis, N., Pérez, P., Cord, M.: Boosting few-shot visual learning with self-supervision. In: ICCV, pp. 8059–8068 (2019)
14. Hendrycks, D., Mazeika, M., Kadavath, S., Song, D.: Using self-supervised learning can improve model robustness and uncertainty. In: NeurIPS 32 (2019)
15. Hinton, G., Vinyals, O., Dean, J.: Distilling the knowledge in a neural network. In: NeurIPS Workshop (2014)

16. Hou, S., Pan, X., Loy, C.C., Wang, Z., Lin, D.: Learning a unified classifier incrementally via rebalancing. In: CVPR, pp. 831–839 (2019)
17. Komodakis, N., Gidaris, S.: Unsupervised representation learning by predicting image rotations. In: ICLR (2018)
18. Krizhevsky, A., Hinton, G.: Learning multiple layers of features from tiny images. Master's thesis, Department of Computer Science, University of Toronto (2009)
19. Krizhevsky, A., Sutskever, I., Hinton, G.E.: ImageNet classification with deep convolutional neural networks. In: NeurIPS 25, pp. 1097–1105 (2012)
20. Larsson, G., Maire, M., Shakhnarovich, G.: Learning Representations for automatic colorization. In: Leibe, B., Matas, J., Sebe, N., Welling, M. (eds.) ECCV 2016. LNCS, vol. 9908, pp. 577–593. Springer, Cham (2016). https://doi.org/10.1007/978-3-319-46493-0_35
21. Lee, E., Huang, C.H., Lee, C.Y.: Few-shot and continual learning with attentive independent mechanisms. In: ICCV, pp. 9455–9464 (2021)
22. Lee, H., Hwang, S.J., Shin, J.: Self-supervised label augmentation via input transformations. In: ICML, pp. 5714–5724. PMLR (2020)
23. Li, Z., Hoiem, D.: Learning without forgetting. TPAMI 40(12), 2935–2947 (2017)
24. Lu, Z., Yang, Y., Zhu, X., Liu, C., Song, Y.Z., Xiang, T.: Stochastic classifiers for unsupervised domain adaptation. In: CVPR, pp. 9111–9120 (2020)
25. Mazumder, P., Singh, P., Rai, P.: Few-shot lifelong learning. In: AAAI (2021)
26. Neal, R.M.: Bayesian Learning for Neural Networks, vol. 118. Springer, New York (2012). https://doi.org/10.1007/978-1-4612-0745-0
27. Noh, H., Hong, S., Han, B.: Learning deconvolution network for semantic segmentation. In: ICCV, pp. 1520–1528 (2015)
28. Noroozi, M., Favaro, P.: Unsupervised learning of visual representations by solving jigsaw puzzles. In: Leibe, B., Matas, J., Sebe, N., Welling, M. (eds.) ECCV 2016. LNCS, vol. 9910, pp. 69–84. Springer, Cham (2016). https://doi.org/10.1007/978-3-319-46466-4_5
29. Ouyang, W., et al.: DeepID-Net: object detection with deformable part based convolutional neural networks. TPAMI 39(7), 1320–1334 (2016)
30. Pennington, J., Socher, R., Manning, C.D.: GloVe: global vectors for word representation. In: EMNLP, pp. 1532–1543 (2014)
31. Rebuffi, S.A., Kolesnikov, A., Sperl, G., Lampert, C.H.: iCaRL: incremental classifier and representation learning. In: CVPR, pp. 2001–2010 (2017)
32. Shi, G., Chen, J., Zhang, W., Zhan, L.M., Wu, X.M.: Overcoming catastrophic forgetting in incremental few-shot learning by finding flat minima. In: NeurIPS 34, pp. 6747–6761 (2021)
33. Subedar, M., Krishnan, R., Meyer, P.L., Tickoo, O., Huang, J.: Uncertainty-aware audiovisual activity recognition using deep Bayesian variational inference. In: ICCV, pp. 6301–6310 (2019)
34. Tan, Z., Ding, K., Guo, R., Liu, H.: Graph few-shot class-incremental learning. In: WSDM (2022)
35. Tao, X., Hong, X., Chang, X., Dong, S., Wei, X., Gong, Y.: Few-shot class-incremental learning. In: CVPR, pp. 12183–12192 (2020)
36. Veličković, P., Cucurull, G., Casanova, A., Romero, A., Liò, P., Bengio, Y.: Graph attention networks. In: ICLR (2017)
37. Wah, C., Branson, S., Welinder, P., Perona, P., Belongie, S.: The Caltech-UCSD birds-200-2011 dataset (2011). http://www.vision.caltech.edu/visipedia/CUB-200.html
38. Wu, Y., et al.: Large scale incremental learning. In: CVPR, pp. 374–382 (2019)

39. Xian, Y., Schiele, B., Akata, Z.: Zero-shot learning-the good, the bad and the ugly. In: CVPR, pp. 4582–4591 (2017)
40. Yang, Y., Xu, Z.: Rethinking the value of labels for improving class-imbalanced learning. In: NeurIPS 33, pp. 19290–19301 (2020)
41. Yu, L., et al.: Semantic drift compensation for class-incremental learning. In: CVPR, pp. 6982–6991 (2020)
42. Yu, T., Li, D., Yang, Y., Hospedales, T.M., Xiang, T.: Robust person re-identification by modelling feature uncertainty. In: ICCV, pp. 552–561 (2019)
43. Zhai, X., Oliver, A., Kolesnikov, A., Beyer, L.: S4L: self-supervised semi-supervised learning. In: ICCV, pp. 1476–1485 (2019)
44. Zhang, C., Song, N., Lin, G., Zheng, Y., Pan, P., Xu, Y.: Few-shot incremental learning with continually evolved classifiers. In: CVPR, pp. 12455–12464 (2021)
45. Zhao, B., Xiao, X., Gan, G., Zhang, B., Xia, S.T.: Maintaining discrimination and fairness in class incremental learning. In: CVPR, pp. 13208–13217 (2020)
46. Zhu, F., Cheng, Z., Zhang, X.y., Liu, C.l.: Class-incremental learning via dual augmentation. In: NeurIPS 34 (2021)
47. Zhu, F., Zhang, X.Y., Wang, C., Yin, F., Liu, C.L.: Prototype augmentation and self-supervision for incremental learning. In: CVPR, pp. 5871–5880 (2021)
48. Zhu, K., Cao, Y., Zhai, W., Cheng, J., Zha, Z.J.: Self-promoted prototype refinement for few-shot class-incremental learning. In: CVPR, pp. 6801–6810 (2021)

# Improving Fine-Grained Visual Recognition in Low Data Regimes via Self-boosting Attention Mechanism

Yangyang Shu[1], Baosheng Yu[2], Haiming Xu[1], and Lingqiao Liu[1]([envelope])

[1] School of Computer Science, The University of Adelaide, Adelaide, Australia
{yangyang.shu,hai-ming.xu,lingqiao.liu}@adelaide.edu.au
[2] School of Computer Science, The University of Sydney, Camperdown, Australia
baosheng.yu@sydney.edu.au

**Abstract.** The challenge of fine-grained visual recognition often lies in discovering the key discriminative regions. While such regions can be automatically identified from a large-scale labeled dataset, a similar method might become less effective when only a few annotations are available. In low data regimes, a network often struggles to choose the correct regions for recognition and tends to overfit spurious correlated patterns from the training data. To tackle this issue, this paper proposes the self-boosting attention mechanism, a novel method for regularizing the network to focus on the key regions shared across samples and classes. Specifically, the proposed method first generates an attention map for each training image, highlighting the discriminative part for identifying the ground-truth object category. Then the generated attention maps are used as pseudo-annotations. The network is enforced to fit them as an auxiliary task. We call this approach the self-boosting attention mechanism (SAM). We also develop a variant by using SAM to create multiple attention maps to pool convolutional maps in a style of bilinear pooling, dubbed SAM-Bilinear. Through extensive experimental studies, we show that both methods can significantly improve fine-grained visual recognition performance on low data regimes and can be incorporated into existing network architectures. The source code is publicly available at: https://github.com/GANPerf/SAM.

**Keywords:** Self-boosting attention mechanism · Fine-grained visual recognition · Low data regimes

## 1 Introduction

Fine-Grained Visual Recognition (FGVR) aims to distinguish subcategories of objects under basic-level category, such as bird species [1,24], vehicle models [10, 26], aircraft models [14]. The key challenge of FGVR is to discover the key object parts that can be used to identify object categories. In the existing works, such

This work is supported by the Centre for Augmented Reasoning.

a discovery is either explicitly achieved through part-mining [6,23] or implicitly learned in end-to-end training [15,32]. The latter strategy is the current state-of-the-art, which usually relies on special designs of the network, e.g., bilinear networks [4,9,12,29], to impose certain inductive bias.

Existing FGVR research is often based on a dataset with sufficient annotations, generally with more than 5,000 images and hundreds of categories. However, many practical FGVR problems do not have such a large dataset since annotating fine-grained data is a time-consuming, costly, and error-prone task. For example, labeling different bird species requires an expert in zoology. It remains unclear if the existing end-to-end learning methods can generalize well in the low data regime.

Unfortunately, from our empirical study (shown in Sect. 5.3), we found that the existing solutions for FGVR may become less effective. It seems that when the number of training samples becomes smaller, the network tends to overfit the spurious patterns that happen to correlate with object categories. For example, when distinguishing different types of birds, the network may pay more attention to the surrounding environment rather than the bird body.

To overcome this issue, in this paper, we propose a novel solution called the self-boosting attention mechanism (SAM) to regularize the network to make the decision based on regions that are shared across instances and categories. Specifically, we first use existing visual explanation approaches such as CAM [30] and GradCAM [18] to obtain attention maps to highlight the key regions supporting the prediction of the ground-truth class. Then we use the generated attention maps as prediction targets and fit them with a class-agnostic projection from the convolutional feature map. In this way, we could encourage the network to use the features from the commonly attended regions to make a prediction. To further strengthen the regularization, we further developed a variant by using the above auxiliary task to regularize a set of projections, with each projection working as a part detector. Those projections allow us to leverage a bilinear pooling operation to obtain a new representation of the image. Through extensive experiments, we show that the proposed two strategies achieve superior performance than the competitive approaches for FGVR in a low data regime. Also, we demonstrate that the proposed method can be easily incorporated into the existing approach and achieve further performance boost.

## 2    Related Work

### 2.1    Fine-Grained Visual Recognition

Locating distinctive regions plays an important and fundamental role in fine-grained visual recognition. In early researches, manually defined object and part annotations are extensively studied for fine-grained visual recognition. For example, Zhang et al. [28] use the trained R-CNN model to learn whole-object and part detectors with the help of part-level bounding boxes. Branson et al. [2] propose a method which is based on part detection. They use part and object bounding boxes to estimate a similarity-based warping function for improving the performance in fine-grained recognition tasks. However, manually defining object and part annotations requires additional human cost, largely limited in practical application. In the visual attention models community, Sermanet *et al.* [19] first propose to use attention models in FGVR. They use an attention-based RNN structure to direct high-resolution attention to the discriminative regions. However, the computational cost in their method is higher because they forward GoogLeNet three times. Xiao *et al.* [25] propose to use three types of attention in a deep neural network for the fine-grained classification task. The three types of attention are combined to train domain-specific deep nets: bottom-up attention, object-level top-down attention, and part-level top-down attention. Hu *et al.* [7] use weakly supervised learning to generate attention maps only by image-level annotation. The generated attention maps in their proposed WS-DAN network ensure the model looks at the object better and closer. The main drawback is that attention models will be vulnerable and prone to over-fitting when the image-level annotation is quite a few.

Bilinear-based methods are very popular in fine-grained visual recognition. Lin *et al.* [12] first propose bilinear CNN models by two feature extractors to model local pairwise feature interactions for fine-grained visual recognition. Because original bilinear CNN models are high-dimensional and computationally expensive to train due to calculating pairwise interaction between channels, various studies of dimension reduction techniques have been proposed. Gao *et al.* [4] propose two compact bilinear pooling methods using two low-dimensional approximations of the polynomial kernel, Random Maclaurin [8] and Tensor Sketch [17] to generate the compact bilinear representations and reduce feature dimensions. Kong *et al.* [9] present a compact low-rank classification model and use the low-rank approximation to the covariance matrix to address the computational demands of high feature dimensionality. Zheng *et al.* [29] propose a deep bilinear transformation (DBT) block to uniformly divide input channels into several semantic groups. The computational cost can be relieved via calculating pairwise interactions within each group. For our method, the feature dimensions can be reduced via controlling the number of the predicted attention maps when the element-wise multiplication.

## 2.2 Low-Supervised FGVR

To reduce the dependence on training data, some studies distinguish different categories with very little supervision, e.g., few-shot fine-grained visual recognition and semi-supervised learning for fine-grained visual recognition. Zhu *et al.* [31] propose a multi-attention meta-learning (MattML) method to capture discriminative parts of images for few-shot FGVR. The proposed MattML consists of the base learner and task learner, where the base learner is used for general feature learning, and the task learner uses a task embedding network to learn task representations. Wei *et al.* [22] proposed an end-to-end trainable deep network to solve few-shot FGVR. They use a bilinear feature learning module to capture the discriminative information of an exemplar image and use a classifier mapping module to map the intermediate feature into the decision boundary of the novel category. Lai *et al.* [11] propose an efficient method of semi-supervised learning, voted pseudo label (VPL), to improve the performance of classification in FGVR task when only a few samples are available. VPL is applied in unlabeled data to pick up their classes with non-confused labels, verified by the consensus prediction of different classification models. Mugnai *et al.* [16] exploit semi-supervised learning to improve the performance of FGVR. They adopt an adversarial optimization strategy to combine the conditional entropy of unlabeled data with a second-order feature encoder to reduce the prohibitive annotation cost of FGVR. Our method works in a different setting to the above methods. Specifically, unlike semi-supervised FGVR, we do not assume the availability of unlabeled data; unlike few-shot FGVR, we do not require a relatively large amount of labeled samples from different categories as "base class samples".

## 3    Background

In this section, we briefly review Class Activation Maps (CAM) [30] and Gradient-weighted Class Activation Mapping (Grad-CAM) [18], which underpins the proposed Self-boosting Attention Mechanism.

### 3.1    Class Activation Maps

Class Activation Maps (CAM) are proposed to identify the importance of the image regions by projecting back the weights of the output layer onto the convolutional feature maps. CAM is applicable for the neural network architecture that uses Global Average Pooling (GAP) layer and classifier layers as the last two layers.

Let $\phi(I) \in \mathbb{R}^{H \times W \times D}$ represents the activation feature map of the last convolutional layer, where $I$ is the input image and $H$, $W$ and $D$ are the height, width and the number of channels of the feature map, respectively. Thus the logits for class $y$, i.e., the decision value before the softmax, can be calculated as:

$$l(y) = \mathbf{w_y}^\top GAP(\phi(I)) = \mathbf{w_y}^\top \frac{1}{HW} \sum_{i=1}^{H} \sum_{j=1}^{W} [\phi(I)]_{i,j} = \frac{1}{HW} \sum_{i=1}^{H} \sum_{j=1}^{W} \mathbf{w_y}^\top [\phi(I)]_{i,j},$$

(1)

where $\mathbf{w_y}$ is the classifier for the $y$-th class. $GAP$ represents Global Average Pooling and $[\phi(I)]_{i,j} \in \mathbb{R}^D$ denotes the feature vector located at the $(i, j)$-th grid. The class activation map (CAM) for class $y$ is defined as:

$$[\text{CAM}(y)]_{i,j} = \mathbf{w_y}^\top [\phi(I)]_{i,j},$$

(2)

where $\text{CAM}(y)$ denotes CAM for the $y$-th class. $[\text{CAM}(y)]_{i,j}$ indicates the importance value of the $(i, j)$th spatial grid.

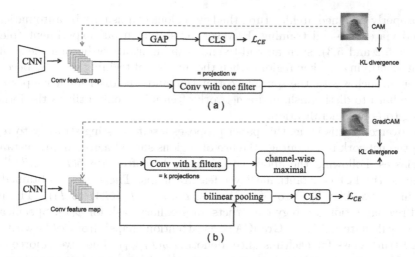

**Fig. 1.** The overview of our SAM network architecture. In the top half-section (a), the last convolutional layer feature maps in CNN network are used to obtain the cross-entropy loss function $\mathcal{L}_{CE}$ via global average pooling (GAP) and classifier (CLS). These feature maps via a linear projection are also enforced to fit the attention maps generated by CAM. The bottom half section (b) represents the method developed in bilinear pooling. The multiple projections are applied in convolutional feature maps to obtain multiple part detectors. Then a bilinear pooling operation is used to obtain a new feature representation. The feature maps after multi-projection and channel-wise maximal operation are also enforced to fit the attention maps generated by GradCAM.

### 3.2 Gradient-Weighted Class Activation Mapping

Gradient-weighted class activation mapping (GradCAM) extends CAM by using the gradient information to calculate the importance of the activation. Unlike CAM, GradCAM could be applied to any convolutional layer or the input image, and is applicable to any neural network architecture. Formally, the GradCAM for the $y$-th class is calculated via:

$$[\text{Grad-CAM}(y)]_{i,j} = ReLU\left([\frac{\partial l(y)}{\partial [\phi(I)]_{i,j}}]^{\top}[\phi(I)]_{i,j}\right), \tag{3}$$

where Grad-CAM($y$) denotes GradCAM for the $y$-th class. $[\text{Grad-CAM}(y)]_{i,j}$ refers to the importance value of the $(i,j)$th spatial grid. $l(y)$ is the logits for class $y$. $\frac{\partial l(y)}{\partial \phi(I)}$ is the gradient of the logits for class $y$ w.r.t. the feature map $\phi(I)$.

## 4    Our Methods

### 4.1 Self-boosting Attention Mechanism

As introduced in the Introduction, the challenge of a fine-grained visual recognition system is to identify the key regions that can be discriminative for distinguishing the subtle difference across categories. With abundant training data and properly designed architecture, the key regions can usually be automatically learned via end-to-end training. However, as shown in our experiment (please see Sect. 5.2 and 5.3), such an end-to-end training strategy becomes less effective in identifying the key regions when the number of training samples becomes smaller. In such a case, the spurious correlation and true discriminative patterns become hard to distinguish, and a network often mistakenly utilizes the former, leading to poor generalization.

To overcome this issue, this paper proposes a self-boosting strategy to regularize the network to encourage the use of regions shared across many instances and classes. Following the above notation, we hereafter use $\phi(I) \in \mathbb{R}^{H \times W \times D}$ to denote the last convolutional layer feature maps. The logits is obtained by applying a classifier $h_p(\cdot)$ to $\phi(I)$, that is, $p(y|I) = h_p(GAP(\phi(I)))$. The proposed regularization strategy constructs an auxiliary task for $\phi(I)$. Specifically, we first calculate CAM or GradCAM as attention maps[1] from $\phi(I)$ w.r.t the ground-truth class for each instance, denoting $g(I_n, y_n)$. Then we enforce $\phi(I)$ to fit $g(I_n, y_n)$ via a linear projection $\mathbf{w} \in \mathbb{R}^D$ without providing the ground-truth class information to the network, which could be implemented as applying a convolutional layer with a single filter. Specifically, we first normalize $g(I_n, y_n)$ and $\mathbf{w}^T \phi(I) \in \mathbb{R}^{H \times W}$ via the softmax function:

$$\bar{\mathbf{G}} = \frac{\exp\left(g(I_n, y_n)/\tau\right)}{\sum_{i=1}^{H} \sum_{j=1}^{W} \exp\left([g(I_n, y_n)]_{i,j}/\tau\right)} \in \mathbb{R}^{H \times W},$$

$$\bar{\mathbf{A}} = \frac{\exp\left(\mathbf{w}^T \phi(I)/\tau\right)}{\sum_{i=1}^{H} \sum_{j=1}^{W} \exp\left([\mathbf{w}^T \phi(I)]_{i,j}/\tau\right)} \in \mathbb{R}^{H \times W}, \quad (4)$$

where $[\cdot]_{i,j}$ denotes the $i, j$-th element of the feature map. $\tau$ is an empirical temperature parameter and we set it to 0.4 for all our experiments. For the simplistic of notations, we also slightly abuse the notation $\mathbf{w}^T \phi(I)$ to denote the feature map obtained by projecting the vector at each location of $\phi(I)$ through $\mathbf{w}$. This normalization will highlight the most important regions and we can also view the normalized feature maps are probability distributions. Then we can use Kullback-Leibler divergence, denoted as $\mathrm{KL}(\cdot, \cdot)$ to measure the compatibility between $g'$ and $p'$. Thus the final loss function could be written as

$$\mathcal{L} = \mathcal{L}_{CE} + \lambda \mathcal{L}_{SAM} = \mathcal{L}_{CE} + \lambda \mathrm{KL}(vec(\bar{\mathbf{A}}), vec(\bar{\mathbf{G}})). \quad (5)$$

At the first glance, the introduction of $\mathcal{L}_{SAM}$ seems to be slightly counter-intuitive. The attention map is generated from the current model, why allowing model to fit it will lead to any benefit? To understand its effect, one should notice that the attention map is calculated based on the ground-truth class. For example, if we use CAM to calculate the attention map, the CAM is calculated via $\mathbf{w}_{y_n}^\top [\phi(I_n)]_{i,j}$, that is, the classifier corresponding to the ground-truth class $y_n$ is chosen to produce the CAM. In contrast, the projection vector $\mathbf{w}$ is class-agnostic. Thus, $\mathbf{w}^\top \phi(I)$ tends to fit the common part that are shared across all

---

[1] Once calculated, the attention map is detached from the back-propagation.

classes and instances. Also in this process, $\phi(I)$ will be learned to produce a good feature presentation for those common key parts. This in effect creates an inductive bias for encouraging the network to use the patterns from the common key parts to make prediction. We call this mechanism as self-boosting attention mechanism since the model will be boosted by fitting its own attention map. The illustration of this scheme can be seen in Fig. 1 (a).

## 4.2   A Bilinear Pooling Extension of SAM

The rationale of the aforementioned SAM is that if $\phi(I)$ is learned to support detecting common parts via the auxiliary task, the network will also prefer to use the feature from the common parts to make a prediction. In such a design, we do not have hard constraints to enforce the network to only use features extracted from those common parts. In this section, we present an extension of SAM by explicitly introducing such a constraint.

The most straightforward approach is to use $A = \mathbf{w}^\top \phi(I)$ as an attention map to weight $\phi(I)$. In other words, instead of directly applying global average pooling to $\phi(I)$ to obtain image representation, we use the following attentive pooling scheme:

$$\mathbf{f} = \sum_{i,j}[A]_{i,j}[\phi(I)]_{i,j} \in \mathbb{R}^D. \tag{6}$$

With such a pooling scheme, the feature from un-attended regions, i.e. $[A]_{i,j} = 0$, will not be preserved into the pooled representation.

We notice that using attentive pooling is akin to the operation in bilinear pooling while the later is equivalent to using multiple attentions. Inspired by this analogy, we further create multiple attention maps $\{A_k | A_k = \mathbf{w}_k^\top \phi(I)\}, k = 1 \cdots K$ via multiple projections $\{\mathbf{w}_k\}$. Intuitively, we expect each attention map highlights one object part, and the union of them should fit the attention map calculated from GradCAM for the current image, as the latter showing all important regions contributing to the decision. In our method, we approximate the union of identified object key parts via taking the maximal value across all $K$ attention maps, that is,

$$[A_u]_{i,j} = \max_k[A_k]_{i,j} \tag{7}$$

Then for each attention map, we can create a pooled feature via Eq. 6. We then concatenate the pooled features from all $K$ feature maps as the final image representation:

$$\mathbf{f} = cat(\mathbf{f}_1, \mathbf{f}_2, \cdots, \mathbf{f}_K) \in \mathbb{R}^{DK}$$
$$\mathbf{f}_k = \sum_{i,j}[A_k]_{i,j}[\phi(I)]_{i,j}, \tag{8}$$

where $cat()$ denotes concatenation of vectors. Note that Eq. 8 is identical to the bilinear pooling [13]. So we call this extension SAM-Bilinear.

**Table 1.** Category and data splits on the CUB-200-2011, Stanford Cars and FGVC-Aircraft datasets

| Datasets | Category | No. of training | No. of testing |
|----------|----------|-----------------|----------------|
| CUB-200-2011 | 200 | 5994 | 5794 |
| Stanford Cars | 196 | 8144 | 8041 |
| FGVC-Aircraft | 100 | 6667 | 3333 |

The above idea can be implemented by following a bilinear neural network structure. The illustration of this scheme is shown in Fig. 1 (b). To summarize, the network introduces a bilinear pooling module with one input being the last convolutional layer feature map $\phi(I)$ and the other input being $K$ projections of $\mathbf{w}_k^\top \phi(I)$. This could be implemented by adding a convolutional layer with $K$ filters after $\phi(I)$. The attention map is calculated by using GradCAM with respect to $\phi(I)$. Then a channel-wise max-pooling (Eq. 7) is applied after the added convolutional layer to obtain a predicted attention map. We then normalized both the predicted attention map and the generated attention map by following the scheme in Eq. 4.

## 5    Experiments

In this section, we conduct experiments to evaluate the performance of the SAM model for FGVR. The experimental conditions, including datasets, implementation Details etc. are firstly given in Sect. 5.1. In Sect. 5.2, ablation analysis are performed to investigate the effectiveness of each component in our model. We give the comparison with state-of-the-art methods in Sect. 5.3. In Sect. 5.4, we conduct experiments to exploit the effect of the number of line projections. Lastly, we use the visualization to explain our model in Sect. 5.5.

### 5.1    Experimental Conditions

**Datasets.** In our experiments, we use three publicly available fine-grained visual datasets: Caltech-UCSD Birds (CUB-200-2011) [21], Stanford Cars [10] and FGVC-Aircraft [14]. The details of category and data splits in these three datasets are shown in Table 1. We reduce the number of labeled annotations, i.e., 10% to 50% for each category and the number of categories in our experiments to simulate the scenarios of low data regimes.

**Implementation Details.** We implement our method using the PyTorch framework. In our experiments, the input images are resized to $256 \times 256$. Then a $224 \times 224$ patch is cropped randomly from the rescaled images on the three datasets for the purpose of data augmentation. ResNet-50 [5] is used as the architecture, and layer four is chosen as feature maps. The pre-trained weights of ResNet-50 on Imagenet are used for initialization. SGD optimizer with a mini-batch size of 24, weight decay of $1 \times 10^{-4}$, and a momentum of 0.9 are used to optimize the proposed network in our experiments. The learning rate of the classifier is 0.001. The parameter $\lambda$ is 0.01.

**Baselines.** We now compare our method to bilinear pooling-based methods. We choose the following four popular methods for comparison. For a fair comparison, we re-implement the method by changing VGG [20] with the ResNet framework.

- **Full Bilinear Pooling (FBP)** [13] uses an image as the input of two CNNs, and their outputs at each location are combined to obtain the bilinear feature representation. In [13], the $relu5\_3$ layer and $relu5$ layer truncated in a VGG-D [20] and VGG-M [3] networks respectively are used for obtaining bilinear. In this paper, we re-implement the method by following the identical structures as SAM-Bilinear for fair comparison. Specifically, we truncate at layer four of ResNet framework and apply $K$ projections into the truncated layer four. The last convolutional feature maps and the outputs of projections are used to obtain the bilinear feature representation.
- **Compact Bilinear Pooling (CBP-TS)** [4] with Tensor Sketch projection is used in the same extract experimental setup as FBP. The projection dimension in [4] is found as $d = 8000$ to reach close-to maximum accuracy. We set d=500 to reach the maximum accuracy in our experiments.
- **Hierarchical Bilinear Pooling (HBP)** [27] integrates multiple cross-layer bilinear features to improve their representation capability. $relu5\_1$, $relu5\_2$ and $relu5\_3$ in VGG-16 in [27] are used because deeper layers contain more part semantic information. This paper applies HBP to ResNet network structures in the deeper layers (layer four). The dimension of joint embedding $D$ in [27] is $8192 * 3$. Given the computational complexity and classification performance, we set the same value as HBP in ResNet network structures.
- **Deep Bilinear Transformation (DBTNet-50)** [29] divides input channels into several semantic groups according to their semantic information and calculates pairwise interaction within semantic groups to obtain bilinear features efficiently. This also results in large saving in computation cost.

**Experimental Design.** To meet the situation of a few annotations, we set the image-level annotations with four ratios, i.e., 10%, 15%, 30%, and 50%. Although only a few annotations are available, the proposed method employs a self-boosting attention mechanism to regularize the network and improve the classification performance of fine-grained tasks.

### 5.2   Main Results

To thoroughly investigate the proposed method, we conduct experiments to provide a detailed ablation analysis with different label proportions and categories on the three databases shown in Table 2. Our Resnet-50 method only uses the

**Table 2.** Evaluation of our method with four label proportions and four label categories on the CUB200-2011 (Bird), Stanford Cars (Car) and FGVC aircraft (Aircraft) databases. SAM ResNet-50 applies the proposed SAM to the Resnet-50. Similarly, SAM-Bilinear combines the proposed SAM with FBP. (Bold numbers indicate the best performance. ↑ is the amount of increase compared to the respective baseline of SAM and SAM-Bilinear, i.e., ResNet-50 for SAM and FBP for SAM-Bilinear.)

| Dataset | Category | Method | Label Proportion | | | |
|---|---|---|---|---|---|---|
| | | | 10% | 15% | 30% | 50% |
| Bird | 30 | ResNet-50 | 55.56% | 61.55% | 69.16% | 77.65% |
| | | SAM ResNet-50 | 58.76%↑3.20% | **65.79%**↑4.24% | 70.16%↑1.00% | 77.75%↑0.10% |
| | | FBP | 56.55% | 61.93% | 69.79% | 77.86% |
| | | SAM bilinear | **60.18%**↑3.63% | 65.65%↑3.72% | **70.79%**↑1.00% | **78.28%**↑0.42% |
| | 50 | ResNet-50 | 45.72% | 58.53% | 68.47% | 73.94% |
| | | SAM ResNet-50 | **51.14%**↑5.42% | 61.80%↑3.27% | 71.43%↑2.76% | 75.19%↑1.25% |
| | | FBP | 42.82% | 58.24% | 68.67% | 74.37% |
| | | SAM bilinear | 50.46%↑7.64% | **61.92%**↑3.68% | **72.07%**↑3.40% | **77.18%**↑2.81% |
| | 100 | ResNet-50 | 42.18% | 56.28% | 67.85% | 75.39% |
| | | SAM ResNet-50 | 46.27%↑4.09% | **60.16%**↑3.88% | 70.82%↑ 2.97% | 78.25%↑2.86% |
| | | FBP | 42.52% | 55.94% | 68.85% | 75.71% |
| | | SAM bilinear | **47.07%**↑4.55% | 59.60%↑3.66% | **70.98%**↑2.13% | **78.53%**↑2.82% |
| | 200 | ResNet-50 | 36.99% | 48.88% | 62.60% | 73.23% |
| | | SAM ResNet-50 | 40.24%↑3.25% | 52.05%↑3.17% | 64.07%↑1.47% | 73.92%↑0.69% |
| | | FBP | 37.88% | 49.12% | 63.27% | 73.70% |
| | | SAM bilinear | **41.83%**↑3.95% | **52.35%**↑3.23% | **65.19%**↑1.92% | **74.54%**↑0.84% |
| Car | 30 | ResNet-50 | 35.09% | 45.72% | 58.65% | 68.53% |
| | | SAM ResNet-50 | 39.95%↑4.86% | 49.98%↑4.26% | 61.90%↑3.25% | **75.86%**↑2.33% |
| | | FBP | 36.24% | 46.14% | 62.98% | 73.92% |
| | | SAM bilinear | **41.76%**↑5.52% | **50.49%**↑4.35% | **66.89%**↑3.91% | 75.37%↑1.43% |
| | 50 | ResNet-50 | 34.38% | 45.32% | 62.64% | 76.67% |
| | | SAM ResNet-50 | 42.39%↑8.01% | **54.23%**↑8.91% | 69.00%↑6.36% | 79.14%↑2.47% |
| | | FBP | 37.76% | 44.53% | 63.43% | 77.27% |
| | | SAM bilinear | **43.23%**↑5.47% | 54.18%↑9.65% | 69.15%↑5.72% | **79.40%**↑2.13% |
| | 100 | ResNet-50 | 36.56% | 47.46% | 69.77% | 79.86% |
| | | SAM ResNet-50 | 47.42%↑10.86% | **59.18%**↑11.72% | 75.75%↑5.98% | 84.96%↑5.10% |
| | | FBP | 38.55% | 50.32% | 71.96% | 81.51% |
| | | SAM bilinear | **47.69%**↑9.14% | 58.74%↑8.42% | **76.86%**↑4.9% | **85.23%**↑3.72% |
| | 196 | ResNet-50 | 37.45% | 53.01% | 75.26% | 83.56% |
| | | SAM ResNet-50 | 39.96%↑2.51% | 55.02%↑2.01% | 76.69%↑1.43% | 84.85%↑1.29% |
| | | FBP | 40.13% | 55.07% | 76.42% | 85.10% |
| | | SAM bilinear | **43.19%**↑3.06% | **57.42%**↑2.35% | **77.63%**↑1.21% | **85.71%**↑0.61% |
| Aircraft | 30 | ResNet-50 | 26.70% | 33.50% | 47.00% | 63.00% |
| | | SAM ResNet-50 | 31.80%↑5.10% | 37.70%↑4.20% | 49.15%↑2.15% | 65.10%↑2.10% |
| | | FBP | 26.90% | 33.60% | 46.70% | 61.90% |
| | | SAM bilinear | **32.50%**↑5.60% | **39.20%**↑5.60% | **51.80%**↑5.10% | **65.80%**↑3.90% |
| | 50 | ResNet-50 | 38.60% | 45.20% | 61.16% | 70.29% |
| | | SAM ResNet-50 | 43.58%↑4.98% | 49.88%↑4.68% | 63.79%↑2.63% | 72.25%↑1.96% |
| | | FBP | 37.94% | 45.44% | 61.48% | 71.79% |
| | | SAM bilinear | **43.70%**↑5.76% | **50.84%**↑5.40% | **65.33%**↑3.85% | **72.95%**↑1.16% |
| | 100 | ResNet-50 | 43.52% | 53.17% | 71.32% | 78.61% |
| | | SAM ResNet-50 | 46.73%↑2.21% | 56.02%↑2.85% | 72.59%↑1.27% | 79.21%↑0.60% |
| | | FBP | 45.16% | 55.06% | 72.12% | 79.93% |
| | | SAM bilinear | **47.97%**↑2.81% | **57.47%**↑2.41% | **73.43%**↑1.31% | **80.86%**↑0.93% |

2048D features representation extracted from the pre-trained ResNet-50 architecture without bilinear pooling and SAM operation. Our FBP is the method that uses bilinear pooling features representation. The method of SAM ResNet-50 uses the proposed self-boosting attention mechanism in ResNet-50, where the model does not use bilinear pooling features and only uses the last convolutional feature as the classifier's input. The method of SAM bilinear uses the proposed self-boosting attention mechanism in FBP.

From Table 2, we make the following observations: First, compared to the method of ResNet-50, SAM ResNet-50 increases the classification accuracy. For example, with the label proportion of 10%, 15%, 30% and 50% and the category of 200, the classification accuracy of SAM ResNet-50 are 40.24%, 52.05%, 64.07% and 73.92% respectively, which are 3.25%, 3.17%, 1.47% and 0.69% higher than ResNet-50 method on the CUB200-2011 datasets. Similarly, significant improvement can also be found on the Stanford Cars and FGVC Aircraft datasets. This demonstrates the superiority of the proposed self-boosting attention mechanism. The model with a few label proportions is prone to overfit spurious correlated patterns. The proposed self-boosting attention mechanism regularizes the network and improves the classification performance in the testing set. A similar conclusion can also be found in comparing FBP and SAM bilinear. Second, compared to the method of ResNet-50, FBP has a better performance in most cases. This is because the method of FBP uses the bilinear pooling feature representation, which is more discriminative features for fine-grained visual recognition. Third, when the label proportion reduces from 50% to 10%, the gap performances between SAM ResNet-50/SAM bilinear and ResNet-50/FBP become larger. Fourth, with the category of label reduced from 200 to 30 on the CUB200-2011 datasets, 196 to 30 on the Stanford Cars dataset, and 100 to 30 on the FGVC Aircraft dataset, respectively, there is generally a better improvement in the performance of the proposed model. The proposed self-boosting attention mechanism effectively regularizes the network and reduces over-fitting under smaller label proportions or category labels, which is more beneficial for fine-grained visual recognition.

## 5.3   Comparison with State-of-the-Art

We compare our method with state-of-the-art bilinear pooling methods on the CUB200-2011, Stanford Cars and FGVC Aircraft datasets shown in the Table 3. We can see that our SAM-based methods achieve state-of-the-art accuracy on the few label proportions on all these fine-grained datasets. Especially, we more significantly improve the classification accuracy on 10% and 15% label proportions compared to the improvement in 30%, 50% and 100% label proportions. We also incorporate the proposed SAM into the existing method of DBTNet-50 [29], which improves the performance when only a few annotations are available compared to the original DBTNet-50 method.

For the computational complexity, the bilinear feature dimensions in the method of FBP [13] in our experiments is $2048 * 16$. The method of CBP-TS [4]

**Table 3.** Comparison with state-of-the-art FGVC methods with three label proportions on the three datasets. We also apply the proposed SAM to the state-of-the-art method DBTNet [29], creating a method dubbed SAM DBTNet-50, which shows compelling results with low feature dimension.

| Dataset | Method | Dimension $D$ | Label proportion | | | | |
|---|---|---|---|---|---|---|---|
| | | | 10% | 15% | 30% | 50% | 100% |
| Bird | Fine-Tuning | 2048 | 36.99% | 48.88% | 62.60% | 73.23% | 81.34% |
| | FBP [13] | 2048 * 16 | 37.88% | 49.12% | 63.27% | 73.70% | 82.52% |
| | CBP-TS [4] | 500 | 37.12% | 47.82% | 62.24% | 72.37% | 81.48% |
| | HBP [27] | $8192 * \frac{n(n-1)}{2}$† | 38.57% | 50.12% | 63.86% | 74.18% | 86.12% |
| | DBTNet-50 [29] | 2048 | 37.67% | 49.52% | 63.16% | 73.28 % | 86.04% |
| | SAM ResNet-50 | 2048 | 40.24% | 52.05% | 64.07% | 73.92% | 81.62% |
| | SAM DBTNet-50 | 2048 | 40.38% | 52.02% | 64.82% | 74.12% | **87.26%** |
| | SAM bilinear | 2048 * 16 | **41.83%** | **52.35%** | **65.19%** | **74.54%** | 81.86% |
| Car | Fine-Tuning | 2048 | 37.45% | 53.01% | 75.26% | 83.56% | 91.02% |
| | FBP [13] | 2048 * 16 | 40.13% | 55.07% | 76.42% | 85.10% | 91.63% |
| | CBP-TS [4] | 500 | 37.77% | 54.87% | 75.51% | 84.80% | 89.52% |
| | HBP [27] | $8192 * \frac{n(n-1)}{2}$† | 40.02% | 55.82% | 76.81% | 85.31% | 92.73% |
| | DBTNet-50 [29] | 2048 | 39.48% | 55.24% | 76.52% | 86.52% | **94.32%** |
| | SAM ResNet-50 | 2048 | 39.96 | 55.02% | 76.69% | 84.85% | 91.06% |
| | SAM DBTNet-50 | 2048 | 42.47% | 56.06% | **78.06%** | **86.86%** | 94.18% |
| | SAM bilinear | 2048 * 16 | **43.19%** | **57.42%** | 77.63% | 85.71% | 91.48% |
| Aircraft | Fine-Tuning | 2048 | 43.52% | 53.17% | 71.32% | 78.61% | 87.13% |
| | FBP [13] | 2048 * 16 | 45.16% | 55.06% | 72.12% | 79.93% | 87.32% |
| | CBP-TS [4] | 500 | 44.63% | 54.79% | 71.32% | 79.60% | 84.58% |
| | HBP [27] | $8192 * \frac{n(n-1)}{2}$† | 45.28% | 56.12% | 72.58% | 81.47% | 89.74% |
| | DBTNet-50 [29] | 2048 | 45.35% | 56.36% | 73.06% | 81.26% | 90.86% |
| | SAM ResNet-50 | 2048 | 46.73% | 56.02% | 72.59% | 79.21% | 86.74% |
| | SAM DBTNet-50 | 2048 | 47.56% | **58.24%** | 73.36% | **81.62%** | **91.18%** |
| | SAM bilinear | 2048 * 16 | **47.97%** | 57.47% | **73.43%** | 80.86% | 87.46% |

†$n$ is the number of convolution layers features.

is proposed to reduce the bilinear feature dimension. Setting the reduced dimension as 500 in our experiments can achieve the best performance. The dimension on the method of HBP [27] is $8192 * \frac{n(n-1)}{2}$ where 8192 is the embedding dimension obtained by the project layer in [27], and $n$ is the number of convolution layers features. We can find that with the increase of $n$, the dimension of the bilinear feature is higher. The dimension on the method of DBTNet-50 [29] is 2048 to keep feature dimensions unchanged. In our method, the proposed SAM can be used in DBTNet-50, demonstrating that SAM DBTNet-50 has a better performance when only a few annotations are available than the original DBTNet-50. In the proposed SAM bilinear, the dimension of bilinear pooling features in our method is $2048 * 16$, ensuring an acceptable dimension and high classification performance. In the proposed SAM ResNet-50, the feature dimension is unchanged and equal to 2048, resulting in large computation cost savings.

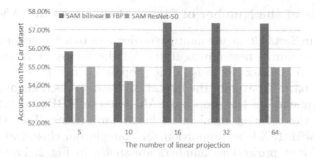

**Fig. 2.** Comparison of SAM bilinear, FBP and SAM ResNet-50 with different number of linear projections on the Stanford Cars dataset.

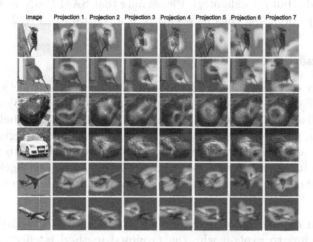

**Fig. 3.** Visualization of each part detector in the multi-projection on the three datasets. The first column is the original input images. The 2–8 columns are the visualization of the seven detected attention regions in seven linear projections.

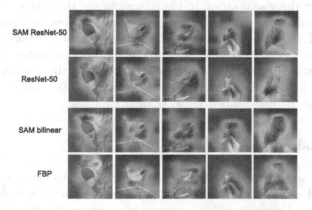

**Fig. 4.** Visualization of the attention regions in the method of SAM ResNet-50 vs ResNet-50 and SAM bilinear vs FBP with 15% label proportion.

## 5.4   Analysis of the Number of Linear Projections in SAM-Bilinear

As elaborated in Sect. 4.2, we use multiple projections to leverage bilinear pooling operations to obtain a new representation of the image. It is also vital and can be used as part detectors to help the proposed network locate the object's discriminative part. To explore the impact of linear projections number $K$, we conduct experiments on the proposed SAM bilinear, FBP and SAM ResNet-50 by setting the different numbers of linear projections. Take the Stanford Cars datasets with 15% label proportion, for example, our classification accuracy w.r.t. five different projections numbers are shown in Fig. 2. From Fig. 2, the accuracy significantly increases then gradually becomes stable in the method of SAM bilinear and FBP. The accuracy is peaked around 16, then slowly decrease with more heads (but only slightly). Please note that SAM ResNet-50 only needs one linear projection, and thus its accuracy is a constant in Fig. 2.

## 5.5   Visualization

**Visualization of Each Linear Projection.** The multi-projection has some practical implications. In our method, the number of linear projections is 16, and we visualize each result of linear projection under 15% label proportion and show them partly in Fig. 3. As we can see, the highlighted regions of multi-projection reveal the significant parts that humans also rely on to improve the discriminative image representation, e.g., the head, body, and back for a bird, the head, tire and light for cars, and wings, head, and tail for aircraft.

**Visualization of Attention Regions for SAM and SAM-Bilinear.** This visualization aims to explain why the proposed method is effective when the number of training data becomes small. We compare the method of ResNet-50 with the proposed SAM ResNet-50, FBP with the proposed SAM bilinear, and visualize their attention regions on the CUB200-2011 dataset with 15% label proportions. From the visualization in Fig. 4, we can see that the existing method may not attend to the correct regions when the number of training samples becomes small. In contrast, the proposed methods, either SAM or SAM-Bilinear can produce a more reasonable attention map. This indicates that the self-boosting attention mechanism can be used to correct the predicted attention regions when the number of training data becomes smaller, thus improving the performance of the fine-grained visual recognition task.

## 6   Conclusions

In this paper, we propose a self-boosting attention mechanism (SAM) for fine-grained visual recognition to regularize the network with low data regimes. The proposed SAM enforces the network to focus on the key regions shared across samples and classes. These key regions are constrained to fit the attention maps generated from CAM/GradCAM. Unlike previous work identifying the key regions that rely on abundant training data, our self-boosting attention mechanism is still effective when the number of training samples becomes smaller. Furthermore, we extend the proposed SAM with the bilinear model to further strengthen the regularization. The proposed SAM effectively regularize the network when image-level annotations are quite a few, and outperforms existing state-of-the-art on the CUB200-2011, Stanford Cars and FGVC Aircraft datasets.

# References

1. Berg, T., Liu, J., Woo Lee, S., Alexander, M.L., Jacobs, D.W., Belhumeur, P.N.: Birdsnap: large-scale fine-grained visual categorization of birds. In: Proceedings of the IEEE Conference on Computer Vision and Pattern Recognition, pp. 2011–2018 (2014)
2. Branson, S., Van Horn, G., Belongie, S., Perona, P.: Bird species categorization using pose normalized deep convolutional nets. arXiv preprint arXiv:1406.2952 (2014)
3. Chatfield, K., Simonyan, K., Vedaldi, A., Zisserman, A.: Return of the devil in the details: Delving deep into convolutional nets. arXiv preprint arXiv:1405.3531 (2014)
4. Gao, Y., Beijbom, O., Zhang, N., Darrell, T.: Compact bilinear pooling. In: Proceedings of the IEEE Conference on Computer Vision and Pattern Recognition, pp. 317–326 (2016)
5. He, K., Zhang, X., Ren, S., Sun, J.: Deep residual learning for image recognition. In: Proceedings of the IEEE Conference on Computer Vision and Pattern Recognition, pp. 770–778 (2016)
6. He, X., Peng, Y.: Weakly supervised learning of part selection model with spatial constraints for fine-grained image classification. In: Thirty-First AAAI Conference on Artificial Intelligence (2017)
7. Hu, T., Qi, H., Huang, Q., Lu, Y.: See better before looking closer: weakly supervised data augmentation network for fine-grained visual classification. arXiv preprint arXiv:1901.09891 (2019)
8. Kar, P., Karnick, H.: Random feature maps for dot product kernels. In: Artificial Intelligence and Statistics, pp. 583–591. PMLR (2012)
9. Kong, S., Fowlkes, C.: Low-rank bilinear pooling for fine-grained classification. In: Proceedings of the IEEE Conference on Computer Vision and Pattern Recognition, pp. 365–374 (2017)
10. Krause, J., Stark, M., Deng, J., Fei-Fei, L.: 3D object representations for fine-grained categorization. In: Proceedings of the IEEE International Conference on Computer Vision Workshops, pp. 554–561 (2013)
11. Lai, D., Tian, W., Chen, L.: Improving classification with semi-supervised and fine-grained learning. Pattern Recogn. **88**, 547–556 (2019)
12. Lin, T.Y., RoyChowdhury, A., Maji, S.: Bilinear CNN models for fine-grained visual recognition. In: Proceedings of the IEEE International Conference on Computer Vision, pp. 1449–1457 (2015)
13. Lin, T.Y., RoyChowdhury, A., Maji, S.: Bilinear convolutional neural networks for fine-grained visual recognition. IEEE Trans. Pattern Analy. Mach. Intell. **40**(6), 1309–1322 (2017)

14. Maji, S., Rahtu, E., Kannala, J., Blaschko, M., Vedaldi, A.: Fine-grained visual classification of aircraft. arXiv preprint arXiv:1306.5151 (2013)
15. Min, S., Yao, H., Xie, H., Zha, Z.J., Zhang, Y.: Multi-objective matrix normalization for fine-grained visual recognition. IEEE Trans. Image Process. **29**, 4996–5009 (2020)
16. Mugnai, D., Pernici, F., Turchini, F., Del Bimbo, A.: Fine-grained adversarial semi-supervised learning. ACM Trans. Multimedia Comput. Commun. Appl. (TOMM) **18**(1s), 1–19 (2022)
17. Pham, N., Pagh, R.: Fast and scalable polynomial kernels via explicit feature maps. In: Proceedings of the 19th ACM SIGKDD International Conference on Knowledge Discovery and Data Mining, pp. 239–247 (2013)
18. Selvaraju, R.R., Cogswell, M., Das, A., Vedantam, R., Parikh, D., Batra, D.: Grad-cam: Visual explanations from deep networks via gradient-based localization. In: Proceedings of the IEEE International Conference on Computer Vision, pp. 618–626 (2017)
19. Sermanet, P., Frome, A., Real, E.: Attention for fine-grained categorization. arXiv preprint arXiv:1412.7054 (2014)
20. Simonyan, K., Zisserman, A.: Very deep convolutional networks for large-scale image recognition. arXiv preprint arXiv:1409.1556 (2014)
21. Wah, C., Branson, S., Welinder, P., Perona, P., Belongie, S.: The Caltech-UCSD birds-200-2011 dataset (2011)
22. Wei, X.S., Wang, P., Liu, L., Shen, C., Wu, J.: Piecewise classifier mappings: learning fine-grained learners for novel categories with few examples. IEEE Trans. Image Process. **28**(12), 6116–6125 (2019)
23. Wei, X.S., Xie, C.W., Wu, J., Shen, C.: Mask-CNN: localizing parts and selecting descriptors for fine-grained bird species categorization. Pattern Recogn. **76**, 704–714 (2018)
24. Welinder, P., et al.: Caltech-UCSD birds 200. Technical report CNS-TR-2010-001, California Institute of Technology (2010)
25. Xiao, T., Xu, Y., Yang, K., Zhang, J., Peng, Y., Zhang, Z.: The application of two-level attention models in deep convolutional neural network for fine-grained image classification. In: Proceedings of the IEEE Conference on Computer Vision and Pattern Recognition, pp. 842–850 (2015)
26. Yang, L., Luo, P., Change Loy, C., Tang, X.: A large-scale car dataset for fine-grained categorization and verification. In: Proceedings of the IEEE Conference on Computer Vision and Pattern Recognition, pp. 3973–3981 (2015)
27. Yu, C., Zhao, X., Zheng, Q., Zhang, P., You, X.: Hierarchical bilinear pooling for fine-grained visual recognition. In: Ferrari, V., Hebert, M., Sminchisescu, C., Weiss, Y. (eds.) ECCV 2018. LNCS, vol. 11220, pp. 595–610. Springer, Cham (2018). https://doi.org/10.1007/978-3-030-01270-0_35
28. Zhang, N., Donahue, J., Girshick, R., Darrell, T.: Part-based R-CNNs for fine-grained category detection. In: Fleet, D., Pajdla, T., Schiele, B., Tuytelaars, T. (eds.) ECCV 2014. LNCS, vol. 8689, pp. 834–849. Springer, Cham (2014). https://doi.org/10.1007/978-3-319-10590-1_54
29. Zheng, H., Fu, J., Zha, Z.J., Luo, J.: Learning deep bilinear transformation for fine-grained image representation. In: Advances in Neural Information Processing Systems 32 (2019)
30. Zhou, B., Khosla, A., Lapedriza, A., Oliva, A., Torralba, A.: Learning deep features for discriminative localization. In: Proceedings of the IEEE Conference on Computer Vision and Pattern Recognition, pp. 2921–2929 (2016)

31. Zhu, Y., Liu, C., Jiang, S.: Multi-attention meta learning for few-shot fine-grained image recognition. In: IJCAI, pp. 1090–1096 (2020)
32. Zhuang, P., Wang, Y., Qiao, Y.: Learning attentive pairwise interaction for fine-grained classification. In: Proceedings of the AAAI Conference on Artificial Intelligence, vol. 34, pp. 13130–13137 (2020)

# VSA: Learning Varied-Size Window Attention in Vision Transformers

Qiming Zhang[1](✉)(iD), Yufei Xu[1](iD), Jing Zhang[1](iD), and Dacheng Tao[1,2](iD)

[1] University of Sydney, Camperdown, Australia
{qzha2506,yuxu7116}@uni.sydney.edu.au, jing.zhang1@sydney.edu.au
[2] JD Explore Academy, Beijing, China
dacheng.tao@gmail.com

**Abstract.** Attention within windows has been widely explored in vision transformers to balance the performance, computation complexity, and memory footprint. However, current models adopt a hand-crafted fixed-size window design, which restricts their capacity of modeling long-term dependencies and adapting to objects of different sizes. To address this drawback, we propose **V**aried-**S**ize Window **A**ttention (VSA) to learn adaptive window configurations from data. Specifically, based on the tokens within each default window, VSA employs a window regression module to predict the size and location of the target window, *i.e.*, the attention area where the key and value tokens are sampled. By adopting VSA independently for each attention head, it can model long-term dependencies, capture rich context from diverse windows, and promote information exchange among overlapped windows. VSA is an easy-to-implement module that can replace the window attention in state-of-the-art representative models with minor modifications and negligible extra computational cost while improving their performance by a large margin, e.g., 1.1% for Swin-T on ImageNet classification. In addition, the performance gain increases when using larger images for training and test. Experimental results on more downstream tasks, including object detection, instance segmentation, and semantic segmentation, further demonstrate the superiority of VSA over the vanilla window attention in dealing with objects of different sizes. The code is available at https://github.com/ViTAE-Transformer/ViTAE-VSA.

## 1 Introduction

Recent Vision transformers have shown great potential in various vision tasks. By stacking multiple transformer blocks with vanilla attention, ViT [14] processes non-overlapping image patches and obtain superior classification performance.

---

Q. Zhang and Y. Xu—Equal contribution.

---

**Supplementary Information** The online version contains supplementary material available at https://doi.org/10.1007/978-3-031-19806-9_27.

S. Avidan et al. (Eds.): ECCV 2022, LNCS 13685, pp. 466–483, 2022.
https://doi.org/10.1007/978-3-031-19806-9_27

However, vanilla attention with quadratic complexity over the input length is hard to adapt to vision tasks with high-resolution images as input due to the expensive computational cost. To alleviate such issues, window-based attention [29] is proposed to partition the images into local windows and conduct attention within each window to balance the performance, computation complexity, as well as memory footprint. This mechanism enables vision transformers to make a great success in many downstream visual tasks [13, 29, 32, 40, 41, 43, 44, 50]. However, it also enforces a spatial constraint on transformers' attention distance, i.e., within the predefined window at each layer, thereby limiting the transformer's ability to deal with objects at different scales.

Recent works have explored heuristic designs of attending to more tokens to alleviate such a spatial constraint. For example, Swin transformer [29] enlarges the window sizes from $7 \times 7$ to $12 \times 12$ when varying the image size from $224 \times 224$ to $384 \times 384$, and sets the window size as $32 \times 32$ to deal with image size $640 \times 640$ in SwinV2 [28]. Some other methods try to find a good trade-off between attending to more tokens and increasing attention distance, e.g., multiple window mechanisms have been explored in Focal attention [43], where coarse granularity tokens are involved in capturing long-distance information. Cross-shaped window attention [13] relaxes the spatial constraint of the window in vertical and horizontal directions and allows the transformer to attend to far-away relevant tokens along with the two directions while keeping the constraint along the diagonal direction. Pale [36] further increases the diagonal-direction attention distance by attending to tokens in the dilated vertical/horizontal directions. These methods have achieved superior performance in image classification tasks by enlarging the attention distance. However, they sacrifice computational efficiency and consume more memory, especially when training large models with high-resolution images. Besides, all these methods determine the window sizes heuristically. Intuitively, using a fixed-size window may be sub-optimal for dealing with objects of different sizes, although stacking more layers could mitigate this issue to some extent, which may also result in more parameters and optimization difficulty. In this paper, we argue that if the window can be relaxed to a varied-size rectangular one, whose size and position are learned directly from data, the transformer can capture rich context from diverse windows and learn more powerful object feature representation.

To this end, we propose a novel **V**aried-**S**ize Window **A**ttention (VSA) mechanism to learn adaptive window configurations from data. Different from the previous window-based transformers where query, key, and value tokens are all sampled from the same window as shown in Fig. 1(a), VSA employs a window regression module to predict the size and location of the target window based on the tokens within each default window. Then, the key and values tokens are sampled from the target window. By adopting VSA independently for each attention head, it enables the attention layers to model long-term dependencies, capture rich context from diverse windows, and promote information exchange among overlapped windows, as illustrated in Fig. 1(b). VSA is an easy-to-implementation module that can replace the window attention in state-of-the-art representative models with minor modifications and negligible extra

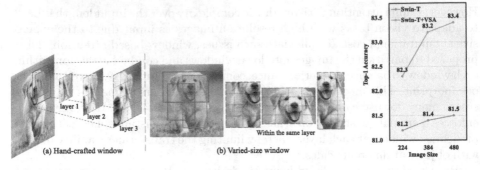

**Fig. 1.** The comparison of the current works (hand-crafted windows) and the proposed VSA (varied-size windows).

**Fig. 2.** The performance with different image sizes.

computational cost while improving their performance by a large margin, e.g., 1.1% for Swin-T on ImageNet classification. In addition, the performance gain increases when using larger images for training and test, as shown in Fig. 2. With the larger images as input, Swin-T with predefined window sizes cannot adapt to large objects well, and the improvement brought by enlarging image sizes is marginal, i.e., a gain of 0.3% from $224 \times 224$ to $480 \times 480$. In contrast, the performance gain of VSA over Swin-T increases significantly from 1.1% to 1.9%, owing to the varied-size window attention. Besides, as VSA can effectively promote information exchange across overlapped windows via token sampling, it does not need the shifted windows mechanism in Swin.

In conclusion, the contribution of this study is threefold. (1) We introduce a novel VSA mechanism that can directly learn adaptive window size and location from data. It breaks the spatial constraint of the fixed-size window in existing works and makes it easier for window-based transformers to adapt to objects at different scales. (2) VSA can serve as an easy-to-implement module to improve various window-based transformers, including but not limited to Swin [28,29] and ViTAEv2 [41,50], with minor modifications and negligible extra computational cost. (3) Extensive experimental results on public benchmarks demonstrate the superiority of VSA over the vanilla window attention on various visual tasks, including image classification, object detection, and semantic segmentation.

## 2    Related Work

### 2.1    Window-Based Vision Transformers

Vision transformers [14] have demonstrated superior performance in many vision tasks by modeling long-term dependencies among local image patches (a.k.a. tokens) [23,24,40]. However, vanilla full attention performs poorly in training efficiency due to the shortage of inductive bias. To improve the efficiency, the following works either implicitly or explicitly introduce inductive bias into vision transformers [11,31,41,42] and obtain superior classification performance. After that, multi-stage design has been explored in [29,33–35,50] to better adapt vision transformers to downstream vision tasks. Among them, Swin [29] is a representative work. By partitioning the tokens into non-overlapping windows and conducting attention within each window, Swin alleviates the huge computational cost caused by attention when dealing with larger input images. Although it balances the performance, computational cost, and memory footprints well, window-based attentions bring a spatial constraint on the attention distance due to the constant maximum size of windows. To alleviate such issues, different techniques have been explored to recover the transformer's ability to model long-term dependency gradually, *e.g.*, using additional tokens for efficient cross-window feature exchange or designing delicate windows to allow the transformer layers to attend to far-away tokens in specific directions [13,16,22,36]. However, they still 1) rely on heuristic-designed windows for attention computation and 2) need to stack the transformers layers sequentially to enable feature exchange across all windows and model long-term dependencies. Thus, they lack the flexibility to adapt well to inputs of various sizes since their maximum attention distances are restricted by the constant and data-agnostic window size and model depth.

Unlike them, the proposed VSA estimates window sizes and locations adaptively based on input features and calculates attention within such windows. Therefore, VSA allows transformer layers to model long-term dependencies, capture rich context, and promote cross-window information exchange from diverse varied-size windows. As VSA learns the window sizes in a data-driven manner, it can benefit window-based vision transformers to adapt to objects at various scales and thus helps boost their performance on image classification, object detection, and semantic segmentation.

## 2.2 Deformable Sampling

Deformable sampling has been widely explored previously to help the convolution networks [10,52] to focus on regions of interest and extract better features. Similar mechanisms have been exploited in deformable-DETR [53] to help the transformer detector to find and utilize the most valuable token features for object detection in a sparse manner. Recently, DPT [6] designs deformable patch merging layers based on PVT [34] to help the transformer to preserve better features after downsampling. VSA, from another perceptive, introduces learnable varied-size window attention into transformers. By flexibly estimating the window sizes and locations for attention calculation, VSA breaks the spatial constraint of fixed-size windows and makes it easier for window-based transformers to better adapt to the objects at various scales.

## 3    Method

In this section, we will take Swin transformer [29] as an example and give a detailed description of applying VSA in Swin. The details of incorporating VSA into ViTAE [50] will be presented in the supplementary.

## 3.1 Preliminary

We will first briefly review the window attention operation in the baseline method Swin transformer. Given the input features $X \in \mathcal{R}^{H \times W \times C}$ as input, Swin transformer employs several window-based attention layers for feature extraction. In each window-based attention layer, the input features are firstly partitioned into several non-overlapping windows, i.e., $\{X_w^i \in \mathcal{R}^{w \times w \times C} | i \in [1, \ldots, \frac{H \times W}{w^2}]\}$, where $w$ is the predefined window size. After that, the partitioned tokens are flatten along the spatial dimension and projected to query, key, and value tokens, i.e., $\{Q_{w,f}^i, K_{w,f}^i, V_{w,f}^i \in \mathcal{R}^{w^2 \times N \times C'} | i \in [1, \ldots, \frac{H \times W}{w^2}]\}$, where $Q, K, V$ represent the query, key, and value tokens, respectively, $N$ denotes the head number and $C'$ is the channel dimension along each head. It is noted that $N \times C'$ equals the channel dimension $C$ of the given feature. Given the flattened query, key, and value tokens from the same default window, the window-based attention layers conduct full attention within the window, i.e.,

$$F_{w,f}^i = MHSA(Q_{w,f}^i, K_{w,f}^i, V_{w,f}^i). \tag{1}$$

The $F_{w,f}^i \in \mathcal{R}^{w^2 \times N \times C'}$ is the features after attention and $MHSA$ represents the vanilla multi-head self-attention operation [14]. The relative position embeddings are utilized during the attention calculation to encode spatial information into the features. The extracted features $F$ are reshaped back to the window shape, i.e., $F_w^i \in \mathcal{R}^{w \times w \times C}$, and added with the input feature $X_w^i$. The same operation is individually repeated for each window and the generated features from all windows are then concatenated to recover the shape of input features. After that, an FFN module is employed to refine the extracted features, which contains two linear layers with hidden dimension $\alpha C$, where $\alpha$ is the expansion ratio. For notation simplification, we dismiss the window index notation $i$ in the following since each window's operations are the same.

With the usage of window-based attention, the computational complexity decreases to linear to the input size, i.e., each window attention's complexity is $\mathcal{O}(w^4 C)$ and the computation complexity of window attention for each image is $\mathcal{O}(w^2 HWC)$. To bridge connections between different windows, shifted operations are used between two adjacent transformer layers in Swin [29]. As a result, the receptive field of the model is gradually enlarged with layers stacking in sequence. However, current window-based attentions restrict the attention area of the tokens within the corresponding hand-crafted window at each transformer layer. It limits the model's ability to capture far-away contextual information and learn better feature representations for objects at different scales.

## 3.2 Varied-Size Window Attention

**Base Window Generation.** Rather than stacking layers with hand-crafted windows to gradually enlarge the receptive field, our VSA allows the query tokens to attend to far-away regions and empower the network with the flexibility to determine the target window size, i.e., attention area, given specific

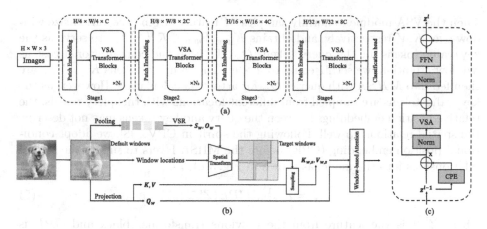

**Fig. 3.** The pipeline of the transformer with our proposed varied-size window attention. (a) The overall structure of stacking VSA transformers blocks; (b) The details of the proposed VSA module; (c) The pipeline of the VSA transformer block.

input data at each layer. VSA only needs to make minor modifications to the basic structure of backbone networks and serves as an easy-to-implement module to replace the vanilla window attention in window-based transformers as in Fig. 3(a). Technically, given the input features $X$, VSA first partitions these tokens into several windows $X_w$ with the predefined window size $w$, following the baseline methods' routine. We refer to these windows as default windows and get the query features from the default windows, $i.e.$,

$$Q_w = Linear(X_w). \tag{2}$$

**Varied-Size Window Regression Module.** To estimate the size and location of the target window for each default window, VSA considers the size and location of the default window as a reference and adopts a varied-size window regression ($VSR$) module to predict the scale and offset upon the references as shown in Fig. 3(b). The $VSR$ module consists of an average pooling layer, a LeakyReLU [39] activation layer, and a $1 \times 1$ convolutional layer with stride 1 in sequence. The kernel size and stride of the pooling layer follow the default window size, $i.e.$,

$$S_w, O_w = Conv \circ LeakyReLU \circ AveragePool(X_w), \tag{3}$$

where $S_w$ and $O_w \in \mathcal{R}^{2 \times N}$ represent the estimated scales and offsets in the horizontal and vertical directions w.r.t. the default window locations, independently for $N$ attention heads. The generated windows are referred to as target windows.

**Varied-Size Window-Based Attention.** We first get the key and value tokens $K, V \in \mathcal{R}^{H \times W \times C}$ from the feature map $X$, $i.e.$,

$$K, V = Reshape \circ Linear(X). \tag{4}$$

Then the VSA module uniformly samples $M$ features from each varied-size window over $K, V$ respectively, and obtains $K_{w,v}, V_{w,v} \in \mathcal{R}^{M \times N \times C'}$ to serve as the key/value tokens for the query tokens $Q_w$. To keep the computational cost as window attention, we set $M$ equal to $w \times w$. The sampled tokens $K_{w,v}, V_{w,v}$ are then fed into $MHSA$ with queries $Q_w$ for attention calculation. However, as the key/value tokens are sampled from different locations with the query tokens, the relative position embeddings between the query and key tokens may not describe the spatial relationship well. Following the spirit in CPVT [8], we adopt conditional position embedding (CPE) before the MHSA layers to supply the spatial relationships into the model as shown in Fig. 3(c), *i.e.*,

$$X = Z^{l-1} + CPE(Z^{l-1}), \tag{5}$$

where $Z^{l-1}$ is the feature from the previous transformer block and $CPE$ is implemented by a depth-wise convolution layer with kernel size equal the window size, *i.e.*, $7 \times 7$ by default, and stride 1.

### 3.3   Computation Complexity Analysis

The extra computations caused by VSA come from the $CPE$ and $VSR$ module, while the other parts, including the window-based multi-head self-attention and FFN network, are exactly the same as the baseline models. Given the input features $X \in \mathcal{R}^{H \times W \times C}$, VSA firstly uses a depth-wise convolutional layer with $7 \times 7$ kernels to generate CPE, which brings extra $\mathcal{O}(49 \cdot HWC)$ computations. In the $VSR$ module, we first employ an average pooling layer with kernel size and stride equal to the window size to aggregate features from the default windows, whose complexity is $\mathcal{O}(HWC)$. The following activation function does not introduce extra computations, and the last convolutional layer with kernel size $1 \times 1$ takes $X_{pool} \in \mathcal{R}^{\frac{H}{w} \times \frac{W}{w} \times C}$ as the input and estimates the scales $S_w$ and offsets $O_w$. Both the scales and offsets belong to $\mathcal{R}^{2 \times N}$. Thus, the computational complexity of the convolutional layer is $\mathcal{O}(\frac{4N}{w^2} HWC)$, where $N$ is the number of the attention heads in the transformer layers, and $w$ is the window size. After obtaining the scales and offsets, we transform the default windows to the varied-size windows and uniformly sample $w \times w$ tokens within each target window. The computational complexity for each window is $w^2 \times 4 \times C$, and the total computational complexity for the sampling operation is $\mathcal{O}(4 \cdot HWC)$. Thus, the total extra computations brought by VSA is $\mathcal{O}\{(54 + \frac{4N}{w^2})HWC\}$, which is far less ($\leq 5\%$) than the total computational cost of the baseline models, regarding the complexity of FFN is $\mathcal{O}(2\alpha HWC^2)$ and $C$ is always larger than 96.

## 4   Experiments

### 4.1   Implementation Details

We evaluate the performance of the proposed VSA based on Swin [29] and ViTAEv2 [50]. The former is a pure transformer model with shifted windows between two adjacent layers, while the latter is an improved transformer model by introducing convolution inductive bias, which models long- and short-term dependencies jointly. In this paper, we adopt the full-window version of ViTAEv2 as the baseline. All the models are trained for 300 epochs from scratch on the standard ImageNet-1k [12] dataset with input resolution $224 \times 224$. We follow the hyper-parameters setting in the baseline methods to train the variants with VSA, e.g., we use AdamW [30] optimizer with cosine learning rate schedulers during training. A 20-epochs linear warm-up is utilized following Swin [29] to stabilize training. The initial learning rate is set to 0.001 for 1024 batch size during training. The data augmentation is the same as [29] and [50], i.e., random cropping, auto-augmentation [25], CutMix [47], MixUp [48], and random erasing are used to augment the input images. Besides, label smoothing with a weight of 0.1 is adopted. It is also noteworthy that there is no shifted window mechanism in the models with VSA, since VSA enables cross-window information exchange among overlapped varied-size windows.

### 4.2 Image Classification on ImageNet

We evaluate the classification performance of different models on the ImageNet [12] validation set. As shown in Table 1, the proposed VSA helps boost the classification accuracy of Swin transformer by 1.1% absolute Top-1 accuracy, i.e. from 81.2% to 82.3%, even without the shifted window mechanisms. It indicates that VSA can flexibly determine the appropriate window sizes and locations given the input features, allow the tokens to effectively attend far-away but relevant tokens outside the default windows to extract rich context, and learn better feature representations. Besides, Swin-T with VSA obtains comparable performance with MSG-T [16], which adopts extra messenger tokens for feature exchange across windows, i.e., 82.3% v.s. 82.4%, demonstrating that our varied-size window mechanism can enable sufficient feature exchange across windows without the need of using extra tokens. For ViTAEv2 [50], ViTAEv2-S with VSA obtains 82.7% (+0.5%) classification accuracy with only 20M parameters, demonstrating that the proposed varied-size window attention is compatible with not only the transformers with vanilla window attentions but also those with convolutions for feature exchange across windows.

When scaling the input images to higher resolutions, i.e., from $224 \times 224$ to $384 \times 384$ and $480 \times 480$, the performance gains from VSA become larger owing to its ability to learn adaptive target window sizes from data. Specifically, the performance gain brought by VSA increases from 1.1% to 1.8% absolute accuracy over Swin-T when scaling the input size from 224 to 384, respectively. For the $480 \times 480$ input resolution, the performance gain of VSA further increases to 1.9%, while the Swin transformers only benefit from the higher resolution marginally (i.e., 0.2%). The reason is that the fixed-size window attention in Swin limits the attention region at each transformer layer, which brings difficulty in handling objects at different scales. In contrast, VSA can learn to vary the window size to adapt to the objects and capture rich contextual information from different attention heads at each layer, which is beneficial for learning powerful object feature representations.

**Table 1.** Image classification results on ImageNet. 'Input Size' denotes the image size used for training and test.

| Model | Params (M) | FLOPs (G) | Input size | ImageNet [12] Top-1 | Top-5 | Real [1] Top-1 |
|---|---|---|---|---|---|---|
| DeiT-S [31] | 22 | 4.6 | 224 | 81.2 | 95.4 | 86.8 |
| PVT-S [34] | 25 | 3.8 | 224 | 79.8 | – | – |
| ViL-S [49] | 25 | 4.9 | 224 | 82.4 | – | – |
| PiT-S [21] | 24 | 4.8 | 224 | 80.9 | – | – |
| TNT-S [18] | 24 | 5.2 | 224 | 81.3 | 95.6 | – |
| MSG-T [16] | 25 | 3.8 | 224 | 82.4 | – | – |
| Twins-PCPVT-S [7] | 24 | 3.8 | 224 | 81.2 | – | – |
| Twins-SVT-S [7] | 24 | 2.9 | 224 | 81.7 | – | – |
| T2T-ViT-14 [46] | 22 | 5.2 | 224 | 81.5 | 95.7 | 86.8 |
| Swin-T [29] | 29 | 4.5 | 224 | 81.2 | – | – |
| **Swin-T+VSA** | **29** | **4.6** | **224** | **82.3** | **96.1** | **87.5** |
| ViTAEv2-S[a] [50] | 20 | 5.4 | 224 | 82.2 | 96.1 | 87.5 |
| **ViTAEv2-S[a] +VSA** | **20** | **5.6** | **224** | **82.7** | **96.3** | **87.8** |
| Swin-T [29] | 29 | 14.2 | 384 | 81.4 | 95.4 | 86.4 |
| **Swin-T+VSA** | **29** | **14.9** | **384** | **83.2** | **96.5** | **88.0** |
| Swin-T [29] | 29 | 23.2 | 480 | 81.5 | 95.7 | 86.3 |
| **Swin-T+VSA** | **29** | **24.0** | **480** | **83.4** | **96.7** | **88.0** |
| PiT-B [21] | 74 | 12.5 | 224 | 82.0 | – | – |
| TNT-B [18] | 66 | 14.1 | 224 | 82.8 | 96.3 | – |
| Focal-B [43] | 90 | 16.0 | 224 | 83.8 | – | – |
| ViL-B [49] | 56 | 13.4 | 224 | 83.7 | – | – |
| MSG-S [16] | 56 | 8.4 | 224 | 83.4 | – | – |
| PVTv2-B5 [33] | 82 | 11.8 | 224 | 83.8 | – | – |
| Swin-S [29] | 50 | 8.7 | 224 | 83.0 | – | – |
| **Swin-S+VSA** | **50** | **8.9** | **224** | **83.8** | **96.8** | **88.54** |
| Swin-B [29] | 88 | 15.4 | 224 | 83.3 | – | 88.0 |
| **Swin-B+VSA** | **88** | **16.0** | **224** | **83.9** | **96.7** | **88.6** |

[a] The full window version.

### 4.3   Object Detection and Instance Segmentation on MS COCO

**Settings.** We evaluate the backbone models for the object detection and instance segmentation tasks on the MS COCO [27] dataset, which contains 118K training, 5K validation, and 20K test images with full annotations. We adopt the models trained on ImageNet with 224 × 224 input resolutions as backbones and use three typical object detection frameworks, *i.e.*, the two-stage frameworks Mask RCNN [19] and Cascade RCNN [2,3], and the one-stage framework RetinaNet [26]. We follow the common practice in mmdetection [5], *i.e.*, multi-scale training with an AdamW optimizer and a batch size of 16. The initial learning rate is 0.0001 and the weight decay is 0.05. We adopt both 1× (12 epochs) and 3× (36 epochs) training schedules for the Mask RCNN framework to evaluate

**Table 2.** Object detection results on MS COCO with Mask RCNN.

| | Params (M) | Mask RCNN 1x | | | | | | Mask RCNN 3x | | | | | |
|---|---|---|---|---|---|---|---|---|---|---|---|---|---|
| | | $AP^{bb}$ | $AP^{bb}_{50}$ | $AP^{bb}_{75}$ | $AP^{mk}$ | $AP^{mk}_{50}$ | $AP^{mk}_{75}$ | $AP^{bb}$ | $AP^{bb}_{50}$ | $AP^{bb}_{75}$ | $AP^{mk}$ | $AP^{mk}_{50}$ | $AP^{mk}_{75}$ |
| ResNet50 [20] | 44 | 38.6 | 59.5 | 42.1 | 35.2 | 56.3 | 37.5 | 40.8 | 61.2 | 44.4 | 37.0 | 58.4 | 39.3 |
| ViL-S [45] | 45 | 44.9 | 67.1 | 49.3 | 41.0 | 64.2 | 44.1 | 47.1 | 68.7 | 51.5 | 42.7 | 65.9 | 46.2 |
| PVT-M [34] | 64 | 42.0 | 64.4 | 45.6 | 39.0 | 61.6 | 42.1 | – | – | – | – | – | – |
| PVT-L [34] | 81 | 42.9 | 65.0 | 46.6 | 39.5 | 61.9 | 42.5 | | | | | | |
| PVTv2-B2 [33] | 45 | 45.3 | 67.1 | 49.6 | 41.2 | 64.2 | 44.4 | – | – | – | – | – | |
| CMT-S [17] | 45 | 44.6 | 66.8 | 48.9 | 40.7 | 63.9 | 43.4 | – | – | – | – | – | – |
| RegionViT-S [4] | 50 | 42.5 | – | – | 39.5 | – | – | 46.3 | – | – | 42.3 | – | – |
| XCiT-S12/16 [15] | 44 | – | – | – | – | – | – | 45.3 | 67.0 | 49.5 | 40.8 | 64.0 | 43.8 |
| DPT-M [6] | 66 | 43.8 | 66.2 | 48.3 | 40.3 | 63.1 | 43.4 | 44.3 | 65.6 | 48.8 | 40.7 | 63.1 | 44.1 |
| ResT-Base [51] | 50 | 41.6 | 64.9 | 45.1 | 38.7 | 61.6 | 41.4 | – | – | – | – | – | – |
| Shuffle-T [22] | 48 | – | – | – | – | – | – | 46.8 | 68.9 | 51.5 | 42.3 | 66.0 | 45.6 |
| Focal-T [43] | 49 | 44.8 | – | – | 41.0 | – | – | 47.2 | 69.4 | 51.9 | 42.7 | 66.5 | 45.9 |
| Swin-T [29] | 48 | 43.7 | 66.6 | 47.7 | 39.8 | 63.3 | 42.7 | 46.0 | 68.1 | 50.3 | 41.6 | 65.1 | 44.9 |
| **Swin-T+VSA** | **48** | **45.6** | **68.4** | **50.1** | **41.4** | **65.2** | **44.4** | **47.5** | **69.4** | **52.3** | **42.8** | **66.3** | **46.0** |
| ViTAEv2-S[a] [50] | 39 | 43.5 | 65.8 | 47.4 | 39.4 | 62.6 | 41.8 | 44.7 | 65.8 | 49.1 | 40.0 | 62.6 | 42.8 |
| **ViTAEv2-S[a]+VSA** | **39** | **45.9** | **68.2** | **50.4** | **41.4** | **65.1** | **44.5** | **48.1** | **69.8** | **52.9** | **42.9** | **66.9** | **46.2** |

[a] The full window version.

the object detection performance w.r.t. different backbones. For RetinaNet and Cascade RCNN, the models are trained with 1× and 3× schedules, respectively. The results on other settings are reported in the supplementary.

**Results.** The results of baseline models and those with VSA on the MS COCO dataset with Mask RCNN, RetinaNet, and Cascade RCNN are reported in Tables 2, 3, and 4, respectively. Compared to the baseline method Swin-T [29] and ViTAEv2 [50], their VSA variants obtain better performance on both object detection and instance segmentation tasks with all detection frameworks, e.g., VSA brings a gain of 1.9 and 2.4 $mAP^{bb}$ for Swin-T and ViTAEv2-S with Mask RCNN 1× training schedule, confirming that VSA learns better object features than the vanilla window attention via the varied-size window attention that can better deal with objects at different scales for object detection. Besides, a longer training schedule (3×) also sees a significant performance gain from VSA over the vanilla window attention. For example, the performance gain of VSA on Swin-T and ViTAEv2 reaches 1.5 $mAP^{bb}$ and 3.4 $mAP^{bb}$, respectively. We attribute this to the better attention regions learned by the VSR module in our VSA under longer training epochs. Similar conclusions can also be drawn when using RetinaNet [26] and Cascade RCNN [2] as detection frameworks, where VSA brings a gain of at least 2.0 and 1.2 $mAP^{bb}$, respectively. It is also noteworthy that the performance gains on ViTAEv2 are more significant than those on Swin-T. This is because there is no shifted window mechanism existing in ViTAEv2, and thus the ability to model long-range dependencies via attention is constrained within each window. In contrast, the varied size window attention in VSA empowers ViTAEv2 models to have such an ability and efficiently exchange rich contextual information across windows.

## 4.4   Semantic Segmentation on Cityscapes

**Settings.** The Cityscapes [9] dataset is adopted to evaluate the performance of different backbones for semantic segmentation. The dataset contains over 5K well-annotated images of street scenes from 50 different cities. UperNet [38] is adopted as the segmentation framework. The training and evaluation of the models follow the common practice, *i.e.*, using the Adam optimizer with polynomial learning rate schedulers. The models are trained for 40k iterations and 80k iterations separately with both $512 \times 1024$ and $769 \times 769$ input resolutions.

**Table 3.** Object detection results on MS COCO [27] with RetinaNet [26].

| | Params | RetinaNet | | |
|---|---|---|---|---|
| | (M) | $AP^{bb}$ | $AP^{bb}_{50}$ | $AP^{bb}_{75}$ |
| ResNet50 [20] | 38 | 36.3 | 55.3 | 38.6 |
| PVTv2-B1 [33] | 24 | 41.2 | 61.9 | 43.9 |
| ResT-Base [51] | 41 | 42.0 | 63.2 | 44.8 |
| DAT-T [37] | 39 | 42.8 | 64.4 | 45.2 |
| Twins-SVT-S [7] | 34 | 42.3 | 63.4 | 45.2 |
| Swin-T [29] | 39 | 41.6 | 62.1 | 44.2 |
| **Swin-T+VSA** | **39** | **43.6** | **64.8** | **46.6** |
| ViTAEv2-S[1] [50] | 30 | 42.1 | 62.7 | 44.8 |
| **ViTAEv2-S[1]+VSA** | **30** | **44.3** | **65.2** | **47.6** |

[1] The full window version.

**Table 4.** Object detection results on MS COCO [27] with Cascade RCNN [2].

| | Params | Cascade RCNN | | |
|---|---|---|---|---|
| | (M) | $AP^{bb}$ | $AP^{bb}_{50}$ | $AP^{bb}_{75}$ |
| ResNet50 [20] | 82 | 44.3 | 62.4 | 48.5 |
| PVTv2-B2 [33] | 83 | 51.1 | 69.8 | 55.3 |
| PVTv2-B2-Li [33] | 80 | 50.9 | 69.5 | 55.2 |
| MSG-T [16] | 83 | 51.4 | 70.1 | 56.0 |
| Swin-T [29] | 86 | 50.2 | 68.8 | 54.7 |
| **Swin-T+VSA** | **86** | **51.4** | **70.4** | **55.9** |
| ViTAEv2-S[1] [50] | 77 | 48.0 | 65.7 | 52.5 |
| **ViTAEv2-S[1]+VSA** | **77** | **51.9** | **70.6** | **56.2** |

[1] The full window version.

**Results.** The results are available in Table 5. With $512 \times 1024$ input size, VSA brings over 1.3 mIoU and 1.4 mAcc gains for both Swin-T [29] and ViTAEv2-S [50], no matter with 40k or 80k training schedules. This observations hold with $769 \times 769$ resolution images as input, where VSA brings over 1.0 mIoU and 1.0 mAcc gains for both models. Such phenomena validates the effectiveness of the proposed VSA in improving the baseline models' performance on semantic segmentation tasks. With more training iterations (80k), the performance gains of VSA over Swin-T increases from 1.9 to 2.2 mIoU with $512 \times 1024$ and from 1.7

**Table 5.** Semantic segmentation results on Cityscapes [9] with UperNet [38]. * denotes results are obtained with multi-scale test.

| | $512 \times 1024$ | | | | | | $769 \times 769$ | | | | | |
|---|---|---|---|---|---|---|---|---|---|---|---|---|
| | 40k | | | 80k | | | 40k | | | 80k | | |
| | mIoU | mAcc | mIoU* | mIoU | mAcc | mIoU* | mIoU | mAcc | mIoU* | mIoU | mAcc | mIoU* |
| ResNet50 [20] | 77.1 | 84.0 | 78.4 | 78.2 | 84.6 | 79.2 | 78.0 | 86.7 | 79.7 | 79.4 | 87.2 | 80.9 |
| Swin-T [29] | 78.9 | 85.3 | 79.9 | 79.3 | 85.7 | 80.2 | 79.3 | 86.7 | 79.8 | 79.6 | 86.6 | 80.1 |
| **Swin-T+VSA** | **80.8** | **87.6** | **81.7** | **81.5** | **87.8** | **82.4** | **81.0** | **88.0** | **81.9** | **81.6** | **88.3** | **82.5** |
| ViTAEv2-S [50] | 80.1 | 86.5 | 80.9 | 80.8 | 87.0 | 81.0 | 79.6 | 86.1 | 80.6 | 80.5 | 86.8 | 81.2 |
| **ViTAEv2-S+VSA** | **81.4** | **87.9** | **82.3** | **82.2** | **88.6** | **83.0** | **80.6** | **87.1** | **81.4** | **81.5** | **88.0** | **82.4** |
| Swin-S [29] | 80.7 | 87.3 | 82.0 | 81.2 | 87.4 | 82.2 | 80.9 | 87.8 | 81.6 | 81.5 | 88.1 | 82.3 |
| **Swin-S+VSA** | **82.1** | **88.5** | **83.2** | **82.8** | **88.9** | **83.6** | **82.0** | **88.7** | **83.0** | **82.8** | **89.5** | **83.6** |

to 2.0 mIoU with $769 \times 769$, owing to the better attention regions learned by the VSR module. Besides, with multi-scale testing, the performance of using VSA further improves, indicating that VSA can implicit capture multi-scale features as the target windows have different scales and locations for each head.

## 4.5  Ablation Study

We adopt Swin-T [29] with VSA for ablation studies. The models are trained for 300 epochs with AdamW optimizer. To find the optimal configuration of VSA, we gradually substitute the window attention in different stages of Swin with VSA. The results are shown in Table 6, where ✓ indicates that VSA replaces the vanilla window attention. We can see that the performance gradually improves with more VSA used and reaches the best when using VSA in all four stages. Meanwhile, it only takes a few extra parameters and FLOPs. Therefore, we choose to use VSA at all stages as the default setting in this paper.

**Table 6.** The ablation study of using VSA in each stage of Swin-T [29].

| VSA at stages | | | | FLOPs | Param | Acc. |
|---|---|---|---|---|---|---|
| Stage 1 | Stage 2 | Stage 3 | Stage 4 | (G) | (M) | (%) |
| | | | | 4.5 | 28.2 | 81.2 |
| | | | ✓ | 4.5 | 28.3 | 81.4 |
| | | ✓ | ✓ | 4.6 | 28.7 | 81.9 |
| | ✓ | ✓ | ✓ | 4.6 | 28.7 | 82.1 |
| ✓ | ✓ | ✓ | ✓ | 4.6 | 28.7 | 82.3 |

**Table 7.** The ablation study of each component in VSA based on Swin-T [29].

| CPE | VSR | Shift | Acc. |
|---|---|---|---|
| | | ✓ | 81.2 |
| | ✓ | | 81.6 |
| ✓ | | ✓ | 81.6 |
| ✓ | ✓ | | 82.3 |
| ✓ | ✓ | ✓ | 82.3 |

We take Swin-T as the baseline and further validate the contribution of each component in VSA. The results are available in Table 7, where ✓ denotes using the specific component. 'Shift' is short for the shifted window mechanism. With only 'Shift' marked, the model becomes the baseline Swin-T. As can be seen, the model with 'VSR' alone outperforms Swin-T by 0.3% absolute accuracy, implying (1) the effectiveness of varied-size windows in cross-window information exchange and (2) the advantage of adapting the window sizes and locations, *i.e.*, attention regions, to the objects at different scales. Besides, using CPE and VSR in VSA further boosts to 82.3%, which outperforms the variant of 'CPE' + 'Shift' by 0.6% accuracy. It indicates that CPE is better compatible with varied size windows by providing local positional information. It is also noteworthy that there is no need to use the shifted-window mechanism in VSA according to the results in the last two rows, confirming that varied-size windows can guarantee the feature exchange across overlapped windows.

## 4.6   Throughputs and GPU Memory Comparison

**Table 8.** Throughput & GPU memory comparison with VSA.

|  | Throughputs on A100 (fps) | Throughputs on V100 (fps) | Memory (G) |
|---|---|---|---|
| Swin-T | 1557 | 679 | 15.8 |
| Swin-T+VSA | 1297 | 595 | 16.1 |
| Swin-S | 961 | 401 | 23.0 |
| Swin-S+VSA | 769 | 352 | 23.5 |

We also evaluate the model's throughputs during inference and GPU memory consumption during training, with batch size 128 and input resolution $224 \times 224$. We run each model 20 times firstly as warmup and count the average throughputs of the subsequent 30 runs as the throughputs of the models. All of the experiments are conducted on the NVIDIA A100 and V100 GPUs. As shown in Table 8, VSA slows down the Swin model by about 12%–17% on different hardware platforms and consumes 2% more GPU memory, with much better performance on both classification and downstream dense prediction tasks. Such slow-down and extra memory consumption is mainly due to the sub-optimal optimization of sampling operations compared with the matrix multiply operations in the PyTorch framework, where the latter is sufficiently optimized with cuBLAS. Integrating the sampling operation with following linear projection operations with CUDA optimization can help alleviate the speed concerns, which we leave as our future work to implement the proposed VSR module better.

### 4.7   Visual Inspection and Analysis

**Visualization of Target Windows.** We visualize the default windows used in Swin-T [29] and the varied-size windows generated by VSA on images from the ImageNet [12] and MS COCO [27] datasets to see where VSA learns to attend for different images. The results are visualized in Fig. 4. As shown in Fig. 4(a), the generated windows from VSA can better cover the target objects in the images while the fixed-size windows adopted in Swin can only capture part of the targets. It can also be inferred from Fig. 4(b) that the windows generated by different heads in VSA have different sizes and locations to focus on different parts of the targets, which helps to capture rich contextual information and learn better object feature representations. Besides, the windows that cover the target objects have more variance in size and location compared with those covering background as shown in (b), *e.g.*, the windows on the zebra and elephant vary (the blue, red, orange, pink, *etc.*.) significantly while others in the background are less varied. In addition, the target windows are overlapped with each other,

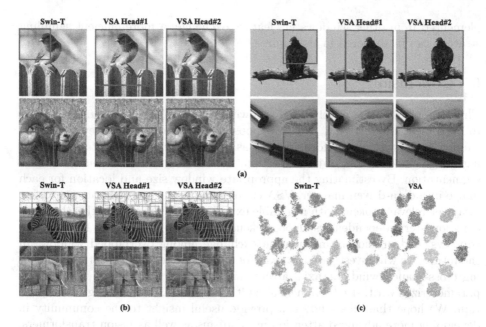

**Fig. 4.** Visualization of the varied-size windows generated by VSA from ImageNet (a) and MS COCO (b). The t-SNE analysis is also provided in (c). (Color figure online)

thus enabling abundant cross-window feature exchange and making it possible to drop the shifted window mechanism in VSA.

**t-SNE Analysis.** We further use t-SNE to analyze the features generated by Swin-T models with and without VSA. We randomly select 20 categories from the ImageNet dataset and use t-SNE to visualize the extracted features. As shown in Fig. 4(c), the features generated by Swin-T with VSA are better clustered, demonstrating that VSA can help the models deal with objects of different sizes and learn more discriminative features.

## 5   Limitation and Discussion

Although VSA has been proven efficient in dealing with images of varied resolutions and has shown its effectiveness on various vision tasks, including classification, detection, instance segmentation, and semantic segmentation, we only evaluate VSA with Swin [29] and ViTAEv2 [50] in this paper. It will be our future work to explore the usage of VSA on other transformers with window-based attentions, *e.g.*, CSwin [13] and Pale [36], which use cross-shaped attentions. Besides, to keep the computational cost as the vanilla window attention, we only sample sparse tokens from each target window, *i.e.*, the number of sampled tokens equals the default window size, which may ignore some details when the window becomes extremely large. Although the missed details may be complemented from other windows via feature exchange, a more efficient sampling strategy can be explored in the future study.

## 6 Conclusion

This paper presents a novel varied-size window attention (VSA), *i.e.*, an easy-to-implement module that can help boost the performance of representative window-based vision transformers such as Swin in various vision tasks, including image classification, object detection, instance segmentation, and semantic segmentation. By estimating the appropriate window size and location for each image in a data-driven manner, VSA enables the transformers to attend to faraway yet relevant tokens with negligible extra computational cost, thereby modeling long-term dependencies among tokens, capturing rich context from diverse windows, and promoting information exchange among overlapped window. In the future, we will investigate the usage of VSA in more attentions types including cross-shaped windows, axial attentions, and others as long as they can be parameterized w.r.t. size (*e.g.*, height, width, or radius), rotation angle, and position. We hope that this study can provide useful insight to the community in developing more advanced attention mechanisms as well as vision transformers.

**Acknowledgement.** Mr. Qiming Zhang, Mr. Yufei Xu, and Dr. Jing Zhang are supported by ARC FL-170100117.

## References

1. Beyer, L., Hénaff, O.J., Kolesnikov, A., Zhai, X., van den Oord, A.: Are we done with ImageNet? arXiv preprint arXiv:2006.07159 (2020)
2. Cai, Z., Vasconcelos, N.: Cascade R-CNN: delving into high quality object detection. In: Proceedings of the IEEE/CVF Conference on Computer Vision and Pattern Recognition (CVPR), pp. 6154–6162 (2018)
3. Cai, Z., Vasconcelos, N.: Cascade R-CNN: high quality object detection and instance segmentation. IEEE Trans. Pattern Anal. Mach. Intell. **43**, 1483–1498 (2019)
4. Chen, C.F., Panda, R., Fan, Q.: RegionViT: regional-to-local attention for vision transformers. In: International Conference on Learning Representations (2022)
5. Chen, K., et al.: MMDetection: open MMLab detection toolbox and benchmark. arXiv preprint arXiv:1906.07155 (2019)
6. Chen, Z., et al.: DPT: deformable patch-based transformer for visual recognition. In: Proceedings of the 29th ACM International Conference on Multimedia, pp. 2899–2907 (2021)
7. Chu, X., et al.: Twins: revisiting the design of spatial attention in vision transformers. In: Advances in Neural Information Processing Systems (2021)
8. Chu, X., et al.: Conditional positional encodings for vision transformers. arXiv preprint arXiv:2102.10882 (2021)
9. Cordts, M., et al.: The cityscapes dataset for semantic urban scene understanding. In: Proceedings of the IEEE/CVF Conference on Computer Vision and Pattern Recognition (CVPR) (2016)

10. Dai, J., et al.: Deformable convolutional networks. In: Proceedings of the IEEE/CVF International Conference on Computer Vision (ICCV), pp. 764–773 (2017)
11. Dai, Z., Liu, H., Le, Q.V., Tan, M.: CoATNet: marrying convolution and attention for all data sizes. In: Advances in Neural Information Processing Systems (2021)
12. Deng, J., Dong, W., Socher, R., Li, L.J., Li, K., Fei-Fei, L.: ImageNet: a large-scale hierarchical image database. In: Proceedings of the IEEE/CVF Conference on Computer Vision and Pattern Recognition (CVPR), pp. 248–255. IEEE (2009)
13. Dong, X., et al.: CSWin transformer: backbone with cross-shaped windows. arXiv preprint arXiv:2107.00652 (2021)
14. Dosovitskiy, A., et al.: An image is worth $16 \times 16$ words: transformers for image recognition at scale. In: International Conference on Learning Representations (2021)
15. El-Nouby, A., et al.: XCiT: cross-covariance image transformers. arXiv preprint arXiv:2106.09681 (2021)
16. Fang, J., Xie, L., Wang, X., Zhang, X., Liu, W., Tian, Q.: MSG-transformer: exchanging local spatial information by manipulating messenger tokens. arXiv preprint arXiv:2105.15168 (2021)
17. Guo, J., et al.: CMT: convolutional neural networks meet vision transformers. arXiv preprint arXiv:2107.06263 (2021)
18. Han, K., Xiao, A., Wu, E., Guo, J., Xu, C., Wang, Y.: Transformer in transformer. In: Advances in Neural Information Processing Systems 34 (2021)
19. He, K., Gkioxari, G., Dollár, P., Girshick, R.: Mask R-CNN. In: Proceedings of the IEEE/CVF International Conference on Computer Vision (ICCV), pp. 2961–2969 (2017)
20. He, K., Zhang, X., Ren, S., Sun, J.: Deep residual learning for image recognition. In: Proceedings of the IEEE/CVF Conference on Computer Vision and Pattern Recognition (CVPR), pp. 770–778 (2016)
21. Heo, B., Yun, S., Han, D., Chun, S., Choe, J., Oh, S.J.: Rethinking spatial dimensions of vision transformers. In: Proceedings of the IEEE/CVF International Conference on Computer Vision (ICCV) (2021)
22. Huang, Z., Ben, Y., Luo, G., Cheng, P., Yu, G., Fu, B.: Shuffle transformer: rethinking spatial shuffle for vision transformer. arXiv preprint arXiv:2106.03650 (2021)
23. Jing, Y., et al.: Dynamic instance normalization for arbitrary style transfer. In: AAAI (2020)
24. Li, Y., Mao, H., Girshick, R., He, K.: Exploring plain vision transformer backbones for object detection. arXiv preprint arXiv:2203.16527 (2022)
25. Lin, C., et al.: Online hyper-parameter learning for auto-augmentation strategy. In: Proceedings of the IEEE/CVF International Conference on Computer Vision (ICCV), pp. 6579–6588 (2019)
26. Lin, T.Y., Goyal, P., Girshick, R., He, K., Dollár, P.: Focal loss for dense object detection. In: Proceedings of the IEEE/CVF International Conference on Computer Vision (ICCV), pp. 2980–2988 (2017)
27. Lin, T.-Y., et al.: Microsoft COCO: common objects in context. In: Fleet, D., Pajdla, T., Schiele, B., Tuytelaars, T. (eds.) ECCV 2014. LNCS, vol. 8693, pp. 740–755. Springer, Cham (2014). https://doi.org/10.1007/978-3-319-10602-1_48
28. Liu, Z., et al.: Swin transformer V2: scaling up capacity and resolution. arXiv preprint arXiv:2111.09883 (2021)
29. Liu, Z., et al.: Swin transformer: hierarchical vision transformer using shifted windows. In: Proceedings of the IEEE/CVF International Conference on Computer Vision (ICCV), pp. 10012–10022 (2021)

30. Loshchilov, I., Hutter, F.: Decoupled weight decay regularization. In: International Conference on Learning Representations (2018)
31. Touvron, H., Cord, M., Douze, M., Massa, F., Sablayrolles, A., Jegou, H.: Training data-efficient image transformers; distillation through attention. In: International Conference on Machine Learning. PMLR (2021)
32. Wang, P., et al.: KVT: k-NN attention for boosting vision transformers. arXiv preprint arXiv:2106.00515 (2021)
33. Wang, W., et al.: PVT v2: improved baselines with pyramid vision transformer. Comput. Vis. Media **8**, 415–424 (2022). https://doi.org/10.1007/s41095-022-0274-8
34. Wang, W., et al.: Pyramid vision transformer: a versatile backbone for dense prediction without convolutions. In: Proceedings of the IEEE/CVF International Conference on Computer Vision (ICCV), pp. 568–578 (2021)
35. Wang, W., et al.: CrossFormer: a versatile vision transformer hinging on cross-scale attention. In: International Conference on Learning Representations (2022)
36. Wu, S., Wu, T., Tan, H., Guo, G.: Pale transformer: a general vision transformer backbone with pale-shaped attention. In: Proceedings of the AAAI Conference on Artificial Intelligence (2022)
37. Xia, Z., Pan, X., Song, S., Li, L.E., Huang, G.: Vision transformer with deformable attention (2022)
38. Xiao, T., Liu, Y., Zhou, B., Jiang, Y., Sun, J.: Unified perceptual parsing for scene understanding. In: Ferrari, V., Hebert, M., Sminchisescu, C., Weiss, Y. (eds.) ECCV 2018. LNCS, vol. 11209, pp. 432–448. Springer, Cham (2018). https://doi.org/10.1007/978-3-030-01228-1_26
39. Xu, B., Wang, N., Chen, T., Li, M.: Empirical evaluation of rectified activations in convolutional network. arXiv preprint arXiv:1505.00853 (2015)
40. Xu, Y., Zhang, J., Zhang, Q., Tao, D.: ViTPose: simple vision transformer baselines for human pose estimation. arXiv preprint arXiv:2204.12484 (2022)
41. Xu, Y., ZHANG, Q., Zhang, J., Tao, D.: ViTAE: Vision transformer advanced by exploring intrinsic inductive bias. In: Advances in Neural Information Processing Systems (2021)
42. Yan, H., Li, Z., Li, W., Wang, C., Wu, M., Zhang, C.: ConTNet: why not use convolution and transformer at the same time? arXiv preprint arXiv:2104.13497 (2021)
43. Yang, J., et al.: Focal attention for long-range interactions in vision transformers. In: Advances in Neural Information Processing Systems (2021)
44. Yang, Z., Liu, D., Wang, C., Yang, J., Tao, D.: Modeling image composition for complex scene generation. In: Proceedings of the IEEE/CVF Conference on Computer Vision and Pattern Recognition, pp. 7764–7773 (2022)
45. Yu, F., Koltun, V.: Multi-scale context aggregation by dilated convolutions. In: International Conference on Learning Representations (2016)
46. Yuan, L., et al.: Tokens-to-token ViT: training vision transformers from scratch on ImageNet. In: Proceedings of the IEEE/CVF International Conference on Computer Vision (ICCV), pp. 558–567 (2021)
47. Yun, S., Han, D., Oh, S.J., Chun, S., Choe, J., Yoo, Y.: CutMix: regularization strategy to train strong classifiers with localizable features. In: Proceedings of the IEEE/CVF International Conference on Computer Vision (ICCV), pp. 6023–6032 (2019)
48. Zhang, H., Cisse, M., Dauphin, Y.N., Lopez-Paz, D.: mixup: beyond empirical risk minimization. arXiv preprint arXiv:1710.09412 (2017)

49. Zhang, P., et al.: Multi-scale vision Longformer: a new vision transformer for high-resolution image encoding. In: Proceedings of the IEEE/CVF International Conference on Computer Vision (ICCV), pp. 2998–3008, October 2021

50. Zhang, Q., Xu, Y., Zhang, J., Tao, D.: VITAEv2: vision transformer advanced by exploring inductive bias for image recognition and beyond. arXiv preprint arXiv:2202.10108 (2022)

51. Zhang, Q., Yang, Y.B.: Rest: An efficient transformer for visual recognition. In: Advances in Neural Information Processing Systems 34 (2021)

52. Zhu, X., Hu, H., Lin, S., Dai, J.: Deformable ConvNets v2: more deformable, better results. In: Proceedings of the IEEE/CVF Conference on Computer Vision and Pattern Recognition (CVPR), pp. 9308–9316 (2019)

53. Zhu, X., Su, W., Lu, L., Li, B., Wang, X., Dai, J.: Deformable DETR: deformable transformers for end-to-end object detection. In: International Conference on Learning Representations (2021)

# Unbiased Manifold Augmentation
# for Coarse Class Subdivision

Baoming Yan, Ke Gao$^{(\boxtimes)}$, Bo Gao, Lin Wang, Jiang Yang, and Xiaobo Li

Alibaba Group, Hangzhou, China
{andy.ybm,gaoke.gao,leo.gb,youlin.wl,yangjiang.yj,
xiaobo.lixb}@alibaba-inc.com

**Abstract.** Coarse Class Subdivision (CCS) is important for many practical applications, where the training set originally annotated for a coarse class (e.g. bird) needs to further support its sub-classes recognition (e.g. swan, crow) with only very few fine-grained labeled samples. From the perspective of causal representation learning, these sub-classes inherit the same determinative factors of the coarse class, and their difference lies only in values. Therefore, to support the challenging CCS task with minimum fine-grained labeling cost, an ideal data augmentation method should generate abundant variants by manipulating these sub-class samples at the granularity of generating factors. For this goal, traditional data augmentation methods are far from sufficient. They often perform in highly-coupled image or feature space, thus can only simulate global geometric or photometric transformations. Leveraging the recent progress of factor-disentangled generators, Unbiased Manifold Augmentation (UMA) is proposed for CCS. With a controllable StyleGAN pre-trained for a coarse class, an approximate unbiased augmentation is conducted on the factor-disentangled manifolds for each sub-class, revealing the unbiased mutual information between the target sub-class and its determinative factors. Extensive experiments have shown that in the case of small data learning (less than 1% fine-grained samples of commonly used), our UMA can achieve 10.37% average improvement compared with existing data augmentation methods. On challenging tasks with severe bias, the accuracy is improved by up to 16.79%. We release our code at https://github.com/leo-gb/UMA.

**Keywords:** Coarse class subdivision · Causal representation learning · Factor-disentangled generator · Unbiased manifold augmentation

## 1 Introduction

Different from the conventional classification tasks where the original class and the new target are of similar level of semantic granularity, this paper focuses on Coarse Class Subdivision (CCS) which is a very practical problem. Given an existing training set for a coarse class, the target of CCS is to further recognize

S. Avidan et al. (Eds.): ECCV 2022, LNCS 13685, pp. 484–499, 2022.
https://doi.org/10.1007/978-3-031-19806-9_28

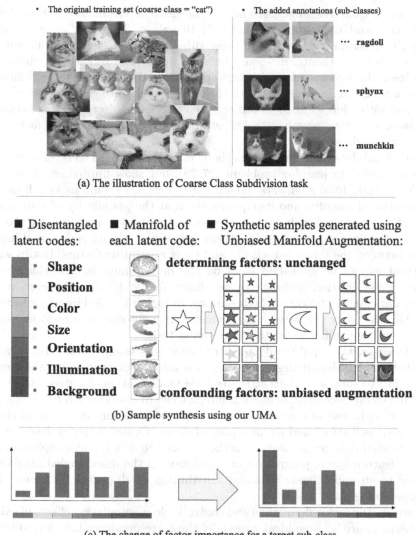

(a) The illustration of Coarse Class Subdivision task

■ Disentangled latent codes:    ■ Manifold of each latent code:    ■ Synthetic samples generated using Unbiased Manifold Augmentation:

- Shape
- Position
- Color
- Size
- Orientation
- Illumination
- Background

determining factors: unchanged

confounding factors: unbiased augmentation

(b) Sample synthesis using our UMA

(c) The change of factor importance for a target sub-class before/after using UMA

**Fig. 1.** The proposed Unbiased Manifold Augmentation (UMA) for coarse class subdivision task. (a) An example of task overview: given a training set for coarse class, and only very few samples for each sub-class. (b) Abundant and unbiased samples generation using our UMA. It should be noted that the semantic of each latent-code manifold is implicit. (c) The problem caused by limited and biased fine-grained data, and the effect of our UMA.

its sub-classes with minimum fine-grained labeling cost, as shown in Fig. 1(a). From the perspective of causal representation learning [17,20,26], the generating factors of images are composed of determinative factors and confounding factors.

In the case of CCS, the sub-classes inherit the same determinative factors of the coarse class, and their difference lies only in values. This task requires identifying the determinative factors of these sub-classes and distinguishing subtle differences between them. Fine-grained classification [10,16,17] is very challenging in itself, limited samples with agnostic bias make the task more difficult. For instance, given a training set with the coarse label "bird", a sub-class model fine-tuned with a few white-swan images often fails while discriminating between black swan and crow, revealing "color" as an unreliable determinative factor for the target sub-class.

Traditional data augmentation methods have been proved to be effective for common small data learning problems [27,28], but show limited effect on this challenging task. Ideal augmentation strategies for CCS should make full use of the fine-grained samples, and manipulate them at the granularity of generating factors. Even if their distribution on the generating factors is biased, we should generate abundant variants based on them, revealing the unbiased mutual information between the target sub-classes and their generating factors. In this way, the classifiers can be guided to focus on the determining factors which have the best generalization performance, as shown in Fig. 1(b)(c). However, most existing data augmentation methods perform in highly-coupled image or feature space, thus can only simulate global geometric or photometric transformations, which is far from sufficient for this challenging task.

Fortunately, the rapid development of factors-disentangled and controllable generative models illuminates an entirely new avenue for overcoming this problem [18,23]. To support various attribute-level manipulation of a given image, an idea controllable generative network is forced to learn disentangled manifolds for all generating factors of the target class, thus can model any variations of these factors with well-structured latent representations. Consequently, different from the traditional data augmentation methods conducted in highly-coupled image space or feature space, progressive manipulation in the disentangled manifolds can lead to an approximate unbiased distribution of all generating factors for the target category.

However, the factor-decoupling and controllable-manipulation effects of existing generators are far from ideal, especially the correspondence between editable latent-codes and the generating factors are implicit. Despite there are many methods aiming to find out these relations [8,15], most of them are too costly to be a practical option. In this paper, we propose a novel method called Unbiased Manifold Augmentation method (UMA), which is a simple and effective solution for the above difficult problems.

It should be noted that although the editable generator is essential for our UMA, there are many off-the-shelf generic generators can be utilized directly. For example, a generic face generator trained on the well-known datasets FFHQ [3] or CelebA [1]can be used in our UMA for any facial attribute recognition task. And any general bird generator trained on LSUN [25] or [2] can be used to improve the recognition of "swan" or "gull".

Our main contributions are as follows:

– A novel and systematic data augmentation mechanism called Unbiased Manifold Augmentation (UMA) is proposed for coarse class subdivision problem. Given an existing training set for a coarse class, our UMA can support subclasses recognition with minimum fine-grained labeling cost.
– The UMA is conducted on latent-code manifolds of a controllable generator pretrained for a coarser category, instead of the traditional highly-coupled image or feature space. Using a simple and effective progressive synthesis strategy, an approximate unbiased augmentation at the granularity of generating factors is achieved, even with limited labeled samples and agnostic bias. By revealing the unbiased mutual information between the target class and all of its impact factors, the classifier can be guided to focus on the right determining factors of the target sub-classes. In conjunction with it, a phase of progressive robust learning is further integrated, to keep a good balance of the diversity and reliability of these synthetic samples.
– Extensive experiments have shown that in the case of small data learning (less than 1% fine-grained samples of commonly used), our UMA can achieve 10.37% average improvement compared with existing data augmentation methods. On challenging tasks with severe bias, the accuracy is improved by up to 16.79%.

## 2    Related Work

Although the coarse class subdivision task has rarely been formally defined, it is a very practical problem and the related research is ubiquitous in deep learning. An exhaustive list of these work is out of the scope of this paper. Here we highlight data-augmentation strategies, especially based on the exploration of the recent progress of controllable generators with disentangled manifolds.

**Data Augmentation.** As one of the most hopeful means to alleviate small data learning problem in CCS task, the data augmentation methods have been actively studied [5,6,9,13,24,27,28,30]. Considering the different spaces in which the operations are performed, most of the widely used methods can be roughly divided into three categories. 1) Image Augmentation: given two training samples, Mixup [28] interpolates both the image and labels, while CutMix [27] partially mixes the patches and labels. The approaches conducted in the original image space [5,27,28] can improve the DNNs' robustness over some common noise, but the effects are often limited due to these simple variants of global geometric or photometric. 2) Feature Augmentation: Some methods such as [10,24] regularizes the DNNs by random interpolation of feature maps. It should be noted that the manifolds mentioned in Manifold Mixup [24] are actually the traditional feature maps in classification networks, not the manifolds of latent codes derived from controllable generative models, as adopted in this paper. 3) Style Augmentation: Since [7,9] decomposed the feature maps of the DNNs into separated representations of image content and style, many data augmentation methods using style or content manipulation has been proposed [8–10,14,29].

However, the diversity and reasonableness of the above synthetic data are difficult to guarantee, because both the feature space and style space are still highly coupled in semantic. Different from them, Our UMA is conducted in a well-structured latent space of disentangled generating factors, leveraging the recent progress of controllable generative models.

**Controllable Generative Models.** In recent years, controllable generators have witnessed great progress. It has been demonstrated that StyleGAN and StyleGAN2 [4] can offer strong editing capabilities with a disentangled latent space. Motivated by it, various methods have used StyleGAN to perform some specific manipulation for any given image [18,19,23]. They first encode an image into the latent space W of a pre-trained StyleGAN, then edit the latent code in a semantically meaningful way to obtain a new code, according to different image editing requirements. A desired image is then generated with this new code using the StyleGAN. An extended latent space W+ as the concatenation of 18 different W vectors is often used, one for each input layer of StyleGAN [18,23]. The latent space is considered as an ideal model of natural images' inherent distribution [4,18,19,23]. Sample synthesis in these disentangled semantic manifolds can lead to an approximate unbiased distribution of all generating factors of the target category, thus will guide the classifier to correctly focus on the determining factors which have the best generalization performance.

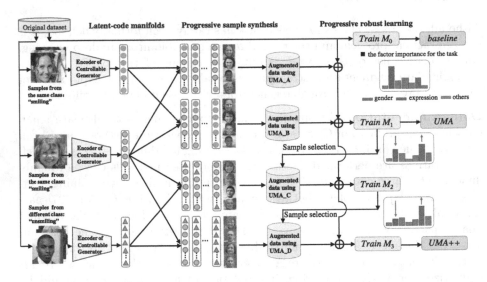

**Fig. 2.** The architecture of the proposed Unbiased Manifold Augmentation (UMA) for coarse class subdivision task. Take the coarse class "face" for example, here the target sub-classes are "smiling" and "unsmiling". Randomly selected fine-grained samples often have inevitable bias on the confounding factor "gender", instead of the determining factor "expression" for the target task. Our UMA can generate unbiased samples for each sub-class and lead the classifier to focus on determining factors with better generalization.

# 3    The UMA Method

Although the advanced controllable generative models can support image manipulations at the granularity of generating factors, as for coarse class subdivision task, there are still three questions need to be answered:

1. *How to synthetize abundant variants with only very few fine-grained samples?*
2. *How to synthetize unbiased variants without knowing what factors are the determinative ones?*
3. *How to guarantee that these synthetic variants are fine-grained-label preserving?*

The key idea of our approach is based on an important observation: From the perspective of causal representation learning, the generating factors of images are composed of determinative factors and confounding factors. From the perspective of information theory, the determinative factors often have consistently high mutual information with the target class under most scenarios, whereas the confounding factors vary wildly, thus determinative factors have better generalization ability. In the case of coarse class subdivision, the sub-classes inherit the same determinative factors of the coarse class, and their difference lies only in values. Consequently, given two samples within the same sub-class, if we exchange their correspondence factors, even without knowing their semantic or whether they are determinative factors of the target class, the generated samples will still fall into the same sub-class. This observation is consistent with the experimental results.

Furthermore, the progress of controllable generators illuminates a new avenue for overcoming these problems, because the semantic-disentangled manifolds have excellent properties of local linearity to support abundant and unbiased augmentation even with limited and biased samples for each sub-class.

Based on the above observations, the Unbiased Manifold Augmentation (UMA) is proposed. It consists of a simple and effective progressive synthesis strategy, and a phase of progressive robust learning.

## 3.1    Progressive Sample Synthesis

As shown in Fig. 2, the proposed UMA consists of two complementary phases to ensure the diversity and credibility of the generated samples respectively. We now first turn to describe the details of the progressive sample synthesis strategy. In the phase of progressive sample synthesis, given a target category and only a few training samples, a series of simple and effective synthesis strategies is conducted, in the latent-code manifolds of a pretrained editable generator.

It should be noted that the controllable generator needed by UMA is any StyloGAN or similar architecture whose latent codes containing the generating factors of the target class, so the editable generator can be trained at a much coarser granularity. E.g., a generic face generator can support any facial attribute recognition task with UMA, while the recognition of "swan" or "gull"

**Fig. 3.** Examples of the progressive diversity of synthetic samples for sub-class "smiling face", corresponding to UMA_A to UMA_D. The full version of UMA and UMA++ are different integration of them.

can be improved with any generic bird generator. Since the controllable generative models have seen rapid improvement recently, there are many off-the-shelf models pretrained on well-known large datasets for coarse categories. They can be adopted as the cornerstone as our UMA, to support the unbiased manifold augmentation of any subclass of them, which meets the needs of many practical applications.

The advanced controllable generators often consist of two components, named the encoder-decoder architecture. First, a mapping network converts a given image into the latent code vectors $(W^0 \cdots W^{17})$ of a pre-trained StyleGAN, corresponding to its 18 layers of progressive generator with different resolutions. Second, after some manipulations, the modified latent vectors are then fed into the synthesis network to generate a new image. It has been demonstrated that different layers correspond to different semantic levels of image attributes from coarse to fine, taking facial attributes manipulation for example, from global pose to local details of the hair.

However, most existing manipulation methods are not suitable for unbiased augmentation due to the lack of safety and diversity guarantee. The generated images must still fall into the same class, and variants of the generating factors should be covered as many as possible, even with limited and biased training samples of this category.

For the purpose of coarse class classification, the progressive sample synthesis is proposed, based on the full exploration of the controllable generators' underlying properties.

Based on the observation introduced before, a series of progressive sample synthesis strategy denoted as UMA_A to UMA_D is proposed. Given a pair of samples $x_i$ and $x_j$, the corresponding operations are as following:

$$W_i^k = e(x_i), \ W_j^k = e(x_j), \ k \in [0, 17] \tag{1}$$

$$\left\{ W_i^k \odot W_j^k \right\}_t = \left\{ W_j^k \mid_{t=k}, W_i^k \mid_{t \neq k} \right\}_t, \ t \in [0, 17] \tag{2}$$

$$\{\widehat{x}_{ij\_single}\}_t = \left\{ g \left( W_i^k \odot W_j^k \right) \right\}_t \tag{3}$$

$$\left\{ W_i^k \oplus W_j^k \right\}_t = \left\{ W_j^k \mid_{t \leq k}, W_i^k \mid_{t > k} \right\}_t, \ t \in [0, 17] \tag{4}$$

$$\{\widehat{x}_{ij\_multiple}\}_t = \left\{ g \left( W_i^k \oplus W_j^k \right) \right\}_t \tag{5}$$

Here $e$ and $g$ denote the encoder and decoder of the used controllable generator, while k means 18 latent-code layers. For UMA_A, the pair of seed images is randomly sampled from the target category, and new codes are generated by single layer switching, leading to 18 new images in all. UMA_B uses progressive switching layer by layer. Figure 3 shows that the simple operation is very useful to guarantee the safety of the synthetic samples, as it only swaps the real attribute values within the same class, thus the determining factors and their manifolds are kept unchanged. Meanwhile, the progressive switching also brings in many reasonable variants of other factors. To further improve diversity, UMA_C and UMA_D use one sample in the target class and another from the coarser category, conducting single or multiple layers swapping respectively. We can see from Fig. 3 that the diversity and reliability of the synthetic samples gradually change from UMA_A to UMA_D.

---

**Algorithm 1** : UMA (Unbiased Manifold Augmentation)

---

**Input:** a source dataset $S(s+, s-)$ for the target category $c$;
         a controllable generator $G(e, g)$ for a coarser category $C$
**Output:** learned classification model $M$ for task $c$
1: **Initialize:** $S_{training} \leftarrow S$
2: **for** $n = 1, ..., N$ **do**
3:     sample a pair of seed images $(x_i, x_j)$ from $s+$:
4:     $S_{training} \leftarrow \{(\widehat{x}_{ij\_single}, y+)\}_t$, using $Eq.(1)(2)(3)$
5:     $S_{training} \leftarrow \{(\widehat{x}_{ij\_multiple}, y+)\}_t$, using $Eq.(1)(4)(5)$
6:     sample a pair of seed images $(x_i, x_j)$ from $s-$:
7:     $S_{training} \leftarrow \{(\widehat{x}_{ij\_single}, y-)\}_t$, using $Eq.(1)(2)(3)$
8:     $S_{training} \leftarrow \{(\widehat{x}_{ij\_multiple}, y-)\}_t$, using $Eq.(1)(4)(5)$
9: **end for**
10: train $M_{UMA}$ using $S_{training}$
11: **for** $n = 1, ..., N$ **do**
12:     sample seed pair $(x_i, x_j)$, $x_i$ from $s+$, $x_j$ from $C$:
13:     $S_{training} \leftarrow \{(\widehat{x}_{ij\_single}, \widehat{y})\}_t$, using $Eq.(1)(2)(3)$
14:     $S_{training} \leftarrow \{(\widehat{x}_{ij\_multiple}, y)\}_t$, using $Eq.(1)(4)(5)$
15:     $\widehat{y}$ (or weight ) is determined using robust learning
16: **end for**
17: train $M_{UMA++}$ using $S_{training}$
18: **return** $M_{UMA}$ or $M_{UMA++}$

---

### 3.2    Progressive Robust Learning

Theoretically, using the proposed progressive sample synthesis strategy mentioned above, infinite new samples can be generated. But the trustworthiness of their pseudo labels should also be taken into account.

We can see from Fig. 3 that based on the underlying properties of the controllable generators, using seed images sampled from the target category, UMA_A and UMA_B can generate label-preserving samples. To further improve diversity, UMA_C and UMA_D are also introduced, but they often result in unreliable labels. For example, the layer swapping between images of a smiling person and a person who doesn't smile, may lead to a new one without obvious expression. Consequently, the phase of progressive robust learning is further integrated, to keep a good balance of the diversity and reliability for the synthetic samples.

As noisy labels may severely degrade the generalization, robust learning with noisy samples has gained significant attention in the machine learning community. Please refer to the comprehensive survey [22] for more information.

As introduced before, the diversity and reliability of the synthetic samples gradually change with UMA_A to D. In conjunction with it, a progressive robust learning strategy is proposed to cope with different scenarios. For datasets with random distribution, a classifier for the target category is trained on augmented dataset with label-preserving synthetic samples using UMA_A and B, which is called UMA in this paper. For a dataset with severe bias, only using UMA may still generate biased samples. To cope with it, UMA++ should be used. It consists of the complete series of progressive synthesis strategies and the progressive robust learning strategy. Here a simple method wildly used in semi-supervised learning [12,21,22] is adopted. A classifier is trained using UMA first. Then the classifier itself can be used to filter out unreliable samples obtained with UMA_C and D, and fine-tune in an iterative manner. The appropriate combination of the progressive sample synthesis and selection makes UMA a flexible mechanism. Thus, a good balance of the diversity and reliability of the synthetic samples can be achieved.

## 4    Experiments

To verify the effectiveness of the proposed UMA and UMA++ methods, extensive experiments are conducted on three publicly available datasets, CelebA [1], Stanford-Cars [11] and LSUN-Horses [25]. The performance of classification accuracy is compared with ten widely used data augmentation methods [5,6,9,13,24,27,28,30], on various settings including random distribution and severe bias.

### 4.1    Datasets and Settings

Different from traditional data augmentation methods which simulate global transformations, UMA can support the unbiased augmentation at the granularity of generating factors, thus we perform experiments on a diverse set of challenging domains to illustrate the generalization of our approach. For facial domain, we perform various facial attributes recognition tasks from CelebA dataset [1]. Recognition tasks on Stanford Cars dataset [11] and LSUN horse dataset [25] are also conducted.

For sample synthesis, we start with the pretrained StyleGAN [4] generator for each coarse domain, e.g., a generic face generator pretrained on FFHQ dataset [3]. Then the latent-code encoder is further obtained by e4e [23] framework through image manipulation (or StyleGAN inversion) task. Hence, the latent code of each image could be extracted, which contains 18 layers with 512 dimensions. For the UMA_A and UMA_B synthesis mode, the source image and reference image are from the same class. In mode A, the latent code of the two images is extracted, and single layer is switched, then fed into the StyleGAN [4] generator to synthesis a new image. For B mode, the latent code of source image is replaced by the reference image from the first layer to the 18th layer. For the UMA_C and UMA_D synthesis mode, the source image and reference image are from the different class. In mode C, single layer of the latent code is switched, while the latent code is gradually replaced in mode D.

For these recognition tasks, we train the model from scratch, and no extra data or pretrained models are used. ResNet-18 is used as the default CNN backbone for feature extraction, and all images are resized to $224 \times 224$ size. The training batch size is 32 for all the tasks, and Adam optimizer is used during training with initial learning rate 0.004. We perform warm-up schedule in the first 5 epochs, then the learning rate is decayed by 0.1 every 20 epochs and total 50 epochs are trained. The training set is 256, and the test set is 1024. To train all the parameters in our model, we compute the cross-entropy between the prediction and target as the loss function. In the robust learning process, the probability distribution over the classes of the synthesized image is predicted. If the probability of the most likely class is higher than a predetermined threshold of 0.95, it would be added to the training dataset. The label of the sample would be assigned to its most likely class.

## 4.2   Evaluation of Datasets with Agnostic Bias

For datasets with agnostic bias, we validate the effective ness of UMA by measuring classification accuracies on 11 challenging recognition tasks, across facial, car and horse domains [1,11,25], and compare the performance with 10 widely used data augmentation methods [5,6,9,13,24,27,28,30]. All the results in Table 1 and Fig. 4 show that the UMA is very effective, and consistently outperforms other augmentation methods significantly.

As shown in Table 1, we perform five single attributes recognition tasks (black hair, eyeglasses, heavy makeup, smiling and bald) and two tasks for combined attributes recognition (CA #1 is heavy makeup and smiling, CA #2 is male with black hair) in facial domain. The subclass recognition tasks in car or horse domain are also included. We can see that the performances of other methods are not stable, revealing that they are not suitable for all scenarios. By contrast,

**Table 1.** Accuracy comparison on 11 coarse class subdivision tasks with 10 widely used data augmentation methods. All methods use an identical backbone architecture and the same default parameters. The number of training samples is only 32. More details of the task settings please refer to Sect. 4.

| Method | Publication | Black hair | Eye-glasses | Makeup | Smilling | Bald | CA#1 | CA#2 | Sedan | SUV | Brown Horse | White Horse | Average |
|---|---|---|---|---|---|---|---|---|---|---|---|---|---|
| MixUp [28] | ICLR'18 | 74.28 | 77.39 | 67.58 | 55.76 | 76.56 | 64.45 | 74.51 | 62.89 | 62.30 | 79.69 | 84.38 | 70.89 |
| CutMix [27] | ICCV'19 | 70.68 | 74.45 | 62.89 | 51.76 | 76.17 | 65.82 | 71.00 | 65.04 | 62.50 | 79.69 | 79.69 | 69.06 |
| Auto Augment [5] | CVPR'19 | 71.55 | 77.76 | 59.67 | 54.98 | 74.22 | 63.77 | 72.75 | 68.75 | 66.99 | 85.94 | 78.91 | 70.48 |
| Manifold Mixup [24] | ICML'19 | 75.76 | 75.74 | 67.29 | 58.40 | 76.95 | 66.70 | 74.32 | 63.96 | 61.91 | 76.56 | 80.47 | 70.73 |
| Random Erasing [30] | AAAI'20 | 74.24 | 75.55 | 60.94 | 50.78 | 73.05 | 62.79 | 72.07 | 61.52 | 59.08 | 78.91 | 78.12 | 67.91 |
| Random Augment [6] | NIPS'20 | 71.52 | 72.06 | 59.28 | 54.69 | 73.83 | 59.18 | 71.78 | 66.99 | 68.55 | 81.25 | 81.25 | 69.13 |
| MoEx [13] | CVPR'21 | 74.09 | 78.68 | 69.73 | 53.22 | 81.64 | 66.80 | 71.97 | 60.16 | 57.62 | 85.16 | 86.72 | 71.44 |
| StyleMix [9] | CVPR'21 | 68.71 | 78.86 | 63.67 | 61.23 | 71.88 | 51.76 | 73.34 | 63.96 | 62.50 | 78.12 | 81.25 | 68.66 |
| StyleCutMix [9] | CVPR'21 | 72.34 | 69.30 | 64.84 | 60.94 | 75.39 | 66.11 | 72.75 | 64.36 | 59.57 | 75.00 | 78.91 | 69.05 |
| StyleCutMix (auto-$\gamma$) [9] | CVPR'21 | 68.67 | 71.32 | 63.09 | 58.98 | 74.21 | 67.09 | 72.27 | 64.84 | 62.65 | 76.56 | 85.16 | 69.53 |
| **UMA** | – | **79.20**(3.44↑) | **90.99**(12.13↑) | **74.41**(4.68↑) | **67.87**(6.64↑) | **84.77**(3.13↑) | **76.95**(9.86↑) | **76.86**(2.35↑) | **72.56**(3.81↑) | **71.29**(2.74↑) | **89.84**(3.90↑) | **88.28**(1.56↑) | **79.37**(7.93↑) |
| **UMA++** | – | **79.89**(4.13↑) | **93.01**(14.15↑) | **77.05**(7.32↑) | **69.53**(8.30↑) | **87.50**(5.86↑) | **78.03**(10.94↑) | **81.74**(7.23↑) | **74.61**(5.86↑) | **74.90**(6.35↑) | **91.41**(5.47↑) | **92.19**(5.47↑) | **81.81**(10.37) |

UMA performs best in all tasks. Especially, in the eyeglass-wearing recognition task, our UMA and UMA++ are superior to the best one with a large margin of 12.13% and 14.15%. On average, UMA and UMA++ gain 7.93% and 10.37% improvement than the best method.

Figure 4 shows the details of accuracy varying with different number of training samples. In general, the accuracy substantially improves with the increase of training data, whereas the marginal gain decreases gradually. This means that the less data, the more important data augmentation is. UMA has a greater advantage with limited training data. With the whole training data, 2% improvement is obtained. While using only 12.5% training data, UMA can achieve up to 7% improvement in smiling recognition and 9.8% improvement in combined

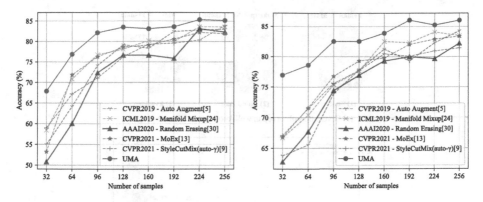

**Fig. 4.** Accuracy comparison on various sub-class recognition tasks, with different number of training samples. To simulate the challenging small-data-learning scenario of coarse class subdivision task, we only provide less than 1% fine-grained samples of commonly used.

attribute recognition task of heavy makeup with smiling. This is a compelling proof of the diversity and reliability of the progressive synthesis and selection method in UMA.

### 4.3  Evaluation of Datasets with Severe Bias

For a dataset with severe bias, only UMA is not enough, and UMA++ is very suitable for this problem. Severe bias is very common in many well-known datasets. As shown in Fig. 5(a), 70% of the annotation samples in [1] with smiling are female, while 73% annotated blond hair are heavily makeup, and 83% person with eyeglasses are male. The highly-coupled attributes can become the confounding factors during recognition. E.g., "smiling" would hinder the discrimination of "gender" attribute.

To study the effectiveness of UMA++ with severe bias, we conduct gender recognition on a biased dataset. In the training dataset, 95% of the male samples are wearing eyeglasses, and 5% of the female samples are wearing eyeglasses, while in the test dataset, 50% of the samples are wearing eyeglasses for all genders.

We start with a baseline classification model with only random horizontal flip augmentation, and achieves 66.02% accuracy. Because of the severe bias in the training dataset, the model heavily relies on the factors of eyeglasses, while the intrinsic factors of gender are neglected. To relieve this problem, samples of male without eyeglasses and female with eyeglasses are desired. Hence, we generate samples using UMA_C and UMA_D, which selects reference images outside the target class. It can introduce valuable variants, e.g., male samples without eyeglasses and female samples with eyeglasses. In UMA++, samples synthesized by UMA_C are assigned with the same label with the source image, and added to the original dataset to train a base classifier. Then samples are further synthe-

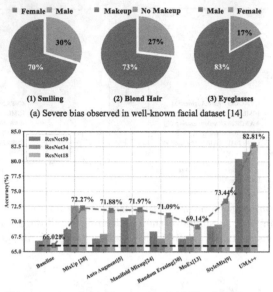

(a) Severe bias observed in well-known facial dataset [14]

(b) Accuracy comparison on the recognition task of "gender" with severe bias on "wearing eyeglasses", using three different backbones.

**Fig. 5.** The observation of severe bias in wildly-used datasets, and the accuracy comparison between our UMA and the state-of-the-art data augmentation methods.

sized by UMA_D and selected with robust learning such as [12], achieving 16.79% improvement compared with baseline, as shown in Fig. 5(b). Compared with the state-of-the-art methods, the UMA++ still outperforms them by 9.37%.

We also conduct experiments with different backbones, Fig. 5(b) shows that UMA++ outperforms others consistently with various backbones. With limited and biased datasets, ResNet-18 achieves the best performance, which implies that deeper backbone could learn to fit the confounding factors much easier and reduce the performance.

**Table 2.** Performance comparison with several state-of-the-art FGVC methods, on a dataset with severe bias. Baseline stands for resnet-18 backbone with one fully connected layers. UMA++ and various FGVC methods are added to evaluate the performance.

| Method | Publication | Baseline | Baseline+ UMA++ | Baseline+ FGVC | Baseline+ FGVC+UMA++ |
|---|---|---|---|---|---|
| SPS [16] | ICCV'21 | 66.02% | 82.81% | 72.27% | 83.59%(**11.31**↑) |
| ProtoTree [10] | CVPR'21 | | | 66.80% | 84.38%(**17.58**↑) |
| CAL [17] | CVPR'21 | | | 73.05% | 84.77%(**11.72**↑) |

**Fig. 6.** Visualization of the proposed UMA and other wildly used data augmentation methods. The reliability and diversity of the synthetic samples using the UMA are better than other augmentation methods conducted in image space or feature space

For sub-class recognition tasks, many Fine-Grained Visual Classification(FGVC) methods have been proposed [10,16,17], focusing on the design of networks or attention mechanism, complementary with data augmentation discussed in this paper. Table 2 shows that compared with the state-of-the-art FGVC strategies, our UMA can still perform best with dataset bias. Besides, our UMA is complementary with these FGVC strategies, and further improve the performance by over 11.31% (Fig. 6).

## 5    Conclusion

To support the challenging CCS task with minimum fine-grained labeling cost, the Unbiased Manifold Augmentation (UMA) is proposed. Leveraging the recent progress of controllable generators, unbiased and reliable sample synthesis is conducted in the disentangled latent-code manifolds, at the granularity of generating factors or called attributes, different from traditional augmentation in highly-coupled image or feature space. UMA can reveal the approximate unbiased mutual information between the target class and all of its impact factors, thus guides the classifier to focus on causal factors.The proposed framework is independent of the adopted editable generator or the specific robust learning method. Experiments have shown that with a generator for a coarser category, our UMA can greatly improve the generalization ability of the DNNs for sub-classes recognition, on datasets with agnostic even severe bias.

# References

1. Celeba. https://mmlab.ie.cuhk.edu.hk/projects/CelebA.html
2. Cub-200-2011. https://www.vision.caltech.edu/visipedia/CUB-200-2011.html
3. ffhq-dataset. https://github.com/NVlabs/ffhq-dataset
4. Choi, Y., Uh, Y., Yoo, J., Ha, J.W.: StarGAN v2: diverse image synthesis for multiple domains. In: Proceedings of the IEEE/CVF Conference on Computer Vision and Pattern Recognition, pp. 8188–8197 (2020)
5. Cubuk, E.D., Zoph, B., Mane, D., Vasudevan, V., Le, Q.V.: AutoAugment: learning augmentation strategies from data. In: Proceedings of the IEEE/CVF Conference on Computer Vision and Pattern Recognition, pp. 113–123 (2019)
6. Cubuk, E.D., Zoph, B., Shlens, J., Le, Q.V.: RandAugment: practical automated data augmentation with a reduced search space. In: Proceedings of the IEEE/CVF Conference on Computer Vision and Pattern Recognition Workshops, pp. 702–703 (2020)
7. Gatys, L.A., Ecker, A.S., Bethge, M.: Image style transfer using convolutional neural networks. In: Proceedings of the IEEE Conference on Computer Vision and Pattern Recognition, pp. 2414–2423 (2016)
8. Härkönen, E., Hertzmann, A., Lehtinen, J., Paris, S.: GANSpace: discovering interpretable GAN controls. In: Advances in Neural Information Processing Systems 33, pp. 9841–9850 (2020)
9. Hong, M., Choi, J., Kim, G.: StyleMix: separating content and style for enhanced data augmentation. In: Proceedings of the IEEE/CVF Conference on Computer Vision and Pattern Recognition, pp. 14862–14870 (2021)
10. Huang, S., Wang, X., Tao, D.: Stochastic partial swap: enhanced model generalization and interpretability for fine-grained recognition. In: Proceedings of the IEEE/CVF International Conference on Computer Vision, pp. 620–629 (2021)
11. Krause, J., Stark, M., Deng, J., Fei-Fei, L.: 3D object representations for fine-grained categorization. In: Proceedings of the IEEE International Conference on Computer Vision Workshops, pp. 554–561 (2013)
12. Lee, D.H., et al.: Pseudo-label: the simple and efficient semi-supervised learning method for deep neural networks. In: Workshop on Challenges in Representation Learning, ICML, vol. 3, p. 896 (2013)
13. Li, B., Wu, F., Lim, S.N., Belongie, S., Weinberger, K.Q.: On feature normalization and data augmentation. In: Proceedings of the IEEE/CVF Conference on Computer Vision and Pattern Recognition, pp. 12383–12392 (2021)
14. Li, Y., et al.: Shape-texture debiased neural network training. arXiv preprint arXiv:2010.05981 (2020)
15. Lin, J., Zhang, R., Ganz, F., Han, S., Zhu, J.Y.: Anycost GANs for interactive image synthesis and editing. In: Proceedings of the IEEE/CVF Conference on Computer Vision and Pattern Recognition, pp. 14986–14996 (2021)
16. Nauta, M., van Bree, R., Seifert, C.: Neural prototype trees for interpretable fine-grained image recognition. In: Proceedings of the IEEE/CVF Conference on Computer Vision and Pattern Recognition, pp. 14933–14943 (2021)
17. Rao, Y., Chen, G., Lu, J., Zhou, J.: Counterfactual attention learning for fine-grained visual categorization and re-identification. In: Proceedings of the IEEE/CVF International Conference on Computer Vision, pp. 1025–1034 (2021)
18. Richardson, E., et al.: Encoding in style: a StyleGAN encoder for image-to-image translation. In: Proceedings of the IEEE/CVF Conference on Computer Vision and Pattern Recognition, pp. 2287–2296 (2021)

19. Roich, D., Mokady, R., Bermano, A.H., Cohen-Or, D.: Pivotal tuning for latent-based editing of real images. arXiv preprint arXiv:2106.05744 (2021)
20. Schölkopf, B., et al.: Toward causal representation learning. Proc. IEEE **109**(5), 612–634 (2021)
21. Sohn, K., et al.: FixMatch: simplifying semi-supervised learning with consistency and confidence. In: Advances in Neural Information Processing Systems 33, pp. 596–608 (2020)
22. Song, H., Kim, M., Park, D., Shin, Y., Lee, J.G.: Learning from noisy labels with deep neural networks: a survey. arXiv preprint arXiv:2007.08199 (2020)
23. Tov, O., Alaluf, Y., Nitzan, Y., Patashnik, O., Cohen-Or, D.: Designing an encoder for StyleGAN image manipulation. ACM Trans. Graph. (TOG) **40**(4), 1–14 (2021)
24. Verma, V., et al.: Manifold mixup: better representations by interpolating hidden states. In: International Conference on Machine Learning, pp. 6438–6447. PMLR (2019)
25. Yu, F., Seff, A., Zhang, Y., Song, S., Funkhouser, T., Xiao, J.: LSUN: construction of a large-scale image dataset using deep learning with humans in the loop. arXiv preprint arXiv:1506.03365 (2015)
26. Yue, Z., Wang, T., Sun, Q., Hua, X.S., Zhang, H.: Counterfactual zero-shot and open-set visual recognition. In: Proceedings of the IEEE/CVF Conference on Computer Vision and Pattern Recognition, pp. 15404–15414 (2021)
27. Yun, S., Han, D., Oh, S.J., Chun, S., Choe, J., Yoo, Y.: CutMix: regularization strategy to train strong classifiers with localizable features. In: Proceedings of the IEEE/CVF International Conference on Computer Vision, pp. 6023–6032 (2019)
28. Zhang, H., Cisse, M., Dauphin, Y.N., Lopez-Paz, D.: mixup: beyond empirical risk minimization. arXiv preprint arXiv:1710.09412 (2017)
29. Zheng, X., Chalasani, T., Ghosal, K., Lutz, S., Smolic, A.: STaDA: Style transfer as data augmentation. arXiv preprint arXiv:1909.01056 (2019)
30. Zhong, Z., Zheng, L., Kang, G., Li, S., Yang, Y.: Random erasing data augmentation. In: Proceedings of the AAAI Conference on Artificial Intelligence, vol. 34, pp. 13001–13008 (2020)

# DenseHybrid: Hybrid Anomaly Detection for Dense Open-Set Recognition

Matej Grcić$^{(\boxtimes)}$ [iD], Petra Bevandić [iD], and Siniša Šegvić [iD]

Faculty of Electrical Engineering and Computing, University of Zagreb,
Unska 3, 10000 Zagreb, Croatia
{matej.grcic,petra.bevandic,sinisa.segvic}@fer.hr

**Abstract.** Anomaly detection can be conceived either through generative modelling of regular training data or by discriminating with respect to negative training data. These two approaches exhibit different failure modes. Consequently, hybrid algorithms present an attractive research goal. Unfortunately, dense anomaly detection requires translational equivariance and very large input resolutions. These requirements disqualify all previous hybrid approaches to the best of our knowledge. We therefore design a novel hybrid algorithm based on reinterpreting discriminative logits as a logarithm of the unnormalized joint distribution $\hat{p}(\mathbf{x}, \mathbf{y})$. Our model builds on a shared convolutional representation from which we recover three dense predictions: i) the closed-set class posterior $P(\mathbf{y}|\mathbf{x})$, ii) the dataset posterior $P(d_{in}|\mathbf{x})$, iii) unnormalized data likelihood $\hat{p}(\mathbf{x})$. The latter two predictions are trained both on the standard training data and on a generic negative dataset. We blend these two predictions into a hybrid anomaly score which allows dense open-set recognition on large natural images. We carefully design a custom loss for the data likelihood in order to avoid backpropagation through the untractable normalizing constant $Z(\theta)$. Experiments evaluate our contributions on standard dense anomaly detection benchmarks as well as in terms of open-mIoU - a novel metric for dense open-set performance. Our submissions achieve state-of-the-art performance despite neglectable computational overhead over the standard semantic segmentation baseline. Official implementation: https://github.com/matejgrcic/DenseHybrid

**Keywords:** Dense anomaly detection · Dense open-set recognition · Out-of-distribution detection · Semantic segmentation

## 1 Introduction

High accuracy, fast inference and small memory footprint of modern neural networks steadily expand the horizon of downstream applications. Many exciting applications require advanced image understanding functionality provided by

**Supplementary Information** The online version contains supplementary material available at https://doi.org/10.1007/978-3-031-19806-9_29.

semantic segmentation [17]. These models associate each pixel with a class from a predefined taxonomy. They can accurately segment two megapixel images in real-time on low-power embedded hardware [11,26,43]. However, the standard training procedures assume the closed-world setup which may raise serious safety issues in real-world deployments. For example, if a segmentation model miss-classifies an unknown object (e.g. lost cargo) as road, the autonomous car may experience a serious accident. Such hazards can be alleviated by complement-ing semantic segmentation with dense anomaly detection. The resulting dense open-set recognition models are more suitable for real-world applications due to ability to decline the decision in anomalous pixels.

Previous approaches for dense anomaly detection either use a generative or a discriminative perspective. Generative approaches are based on density esti-mation [6] or image resynthesis [4,36]. Discriminative approaches use classifica-tion confidence [23], a binary classifier [2] or Bayesian inference [29]. These two perspectives exhibit different failure modes. Generative detectors inaccurately disperse the probability volume [38,41,47,53] or rely on risky image resynthesis. On the other hand, discriminative detectors assume training on full span of the input space, even including unknown unknowns [25].

In this work we combine the two perspectives into a hybrid anomaly detector. The proposed approach complements a standard semantic segmentation model with two additional predictions: i) unnormalized dense data likelihood $\hat{p}(\mathbf{x})$ [6], and ii) dense data posterior $P(d_{in}|\mathbf{x})$ [2]. Both predictions require training with negative data [2,4,10,25]. Joining these two outputs yields an accurate yet effi-cient dense anomaly detector which we refer to as DenseHybrid (Fig. 1).

We summarize our contributions as follows. We propose the first hybrid anomaly detector which allows end-to-end training and operates at pixel level. Our approach combines likelihood evaluation and discrimination with respect to an off-the-shelf negative dataset. Our experiments reveal accurate anomaly detection despite minimal computational overhead. We complement semantic segmentation with DenseHybrid to achieve dense open-set recognition. We report state-of-the-art dense open-set recognition performance according to a novel per-formance metric which we refer to as *open-mIoU*.

**Fig. 1.** Qualitative performance of the proposed DenseHybrid approach on standard datasets. Top: input images. Bottom: dense maps of the proposed anomaly score

## 2    Related Work

Detecting samples which deviate from the generative process of the training data is a decades old problem [22]. In the machine learning community this task is also known as anomaly detection or out-of-distribution (OOD) detection [24]. Early image-wide approaches utilize max-softmax probability [24], input perturbations [34] ensembling [31] or Bayesian uncertainty [40]. More encouraging performance has been reported by discriminative training against a broad negative dataset [2,14,25,37] or an appropriately trained generative model [21,32,54].

Another line of work detects anomalies by estimating the likelihood with a generative model. Surprisingly, this research revealed that anomalies may give rise to higher likelihood than inliers [41,47,53]. Further works suggest that better performance can be hoped for group-wise anomaly detection [27], however, this case has less practical importance. Generative models can be encouraged to assign low likelihood in negative training data [25]. This practice may mitigate sub-optimal dispersion of the probability volume [38].

Image-wide anomaly detection approaches can be adapted for dense prediction with variable success. None of the existing generative approaches can deliver dense likelihood estimates. On the other hand, concepts such as max-softmax and discriminative training with negative data are easily ported to dense prediction. Many dense anomaly detectors are trained on mixed-content images obtained by pasting negatives (e.g. ImageNet, COCO, ADE20k) over regular training images [2,4,10]. Discriminative anomaly detections may be produced by a dedicated OOD head which shares features with the standard classification head. Shared features improve OOD performance and incur neglectable computational overhead with respect to the baseline semantic segmentation model [2]. Recent approach [10] encourages large softmax entropy in negative pixels.

Anomalies can also be recognized in feature space [6]. However, this approach complicates the detection of small objects due to subsampled feature represenations and feature collapse [1,38]. Orthogonally to previous approaches, anomaly detector can be implemented according to dissimilarity between the input and a resynthesised image [4,36,50]. The resynthesis is performed by a generative model conditioned on the predicted labels. However, this approach is suitable only for uniform backgrounds such as roads [36]. Furthermore, it adds significant computational overhead making it inapplicable for real-time applications.

Our approach to dense anomaly detection is a hybrid combination of discriminative detection and likelihood evaluation. Discriminative OOD detection has been introduced in [2,14,25]. Contrary to all these approaches, we improve discriminative OOD detection through synergy with likelihood testing. Dense likelihood evaluation has been accomplished by fitting a generative model to discriminative features [6]. However, their approach is vulnerable to feature collapse [1,38] due to two-phase training. Moreover, detection of small outliers is jeopardized due to subsampling. Contrary to their approach, our method allows joint training with the standard dense prediction model and anomaly detection at full resolution.

We perform dense likelihood evaluation by reinterpreting logits as unnormalized joint likelihood [20]. However, the method [20] is completely unsuitable for dense prediction due to intractability of Langevin sampling at large resolutions. We reformulate their method in order to allow training on mixed-content images and show that such adaptation dramatically simplifies the training by precluding backpropagation through intractable normalizing constant $Z(\theta)$. To the best of our knowledge, the proposed design offers the first approach for dense likelihood evaluation that is suitable for end-to-end training.

We build an open-set recognition model by thresholding our hybrid anomaly score and combining it with the standard semantic segmentation predictions [7]. The resulting model is suitable for simultaneous anomaly detection and recognition of inlier scenery. We note that standard metrics for dense recognition performance [16] do not take into account the accuracy in anomalous samples. This is not surprising since outlier pixels have been introduced only in recent dense prediction benchmarks [5,9,52]. Also, previous work on discrimination in presence of anomalous pixels was more focused on robustness of algorithms rather than on recognition performance [52]. Hence, we propose a novel anomaly-aware metric (open-mIoU) which measures the prediction quality both in inliers and the outliers, similarly to previous image-wide metrics [46,48].

# 3    Dense Recognition with Hybrid Anomaly Detector

We propose a hybrid algorithm for dense anomaly detection based on unnormalized data likelihood and dataset posterior (Sect. 3.1). The proposed hybrid anomaly detector extends the standard dense classifier to form dense open-set recognition model (Sect. 3.2). The resulting recognition model trains on mixed content images.

## 3.1    Hybrid Anomaly Detection for Dense Prediction

We represent RGB images with a random variable $\underline{x}$. Variable $\underline{y}$ denotes the corresponding pixel-level predictions, while the binary random variable $\underline{d}$ models whether a given pixel belongs to the inliers or outliers. We denote a realization of a random variable without the underline. Thus, $P(\mathbf{y}|\mathbf{x})$ is a shortcut for $P(\underline{\mathbf{y}} = \mathbf{y}|\underline{\mathbf{x}} = \mathbf{x})$. We write $d_{in}$ for inliers and $d_{out}$ for outliers. Thus, $P(d_{in}|\mathbf{x})$ denotes a dense posterior probability that a given pixel is an inlier [2,25]. Conversely, $p(\mathbf{x})$ denotes dense likelihoods of patches centered at a given pixel.

We build upon reinterpretation of logits $\mathbf{s}$ produced by a discriminative model $P(\mathbf{y}|\mathbf{x}) = \mathrm{softmax}(f_{\theta_2}(q_{\theta_1}(\mathbf{x})))$ [20]. We reinterpret the logits as unnormalized joint log-density of input and labels:

$$p(\mathbf{y}, \mathbf{x}) = \frac{1}{Z}\hat{p}(\mathbf{y}, \mathbf{x}) := \frac{1}{Z}\exp \mathbf{s}, \quad \mathbf{s} = f_{\theta_2}(q_{\theta_1}(\mathbf{x})). \tag{1}$$

Note that $q_{\theta_1}$ produces pre-logits $\mathbf{t}$ based on which $f_{\theta_2}$ computes logits $\mathbf{s}$. Hence, $q_{\theta_1}$ and $f_{\theta_2}$ form the standard discriminative model. $\hat{p}(\mathbf{y}, \mathbf{x})$ denotes unnormalized joint density across data $\underline{\mathbf{x}}$ and labels $\underline{\mathbf{y}}$, while $Z$ denotes the corresponding normalization constant. As usual, computing $Z$ is intractable since it requires evaluating the unnormalized distribution for all realizations of $\mathbf{y}$ and $\mathbf{x}$. Throughout this work we conveniently eschew the evaluation of $Z$ in order to enable efficient training and inference.

Standard discriminative predictions are easily obtained through Bayes rule:

$$P(\mathbf{y}|\mathbf{x}) = \frac{p(\mathbf{y},\mathbf{x})}{\sum_{\mathbf{y}} p(\mathbf{y},\mathbf{x})} = \frac{\exp \mathbf{s}}{\sum_i \exp \mathbf{s}_i} = \text{softmax}(\mathbf{s}). \tag{2}$$

Hence, we can recover the unnormalized joint density (1) through the standard closed-world discriminative learning over K classes. Moreover, we can share the logits with the primary discriminative task and even exploit pretrained classifiers. We can express the dense likelihood $p(\mathbf{x})$ by marginalizing out $\mathbf{y}$:

$$p(\mathbf{x}) = \sum_y p(\mathbf{y},\mathbf{x}) = \frac{1}{Z} \sum_y \hat{p}(\mathbf{y},\mathbf{x}) = \frac{1}{Z} \sum_i \exp \mathbf{s}_i. \tag{3}$$

One could argue for detecting anomalies with $p(\mathbf{x})$ directly: if a given input is unlikely under the $p(\mathbf{x})$, it should likely be an anomaly. However, this approach may not work very well in practice due to tendency of maximum likelihood optimization towards over-generalization [38]. In simple words, some outliers will have higher likelihood than the inliers [41, 47]. We discourage such behaviour by minimizing the likelihood of negatives during the training [25].

Besides logit reinterpretation, we define the dataset posterior $P(d_{in}|\mathbf{x})$ as a non-linear transformation based on pre-logit activations $q_{\theta_1}(\mathbf{x})$ [2]:

$$P(d_{in}|\mathbf{x}) := \sigma(g_\gamma(q_{\theta_1}(\mathbf{x}))). \tag{4}$$

In our case, the function $g$ is BN-ReLU-Conv1x1 of pre-logits, followed by a sigmoid non-linearity. Anomalies can be detected solely with $P(d_{in}|\mathbf{x})$ [13]: inlier samples should give rise to high posterior of the inlier dataset. However, our experiments show that this is suboptimal compared to our hybrid approach.

Figure 2 illustrates shortcomings of generative and discriminative anomaly detectors on a toy problem. Blue dots designate inlier data. Green triangles designate the negative data used for training. Red squares denote anomalous test data. Discriminative detectors which model $P(d_{in}|\mathbf{x})$ can't differentiate inliers if the negative data seen during the training insufficiently covers the sample space (left). On the other hand, generative detectors which model $p(\mathbf{x})$ tend to inaccurately distribute probability volume over sample space [38] (center). Joining discriminative and generative approach into a hybrid detector we mitigate the aforementioned limitations (right).

We build our hybrid anomaly detector upon the discriminative dataset posterior $P(d_{in}|\mathbf{x})$ and the generative data likelihood $p(\mathbf{x})$. We express a novel hybrid anomaly score as log-ratio between $P(d_{out}|\mathbf{x}) = 1 - P(d_{in}|\mathbf{x})$ and $p(\mathbf{x})$:

$$s(\mathbf{x}) := \ln \frac{P(d_{out}|\mathbf{x})}{p(\mathbf{x})} = \ln P(d_{out}|\mathbf{x}) - \ln \hat{p}(\mathbf{x}) + \ln Z \tag{5}$$

$$\cong \ln P(d_{out}|\mathbf{x}) - \ln \hat{p}(\mathbf{x}). \tag{6}$$

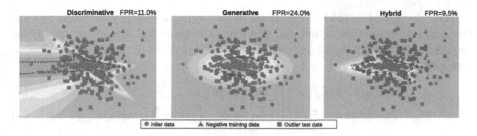

**Fig. 2.** Anomaly detection on a toy dataset. The discriminative approach (left) models $P(d_{in}|\mathbf{x})$. It fails if the negative training dataset does not cover all modes of the test anomalies. The generative approach (middle) models $p(\mathbf{x})$. It often assigns high likelihoods to test anomalies due to over-generalization [38]. The hybrid approach achieves a synergy between discriminative and generative modelling (Color figure online)

We can neglect $Z$ since ranking performance [24] is invariant to monotonic transformations such as taking a logarithm or adding a constant. Other formulations of $s(\mathbf{x})$ may also be effective which is an interesting direction for future work.

### 3.2 Dense Open-Set Recognition Based on Hybrid Anomaly Detection

Figure 3 illustrates the inference with the proposed open-set recognition setup. RGB input is fed to a hybrid dense model which produces pre-logit activations $\mathbf{t}$ and logits $\mathbf{s}$. Then, we obtain the closed-set class posterior $P(\mathbf{y}|\mathbf{x}) = \mathrm{softmax}(\mathbf{s})$ (designated in yellow) and the unnormalized data likelihood $\hat{p}(\mathbf{x})$ (designated in green). A distinct head $g$ transforms pre-logits $\mathbf{t}$ into the dataset posterior $P(d_{out}|\mathbf{x})$. The anomaly score $s(\mathbf{x})$ is a log-ratio between latter two distributions. The resulting anomaly map is thresholded and fused with the discriminative output into the final dense open-set recognition map.

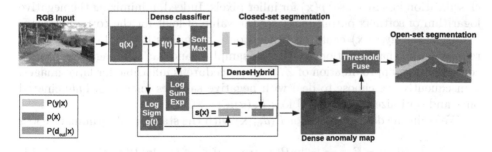

**Fig. 3.** The proposed dense open-set recognition approach. Our anomaly score is a log-ratio of outputs derived from the hybrid model. We fuse the thresholded anomaly score with the closed-set segmentation map to obtain the open-set segmentation map (Color figure online)

The developed hybrid model aims at achieving a synergy between generative and discriminative modelling. However, the proposed hybrid interpretation requires specific training objectives. Dense class posteriors require a discriminative loss over the inlier data $D_{in}$:

$$L_{\text{cls}}(\theta) = \mathbb{E}_{\mathbf{x},\mathbf{y} \in D_{in}}[-\ln P(\mathbf{y}|\mathbf{x})] \tag{7}$$

$$= -\mathbb{E}_{\mathbf{x},\mathbf{y} \in D_{in}}[\mathbf{s}_y] + \mathbb{E}_{\mathbf{x},\mathbf{y} \in D_{in}}[\ln \sum_i \exp \mathbf{s}_i]. \tag{8}$$

The discriminative loss (7) corresponds to the standard training in the closed world. We introduce the negative data $D_{out}$ into the training procedure to ensure the desired behaviour of $P(d_{in}|\mathbf{x})$ and $p(\mathbf{x})$ [2,25]. Both distributions should yield low probability in negative pixels. We propose to train $p(\mathbf{x})$ to maximize the likelihood in inliers and to minimize the likelihood in outliers. We derive the upper bound of the desired loss as follows:

$$L_{\mathbf{x}}(\theta) = \mathbb{E}_{\mathbf{x} \in D_{in}}[-\ln p(\mathbf{x})] - \mathbb{E}_{\mathbf{x} \in D_{out}}[-\ln p(\mathbf{x})] \tag{9}$$

$$= \mathbb{E}_{\mathbf{x} \in D_{in}}[-\ln \hat{p}(\mathbf{x})] + \ln Z - \mathbb{E}_{\mathbf{x} \in D_{out}}[-\ln \hat{p}(\mathbf{x})] - \ln Z \tag{10}$$

$$= -\mathbb{E}_{\mathbf{x} \in D_{in}}\left[\ln \sum_i \exp(\mathbf{s}_i)\right] + \mathbb{E}_{\mathbf{x} \in D_{out}}\left[\ln \sum_i \exp(\mathbf{s}_i)\right] \tag{11}$$

$$\leq -\mathbb{E}_{\mathbf{x},\mathbf{y} \in D_{in}}[\mathbf{s}_y] + \mathbb{E}_{\mathbf{x} \in D_{out}}[\ln \sum_i \exp(\mathbf{s}_i)]. \tag{12}$$

Note that we eschew the backpropagation into the normalization constant $Z$, and derive the upper bound according to the following inequality:

$$\ln \sum_i \exp \mathbf{s}_i \geq \max_i \mathbf{s}_i \geq \mathbf{s}_y. \tag{13}$$

Proof of inequality (13) can be easily derived by recalling that log-sum-exp is a smooth upper bound of the max function. By comparing the standard classification loss (7) and the upper bound (12) we realize that minimizing the standard classification loss increases $p(\mathbf{x})$ for inlier pixels. Indeed, minimizing the negative logarithm of softmax output increases the value of logit for the correct class.

Alternatively, $p(\mathbf{x})$ could be trained only on inliers [15,20,45]. This would require sample hallucination via MCMC sampling and back-propagation into the corresponding approximation of $Z$. Such procedure is infeasible for large images. Consequently, we choose to deal with negative samples instead of hallucinated ones and optimize the proposed loss $L_{\mathbf{x}}(\theta)$.

We train the dataset posterior $P(d_{in}|\mathbf{x})$ with the standard discriminative loss [2]:

$$L_{\mathbf{d}}(\theta, \gamma) = \mathbb{E}_{\mathbf{x} \in D_{in}}[-\ln P(d_{in}|\mathbf{x})] + \mathbb{E}_{\mathbf{x} \in D_{out}}[-\ln(P(d_{out}|\mathbf{x}))]. \tag{14}$$

By joining losses $L_{\text{cls}}$, $L_{\mathbf{x}}$ and $L_{\mathbf{d}}$ we obtain the final loss:

$$L(\theta, \gamma) = -\mathbb{E}_{\mathbf{x},\mathbf{y} \in D_{in}}[\ln P(\mathbf{y}|\mathbf{x}) + \ln P(d_{in}|\mathbf{x})]$$
$$- \beta \cdot \mathbb{E}_{\mathbf{x} \in D_{out}}[\ln(P(d_{out}|\mathbf{x})) - \ln \hat{p}(\mathbf{x})]. \tag{15}$$

Hyperparameter $\beta$ controls the impact of negative data to the primary classification task. Note that the final loss (15) omits the first term from $L_{\mathbf{x}}$ (12) in positive pixels. We choose to do so since $\hat{p}(\mathbf{x})$ is implicitly optimized through $L_{cls}$.

Figure 4 illustrates the described training procedure of the proposed open-set recognition model. We prepare the training images by pasting the negative instances atop the standard training images. The resulting mixed-content image [2] is fed to the hybrid model. We obtain the classification output $P(\mathbf{y}|\mathbf{x})$ with softmax. The unnormalized likelihood $\hat{p}(\mathbf{x})$ is obtained through sum-exp operator. We recover $p(d_{in}|\mathbf{x})$ by branching from pre-logit activations. The model outputs are trained by applying the dicriminative loss $L_{cls}$ (7), likelihood loss $L_{\mathbf{x}}$ (12) and dataset posterior loss $L_{\mathbf{d}}$ (14). As proposed, these losses are conveniently joined into a single loss $L(\theta, \gamma)$ (15).

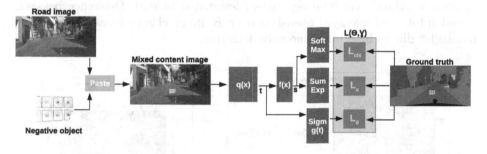

**Fig. 4.** The training procedure of the proposed open-set recognition model. Mixed-content images are fed to the open-set model with three outputs. Each output is optimized according to the compound loss (15)

## 4    Measuring Dense Open-Set Performance

Test datasets for anomaly segmentation either exclusively measure the performance of anomaly detectors [9, 44] or simply report the classification performance [5]. In the latter case, the reported drop in segmentation performance is usually negligible and is explained away by allocation of model capacity for the anomaly detection. We will show that the real impact of anomaly detector on the segmentation performance can be clearly seen only in the open world. Also, the impact is more severe than the small performance drop visible in the closed world.

To properly measure open-set recognition performance, we first select threshold at which the anomaly detector achieves TPR of 95%. This ensures high safety standards for the recognition model. Then, we override the classification in pixels which raise concern according to the thresholded anomaly map. The resulting recognition map has $K + 1$ labels. We compute the recognition performance in open-world using open intersection over union (open-IoU). For the $k$-th class we can compute the proposed open-IoU as:

$$\text{open-IoU}_k = \frac{\text{TP}_k}{\text{TP}_k + \text{FP}_k^{\text{ow}} + \text{FN}_k^{\text{ow}}}, \ \text{FP}_k^{\text{ow}} = \sum_{\substack{i \neq k \\ i=1}}^{K+1} \text{FP}_k^i, \ \text{FN}_k^{\text{ow}} = \sum_{\substack{i \neq k \\ i=1}}^{K+1} \text{FN}_k^i \quad (16)$$

Different that the standard IoU formulation, open-IoU also takes into account false positives and false negatives caused by imperfect anomaly detector. However, we still average open-IoU over $K$ inlier classes. This means that a recognition model which uses a perfect anomaly detector would match segmentation performance in the closed world. This property would not be preserved if we averaged IoU over K+1 classes.

Figure 5 (right) shows the open world confusion matrix. Imperfect anomaly detection impacts recognition performance through increased false positives (designated in yellow) and false negatives (designated in red). Difference between closed mIoU and averaged open-IoU over $K$ inlier classes reveals the performance hit due to inaccurate anomaly detection.

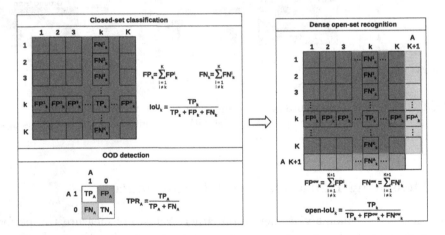

**Fig. 5.** The proposed open intersection over union (open-IoU) takes into account missclassifications in anomalous pixels to accurately measure dense recognition performance in open world (Color figure online)

Measuring performance using the proposed open-IoU requires datasets with K+1 labels. Creating such taxonomy requires substantial resources. Currently, only StreetHazards [23] offers appropriate taxonomy for measuring open-IoU.

## 5  Experiments

We report dense anomaly detection and open-set recognition performance of the proposed DenseHybrid approach, and compare them with the state of the art.

We also explore influence of distance, show computational requirements of the proposed module, and ablate the design choices.

## 5.1  Benchmarks and Datasets

We evaluate performance on standard benchmarks for dense anomaly detection. Fishyscapes [5] considers urban scenarios on a subset of LostAndFound [44] and on Cityscapes validation images with pasted anomalies (FS Static). SegmentMeIfYouCan (SMIYC) [9] moves away from anomaly injection. Instead, appropriate images are collected from the real world and grouped based on the anomaly size into AnomalyTrack (large) and ObstacleTrack (small). Additionally, the benchmark encapsulates all LostAndFound images. Unfortunately, both benchmarks only have binary labels which makes them insufficient for measuring the recognition performance as proposed in Sect. 4. StreetHazards [23] is a synthetic dataset created by CARLA virtual environment. The simulated environment enables smooth anomaly injection and low-cost label extraction. Consequently, the dataset contains $K+1$ labels which makes it suitable for measuring both anomaly detection and dense recognition.

## 5.2  Dense Anomaly Detection

Table 1 shows performance of the proposed hybrid anomaly detector on the SMIYC benchmark [9]. DenseHybrid outperforms contemporary approaches on both AnomalyTrack and ObstacleTrack by a wide margin. Also, the proposed anomaly detector achieves the best FPR on LostAndFound.

**Table 1.** Performance evaluation on the SMIYC benchmark [9]. DenseHybrid outperforms contemporary approaches on Anomaly and Obstacle track by a wide margin, while also achieving the best FPR on LostAndFound

| Method | Aux data | Img rsyn. | AnomalyTrack | | ObstacleTrack | | LAF-noKnown | |
|---|---|---|---|---|---|---|---|---|
| | | | AP | FPR$_{95}$ | AP | FPR$_{95}$ | AP | FPR$_{95}$ |
| SynBoost [4] | ✓ | ✓ | 56.4 | 61.9 | 71.3 | 3.2 | 81.7 | 4.6 |
| Image Resyn. [36] | ✗ | ✓ | 52.3 | 25.9 | 37.7 | 4.7 | 57.1 | 8.8 |
| JSRNet [50] | ✗ | ✓ | 33.6 | 43.9 | 28.1 | 28.9 | 74.2 | 6.6 |
| Road Inpaint. [35] | ✗ | ✓ | – | – | 54.1 | 47.1 | **82.9** | 35.8 |
| Embed. Dens. [5] | ✗ | ✗ | 37.5 | 70.8 | 0.8 | 46.4 | 61.7 | 10.4 |
| ODIN [34] | ✗ | ✗ | 33.1 | 71.7 | 22.1 | 15.3 | 52.9 | 30.0 |
| MC Dropout [29] | ✗ | ✗ | 28.9 | 69.5 | 4.9 | 50.3 | 36.8 | 35.6 |
| Max softmax [24] | ✗ | ✗ | 28.0 | 72.1 | 15.7 | 16.6 | 30.1 | 33.2 |
| Mahalanobis [33] | ✗ | ✗ | 20.0 | 87.0 | 20.9 | 13.1 | 55.0 | 12.9 |
| Void Classifier [5] | ✓ | ✗ | 36.6 | 63.5 | 10.4 | 41.5 | 4.8 | 47.0 |
| DenseHybrid (ours) | ✓ | ✗ | **78.0** | **9.8** | **87.1** | **0.2** | 78.7 | **2.1** |

Table 2 shows performance of the proposed DenseHybrid on Fishyscapes [5]. Our anomaly detector achieves the best results on FS LostAndFound, and the best FPR on FS Static. We achieve these results while having negligible impact on classification task in closed-world. However, in the next section we show that the impact of anomaly detection to recognition performance is much more significant than in the closed world.

**Table 2.** Performance evaluation on the Fishyscapes benchmark [5]. DenseHybrid achieves the best performance on FS LostAndFound and the best FPR on FS Static

| Method | Aux data | Img rsyn. | LostAndFound | | Static | | Closed world |
|---|---|---|---|---|---|---|---|
| | | | AP | FPR$_{95}$ | AP | FPR$_{95}$ | Cityscapes mIoU |
| SynBoost [4] | ✓ | ✓ | 43.2 | 15.8 | 72.6 | 18.8 | **81.4** |
| Image Resyn. [36] | ✗ | ✓ | 5.7 | 48.1 | 29.6 | 27.1 | 81.4 |
| Standardized ML [28] | ✗ | ✗ | 31.1 | 21.5 | 53.1 | 19.6 | 80.3 |
| Embed. Dens. [5] | ✗ | ✗ | 4.7 | 24.4 | 62.1 | 17.4 | 80.3 |
| Max softmax [24] | ✗ | ✗ | 1.77 | 44.9 | 12.9 | 39.8 | 80.3 |
| Dirichlet prior [39] | ✓ | ✗ | 34.3 | 47.4 | **84.6** | 30.0 | 70.5 |
| OOD Head [2] | ✓ | ✗ | 30.9 | 22.2 | 84.0 | 10.3 | 77.3 |
| Void Classifier [5] | ✓ | ✗ | 10.3 | 22.1 | 45.0 | 19.4 | 70.4 |
| Mutual information [40] | ✓ | ✗ | 9.8 | 38.5 | 48.7 | 15.5 | 73.8 |
| DenseHybrid (ours) | ✓ | ✗ | **43.9** | **6.2** | 72.3 | **5.5** | 81.0 |

Table 3 explores sensitivity of anomaly detection with respect to distance from the camera. We perform all these experiments on LostAndFound since it includes disparity maps. Still, due to errors in available disparities, we limit our analysis to the first 50 m from the camera. The proposed DenseHybrid approach achieves accurate results even at large distances from the vehicle.

**Table 3.** Anomaly detection performance at different distances from camera. Our DenseHybrid based on DeeplabV3+ with WRN38 backbone [55] accurately detects anomalies at different ranges

| Method | Metric | Range in meters | | | | | | | | |
|---|---|---|---|---|---|---|---|---|---|---|
| | | 5–10 | 10–15 | 15–20 | 20–25 | 25–30 | 30–35 | 35–40 | 40–45 | 45–50 |
| Max-softmax [24] | AP | 28.7 | 28.8 | 26.0 | 25.1 | 29.0 | 26.2 | 29.6 | 31.7 | 33.7 |
| | FPR$_{95}$ | 16.4 | 29.7 | 28.8 | 44.2 | 41.3 | 47.8 | 44.7 | 43.2 | 45.3 |
| Max-logit [23] | AP | 76.1 | 73.9 | 78.2 | 69.6 | 72.6 | 70.2 | 71.0 | 74.0 | 73.9 |
| | FPR$_{95}$ | 5.4 | 16.2 | 5.9 | 12.8 | 9.5 | 10.0 | 9.8 | 9.8 | 11.0 |
| SynBoost [4] | AP | **93.7** | 78.7 | 76.9 | 70.0 | 65.6 | 58.5 | 59.8 | 60.0 | 53.3 |
| | FPR$_{95}$ | **0.2** | 17.7 | 25.0 | 23.3 | 18.8 | 27.4 | 25.4 | 25.8 | 29.9 |
| DenseHybrid (ours) | AP | 90.7 | **89.8** | **92.9** | **89.1** | **89.5** | **87.7** | **85.0** | **85.6** | **82.1** |
| | FPR$_{95}$ | 0.3 | **1.1** | **0.6** | **1.4** | **1.4** | **2.5** | **3.7** | **4.7** | **6.3** |

## 5.3  Dense Open-Set Recognition

By fusing a properly thresholded anomaly detector with the dense classifier, we obtain a dense open-set recognition model (Fig. 3). The resulting model detects anomalous scene parts, while correctly classifying the rest of the scene.

To measure the dense recognition performance, we create two test folds based on towns t5 and t6 from StreetHazards test. Then, we select anomaly threshold on t6 and use it to measure the proposed open-mIoU on t5. We switch the folds and repeat the procedure. We compute the weighted average based on image count to obtain the final test set open-mIoU.

Table 4 shows performance of our dense recognition models on StreetHazards. The left part of the table considers anomaly detection where DenseHybrid achieves the best performance. The right part of the table considers dense recognition performance. Our model outperforms other contemporary approaches despite lower classification performance in the closed world. Note that the performance drop between the closed and the open set is significant. The models achieve over 60% mIoU in closed world while the open world performance peeks at 46%. Hence, we conclude that even the best anomaly detectors are still insufficient for matching the closed world performance in open-world. Researchers should strive to close this gap in order to improve the safety of recognition systems in the real world.

**Table 4.** Performance evaluation on StreetHazards [23]. DenseHybrid achieves the best anomaly detection performance. The corresponding open-set recognition model yields the best performance measured by open-mIoU (Sect. 4)

| Method | Aux. data | Anomaly detection | | | Closed world | Open world | | |
|---|---|---|---|---|---|---|---|---|
| | | AP | FPR$_{95}$ | AUC | $\overline{IoU}$ | o-$\overline{IoU}$-t5 | o-$\overline{IoU}$-t6 | o-$\overline{IoU}$ |
| SynthCP [51] | ✗ | 9.3 | 28.4 | 88.5 | – | – | – | – |
| Dropout [29] [51] | ✗ | 7.5 | 79.4 | 69.9 | – | – | – | – |
| TRADI [19] | ✗ | 7.2 | 25.3 | 89.2 | – | – | – | – |
| OVNNI [18] | ✗ | 12.6 | 22.2 | 91.2 | 54.6 | – | – | – |
| SO+H [21] | ✗ | 12.7 | 25.2 | 91.7 | 59.7 | – | – | – |
| DML [8] | ✗ | 14.7 | 17.3 | 93.7 | – | – | – | – |
| MSP [24] | ✗ | 7.5 | 27.9 | 90.1 | 65.0 | 32.7 | 40.2 | 35.1 |
| ML [23] | ✗ | 11.6 | 22.5 | 92.4 | 65.0 | 39.6 | 44.5 | 41.2 |
| ODIN [34] | ✗ | 7.0 | 28.7 | 90.0 | 65.0 | 26.4 | 33.9 | 28.8 |
| ReAct [49] | ✗ | 10.9 | 21.2 | 92.3 | 62.7 | 33.0 | 36.2 | 34.0 |
| Energy [37] | ✓ | 12.9 | 18.2 | 93.0 | 63.3 | 41.7 | 44.9 | 42.7 |
| Outlier Exposure [25] | ✓ | 14.6 | 17.7 | 94.0 | 61.7 | 43.7 | 44.1 | 43.8 |
| OOD-Head [3] | ✓ | 19.7 | 56.2 | 88.8 | **66.6** | 33.7 | 34.3 | 33.9 |
| OH*MSP [2] | ✓ | 18.8 | 30.9 | 89.7 | **66.6** | 43.3 | 44.2 | 43.6 |
| DenseHybrid (ours) | ✓ | **30.2** | **13.0** | **95.0** | 63.0 | **46.1** | **45.3** | **45.8** |

Figure 6 visualises dense anomaly and recognition maps on StreetHazards. Our recognition model significantly outperforms the max-logit baseline [23].

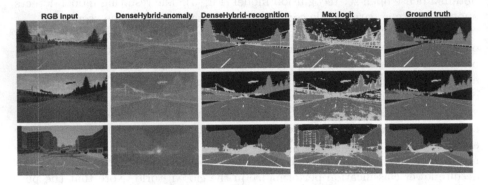

**Fig. 6.** Visualisation of dense open-set recognition performance on StreetHazards. DenseHybrid significantly outperforms the max-logit baseline [23]

### 5.4 Inference Speed

Table 5 shows computational overhead of the proposed DenseHybrid anomaly detector over the baseline segmentation model on two megapixels images. Dense-Hybrid has negligible computational overhead of 0.1 GFLOPs and 2.8 ms. Our results are averaged over 200 runs on NVIDIA RTX3090. These experiments also suggest that image resynthesis is not applicable for real-time inference.

**Table 5.** Computational overhead of the proposed DenseHybrid anomaly detector when inferring with RTX3090 on two megapixel images

| Method | Resynth. | Infer. time (ms) | Frames per sec. | GFLOPs |
|---|---|---|---|---|
| SynBoost [4] | ✓ | 1055.5 | <1 | – |
| SynthCP [51] | ✓ | 146.9 | <1 | 4551.1 |
| LDN-121 [30] | ✗ | 60.9 | 16.4 | 202.3 |
| LDN-121 + SML [28] | ✗ | 75.4 | 13.3 | 202.6 |
| LDN-121 + DenseHybrid (ours) | ✗ | **63.7** | **15.7** | **202.4** |

### 5.5 Impact of Anomaly Detector Design

Table 6 compares the proposed DenseHybrid approach with its generative and discriminative components – $\hat{p}(\mathbf{x})$ and $P(d_{in}|\mathbf{x})$. The hybrid anomaly score based on the ratio of these two distributions outperforms each of the two components. The results are averaged over the last three epochs.

**Table 6.** Validation of DenseHybrid components on Fishyscapes validation set

| Anomaly detector | FS LostAndFound | | FS static | |
|---|---|---|---|---|
| | AP | FPR$_{95}$ | AP | FPR$_{95}$ |
| Discriminative $(1 - P(d_{in}|\mathbf{x}))$ | $42.9 \pm 4.2$ | $42.1 \pm 7.0$ | $47.8 \pm 5.0$ | $41.6 \pm 8.3$ |
| Generative $\hat{p}(\mathbf{x})$ | $60.5 \pm 2.6$ | $7.4 \pm 0.8$ | $54.2 \pm 2.1$ | $6.2 \pm 0.7$ |
| Hybrid $(1 - P(d_{in}|\mathbf{x}))/\hat{p}(\mathbf{x})$ | $\mathbf{63.8 \pm 2.9}$ | $\mathbf{6.1 \pm 0.7}$ | $\mathbf{60.0 \pm 2.0}$ | $\mathbf{4.9 \pm 0.6}$ |

## 5.6   Implementation Details

We adapt the standard segmentation networks [30,55] to enable co-operation with our hybrid anomaly detector. We append an additional branch $g_\gamma$ which is in our case BN-ReLU-Conv1x1. The additional branch computes the discriminative anomaly output. We obtain generative anomaly output by computing sum of exponentiated logits. We build our recognition models based on dense classifiers. We fine-tune all our models on mixed content images with pasted negative instances from ADE20k. In the case of SMIYC we fine-tune LDN-121 [30] for 10 epochs on images from Cityscapes [12], Vistas [42] and Wilddash2 [52]. In the case of Fishyscapes we use DeepLabV3+ with WideResNet38 [55]. We fine-tune the model for 10 epochs on Cityscapes. We train LDN-121 on Street-Hazards for 120 epochs in closed world and then fine-tune the recognition model on mixed-content images. Other details are available in the supplement.

## 6   Conclusion

Discriminative and generative approaches to dense anomaly detection assume different failure modes. We propose to achieve a synergy of these two approaches by fusing the data posterior and the data likelihood derived from the standard discriminative model. The proposed hybrid setup relies on unnormalized distributions. Hence, we try to eschew evaluation of the intractable normalization constant both during training and inference. The proposed DenseHybrid architecture yields state-of-the-art performance on the standard anomaly segmentation benchmarks as well as competitive dense recognition performance in the open world. The latter is measured with the novel open-mIoU score which takes into account classification in both inliers and anomalous pixels. Future work should focus on reducing the revealed performance gap between closed-world and open-world recognition in order to improve the progress toward safe autonomous driving systems.

**Acknowledgement.** This work has been supported by Croatian Science Foundation grant IP-2020-02-5851 ADEPT, as well as by European Regional Development Fund grants KK.01.1.1.01.0009 DATACROSS and KK.01.2.1.02.0119 A A-Unit. We thank Marin Oršić for insightful discussions during early stages of this work.

# References

1. van Amersfoort, J., Smith, L., Jesson, A., Key, O., Gal, Y.: On feature collapse and deep kernel learning for single forward pass uncertainty. arXiv preprint arXiv:2102.11409 (2021)
2. Bevandić, P., Krešo, I., Oršić, M., Šegvić, S.: Dense open-set recognition based on training with noisy negative images. Image Vis. Comput. **124**, 104490 (2022)
3. Bevandic, P., Kreso, I., Orsic, M., Segvic, S.: Simultaneous semantic segmentation and outlier detection in presence of domain shift. In: 41st DAGM German Conference, DAGM GCPR (2019). https://doi.org/10.1007/978-3-030-33676-9_3
4. Biase, G.D., Blum, H., Siegwart, R., Cadena, C.: Pixel-wise anomaly detection in complex driving scenes. In: Computer Vision and Pattern Recognition, CVPR (2021)
5. Blum, H., Sarlin, P.-E., Nieto, J., Siegwart, R., Cadena, C.: The Fishyscapes benchmark: measuring blind spots in semantic segmentation. Int. J. Comput. Vis. **129**(11), 3119–3135 (2021). https://doi.org/10.1007/s11263-021-01511-6
6. Blum, H., Sarlin, P., Nieto, J.I., Siegwart, R., Cadena, C.: Fishyscapes: a benchmark for safe semantic segmentation in autonomous driving. In: 2019 IEEE/CVF International Conference on Computer Vision Workshops, pp. 2403–2412. IEEE (2019). https://doi.org/10.1109/ICCVW.2019.00294
7. Boult, T.E., Cruz, S., Dhamija, A.R., Günther, M., Henrydoss, J., Scheirer, W.J.: Learning and the unknown: surveying steps toward open world recognition. In: The Thirty-Third AAAI Conference on Artificial Intelligence, AAAI 2019, The Thirty-First Innovative Applications of Artificial Intelligence Conference, IAAI 2019, The Ninth AAAI Symposium on Educational Advances in Artificial Intelligence, EAAI 2019, Honolulu, Hawaii, USA, January 27–1 February 2019, pp. 9801–9807. AAAI Press (2019)
8. Cen, J., Yun, P., Cai, J., Wang, M.Y., Liu, M.: Deep metric learning for open world semantic segmentation. In: Proceedings of the IEEE/CVF International Conference on Computer Vision (ICCV), pp. 15333–15342, October 2021
9. Chan, R., et al.: Segmentmeifyoucan: a benchmark for anomaly segmentation. CoRR abs/2104.14812 (2021)
10. Chan, R., Rottmann, M., Gottschalk, H.: Entropy maximization and meta classification for out-of-distribution detection in semantic segmentation. In: International Conference on Computer Vision ICCV (2021)
11. Chao, P., Kao, C., Ruan, Y., Huang, C., Lin, Y.: HarDNet: a low memory traffic network. In: 2019 IEEE/CVF International Conference on Computer Vision, ICCV, pp. 3551–3560. IEEE (2019). https://doi.org/10.1109/ICCV.2019.00365
12. Cordts, M., et al.: The cityscapes dataset for semantic urban scene understanding. In: IEEE Conference on Computer Vision and Pattern Recognition CVPR (2016)
13. DeVries, T., Taylor, G.W.: Learning confidence for out-of-distribution detection in neural networks. CoRR abs/1802.04865 (2018)
14. Dhamija, A.R., Günther, M., Boult, T.E.: Reducing network agnostophobia. In: Annual Conference on Neural Information Processing Systems 2018 NeurIPS (2018)

15. Du, Y., Mordatch, I.: Implicit generation and modeling with energy based models. In: Wallach, H.M., Larochelle, H., Beygelzimer, A., d'Alché-Buc, F., Fox, E.B., Garnett, R. (eds.) Advances in Neural Information Processing Systems 32: Annual Conference on Neural Information Processing Systems 2019, NeurIPS 2019, 8–14 December 2019, Vancouver, BC, Canada, pp. 3603–3613 (2019). https://proceed ings.neurips.cc/paper/2019/hash/378a063b8fdb1db941e34f4bde584c7d-Abstract. html

16. Everingham, M., Eslami, S.M.A., Gool, L.V., Williams, C.K.I., Winn, J.M., Zisserman, A.: The pascal visual object classes challenge: a retrospective. Int. J. Comput. Vis. **111**(1), 98–136 (2015)

17. Farabet, C., Couprie, C., Najman, L., LeCun, Y.: Learning hierarchical features for scene labeling. IEEE Trans. Pattern Anal. Mach. Intell. **35**(8), 1915–1929 (2013)

18. Franchi, G., Bursuc, A., Aldea, E., Dubuisson, S., Bloch, I.: One versus all for deep neural network incertitude (OVNNI) quantification. CoRR abs/2006.00954 (2020)

19. Franchi, G., Bursuc, A., Aldea, E., Dubuisson, S., Bloch, I.: TRADI: tracking deep neural network weight distributions. In: Vedaldi, A., Bischof, H., Brox, T., Frahm, J.-M. (eds.) ECCV 2020. LNCS, vol. 12362, pp. 105–121. Springer, Cham (2020). https://doi.org/10.1007/978-3-030-58520-4_7

20. Grathwohl, W., Wang, K., Jacobsen, J., Duvenaud, D., Norouzi, M., Swersky, K.: Your classifier is secretly an energy based model and you should treat it like one. In: 8th International Conference on Learning Representations, ICLR 2020, 26–30 April 2020, Addis Ababa, Ethiopia (2020)

21. Grcić, M., Bevandić, P., Šegvić, S.: Dense open-set recognition with synthetic outliers generated by real NVP. In: 16th International Joint Conference on Computer Vision, Imaging and Computer Graphics Theory and Applications, VISIGRAPP (2021)

22. Hawkins, D.M.: Identification of Outliers. Monographs on Applied Probability and Statistics, Springer (1980). https://doi.org/10.1007/978-94-015-3994-4, https://doi.org/10.1007/978-94-015-3994-4

23. Hendrycks, D., Basart, S., Mazeika, M., Mostajabi, M., Steinhardt, J., Song, D.: Scaling out-of-distribution detection for real-world settings. arXiv preprint arXiv:1911.11132 (2019)

24. Hendrycks, D., Gimpel, K.: A baseline for detecting misclassified and out-of-distribution examples in neural networks. In: 5th International Conference on Learning Representations, ICLR (2017)

25. Hendrycks, D., Mazeika, M., Dietterich, T.G.: Deep anomaly detection with outlier exposure. In: 7th International Conference on Learning Representations ICLR (2019)

26. Hong, Y., Pan, H., Sun, W., Jia, Y.: Deep dual-resolution networks for real-time and accurate semantic segmentation of road scenes. CoRR abs/2101.06085 (2021)

27. Jiang, D., Sun, S., Yu, Y.: Revisiting flow generative models for out-of-distribution detection. In: International Conference on Learning Representations (2022)

28. Jung, S., Lee, J., Gwak, D., Choi, S., Choo, J.: Standardized max logits: a simple yet effective approach for identifying unexpected road obstacles in urban-scene segmentation. In: International Conference on Computer Vision, ICCV (2021)

29. Kendall, A., Gal, Y.: What uncertainties do we need in Bayesian deep learning for computer vision? In: Neural Information Processing Systems (2017)

30. Kreso, I., Krapac, J., Segvic, S.: Efficient ladder-style DenseNets for semantic segmentation of large images. IEEE Trans. Intell. Transp. Syst. **22**, 4951–4961 (2021)

31. Lakshminarayanan, B., Pritzel, A., Blundell, C.: Simple and scalable predictive uncertainty estimation using deep ensembles. In: Advances in Neural Information Processing Systems 30: Annual Conference on Neural Information Processing Systems, pp. 6402–6413 (2017)
32. Lee, K., Lee, H., Lee, K., Shin, J.: Training confidence-calibrated classifiers for detecting out-of-distribution samples. In: 6th International Conference on Learning Representations, ICLR (2018)
33. Lee, K., Lee, K., Lee, H., Shin, J.: A simple unified framework for detecting out-of-distribution samples and adversarial attacks. In: Neural Information Processing Systems, NeurIPS (2018)
34. Liang, S., Li, Y., Srikant, R.: Enhancing the reliability of out-of-distribution image detection in neural networks. In: 6th International Conference on Learning Representations, ICLR (2018)
35. Lis, K., Honari, S., Fua, P., Salzmann, M.: Detecting road obstacles by erasing them. CoRR abs/2012.13633 (2020)
36. Lis, K., Nakka, K.K., Fua, P., Salzmann, M.: Detecting the unexpected via image resynthesis. In: International Conference on Computer Vision, ICCV (2019)
37. Liu, W., Wang, X., Owens, J.D., Li, Y.: Energy-based out-of-distribution detection. In: NeurIPS (2020)
38. Lucas, T., Shmelkov, K., Alahari, K., Schmid, C., Verbeek, J.: Adaptive density estimation for generative models. In: Neural Information Processing Systems (2019)
39. Malinin, A., Gales, M.J.F.: Predictive uncertainty estimation via prior networks. In: Annual Conference on Neural Information Processing Systems (2018)
40. Mukhoti, J., Gal, Y.: Evaluating Bayesian deep learning methods for semantic segmentation. CoRR abs/1811.12709 (2018)
41. Nalisnick, E.T., Matsukawa, A., Teh, Y.W., Görür, D., Lakshminarayanan, B.: Do deep generative models know what they don't know? In: 7th International Conference on Learning Representations, ICLR (2019)
42. Neuhold, G., Ollmann, T., Bulò, S.R., Kontschieder, P.: The mapillary vistas dataset for semantic understanding of street scenes. In: IEEE International Conference on Computer Vision, ICCV (2017)
43. Orsic, M., Segvic, S.: Efficient semantic segmentation with pyramidal fusion. Patt. Recognit. **110**, 107611 (2021). https://doi.org/10.1016/j.patcog.2020.107611
44. Pinggera, P., Ramos, S., Gehrig, S., Franke, U., Rother, C., Mester, R.: Lost and found: detecting small road hazards for self-driving vehicles. In: International Conference on Intelligent Robots and Systems, IROS (2016)
45. Salakhutdinov, R., Hinton, G.: Deep Boltzmann machines. In: Twelth International Conference on Artificial Intelligence and Statistics. PMLR (2009)
46. Scherreik, M.D., Rigling, B.D.: Open set recognition for automatic target classification with rejection. IEEE Trans. Aerosp. Electron. Syst. **52**(2), 632–642 (2016)
47. Serrà, J., Álvarez, D., Gómez, V., Slizovskaia, O., Núñez, J.F., Luque, J.: Input complexity and out-of-distribution detection with likelihood-based generative models. In: 8th International Conference on Learning Representations, ICLR (2020)
48. Sokolova, M., Lapalme, G.: A systematic analysis of performance measures for classification tasks. Inf. Process. Manag. **45**(4), 427–437 (2009)
49. Sun, Y., Guo, C., Li, Y.: React: Out-of-distribution detection with rectified activations. In: NeurIPS (2021)
50. Vojir, T., Šipka, T., Aljundi, R., Chumerin, N., Reino, D.O., Matas, J.: Road anomaly detection by partial image reconstruction with segmentation coupling. In: International Conference on Computer Vision, ICCV (2021)

51. Xia, Y., Zhang, Y., Liu, F., Shen, W., Yuille, A.L.: Synthesize then compare: detecting failures and anomalies for semantic segmentation. In: Vedaldi, A., Bischof, H., Brox, T., Frahm, J.-M. (eds.) ECCV 2020. LNCS, vol. 12346, pp. 145–161. Springer, Cham (2020). https://doi.org/10.1007/978-3-030-58452-8_9

52. Zendel, O., Honauer, K., Murschitz, M., Steininger, D., Dominguez, G.F.: Wilddash - creating hazard-aware benchmarks. In: European Conference on Computer Vision (ECCV) (2018)

53. Zhang, L.H., Goldstein, M., Ranganath, R.: Understanding failures in out-of-distribution detection with deep generative models. In: 38th International Conference on Machine Learning, ICML (2021)

54. Zhao, Z., Cao, L., Lin, K.: Revealing distributional vulnerability of explicit discriminators by implicit generators. CoRR abs/2108.09976 (2021)

55. Zhu, Y., Sapra, K., Reda, F.A., Shih, K.J., Newsam, S.D., Tao, A., Catanzaro, B.: Improving semantic segmentation via video propagation and label relaxation. In: IEEE Conference on Computer Vision and Pattern Recognition, CVPR 2019, 16–20 June 2019, Long Beach, CA, USA, pp. 8856–8865. Computer Vision Foundation/IEEE (2019)

# Rethinking Confidence Calibration
# for Failure Prediction

Fei Zhu[1,2], Zhen Cheng[1,2], Xu-Yao Zhang[1,2(✉)], and Cheng-Lin Liu[1,2]

[1] NLPR, Institute of Automation, Chinese Academy of Sciences,
Beijing 100190, China
{zhufei2018,chengzhen2019}@ia.ac.cn, {xyz,liucl}@nlpr.ia.ac.cn
[2] University of Chinese Academy of Sciences, Beijing 100049, China

**Abstract.** Reliable confidence estimation for the predictions is important in many safety-critical applications. However, modern deep neural networks are often overconfident for their incorrect predictions. Recently, many calibration methods have been proposed to alleviate the overconfidence problem. With calibrated confidence, a primary and practical purpose is to detect misclassification errors by filtering out low-confidence predictions (known as failure prediction). In this paper, we find a general, widely-existed but actually-neglected phenomenon that most confidence calibration methods are useless or harmful for failure prediction. We investigate this problem and reveal that popular confidence calibration methods often lead to worse confidence separation between correct and incorrect samples, making it more difficult to decide whether to trust a prediction or not. Finally, inspired by the natural connection between flat minima and confidence separation, we propose a simple hypothesis: flat minima is beneficial for failure prediction. We verify this hypothesis via extensive experiments and further boost the performance by combining two different flat minima techniques. Our code is available at https://github.com/Impression2805/FMFP.

**Keywords:** Failure prediction · Confidence calibration · Flat minima · Uncertainty · Misclassification detection · Selective classification

## 1 Introduction

Deep neural networks (DNNs), especially vision models, has been widely deployed in risk-sensitive applications such as computer-aided medical diagnosis [11,44], autonomous driving [2,29], and robotics [38]. For such applications, besides the prediction accuracy, another crucial requirement is to provide *reliable confidence* for users to make safe decisions. For example, an autonomous driving car should rely more on other sensors or trigger an alarm when the detection

**Supplementary Information** The online version contains supplementary material available at https://doi.org/10.1007/978-3-031-19806-9_30.

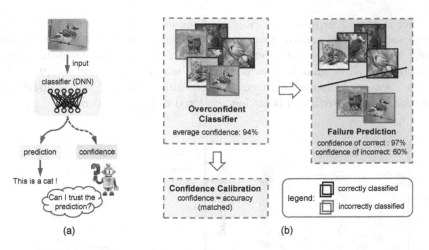

**Fig. 1.** Confidence calibration aims to reduce the mismatch between a model's confidence and accuracy from the perspective of global statistics, while failure prediction is to distinguish correct from incorrect predictions from the perspective of confidence separability. They both focus on in-distribution data and share the same motivation to provide reliable confidence for trustworthy AI. Therefore, we explore a natural but ignored question: is calibrated confidence useful for failure prediction?

network is unable to confidently predict obstructions [29]. Another example is the control should be handed over to human doctors when the confidence of a disease diagnosis network is low [44]. Unfortunately, modern DNNs are generally *overconfident* for their predictions, and can easily assign high confidence for misclassified samples [7,15,17,22]. The overconfident issue makes DNNs models untrustworthy, and therefore brings great concerns when DNNs are deployed in practical applications.

Recently, many approaches have been developed to alleviate the overconfidence problem by calibrating the confidence, *i.e.*, matching the accuracy and confidence scores to reflect the predictive uncertainty [43]. Specifically, one category of approaches [20,41,47,48,54,61,66,68,70,75] aim to learn well-calibrated models during training. For instance, mixup [61], label smoothing [48] and focal loss [47] have been demonstrated to be effective for confidence calibration. Another class of approaches [15,16,35,53,56,58] use post-processing techniques to calibrate DNNs. The most famous post-processing calibration method is temperature scaling [15] which learns a single scalar parameter to calibrate the probabilities.

In this paper, we study a natural but ignored question: *can we use calibrated confidence to detect misclassified samples by filtering out low-confidence predictions?* This, perhaps, is the most direct and practical way to evaluate the quality of the uncertainty. Actually, this problem is studied in the literature as *failure prediction* (also known as misclassification detection or selective classification) [7,14,22], whose purpose is to determine whether the prediction yielded by a classifier is correct or incorrect. Note that failure prediction aims to detect the erroneously classified natural example from seen class (*e.g.*, misclassified samples in test dataset), which is different from the widely studied out-of-distribution detection [23,37,39] that focuses on judging whether an input sample is from unseen classes. Compared with confidence calibration and out-of-distribution detection, failure prediction is far less explored in the literature.

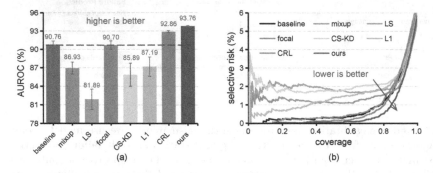

**Fig. 2.** A comparison of (a) AUROC and (b) risk-coverage curves. We observed that many popular confidence calibration methods are useless or harmful for failure prediction. We propose a simple flat minima based method that can outperform the state-of-the-art failure prediction method CRL [45]. ResNet110 [19] on CIFAR-10 [33].

As shown in Fig. 1, confidence calibration and failure prediction both focus on the confidence of in-distribution data and share the same motivation that enables the model to provide reliable confidence to make safe decisions. Therefore, common wisdom in the community suggests that calibrated confidence could be useful for failure prediction. However, we find a surprising pathology: many popular confidence calibration methods (including both training-time [24,48,54,61,68,70] and post-processing [15] calibration methods) are more of a hindrance than a help for failure prediction, as illustrated in Fig. 2. Empirical study shows that those methods often reduce overconfidence by simply aligning the accuracy and average confidence. Such calibration could lead to worse separability between correct and misclassified samples, which is harmful for failure prediction. Consequently, one can not effectively detect misclassified samples by filtering out low-confidence predictions based on the calibrated confidence.

Finally, how can we improve the failure prediction performance of DNNs? Intuitively, failure prediction requires better discrimination between the confidence of correct and incorrect samples, which would increase the difficulty of changing the correct samples to be incorrect due to the larger confidence margins. Interestingly, this is closely related to the notion of *"flatness"* in DNNs, which reflects how sensitive the correct samples become misclassified when perturbing the model parameters [12,27,28]. Inspired by the natural connection between flat minima and confidence separation, we propose a simple hypothesis: *flat minima is beneficial for failure prediction*. We verify this hypothesis by extensive experiments and propose a simple and effective technique that combines different kinds of flat methods to achieve state-of-the-art performance on failure prediction.

**Contributions.** Motivated by the widely confirmed confidence calibration effect of recently proposed techniques, we rethink the confidence reliability by evaluating them on the challenging and practical failure prediction task. Surprisingly, we find that they often have negative effect on failure prediction. From a detailed analysis, we identify a compounding less-separability effect of training-time calibration methods [31,40,48,61,70], and further find that failure prediction can not be improved by post-hoc calibration strategies like temperature scaling [15]. Finally, inspired by the connection between flat minima [12,27,28] and confidence separation, we propose to find flat minima to significantly reduce the confidence of misclassified samples while maintaining the confidence of correct samples. Extensive experiments show the strong performance of our method on both failure prediction and confidence calibration.

## 2 Problem Formulation and Background

Considering the multi-class classification problem, we assume a sample $(x, y)$ is drawn *i.i.d.* from an unknown joint distribution over $\mathcal{X} \times \mathcal{Y}$ where $\mathcal{X} = \mathbb{R}^d$ donates the feature space and $\mathcal{Y} = \{1, 2, ..., k\}$ is a label space. Utilizing a standard softmax function, a deep neural network classifier $f : \mathcal{X} \to \mathcal{Y}$ produces a probability distribution over $k$ classes. Specifically, given an input $x$, $f$ produces the predicted class probabilities $\hat{p} = \hat{P}(y|x, \theta)$, where $\theta$ is the parameters of the classification model. With these probabilities, $\hat{y} = \arg\max_{y \in \mathcal{Y}} \hat{P}(y|x, \theta)$ can be returned as the predicted class and the associated probability $\hat{p} = \max_{y \in \mathcal{Y}} \hat{P}(y|x, \theta)$, *i.e.*, the maximum class probability, can be viewed as the predicted confidence.

### 2.1 Confidence Calibration

**Definitions and Notation.** Intuitively, the predictive confidence of a well-calibrated model could be indicative of the actual likelihood of correctness [15]. For example, if a calibrated model predicts a set of inputs $x$ to be class $y$ with 40% probability, then we expect 40% of the inputs indeed belong to class $y$. Formally, a model is perfectly calibrated if [15,36]:

$$P(\hat{y} = y|\hat{p} = p^*) = p^*, \forall p^* \in [0, 1]. \tag{1}$$

The most commonly used calibration metric is the Expected Calibration Error (ECE) [50], which approximates the miscalibration by binning the confidence in $[0, 1]$ under $M$ equally-spaced intervals *i.e.*, $\{B_m\}_{m=1}^M$. Then the miscalibration is estimated by taking the expectation of the mismatch between the accuracy and averaged confidence in each bin: $\text{ECE} = \sum_{m=1}^M \frac{|B_m|}{n} |\text{acc}(B_m) - \text{avgConf}(B_m)|$, where $n$ is the number of all samples. Alternatives to ECE include the negative log likelihood (NLL) and brier score [3].

**Improving Calibration.** Many strategies have been proposed to address the miscalibration of modern DNNs. (1) One category of approaches [47,48,54,61, 66,68,70,75] aim to learn well-calibrated models during training. For example, several works [61,73,74] found that the predicted scores of DNNs trained with mixup [72] are better calibrated. Muller et al. [48] showed the favorable calibration effect of label smoothing. Mukhoti et al. [47] demonstrated that focal loss [40] can automatically learn well-calibrated models. CS-KD [70] calibrates over-confident predictions by penalizing the predictive distribution between the samples within the same class. Recently, Joo et al. [31] explored the effect of explicit regularization strategies (e.g., $L_p$ norm in the logits space) for calibration. (2) Another class of approaches [15,16,35,53,56,58] rescal the predictions in a post-hoc manner. Among them, temperature scaling [15] is a effective and simple technique, which has inspired various post-processing approaches [34,46,58].

**Empirical Studies of Calibration.** In addition to the calibration strategies, there have been some empirical studies on calibration. Guo et al. [15] observed that larger networks tend to be less calibrated, even as classification accuracy is improved. Ovadia et al. [52] studied the calibration under distribution shift and empirically found the generally existing performance drop of different calibration methods under distribution shift. More recently, Wang et al. [65] found that it is harder to further calibrate the model with temperature scaling if it has been trained with regularization methods. Minderer et al. [43] found that the most recent non-convolutional models [10,62] are well-calibrated, suggesting that architecture is a major factor of calibration performance. Differently from those works, we rethink the confidence calibration for failure prediction.

## 2.2 Failure Prediction

**Definitions and Notation.** Failure prediction, also known as misclassification detection [22] or ordinal ranking [45], focus on distinguishing incorrect from correct predictions based on their confidence ranking. Intuitively, if the associated confidence of each misclassified sample is lower than that of any correctly classified samples, we can successfully predict each error made by the classification model at inference time. Formally, an optimal ordinal ranking model should reflect the following relationship for every two samples $(\boldsymbol{x}_i, y_i)$ and $(\boldsymbol{x}_j, y_j)$:

$$\kappa(\hat{\boldsymbol{p}}_i|\boldsymbol{x}_i, \boldsymbol{\theta}) \geq \kappa(\hat{\boldsymbol{p}}_j|\boldsymbol{x}_j, \boldsymbol{\theta}) \iff P(\hat{y}_i = y_i|\boldsymbol{x}_i) \geq P(\hat{y}_j = y_j|\boldsymbol{x}_j), \qquad (2)$$

where $\kappa$ denotes a confidence-rate function (e.g., the maximum class probability) that assess the degree of confidence of the predictions. Then, with a predefined threshold $\delta \in \mathbb{R}^+$, the users can reject the erroneously classification results based on the following decision function $g$:

$$g(\boldsymbol{x}) = \begin{cases} \text{accept, if } \kappa(\boldsymbol{x}) \geq \delta, \\ \text{reject, otherwise.} \end{cases} \qquad (3)$$

Common metrics for failure prediction are the risk-coverage curve (AURC), the normalized AURC (E-AURC) [14,45], the false positive rate at 95% true positive rate (FPR-95%TPR), and the area under the receiver operating characteristic curve (AUROC). In addition, there are some other metrics [22] to imply how the correct and incorrect predictions are separated.

**Improving Failure Prediction.** For DNNs, Hendrycks *et al.* [22] firstly established a standard **baseline** for failure prediction by using maximum softmax probability. Trust-Score [30] adopts the similarity between the classifier and a nearest-neighbor classifier as a confidence measure. The main drawback of Trust-Score is the lack of practicality and scalability in high-dimensional spaces. Some works [7,42] formulate the failure prediction as a supervised binary classification problem. Technically, ConfidNet [7,8] and SS [42] train auxiliary models to predict confidence by learning the misclassified samples in training set. However, they may fail when the model has a high training accuracy, in which few or even no misclassified examples will exist in the training set. CRL [45] improves failure prediction by regularizing the model to learn an ordinal ranking relationship based on the historical correct rate during training. To the best of our knowledge, there are only a few works for failure prediction and no method can significantly or fairly outperform the baseline [22].

**Why Revisit Confidence Calibration for Failure Prediction?** On the one hand, confidence calibration and failure prediction both focus on the confidence of in-distribution data and share the same motivation to provide reliable confidence for making safer decisions. From a practical perspective, with a calibrated classifier in hand, one natural way to verify its trustworthiness is to filter out predictions with low confidence. On the other hand, confidence calibration has drawn significant attention from the machine learning community, including improving calibration [15,48,61,70], empirical studies of model calibration [15,43,52,66] and measures of model calibration [3,16,51,64]. However, there are few works for failure prediction, which is a practical, important, yet somewhat under-appreciated area of research. Therefore, revisiting calibration from the perspective of failure prediction not only helps understand the effect of calibration but also benefits the investigation of failure prediction.

## 3    Does Calibration Help Failure Prediction?

In recent years, there is a surge of research focused on alleviating the overconfidence problem of modern DNNs. As shown by many empirical results, existing methods do help the calibration of DNNs. In this section, we empirically investigate the reliability of the calibrated confidence for failure prediction.

### 3.1    Experimental Setup

**Datasets and Network Architectures.** We thoroughly conduct experiments on benchmark datasets CIFAR-10 and CIFAR-100 [33], and large-scale ImageNet

**Table 1.** Failure prediction performance on CIFAR-10 and CIFAR-100 datasets. AURC and E-AURC values are multiplied by $10^3$, and all remaining values are percentage.

| Network | Method | AURC (↓) | E-AURC (↓) | FPR-95% TPR (↓) | AUROC (↑) | AUPR-Success (↑) | AUPR-Error (↑) |
|---|---|---|---|---|---|---|---|
| **lIFAR-10** | | | | | | | |
| ResNet110 | baseline [22] | **9.94 ± 1.29** | **7.94 ± 1.23** | 45.01 ± 2.55 | **90.76 ± 0.60** | **99.16 ± 0.13** | 43.66 ± 1.86 |
| | mixup [61] | 15.05 ± 0.09 | 13.31 ± 0.29 | **41.18 ± 2.54** | 86.93 ± 0.98 | 98.60 ± 0.03 | 43.19 ± 3.52 |
| | LS [48] | 24.50 ± 2.73 | 22.57 ± 2.77 | 44.76 ± 3.76 | 81.89 ± 1.64 | 97.63 ± 0.29 | 39.57 ± 1.00 |
| | Focal [47] | 10.70 ± 1.32 | 8.30 ± 1.25 | 45.85 ± 0.75 | 90.70 ± 0.69 | 99.12 ± 0.13 | **44.32 ± 1.40** |
| | CS-KD [70] | 18.02 ± 3.47 | 15.81 ± 3.43 | 43.98 ± 3.86 | 85.89 ± 1.87 | 98.33 ± 0.36 | 41.17 ± 4.09 |
| | L1 [70] | 14.21 ± 1.93 | 12.11 ± 1.92 | 45.71 ± 0.60 | 87.19 ± 1.56 | 98.72 ± 0.20 | 41.93 ± 1.51 |
| WRNet | baseline [22] | **4.89 ± 0.25** | **3.93 ± 0.22** | 32.85 ± 0.36 | **93.24 ± 0.15** | **99.59 ± 0.02** | **43.38 ± 1.12** |
| | mixup [61] | 6.24 ± 0.79 | 5.52 ± 0.80 | **31.27 ± 0.63** | 91.18 ± 0.66 | 99.43 ± 0.08 | 41.86 ± 0.79 |
| | LS [48] | 16.69 ± 2.86 | 15.69 ± 2.86 | 34.24 ± 2.84 | 85.30 ± 1.79 | 98.38 ± 0.29 | 43.19 ± 1.27 |
| | Focal [47] | 6.91 ± 0.56 | 5.83 ± 0.55 | 35.43 ± 2.52 | 91.86 ± 0.66 | 99.39 ± 0.06 | 43.11 ± 0.37 |
| | CS-KD [70] | 10.29 ± 0.35 | 9.22 ± 0.38 | 38.65 ± 2.67 | 88.13 ± 0.74 | 99.04 ± 0.04 | 38.88 ± 0.66 |
| | L1 [70] | 7.01 ± 1.63 | 5.99 ± 1.66 | 34.19 ± 0.78 | 91.08 ± 1.91 | 99.38 ± 0.17 | 42.25 ± 1.51 |
| DenseNet | baseline [22] | **6.2 ± 0.29** | **4.66 ± 0.27** | 38.20 ± 2.48 | **92.87 ± 0.44** | **99.51 ± 0.03** | 43.74 ± 2.44 |
| | mixup [61] | 8.57 ± 0.54 | 7.08 ± 0.51 | **37.88 ± 3.73** | 91.17 ± 0.84 | 99.26 ± 0.05 | **44.35 ± 1.16** |
| | LS [48] | 19.35 ± 2.29 | 17.67 ± 2.19 | 40.20 ± 2.10 | 84.45 ± 1.45 | 98.15 ± 0.23 | 41.35 ± 1.18 |
| | Focal [47] | 7.17 ± 0.28 | 5.35 ± 0.19 | 41.75 ± 0.88 | 92.31 ± 0.17 | 99.44 ± 0.02 | 43.27 ± 2.04 |
| | CS-KD [70] | 13.55 ± 1.02 | 11.64 ± 0.92 | 43.11 ± 3.75 | 88.02 ± 0.46 | 98.77 ± 0.10 | 40.08 ± 4.30 |
| | L1 [70] | 8.34 ± 1.24 | 6.94 ± 1.07 | 37.02 ± 0.97 | 91.40 ± 0.63 | 99.27 ± 0.13 | 44.19 ± 0.55 |
| ConvMixer | baseline [22] | **8.33 ± 1.44** | **6.29 ± 1.30** | 42.32 ± 3.26 | **92.02 ± 0.96** | **99.34 ± 0.14** | 43.80 ± 1.49 |
| | mixup [61] | 9.87 ± 0.14 | 8.40 ± 0.25 | **37.57 ± 2.10** | 90.25 ± 0.81 | 99.12 ± 0.02 | **45.01 ± 2.40** |
| | LS [48] | 18.45 ± 1.12 | 16.41 ± 1.08 | 40.99 ± 1.91 | 86.01 ± 0.24 | 98.27 ± 0.11 | 43.32 ± 0.70 |
| | Focal [47] | 9.59 ± 1.02 | 7.17 ± 1.03 | 46.18 ± 1.66 | 91.32 ± 0.87 | 99.24 ± 0.11 | 44.03 ± 0.57 |
| | CS-KD [70] | 13.62 ± 0.86 | 11.69 ± 0.93 | 43.06 ± 0.35 | 88.02 ± 0.53 | 98.77 ± 0.10 | 41.35 ± 0.78 |
| | L1 [70] | 12.92 ± 2.41 | 11.07 ± 2.36 | 41.39 ± 0.91 | 88.35 ± 1.57 | 98.83 ± 0.25 | 42.91 ± 1.60 |
| **CIFAR-100** | | | | | | | |
| ResNet110 | baseline [22] | **93.90 ± 2.37** | **50.88 ± 2.03** | 66.02 ± 1.53 | **85.00 ± 0.35** | **93.42 ± 0.28** | **66.54 ± 0.29** |
| | mixup [61] | 95.03 ± 2.77 | 57.57 ± 3.33 | **63.68 ± 0.36** | 84.03 ± 0.80 | 92.65 ± 0.40 | 64.55 ± 1.46 |
| | LS [48] | 111.18 ± 0.36 | 69.46 ± 1.08 | 63.93 ± 0.65 | 82.85 ± 0.34 | 91.00 ± 0.11 | 65.19 ± 0.32 |
| | Focal [47] | 96.60 ± 2.81 | 52.97 ± 1.96 | 66.60 ± 0.64 | 84.22 ± 0.17 | 93.16 ± 0.28 | 65.23 ± 0.53 |
| | CS-KD [70] | 100.68 ± 2.83 | 58.89 ± 1.94 | 66.15 ± 1.69 | 83.98 ± 0.21 | 92.39 ± 0.27 | 65.09 ± 0.55 |
| | L1 [70] | 119.49 ± 4.04 | 71.47 ± 3.31 | 65.78 ± 0.96 | 82.73 ± 0.51 | 90.55 ± 0.44 | 66.44 ± 0.59 |
| WRNet | baseline [22] | 51.97 ± 1.74 | **30.18 ± 1.09** | 59.19 ± 0.20 | **87.75 ± 0.30** | **96.38 ± 0.14** | **62.99 ± 0.98** |
| | mixup [61] | **50.54 ± 0.98** | 32.00 ± 0.92 | **57.29 ± 1.57** | 87.47 ± 0.43 | 96.21 ± 0.10 | 61.72 ± 1.25 |
| | LS [48] | 58.29 ± 3.46 | 36.69 ± 2.66 | 58.47 ± 0.98 | 86.76 ± 0.19 | 95.59 ± 0.34 | 61.95 ± 0.72 |
| | Focal [47] | 54.54 ± 1.44 | 32.40 ± 1.28 | 61.87 ± 1.06 | 86.89 ± 0.22 | 96.12 ± 0.16 | 60.56 ± 0.65 |
| | CS-KD [70] | 58.30 ± 1.29 | 35.62 ± 0.68 | 60.44 ± 0.95 | 86.98 ± 0.19 | 95.70 ± 0.09 | 62.23 ± 1.17 |
| | L1 [70] | 61.63 ± 0.46 | 38.78 ± 0.45 | 59.48 ± 2.07 | 86.21 ± 0.28 | 95.31 ± 0.05 | 62.55 ± 0.77 |
| DenseNet | baseline [22] | 67.41 ± 0.67 | **35.82 ± 0.54** | 61.55 ± 2.01 | **86.46 ± 0.31** | **95.55 ± 0.05** | **65.60 ± 1.26** |
| | mixup [61] | **64.84 ± 4.26** | 37.06 ± 2.74 | 62.94 ± 2.55 | 86.26 ± 0.63 | 95.47 ± 0.36 | 62.64 ± 0.81 |
| | LS [48] | 76.24 ± 2.31 | 44.40 ± 1.01 | 62.41 ± 0.51 | 85.32 ± 0.10 | 94.47 ± 0.15 | 63.59 ± 0.43 |
| | Focal [47] | 73.43 ± 2.05 | 40.70 ± 1.40 | 65.67 ± 1.48 | 85.62 ± 0.30 | 94.95 ± 0.19 | 62.76 ± 0.61 |
| | CS-KD [70] | 75.22 ± 1.02 | 41.38 ± 1.28 | 62.75 ± 0.85 | 86.20 ± 0.40 | 94.82 ± 0.15 | 64.50 ± 0.30 |
| | L1 [70] | 68.73 ± 1.10 | 40.47 ± 1.37 | 63.39 ± 0.92 | 85.46 ± 0.50 | 95.06 ± 0.22 | 61.90 ± 0.44 |
| ConvMixer | baseline [22] | 76.96 ± 1.64 | 41.20 ± 1.64 | **63.57 ± 0.52** | **86.28 ± 0.18** | 94.81 ± 0.06 | **65.39 ± 0.83** |
| | mixup [61] | **70.87 ± 2.25** | **39.38 ± 2.65** | 63.80 ± 1.72 | 86.12 ± 0.75 | **95.12 ± 0.75** | 63.71 ± 0.75 |
| | LS [48] | 83.50 ± 3.88 | 47.37 ± 2.45 | 66.49 ± 1.50 | 84.69 ± 0.62 | 94.03 ± 0.33 | 62.87 ± 1.24 |
| | Focal [47] | 83.79 ± 2.03 | 45.51 ± 0.88 | 66.26 ± 1.50 | 85.17 ± 0.34 | 94.24 ± 0.12 | 64.36 ± 1.76 |
| | CS-KD [70] | 74.02 ± 1.18 | 42.18 ± 0.56 | 64.83 ± 1.46 | 85.44 ± 0.14 | 94.76 ± 0.09 | 62.64 ± 0.69 |
| | L1 [70] | 82.68 ± 0.35 | 46.62 ± 0.50 | 65.03 ± 0.44 | 85.02 ± 0.14 | 94.12 ± 0.05 | 64.01 ± 0.42 |

[9] dataset. In terms of network architectures, we consider a range of models: PreAct-ResNet110 [19], WideResNet [71], DenseNet [26] and more recent architecture ConvMixer [63] for experiments on CIFAR-10 and CIFAR-100. For ImageNet, we used a ResNet-18 [18] model. Due to space limitation, we provide the results of more networks like MobileNet [25], EfficientNet [60] and dataset like Tiny-ImageNet [69] in the supplementary material.

**Evaluation Metrics.** We adopt the standard metrics in [22] and [14,45] to measure failure prediction: AURC, E-AURC, AUROC, FPR-95%TPR, AUPR-Success and AUPR-Error. Lower values of AURC, E-AURC, FPR-95%TPR and higher values of AUROC, AUPR-Success, AUPR-Error indicate better failure prediction ability. Supplementary material provides definitions of these metrics.

**Implementation Details.** All models are trained using SGD with a momentum of 0.9, an initial learning rate of 0.1, and a weight decay of 5e-4 for 200 epochs with the mini-batch size of 128 on CIFAR-10 and CIFAR-100. The learning rate is reduced by a factor of 10 at 80, 130, and 170 epochs. We randomly sample 10% of training samples as a validation dataset for each task because it is a requirement for post-calibration methods like temperature scaling [15]. For each experiment, the mean and standard deviation over three random runs are reported.

**Evaluated Calibration Methods.** We evaluate various calibration methods include training-time regularization like mixup [61], label-smoothing (LS) [48], focal loss [40], CS-KD [70], $L_1$ norm [31] and post-hoc method like temperature scaling (TS) [15]. Those methods have been verified to be effective to address the miscalibration problem of DNNs. Particularly, compared with post-hoc methods, the effect of training-time regularization is irreversible. Therefore, we mainly focus on their performance on failure prediction. Supplementary material provides detail introduction and hyperparameter setting of each method.

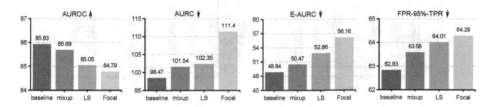

**Fig. 3.** Large-scale experiments on ImageNet. AURC and E-AURC values are multiplied by $10^3$ for clarity, and all remaining values are percentage.

## 3.2  Results and Analysis

In our experiments, we confirmed the positive calibration effects of the evaluated methods. For example, on CIFAR-10, with mixup, the ECE (%) can be reduced from 4.14 to 2.97 for ResNet110 and from 2.96 to 1.39 for DenseNet; with focal loss, the ECE (%) can be reduced from 4.14 to 1.60 for ResNet110 and from 2.96 to 1.36 for DenseNet. These observations are consistent with that in [40,61].

**Popular Calibration Methods Can Harm Failure Prediction.** In practice, users would naturally expect that the calibrated confidence can be used to filter out low-confidence predictions in risk-sensitive applications. However, if we shift focus to Table 1, it is evident that those methods generally lead to *worse* failure prediction performance under various metrics. For example, when training with mixup and LS on CIFAR-10/ResNet110, the AUROC ($\uparrow$) drops 3.83 and 9.07 percentages, respectively. And the AURC ($\downarrow$) increases 5.51 and 14.56 percentages, respectively. This is counter-intuitive as we expect those methods, which successfully calibrate the confidence, could be useful for failure prediction.

**The Same Observations Generalize to Large-Scale Dataset.** Here we verify our observation that calibration methods often harm failure prediction on ImageNet [9] dataset, which comprises 1000 classes and over 1.2 million images. We train a ResNet-18 [18] that achieve a 70.20% top-1 classification accuracy. The results are shown in Fig. 3, from which we can observe similar negative effect of calibration methods on failure prediction. More results on other networks, which exhibit similar pattern, can be found in supplementary material.

**Selective Risk Analysis.** To make intuitive sense of the effect of those calibration methods on failure prediction, Fig. 2(b) plots the risk-coverage curve. Specifically, selective risk is the empirical loss or error rate that trust the prediction, while coverage is the probability mass of non-rejected predictions [14,45]. Intuitively, a better failure predictor should have low risk at a given coverage. As can be seen from Fig. 2(b), the baseline has the lowest risks compared to other calibration methods, which indicates that using the confidence calibrated by those methods would unfortunately increase the risk when making decisions.

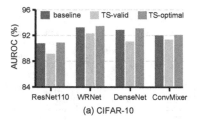 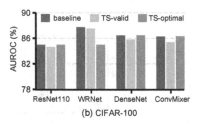

Fig. 4. Temperature scaling can hardly improve failure prediction.

**Does Temperature Scaling Improve Failure Prediction?** As a representative post-hoc calibration technique, TS [15] is simple and effective. Specifically, TS calibrates probabilities by learning a single scalar parameter $T$ for all classes on a hold-out validation set. In Fig. 4, we show the failure prediction performance of TS on different networks and datasets. Specifically, using validation set and test set to learn the parameter $T$ are donated as *TS-valid* and *TS-optimal*, respectively. By directly using test set, TS-optimal yields the optimal

$T$ for failure prediction. As shown in Fig. 4, compared with baseline, TS-valid has negative effectiveness while TS-optimal has negligible improvement.

### 3.3    Calibration Harms Failure Prediction: A Closer Look

**Illustrative Experiments.** To empirically understand the negative effect of those calibration methods, Fig. 5 shows the confidence distribution of test samples. It can be seen that LS leads to a more severe overlap between the confidence of correct and incorrect samples. Figure 6(a) plots the average confidence of correctly classified samples during training, where their confidences are obviously reduced. This can also be seen from Fig. 6(b–c), in which mixup and LS lead to better overall ECE but worse ECE of correct samples. This indicates that those calibration methods yield under-confident correct prediction. In conclusion, those calibration methods reduce the overconfident of DNNs, but lead to worse separability between correct and misclassified samples, making it hard to detect misclassified samples based on the calibrated confidence.

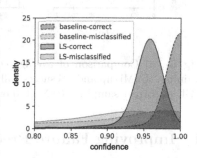

**Fig. 5.** LS results in under-confident of correct samples. ResNet110 on CIFAR-10.

**Discussion on Calibration for Failure Prediction.** The best failure prediction is achieved when correct and wrong predictions are clearly separated according to the confidence level. However, calibration focuses on matching the average accuracy and confidence, and the best ECE score is achieved when correct and wrong predictions are "mixed" in the right way such that those with confidence at level $[c, c + w)$ (confidence window in a bin, where $c$ donates the value of confidence) should have a mix of correct and wrong predictions with ratios $c : 1 - c$. Regularization methods such as mixup [61], LS [48], focal loss [40], CS-KD [70] and $L_p$ norm [31] typically improve calibration by penalizing the confidence of the whole samples to a low level. However, this will lead to undesirable effects: erasing important information about the hardness of samples [59], which would introduce an undesired mixing in ranking, and thus result in drops in failure prediction qualities. Nevertheless, this does not mean that a better ECE must lead to worse failure prediction. A proper strategy might benefit both confidence-accuracy matching and confidence separability. As shown in Sect. 4, calibration and failure prediction could be improved concurrently.

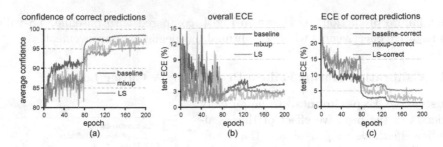

**Fig. 6.** (a) Comparison of average confidence of correctly classified samples during training. (b) Mixup and LS successfully reduce the overall ECE, (c) but result in worse ECE of correct samples. ResNet110 on CIFAR-10.

# 4    Improving Failure Prediction by Finding Flat Minima

As reported in Sect. 3, none of those popular calibration methods seem to address failure prediction problem (stably) better than simple baseline [22]. Does there exist a more principled and hassle-free strategy to improve failure prediction?

## 4.1    Motivation and Methodology

**Rationale: Why.** Confidence separability between correct and incorrect samples is crucial for failure prediction. Let us consider how confidence separability affects the confidence robustness of correct samples. Specifically, for a correctly classified sample, to become misclassified, it must reduce the probability on the ground truth class and increase its probability on another (wrong) class. During this process, the confidence margin plays a crucial role: a larger confidence margin could make it harder to change the predicted class label. Interestingly, flatness of a model reflects how sensitive the correctly classified samples become misclassified when perturbing the weights of a model [12,27,28]. As illustrated in Fig. 7, with flat minima, a correct sample is difficult to be misclassified under weight perturbations and vice versa. Therefore, we conjecture that the confidence gap between correct and incorrect samples of a flat minima is larger than that of a sharp minima.

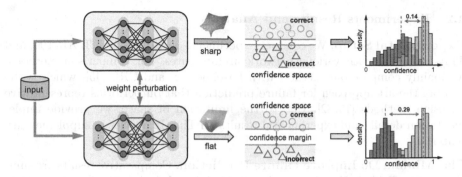

**Fig. 7.** An intuitive relationship between flatness and failure prediction. The stability of predictions to parameter perturbations can be seen as a *confidence margin* condition. This inspires us to improve failure prediction by finding flat minima.

**Reliable Overfitting Phenomenon.** As shown in Fig. 8, we observed an interesting phenomenon that the AUROC can be easily overfitting during the training of a model (ResNet110 on CIFAR-10). Concretely, the test accuracy continually increases while the AUROC decreases at the last phases, making it difficult for failure prediction. We term this phenomenon as *"reliable overfitting"*, which exists on different model and dataset settings and somewhat similar to the *robust overfitting* [57] in adversarial robustness literature. Since flat minima has been verified to be effective for alleviating robust overfitting [6,67], we expect that flat minima could also benefit failure prediction.

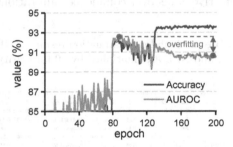

**Fig. 8.** *Reliable overfitting* phenomenon.

**Approach: How.** There are several methods have been proposed to seek flat minima for DNNs [5,12,28,55]. We select *stochastic weight averaging* (SWA) [28] and *sharpness-aware minimization* (SAM) [12] as two representative methods due to the simplicity for proofs-of-concept. Specifically, SWA simply averages multiple parameters of the model along the training trajectory: $\theta_{swa}^t = \frac{\theta_{swa}^{t-1} \times n + \theta^t}{n+1}$, where $n$ indexes the number of past checkpoints to be averaged, $t$ is the training epoch, $\theta$ is the current weights, $\theta_{swa}$ is the averaged weights. While SAM finds the flat minima by directly perturbing the weights: $\min_{\theta} \max_{||\epsilon||_p \leq \rho} \mathcal{L}(\theta + \epsilon) + \frac{\lambda}{2}||\theta||$. Although the SWA and SAM find flat minima based on different mechanism, we find they both improve the failure prediction performance. This also motivates us to combine them to get better performance. We refer the combine of them as **FMFP** (*Flat Minima for Failure Prediction*). Supplementary material presents pseudo-code for the FMFP algorithm.

## 4.2 Experiments Results and Analysis

**Experimental Setup.** We conduct experiments on CIFAR-10, CIFAR-100, and Tiny-ImageNet with various network architectures. For comparison methods, we mainly compare our method with baseline [22] and CRL [45], which is the state-of-the-art approach for failure prediction that outperforms representative bayesian methods [13,32]. Due to the limitation of space, we provide implementation details and experimental results on Tiny-ImageNet in supplementary material.

**Flat Minima Do Improve Failure Prediction.** Comparative results are summarized in Table 2. We observe that flat minima based methods: SAM, SWA, and FMFP (ours) consistently outperform the strong baseline and CRL on various metrics of failure prediction. Particularly, FMFP generally yields the best results. For example, in the case of ResNet110, our method has 3.00% and 2.24% higher values of AUROC on CIFAR-10 and CIFAR-100, respectively. In addition, flat minima based methods, especially the proposed FMFP, can achieve effective gains over confidence calibration (the last three columns in Table 2).

**Table 2.** Confidence estimation results. AURC and E-AURC values are multiplied by $10^3$, and NLL are multiplied by 10 for clarity. Remaining values are percentages.

**CIFAR-10**

| Network | Method | AURC (↓) | E-AURC (↓) | FPR-95% TPR (↓) | AUROC (↑) | AUPR-Success(↑) | AUPR-Error (↑) | ECE (↓) | NLL (↓) | Brier (↓) |
|---|---|---|---|---|---|---|---|---|---|---|
| ResNet110 | baseline [22] | 9.94±1.29 | 7.94±1.23 | 45.01±2.55 | 90.76±0.60 | 99.16±0.13 | 43.66±1.86 | 4.14±0.06 | 2.88±0.08 | 10.47±0.28 |
| | CRL [45] | 7.54±0.20 | 5.29±0.16 | 45.25±3.24 | 92.86±0.17 | 99.44±0.02 | 44.93±1.31 | 1.65±0.08 | 2.05±0.03 | 10.01±0.09 |
| | SAM | 5.31±0.13 | 3.74±0.17 | 39.44±2.75 | 93.73±0.45 | 99.61±0.02 | 45.23±2.88 | 1.86±0.12 | 1.76±0.02 | 8.55±0.19 |
| | SWA | 6.38±0.18 | 4.38±0.07 | 39.36±0.29 | 93.69±0.08 | 99.54±0.01 | 47.49±2.03 | 1.33±0.10 | 1.83±0.03 | 9.17±0.15 |
| | ours | 5.57±0.11 | 3.92±0.09 | 39.50±0.52 | 93.76±0.10 | 99.58±0.01 | 44.45±1.89 | 0.50±0.13 | 1.68±0.02 | 8.50±0.13 |
| WRNet | baseline [22] | 4.89±0.25 | 3.93±0.22 | 32.85±0.36 | 93.24±0.15 | 99.53±0.02 | 43.38±1.12 | 2.71±0.06 | 1.82±0.03 | 7.15±0.07 |
| | CRL [45] | 4.52±0.10 | 3.23±0.10 | 32.92±2.18 | 94.24±0.23 | 99.66±0.01 | 44.07±1.61 | 0.44±0.14 | 1.52±0.02 | 7.41±0.14 |
| | SAM | 2.85±0.04 | 2.15±0.07 | 26.07±0.96 | 95.10±0.19 | 99.78±0.01 | 44.50±1.20 | 1.58±0.05 | 1.25±0.01 | 5.76±0.07 |
| | SWA | 2.84±0.04 | 2.06±0.05 | 28.60±0.08 | 95.31±0.12 | 99.79±0.01 | 44.62±2.14 | 1.22±0.05 | 1.22±0.01 | 5.92±0.05 |
| | ours | 2.60±0.06 | 1.90±0.03 | 27.80±2.19 | 95.43±0.07 | 99.80±0.01 | 44.36±3.46 | 0.43±0.14 | 1.12±0.01 | 5.57±0.03 |
| DenseNet | baseline [22] | 6.20±0.29 | 4.66±0.27 | 38.20±2.48 | 92.87±0.44 | 99.51±0.03 | 43.74±2.44 | 2.96±0.12 | 2.10±0.06 | 8.77±0.17 |
| | CRL [45] | 6.17±0.26 | 4.29±0.09 | 39.76±0.24 | 93.64±0.18 | 99.55±0.01 | 46.51±1.88 | 0.95±0.18 | 1.81±0.06 | 8.98±0.35 |
| | SAM | 4.56±0.17 | 3.06±0.14 | 33.69±1.68 | 94.55±0.20 | 99.68±0.01 | 47.32±1.03 | 1.37±0.13 | 1.53±0.05 | 7.45±0.20 |
| | SWA | 5.02±0.20 | 3.48±0.04 | 37.87±2.71 | 94.31±0.24 | 99.64±0.01 | 44.48±1.38 | 1.13±0.11 | 1.61±0.03 | 8.12±0.24 |
| | ours | 4.48±0.13 | 3.01±0.12 | 31.41±1.29 | 94.92±0.19 | 99.69±0.01 | 48.12±0.88 | 0.52±0.08 | 1.51±0.01 | 7.68±0.06 |
| ConvMixer | baseline [22] | 8.33±1.44 | 6.29±1.30 | 42.32±3.26 | 92.02±0.96 | 99.34±0.14 | 43.80±1.49 | 3.43±0.51 | 2.53±0.27 | 10.15±0.65 |
| | CRL [45] | 6.89±0.51 | 4.78±0.35 | 41.47±1.38 | 93.27±0.21 | 99.50±0.04 | 45.99±1.38 | 0.99±0.22 | 1.98±0.07 | 9.57±0.31 |
| | SAM | 5.52±0.22 | 3.88±0.16 | 36.16±1.35 | 93.92±0.32 | 99.59±0.02 | 46.66±2.60 | 2.16±0.21 | 1.84±0.06 | 8.55±0.29 |
| | SWA | 4.68±0.26 | 3.35±0.17 | 34.73±2.04 | 94.54±0.16 | 99.65±0.02 | 45.62±1.17 | 1.31±0.17 | 1.59±0.07 | 7.90±0.30 |
| | ours | 4.98±0.23 | 3.47±0.13 | 32.88±1.77 | 94.75±0.19 | 99.63±0.02 | 49.02±1.36 | 0.89±0.20 | 1.58±0.05 | 7.86±0.28 |

**CIFAR-100**

| Network | Method | AURC (↓) | E-AURC (↓) | FPR-95% TPR(↓) | AUROC (↑) | AUPR-Success (↑) | AUPR-Error (↑) | ECE (↓) | NLL (↓) | Brier (↓) |
|---|---|---|---|---|---|---|---|---|---|---|
| ResNet110 | baseline [22] | 93.90±2.37 | 50.88±2.03 | 66.02±1.53 | 85.00±0.35 | 93.42±0.28 | 66.34±0.29 | 15.71±0.15 | 13.54±0.12 | 42.88±0.27 |
| | CRL [45] | 81.02±2.06 | 41.82±0.94 | 64.37±0.43 | 86.32±0.24 | 94.68±0.13 | 66.26±0.32 | 10.96±0.53 | 11.02±0.09 | 38.82±0.57 |
| | SAM | 78.35±1.32 | 41.01±0.61 | 63.86±0.52 | 86.38±0.14 | 94.82±0.09 | 66.21±0.72 | 10.58±0.15 | 10.54±0.18 | 37.89±0.44 |
| | SWA | 71.94±0.60 | 37.23±0.67 | 63.98±0.68 | 86.86±0.21 | 95.35±0.08 | 65.59±0.88 | 5.38±0.13 | 8.81±0.02 | 34.95±0.08 |
| | ours | 69.51±0.56 | 35.51±0.68 | 62.57±0.81 | 87.24±0.12 | 95.57±0.02 | 66.52±1.04 | 3.41±0.35 | 8.51±0.07 | 34.10±0.19 |
| WRNet | baseline [22] | 51.97±1.74 | 30.18±1.09 | 59.19±0.20 | 87.75±0.30 | 96.38±0.14 | 62.99±0.98 | 7.19±0.36 | 8.43±0.11 | 29.67±0.45 |
| | CRL [45] | 46.17±0.20 | 25.28±0.34 | 58.32±0.48 | 88.77±0.35 | 97.00±0.03 | 63.34±0.98 | 3.93±0.06 | 7.33±0.06 | 27.98±0.17 |
| | SAM | 43.21±0.22 | 24.51±0.65 | 57.56±0.91 | 88.82±0.26 | 97.11±0.07 | 62.69±0.72 | 4.97±0.38 | 7.15±0.03 | 26.99±0.16 |
| | SWA | 41.62±0.18 | 22.73±0.02 | 57.19±0.87 | 89.23±0.03 | 97.33±0.01 | 62.17±0.27 | 7.61±0.14 | 7.29±0.05 | 27.64±0.06 |
| | ours | 40.80±0.31 | 22.00±0.15 | 56.13±0.44 | 89.53±0.10 | 97.41±0.01 | 63.11±0.12 | 6.07±0.34 | 6.83±0.01 | 26.78±0.20 |
| DenseNet | baseline [22] | 67.41±0.67 | 35.82±0.54 | 61.55±2.01 | 86.46±0.31 | 95.55±0.05 | 65.60±1.26 | 9.04±0.31 | 9.60±0.08 | 35.11±0.39 |
| | CRL [45] | 64.30±1.26 | 34.59±0.33 | 61.42±1.74 | 87.19±0.25 | 95.74±0.06 | 64.67±1.45 | 5.38±0.34 | 8.50±0.14 | 32.85±0.32 |
| | SAM | 63.52±2.41 | 34.51±1.07 | 61.46±0.32 | 87.01±0.13 | 95.76±0.15 | 64.41±1.04 | 5.91±0.39 | 8.53±0.18 | 32.75±0.71 |
| | SWA | 59.88±1.40 | 32.08±0.25 | 63.11±0.73 | 87.34±0.18 | 96.09±0.05 | 62.88±1.39 | 4.89±0.28 | 7.82±0.10 | 31.63±0.47 |
| | ours | 56.62±0.18 | 30.33±0.42 | 61.34±1.59 | 87.75±0.20 | 96.32±0.05 | 63.45±0.70 | 3.16±0.08 | 7.53±0.04 | 30.55±0.10 |
| ConvMixer | baseline [22] | 76.96±1.64 | 41.20±1.64 | 63.57±0.52 | 86.28±0.18 | 94.81±0.06 | 65.39±0.83 | 7.42±0.19 | 9.98±0.33 | 36.27±0.83 |
| | CRL [45] | 64.20±0.50 | 33.57±0.56 | 60.11±2.62 | 87.59±0.31 | 95.85±0.06 | 65.78±1.73 | 3.99±0.43 | 8.55±0.02 | 32.84±0.06 |
| | SAM | 64.47±2.10 | 34.05±1.19 | 64.58±1.44 | 87.11±0.24 | 95.43±0.17 | 63.52±0.66 | 7.96±0.10 | 8.34±0.10 | 33.36±0.38 |
| | SWA | 69.73±2.51 | 37.47±1.14 | 63.43±1.24 | 86.56±0.15 | 95.35±0.17 | 64.57±0.64 | 6.29±0.35 | 9.13±0.24 | 34.54±0.67 |
| | ours | 57.15±1.92 | 29.96±0.59 | 60.49±2.22 | 88.04±0.35 | 96.35±0.09 | 64.57±2.05 | 6.40±0.62 | 8.05±0.18 | 31.52±0.63 |

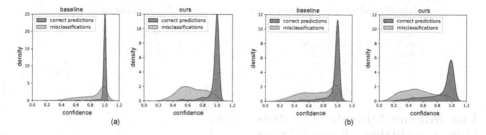

**Fig. 9.** Confidence distribution on correct and misclassified samples. Our method leads to a better separation for failure prediction.

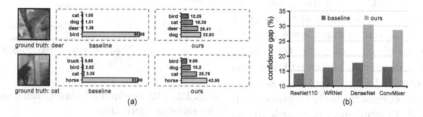

**Fig. 10.** (a) Predictive distribution on misclassified samples. (b) Our method (FMFP) significantly enlarges the average confidence gap between correct and incorrect samples.

In Fig. 9, we observe that correct predictions and erroneous predictions overlap severely, making it difficult to distinguish them. Our method remarkably shifts the errors' confidence distributions to smaller values and maintains the confidence of correct samples, leading to a better separation for failure prediction. Figure 10(a) presents some examples of misclassified samples and their corresponding confidence distribution. Ours outputs much lower confidence on the erroneously pre-

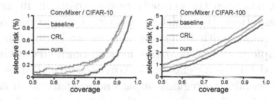

**Fig. 11.** Comparison of risk-coverage curves.

dicted class. In Fig. 10(b), our method significantly enlarges the confidence gap between correct and incorrect samples. Besides, the risk-coverage curves in Fig. 11 and Fig. 2(b) also demonstrate the confidence reliability of our method.

**Failure Prediction Under Distribution Shift.** In real-world applications, the model may encoder inputs subject to various kinds of distributional shifts. Thus, it becomes necessary to evaluate the confidence estimation performance to distributional shifts. The model is trained on CIFAR-10 and evaluated on corrupted dataset CIFAR-10-C [21]. The average results for 15 kinds of corruption under 5 different levels of perturbation severity are reported in Table 3. Our method consistently performs better than baseline and CRL methods.

**Table 3.** Failure prediction performance under distributional shifts.

| Method | AUROC ↑ | | | | AURC ↓ | | | | FPR-95%TPR ↓ | | | |
|---|---|---|---|---|---|---|---|---|---|---|---|---|
| | ResNet110 | WRNet | DenseNet | ConvMixer | ResNet110 | WRNet | DenseNet | ConvMixer | ResNet110 | WRNet | DenseNet | ConvMixer |
| Baseline [22] | 79.45 | 83.81 | 81.97 | 81.28 | 157.46 | 112.46 | 148.91 | 168.39 | 71.29 | 64.05 | 69.26 | 71.07 |
| CRL [45] | 82.54 | 85.91 | 83.51 | 82.46 | 133.73 | 104.95 | 133.58 | 163.68 | 68.86 | 63.35 | 67.73 | 69.34 |
| Ours | **84.72** | **87.34** | **84.90** | **84.93** | **119.79** | **94.34** | **130.42** | **145.21** | **65.51** | **58.87** | **64.95** | **65.29** |

**Flat Minima Mitigates the Reliable Overfitting.** Figure 12 plots the AUROC curves during training. Although the failure prediction performance can be improved by early stopping, the classification accuracy of early checkpoint is much lower (Fig. 8). We can clearly observe that with flat minima, reliable overfitting has been diminished significantly, and the AUROC curves robustly improve until the end. Flat minima further leads to better classification accuracy, avoiding the trade-off between AUROC and accuracy when applying early stopping.

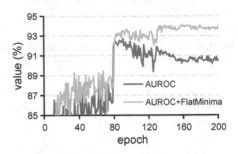

**Fig. 12.** Flat minima effectively mitigates the reliable overfitting.

**Further Understanding Flat Minima for Failure Prediction.** ① *Representation learning.* Misclassification with high confidence is often attributed to spurious correlations appearing in the sample and the wrong class. Flat minima has been theoretically proved to result in invariant and disentangled representations [1], which is effective for spurious representations mitigation [4]. Therefore, with fewer spurious or irrelevant representations, the misclassified sample would be near the decision boundary with low confidence and less activated for wrong classes. ② *Uncertainty.* It has been shown that flat minima corresponds to regions in parameter space with rich posterior uncertainty [49]. Therefore, flat minima has the advantage to indicate the uncertainty of an input.

## 5    Concluding Remarks

Failure prediction is an important yet far less explored problem for safety-critical applications. This paper evaluates the effect of popular calibration methods for failure prediction. To our surprise, they have no or negative effect on failure prediction. We further find the under-confident issue of correctly classified samples, which leads to worse separation between the confidence of correct and incorrect samples. Finally, we propose to enlarge the confidence gap by finding flat minima, which yields strong performance on extensive experiments.

**Acknowledgement.** This work has been supported by the National Key Research and Development Program under Grant No. 2018AAA0100400, the National Natural

Science Foundation of China grants U20A20223, 62076236, 61721004, the Key Research Program of Frontier Sciences of CAS under Grant ZDBS-LY-7004, and the Youth Innovation Promotion Association of CAS under Grant 2019141.

# References

1. Achille, A., Soatto, S.: Emergence of invariance and disentanglement in deep representations. J. Mach. Learn. Res. **19**, 50:1–50:34 (2018)
2. Bojarski, M., et al.: End to end learning for self-driving cars. arXiv preprint arXiv:1604.07316 (2016)
3. Brier, G.W., et al.: Verification of forecasts expressed in terms of probability. Mon. Weather Rev. **78**(1), 1–3 (1950)
4. Cha, J., et al.: SWAD: domain generalization by seeking flat minima. In: NeurIPS (2021)
5. Chaudhari, P., et al.: Entropy-SGD: biasing gradient descent into wide valleys. J. Stat. Mech. Theory Exp. **2019**(12), 124018 (2019)
6. Chen, T., Zhang, Z., Liu, S., Chang, S., Wang, Z.: Robust overfitting may be mitigated by properly learned smoothening. In: ICLR (2021)
7. Corbière, C., Thome, N., Bar-Hen, A., Cord, M., Pérez, P.: Addressing failure prediction by learning model confidence. In: NeurIPS, pp. 2898–2909 (2019)
8. Corbière, C., Thome, N., Saporta, A., Vu, T.H., Cord, M., Perez, P.: Confidence estimation via auxiliary models. IEEE Trans. Pattern Anal. Mach. Intell. **44**, 6043–6055 (2021)
9. Deng, J., Dong, W., Socher, R., Li, L.J., Li, K., Fei-Fei, L.: ImageNet: a large-scale hierarchical image database. In: CVPR, pp. 248–255 (2009)
10. Dosovitskiy, A., et al.: An image is worth $16 \times 16$ words: transformers for image recognition at scale. In: ICLR (2020)
11. Esteva, A., et al.: Dermatologist-level classification of skin cancer with deep neural networks. Nature **542**(7639), 115–118 (2017)
12. Foret, P., Kleiner, A., Mobahi, H., Neyshabur, B.: Sharpness-aware minimization for efficiently improving generalization. In: ICLR (2020)
13. Gal, Y., Ghahramani, Z.: Dropout as a Bayesian approximation: representing model uncertainty in deep learning. In: ICML, vol. 48, pp. 1050–1059 (2016)
14. Geifman, Y., El-Yaniv, R.: Selective classification for deep neural networks. In: NeurIPS, pp. 4878–4887 (2017)
15. Guo, C., Pleiss, G., Sun, Y., Weinberger, K.Q.: On calibration of modern neural networks. In: ICML, pp. 1321–1330 (2017)
16. Gupta, K., Rahimi, A., Ajanthan, T., Mensink, T., Sminchisescu, C., Hartley, R.: Calibration of neural networks using splines. In: ICLR (2020)
17. Havasi, M., et al.: Training independent subnetworks for robust prediction. In: ICLR (2020)
18. He, K., Zhang, X., Ren, S., Sun, J.: Deep residual learning for image recognition. In: CVPR, pp. 770–778 (2016)
19. He, K., Zhang, X., Ren, S., Sun, J.: Identity mappings in deep residual networks. In: Leibe, B., Matas, J., Sebe, N., Welling, M. (eds.) ECCV 2016. LNCS, vol. 9908, pp. 630–645. Springer, Cham (2016). https://doi.org/10.1007/978-3-319-46493-0_38
20. Hebbalaguppe, R., Prakash, J., Madan, N., Arora, C.: A stitch in time saves nine; a train-time regularizing loss for improved neural network calibration. In: CVPR, pp. 16081–16090, June 2022

21. Hendrycks, D., Dietterich, T.G.: Benchmarking neural network robustness to common corruptions and perturbations. In: ICLR (2019)
22. Hendrycks, D., Gimpel, K.: A baseline for detecting misclassified and out-of-distribution examples in neural networks. In: ICLR (2017)
23. Hendrycks, D., Mazeika, M., Dietterich, T.G.: Deep anomaly detection with outlier exposure. In: ICLR (2019)
24. Hendrycks, D., Mu, N., Cubuk, E.D., Zoph, B., Gilmer, J., Lakshminarayanan, B.: AugMix: a simple data processing method to improve robustness and uncertainty. In: ICLR (2020)
25. Howard, A.G., et al.: MobileNets: efficient convolutional neural networks for mobile vision applications. arXiv preprint arXiv:1704.04861 (2017)
26. Huang, G., Liu, Z., van der Maaten, L., Weinberger, K.Q.: Densely connected convolutional networks. In: CVPR, pp. 2261–2269 (2017)
27. Huang, W.R., et al.: Understanding generalization through visualizations. In: "I Can't Believe It's Not Better!" NeurIPS 2020 Workshop (2020)
28. Izmailov, P., Wilson, A., Podoprikhin, D., Vetrov, D., Garipov, T.: Averaging weights leads to wider optima and better generalization. In: UAI, pp. 876–885 (2018)
29. Janai, J., Güney, F., Behl, A., Geiger, A., et al.: Computer vision for autonomous vehicles: Problems, datasets and state of the art. Found. Trends® Comput. Graph. Vis. **12**(1–3), 1–308 (2020)
30. Jiang, H., Kim, B., Gupta, M.R.: To trust or not to trust a classifier. In: NeurIPS (2018)
31. Joo, T., Chung, U.: Revisiting explicit regularization in neural networks for well-calibrated predictive uncertainty. arXiv preprint arXiv:2006.06399 (2020)
32. Kendall, A., Gal, Y.: What uncertainties do we need in Bayesian deep learning for computer vision? In: NeurIPS, pp. 5574–5584 (2017)
33. Krizhevsky, A., Hinton, G., et al.: Learning multiple layers of features from tiny images. Technical report, Citeseer (2009)
34. Kull, M., Perelló-Nieto, M., Kängsepp, M., de Menezes e Silva Filho, T., Song, H., Flach, P.A.: Beyond temperature scaling: Obtaining well-calibrated multi-class probabilities with Dirichlet calibration. In: NeurIPS, pp. 12295–12305 (2019)
35. Kull, M., de Menezes e Silva Filho, T., Flach, P.A.: Beta calibration: a well-founded and easily implemented improvement on logistic calibration for binary classifiers. In: AISTATS, pp. 623–631 (2017)
36. Kumar, A., Liang, P.S., Ma, T.: Verified uncertainty calibration. In: NeurIPS (2019)
37. Lee, K., Lee, K., Lee, H., Shin, J.: A simple unified framework for detecting out-of-distribution samples and adversarial attacks. In: NeurIPS, pp. 7167–7177 (2018)
38. Leidner, D., Borst, C., Dietrich, A., Beetz, M., Albu-Schäffer, A.: Classifying compliant manipulation tasks for automated planning in robotics. In: 2015 IEEE/RSJ International Conference on Intelligent Robots and Systems (IROS), pp. 1769–1776 (2015)
39. Liang, S., Li, Y., Srikant, R.: Enhancing the reliability of out-of-distribution image detection in neural networks. In: ICLR (2018)
40. Lin, T., Goyal, P., Girshick, R.B., He, K., Dollár, P.: Focal loss for dense object detection. IEEE Trans. Pattern Anal. Mach. Intell. **42**, 318–327 (2020)
41. Liu, B., Ben Ayed, I., Galdran, A., Dolz, J.: The devil is in the margin: margin-based label smoothing for network calibration. In: CVPR, pp. 80–88, June 2022
42. Luo, Y., Wong, Y., Kankanhalli, M.S., Zhao, Q.: Learning to predict trustworthiness with steep slope loss. NeurIPS (2021)

43. Minderer, M., et al.: Revisiting the calibration of modern neural networks. In: NeurIPS (2021)
44. Miotto, R., Li, L., Kidd, B.A., Dudley, J.T.: Deep patient: an unsupervised representation to predict the future of patients from the electronic health records. Sci. Rep. **6**, 26094 (2016)
45. Moon, J., Kim, J., Shin, Y., Hwang, S.: Confidence-aware learning for deep neural networks. In: ICML, pp. 7034–7044 (2020)
46. Mozafari, A.S., Gomes, H.S., Leão, W., Gagné, C.: Unsupervised temperature scaling: an unsupervised post-processing calibration method of deep networks. arXiv: Computer Vision and Pattern Recognition (2019)
47. Mukhoti, J., Kulharia, V., Sanyal, A., Golodetz, S., Torr, P.H.S., Dokania, P.K.: Calibrating deep neural networks using focal loss. In: NeurIPS (2020)
48. Müller, R., Kornblith, S., Hinton, G.: When does label smoothing help? In: NeurIPS, pp. 4696–4705 (2019)
49. Murphy, K.P.: Probabilistic Machine Learning: An introduction. MIT Press, Cambridge (2022). probml.ai
50. Naeini, M.P., Cooper, G.F., Hauskrecht, M.: Obtaining well calibrated probabilities using Bayesian binning. In: AAAI, pp. 2901–2907 (2015)
51. Nixon, J., Dusenberry, M.W., Zhang, L., Jerfel, G., Tran, D.: Measuring calibration in deep learning. In: CVPR Workshops, vol. 2 (2019)
52. Ovadia, Y., et al.: Can you trust your model's uncertainty? Evaluating predictive uncertainty under dataset shift. In: NeurIPS (2019)
53. Patel, K., Beluch, W.H., Yang, B., Pfeiffer, M., Zhang, D.: Multi-class uncertainty calibration via mutual information maximization-based binning. In: ICLR (2020)
54. Pereyra, G., Tucker, G., Chorowski, J., Kaiser, L., Hinton, G.: Regularizing neural networks by penalizing confident output distributions. arXiv preprint arXiv:1701.06548 (2017)
55. Pittorino, F., et al.: Entropic gradient descent algorithms and wide flat minima. J. Stat. Mech. Theory Exp. **2021**(12), 124015 (2021)
56. Rahimi, A., Shaban, A., Cheng, C., Hartley, R., Boots, B.: Intra order-preserving functions for calibration of multi-class neural networks. In: NeurIPS (2020)
57. Rice, L., Wong, E., Kolter, Z.: Overfitting in adversarially robust deep learning. In: ICML, pp. 8093–8104 (2020)
58. Shehzad, M.N., et al.: Threshold temperature scaling: Heuristic to address temperature and power issues in MPSoCs. Microprocess. Microsyst. **77**, 103124 (2020)
59. Shen, Z., Liu, Z., Xu, D., Chen, Z., Cheng, K.T., Savvides, M.: Is label smoothing truly incompatible with knowledge distillation: an empirical study. In: ICLR (2020)
60. Tan, M., Le, Q.: EfficientNet: rethinking model scaling for convolutional neural networks. In: ICML, pp. 6105–6114 (2019)
61. Thulasidasan, S., Chennupati, G., Bilmes, J., Bhattacharya, T., Michalak, S.: On mixup training: Improved calibration and predictive uncertainty for deep neural networks. In: NeurIPS, pp. 13888–13899 (2019)
62. Tolstikhin, I.O., et al.: MLP-mixer: an all-MLP architecture for vision. In: NeurIPS (2021)
63. Trockman, A., Kolter, J.Z.: Patches are all you need? arXiv preprint arXiv:2201.09792 (2022)
64. Vaicenavicius, J., Widmann, D., Andersson, C., Lindsten, F., Roll, J., Schön, T.: Evaluating model calibration in classification. In: AISTATS, pp. 3459–3467 (2019)
65. Wang, D., Feng, L., Zhang, M.: Rethinking calibration of deep neural networks: do not be afraid of overconfidence. In: NeurIPS (2021)

66. Wen, Y., et al.: Combining ensembles and data augmentation can harm your calibration. In: ICLR (2020)
67. Wu, D., Xia, S., Wang, Y.: Adversarial weight perturbation helps robust generalization. In: NeurIPS (2020)
68. Xing, C., Arik, S.Ö., Zhang, Z., Pfister, T.: Distance-based learning from errors for confidence calibration. In: ICLR (2020)
69. Yao, L., Miller, J.: Tiny ImageNet classification with convolutional neural networks. CS 231N
70. Yun, S., Park, J., Lee, K., Shin, J.: Regularizing class-wise predictions via self-knowledge distillation. In: CVPR, pp. 13873–13882 (2020)
71. Zagoruyko, S., Komodakis, N.: Wide residual networks. In: BMVC (2016)
72. Zhang, H., Cisse, M., Dauphin, Y.N., Lopez-Paz, D.: Mixup: beyond empirical risk minimization. In: ICLR (2018)
73. Zhang, L., Deng, Z., Kawaguchi, K., Zou, J.: When and how mixup improves calibration. In: ICML, pp. 26135–26160 (2022)
74. Zhang, W., Vaidya, I.: Mixup training leads to reduced overfitting and improved calibration for the transformer architecture. CoRR (2021)
75. Zhong, Z., Cui, J., Liu, S., Jia, J.: Improving calibration for long-tailed recognition. In: CVPR, pp. 16489–16498 (2021)

# Uncertainty-Guided Source-Free Domain Adaptation

Subhankar Roy[1,2(✉)], Martin Trapp[3], Andrea Pilzer[4], Juho Kannala[3],
Nicu Sebe[1], Elisa Ricci[1,2], and Arno Solin[3]

[1] University of Trento, Trento, Italy
subhankar.roy@unitn.it
[2] Fondazione Bruno Kessler, Trento, Italy
[3] Aalto University, Espoo, Finland
[4] NVIDIA, Santa Clara, USA

**Abstract.** Source-free domain adaptation (SFDA) aims to adapt a classifier to an unlabelled target data set by only using a pre-trained source model. However, the absence of the source data and the domain shift makes the predictions on the target data unreliable. We propose quantifying the uncertainty in the source model predictions and utilizing it to guide the target adaptation. For this, we construct a probabilistic source model by incorporating priors on the network parameters inducing a distribution over the model predictions. Uncertainties are estimated by employing a Laplace approximation and incorporated to identify target data points that do not lie in the source manifold and to downweight them when maximizing the mutual information on the target data. Unlike recent works, our probabilistic treatment is computationally lightweight, decouples source training and target adaptation, and requires no specialized source training or changes of the model architecture. We show the advantages of uncertainty-guided SFDA over traditional SFDA in the closed-set and open-set settings and provide empirical evidence that our approach is more robust to strong domain shifts even without tuning.

**Keywords:** Source-free domain adaptation ·
Uncertainty quantification

## 1 Introduction

Deep neural networks have proven to be very successful in a myriad of computer vision tasks such as categorization, detection, and retrieval. However, much of the success has come at the price of excessive human effort put into the manual data-labelling process. Since collecting annotated data can be prohibitive and

**Supplementary Information** The online version contains supplementary material available at https://doi.org/10.1007/978-3-031-19806-9_31.

impossible at times, domain adaptation (DA, see [8] for an overview) methods
have gained increasing attention. They enable training on unlabelled target data
by conjointly leveraging a previously labelled yet related source data set while
mitigating *domain-shift* [60] between the two. Such methods predominantly
comprise of minimizing statistical moments between distributions [37,53,57,62],
using adversarial objectives to maximize domain confusion [14,61], or reconstructing data with generative methods [23].

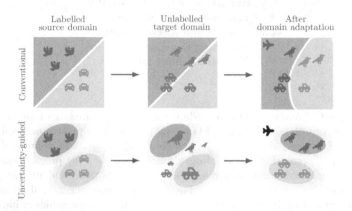

**Fig. 1.** Illustrative sketch of source-free domain adaptation (SFDA) on a labelled source
domain (🐦, 🚗) and an *unlabelled* target domain (🐦, 🚲) potentially containing additional classes (✈) . The **top-row** shows conventional methods which ignore model
uncertainties; the **bottom-row** shows our method which incorporates uncertainties
about the predictive model, enabling uncertainty-guided SFDA that is more robust to
distribution shifts

Albeit successful, the preceding methods mandate access to the source data
set during the target adaptation phase as they require an estimate of the source
distribution for the alignment. With the emergence of regulations on data privacy and bottleneck in data transmission for large data sets, access to the source
data can not always be guaranteed. Thus, paving the way to a relatively new
and more realistic DA setting, called *source-free* DA (SFDA, [8]), where the
task is to adapt to the target data set when the only source of supervision is a
source-trained model. SFDA facilitates maintaining data anonymity in privacy-
sensitive applications (*e.g.*, surveillance or medical applications) and at the same
time reduces data transmission and storage overhead. Towards this goal, recently,
several SFDA methods have been proposed that utilize the hypotheses learned
from the source data [27,33,58]. Notably, SHOT [33] – an information maximization (IM) [17] based SFDA method – has demonstrated to work reasonably well
on DA benchmarks, sometimes outperforming traditional DA methods. While
promising, these conventional SFDA techniques do not account for the uncertainty in the predictions of the source model on the target data. As a by-product,

solely maximizing mutual information [17] on the target data can lead to erroneous decision surfaces (see Fig. 1 top).

This work argues that quantification of the uncertainty in predictions is essential in SFDA. Depending on the inductive biases of the model, the source model may predict incorrect target pseudo-labels with high confidence, *e.g.*, due to the extrapolation property in ReLU networks [22] (see Fig. 2b left). In the literature, uncertainty-guided methods have been proposed in the context of traditional UDA and SFDA settings, employing Monte Carlo (MC) dropout to estimate the uncertainties in the model predictions [51, 72]. However, MC dropout requires specialized training and specialized model architecture, suffers from manual hyperparameter tuning [13], and is known to provide a poor approximation even for simple (*e.g.*, linear) models [10, 46, 47].

In this work, we propose to construct a probabilistic source model by incorporating priors on the network parameters, inducing a distribution over the model predictions, on the last layer of the source model. This enables us to perform an efficient local approximation to the posterior using a *Laplace approximation* (LA, [41, 59]), see Fig. 2a. This principled Bayesian treatment leads to more robust predictions, especially when the target data set contains out-of-distribution (OOD) classes (see Fig. 1 bottom) or in case of strong domain shifts. Once the uncertainty in predictions is estimated, we selectively guide the target model to maximize the mutual information [17] in the target predictions. This alleviates the alignment of the target features with the wrong source hypothesis, resulting in a domain adaptation scheme that is robust to mild and strong domain shifts without tuning. We call our proposed method **U**ncertainty-guided **S**ource-**F**ree **A**daptatio**N** (U-SFAN). Our approach requires no specialized source training or specialized architecture, opposed to exiting works (*e.g.*, [30, 72]), introduces little computational overhead, and decouples source training and target adaptation.

We summarize our contributions as follows. *(i)* We emphasize the need to quantify uncertainty in the predictions for SFDA and propose to account for uncertainties by placing priors on the parameters of the source model. Our approach is computationally efficient by employing a last-layer Laplace approximation and greatly decouples the training of the source and target. *(ii)* We demonstrate that our proposed U-SFAN successfully guides the target adaptation without specialized loss functions or a specialised architecture. *(iii)* We empirical show the advantage of our method over SHOT [33] in the closed-set and the open-set setting for several benchmarks tasks and provide evidence for the improved robustness against mild and strong domain shifts.

## 2   Related Work

**Closed-set Domain Adaptation**, often abbreviated as UDA, refers to the family of DA methods that aim to learn a classifier for an unlabelled target data set while simultaneously using the labelled source data set, which differ in their underlying data distributions. In the literature [64] mainly three categories of UDA methods can be found. First, discrepancy-based UDA methods

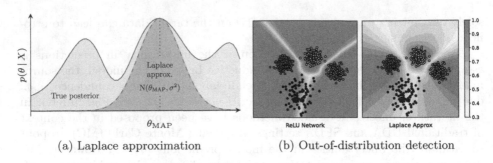

(a) Laplace approximation  (b) Out-of-distribution detection

**Fig. 2.** (a) The Laplace approximation is mode-seeking and adapts to the local curvature around the mode $\theta_{MAP}$. It does not necessarily capture the (intractable) full posterior, but gives a proxy for it, is principled, and efficient to evaluate. (b) Example of predictive uncertainty (un■■■certain) captured by a ReLU network vs. a Laplace approximation that assigns higher uncertainty to inputs (⠶) of an unseen class

aim to diminish the domain-shift between the two domains with maximum mean discrepancy (MMD, [37,39,62]), or with correlation alignment [43,53,57]. The second category of UDA methods exploits the adversarial objective [18] to promote domain confusion between the two data distributions by using domain discriminator [14,38,61]. Finally, the third category comprises reconstruction-based UDA methods [4,16,23] that casts data reconstruction as an auxiliary objective in order to ensure invariance in the feature space. However, these methods can only work in the presence of the source data set during the adaptation stage, which might be limited in practice due to data privacy or storage concerns.

**Open-set Domain Adaptation** (OSDA), originally proposed in [48], refers to the DA setting where both the domains have some shared and private classes, with explicit knowledge about the shared classes. However, such a setting was deemed impractical, and later Saito *et al.* [56] proposed the open-set setting where the source labels are a subset of the target labels. Thereon, several OSDA methods have been proposed which use image-to-image translations [71], progressive filtering [36], ensemble of multiple classifiers [11] and one-vs-all classifiers [55] to detect OOD samples. Similar to the UDA, the OSDA methods also require support from the source data to detect target private classes, which make them unsuitable for source-free DA.

**Source-free Domain Adaptation** (SFDA) aims to adapt a model to the unlabelled target domain when only the source model is available and the source data set is absent during target adaptation. Existing SFDA methods use pseudo-label refinement [1,5,33], latent source feature generation using variational inference [70], or disparity among an ensemble of classifiers [30]. Certain SFDA methods resort to *ad hoc* source training protocols to enable the source model to be adapted on the target data. For instance, [30] requires an ensemble of classifiers to be trained during source training so that the disparity among them could be utilized for target adaptation. Similarly, USFDA [27] requires artificially generated negative samples in the source training stage for the model to detect OOD samples. Such coupled source and target training procedures make these SFDA methods less viable for practical applications. On the other hand, our proposed U-SFAN does not require specialized source training except a computationally lightweight approximate inference, which can be done with a single pass of the source data during the source training. Moreover, unlike [1,30], our U-SFAN works well on both closed-set and open-set SFDA without *ad hoc* modifications.

**Uncertainty Quantification** in the form of Bayesian deep learning (*e.g.*, [24,45]) is concerned with formalizing prior knowledge and representing uncertainty in model predictions, especially under domain-shift or out-of-distribution samples. Even though the Bayesian methodology gives an explicit way of formalizing uncertainty, computation is often intractable. Thus, approximate inference methods such as Monte Carlo (MC) dropout [12], deep ensembles [29,66], other stochastic methods (*e.g.*, [42]), variational methods [3], or the Laplace approximation [52] are typically employed in practice. Prior works in semantic segmentation [72] and UDA [20,28,30,51,65] applied MC dropout or deep ensembles, respectively, for uncertainty quantification if DA. However, none of those above approaches can be considered practical for the more challenging source-free DA scenario as MC dropout, ensembles, and other stochastic methods do not lend themselves well to the source-free case. In particular, they either require retraining several models on the source, changing the model architecture or requiring a tailored learning procedure on the source data. Thus we take a Laplace approach which allows re-using the source model by linearizing around a point-estimate (see Fig. 2), which is *post hoc*, yet grounded in classical statistics [15].

## 3   Methods

**Problem Definition and Notation.** We are given a labelled source data set, having $n^{[S]}$ instances, $\mathcal{D}^{[S]} = \{(\mathbf{x}_i^{[S]}, \mathbf{y}_i^{[S]})\}_{i=1}^{n^{[S]}}$, where $\mathbf{x}^{[S]} \in \mathcal{X}^{[S]}$ are $D$-dimensional inputs and $\mathbf{y}^{[S]} \in \mathcal{Y}^{[S]}$ where we assume $K$-dimensional one-hot encoded class labels, *i.e.*, $\mathcal{Y}^{[S]} = \mathbb{B}^K$. Moreover, we have $n^{[T]}$ unlabelled target observations $\mathcal{D}^{[T]} = \{\mathbf{x}_j^{[T]}\}_{j=1}^{n^{[T]}}$, where $\mathbf{x}^{[T]} \in \mathcal{X}^{[T]}$ are $D$-dimensional unlabelled inputs. As in any DA scenario, the assumption made is that the marginal distributions of the source and the target are different, but the semantic concept represented through class labels does not change. Formally, we assume that $p(\mathbf{y}^{[S]} \mid \mathbf{x}^{[S]}) \approx p(\mathbf{y}^{[S]} \mid \mathbf{x}^{[T]})$ and $p(\mathbf{x}^{[S]}) \neq p(\mathbf{x}^{[T]})$. In the SFDA scenario we further assume that the source data set is only available while learning the source function $f \colon \mathcal{X}^{[S]} \to \mathcal{Y}^{[S]}$ and becomes unavailable while adapting on the unlabelled data. The goal of SFDA is to adapt the source function $f$ to the target domain solely by using the data in $\mathcal{D}^{[T]}$. The resulting target function, denoted as $f' \colon \mathcal{X}^{[T]} \to \mathcal{Y}^{[T]}$, can then be used to infer the class assignment for $\mathbf{x}^{[T]} \in \mathcal{X}^{[T]}$. In this work we have considered two settings of the SFDA: i) *vanilla closed-set* SFDA where the label space of the source S and the target T is the same, $L^{[S]} = L^{[T]}$; and ii) *open-set* SFDA where the label space of the S is a subset of the T, *i.e.*, $L^{[S]} \subset L^{[T]}$, and $L^{[T]} \setminus L^{[S]}$ are denoted as *target-private* or OOD classes.

We model the source and target functions $f$ with a neural network that is composed of two sub-networks: feature extractor $g$ and hypothesis function $h$, such that $f = h \circ g$. The feature extractor $g$ and the hypothesis function $h$ are parameterized by parameters $\beta$ and $\theta$, respectively. During target adaptation, the model is initialized with parameters learned on $\mathcal{D}^{[S]}$ and subsequently the feature extractor parameters are updated using backpropagation, *i.e.*, the hypothesis function is kept frozen.

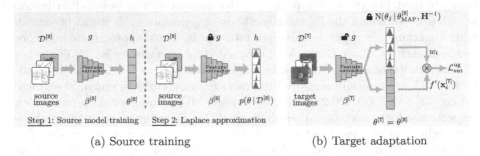

(a) Source training          (b) Target adaptation

**Fig. 3.** The pipeline for U-SFAN: (a) Initial source model training (1) and the additional step (2) of composing a Laplace approximation for assessing the posterior over model parameters, $p(\theta \mid \mathcal{D}^{[S]})$. (b) At target adaptation, we keep the posterior over the parameters fixed (🔒) and train $g$ under a uncertainty-aware composite loss that weights samples according to predictive uncertainty

**Overall Idea.** Our proposed method for SFDA operates in two stages. We begin the first stage (see Fig. 3a) by training a source model on the data set $\mathcal{D}^{[S]}$, which gives us the maximum-a-posteriori probability (MAP) estimate of the source network parameters ($\{\beta_{\text{MAP}}^{[S]}, \theta_{\text{MAP}}^{[S]}\}$). The second stage (see Fig. 3b) comprises of maximization of mutual information [17] in the predictions for the target inputs $\mathcal{D}^{[T]}$. However, due to the overconfidence of ReLU networks [22], maximizing mutual information for all inputs equally, including those that are far away from the source data, could be detrimental. To overcome this pathology, we derive a per-sample weight using the model's uncertainty and use it to modulate the mutual information objective in SHOT. To estimate the uncertainty in the predictions on the target data, we perform approximate posterior inference over the parameters of the hypothesis function, *i.e.*, $p(\theta^{[S]} \mid \mathcal{D}^{[S]})$. Inspired by recent works on approximate inference in Bayesian neural networks [25,40,59], we propose to estimate the posterior predictive distribution $p(\mathbf{y} \mid \mathbf{x}, \mathcal{D})$ using a Laplace approximation, introducing little computational overhead and without the need for specialized source training. We briefly describe the preliminaries to our approach in the following section.

### 3.1  Preliminaries

Liang *et al.* [33] proposed SHOT (**S**ource **H**yp**O**thesis **T**ransfer) for the task of SFDA, where the goal is to find a parameterization $\beta^{[T]}$ of the feature extractor $g$ such that the distribution of latent features $\mathbf{z}^{[T]} = g_{\beta^{[T]}}(\mathbf{x}^{[T]})$ matches the distribution of the latent source features. This enables that the target data can be accurately classified by the hypothesis function parameterized by $\theta^{[S]}$. To this end, the authors address the SFDA task in two stages where the first and second stage comprise of source model training and maximizing the mutual information [17] between the latent representations and the classifier output, respectively.

The source model $f\colon \mathcal{X}^{[S]} \to \mathcal{Y}^{[T]}$ for a $K$-way classification task is learned using a label-smoothed cross-entropy objective [44], *i.e.*,

$$\mathcal{L}_{\mathrm{src}} = -\, \mathbb{E}_{p(\mathbf{x}^{[S]}, \mathbf{y}^{[S]})} \sum_{k=1}^{K} \tilde{y}_k^{[S]} \log \phi_k(f(\mathbf{x}^{[S]})), \tag{1}$$

where $\phi_k(\mathbf{a}) = \exp(a_k)/\sum_j \exp(a_j)$ denotes the likelihood for the $k^{\mathrm{th}}$ component of the model output and $\tilde{y}_{i,k}^{[S]} = y_{i,k}^{[S]}(1-\alpha) + \alpha/K$ the class label for the $i^{\mathrm{th}}$ label smoothed datum.

After the source training, the $\mathcal{D}^{[S]}$ is discarded and the target adaptation is conducted on $\mathcal{D}^{[T]}$ only. To adapt on the target domain, the target function $f'$ is initialized based on the learned source function $f$ and learned with the information maximization (IM) loss [17]. The IM loss ensures that the function mapping will produce one-hot predictions while at the same time enforcing diverse assignments, *i.e.*,

$$\mathcal{L}_{\mathrm{ent}} = -\mathbb{E}_{p(\mathbf{x}^{[T]})} \sum_{k=1}^{K} \phi_k(f'(\mathbf{x}^{[T]})) \log \phi_k(f'(\mathbf{x}^{[T]})), \tag{2}$$

$$\mathcal{L}_{\mathrm{div}} = \mathrm{D}_{\mathrm{KL}}(\hat{\mathbf{p}} \,\|\, K^{-1}\mathbf{1}_K) - \log K, \tag{3}$$

where $\mathbf{1}_K$ is a vector of all ones, and $\hat{p}_k = \mathbb{E}_{p(\mathbf{x}^{[T]})}[\phi_k(f'(\mathbf{x}^{[T]}))]$ is the expected network output for the $k^{\mathrm{th}}$ class. Intuitively, $\mathcal{L}_{\mathrm{ent}}$ is in charge of making the network output one-hot, while $\mathcal{L}_{\mathrm{div}}$ is responsible for equally partitioning the network prediction into $K$ classes. In practice $\mathcal{L}_{\mathrm{div}}$ operates on a mini-batch level. In this work we start from SHOT-IM to adapt to the target domain.

### 3.2  Uncertainty-Guided Source-Free DA

Distributional shift between source and target data sets causes the network outputs to differ, even for the same underlying semantic concept [8]. In a standard UDA scenario, where the source data is available during target adaptation, it is still possible to align the marginal distributions by using a quantifiable discrepancy metric. The task becomes more challenging in the SFDA scenario because it is not possible to align the target feature distribution to a reference (or source) distribution. Moreover, standard ReLU networks are known to yield overconfident predictions for data points which lie far away from the training (source) data [22]. In other words, the MAP estimates of a neural network has no notion of uncertainty over the learned weights. Thus, blindly trusting the source model predictions for $\mathbf{x}^{[\mathrm{T}]} \in \mathcal{D}^{[\mathrm{T}]}$ while performing information maximization [33] or entropy minimization [19] can potentially lead to misalignment of clusters between the source and target.

In this work we propose to incorporate the uncertainty of the neural network's weights into the predictions. This mandates a Bayesian treatment of the networks parameters ($\theta$), which gives a posterior distribution over the model parameters by conditioning onto observed data ($\mathcal{D}$), i.e., $p(\theta \mid \mathcal{D}) = \frac{p(\theta)\, p(\mathcal{D} \mid \theta)}{p(\mathcal{D})} \propto p(\theta)\, p(\mathcal{D} \mid \theta)$. The prediction of the network $h_\theta$ for an observation $\mathbf{x}$ is given by the predictive posterior distribution, i.e.,

$$p(y_k \mid \mathbf{x}, \mathcal{D}) = \int_\theta \phi_k(h_\theta(\mathbf{x}))\, p(\theta \mid \mathcal{D})\, \mathrm{d}\theta. \tag{4}$$

Note that the posterior $p(\theta \mid \mathcal{D})$ in Eq. (4) does not have an analytical solution in general and need to be approximated. For this, we employ a local approximation to the posterior using a Laplace approximation (LA, [59]). The LA locally approximates the true posterior using a multivariate Gaussian distribution centred at a local maximum and with covariance matrix given by the inverse of the Hessian $\mathbf{H}$ of the negative log-posterior, i.e., $p(\theta \mid \mathcal{D}) \approx \mathrm{N}(\theta \mid \theta_{\mathrm{MAP}}, \mathbf{H}^{-1})$ with $\mathbf{H} := -\nabla_\theta^2 \log p(\theta \mid \mathcal{D}) \mid_{\theta_{\mathrm{MAP}}}$. Details can be found in the appendix. Note that the LA is a principled and simple, yet effective, approach to approximate posterior inference stemming from a second-order Taylor expansion of the true posterior around $\theta_{\mathrm{MAP}}$. Next we will discuss LA in the context of SFDA.

**Bayesian Source Model Generation.** In the source training stage (see Fig. 3a), by optimizing Eq. (1), we obtain a MAP estimate of the weights for our source model, comprising $\beta_{\mathrm{MAP}}$ and $\theta_{\mathrm{MAP}}$ for $g$ and $h$, respectively. Since $f$ is often modelled by a very deep neural network (e.g., ResNet-50), computing the Hessian can be computationally infeasible owing to the large number of parameters. So we make another simplification by applying a Bayesian treatment only to hypothesis function $h$, known as the *last-layer* Laplace approximation [25]. This gives us a probabilistic source hypothesis with posterior distribution $p(\theta \mid \mathcal{D}^{[\mathrm{S}]})$ for the parameters. The feature extractor $g$ remains deterministic. Formally, let $\mathbf{z} = g_{\beta^{[\mathrm{S}]}}(\mathbf{x})$ be the latent feature representation from the feature extractor. Following Eq. (4), the predictive posterior distribution is given as:

$$p(y_k \mid \mathbf{z}, \mathcal{D}^{[\mathrm{S}]}) \approx \int_\theta \phi_k(h_\theta(\mathbf{z}))\, \mathrm{N}(\theta \mid \theta_{\mathrm{MAP}}, \mathbf{H}^{-1})\, \mathrm{d}\theta. \tag{5}$$

While the *last-layer* LA greatly simplifies the computational overhead for large networks, the Hessian can still be difficult to compute in the case the number of classes is large. To simplify computations, we assume that $\mathbf{H}$ can be Kronecker-factored $\mathbf{H} := \mathbf{V} \otimes \mathbf{U}$ and the resulting approximation is referred to as Kronecker-factored Laplace approximation (KFLA, [52]). Such probabilistic treatment allows us to quantify uncertainty in the predictions for data points from the target with little computational overhead. Also, the LA can be readily computed using a single forward pass of the source data through the network. Next, we describe how to use the uncertainty estimates during target adaptation.

**Uncertainty-Guided Information Maximization.** Upon completion of the source model generation stage, we exploit the probabilistic source hypothesis to guide the information maximization in the target adaptation stage. SHOT puts equal confidence on all the target predictions and do not make any distinction for the target feature that lies outside of the source manifold. We emphasize that in case of strong domain-shift naïvely maximizing the IM loss could lead to cluster misalignment. For that reason, we propose to weigh the entropy minimization objective (Eq. (2)) with a weight which is proportional to the certainty in the target predictions (see Fig. 3b). To get the per-sample weight for a $\mathbf{x}^{[T]}$ we need to compute the predictive posterior distribution, as outlined in Eq. (5). However, exactly solving the integration is intractable in many cases and we, therefore, resort to Monte Carlo (MC) integration. Let $\mathbf{z}^{[T]} = g_{\beta^{[T]}}(\mathbf{x}^{[T]})$, the approximate predictive posterior distributions is:

$$p(y_k \mid \mathbf{z}^{[T]}, \mathcal{D}^{[S]}) \approx \frac{1}{M} \sum_{j=1}^{M} \phi_k \left( h_{\theta_j}(\mathbf{z}^{[T]}) \right), \tag{6}$$

where $\theta_j \sim \mathrm{N}(\theta_j \mid \theta_{\mathrm{MAP}}, \mathbf{H}^{-1})$ and $M$ denotes the number of MC steps. To encourage low entropy predictions we additionally scale the outputs of the hypothesis by $1/\tau$, where $0 < \tau \leq 1$. The final weight of each observation $\mathbf{x}_i^{[T]}$ is then computed as $w_i = \exp(-H)$ where $H$ denotes the entropy of the predictive mean. The *uncertainty-guided entropy loss* is then given as:

$$\mathcal{L}_{\mathrm{ent}}^{\mathrm{ug}} = -\mathbb{E}_{p(\mathbf{x}^{[T]})} \sum_{k=1}^{K} w\, \sigma_k(f'(\mathbf{x}^{[T]})) \log \sigma_k(f'(\mathbf{x}^{[T]})). \tag{7}$$

The final training objective is then given as: $\mathcal{L}_{\mathrm{U\text{-}SFAN}} = (1 - \gamma)\mathcal{L}_{\mathrm{ent}}^{\mathrm{ug}} + \gamma\, \mathcal{L}_{\mathrm{div}}$. Pseudocode for our U-SFAN can be found in the appendix.

**How Does this Differ from Conventional Uncertainty Estimation?** The importance and advantages of adopting a Laplace approximation (LA) over Monte Carlo (MC) dropout to estimate uncertainty in SFDA can be summarized as follows: *(i)* LA does not require specialized network architecture (*e.g.*, dropout layers), loss function, or re-training (as in MC dropout) to estimate predictive uncertainties. This greatly decouples the source training from target adaptation, which is essential to be applicable in SFDA; *(ii)* To have well-calibrated uncertainties, MC dropout requires a grid search over the dropout probabilities [13], a prohibitive operation in deep neural networks, especially as the future target data is not available at source training. LA is a more principled approach that does not require a grid search, making it better suited for SFDA. *(iii)* LA is computationally lightweight since it requires just a single forward pass of the source data through the network after the source training to estimate the posterior over the parameters of the sub-network. *(iv)* LA does not impact the training time during target adaptation because, unlike MC dropout, only a single forward pass is needed to quantify the predictive uncertainties. Because LA employs a Gaussian approximation to the posterior, MC integration is cheap and efficient to compute. *(v)* As used in our work, LA estimates the full posterior over the weights and biases, while MC dropout can only account for the uncertainties over the weights [12] and is known to be a poor approximation to the posterior [10,46,47]. *(vi)* LA preserves the decision boundary induced by the MAP estimate, which is not the case for MC dropout [25]. In summary, our contribution goes beyond the uncertainty re-weighting scheme [32,35] commonly used in UDA, while carrying many advantages over existing works.

## 4   Experiments

We conduct experiments on four standard DA benchmarks: OFFICE31 [54], OFFICE-HOME [63], VISDA-C [50], and the large-scale DOMAINNET [49] (**0.6 million** images). The details of the benchmarks are summarized in appendix. For the experiments in the open-set DA setting we follow the split of [33] for shared and target-private classes.

**Evaluation Protocol.** We report the classification accuracy for every possible pair of *source* $\mapsto$ *target* directions, except for the VISDA-C where we are only concerned with the transfer from *synthetic* $\mapsto$ *real* domain. For the open-set experiments, following the evaluation protocol in [33], we report the OS accuracy which includes the per-class accuracy of the known and the unknown class and is computed as OS $= \frac{1}{K+1} \sum_{k=1}^{K+1} \mathrm{acc}_k$, where $k = \{1, 2, \ldots, K\}$ denote the shared classes and $(K+1)^{\mathrm{th}}$ is the target-private or OOD classes. This metric is preferred over the known class accuracy, OS$^* = \frac{1}{K} \sum_{k=1}^{K} \mathrm{acc}_k$, as it does not take into account the OOD classes.

**Implementation Details.** We adopted the network architectures used in the SFDA literature, which are ResNet-50 or ResNet-101 [21]. Following [33], we added a bottleneck layer containing 256 neurons which is then followed by a batch normalization layer. The network finally ends with a weight normalized linear classifier that is kept frozen during the target adaptation. Details about hyperparameters can be found in the appendix. For computing the KFLA we use the PyTorch package of Dangel *et al.* [9]. Our code is available at https://github.com/roysubhankar/uncertainty-sfda

### 4.1   Ablation Studies

As discussed in Sect. 3.2, conventional SFDA methods that rely on optimizing the IM loss on the unlabelled target data (*e.g.*, SHOT) are prone to misalignment of the target data with the source hypothesis under strong domain shift. To visually demonstrate this phenomenon, we design an experiment of a 3-way classification task on toy data (see Fig. 4). Given a set of source data points, belonging to three classes, we simulate two kinds of domain-shift: *mild* shift (Fig. 4a) and *strong* shift (Fig. 4b). In the case of mild shift, the target data points stay very close to the source manifold, and the conventional approach (only using the MAP estimate) can classify a majority of target data points without the need of adaptation. Whereas, in the case of strong shift, the target data points for the blue class, in particular, shift drastically away from the source points. The source model based on the MAP estimate misclassifies most of the target data points with high confidence. On the other hand, our uncertainty-guided source model remains certain only for those target points which lie within the source support and assigns low certainty otherwise (proportional to the strength of colours depicting the decision surface in Fig. 4), robustifying the adaptation on the target data in case of domain shift.

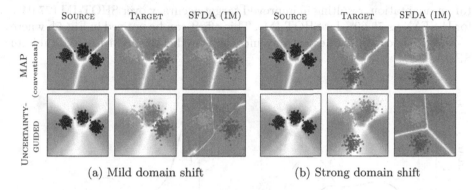

(a) Mild domain shift                    (b) Strong domain shift

**Fig. 4.** Comparison of conventional IM (MAP) with our uncertainty-guided IM on target data under mild and strong domain-shift. The solid • vs. hollow ○ circles represent the source and the target data, respectively. Each class is colour coded and the decision boundaries are shaded with the corresponding colours. Under strong domain-shift, IM, when used with a MAP estimate, finds a **completely flipped** decision boundary. U-SFAN finds the decision boundary by down-weighting the *far away* target data

Given such a set-up, we optimize the IM loss (*i.e.*, SHOT-IM) for both the conventional and the uncertainty-guided source models. In the case of mild shift, both can reliably partition the target data points under the right decision surfaces (see Fig. 4a (right)). This is intuitive because the decision boundary of the target model already passes through the low-density regions. Hence, the optimization of the IM loss leads to correct target classification with both methods. However, when the domain shift is more substantial, the conventional approach results in *completely flipped* decision boundaries. This happens because most blue target points fall under the red decision surface, and thus, the IM loss assigns them to class 'red'. On the contrary, our uncertainty-guided approach down-weights the blue points, and *safely* optimizes the IM loss as the model is uncertain about the class assignment for those points (Fig. 4b (right)). This protects from major changes in the decision boundaries and allows the optimization to find the correct decision boundaries for the target data. Therefore, highlighting the importance of having a notion of uncertainty in the model predictions during adaptation. We show later that this intuition also holds well for real-world data sets where our U-SFAN offers more robustness when the domain-shift in a data set becomes challenging.

To gain further insights, we visualize the entropy density plots of the source model predictions before and after adaptation with conventional (MAP estimate) and uncertainty-guided models on an image data set (CIFAR [26] as source data set and STL [7] as target). As shown in Fig. 5a, the MAP estimate has lower entropy predictions for both the correct and incorrect predictions, when compared to our uncertainty-guided model. Reduced over-confidence for our approach is expected before the adaptation phase, however, it is non-trivial that this behavior also bears in the post-adaptation phase. The reduced over-confident allows our U-SFAN to down-weight the incorrect predictions during target adaptation, resulting in improved target accuracy over SHOT-IM (77.04% for U-SFAN vs 75.69% for SHOT-IM). This effect can be noticed in Fig. 5b where U-SFAN has overall higher entropy incorrect predictions, which is desirable in SFDA.

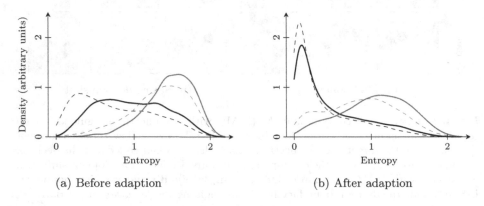

(a) Before adaption       (b) After adaption

**Fig. 5.** Entropy density plots for CIFAR9 → STL9 in the closed-set SFDA setting using the MAP estimate (- - - correct, - - - incorrect) or our approach (—— correct,—— incorrect). Our uncertainty-guided SFDA approach places less mass on low-entropy incorrect samples before and after adaptation

**Table 1.** Comparison of model performance using entropy weighting during target adaptation on the OFFICE-HOME data set. The weights computed using the LA is more beneficial than the weights computed with a MAP network

| METHOD | SOURCE-ONLY | SHOT-IM [33] | SHOT-IM + ENT. WEIGHTING | U-SFAN (OURS) |
|---|---|---|---|---|
| AVG. ACC. | 60.3 | 70.5 | 71.2 | **71.8** |

To further understand the contribution of our uncertainty-guided re-weighting, we run an ablation where the approximate posterior distribution of our method (Eq. (7)) is replaced by a weight computed from a point estimate from a MAP source model. This model is denoted as SHOT-IM +

**Table 2.** Comparison of the classification accuracy on the OFFICE-HOME for the closed-set setting using ResNet-50. High overall performance signifies *milder* distributional shift between domains. The improvement of U-SFAN upon SHOT is moderate, but competitive w.r.t. A$^2$Net [67] or SHOT++ [34], which require complex training objectives

| METHOD | A→C | A→P | A→R | C→A | C→P | C→R | P→A | P→C | P→R | R→A | R→C | R→P | AVG. |
|---|---|---|---|---|---|---|---|---|---|---|---|---|---|
| ResNet-50 | 34.9 | 50.0 | 58.0 | 37.4 | 41.9 | 46.2 | 38.5 | 31.2 | 60.4 | 53.9 | 41.2 | 59.9 | 46.1 |
| DANN [14] | 45.6 | 59.3 | 70.1 | 47.0 | 58.5 | 60.9 | 46.1 | 43.7 | 68.5 | 63.2 | 51.8 | 76.8 | 57.6 |
| DWT [53] | 50.3 | 72.1 | 77.0 | 59.6 | 69.3 | 70.2 | 58.3 | 48.1 | 77.3 | 69.3 | 53.6 | 82.0 | 65.6 |
| CDAN [38] | 50.7 | 70.6 | 76.0 | 57.6 | 70.0 | 70.0 | 57.4 | 50.9 | 77.3 | 70.9 | 56.7 | 81.6 | 65.8 |
| SAFN [68] | 52.0 | 71.7 | 76.3 | 64.2 | 69.9 | 71.9 | 63.7 | 51.4 | 77.1 | 70.9 | 57.1 | 81.5 | 67.3 |
| SHOT-IM [33] | 55.4 | 76.6 | 80.4 | 66.9 | 74.3 | 75.4 | 65.6 | 54.8 | 80.7 | 73.7 | 58.4 | 83.4 | 70.5 |
| LSC [69] | 57.9 | 78.6 | 81.0 | 66.7 | 77.2 | 77.2 | 65.6 | 56.0 | 82.2 | 72.0 | 57.8 | 83.4 | 71.3 |
| U-SFAN (Ours) | 58.5 | 78.6 | 81.1 | 66.6 | 75.2 | 77.9 | 66.3 | 57.9 | 80.6 | 73.6 | 61.4 | 84.1 | 71.8 |
| A$^2$Net[67] | 58.4 | 79.0 | 82.4 | 67.5 | 79.3 | 78.9 | 68.0 | 56.2 | 82.9 | 74.1 | 60.5 | 85.0 | 72.8 |
| SHOT++ [34] | 57.9 | 79.7 | 82.5 | 68.5 | 79.6 | 79.3 | 68.5 | 57.0 | 83.0 | 73.7 | 60.7 | 84.9 | 73.0 |
| SHOT [33] | 57.1 | 78.1 | 81.5 | 68.0 | 78.2 | 78.1 | 67.4 | 54.9 | 82.2 | 73.3 | 58.8 | 84.3 | 71.8 |
| U-SFAN+ (Ours) | 57.8 | 77.8 | 81.6 | 67.9 | 77.3 | 79.2 | 67.2 | 54.7 | 81.2 | 73.3 | 60.3 | 83.9 | 71.9 |

**Table 3.** Comparison of the OS classification accuracy on the OFFICE-HOME for the open-set setting using ResNet-50. U-SFAN improves over SHOT without the need for nearest-centroid pseudo-labelling in the case of open-set SFDA

| METHOD | A→C | A→P | A→R | C→A | C→P | C→R | P→A | P→C | P→R | R→A | R→C | R→P | AVG. |
|---|---|---|---|---|---|---|---|---|---|---|---|---|---|
| ResNet-50 | 53.4 | 52.7 | 51.9 | 69.3 | 61.8 | 74.1 | 61.4 | 64.0 | 70.0 | 78.7 | 71.0 | 74.9 | 65.3 |
| ATI-λ[48] | 55.2 | 52.6 | 53.5 | 69.1 | 63.5 | 74.1 | 61.7 | 64.5 | 70.7 | 79.2 | 72.9 | 75.8 | 66.1 |
| OpenMax [2] | 56.5 | 52.9 | 53.7 | 69.1 | 64.8 | 74.5 | 64.1 | 64.0 | 71.2 | 80.3 | 73.0 | 76.9 | 66.7 |
| STA [36] | 58.1 | 53.1 | 54.4 | 71.6 | 69.3 | 81.9 | 63.4 | 65.2 | 74.9 | 85.0 | 75.8 | 80.8 | 69.5 |
| SHOT-IM [33] | 62.5 | 77.8 | 83.9 | 60.9 | 73.4 | 79.4 | 64.7 | 58.7 | 83.1 | 69.1 | 62.0 | 82.1 | 71.5 |
| SHOT [33] | 64.5 | 80.4 | 84.7 | 63.1 | 75.4 | 81.2 | 65.3 | 59.3 | 83.3 | 69.6 | 64.6 | 82.3 | 72.8 |
| U-SFAN (Ours) | 62.9 | 77.9 | 84.0 | 67.9 | 74.6 | 79.6 | 68.8 | 61.3 | 83.3 | 76.0 | 63.9 | 82.3 | 73.5 |

ENT. WEIGHTING in Table 1. We observe that such weighting scheme indeed improves the performance over SHOT-IM. However, it still lacks behind our proposed U-SFAN which uses weights computed from the uncertainty-guided model. This clearly shows that the improvement in performance with U-SFAN is not simply caused by the re-weighting but also due to better identification of target samples that are not well explained under the source model.

## 4.2   State-of-the-Art Comparison

We compare our U-SFAN with UDA and SFDA methods on multiple data sets for closed-set and open-set settings. First, we compare U-SFAN with the baselines on the most common benchmark of OFFICE-HOME for both closed-set and open-set settings. As can be seen from Table 2 and Table 3 we improve the performance over majority of the baselines. Especially, we consistently improve over SHOT-IM with our method. We also combine the nearest centroid pseudo-labelling, used in

**Table 4.** (a) Comparison of the classification accuracy on the VISDA-C for the closed-set DA, pertaining to the *Synthetic* → *Real* direction, using ResNet-101. † indicates the numbers of [33] that are obtained using the official code from the authors. Note that several SFDA methods perform equally well for VISDA-C, hinting at saturating performance. (b) Comparison of the average accuracy on the DOMAINNET for the closed-set SFDA using ResNet-50. The SOURCE column indicates the domain where the source model has been trained. The data set being challenging (exhibiting *strong* domain-shift), the improvement with our U-SFAN over [33] is substantial

(a) VISDA-C

| METHOD | ACC. |
|---|---|
| ResNet-101 | 52.4 |
| CDAN+BSP [6] | 75.9 |
| SAFN [68] | 76.1 |
| SHOT-IM† [33] | 80.3 |
| U-SFAN (Ours) | 81.2 |
| 3C-GAN [31] | 81.6 |
| $A^2$Net[67] | 84.3 |
| SHOT† [33] | 82.4 |
| U-SFAN+ (Ours) | 82.7 |

(b) VISDA-C

| SOURCE | SHOT-IM [33] | U-SFAN |
|---|---|---|
| CLIPART | 25.04 | 30.88 |
| INFOGRAPH | 21.58 | 26.44 |
| PAINTING | 23.89 | 29.91 |
| QUICKDRAW | 10.76 | 10.44 |
| REAL | 21.74 | 29.32 |
| SKETCH | 28.87 | 29.99 |
| AVG. | 21.98 | 26.13 |

SHOT [33], with U-SFAN (indicated as U-SFAN+ in Table 2 and Table 4a), and we find that it further helps improving the performance. Notably, the recently proposed $A^2$Net [67] (which just addresses closed-set SFDA) outperforms our U-SFAN in a couple of data sets, but uses a combination of several loss functions. Interplay of multiple losses can be hard to tune in practice. On the other hand, our method is simpler, more versatile and works for both the SFDA settings. Due to lack of space, we report the numbers for OFFICE31 in the appendix. Given the performance of the SFDA baseline methods in OFFICE-HOME and VISDA-C are relatively high and closer to each other, the domain shift can be considered milder with respect to more challenging data set like DOMAIN-NET.

When we compare U-SFAN with SHOT-IM on the challenging SFDA benchmark DOMAIN-NET the advantage of our U-SFAN over SHOT-IM becomes imminent (*cf.* Table 4b), which is in line with the ablation study in Sect. 4.1. Different from the previous data sets, the difficulty in mitigating domain-shift for DOMAIN-NET is evident from the low overall performance of both SHOT-IM and U-SFAN. This data set can be seen as a real-world example of strong domain-shift. The improvement in the performance of U-SFAN over SHOT-IM for DOMAIN-NET demonstrates that incorporating the uncertainty in the model's predictions plays a crucial role in SFDA. The conventional approach may overfit to noisy model predictions, leading to poor performance. Whereas, U-SFAN can capture the uncertainty in predictions and down-weight the impact of noisy predictions.

# 5   Discussion and Conclusion

In this work, we demonstrated the need for uncertainty quantification in SFDA and proposed U-SFAN for leveraging it during target adaptation. Our uncertainty-guided approach employs a Laplace approximation to the posterior, does not require specialized source training, and allows for efficient computation of predictive uncertainties. Our experiments showed that down-weighting *distant* target data points in our novel uncertainty-weighted IM loss alleviates the misalignment of target data with the source hypothesis. We ran experiments on closed and open-set SFDA settings and show that U-SFAN consistently improves upon the existing methods. Moreover, U-SFAN has shown to be robust under mild distribution shifts and shows promising results under severe distribution shifts.

While we mainly focused on the popular IM-based SFDA methods, our proposed uncertainty-guided adaptation is also applicable to other SFDA frameworks, *e.g.*, neighbourhood clustering [69] or extensions to the multi-source SFDA problem. Moreover, the principles we build upon are general, interpretable, and have strong backing in classical statistics. We believe that uncertainty-guided SFDA will become a backbone tool for future methods in DA that generalize over different problem domains, are less sensitive to the training setup, and will provide good results without extensive *ad hoc* tuning to each problem.

**Acknowledgements.** We acknowledge funding from EU H2020 projects SPRING (No. 871245) and AI4Media (No. 951911); the EUREGIO project OLIVER; Academy of Finland (No. 339730, 308640), and the Finnish Center for Artificial Intelligence (FCAI). We acknowledge the computational resources by the Aalto Science-IT project and CSC – IT Center for Science, Finland.

# References

1. Ahmed, W., Morerio, P., Murino, V.: Adaptive pseudo-label refinement by negative ensemble learning for source-free unsupervised domain adaptation. In: Proceedings of the Winter Conference on Applications of Computer Vision (WACV) (2022)
2. Bendale, A., Boult, T.E.: Towards open set deep networks. In: Proceedings of the IEEE Conference on Computer Vision and Pattern Recognition (CVPR), pp. 1563–1572 (2016)
3. Blei, D.M., Kucukelbir, A., McAuliffe, J.D.: Variational inference: a review for statisticians. J. Am. Stat. Assoc. **112**(518), 859–877 (2017)
4. Bousmalis, K., Trigeorgis, G., Silberman, N., Krishnan, D., Erhan, D.: Domain separation networks. In: Advances in Neural Information Processing Systems (NeurIPS), pp. 343–351 (2016)
5. Chen, W., et al.: Self-supervised noisy label learning for source-free unsupervised domain adaptation. arXiv preprint arXiv:2102.11614 (2021)
6. Chen, X., Wang, S., Long, M., Wang, J.: Transferability vs. discriminability: batch spectral penalization for adversarial domain adaptation. In: Proceedings of the International Conference on Machine Learning (ICML), pp. 1081–1090 (2019)

7. Coates, A., Ng, A., Lee, H.: An analysis of single-layer networks in unsupervised feature learning. In: Proceedings of the Fourteenth International Conference on Artificial Intelligence and Statistics (AISTATS), pp. 215–223. Journal of Machine Learning Research Workshop and Conference Proceedings (2011)

8. Csurka, G.: A comprehensive survey on domain adaptation for visual applications. In: Domain Adaptation in Computer Vision Applications, pp. 1–35 (2017)

9. Dangel, F., Kunstner, F., Hennig, P.: Backpack: packing more into backprop. In: Proceedings of the International Conference on Learning Representations (ICLR) (2020)

10. Foong, A., Burt, D., Li, Y., Turner, R.: On the expressiveness of approximate inference in bayesian neural networks. In: Advances in Neural Information Processing Systems (NeurIPS), pp. 15897–15908 (2020)

11. Fu, B., Cao, Z., Long, M., Wang, J.: Learning to detect open classes for universal domain adaptation. In: Vedaldi, A., Bischof, H., Brox, T., Frahm, J.-M. (eds.) ECCV 2020. LNCS, vol. 12360, pp. 567–583. Springer, Cham (2020). https://doi.org/10.1007/978-3-030-58555-6_34

12. Gal, Y., Ghahramani, Z.: Dropout as a Bayesian approximation: representing model uncertainty in deep learning. In: Proceedings of the International Conference on Machine Learning (ICML), pp. 1050–1059 (2016)

13. Gal, Y., Hron, J., Kendall, A.: Concrete dropout. In: Advances in Neural Information Processing Systems (NeurIPS), pp. 3581–3590 (2017)

14. Ganin, Y., Ustinova, E., Ajakan, H., Germain, P., Larochelle, H., Laviolette, F., Marchand, M., Lempitsky, V.: Domain-adversarial training of neural networks. J. Mach. Learn. Res. **17**(59), 1–35 (2016)

15. Gelman, A., Carlin, J.B., Stern, H.S., Dunson, D.B., Vehtari, A., Rubin, D.B.: Bayesian Data Analysis. FL, 3rd edn. Chapman and Hall/CRC, Boca Raton (2013)

16. Ghifary, M., Kleijn, W.B., Zhang, M., Balduzzi, D., Li, W.: Deep reconstruction-classification networks for unsupervised domain adaptation. In: Leibe, B., Matas, J., Sebe, N., Welling, M. (eds.) ECCV 2016. LNCS, vol. 9908, pp. 597–613. Springer, Cham (2016). https://doi.org/10.1007/978-3-319-46493-0_36

17. Gomes, R., Krause, A., Perona, P.: Discriminative clustering by regularized information maximization. In: Advances in Neural Information Processing Systems (NeurIPS) (2010)

18. Goodfellow, I., et al.: Generative adversarial nets. In: Advances in Neural Information Processing Systems (NeurIPS) (2014)

19. Grandvalet, Y., Bengio, Y., et al.: Semi-supervised learning by entropy minimization. In: Advances in Neural Information Processing Systems (NeurIPS), pp. 281–296 (2005)

20. Han, L., Zou, Y., Gao, R., Wang, L., Metaxas, D.: Unsupervised domain adaptation via calibrating uncertainties. In: CVPR Workshops (2019)

21. He, K., Zhang, X., Ren, S., Sun, J.: Deep residual learning for image recognition. In: Proceedings of the IEEE Conference on Computer Vision and Pattern Recognition (CVPR), pp. 770–778 (2016)

22. Hein, M., Andriushchenko, M., Bitterwolf, J.: Why relu networks yield high-confidence predictions far away from the training data and how to mitigate the problem. In: Proceedings of the IEEE Conference on Computer Vision and Pattern Recognition (CVPR), pp. 41–50 (2019)

23. Hoffman, J., et al.: Cycada: cycle-consistent adversarial domain adaptation. In: Proceedings of the International Conference on Machine Learning (ICML), pp. 1989–1998 (2018)

24. Kendall, A., Gal, Y.: What uncertainties do we need in Bayesian deep learning for computer vision? In: Advances in Neural Information Processing Systems (NeurIPS), pp. 5574–5584 (2017)
25. Kristiadi, A., Hein, M., Hennig, P.: Being Bayesian, even just a bit, fixes overconfidence in relu networks. In: Proceedings of the International Conference on Machine Learning (ICML), pp. 5436–5446 (2020)
26. Krizhevsky, A.: Learning Multiple Layers of Features from Tiny Images. Master's thesis, University of Tronto, Toronto, Canada (2009)
27. Kundu, J.N., Venkat, N., Babu, R.V., et al.: Universal source-free domain adaptation. In: Proceedings of the IEEE Conference on Computer Vision and Pattern Recognition (CVPR), pp. 4544–4553 (2020)
28. Kurmi, V.K., Kumar, S., Namboodiri, V.P.: Attending to discriminative certainty for domain adaptation. In: Proceedings of the IEEE/CVF Conference on Computer Vision and Pattern Recognition (CVPR), pp. 491–500 (2019)
29. Lakshminarayanan, B., Pritzel, A., Blundell, C.: Simple and scalable predictive uncertainty estimation using deep ensembles. In: Advances in Neural Information Processing Systems (NeurIPS) (2017)
30. Lao, Q., Jiang, X., Havaei, M.: Hypothesis disparity regularized mutual information maximization. In: Proceedings of the AAAI Conference on Artificial Intelligence (2021)
31. Li, R., Jiao, Q., Cao, W., Wong, H.S., Wu, S.: Model adaptation: unsupervised domain adaptation without source data. In: Proceedings of the IEEE Conference on Computer Vision and Pattern Recognition (CVPR), pp. 9641–9650 (2020)
32. Liang, J., He, R., Sun, Z., Tan, T.: Exploring uncertainty in pseudo-label guided unsupervised domain adaptation. Pattern Recogn. **96**, 106996 (2019)
33. Liang, J., Hu, D., Feng, J.: Do we really need to access the source data? source hypothesis transfer for unsupervised domain adaptation. In: Proceedings of the International Conference on Machine Learning (ICML), pp. 6028–6039 (2020)
34. Liang, J., Hu, D., Wang, Y., He, R., Feng, J.: Source data-absent unsupervised domain adaptation through hypothesis transfer and labeling transfer. IEEE Trans. Pattern Anal. Mach. Intell. (2021)
35. Liang, J., Wang, Y., Hu, D., He, R., Feng, J.: A balanced and uncertainty-aware approach for partial domain adaptation. In: Vedaldi, A., Bischof, H., Brox, T., Frahm, J.-M. (eds.) ECCV 2020. LNCS, vol. 12356, pp. 123–140. Springer, Cham (2020). https://doi.org/10.1007/978-3-030-58621-8_8
36. Liu, H., Cao, Z., Long, M., Wang, J., Yang, Q.: Separate to adapt: open set domain adaptation via progressive separation. In: Proceedings of the IEEE Conference on Computer Vision and Pattern Recognition (CVPR), pp. 2927–2936 (2019)
37. Long, M., Cao, Y., Wang, J., Jordan, M.: Learning transferable features with deep adaptation networks. In: Proceedings of the International Conference on Machine Learning (ICML), pp. 97–105 (2015)
38. Long, M., Cao, Z., Wang, J., Jordan, M.I.: Conditional adversarial domain adaptation. In: Advances in Neural Information Processing Systems (NeurIPS), pp. 1647–1657 (2018)
39. Long, M., Zhu, H., Wang, J., Jordan, M.I.: Deep transfer learning with joint adaptation networks. In: Proceedings of the International Conference on Machine Learning (ICML), pp. 2208–2217 (2017)
40. MacKay, D.J.: A practical Bayesian framework for backpropagation networks. Neural Comput. **4**(3), 448–472 (1992)
41. MacKay, D.J.: Information Theory. Cambridge University Press, Inference and Learning Algorithms (2003)

42. Maddox, W.J., Izmailov, P., Garipov, T., Vetrov, D.P., Wilson, A.G.: A simple baseline for Bayesian uncertainty in deep learning. In: Advances in Neural Information Processing Systems (NeurIPS), pp. 13132–13143 (2019)

43. Morerio, P., Cavazza, J., Murino, V.: Minimal-entropy correlation alignment for unsupervised deep domain adaptation. In: Proceedings of the International Conference on Learning Representations (ICLR) (2018)

44. Müller, R., Kornblith, S., Hinton, G.: When does label smoothing help? In: Advances in Neural Information Processing Systems (NeurIPS), pp. 4694–4703 (2019)

45. Neal, R.M.: Bayesian Learning for Neural Networks. Springer Science & Business Media (2012)

46. Osband, I.: Risk versus uncertainty in deep learning: Bayes, bootstrap and the dangers of dropout. In: NeurIPS Workshop on Bayesian Deep Learning (2016)

47. Osband, I., Aslanides, J., Cassirer, A.: Randomized prior functions for deep reinforcement learning. In: Advances in Neural Information Processing Systems (NeurIPS), pp. 8617–8629 (2018)

48. Panareda Busto, P., Gall, J.: Open set domain adaptation. In: Proceedings of the IEEE International Conference on Computer Vision (ICCV), pp. 754–763 (2017)

49. Peng, X., Bai, Q., Xia, X., Huang, Z., Saenko, K., Wang, B.: Moment matching for multi-source domain adaptation. In: Proceedings of the IEEE International Conference on Computer Vision (ICCV), pp. 1406–1415 (2019)

50. Peng, X., Usman, B., Kaushik, N., Hoffman, J., Wang, D., Saenko, K.: Visda: the visual domain adaptation challenge. arXiv preprint arXiv:1710.06924 (2017)

51. Ringwald, T., Stiefelhagen, R.: Unsupervised domain adaptation by uncertain feature alignment. In: The British Machine Vision Conference (BMVC) (2020)

52. Ritter, H., Botev, A., Barber, D.: A scalable laplace approximation for neural networks. In: Proceedings of the International Conference on Learning Representations (ICLR) (2018)

53. Roy, S., Siarohin, A., Sangineto, E., Bulo, S.R., Sebe, N., Ricci, E.: Unsupervised domain adaptation using feature-whitening and consensus loss. In: Proceedings of the IEEE Conference on Computer Vision and Pattern Recognition (CVPR), pp. 9471–9480 (2019)

54. Saenko, K., Kulis, B., Fritz, M., Darrell, T.: Adapting visual category models to new domains. In: Daniilidis, K., Maragos, P., Paragios, N. (eds.) ECCV 2010. LNCS, vol. 6314, pp. 213–226. Springer, Heidelberg (2010). https://doi.org/10.1007/978-3-642-15561-1_16

55. Saito, K., Saenko, K.: Ovanet: one-vs-all network for universal domain adaptation. In: Proceedings of the IEEE International Conference on Computer Vision (ICCV), pp. 9000–9009 (2021)

56. Saito, K., Yamamoto, S., Ushiku, Y., Harada, T.: Open set domain adaptation by backpropagation. In: Ferrari, V., Hebert, M., Sminchisescu, C., Weiss, Y. (eds.) ECCV 2018. LNCS, vol. 11209, pp. 156–171. Springer, Cham (2018). https://doi.org/10.1007/978-3-030-01228-1_10

57. Sun, B., Saenko, K.: Deep coral: Correlation alignment for deep domain adaptation. In: Proceedings of the European Conference on Computer Vision (ECCV). pp. 443–450 (2016)

58. Tian, J., Zhang, J., Li, W., Xu, D.: VDM-DA: virtual domain modeling for source data-free domain adaptation. IEEE Trans. Circuits Syst. Video Technol. (2021)

59. Tierney, L., Kadane, J.B.: Accurate approximations for posterior moments and marginal densities. J. Am. Stat. Assoc. **81**(393), 82–86 (1986)

60. Torralba, A., Efros, A.A.: Unbiased look at dataset bias. In: Proceedings of the IEEE Conference on Computer Vision and Pattern Recognition (CVPR), pp. 1521–1528 (2011)
61. Tzeng, E., Hoffman, J., Darrell, T., Saenko, K.: Adversarial discriminative domain adaptation. In: Proceedings of the IEEE Conference on Computer Vision and Pattern Recognition (CVPR), pp. 7167–7176 (2017)
62. Tzeng, E., Hoffman, J., Zhang, N., Saenko, K., Darrell, T.: Deep domain confusion: maximizing for domain invariance. arXiv preprint arXiv:1412.3474 (2014)
63. Venkateswara, H., Eusebio, J., Chakraborty, S., Panchanathan, S.: Deep hashing network for unsupervised domain adaptation. In: Proceedings of the IEEE Conference on Computer Vision and Pattern Recognition (CVPR), pp. 5018–5027 (2017)
64. Wang, M., Deng, W.: Deep visual domain adaptation: a survey. Neurocomputing **312**, 135–153 (2018)
65. Wen, J., Zheng, N., Yuan, J., Gong, Z., Chen, C.: Bayesian uncertainty matching for unsupervised domain adaptation. In: International Joint Conference on Artificial Intelligence (IJCAI) (2019)
66. Wilson, A.G.: The case for Bayesian deep learning. New York University, Tech. rep. (2019)
67. Xia, H., Zhao, H., Ding, Z.: Adaptive adversarial network for source-free domain adaptation. In: Proceedings of the IEEE International Conference on Computer Vision (ICCV), pp. 9010–9019 (2021)
68. Xu, R., Li, G., Yang, J., Lin, L.: Larger norm more transferable: an adaptive feature norm approach for unsupervised domain adaptation. In: Proceedings of the IEEE International Conference on Computer Vision (ICCV), pp. 1426–1435 (2019)
69. Yang, S., Wang, Y., van de Weijer, J., Herranz, L., Jui, S.: Generalized source-free domain adaptation. In: Proceedings of the IEEE International Conference on Computer Vision (ICCV), pp. 8978–8987 (2021)
70. Yeh, H.W., Yang, B., Yuen, P.C., Harada, T.: Sofa: source-data-free feature alignment for unsupervised domain adaptation. In: Proceedings of the IEEE Winter Conference on Applications of Computer Vision (WACV), pp. 474–483 (2021)
71. Zhang, H., Li, A., Han, X., Chen, Z., Zhang, Y., Guo, Y.: Improving open set domain adaptation using image-to-image translation. In: IEEE International Conference on Multimedia and Expo (ICME), pp. 1258–1263. IEEE (2019)
72. Zheng, Z., Yang, Y.: Rectifying pseudo label learning via uncertainty estimation for domain adaptive semantic segmentation. Int. J. Comput. Vis. (IJCV) **129**, 1106–1120 (2021)

# Should All Proposals Be Treated Equally in Object Detection?

Yunsheng Li[1,2]($\boxtimes$), Yinpeng Chen[1], Xiyang Dai[1], Dongdong Chen[1],
Mengchen Liu[1], Pei Yu[1], Ying Jin[1], Lu Yuan[1], Zicheng Liu[1],
and Nuno Vasconcelos[2]

[1] Microsoft Corporation, Redmond, WA 98052, USA
{yunshengli,yiche,xidai,dochen,mengcliu,pei.yu,ying.jin,
luyuan,zliu}@microsoft.com, nvasconcelos@ucsd.edu
[2] UC San Diego, La Jolla, CA 92093, USA

**Abstract.** The complexity-precision trade-off of an object detector is a critical problem for resource constrained vision tasks. Previous works have emphasized detectors implemented with efficient backbones. The impact on this trade-off of proposal processing by the detection head is investigated in this work. It is hypothesized that improved detection efficiency requires a paradigm shift, towards the unequal processing of proposals, assigning more computation to good proposals than poor ones. This results in better utilization of available computational budget, enabling higher accuracy for the same FLOPS. We formulate this as a learning problem where the goal is to assign operators to proposals, in the detection head, so that the total computational cost is constrained and the precision is maximized. The key finding is that such matching can be learned as a function that maps each proposal embedding into a one-hot code over operators. While this function induces a complex dynamic network routing mechanism, it can be implemented by a simple MLP and learned end-to-end with off-the-shelf object detectors. This *dynamic proposal processing* (DPP) is shown to outperform state-of-the-art end-to-end object detectors (DETR, Sparse R-CNN) by a clear margin for a given computational complexity. Source code is at https://github.com/liyunsheng13/dpp.

**Keywords:** Object detection · Proposal processing · Dynamic network

## 1 Introduction

Object detection is a challenging but fundamental task in computer vision, which aims to predict a bounding box and category label for each object instance in an image. A popular strategy, introduced by the Faster RCNN [25], is to rely on a backbone network to produce a relatively large set of object proposals and a detection head to derive a final prediction from these. Since then, the design trend for this two-stage detection framework, e.g. the path Faster RCNN

S. Avidan et al. (Eds.): ECCV 2022, LNCS 13685, pp. 556–572, 2022.
https://doi.org/10.1007/978-3-031-19806-9_32

[25] → Cascade RCNN [2] → DETR [3] → Sparse RCNN [27], has been to sparsify the proposal density. Recent approaches, such as the Sparse R-CNN [27], successfully reduce the thousands of proposals of the Faster RCNN [25] to a few hundred. However, because the per proposal computation of the detection head is substantially increased by the use of a much more complicated architecture, the overall computational benefits of reducing the number of proposals are limited. While the aggregate effect has been to make detectors more efficient, in general, these approaches are still not suitable for use with lighter backbones, since the head complexity becomes a larger fraction of the overall computation.

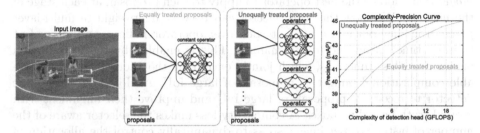

**Fig. 1.** Existing object detectors treat proposals equally, applying the same operator to all proposals. Dynamic Proposal Processing (DPP) instead argues for an unequal treatment, by learning to dynamically assign different proposals to operators of different complexities. This enables the allocation of more (less) computation to high (low) IoU proposals and enables improved complexity-precision curves.

While efficient object detection is now an extensively researched problem in computer vision, this literature has mostly focused on the design of computationally efficient backbones. The introduction of heavy detection heads would reverse the computational gains that have been achieved with lightweight models [8,23,26]. For example, the detection head of the Sparse RCNN [27] with 300 proposals consumes 4× the computation of the entire MobileNetV2 [26] (25 GFLOPS vs 5.5 GFLOPS). In this work, we investigate whether it is possible to retain the accuracy gains and proposal sparsity of modern detection heads while reducing their computational cost, so as to make them applicable to efficient object detection design. We note that a main limitation of existing high-end detectors is that they treat all proposals equally, in the sense that the detection head applies to all proposals an operator of identical complexity, maintaining a constant cost per proposal. This, however, is unintuitive. While it seems appropriate to spend significant computation on good proposals, it is wasteful to allocate equal resources to poor proposals. Since the IoU of each proposal is known during training, the detector could, in principle, learn to allocate different amounts of computation to different proposals. This, however, requires a paradigm shift for detector design, illustrated in Fig. 1: *that different proposals should be treated unequally in terms of resource allocation, reserving more computation for high quality proposals than low quality ones.*

The difficulty is that, because IoUs are not available at inference, the network has to *learn* to perform the resource allocation on the fly. This implies the need for a *resource allocation function* that depends on the proposal itself and has to be learned, i.e. a dynamic network module. To address this problem, we propose the *dynamic proposal processing* (DPP) framework, where the single operator used by current detection heads is replaced by an *operator set*, composed of multiple operators of different complexities. The benefit of this approach is to allow the detector to operate on multiple points of the complexity-precision curve, on a proposal by proposal basis, so as to optimize the overall trade-off between the two objectives. This is implemented by the addition of a *selection model* that chooses the best operator to apply to each proposal, at each stage of the network. We show that this selector can be very lightweight, a multi-layer perceptron that outputs a one-hot code over operator indices, and learned at training time, in an end-to-end manner. This is enabled by the introduction of two novel loss functions, which jointly encourage the allocation of the available computational budget to proposals of large IoU. An IoU loss teaches the detector to recognize proposals of large IoU and improve their alignment with ground truth bounding boxes. A complexity loss makes the selector aware of the number of instances, per image, so as to dynamically control the allocation of computational resources and meet the overall computational target.

Experimental results on the COCO dataset show that DPP achieves a better complexity-precision curve (see Fig. 1) than designs that treat proposals equally, especially in the low complexity regime, confirming the effectiveness of treating proposals unequally. For large backbones (ResNet [9]), DPP achieves the best precision-complexity curves in the literature, achieving state-of-the-art precision with 60% of the computation of current models. For low-complexity networks (MobileNet [26]), the gains are even more significant, in that DPP establishes a new state-of-the-art in terms of both precision and computation and produces the best latency-precision curves.

## 2   Related Work

**Object Detection.** Object detection frameworks can be mainly categorized into one-stage [13,16,19,22,28,33] vs two-stage [1,2,5,6,25], depending on the approach used to generate proposals. One-stage detectors can be anchor-based or not, but all rely on the very dense generation of proposals, which means each feature vector in the feature map is leveraged as a proposal. Two-stage detectors rely on a region proposal network [25] to filter out the majority of regions that are unlikely to contain an object instance. All the aforementioned methods require a post-processing step (non-maximum suppression) to remove a large number of duplicate proposals. More recently, an attention based framework [3,21,32, 34] has been proposed to overcome this problem, eliminating the need to post-process candidate predictions. By resorting to an attention mechanism, [27] even showed that it is possible to rely on a very sparse proposal density. In result, existing methods differ significantly in terms of proposal density. However, within each framework, all proposals are treaty equally. In this paper, we show that, by diversifying the complexity of proposal processing dynamically, it is possible to reduce detection complexity without decreasing precision.

**Dynamic Network.** Dynamic networks are a family of networks with input dependent structures or parameters derived from dynamic branches [11]. For classical convolutional networks, this can be done by using input-dependent rather than static filters [4,14,15,17,29,31] or reweighing features spatially or in a channel-wise manner [10,11]. Transformers are by definition dynamic networks, due to their extensive reliance on attention. Beyond that, [24,30] dynamically discard uninformative tokens to reduce computational cost. While previous methods show remarkable improvements in network efficiency, they mainly focus on backbones. This cannot fully address the problem of object detection, namely the heavy computation required to process proposals. Dynamic DETR [7] attempts to address the problem by building dynamic blocks on the detection head. However, it still processes all proposals with a common operator, inducing a constant complexity per proposal. In this work, we propose to leverage the power of dynamic networks by matching proposals to operators of variable complexity in a dynamic manner.

## 3  Complexity and Precision of Proposals

In this section, we compare the complexity of treating proposals equally or unequally. We assume that a backbone produces a set $X = \{x_1, x_2, ..., x_N\}$ of proposals and focus on the cost of the detection head, i.e. ignore backbone costs. We further assume that the computation of the detection head can be decomposed into a per-proposal operator $h$, e.g. a network block, and a pairwise component $p$ that accounts for the cost of inter-proposal computations. For example, the NMS operation of classical detectors or a self-attention mechanism between proposals for transformers.

**Complexity of Equally Treated Proposals.** In prior works, all proposals are processed by the same operator $h$. This has complexity

$$C(\psi) = NC_h + \frac{N(N-1)}{2}C_p, \tag{1}$$

where $\psi = \{h, p\}$, and $C_h$ and $C_p$ are the per proposal complexity of $h$ and $p$, respectively.

**Complexity of Unequally Treated Proposals.** We propose to treat proposals unequally. Rather than applying the same operator $h$ to all proposals, we propose to leverage an operator set $\mathcal{G} = \{h_j\}_{j=1}^{J}$ of $J$ operators of different architectures and complexity, which are assigned to the proposals $x_i$ by a dynamic selector $s$. This has complexity

$$C(\psi) = \sum_{i=1}^{N} C_{h_{s_i}} + \frac{N(N-1)}{2}C_p, \tag{2}$$

where $s_i = s(\boldsymbol{x}_i)$, $h_{s_i} \in \mathcal{G}$ represents the operator from $\mathcal{G}$ that is assigned to the proposal $\boldsymbol{x}_i$ by the selector $s$, $\psi = \{\{h_{s_i}\}_i, s, p\}$, and $C_{h_{s_i}}$ is the complexity of the entire per proposal operation (selector plus operator). For simplicity, the pairwise complexity is still considered constant.

**Precision over Proposals.** When the detection head treats proposals unequally, the optimal detector precision for a given complexity constraint $C$ can be determined by optimizing the assignment of operators to proposals

$$P(\psi^*|C) = \max_{\substack{h_{s_i} \in \mathcal{G} \\ C(\psi) < C}} \mathcal{P}(\{h_{s_i}\}_i), \tag{3}$$

where $\mathcal{P}(\{h_{s_i}\}_i)$ is the precision of a specific operator assignment $\{h_{s_i}\}_i$. As $C$ changes, $P(\psi^*|C)$ forms a complexity-precision (C-P) curve that characterizes the optimal performance, in terms of the trade-off between cost and precision, of the object detectors implementable with $\mathcal{G}$. In this work, we use both precision (mAP) and the C-P curve as criteria to justify the effectiveness of treating proposals unequally. Note that the assignment of operators to proposals is the key to optimize the precision under a given computation budget $C$. This is formulated as a learning function implementable with a simple network branch and solved via suitable loss functions, as discussed next.

## 4 Dynamic Proposal Processing

In this section, we proposed a *dynamic proposal processing* (DPP) framework for the solution of (3). Following the design of prior works [3,27,34], we assume a detector head composed of multiple stages ($\psi = \phi_1 \circ \ldots \circ \phi_K$) that process proposals sequentially. Each stage $\phi_k$ is implemented with an operator chosen from $\mathcal{G}$ by a selector $s$. To minimize complexity, the selector can be applied only to a subset $k \in \mathcal{K} \subset \{1, \ldots, K\}$ of the stages, with the remaining stages using the operator chosen for their predecessor, i.e. $\phi_k = \phi_{k-1}, \forall k \notin \mathcal{K}$.

### 4.1 Operator Set

In this paper, we consider an operator set $\mathcal{G} = \{g_0, g_1, g_2\}$ composed of three operators of very different computational cost. Specifically, $g_0$ is a high complexity operator, implemented with a dynamic convolutional layer (DyConv) of proposal dependent parameters and a feed forward network (FFN) [3]. This operator is based on the dynamic head architecture employed in the recent Sparse R-CNN [27]. $g_1$ is a medium complexity operator, implemented with a static FFN [3]. Finally, $g_2$ is a light operator formed by an identity block, which simply feeds the proposal forward with no further refinement.

### 4.2 Selector

In DPP, the selector is the key component to control the trade-off between precision and complexity, by controlling the assignment of operators to proposals.

Let $z_i^k$ be the embedding of proposal $x_i$ at the input of stage $\phi_k$. The selector is implemented with a 3-layer MLP that associates a 3 dimensional vector $\epsilon_i^k \in [0,1]^3$ with $z_i^k$ according to

$$\epsilon_i^k = \text{MLP}(z_i^k) \tag{4}$$

where $\epsilon_{i,j}^k$ is the selection variable in $\epsilon_i^k$ that represents the strength of the assignment of operator $g_j$ to proposal $x_i$. During training, the selection vector is a one hot code over three variables and the Gumble-Softmax function [12] is used as activation of the MLP to generate the selection vector. For inference, the selection variables have soft values and the operator that matches the index of the selection variable with largest value is chosen. The flow graph of the operator assignment process is illustrated in Fig. 2. Please note that the proposed selector is very light (using $4e-3$ GFLOPS for 100 proposals in our experimental setting), in fact negligible in complexity when compared to the detection head.

It is clear from (4) that the chosen operator varies both across proposals $i$ and head stages $k$, enabling the unequal treatment of proposals in a dynamic manner. Furthermore, while $\mathcal{G}$ has cardinality three, the cardinality of the set of network architectures that can be used to implement the detector head is $3^{|\mathcal{K}|}$. Finally, because the selector is trainable, the assignment function can be learned end-to-end.

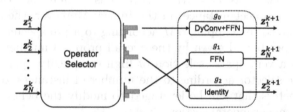

**Fig. 2. Flow graph of operator assignments to proposals.** The selector takes the proposal embeddings, i.e. $\{z_1^k, z_2^k, ..., z_N^k\}$ in the $k^{th}$ stage as input and outputs a selection vector per proposal. The operator that matches the index of largest value in the selection vector is selected to process the proposal. In the operator set, operator $g_0$ contains a high complexity dynamic convolution (DyConv) followed by a FFN [3]. $g_1$ consists of a feed forward network (FFN), while $g_2$ is implemented with an identity function (Identity).

### 4.3   Loss Functions

To assure that, given a complexity budget, DPP selects the optimal sequence of operators for each proposal, a selection loss is applied to the selector of each stage in $\mathcal{K}$. This selection loss is designed to encourage two goals. First, complex operators should be assigned to high quality proposals (large IoU), since these require most additional work by the detection head. This is enforced through the IoU loss

$$L_{iou} = \frac{1}{N} \sum_{i=1}^{N} \sum_{k \in \mathcal{K}} \sum_{j \in \{0,1\}} (1 - u_i^k)\epsilon_{i,j}^k + u_i^k(1 - \epsilon_{i,j}^k), \tag{5}$$

where $u_i^k$ is the IoU of the $i^{th}$ proposal in $k^{th}$ stage. $L_{iou}$ pushes the selector to turn $\epsilon_{i,0}^k$ and $\epsilon_{i,1}^k$ into '0' for proposals of IoU smaller than 0.5 and into '1' otherwise. This encourages the use of more complex operators in stage $k$ for the high quality proposals, which require more efforts for classifying categories and regressing bounding boxes. Moreover, the loss magnitude is determined by the IoU value, originating larger gradients when the selector predicts $\epsilon_{i,0}^k$ or $\epsilon_{i,1}^k$ as '1' for tiny IoU proposals or as '0' for large proposals. Second, the selector should be aware of the total number of instances in each image and adjust the overall complexity according to it, i.e., selecting more complex operators when instances are dense. This is enforced through the complexity loss

$$L_c = \frac{1}{N} \sum_{k \in \mathcal{K}} \left| \sum_{i=1}^{N} \epsilon_{i,0}^k - T \right|, \tag{6}$$

where $T$ is the target number of times that operator $g_0$ is selected for a particular image. This is defined as $T = \alpha M$ where $\alpha$ is a multiplier that specifies a multiple of the $M$ object instances in the image. Moreover, the condition $T \in [T_{min}, N]$ is enforced, by clipping $\alpha M$ according to a pre-specified lower bound $T_{min}$ and an upper bound given by the overall proposal number $N$. The lower bound prevents a very sparse selection of high complexity operators $g_0$ and $\alpha$ then adjusts the selector according to the number of instances. $\alpha$, $T_{min}$ and $N$ are hyperparameters that can be leveraged to modify the behavior of DPP, as discussed in the experimental section.

The overall selection loss is finally

$$L_s = L_{iou} + \lambda L_c, \tag{7}$$

where $\lambda$ is the hyperparameter that controls the trade-off between the loss components. Note that the selection loss is a plug-and-play loss that can be applied to different object detectors. In this paper, $L_s$ is combined with all the losses of the original detector to which DPP is applied, including the cross entropy loss and the bounding box regression loss, which are omitted from our discussion.

## 5   Experiments

**Dataset.** DPP is evaluated on the COCO dataset [20]. It is trained on the train2017 split and mainly tested on the val2017 split with mAP.

**Network.** DPP is applied to detectors whose backbone is built on MobileNet V2 [26] or ResNet-50 [9], using Feature Pyramid Networks (FPN) [18], on top of which proposals are generated using the strategies of [27]. For MobileNetV2 [26], the FPN only considers features with strides 16 and 32 and the $3 \times 3$ FPN convolution is decomposed into an $1 \times 1$ pointwise convolution and a $3 \times 3$ depthwise convolution for efficiency. For ResNet-50, FPN is implemented on features with the standard 4 different strides. Following [27], the detection head is a decoder only transformer of 6 stages. For simplicity, the selector is only applied in stages $\mathcal{K} = \{2, 4, 6\}$. In the first stage, all proposals are processed with the high complexity operator $(g_0)$. The full operator set $\mathcal{G}$ is used in all remaining stages.

**Table 1. Contribution of each operator to proposal processing.** Performance is evaluated on the COCO validation set. $N_{eval}$ is the average number of proposals matched to the checkmarked operator(s).

| $g_0$ | $g_1$ | $g_2$ | AP | $AP_{50}$ | $AP_{75}$ | $N_{eval}$ |
|---|---|---|---|---|---|---|
| ✓ | | | 41.0 | 58.5 | 44.4 | 15 |
| | ✓ | | 2.4 | 5.1 | 2.1 | 7 |
| | | ✓ | 0.8 | 2.2 | 0.5 | 78 |
| ✓ | ✓ | | 41.7 | 59.9 | 45.2 | 22 |
| ✓ | ✓ | ✓ | **42.2** | **60.6** | **45.5** | 100 |

**Experimental Setting.** DPP is pretrained without selectors, using the hyper-parameters and data augmentations of [3,25,27] on COCO. The selectors are then added and trained with learning rate 2e−5, while 2e−6 is used for other layers. The training process lasts 36 (3×) epochs and the learning rate is divided by 10 at 27 and 33 epochs. The selection loss $L_s$ is combined with all the losses used in [3,25,27], i.e. cross entropy loss $L_{ce}$, GIoU loss $L_{giou}$ and bounding boxes regression loss $L_{bbox}$ and $\lambda = 10$ is used for all selectors. The lower bound $T_{min}$ for the target number of times that $g_0$ is selected is manually set to $T_{min}^{last}$ for the last selector. For the remaining selectors, $T_{min}$ is derived automatically, so that it decreases exponentially from $N$ (number of proposals) to $T_{min}^{last}$. Hence we omit the subscript of the lower bound for conciseness in the following sections. The multiplier $\alpha$ is constant across all selectors.

## 5.1    Proposal Processing by DPP

We start by discussing experiments that illustrate the unequal processing of proposals by DPP and how this impacts complexity. In these experiments, we analyze how each operator contributes to the processing of proposals produced by a ResNet-50 backbone. DPP training uses a lower bound $T_{min} = 1$, a multiplier $\alpha = 2$, and $N = 100$ proposals.

**Contribution of Each Operator.** The influence of each operator in $\mathcal{G} = \{g_0, g_1, g_2\}$ is investigated separately. For this, we manually split the proposals into three groups, according to the operator that process them, and evaluate precision for each group. For simplicity, the split is only based on the selector of the last DPP stage, i.e. the analysis is limited to this stage.

Table 1 shows the precision of proposals processed by the different operators. $N_{eval}$ represents the average number of proposals evaluated across the COCO validation set. This is equivalent to the number of times that the operators checkmarked in the table were used. Clearly, the proposals processed by $g_0$ are the main contributors to the overall precision (41.0 vs 42.2), even though only 15 such proposals are evaluated on average. For proposals processed by $g_1$ or $g_2$ the performance is quite poor. This shows that the selector successfully allocates operators to proposals, assigning the operators of large complexity to the proposals that have higher chance of being associated with objects and devoting much less computation to the remaining.

Interestingly, the vast majority of proposals (78%) are assigned to $g_2$, i.e. use *no* computation in the final DPP stage. These are very poor proposals (almost zero AP), showing that the DPP detector learns to "give up" on such proposals, simply shipping them to the output. When the proposals processed by $g_0$ and $g_1$ are merged, the precision is promoted by 0.7% (41.0 vs 41.7). This shows, that the two types of proposals are complementary and confirms that $g_1$ is important although sparsely used.

**Performance of Each Stage in DPP.** Precision is tested across all stages ($k = 1 \sim 6$) and we obtain the AP as $\{15.6, 32.1, 39.3, 41.7, 42.0, 42.2\}$. The results show that the precision increases quickly in the first 4 stages and then saturates. Among the 6 stages, the selector is applied in stages $\{2, 4, 6\}$. The IoU distribution of the proposals selected by different operators is shown in Fig. 3. The total number of proposals processed by each operator is illustrated as a subplot. Note that the proposals of larger IoU are mostly processed by $g_0$ (blue curve) even though the overall number of proposals processed by $g_0$ decreases drastically for the later stages (blue bar). In these stages, most proposals are simply "shipped to the next stage" without any computation ($g_2$). Conversely, most low IoU proposals are processed by operator $g_2$ (green curve) and the number of such proposals increases drastically with the stage (green bar). This illustrates how DPP is quite successful at trading off complexity for precision.

**Visualization.** Figure 4 shows some qualitative results, in the form of bounding boxes predicted by the high complexity operator $g_0$ in stages 4 and 6. Note that the boxes predicted in stage 6 (right column) have a good overlap with the ground truth (left column) with limited duplication. By comparing the boxes predicted in different stages, we can observe that they are refined in the deeper stages. More importantly, duplication is removed to a remarkable extent, indicating that not only the selector prevents poor proposals from being processed by operator $g_0$ but the network gradually transforms duplicates into bad proposals, in order to meet the complexity constraint.

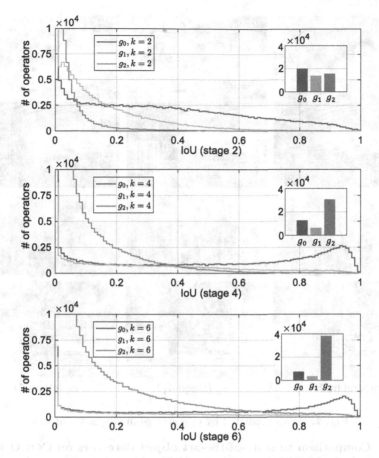

**Fig. 3. IoU distribution of proposals matched to the three operators across DPP stages** (stage indexes $k \in \{2, 4, 6\}$). Within each plot, the number of proposals processed per operator is shown as a subplot.

## 5.2  Main Results

DPP is compared to the state-of-the-arts for two backbones, ResNet-50 [9] and MobileNetV2 [26], with the results shown in Table 2 and 3 respectively. In Table 2 and 3, $\bar{N}$ represents the number of proposals for the Faster R-CNN [25] and Sparse R-CNN [27] and the number of queries (which play identical roles to proposals for final prediction) for attention baselines. For DPP, where proposals are processed by different operators, $\bar{N}$ is the equivalent proposal number, defined as the ratio between the overall FLOPS spent by the detector head and the FLOPS spent by the high complexity operator $g_0$. For ResNet-50 the results of the baselines are copied from the original papers. For MobileNetV2 baselines, they are obtained with the official code, using the recommended hyperparameters.

**ResNet.** When ResNet-50 is used as backbone, four variants of DPP are used as the detection head. DPP-S, DPP-M and DPP-L use different overall

| ground truth | $g_0$ (stage 4) | $g_0$ (stage 6) |

**Fig. 4.** Boxes predicted by operator $g_0$ in stages 4 and 6.

**Table 2. Comparison to state-of-the-art object detectors on COCO validation set with ResNet-50.** Four variants of DPP with various sizes are shown, based on FPN. For DPP, $\bar{N}$ is the equivalent proposal number, defined as the ratio between the overall FLOPS spent by the detector head and the FLOPS spent by each high complexity operator $g_0$ ($\bar{N} = C(\psi)/C_{g_0}$ in (2)), while for baselines $\bar{N}$ is either the proposal number or the number of queries. The complexity (GFLOPS) is only that of the detection head.

| Method | $\bar{N}$ | Epochs | AP | $AP_{50}$ | $AP_{75}$ | $AP_s$ | $AP_m$ | $AP_l$ | GFLOPS |
|---|---|---|---|---|---|---|---|---|---|
| Faster RCNN-FPN [25] | 2000 | 36 | 40.2 | 43.8 | 43.8 | 24.2 | 43.5 | 52.0 | 14 |
| RetinaNet [19] | – | 36 | 38.7 | 58.0 | 41.5 | 23.3 | 42.3 | 50.3 | 90 |
| DETR-DC5 [3] | 100 | 500 | 43.3 | 63.1 | 45.9 | 22.5 | 47.3 | **61.1** | 76 |
| Deformable Detr [34] | 300 | 50 | 43.8 | 62.6 | 44.2 | 20.5 | 47.1 | 58.0 | 98 |
| Sparse R-CNN [27] | 300 | 36 | **45.0** | **64.1** | **49.0** | 27.8 | **47.6** | 59.7 | 25 |
| DPP-XL (ours) | 182.3 | 36 | **45.0** | 63.8 | 48.8 | **28.2** | 47.4 | 59.9 | 15 |
| DPP-L (ours) | 82.6 | 36 | 43.7 | 62.4 | 47.5 | 27.2 | 46.0 | 59.1 | 6.8 |
| DPP-M (ours) | 38.8 | 36 | 42.2 | 60.6 | 45.5 | 23.9 | 44.6 | 58.5 | 3.2 |
| DPP-S (ours) | 25.5 | 36 | 40.4 | 58.2 | 43.4 | 22.0 | 42.8 | 57.0 | 2.1 |

**Table 3. Comparison to state-of-the-art object detectors on COCO valida-tion set with MobileNetV2.** Four variants of DPP with various sizes are shown, based on light FPN for features with 2 strides (16, 32). For DPP, $\bar{N}$ is the equivalent proposal number, defined same as that in Table 2, while for baselines $\bar{N}$ is either the proposal number or the number of queries. The complexity (GFLOPS) is only that of the detection head.

| Method | $\bar{N}$ | Epochs | AP | $AP_{50}$ | $AP_{75}$ | $AP_s$ | $AP_m$ | $AP_l$ | GFLOPS |
|---|---|---|---|---|---|---|---|---|---|
| Faster RCNN-FPN [25] | 2000 | 36 | 28.7 | 47.1 | 30.3 | 12.7 | 32.6 | 39.6 | 14 |
| DETR [3] | 100 | 150 | 29.3 | 49.0 | 29.1 | 9.8 | 30.9 | 47.5 | 12 |
| Deformable Detr [34] | 100 | 50 | 35.8 | 54.4 | 37.8 | 17.6 | 38.8 | 51.0 | 25 |
| Sparse R-CNN [27] | 100 | 36 | 36.6 | 55.3 | 39.1 | 18.0 | 39.3 | **52.9** | 8.2 |
| DPP-XL (ours) | 94.8 | 36 | **36.9** | **55.8** | **39.3** | **18.8** | **40.3** | 51.9 | 7.8 |
| DPP-L (ours) | 78.9 | 36 | 36.7 | 55.3 | 39.0 | 18.4 | 39.8 | 52.2 | 6.5 |
| DPP-M (ours) | 54.5 | 36 | 36.1 | 54.5 | 38.3 | 17.5 | 38.8 | 52.1 | 4.5 |
| DPP-S (ours) | 43.7 | 36 | 35.7 | 54.2 | 37.9 | 16.9 | 38.2 | 52.1 | 3.6 |

numbers of proposals ($N \in \{50, 100, 300\}$). The other hyperparameters, i.e. $T_{min}$ and $\alpha$, are set to 1 and 2 respectively. In this way, $L_c$ can assure there is at least 1 high complexity operator and assign 2 high complexity operators per instance, on average. DPP-XL, is equivalent to DPP-L but further increases the hyperparameter $T_{min}$ to 100. Table 2 shows that DPP achieves a good trade-off between complexity and precision. At the high end, DPP-XL performs on par with the Sparse R-CNN [27] with a much lighter detection head (15 vs 25 GFLOPS). The prior method with this level of complexity (Faster RCNN-FPN) has an AP loss of close to 5 points (40.2% vs 45.0%). At the low end, DPP-S reduces the Sparse R-CNN computation by 12.5×, for a decrease of 4.6 points in AP. This is equivalent to the Faster RCNN-FPN, but saving 7× computa-tion. Figure 5 shows that the complexity-precision (C-P) curve of DPP is better than those of all other baselines. This confirms the benefits of treating proposals unequally. Finally, DPP is evaluated on the COCO test set and we achieve the AP as $\{44.7, 43.8, 42.5, 40.7\}$ for the four variants of DPP (44.7 is obtained for SparseRCNN [27]), which further justifies the effectiveness and stability of DPP.

**MobileNetV2.** For MobileNetV2 we consider a lighter detection head, by decreasing the number of proposals for both DPP and baselines. Similar to ResNet, four variants of DPP are proposed. Given the more important role played by the detection head in this case, we force the selector to choose more high complexity operators, by increasing the lower bound $T_{min}$ for the target number of the operators $g_0$. When comparing DPP to the state-of-the-arts, the results shown in Table 3 and Fig. 6 enable even stronger conclusions than those drawn for the ResNet. In this case, DPP-XL outperforms the Sparse R-CNN, establishing a new state of the art, and even DPP-S has a small AP loss (less than 1%) compared to the latter. These results confirm that DPP is a generic framework, which can perform well with different types of backbones.

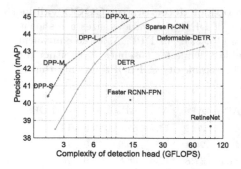

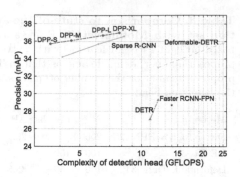

**Fig. 5. Comparison of complexity-precision curve on ResNet-50** between DPP and state-of-the-arts (MAdds only reflects the computational cost of the detector head).

**Fig. 6. Comparison of complexity-precision curve on MobileNetV2** between DPP and state-of-the-arts (MAdds only reflects the computational cost of the detector head).

**Inference Speed.** Inference speed is measured for DPP and baselines on MobileNetV2 with a single-threaded core Intel(R) Xeon(R) CPU E5-2470 (2.4 GHz) (Deformable DETR [34] does not support CPU implementation). Results are obtained by averaging inference time of all images in the COCO validation split and shown in Fig. 7. The latency is for the whole network, not just the head. It can be seen that DPP achieves a consistently better latency-precision curve and its savings in computation are clearly reflected in savings of inference time.

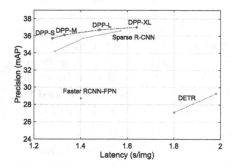

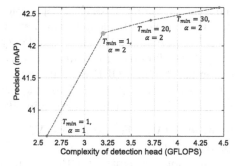

**Fig. 7. Comparison of latency-precision curve.** Latency is tested by using MobileNetV2 implemented on a CPU, across the COCO validation set. Latency reflects the inference time of the whole network instead of only the detection head.

**Fig. 8. Effect of the hyperparameters for the target usage of** $g_0$, i.e. lower bound ($T_{min}$) and multiplier ($\alpha$), on the complexity-precision trade-off. The performance of four variants of DPP model are illustrated via varying $T_{min}$ and $\alpha$.

## 5.3    Ablation Study

In this section, we present some ablation studies for the proposed loss function and hyperparameters used by DPP. The backbone is based on ResNet-50 and, by default, 100 proposals ($N = 100$) are used by all models. The lower bound $T_{min}$ and multiplier $\alpha$ for the operator $g_0$ are 1 and 2. All experiments are performed on the COCO dataset.

**Selection Loss.** We start by exploring the influence of the selection loss $L_s$ on DPP performance. Table 4 shows that using either component, IoU loss $L_{iou}$ or complexity loss $L_c$, alone degrades the precision of DPP. Without $L_{iou}$ the precision drops by 0.4% (41.8% vs 42.2%), because the selector can no longer fully match the proposal qualities to the operator complexities. Without $L_c$, the precision is 1.1% worse (41.1% vs 42.2%). This is because, during training without $L_c$, the model is more prone to assign the light operator ($g_2$) to proposals. Beyond weakening precision, this more critically prevents the complexity of DPP from being modified as needed. Table 5 studies the trade-off between $L_{iou}$ and $L_c$ as a function of $\lambda$. The performance is similar for $\lambda = 1$ and $\lambda = 10$, but further increasing $\lambda$ makes DPP focus too much on complexity and ignore the importance of IoU matching, degrading performance. We thus set $\lambda = 10$ in all subsequent experiments.

**Target Number of Heavy Operators.** The target number $T$ of useage of heavy operator $g_0$ is leveraged in $L_c$ to control the complexity of DPP. $T$ is determined by two hyperparameters, the lower bound $T_{min}$ and the multiplier $\alpha$. Four DPP variants are implemented by varying these hyperparameters as shown in Fig. 8. The average number of times the operator $g_0$ is selected per image is $\{8, 15, 22, 31\}$ in the COCO validation set, for models ranging from small to large FLOPS in Fig. 8. It can be seen that the precision of the model with $T_{min} = 1$ and $\alpha = 2$ is at the inflection point of the curve, beyond which the precision grows slowly for a large increase of the computational cost. When $\alpha = 2$ and $T_{min} = 1$, the model selects the $g_0$ operator 15 times on average. This is only twice the average instance number in COCO (7), confirming the effectiveness of loss function $L_c$. This result also suggests that using twice as many high complexity proposals as the number of object instances is a very effective choice in terms of the complexity-precision trade-off for the detection head.

In summary, the number of high complexity operators used on average can be very smaller than the overall number of proposals ($N = 100$). Moreover, both hyperparameters can be used to modify the complexity of the detection head. The multiplier is more useful when the best complexity-precision trade-off is desired while the lower bound is more effective when the goal is to achieve the best precision irrespective of complexity.

**Table 4. Effect of the loss functions**, i.e. the IoU loss $L_{iou}$ and the complexity loss $L_c$ on DPP.

| $L_{iou}$ | $L_c$ | AP | $AP_{50}$ | $AP_{75}$ | $AP_s$ | $AP_m$ | $AP_l$ |
|---|---|---|---|---|---|---|---|
| ✓ | | 41.1 | 59.2 | 44.2 | 23.1 | 43.1 | 57.0 |
| | ✓ | 41.8 | 60.2 | 45.1 | 23.7 | 44.0 | 58.2 |
| ✓ | ✓ | **42.2** | **60.6** | **45.5** | **23.9** | **44.6** | **58.5** |

**Table 5. Effect of the hyperparameter** $\lambda$ in the selection loss ($L_s = L_{iou} + \lambda L_c$) of DPP.

| $\lambda$ | AP | $AP_{50}$ | $AP_{75}$ | $AP_s$ | $AP_m$ | $AP_l$ |
|---|---|---|---|---|---|---|
| 1 | 42.1 | **60.7** | **45.6** | **24.1** | 44.5 | 58.3 |
| 10 | **42.2** | 60.6 | 45.5 | 23.9 | **44.6** | **58.5** |
| 100 | 41.7 | 60.3 | 44.9 | 23.4 | 44.1 | 57.5 |
| 300 | 41.0 | 59.4 | 44.3 | 22.2 | 43.5 | 57.2 |

## 6    Conclusion

In this paper, we propose to treat proposals of object detection unequally. A matching problem between proposals and operators is designed and optimized via a dynamic proposal processing (DPP) framework that contains a simple selector supervised with two loss functions, the IoU loss and the complexity loss. Experimental results show that the DPP framework achieves the state-of-the-art complexity-precision trade-off for the object detection on different types of backbones under a wide complexity range. We hope this paper can provide inspiration for different approaches of proposal processing by future research as well as research in deeper questions, such as the role of computational constraints in the development of effective vision systems.

## References

1. Cai, Z., Fan, Q., Feris, R.S., Vasconcelos, N.: A unified multi-scale deep convolutional neural network for fast object detection. In: Leibe, B., Matas, J., Sebe, N., Welling, M. (eds.) ECCV 2016. LNCS, vol. 9908, pp. 354–370. Springer, Cham (2016). https://doi.org/10.1007/978-3-319-46493-0_22
2. Cai, Z., Vasconcelos, N.: Cascade R-CNN: delving into high quality object detection. In: Proceedings of the IEEE Conference on Computer Vision and Pattern Recognition, pp. 6154–6162 (2018)
3. Carion, N., Massa, F., Synnaeve, G., Usunier, N., Kirillov, A., Zagoruyko, S.: End-to-end object detection with transformers. In: Vedaldi, A., Bischof, H., Brox, T., Frahm, J.-M. (eds.) ECCV 2020. LNCS, vol. 12346, pp. 213–229. Springer, Cham (2020). https://doi.org/10.1007/978-3-030-58452-8_13

4. Chen, Y., Dai, X., Liu, M., Chen, D., Yuan, L., Liu, Z.: Dynamic convolution: Attention over convolution kernels. In: Proceedings of the IEEE/CVF Conference on Computer Vision and Pattern Recognition, pp. 11030–11039 (2020)
5. Chen, Z., Huang, S., Tao, D.: Context refinement for object detection. In: Ferrari, V., Hebert, M., Sminchisescu, C., Weiss, Y. (eds.) ECCV 2018. LNCS, vol. 11212, pp. 74–89. Springer, Cham (2018). https://doi.org/10.1007/978-3-030-01237-3_5
6. Dai, J., Li, Y., He, K., Sun, J.: R-FCN: object detection via region-based fully convolutional networks. In: Advances in Neural Information Processing Systems, pp. 379–387 (2016)
7. Dai, X., Chen, Y., Yang, J., Zhang, P., Yuan, L., Zhang, L.: Dynamic DETR: end-to-end object detection with dynamic attention. In: Proceedings of the IEEE/CVF International Conference on Computer Vision, pp. 2988–2997 (2021)
8. Han, K., Wang, Y., Tian, Q., Guo, J., Xu, C., Xu, C.: GhostNet: more features from cheap operations. In: Proceedings of the IEEE/CVF Conference on Computer Vision and Pattern Recognition, pp. 1580–1589 (2020)
9. He, K., Zhang, X., Ren, S., Sun, J.: Deep residual learning for image recognition. In: Proceedings of the IEEE Conference on Computer Vision and Pattern Recognition, pp. 770–778 (2016)
10. Hou, Q., Zhou, D., Feng, J.: Coordinate attention for efficient mobile network design. In: Proceedings of the IEEE/CVF Conference on Computer Vision and Pattern Recognition, pp. 13713–13722 (2021)
11. Hu, J., Shen, L., Sun, G.: Squeeze-and-excitation networks. In: Proceedings of the IEEE Conference on Computer Vision and Pattern Recognition, pp. 7132–7141 (2018)
12. Jang, E., Gu, S., Poole, B.: Categorical reparameterization with Gumbel-softmax. arXiv preprint arXiv:1611.01144 (2016)
13. Law, H., Deng, J.: CornerNet: detecting objects as paired keypoints. Int. J. Comput. Vis. **128**(3), 642–656 (2019). https://doi.org/10.1007/s11263-019-01204-1
14. Li, C., Wang, G., Wang, B., Liang, X., Li, Z., Chang, X.: Dynamic slimmable network. In: Proceedings of the IEEE/CVF Conference on Computer Vision and Pattern Recognition, pp. 8607–8617 (2021)
15. Li, F., Li, G., He, X., Cheng, J.: Dynamic dual gating neural networks. In: Proceedings of the IEEE/CVF International Conference on Computer Vision, pp. 5330–5339 (2021)
16. Li, X., Wang, W., Hu, X., Li, J., Tang, J., Yang, J.: Generalized focal loss V2: learning reliable localization quality estimation for dense object detection. In: Proceedings of the IEEE/CVF Conference on Computer Vision and Pattern Recognition, pp. 11632–11641 (2021)
17. Li, Y., et al.: Revisiting dynamic convolution via matrix decomposition. arXiv preprint arXiv:2103.08756 (2021)
18. Lin, T.Y., Dollár, P., Girshick, R., He, K., Hariharan, B., Belongie, S.: Feature pyramid networks for object detection. In: Proceedings of the IEEE Conference on Computer Vision and Pattern Recognition, pp. 2117–2125 (2017)
19. Lin, T.Y., Goyal, P., Girshick, R., He, K., Dollár, P.: Focal loss for dense object detection. In: Proceedings of the IEEE International Conference on Computer Vision, pp. 2980–2988 (2017)
20. Lin, T.-Y., et al.: Microsoft COCO: common objects in context. In: Fleet, D., Pajdla, T., Schiele, B., Tuytelaars, T. (eds.) ECCV 2014. LNCS, vol. 8693, pp. 740–755. Springer, Cham (2014). https://doi.org/10.1007/978-3-319-10602-1_48

21. Liu, F., Wei, H., Zhao, W., Li, G., Peng, J., Li, Z.: WB-DETR: transformer-based detector without backbone. In: Proceedings of the IEEE/CVF International Conference on Computer Vision, pp. 2979–2987 (2021)
22. Liu, W., et al.: SSD: single shot multibox detector. In: Leibe, B., Matas, J., Sebe, N., Welling, M. (eds.) ECCV 2016. LNCS, vol. 9905, pp. 21–37. Springer, Cham (2016). https://doi.org/10.1007/978-3-319-46448-0_2
23. Ma, N., Zhang, X., Zheng, H.-T., Sun, J.: ShuffleNet V2: practical guidelines for efficient CNN architecture design. In: Ferrari, V., Hebert, M., Sminchisescu, C., Weiss, Y. (eds.) Computer Vision – ECCV 2018. LNCS, vol. 11218, pp. 122–138. Springer, Cham (2018). https://doi.org/10.1007/978-3-030-01264-9_8
24. Rao, Y., Zhao, W., Liu, B., Lu, J., Zhou, J., Hsieh, C.J.: DynamicViT: efficient vision transformers with dynamic token sparsification. arXiv preprint arXiv:2106.02034 (2021)
25. Ren, S., He, K., Girshick, R., Sun, J.: Faster R-CNN: towards real-time object detection with region proposal networks. In: Advances in Neural Information Processing Systems, vol. 28, pp. 91–99 (2015)
26. Sandler, M., Howard, A., Zhu, M., Zhmoginov, A., Chen, L.C.: MobileNetV 2: inverted residuals and linear bottlenecks. In: Proceedings of the IEEE Conference on Computer Vision and Pattern Recognition, pp. 4510–4520 (2018)
27. Sun, P., et al.: Sparse R-CNN: end-to-end object detection with learnable proposals. In: Proceedings of the IEEE/CVF Conference on Computer Vision and Pattern Recognition, pp. 14454–14463 (2021)
28. Tian, Z., Shen, C., Chen, H., He, T.: FCOS: fully convolutional one-stage object detection. In: Proceedings of the IEEE/CVF International Conference on Computer Vision, pp. 9627–9636 (2019)
29. Verelst, T., Tuytelaars, T.: Dynamic convolutions: exploiting spatial sparsity for faster inference. In: Proceedings of the IEEE/CVF Conference on Computer Vision and Pattern Recognition, pp. 2320–2329 (2020)
30. Wang, Y., Huang, R., Song, S., Huang, Z., Huang, G.: Not all images are worth 16x16 words: dynamic vision transformers with adaptive sequence length. arXiv preprint arXiv:2105.15075 (2021)
31. Yang, B., Bender, G., Le, Q.V., Ngiam, J.: CondConv: conditionally parameterized convolutions for efficient inference. arXiv preprint arXiv:1904.04971 (2019)
32. Zhang, J., Huang, J., Luo, Z., Zhang, G., Lu, S.: DA-DETR: domain adaptive detection transformer by hybrid attention. arXiv preprint arXiv:2103.17084 (2021)
33. Zhang, S., Chi, C., Yao, Y., Lei, Z., Li, S.Z.: Bridging the gap between anchor-based and anchor-free detection via adaptive training sample selection. In: Proceedings of the IEEE/CVF Conference on Computer Vision and Pattern Recognition, pp. 9759–9768 (2020)
34. Zhu, X., Su, W., Lu, L., Li, B., Wang, X., Dai, J.: Deformable DETR: deformable transformers for end-to-end object detection. arXiv preprint arXiv:2010.04159 (2020)

# ViP: Unified Certified Detection and Recovery for Patch Attack with Vision Transformers

Junbo Li[1], Huan Zhang[2], and Cihang Xie[1(✉)]

[1] University of California Santa Cruz, Santa Cruz, CA, USA
cixie@ucsc.edu
[2] Carnegie Mellon University, Pittsburgh, PA, USA

**Abstract.** Patch attack, which introduces a perceptible but localized change to the input image, has gained significant momentum in recent years. In this paper, we present a unified framework to analyze certified patch defense tasks, including both *certified detection* and *certified recovery*, leveraging the recently emerged Vision Transformers (ViTs). In addition to the existing patch defense setting where only one patch is considered, we provide the very first study on developing certified detection against the *dual patch attack*, in which the attacker is allowed to adversarially manipulate pixels in two different regions.

By building upon the latest progress in self-supervised ViTs with masked image modeling (*i.e.*, masked autoencoder (MAE)), our method achieves state-of-the-art performance in both certified detection and certified recovery of adversarial patches. Regarding certified detection, we improve the performance by up to ~16% on ImageNet without training on a single adversarial patch, and for the first time, can also tackle the more challenging dual patch setting. Our method largely *closes the gap* between detection-based certified robustness and clean image accuracy. Regarding certified recovery, our approach improves certified accuracy by ~2% on ImageNet across all attack sizes, attaining the new state-of-the-art performance.

**Keywords:** Certified defense · Patch attacks · Vision transformer

## 1 Introduction

Deep neural networks (DNNs) are vulnerable to adversarial attacks [9,22]. Researchers have come up with various attacks to craft visually imperceptible adversarial examples that can lead to a model failing in a set of image recognition tasks, including classification [22], object detection [29], semantic segmentation [4,29], *etc.* Among these attack methods, patch attack [2,8,13,25,30] considers

---

**Supplementary Information** The online version contains supplementary material available at https://doi.org/10.1007/978-3-031-19806-9_33.

arbitrarily modifying a small and continuous region in an image, which utilizes characteristics of physical objects. Due to arbitrary location and small size of the patch attack, it is more challenging to defend against such an attack. Existing empirical methods designed for defending against patch attacks [11,20] reported ~70% robust accuracy on ImageNet [6]. However, if we consider a stronger attacker who is aware of the pre-processing step, the robustness of these defenses will severely drop to ~50% [3].

To fix such issues, another series of works focus on designing provable mechanisms, which aim to provide a provable defense against adversarial attacks. Specifically, on account of different levels of provable defense, there are usually two kinds of tasks: certified detection [10,14,17,28] and certified recovery [15,18,21,26] for adversarial patches. The former task is to detect whether an image was successfully attacked or not, while the latter one aims to classify an image correctly under any patch attacks smaller than a particular size. In general, certified recovery is considered as a much more challenging task than certified detection in the real-world scenario.

In certified detection, a small mask is applied on a clean image and slides from upper left to lower right (*i.e.*, acting like a convolution kernel). We have a partially occluded image for a patch mask applied on each position. All these different images are sent to a DNN. Finally, the original image can be certifiably detected for any patch attacks if all the output prediction results are strictly consistent. Related works include Minority Reports Defense [17], PatchGuard++ [28], and ScaleCert [10]. However, these methods are either computationally intractable for large-scale data or rely on CNNs with a small reception field to extract features, restricting their further applications. Recently, Huang *et al.* [14] introduces ViTs for certified detection and substantially improves performance, even for defending against larger patch attacks.

We find that methods for certified recovery based on randomized smoothing [5,16] are similar to certified detection. In this setting, we first forward a small subset of an image each time and then make a majority voting for the outputs of all these small subsets. Appropriate geometry structures provide that a patch can only intersect with restricted small subsets. Therefore if the gap between the majority prediction and the sub-majority prediction is large enough, we can guarantee that the voting result will not change regardless of where the attacker put the patch attack.

The current state-of-the-art methods for these two tasks are both achieved with vision transformers [14,21]. Interestingly, we find that these two tasks can actually be solved in a unified framework with vision transformer structures and a strategy of dropping patches. A patch attack can be certifiably detected if we drop a few patches each time and all the predictions are strictly consistent. In comparison, an image can be certifiably recovered if we drop many patches each time, and the gap between the majority voting predictions and the sub-majority voting predictions is big enough. Due to the similarity of the two tasks, we can use the same framework and network structure to solve these problems. Moreover, in real-world attack settings, we cannot restrict how many patches an attacker can use, so it is necessary to design general defense algorithms beyond single-patch attack.

In this work, we present ViP, a unified analysis framework for certified robustness including both certified detection certified recovery. Benefited by the recent progress in self-supervised vision transformers, especially the powerful masked autoencoder (MAE) [12], we achieve the state-of-the-art performance on all related tasks. By evaluating certified detection in a zero-shot manner, our method improves the certified detection rate by up to ~16% on ImageNet over the prior art [14]. Moreover, we develop the first theoretical guarantee for dual-patch attack detection. As a byproduct of improvement on single-patch attack, we successfully generalize the dual-patch detection to the large-scale dataset like ImageNet. In addition, our methods improves the certified accuracy by ~2% on all tasks in certified recovery compared to the state-of-the-art [21].

## 2 Related Works

### 2.1 Certified Detection

McCoyd *et al.* [17] is the first work on certified detection for adversarial patches. Their certification is achieved by generating a prediction grid. However, this method is computationally infeasible on large-scale dataset like ImageNet. To reduce computational complexity, Xiang *et al.* [28] uses CNNs with small reception field and conducts masking on feature level. However, they still cannot get a good performance on ImageNet. The performance is restricted due to locality information. Moreover, Han *et al.* [10] proposes to only forward the top $k$ of SIN, Superficial Important Neurons. Recently, Huang *et al.* [14] proposes to use vision transformer structures to do certified detection, which improves a lot on both performance and speed.

### 2.2 Certified Recovery

Earlier works on certified recovery include [3,19], which rely on the bound of activation value. However they are infeasible to extend to large-scale datasets. Based on traditional randomized smoothing method [5,16], Levine *et al.* [15] first proposes the (de)randomized smoothing method designed for patch attack, and scales to ImageNet. The follow-up work [21] changes to use vision transformers, but it remains unclear why vision transformers work better than CNNs. If assuming information of patch size is known, PatchCleanser in [27] designs a two-stage certification process that enjoys a much better recovery rate.

### 2.3 Vision Transformers

Application of self-attention blocks in vision transformers has achieved a huge success these years [7,23]. Due to patchfying an image to be a token sequence, a vision transformer can accept almost arbitrary subparts of an image as the input. This greatly helps self-supervision, especially using masked-image-modeling strategy [1,12,24,31]. These works demonstrate the great potential of vision transformers. Especially for the task of certified detection or recovery of adversarial patches, vision transformers are a better choice compared to traditional CNNs, because vision transformers intrinsically use patches as their inputs.

## 3   Certified Patch Defense

### 3.1   Problem Setup

We consider the $L_0$ patch attack in this work, which shares the same setting as many previous works. Specifically, for a classifier $F : \mathbb{R}^{C \times H \times W} \rightarrow \{1, \cdots, N\}$ and an image $x \in \mathbb{R}^{C \times H \times W}$ with channel $C$, height $H$ and width $W$, the attacker can adversarially choose $(a, b)$ as the upper left position, and arbitrarily change pixels within the corresponding square patch of size $p$. For an attack set $\mathcal{A}$ and $A \in \mathcal{A}$, denote $\mathcal{K}(A)$ to be the set of pixels that are changeable by $A$. Denote $\mathcal{A}_p$ to be the set of attacks that can arbitrarily change pixels inside a $p \times p$ square. So for any $A \in \mathcal{A}_p$, $\mathcal{K}(A)$ is a $p \times p$ square. Since an arbitrary rectangular can be covered by a larger square, here we only consider a square patch attack.

In our defense framework, the classifier $F$ is based on base classifiers, and we denote these base classifiers as $f_1, \cdots, f_n$. Moreover, since the certification framework relies on mask strategy, here we make some additional notations. Suppose $M$ is a $0 - 1$ mask matrix that shares the same height and width with image $x$, where masked pixels are 0 and others are 1. Denote $\mathcal{O}(M)$ to be the positions of pixels that are masked. For a classifier $f$, define $f_M(x) = f(M \odot x)$.

### 3.2   Certified Detection for Patch Defense

In this task, our goal is to decide whether an image is successfully attacked or not. This can be achieved by choosing base classifiers $f_1, \cdots, f_n$ and $F$ properly. Our algorithms are based on the following theorem.

**Definition 1.** *For an attack set $\mathcal{A}$, the base classifiers $f_1, \cdots, f_n$ are called* **compatible** *to $\mathcal{A}$, if they satisfy that for any image $x \in \mathbb{R}^{C \times H \times W}$ and any attack $A \in \mathcal{A}$, there exists $1 \le i \le n$ such that $f_i(x) = f_i(A(x))$.*

**Theorem 1.** *For an attack set $\mathcal{A}$, suppose the base classifiers $f_1, \cdots, f_n$ are compatible to $\mathcal{A}$. For an image $x \in \mathbb{R}^{C \times H \times W}$, an attack from $\mathcal{A}$ can be either certified detected or regarded as "harmless" if no warning is raised under the following definition of $F$:*

$$F(x) := \begin{cases} a, & \text{if } f_1(x) = \cdots f_n(x) = a \\ warning, & else \end{cases}$$

*Proof.* Suppose $x$ is an image that satisfies

$$f_1(x) = \cdots = f_n(x) = a.$$

For any attack $A \in \mathcal{A}$, denote $U = unique(f_1(A(x)), \cdots, f_n(A(x)))$ to be the deduplication of the set $\{f_1(A(x)), \cdots, f_n(A(x))\}$, and $\#U$ to be the number of elements of $U$. If $\#U \geq 2$, then obviously $x$ is attacked. If $\#U = 1$, suppose we have $f_1(A(x)) = \cdots = f_n(A(x)) = b$. However, there exist $1 \leq i \leq n$ such that $f_i(x) = f_i(A(x))$ because $f_1, \cdots, f_n$ are compatible to $\mathcal{A}$. Since $f_i(x) = a$ and $f_i(A(x)) = b$, we have $a = b$. So this attack fails to make any changes to the prediction result.

**Fig. 1.** (a)-(d) is certified detection process. (a) is the original image. We slide a square mask from upper left to lower right. (b), (c) and (d) are three different positions. The black patch "A" is an adversarial attack. One of such gray square masks can fully cover the adversarial patch.

Our theorem is a more general version of previous certification [14, 17]. We have no restrictions of base classifiers constructions, and can be adapted to any attack set out of single-patch attack. For example, we can also solve dual-patch attack or more generally, sparse adversarial attack proposed in [16].

**Base Classifiers Design.** Denote $\mathcal{A}_p$ to be the set of square patch attacks with size smaller than $p$. When attacks are restricted to $\mathcal{A}_p$, it is not hard to design the base classifiers. Fixed a known classifier $f$, we consider classifiers $\tilde{f} \in \mathcal{F} = \{f_M, M : \text{0-1} mask\}$. So we only need to choose $n$ masked areas $M_1, \cdots, M_n$ such that for any $A \in \mathcal{A}_p$, there exists $1 \leq i \leq n$ such that $M_i \odot x = M_i \odot A(x)$, which means $\mathcal{K}(A) \subset \mathcal{O}(M_i)$.

Therefore, it is sufficient to assign a $M_i$ for every possible position of $p \times p$ area. Moreover, since we need $f_{M_1}(x) = \cdots = f_{M_n}(x)$, we should make $\mathcal{O}(M_i)$ as small as possible, so that the unmasked area is big enough to achieve consistency for all these classifiers. Based on these analysis and the principles of simplicity, we first set a proper size $m \geq p$ and a proper stride $s$. We can have two straight solutions. Firstly, we can slide the $m \times m$ square area with stride $s$ from upper left to lower right. Each $m \times m$ area acts as $\mathcal{O}(M_i)$ for some $M_i$. Recent works based on CNNs have similar ideas [10, 17, 28]. However, the complexity increases quadratically as image size increases. So it is impractical to make a certification for high resolution like 224. Second, we can slide a band of width $m$ with stride $s$ from left to right. Each band acts as $\mathcal{O}(M_i)$ for some $M_i$. This is a linear-complexity algorithm that hasn't been explored before for certified detection.

Although the above ideas are restricted to use due to the high complexity, we find that vision transformers can perfectly solve this problem. Figure 1 and 2 (a)(b) show how we can take advantage of vision transformers for quadratic and linear complexity respectively. First, the natural square patch structure can act as the role of a sliding window with a big size and stride. For any $A \in \mathcal{A}_p$, it will only intersect with restricted patches. For example, if we use regular vision transformers with patch size 16, the attack $A$ only influences $r_p^2$ patches, where $r_p = \lceil (p-1)/16 \rceil + 1$. Second, after patchifying the image to be a sequence of patches, we can take the tokens that are not influenced by $A$, and drop others. This can additionally reduce complexity. Finally, with a large kernel size and stride, the certification process can be two-magnitude faster than previous methods. So we can certify ImageNet data with a high speed. This method using vision transformers with quadratic complexity is also illustrated in [14].

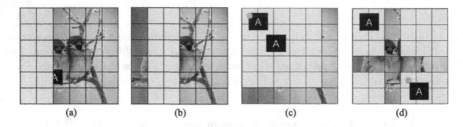

**Fig. 2.** (a) and (b) are the illustration of linear-complexity certification. We slide a band mask from left to right. At least one gray mask will fully cover the adversarial patch (Figure (b)). In (c) and (d), we can see that when two adversarial patches are close enough, we can certainly cover them with a reasonable bigger area. However, they can distribute arbitrarily far from each other in the image. Our generalized window solve this problem as shown in (d). Here we mark the start position of a generalized window with a smiley face.

**Certified Detection for Dual-Patch Attack.** Dual-patch attack is considered to be challenging for certified defense. In this setting, the attacker is allowed to attack two arbitrary patches. Naturally, we hope to use what we do in the defense of a single-patch attack: finding some $i$ such that $\mathcal{K}(A) \subset \mathcal{O}(M_i)$. It is natural when two adversarial patches are close to each other enough. However, what if they are far from each other since we allow the attacker to choose patches arbitrarily? What kind of masks should we choose to make the base classifiers compatible to the attack set?

Does our theoretical guarantee fail completely? The answer is no. Actually, we can still certify dual-patch attack cases with slight modification. The first key is to modify the topological structure of an image. For image size $H \times W$, we define the generalized window as follows:

**Definition 2.** *(Generalized Window).* *For any* $1 \leq a \leq H, 1 \leq b \leq W$, *a generalized window* $M$ *of size* $(m_1, m_2)$ *starting from position* $(a, b)$ *is defined to be* $M = \{((a+i)\%H, (b+j)\%W)\}_{i=1,j=1}^{m_1, m_2}$. *Here* % *means taking the remainder.*

Obviously, when $a, b$ are small, generalized windows are just the same as the regular square windows. With generalized windows, we can say the left and right sides of an image are connected, and the upper and lower sides are also connected. Our certification is based on generalized windows.

**Theorem 2.** *For an even number* $q$ *and a square grid of size* $q \times q$, *any two sub-areas of size* $p_n \times p_n$ *can be covered by a generalized window of size* $(p_n + q/2, p_n + q/2)$.

Actually the geometric understanding is quite straightforward. Please refer to Fig. 2. We leave the formal proof of Theorem 2 to appendix. Now we can do certification for dual-patch cases totally same as single-patch case. Here $q$ is the patch number typically set to be $224/16 = 14$, also denote $p_s$ is the patch size. Denote $\mathcal{A}_p \times \mathcal{A}_p$ to be the set of dual-patch attacks of size $p$. By Theorem 2, for any $A \in \mathcal{A}_p \times \mathcal{A}_p$, there exists a generalized window $M$ of size $((p_n + q/2)p_s, (p_n + q/2)p_s)$, where $p_n = \lceil (p-1)/p_s \rceil + 1$, that fully covers areas influenced by $A$. So let $\{M_i\}_{i=1}^{q^2}$ satisfy that $\{\mathcal{O}(M_i)\}_{i=1}^{q^2}$ are all the generalized windows of size $((p_n + q/2)p_s, (p_n + q/2)p_s)$, which are exact combinations of some patches. Then define $f_i = f_{M_i}$ for $1 \leq i \leq n$ and a known classifier $f$. Theorem 1 provides that we can certified detect every successful attack from $\mathcal{A}_p \times \mathcal{A}_p$ if the predictions of $f_i$ are consistent.

### 3.3 Certified Recovery for Patch Defense

This task is more challenging because we aim to directly make a correct prediction no matter an adversarial attack is successful or not. This task also highly relies on the choices of $f_1, \cdots, f_n$ and $F$.

**Definition 3.** *For an attack set* $\mathcal{A}$, *the base classifiers* $f_1, \cdots, f_n$ *are called* $m$-*compatible to* $\mathcal{A}$, *if*

$$\sup_{x \in \mathbb{R}^{C \times H \times W}} \sum_{i=1}^{n} \mathbb{I}\{f_i(x) \neq f_i(A(x))\} = m.$$

**Theorem 3.** *For an attack set* $\mathcal{A}$, *suppose the base classifiers* $f_1, \cdots, f_n$ *are* $m$-*compatible to* $\mathcal{A}$. *For an image* $x$, *and all labels* $\mathcal{Y} = \{1, \cdots, N\}$, *denote* $n_j(x)$ *to be the number of base classifiers that return label* $j \in \mathcal{Y}$. *Also, denote* $\{n_{i_j}(x)\}_{j=1}^{N}$ *to be the descending sort of* $\{n_j(x)\}_{j=1}^{N}$. *Define*

$$F(x) = \arg\max_{1 \leq j \leq N} n_j(x).$$

*If* $n_{i_1}(x) > n_{i_2}(x) + 2m$, *then* $F(x) = F(A(x))$ *for any* $A \in \mathcal{A}$

*Proof.* Our goal is to prove that if $n_{i_1}(x) > n_{i_2}(x) + 2m$, then for any $A \in \mathcal{A}$, $n_{i_1}(A(x)) = \max_{1 \leq j \leq n} n_j(A(x))$. By definition, we have

$$n_{i_1}(A(x)) = \sum_{i=1}^{n} \mathbb{I}\{f_i(A(x)) = i_1\}$$

$$= \sum_{i=1}^{n} \mathbb{I}\{f_i(x) = i_1\} + \sum_{i=1}^{n} \left( \mathbb{I}\{f_i(A(x)) = i_1\} - \mathbb{I}\{f_i(x) = i_1\} \right)$$

$$= n_{i_1}(x) +$$

$$\sum_{i=1}^{n} \left( \mathbb{I}\{f_i(A(x)) = i_1, f_i(x) \neq i_1\} - \mathbb{I}\{f_i(A(x)) \neq i_1, f_i(x) = i_1\} \right)$$

$$\geq n_{i_1}(x) - \sum_{i=1}^{n} \mathbb{I}\{f_i(A(x)) \neq i_1, f_i(x) = i_1\}$$

$$\geq n_{i_1}(x) - \sum_{i=1}^{n} \mathbb{I}\{f_i(A(x)) \neq f_i(x)\}$$

$$\geq n_{i_1}(x) - \sup_{x \in \mathbb{R}^{C \times H \times W}} \sum_{i=1}^{n} \mathbb{I}\{f_i(A(x)) \neq f_i(x)\} = n_{i_1}(x) - m.$$

Due to $n_{i_1}(x) > n_{i_2}(x) + 2m$, this gives for any $j \neq i_1$,

$$n_{i_1}(A(x)) \geq n_{i_1}(x) - m > n_{i_2}(x) + m \geq n_j(x) + m.$$

Moreover,

$$n_{i_1}(A(x)) > n_j(x) + m = \sum_{i=1}^{n} \mathbb{I}\{f_i(x) = j\} + m$$

$$= \sum_{i=1}^{n} \mathbb{I}\{f_i(A(x)) = j\} + \sum_{i=1}^{n} \left( \mathbb{I}\{f_i(x) = j\} - \mathbb{I}\{f_i(A(x)) = j\} \right) + m$$

$$= n_j(A(x)) +$$

$$\sum_{i=1}^{n} \mathbb{I}\{f_i(x) = j, f_i(A(x)) \neq j\} - \sum_{i=1}^{n} \mathbb{I}\{f_i(x) \neq j, f_i(A(x)) = j\} + m$$

$$\geq n_j(A(x)) - \sum_{i=1}^{n} \mathbb{I}\{f_i(x) \neq j, f_i(A(x)) = j\} + m$$

$$\geq n_j(A(x)) - \sup_{x \in \mathbb{R}^{C \times H \times W}} \sum_{i=1}^{n} \mathbb{I}\{f_i(x) \neq j, f_i(A(x)) = j\} + m = n_j(A(x)).$$

Hence, for any $j \neq i_1$, we have

$$n_{i_1}(A(x)) > n_j(A(x)).$$

Therefore, for any $A \in \mathcal{A}$, we have $n_{i_1}(A(x)) = \max_{1 \leq j \leq n} n_j(A(x))$ and $f(x) = f(A(x))$.

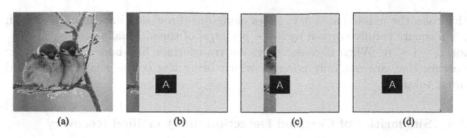

**Fig. 3.** Certification process using derandomized smoothing. (a) is the original full image. We slide the band of size $(224, w)$ from left to right with stride $s$. (b), (c), (d) are three positions. The black patch "A" is an adversarial patch with size $p$. The band in (c) intersect with the adversarial patch, and the adversarial patch only intersects bands close to (c).

Similar to Theorem 1, Theorem 3 is also very flexible. Actually for any base classifiers, at least we have $f_1, \cdots, f_n$ is $m$−compatible for $m = n$. So all we need to do is to make $m$ small enough.

**Base Classifiers Design.** When it comes to square patch attack set $\mathcal{A}_p$, we also choose base classifiers based on the mask strategy. The goal is different from the first task. Previously, we want a consistency so we keep as many as possible unmasked area. Now we need the gap between $n_{i_1}$ and $n_{i_2}$ is bigger than the 'inconsistency' of predictions between clean image and attacked image, which means we need to minimize the influence of any attack $A \in \mathcal{A}_p$. Therefore, we need to mask as large as possible areas. Notice that there exists a trade-off since masking more area will reduce $m$ in Theorem 3, but decrease the accuracy of a single classifier.

Because the mask is big here, we also need to use generalized windows otherwise there will be only limited areas to choose. However, square masks do not work in recovery, we show this through an example. Considering patch attack that can change about $32 \times 32$ pixels of a $224 \times 224$ image (approximately 2%). For $m \geq 32$, there are $[(m - 32 + 1)/s]^2$ masks that can fully cover a $32 \times 32$ attack. This means for stride $s$, about

$$\left(\frac{224}{s}\right)^2 - \left(\frac{m-31}{s}\right)^2$$

base classifiers could be influenced by $32 \times 32$ attack. Suppose $m$ is approximately 200, then the above term is approximately $20000/s^2$. But the number of total base classifiers is only $224^2/s^2 \approx 50000/s^2$. So it is hard to make the gap larger than $40000/s^2$. Therefore, if we use mask-based classifiers, we should consider choices out of squares. Actually rectangular mask whose either height or width equals to the original image works. That's what recent works focusing on (de)randomized smoothing did. Figure 3 shows this process. Let $M_1, \cdots, M_n$ be generalized windows of size $(H, m)$ (or similarly, $(m, W)$) and stride $s$. In this case, the masked area only slides along one dimension instead of two. Each $p \times p$ square is fully covered by $[(m - p + 1)/s]$ of them. Finally, we let $f_i = f_{M_i}$ for $1 \leq i \leq n$. When it comes to vision transformer backbones, we only take patches that are not fully covered, which bring less complexity with reduced input tokens.

### 3.4  Similarities of Certified Detection and Certified Recovery

Recently, both tasks achieve the state-of-the-art result using vision transformer structures, but it remains unclear why vision transformers work well. From the above analysis, we can find that there does exist many similarities in these two tasks. In both, we find a masked area and slide them around the image. After obtaining predictions using masked part, we either analyze consistency or vote. Since our model either does zero-shot certification or slightly finetunes with target size of unmasked area, the training recipe acts an important role. The recent progress of self-supervised vision transformers inspires us to choose vision transformers pretrained with the mask-image-modeling (MIM) method as our backbone, to additionally generate base classifiers in both tasks.

## 4  Results

In this section, we compare ViP and previous methods for various certified robustness tasks on ImageNet, which is challenging for most of the previous certification methods. Our methods with masked autoencoder (MAE) achieves state-of-the-art performance on all related tasks.

### 4.1  Certified Detection

**Single-Patch Detection.** We first evaluate our certified detection methods on single-patch detection in a zero-shot manner.Results are shown in Table 1. We range the possible influenced patch number from $2 \times 2$ to $8 \times 8$ following [14]. We also compare with methods based on CNNs [10,28] on pixel level. Results are shown in Table 2.

Both DeiT and MAE surpass results in [14] a lot. Although DeiT and the original ViT model in [14] shares similar accuracy on clean images, we find that DeiT has a very big improvement about $3 \sim 11\%$ over the original ViT model. This illustrates that data augmentation in training helps a lot. Additionally, MAE makes further improvement, about $6 \sim 16\%$ compared to [14]. At the first time, detection-based certified robustness is approaching the clean accuracy, even with a zero-shot manner.

We also show the results of linear-complexity certified detection in the last line of Table 1. This new linear time detection algorithm produces slightly worst results compared to our original quadratic time algorithm, yet being much faster. Furthermore, our linear time algorithm outperforms the quadratic algorithm in

**Table 1.** Results of single-patch certified detection on ImageNet. Here $2 \times 2$ means that an adversarial patch attack can at most influence $2 \times 2$ square patches of size $16 \times 16$. So $2 \times 2$ actually corresponds to patch attack of size not larger than $17 \times 17$ in the original $224 \times 224$ image. The same is true for $3 \times 3$ to $8 \times 8$. For example, $3 \times 3$ corresponds to patch attack of size $18 \times 18 \sim 33 \times 33$, and so on.

| Methods | Complexity | Speed | Clean acc. | Certified robustness | | | | | | |
|---|---|---|---|---|---|---|---|---|---|---|
| | | | | $2\times2$ | $3\times3$ | $4\times4$ | $5\times5$ | $6\times6$ | $7\times7$ | $8 \times 8$ |
| PatchVeto [14] | quadratic | 0.92s | 81.8 | 72.0 | 67.2 | 61.9 | 56.4 | 50.5 | 44.1 | 37.1 |
| ViP_DeiT_base | quadratic | 0.92s | 81.9 | 75.0 | 71.4 | 67.4 | 63.2 | 58.6 | 53.8 | 48.4 |
| ViP_MAE_base | quadratic | 0.92s | 83.7 | **77.7** | **74.6** | **70.9** | **67.2** | **62.9** | **58.4** | **53.4** |
| ViP_MAE_base | linear | 0.11s | 83.7 | 74.5 | 70.6 | 66.2 | 61.6 | 56.8 | 52.1 | 46.7 |

**Table 2.** Results of single-patch certified detection compared to previous CNN-based methods on ImageNet. MRD [17] cannot scale to ImageNet.

| Methods | 1% pixels | | 2% pixels | | 3% pixels | |
|---|---|---|---|---|---|---|
| | acc | rob | acc | rob | acc | rob |
| MRD [17] | - | - | - | - | - | - |
| PatchGuard++[28] | 61.8 | 36.3 | 61.6 | 33.9 | 61.5 | 31.1 |
| ScaleCert[10] | 62.8 | 60.4 | 58.5 | 55.4 | 56.4 | 52.8 |
| ViP_MAE_base | **83.66** | **74.56** | **83.66** | **74.56** | **83.66** | **70.9** |

[9] with an improvement about $3 \sim 9\%$. Our certification time for one image against $2 \times 2$ attack is reduced from 0.92 seconds to 0.11 seconds.

We then compare on pixel level. Here we choose patch size from $\{24, 32, 40\}$, which corresponds to $1 \sim 3\%$ pixels respectively.

**Dual-Patch Detection.** This task of detecting attacks with two patches is much more challenging and was never demonstrated in prior works. We are the first to make this practical on large-scale dataset like ImageNet as far as we know. Table 3 compares different training recipe with certification in our framework. Conclusions are similar as the single-patch case. MAE-based model improves about 20% under two $2 \times 2$ adversarial patches. This also illustrates the effect of MIM-based pretraining methods; when the adversarial patch sizes are bigger, the detection rate is lower however the MAE-based model is consistently better. The low detection rate is reasonable since two big patches like $6 \times 6$ can actually cover most of the key information of an image. Note that these results are also obtained *without additional training* and we can potentially further improve performance by finetuning on target image size.

**Table 3.** Results of dual-patch certified detection on ImageNet. This setting is much more challenging and is not handled by existing works. Here $2 \times 2$ means each of these two patches can at most influence $2 \times 2$ square patches of size $16 \times 16$. So are $3 \times 3$ to $6 \times 6$.

| Model | Clean acc. | Robustness | | | | |
|---|---|---|---|---|---|---|
| | | 2×2 | 3×3 | 4×4 | 5×5 | 6×6 |
| ViP_ViT_base | 81.8 | 22.2 | 12.5 | 4.3 | 0.6 | 0.03 |
| ViP_DeiT_base | 81.9 | 35.5 | 26.4 | 16.6 | 6.3 | 0.4 |
| ViP_MAE_base | 83.66 | **42.0** | **33.3** | **23.9** | **14.1** | **4.8** |

## 4.2 Certified Recovery

Finally, we evaluate different certified recovery methods compared with previous CNN-based methods (Fig. 2) and current state-of-the-art method [21] when adversarial patch size is unknown. Following the same setting in [21], we choose same training parameters and test with same width of unmasked area. In detail, for width $w \in \{19, 25, 37\}$, we randomly choose an unmasked area of size $(224, w)$. After patch embedding, we drop tokens that are fully masked. We train for 30 epochs, using SGD optimizer with momentum 0.9, fixed learning rate 1e-3 for batch size 256, with a weight decay 1e-4. We only use random resized crop, horizontal flip and color jitter for data augmentation. Our method using MAE_base all achieve a better performance with about 2% improvement over all different width and stride.

Moreover, we test the influence of fintuning epoch and model size for width 19. If we train for longer epochs like 60, the recovery rate can additionally gain for about 1%. So we have not achieved the limit. Also, we test MAE_large with 30-epoch finetuning. This can further give about 5% improvement compared with MAE_base, and nearly 10% improvement compared with DeiT_base. Compared with about 2% improvement over MAE_base and 5% improvement over DeiT on clean accuracy, we find that certified robustness benefits more from larger model.

**Table 4.** Results of certified recovery compared to previous CNN-based methods on ImageNet. Here we use ViP_MAE_base with width 19 and stride 1.

| Methods | Complexity | Speed | Clean acc. | Certified robustness | | | | | | |
|---|---|---|---|---|---|---|---|---|---|---|
| | | | | 2×2 | 3×3 | 4×4 | 5×5 | 6×6 | 7×7 | 8 × 8 |
| PatchVeto [14] | quadratic | 0.92s | 81.8 | 72.0 | 67.2 | 61.9 | 56.4 | 50.5 | 44.1 | 37.1 |
| ViP_DeiT_base | quadratic | 0.92s | 81.9 | 75.0 | 71.4 | 67.4 | 63.2 | 58.6 | 53.8 | 48.4 |
| ViP_MAE_base | quadratic | 0.92s | 83.7 | **77.7** | **74.6** | **70.9** | **67.2** | **62.9** | **58.4** | **53.4** |
| ViP_MAE_base | linear | 0.11s | 83.7 | 74.5 | 70.6 | 66.2 | 61.6 | 56.8 | 52.1 | 46.7 |

**Table 5.** Results of certified recovery.

| Method | Epoch | Width | Stride | Clean acc | Adversarial robustness | | |
|---|---|---|---|---|---|---|---|
| | | | | | $24 \times 24$ | $32 \times 32$ | $40 \times 40$ |
| ViP_DeiT_base [21] | 30 | 19 | 10 | 68.3 | 36.9 | 36.9 | 31.4 |
| | | | 5 | 69.0 | 40.6 | 37.7 | 32.0 |
| | | | 1 | 69.3 | 43.8 | 38.3 | 34.3 |
| | | 25 | 10 | 70.3 | 40.9 | 35.2 | 29.8 |
| | | | 5 | 70.8 | 41.6 | 36.0 | 33.0 |
| | | | 1 | 72.1 | 44.0 | 38.8 | 34.8 |
| | | 37 | 10 | 72.6 | 41.3 | 36.1 | 30.8 |
| | | | 5 | 73.1 | 41.9 | 36.4 | 33.5 |
| | | | 1 | 73.2 | 43.0 | 38.2 | 34.1 |
| ViP_MAE_base | 30 | 19 | 10 | 69.5 | 38.8 | 38.8 | 33.1 |
| | | | 5 | 70.1 | 42.5 | 39.6 | 33.7 |
| | | | 1 | 70.4 | 45.0 | 40.3 | 35.6 |
| | | 25 | 10 | 71.1 | 42.8 | 37.3 | 31.6 |
| | | | 5 | 72.3 | 43.7 | 37.8 | 34.9 |
| | | | 1 | 72.5 | 45.6 | 40.9 | 36.2 |
| | | 37 | 10 | 75.3 | 43.9 | 38.3 | 32.8 |
| | | | 5 | 75.7 | 44.5 | 38.7 | 32.9 |
| | | | 1 | 75.8 | 45.1 | 40.4 | 35.7 |
| ViP_MAE_base | 60 | 19 | 10 | 69.9 | 39.8 | 39.8 | 34.2 |
| | | | 5 | 70.4 | 43.5 | 40.6 | 34.8 |
| | | | 1 | 70.8 | 46.0 | 41.4 | 36.7 |
| ViP_MAE_large | 30 | 19 | 10 | 73.6 | 44.6 | 44.6 | 38.6 |
| | | | 5 | 74.1 | 48.3 | 45.4 | 39.3 |

## 5  Conclusion

In this work, we propose a unified analysis framework for certified robustness tasks including both certified detection and certified recovery. For $L_0$ patch attack, these two tasks both rely on the choices of the masks. Our work illustrate the great potential of using recent progress on vision transformers, especially cutting-edge self-supervised masked-image-modeling methods, to promote patch defense. With our defense framework, certified robustness for both tasks are approaching the clean accuracy. Compared with earlier works which only have about $20 \sim 30\%$ certified robustness, we make a progress on making certification practical in real world.

**Acknowledgment.** This work is supported by a gift from Open Philanthropy, TPU Research Cloud (TRC) program, and Google Cloud Research Credits program.

# References

1. Bao, H., Dong, L., Wei, F.: Beit: BERT pre-training of image transformers. In: ICLR (2022)
2. Brown, T.B., Mané, D., Roy, A., Abadi, M., Gilmer, J.: Adversarial patch. arXiv preprint arXiv:1712.09665 (2017)
3. Chiang, P.Y., Ni, R., Abdelkader, A., Zhu, C., Studer, C., Goldstein, T.: Certified defenses for adversarial patches. In: ICLR (2020)
4. Cisse, M.M., Adi, Y., Neverova, N., Keshet, J.: Houdini: fooling deep structured visual and speech recognition models with adversarial examples. In: NeurIPS (2017)
5. Cohen, J., Rosenfeld, E., Kolter, Z.: Certified adversarial robustness via randomized smoothing. In: ICML (2019)
6. Deng, J., Dong, W., Socher, R., Li, L.J., Li, K., Fei-Fei, L.: ImageNet: a large-scale hierarchical image database. In: CVPR (2009)
7. Dosovitskiy, A., et al.: An image is worth $16 \times 16$ words: transformers for image recognition at scale. In: ICLR (2021)
8. Eykholt, K., et al.: Robust physical-world attacks on deep learning visual classification. In: CVPR (2018)
9. Goodfellow, I.J., Shlens, J., Szegedy, C.: Explaining and harnessing adversarial examples. In: ICLR (2015)
10. Han, H., X., et al.: ScaleCert: scalable certified defense against adversarial patches with sparse superficial layers. In: NeurIPS (2021)
11. Hayes, J.: On visible adversarial perturbations & digital watermarking. In: CVPR Workshops (2018)
12. He, K., Chen, X., Xie, S., Li, Y., Dollár, P., Girshick, R.: Masked autoencoders are scalable vision learners. In: CVPR (2021)
13. Huang, L., et al.: Universal physical camouflage attacks on object detectors. In: CVPR (2020)
14. Huang, Y., Li, Y.: Zero-shot certified defense against adversarial patches with vision transformers. arXiv preprint arXiv:2111.10481 (2021)
15. Levine, A., Feizi, S.: (De) Randomized smoothing for certifiable defense against patch attacks. In: NeurIPS (2020)
16. Levine, A., Feizi, S.: Robustness certificates for sparse adversarial attacks by randomized ablation. In: AAAI (2020)
17. McCoyd, M., et al.: Minority reports defense: defending against adversarial patches. In: ACNS (2020)
18. Metzen, J.H., Yatsura, M.: Efficient certified defenses against patch attacks on image classifiers. In: ICLR (2021)
19. Mirman, M., Gehr, T., Vechev, M.: Differentiable abstract interpretation for provably robust neural networks. In: ICML (2018)
20. Naseer, M., Khan, S., Porikli, F.: Local gradients smoothing: defense against localized adversarial attacks. In: WACV (2019)
21. Salman, H., Jain, S., Wong, E., Madry, A.: Certified patch robustness via smoothed vision transformers. In: CVPR (2022)
22. Szegedy, C., et al.: Intriguing properties of neural networks. In: ICLR (2014)
23. Touvron, H., Cord, M., Douze, M., Massa, F., Sablayrolles, A., Jégou, H.: Training data-efficient image transformers & distillation through attention. In: ICML (2021)
24. Wei, C., Fan, H., Xie, S., Wu, C.Y., Yuille, A., Feichtenhofer, C.: Masked feature prediction for self-supervised visual pre-training. In: CVPR (2022)

25. Wu, Z., Lim, S.N., Davis, L.S., Goldstein, T.: Making an invisibility cloak: real world adversarial attacks on object detectors. In: ECCV (2020)
26. Xiang, C., Bhagoji, A.N., Sehwag, V., Mittal, P.: PatchGuard: a provably robust defense against adversarial patches via small receptive fields and masking. In: USENIX Security Symposium (2021)
27. Xiang, C., Mahloujifar, S., Mittal, P.: PatchCleanser: certifiably robust defense against adversarial patches for any image classifier. In: USENIX Security Symposium (2022)
28. Xiang, C., Mittal, P.: Patchguard++: efficient provable attack detection against adversarial patches. arXiv preprint arXiv:2104.12609 (2021)
29. Xie, C., Wang, J., Zhang, Z., Zhou, Y., Xie, L., Yuille, A.: Adversarial examples for semantic segmentation and object detection. In: ICCV (2017)
30. Yang, C., Kortylewski, A., Xie, C., Cao, Y., Yuille, A.: PatchAttack: a black-box texture-based attack with reinforcement learning. In: ECCV (2020)
31. Zhou, J., et al.: IBOT: image BERT pre-training with online tokenizer. In: ICLR (2022)

# incDFM: Incremental Deep Feature Modeling for Continual Novelty Detection

Amanda Rios[1,2]([✉]), Nilesh Ahuja[2], Ibrahima Ndiour[4], Utku Genc[3],
Laurent Itti[1], and Omesh Tickoo[3]

[1] University of Southern California, Los Angeles, CA 90089, USA
amanda.rios@intel.com
[2] Intel Labs, Santa Clara, USA
[3] Intel Labs, Hillsboro, USA
[4] Intel Labs, Chandler, USA

**Abstract.** Novelty detection is a key capability for practical machine
learning in the real world, where models operate in non-stationary conditions and are repeatedly exposed to new, unseen data. Yet, most current
novelty detection approaches have been developed exclusively for static,
offline use. They scale poorly under more realistic, continual learning
regimes in which data distribution shifts occur. To address this critical
gap, this paper proposes incDFM (incremental Deep Feature Modeling),
a self-supervised continual novelty detector. The method builds a statistical model over the space of intermediate features produced by a deep
network, and utilizes feature reconstruction errors as uncertainty scores
to guide the detection of novel samples. Most importantly, incDFM estimates the statistical model incrementally (via several iterations within a
task), instead of a single-shot. Each time it selects only the most confident
novel samples which will then guide subsequent recruitment incrementally. For a certain task where the ML model encounters a mixture of
old and novel data, the detector flags novel samples to incorporate them
to old knowledge. Then the detector is updated with the flagged novel
samples, in preparation for a next task. To quantify and benchmark performance, we adapted multiple datasets for continual learning: CIFAR-
10, CIFAR-100, SVHN, iNaturalist, and the 8-dataset. Our experiments
show that incDFM achieves state of the art continual novelty detection
performance. Furthermore, when examined in the greater context of continual learning for classification, our method is successful in minimizing
catastrophic forgetting and error propagation.

**Keywords:** Continual learning · Out-of-distribution detection

---

**Supplementary Information** The online version contains supplementary material
available at https://doi.org/10.1007/978-3-031-19806-9_34.

# 1    Introduction

Deep Neural network models excel at learning complex mappings between inputs and outputs, so long as the data is drawn from a stationary distribution. Yet, when these models are deployed in the real-world, they may encounter out-of-distribution (OOD, "novel") inputs, i.e. input data that does not resemble the training data (in-distribution, "ID"), prompting misleading predictions. This is a strong limitation because many real world applications require handling non-stationary data. Models deployed in self-driving cars, for instance, will inevitably encounter novel out-of-distribution data (e.g. new terrains, objects, weather) that they have to adapt to. Hence, continual novelty detection is critical for operating in real-world, non-stationary conditions. However, most novelty detection methods were developed for and evaluated against a single fixed split of ID/OOD data. They do not integrate the detected OOD data into the learnt knowledge and perform poorly in dynamic, non-stationary conditions. On the other hand, most approaches in continual learning (CL) focus on mitigating *catastrophic forgetting*, a phenomenon in which training a neural network on a new task with novel data typically destroys the fixed mapping learned from the previous tasks. Most importantly, they use an oracle to identify novel data, leaving the question of continual novelty detection largely unaddressed.

We seek to bridge the divide between the continual learning and novelty detection fields by addressing novelty detection in continual learning, a much more challenging evaluation and deployment paradigm. Specifically, we focus on the task-incremental continual learning setting, where the model increasingly encounters new, additional classes of data without significant distribution shift for the already-seen classes of previous tasks. In this setting, a novelty detector is presented with several OOD/ID separation tasks through time. This can bring about several challenges: (1) *Novelty consolidation*: integrating detected novel samples to knowledge (to avoid treating them as novel in subsequent tasks) (2) *Catastrophic forgetting*: remembering this cumulative knowledge through tasks, and (3) *Error propagation*: minimizing the number of samples falsely flagged as novel to avoid impairing knowledge consolidation.

**Contribution:** We propose a novelty detection algorithm, "incremental Deep Feature Modeling" (incDFM) that addresses these three challenges. It is trained using only ID data and designed to operate under the continual learning setting. incDFM builds a per-class or per-task statistical model over the space of intermediate features produced by the deep network and computes a feature reconstruction score to flag the OOD samples. Most importantly, with the goal of minimizing continual error propagation, incDFM estimates this statistical model incrementally (via several iterations within a task) for each novel task. At each iteration within a novel task, it recruits the top most "certain" novel samples that will then improve subsequent recruitments incrementally. incDFM can be used to substitute the novelty oracle used in traditional supervised CL. Finally, we show that incDFM achieves state of the art novelty detection performance when evaluated on multiple datasets adapted for task-based continual learning, such as CIFAR-10, CIFAR-100, SVHN, iNaturalist and the 8-dataset.

## 2   Background and Motivation

**Novelty Detection:** Also known as outlier or out-of-distribution (OOD) detection, novelty detection is a very active research area. It is typically performed by making the network provide an uncertainty score (along with the output) for each input. Common methods include the Softmax score [15] and its temperature-scaled variants such as ODIN [24]. Bayesian neural networks [12] and ensembles of discriminative classifiers [22] can generate high quality uncertainty, but at the cost of complex model representations, and substantial compute and memory. Deep generative models learn distributions over the input data, and then evaluate the likelihood of new inputs with respect to the learnt distributions [16,32,37]. Gradient-based characterization of abnormality in autoencoders is highlighted in [21]. Finally, there are methods [1,23] that learn parametric class-conditional probability distributions over the features and use the likelihoods (w.r.t the learnt distributions) as uncertainty scores.

**Continual Learning:** This paper focuses on *task incremental learning*, a paradigm where a model continually learns from a sequence of tasks that each introduce novel data but with no or limited access to past, labeled data. The majority of the CL literature has focused on *catastrophic forgetting* [11,33] while mostly offloading the task transition detection duty to a so-called *novelty oracle*. Overall, [39] proposes that current continual learning algorithms can be grouped into *task-dependent* and *task-independent* models by their reliance on task labels at test time. *Task-independent* algorithms do not require task labels and typically employ a single shared classification layer which has as many output nodes as the number of learned classes over all tasks. One subclass consists of *regularization-based* approaches which aim to mitigate forgetting by constraining the change of learnable parameters. Alternatively, *replay-based* algorithms approximate the CL problem to a multi-task setting by either storing [25,36] or learning to generate [38,41,46] past data. Broadly, task-independent models solve a more challenging CL formulation since task-specific parameters are not exploited for test time performance. *Task-dependent* methods, on the other hand, require the availability of task labels which are usually provided by a *task oracle* and utilize this information by employing task-specific classification heads and other task-dependent parameters to share the rest of the network for different tasks, e.g. partitioning with context [5,47,48] or mask matrices [9,27]. Dependence on an oracle limits their applicability as determining tasks and detecting task transitions are challenging and also prone to *forgetting* [39].

**Continual Novelty Detection:** The problem of novelty detection in the continual learning setting has not been extensively studied or discussed in the literature. Most CL literature has assumed the use of a novelty oracle to indicate fully-labeled task transitions. Incipient proposals and discussions for novelty detection have occurred in [3,28,42]. Yet, most of these works do not propose novel OOD algorithms, rather, they adapt existing OOD approaches and to a limited success. For instance, the closest work, by [3], compares among several existing OOD detectors. However, their best results occur under a task-oracle-dependent continual learning setting and using task-dependent CL algorithms to mitigate novelty detection forgetting. We argue that this limits real-world applicability since it is not realistic to assume that at deployment, unlabeled test samples will be accompanied by their respective task IDs, which would obviate the need for OOD detection in the first place. To our knowledge, no work has yet proposed a reliable OOD detection solution for oracle-less continual learning over several tasks, a more realistic but also more challenging setting.

# 3  Methodology for Continual Novelty Detection

To bridge the gap between the CL and OOD fields, we first establish a novelty detection methodology suited to continual learning. In our framework, each incoming task $t$ is an unsupervised mixture of unseen $ID_t$ samples ("old" classes) and $OOD_t$ samples ("new" unseen classes):

$$ID_t = \{u^{old,unseen}|u^{old,unseen} \sim D_k\}, k = 1, ..., t-1$$
$$OOD_t = \{u^{new,unseen}|u^{new,unseen} \sim D_t\}$$

$ID_t$ comprises unseen samples that were never used in training, but come from the same source distributions $D_k, k = 1, ..., t-1$ that were used to train past tasks, while $OOD_t$ consists of samples from an entirely new distribution $D_t$. In our experiments, we simulate this by using 80% of original training samples as novel data at each task and leaving the remainder for introduction at later tasks (at which point they will be old ID data). The goal for the novelty detector is to accurately differentiate between $ID_t$ and $OOD_t$ to produce an estimate of the novel samples which we denote as $\widehat{OOD_t}$. This then becomes the training data to consolidate knowledge of novel samples.

This methodology leads to the additional challenges of *catastrophic forgetting* and *error propagation* (alluded to in Sect. 1) that aren't present in conventional offline OOD detection. First, as more and more classes/tasks are encountered, incDFM has to increasingly add to its stored representation of what is ID and remember the cumulative $\{D_k\}, k \leq t$ going forward. If past $D_k$'s are not properly remembered and represented in knowledge, this can result in catastrophic forgetting and failure to identify incoming old samples as ID. incDFM addresses this by building a per-class or per-task statistical model to detect novel samples at each task. The per-task parameters once stored are not interfered with in future tasks, minimizing forgetting (refer to Sect. 3.1.2). Second, as already mentioned, whenever the novelty detector finalizes its selection of novel samples $\widehat{OOD_t}$, these are then used as training data to consolidate knowledge and expand what is considered as $ID_{t+1}$ for the following task. However, since $\widehat{OOD_t}$ can contain misclassified samples, this could result in an inaccurate representation of $D_t$ during consolidation, which will lead to error propagation that grows progressively worse. Cumulatively, these two aspects can lead to severe performance degradation. We show incDFM's incremental recruitment strategy (Sect. 3.1.2) minimizes error propagation.

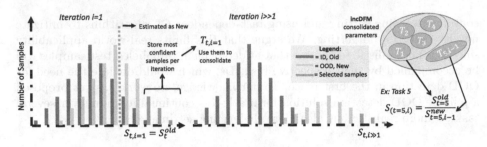

**Fig. 1.** incDFM estimates novelty incrementally per task. A tasks's unlabeled data mixture is shown here with ID/old samples in blue and OOD/novel samples in orange. At each iteration within one novel task, incDFM recruits the top most "certain" novel samples (in red) according to the evaluation function $S_i$. It then removes them from the unlabeled pool. At iteration 1 we can see new and old distributions are entangled but tend to separate in later tasks, as incDFM improves its estimate of novelty.

Lastly, we also evaluate continual OOD detection in an inherently more difficult experimental paradigm where ID and OOD sets are drawn from different splits of the same dataset (intra-dataset). In particular, we propose experiments of intra-dataset class-incremental learning where, at each task, only one novel class is introduced, up until all classes of a dataset are covered. ID and OOD splits sampled from the same dataset tend to be close and harder to disentangle [39]. In contrast, most offline OOD detection literature has focused on OOD/ID splits between different datasets (inter-dataset, e.g., CIFAR-10 as ID vs. SVHN as OOD) - these are typically comprised of highly divergent data distributions, causing the model to first explore accidental low-level statistical differences instead of more meaningful semantic variances. Overall, combining a naturally harder ID/OOD setting per task with having to remember what is ID through time makes most conventional OOD detectors underperfom. In incDFM, iterative estimation and recruitment algorithm is better suited to continual and challenging ID/OOD splits.

## 3.1  incDFM Model

### 3.1.1  Deep Feature Modeling

incDFM is built upon the OOD detection technique proposed in [1] based on probabilistic modeling of deep features. Consider a deep neural network (DNN) trained on an $N$-class classification problem. For an input $\mathbf{x}$, let $\mathbf{u} \triangleq \mathcal{F}_l(\mathbf{x})$ denote the output at an intermediate layer $l$ of the network. In [1], class-conditional probability densities are learnt on this set of intermediate deep-features and the likelihood scores from these are used to discriminate between ID and OOD samples. A principal component analysis (PCA) transformation, $\mathcal{T} : \mathcal{H} \to \mathcal{L}$, is simultaneously learnt to map the high-dimensional features onto an appropriate lower-dimensional subspace, $dim(\mathcal{L}) \ll dim(\mathcal{H})$, prior to density estimation. The PCA transformations are also learnt on a per-class basis. For incDFM, this implies that a separate PCA transformation, $\mathcal{T}_t$, is learnt for each task $t$. In [29], it was shown that the *feature reconstruction error* (FRE) score, defined as

$$FRE(\mathbf{u}, \mathcal{T}) = \|\mathbf{u} - (\mathcal{T}^\dagger \circ \mathcal{T})\mathbf{u}\|_2 \tag{1}$$

is highly effective at discriminating between ID and OOD samples, where $\mathcal{T}^\dagger$ is the inverse PCA transformation (computed as the Moore-Penrose pseudo-inverse of $\mathcal{T}$). The intuition behind FRE is that OOD samples will lie outside the subspace of ID samples and will hence result in higher FRE scores.

### 3.1.2  Knowledge Consolidation and Storage

To obtain deep features, incDFM employs a frozen feature extractor pre-trained via unsupervised contrastive learning on an independent large dataset - e.g., imagenet. Using a frozen pre-trained deep feature extractor showed superior performance to fine-tuning, which is in line with recent findings in the adaptive learning field [8,34]. At each task $t$, we process all unlabeled samples, $\mathbf{x_t} = OOD_t \cup ID_t$ through the feature extractor and collect deep features $\mathbf{u_t} = \mathcal{F}_l(\mathbf{x_t})$ which are used as input to the main incDFM algorithm. Further, as mentioned earlier, we learn and store the parameters for $\mathcal{T}_t$ for each task separately (Procedure *Consolidate* in Algorithm 1 Fig 2). This consolidation approach has two advantages for continual learning. First, by modeling $OOD_t$ via isolated per-task (per-class) parameters, we minimize catastrophic interference when new classes are introduced later on. The consolidated per-class parameters are never altered so cannot actually be "forgotten", assuming no distribution shift for old tasks. In deep neural networks (DNNs), by contrast, the majority, if not all, of parameters are shared between the classes and per-class importance of each weight is not as easily assessed. As such, when new classes are introduced, it is naturally much more difficult to isolate inter-class interference in DNN weight space. This is one of the reasons most CL approaches tackling single-headed classification require a replay strategy to not "forget", which can quickly escalate in memory usage. This brings us to the second advantage: our consolidation approach is both fast and memory-efficient. More specifically, it is fast because it requires a single PCA fitting operation per task. Additionally, it entails a low memory usage since it only retains the PCA transformation $\mathcal{T}_t$ per task, which is almost always less memory expensive than storing raw image samples for replay typical in task-independent CL approaches.

### 3.1.3  Novelty Detection and Selection: Incremental Recruitment

When a new task arrives, the stored consolidation parameters ($\{\mathcal{T}_k\}$ for $k = 1 : t - 1$) are used to initialize an incremental recruitment of novel samples. We express the unlabeled deep features from incoming task $t$ as $\mathbf{u_t} = \mathcal{F}_l(\mathbf{x_t}), \mathbf{x_t} = ID_t \cup OOD_t$. For all unlabeled samples $u_t$, we first compute the FRE scores for all $k = t - 1$ stored sets of transforms and then take the minimum FRE:

$$S^{old}(\mathbf{u_t}) = \min_k(FRE(\mathbf{u_t}, \mathcal{T}_k)), k = 1, ..., t - 1 \tag{2}$$

**Algorithm 1:** incDFM - Incremental Novelty Recruitment per Task

| | |
|---|---|
| **Input** | : $u_t$ - Deep Features of current Task |
| **Require** | : $I$ - Maximum Number of iterations; $R$ - Recruitment per iteration; |
| **Initialize** | : $S^{old} \leftarrow$ KnowledgeScores$(X_t, \{\mathcal{T}_k\}$ for $k < t)$; |

                        $i \leftarrow 1$; $N^{new}_{1,left} \leftarrow length(X_t)$; $S_1 \leftarrow S^{old}$;

                        Indices$_t = [1, ..., length(X_t)]$; Indices$^{new}_1 = []$;

    // Select most certain novel samples per iteration until stopping criterion

1  **while** $(i < I)$ *and* $(N^{new}_{i,left} > 0)$ **do**

       // Concatenate newly selected indices to previously selected

2       Indices$^{new}_i$, $N^{new}_{i,left} \leftarrow$ SelectTop$(S_i, R)$

       // Remove selected indices from unlabeled pool

3       Indices$^{new} \leftarrow$ [Indices$^{new}_i$, Indices$^{new}$]

4       Indices$_t \leftarrow$ Indices$_t$ − Indices$^{new}_i$

5       $\mathcal{T}_i \leftarrow$ Consolidate(Indices$^{new}$, $X_t$)

6       $S^{new}_i \leftarrow FRE(u_t, \mathcal{T}_i)$

7       $S_i \leftarrow \frac{S^{old}}{\lambda S^{new}_i}$

8       $i \leftarrow i + 1$

9  $\{\mathcal{T}_k\}, k = 1, .., t \leftarrow$ Store$(\mathcal{T}_{t,I})$

**Fig. 2.** Procedures *KnowledgeScores* and *SelectTop* are described in Sect. 3.1.3; *Consolidate* in 3.1.2

Intuitively, this indicates which of the older classes/tasks each sample is closest to. We sort the set of unlabeled samples by their FRE scores with the intuition that $ID_t$ samples will tend to yield lower values of FRE than $OOD_t$. We could presumably set a threshold and select samples whose scores exceed that to constitute $\widehat{OOD_t}$ and then estimate $\mathcal{T}_t$ from those. A relaxed threshold could result in $\widehat{OOD_t}$ containing a large number of ID samples misclassified as novel, whereas a high threshold might result in very few novel samples being available for computation of $\mathcal{T}_t$. Either way, this could lead to poor estimates of $\mathcal{T}_t$ and the error from this would propagate and progressively worsen for subsequent tasks.

Hence, we propose an iterative method to estimate the novel samples in an incremental fashion as outlined in Fig 2. In the first iteration, $i = 0$, we compute $S^{old}(u_t)$ as previously described in Eq. 2 (Procedure *KnowledgeScores*) and select only the highest $R$ percent of the $S_{old}$ scores, corresponding to the most confident "novel" samples until now (farthest from old). These samples constitute a first estimate, $\widehat{OOD}_{t,0}$, of what is OOD. They are used to consolidate knowledge by computing $\mathcal{T}_{t,0}$ and using the latter to obtain $S^{new}_0 \triangleq FRE(u_t, \mathcal{T}_{t,0})$. For all subsequent iterations $i \geq 1$, we compute a composite evaluation score function $S_i$ which combines $S_{old}$ and the previous iteration's $S^{new}_{i-1}$

$$S_i = \frac{S^{old}}{\lambda S^{new}_{i-1}}, \quad S^{new}_{i-1} \triangleq FRE(u_t, \mathcal{T}_{i-1}) \tag{3}$$

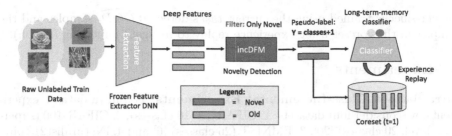

**Fig. 3.** Full Pipeline - unsupervised class incremental learning with incDFM

and use this composite score to select the next R top percent, $indices_i^{new}$ (Procedure *SelectTop* in Algorithm 1), which are then concatenated to all previous iteration's indices, $indices^{new}$, and used to compute the next estimate of $\mathcal{T}_{t,i}$. The idea behind this algorithm is to increasingly separate hard ID/OOD splits (Fig 1). At each iteration, OOD (novel) samples will tend to have low scores $S_{i-1}^{new}$ and high $S_{old}$, resulting in the highest composite $S_i$ values. To minimize errors, we set $R$ conservatively to recruit only the most confident OOD detections. Moroever, as more and more confident OOD estimated samples are recruited, i.e. $Indices^{new}$ grows in size, the better will be the subsequent estimate of PCA parameters $\mathcal{T}_i$. This in turn will yield progressively more reliable $S_i^{new}$ scores.

To estimate a stopping point to incremental recruitment, we set a total maximum number of iterations and employ a small validation set with only in-distribution (old) samples, $(\{V_k\}, k < t)$, to estimate if there is still a probability of having non-recruited novel samples left (suppl.). In practice, at each task we reserve a small percentage of detected novel samples for validation and do not use them for fitting any parameters. For fairness, the same validation set is used across all baselines that we compare with.

## 3.2 Full Pipeline: Unsupervised Class-Incremental Learning Using incDFM for Continual Novelty Detection

We show that incDFM can be coupled onto an unsupervised class incremental classification pipeline, Fig. 3. We take the same experimental setting previously described, where at each task we have a mixture of holdout samples of old classes and one new class at a time, all unlabeled. Over tasks, we keep a counter of how many novelties have been introduced so far, $\mathcal{C}_t$ (equivalent to number of classes in this case). At each task, after incDFM has selected a final estimate of novel samples $\widehat{OOD_t}$, these are pseudolabeled as $\mathcal{C}_{t-1} + 1$ and the counter is also incremented. As the classifier we use a perceptron on top of the frozen feature extractor that is also shared with incDFM, similarly to [39,45]. The detected novel samples are then used to train the classifier using the pseudolabels as targets and are stored in a coreset for replay at future tasks. We employ a fixed size coreset with the same building strategy as in [38]. Thus, at each task, the classifier is trained using the current tasks detected $\widehat{OOD}_t$ samples and the samples in the coreset using experience replay to mitigate forgetting (suppl.).

## 4  Experiments

**Intra-dataset Class-Incremental Experiments:** For intra-dataset experiments, we consider four datasets: 1. CIFAR-10 (10 classes), 2. CIFAR-100 (superclass level, 20 classes) [20], 3. EMNIST (26 classes) [6] and 4. iNaturalist21 (phylum level, 9 classes) [43]. We adapt all datasets for class-incremental learning by starting with 2 classes for the first task and adding one class at each incremental task until all classes are covered.

**Inter-dataset Experiment:** In this experiment, the novelty per task is an entire novel dataset (with multiple new classes). This is a CL version of the conventional ID/OOD setting. We compare how much easier it is to detect ID/OOD shifts in this CL inter-dataset paradigm versus the previous CL intra-dataset class incremental experiment. We consider a sequence of eight tasks each being one of 8 object recognition datasets (Flowers [31]; Scenes [35]; Birds [44]; Cars [19]; Aircrafts [26]; VOC Actions [10]; Letters [7]; svhn [30]) as in [2] (see suppl.).

**Baselines:** We compare and benchmark our method against the various commonly used offline OOD detectors: (i) Mahalanobis based OOD detector [23] (ii) Softmax based OOD detector [15] which uses softmax output as a confidence score, and (iii) Generalized ODIN [17] which introduces a decomposed softmax scoring function as an improvement of Softmax. Note that while Softmax and ODIN both rely on classification layers to detect novelties, Mahalanobis relies on distance scores computed from intermediate features of a DNN. For ODIN and Softmax we use the same classifier architecture as in our full-pipeline (Sect. 5.3.), i.e. a perceptron (MLP) on top of the frozen feature extractor. Since these baselines were developed for offline OOD detection, we make the necessary adaptations to use them in continual learning: First, for Mahalanobis we keep a coreset with select past ID samples to estimate the joint covariance needed for the metric. Second, because the MLP classifier in both Softmax and in ODIN is plastic and updated continually, *catastrophic forgetting* is expected to have a degrading effect on continual novelty detection performance unless an alleviation mechanism is employed. In the intra-dataset class incremental experiments, we apply *coreset-based experience replay* [40], the same CL strategy as in our full-pipeline. Task-dependent algorithms cannot be applied in this case since each task is only one class. Alternatively, to mitigate forgetting in the inter-dataset experiment, we use PSP [5](a task-dependent CL algorithm) and separate readout heads per task, similar to [39]. The original PSP formulation requires a task oracle. Hence, we also propose a version of PSP that is oracle-less: we loop through all PSP task-conditioned MLP partitions and output heads collecting task-dependent Softmax/ODIN scores. We then select the task-dependent score yielding maximum certainty among them as a final task-independent score. Finally, we also compare against a direct implementation of DFM, which uses the same per-task knowledge consolidation strategy as described in Sect. 3.1.2. but does not employ our proposed incremental recruitment algorithm. This serves as an ablated version of incDFM. For all four baselines, we select $\widehat{OOD}_t$ by applying a single threshold per task on the corresponding generated uncertainty scores. The threshold is chosen based on a validation set containing ID samples. For fairness, we employ the same validation set $\{V_k\}, k < t$ used by incDFM. Refer to suppl. for more implementation details.

**Architecture and Training Parameters:** For all methods considered, including ours, we use a ResNet50 [14] backbone pre-trained on ImageNet using SwAV [4], a contrastive learning algorithm. For OOD methods which rely on classification (*ODIN, Softmax*) and also for the end-to-end class incremental learning pipeline, we use an MLP, with 4096-dimensional hidden layer, as the classifier. The backbone is kept frozen for all tasks and only the classifier is fine-tuned over the course of an experiment. We compared to fine-tuning the backbone continually using experience replay but the reported frozen backbone approach worked best for incDFM and baselines (see suppl.), in line with the results reported in [13]. We optimize using ADAM [18] with a learning rate of 0.001 and decrease the learning rate when on a plateau. Finally, for all methods requiring a coreset, e.g., our end-to-end incremental learning pipeline (Sect. 5.3), ODIN, Softmax and Mahalanobis, we keep between 5–10% of the dataset converted to deep embeddings (output of frozen feature extractor) into a fixed-size coreset. For the end-to-end-pipeline, we train until convergence using 40 epochs per task for ODIN and 20 epochs per task for all others.

# 5   Results

## 5.1   Preliminary Offline Evaluation of IncDFM and Baselines

**Table 1.** AUROC scores for offline OOD estimation

| ID → OOD | incDFM | DFM | Mahal | Softmax | ODIN |
|---|---|---|---|---|---|
| CIFAR-10 → SVHN | **99.9** | 93.4 | 93.1 | 88.2 | 95.8 |
| CIFAR-100 → SVHN | **99.9** | 93.6 | 87.7 | 83.5 | 88.4 |

In Table 1 we evaluate incDFM performance in a conventional offline interdataset setting: training on one ID dataset (one task) and evaluating once on another OOD dataset. We use CIFAR-10 and CIFAR-100 as ID datasets and SVHN as OOD. We implemented each baseline (DFM, ODIN, Softmax and Mahalanobis) using the same architecture as described in Sect. 4.1 - a frozen Resnet50 backbone followed by trainable MLP. The latter in the case of methods that perform classification (i.e. ODIN and Softmax). We show that incDFM overperforms the compared baselines as measured by AUROC scores. AUROC stands for area under the receiver operating characteristic curve, which plots the

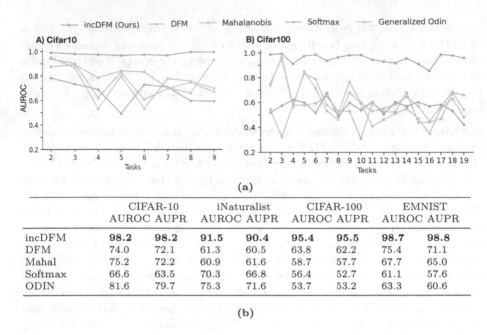

(a)

|  | CIFAR-10 | | iNaturalist | | CIFAR-100 | | EMNIST | |
| --- | --- | --- | --- | --- | --- | --- | --- | --- |
|  | AUROC | AUPR | AUROC | AUPR | AUROC | AUPR | AUROC | AUPR |
| incDFM | **98.2** | **98.2** | **91.5** | **90.4** | **95.4** | **95.5** | **98.7** | **98.8** |
| DFM | 74.0 | 72.1 | 61.3 | 60.5 | 63.8 | 62.2 | 75.4 | 71.1 |
| Mahal | 75.2 | 72.2 | 60.9 | 61.6 | 58.7 | 57.7 | 67.7 | 65.0 |
| Softmax | 66.6 | 63.5 | 70.3 | 66.8 | 56.4 | 52.7 | 61.1 | 57.6 |
| ODIN | 81.6 | 79.7 | 75.3 | 71.6 | 53.7 | 53.2 | 63.3 | 60.6 |

(b)

**Fig. 4.** Intra-dataset Novelty Detection: (a) AUROC scores per task using detected samples for model update. (b) Average AUROC and AUPR scores after all tasks.

true positive rate (TPR) of in-distribution data against the false positive rate (FPR) of OOD data by varying a threshold. It can be regarded as an averaged score.

## 5.2   Continual Novelty Detection

**Intra-dataset OOD, Class Incremental Novelty Detection:** Figure 4(a) displays the performance per task of incDFM when evaluated on intra-dataset class incremental novelty detection, shown for CIFAR-10 and CIFAR-100. Additionally, Fig. 4(b) shows the average performance across tasks for all datasets. We evaluate performance using AUROC and AUPR scores. The latter refers to the area under precision recall curve with respect to the novelty class. Overall, our approach over-performs the competing methods. incDFM shows consistent performance over tasks, with minimal to no degradation. We can directly observe the advantage of incDFM's incremental recruitment algorithm by comparing it to DFM (our ablated baseline) which employs a single threshold for OOD selection instead. Additionally, we can observe that the performance gap between incDFM and compared methods is much larger in this class incremental setting then those shown in Table 1 for the offline setting. When $ID_t$ and $OOD_t$ sets are drawn from the same dataset, as is the case in our class-incremental setting, OOD detectors cannot explore low-level statistics to arrive at a prediction. Instead, the distinction must come from more conceptual class-defining proper-

**Table 2.** Inter-dataset continual learning (8-dataset) with and without Task Oracle.

| Task-Oracle | incDFM | | DFM | | Mahal | | Softmax | | ODIN | |
|---|---|---|---|---|---|---|---|---|---|---|
| | AUROC | AUPR | AUROC | AUPR | AUROC | AUPR | AUROC | AUPR | AUROC | AUPR |
| Yes | – | - | – | - | – | – | 99.9 | 99.9 | 99.8 | 99.6 |
| No | 99.9 | 99.9 | 95.0 | 94.5 | 94.7 | 94.3 | 69.4 | 70.1 | 64.2 | 64.0 |

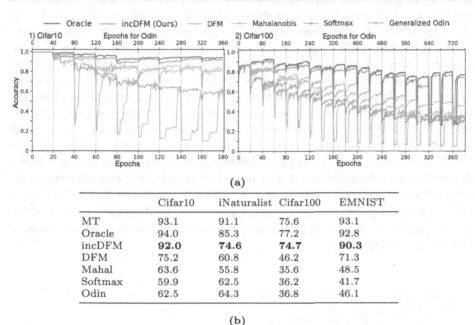

(a)

| | Cifar10 | iNaturalist | Cifar100 | EMNIST |
|---|---|---|---|---|
| MT | 93.1 | 91.1 | 75.6 | 93.1 |
| Oracle | 94.0 | 85.3 | 77.2 | 92.8 |
| incDFM | **92.0** | **74.6** | **74.7** | **90.3** |
| DFM | 75.2 | 60.8 | 46.2 | 71.3 |
| Mahal | 63.6 | 55.8 | 35.6 | 48.5 |
| Softmax | 59.9 | 62.5 | 36.2 | 41.7 |
| Odin | 62.5 | 64.3 | 36.8 | 46.1 |

(b)

**Fig. 5.** Unsupervised incremental classification pipeline - (a) Average incremental classification accuracy over tasks. (b) Final classification accuracy after all tasks.

ties, arguably harder. Moreover, in this continual setting, other factors such as forgetting and error propagation pose a further challenge.

**Inter-dataset OOD, Dataset Incremental Novelty Detection:** Table 2 shows results for incDFM in a different continual learning setting, where each task now corresponds to a fully novel dataset (experiment described in Sect. 4). In general, all OOD detectors, including incDFM, show higher performance in this experiment than in the previous intra-dataset experiments (refer to Fig 4). This again reaffirms the notion that inter-dataset ID/OOD splits are easier to disentangle than splits within the same dataset. Additionally, we show that baselines Softmax and ODIN really suffer in performance when they don't have access to ground-truth task labels (second row). This finding is in line with other works that have explored task oracle substitutions in CL [39]. In fact, having access to task labels for unlabeled ID samples is unrealistic in novelty detection since if a task-label is known, it obviates the need for novelty detection in the first place.

### 5.3   Full Pipeline Results

Figure 5 shows results for our end-to-end pipeline for unsupervised incremental class learning. In incDFM, the experience replay coreset stores $\widehat{OOD}_t$ samples and their assigned pseudolabels, see Sect. 3.2. Thus, we propose an upper-bound baseline, *Oracle*, which employs the same classifier and experience replay strategy but uses real ground truth novelties($OOD_t$) for training and for populating the coreset. This is equivalent to stopping error propagation. We also compare to the multi-task (MT) upper-bound which trains all classes for the dataset jointly, without continual learning. Firstly, Fig. 5(b) shows that our experience replay baseline using ground-true labels (*Oracle* - dark gray) is reliably close to upper bound MT for all datasets, suggesting a consistent mitigation of forgetting through time by using coreset-based replay only. Yet, most importantly, we see that incDFM (red) is very close to the upper-bound *Oracle* for all tasks and datasets, despite using only pseudolabels. In contrast, all other baselines incur a significant drop in classification performance through time. The reason is likely due to the compounded effect of error propagation since they provide a very suboptimal novelty detection performance across tasks (refer back to Fig. 4). Poorer $\widehat{OOD}_t$ estimates per task will propagate wrong pseudolabels for training and for coreset storage, adding detrimental noise to the overall training and increasingly hurting performance through time.

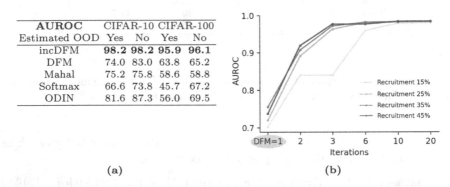

| AUROC | CIFAR-10 | | CIFAR-100 | |
|---|---|---|---|---|
| Estimated OOD | Yes | No | Yes | No |
| incDFM | **98.2** | **98.2** | **95.9** | **96.1** |
| DFM | 74.0 | 83.0 | 63.8 | 65.2 |
| Mahal | 75.2 | 75.8 | 58.6 | 58.8 |
| Softmax | 66.6 | 73.8 | 45.7 | 67.2 |
| ODIN | 81.6 | 87.3 | 56.0 | 69.5 |

(a)                                                 (b)

**Fig. 6.** (a) Error Propagation from using $\widehat{OOD}_t$/(yes) vs. ground-truth $OOD_t$/(no). (b) incDFM iterations and recruitment % (Cifar10 averaged across tasks).

### 5.4   Ablation and Hyper-parameter Sensitivity Study in IncDFM

**Error Propagation in Continual OOD Detection:** We analyze the effect of using estimated novel samples, $\widehat{OOD}_t$, versus ground truth novel samples, $OOD_t$, for knowledge consolidation (Fig. 6(a)). Note that estimated $\widehat{OOD}_t$ will contain a degree of error, i.e., ID samples that are erroneously pseudolabeled as novel. Or, instead, too many OOD samples labeled as old. When this error percentage grows too large (as is often the case for hard OOD/ID splits), it begins to detrimentally and progressively affect the ability to perform OOD detection at subsequent tasks. We call this continual compounded effect "error propagation". In incDFM error propagation is largely minimized due to incremental recruitment, which maintains prediction errors low throughout tasks. In contrast, we can see that classification based OOD detectors, e.g. ODIN and Softmax, are particularly vulnerable to error propagation.

**Incremental Recruitment Sensitivity in incDFM:** The number of maximum iterations within a task and the percentage of recruitment of estimated novel remaining samples at each iteration are both hyperparameters in incDFM. We analyze the sensitivity to each in Fig. 6(b). Note that when maximum iterations is equal to 1 in the x axis, we fall back to single thresholding per task, same as in our ablated baseline DFM. Iterative recruitment seems to peak in performance roughly at about 5 iterations for CIFAR-10 and we observed a similar trend across all datasets. Moreover, performing two iterations is already a 22% improvement when compared to single thresholding as in simple DFM. Alternatively, incDFM is less sensitive to the recruitment percentage and follows an intuitive trend where, for very low recruitment percentages, it takes more iterations to converge (yellow line - 15% recruitment rate). Overall, incDFM with 10 maximum iterations achieves up to a 39.4% improvement over simple DFM.

**Table 3.** AUPR Scores with task data imbalanced towards more old samples (Cifar10).

| New: Old | incDFM | DFM | Mahal | Softmax | ODIN |
|----------|--------|------|-------|---------|------|
| 1:1 | **98.2** | 72.1 | 72.2 | 63.5 | 79.7 |
| 1:2 | **97.0** | 56.6 | 59.5 | 46.2 | 62.0 |
| 1:3 | **95.9** | 49.3 | 52.4 | 39.3 | 51.7 |
| 1:4 | **95.0** | 44.2 | 48.1 | 34.6 | 45.1 |

**Mixing Ratio of New/Old in Each Task:** In previous experiments we kept each task with a balanced number of old and new data samples. However, increasing the ratio of old to new data can have a detrimental effect in precision and recall performance. Old classes can be interpreted as distractors and more distractors can make novelty detection harder. We show the effect of data imbalance on performance in Table 3. Overall incDFM is much more robust to imbalances than other baseline methods. From a 1:1 to a 1:4 new to old ratio in the unlabeled pool, incDFM decreases only 3.3% in performance (AUPR scores) whereas baselines have a decrease between 33% (ODIN) to 41.4% (Softmax).

# 6 Conclusion

This paper presented a novel, self-supervised continual novelty detector. In contrast to the prevailing novelty detection approaches that operate in a static setting, we designed a method capable of handling realistic, non-stationary conditions with recurrent exposure to new classes of data. Using cumulative consolidated knowledge of what is in-distribution up until the new task, our method incrementally estimates a statistical novelty detection model associated to the new task by iteratively recruiting the most certain novel samples and updating itself to progressively enable better estimates. Extensive experimentation in the challenging task-incremental continual learning setting shows state of the art performance in continual novelty detection, minimizing catastrophic forgetting and error propagation at each task through time.

**Acknowledgements:.** This work was supported by the Intel corporation, C-BRIC (part of JUMP, a Semiconductor Research Corporation (SRC) program sponsored by DARPA), DARPA (HR00112190134) and the Army Research Office (W911NF2020053).

# References

1. Ahuja, N.A., Ndiour, I.J., Kalyanpur, T., Tickoo, O.: Probabilistic modeling of deep features for out-of-distribution and adversarial detection. In: Bayesian Deep Learning workshop, NeurIPS (2019)
2. Aljundi, R., Babiloni, F., Elhoseiny, M., Rohrbach, M., Tuytelaars, T.: Memory aware synapses: learning what (not) to forget. In: Ferrari, V., Hebert, M., Sminchisescu, C., Weiss, Y. (eds.) ECCV 2018. LNCS, vol. 11207, pp. 144–161. Springer, Cham (2018). https://doi.org/10.1007/978-3-030-01219-9_9
3. Aljundi, R., Reino, D.O., Chumerin, N., Turner, R.E.: Continual novelty detection. arXiv preprint arXiv:2106.12964 (2021)
4. Caron, M., Misra, I., Mairal, J., Goyal, P., Bojanowski, P., Joulin, A.: Unsupervised learning of visual features by contrasting cluster assignments. In: Advances in Neural Information Processing Systems, vol. 33, pp. 9912–9924 (2020)
5. Cheung, B., Terekhov, A., Chen, Y., Agrawal, P., Olshausen, B.: Superposition of many models into one. In: Advances in Neural Information Processing Systems 32 (2019)
6. Cohen, G., Afshar, S., Tapson, J., Van Schaik, A.: EMNIST: Extending MNIST to handwritten letters. In: 2017 International Joint Conference on Neural Networks (IJCNN), pp. 2921–2926. IEEE (2017)
7. De Campos, T.E., Babu, B.R., Varma, M., et al.: Character recognition in natural images. VISAPP (2), 7 (2009)
8. Dhillon, G.S., Chaudhari, P., Ravichandran, A., Soatto, S.: A baseline for few-shot image classification. arXiv preprint arXiv:1909.02729 (2019)
9. Du, X., Charan, G., Liu, F., Cao, Y.: Single-net continual learning with progressive segmented training. In: 2019 18th IEEE International Conference on Machine Learning and Applications (ICMLA), pp. 1629–1636. IEEE (2019)
10. Everingham, M., Eslami, S.A., Van Gool, L., Williams, C.K., Winn, J., Zisserman, A.: The pascal visual object classes challenge: a retrospective. Int. J. Comput. Vis. **111**(1), 98–136 (2015)
11. French, R.M.: Catastrophic forgetting in connectionist networks. Trends Cognit. Sci. **3**(4), 128–135 (1999)

12. Gal, Y., Ghahramani, Z.: Dropout as a Bayesian approximation: representing model uncertainty in deep learning. In: International Conference on Machine Learning, pp. 1050–1059 (2016)
13. Gallardo, J., Hayes, T.L., Kanan, C.: Self-supervised training enhances online continual learning. arXiv preprint arXiv:2103.14010 (2021)
14. He, K., Zhang, X., Ren, S., Sun, J.: Deep residual learning for image recognition. In: Proceedings of the IEEE Conference on Computer Vision and Pattern Recognition, pp. 770–778 (2016)
15. Hendrycks, D., Gimpel, K.: A baseline for detecting misclassified and out-of-distribution examples in neural networks (2017)
16. Hendrycks, D., Mazeika, M., Dietterich, T.: Deep anomaly detection with outlier exposure. In: International Conference on Learning Representations (2019)
17. Hsu, Y.C., Shen, Y., Jin, H., Kira, Z.: Generalized ODIN: detecting out-of-distribution image without learning from out-of-distribution data. In: Proceedings of the IEEE/CVF Conference on Computer Vision and Pattern Recognition, pp. 10951–10960 (2020)
18. Kingma, D.P., Ba, J.: Adam: a method for stochastic optimization. arXiv preprint arXiv:1412.6980 (2014)
19. Krause, J., Stark, M., Deng, J., Fei-Fei, L.: 3D object representations for fine-grained categorization. In: Proceedings of the IEEE International Conference on Computer Vision Workshops, pp. 554–561 (2013)
20. Krizhevsky, A., Hinton, G., et al.: Learning multiple layers of features from tiny images (2009)
21. Kwon, G., Prabhushankar, M., Temel, D., AlRegib, G.: Novelty detection through model-based characterization of neural networks. In: IEEE International Conference on Image Processing, pp. 3179–3183 (2020)
22. Lakshminarayanan, B., Pritzel, A., Blundell, C.: Simple and scalable predictive uncertainty estimation using deep ensembles. In: Advances in Neural Information Processing Systems, pp. 6402–6413 (2017)
23. Lee, K., Lee, K., Lee, H., Shin, J.: A simple unified framework for detecting out-of-distribution samples and adversarial attacks. In: Advances in Neural Information Processing Systems, pp. 7167–7177 (2018)
24. Liang, S., Li, Y., Srikant, R.: Enhancing the reliability of out-of-distribution image detection in neural networks (2018)
25. Lopez-Paz, D., Ranzato, M.: Gradient episodic memory for continual learning. In: Advances in Neural Information Processing Systems 30 (2017)
26. Maji, S., Rahtu, E., Kannala, J., Blaschko, M., Vedaldi, A.: Fine-grained visual classification of aircraft. arXiv preprint arXiv:1306.5151 (2013)
27. Mallya, A., Lazebnik, S.: PackNet: adding multiple tasks to a single network by iterative pruning. In: Proceedings of the IEEE Conference on Computer Vision and Pattern Recognition, pp. 7765–7773 (2018)
28. Mundt, M., Hong, Y.W., Pliushch, I., Ramesh, V.: A wholistic view of continual learning with deep neural networks: forgotten lessons and the bridge to active and open world learning. arXiv preprint arXiv:2009.01797 (2020)
29. Ndiour, I., Ahuja, N.A., Tickoo, O.: Out-of-distribution detection with subspace techniques and probabilistic modeling of features. arXiv preprint arXiv:2012.04250 (2020)
30. Netzer, Y., Wang, T., Coates, A., Bissacco, A., Wu, B., Ng, A.Y.: Reading digits in natural images with unsupervised feature learning (2011)

31. Nilsback, M.E., Zisserman, A.: Automated flower classification over a large number of classes. In: 2008 Sixth Indian Conference on Computer Vision, Graphics & Image Processing, pp. 722–729. IEEE (2008)
32. Van den Oord, A., Kalchbrenner, N., Espeholt, L., Vinyals, O., Graves, A., et al.: Conditional image generation with PixelCNN decoders. In: Advances in Neural Information Processing Systems, pp. 4790–4798 (2016)
33. Parisi, G., Kemker, R., Part, J., Kanan, C., Wermter, S.: Continual lifelong learning with neural networks: a review. Neural Netw. **113**, 54–71 (2019)
34. Petrov, A.A., Dosher, B.A., Lu, Z.L.: The dynamics of perceptual learning: an incremental reweighting model. Psychol. Rev. **112**(4), 715 (2005)
35. Quattoni, A., Torralba, A.: Recognizing indoor scenes. In: 2009 IEEE Conference on Computer Vision and Pattern Recognition, pp. 413–420. IEEE (2009)
36. Rebuffi, S.A., Kolesnikov, A., Sperl, G., Lampert, C.H.: iCaRL: incremental classifier and representation learning. In: Proceedings of the IEEE Conference on Computer Vision and Pattern Recognition, pp. 2001–2010 (2017)
37. Ren, J., et al.: Likelihood ratios for out-of-distribution detection. In: Advances in Neural Information Processing Systems, pp. 14707–14718 (2019)
38. Rios, A., Itti, L.: Closed-loop memory GAN for continual learning. arXiv preprint arXiv:1811.01146 (2018)
39. Rios, A., Itti, L.: Lifelong learning without a task oracle. In: 2020 IEEE 32nd International Conference on Tools with Artificial Intelligence (ICTAI), pp. 255–263. IEEE (2020)
40. Rolnick, D., Ahuja, A., Schwarz, J., Lillicrap, T., Wayne, G.: Experience replay for continual learning. In: Advances in Neural Information Processing Systems 32 (2019)
41. Shin, H., Lee, J.K., Kim, J., Kim, J.: Continual learning with deep generative replay. In: Advances in Neural Information Processing Systems 30 (2017)
42. Sun, J., et al.: Gradient-based novelty detection boosted by self-supervised binary classification. arXiv preprint arXiv:2112.09815 (2021)
43. Van Horn, G., Cole, E., Beery, S., Wilber, K., Belongie, S., Mac Aodha, O.: Benchmarking representation learning for natural world image collections. In: Proceedings of the IEEE/CVF Conference on Computer Vision and Pattern Recognition, pp. 12884–12893 (2021)
44. Wah, C., Branson, S., Welinder, P., Perona, P., Belongie, S.: The caltech-ucsd birds-200-2011 dataset (2011)
45. Wen, S., Rios, A., Ge, Y., Itti, L.: Beneficial perturbation network for designing general adaptive artificial intelligence systems. IEEE Trans. Neural Netw. Learn. Syst. (2021)
46. Wu, C., Herranz, L., Liu, X., van de Weijer, J., Raducanu, B., et al.: Memory replay GANs: learning to generate new categories without forgetting. In: Advances in Neural Information Processing Systems 31 (2018)
47. Yoon, J., Yang, E., Lee, J., Hwang, S.J.: Lifelong learning with dynamically expandable networks (2018)
48. Zeng, G., Chen, Y., Cui, B., Yu, S.: Continual learning of context-dependent processing in neural networks. Nat. Mach. Intell. **1**(8), 364–372 (2019)

# IGFormer: Interaction Graph Transformer for Skeleton-Based Human Interaction Recognition

Yunsheng Pang[1], Qiuhong Ke[1,2(✉)], Hossein Rahmani[3], James Bailey[1], and Jun Liu[4]

[1] The University of Melbourne, Melbourne, Australia
yunshengp@student.unimelb.edu.au, baileyj@unimelb.edu.au
[2] Monash University, Melbourne, Australia
Qiuhong.Ke@monash.edu
[3] Lancaster University, Lancaster, UK
h.rahmani@lancaster.ac.uk
[4] Singapore University of Technology and Design, Singapore, Singapore
jun_liu@sutd.edu.sg

**Abstract.** Human interaction recognition is very important in many applications. One crucial cue in recognizing an interaction is the interactive body parts. In this work, we propose a novel Interaction Graph Transformer (IGFormer) network for skeleton-based interaction recognition via modeling the interactive body parts as graphs. More specifically, the proposed IGFormer constructs interaction graphs according to the semantic and distance correlations between the interactive body parts, and enhances the representation of each person by aggregating the information of the interactive body parts based on the learned graphs. Furthermore, we propose a Semantic Partition Module to transform each human skeleton sequence into a Body-Part-Time sequence to better capture the spatial and temporal information of the skeleton sequence for learning the graphs. Extensive experiments on three benchmark datasets demonstrate that our model outperforms the state-of-the-art with a significant margin.

**Keywords:** Transformer · Skeleton-based human action recognition · Human interaction recognition

## 1 Introduction

Human interaction recognition plays a significant role in a wide range of applications [1,24,29,34]. For example, it can be used in visual surveillance to detect dangerous events such as "kicking" and "punching". It can also be used for robot controlling for human-robot interaction. This paper addresses human interaction recognition from skeleton sequences [15,26]. Compared with RGB videos, skeleton sequences provide only 3D coordinates of human joints, which are more robust to unconventional and variable conditions, such as unusual viewpoints and cluttered backgrounds.

S. Avidan et al. (Eds.): ECCV 2022, LNCS 13685, pp. 605–622, 2022.
https://doi.org/10.1007/978-3-031-19806-9_35

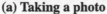

(a) Taking a photo               (b) Shaking hands

**Fig. 1.** (a) In the interaction of "Taking a photo", there is strong semantic correlation between the hands holding the camera of one person and the hands with "yeah" of the other person. (b) In the interaction of "Shaking hands", the interactive body parts demonstrate both semantic correlation and distance evolution, i.e., the hands of two interactive persons correspond to each other and are gradually close to each other when they are shaking hands.

Compared with single-person action recognition, one additional crucial cue in recognizing a human interaction is the interactive body parts of the interactive persons. For example, the interactive hands of two persons are critical in understanding a "shaking hands" interaction. Generally, the interactive body parts in interactions demonstrate semantic correlations and correspondence. For example, in the interaction of "Taking a photo" shown in Fig. 1 (a), the hands holding the camera of one person and the hands with "yeah" of the other person demonstrate a strong correlation. Similarly, in "Shaking hands" shown in Fig. 1 (b), the interactive hands of the two persons correspond to each other. In these cases, exploring the semantic correlation between the interactive body parts is crucial for interaction understanding. In addition, for some interactions, the interactive body parts demonstrate distance evolution. For example, the hands of the two persons gradually approach each other when the two persons are "shaking hands". Measuring the distance between body parts of the interactive persons can provide additional useful information to the semantic correlation for better interaction recognition.

Inspired by the above observation and the successful application of Transformer in many fields [4,5,35,38], we propose a novel Transformer-based model named Interaction Graph Transformer (IGFormer) for interaction recognition from skeleton sequences. In particular, the proposed IGFormer consists of a Graph Interaction Multi-head Self-Attention (GI-MSA) module, which aims at modeling the relationship of interactive persons from both semantic and distance levels to recognize actions. More specifically, the GI-MSA module learns a semantic-based graph and a distance-based interaction graph to represent the mutual relationship between body parts of the interactive persons. The semantic-based graph is learned by the attention mechanism in a data-driven manner to capture the semantic correlations of the interactive body parts. The distance-based graph is constructed by measuring the distance between pairs of body parts to excavate the distance information between interactive body parts. The two interaction graphs are combined to complement each other in a refinement way, making the model suitable for modeling different interactions.

To feed skeleton sequences to the IGFormer, one straightforward solution is to transform each skeleton sequence to a pseudo-image and divide the image into a sequence of patches, similar to the manner of ViT [5]. However, this may destroy the spatial relationship among the skeleton joints in each body part, which could hinder effective modeling of the interactive body parts for interaction recognition. To tackle this problem, we propose a Semantic Partition Module (SPM) to transform the skeleton sequence of each subject into a new format, i.e., a Body-Part-Time (BPT) sequence, each of which is the representation of one body part during a short period. The BPT sequence encodes semantic information and temporal dynamics of the body parts, enhancing the capability of the network for modeling interactive body parts for interaction recognition.

We summarize the contributions of this paper as follows:

- We introduce a Transformer-based model named IGFormer, which contains a novel GI-MSA module to learn the relationships of the interactive persons from both semantic and distance levels for skeleton-based human interaction recognition.
- We introduce a Semantic Partition Module (SPM) transforming each skeleton sequence into a BPT sequence to enhance the modeling of interactive body parts.
- We conduct extensive experiments on three challenging datasets and achieve state-of-the-art performance.

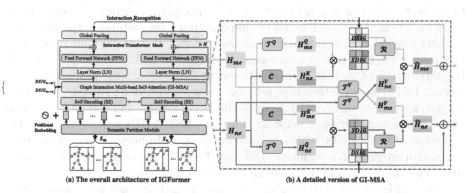

(a) The overall architecture of IGFormer          (b) A detailed version of GI-MSA

**Fig. 2.** (a) The overall architecture of the proposed IGFormer for skeleton-based human interaction recognition. Given the skeleton sequences of two subjects, they are first fed into the Semantic Partition Module (SPM) to generate two Body-part-time (BPT) sequences. The BPT sequences are then fed into the Interaction Transformer Block (ITB) for interactive learning. The ITB contains three main components: two self-encoding (SE) modules, the proposed GI-MSA module and two-layer Feed-Forward Networks (FFN). Finally, a global average pooling followed by a softmax classifier is applied to the outputs of the last ITB to predict interaction labels. (b) The structure of the proposed Graph Interaction Multi-head Self-Attention (GI-MSA) module (DSIG: distance-based sparse interaction graph, SDIG: semantic-based dense interaction graph).

## 2    Related Work

### 2.1    Skeleton-Based Action Recognition

Conventional deep learning-based methods model the human skeleton as a sequence of joint-coordinate vectors [7,13,17,26,28,33] or a pseudo-image [6,9–11,14], which is then fed into RNNs or CNNs to predict the actions. However, representing the skeleton data as a vector sequence or a 2D grid cannot fully express the dependency between correlated joints since the human skeleton is naturally structured as a graph. Recently, GCN-based methods [12,21,27] consider the human skeleton as a graph whose vertices are joints and edges are bones and apply graph convolutional networks (GCN) on the human graph to extract correlated features. These methods achieve better performance than RNN- and CNN-based methods, and become the mainstream methods in skeleton-based action recognition. However, these methods consider each person as an independent entity and cannot effectively capture human interaction. In this work, we focus on skeleton-based human interaction recognition and propose to model the interactive relationship of persons from both semantic and distance levels.

### 2.2    Human Interaction Recognition

Human interaction recognition [25,29,34] is a sub-field of action recognition. Compared with single-person action recognition, human interaction methods should not only be able to model the behavior of each individual but also capture the interaction between them. Yun et al. [32] evaluated several geometric relational body-pose features including joint features, plane features and velocity features for interaction modeling, and found out that joint features outperform others, whereas velocity features are sensitive to noise. Ji et al. [8] built poselets by grouping joints that belong to the same body part of each individual to describe the interaction of each body part. Recently, Perez et al. [22] proposed a two-stream LSTM-based interaction relation network called LSTM-IRN to model the intra relations of body joints from the same person and the inter relations of the joints from different persons. However, LSTM-IRN ignores the distance evolution of body parts, which is considered as an important prior knowledge for human interaction recognition. Different from the above-mentioned methods, we model the interaction relationship of interactive humans as two interaction graphs, which are constructed from the semantic and distance levels respectively to capture the semantic correlation and distance evolution between body parts.

### 2.3    Visual Transformer

Transformer was first proposed in [30] for machine translation task and since then has been widely adopted in various natural language processing (NLP) tasks. Inspired by the successful application in NLP, Transformer has been applied to the computer vision and demonstrated its scalability and effectiveness in many vision tasks. Vision Transformer (ViT) [5] was the first pure Transformer architecture for image recognition and obtained better performance and generalization than traditional convolutional neural networks (CNNs). After that, Transformer-based models with carefully designed and complicated architectures have been applied to various downstream vision tasks, such as object detection [37], semantic segmentation [35] and video classification [2]. In skeleton-based action recognition, Plizzari et al. [23] proposed ST-TR to model the dependencies between joints by substituting the graph convolution operator with the self-attention operator. Different from ST-TR, we focus on human interaction modeling and propose a novel self-attention-based GI-MSA module to model the correlations between body parts of interactive persons.

## 3    Interaction Graph Transformer

One important cue in recognizing human interaction is the interactive body parts. In this section, we introduce an Interaction Graph Transformer (IGFormer), which contains a Graph Interaction Multi-head Self-Attention (GI-MSA) module to model the interactive body parts at both semantic and distance levels for skeleton-based interaction recognition. The proposed IGFormer is also equipped with a Semantic Partition Module (SPM), which aims at retaining the semantic and temporal information of each body part within the input skeleton sequences for better learning of the interactive body parts.

The overall architecture of the proposed IGFormer is shown in Fig. 2 (a). Given the skeleton sequences of two interactive subjects $\mathbf{S}_m, \mathbf{S}_n \in \mathbb{R}^{T \times J \times C}$, where $T$ and $J$ represent the numbers of frames and joints in each frame, respectively, and $C = 3$ represents the dimension of the 3D coordinates of each joint, we first feed the two skeletons into the proposed SPM to generate two Body-Part-Time (BPT) sequences, $\mathbf{H}_m, \mathbf{H}_n$, which are then fed into a stack of *Interaction Transformer Blocks (ITBs)* for interaction modeling. Finally, a global average pooling followed by a softmax classifier is applied to the output of the last ITB to predict the interaction class.

More specifically, each ITB contains three components including two shared-weight self-encoding (SE) modules, the Graph Interaction Multi-head Self-Attention (GI-MSA) module, and two Feed-Forward Networks (FFN). Each SE module is a standard one-layer Transformer [5], which aims at modeling the interaction among the body parts within each individual skeleton. The two outputs of the SE are fed into the GI-MSA to model the interactive body parts and generate an enhanced representation for each interactive person. Finally, each output of the GI-MSA is fed to a Layer Normalization (LN) followed by a FFN. We add an addition operation between the output of GI-MSA and FFNs to improve the representation capability of the model. The ITB can be formulated as follows:

$$
\begin{aligned}
\mathbf{H}_{me}, \mathbf{H}_{ne} &= \text{SE}(\mathbf{H}_m), \text{SE}(\mathbf{H}_n), \\
\hat{\mathbf{H}}_{me}, \hat{\mathbf{H}}_{ne} &= \text{GI-MSA}(\mathbf{H}_{me}, \mathbf{H}_{ne}), \\
\hat{\mathbf{H}}_{mo} &= \text{FFN}(\text{LN}(\hat{\mathbf{H}}_{me})) + \hat{\mathbf{H}}_{me}, \\
\hat{\mathbf{H}}_{no} &= \text{FFN}(\text{LN}(\hat{\mathbf{H}}_{ne})) + \hat{\mathbf{H}}_{ne},
\end{aligned}
\tag{1}
$$

where $\mathbf{H}_{me}$ and $\mathbf{H}_{ne}$ denote the outputs of the SE, $\hat{\mathbf{H}}_{me}$ and $\hat{\mathbf{H}}_{ne}$ denote the outputs of the GI-MSA module, and $\hat{\mathbf{H}}_{mo}$ and $\hat{\mathbf{H}}_{no}$ are the outputs of the ITB.

The two SE modules in the first ITB take the Body-Part-Time (BPT) representations of two interactive subjects, i.e., $\mathbf{H}_m$ and $\mathbf{H}_n$, as input. The inputs of the SE in the following ITB are the outputs of the previous ITB. In the following subsections, we introduce the proposed SPM and GI-MSA in detail.

### 3.1 Semantic Partition Module

Different from natural 2D images that can be directly divided into a sequence of patches to feed to the Transformer [5], human skeleton sequences are represented as a set of 3D joints. Transforming the 3D skeleton sequences to 2D pseudo-images and passing them through a vision Transformer such as ViT [5] may result in losing the temporal dependency between frames as well as the correlation between joints. To better retain both spatial and tem-

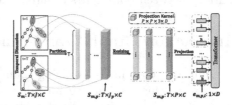

**Fig. 3.** The proposed Semantic Partition Module (SPM) performs three main operations (i.e., Partitioning, Resizing, and Projection) on the input skeleton sequence to generate its Body-Part-Time (BPT) sequence.

poral information of the skeleton sequences, we propose SPM to transform the skeleton sequence of each subject into a sequence of BPT. Each element in the BPT is the representation of one body part during a short temporal period. The overall architecture of the proposed SPM is shown in Fig. 3. There are three main steps in the SPM, i.e., partitioning, resizing, and projection, which are explained below.

**Partitioning.** Given the skeleton sequences of the interactive persons $\mathbf{S}_m, \mathbf{S}_n \in \mathbb{R}^{T \times J \times C}$, we first divide each skeleton sequence into $B = 5$ body parts, i.e., *left arm, right arm, left leg, right leg and torso*, according to the natural structure of the human body. After the partitioning operation, each body part of each subject is represented as $\mathbf{S}_{m,p}, \mathbf{S}_{n,p} \in \mathbb{R}^{T \times J_p \times C}$, where $p \in B$ and $J_p$ is the number of joints of body part $p$.

**Resizing.** Different body parts may have different numbers of joints. In order to adapt these body parts to the input of the Transformer, we adopt the linear interpolation to resize the spatial dimension $J_p$ of all body parts to the same dimension $P$, i.e., $\mathbf{S}_{m,p}, \mathbf{S}_{n,p} \in \mathbb{R}^{T \times J_p \times C} \to \mathbf{S}_{m,p}, \mathbf{S}_{n,p} \in \mathbb{R}^{T \times P \times C}$, where $p \in B$. After the resizing operation, all $B$ body parts have the same dimension.

**Projection.** The projection operation aims to transform the resized body parts of each person into a BPT sequence to feed to the Transformer. Specifically, we apply a 2D convolution with kernel size of $P \times P$ on $\mathbf{S}_{m,p}$ and $\mathbf{S}_{n,p}$ to generate 2D feature maps, respectively. The size of each output feature map is $L \times D$, where $L = \lceil (T + 2 \times padding - P + 1)/stride \rceil$ and $D$ denotes the number of output channels. *"padding"* and *"stride"* denote the padding size and the stride of the convolutional filter. Each 2D feature map can then be split into a sequence of $L$ steps, where each step is a feature vector of dimension $D$. The projection can be formulated as follows:

$$\mathbf{e}_{m,p,1}, \mathbf{e}_{m,p,2}, ..., \mathbf{e}_{m,p,L} = \text{Split}(\text{Conv}(\mathbf{S}_{m,p})),$$
$$\mathbf{e}_{n,p,1}, \mathbf{e}_{n,p,2}, ..., \mathbf{e}_{n,p,L} = \text{Split}(\text{Conv}(\mathbf{S}_{n,p})), \tag{2}$$

where $\mathbf{e}_{m,p,j}, \mathbf{e}_{n,p,j} \in \mathbb{R}^D$ denote the embedding of the body part $p$ at temporal step $j$ for interactive person $m$ and $n$, respectively. $j \in [1, \cdots, L]$, and $D$ is the dimension of the embedding. $L$ is the number of time steps of each body part. After projection, we concatenate the embedding of all the $B$ body parts step by step for all the $L$ time steps to generate a sequence with $M = B * L$ time steps. The sequence is referred to as the BPT sequence. As shown in Fig. 3, the BPT sequence can be considered as a combination of $L$ sub-sequences, each of which is formed by the features of the $B$ body part. We denote the BPT sequences generated from the skeleton sequences of the two interactive persons as $\mathbf{H}_m, \mathbf{H}_n \in \mathbb{R}^{M \times D}$. A learnable positional encoding [5] is added to $\mathbf{H}_m$ and $\mathbf{H}_n$ to form the inputs of two shared-weight Self Encoding (SE) modules, which are standard one-layer Transformers [5]. The output sequences of SE are denoted as $\mathbf{H}_{me}, \mathbf{H}_{ne} \in \mathbb{R}^{M \times D}$, which are then fed to the Graph Interaction Multi-head Self-Attention (GI-MSA) module to model the interactive body parts and generate an enhanced representation for each interactive subject.

## 3.2   Graph Interaction Multi-head Self-attention

To accurately recognize human interaction, one critical cue is the interactive body parts. Considering the semantic correspondence and the distance characteristics that may exist in the interactive body parts, we propose a Graph Interaction Multi-head Self-attention (GI-MSA) module to model the interactive body parts as two interaction graphs as shown in Fig. 2 (b). Specifically, GI-MSA contains a Semantic-based Dense Interaction Graph (SDIG) and a Distance-based Sparse Interaction Graph (DSIG). The SDIG is learned by exploring the semantic correlations of the interactive body parts in a data-driven manner while the DSIG is constructed based on the prior knowledge that the physically close body parts of the interactive persons are generally interactive body parts and should be connected. With the SDIG and DSIG, the proposed GI-MSA models the interaction relationships of humans from both semantic and distance spaces to capture critical interactive information. Finally, the representation of each individual is enhanced by aggregating interactive features from the other person.

**Semantic-Based Dense Interaction Graph.** In order to capture the semantic correlations between interactive body parts of people (e.g., the hands holding the camera of one person and the hand with "yeah" of the other person in the action of "taking a photo"), we construct a Semantic-based Dense Interaction

Graph (SDIG) for each interactive person. We take the learning of SDIG of person $m$ (which is denoted as $\text{SDIG}_{m \to n}$) as an example. As shown in Fig. 2 (b), given the representations of two interactive persons $\mathbf{H}_{me}, \mathbf{H}_{ne} \in \mathbb{R}^{M \times D}$, which are the outputs of the SE module, we first transform $\mathbf{H}_{me}$ into the latent space by a linear transformation function $\mathcal{T}^Q$:

$$\mathbf{H}_{me}^Q = \mathcal{T}^Q(\mathbf{H}_{me}) = \mathbf{H}_{me}\mathbf{W}^Q, \tag{3}$$

where $\mathbf{H}_{me}^Q \in \mathbb{R}^{M \times D}$ is the transformed query feature and $\mathbf{W}^Q \in \mathbb{R}^{D \times D}$ is the weight matrix. Then, we propose a context transformation function $\mathcal{C}$ to transform the representation of the other person $\mathbf{H}_{ne}$ into a high-level space as the key features,

$$\mathbf{H}_{ne}^K = \mathcal{C}(\mathbf{H}_{ne}) = (\mathbf{H}_{ne} + \mathbf{H}_{ne}^{tc} + \mathbf{H}_{ne}^{sc})\mathbf{W}^K, \tag{4}$$

where $\mathbf{H}_{ne}^K \in \mathbb{R}^{M \times D}$ is the key features. $\mathbf{W}^K \in \mathbb{R}^{D \times D}$ is the learned weight matrix. $\mathbf{H}_{ne}^{tc} \in$ and $\mathbf{H}_{ne}^{sc}$ are temporal and spatial contexts of $\mathbf{H}_{ne}$. To compute $\mathbf{H}_{ne}^{tc}$ and $\mathbf{H}_{ne}^{sc}$, we first compute $\mathbf{H}_{ne,p}^{tc}$ and $\mathbf{H}_{ne,t}^{sc}$ as follows, which denote the temporal context of each body part $p$ and spatial context at time step $t$ in $\mathbf{H}_{ne}$.

$$\begin{aligned} \mathbf{H}_{ne,p}^{tc} &= \tfrac{1}{L} \sum_{j=1}^{L} \mathbf{H}_{ne,p,j}, \\ \mathbf{H}_{ne,t}^{sc} &= \tfrac{1}{B} \sum_{i=1}^{B} \mathbf{H}_{ne,i,t}, \end{aligned} \tag{5}$$

where $L$ denotes the temporal steps of each body part in $\mathbf{H}_{ne}$, and $B$ is the number of body parts. $\mathbf{H}_{ne,p,j} \in \mathbb{R}^D$ and $\mathbf{H}_{ne,i,t} \in \mathbb{R}^D$ denote the feature encoding of body part $p$ at time step $j$ and the feature encoding of body part $i$ at time step $t$ in the sequence $\mathbf{H}_{ne}$, respectively. By stacking the temporal context of all $B$ body parts and repeating $L$ times, and repeating the spatial context of each time step $B$ times and stacking the repetition of all $L$ time steps, respectively, we obtain $\mathbf{H}_{ne}^{tc}, \mathbf{H}_{ne}^{sc} \in \mathbb{R}^{M \times D}$. Finally, $\text{SDIG}_{m \to n}$ can be obtained by performing the matrix multiplication operation between $\mathbf{H}_{me}^Q$ and $\mathbf{H}_{ne}^K$:

$$\text{SDIG}_{m \to n} = \frac{\mathbf{H}_{me}^Q (\mathbf{H}_{ne}^K)^\top}{\sqrt{D}}, \tag{6}$$

where $\top$ is the transpose operation, $\text{SDIG}_{m \to n} \in \mathbb{R}^{M \times M}$. $\text{SDIG}_{n \to m}$ can be obtained in a similar way, and the learnable weight matrices $\mathbf{W}^Q$ and $\mathbf{W}^K$ are shared for learning both $\text{SDIG}_{m \to n}$ and $\text{SDIG}_{n \to m}$.

**Distance-Based Sparse Interaction Graph.** In addition to modeling the interaction relationship from the semantic level, we also compute the distance correlation between body parts of the interactive persons. The DSIG is a predefined graph and could be constructed in the data pre-processing stage. The idea of DSIG is to leverage the distance between body parts to construct an adjacency matrix that contains the connection information between body parts of the interactive persons. More specifically, if the distance between two body parts of the interactive persons is small, then the two body parts are connected. Given the original skeleton sequences of two interactive humans $\mathbf{S}_m, \mathbf{S}_n \in \mathbb{R}^{T \times J \times C}$, we first divide the skeleton sequences into $B$ body parts $\mathbf{S}_{m,p}, \mathbf{S}_{n,p} \in \mathbb{R}^{T \times J_p \times C}$ via the same Partitioning process in SPM. To estimate the distance between body parts, we first compute the representations of body parts by averaging the coordinates of joints within each body part:

$$\overline{\mathbf{S}}_{m,p} = \tfrac{1}{J_p} \sum_{i=1}^{J_p} \mathbf{S}_{m,p}[i], i \in J_p, p \in B,$$

$$\overline{\mathbf{S}}_{n,p} = \tfrac{1}{J_p} \sum_{j=1}^{J_p} \mathbf{S}_{n,p}[j], j \in J_p, p \in B, \tag{7}$$

where $\overline{\mathbf{S}}_{m,p}, \overline{\mathbf{S}}_{n,p} \in \mathbb{R}^{T \times C}$ are the representations of body part $p$ of two inter-active persons respectively. $\mathbf{S}_{m,p}[i]$ and $\mathbf{S}_{n,p}[j]$ denote the $i$-th joint in $\mathbf{S}_{m,p}$ and the $j$-th joint in $\mathbf{S}_{n,p}$, respectively. $J_p$ is the number of joints within body part $p$. We downsample the temporal dimension of $\overline{\mathbf{S}}_{m,p}$ and $\overline{\mathbf{S}}_{n,p}$ from $T$ to $L$, i.e., $\overline{\mathbf{S}}_{m,p}, \overline{\mathbf{S}}_{n,p} \in \mathbb{R}^{T \times C} \to \overline{\mathbf{S}}_{m,p}, \overline{\mathbf{S}}_{n,p} \in \mathbb{R}^{L \times C}$. Then combining the representations of $B$ body parts, we get the representations of two persons $\overline{\mathbf{S}}_m, \overline{\mathbf{S}}_n \in \mathbb{R}^{M \times C}$ in the distance space, where $M = L \times B$. $\overline{\mathbf{S}}_m, \overline{\mathbf{S}}_n$ can be treated as sequences with $M$ time steps with dimension $C$. Each time step corresponds to a body part at a particular time step of the original sequence. For human $m$, we compute the Euclidean distance of each time step $a$ in $\overline{\mathbf{S}}_m$ ($\overline{\mathbf{S}}_m[a]$) with each time step $b$ in $\overline{\mathbf{S}}_n$ ($\overline{\mathbf{S}}_n[b]$):

$$\mathbf{A}_{m \to n}[a, b] = \sqrt{\sum_{c=1}^{C} (\overline{\mathbf{S}}_m[a] - \overline{\mathbf{S}}_n[b])^2}, \tag{8}$$

where $a, b \in [1, \cdots, M]$, and $\mathbf{A}_{m \to n} \in \mathbb{R}^{M \times M}$ records the distance between the body parts of two people. We finally connect each time step $a$ in human $m$ to the $k$ nearest time step in human $n$ to build the $\mathrm{DSIG}_{m \to n} \in \mathbb{R}^{M \times M}$ as below:

$$\mathrm{DSIG}_{m \to n}[a, b] = \begin{cases} 1, & \mathbf{A}_{m \to n}[a, b] <= \mathbf{A}_{m \to n}^k[a] \\ 0, & \mathbf{A}_{m \to n}[a, b] > \quad \mathbf{A}_{m \to n}^k[a] \end{cases} \tag{9}$$

where $\mathbf{A}_{m \to n}^k[a]$ is the $k$-th smallest value in $a$-th row of $\mathbf{A}_{m \to n}$. The $\mathrm{DSIG}_{n \to m} \in \mathbb{R}^{M \times M}$ is built in a similar way to encode the distance between each part of the interactive person $n$ to all body parts of person $m$.

**Interaction-Based Feature Generation.** Given the semantic- and distance-based interaction graphs, we aggregate the interactive information of the graphs with the individual features of the interactive persons to generate an enhanced representation for better interaction recognition as shown in Fig. 2 (b). Specifically, we first transform the input individual representation $\mathbf{H}_{ne}$, which is the output of the SE module for person $n$, into the value features $\mathbf{H}_{ne}^V$:

$$\mathbf{H}_{ne}^V = \mathcal{T}^V(\mathbf{H}_{ne}) = \mathbf{H}_{ne} \mathbf{W}^V, \tag{10}$$

where $\mathbf{H}_{ne}^V \in \mathbb{R}^{M \times D}$, and $\mathbf{W}^V$ is the weight matrix. Then we perform the matrix multiplication operation on $\mathbf{H}_{ne}^V$ and the combination of $\mathrm{DSIG}_{m \to n}$ and

$\mathrm{SDIG}_{m \to n}$, followed by an addition operation with $\mathbf{H}_{me}$ to obtain the interactive representation of person $m$:

$$\hat{\mathbf{H}}_{me} = \mathcal{R}(\mathrm{DSIG}_{m \to n}, \mathrm{SDIG}_{m \to n})\mathbf{H}_{ne}^{V} + \mathbf{H}_{me} \tag{11}$$

where $\hat{\mathbf{H}}_{me} \in \mathbb{R}^{M \times D}$, and $\mathcal{R}$ is the combination function:

$$\mathcal{R}(\mathrm{DSIG}, \mathrm{SDIG}) = \mathrm{Softmax}(\mathrm{DSIG}_{m \to n} + \alpha \cdot \mathrm{SDIG}_{m \to n}), \tag{12}$$

where $\alpha$ is a trainable scalar to adjust the intensity of each graph enabling the network to be adaptively adjustable between distance evolution and semantic correlation of body parts. Similarly, $\hat{\mathbf{H}}_{ne}$ can be obtained in the same way.

We define the above steps of generating $\hat{\mathbf{H}}_{me}$ and $\hat{\mathbf{H}}_{ne}$ from $\mathbf{H}_{me}$ and $\mathbf{H}_{ne}$ as Graph Interaction Self-Attention (GI-SA), which is formulated as:

$$\hat{\mathbf{H}}_{me}, \hat{\mathbf{H}}_{ne} = \mathbf{GI\text{-}SA}(\mathbf{H}_{me}, \mathbf{H}_{ne}). \tag{13}$$

Finally, GI-MSA is defined by considering $h$ attention "heads", i.e., $h$ self-attention functions are applied to the input in parallel. Each head provides a sequence of size $M \times d$, where $d = D/h$. The outputs of the $h$ self-attention functions are concatenated to form an $M \times D$ sequence to be fed to the a Layer Normalization (LN) followed by a FFN. The GI-MSA can be formulated as:

$$\begin{aligned} \mathrm{GI\text{-}MSA}(\mathbf{H}_{me}, \mathbf{H}_{ne}) &= \mathrm{Concat}(\hat{\mathbf{H}}_{me,1}, ..., \hat{\mathbf{H}}_{me,h})\mathbf{W}^{m}, \\ &\quad \mathrm{Concat}(\hat{\mathbf{H}}_{ne,1}, ..., \hat{\mathbf{H}}_{ne,h})\mathbf{W}^{n} \\ \hat{\mathbf{H}}_{me,i}, \hat{\mathbf{H}}_{ne,i} &= \mathbf{GI\text{-}SA}(\mathbf{H}_{me,i}, \mathbf{H}_{ne,i}), \end{aligned} \tag{14}$$

where $h$ is the number of heads, $\hat{\mathbf{H}}_{me,i}, \hat{\mathbf{H}}_{ne,i} \in \mathbb{R}^{M \times d}$ are output representations of $i$-th head of GI-SA, and $\mathbf{W}^{m}, \mathbf{W}^{n}$ are the weight matrices. $\mathbf{H}_{me,i}, \mathbf{H}_{ne,i} \in \mathbb{R}^{M \times d}$ are $i$-th head representations of $\mathbf{H}_{me}$ and $\mathbf{H}_{ne}$.

## 4    Experiments

The proposed IGFormer is evaluated on three benchmark datasets, i.e., SBU [32], NTU-RGB+D [26] and NTU-RGB+D120 [15], and is compared with state-of-the-art RNN-, CNN- and GCN-based human action and interaction recognition methods, including Co-LSTM [36], ST-LSTM [17], GCA-LSTM [19], 2s-GCA [18], FSNET [16], VA-LSTM [33], LSTM-IRN [22], ST-GCN [31], AS-GCN [12] and CTR-GCN [3]. Furthermore, to demonstrate the improvement of the proposed IGFormer over the standard Transformer model, we design a Transformer-based baseline named ViT-baseline, which is a ViT-base [5] model taking the pseudo-image representation of the skeleton sequence as input.

## 4.1   Datasets

**SBU** [32] is a two-person interaction dataset, which contains eight classes of human interactions including *approaching, departing, pushing, kicking, punching, exchanging objects, hugging,* and *shaking hands.* Seven participants (pairing up to 21 different permutations) performed all eight interactions. In total, the dataset contains 282 short videos. Each video contains 3D coordinates of 15 joints per person at each frame. Following [32], we use the 5-fold cross validation protocol to evaluate our method.

**NTU-RGB+D** [26] is a large-scale action dataset containing 56,578 skeleton sequences from 60 action classes. Each action is captured by 3 cameras at the same height but from different horizontal angles. Each human skeleton contains 3D coordinates of 25 body joints. There are two standard evaluation protocols for this dataset including 1) Cross-Subject, where half of the subjects are used for training and the remaining ones are used for testing, and 2) Cross-View, where two cameras are used for training, and the third one is used for testing. This dataset contains 11 human interaction classes including *punch/slap, pat on the back, giving something, walking towards, kicking, point finger, touch pocket, walking apart, pushing, hugging* and *handshaking.* The maximum number of frames in each sample is 256.

**NTU-RGB+D120** [15] extends NTU-RGB+D with an additional 57,367 samples from 60 extra action classes. In total, it contains 113,945 skeleton sequences from 120 action classes. There are two standard evaluation protocols for this dataset including 1) Cross-Subject, where half of the subjects are employed for training and the rest are left for testing, 2) Cross-Setup, where half of the setups are used for training, and the remaining ones are used for testing. In addition to the 11 interaction classes in the NTU-RGB+D, This dataset contains 15 additional human interaction classes including *hit with object, wield knife, knock over, grab stuff, shoot with gun, step on foot, high-five, cheers and drink, carry object, take a photo, follow, whisper, exchange things, support somebody* and *rock-paperscissors,* resulting a total of 26 interaction classes. In both NTU-RGB+D120 and NTU-RGB+D datasets, for samples with less than 256 frames, we repeat the sample until it reaches 256 frames.

## 4.2   Implementation Details

**Transformer Architecture.** We use a variant of ViT-Base [5] as the backbone of our proposed IGFormer model. The original ViT-base model contains 12 Transformer layers with the hidden size of 768 ($D = 768$). The dimension of each MLP layer is four times the hidden size. However, due to the small number of samples in the human interaction recognition datasets, a lighter model is more suitable to avoid overfitting. Therefore, we reduce the number of Transformer layers to 3 ($N = 3$) and initialize them with the pre-trained weights of the first three layers of the ViT-base model. We also remove the classification

**Table 1.** Performance comparison of different types of inputs and different lengths of the sequences on NTU-RGB+D and NTU-RGB+D 120. "PI" denotes "Pseudo-Image".

| Input | Length | NTU 60 (%) | | NTU 120(%) | |
|---|---|---|---|---|---|
| | | X-Sub | X-View | X-Sub | X-Set |
| Sequence from PI | 80 | 90.8 | 94.1 | 83.2 | 84.2 |
| | 125 | 91.8 | 95.2 | 83.7 | 85.0 |
| | 200 | 89.7 | 93.9 | 81.9 | 83.1 |
| BPT sequence | 80 | 92.8 | 96.0 | 84.8 | 86.1 |
| | 125 | **93.6** | **96.5** | **85.4** | **86.5** |
| | 200 | 91.9 | 95.1 | 83.8 | 83.9 |

**Table 2.** Performance comparison of different interaction learning methods

| Methods | NTU 60 (%) | | NTU 120(%) | |
|---|---|---|---|---|
| | X-Sub | X-View | X-Sub | X-Set |
| Input fusion | 90.8 | 94.3 | 82.9 | 83.8 |
| Late fusion | 91.2 | 94.8 | 83.0 | 84.1 |
| IGFormer | **93.6** | **96.5** | **85.4** | **86.5** |

token (CLS) and adopt the average pooling operation to obtain the final representation from each sequence of patches. We set the patch size $P$ in the Resizing step of SPM to 16 and the stride of convolution in the Projection step to 10, which results in BPT sequences with M = 125 for each person in all datasets. In each body part, L equals to 25. $k$ in Eq. (9) is set to 15.

**Training Details.** The experiments are conducted on NVIDIA P100 GPU. We adopt SGD algorithm with Nesterov momentum of 0.9 as the optimizer. The initial learning rate is set to 0.01 and is divided by 10 at the $30^{th}$ and $40^{th}$ epochs. The training process is terminated at the $60^{th}$ epoch, batch size is 32.

### 4.3   Ablation Study

In this section, we conduct extensive ablation studies on both NTU RGB+D and NTU RGB+D 120 datasets to validate the effectiveness of the proposed SPM (Sect. 3.1) and GI-MSA (Sect. 3.2) modules.

**Impacts of SPM.** We compare two different representations of the skeleton sequences as the input of the proposed IGFormer to validate the effectiveness of the proposed SPM. The first one is **Pseudo-Image** representation, which have been widely used in CNN-based models [9–11] by transforming each 3D skeleton sequence to a 2D pseudo-image. We define the numbers of frames $T$ and joints $J$ of a skeleton sequence as the width and height of the image and then perform a linear projection on the image as ViT [5]. The second representation is the

**Table 3.** Performance comparison of different components of the proposed GI-MSA module. *sc* and *tc* represent spatial context and temporal context in Eq. (5).

| Methods | NTU 60 (%) | | NTU 120(%) | |
|---|---|---|---|---|
| | X-Sub | X-View | X-Sub | X-Set |
| Baseline | 90.2 | 93.3 | 82.1 | 83.6 |
| DSIG | 90.4 | 92.9 | 82.2 | 83.5 |
| SDIG w/o sc | 92.4 | 95.5 | 84.6 | 85.4 |
| SDIG w/o tc | 92.3 | 95.1 | 84.3 | 85.0 |
| SDIG | 92.8 | 95.7 | 84.8 | 85.5 |
| SDIG + DSIG | **93.6** | **96.5** | **85.4** | **86.5** |

BPT sequence, which is generated by the proposed SPM. Moreover, skeletons are transformed into the different lengths by changing the stride of convolution projection in ViT and SPM to validate the robustness of the proposed SPM under different input configurations. The experimental results are shown in Table 1. We observe that the BPT representation outperforms Pseudo-Image representation at all three configurations, which validates the effectiveness of the proposed SPM. We also evaluate a baseline that models each skeleton joint as a token of the Transformer sequence and fuses features of two persons, but the performance drops by 2.2% compared with our SPM on X-Sub of NTU-RGB+D.

**GI-MSA versus Input/Late Fusion.** We design two interaction learning baselines, i.e., **Input Fusion** and **Late Fusion**, to compare with our proposed GI-MSA module. The **Input Fusion** baseline merges the BPT sequences of two subjects to form a single sequence and passes it through a standard Transformer to learn the interactions between two subjects. The **Late Fusion** baseline feeds the BPT sequences of two subjects individually through a Transformer model to extract their representations, which are then fused to model the interaction. As shown in Table 2, we observe that the performance of both input fusion and late fusion methods are worse than our proposed IGFormer on both datasets, demonstrating the efficacy of the proposed GI-MSA module for interactive learning.

**Impacts of SDIG and DSIG.** We evaluate the impacts of different components of the proposed GI-MSA, including SDIG, DSIG, the spatial and temporal context for learning SDIG. Here, we employ IGFormer without GI-MSA module as our baseline. Based on the results in Table 3, we draw three conclusions: (1) Both spatial and temporal context in Eq. (5) are important

**Table 4.** Performance comparison of number of ITB layers on NTU-RGB+D and NTU-RGB+D 120 datasets.

| ITB | NTU 60 (%) | | NTU 120(%) | |
|---|---|---|---|---|
| | X-Sub | X-View | X-Sub | X-Set |
| 2 | 92.7 | 95.3 | 84.0 | 85.2 |
| 3 | **93.6** | **96.5** | **85.4** | **86.5** |
| 4 | 92.6 | 95.1 | 84.2 | 85.7 |
| 5 | 91.9 | 94.7 | 83.5 | 84.8 |

for learning key contextual features, i.e., the performance drops significantly by removing any of them. (2) The GI-MSA containing only SDIG can improve the performance of human interaction recognition, which validates the effectiveness of the proposed SDIG. (3) The DSIG, which serves as the prior knowledge of human interaction, does not perform well individually but provides extra information for interaction learning, leading to improved performance after being combined with SDIG.

**Impacts of Number of ITB Layers.** Our IGFormer is built by stacking several Interaction Transformer Blocks (ITBs) to enhance the capability of interaction modeling. Here, we evaluate the influence of different number of ITBs on the performance of IGFormer. As shown in Table 4, stacking 3 layers of ITB achieves the best results on both NTU-RGB+D and NTU-RGB+D 120. Increasing the number of ITBs degrades the accuracy due to over-fitting problem.

**Impacts of the Joint Noise on Human Interaction.** The skeletons in NTU-RGB+D are usually noisy, e.g., some joints are missing. We evaluate the performance of our IGFormer on X-Sub of NTU-RGB+D by adding zero-mean noise to the skeleton sequences. IGFormer achieves 93.6%, 93.1%, 92.0%, 90.4% accuracy when the standard deviation ($\sigma$) is set to 0 cm, 1 cm, 2 cm, 4 cm, respectively, which demonstrates that IGFormer is robust against the input noise.

**Table 5.** Performance comparison on SBU, NTU-RGB+D and NTU-RGB+D 120.

| Methods | SBU (%) | NTU-RGB+D | | NTU-RGB+D 120 | |
|---|---|---|---|---|---|
| | | X-Sub (%) | X-View (%) | X-Sub (%) | X-Set (%) |
| Co-LSTM [36] | 90.4 | – | – | – | – |
| ST-LSTM [17] | 93.3 | 83.0 | 87.3 | 63.0 | 66.6 |
| GCA [20] | – | 85.9 | 89.0 | 70.6 | 73.7 |
| 2s-GCA [18] | 94.9 | 87.2 | 89.9 | 73.0 | 73.3 |
| VA-LSTM [33] | 97.2 | – | – | - | – |
| FSNET [16] | – | 74.0 | 80.5 | 61.2 | 69.7 |
| LSTM-IRN [22] | 98.2 | 90.5 | 93.5 | 77.7 | 79.6 |
| ST-GCN [31] | – | 83.3 | 87.1 | 78.9 | 76.1 |
| AS-GCN [12] | – | 89.3 | 93.0 | 82.9 | 83.7 |
| CTR-GCN [3] | – | 91.6 | 94.3 | 83.2 | 84.4 |
| ViT-baseline | 93.1 | 89.7 | 92.5 | 81.5 | 82.5 |
| **IGFormer** | **98.4** | **93.6** | **96.5** | **85.4** | **86.5** |

### 4.4 Comparison with State-of-the-Arts

The experimental results on the interaction classes of SBU, NTU-RGB+D and NTU-RGB+D 120 datasets are shown in Table 5. The proposed IGFormer achieves state-of-the-art performance compared with other skeleton-based human interaction recognition methods. Benefiting from the proposed SPM and GI-MSA modules, IGFormer outperforms the CNN- and RNN-based methods by a large margin. IGFormer also outperforms state-of-the-art GCN-based method, CTR-GCN [3], by 2.0% and 2.2% on X-Sub and X-View of NTU-RGB+D, and 2.2% and 2.1% on X-Sub and X-set of NTU-RGB+D 120. Compared with the baseline Transformer-based method, ViT-baseline, our IGFormer achieves 3.4% and 3.2% gains on X-Sub and X-View of NTU-RGB+D, and 3.9% and 4.0% gains on X-Sub and X-Set of NTU-RGB+D 120.

## 5  Conclusion

In this work, we presented IGFomer, which consists of a GI-MSA module to model the interaction of persons as graphs. The GI-MSA learns an SDIG and DSIG to capture the semantic and distance correlations between body parts of interactive persons. We also presented a SPM to transform each human skeleton into a BPT sequence for retaining interactive information of body parts. The proposed IGFormer outperformed state-of-the-art methods on three datasets.

**Acknowledgment.** The research is partially supported by University of Melbourne Early Career Researcher Grant (No: 2022ECR008). This research is also partially supported by TAILOR, a project funded by EU Horizon 2020 research and innovation programme under GA No 952215. This work is also partially supported by National Research Foundation, Singapore under its AI Singapore Programme (AISG Award No: AISG-100E-2020-065), SUTD Startup Research Grant and MOE Tier 1 Grant.

## References

1. Aggarwal, J.K., Ryoo, M.S.: Human activity analysis: a review. ACM Comput. Surv. **43**(3), 16:1–16:43 (2011). https://doi.org/10.1145/1922649.1922653
2. Arnab, A., Dehghani, M., Heigold, G., Sun, C., Lučić, M., Schmid, C.: ViViT: a video vision transformer (2021)
3. Chen, Y., Zhang, Z., Yuan, C., Li, B., Deng, Y., Hu, W.: Channel-wise topology refinement graph convolution for skeleton-based action recognition. In: Proceedings of the IEEE/CVF International Conference on Computer Vision, pp. 13359–13368 (2021)
4. Devlin, J., Chang, M.W., Lee, K., Toutanova, K.: BERT: pre-training of deep bidirectional transformers for language understanding. In: Proceedings of the 2019 Conference of the North American Chapter of the Association for Computational Linguistics: Human Language Technologies, Volume 1 (Long and Short Papers), pp. 4171–4186. Association for Computational Linguistics, June 2019. https://doi. org/10.18653/v1/N19-1423. https://aclanthology.org/N19-1423
5. Dosovitskiy, A., et al.: An image is worth 16x16 words: transformers for image recognition at scale. arXiv preprint arXiv:2010.11929 (2020)
6. Du, Y., Fu, Y., Wang, L.: Skeleton based action recognition with convolutional neural network. In: 2015 3rd IAPR Asian Conference on Pattern Recognition (ACPR), pp. 579–583. IEEE (2015)

7. Du, Y., Wang, W., Wang, L.: Hierarchical recurrent neural network for skeleton based action recognition. In: Proceedings of the IEEE Conference on Computer Vision and Pattern Recognition, pp. 1110–1118 (2015)
8. Ji, Y., Ye, G., Cheng, H.: Interactive body part contrast mining for human interaction recognition. In: 2014 IEEE International Conference on Multimedia and Expo Workshops (ICMEW), pp. 1–6 (2014). https://doi.org/10.1109/ICMEW.2014.6890714
9. Ke, Q., Bennamoun, M., An, S., Sohel, F., Boussaid, F.: A new representation of skeleton sequences for 3D action recognition. In: Proceedings of the IEEE Conference on Computer Vision And Pattern Recognition, pp. 3288–3297 (2017)
10. Kim, T.S., Reiter, A.: Interpretable 3D human action analysis with temporal convolutional networks. In: 2017 IEEE Conference on Computer Vision and Pattern Recognition Workshops (CVPRW), pp. 1623–1631. IEEE (2017)
11. Li, B., Dai, Y., Cheng, X., Chen, H., Lin, Y., He, M.: Skeleton based action recognition using translation-scale invariant image mapping and multi-scale deep CNN. In: 2017 IEEE International Conference on Multimedia & Expo Workshops (ICMEW), pp. 601–604. IEEE (2017)
12. Li, M., Chen, S., Chen, X., Zhang, Y., Wang, Y., Tian, Q.: Actional-structural graph convolutional networks for skeleton-based action recognition. In: Proceedings of the IEEE/CVF Conference on Computer Vision and Pattern Recognition, pp. 3595–3603 (2019)
13. Li, S., Li, W., Cook, C., Zhu, C., Gao, Y.: Independently recurrent neural network (IndRNN): building a longer and deeper RNN. In: Proceedings of the IEEE Conference on Computer Vision and Pattern Recognition, pp. 5457–5466 (2018)
14. Liu, H., Tu, J., Liu, M.: Two-stream 3D convolutional neural network for skeleton-based action recognition. arXiv preprint arXiv:1705.08106 (2017)
15. Liu, J., Shahroudy, A., Perez, M., Wang, G., Duan, L.Y., Kot, A.C.: NTU RGB+D 120: a large-scale benchmark for 3D human activity understanding. IEEE Trans. Pattern Anal. Mach. Intell. **42**(10), 2684–2701 (2019)
16. Liu, J., Shahroudy, A., Wang, G., Duan, L.Y., Kot, A.C.: Skeleton-based online action prediction using scale selection network. IEEE Trans. Pattern Anal. Mach. Intell. **42**(6), 1453–1467 (2019)
17. Liu, J., Shahroudy, A., Xu, D., Wang, G.: Spatio-temporal LSTM with trust gates for 3D human action recognition. In: Leibe, B., Matas, J., Sebe, N., Welling, M. (eds.) ECCV 2016. LNCS, vol. 9907, pp. 816–833. Springer, Cham (2016). https://doi.org/10.1007/978-3-319-46487-9_50
18. Liu, J., Wang, G., Duan, L.Y., Abdiyeva, K., Kot, A.C.: Skeleton-based human action recognition with global context-aware attention LSTM networks. IEEE Trans. Image Process. **27**(4), 1586–1599 (2017). https://doi.org/10.1109/tip.2017.2785279
19. Liu, J., Wang, G., Hu, P., Duan, L.Y., Kot, A.C.: Global context-aware attention LSTM networks for 3D action recognition. In: 2017 IEEE Conference on Computer Vision and Pattern Recognition (CVPR), pp. 3671–3680 (2017). https://doi.org/10.1109/CVPR.2017.391
20. Liu, J., Wang, G., Hu, P., Duan, L.Y., Kot, A.C.: Global context-aware attention LSTM networks for 3D action recognition. In: Proceedings of the IEEE Conference on Computer Vision and Pattern Recognition, pp. 1647–1656 (2017)
21. Liu, Z., Zhang, H., Chen, Z., Wang, Z., Ouyang, W.: Disentangling and unifying graph convolutions for skeleton-based action recognition. In: Proceedings of the IEEE/CVF Conference on Computer Vision and Pattern Recognition, pp. 143–152 (2020)

22. Perez, M., Liu, J., Kot, A.C.: Interaction relational network for mutual action recognition. IEEE Trans. Multimedia **24**, 366–376 (2021)
23. Plizzari, C., Cannici, M., Matteucci, M.: Skeleton-based action recognition via spatial and temporal transformer networks. Comput. Vis. Image Underst. **208–209**, 103219 (2021). https://doi.org/10.1016/j.cviu.2021.103219. https://www.sciencedirect.com/science/article/pii/S1077314221000631
24. Poppe, R.: A survey on vision-based human action recognition. Image Vis. Comput. **28**(6) 976–990 (2010). https://doi.org/10.1016/j.imavis.2009.11.014
25. Raptis, M., Sigal, L.: Poselet key-framing: a model for human activity recognition. In: Proceedings of the IEEE Conference on Computer Vision and Pattern Recognition, pp. 2650–2657 (2013)
26. Shahroudy, A., Liu, J., Ng, T.T., Wang, G.: nTU RGB+D: a large scale dataset for 3D human activity analysis. In: Proceedings of the IEEE Conference on Computer Vision and Pattern Recognition (CVPR) (2016)
27. Shi, L., Zhang, Y., Cheng, J., Lu, H.: Two-stream adaptive graph convolutional networks for skeleton-based action recognition. In: Proceedings of the IEEE/CVF Conference on Computer Vision and Pattern Recognition, pp. 12026–12035 (2019)
28. Song, S., Lan, C., Xing, J., Zeng, W., Liu, J.: An end-to-end spatio-temporal attention model for human action recognition from skeleton data. In: Proceedings of the AAAI Conference on Artificial Intelligence, vol. 31 (2017)
29. Vahdat, A., Gao, B., Ranjbar, M., Mori, G.: A discriminative key pose sequence model for recognizing human interactions. In: 2011 IEEE International Conference on Computer Vision Workshops (ICCV Workshops), pp. 1729–1736. IEEE (2011)
30. Vaswani, A., et al.: Attention is all you need. In: Advances in Neural Information Processing Systems, pp. 5998–6008 (2017)
31. Yan, S., Xiong, Y., Lin, D.: Spatial temporal graph convolutional networks for skeleton-based action recognition. In: Thirty-Second AAAI Conference on Artificial Intelligence (2018)
32. Yun, K., Honorio, J., Chattopadhyay, D., Berg, T.L., Samaras, D.: Two-person interaction detection using body-pose features and multiple instance learning. In: 2012 IEEE Computer Society Conference on Computer Vision and Pattern Recognition Workshops, pp. 28–35 (2012). https://doi.org/10.1109/CVPRW.2012.6239234
33. Zhang, P., Lan, C., Xing, J., Zeng, W., Xue, J., Zheng, N.: View adaptive recurrent neural networks for high performance human action recognition from skeleton data. In: Proceedings of the IEEE International Conference on Computer Vision, pp. 2117–2126 (2017)
34. Zhang, Y., Liu, X., Chang, M.-C., Ge, W., Chen, T.: Spatio-temporal phrases for activity recognition. In: Fitzgibbon, A., Lazebnik, S., Perona, P., Sato, Y., Schmid, C. (eds.) ECCV 2012. LNCS, vol. 7574, pp. 707–721. Springer, Heidelberg (2012). https://doi.org/10.1007/978-3-642-33712-3_51
35. Zheng, S., et al.: Rethinking semantic segmentation from a sequence-to-sequence perspective with transformers. In: Proceedings of the IEEE/CVF Conference on Computer Vision and Pattern Recognition, pp. 6881–6890 (2021)
36. Zhu, W., et al.: Co-occurrence feature learning for skeleton based action recognition using regularized deep LSTM networks. In: Proceedings of the AAAI Conference on Artificial Intelligence, vol. 30 (2016)

37. Zhu, X., Su, W., Lu, L., Li, B., Wang, X., Dai, J.: Deformable DETR: deformable transformers for end-to-end object detection. arXiv preprint arXiv:2010.04159 (2020)
38. Zhu, X., Su, W., Lu, L., Li, B., Wang, X., Dai, J.: Deformable DETR: deformable transformers for end-to-end object detection. In: International Conference on Learning Representations (2021). https://openreview.net/forum?id=gZ9hCDWe6ke

# PRIME: A Few Primitives Can Boost Robustness to Common Corruptions

Apostolos Modas[1(✉)], Rahul Rade[2], Guillermo Ortiz-Jiménez[1], Seyed-Mohsen Moosavi-Dezfooli[3], and Pascal Frossard[1]

[1] Ecole Polytechnique Fédérale de Lausanne (EPFL), Lausanne, Switzerland
apostolos.modas@gmail.com
[2] ETH Zürich, Zürich, Switzerland
[3] Imperial College London, London, UK

**Abstract.** Despite their impressive performance on image classification tasks, deep networks have a hard time generalizing to unforeseen corruptions of their data. To fix this vulnerability, prior works have built complex data augmentation strategies, combining multiple methods to enrich the training data. However, introducing intricate design choices or heuristics makes it hard to understand which elements of these methods are indeed crucial for improving robustness. In this work, we take a step back and follow a principled approach to achieve robustness to common corruptions. We propose PRIME, a general data augmentation scheme that relies on simple yet rich families of max-entropy image transformations. PRIME outperforms the prior art in terms of corruption robustness, while its simplicity and plug-and-play nature enable combination with other methods to further boost their robustness. We analyze PRIME to shed light on the importance of the mixing strategy on synthesizing corrupted images, and to reveal the robustness-accuracy trade-offs arising in the context of common corruptions. Finally, we show that the computational efficiency of our method allows it to be easily used in both on-line and off-line data augmentation schemes. Our code is available at https://github.com/amodas/PRIME-augmentations.

## 1 Introduction

Deep image classifiers do not work well in the presence of various types of distribution shifts [14,18,39]. Most notably, their performance can severely drop when the input images are affected by common corruptions that are not contained in the training data, such as digital artefacts, low contrast, or blurs [21,29]. In general, "common corruptions" is an umbrella term coined to describe the set of all possible distortions that can happen to natural images during their acquisition, storage, and processing lifetime, which can be very diverse. Nevertheless, while the space of possible perturbations is huge, the term "common corruptions" is generally used

---

A. Modas and R. Rade—Contributed equally to this work.

**Supplementary Information** The online version contains supplementary material available at https://doi.org/10.1007/978-3-031-19806-9_36.

**Fig. 1.** Images generated with PRIME, a simple method that uses a family of max-entropy transformations in different visual domains to create diverse augmentations.

to refer to image transformations that, while degrading the quality of the images, still preserve their semantic information.

Building classifiers that are robust to common corruptions is far from trivial. A naive solution is to include data with all sorts of corruptions during training, but the sheer scale of all possible types of typical perturbations that might affect an image is simply too large. Moreover, the problem is per se ill-defined since there exists no formal description of all possible common corruptions.

To overcome this issue, the research community has recently favoured increasing the "diversity" of the training data via data augmentation schemes [10,20,22]. Intuitively, the hope is that showing very diverse augmentations of an image to a network would increase the chance that the latter becomes invariant to some common corruptions. Still, covering the full space of common corruptions is hard. Hence, current literature has mostly resorted to increasing the diversity of augmentations by designing intricate data augmentation pipelines, e.g., introducing DNNs for generating varied augmentations [5,20], or coalescing multiple techniques [41], and thus achieve good performance on different benchmarks. This strategy, though, leaves a big range of unintuitive design choices, making it hard to pinpoint which elements of these methods meaningfully contribute to the overall robustness. Meanwhile, the high complexity of recent methods [5,41] makes them impractical for large-scale tasks. Whereas, some methods are tailored to particular datasets and might not be general enough. Nonetheless, the problem of building robust classifiers is far from completely solved, and the gap between robust and standard accuracy is still large.

In this work, we take a step back and provide a systematic way for designing a simple, yet effective data augmentation scheme. By focusing on first principles, we formulate a new mathematical model for semantically-preserving corruptions, and build on basic concepts to characterize the notions of transformation strength and diversity using a few transformation primitives. Relying on this model, we propose *PRIME*, a data augmentation scheme that draws transformations from a max-entropy distribution to efficiently sample from a large space of possible distortions (see Fig. 1). The performance of PRIME, alone, already tops the current baselines on different common corruption datasets, whilst it can also be combined with other methods to further boost their performance. Moreover, the simplicity and flexibility of PRIME allows to easily understand how each of its components contributes to improving robustness.

Altogether, the main contributions of our work include:

- We introduce PRIME, a simple method that is built on a few guiding principles, which efficiently boosts robustness to common corruptions.
- We experimentally show that PRIME, despite its simplicity, achieves state-of-the-art robustness on multiple corruption benchmarks.
- Last, our thorough ablation study sheds light on the necessity of having diverse transformations, on the role of mixing in the success of current methods, on the potential robustness-accuracy trade-off, and on the importance of online augmentations.

Overall, PRIME is a simple model-based scheme that can be easily understood, ablated, and tuned. Our work is an important step in the race for robustness against common corruptions, and we believe that it has the potential to become the new baseline for learning robust classifiers.

## 2    General Model of Visual Corruptions

In this work, motivated by the "semantically-preserving" nature of common corruptions, we leverage the long tradition of image processing in developing techniques to manipulate images while retaining their semantics, and construct a principled framework to characterize a large space of visual corruptions.

Let $x : [0, 1]^2 \to [0, 1]^3$ be a continuous image[1] mapping pixel coordinates $r = (r_1, r_2)$ to RGB values. We define our model of common corruptions as the action on $x$ of the following additive subgroup of the near-ring of transformations [4]

$$\mathcal{T}_x = \left\{ \sum_{i=1}^{n} \lambda_i \, g_1^i \circ \cdots \circ g_m^i(x) : g_j^i \in \{\omega, \tau, \gamma\}, \lambda_i \in \mathbb{R} \right\}, \qquad (1)$$

where $\omega, \tau$ and $\gamma$ are random primitive transformations which distort $x$ along the spectral ($\omega$), spatial ($\tau$), and color ($\gamma$) domains. As we will see, defining each of these primitives in a principled and coherent fashion will be enough to construct a set of perturbations which covers most types of visual corruptions.

To guarantee as much diversity as possible in our model, we follow the principle of maximum entropy to define our distributions of transformations [8]. Note that using a set of augmentations that guarantees maximum entropy comes naturally when trying to optimize the sample complexity derived from certain information-theoretic generalization bounds, both in the clean [42] and corrupted settings [28]. Specifically, the principle of maximum entropy postulates favoring those distributions that are as unbiased as possible given the set of constraints that define a family of distributions. In our case, these constraints are given in the form of an expected strength $\sigma^2$, some boundary conditions, e.g., the displacement field must be zero at the borders of an image, and finally the desired smoothness level $K$. The

---

[1] In practice, we will work with discrete images on a regular grid.

principle of smoothness helps formalize the notion of physical plausibility, as most naturally occurring processes are smooth.

Let $\mathcal{I}$ denote the space of all images, and let $f : \mathcal{I} \to \mathcal{I}$ be a random image transformation distributed according to the law $\mu$. Further, let $\mathcal{C} \subseteq \mathcal{F}$ be a set of constraints that restricts the domain of applicability of $f$, i.e., $f \in \mathcal{C}$, with $\mathcal{F}$ denoting the space of functions $\mathcal{I} \to \mathcal{I}$. The maximum entropy principle postulates using the distribution $\mu$ which has maximum entropy given the constraints:

$$\underset{\mu}{\text{maximize}} \quad H(\mu) = -\int_{\mathcal{F}} \mathrm{d}\mu(f) \log(\mu(f)) \tag{2}$$
$$\text{subject to} \quad f \in \mathcal{C} \quad \forall f \in \mathrm{supp}(\mu),$$

where $H(\mu)$ represents the entropy of the distribution $\mu$ [8]. In its general form, solving Eq. (2) for any set of constraints $\mathcal{C}$ is intractable. In Appendix A, we formally derive the analytical expressions for the distributions of each of our family of transformations, by leveraging results from statistical physics [1].

In what follows, we describe the analytical solutions to Eq. (2) for each of our basic primitives. In general, these distributions are governed by two parameters: $K$ to control smoothness, and $\sigma^2$ to control strength. These transformations fall back to identity mappings when $\sigma^2 = 0$, independently of $K$.

**Spectral Domain.** We parameterize the distribution of random spectral transformations using random filters $\omega(r)$, such that the transformation output follows

$$\omega(x)(r) = (x * (\delta + \omega')) (r), \tag{3}$$

where, $*$ is the convolution operator, $\delta(r)$ represents a Dirac delta, i.e., identity filter, and $\omega'(r)$ is implemented in the discrete grid as an FIR filter of size $K_\omega \times K_\omega$ with i.i.d random entries distributed according to $\mathcal{N}(0, \sigma_\omega^2)$. Here, $\sigma_\omega^2$ governs the transformation strength, while larger $K_\omega$ yields filters of higher spectral resolution. The bias $\delta(r)$ retains the output close to the original image.

**Spatial Domain.** We model our distribution of random spatial transformations, which apply random perturbations over the coordinates of an image, as

$$\tau(x)(r) = x(r + \tau'(r)). \tag{4}$$

This model has been recently proposed in [32] to define a distribution of random smooth diffeomorphisms in order to study the stability of neural networks to small spatial transformations. To guarantee smoothness but preserve maximum entropy, the authors propose to parameterize the vector field $\tau'$ as

$$\tau'(r) = \sum_{i^2+j^2 \leq K_\tau^2} \beta_{i,j} \sin(\pi i r_1) \sin(\pi j r_2), \tag{5}$$

where $\beta_{i,j} \sim \mathcal{N}(0, \sigma_\tau^2/(i^2 + j^2))$. Such choice guarantees that the resulting mapping is smooth according to the cut frequency $K_\tau$, while $\sigma_\tau^2$ determines its strength.

---

**Algorithm 1. PRIME**

---

**Input**: Image $x$, primitives $\mathcal{G} = \{\mathrm{Id}, \omega, \tau\,\gamma\}$, where Id is the identity operator
**Output**: Augmented image $\tilde{x}$

1  $\tilde{x}_0 \leftarrow x$
2  **for** $i \in \{1, \ldots, n\}$ **do**
3     $\tilde{x}_i \leftarrow x$
4     **for** $j \in \{1, \ldots, m\}$ **do**
5          $g \sim \mathcal{U}(\mathcal{G})$                       ▷ Strength $\sigma \sim \mathcal{U}(\sigma_{\min}, \sigma_{\max})$
6          $\tilde{x}_i \leftarrow g(\tilde{x}_i)$
7     **end**
8  **end**
9  $\tilde{x} \leftarrow \sum_{i=0}^{n} \lambda_i \tilde{x}_i$           ▷ $\lambda \sim \mathrm{Dir}(1)$: Random Dirichlet convex coefficients

---

**Color Domain.** Following a similar approach, we define the distribution of random color transformations as random mappings $\gamma$ between color spaces

$$\gamma(x)(r) = x(r) + \sum_{n=0}^{K_\gamma} \beta_n \odot \sin\left(\pi n\, x(r)\right), \tag{6}$$

where $\beta_n \sim \mathcal{N}(0, \sigma_\gamma^2 I_3)$, with $\odot$ denoting elementwise multiplication. Again, $K_\gamma$ controls the smoothness of the transformations and $\sigma_\gamma^2$ their strength. Compared to Eq. (5), the coefficients in Eq. (6) are not weighted by the inverse of the frequency, and have constant variance. In practice, we observe that reducing the variance of the coefficients for higher frequencies creates color mappings that are too smooth and almost imperceptible, so we decided to drop this dependency.

Finally, we note that our model can be easily extended to include other distributions of maximum entropy transformations that suit an objective task. For example, one might add the distribution of maximum entropy additive perturbations given by $\eta(x)(r) = x(r) + \eta'(r)$, where $\eta'(r) \sim \mathcal{N}(0, \sigma_\eta^2)$. Nonetheless, since most benchmarks of visual corruptions disallow the use of additive perturbations during training [21], we do not include an additive perturbation category.

Overall, as demonstrated by our results in Sects. 4.2 and 5.2, our model is very flexible and can cover a large part of the semantic-preserving distortions. It also allows to easily control the strength and style of the transformations with just a few parameters. Moreover, changing the transformation strength enables to control the trade-off between corruption robustness and standard accuracy, as shown in Sect. 5.3. In what follows, we use this model to design an efficient augmentation scheme to build classifiers robust to common corruptions.

## 3    PRIME: A Simple Augmentation Scheme

We now introduce PRIME, a simple yet efficient augmentation scheme that uses our **PRI**mitives of **M**aximum **E**ntropy to confer robustness against common corruptions. The pseudo-code of PRIME is given in Algorithm 1, which draws a random sample from Eq. (1) using a convex combination of a composition of basic primitives. Below we describe the main implementation details.

**Parameter Selection.** It is important to ensure that the semantic information of an image is preserved after it goes through PRIME. As measuring semantic preservation quantitatively is not simple, we subjectively select each primitive's parameters based on visual inspection, ensuring maximum permissible distortion while retaining the semantic content of the image. However, to avoid relying on a specific strength for each transformation, PRIME stochastically generates augmentations of different strengths by sampling $\sigma$ from a uniform distribution, with different minimum and maximum values for each primitive. Figure 2 shows some visual examples for each kind of transformation, while additional visual examples along with the details of all the parameters can be found in Appendix B.

For the color primitive, we observed that fairly large values for $K_\gamma$ (in the order of 500) are important for covering a large space of visual distortions. Unfortunately, implementing such a transformation can be memory inefficient. To avoid this issue, PRIME uses a slight modification of Eq. (6) and combines a fixed number $\Delta$ of consecutive frequencies randomly chosen in the range $[0, K_\gamma]$.

**Mixing Transformations.** The concept of mixing has been a recurring theme in the augmentation literature [22,41,44,45] and PRIME follows the same trend. In particular, Algorithm 1 uses a convex combination of $n$ basic augmentations consisting of the composition of $m$ of our primitive transformations. In general, the convex mixing procedure (i) broadens the set of possible training augmentations, and (ii) ensures that the augmented image stay close to the original one. We later provide empirical results which underline the efficacy of mixing in Sect. 5.2. Overall, the exact mixing parameters are provided in Appendix B. Note that, the basic skeleton of PRIME is similar to that of AugMix. However, as we will see next, incorporating our maximum entropy transformations leads to significant gains in common corruptions robustness over AugMix.

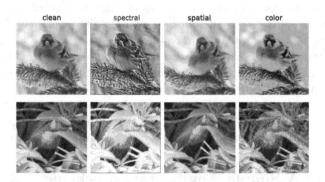

**Fig. 2.** Images generated with the transformations of our common corruptions model. Despite the perceptibility of the distortion, the image semantics are preserved.

## 4     Performance Analysis

In this section, we compare the classification performance of our method on multiple datasets with that of two current approaches: AugMix and DeepAugment (DA). In Appendix L, we also compare PRIME with additional baselines. We illustrate that PRIME significantly advances the corruption robustness over that of AugMix and DeepAugment on all the benchmarks[2].

**Table 1.** Clean and corruption accuracy, and mean corruption error (mCE) for different methods with ResNet-18 on C-10, C-100, IN-100 and ResNet-50 on IN. mCE is the mean corruption error on common corruptions un-normalized for C-10 and C-100; normalized relative to standard model on IN-100 and IN. [†]indicates that JSD consistency loss is not used. [*]Models taken from [9].

| Dataset | Method | Clean | Common Corruption | |
|---------|--------|-------|-------|-------|
| | | Acc (↑) | Acc (↑) | mCE (↓) |
| C-10 | Standard | 95.0 | 74.0 | 24.0 |
| | AugMix | 95.2 | 88.6 | 11.4 |
| | PRIME | 94.2 | **89.8** | **10.2** |
| C-100 | Standard | 76.7 | 51.9 | 48.1 |
| | AugMix | 78.2 | 64.9 | 35.1 |
| | PRIME | 78.4 | **68.2** | **31.8** |
| IN-100 | Standard | 88.0 | 49.7 | 100.0 |
| | AugMix | 88.7 | 60.7 | 79.1 |
| | DA | 86.3 | 67.7 | 68.1 |
| | PRIME | 85.9 | **71.6** | **61.0** |
| | DA+AugMix | 86.5 | 73.1 | 57.3 |
| | DA+PRIME | 84.9 | **74.9** | **54.6** |
| IN | Standard[*] | 76.1 | 38.1 | 76.7 |
| | AugMix[*] | 77.5 | 48.3 | 65.3 |
| | DA[*] | 76.7 | 52.6 | 60.4 |
| | PRIME[†] | 77.0 | **55.0** | **57.5** |
| | DA+AugMix | 75.8 | 58.1 | 53.6 |
| | DA+PRIME[†] | 75.5 | **59.9** | **51.3** |

### 4.1     Training Setup

We consider the CIFAR-10 (C-10), CIFAR-100 (C-100) [25], ImageNet-100 (IN-100) and ImageNet (IN) [11] datasets. IN-100 is a 100-class subset of IN obtained

---

[2] In Appendix K, we also show that our method yields additional benefits when employed in concert with unsupervised domain adaptation [37].

by selecting every 10$^{th}$ class in WordNet ID order. We train a ResNet-18 [19] on C-10, C-100 and IN-100; and a ResNet-50 on IN for 100 epochs. Following AugMix, and for a complete comparison, we also integrate the Jensen-Shannon divergence (JSD)-based consistency loss in PRIME which compels the network to learn similar representations for differently augmented versions of the same input image. Detailed training setup appears in Appendix C. We evaluate our trained models on the common corrupted versions (C-10-C, C-100-C, IN-100-C, IN-C) of the aforementioned datasets. The common corruptions [21] constitute 15 image distortions each applied with 5 different severity levels. These corruptions can be grouped into four categories, viz. noise, blur, weather and digital.

## 4.2   Robustness to Common Corruptions

In order to assess the effectiveness of PRIME, we evaluate its performance against C-10, C-100, IN-100 and IN common corruptions. The results are summarized in Table 1[3]. Amongst individual methods, PRIME yields superior results compared to those obtained by AugMix and DeepAugment alone and advances the baseline performance on the corrupted counterparts of the four datasets. As listed, PRIME pushes the corruption accuracy by 1.2% and 3.3% on C-10-C and C-100-C respectively over AugMix. On IN-100-C, a more complicated dataset, we observe significant improvements wherein PRIME outperforms AugMix by 10.9%. In fact, this increase in performance hints that our primitive transformations are actually able to cover a larger space of image corruptions, compared to the restricted set of AugMix. Interestingly, the random transformations in PRIME also lead to a 3.9% boost in corruptions accuracy over DeepAugment despite the fact that DeepAugment leverages additional knowledge to augment the training data via its use of pre-trained architectures. Moreover, PRIME provides cumulative gains when combined with DeepAugment, reducing the mean corruption error (mCE) of prior art (DA+AugMix) by 2.7% on IN-100-C. Lastly, we also evaluate the performance of PRIME on full IN-C. However, we do not use JSD in order to reduce computational complexity. Yet, even without the JSD loss, PRIME outperforms, in terms of corruption accuracy, both AugMix (with JSD) and DeepAugment by 6.7% and 2.4% respectively, while the mCE is reduced by 7.8% and 2.9%. And last, when PRIME is combined with DeepAugment, it also surpasses the performance of DA+AugMix (with JSD), reaching a corruption accuracy of almost 60% and an mCE of 51.3%. Note here, that, not only PRIME achieves superior robustness, but it does so efficiently. Compared to standard training on IN-100, AugMix requires 1.20x time and PRIME requires 1.27x. In contrast, DA is tedious and we do not measure its runtime since it also requires the training of two large image-to-image networks for producing augmentations, and can only be applied offline.

---

[3] We provide the per-corruption performance of every method in Appendix H.

# 5    Robustness Insights Using PRIME

In this section, we exploit the simplicity and the controllable nature of PRIME to investigate different aspects behind robustness to common corruptions. We first analyze how each transformation domain contributes to the overall robustness of the network. Then, we empirically locate and justify the benefits of mixing the transformations of each domain. Moreover, we demonstrate the existence of a robustness-accuracy trade-off, and, finally, we comment on the low-complexity benefits of PRIME in different data augmentation settings.

## 5.1    Contribution of Transformations

We want to understand how the transformations in each domain of Eq. (1) contribute to the overall robustness. To that end, we conduct an ablation study on IN-100-C by training a ResNet-18 with the max-entropy transformations of PRIME individually or in combination. As shown in Table 2, spectral transformations mainly help against blur, weather and digital corruptions. Spatial operations also improve on blurs, but on elastic transforms as well (digital). On the contrary, color transformations excel on noises and certain high frequency digital distortions, e.g., pixelate and JPEG artefacts, and have minor effect on weather changes. Besides, incrementally combining the transformations lead to cumulative gains e.g., spatial+color help on both noises and blurs. Yet, for obtaining the best results, the combination of all transformations is required. This means that each transformation increases the coverage over the space of possible distortions and the increase in robustness comes from their cumulative contribution.

**Table 2.** Impact of the different max-entropy primitives ($\omega$: spectral, $\gamma$: color, $\tau$: spatial) in PRIME on common corruption accuracy ($\uparrow$) of a ResNet-18. All the transformations are essential for the performance of PRIME. The JSD loss is *not* used.

| Transform | IN-100-C | Noise | Blur | Weather | Digital | IN-100 |
|---|---|---|---|---|---|---|
| None | 49.7 | 27.3 | 48.6 | 54.8 | 62.6 | **88.0** |
| $\omega$ | 64.1 | 60.7 | 55.4 | 66.6 | 72.9 | 87.3 |
| $\tau$ | 53.8 | 30.1 | 56.2 | 57.6 | 65.4 | 87.0 |
| $\gamma$ | 59.9 | 67.4 | 52.6 | 54.4 | 67.1 | 86.9 |
| $\omega+\tau$ | 64.5 | 58.5 | 57.3 | **66.8** | 73.9 | 87.7 |
| $\omega+\gamma$ | 67.5 | 77.2 | 55.7 | 65.3 | 74.2 | 87.1 |
| $\tau+\gamma$ | 63.3 | 74.7 | 57.4 | 56.2 | 67.8 | 86.2 |
| $\omega+\tau+\gamma$ | **68.8** | **78.8** | **58.3** | 66.0 | **74.8** | 87.1 |

## 5.2    The Role of Mixing

In most data augmentation methods, besides the importance of the transformations themselves, mixing has been claimed as an essential module for increasing diversity in the training process [22,41,44,45]. In our attempt to provide insights on the role of mixing in the context of common corruptions, we found out that it is capable of constructing augmented images that look perceptually similar to their corrupted counterparts. In fact, the improvements on specific corruption types observed in Table 2 can be largely attributed to mixing. As exemplified in Fig. 3, careful combinations of spectral transformations with the clean image introduce brightness and contrast-like artefacts that look similar to the corresponding corruptions in IN-C. Also, combining spatial transformations creates blur-like artefacts that look identical to zoom blur in IN-C. Finally, notice how mixing color transformations helps fabricate corruptions of the "noise" category. This means that the max-entropy color model of PRIME enables robustness to different types of noise without explicitly adding any during training.

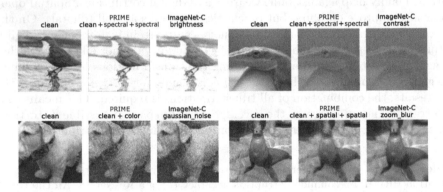

**Fig. 3.** Mixing produces images that are visually similar to the test-time corruptions. Each example shows the clean image, the PRIME image and the common corruption that resembles the image produced by mixing. We also report the mixing combination used for recreating the corruption. See Appendix D for additional examples.

Note that one of the main goals of data augmentation is to achieve maximum coverage of the space of possible distortions using a limited transformation budget, i.e., within a few training epochs. The principle of max-entropy guarantees this within each primitive, but the effect of mixing on the overall space is harder to quantify. In this regard, we can use the distance in the embedding space, $\phi$, of a SimCLRv2 [7] model as a proxy for visual similarity [30,46]. We are interested in measuring how mixing the base transformations changes the likelihood that an augmentation scheme generates some sample during training that is visually similar to some of the common corruptions. To that end, we randomly select $N = 1000$ training images $\{x_n\}_{n=1}^{N}$ from IN, along with their $C = 75$ (15 corruptions of 5 severity levels) associated common corruptions $\{\hat{x}_n^c\}_{c=1}^{C}$, and generate for each of the clean images another $T = 100$ transformed samples $\{\tilde{x}_n^t\}_{t=1}^T$ using each augmentation scheme. Moreover, for each corruption $\hat{x}_n^c$ we find its closest neighbor $\tilde{x}_n^t$ from the set of generated samples using the cosine distance in the embedding space. Our overall measure of fitness is

$$\frac{1}{NC}\sum_{n=1}^N\sum_{c=1}^C \min_t\left\{1 - \left(\frac{\phi(\hat{x}_n^c)^\top \phi(\tilde{x}_n^t)}{\|\phi(\hat{x}_n^c)\|_2 \, \|\phi(\tilde{x}_n^t)\|_2}\right)\right\}. \tag{7}$$

**Table 3.** Minimum cosine distances in the ResNet-50 SimCLRv2 embedding space between 100 augmented samples from 1000 ImageNet images, and their corresponding common corruptions.

| Method | Min. cosine distance ($\times 10^{-3}$) | |
|---|---|---|
| | Avg. ($\downarrow$) | Median ($\downarrow$) |
| None (clean) | 25.38 | 6.44 |
| AugMix (w/o mix) | 20.57 | 3.56 |
| PRIME (w/o mix) | **10.61** | **1.88** |
| AugMix | 17.48 | 2.61 |
| PRIME | **7.71** | **1.61** |

Table 3 shows the values of this measure applied to AugMix and PRIME, with and without mixing. For reference, we also report the values of the clean (no transform) images $\{x_n\}_{n=1}^N$. More percentile scores can be found in Appendix F. Clearly, mixing helps reduce the distance between the common corruptions and the augmented samples from both methods. We also observe that PRIME, even with only 100 augmentations per image – in the order of the number of training epochs – can generate samples that are twice as close to the common corruptions as AugMix. In fact, the feature similarity between training augmentations and test corruptions was also studied in [29], with an attempt to justify the good performance of AugMix on C-10. Yet, we see that the fundamental transformations of AugMix are not enough to span a broad space guaranteeing high perceptual similarity to IN-C. The significant difference in terms of perceptual similarity in Table 3 between AugMix and PRIME may explain the superior performance of PRIME on IN-100-C and IN-C (cf. Table 1)[4].

## 5.3   Robustness vs. Accuracy Trade-Off

An important phenomenon observed in the literature of adversarial robustness is the so-called robustness-accuracy trade-off [16,33,40], where technically adversarial training [27] with smaller perturbations (typically smaller $\epsilon$) results in

---

[4] A visualization of the augmented space using PCA can be found in Appendix G.

models with higher standard but lower adversarial accuracy, and vice versa. In this sense, we want to understand if the strength of the image transformations introduced through data augmentations in PRIME can also cause such phenomenon in the context of robustness to common corruptions. As described in Sect. 2, each of the transformations of PRIME has a strength parameter $\sigma$, which can be seen as the analogue of $\varepsilon$ in adversarial robustness. Hence, we can easily reduce or increase the strength of the transformations by setting $\hat{\sigma} = \alpha\sigma$, where $\alpha \in \mathbb{R}^+$. Then, by training a network for different values of $\alpha$ we can monitor its accuracy on the clean and the corrupted datasets.

We train a ResNet-18 on C-10 and IN-100 using the setup of Sect. 4.1. For reducing complexity, we do not use the JSD loss and train for 30 epochs. This sub-optimal setting could cause some performance drop compared to the results of Table 1, but we expect the overall trends in terms of accuracy and robustness to be preserved. Regarding the scaling of the parameters' strength, for C-10 we set $\alpha \in [10^{-3}, 10^2]$ and sample 100 values spaced evenly on a log-scale, while for IN-100 we set $\alpha \in [10^{-2}, 10^2]$ and we sample 20 values.

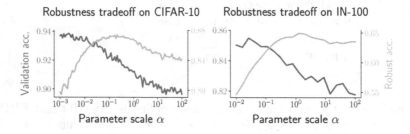

**Fig. 4.** Robustness vs. accuracy of a ResNet-18 (w/o JSD) on CIFAR-10 (left) and ImageNet-100 (right), when trained multiple times with PRIME. On each training instance, the transformation strength is scaled by $\alpha$. Note the different scale in axes.

The results are presented in Fig. 4. For both C-10 and IN-100, it seems that there is a sweet spot for the scale around $\alpha = 0.2$ and $\alpha = 1$ respectively, where the accuracy on common corruptions reaches its maximum. For $\alpha$ smaller than these values, we observe a clear trade-off between validation and robust accuracy. While the robustness to common corruptions increases, the validation accuracy decays. However, for $\alpha$ greater than the sweet-spot values, we observe that the trade-off ceases to exist since both the validation and robust accuracy present similar behaviour (slight decay). In fact, these observations indicate that robust and validation accuracies are not always positively correlated and that one might have to slightly sacrifice validation accuracy in order to achieve robustness.

## 5.4   Sample Complexity

Finally, we investigate the necessity of performing augmentation during training (on-line augmentation), compared to statically augmenting the dataset before training (off-line augmentation). On the one hand, on-line augmentation is use-ful when the dataset is huge and storing augmented versions requires a lot of memory. Besides, there are cases where offline augmentation is not feasible as it relies on pre-trained or generative models which are unavailable in certain sce-narios, e.g., DeepAugment [20] or AdA [5] cannot be applied on C-100. On the other hand, off-line augmentation may be necessary to avoid the computational cost of generating augmentations during training.

To this end, for each of the C-10 and IN-100 training sets, we augment them off-line with $k = 1, 2, \ldots, 10$ i.i.d. PRIME transformed versions. Then, for different values of $k$, we train a ResNet-18 on the corresponding augmented dataset and report the validation and common corruption accuracy. For the training setup, we follow the settings of Sect. 4.1, but without JSD loss. Finally, since we increase the training set size by $(k+1)$, we divide the number of training epochs by the same factor to keep the same overall number of gradient updates.

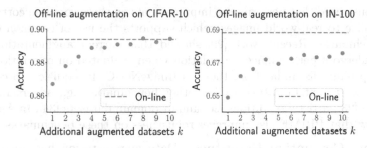

**Fig. 5.** Accuracy of a ResNet-18 (w/o JSD) on CIFAR-10 (left) and ImageNet-100 (right) when augmenting the training sets with additional PRIME counterparts off-line. Dashed lines represent the accuracy achieved by training under the same setup, but generating the transformed samples during training (on-line augmentation). Validation accuracy is omitted because it is rather constant: around 93.4% for CIFAR-10 and around 87% for ImageNet-100.

The performance on common corruptions is presented in Fig. 5. Notice that, even for $k = 1$, the robustness to common corruptions is already quite good. In fact, for IN-100 the accuracy (65%) is already better than AugMix (60.7% with JSD loss cf. Table 1). Regarding C-10, we see that for $k = 4$ the actual difference with respect to the on-line augmentation is almost negligible (88.8% vs. 89.3%), especially considering the overhead of transforming the data at every epoch. Technically, this means that augmenting C-10 with 4 PRIME counterparts is enough for achieving good robustness to common corruptions. Finally, we also see in Fig. 5 that the corruption accuracy on IN-100 presents a very slow improve-ment after $k = 4$. Comparing the accuracy at $k = 4$ (67.2%) to the one obtained with on-line augmentation and without JSD (68.8% cf. Table 2) we observe a gap of 1.6%. Hence, given the cost of on-line augmentation on such large scale datasets, simply augmenting the training with 4 extra PRIME samples presents a good compromise for achieving competitive robustness. Still, the 1.6% increase introduced by on-line augmentation is rather significant, hinting that generating transformed samples during training might be necessary for maximizing performance. In this regard, the lower computational complexity of PRIME allows it to easily achieve this +1.6% gain through on-line augmentation, as it only requires 1.27× additional training time compared to standard training, and only 1.06× compared to AugMix, but with much better performance. This can be a significant advantage with respect to complex methods, like DeepAugment, that cannot be even applied on-line (require heavy pretraining).

# 6   Related Work

**Common Corruptions.** Towards evaluating the robustness of deep neural networks (DNNs) to natural distribution shifts, the authors in [21] proposed common corruptions benchmarks (CIFAR-10-C and ImageNet-C) constituting 15 realistic image distortions. Later studies [20] considered the example of blurring and demonstrated that performance improvements on these common corruptions do generalize to real-world images, which supports the use of common corruptions benchmarks. Recent work [29] showed that current augmentation techniques undergo a performance degradation when evaluated on corruptions that are perceptually dissimilar from those in ImageNet-C. In addition to common corruptions, current literature studies other benchmarks e.g., adversarially filtered data [23], artistic renditions [20] and in-domain datasets [34]. In Appendix J, we show that PRIME also improves robustness on these benchmarks.

**Improving Corruption Robustness.** Data augmentation has been a central pillar for improving the generalization of DNNs [10,12,26,44,45]. A notable augmentation scheme for endowing corruption robustness is AugMix [22], which employs a careful combination of stochastic augmentation operations and mixing. AugMix attains significant gains on CIFAR-10-C, but it does not perform as well on larger benchmarks like ImageNet-C. DeepAugment (DA) [20] addresses this issue and diversifies the space of augmentations by introducing distorted images computed by perturbing the weights of image-to-image networks. DA, combined with AugMix, achieves the current state-of-the-art on ImageNet-C. Other schemes include: (i) worst-case noise training [35] or data augmentation through Fourier-based operations [38], (ii) inducing shape bias through stylized images [17], (iii) adversarial counterparts of DeepAugment [5] and AugMix [41], (iv) pre-training and/or adversarial training [24,43], (v) constraining the total variation of convolutional layers [36] or compressing the model [13] and (vi) learning the image information in the phase rather than amplitude [6] Besides, Vision Transformers [15] have been shown to be more robust to common corruptions than standard CNNs [3,31] when trained on big data. It would thus be interesting to study the effect of extra data alongside PRIME in future works. Finally, unsupervised domain adaptation [2,37] using a few corrupted samples has also been shown to provide a considerable boost in corruption robustness. Nonetheless, domain adaptation is orthogonal to this work as it requires knowledge of the target distribution.

# 7  Concluding Remarks

We took a systematic approach to understand the notion of common corruptions and formulated a universal model that encompasses a wide variety of semantic-preserving image transformations. We then proposed a novel data augmentation scheme called *PRIME*, which instantiates our model of corruptions, to confer robustness against common corruptions. From a practical perspective, our method is principled yet efficient and can be conveniently incorporated into existing training procedures. Moreover, it yields a strong baseline on existing corruption benchmarks outperforming current standalone methods. Additionally, our thorough ablations demonstrate that diversity among basic augmentations (primitives) – which AugMix and other approaches lack – is essential, and that mixing plays a crucial role in the success of both prior methods and PRIME. In general, while complicated methods like DeepAugment perform well, it is difficult to understand, ablate and apply these online. Instead, we show that a simple model-based stance with a few guiding principles can be used to build a very effective augmentation scheme that can be easily understood, ablated and tuned. We believe that our insights and PRIME pave the way for building robust models in real-life scenarios. PRIME, for instance, provides a ready-to-use recipe for data-scarce domains such as medical imaging.

**Acknowledgment.** We thank Alessandro Favero for the fruitful discussions and feedback. This work has been partially supported by the CHIST-ERA program under Swiss NSF Grant 20CH21_180444, and partially by Google via a Postdoctoral Fellowship and a GCP Research Credit Award.

# References

1. Beale, P.: Statistical Mechanics. Elsevier (1996)
2. Benz, P., Zhang, C., Karjauv, A., Kweon, I.S.: Revisiting batch normalization for improving corruption robustness. In: Proceedings of the IEEE/CVF Winter Conference on Applications of Computer Vision (2021)
3. Bhojanapalli, S., Chakrabarti, A., Glasner, D., Li, D., Unterthiner, T., Veit, A.: Understanding robustness of Transformers for image classification. In: Proceedings of the IEEE/CVF International Conference on Computer Vision (ICCV) (2021)
4. Binder, F., Aichinger, E., Ecker, J., Nöbauer, C., Mayr, P.: Algorithms for near-rings of non-linear transformations. In: Proceedings of the International Symposium on Symbolic and Algebraic Computation. Association for Computing Machinery (2000)
5. Calian, D.A., Stimberg, F., Wiles, O., Rebuffi, S.A., Gyorgy, A., Mann, T., Gowal, S.: Defending against image corruptions through adversarial augmentations. arXiv preprint arXiv:2104.01086 (2021)
6. Chen, G., Peng, P., Ma, L., Li, J., Du, L., Tian, Y.: Amplitude-phase recombination: Rethinking robustness of convolutional neural networks in frequency domain. In: Proceedings of the IEEE/CVF International Conference on Computer Vision (ICCV) (2021)

7. Chen, T., Kornblith, S., Swersky, K., Norouzi, M., Hinton, G.E.: Big self-supervised models are strong semi-supervised learners. In: Advances in Neural Information Processing Systems (2020)

8. Cover, T.M., Thomas, J.A.: Elements of Information Theory. Wiley, Hoboken (2006)

9. Croce, F., Andriushchenko, M., Sehwag, V., Debenedetti, E., Flammarion, N., Chiang, M., Mittal, P., Hein, M.: RobustBench: a standardized adversarial robustness benchmark. In: Thirty-Fifth Conference on Neural Information Processing Systems Datasets and Benchmarks Track (2021)

10. Cubuk, E.D., Zoph, B., Mané, D., Vasudevan, V., Le, Q.V.: AutoAugment: learning augmentation strategies from data. In: 2019 IEEE/CVF Conference on Computer Vision and Pattern Recognition (2019)

11. Deng, J., Dong, W., Socher, R., Li, L.J., Li, K., Fei-Fei, L.: ImageNet: a large-scale hierarchical image database. In: 2009 IEEE Conference on Computer Vision and Pattern Recognition (2009)

12. DeVries, T., Taylor, G.W.: Improved regularization of convolutional neural networks with cutout. arXiv preprint arXiv:1708.04552 (2017)

13. Diffenderfer, J., Bartoldson, B.R., Chaganti, S., Zhang, J., Kailkhura, B.: A winning hand: Compressing deep networks can improve out-of-distribution robustness. In: Advances in Neural Information Processing Systems, December 2021

14. Dodge, S., Karam, L.: Understanding how image quality affects deep neural networks. In: 2016 Eighth International Conference on Quality of Multimedia Experience (QoMEX) (2016)

15. Dosovitskiy, A., Beyer, L., Kolesnikov, A., Weissenborn, D., Zhai, X., Unterthiner, T., Dehghani, M., Minderer, M., Heigold, G., Gelly, S., Uszkoreit, J., Houlsby, N.: An image is worth 16x16 words: transformers for image recognition at scale. In: International Conference on Learning Representations (2021)

16. Fawzi, A., Fawzi, O., Frossard, P.: Analysis of classifiers' robustness to adversarial perturbations. Mach. Learn. **107**(3), 481–508 (2018)

17. Geirhos, R., Rubisch, P., Michaelis, C., Bethge, M., Wichmann, F.A., Brendel, W.: ImageNet-trained CNNs are biased towards texture; increasing shape bias improves accuracy and robustness. In: International Conference on Learning Representations (2019)

18. Geirhos, R., Temme, C.R.M., Rauber, J., Schütt, H.H., Bethge, M., Wichmann, F.A.: Generalisation in humans and deep neural networks. In: Advances in Neural Information Processing Systems (2018)

19. He, K., Zhang, X., Ren, S., Sun, J.: Deep residual learning for image recognition. In: 2016 IEEE Conference on Computer Vision and Pattern Recognition (2016)

20. Hendrycks, D., Basart, S., Mu, N., Kadavath, S., Wang, F., Dorundo, E., Desai, R., Zhu, T., Parajuli, S., Guo, M., Song, D., Steinhardt, J., Gilmer, J.: The many faces of robustness: a critical analysis of out-of-distribution generalization. In: IEEE Conference on Computer Vision and Pattern Recognition (2021)

21. Hendrycks, D., Dietterich, T.: Benchmarking neural network robustness to common corruptions and perturbations. In: International Conference on Learning Representations (2019)

22. Hendrycks, D., Mu, N., Cubuk, E.D., Zoph, B., Gilmer, J., Lakshminarayanan, B.: AugMix: a simple method to improve robustness and uncertainty under data shift. In: International Conference on Learning Representations (2020)

23. Hendrycks, D., Zhao, K., Basart, S., Steinhardt, J., Song, D.: Natural adversarial examples. In: Proceedings of the IEEE/CVF Conference on Computer Vision and Pattern Recognition (2021)

24. Kireev, K., Andriushchenko, M., Flammarion, N.: On the effectiveness of adversarial training against common corruptions. arXiv preprint arXiv:2103.02325 (2021)
25. Krizhevsky, A.: Learning multiple layers of features from tiny images (2009)
26. Lopes, R.G., Yin, D., Poole, B., Gilmer, J., Cubuk, E.D.: Improving robustness without sacrificing accuracy with patch gaussian augmentation. arXiv preprint arXiv:1906.02611 (2019)
27. Madry, A., Makelov, A., Schmidt, L., Tsipras, D., Vladu, A.: Towards deep learning models resistant to adversarial attacks. In: International Conference on Learning Representations, April 2018
28. Masiha, M.S., Gohari, A., Yassaee, M.H., Aref, M.R.: Learning under distribution mismatch and model misspecification. In: IEEE International Symposium on Information Theory (ISIT) (2021)
29. Mintun, E., Kirillov, A., Xie, S.: On interaction between augmentations and corruptions in natural corruption robustness. arXiv preprint arXiv:2102.11273 (2021)
30. Moayeri, M., Feizi, S.: Sample efficient detection and classification of adversarial attacks via self-supervised embeddings. In: Proceedings of the IEEE/CVF International Conference on Computer Vision (ICCV) (2021)
31. Morrison, K., Gilby, B., Lipchak, C., Mattioli, A., Kovashka, A.: Exploring corruption robustness: inductive biases in vision transformers and MLP-mixers. arXiv preprint arXiv:2106.13122 (2021)
32. Petrini, L., Favero, A., Geiger, M., Wyart, M.: Relative stability toward diffeomorphisms indicates performance in deep nets. In: Advances in Neural Information Processing Systems (2021)
33. Raghunathan, A., Xie, S.M., Yang, F., Duchi, J., Liang, P.: Understanding and mitigating the tradeoff between robustness and accuracy. In: Proceedings of the 37th International Conference on Machine Learning, July 2020
34. Recht, B., Roelofs, R., Schmidt, L., Shankar, V.: Do ImageNet classifiers generalize to ImageNet? In: Proceedings of the 36th International Conference on Machine Learning (2019)
35. Rusak, E., Schott, L., Zimmermann, R.S., Bitterwolf, J., Bringmann, O., Bethge, M., Brendel, W.: A simple way to make neural networks robust against diverse image corruptions. In: Vedaldi, A., Bischof, H., Brox, T., Frahm, J.-M. (eds.) ECCV 2020. LNCS, vol. 12348, pp. 53–69. Springer, Cham (2020). https://doi.org/10.1007/978-3-030-58580-8_4
36. Saikia, T., Schmid, C., Brox, T.: Improving robustness against common corruptions with frequency biased models. In: Proceedings of the IEEE/CVF International Conference on Computer Vision (ICCV) (2021)
37. Schneider, S., Rusak, E., Eck, L., Bringmann, O., Brendel, W., Bethge, M.: Improving robustness against common corruptions by covariate shift adaptation. In: Advances in Neural Information Processing Systems (2020)
38. Sun, J., Mehra, A., Kailkhura, B., Chen, P.Y., Hendrycks, D., Hamm, J., Mao, Z.M.: Certified adversarial defenses meet out-of-distribution corruptions: benchmarking robustness and simple baselines. arXiv preprint arXiv:arXiv:2112.00659 (2021)
39. Taori, R., Dave, A., Shankar, V., Carlini, N., Recht, B., Schmidt, L.: Measuring robustness to natural distribution shifts in image classification. In: Advances in Neural Information Processing Systems (2020)
40. Tsipras, D., Santurkar, S., Engstrom, L., Turner, A., Madry, A.: Robustness may be at odds with accuracy. In: International Conference on Learning Representations, May 2019

41. Wang, H., Xiao, C., Kossaifi, J., Yu, Z., Anandkumar, A., Wang, Z.: AugMax: adversarial composition of random augmentations for robust training. In: Advances in Neural Information Processing Systems (2021)

42. Xu, A., Raginsky, M.: Information-theoretic analysis of generalization capability of learning algorithms. In: Advances in Neural Information Processing Systems (2017)

43. Yi, M., Hou, L., Sun, J., Shang, L., Jiang, X., Liu, Q., Ma, Z.: Improved OOD generalization via adversarial training and pretraining. In: Proceedings of the 86th International Conference on Machine Learning (2021)

44. Yun, S., Han, D., Chun, S., Oh, S.J., Yoo, Y., Choe, J.: CutMix: regularization strategy to train strong classifiers with localizable features. In: 2019 IEEE/CVF International Conference on Computer Vision (2019)

45. Zhang, H., Cisse, M., Dauphin, Y.N., Lopez-Paz, D.: mixup: Beyond empirical risk minimization. In: International Conference on Learning Representations (2018)

46. Zhang, R., Isola, P., Efros, A.A., Shechtman, E., Wang, O.: The unreasonable effectiveness of deep features as a perceptual metric. In: 2018 IEEE/CVF Conference on Computer Vision and Pattern Recognition (2018)

# Rotation Regularization Without Rotation

Takumi Kobayashi[1,2]([✉])([iD])

[1] National Institute of Advanced Industrial Science and Technology,
Tsukuba 305 -8560, Japan
takumi.kobayashi@aist.go.jp
[2] University of Tsukuba, Tsukuba 305-8577, Japan

**Abstract.** In various visual classification tasks, we enjoy significant performance improvement by deep convolutional neural networks (CNNs). To further boost performance, it is effective to regularize feature representation learning of CNNs such as by considering margin to improve feature distribution across classes. In this paper, we propose a regularization method based on random rotation of feature vectors. Random rotation is derived from cone representation to describe angular margin of a sample. While it induces geometric regularization to randomly rotate vectors by means of rotation matrices, we theoretically formulate the regularization in a statistical form which excludes costly geometric rotation as well as effectively imposes rotation-based regularization on classification in training CNNs. In the experiments on classification tasks, the method is thoroughly evaluated from various aspects, while producing favorable performance compared to the other regularization methods. Codes are available at https://github.com/tk1980/StatRot.

**Keywords:** Regularization · Random rotation · CNN · Classification

## 1 Introduction

The last decade has witnessed great success of deep convolutional neural networks (CNNs) in computer vision fields [14,31]. For training deep models equipped with huge amount of parameters, regularization methods effectively work to remedy such as over fitting on scarce training data. Those models are also regularized so as to improve feature representation even on biased learning scenarios [4].

Regularization in training CNNs is roughly categorized into two groups. One is for input signals, i.e., images in computer vision. Injecting perturbation into images increases robustness against such as image noises, object deformation and occlusion [9,40]. While regularization on input signals is designed on the

**Supplementary Information** The online version contains supplementary material available at https://doi.org/10.1007/978-3-031-19806-9_37.

basis of prior knowledge about the input patterns, the other type of regularization is rather generally applicable to feature representation (neuron activations) and weights in deep models. The most common approach is to impose $L_2$-norm regularization on weights in the form of weight decay in optimizers [23]. Features composed of neuron activations are subject to normalization such as BatchNorm [20] and its variants [1,33,35] for stabilizing the training process. It is also effective to inject perturbation into features as in input regularization such as by randomly adding noises [13] and masking some feature components via DropOut [34] in a *stochastic* manner. From the geometrical viewpoint in a feature space, there are regularization approaches to improve feature representation by addressing intra-class compactness and between-class separability. While center loss [38] is simply formulated to reduce within-class variance, the large-margin approaches [8,36] provide effective feature representation through introducing margin into a classification loss. The margin-based losses focus on *angular* margin between an input feature vector and its target classifier vector to enhance margin from the classification boundary.

In this work, we integrate the stochastic and margin-based approaches by means of *rotation*. Rotating a feature vector in any random directions by an angle $\alpha$ is naturally derived from a cone centered on the feature vector (Fig. 1ab). From the geometrical viewpoint, the cone exhibits an angular margin of angle $\alpha$ around the feature vector and thus classification of the cones contributes to improving classification margin. Though the random rotation applies stochastic perturbation across feature components [17], geometric operation of rotating vector in higher dimensional feature space demands considerable amount of computation cost. Thus, we theoretically propose an efficient formulation through reparameterization of geometric rotation. The proposed method imposes rotation regularization on classification as in geometric random rotation while excluding costly geometric operation of rotation to significantly reduce the computation cost. Our contributions are summarized as follows.

- Through analyzing geometric random rotation of feature vectors, we theoretically formulate an efficient rotation-based regularization *without geometric rotation* for improving feature representation from the viewpoint of margin.
- The proposed method works with a low computation cost to regularize classifier logits by using a parameter of rotation angle which is so interpretable as to be set in advance based on general geometric characteristics of classifiers.
- We thoroughly analyze the proposed method through empirical evaluation from various aspects as well as performance comparison to the other regularization methods on various visual classification tasks.

## 2   Related Works

This paper addresses regularization on feature vectors in linear classification; those features are produced at the penultimate layer of CNN models which is followed by the (fully-connected) linear classifier. This section briefly reviews related regularization approaches which cope with the feature vectors.

**Stochastic Regularization.** DropOut [34] is a representative stochastic regularization to randomly mask (drop) feature components for increasing generalization performance via preventing co-adaptation; it is applicable not only to neuron activations at intermediate layers but also the final feature representation at the penultimate layer [25]. The DropOut has some variants to target such as feature maps [11] and residual paths [18]. In contrast to the component-wise perturbation, our angular perturbation is applied to a whole feature vector via rotation and the stochasticity is derived from random directions of the rotation. Thus, the method is orthogonal to DropOut and their combination could further regularize networks from two distinctive aspects.

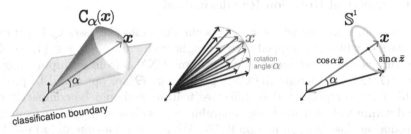

(a) Angular-margin cone $\mathsf{C}_\alpha$    (b) Random rotation    (c) Reparameterization

**Fig. 1.** Angular-margin cone of a vector $x \in \mathbb{R}^3$ (a) induces random rotation by an angle $\alpha$ (b) and is also reparameterized by using $\bar{z} \in \mathbb{S}^1$ (circle) (c).

**Margin-based Regularization.** In the process of classifying feature vectors, margin-based losses are constructed from a geometrical viewpoint by underestimating (degrading) the angle between the feature vector and the target classifier vector of the assigned class [8,26,27,36]. The regularization further encourages feature vectors to be close to the target classifier, which is also contributive to alleviate saturation of softmax loss [5]. While the margin-based methods pay special attention to the target class by leaving the others untouched, the proposed regularization works symmetrically across classes without requiring class labels assigned to samples. Meanwhile, our statistical formulation of the regularization includes slight connection to the margin-based loss, especially noisy softmax [5] which stochastically degrades the target angle in a large-margin framework.

**Rotation.** In the literature of computer vision, some works have payed attention to rotation of input *images* from theoretical viewpoints [6,24]. In contrast to 2D image rotation, we focus on rotating feature *vectors* of higher dimension. Rotating features has been addressed in a learning framework [3,17], though rotation is also utilized to analyze interpretability of CNN features [2]. In ensemble learning, rotation is effectively applied to construct diverse base learners of decision trees [3]. RotationOut [17] randomly injects rotation variation into feature representation via sparse rotation matrices in a manner similar to DropOut [34]. Though it is based on the regularization of random rotation similarly to ours, we analyze dense random rotation to theoretically formulate the proposed regularization in a clearly different form than [17].

## 3   Method

We first define a rotation regularization from a geometrical viewpoint by showing its connection to angular margin of feature representation. Then, the geometric formulation of the rotation regularization is theoretically relaxed via statistical analysis into the efficient one *without* geometrically rotating vectors.

### 3.1   Geometrical Rotation Regularization

Suppose an input feature vector $x \in \mathbb{R}^d$ is classified into $C$ classes by linear classifiers, each of which is equipped with a weight vector $w_c \in \mathbb{R}^d$, $c \in \{1, \cdots, C\}$. The feature vector is produced by a backbone CNN $\phi$ from an input image $\mathcal{I}$ as $x = \phi(\mathcal{I}; \Theta)$ and thereby the CNN parameters $\Theta$ are optimized to provide favorable feature representation. Effective feature $x$ should be compactly distributed within a class while being separable across classes, which is encouraged by introducing classification margin [8, 36]. We introduce a *cone* $\mathsf{C}_\alpha(x)$ pointing toward $x$ which geometrically describes angular margin around $x$:

$$\mathsf{C}_\alpha(x) = \left\{ z \,\middle|\, \frac{z^\top x}{\|z\|_2 \|x\|_2} = \cos\alpha, \ \|z\|_2 = \|x\|_2, \ z \in \mathbb{R}^d \right\}, \tag{1}$$

where $0 \le \alpha < \frac{\pi}{2}$ is a half cone angle, equivalent to angular margin, as shown in Fig. 1a. Instead of a feature vector $x$, we consider to classify a cone $\mathsf{C}_\alpha(x)$ as

$$w_y^\top x > w_c^\top x, \forall c \ne y \quad \Rightarrow \quad w_y^\top z > w_c^\top z, \ \forall c \ne y, \forall z \in \mathsf{C}_\alpha(x), \tag{2}$$

where $y$ is the class label of $x$. To correctly classify the cone $\mathsf{C}_\alpha(\alpha)$, the vector $x$ is forced to exhibit angular margin larger than $\alpha$ from classification boundaries (Fig. 1a). The cone representation (1) is only dependent on a vector $x$ in disregard of a class label $y$, being contrastive with margin-based losses [5, 8, 36] which focuses on the angle to the target class $y$.

We relax the cone classification (1) by means of sampling to facilitate training. A cone $\mathsf{C}_\alpha(x)$ is approximated by randomly *rotating* a vector $x$ with an angle $\alpha$ during training since random rotation is equivalent to random sampling from the cone. Therefore, by using a random rotation matrix $R_\alpha \in \mathbb{R}^{d \times d}$ of a rotation angle $\alpha$, a backbone CNN $\Theta$ and a classifier $W = [w_1, \cdots, w_C]$ are optimized through minimizing the following loss:

$$\mathop{\mathbb{E}}_{(x=\phi(\mathcal{I}),y)} \mathop{\mathbb{E}}_{R_\alpha \in \mathcal{R}_\alpha} [\ell(W^\top R_\alpha x, y)], \tag{3}$$

where $\ell$ is a classification loss of softmax cross-entropy based on *rotated* logits $W^\top R_\alpha x$ and $\mathcal{R}_\alpha$ is a set of rotation matrices with rotation angle $\alpha$.

**Random rotation matrix** $R_\alpha$ can be computed based on Givens rotation [12]. Let random rotation orientation be described by orthonormal matrix $V \in \mathbb{R}^{d \times d}$. A rotation matrix toward the orientation $V$ by an angle $\alpha$ is represented as

$$R_\alpha = V \, \texttt{blkdiag}\left[\left\{\begin{pmatrix} \cos\alpha & -\sin\alpha \\ \sin\alpha & \cos\alpha \end{pmatrix}\right\}_{i=1}^{d/2}\right] V^\top, \tag{4}$$

where `blkdiag` concatenates $d/2$ small rotation matrices of $2 \times 2$ in a block-diagonal manner[1]. To embed stochasticity into the rotation matrix $R_\alpha$, the orthonormal matrix $V$ is randomly drawn in a rather dense manner. In contrast, to reduce the computation cost of projection via $V$, in [17] sparse orthonormal matrix is sampled so that $\text{card}(V) = d$, identical to swapping feature components, though lacking the following analysis about subspace of the classifier $W$.

The matrix (4) rotates vectors in a (full) $d$-dimensional feature space, effectively working in the case that the classifier $W$ spans the full space, i.e., $\text{rank}(W) = d$ requiring $d \leq C$. It, however, degrades efficacy if $W$ occupies only a subspace of $d$-dimensional feature space by $\text{rank}(W) < d$ such as due to $d > C$. In that case, a rotation by $R_\alpha$ would project vectors onto orthogonal space of $W$ and the orthogonal space gives no interferences in the classification (3) by $W$. Thus, we consider an essential rotation in the space spanned by $W$, reformulating the rotation matrix into

$$R_\alpha = U \tilde{R}_\alpha U^\top + U_\perp U_\perp^\top \text{ where } \tilde{R}_\alpha = \tilde{V} \, \texttt{blkdiag}\left[\left\{\begin{pmatrix} \cos\alpha & -\sin\alpha \\ \sin\alpha & \cos\alpha \end{pmatrix}\right\}_{i=1}^{D/2}\right] \tilde{V}^\top, \tag{5}$$

where $U \in \mathbb{R}^{d \times D}$ is an orthonormal basis matrix of the subspace spanned by $W$ and $D = \text{rank}(W)$ is the essential dimension for rotation; $W = UU^\top W$ and $U_\perp^\top U = \mathbf{0}$ for $U_\perp \in \mathbb{R}^{d \times d - D}$. The essential rotation matrix $\tilde{R} \in \mathbb{R}^{D \times D}$ is produced by the random orthonormal matrix $\tilde{V}$ in the $D$-dimensional space. The rotation matrix (5) is reduced into (4) in case of $D = d$; considering $D = \min(d, C)$ in most cases, it is the case of $d \leq C$.

## 3.2 Statistical Rotation Regularization

The geometric rotation (5) requires considerable amount of computation for matrix-vector multiplication $R_\alpha x$. Apart from such a geometrical point of view, we shed light on statistical aspect of the random rotation, leading to a novel rotation regularization formulation which excludes the geometrical rotation of vectors and thus is computationally efficient.

We consider normalized representation $\bar{x} = \frac{x}{\|x\|_2} \in \mathbb{S}^{D-1}$ and $\bar{w} = \frac{w}{\|w\|_2} \in \mathbb{S}^{D-1}$ of a feature vector $x \in \mathbb{R}^D$ and a classifier weight vector $w \in \mathbb{R}^D$ in the essential $D$-dimensional space since the rotation essentially affects them;

$$w^\top R_\alpha x = \|w\|_2 \|x\|_2 \bar{w}^\top R_\alpha \bar{x}. \tag{6}$$

---

[1] For odd $d$, we apply $(d-1)/2$ with $V \in \mathbb{R}^{d \times d - 1}$.

We begin with *reparameterization* of rotating vectors as follows.

**Lemma 1.** *A vector $\bar{\boldsymbol{x}}$ is rotated by an angle $\alpha$ through a rotation matrix $\boldsymbol{R}_\alpha$. As shown in Fig. 1c, so rotated vector is described by using a differential vector $\exists \bar{\boldsymbol{z}} \in \mathbb{S}^{D-2}$ which is in the orthogonal complement space to the input vector $\bar{\boldsymbol{x}}$ as*

$$\boldsymbol{R}_\alpha \bar{\boldsymbol{x}} = \cos \alpha \, \bar{\boldsymbol{x}} + \sin \alpha \, \bar{\boldsymbol{z}}, \ where \ \|\bar{\boldsymbol{z}}\|_2 = 1, \ \bar{\boldsymbol{x}}^\top \bar{\boldsymbol{z}} = 0. \tag{7}$$

We then focus on the rotated logits $\bar{\boldsymbol{w}}^\top \boldsymbol{R}_\alpha \bar{\boldsymbol{x}}$ through projection by a classifier vector $\boldsymbol{w}$. The following statistical representation is useful for characterizing the projection.

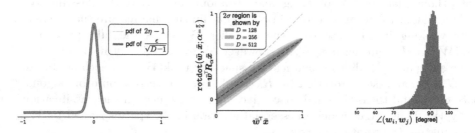

**Fig. 2.** PDF of Beta $\eta$ and Gaussian $\epsilon$ by $D = 256$.

**Fig. 3.** Rotated logits rotdat (13) or equivalently $\bar{\boldsymbol{w}}^\top \boldsymbol{R}_\alpha \bar{\boldsymbol{x}}$.

**Fig. 4.** Angles between classifiers in Sect. 5.1.

**Lemma 2.** *Projection of random vectors $\bar{\boldsymbol{a}}$ uniformly distributed on a unit hyper sphere $\mathbb{S}^{m-1}$ into a unit-length vector $\bar{\boldsymbol{b}} \in \mathbb{S}^{m-1}$ follows Beta distribution.*

$$\bar{\boldsymbol{a}} \in \mathbb{S}^{m-1}, \ \bar{\boldsymbol{b}} \sim Unif(\mathbb{S}^{m-1}), \ u = \frac{1 + \bar{\boldsymbol{a}}^\top \bar{\boldsymbol{b}}}{2} \Rightarrow u \sim Beta(\frac{m-1}{2}, \frac{m-1}{2}). \tag{8}$$

*For the higher dimensional case $m \gg 1$, it approaches Gaussian distribution as*

$$\bar{\boldsymbol{a}}^\top \bar{\boldsymbol{b}} \sim \mathcal{N}(0, \frac{1}{\sqrt{m}}). \tag{9}$$

We apply Lemma 1 & 2 to the rotated logit $\bar{\boldsymbol{w}} \boldsymbol{R}_\alpha \bar{\boldsymbol{x}}$ to construct the following statistical representation.

**Theorem 1.** *Random rotation matrix $\boldsymbol{R}_\alpha$ of an angle $\alpha$ is applied to an inner product between two unit-length vectors $\bar{\boldsymbol{w}}$ and $\bar{\boldsymbol{x}}$ where $\bar{\boldsymbol{w}}^\top \bar{\boldsymbol{x}} = \cos \theta$. Then, the inner product is endowed with stochasticity by the random $\boldsymbol{R}_\alpha$ and is statistically described by*

$$\bar{\boldsymbol{w}}^\top \boldsymbol{R}_\alpha \bar{\boldsymbol{x}} = \cos \alpha \cos \theta + (2\eta - 1) \sin \alpha \sin \theta \ where \ \eta \sim Beta\left(\frac{D-2}{2}, \frac{D-2}{2}\right). \tag{10}$$

*For the higher dimensional case $D \gg 1$, it approaches Gaussian distribution as*

$$\bar{\boldsymbol{w}}^\top \boldsymbol{R}_\alpha \bar{\boldsymbol{x}} = \cos\alpha\cos\theta + \frac{\epsilon}{\sqrt{D-1}}\sin\alpha\sin\theta \; \text{where } \epsilon \sim \mathcal{N}(0,1). \tag{11}$$

It is noteworthy that the statistical representation (11) is simply computed by using a Gaussian random number $\epsilon$ without geometrically rotating vectors; the correspondence between Guassian and Beta distributions are depicted in Fig. 2. The inner product (logit) degraded by random rotation is shown in Fig. 3. By using this efficient formulation of random rotation, an objective loss (3) can be rewritten into

$$\mathop{\mathbb{E}}_{(\boldsymbol{x}=\phi(\mathcal{I}),y)} \mathop{\mathbb{E}}_{\epsilon\sim\mathcal{N}(0,1)} [\ell(\{\mathtt{rotdot}(\boldsymbol{w}_c, \boldsymbol{x}; \epsilon_c, \alpha)\}_{c=1}^C, y)], \tag{12}$$

$$\mathtt{rotdot}(\boldsymbol{w}, \boldsymbol{x}; \epsilon, \alpha) = \cos\alpha\,\boldsymbol{w}^\top\boldsymbol{x} + \frac{\epsilon}{\sqrt{D-1}}\sin\alpha\sqrt{\|\boldsymbol{w}\|_2^2\|\boldsymbol{x}\|_2^2 - (\boldsymbol{w}^\top\boldsymbol{x})^2}, \tag{13}$$

where $D = \min(d, C)$ indicates an essential dimensionality in the linear classification as described in Sect. 3.1. In (13), we assume less correlation among classifier vectors $\{\boldsymbol{w}_c\}_{c=1}^C$ to simply draw a random number $\epsilon_c$ in an *i.i.d.* manner. It practically holds since the learned classifier vectors are close to orthogonal as shown in Fig. 4. This orthogonality of classifiers also inspires us to set the rotation angle as half of the orthogonality, $\alpha = \frac{\pi}{4}$, so as to maximize the angular margin $\alpha$ within a gap $(\frac{\pi}{2})$ between classifiers. Fig. 5 shows a computational procedure of the proposed method, which first computes the logit by (13) and then feeds it into a loss function such as softmax cross-entropy loss.

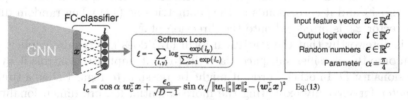

1. Sample $C$ normal random numbers $\{\epsilon_c\}_{c=1}^C$.
2. Compute logits $\{l_c\}_{c=1}^C$ by (13) based on $\boldsymbol{w}_c^\top\boldsymbol{x}$ and $\epsilon_c$ with $\alpha = \frac{\pi}{4}$.
3. Feed the logits into a softmax cross-entropy loss.

**Fig. 5.** Computational procedure of the proposed method.

# 4   Discussion

We analyze the proposed regularization (13) through comparing it with its variants and related margin losses [5,8]. The methods mentioned in this section are also empirically evaluated in Sect. 5.

## 4.1   Comparison to Geometric Regularization

The geometrical formulation (3) is different from the statistical one (13) due to reparameterization, though both of them are derived from the regularization of randomly rotating input vector $\boldsymbol{x}$. We delve deeper into the difference by contrasting gradients of the $c$-th logit $l_c$ with respect to input vector $\boldsymbol{x}$ as

$$(3) \Rightarrow \frac{\partial l_c}{\partial \boldsymbol{x}} = \boldsymbol{R}_\alpha^\top \boldsymbol{w}_c = \|\boldsymbol{w}_c\|_2 \left[\cos\alpha\, \bar{\boldsymbol{w}}_c + \sin\alpha\, \bar{\boldsymbol{z}}_w\right], \tag{14}$$

$$(13) \Rightarrow \frac{\partial l_c}{\partial \boldsymbol{x}} = \cos\alpha\, \boldsymbol{w}_c + \sin\alpha\frac{\epsilon}{\sqrt{D-1}}\frac{\|\boldsymbol{w}_c\|_2^2\boldsymbol{x} - \boldsymbol{w}_c\boldsymbol{w}_c^\top\boldsymbol{x}}{\sqrt{\|\boldsymbol{w}_c\|_2^2\|\boldsymbol{x}\|_2^2 - (\boldsymbol{w}_c^\top\boldsymbol{x})^2}} \tag{15}$$

$$= \|\boldsymbol{w}_c\|_2 \left[\cos\alpha\, \bar{\boldsymbol{w}}_c + \sin\alpha\frac{\epsilon}{\sqrt{D-1}}\frac{\hat{\boldsymbol{x}}_c}{\|\hat{\boldsymbol{x}}_c\|_2}\right], \tag{16}$$

where we apply Lemma 1 to (14) with a rotation matrix $\boldsymbol{R}_\alpha^\top = \boldsymbol{R}_{-\alpha}$ and $\hat{\boldsymbol{x}}_c = (\boldsymbol{I} - \bar{\boldsymbol{w}}_c\bar{\boldsymbol{w}}_c^\top)\boldsymbol{x}$ as shown in Fig. 6a. A critical difference between (14) and (16) is found in $\bar{\boldsymbol{z}}_w$ and $\frac{\epsilon}{\sqrt{D-1}}\frac{\hat{\boldsymbol{x}}}{\|\hat{\boldsymbol{x}}\|_2}$ which involve randomness of $\bar{\boldsymbol{z}}_w$ on $\mathbb{S}^{D-2}$ and $\epsilon$ from $\mathcal{N}$, respectively. Updating feature representation $\boldsymbol{x}$ based on the logit $l_c$ connected to the classifier $\boldsymbol{w}_c$ is supposed to be essentially performed on the plane spanned by $\boldsymbol{w}_c$ and $\boldsymbol{x}$, or equivalently $\hat{\boldsymbol{x}}_c$. It inspires us to consider the projection of $\bar{\boldsymbol{z}}_w$ onto $\hat{\boldsymbol{x}}_c$ (Fig. 6b) as

$$\frac{\hat{\boldsymbol{x}}_c\hat{\boldsymbol{x}}_c^\top\bar{\boldsymbol{z}}_w}{\|\hat{\boldsymbol{x}}_c\|_2^2} \approx \frac{\epsilon}{\sqrt{D-1}}\frac{\hat{\boldsymbol{x}}_c}{\|\hat{\boldsymbol{x}}_c\|_2}, \tag{17}$$

where we apply Lemma 2 to $\bar{\boldsymbol{z}}_w$ uniformly drawn from $\mathbb{S}^{D-2}$. From this viewpoint, the statistical formulation (13) provides an effective updating on the plane of $\boldsymbol{w}_c$ and $\hat{\boldsymbol{x}}_c$ and it corresponds to the geometric one (14) when random differential vector $\bar{\boldsymbol{z}}_w$ is projected onto the direction of $\hat{\boldsymbol{x}}_c$.

It is noteworthy that the statistical form (13) does not require explicit projection onto the classifier subspace via $\boldsymbol{U}$ in (5) but implicitly controls it by the dimensionality $D$. In other words, it might be possible to regard $D$ as a tunable *parameter* for virtually exploiting the more essential feature dimensionality in the classification; such an approach is empirically evaluated in Sect. 5.1.

## 4.2   Correlated Stochasticity

In (13), we apply *i.i.d.* random number $\epsilon \sim \mathcal{N}(0,1)$ on the assumption of less correlation among classifiers which is practically plausible (Fig. 4). Meanwhile, to take into account the correlation among $\boldsymbol{W}$, we can explicitly draw random unit vector $\bar{\boldsymbol{z}}$ in (7) to modify the regularization into

$$\texttt{rotdot}_{corr}(\boldsymbol{w}, \boldsymbol{x}; \bar{\boldsymbol{z}}, \alpha) = \cos\alpha\, \boldsymbol{w}^\top\boldsymbol{x} + \frac{\hat{\boldsymbol{w}}^\top\bar{\boldsymbol{z}}}{\|\hat{\boldsymbol{w}}\|_2}\sin\alpha\sqrt{\|\boldsymbol{w}\|_2^2\|\boldsymbol{x}\|_2^2 - (\boldsymbol{w}^\top\boldsymbol{x})^2}, \tag{18}$$

where $\hat{\boldsymbol{w}} = (\boldsymbol{I} - \bar{\boldsymbol{x}}\bar{\boldsymbol{x}}^\top)\boldsymbol{w}$ and a random vector $\bar{\boldsymbol{z}}$ satisfies $\|\bar{\boldsymbol{z}}\|_2 = 1$ and $\bar{\boldsymbol{x}}^\top\bar{\boldsymbol{z}} = 0$.

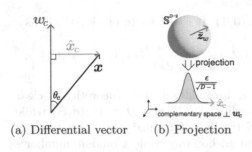

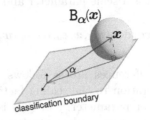

(a) Differential vector    (b) Projection

classification boundary

**Fig. 6.** Gradient of rotated logits w.r.t. $x$ is essentially on the plane of $w_c$ and a differential vector $\hat{x}_c$ (a) through projecting random unit vector $\bar{z}_w$ onto it (b).

**Fig. 7.** Margin ball $B_\alpha$ in accordance with cone $C_\alpha$.

### 4.3 Margin Ball

Section 3.1 introduces a *cone* $C_\alpha(x)$ to assign an angular margin with each sample $x$. Sample-wise margin can be embedded by a *ball* $B_\alpha(x) = \{z | \|z - x\|_2 = \sin \alpha \|x\|_2\}$ as shown in Fig. 7. Similarly to Sect. 3, classifying the ball leads to the following regularization on logits through reparameterization of the ball.

$$z = x + \sin \alpha \, \|x\|_2 \, \bar{z} \in B_\alpha \text{ where } \bar{z} \in \mathbb{S}^{D-1}, \tag{19}$$

$$w^\top z = w^\top x + \sin \alpha \, \|x\|_2 \, (w^\top \bar{z}) = w^\top x + \frac{\epsilon}{\sqrt{D}} \sin \alpha \, \|x\|_2 \|w\|_2, \tag{20}$$

where we apply Lemma 2 to $w^\top \bar{z}$ and $\epsilon \sim \mathcal{N}(0, 1)$. From geometrical viewpoint, a ball $B_\alpha$ contains perturbation that exhibits $\angle(z, x) < \alpha$ while a cone $C_\alpha$ strictly imposes $\angle(z, x) = \alpha$, which implies that balls provide modest regularization than cones in terms of angular margin. From the arithmetic viewpoint, the stochastic term in (20) is simply composed of norms $\|w\|_2$ and $\|x\|_2$ in contrast to (13) containing correlation $w^\top x$ similarly to margin-based losses as discussed next.

### 4.4 Comparison to Margin-Based Losses

The statistical form (13) is rewritten in

$$\texttt{rotdot}(w_c, x; \epsilon_c, \alpha) = \|w_c\|_2 \|x\|_2 \left( \cos \alpha \cos \theta_c + \frac{\epsilon_c}{\sqrt{D-1}} \sin \alpha \sin \theta_c \right), \tag{21}$$

where $w_c^\top x = \|w_c\|_2 \|x\|_2 \cos \theta_c$ and $c \in \{1, \cdots, C\}$. Thus, $\texttt{rotdot}(w_y, x; \epsilon_y, \alpha)$ is reduced to $\cos(\theta_y + \alpha)$ when $\epsilon_y = -\sqrt{D-1}$ which is the degraded logit in the margin-based loss [8] underestimating the angle to the target class $y$. The margin-based loss computes the degraded logits in a deterministic way with a margin parameter, while our regularization works in a stochastic fashion.

Noisy softmax loss [5] introduces stochasticity into the margin-based loss by

$$\texttt{noisydot}(w_y, x; \epsilon, \gamma) = \|w_y\|_2 \|x\|_2 \{\cos \theta_y - \gamma|\epsilon|(1 - \cos \theta_y)\}, \tag{22}$$

where $\gamma$ is a scale parameter and $\epsilon \sim \mathcal{N}(0, 1)$. It is similar to our logit (21) as

$$\frac{1}{\cos\alpha}\text{rotdot}(\boldsymbol{w}_y, \boldsymbol{x}; \epsilon_y, \alpha) = \|\boldsymbol{w}_y\|_2\|\boldsymbol{x}\|_2\left\{\cos\theta_y + \frac{\tan\alpha}{\sqrt{D-1}}\epsilon_y(1 - \cos^2\theta_y)^{\frac{1}{2}}\right\}.$$

(23)

Their differences are as follows. (i) Our formulation gives theoretically clear interpretation to the scaling factor regarding $\alpha = \frac{\pi}{4}$ and $D = \min(d, C)$ while the hyper parameter $\gamma$ in (22) is heuristically determined. (ii) Noisy softmax assigns positive random number $|\epsilon|$ in an ad-hoc way while a random number $\epsilon$ in our regularization is derived from random rotation in a theoretical manner.

It should be noted that our regularization works on any classes symmetrically while the margin-based losses [5, 8, 36] touch only the target logit of class $y$ in an asymmetric way. Such a difference might also motivate us to modify the target random number $\epsilon_y$ into $-|\epsilon_y|$ as in (22) to follow the asymmetric approach toward larger margin.

**Table 1.** Ablation study of the proposed statistical rotation regularization (13) on IMAGENET-LT dataset of long-tailed recognition using ResNet10.

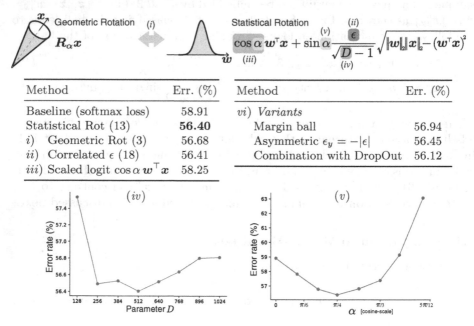

| Method | Err. (%) | Method | Err. (%) |
|---|---|---|---|
| Baseline (softmax loss) | 58.91 | *vi) Variants* | |
| Statistical Rot (13) | **56.40** | Margin ball | 56.94 |
| *i)* Geometric Rot (3) | 56.68 | Asymmetric $\epsilon_y = -|\epsilon|$ | 56.45 |
| *ii)* Correlated $\epsilon$ (18) | 56.41 | Combination with DropOut | 56.12 |
| *iii)* Scaled logit $\cos\alpha\,\boldsymbol{w}^\top\boldsymbol{x}$ | 58.25 | | |

## 5    Experimental Results

The proposed method is applied to regularize training CNN models on classification tasks of long-tailed recognition, transfer learning and person reidentification, which follows ablation study to analyze the method in detail.

## 5.1   Ablation Study

The proposed rotation regularization is analyzed on long-tailed recognition [21] by applying ResNet-10 [14] to IMAGENET-LT [28]; the detail of training protocol is shown in Sect. 5.2. We can analyze the method (13) with $\alpha = \frac{\pi}{4}$ from various aspects outlined in Table 1 following the discussion in Sect. 4.

$i$) **Rotation formulation** Sect. 3 presents two formulations from geometrical (3) and statistical (13) viewpoints, performances of which are compared in Table 1$i$. Both approaches improve performance of baseline using softmax loss and particularly, the statistical formulation outperforms the geometric one, implying that the effective updating discussed in Sect. 4.1 works in training. It is noteworthy that the statistical approach is computationally efficient without applying rotation matrix; rotating logits (13) requires $O(Cd)$ while the geometrical rotation (3) performs in $O(Cd+d^3)$. Actually, our statistical rotation requires 0.72 ms while the geometrical one takes 160 ms for batch size of 256 on TitanV GPU.

$ii$) **Correlation among classifiers** Stochasticity $\epsilon$ in the statistical formulation (13) is built upon a simple assumption that classifiers $W$ are less correlated. It is contrasted with the correlated form (18) which directly considers random unit vector. Those two approaches are different only in terms of stochasticity and are compared in Table 1$ii$ without showing performance difference. This result validates our assumption about the correlation from the performance viewpoint, which is also plausible according to the observation of $\angle(w_i, w_j)$ in Fig. 4.

$iii$) **Scaled logits** The formulation (13) is composed of two parts. One is a deterministic scaling of logit via $\cos\alpha\, w_c^\top x$ and the other gives stochasticity derived from random rotation via a random number $\epsilon$. The former scaling term can be regarded as changing temperature of softmax loss by $\cos\alpha$. To disentangle its effect, Table 1$iii$ shows performance of the scaled logits $\cos\alpha\, w_c^\top x$ which is significantly inferior to that of the proposed method, being close to the baseline performance. Therefore, the performance improvement of our method is actually brought by the random rotation regularization beyond a trivial logit scaling.

$iv$) **Stochasticity scale** $\frac{1}{\sqrt{D-1}}$ Given an angle $\alpha = \frac{\pi}{4}$, scale of the stochastic term is theoretically determined by $\frac{1}{\sqrt{D-1}}$ based on random rotation; $D = \min(d, C) = 512$ in this experiment[2]. To validate this theoretical scale, we regard $D$ as a tunable *hyper-parameter* and evaluate performances across various $D$ as shown in Table 1$iv$. Increasing $D$ means that random rotation is performed in a higher dimensional feature space by padding redundant features. Decreasing $D$ indicates that the classifiers are shrunk into a lower dimensional subspace, reducing rank($W$). In Table 1$iv$, one can see effectiveness of the theoretical $D = \min(d, C) = 512$ improving performance. On the other hand, smaller $D = 128$ imposes an impractical assumption that the classifiers can be packed into a fewer dimensional subspace, thereby degrading performance.

$v$) **Rotation angle** $\alpha$ While the angle $\alpha = \frac{\pi}{4}$ is determined based on the geometrical analysis of classifier orthogonality, we evaluate performances over

---

[2] ResNet10 produces $d = 512$-dimensional features for $C = 1000$ IMAGENET classes.

various $0 < \alpha < \frac{\pi}{2}$. The smaller $\alpha$ works as weak regularization while the larger $\alpha$ highly regularize training. The favorable performance is found at $\alpha = \frac{\pi}{4}$ which is half of orthogonality of classifiers, while the larger $\alpha$ significantly degrades performance. The setting of $\alpha = \frac{\pi}{4}$ is applied to the other experiments as well.
*vi*) **Variants** Some variants of the method are conceivable as discussed in Sect. 4. In contrast to the angular margin *cone* $C_\alpha$ (Fig. 1a), the margin *ball* (Fig. 7) could endow regularization regarding Euclidean margin as described in Sect. 4.3. Table 1*vi* shows that the ball approach is inferior to our cone-based method. A margin ball contains not only perturbation affecting angles but also variations of norm $\|x\|_2$ irrelevant to angular margin.

Our symmetric formulation can also be transformed into an asymmetric one in a manner similar to margin-based losses [5,8,36] by touching only the target logit via $\epsilon_y \rightarrow -|\epsilon_y|$ as in (22). The performance result in Table 1*vi* shows that the asymmetric approach is competitive with the simple symmetric one (13). Thus, the symmetric regularization form derived from random rotation even works well without requiring label information.

Our simple regularization is compatible with the others such as DropOut [34] to impose regularization from various aspects, further improving performance as shown in Table 1*vi*. For fair comparison in the following experiments, however, we apply only the proposed method (13) without such a combination technique.

## 5.2 Performance Comparison

We evaluate the proposed method in comparison with the other regularization methods. On the basis of the baseline softmax cross-entropy loss, we apply DropOut [34] as stochastic regularization and CosFace [36], ArcFace [8] and NoisySoftmax [5] for large-margin losses; their parameter settings are shown in the supplementary material. The proposed statistical rotation (StatRot) (13) is also compared to the geometrical rotation regularization which is formulated by means of geometrical rotation (GeoRot) using a random orthonormal matrix (3) and a sparse matrix [17]; they are equipped with $\alpha = \frac{\pi}{4}$ for fair comparison.
**Long-tailed Recognition.** In a real-world scenario, the number of available samples per category is occasionally biased across class categories to form a long-tailed distribution, in contrast to the standard benchmark datasets composed of well balanced number of training samples. The imbalanced training dataset biases CNNs toward majority classes through disregarding minority ones. To cope with the imbalance issue, we follow the two-stage training procedure [21] which first leans feature representation in a standard training protocol and then finetunes only the linear classifier by balanced batch sampling while freezing the backbone feature extractor. Regularization methods are compatible with the first-stage training to improve feature representation.

We evaluate the methods on IMAGENET-LT dataset [28] using ResNet10 [14], iNaturalist2018 (*i*NAT2018) [19] using ResNet50 and PLACES-LT [28] using ResNet10 and ResNet152. While IMAGENET-LT and PLACES-LT are artificially constructed from large-scale IMAGENET [7] and PLACES365 [42], respectively, *i*NAT2018 is a real-world long-tailed dataset. At the first-stage learning,

ResNet10 and ResNet50 are trained from random initial weights by SGD optimizer with momentum 0.9, weight decay $10^{-4}$ and cosine-scheduled learning rates starting from 0.2 over 180 epochs; the second-stage training is similarly performed over 30 epochs. In PLACES-LT, we apply ResNet152 pre-trained on IMAGENET and then trained it at the first stage over 30 epochs by SGD with cosine-scheduled learning rate starting from 0.1 on a linear classifier and 0.001 on the backbone ResNet152; the second-stage training takes 10 epochs. The performance results are shown in Table 2 demonstrating the effectiveness of the proposed statistical rotation regularization compared to the other approaches. It also works for training the pre-trained ResNet152 on PLACES-LT.

**Transfer Learning.** The methods are then evaluated on transfer learning. Deeper CNN models pretrained on a large-scale dataset are transferable to downstream tasks which are equipped with limited amount of training samples. The regularization methods contribute to exploit the discriminative power of the deeper models even on those scarce training data.

**Table 2.** Performance results (error rates %) on long-tailed recognition in the two-stage learning framework [21].

|  | IMAGENET-LT [28] | iNAT2018 [19] | PLACES-LT [28] | |
| --- | --- | --- | --- | --- |
|  | ResNet10 [14] | ResNet50 | ResNet10 | ResNet152 |
| SoftmaxLoss [21] | 58.91 | 32.82 | 72.99 | 61.14 |
| ArcFace [8] | 59.68 | 32.79 | 75.40 | 60.21 |
| CosFace [36] | 59.40 | 32.59 | 75.59 | 60.23 |
| NoisySoftmax [5] | 57.42 | 34.41 | 72.92 | 70.57 |
| DropOut [34] | 56.82 | 31.05 | 72.30 | 60.98 |
| GeoRot sparse [17] | 56.53 | 30.98 | 71.96 | 60.41 |
| GeoRot dense (3) | 56.68 | 30.92 | 71.89 | 60.09 |
| StatRot (13) | **56.40** | **30.39** | **71.85** | **59.93** |

**Table 3.** Performance results (error rates %) on transfer learning by applying RegNetY-32gf [31] pre-trained on IMAGENET. The last column shows performance gain compared to the baseline.

|  | CUB [37] | AIRCRAFT [30] | CAR [22] | SUN [39] | C101 [10] | Avg.Gain |
| --- | --- | --- | --- | --- | --- | --- |
| SoftmaxLoss | 16.05 | 17.61 | 11.07 | 33.31 | 5.91 | – |
| ArcFace [8] | 14.67 | 19.78 | 12.00 | 33.86 | **4.64** | −0.20 |
| CosFace [36] | 14.46 | 19.89 | 12.32 | 33.87 | 4.75 | −0.27 |
| NoisySoftmax [5] | 14.77 | 22.89 | 10.43 | 34.36 | 5.65 | −0.83 |
| DropOut [34] | 15.52 | 17.16 | 10.72 | 33.09 | 5.76 | 0.34 |
| GeoRot sparse [17] | 15.22 | 16.20 | 10.56 | 32.51 | 5.56 | 0.78 |
| GeoRot dense (3) | **14.00** | 17.79 | 9.87 | 32.28 | 5.15 | 0.97 |
| StatRot (13) | 14.22 | **15.96** | **9.76** | **32.23** | 4.66 | **1.42** |

We finetune RegNetY-32gf [31] pretrained on IMAGENET dataset by means of SGD with 0.9 momentum and $10^{-4}$ weight decay over 60 epochs with 128 batch size by cosine-scheduled learning rate; the initial learning rates are 0.1 for linear classifiers and 0.001 for backbone CNN models. Table 3 shows performance results on various downstream classification tasks, CUB200 [37], AIRCRAFT100 [30], CAR196 [22], SUN397 [39] and CALTECH101 [10]. The deeper models are stably finetuned by the proposed method to improve performance.

**Person Reidentification.** We finally apply the methods to regularize feature representation learning on person re-identification. The task demands CNN backbones to capture effective features from diverse camera images so that identical person images are matched across multiple cameras. We follow the baseline procedure [29] integrating three types of losses, triple loss [15], softmax loss and center loss [38], in which the regularization method is applicable to replace the center loss while keeping the other modules and training protocols the same.

The CNN backbones of ResNet50 [14] and SE-ResNeXt50 [16] pretrained on IMAGENET dataset [7] are applied to extract features from $128 \times 256$ bounding-box images. We evaluate performance by rank-1 accuracy (Rank1) and mean average precision (mAP) [41] on MARKET1501 [41] and DUKEMTMC [32] datasets as shown in Table 4. The proposed method effectively improves performance on both metrics of Rank1 and mAP which comprehensively evaluate matching performance, i.e., feature representation.

As shown in these experimental results, the proposed regularization theoretically derived from random rotation of feature vectors is stably contributive to performance improvement on various tasks outperforming the other types of regularization. Besides, it is also demonstrated that the statistical formulation effectively connects the geometric formulation with regularizing CNNs at classification in a superior manner to the naive geometric formulations.

**Table 4.** Performance results (accuracy %) on person re-identification.

| | MARKET1501 [41] | | | | DUKEMTMC [32] | | | |
| | ResNet50 [14] | | SE-ResNeXt50 [16] | | ResNet50 | | SE-ResNeXt50 | |
| Method | Rank1 | mAP | Rank1 | mAP | Rank1 | mAP | Rank1 | mAP |
|---|---|---|---|---|---|---|---|---|
| SoftmaxLoss [29] | 94.1 | 85.7 | 94.9 | 87.8 | 86.2 | 75.9 | 88.7 | 78.7 |
| CenterLoss [29] | 94.5 | 85.9 | 94.7 | 87.7 | 86.4 | 76.4 | 88.8 | 78.9 |
| ArcFace [8] | 89.2 | 72.4 | 82.2 | 67.6 | 79.6 | 60.6 | 72.9 | 53.5 |
| CosFace [8] | 85.2 | 72.4 | 85.0 | 71.0 | 79.5 | 62.0 | 76.2 | 56.9 |
| NoisySoftmax [5] | 94.7 | 87.1 | 94.9 | 87.7 | 86.7 | 75.3 | 88.0 | 76.9 |
| DropOut [34] | 93.8 | 85.3 | 94.8 | 87.7 | 86.0 | 75.9 | 88.5 | 78.8 |
| GeoRot sparse [17] | 94.1 | 85.5 | 95.2 | 87.6 | 86.7 | 76.1 | 89.1 | 78.5 |
| GeoRot dense (3) | 93.8 | 85.9 | 95.1 | 88.5 | 87.0 | 76.7 | 88.7 | 79.5 |
| StatRot (13) | **94.8** | **87.2** | **95.6** | **89.1** | **87.9** | **77.8** | **89.9** | **80.2** |

# 6   Conclusion

We have proposed a regularization method based on random rotation of feature vectors. The random rotation is derived from sample-wise cone representation to geometrically embed angular margin into classification. Beyond straightforward geometric formulation to rotate vectors by random rotation matrices, we established a novel regularization formulation through theoretically analyzing the random rotation from a statistical viewpoint. It excludes laborious operation of rotating vectors as well as improves backward updating for effective training with only one hyper-parameter of a rotation angle $\alpha$ which can be geometrically set as $\alpha = \frac{\pi}{4}$. The experimental results on various visual classification tasks demonstrate that the method effectively contributes to performance improvement.

# References

1. Ba, J.L., Kiros, J.R., Hinton, G.E.: Layer normalization. arXiv **1607**, 06450 (2016)
2. Bau, D., Zhou, B., Khosla, A., Oliva, A., Torralba, A.: Network dissection: quantifying interpretability of deep visual representations. In: CVPR, pp. 6541–6549 (2017)
3. Blaser, R., Fryzlewicz, P.: Random rotation ensembles. J. Mach. Learn. Rese. **17**(4), 1–26 (2016)
4. Cao, K., Wei, C., Gaidon, A., Arechiga, N., Ma, T.: Learning imbalanced datasets with label-distribution-aware margin loss. In: NeurIPS (2019)
5. Chen, B., Deng, W., Du, J.: Noisy softmax: improving the generalization ability of DCNN via postponing the early softmax saturation. In: CVPR, pp. 4021–4030 (2017)
6. Cohen, T.S., Welling, M.: Group equivariant convolutional networks. In: ICML, pp. 2990–2999 (2016)
7. Deng, J., Dong, W., Socher, R., Li, L.J., Li, K., Fei-Fei, L.: Imagenet: a large-scale hierarchical image database. In: CVPR, pp. 248–255 (2009)
8. Deng, J., Guo, J., Niannan, X., Zafeiriou, S.: Arcface: additive angular margin loss for deep face recognition. In: CVPR, pp. 4690–4699 (2019)
9. DeVries, T., Taylor, G.W.: Improved regularization of convolutional neural networks with cutout. arXiv. 1708.04552 (2017)
10. Fei-Fei, L., Fergus, R., Perona, P.: Learning generative visual models from few training examples: an incremental Bayesian approach tested on 101 object categories. In: Computer Vision and Pattern Recognition Workshop, pp. 178–178 (2004)
11. Ghiasi, G., Lin, T.Y., Le, Q.V.: Dropblock: a regularization method for convolutional networks. In: NeurIPS, pp. 3917–3924 (2018)
12. Golub, G.H., Loan, C.F.V.: Matrix Computations, 3rd edn. Johns Hopkins Univ. Press, London (1996)
13. Goodfellow, I., Bengio, Y., Courville, A.: Deep Learning. MIT Press (2016). http://www.deeplearningbook.org
14. He, K., Zhang, X., Ren, S., Sun, J.: Deep residual learning for image recognition. In: CVPR, pp. 770–778 (2016)

15. Hermans, A., Beyer, L., Leibe, B.: In defense of the triplet loss for person re-identification. arXiv:1703.07737 (2017)
16. Hu, J., Shen, L., Sun, G.: Squeeze-and-excitation networks. In: CVPR, pp. 7132–7141 (2018)
17. Hu, K., Póczos, B.: Rotationout as a regularization method for neural network. arXiv:1911.07427 (2019)
18. Huang, G., Sun, Yu., Liu, Z., Sedra, D., Weinberger, K.Q.: Deep networks with stochastic depth. In: Leibe, B., Matas, J., Sebe, N., Welling, M. (eds.) ECCV 2016. LNCS, vol. 9908, pp. 646–661. Springer, Cham (2016). https://doi.org/10.1007/978-3-319-46493-0_39
19. iNatrualist: The inaturalist 2018 competition dataset. https://github.com/visipedia/inat_comp/tree/master/2018 (2018)
20. Ioffe, S., Szegedy, C.: Batch normalization: accelerating deep network training by reducing internal covariate shift. J. Mach. Learn. Res. **37**, 448–456 (2015)
21. Kang, B., Xie, S., Rohrbach, M., Yan, Z., Gordo, A., Feng, J., Kalantidis, Y.: Decoupling representation and classifier for long-tailed recognition. In: ICLR (2020)
22. Krause, J., Stark, M., Deng, J., Fei-Fei, L.: 3D object representations for fine-grained categorization. In: Workshop on 3D Representation and Recognition, pp. 554–561 (2013)
23. Krogh, A., Hertz, J.A.: A simple weight decay can improve generalization. In: NeurIPS, pp. 950–957 (1991)
24. Lenc, K., Vedaldi, A.: Understanding image representations by measuring their equivariance and equivalence. In: CVPR, pp. 991–999 (2015)
25. Li, X., Chen, S., Hu, X., Yang, J.: Understanding the disharmony between dropout and batch normalization by variance shift. In: CVPR, pp. 2682–2690 (2019)
26. Liu, W., Wen, Y., Yu, Z., Li, M., Raj, B., Song, L.: Sphereface: deep hypersphere embedding for face recognition. In: CVPR, pp. 212–220 (2017)
27. Liu, W., Wen, Y., Yu, Z., Yang, M.: Large-margin softmax loss for convolutional neural networks. In: ICML, pp. 507–516 (2016)
28. Liu, Z., Miao, Z., Zhan, X., Wang, J., Gong, B., Yu, S.X.: Large-scale long-tailed recognition in an open world. In: CVPR, pp. 2537–2546 (2019)
29. Luo, H., Gu, Y., Liao, X., Lai, S., Jiang, W.: Bag of tricks and a strong baseline for deep person re-identification. In: CVPR workshop (2019)
30. Maji, S., Rahtu, E., Kannala, J., Blaschko, M.B., Vedaldi, A.: Fine-grained visual classification of aircraft. arXiv:1306.5151 (2013)
31. Radosavovic, I., Kosaraju, R.P., Girshick, R., He, K., Dollár, P.: Designing network design spaces. In: CVPR, pp. 10428–10436 (2020)
32. Ristani, E., Solera, F., Zou, R., Cucchiara, R., Tomasi, C.: Performance measures and a data set for multi-target, multi-camera tracking. In: Hua, G., Jégou, H. (eds.) ECCV 2016. LNCS, vol. 9914, pp. 17–35. Springer, Cham (2016). https://doi.org/10.1007/978-3-319-48881-3_2
33. Salimans, T., Kingma, D.P.: Weight normalization: a simple reparameterization to accelerate training of deep neural networks. In: NeurIPS (2016)
34. Srivastava, N., Hinton, G.E., Krizhevsky, A., Sutskever, I., Salakhutdinov, R.: Dropout?: a simple way to prevent neural networks from overfitting. J. Mach. Learn. Res. **15**, 1929–1958 (2014)
35. Ulyanov, D., Vedaldi, A., Lempitsky, V.: Instance normalization: The missing ingredient for fast stylization. arXiv:1607.08022 (2016)
36. Wang, H., et al.: Cosface: large margin cosine loss for deep face recognition. In: CVPR, pp. 5265–5274 (2018)

37. Welinder, P., Branson, S., Mita, T., Wah, C., Schroff, F., Belongie, S., Perona, P.: Caltech-UCSD Birds 200. Tech. Rep. CNS-TR-2010-001, California Institute of Technology (2010)

38. Wen, Y., Zhang, K., Li, Z., Qiao, Yu.: A discriminative feature learning approach for deep face recognition. In: Leibe, B., Matas, J., Sebe, N., Welling, M. (eds.) ECCV 2016. LNCS, vol. 9911, pp. 499–515. Springer, Cham (2016). https://doi.org/10.1007/978-3-319-46478-7_31

39. Xiao, J., Hays, J., Ehinger, K.A., Oliva, A., Torralba, A.: Sun database: large-scale scene recognition from abbey to zoo. In: CVPR, pp. 3485–3492 (2010)

40. Yun, S., Han, D., Oh, S.J., Chun, S., Choe, J., Yoo, Y.: Cutmix: regularization strategy to train strong classifiers with localizable features. In: ICCV, pp. 6023–6032 (2019)

41. Zheng, L., Shen, L., Tian, L., Wang, S., Wang, J., Tian, Q.: Scalable person re-identification: a benchmark. In: ICCV, pp. 1116–1124 (2015)

42. Zhou, B., Lapedriza, A., Khosla, A., Oliva, A., Torralba, A.: Places: a 10 million image database for scene recognition. IEEE Trans. Pattern Anal. Mach. Intell. 40(6), 1452–1464 (2018)

# Towards Accurate Open-Set Recognition via Background-Class Regularization

Wonwoo Cho[1,2] and Jaegul Choo[1,2(✉)]

[1] KAIST AI, Daejeon, Republic of Korea
{wcho,jchoo}@kaist.ac.kr
[2] Letsur Inc., Daejeon, Republic of Korea

**Abstract.** In open-set recognition (OSR), classifiers should be able to reject unknown-class samples while maintaining high closed-set classification accuracy. To effectively solve the OSR problem, previous studies attempted to limit latent feature space and reject data located outside the limited space via offline analyses, *e.g.*, distance-based feature analyses, or complicated network architectures. To conduct OSR via a simple inference process (without offline analyses) in standard classifier architectures, we use distance-based classifiers instead of conventional Softmax classifiers. Afterwards, we design a background-class regularization strategy, which uses background-class data as surrogates of unknown-class ones during training phase. Specifically, we formulate a novel regularization loss suitable for distance-based classifiers, which reserves sufficiently large class-wise latent feature spaces for known classes and forces background-class samples to be located far away from the limited spaces. Through our extensive experiments, we show that the proposed method provides robust OSR results, while maintaining high closed-set classification accuracy.

**Keywords:** Generalized open-set recognition · Distance-based classifiers · Background-class regularization · Probability of inclusion

## 1 Introduction

In machine learning (ML), classification algorithms have achieved great success. Through recent advances in convolutional neural networks, their classification performance already surpassed the human-level performance in image classification [8]. However, such algorithms have usually been developed under a *closed-set* assumption, *i.e.*, the class of each test sample is assumed to always belong to one of the pre-defined set of classes. Although this conventional assumption can be easily violated in real-world applications (classifiers can face unknown-class

**Supplementary Information** The online version contains supplementary material available at https://doi.org/10.1007/978-3-031-19806-9_38.

data), traditional classification algorithms are highly likely to force unknown-class samples to be classified into one of the known classes. To tackle this problem, the *open-set recognition (OSR)* problem [34] aims to properly classify unknown-class samples as "unknown" and known-class samples as one of the known classes.

According to the definition of OSR [34], it is required to properly limit the latent feature space of known-class data. To satisfy the requirement, various OSR methods were developed based on traditional ML models. Previously, Scheirer *et al.* [33] calibrated the decision scores of support vector machines (SVMs). Based on the intuition that a large set of data samples of unknown classes can be rejected if those of known classes are accurately modeled, Jain *et al.* [13] proposed $P_I$-SVM, which utilized the statistical modeling of known-class samples located near the decision boundary of SVMs. Afterwards, it was attempted to solve the OSR problem based on the principle of the nearest neighbors [14]. Taking distribution information of data into account, Rudd *et al.* [29] proposed the extreme value machine which utilizes the concept of margin distributions.

Since deep neural networks (DNNs) have robust classification performance by learning high-level representations of data, OSR methods for DNNs have received great attention. Based on the theoretical foundations studied in traditional ML-based OSR methods, Bendale and Boult [1] proposed the first OSR strategy for DNNs called Openmax, which calibrates the output logits of pre-trained Softmax classifiers. To improve Openmax, Yoshihashi *et al.* [41] proposed the classification-reconstruction learning to make robust latent feature vectors. Afterwards, Oza and Patel [27] proposed to exploit a class-conditioned autoencoder and use its reconstruction error to assess each input sample. Sun *et al.* [37] employed several class-conditioned variational auto-encoders for generative modeling.

Although previous methods applied *offline analyses* to pre-trained Softmax classifiers or employed complicated DNN architectures, they have limited performance since the classifiers were trained solely based on known-class data. To mitigate the problem, this paper designs an simple and effective open-set classifier in the *generalized OSR setting*, which uses background-class regularization (BCR) at training time. Despite its effectiveness, BCR has received a little attention in OSR and previous BCR methods [5,11,21] are insufficient to properly solve the OSR problem. In this paper, we denote the infinite label space of all classes as $\mathcal{Y}$ and use the following class categories, whose definition is also provided in [5,7].

- **Known known classes** (KKCs; $\mathcal{K} = \{1, \cdots, C\} \subset \mathcal{Y}$) include distinctly labeled positive classes, where $\mathcal{U} = \mathcal{Y} \setminus \mathcal{K}$ is the entire unknown classes.
- **Known unknown classes** (KUCs; $\mathcal{B} \subset \mathcal{U}$) include background classes, *e.g.*, labeled classes which are not necessarily grouped into a set of KKCs $\mathcal{K}$.
- **Unknown unknown classes** (UUCs; $\mathcal{A} = \mathcal{U} \setminus \mathcal{B}$) represent the rest of $\mathcal{U}$, where UUCs are not available at training time, but occur at inference time.

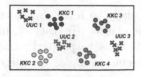 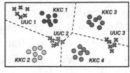 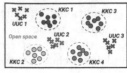

(a) Latent feature space     (b) Closed-set problem     (c) Open-set problem

**Fig. 1.** Given (a) a latent feature space, we demonstrate (b) closed-set and (c) open-set problems, where KKCs and UUCs are known and unknown classes, respectively.

Also, we denote $\mathcal{D}_t$ as a training set consisting of multiple pairs of a KKC data sample and the corresponding class label $y \in \{1, \cdots, C\}$. $\mathcal{D}_{test}^k$ and $\mathcal{D}_{test}^u$ are test sets of KKCs and UUCs, respectively. $\mathcal{D}_b$ is a background dataset of KUCs.

## 2    Preliminary Studies

### 2.1    The Open-Set Recognition Problem

The OSR problem addresses a classification setting that can face test samples from classes unseen during training (UUCs). In this setting, open-set classifiers aim to properly classify KKC samples while rejecting UUC ones simultaneously. A similar problem to OSR is out-of-distribution (OoD) detection [10], which typically aims to reject data items drawn far away from the training data distribution. Conventionally, previous studies such as [10,17,18,20] assumed that OoD samples are drawn from other datasets or can be even noise data. In this paper, we aim to reject test data whose classes are unknown but related to the training data, which narrows down the scope of conventional OoD detection tasks.

Previously, Scheirer et al. [34] introduced a formal definition of OSR based on the notion of open-space risk $R_\mathcal{O}$, which is a relative measure of a positively labeled union of balls $\mathcal{S}_V$ and open space $\mathcal{O}$ located far from $\mathcal{S}_V$. Since labeling any data item in $\mathcal{O}$ incurs open-space risk, it is straightforward that a classifier cannot be a solution for the OSR problem if the classifier accepts data in infinitely wide regions, i.e., its open-space risk is unbounded ($R_\mathcal{O} = \infty$). The definition implies that essential requirements to solve the OSR problem are 1) *bounding open-space risk* and 2) *ideally balancing it with empirical risk*.

Unlike traditional classifier models, open-set classifiers are required to limit the latent feature space of KKC data to bound their open-space risk. To ensure open-space risk to be bounded, Scheirer et al. [33] introduced compact abating probability (CAP) models. The principle of CAP models is that if the support region of a classifier decays in all directions from the training data, thresholding the region will bound the classifier's open-space risk [2]. As depicted in Fig. 1, which compares traditional closed-set and open-set classification problems [7], building proper *class-wise* CAP models is an effective strategy for OSR.

## 2.2  Post-Classification Analysis for Pre-Trained Softmax Classifier

This paper aims to solve the OSR problem solely based on a standard DNN-based classifier architecture $f$ as a latent feature extractor. Applying a fully-connected layer to $f$, a conventional Softmax classifier computes the posterior probability of an input $\mathbf{x}$ belonging to the $c$-th known class by

$$P_s(y = c | \mathbf{x}) = \frac{\exp(\mathbf{w}_c^T f(\mathbf{x}) + b_c)}{\sum_{i=1}^{C} \exp(\mathbf{w}_i^T f(\mathbf{x}) + b_i)}, \tag{1}$$

where $c \in \{1, \cdots, C\}$, $f(\mathbf{x}) \in \mathbb{R}^n$ is the latent feature vector of $\mathbf{x}$, and $\mathbf{w}_c$ and $b_c$ are the weight and bias for the $c$-th class, respectively. For pre-trained Softmax classifiers, Hendrycks and Gimpel [10] proposed a baseline technique to detect anomalous samples, which imposes a threshold on the predictive confidence of Eq. (1). When using the baseline approach to solve the OSR problem, one can estimate the class of each KKC sample and recognize UUC data by

$$\hat{y} = \begin{cases} \arg\max_{c \in \{1, \cdots, C\}} P_s(y = c | \mathbf{x}), & \text{if } \max_{c \in \{1, \cdots, C\}} P_s(y = c | \mathbf{x}) \geq \tau, \\ C + 1 \text{ (unknown class)}, & \text{otherwise.} \end{cases} \tag{2}$$

However, Eq. (2) cannot formally bound open-space risk and formulate class-wise CAP models since it only rejects test data near the decision boundary of classifiers, thus having infinitely wide regions of acceptance [2]. Therefore, *post-classification analysis* methods using an auxiliary measure other than the Softmax probability are necessary to build auxiliary CAP models in the latent feature space of $f$, where *distance measures* have been widely employed in previous studies [1,18].

To build class-wise CAP models, Openmax [1] defined radial-basis decaying functions $\{s(\mathbf{x}, i)\}_{i=1}^{C}$, each of which measures the class-belongingness of $\mathbf{x}$ for the $c$-th class, in the latent feature space of $f$. For each $s(\mathbf{x}, c)$, the authors employed distance measures between $f(\mathbf{x})$ and an empirical class mean vector $\boldsymbol{\mu}_c$, e.g., $s(\mathbf{x}, c) = D_E^2(f(\mathbf{x}), \boldsymbol{\mu}_c) = (f(\mathbf{x}) - \boldsymbol{\mu}_c)^T(f(\mathbf{x}) - \boldsymbol{\mu}_c)$. To formulate more effective CAP models, they statistically analyzed the distribution of $s(\mathbf{x}, c)$ based on the extreme value theory (EVT) [32], which provides a theoretical foundation that the Weibull distribution is suitable for modeling KKC samples located far from the class mean vectors (extreme samples). To be specific, Openmax fits a Weibull distribution on extreme samples of the $c$-th class having the highest $D_E(f(\mathbf{x}), \boldsymbol{\mu}_c)$ values, where its cumulative distribution function (CDF) formulates the *probability of inclusion* $P_I(\mathbf{x}, c)$ [13,29], i.e., $P_I(\mathbf{x}, c) = 1 - \texttt{WeibullCDF}$, which rapidly decays near the extreme samples. Based on $P_I(\mathbf{x}, c)$, the decision rule of Eq. (2) can be calibrated to conduct OSR with Softmax classifiers.

## 2.3  Background-Class Regularization

Although they need additional inference procedures (*e.g.*, EVT modeling), previous offline analyses may have limited OSR performance since the classifiers were trained solely based on known-class data. To obtain robust empirical results without complicated analyses, one can use the strategy of BCR at the training phase, which exploits background-class (KUC) samples as surrogates of UUC data. Geng $et$ $al.$ [7] argued that the generalized OSR setting that utilizes KUC samples is still less-explored and an important research direction for robust OSR.

Conventionally, a loss function for training classifiers with BCR can be

$$\mathcal{L} = \mathcal{L}_{cf} + \lambda\mathcal{L}_{bg} = \mathbb{E}_{(\mathbf{x}^k, y)\sim\mathcal{D}_t}\left[-\log P_s(y|\mathbf{x}^k) + \lambda\mathbb{E}_{\mathbf{x}^b\sim\mathcal{D}_b}\left[f_{reg}\left(\mathbf{x}^k, y, \mathbf{x}^b\right)\right]\right], \quad (3)$$

where $\mathcal{L}_{cf}$ and $\mathcal{L}_{bg}$ are the loss terms for closed-set classification and BCR, respectively, and $\lambda$ is a hyperparameter. For $\mathcal{L}_{bg}$, previous studies designed their own $f_{reg}$, where [5] proposed the objectosphere loss for OSR, and [11] and [21] employed the uniformity and the energy losses for OoD detection, respectively.

In this paper, we tackle the following limitations of the previous BCR methods.

- In the previous BCR methods, $\mathcal{L}_{bg}$ were designed to make normal data and anomalies more distinguishable in terms of the corresponding anomaly scores. Since they categorized normal data into a single group (did not consider the classes) in $\mathcal{L}_{bg}$, the previous methods may have limited performance in rejecting UUC data and maintaining robust closed-set classification results.
- The previous methods using the decision rule of Eq. (2) ($e.g.$, objectosphere [5] and uniformity [11]) cannot bound open-space risk. Although one can use post-classification analyses to bound open-space risk, trained latent feature space can be inappropriate for using another metric such as distance measures.
- To increase the gap between KKC and KUC data in terms of latent feature magnitude and energy in the objectosphere [5] and the energy [21] losses, respectively, it is necessary to find proper margin parameters for each dataset.

## 3   Proposed Method

### 3.1   Overview

Using a standard classifier $f$, this paper aims to design open-set classifiers having simple yet effective inference steps. In the following, we summarize our method.

- Instead of applying fully-connected layers to feature extractors $f$, we use the principle of linear discriminant analysis (LDA) [24] to classify images based on a distance measure. By simply imposing a threshold on the distance as in Eq. (2), our classifiers can easily build class-wise CAP models. (Sect. 3.2)
- Afterwards, we propose a novel BCR strategy suitable for the distance-based classifiers. Following the convention of Eq. (3), we design our own $\mathcal{L}_{bg}$ called $class$-$inclusion$ $loss$, where our total loss is function defined by

$$\mathcal{L} = \mathcal{L}_{cf} + \lambda\mathcal{L}_{bg} = \mathcal{L}_{cf} + \lambda(\mathcal{L}_{bg,k} + \mathcal{L}_{bg,u}) \quad (4)$$

The class-inclusion loss first limits the feature space of KKC data by formulating *explicit* class-wise boundaries, and then forces KUC data to be located outside the boundaries at each training iteration. Our loss is designed to increase the distance gaps between KKC and KUC samples while maintaining robust closed-set classification performance. (Sects. 3.3 and 3.4)

For a better understanding of the training and inference processes of our method, we provide their detailed algorithm in our supplementary materials.

## 3.2   Distance-Based Classification Models

**Distance-based Classifiers.** To train a robust open-set classifier, we formulate a *distance-based classifier* as an alternative of Eq. (1):

$$P_d(y = c|\mathbf{x}) = \frac{P_c \cdot \mathcal{N}(f(\mathbf{x})|\boldsymbol{\mu}_c, \mathbf{I})}{\sum_{i=1}^{C} P_i \cdot \mathcal{N}(f(\mathbf{x})|\boldsymbol{\mu}_i, \mathbf{I})} = \frac{P_c \cdot \exp\left(-D_E^2(f(\mathbf{x}), \boldsymbol{\mu}_c)\right)}{\sum_{i=1}^{C} P_i \cdot \exp\left(-D_E^2(f(\mathbf{x}), \boldsymbol{\mu}_i)\right)} \quad (5)$$

where Eq. (5) uses the principle of LDA and $\mathcal{L}_{cf} = \mathbb{E}_{(\mathbf{x}^k, y) \sim \mathcal{D}_t}[-\log P_d(y|\mathbf{x}^k)]$. In Eq. (5), we exploit an identity covariance matrix $\mathbf{I}$ and $P_c = P(y = c) = C^{-1}$ for all $c$ for KKCs. The classifier estimates the class of each $\mathbf{x}$ via $D_E^2(f(\mathbf{x}), \boldsymbol{\mu}_c) = (f(\mathbf{x}) - \boldsymbol{\mu}_c)^T(f(\mathbf{x}) - \boldsymbol{\mu}_c)$, the Euclidean distance between $f(\mathbf{x}) \in \mathbb{R}^n$ and $\boldsymbol{\mu}_c \in \mathbb{R}^n$, where we call $\boldsymbol{\mu}_c$ a *class-wise anchor*. To ensure sufficiently large distance gaps between the pairs of initial class-wise anchors, we randomly sample each $\boldsymbol{\mu}_c$ from the standard Gaussian distribution and then set each $\boldsymbol{\mu}_c$ as a trainable vector. For distance analysis results of such randomly sampled vectors, see [12].

**Decision Rule.** At inference time, each KKC sample $\mathbf{x}$ can be classified via $\hat{y} = \arg\min_{c \in \{1, \cdots, C\}} D_E^2(f(\mathbf{x}), \boldsymbol{\mu}_c)$. Furthermore, applying a threshold to $D_E^2(f(\mathbf{x}), \boldsymbol{\mu}_c)$ can bound open-space risk by formulating class-wise CAP models as follows:

$$\hat{y} = \begin{cases} \arg\min_{c \in \{1, \cdots, C\}} D_E^2(f(\mathbf{x}), \boldsymbol{\mu}_c), & \text{if } \max_{c \in \{1, \cdots, C\}} -D_E^2(f(\mathbf{x}), \boldsymbol{\mu}_c) \geq \tau, \\ C + 1 \text{ (unknown class)}, & \text{otherwise.} \end{cases}$$

$$(6)$$

As Eq. (6) employs the same metric $D_E$ for classification and UUC rejection, our method may support more accurate latent feature space analysis for OSR than the previous OSR methods using post-classification analyses.

The concept of distance-based classification was also employed in prototypical networks [36], nearest class mean classifiers [23], and the previous studies of the center loss function [38] and convolutional prototype classifiers [40]. In addition, polyhedral conic classifiers [3] used the idea of returning compact class regions for KKC samples based on distance-based feature analyses. It is noteworthy that our main contribution is a novel BCR method that can effectively utilize KUC samples in a distance-based classification scheme (described in Sect. 3.3 and 3.4), not the distance based classifier method itself. To the best of our knowledge, we are the first to discuss the necessity of distance-based BCR methods for OSR and propose a reasonable regularization method for distance-based classifiers.

### 3.3   Background Class Regularization for Distance-based Classifiers

**Intuition and Hypersphere Classifiers.** To obtain robust OSR performance via Eq. (6), we aim to design a BCR method suitable for distance-based classifiers, which uses $\mathcal{D}_t$ and $\mathcal{D}_b$ as surrogates of $\mathcal{D}_{test}^k$ and $\mathcal{D}_{test}^u$ at training time, respectively. Although it cannot provide any information of $\mathcal{D}_{test}^u$, $\mathcal{D}_b$ can be effective to limit the latent feature space of KKCs, while reserving space for UUCs. With $\mathcal{D}_b$, it is intuitive that the primary objective of BCR for Eq. (6) is to make KUC samples located far away from $\boldsymbol{\mu}_i$ for all classes $i \in \{1, \cdots, C\}$.

Before we illustrate our BCR method, we first introduce hypersphere classifiers (HSCs) [30]. An HSC conducts anomaly detection by using a feature extractor $g$, where its anomaly score for an input $\mathbf{x}$ is the Euclidean distance between a single center vector $\boldsymbol{\mu}$ and $g(\mathbf{x})$. When training the HSC model, the authors used normal and background data, $\mathcal{D}_t$ and $\mathcal{D}_b$, respectively, and a loss function

$$\mathbb{E}_{\mathbf{x}^k \sim \mathcal{D}_t} \left[ h \left( D_E^2 \left( g(\mathbf{x}^k), \boldsymbol{\mu} \right) \right) \right] - \mathbb{E}_{\mathbf{x}^b \sim \mathcal{D}_b} \left[ \log \left( 1 - \exp \left( -h \left( D_E^2 \left( g(\mathbf{x}^b), \boldsymbol{\mu} \right) \right) \right) \right) \right]. \tag{7}$$

The loss function is designed to decrease the Euclidean distances between normal samples $\mathbf{x}^k$ and $\boldsymbol{\mu}$ while increasing the distances for background samples $\mathbf{x}^b$. In Eq. (7), $h(x) = \sqrt{x+1} - 1$, which implies that the Euclidean distance $D_E^2(g(\mathbf{x}), \boldsymbol{\mu})$ is scaled into the range of $(0, 1]$ via $\exp(-h(D_E^2(g(\mathbf{x}), \boldsymbol{\mu})))$.

**Background-class Regularization Strategy.** It is straightforward that the decision rule of Eq. (6) employs the principle of HSCs in a class-wise manner. In other words, the class-wise HSC for the $c$-th class determines whether a test sample belongs to the $c$-th class by computing $D_E^2(f(\mathbf{x}), \boldsymbol{\mu}_c)$, where the input is determined as UUC if the entire class-wise HSCs reject the data item. Thus, a proper BCR strategy for distance-based classifiers should force each KUC sample $\mathbf{x}^b$ to be rejected by the entire class-wise HSCs (increase $D_E^2(f(\mathbf{x}^b), \boldsymbol{\mu}_i)$ for all $i$). Since it is inefficient to consider the entire KKCs to regularize $f$ with $\mathbf{x}^b$ at each iteration, we approximate the process by only taking the *closest* class-wise HSC into account (increase $\min_{i \in \{1, \cdots, C\}} D_E^2(f(\mathbf{x}^b), \boldsymbol{\mu}_i)$).

Although one can adopt Eq. (7) to formulate $\mathcal{L}_{bg}$ for distance-based classifiers, scaling $D_E^2(f(\mathbf{x}), \boldsymbol{\mu}_c)$ into $(0, 1]$ via $\exp(-h(D_E^2(f(\mathbf{x}), \boldsymbol{\mu}_c)))$, which rapidly decays near $\boldsymbol{\mu}_c$, can be insufficient to move KUC data far away from class-wise anchors. Therefore, we design $\mathcal{L}_{bg}$ that can guarantee sufficient spaces for KKC data and simultaneously force KUC samples located outside the limited class-wise spaces.

### 3.4   Probability of Inclusion and Class-Inclusion Loss

As we described in Sect. 2.2, the probability of inclusion builds effective CAP models, since it is designed to rapidly decay near extreme data, *i.e.*, $P_I(\mathbf{x}, c) \approx 1$ in the region that a majority of class-$c$ KKC samples are located. In the following, we introduce a novel regularization method for distance-based classifiers based on the principle of the probability of inclusion, and then design a loss function.

**Probability of Inclusion for Distance-Based Classifiers.** For pre-trained Softmax classifiers, Openmax [1] formulated the probability of inclusion via EVT modeling at inference time, where the strategy is to find *implicit* class-wise boundaries that distinguish KKCs from UUCs. However, such EVT-based analysis can be intractable at each training iteration, since it requires computationally-expensive and parameter-sensitive processes. In addition, it is inappropriate to make boundaries by analyzing features which are not properly trained yet.

Thus, we build *explicit* class-wise boundaries by formulating $P_I(\mathbf{x}, c)$ based on the underlying assumption of LDA, and then use the boundaries for regularization without additional analysis of latent feature distribution. Under the assumption of LDA that each class-$c$ latent feature vector is drawn from a unimodal Gaussian distribution $\mathcal{N}(f(\mathbf{x})|\boldsymbol{\mu}_c, \mathbf{I})$, the Euclidean distance $D_E^2(f(\mathbf{x}), \boldsymbol{\mu}_c)$, a simplified version of the Mahalanobis distance, can be assumed to follow the Chi-square distribution having the degree of freedom $n$. Then, we have

$$P\left(D_E^2(f(\mathbf{x}), \boldsymbol{\mu}_c) = t\right) = \frac{t^{\frac{n}{2}-1}}{2^{\frac{n}{2}} \cdot \Gamma(n/2)} \cdot \exp\left(-\frac{t}{2}\right), \tag{8}$$

where $t \geq 0$, $\Gamma(\cdot)$ is the Gamma function, and $n$ is the dimension of $f(\mathbf{x})$.

As previous studies [1,13,29] formulated the probability of inclusion by computing the CDF of the Weibull distribution, *i.e.*, $P_I(\mathbf{x}, c) = 1 - \texttt{WeibullCDF}$, we define our $P_I(\mathbf{x}, c)$ by using the CDF of Eq. (8) as follows:

$$P_I(\mathbf{x}, c) = 1 - \int_0^{D_E^2(\mathbf{x}, c)/2} \frac{t^{n/2-1}}{\Gamma(n/2)} \cdot \exp\left(-t\right) dt = \frac{\Gamma(n/2, D_E^2(f(\mathbf{x}), \boldsymbol{\mu}_c)/2)}{\Gamma(n/2)}, \tag{9}$$

where $\Gamma(\cdot, \cdot)$ is the upper incomplete Gamma function. It is noteworthy that Eq. (9) can be easily computable via `igammac` function in PyTorch [28].

**Class-inclusion Loss Function.** Based on $\mathcal{D}_t$, $\mathcal{D}_b$, and our $P_I(\mathbf{x}, c)$ of Eq. (9), the primary objective of the proposed BCR strategy, which aims to force each KUC data sample to be located far away from the closest class-wise HSC, can be achieved by employing a loss function $\mathcal{L}_{bg,u} = \mathbb{E}_{\mathbf{x}^b \sim \mathcal{D}_b}[-\log(1 - \max_{i \in \{1,\cdots,C\}} P_I(\mathbf{x}^b, i))]$. To compare $P_I(\mathbf{x}, c)$ and $P_H(\mathbf{x}, c) = \exp(-h(D_E^2(f(\mathbf{x}), \boldsymbol{\mu}_c)))$, which was used in Eq. (7), we plot $P_I(\mathbf{x}, c)$ and $P_H(\mathbf{x}, c)$ in

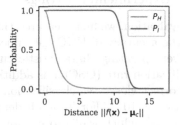

**Fig. 2.** $P_H$ and $P_I$ (Ours).

Fig. 2 with respect to $\|f(\mathbf{x}) - \boldsymbol{\mu}_c\|$ by assuming $n = 128$. The figure implies that unlike $P_H(\mathbf{x}, c)$, our $P_I(\mathbf{x}, c)$ can assign sufficiently large space for KKC data and force KUC samples to be located outside the space. Also, it is noteworthy that our regularization method based on $P_I(\mathbf{x}, c)$ does not require any margin parameters dependent on datasets or the dimension of latent features.

At training time, $P_I(\mathbf{x}, c) = 0.5$ constructs an auxiliary decision boundary between the $c$-th class KKC data and the other data items, where $\mathcal{L}_{bg,u}$

makes a majority of KUC data to be located outside the entire class-wise boundaries. However, $\mathcal{L}_{bg,u}$ can be insufficient to achieve robust UUC rejection and closed-set classification results, since it does not control correctly classified KKC samples to be located inside the corresponding class-wise boundaries. Therefore, in addition to $\mathcal{L}_{cf} = \mathbb{E}_{(\mathbf{x}^k,y)\sim\mathcal{D}_t}[-\log P_d(y|\mathbf{x}^k)]$, we apply another loss $\mathcal{L}_{bg,k}$ to KKC data to *maintain* high closed-set classification accuracy and enhance the gap between KKC and KUC samples in terms of the Euclidean distance. By formulating $\mathcal{L}_{bg,k} = \mathbb{E}_{(\mathbf{x}^k,y)\sim\mathcal{D}_t}[-\mathbb{1}(y = \hat{c})\log(P_I(\mathbf{x}^k,\hat{c}))]$, where $\hat{c} = \arg\max_{i\in\{1,\cdots,C\}} P_I(\mathbf{x}^k,i)$, we define our $\mathcal{L}_{bg}$ as $\mathcal{L}_{bg,k} + \mathcal{L}_{bg,u}$ and call $\mathcal{L}_{bg}$ the *class-inclusion loss*.

In our total loss (Eq. (4)), $\mathcal{L}_{cf}$ makes KKC samples be correctly classified, $\mathcal{L}_{bg,u}$ makes KUC samples located outside the explicit class-wise boundaries, and $\mathcal{L}_{bg,k}$ additionally regularizes correctly classified KKC samples. It is noteworthy that we use an additional loss for KKC samples after they are correctly classified, to prevent obstructions in training closed-set classifiers at early iterations.

## 4   Experiments

Through extensive experiments, we compared our class-inclusion loss for distance-based classifiers to the objectosphere [5], the uniformity (also widely known as OE) [11], and the energy [21] losses for conventional Softmax classifiers. This section aims to show that whether our approach provides competitive UUC rejection results, while keeping high closed-set classification accuracy. Furthermore, we conducted additional experiments and provided the corresponding discussions.

### 4.1   Experimental Settings

For evaluation, we first measured the closed-set classification accuracy. To quantify the accuracy of UUC data rejection, we also measured the area under the receiver operating characteristic curve (AUROC). Also, we used the open-set classification rate (OSCR) as additional OSR accuracy measure by quantifying the correct closed-set classification rate when the false positive rate for UUC rejection is $10^{-1}$. For in-depth details of OSCR, see [5]. As $\mathcal{D}_b$, we used ImageNet [31], which was also employed in [19]. To ensure that the classes of $\mathcal{D}_b$ and our test sets are disjoint, we used only the remaining classes of ImageNet, which are not included in the test sets. In our experiments, we considered the following two settings.

**Setting 1.** In Setting 1, a single dataset was split into KKCs and UUCs, where we used the KKCs in the training set as $\mathcal{D}_t$, and the KKCs and UUCs in the test set as $\mathcal{D}_{test}^k$ and $\mathcal{D}_{test}^u$, respectively. Following the protocol in [25], which were also employed in [27,37], we conducted experiments by using the following standard datasets: SVHN [26], CIFAR10 & CIFAR100 [15], and TinyImageNet [16].

*SVHN, CIFAR10*    For SVHN and CIFAR10, each of which consists of images of 10 classes, each dataset was randomly partitioned into 6 KKCs and 4 UUCs.

*CIFAR+10, CIFAR+50*    For CIFAR+$M$, we employed randomly selected 4 classes of CIFAR10 as KKCs and $M$ classes of CIFAR100 as UUCs.

*TinyImageNet*    For a larger number of classes, we randomly selected 20 classes of TinyImageNet as KKCs and then used the remaining 180 classes as UUCs.

**Setting 2.** By using the training and the test sets of a single dataset as $\mathcal{D}_t$ and $\mathcal{D}_{test}^k$, respectively, we employed the test set of another dataset relatively close to $\mathcal{D}_t$ as $\mathcal{D}_{test}^u$ in Setting 2. Adopting the experiment settings in [41] and [20], we used the entire classes of a dataset as KKCs for CIFAR10 & CIFAR100. For UUC dataset, TinyImageNet, LSUN [42], and iSUN [39] were selected. TinyImageNet and LSUN consists of 10,000 test samples each, where the samples in each dataset were resized (R) or cropped (C) into the size $32 \times 32$. The iSUN dataset has 8,925 test samples and they were also resized into the size of $32 \times 32$. The modified datasets can be obtained in the Github repository of [20].

## 4.2   Training Details

**Network Selection.** For $f$, we employed the Wide-ResNet (WRN) [43] and then used its penultimate layer $f(\mathbf{x}) \in \mathbb{R}^n$ for the latent feature vector of each input sample $\mathbf{x}$. For CIFAR10 and TinyImageNet, we used WRN 40-2 with a dropout rate of 0.3, where WRN 28-10 was employed for CIFAR100 with the same dropout rate. For SVHN, we used WRN 16-4 with a dropout rate of 0.4. Such network selection was determined by referring the experiments in [11,43].

**Table 1.** Comparison with the previous BCR methods in the first setting.

| Experiments | Accuracy (↑) | AUROC (↑) | OSCR (↑) |
|---|---|---|---|
| | Objectosphere/Uniformity/ Energy/Class-inclusion (Ours) | | |
| SVHN | 0.968/0.966/0.972/<u>0.974</u> | 0.935/0.927/0.911/<u>0.956</u> | 0.813/0.793/0.774/<u>0.854</u> |
| CIFAR10 | 0.964/0.964/0.956/<u>0.973</u> | 0.942/0.923/0.933/<u>0.948</u> | 0.851/0.814/0.80/<u>0.870</u> |
| CIFAR+10 | 0.958/0.969/0.949/<u>0.976</u> | 0.945/0.950/0.936/<u>0.961</u> | 0.839/0.867/0.808/<u>0.881</u> |
| CIFAR+50 | | 0.944/0.942/0.937/<u>0.957</u> | 0.837/0.837/0.808/<u>0.865</u> |
| TinyImageNet | 0.778/0.779/0.715/<u>0.802</u> | 0.755/0.771/0.727/<u>0.785</u> | 0.484/0.488/0.357/<u>0.493</u> |

**Parameters.** For the entire BCR methods, we set the mini-batch sizes of KKC training samples and KUC samples to 128. We kept $\lambda$ as a constant during training, *i.e.*, each $f$ was trained with the BCR method *from scratch*. To select hyperparameters and margin parameters of the previous regularization methods, we followed the official implementations[1,2,3]. For SVHN, CIFAR10, CIFAR100,

---

[1]  https://github.com/Vastlab/Reducing-Network-Agnostophobia.

[2]  https://github.com/hendrycks/outlier-exposure.

[3]  https://github.com/wetliu/energy_ood.

**Table 2.** Comparison with the previous methods in the second setting. The corresponding classification accuracy values are reported in the first column.

| $\mathcal{D}_t/\mathcal{D}_{test}^k$ | $\mathcal{D}_{test}^u$ | AUROC (↑) | OSCR (↑) |
|---|---|---|---|
| | | Objectosphere/Uniformity/Energy/Class-inclusion (Ours) | |
| CIFAR10 0.940/0.939/0.925/<u>0.947</u> | ImageNet-C | 0.988/0.986/0.981/<u>0.989</u> | 0.929/0.928/0.894/<u>0.932</u> |
| | ImageNet-R | 0.979/0.984/0.972/<u>0.984</u> | 0.923/0.926/0.886/<u>0.927</u> |
| | LSUN-C | <u>0.994</u>/0.990/0.989/0.993 | 0.938/0.931/0.904/<u>0.940</u> |
| | LSUN-R | 0.985/0.988/0.984/<u>0.990</u> | 0.928/0.931/0.897/<u>0.935</u> |
| | iSUN | 0.985/0.989/0.984/ <u>0.991</u> | 0.928/0.932/0.896/<u>0.936</u> |
| | **Average** | 0.986/0.987/0.982/<u>0.989</u> | 0.929/0.930/0.895/<u>0.934</u> |
| CIFAR100 0.727/0.735/0.705/<u>0.779</u> | ImageNet-C | 0.886/0.929/0.925/<u>0.930</u> | 0.641/0.686/0.652/<u>0.696</u> |
| | ImageNet-R | 0.815/0.910/<u>0.934</u>/0.920 | 0.572/0.674/0.658/<u>0.687</u> |
| | LSUN-C | <u>0.967</u>/0.931/0.901/0.965 | 0.685/0.680/0.643/<u>0.751</u> |
| | LSUN-R | 0.844/0.930/<u>0.959</u>/0.945 | 0.608/0.695/0.684/<u>0.731</u> |
| | iSUN | 0.842/0.923/0.954/<u>0.955</u> | 0.603/0.689/0.680/<u>0.734</u> |
| | **Average** | 0.871/0.925/0.935/<u>0.943</u> | 0.621/0.685/0.663/<u>0.720</u> |

and TinyImageNet, we trained the corresponding classifiers for 80, 100, 200, and 200 epochs, respectively, where we used the stochastic gradient descent for optimization. For SVHN and the other datasets, we used initial learning rates of 0.01 and 0.1, respectively, and a cosine learning rate decay [22]. We also used the learning rate warm-up strategy for the first 5 epochs of each training process.

### 4.3 Results

The OSR results of our proposed approach and the previous methods are reported in Tables 1 and 2. All the reported values were averaged over five randomized trials, by randomly sampling seeds, data splits of KKCs and UUCs, and class-wise anchors. In the tables, ↑ and ↓ indicate higher-better and lower-better measures, respectively, where underlined values present the best scores.

**Setting 1.** For the first setting, Table 1 compares our proposed BCR methods for distance-based classifiers with the previous approachs designed for Softmax classifiers. The results demonstrate that our proposed method obtained robust UUC rejection results, which were superior to the results of the previous approaches. It is noteworthy that our method achieved higher classification accuracy values, which were critical in acquiring better OSR results in terms of the OSCR measure, than the previous methods. Such results imply that the proposed framework effectively satisfies the two essential requirements described in Sect. 2.1, bounding open-space risk and ideally balancing it with empirical risk.

**Setting 2.** In Table 2, we present our experiment results of the second setting. When using the CIFAR10 and CIFAR100 datasets as KKC data, our approach achieved the highest closed-set classification accuracy, which is consistent with the experiment results of Setting 1. Furthermore, by averaging the AUROC and the OSCR values over the various UUC datasets, the table shows that our model outperformed the previous methods in the second setting.

**Average Runtime.** We conducted all the experiments with PyTorch and two GeForce RTX 3090 GPUs. At each trial in the CIFAR10 experiment of Setting 1, the running time of each training epoch took 28 s for our method, where its OSR evaluation required approximately 6.5 s. We observed that the other methods take similar running time at their training and inference phases.

### 4.4   Additional Experiments and Discussions

We further analyzed our BCR method by using various $\lambda$ in our loss function. Furthermore, we compared our method by formulating another baseline using the triplet loss [35]. Using the CIFAR10 and TinyImageNet experiments in Setting 1, we present the corresponding OSR results. We also conducted various additional experiments that can show the effectiveness of our proposed method.

*Selecting* $\lambda$. Conducting additional OSR experiments with $\lambda \in \{0.1, 0.5, 1, 5, 10\}$ in our loss function $\mathcal{L} = \mathcal{L}_{cf} + \lambda\mathcal{L}_{bg}$, Table 3 presents that our method provides robust OSR accuracy across a *wide range* of $\lambda$, *e.g.*, $\lambda \in [1, 5]$, which implies that users can flexibly select $\lambda$ in our method. Although such range may depend on datasets, users are not required to carefully adjust the $\lambda$ parameter. In additional experiments, $\lambda = 5$ yielded the best OSR results in the SVHN and CIFAR + $M$ experiments of Setting 1 and the CIFAR10 experiments of Setting 2, where $\lambda = 0.5$ showed the best results in the CIFAR100 experiments. Such empirical results implies that a lower $\lambda$ value can be better when handling more KKCs.

**Table 3.** OSR results with various $\lambda$ in our class-inclusion and the triplet losses. In each cell, the results are presented in the form of (Accuracy/AUROC/OSCR).

| Parameter $\lambda$ | CIFAR10 | | TinyImageNet | |
|---|---|---|---|---|
| | Class inclusion | Triplet | Class inclusion | Triplet |
| 0 (Vanilla) | 0.963/0.759/0.472 | – | 0.785/0.631/0.308 | – |
| 0.1 | 0.966/0.899/0.742 | 0.963/0.820/0.537 | 0.790/0.765/0.442 | 0.787/0.746/0.431 |
| 0.5 | 0.967/0.928/0.810 | 0.968/0.842/0.572 | 0.794/0.775/0.464 | 0.785/0.729/0.426 |
| 1 | 0.973/0.936/0.840 | 0.966/0.860/0.628 | 0.802/0.785/0.493 | 0.793/0.714/0.423 |
| 5 | 0.973/0.948/0.870 | 0.965/0.872/0.628 | 0.798/0.783/0.480 | 0.785/0.707/0.360 |
| 10 | 0.968/0.947/0.863 | 0.958/0.856/0.597 | 0.787/0.701/0.361 | 0.738/0.637/0.220 |

*Triplet Loss.* We propose a distance-based BCR method suitable for the OSR problem, where the proposed method defines explicit class-wise boundaries and then increases the distance gap between KKC and KUC samples based on the boundaries. Another loss function that can separate KKC and KUC data in terms of such distance measure is the triplet loss, where the loss function has

**Table 4.** Comparison with the previous OSR methods (Macro-averaged F1 score).

| Experiments | Setting 1 | | | | Setting 2 | | | |
|---|---|---|---|---|---|---|---|---|
| | SVHN | CIFAR10 | CIFAR+10 | CIFAR+50 | ImageNet-C | ImageNet-R | LSUN-C | LSUN-R |
| Softmax [10] | 0.725 | 0.600 | 0.701 | 0.637 | 0.639 | 0.653 | 0.642 | 0.647 |
| Openmax [1] | 0.737 | 0.623 | 0.731 | 0.676 | 0.600 | 0.684 | 0.657 | 0.668 |
| CROSR [41] | 0.753 | 0.668 | 0.769 | 0.684 | 0.721 | 0.735 | 0.720 | 0.749 |
| CGDL [37] | 0.776 | 0.655 | 0.760 | 0.695 | 0.840 | 0.832 | 0.806 | 0.812 |
| AOSR [6] | 0.842 | 0.705 | 0.773 | 0.706 | 0.798 | 0.795 | 0.839 | 0.838 |
| **Ours** | 0.854 | 0.761 | 0.805 | 0.732 | 0.876 | 0.869 | 0.880 | 0.877 |

been widely employed to control the distances between latent feature vectors effectively. Therefore, we formulated a baseline distance-based BCR method by following the conventional definition of the triplet loss $\mathcal{L}_{tri}$, where we set class-wise anchors, KKC training data, and KUC data as anchors, positive samples, and negative samples, respectively. Since we observed that training classifiers solely based on the triplet loss $\mathcal{L} = \mathcal{L}_{tri}$ yields significantly worse OSR results in comparison with the regularization method $\mathcal{L} = \mathcal{L}_{cf} + \lambda\mathcal{L}_{tri}$, we employed $\mathcal{L}_{tri}$ as a regularization loss function for BCR. In Table 3, we reported experiment results by using the triplet loss as $\mathcal{L}_{bg}$. The results show that our proposed method (class-inclusion loss) outperforms the regularization method based on the triplet loss.

*Vanilla Distance-Based Classifiers.* To show the effectiveness of our method, we assessed the OSR performance of vanilla distance-based classifiers (trained solely based on $\mathcal{L}_{cf}$), where we present the results in the form of (Accuracy/AUROC/OSCR). In the CIFAR10 and TinyImageNet experiments of Setting 1, we obtained (0.962/0.757/0.470) and (0.785/0.629/0.315), respectively. In the CIFAR10 and CIFAR100 experiments of Setting 2, the OSR results averaged over the five UUC datasets in vanilla distance-based classifiers were (0.936/0.838/0.709) and (0.766/0.807/0.549), respectively. Comparing these results to the results in Tables 1 and 2, we show that our regularization strategy can significantly improve the OSR performance of distance-based classifiers.

*Ablation Study on Loss Terms.* Recall our loss function $\mathcal{L}_{cf} + \lambda(\mathcal{L}_{bg,k} + \mathcal{L}_{bg,u})$. As $\mathcal{L}_{bg,u}$ is essential for BCR by making KUC samples located outside explicit class-wise boundaries, we conducted an ablation study to investigate the necessity of $\mathcal{L}_{bg,k}$. In the absence of $\mathcal{L}_{bg,k}$, which additionally regularizes correctly classified KKC data, we obtained the result of (0.963/0.821/0.509) for the (Accuracy/AUROC/OSCR) measures in the CIFAR10 experiment of Setting 1, which is worse than our original result (0.973/0.948/0.870). This result implies that $\mathcal{L}_{bg,k}$ is necessary to increase the distance gap between KKC and KUC data.

Also, by designing $\mathcal{L}_{bg}$ based on the original HSC loss function (Eq. (7)), we obtained the result of (0.950/0.634/0.338) for (Accuracy/AUROC/OSCR) in the CIFAR10 experiment of Setting 1, which supports our hypothesis.

*Previous OSR Approaches.* We additionally compared our proposed approach to previous OSR methods, whose OSR results are already reported in [6,41]. For fair comparison, the entire methods presented in Table 4 (including ours) were implemented by using a VGG backbone and tested based on the codebase of (https://github.com/Anjin-Liu/Openset_Learning_AOSR). The table, which presents OSR results based on the macro-averaged F1 score measure, shows that our distance-based BCR approach can achieve robust OSR results via a simple inference process in standard classifier architectures.

**Table 5.** Comparison with the previous methods in the second setting by using ResNet-18. The corresponding classification accuracy values are reported in the first column.

| $\mathcal{D}_t/\mathcal{D}_{test}^k$ | $\mathcal{D}_{test}^u$ | AUROC (↑) | OSCR (↑) |
|---|---|---|---|
| | | Objectosphere/Uniformity/Energy / Class-inclusion (Ours) | |
| CIFAR10 0.937/0.949/0.933/<u>0.951</u> | ImageNet-CR | 0.982/0.979/0.983/<u>0.987</u> | 0.932/0.928/0.917/<u>0.941</u> |
| | ImageNet-RE | 0.977/0.982/0.975/<u>0.988</u> | 0.918/0.934/0.909/<u>0.945</u> |
| | LSUN-CR | 0.991/0.984/0.987/<u>0.993</u> | 0.934/0.935/0.919/<u>0.946</u> |
| | LSUN-RE | 0.987/0.987/0.986/<u>0.990</u> | 0.932/0.938/0.918/ <u>0.942</u> |
| | iSUN | 0.987/0.986/0.987/<u>0.994</u> | 0.932/0.938/0.919/<u>0.946</u> |
| | **Average** | 0.985/0.984/0.984/<u>0.991</u> | 0.930/0.935/0.916/<u>0.944</u> |

**Table 6.** Comparison with the previous BCR method in text classification experiments.

| $\mathcal{D}_t/\mathcal{D}_{test}^k$ | $\mathcal{D}_{test}^u$ | AUROC (↑) | AUPR (↑) | FPR95 (↓) | OSCR (↑) |
|---|---|---|---|---|---|
| | | Uniformity/Class-inclusion (Ours) | | | |
| 20 Newsgroups 0.719/<u>0.749</u> | Multi30k | 0.997/<u>0.997</u> | <u>0.998</u>/0.997 | <u>0.002</u>/0.010 | 0.715/<u>0.745</u> |
| | WMT16 | <u>0.997</u>/0.996 | <u>0.997</u>/0.995 | <u>0.010</u>/ 0.016 | 0.715/<u>0.742</u> |
| | IMDB | 0.805/<u>0.999</u> | 0.692/<u>0.999</u> | 0.367/ <u>0.003</u> | 0.585/<u>0.747</u> |
| | **Average** | 0.933/<u>0.997</u> | 0.896/<u>0.997</u> | 0.126/<u>0.010</u> | 0.672/<u>0.745</u> |

*ResNet-18 Architecture.* In our main experiments, we used the WRN architectures as feature extractors. To further investigate the effectiveness of our method, we used another standard classifier architecture, ResNet-18 [9]. In the first setting, we obtained the quantitative results of (0.963/0.945/0.844), (0.966/0.950/0.845), (0.967/0.945/0.848), and (0.971/0.947/ 0.850) for the regularization methods using the objectosphere [5], the uniformity [11], the energy [21], and our class-inclusion losses, respectively. In addition to the results, Table 5 shows quantitative results in the second setting, where the results imply that our method can outperform the previous BCR methods with ResNet-18, as we observed in the experiments using the WRN architectures.

*Text Classification.* To show that our proposed BCR method can be applicable in another domain, we compared our class-inclusion loss to the uniformity loss in text classification applications. For text classification, we used 20 Newsgroups and WikiText103 for KKCs and KUCs, respectively, and trained a simple GRU model [4] for $f$ as in [11]. As UUC sets, we used Multi30K, WMT16, and IMDB.

Since the margin parameters of the objectosphere and the energy losses selected for image classification cannot be suitable for the text classification tasks, we only tested the uniformity loss for comparison. In Table 6, we present the results, where we additionally reported the area under the precision-recall curve (AUPR) and the false-positive rate at 95% true-positive rate (FPR95) measures. As it outperformed the uniformity loss in image classification tasks, our method also showed significantly better OSR accuracy in text classification. We provide more training details of our text classification models in our supplementary materials.

## 5   Concluding Remarks

In this paper, we propose a novel BCR method to train open-set classifiers that can provide robust OSR results with a simple inference process. By employing distance-based classifiers with the principle of LDA, we designed a novel class-inclusion loss based on the principle of probability of inclusion, which effectively limits the feature space of KKC data in a class-wise manner and then regularizes KUC samples to be located far away from the limited class-wise spaces. Through our extensive experiments, we present that our method can achieve robust UUC rejection performance, while maintaining high closed-set classification accuracy. As this paper aims to improve the reliability of modern DNN-based classifiers, we hope our work to enhance reliability and robustness in various classification applications by providing a novel methodology of handling UUC samples.

**Acknowledgements.** This work was supported by Institute of Information & communications Technology Planning & Evaluation (IITP) grant funded by the Korea government (MSIT) (No. 2019-0-00075, Artificial Intelligence Graduate School Program (KAIST)) and the National Research Foundation of Korea (NRF) grants funded by the Korea government (MSIT) (No. NRF-2018M3E3A1057305 and No. NRF-2022R1A2B5B02001913).

## References

1. Bendale, A., Boult, T.E.: Towards open set deep networks. In: Proceedings of the IEEE Conference on Computer Vision and Pattern Recognition, pp. 1563–1572 (2016)
2. Boult, T.E., Cruz, S., Dhamija, A.R., Gunther, M., Henrydoss, J., Scheirer, W.J.: Learning and the unknown: surveying steps toward open world recognition. In: Proceedings of the AAAI Conference on Artificial Intelligence. vol. 33, pp. 9801–9807 (2019)
3. Cevikalp, H., Uzun, B., Köpüklü, O., Ozturk, G.: Deep compact polyhedral conic classifier for open and closed set recognition. Pattern Recogn. **119**, 108080 (2021)
4. Cho, K., Van Merriënboer, B., Gulcehre, C., Bahdanau, D., Bougares, F., Schwenk, H., Bengio, Y.: Learning phrase representations using RNN encoder-decoder for statistical machine translation. In: The 2014 Conference on Empirical Methods in Natural Language Processing (2014)
5. Dhamija, A.R., Günther, M., Boult, T.: Reducing network agnostophobia. Adv. Neural Inf. Process. Syst. **31**, 9157–9168 (2018)

6. Fang, Z., Lu, J., Liu, A., Liu, F., Zhang, G.: Learning bounds for open-set learning. In: International Conference on Machine Learning, pp. 3122–3132. PMLR (2021)
7. Geng, C., Huang, S.J., Chen, S.: Recent advances in open set recognition: a survey. IEEE Trans. Pattern Anal. Mach. Intell. **43**(10), 3614–3631 (2020)
8. He, K., Zhang, X., Ren, S., Sun, J.: Delving deep into rectifiers: surpassing human-level performance on imagenet classification. In: Proceedings of the IEEE International Conference on Computer Vision, pp. 1026–1034 (2015)
9. He, K., Zhang, X., Ren, S., Sun, J.: Deep residual learning for image recognition. In: Proceedings of the IEEE Conference on Computer Vision and Pattern Recognition, pp. 770–778 (2016)
10. Hendrycks, D., Gimpel, K.: A baseline for detecting misclassified and out-of-distribution examples in neural networks. In: International Conference on Learning Representations (2017)
11. Hendrycks, D., Mazeika, M., Dietterich, T.: Deep anomaly detection with outlier exposure. In: International Conference on Learning Representations (2019)
12. Izmailov, P., Kirichenko, P., Finzi, M., Wilson, A.G.: Semi-supervised learning with normalizing flows. In: International Conference on Machine Learning, pp. 4615–4630 (2020)
13. Jain, L.P., Scheirer, W.J., Boult, T.E.: Multi-class open set recognition using probability of inclusion. In: Fleet, D., Pajdla, T., Schiele, B., Tuytelaars, T. (eds.) ECCV 2014. LNCS, vol. 8691, pp. 393–409. Springer, Cham (2014). https://doi.org/10.1007/978-3-319-10578-9_26
14. Júnior, P.R.M., Boult, T.E., Wainer, J., Rocha, A.: Specialized support vector machines for open-set recognition. arXiv preprint arXiv:1606.03802 (2016)
15. Krizhevsky, A.: Learning multiple layers of features from tiny images (2009)
16. Le, Y., Yang, X.: Tiny imagenet visual recognition challenge. CS 231N, **7**(7), 3 (2015)
17. Lee, K., Lee, H., Lee, K., Shin, J.: Training confidence-calibrated classifiers for detecting out-of-distribution samples. In: International Conference on Learning Representations (2018)
18. Lee, K., Lee, K., Lee, H., Shin, J.: A simple unified framework for detecting out-of-distribution samples and adversarial attacks. Adv. Neural Inf. Process. Syst. **31**, 7167–7177 (2018)
19. Li, Y., Vasconcelos, N.: Background data resampling for outlier-aware classification. In: Proceedings of the IEEE/CVF Conference on Computer Vision and Pattern Recognition, pp. 13218–13227 (2020)
20. Liang, S., Li, Y., Srikant, R.: Enhancing the reliability of out-of-distribution image detection in neural networks. In: International Conference on Learning Representations (2018)
21. Liu, W., Wang, X., Owens, J., Li, Y.: Energy-based out-of-distribution detection. Adv. Neural Inf. Process. Syst. **33** (2020)
22. Loshchilov, I., Hutter, F.: Sgdr: Stochastic gradient descent with warm restarts. arXiv preprint arXiv:1608.03983 (2016)
23. Mensink, T., Verbeek, J., Perronnin, F., Csurka, G.: Metric learning for large scale image classification: generalizing to new classes at near-zero cost. In: Fitzgibbon, A., Lazebnik, S., Perona, P., Sato, Y., Schmid, C. (eds.) ECCV 2012. LNCS, vol. 7573, pp. 488–501. Springer, Heidelberg (2012). https://doi.org/10.1007/978-3-642-33709-3_35
24. Murphy, K.P.: Machine Larning: a Probabilistic Perspective. MIT Press (2012)

25. Neal, L., Olson, M., Fern, X., Wong, W.K., Li, F.: Open set learning with counterfactual images. In: Proceedings of the European Conference on Computer Vision (ECCV), pp. 613–628 (2018)
26. Netzer, Y., Wang, T., Coates, A., Bissacco, A., Wu, B., Ng, A.Y.: Reading digits in natural images with unsupervised feature learning (2011)
27. Oza, P., Patel, V.M.: C2ae: Class conditioned auto-encoder for open-set recognition. In: Proceedings of the IEEE Conference on Computer Vision and Pattern Recognition, pp. 2307–2316 (2019)
28. Paszke, A., et al.: Pytorch: An imperative style, high-performance deep learning library. In: Wallach, H., Larochelle, H., Beygelzimer, A., d'Alché-Buc, F., Fox, E., Garnett, R. (eds.) Advances in Neural Information Processing Systems, vol. 32, pp. 8024–8035. Curran Associates, Inc. (2019)
29. Rudd, E.M., Jain, L.P., Scheirer, W.J., Boult, T.E.: The extreme value machine. IEEE Trans. Pattern Anal. Mach. Intell. 40(3), 762–768 (2018)
30. Ruff, L., Vandermeulen, R.A., Franks, B.J., Müller, K.R., Kloft, M.: Rethinking assumptions in deep anomaly detection. arXiv preprint arXiv:2006.00339 (2020)
31. Russakovsky, O., Deng, J., Su, H., Krause, J., Satheesh, S., Ma, S., Huang, Z., Karpathy, A., Khosla, A., Bernstein, M., Berg, A.C., Fei-Fei, L.: ImageNet large scale visual recognition challenge. Int. J. Comput. Vis. (IJCV) 115(3), 211–252 (2015). https://doi.org/10.1007/s11263-015-0816-y
32. Scheirer, W.J.: Extreme value theory-based methods for visual recognition. Synth. Lect. Comput. Vis. 7(1), 1–131 (2017)
33. Scheirer, W.J., Jain, L.P., Boult, T.E.: Probability models for open set recognition. IEEE Trans. Pattern Anal. Mach. Intell. 36(11), 2317–2324 (2014)
34. Scheirer, W.J., de Rezende Rocha, A., Sapkota, A., Boult, T.E.: Toward open set recognition. IEEE Trans. Pattern Anal. Mach. Intell. 35(7), 1757–1772 (2013)
35. Schroff, F., Kalenichenko, D., Philbin, J.: Facenet: a unified embedding for face recognition and clustering. In: Proceedings of the IEEE Conference on Computer Vision and Pattern Recognition, pp. 815–823 (2015)
36. Snell, J., Swersky, K., Zemel, R.: Prototypical networks for few-shot learning. Adv. Neural Inf. Process. Syst. 30, 4080–4090 (2017)
37. Sun, X., Yang, Z., Zhang, C., Ling, K.V., Peng, G.: Conditional gaussian distribution learning for open set recognition. In: Proceedings of the IEEE/CVF Conference on Computer Vision and Pattern Recognition, pp. 13480–13489 (2020)
38. Wen, Y., Zhang, K., Li, Z., Qiao, Y.: A comprehensive study on center loss for deep face recognition. Int. J. Comput. Vis. 127(6), 668–683 (2019)
39. Xu, P., Ehinger, K.A., Zhang, Y., Finkelstein, A., Kulkarni, S.R., Xiao, J.: Turkergaze: crowdsourcing saliency with webcam based eye tracking. arXiv preprint arXiv:1504.06755 (2015)
40. Yang, H.M., Zhang, X.Y., Yin, F., Yang, Q., Liu, C.L.: Convolutional prototype network for open set recognition. IEEE Trans. Pattern Anal. Mach. Intell. (2020)
41. Yoshihashi, R., Shao, W., Kawakami, R., You, S., Iida, M., Naemura, T.: Classification-reconstruction learning for open-set recognition. In: Proceedings of the IEEE Conference on Computer Vision and Pattern Recognition, pp. 4016–4025 (2019)
42. Yu, F., Seff, A., Zhang, Y., Song, S., Funkhouser, T., Xiao, J.: LSUN: Construction of a large-scale image dataset using deep learning with humans in the loop. arXiv preprint arXiv:1506.03365 (2015)
43. Zagoruyko, S., Komodakis, N.: Wide residual networks. arXiv preprint arXiv:1605.07146 (2016)

# In Defense of Image Pre-Training
# for Spatiotemporal Recognition

Xianhang Li[1]([✉]), Huiyu Wang[2], Chen Wei[2], Jieru Mei[2], Alan Yuille[2],
Yuyin Zhou[1], and Cihang Xie[1]

[1] University of California, Santa Cruz, US
xli421@ucsc.edu
[2] Johns Hopkins University, Baltimore, US

**Abstract.** Image pre-training, the current de-facto paradigm for a wide
range of visual tasks, is generally less favored in the field of video recognition. By contrast, a common strategy is to directly train with spatiotemporal convolutional neural networks (CNNs) from scratch. Nonetheless,
interestingly, by taking a closer look at these from-scratch learned CNNs,
we note there exist certain 3D kernels that exhibit much stronger appearance modeling ability than others, arguably suggesting appearance information is already well disentangled in learning. Inspired by this observation, we hypothesize that the key to effectively leveraging image pre-
training lies in the decomposition of learning spatial and temporal features, and revisiting image pre-training as the appearance prior to initializing 3D kernels. In addition, we propose Spatial-Temporal Separable (STS) convolution, which explicitly splits the feature channels into
spatial and temporal groups, to further enable a more thorough decomposition of spatiotemporal features for fine-tuning 3D CNNs.

Our experiments show that simply replacing 3D convolution with STS
notably improves a wide range of 3D CNNs without increasing parameters and computation on both Kinetics-400 and Something-Something
V2. Moreover, this new training pipeline consistently achieves better
results on video recognition with significant speedup. For instance, we
achieve +0.6% top-1 of Slowfast on Kinetics-400 over the strong 256-
epoch 128-GPU baseline while fine-tuning for only 50 epochs with 4
GPUs. The code and models are available at https://github.com/UCSC-
VLAA/Image-Pretraining-for-Video.

**Keywords:** Video classification · Imagenet pre-training · 3d
convolution networks

## 1 Introduction

Deep convolutional neural networks (CNNs) pre-trained on large-scale datasets
(*e.g.*, ImageNet [8]) play a vital role in computer vision. The spatial feature rep-

**Supplementary Information** The online version contains supplementary material
available at https://doi.org/10.1007/978-3-031-19806-9_39.

S. Avidan et al. (Eds.): ECCV 2022, LNCS 13685, pp. 675–691, 2022.
https://doi.org/10.1007/978-3-031-19806-9_39

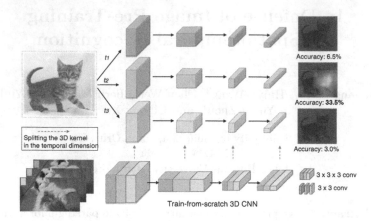

**Fig. 1. Motivation.** By splitting the 3D convolution into several 2D ones along the temporal dimension, we can easily transform a 3D CNN into 2D CNNs. Note the resting 2D parts in the 3D CNN remain the same. Interestingly, we note the 2D CNN along the center temporal direction attains much stronger linear-probing ImageNet accuracy than others, *i.e.*, 33.5% *vs.*6.5% or 3.0%.

resentations acquired by such models can then be transferred to the downstream task of interest via fine-tuning, leading to significant performance improvements especially for small target datasets. This *"pre-training then fine-tuning"* paradigm has gradually become the de-facto standard and established state-of-the-arts for a wide range of vision tasks, such as semantic segmentation [16,27] and object detection [13,29].

The *"Pre-Training then Fine-Tuning"* paradigm is readily used for image recognition, as the two stages usually share the same backbone. However, for video recognition, to model the temporal dynamics and build spatiotemporal features, recent research efforts are dedicated to building video-specific architectures (*e.g.*, Slowfast [12], X3D [11]). However, these structural changes prevent the model from getting image pre-training weights for *free*. One popular method to leverage image pre-training is to inflate 2D kernels pre-trained on ImageNet to 3D ones [4]. However, recent studies such as SlowFast and Multigrid [12,46] suggest that using ImageNet pre-training does not outperform (sometimes even produces worse results than) training from scratch. Hence, the field of video representation learning has witnessed a paradigm shift from pre-training then fine-tuning to training from scratch for today's advanced spatiotemporal 3D CNNs.

As directly training these 3D CNNs from scratch requires enormous computational resources [11,12,38–40,46], many recent research efforts are devoted to designing efficient operations [23,24,43] and architectures [39,40] for 3D video recognition. For instance, R2plus1D [39] is proposed to separate a 3D convolution into a 1D temporal convolution and a 2D spatial convolution. Tran al. propose CSN [38] which operates 3D convolution in the depth-wise manner.

This structural decomposition assumes that we should not treat space and time symmetrically. However, due to the end-to-end characteristic of training from scratch, the spatiotemporal features are still jointly learned in these 3D CNNs in an unconstrained manner. Thus, it remains unclear how spatial and temporal information is exploited in the network.

To better understand what these from-scratch trained 3D kernels learn, as shown in Fig. 1, we split the 3D convolution trained on Kinetics-400 dataset [4] using the CSN-50 network [38] into several 2D counterparts along the temporal dimension, and quantify the appearance modeling power by assessing the linear probing performance of these 2D CNNs on ImageNet-1K. Surprisingly, despite the domain gap between Kinetics-400 and ImageNet-1K, the 2D CNN along the center temporal direction (indicated by the orange branch in Fig. 1) still achieves a non-trivial linear probing performance, indicating its strong appearance modeling ability. Moreover, using the gradients returned from logits in a category [30], we plot the corresponding heat map that highlights the important regions in the image used for prediction, which are also highly correlated with the appearance information (yellow and blue regions).

This interesting phenomenon further inspires us to rethink the value of image pre-training for 3D spatiotemporal recognition—if 3D kernels have such strong appearance modeling power, then the spatial features pre-trained from 2D images should be beneficial for training 3D CNNs. As the appearance information is already well disentangled in 3D CNNs, we hypothesize that the key to harnessing image pre-training lies in properly decomposing the spatiotemporal features learned from 3D kernels into spatial and temporal parts. Based on this principle, we design a new pre-training and fine-tuning pipeline to facilitate feature decomposition. Specifically, image pre-training is leveraged as the appearance prior for only initiating the 2D counterpart along the center temporal direction of the 3D convolution where the strongest appearance modeling power lies. Then in the fine-tuning stage, we propose 3D Spatial-Temporal Separable (STS) convolution which explicitly splits the feature channels into spatial and temporal groups. The former group learns the static appearance while the latter focuses on learning dynamic motion features, thus enabling a more thorough decomposition of spatiotemporal features for fine-tuning 3D CNNs.

Compared with prior solutions which train 3D CNNs from scratch, our method not only enjoys a significant speedup, but also improves 3D video representation learning by carefully tackling the appearance prior from image pre-training models. We evaluate our method on a wide range of advanced 3D CNNs, including SlowFast [12], CSN [38], R2plus1D [39], and X3D [11]. Without using more computation or parameters, our method brings notable improvement on two popular video benchmarks Kinetics-400 [4] (+2.1%) and Something-Something V2 [14] (+5.3%). On Kinetics-400, our proposed training pipeline is at least 2× faster than training from scratch. The empirical analysis and design principles provided in our work will help researchers rethink the value of image pre-training and better understand its role in video recognition.

## 2    Related Works

**Pre-Training and Fine-Tuning for Video Classification.** Pre-training on a large-scale dataset and then fine-tuning on a minor dataset for downstream tasks has been widely used to resist overfitting and get state-of-the-art performance [4,13,16,27,29,31]. This paradigm has also been employed and continuously discussed in video classification [4,6]. Due to the nature of temporal variance in the video, two types of methods can be used to accelerate the learning of video classification algorithms: image-based pre-training and video-based pre-training.

**Image Pre-training.** Video classification models tend to consider both temporal and spatial information, and image pre-training can contribute to preserving spatial properties. There is active research about designing a well-performed video architecture based on a 2D ImageNet pre-trained backbone [17,32,35]. TSN [42] is proposed to sample video frames sparsely that boost 2D image model performance on video classification. Revising a 2D block [18,20,22–24,26,33] or inserting attention-style block [3,5,43,44,49,52] into a 2D model can enhance the ability of spatiotemporal representation. In order to make the 3D model converge faster, I3D [4] is proposed to initialize 3D convolution by inflating the 2D kernels. The recent success of the vision transformer [9,36] has also made significant progress in video classification [1,2,10,21,25], and using larger image datasets such as ImageNet-21K [8], JFT-300M [34] significantly improves the model performance. Compared to these approaches, we find that the improvement from such pre-training strategies are still not well explored in 3D CNNs. Secondly, instead of using larger datasets, we focus on an more efficient and fair setting.

**Efficient 3D Video Recognition.** Expanding a 2D image model is widely adopted in video recognition. First, extending the kernel into 3D increases the spatial and temporal receptive field and brings more parameters and computation [19,28,37,47]. Second, extending the temporal dimension into different resolutions further improves the performance. Recent work X3D [11] considers all these expansions in a video-oriented perspective. Similarly, the decomposition can perform either from the model or the data perspective. R2plus1D [39] is proposed to separate the spatiotemporal convolution. There are other approaches which also separate the 3D convolution along the channel dimension for efficiency [20,38]. From the data perspective, a two-stream architecture [6,12,31,48] is a representative method that divides the input video into appearance and motion, *e.g.*, optical flow [31] and temporal difference [18,41]. In this work, we focus on separating the learning process into efficient image pre-training and fine-tuning. Furthermore, we proposed that the Spatiaotemporal Separable 3D convolution further improves the performance.

## 3    Methodology

In this section, we first reveal that in spatiotemporal recognition, 3D kernels still exhibit strong appearance modeling ability (Sect. 3.1). This observation further inspires us to design a novel pre-training & fine-tuning paradigm for video recognition, where 2D image pre-training serves the appearance prior, guiding the further spatiotemporal fine-tuning process (Sect. 3.2). Finally in Sect. 3.3, we provide two general training settings to conduct a fair comparison with training from scratch.

**Table 1.** ImageNet-1K **Linear Probing** Top1 Accuracy. The weights come from the models trained from scratch on Kinetics-400. We fine tune the linear classification layer for 100 epochs on ImageNet-1K.

|                   | t1-CNN | t2-CNN   | t3-CNN |
| ----------------- | ------ | -------- | ------ |
| CSN-50 [38]       | 3.0    | **33.5** | 6.3    |
| X3D-S [11]        | 5.7    | **41.2** | 5.5    |
| R2plus1D-34 [39]  | 0.8    | **32.3** | 2.2    |
| Slowonly-50 [12]  | 18.3   | **45.1** | 17.6   |

## 3.1  Appearance Modeling in 3D Kernels

Despite numerous variants of 3D CNNs being proposed, it is unclear what these 3D kernels actually learn. In this paper, to better understand the properties of 3D kernels, we aim to examine the relationship between the 3D kernels and 2D appearance modeling by answering the following question: *Do 3D features equally model the 2D appearance across the temporal dimension?*

To answer this question, we propose to split the standard 3D convolution into several 2D ones along the temporal dimension, and quantify the appearance modeling of the 3D CNN by assessing the linear probing performance of these 2D CNNs instead. Specifically, we split a 3D convolution ($3 \times 3 \times 3$ or $3 \times 1 \times 1$) into three 2D convolutions ($3 \times 3$ or $1 \times 1$) at different time stamps t1, t2, t3, as shown in Fig. 1. We then evaluate these 2D CNNs on ImageNet-1k by freezing the weights and only fine-tuning the linear classification layer. As shown in Table 1, we examine four widely-used video classification models: 1) CSN-50 [38], 2) X3D-S [11], 3) R2plus1D-34 [39], 4) Slowonly-50 [12], all of which are trained from scratch on Kinetics-400. Surprisingly, though there is a domain gap between Kinetics-400 and ImageNet-1k, out of the three 2D CNNs, the middle one at t2 consistently achieves a non-trivial linear probing performance, whereas in the other two 2D networks at t1 and t3 time stamps, we observe severe performance degradation. This demonstrates that while spatiotemporal features are not equivalent in terms of appearance modeling, they do exhibit strong appearance modeling ability.

This phenomenon further motivates us to rethink the value of image pre-training in spatiotemporal recognition. Specifically, *can we achieve a better trade-off between performance and training efficiency?* Next, we will elaborate on how image pre-training can be leveraged to improve spatiotemporal recognition.

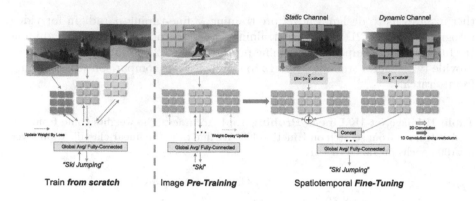

**Fig. 2. Overview of image pre-training and Spatiotemporal Fine-Tuning.** Left: training from scratch learns features in a joint manner. Right: decompose the learning into image pre-training and spatiotemporal fine-tuning.

## 3.2    Image Pre-Training and Spatiotemporal Fine-Tuning

The value of ImageNet pre-training is firstly challenged in He et al. [15]. Later, many recent studies have further demonstrated that compared with training from scratch, ImageNet pre-training even results in performance drop for video action recognition models [11,12,38,39]. However, as shown in Sect. 3.1, by closely examining these from-scratch learned 3D kernels, we find they still exhibit strong appearance modeling power. Based on this interesting observation, we hypothesize that image pre-training is indeed valuable for training video recognition models, when properly decomposing the learning of spatiotemporal features. To this end, we propose a novel pre-training and fine-tuning paradigm. As shown in Fig. 2, compared with the popular train-from-scratch pipeline which learns spatial and temporal features in a joint fashion, our proposed method thoroughly decomposes the spatial and temporal features via the following two steps: 1) image pre-training for appearance modeling, and 2) spatiotemporal fine-tuning.

**Image Pre-Training for Appearance Modeling.** Based on our observation in Sect. 3.1 that 3D kernels usually exhibit strong appearance ability along the center temporal direction, we propose to leverage image pre-training as the appearance prior by only initiating the middle kernel of the 3D convolution. As other parts of the 3D convolution do not have a strong relationship with appearance modeling, the rest of the weights will simply be updated by weight-decay regularization, as shown in Fig. 2. Leveraging the appearance prior from image pre-training plays a key role in facilitating the following fine-tuning stage since 1) it provides better initialization for the 3D kernels, and 2) it helps significantly reduce the fine-tuning schedule. Given that the appearance modeling is already well established, the 3D CNN only needs to focus on learning the temporal information.

**Table 2. Dataset settings.** Each video clip is an instance. Total training images are total number of instances multiply the number of input frames T.

| | # Instance | # Images (frames) | Training epochs | Total training images |
|---|---|---|---|---|
| ImageNet-1K | 1.28 M | 1.28 M | X | $X \times 1.28$ M |
| Kinetics-400 | 0.24 M | 68.89 M | Y | $Y \times T \times 0.24$ M |
| Something-Something V2 | 0.17 M | 18.98 M | Z | $Z \times T \times 0.17$ M |

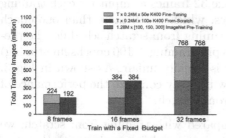
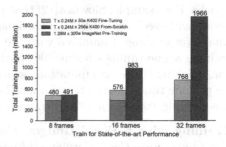

**Fig. 3. Computation budget towards different input frames.** Total numbers of images/frames seen during all training epochs, for pre-training + fine-tuning (blue + yellow bars) vs.from scratch (orange bars). In Fixed-Budget setting (left), we pre-train for 100, 150 and 300 epochs to match total computation. In the train-for-state-of-the-art setting (right), the pre-train is 300 epoch. In both setting, we fine-tune for 50 epochs.

**Spatiotemporal Fine-Tuning.** After acquiring the appearance prior from image pre-training, we then present a novel spatiotemporal fine-tuning method for a more thorough decomposition of spatiotemporal features. Specifically, as shown in Fig. 2, we propose 3D Spatiotemporal Separable (STS) convolution, which splits the 3D convolution along the output channel dimension into two groups, one for the static appearance modeling, and the other for dynamic motion modeling. The motion group builds the spatiotemporal feature by a 3D convolution, while the appearance group focuses on the spatial feature. In the appearance group, we divide the original 3D convolution along the temporal dimension into one 2D convolution (e.g., $3 \times 3$) and two 1D convolutions (e.g., $1 \times 9$ and $9 \times 1$), to enlarge the receptive field. The formal definition of STS can be found in the Appendix. The reason is that if we directly apply a 3D convolution on the spatial feature (e.g., $3 \times 3 \times 3$), the receptive field is limited to the middle 2D spatial convolution ($1 \times 3 \times 3$). By contrast, in the proposed STS, the 1D convolutions can build the spatial feature along each row/column as shown in Fig. 2, which enlarges the original receptive field in the 2D space ($3 \times 3$) to be ($3 \times 3 + 1 \times 9 + 9 \times 1$) without increasing parameters and computation. With a strong appearance prior, STS can significantly boost the performance during the fine-tuning stage benefiting from the more discriminative spatial features.

### 3.3   Training with a Fair Budget

Following the fair comparison setting [15] between pre-training & fine-tuning and training from scratch, we consider total training images as the condition for controlled experiments. We show the comparison on different datasets in Table 2. A typical training from scratch schedule on Kinetics-400 in recent advanced spatiotemporal 3D CNNs [11,12] involves $T \times 0.24M$ frames iterated for 256 epochs. For example, Slowfast[12] that take 32 frames as input for each training epoch will "see" over **7.68** million images, which is $\times 6$ more than one epoch ImageNet training. Compared with the training from scratch schedule, the pre-training & fine-tuning schedule (90 epochs pre-training + 100 epochs fine-tuning) consumes much less computation, which is usually unfair. As shown in Fig. 3, we provide two general settings about how to fairly compare the performance of pre-training & fine-tuning and training from scratch.

**Training with a Fixed Budget.** Compared with training from scratch, we aim to maximize the performance of pre-training and fine-tuning with the same amount of computation. In this setting, we allocate around half of the total training budget to image pre-training, and another half to spatial-temporal fine-tuning, as shown in Fig. 3. Surprisingly, we found that this simple strategy works well no matter the model consumes 8 frames, 16 frames, or 32 frames, according to our experiments.

**Training for State-of-the-art.** In this setting, we provide a more efficient training pipeline to match the previous state-of-the-art CNNs performance. Instead of scaling the image pre-training budget with respect to the total budget, we train our model with images for a long schedule (*e.g.*, 300 epochs) until convergence. As shown in Fig. 3, we then fine-tune our model with a fixed short schedule (50 epochs) for all frame settings. We notice that the total computation cost is still lower than training on videos from scratch but the performance can be significantly improved over a wide range of advanced 3D CNNs on Kinetics-400 (**+2.1%**) and SS-V2 (**+4.1%**).

## 4   Experiments and Results

**Datasets.** We choose ImageNet-1K [8] as our primary image pre-training dataset. It contains around 1.28 million images for training and $50K$ images for validation. We also compare different pre-training datasets in the ablation study, *e.g.*, Kinetics-400. Unless otherwise specified, our default pre-training dataset is ImageNet-1K. Then we fine-tune our models on widely-used Kinetics-400 (abbreviated as K400) [4] and Something-Something V2 (abbreviated as SS-V2) [14]. Kinetics-400 contains about $260K$ videos of 400 different human action categories. We use the training split ($240K$ videos) for training and the validation split ($20K$ videos) for evaluating different models. SS-V2 contains $220K$ videos of 174 predefined human-object interactions with everyday objects.

**Table 3. Comparing Top-1 Accuracy of Common 3D CNNs on K400.** Training time is measured in GPU hours on the same hardware and software implementation for all methods. Baseline performance is obtained by testing the released model. We pre-train all models for 300 epochs on ImageNet.

| | + Image Pre. & STS Conv | Pre-Train (hrs) | Fine-tune (hrs) | Total time | Speedup | K400 | Δ |
|---|---|---|---|---|---|---|---|
| Slowonly50-8f [12] | ✗ | – | 389 | 389 | ×1 | 74.9 | – |
| | ✔ | 182 | 76 | 258 | ×1.5 | 75.6 | +0.7 |
| Slowfast50 (4 × 16) [12] | ✗ | – | 696 | 696 | ×1 | 75.6 | – |
| | ✔ | 237 | 136 | 373 | ×1.9 | 76.2 | +0.6 |
| Slowfast50 (8 × 8) [12] | ✗ | – | 840 | 840 | ×1 | 76.9 | – |
| | ✔ | 237 | 164 | 401 | ×2.1 | 77.2 | +0.3 |
| R2plus1D34-8f [39] | ✗ | – | 778 | 778 | ×1 | 68.7 | – |
| | ✔ | 230 | 152 | 382 | ×2.0 | 76.2 | +7.5 |
| CSN50-32f [38] | ✗ | – | 1106 | 1106 | ×1 | 73.6 | – |
| | ✔ | 176 | 216 | 392 | ×2.8 | 76.7 | +3.1 |
| X3D-S-13f [11] | ✗ | – | 432 | 432 | ×1 | 73.2 | – |
| | ✔ | 121 | 144 | 265 | ×1.6 | 73.5 | +0.3 |

**Training.** We pre-train all models for 100, 150, 300 epochs, respectively, based on different computation budgets. In the 100 and 150 epochs schedule, the model is trained using SGD with a learning rate of 0.4, a momentum of 0.9, a weight decay of 0.0001, and a batch size of 1024. The learning schedule is cosine annealing with a 5-epoch warm-up, and the initial learning rate is 1e-6. For augmentation, we enable the RandAugment [7], Mixup [51], and Cutmix [50]. We only use label smoothing as regularization. In the 300 epochs setting, we follow the training recipe in [45]. In the next fine-tuning stage, we use a dense-sampling strategy for Kinetics-400 [11,12] and an n-segments based method sampling strategy for SS-V2 [24,42]. During training, random resize cropping is utilized for data augmentation, and the cropped region is resized to 224 × 224 for each frame. For K400, the batch size, initial learning rate, weight decay, and dropout rate are set as 128 or 64 (based on input frames), 0.02 or 0.01, 1e-4, and 0.5 respectively. For SS-V2, we change the learning rate to 0.1 and the batch size is 64. Unless otherwise specified, the networks are fine-tuned for 50 epochs using SGD.

**Inference.** For K400, following the common practice [11,12,43] we uniformly sample 10 clips from a video along its temporal axis. We scale the shorter spatial axis to 256 pixels for each clip and take 3 crops of 256 × 256 to cover the spatial dimensions. We average the softmax scores for prediction. For SS-V2, we only sample 1 clip based on the n-segments method and conduct the 3-crop testing following the common recipe in [20,24].

**Table 4. Comparison on Common 3D CNNs on SS-V2.** We show the comparison on training from scratch, image pre-training and applying STS convolution respectively. We use test resolution (T × 256 × 256) to measure GFLOPS.

| | Parameters | GFLOPs | Image Pre. | STS Conv | SS-V2 | Δ |
|---|---|---|---|---|---|---|
| | | | ✗ | ✗ | 58.4 | – |
| Slowonly50-8*f* [12] | 32.0M | 54.9 | ✔ | ✗ | 61.6 | +3.2 |
| | | | ✔ | ✔ | **62.7** | **+4.3** |
| | | | ✗ | ✗ | 49.9 | – |
| Slowfast50 (4 × 16)-32*f* [12] | 34.0M | 36.4 | ✔ | ✗ | 55.8 | +5.9 |
| | | | ✔ | ✔ | **57.2** | **+7.3** |
| | | | ✗ | ✗ | 59.1 | – |
| R2plus1D34-8*f* [39] | 63.6M | 114.8 | ✔ | ✗ | 62.3 | +3.2 |
| | | | ✔ | ✔ | **63.0** | **+3.9** |
| | | | ✗ | ✗ | 57.5 | – |
| CSN50-8*f* [38] | 12.7M | 26.6 | ✔ | ✗ | 60.4 | +2.9 |
| | | | ✔ | ✔ | **61.4** | **+4.0** |
| | | | ✗ | ✗ | 51.9 | – |
| X3D-S-8*f* [11] | 3.3M | 3.2 | ✔ | ✗ | 57.0 | +5.1 |
| | | | ✔ | ✔ | **58.3** | **+6.4** |

## 4.1   Comparison on Common 3D CNN Architectures

**Main Results on K400.** We first demonstrate the evaluation of common 3D CNNs on K400 in Table 3. Firstly, the image pre-training (denoted by **Image Pre.**) and the proposed STS (denoted by **STS Conv**) both improve the video classification accuracy on a wide range of advanced video models, including Slowonly [12], Slowfast [12], R2plus1D [39], CSN [38] and X3D [11], by an average of **2.1 %**. Note that all models are trained with the same pre-training and fine-tuning pipeline (300 epochs pre-training + 50 epochs fine-tuning) described in Sect. 3.3, except for X3D-S. Due to its extremely tiny characteristic we extend the fine-tuning epochs for X3D-S to 100. These results demonstrate the strong generalization ability of our proposed pre-training and fine-tuning pipeline. Secondly, regarding the training efficiency, our method is ×2 faster than training from scratch baseline on average. Note that to be as fair as possible, we take the pre-training time into account of the total training time. In addition, all methods compared in Table 3 use the same hardware and software implementation. More importantly, the training-from-scratch recipe usually includes a large batch size and long training schedule, which requires significant computation resources. For example, X3D-S [11], Slowfast [12] are trained on 128-GPU and R2plus1D-34 [39], CSN-50 [38] are trained on 64-GPU cluster. In our experiments, with our pre-training and fine-tuning pipeline, we can fine-tune the model with a much smaller batch size and achieve better results. Thus, our method requires significantly fewer computational resources. All results are obtained on a single 4-GPU machine.

**Main Results on SS-V2.** SS-V2 is relatively small, therefore training efficiency is not our goal on this dataset. Here we only use the fixed budget setting as described in Sect. 3.3 and fairly train all the methods in our machine within the same setting. We evaluate the temporal modeling ability of our proposed training pipeline and the STS convolution respectively over five common 3D video models in Table 4. First, SS-V2 is known as a temporal-related dataset. The appearance modeling is considered less important than temporal modeling [18, 23, 24]. It is interesting to see that the image pre-training and fine-tuning improve the training from scratch methods by a large margin of **4.1%**. The significant improvements demonstrate the superiority of our proposed training pipeline. Second, the STS convolution can replace any 3D convolution layer (*e.g.*, $3 \times 3 \times 3$ or $3 \times 1 \times 1$) without increasing parameters and computation. Upon image pre-training, using STS convolution can boost the performance by an average of **1.2%**, which clearly shows that the STS convolution is more suitable for temporal modeling. Equipped with both proposed methods, we in total improve the baseline methods by an average of **5.3%**, which indicates that the STS convolution benefits more from the proposed training pipeline.

**Table 5. ResNet3D architectures considered in our exploration experiments.** The backbone is ResNet50 [17]. Note that we set the temporal downsampling rate is 1 by default. *: to reduce computation and parameters, all the $3 \times 3 \times 3$ convolutions are channel-wise.

| layer name | output size | ResNet50-$3\times1\times1$ | ResNet50-$3\times3\times3$* |
|---|---|---|---|
| conv1 | T $\times$ 112 $\times$ 112 | $1 \times 7 \times 7$ or $3 \times 7 \times 7$, 64, stride $1 \times 2 \times 2$ | |
| pool1 | T $\times$ 56 $\times$ 56 | max, $1 \times 3 \times 3$, stride $1 \times 2 \times 2$ | |
| stage 1 | T $\times$ 56 $\times$ 56 | $\begin{bmatrix} 1\times1\times1,\ 256 \\ 1\times3\times3,\ 64 \\ 1\times1\times1,\ 256 \end{bmatrix} \times3$ | $\begin{bmatrix} 1\times1\times1,\ 256 \\ 3\times3\times3,\ 64 \\ 1\times1\times1,\ 256 \end{bmatrix} \times3$ |
| stage 2 | $T\times28\times 28$ | $\begin{bmatrix} 1\times1\times1,\ 512 \\ 1\times3\times3,\ 128 \\ 1\times1\times1,\ 512 \end{bmatrix} \times4$ | $\begin{bmatrix} 1\times1\times1,\ 512 \\ 3\times3\times3,\ 128 \\ 1\times1\times1,\ 512 \end{bmatrix} \times4$ |
| stage 3 | $T\times14 \times 14$ | $\begin{bmatrix} 3\times1\times1,\ 1024 \\ 1\times3\times3,\ 256 \\ 1\times1\times1,\ 1024 \end{bmatrix} \times6$ | $\begin{bmatrix} 1\times1\times1,\ 1024 \\ 3\times3\times3,\ 256 \\ 1\times1\times1,\ 1024 \end{bmatrix} \times6$ |
| stage 4 | $T\times 7\times 7$ | $\begin{bmatrix} 3\times1\times1,\ 2048 \\ 1\times3\times3,\ 512 \\ 1\times1\times1,\ 2048 \end{bmatrix} \times3$ | $\begin{bmatrix} 1\times1\times1,\ 2048 \\ 3\times3\times3,\ 512 \\ 1\times1\times1,\ 2048 \end{bmatrix} \times3$ |
| pool5 | $1 \times 1 \times 1$ | spatial-temporal avg pool, fc layer with softmax | |

## 5   Ablation Study

Next, we fairly perform an in-depth experimental analysis and complete ablation experiments on our proposed training pipeline and STS convolution. We use the fixed budget setting as default pipeline. All the from-scratch baselines are trained for 100 epochs. When evaluating our methods, we only fine-tune 50 epochs.

*Base architecture.* In general, 3D convolution can be divided into temporal 3D convolution and spatial-temporal 3D convolution. We chose two corresponding architectures to verify the generality and effectiveness of our method, presented in Table 5. Their backbone is ResNet 50 [17]. They are distinguished into ResNet50-3×1×1 and ResNet50-3×3×3 depending on whether the convolution of the core bottleneck block is $3 \times 1 \times 1$ or $3 \times 3 \times 3$. It is worth noting that all the 3D convolutions in ResNet50-3 × 3 × 3 are channel-wise to reduce the computation and the number of parameters. Following Slowfast and X3D [11,12], the temporal downsampling rate is always set to 1. Specifically, our model takes clips with a size of T × 224 × 224 where $T = \{8, 16, 32\}$ is the number of frames.

## 5.1 Ablation on Image Pre-Training

**Table 6. Effectiveness.** Ablation study on Image pre-training & fine-tuning and Spatiotemporal separable 3D convolution (STS). We use 8 frames as input and all the models are pre-trained on ImageNet-1K.

| ResNet50-3 ×1 × 1 | K400 | SS-V2 | Training budget | ResNet50-3 × 3 × 3 | K400 | SS-V2 | Training budget |
|---|---|---|---|---|---|---|---|
| From Scratch | 73.1 | 58.4 | 192$M$ | From Scratch | 70.7 | 57.5 | 192$M$ |
| Pre-train&Fine-tune | **74.9** | **61.6** | ×1.16 | Pre-train&Fine-tune | **74.3** | **60.4** | ×1.16 |
| + STS Conv | **75.0** | **62.7** | ×1.16 | + STS Conv | **74.7** | **61.4** | ×1.16 |

**Effectiveness.** We first validate the effectiveness of the proposed method on K400 and SS-V2 in Table 6. First, we control the total training budget to be close to from-scratch (×1.16). On the K400, ResNet50-3 × 1 × 1 trained with our pipeline outperform the from-scratch by **1.8%**. For ResNet50-3 × 3 × 3 it improves the baseline by **3.5%**. Under the tight training computation, image pre-training significantly improves the performance. It shows the importance of appearance modeling in video classification. In addition, replacing all the 3D convolution layer with STS convolution further improve the results. On the SS-V2, the proposed training pipeline can improve the accuracy by **3.2%** from **58.4%** to **61.6%** on ResNet50-3 × 1 × 1. The same-scale improvement of **2.9%** can be found on ResNet50-3 × 3 × 3. Moreover, on both backbones, STS convolution notably improve the pre-trained models by an average of **1.1%** All the results demonstrate that under the same training budget, image pre-training can remarkably boost performance, and the STS convolution can also benefit from the appearance modeling prior to further improve performance.

**Table 7. More frames *vs.*More image pre-training.** Following the fixed budget setting described in Sect. 3.3, we extend the pre-training epochs to match the total computation budget.

| ResNet50-**STS** **3 × 3 × 3** | Input Frames | Pre-Train | Fine-tune | Training budget | K400 Top1 |
|---|---|---|---|---|---|
| From Scratch | 8 | – | 192M | 192M | 71.0 |
| ImageNet Pre. | 8 | 128M | 96M | ×1.16 | **74.7** |
| From scratch | 16 | – | 384M | 384M | 73.5 |
| ImageNet Pre. | 16 | 192M | 192M | ×1 | **76.1** |
| From scratch | 32 | – | 768M | 768M | 74.4 |
| ImageNet Pre. | 32 | 384M | 384M | ×1 | **76.7** |

**More input frames *vs.*more image pre-training epochs.** In this experiment, we aim to compare the capacity of the pre-training schedule when scaling up to different input frames. We use the ResNet50-3 × 3 × 3 equipped with STS convolution as the backbone. To make sure our total computation is consistent, we extend the image pre-training epochs from 100 epochs to 150 or 300 for 16 frames and 32 frames. The fine-tuning epochs remain the same for all models (50 epochs). Surprisingly, this simple scaling works well for more input frames. As shown in Table 7, employing image pre-training improve performance by **3.7%**, **2.6%** and **2.4%** for 8, 16, and 32 frames, respectively. The stable performance gains demonstrate that our method can scale well over different input frames. Furthermore, these results may draw an important clue that why previous default pre-training pipeline does not work well: we should extend the pre-training schedule when our video models take more frames as input.

**Table 8.** Choice of pre-training dataset: imagenet *vs.*K400.

| ResNet50-STS 3 × 3 × 3 | Input Frames | Pre-Train | Fine-tune | Training budget | K400 Top1 |
|---|---|---|---|---|---|
| From Scratch | 8 | – | 192M | 192M | 71.0 |
| ImageNet Pre. | 8 | 128M | 96M | ×1.16 | **74.7** |
| K400/Image Pre. | 8 | 128M | 96M | ×1.16 | 73.4 |

| X3D-S | Input Frames | Pre-Train | Fine-tune | Training budget | K400 Top1 |
|---|---|---|---|---|---|
| From Scratch | 13 | – | 798M | 798M | 73.2 |
| ImageNet Pre. | 13 | 384M | 312M | ×0.87 | **73.5** |
| K400/Image Pre. | 13 | 384M | 312M | ×0.87 | 72.8 |

**Source of Image Pre-Training Dataset.** We next discuss the influence of the dataset used for pre-training. We conduct experiments on two different training budgets (100 epochs *vs.*256 epochs train from scratch). First, in the fixed budget setting, we use ResNet50-STS 3 × 3 × 3 as the backbone. Here we pre-train each frame of all videos in K400, and we match the total training computation with ImageNet by controlling the number of epochs, as shown in Table 8. The performance of the ImageNet pre-train model is better than K400-Image pre-train under the same pre-training setting (**74.7%** *vs.***73.4%**). The k400-image pre-train model also has notable improvement over training from scratch from **71.0%** to **73.4%**, proving the effectiveness of image pre-training. In the train for state-of-the-art setting, the results obtained by pre-training on K400-image are slightly lower than from-scratch by 0.5%. In both settings, the ImageNet pre-training is consistently better than the K400-image. We assume that the label of the K400-image is still an action label, which can lead to confusion. Hence, we choose ImageNet as our source of image pre-training dataset by default.

## 5.2   Ablation on Spatiotemporal Fine-Tuning

**Table 9.** Different initialization strategies.

| ResNet50-**3 × 1 × 1** | K400 | SS-V2 |
|---|---|---|
| Inflation | 74.5 | 61.8 |
| + STS Conv | **74.8** | **62.6** |
| Zero-Init | 74.9 | 61.6 |
| + STS Conv | **75.0** | **62.7** |

| ResNet50-**3 × 3 × 3** | K400 | SS-V2 |
|---|---|---|
| Inflation | 74.0 | 60.0 |
| + STS Conv | **74.6** | **61.7** |
| Zero-Init | 74.3 | 60.4 |
| + STS Conv | **74.7** | **61.4** |

| ResNet50-**3 × 3 × 3** | K400 | SS-V2 |
|---|---|---|
| (1/3, 1/3, 1/3) | 74.0 | 60.0 |
| (1/3, 1/3, 1/9) | 74.3 | 60.0 |
| (1/9, 1/3, 1/9) | 74.3 | 60.2 |
| (0, 1, 0) | **74.3** | **60.4** |

**Initialization Strategy.** Next, we explore how to initialize the model in the fine-tuning phase. Inflation averages the pre-trained 2D model parameters along the temporal dimension [4]. We can initialize the center kernel of 3D convolution with pre-trained weights named as zero-init. Remaining parts are zeros. As shown in Table 9, in most cases, the zero-init approach exceeds inflation. ResNet50-$3 \times 3 \times 3$ zero-init exceeds the inflation by **0.3%** on K400 and **0.2%** on SS-V2. ResNet50-$3 \times 1 \times 1$ zero-init outperforms the inflation by **0.4%** on K400 but slightly lower on SS-V2. These results suggest 3D CNNs prefer 2D image initialization. More importantly, our proposed STS convolution achieves a considerable improvement regardless of the initialization. For example, ResNet50-STS $3 \times 3 \times 3$ improves the inflation baseline by **0.6%** on K400 and **1.7%** on SS-V2. Compared with zero-init, it boosts the performance by **0.4%** on K400 and **1.0%** on SS-V2. Same scale improvement can be found on ResNet50-STS $3 \times 1 \times 1$. It indicates that STS convolution can be optimized very well using different initialization. The performance improvement of STS convolution comes more from the specific design. In the right table, we also evaluate different inflation rates, closer (*e.g.*, (1/9, 1/3, 1/9)) to zero-init rate works better. It also indicates that the initialization strategy is less important than training pipeline setting.

**Table 10.** Details of design in STS convolution.

| ResNet50-$3 \times 3 \times 3$ | ImageNet-1K | K400 | SS-V2 |
|---|---|---|---|
| Baseline | 76.6 | 74.3 | 60.4 |
| w/o splitting | 76.6 | 74.0 | 60.8 |
| w/ splitting | **77.1** | **74.7** | **61.4** |

| ResNet50-$3 \times 3 \times 3$ | ImageNet-1K | K400 | SS-V2 |
|---|---|---|---|
| 1:1 | 77.1 | **74.7** | 61.4 |
| 1:2 | 76.8 | 74.6 | **61.8** |
| 2:1 | **77.2** | 74.7 | 61.4 |

**Ablation on STS Convolution.** Next, we perform ablation on the STS convolution design. The experimental results are shown in Table 10. First of all, our baseline model is ResNet50-3 × 3 × 3. From the table on the left, we can see that the key factor in STS is whether to use splitting or not. Splitting operation utilizes all the weights in the original 3D convolution, increasing the spatial perception field. It can boost the video classification performance as same as image classification. With splitting operation, it improves the without reshaping counterpart on the ImageNet (+ 0.5%), K400 (+0.7%) and SS-V2 (+1.0%). On the right table, we examine how many channels should be divided. For example, ratio of 1 : 2 means 1/3 channels are used for appearance modeling. The results are very close on the K400. Thus we use 1 : 1 as the default ratio.

# 6  Conclusion

We argue that image pre-training has significant potential for 3D video recognition, and should be more commonly adopted since 1) image pre-training models which are widely and freely available, contain enriched appearance information for facilitating temporal reasoning 2) image pre-training enables a large speedup for existing 3D CNN training. Specifically, in this paper, we reveal that the key to exploiting image pre-training lies in properly decomposing the spatiotemporal features into spatial and temporal parts. Based on this principle, we design a new image pre-training and spatiotemporal fine-tuning strategy, which achieves notable performance improvements for a wide range of 3D CNNs on multiple video recognition tasks with significant speedup.

**Acknowledgement.** We thank Chao-yuan Wu and Zeyu Wang for their insightful comments and suggestions. This work is partially supported by ONR N00014-21-1-2812.

# References

1. Arnab, A., Dehghani, M., Heigold, G., Sun, C., Lučić, M., Schmid, C.: Vivit: a video vision transformer. In: ICCV, pp. 6836–6846 (2021)
2. Bertasius, G., Wang, H., Torresani, L.: Is space-time attention all you need for video understanding. In: ICML , vol. 2, no. 3, p. 4 (2021)
3. Cao, Y., Xu, J., Lin, S., Wei, F., Hu, H.: Gcnet: non-local networks meet squeeze-excitation networks and beyond. In: ICCVW (2019)
4. Carreira, J., Zisserman, A.: Quo vadis, action recognition? a new model and the kinetics dataset. In: CVPR, pp. 6299–6308 (2017)
5. Chen, Y., Rohrbach, M., Yan, Z., Shuicheng, Y., Feng, J., Kalantidis, Y.: Graph-based global reasoning networks. In: CVPR, pp. 433–442 (2019)
6. Christoph, R., Pinz, F.A.: Spatiotemporal residual networks for video action recognition. In: NeurIPS, pp. 3468–3476 (2016)
7. Cubuk, E.D., Zoph, B., Shlens, J., Le, Q.V.: Randaugment: practical automated data augmentation with a reduced search space. In: CVPRW, pp. 702–703 (2020)
8. Deng, J., Dong, W., Socher, R., Li, L.J., Li, K., Fei-Fei, L.: Imagenet: a large-scale hierarchical image database. In: CVPR, pp. 248–255 (2009)

9. Dosovitskiy, A., et al.: An image is worth 16 ×16 words: Transformers for image recognition at scale. In: ICLR (2021)
10. Fan, H., Xiong, B., Mangalam, K., Li, Y., Yan, Z., Malik, J., Feichtenhofer, C.: Multiscale vision transformers. In: ICCV (2021)
11. Feichtenhofer, C.: X3D: Expanding architectures for efficient video recognition. In: CVPR, pp. 203–213 (2020)
12. Feichtenhofer, C., Fan, H., Malik, J., He, K.: Slowfast networks for video recognition. In: ICCV, pp. 6202–6211 (2019)
13. Girshick, R.: Fast r-cnn. In: ICCV (2015)
14. Goyal, R., et al.: The something something video database for learning and evaluating visual common sense. In: ICCV, pp. 5842–5850 (2017)
15. He, K., Girshick, R., Dollár, P.: Rethinking imagenet pre-training. In: ICCV, pp. 4918–4927 (2019)
16. He, K., Gkioxari, G., Dollár, P., Girshick, R.: Mask r-CNN. In: ICCV (2017)
17. He, K., Zhang, X., Ren, S., Sun, J.: Deep residual learning for image recognition. In: CVPR, pp. 770–778 (2016)
18. Jiang, B., Wang, M., Gan, W., Wu, W., Yan, J.: Stm: Spatiotemporal and motion encoding for action recognition. In: ICCV, pp. 2000–2009 (2019)
19. Kondratyuk, D., et al.: Movinets: mobile video networks for efficient video recognition. In: CVPR, pp. 16020–16030 (2021)
20. Li, K., Li, X., Wang, Y., Wang, J., Qiao, Y.: CT-net: channel tensorization network for video classification. In: ICLR (2021)
21. Li, K., et al.: Uniformer: unified transformer for efficient spatiotemporal representation learning. In: ICLR (2022)
22. Li, X., Wang, Y., Zhou, Z., Qiao, Y.: Smallbignet: integrating core and contextual views for video classification. In: CVPR, pp. 1092–1101 (2020)
23. Li, Y., Ji, B., Shi, X., Zhang, J., Kang, B., Wang, L.: Tea: temporal excitation and aggregation for action recognition. In: CVPR, pp. 909–918 (2020)
24. Lin, J., Gan, C., Han, S.: Tsm: temporal shift module for efficient video understanding. In: ICCV, pp. 7083–7093 (2019)
25. Liu, Z., Ning, J., Cao, Y., Wei, Y., Zhang, Z., Lin, S., Hu, H.: Video swin transformer. arXiv (2021)
26. Liu, Z., et al.: Teinet: towards an efficient architecture for video recognition. In: AAAI, vol. 34, no. 07, pp. 11669–11676 (2020)
27. Long, J., Shelhamer, E., Darrell, T.: Fully convolutional networks for semantic segmentation. In: CVPR, pp. 3431–3440 (2015)
28. Qiu, Z., Yao, T., Mei, T.: Learning spatio-temporal representation with pseudo-3D residual networks. In: ICCV, pp. 5533–5541 (2017)
29. Ren, S., He, K., Girshick, R., Sun, J.: Faster r-CNN: towards real-time object detection with region proposal networks. In: NeurIPS (2015)
30. Selvaraju, R.R., Cogswell, M., Das, A., Vedantam, R., Parikh, D., Batra, D.: Gradcam: visual explanations from deep networks via gradient-based localization. In: ICCV, pp. 618–626 (2017)
31. Simonyan, K., Zisserman, A.: Two-stream convolutional networks for action recognition in videos. In: NeurIPS (2014)
32. Simonyan, K., Zisserman, A.: Very deep convolutional networks for large-scale image recognition. In: ICLR (2015)
33. Sudhakaran, S., Escalera, S., Lanz, O.: Gate-shift networks for video action recognition. In: CVPR, pp. 1102–1111 (2020)
34. Sun, C., Shrivastava, A., Singh, S., Gupta, A.: Revisiting unreasonable effectiveness of data in deep learning era. In: ICCV, pp. 843–852 (2017)

35. Szegedy, C., et al.: Going deeper with convolutions. In: CVPR (2015)
36. Touvron, H., Cord, M., Douze, M., Massa, F., Sablayrolles, A., Jégou, H.: Training data-efficient image transformers & distillation through attention. In: ICML, pp. 10347–10357 (2021)
37. Tran, D., Bourdev, L., Fergus, R., Torresani, L., Paluri, M.: Learning spatiotemporal features with 3D convolutional networks. In: ICCV, pp. 4489–4497 (2015)
38. Tran, D., Wang, H., Torresani, L., Feiszli, M.: Video classification with channel-separated convolutional networks. In: ICCV, pp. 5552–5561 (2019)
39. Tran, D., Wang, H., Torresani, L., Ray, J., LeCun, Y., Paluri, M.: A closer look at spatiotemporal convolutions for action recognition. In: CVPR, pp. 6450–6459 (2018)
40. Wang, H., Tran, D., Torresani, L., Feiszli, M.: Video modeling with correlation networks. In: CVPR, pp. 352–361 (2020)
41. Wang, L., Tong, Z., Ji, B., Wu, G.: Tdn: Temporal difference networks for efficient action recognition. In: CVPR, pp. 1895–1904 (2021)
42. Wang, L., Xiong, Y., Wang, Z., Qiao, Yu., Lin, D., Tang, X., Van Gool, L.: Temporal segment networks: towards good practices for deep action recognition. In: Leibe, B., Matas, J., Sebe, N., Welling, M. (eds.) ECCV 2016. LNCS, vol. 9912, pp. 20–36. Springer, Cham (2016). https://doi.org/10.1007/978-3-319-46484-8_2
43. Wang, X., Girshick, R., Gupta, A., He, K.: Non-local neural networks. In: CVPR, pp. 7794–7803 (2018)
44. Wang, X., Gupta, A.: Videos as space-time region graphs. In: Proceedings of the European Conference on Computer Vision (ECCV), pp. 399–417 (2018)
45. Wightman, R., Touvron, H., Jégou, H.: Resnet strikes back: an improved training procedure in timm. arXiv (2021)
46. Wu, C.Y., Girshick, R., He, K., Feichtenhofer, C., Krahenbuhl, P.: A multigrid method for efficiently training video models. In: CVPR, pp. 153–162 (2020)
47. Xie, S., Sun, C., Huang, J., Tu, Z., Murphy, K.: Rethinking spatiotemporal feature learning: Speed-accuracy trade-offs in video classification. In: Proceedings of the European Conference on Computer Vision (ECCV), pp. 305–321 (2018)
48. Yang, C., Xu, Y., Shi, J., Dai, B., Zhou, B.: Temporal pyramid network for action recognition. In: CVPR, pp. 591–600 (2020)
49. Yin, M., Yao, Z., Cao, Y., Li, X., Zhang, Z., Lin, S., Hu, H.: Disentangled non-local neural networks. In: Vedaldi, A., Bischof, H., Brox, T., Frahm, J.-M. (eds.) ECCV 2020. LNCS, vol. 12360, pp. 191–207. Springer, Cham (2020). https://doi.org/10.1007/978-3-030-58555-6_12
50. Yun, S., Han, D., Oh, S.J., Chun, S., Choe, J., Yoo, Y.: Cutmix: regularization strategy to train strong classifiers with localizable features. In: ICCV, pp. 6023–6032 (2019)
51. Zhang, H., Cisse, M., Dauphin, Y.N., Lopez-Paz, D.: Mixup: beyond empirical risk minimization. In: ICLR (2018)
52. Zhou, B., Andonian, A., Oliva, A., Torralba, A.: Temporal relational reasoning in videos. In: Proceedings of the European Conference on Computer Vision (ECCV), pp. 803–818 (2018)

# Augmenting Deep Classifiers with Polynomial Neural Networks

Grigorios G. Chrysos[1], Markos Georgopoulos[2]([⊠]), Jiankang Deng[3],
Jean Kossaifi[4], Yannis Panagakis[5], and Anima Anandkumar[4]

[1] EPFL, Ecublens, Switzerland
grigorios.chrysos@epfl.ch
[2] Imperial College London, London, UK
m.georgopoulos@imperial.ac.uk
[3] Huawei, Shenzhen, China
[4] NVIDIA, California, USA
[5] University of Athens, Zografou, Greece

**Abstract.** Deep neural networks have been the driving force behind the
success in classification tasks, e.g., object and audio recognition. Impressive results and generalization have been achieved by a variety of recently
proposed architectures, the majority of which are seemingly disconnected.
In this work, we cast the study of deep classifiers under a unifying framework. In particular, we express state-of-the-art architectures (e.g., residual and non-local networks) in the form of different degree polynomials
of the input. Our framework provides insights on the inductive biases of
each model and enables natural extensions building upon their polynomial nature. The efficacy of the proposed models is evaluated on standard
image and audio classification benchmarks. The expressivity of the proposed models is highlighted both in terms of increased model performance
as well as model compression. Lastly, the extensions allowed by this taxonomy showcase benefits in the presence of limited data and long-tailed data
distributions. We expect this taxonomy to provide links between existing domain-specific architectures. The source code is available at https://
github.com/grigorisg9gr/polynomials-for-augmenting-NNs.

**Keywords:** Polynomial neural networks · Tensor decompositions ·
Polynomial expansions · Classification

## 1 Introduction

The unprecedented performance of AlexNet [37] in ImageNet classification [52]
led to the resurgence of research in the field of neural networks. Since then, an

---

G.G. Chrysos and M. Georgopoulos—Equal contribution

**Supplementary Information** The online version contains supplementary material
available at https://doi.org/10.1007/978-3-031-19806-9_40.

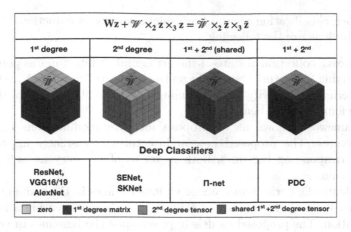

$$\mathbf{W}z + \mathscr{W} \times_2 z \times_3 z = \tilde{\mathscr{W}} \times_2 \tilde{z} \times_3 \tilde{z}$$

| 1st degree | 2nd degree | 1st + 2nd (shared) | 1st + 2nd |
|---|---|---|---|

**Deep Classifiers**

| ResNet, VGG16/19 AlexNet | SENet, SKNet | Π-net | PDC |
|---|---|---|---|

zero   ■ 1st degree matrix   ■ 2nd degree tensor   ■ shared 1st +2nd degree tensor

**Fig. 1.** Parameter interactions for different degrees of polynomials. For visualization purpose we assume a second-degree expansion, where we have folded the learnable parameters into a tensor $\tilde{\mathcal{W}}$ and the input is vectorized. The equation on the top is the second-degree polynomial in a tensor-format, while the $\tilde{z}$ is a padded version of $z$. Notice that first-degree polynomials [24,37,55] have zeros in a large part of the tensor $\tilde{\mathcal{W}}$, while similarly second-degree polynomials [27,38] have the matrices connected to first-order interactions zero. On the contrary, $\Pi$−nets along with the proposed PDC capture both interactions. Importantly, we illustrate how PDC learns a more expressive model without the enforced sharing of the $\Pi$−net. The notation of mode-$m$ product along with the derivation is conducted in sect. B (supplementary).

extensive corpus of papers has been devoted to improving classification performance by modifying the architecture of the neural network. However, only a handful (of seemingly disconnected) architectures, such as ResNet [24] or non-local neural networks [62], have demonstrated impressive generalization across different tasks (e.g., [72]), domains (e.g., [65]) and modalities (e.g., [33]). This phenomenon can be attributed to the challenging nature of devising a network and the lack of understanding regarding the assumptions that come with its design, i.e., its inductive bias.

Demystifying the success of deep neural architectures is of paramount importance. In particular, significant effort has been devoted to the study of neural architectures, e.g., depth versus width of the neural network [19,49] and the effect of residual connections on the training of the network [20,24,28]. In this work, we offer a principled approach to study state-of-the-art classifiers as polynomial expansions. We show that polynomials have been a recurring theme in numerous classifiers and interpret their design choices under a unifying framework.

The proposed framework provides a taxonomy for a collection of deep classifiers, e.g., a non-local neural network is a third-degree polynomial and ResNet is a first-degree polynomial. Thus, we provide an intuitive way to study and extend existing networks as visualized in Fig. 1, as well as interpret their gap in performance. Lastly, we design extensions on existing methods and show that we can improve their classification accuracy or achieve parameter reduction. Concretely, our contributions are the following:

- We express a collection of state-of-the-art neural architectures as polynomials. Our unifying framework sheds light on the inductive bias of each architecture. We experimentally verify the performance of different methods of the taxonomy on four standard benchmarks.
- Our framework allows us to propose intuitive modifications on existing architectures. The proposed new architectures consistently improve upon their corresponding baselines, both in terms of accuracy as well as model compression.
- We evaluate the performance under various changes in the training distribution, i.e., limiting the number of samples per class or creating a long-tailed distribution. The proposed models improve upon the baselines in both cases.
- We release the code as open source to enable the reproduction of our results.

## 2    Fundamentals on Polynomial Expansions

In this section, we provide the notation and an intuitive explanation on how a polynomial expansion emerges on various types of variables.

**Notation:** Below, we symbolize matrices (vectors) with bold capital (lower) letters, e.g. $\boldsymbol{X}(\boldsymbol{x})$. A variable that can be either a matrix or a vector is denoted by $\boldsymbol{\cdot}$. Tensors are considered as the multidimensional equivalent of matrices. Tensors are symbolized by calligraphic boldface letters e.g., $\boldsymbol{\mathcal{X}}$. The symbol $\overrightarrow{\mathbf{1}}$ denotes a vector of ones and $\boldsymbol{\mathcal{I}}$ is a third-order super-diagonal unit tensor. Due to constrained space, the detailed notation is on sect. A, while in Table 1 the core symbols are summarized.

**Table 1.** Symbols

| Symbol | Dimension (s) | Definition |
|--------|---------------|------------|
| $N$ | $\mathbb{N}$ | Degree of polynomial expansion |
| $k$ | $\mathbb{N}$ | Rank of the decompositions |
| $z$ | $\mathbb{R}^d$ | Vector-form input to the expansion |
| $\odot, *$ | - | Khatri-Rao product, Hadamard product |

**Polynomial Expansions:** Below, polynomials express a relationship between an input variable (e.g., a scalar $z$) and (learnable) coefficients; this relationship only involves the two core operations of addition and multiplication. When the input variable is in vector form, e.g., $\boldsymbol{z} \in \mathbb{R}^\delta$ with $\delta \in \mathbb{N}$, then the polynomial captures the relationships between the different elements of the input vector. The

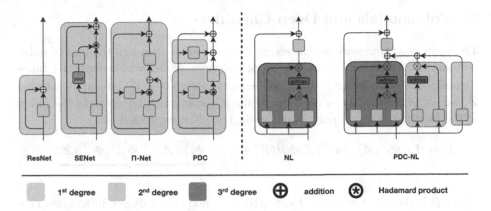

**Fig. 2.** Blocks (up to third-degree) from different architectures. The layers (i.e., blue boxes) denote any linear operation, e.g., a convolution or a fully-connected layer, depending on the architecture. From left to right, the degree of the polynomial is increasing. Our framework enables also to complete the missing terms of the polynomial (i.e., PDC-NL versus NL).

input variable can also be a higher-dimensional structure, e.g., a matrix. This is frequently the case in computer vision, where one dimension can express spatial dimensions, while the other can express the features (channels). The polynomial can either capture the interactions across every element of the matrix with every other element, or it can have higher-order interactions between specific elements, e.g., the interactions of a row with each column.

**Relationship Between Polynomial Expansions and Tensors:** Multivariate polynomial expansions are intertwined with tensors. Specifically, the polynomial expansions of interest involve vector, matrix or tensor form as the input. Let us express the output $y \in \mathbb{R}$ as a $N^{\text{th}}$ degree polynomial expansion of a d-dimensional input $\boldsymbol{z} \in \mathbb{R}^d$:

$$
y = \beta + \sum_{i=1}^{d} w_i^{[1]} z_i + \sum_{i=1}^{d} \sum_{j=1}^{d} w_{i,j}^{[2]} z_i z_j + \ldots + \underbrace{\sum_{i=1}^{d} \cdots \sum_{j=1}^{d}}_{N \ sums} w_{i,\cdots,k}^{[N]} z_i \cdots z_k, \tag{1}
$$

where $\beta \in \mathbb{R}$ is the constant term, and the $w$ terms are the scaling parameters for every degree. Notice that $w^{[n]}$ for $n > 2$ depends on $n$ indices, thus it can be expressed as a tensor. Collecting those tensors, $\{\boldsymbol{\mathcal{W}}^{[n]} \in \mathbb{R}^{\overbrace{d \times \cdots \times d}^{n \ times}}\}_{n=1}^{N}$ represent learnable parameters in (1). Due to the constrained space this relationship is further quantified in sect. B.

# 3 Polynomials and Deep Classifiers

The proposed framework unifies recent deep classifiers through the lens of polynomials. We formalize the framework of polynomials below. Formally, let functions $\boldsymbol{\Phi}_i^{[d]}(\hat{\boldsymbol{Z}})$ define a linear (or multi-linear) function over $\hat{\boldsymbol{Z}}$. The input variable $\hat{\boldsymbol{Z}}$ can either be a vector or a matrix, while $d$ declares the degree and $i$ the index of the function. Then, a polynomial of degree$-N$ is expressed as:

$$\hat{\boldsymbol{Y}} = \hat{\boldsymbol{\beta}} + \boldsymbol{\Phi}_1^{[1]}(\hat{\boldsymbol{Z}}) + \boldsymbol{\Phi}_1^{[2]}(\hat{\boldsymbol{Z}})\boldsymbol{\Phi}_2^{[2]}(\hat{\boldsymbol{Z}}) + \ldots + \underbrace{\boldsymbol{\Phi}_1^{[N]}(\hat{\boldsymbol{Z}})\ldots\boldsymbol{\Phi}_{N-1}^{[N]}\boldsymbol{\Phi}_N^{[N]}(\hat{\boldsymbol{Z}})}_{\text{N terms}} \quad (2)$$

where $\hat{\boldsymbol{\beta}}$ is the constant term. Evidently, each additional degree introduces new parameters that can grow up exponentially with respect to the degree. However, we posit that this introduces a needed inductive bias on the method. In addition, if reduced parameters are required, this can be achieved by using low-rank assumptions or by sharing parameters across different degrees.

Using the formulation in (2), we exhibit how well-established methods can be formulated as polynomials. We present a taxonomy of classifiers based on the degree of the polynomial. In particular, we present first, second, third and higher-degree polynomial expansions. For modeling purposes, we focus on the core block of each architecture, while ignoring any activation functions.

**First-degree polynomials** include the majority of the feed-forward networks, such as AlexNet [37], VGG [55]. Specifically, the networks that include stacked linear operations (fully-connected or convolutional layers) but do not include any matrix or elementwise multiplication of the representations fit in this category. Such networks can be expressed in the form $\hat{\boldsymbol{Y}} = \boldsymbol{C}\hat{\boldsymbol{Z}} + \hat{\boldsymbol{\beta}}$, where the weight matrix $\boldsymbol{C}$ is a learnable parameter. A special case is ResNet [24]. The idea is to introduce shortcut connections that enable residual learning. Notation-wise this is a re-parametrization of the weight matrix $\boldsymbol{C}$ as $\hat{\boldsymbol{Y}}_r = (\boldsymbol{I} + \boldsymbol{C})\hat{\boldsymbol{Z}} + \hat{\boldsymbol{\beta}}$ where $\boldsymbol{I}$ is an identity matrix. Thus, $\boldsymbol{\Phi}_1^{[1]}(\hat{\boldsymbol{Z}}) = (\boldsymbol{I} + \boldsymbol{C})\hat{\boldsymbol{Z}}$.

**Second-degree polynomials** model self-interactions, i.e., they can selectively maximize the related inputs through second-order interactions. Often the interactions emerge in a particular dimension, e.g., correlations of the channels only, based on the particular application.

One special case of the second-degree polynomial is the *Squeeze-and-excitation networks (SENet)* [27]. The motivation lies in improving the channel-wise interactions, since there is already a strong inductive bias for the spatial interactions through convolutional layers. Notation-wise, the squeeze-and-excitation block is expressed as:

$$\boldsymbol{Y}_s = (\boldsymbol{Z}\boldsymbol{C}_1) * r(p(\boldsymbol{Z}\boldsymbol{C}_1)\boldsymbol{C}_2), \quad (3)$$

where $*$ denotes the Hadamard product, $p$ is the global pooling function, $r$ is a function that replicates the channels in the spatial dimensions and $\boldsymbol{C}_1, \boldsymbol{C}_2$ are weight matrices with learnable parameters. For simplicity, we assume the input is a matrix instead of a tensor, i.e., $Z \in \mathbb{R}^{hw \times c}$ with $h$ the height, $w$ the width and $c$ the channels of the image. Then, $Y_s$ expresses a second-degree term with $\Phi_1^{[2]}(Z) = ZC_1$ and $\Phi_2^{[2]}(Z) = \frac{1}{hw}\mathcal{I} \times_3 (C_2^T C_1^T Z^T \overrightarrow{1})$ where $\mathcal{I}$ is a third-order super-diagonal unit tensor and $\overrightarrow{1}$ is a vector of ones.

The Squeeze-and-excitation block has been extended in the literature. The selective kernels networks [38] introduce a variant, where $Z$ is replaced with the transformed $ZU_1 + ZU_2$. The learnable parameters $U_1, U_2$ include different receptive fields. However, the degree of the polynomial remains the same, i.e., second-degree.

The *Factorized Bilinear Model* [39] aim to extend the linear transformations of a convolutional layer by modeling the pairwise feature interactions. In particular, every output $y_{fb} \in \mathbb{R}$ is expressed as the following expansion of the input $z \in \mathbb{R}^d$:

$$y_{fb} = c_1 + c_2^T z + z^T C_3^T C_3 z, \tag{4}$$

where $c_1 \in \mathbb{R}, c_2 \in \mathbb{R}^d, C_3 \in \mathbb{R}^{k \times d}$ are learnable parameters with $k \in \mathbb{N}$.

Arguably, a more general form of second-degree polynomial expansion is proposed in *SORT* [63]. The idea is to combine different branches with multiplicative interactions. SORT is expressed as:

$$Y_t = C_1 \hat{Z} + C_2 \hat{Z} + g((C_1 \hat{Z}) * (C_2 \hat{Z})), \tag{5}$$

where the $C_1, C_2$ are learnable parameters and $g$ an elementwise, differentiable function. When $C_1$ is identity, they $g$ is the elementwise square root function.

**Third-degree polynomials** can encode long-range dependencies that are not captured by local operators, such as convolutions. A popular framework in this category is the *non-local neural networks (NL)* [62]. The non-local block can be expressed as:

$$Y_n = (ZC_1 C_2 Z^T)ZC_3, \tag{6}$$

where the matrices $C_i$ for $i = 1, 2, 3$ are learnable parameters and $Z \in \mathbb{R}^{hw \times c}$ is the input. The third-degree term is then $\Phi_1^{[3]}(Z) = ZC_1$, $\Phi_2^{[3]}(Z) = C_2 Z^T$ and $\Phi_3^{[3]}(Z) = ZC_3$. Recently, *disentangled non-local networks (DNL)* [68] extends the formulation by including a second-degree term and the generated output is:

$$Y_{dn} = ((ZC_1 - \mu_q)(C_2 Z - \mu_k)^T + Zc_4 \overrightarrow{1}^T)ZC_3, \tag{7}$$

where $c_4$ is a weight vector, $\mu_q, \mu_k$ are the mean vectors of the keys and queries representations and $\overrightarrow{1} \in \mathbb{R}^{hw \times 1}$ a vector of ones. This translates to a new second-degree term with $\Phi_1^{[2]}(Z) = Zc_4 \overrightarrow{1}^T$ and $\Phi_2^{[2]}(Z) = ZC_3$.

**Higher-degree polynomials** can (virtually) approximate any smooth functions. The Weierstrass theorem [56] and its extension [45] (pg 19) guarantee that any smooth function can be approximated by a higher-degree polynomial.

A recently proposed framework that leverages high-degree polynomials to approximate functions is *Π-net* [9]. Each $\Pi-$net block is a polynomial expansion with a pre-determined degree. The learnable coefficients of the polynomial are represented with higher-order tensors. One of the drawbacks of this method is that the order of the tensor increases linearly with the degree, hence the parameters explode exponentially. To mitigate this issue, a coupled tensor decomposition that allows for sharing among the coefficients is utilized. Thus, the number of parameters is reduced significantly. Although the method is formulated as a complete polynomial, the proposed sharing of the coefficients suppresses its expressive power in favour of model compression. The model used for the classification can be expressed with the following recursive relationship:

$$x_n = \left(A_{[n]}^T z\right) * \left(S_{[n]}^T x_{n-1} + B_{[n]}^T b_{[n]}\right) + x_{n-1} \tag{8}$$

for an $N^{th}$−degree expansion order with $n = 2, \ldots, N$. The weight matrices $A_{[n]}, S_{[n]}, B_{[n]}$ and the weight vector $b$ are learnable parameters, while $x_1 = \left(A_{[1]}^T z\right) * \left(B_{[1]}^T b_{[1]}\right)$. The recursive equation can be used to express an arbitrary degree of expansion, while the weight matrices are shared across different degree terms. For instance, $A_{[2]}$ is shared by both first and second-degree terms when $N = 2$.

**From Blocks to Architecture:** The core blocks of different architectures, and their polynomial counterparts, are analyzed above. The final network (in each case) is obtained by concatenating the respective blocks in a cascade. That is, the output of the first block is used as the input for the next block and so on. Each block expresses a polynomial expansion, thus, the final architecture expresses a product of polynomials.

## 4    Novel Architectures Based on the Taxonomy

The taxonomy offers a new perspective on how to modify existing architectures in a principled way. We showcase how new architectures arise in a natural way by modifying the popular Non-local neural network and the recent $\Pi$−nets.

### 4.1    Higher-degree ResNet blocks

As shown in the previous section, the ResNet block is a first-degree polynomial. We can extend the polynomial expansion degree in order to enable higher-order correlations. A general $N^{th}$−degree polynomial is expressed as:

$$y = \sum_{n=1}^{N} \left(\mathcal{W}^{[n]} \prod_{j=2}^{n+1} \times_j z\right) + \beta \tag{9}$$

where $z \in \mathbb{R}^{\delta}$, $\times_m$ denotes the mode-m vector product, $\{\mathcal{W}^{[n]} \in \mathbb{R}^{o \times \prod_{m=1}^{n} \times_m \delta}\}_{n=1}^{N}$ are the tensor parameters. To reduce the learnable parameters, we assume a low-rank CP decomposition [34] on each tensor. By applying Lemma 1, we obtain:

$$y = \beta + C_{1,[1]}^T z + \left(C_{1,[2]}^T z\right) * \left(C_{2,[2]}^T z\right) + \ldots + \underbrace{\left(C_{1,[N]}^T z\right) * \ldots * \left(C_{N,[N]}^T z\right)}_{\text{N Hadamard products}}$$

$$\text{(10)}$$

where all $C_i$ are learnable parameters. Our proposed model in (10) is modular and can be designed for arbitrary polynomial degree. A schematic of (10) is depicted in Fig 3. The proposed model differentiates itself from (8) by not assuming any parameter sharing across the different degree terms.

## 4.2    Polynomial Non-local Blocks of Different Degrees

In this section, we demonstrate how the proposed taxonomy can be used to design a new architecture based on non-local blocks (NL). NL includes a third-degree term, while disentangled non-local network (DNL) includes both a third-degree and a second-degree term.

We begin by including an additional first-degree term with learnable weights. The formed PDC-$NL^{[3]}$ block is:

$$Y_{ours}^{[3]} = (ZC_1 C_2 Z^T)ZC_3 + ZC_4 ZC_5 + ZC_6 \tag{11}$$

where $C_i$ are learnable parameters. In practice, a softmax activation function is added for the second and third degree factors, similar to the baseline. Besides the first-degree term, the proposed model differentiates itself from DNL by removing the sharing between the factors of third and second degree (i.e., $C_3$ and $C_5$) as well as utilizing a full factor matrix instead of a vector for the latter (i.e., $C_4$). In our implementation the matrices $C_i$ matrices (for $i \neq 4$) compress the channels of the input by a factor of 4 for all models.

Building on (11), we propose to expand the PDC-$NL^{[3]}$ to a fourth degree polynomial expansion. We multiply the right hand side of (11) with a linear function with respect to the input $Z$. That is, the PDC-$NL^{[4]}$ block is:

$$Y_{ours}^{[4]} = Y_{ours}^{[3]} + Y_{ours}^{[3]} * r(p(ZC_7)C_8), \tag{12}$$

where the term $r(p(ZC_7)C_8)$ is similar to squeeze-and-excitation right hand side term. The new term captures the channel-wise correlations.

## 5    Experimental Evaluation

In this section, we study how the degree of the polynomial expansion affects the expressive power of the model. Our goal is to illustrate how the taxonomy enables improvements in strong-performing models with minimal and intuitive modifications. This approach should also shed light on the inductive bias of each model, as well as the reasons behind the gap in performance and model compression. Unless mentioned otherwise, the degree of the polynomial for each block is considered the second-degree expansion. The proposed variants are referred to as PDC. Experiments with higher-degree polynomials, which are denoted as PDC$^{[k]}$ for $k^{th}$ degree, are also conducted.

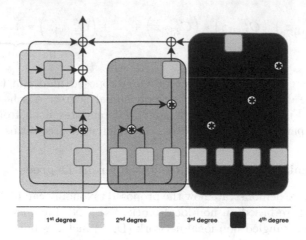

**Fig. 3.** Illustration of the modular nature of the propose polynomial expansion. Notice how we can trivially add new blocks in PDC to reach the pre-determined degree of the complete polynomial. The $N^{th}$-degree term includes $N + 1$ new layers (i.e., blue boxes), which might make it impractical to expand over the fourth-degree. In practice, higher-degree polynomials make the model more expressive and hence allow for reduced number of channels.

**Training Details:** For fair comparison all the aforementioned experiments have the same optimization-related hyper-parameters, e.g., the layer initialization. The training is run for 120 epochs with batch size 128 and the SGD optimizer is used. The initial learning rate is 0.1, while the learning rate is multiplied with a factor of 0.1 in epochs $40, 60, 80, 100$. Classification accuracy is utilized as the evaluation metric.

## 5.1    Image Classification with Residual Blocks

The standard benchmarks of CIFAR10 [36], CIFAR100 [35] and ImageNet [52] are utilized to evaluate our framework on image classification. To highlight the impact of the degree of the polynomial, we experiment with first (ResNet), second (SENet and $\Pi-$net[1]) as well as higher-degree polynomials. PDC relies on eq. 10; that is, we do not assume shared factor matrices across the different degree terms.

The first experiment is conducted on CIFAR100. The ResNet18 and the respective SENet are the baselines, while the $\Pi$-net-ResNet is the main comparison method. To exhibit the efficacy of PDC, we implement various versions: (a) PDC-channels is the variant that retains the same channels as the original ResNet18, (b) PDC-param has approximate the same parameters as the corresponding baselines, (c) PDC-comp has the least parameters that can achieve a

---

[1] The default $\Pi-$net block is designed as second-degree polynomial. Higher-degree blocks are denoted with the symbol $\cdot^{[k]}$.

performance similar to the ResNet18 (which is achieved by reducing the channels), (d) the PDC which is the variant that includes both reduced parameters and increased performance with respect to ResNet18, (e) the higher-degree variants of PDC[3] and PDC[4] that modify the PDC such that the degree of each respective block is three and four respectively (see Fig. 3).

The accuracy of each method is reported in Table 2. SENet improves upon the baseline of ResNet18, which verifies the benefit of second-degree correlations in the channels. This is further demonstrated with $\Pi$-net-ResNet that captures second-degree information on all dimensions and can achieve the same performance with reduced parameters. Our method can further reduce the parameters by 60% over ResNet18 and achieve the same accuracy. This can be attributed to the no-sharing scheme that enables more flexibility in the learned decompositions. The PDC-param further improves the accuracy by increasing the parameters, while the PDC-channels achieves the best accuracy by maintaining the same channels per residual block as ResNet18. The experiment is repeated with ResNet34 as the baseline. The accuracies in Table 9 demonstrate similar pattern, i.e., the parameters can be substantially reduced without sacrificing the accuracy. The results exhibit that the expressive power of PDC can allow it to be used both for compression and for improving the performance by maintaining the same number of parameters.

**Table 2.** Image classification on CIFAR100 with variants of ResNet18. The symbol 'p' denotes parameters.

| Model | #p $\times 10^6$ | Accuracy |
|---|---|---|
| ResNet18 | 11.2 | 0.756 |
| SENet | 11.6 | 0.760 |
| $\Pi$-net-ResNet | 6.1 | 0.760 |
| PDC-comp | **4.3** | 0.760 |
| PDC-channels | 19.2 | **0.773** |
| PDC-param | 11.4 | 0.770 |
| PDC | 8.0 | 0.765 |
| PDC[3] | 16.8 | 0.766 |
| PDC[4] | 28.0 | 0.771 |

**Table 3.** Image classification on CIFAR10. The symbol 'p' denotes parameters.

| Model | #p $\times 10^6$ | Accuracy |
|---|---|---|
| ResNet18 | 11.2 | 0.945 |
| SENet | 11.5 | 0.946 |
| $\Pi$-net-ResNet | 6.0 | 0.945 |
| PDC | 8.0 | **0.946** |
| PDC-comp | **4.3** | 0.945 |
| ResNet34 | 21.3 | 0.948 |
| $\Pi$-net-ResNet | 13.0 | **0.949** |
| PDC | **10.5** | 0.948 |

A similar experiment is conducted on CIFAR10. The same networks as above are used as baselines, i.e., ResNet18 and SENet. The methods $\Pi$-net-ResNet and the PDC variants are also implemented as above. The results in Table 3 verify that both the $\Pi$-net-ResNet and PDC-comp can compress substantially the number of parameters required while retaining the same accuracy. Importantly, our method achieves a parameter reduction of 28% over $\Pi$-net-ResNet.

The last experiment is conducted on ImageNet [13], which contains 1.28M training images and 50K validation images from 1000 classes. We follow the standard settings to train deep networks on the training set and report the single-crop top-1 and the top-5 errors on the validation set. Our pre-processing and augmentation strategy follows the settings of the baseline (i.e., ResNet18). All models are trained for 100 epochs on 8 GPUs with 32 images per GPU (effective batch size of 256) with synchronous SGD of momentum 0.9. The learning rate is initialized to 0.1, and decays by a factor of 10 at the $30^{th}$, $60^{th}$, and $90^{th}$ epochs. The results in Table 4 reflect the patterns that emerged above. The proposed PDC can reduce the number of parameters required while retaining the same accuracy. The variant of PDC that has similar number of parameters to the baseline ResNet18 can achieve an increase in the accuracy. More specifically, we set the stem channel number to 52 for PDC-ResNet18-cmp and 60 for PDC18, respectively. In addition, we also decrease the channel to 1/4 before the Hadamard product in the proposed PDC block to save the computation cost.

**Table 4.** Image classification on ImageNet with variants of ResNet18.

| Model | Top-1 Accuracy | Top-5 Accuracy | Flops | #p $\times 10^6$ |
|---|---|---|---|---|
| ResNet18 | 0.698 | 0.891 | 1.82G | 11.69 M |
| SE-ResNet18 | 0.706 | 0.896 | 1.82G | 11.78 M |
| $\Pi$-net-ResNet | 0.707 | 0.895 | 1.8207G | 11.96 M |
| PDC-cmp | 0.698 | 0.893 | 1.30G | 7.51 M |
| PDC | **0.710** | **0.899** | 1.67G | 10.69 M |

### 5.2   Image Classification with Non-local Blocks

In this section, an experimental comparison and validation is conducted with non-local blocks. The benchmark of CIFAR100 is selected, while ResNet18 is referred as the baseline. The original non-local network (NL) and the disentangled non-local (DNL) are the main compared methods from the literature. As a reminder we perform two extensions in DNL: i) we add a first-degree term (PDC-$NL^{[3]}$), ii) we add a fourth degree term (PDC-$NL^{[4]}$).

Table 5 contains the accuracy of each method. Notice that DNL improves upon the baseline NL, while PDC-$NL^{[3]}$ improves upon both DNL and NL. Interestingly, the fourth-degree variant, i.e., PDC-$NL^{[4]}$ outperforms all the compared methods by a considerable margin without increasing the number of parameters significantly. The results verify our intuition that the different polynomial terms enable additional flexibility to the model.

Besides the experiments on CIFAR100, we also test the proposed Non-local blocks in ImageNet. The training setup remains the same as in sec. 5.1. As shown in Table 6, the proposed Non-local blocks with different polynomial degrees significantly improve the top-1 accuracy on ImageNet while the total parameter numbers are lower than the baseline ResNet18. More specifically, we set the bottleneck ratio of 4 for the proposed PDC-$NL^{[3]}$ and PDC-$NL^{[4]}$, and we apply non-local blocks in multiple layers (c3+c4+c5) to better capture long-range

**Table 5.** Classification on CIFAR100 with non-local blocks.

| Model | #p $\times 10^6$ | Accuracy |
|---|---|---|
| ResNet18 | 11.2 | 0.756 |
| NL | 11.57 | 0.769 |
| DNL | 11.57 | 0.771 |
| PDC-$NL^{[3]}$ | 11.87 | 0.773 |
| PDC-$NL^{[4]}$ | 12.00 | **0.779** |

**Table 6.** Classification on ImageNet with non-local blocks.

| Model | #p $\times 10^6$ | Accuracy |
|---|---|---|
| ResNet18 | 11.69 | 0.698 |
| NL | 12.02 | 0.702 |
| PDC | 10.69 | 0.710 |
| PDC-$NL^{[3]}$ | 11.35 | 0.712 |
| PDC-$NL^{[4]}$ | 11.51 | **0.716** |

dependency with only a slight increase in the computation cost. PDC-$NL^{[4]}$ significantly outperforms NL by 1.03%, showing the advantages of the polynomial information fusion.

## 5.3 Audio Classification

Besides image classification, we conduct a series of experiments on audio classification to test the generalization of the polynomial expansion in different types of signals. The popular dataset of Speech Commands [64] is selected as our benchmark. The dataset consists of 60,000 audio files containing a single word each. The total number of words is 35, while there are at least 1,500 different files for each word. Every audio file is converted into a mel-spectrogram.

ResNet7 includes one residual block per group, while ResNet18 includes two residual blocks per group. The accuracy for each model (in both ResNet7 and ResNet18 comparisons) is reported in Table 7. All the compared methods have accuracy over 0.97, while the polynomial expansions of $\Pi$-net-ResNet and PDC are able to reduce the number of parameters required to achieve the same accuracy, due to their expressiveness.

**Table 7.** Speech classification with ResNet variants. Four residual blocks are used in ResNet7 instead of eight of ResNet18. Nevertheless, the respective PDC7 can reduce even further the parameters to achieve the same performance.

| Model | # param ($\times 10^6$) | Accuracy |
|---|---|---|
| ResNet7 | 4.9 | 0.974 |
| SENet | 5.1 | 0.974 |
| PDC | **3.9** | **0.975** |
| ResNet18 | 11.2 | 0.977 |
| SENet | 11.5 | 0.977 |
| $\Pi$-net-ResNet | **6.0** | 0.977 |
| PDC | 8.0 | **0.978** |

## 5.4   Image Classification on Long-Tailed Distributions

We scrutinize the performance of the proposed models on long-tailed image recognition. We convert CIFAR10, which has $5,000$ number of samples per class, to a long-tailed version, called CIFAR10-LT. The imbalance factor (IF) is defined as the ratio of the largest class to the smallest class. The imbalance factor varies from $10 - 200$, following similar benchmarks tailored to long-tailed distributions [12]. We note that the models are as defined above; the only change is the data distribution. The accuracy of each method is reported in Table 8. The results exhibit the benefits of the proposed models, which outperform the baselines.

**Table 8.** Accuracy on image classification on CIFAR10-LT. Each column corresponds to a different imbalance factor (IF).

| Model \ IF | 200 | 100 | 50 | 20 | 10 |
|---|---|---|---|---|---|
| ResNet18 | 0.645 | 0.696 | 0.784 | 0.844 | 0.877 |
| SENet | 0.636 | 0.713 | 0.784 | 0.844 | 0.878 |
| $\Pi$-net-ResNet | 0.653 | 0.718 | 0.783 | 0.845 | 0.879 |
| PDC-comp | 0.653 | **0.727** | 0.786 | 0.848 | 0.882 |
| PDC-param | **0.665** | 0.726 | **0.792** | **0.851** | **0.886** |

# 6   Related Work

Classification benchmarks [52] have a profound impact in the progress observed in machine learning. Such benchmarks been a significant testbed for new architectures [23,24,27,37] and for introducing novel tasks, such as adversarial perturbations [59]. The architectures originally designed for classification have been applied to diverse tasks, such as image generation [3,72].

ResNet [24] has been among the most influential works of the last few years which can be attributed both in its simplicity and its stellar performance. ResNet has been studied in both its theoretical capacity [2,20,53,70] and its empirical performance [58,66,71]. A number of works focus on modifying the shortcut connection and the concatenation operation [7,28,61].

The Squeeze-and-Excitation network (SENet) [27] has been extended by [50] to capture second-degree correlations in both the spatial and the channel dimensions. [26] extend SENet by replacing the pooling operation with alternative operators that aggregate contextual information. [67] inspired by the SENet propose a gated convolution module. [51] improve SENet by introducing long-range dependencies. SENet has also been used as a drop-in module to improve the performance of residual blocks [15].

Non-local neural networks have been used extensively for capturing long-range interactions in both image-related tasks [30,40,73] and video-related tasks [6,18]. Non-local networks are also related with self-attention [60] that is widely used in both vision [46] and natural language processing [14,44]. [5] study when the long-range interactions emerge in non-local neural networks. They also frame a simplified non-local block, which in our terminology is a second-degree polynomial. Naturally, they observe that this resembles the SENet and merge their simplified non-local block and SENet block.

A promising line of research is that of polynomial activation functions. For instance, the element-wise quadratic activation function $f^2$ applied to a linear operation $C\hat{Z}$ is $(C\hat{Z})^2$. Both the theoretical [32,42] and the empirical results [43,47] support that polynomial activation functions can be beneficial. Our work is orthogonal to the polynomial activation functions, as they express a polynomial expansion of the representation, while we model a polynomial expansion of the input.

A well-established line of research is that of considering second or higher-order moments for various tasks. For instance, second-order statistics have been used for normalization methods [29], learning latent variable models [1]. However, our work focuses on classification methods that can be expresses as polynomials and not on the method of moments.

Tensors and tensor decompositions are related to our work [54]. Tensor decompositions such as the CP or the Tucker decompositions [34] are frequently used for model compression in computer vision. Tensor decompositions have also been used for modeling the components of deep neural networks. [11] interpret a whole convolutional network as a tensor decomposition, while the recent Einconv [21] focus on a single convolutional layer and model them with tensor decompositions. In our work the focus is not in the tensor decomposition used, but on the polynomial expansion that provides insights on the correlations that are captured by each model.

A line of research that is related to ours is that of multiplicative data fusion [8, 16,17,31,33,48,69]. Even though multiplicative interactions can be considered as second-degree polynomials, data fusion of the aforementioned works is not our focus.

# 7    Conclusion

In this work, we study popular classification networks under the unifying perspective of polynomials. Notably, the popular ResNet, SENet and non-local networks are expressed as first, second and third degree polynomials respectively. The common framework provides insights on the inductive biases of each model and enables natural extensions building upon their polynomial nature. We conduct an extensive evaluation on image and audio classification benchmarks. We show how intuitive extensions to existing networks, e.g., converting the third-degree non-local network into a fourth degree, can improve the performance. Such natural extensions can be used for designing new architectures based on the proposed taxonomy. Importantly, our experimental evaluation highlights the dual utility of the polynomial framework: the networks can be used either for model compression or increased model performance. We expect this to be a significant feature when designing architectures for edge devices. Our experimentation in the presence of limited data and long-tailed data distributions highlights the benefits of the proposed taxonomy and provides a link to real-world applications, where massive data annotation is challenging.

## A     Detailed notation

**Products**: The *Hadamard* product of $A, B \in \mathbb{R}^{I \times N}$ is defined as $A * B$ and is equal to $a_{(i,j)} b_{(i,j)}$ for the $(i,j)$ element. The *Khatri-Rao* product of matrices $A \in \mathbb{R}^{I \times N}$ and $B \in \mathbb{R}^{J \times N}$ is denoted by $A \odot B$ and yields a matrix of dimensions $(IJ) \times N$. The Khatri-Rao product for a set of matrices $\{A_{[m]} \in \mathbb{R}^{I_m \times N}\}_{m=1}^{M}$ is abbreviated by $A_{[1]} \odot A_{[2]} \odot \cdots \odot A_{[M]} \doteq \bigodot_{m=1}^{M} A_{[m]}$.

**Tensors**: Each element of an $M^{th}$ order tensor $\mathcal{X}$ is addressed by $M$ indices, i.e., $(\mathcal{X})_{i_1, i_2, \ldots, i_M} \doteq x_{i_1, i_2, \ldots, i_M}$. An $M^{th}$-order tensor $\mathcal{X}$ is defined over the tensor space $\mathbb{R}^{I_1 \times I_2 \times \cdots \times I_M}$, where $I_m \in \mathbb{Z}$ for $m = 1, 2, \ldots, M$. The *mode-m unfolding* of a tensor $\mathcal{X} \in \mathbb{R}^{I_1 \times I_2 \times \cdots \times I_M}$ maps $\mathcal{X}$ to a matrix $X_{(m)} \in \mathbb{R}^{I_m \times \bar{I}_m}$ with $\bar{I}_m = \prod_{\substack{k=1 \\ k \neq m}}^{M} I_k$ such that the tensor element $x_{i_1, i_2, \ldots, i_M}$ is mapped to the matrix element $x_{i_m, j}$ where $j = 1 + \sum_{\substack{k=1 \\ k \neq m}}^{M} (i_k - 1) J_k$ with $J_k = \prod_{\substack{n=1 \\ n \neq m}}^{k-1} I_n$. The *mode-m vector product* of $\mathcal{X}$ with a vector $c \in \mathbb{R}^{I_m}$, denoted by $\mathcal{X} \times_m c \in \mathbb{R}^{I_1 \times I_2 \times \cdots \times I_{m-1} \times I_{m+1} \times \cdots \times I_M}$, results in a tensor of order $M - 1$:

$$(\mathcal{X} \times_m c)_{i_1, \ldots, i_{m-1}, i_{m+1}, \ldots, i_M} = \sum_{i_m = 1}^{I_m} x_{i_1, i_2, \ldots, i_M} u_{i_m}. \tag{13}$$

The *CP decomposition* [34] factorizes a tensor into a sum of component rank-one tensors. The rank-$R$ CP decomposition of an $M^{th}$-order tensor $\mathcal{X}$ is written as:

$$\mathcal{X} \doteq [\![C_{[1]}, C_{[2]}, \ldots, C_{[M]}]\!] = \sum_{r=1}^{R} c_r^{(1)} \circ c_r^{(2)} \circ \cdots \circ c_r^{(M)}, \tag{14}$$

where $\circ$ is the vector outer product. The factor matrices $\{C_{[m]} = [c_1^{(m)}, c_2^{(m)}, \cdots, c_R^{(m)}] \in \mathbb{R}^{I_m \times R}\}_{m=1}^{M}$ collect the vectors from the rank-one components. By considering the mode-1 unfolding of $\mathcal{X}$, the CP decomposition can be written in matrix form as:

$$X_{(1)} \doteq C_{[1]} \left( \bigodot_{m=M}^{2} C_{[m]} \right)^T \tag{15}$$

The following lemma is useful in our method:

**Lemma 1.** ([10]). *For a set of $N$ matrices $\{A_{[\nu]} \in \mathbb{R}^{I_\nu \times K}\}_{\nu=1}^N$ and $\{B_{[\nu]} \in \mathbb{R}^{I_\nu \times L}\}_{\nu=1}^N$, the following equality holds:*

$$\left(\bigodot_{\nu=1}^N A_{[\nu]}\right)^T \cdot \left(\bigodot_{\nu=1}^N B_{[\nu]}\right) = (A_{[1]}^T \cdot B_{[1]}) * \ldots * (A_{[N]}^T \cdot B_{[N]}) \tag{16}$$

# B    Polynomials as a single tensor product

As mentioned in the main paper polynomials and tensors are closely related. To illustrate the differences between the proposed variant of sec. 4.1 and the proposed taxonomy we can formulate them as a single tensor product. We assume a second-degree polynomial expansion of (1). The tensors are then up to third-order, which enables a visualization (as in the Fig. 1). The initial equation is:

$$y = \beta + \left(W^{[1]}\right)^T z + \left(\mathcal{W}^{[2]} \times_2 z \times_3 z\right) \tag{17}$$

The $\tau^{th}$ output of (17) can be written in element-wise form as:

$$y_\tau = \beta_\tau + \sum_{k=1}^\delta w_{\tau,k}^{[1]} z_k + \sum_{k,m=1}^\delta w_{\tau,k,m}^{[2]} z_k z_m \tag{18}$$

We can collect all the parameters of (17) under a single tensor by padding the input $z \in \mathbb{R}^\delta$. Specifically, if we consider the padded version $\tilde{z} = [z_1, \ldots, z_\delta, 1]^T$, then (17) can be written in the format $y = \tilde{\mathcal{W}} \times_2 \tilde{z} \times_3 \tilde{z}$ as we demonstrate below.

The $\tau^{th}$ output of $\tilde{\mathcal{W}} \times_2 \tilde{z} \times_3 \tilde{z}$ is:

$$y_\tau = \sum_{k,m=1}^{\delta+1} \tilde{w}_{\tau,k,m} \tilde{z}_k \tilde{z}_m = \underbrace{\tilde{w}_{\tau,\delta+1,\delta+1}}_{\text{constant term}} +$$

$$\underbrace{\sum_{m=1}^\delta \tilde{w}_{\tau,\delta+1,m} z_m + \sum_{k=1}^\delta \tilde{w}_{\tau,k,\delta+1} z_k}_{\text{first-degree term}} + \underbrace{\sum_{k,m=1}^\delta \tilde{w}_{\tau,k,m} z_k z_m}_{\text{second-degree term}} \tag{19}$$

If we set:

$$\begin{cases} \beta_\tau = \tilde{w}_{\tau,\delta+1,\delta+1} \\ w_{\tau,k}^{[1]} = \tilde{w}_{\tau,\delta+1,k} + \tilde{w}_{\tau,k,\delta+1} & \text{for } k = 1, \ldots, \delta \\ w_{\tau,k,m}^{[2]} = \tilde{w}_{\tau,k,m} & \text{for } k, m = 1, \ldots, \delta \end{cases} \tag{20}$$

then (19) becomes the polynomial expansion of (18).

This enables us to express different degree polynomial expansions with a third-order tensor. The first-degree methods, e.g., ResNet [24], have $w_{\tau,k,m}^{[2]} = 0$, while SENet [27] assumes $w_{\tau,k}^{[1]} = 0$. The $\Pi$-net family assumes low-rank decomposition with shared factors, i.e., the low-rank decompositions of $\mathcal{W}^{[n]}{}_{n=1}^{N}$ share factor matrices. On the contrary, our proposed PDC does not assume a sharing pattern, thus it can express independently the terms $W^{[1]}, \mathcal{W}^{[2]}$.

## C    Proofs

*Claim.* The Squeeze-and-excitation block of (3) is a special form of second-degree polynomial term.

*Proof.* The global pooling function on a matrix $C$ can be expressed as $\frac{1}{hw}\vec{1}^{T}C$. The $r$ function that replicates the channels acts on a vector $c$ and results in the expression $\vec{1}c^{T}$.

The identity $X * ab^{T} = diag(a)X diag(b)$ can be used to convert the Hadamard product of (3) into a matrix multiplication [57]. Then, (3) becomes:

$$Y_s = (ZC_1) * \vec{1}\left(\left(\frac{1}{hw}\vec{1}^{T}ZC_1\right)C_2\right)^{T} = (ZC_1)\frac{1}{hw}diag(C_2^{T}C_1^{T}Z^{T}\vec{1}) =$$

$$(ZC_1)\frac{1}{hw}\mathcal{I}\times_3 (C_2^{T}C_1^{T}Z^{T}\vec{1})$$

$$(21)$$

where as a reminder $\mathcal{I}$ is a third-order super-diagonal unit tensor. The last equation is a second-degree term with $\Phi_1^{[2]}(Z) = ZC_1$ and $\Phi_2^{[2]}(Z) = \frac{1}{hw}\mathcal{I}\times_3 (C_2^{T}C_1^{T}Z^{T}\vec{1})$.

## D    Auxiliary experiments

**Table 9.** Image classification on CIFAR100 with variants of ResNet34.

| Model | # param ($\times 10^6$) | Accuracy |
|---|---|---|
| ResNet34 | 21.3 | 0.769 |
| $\Pi$-net-ResNet | 14.7 | 0.769 |
| PDC-channels | 36.3 | **0.774** |
| PDC | **10.5** | 0.770 |

## D.1    Image classification with limited data

A number of experiments is performed by progressively reducing the number of training samples per class. The number of samples is reduced uniformly from the original 5,000 down to 50 per class, i.e., a 100× reduction, in CIFAR10. The architectures of Table 3 (similar to ResNet18) are used unchanged; only the number of training samples is progressively reduced. The resulting Fig. 4 visualizes the performance as we decrease the training samples. The accuracy of ResNet18 decreases fast for limited training samples. SENet deteriorates at a slower pace, steadily increasing the difference from ResNet18 (note that both share similar number of parameters). $\Pi$-net-ResNet improves upon SENet and performs better even under limited data. However, the proposed PDC-comp outperforms all the compared methods for 50 training samples per class. The difference in the accuracy between PDC and $\Pi$-net-ResNet increases as we reduce the number of training samples. Indicatively, with 50 samples per class, ResNet18 attains accuracy of 0.347, SENet scores 0.355, $\Pi$-net-ResNet scores 0.397 and PDC-comp scores 0.426, which is a 22% increase over the ResNet18 baseline.

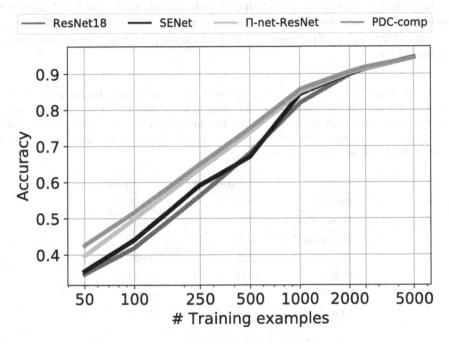

**Fig. 4.** Image classification with limited data. The x-axis declares the number of training samples per class (log-axis). As the number of samples is reduced (i.e., moving from right to the left), the performance gap between $\Pi$-net-ResNet and ResNet18 increases. Similarly, PDC-comp performs better than $\Pi$-net-ResNet, especially in the limited data regimes on the left.

## D.2    Classification without activation functions

Typical feed-forward neural networks, such as CNNs, require activation functions to learn complex functions [25]. However, the proposed view of polynomial expansion enables capturing higher-order correlations even in the absence of activation functions. That is, the expressivity of higher-degree polynomials can be assessed without activation functions. We conduct a series of experiments on all three datasets with higher-degree polynomials. Our core experiments study the higher-degree polynomials of $\Pi$-nets [9], versus the proposed model of (10). We also implement the ResNet without activation functions to assess how first-degree polynomials perform.

For the first experiment, we utilize ResNet18 as the backbone and test the baselines on CIFAR100. Three variations of $Pi$-net are considered as the compared methods: one with second-degree, one with third-degree and one with fourth-degree residual blocks. The same polynomial expansions are used for the proposed PDC. The accuracy of each method is reported in Table 10. All the variants of $\Pi$-net-ResNet and PDC exhibit a high accuracy based solely on the high-degree polynomial expansion. However, $\Pi$-net-ResNet saturates when the residual block is a third or fourth degree polynomial, while the PDC does not suffer from the same issue. On the contrary, the performance of the PDC variant with third and forth degree residual block outperforms the second-degree residual block.

**Table 10.** Image classification on CIFAR100 without activation functions. Both $\Pi$-net-ResNet and PDC use high-degree polynomial expansion to achieve high accuracy even in the absence of activation functions. The proposed PDC achieves both increased performance and improves its performance when each residual block has third or fourth degree polynomial instead of second.

| Model | # param ($\times 10^6$) | Accuracy |
|---|---|---|
| ResNet18 | 11.2 | 0.168 |
| $\Pi$-net-ResNet | 11.9 | 0.667 |
| $\Pi$-net-ResNet[3] | 11.2 | 0.648 |
| $\Pi$-net-ResNet[4] | 11.2 | 0.626 |
| PDC | **5.46** | 0.689 |
| PDC[3] | 11.2 | **0.703** |
| PDC[4] | 18.8 | 0.699 |

The models are also evaluated on CIFAR10 with ResNet18 and three variants of $\Pi$-nets as the backbone. Three variants of PDC with different expansion degrees are designed. The results are tabulated on Table 11. Each variant of $\Pi$-net-ResNet and PDC surpasses the 0.87 accuracy and outperform the ResNet18 by a wide margin. In contrast to $\Pi$-net-ResNet, the performance of PDC does

**Table 11.** Image classification on CIFAR10 without activation functions. The results illustrate the expressiveness of the proposed model even in the absence of activation functions. Notice that PDC[3] improves upon PDC with second-degree blocks. On the contrary, this does not happen to the compared $\Pi$-net-ResNet.

| Model | # param ($\times 10^6$) | Accuracy |
|---|---|---|
| ResNet18 | 11.2 | 0.391 |
| $\Pi$-net-ResNet | 11.9 | 0.907 |
| $\Pi$-net-ResNet[3] | 11.2 | 0.891 |
| $\Pi$-net-ResNet[4] | 11.2 | 0.877 |
| PDC | **5.4** | 0.909 |
| PDC[3] | 11.2 | **0.918** |
| PDC[4] | 18.8 | **0.918** |

**Table 12.** Audio classification without activation functions.

| Model | # param ($\times 10^6$) | Accuracy |
|---|---|---|
| ResNet18 | 11.2 | 0.464 |
| $\Pi$-net-ResNet | 11.9 | 0.971 |
| PDC | **5.4** | **0.972** |

not decrease when the degree of the residual block increases, i.e., from second to fourth-degree. Overall, PDC outperforms $\Pi$−net.

The last experiment is conducted on the Speech Commands dataset. The baseline of ResNet18 is selected, while the $\Pi$-net-ResNet is the compared method. The results in Table 12 depict the same motif: the two polynomial expansions are very expressive. Impressively, in this dataset the result without activation functions is only 0.007 decreased when compared to the respective

**Table 13. COCO object detection and segmentation results** using Mask-RCNN and Cascade Mask-RCNN. The backbone models are pre-trained ResNet18 and PDC-ResNet18 models on ImageNet-1K. We employ MMDetection with 1× schedule.

| backbone | $AP^{box}$ | $AP_{50}^{box}$ | $AP_{75}^{box}$ | $AP^{mask}$ | $AP_{50}^{mask}$ | $AP_{75}^{mask}$ |
|---|---|---|---|---|---|---|
| Mask-RCNN 1× schedule | | | | | | |
| ResNet18 | 33.9 | 53.9 | 36.2 | 31.0 | 50.9 | 33.0 |
| PDC-ResNet18 | 34.8 | 55.2 | 37.4 | 31.8 | 52.2 | 34.1 |
| Cascade Mask-RCNN 1× schedule | | | | | | |
| ResNet18 | 37.3 | 54.8 | 40.4 | 32.6 | 52.2 | 34.9 |
| PDC-ResNet18 | 38.1 | 55.9 | 41.7 | 33.2 | 53.3 | 35.7 |

results with activation functions. This highlights that simple datasets might not always demand activation functions to achieve high-accuracy.

### D.3     Object detection and segmentation

We adopt MS COCO 2017 [41] as the primary benchmark for the experiments of object detection and segmentation. We use the train split (118k images) for training and report the performance on the val split (5k images). We employ standard evaluation metrics for COCO dataset, where multiple IoU thresholds from 0.5 to 0.95 are applied. The detection results are evaluated with mAP.

We use the final model weights from ImageNet-1K pre-training as network initializations and fine-tune Mask R-CNN [22] and Cascade Mask R-CNN [4] on the COCO dataset. Following default settings in MMDetection, we use the 1× schedule (i.e.,12 epochs).

Table 13 shows object detection and instance segmentation results comparing ResNet18 and the proposed PDC-ResNet18. As we can see from the results, the proposed PDC-ResNet18 achieves an obvious better performance than the baseline ResNet18 in terms of the box and mask AP, confirming the effectiveness of the proposed polynomial learning scheme.

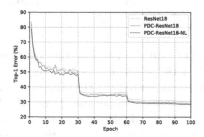

**Fig. 5.** Top-1 validation error on ImageNet with proposed PDC and NL methods throughout the training.

# References

1. Anandkumar, A., Ge, R., Hsu, D., Kakade, S.M., Telgarsky, M.: Tensor decompositions for learning latent variable models. J. Mach. Learn. Res. **15**, 2773–2832 (2014)
2. Balduzzi, D., Frean, M., Leary, L., Lewis, J., Ma, K.W.D., McWilliams, B.: The shattered gradients problem: If resnets are the answer, then what is the question? In: International Conference on Machine Learning (ICML), pp. 342–350 (2017)
3. Brock, A., Donahue, J., Simonyan, K.: Large scale gan training for high fidelity natural image synthesis. In: International Conference on Learning Representations (ICLR) (2019)
4. Cai, Z., Vasconcelos, N.: Cascade R-CNN: Delving into high quality object detection. In: Conference on Computer Vision and Pattern Recognition (CVPR) (2018)

5. Cao, Y., Xu, J., Lin, S., Wei, F., Hu, H.: Gcnet: Non-local networks meet squeeze-excitation networks and beyond. In: International Conference on Computer Vision Workshops (ICCV'W), pp. 0–0 (2019)
6. Chen, Y., Kalantidis, Y., Li, J., Yan, S., Feng, J.: Aˆ 2-nets: Double attention networks. In: Advances in neural information processing systems (NeurIPS), pp. 352–361 (2018)
7. Chen, Y., Li, J., Xiao, H., Jin, X., Yan, S., Feng, J.: Dual path networks. In: Advances in neural information processing systems (NeurIPS), pp. 4467–4475 (2017)
8. Chrysos, G., Georgopoulos, M., Panagakis, Y.: Conditional generation using polynomial expansions. In: Advances in neural information processing systems (NeurIPS) (2021)
9. Chrysos, G., Moschoglou, S., Bouritsas, G., Panagakis, Y., Deng, J., Zafeiriou, S.: $\pi-$nets: Deep polynomial neural networks. In: Conference on Computer Vision and Pattern Recognition (CVPR) (2020)
10. Chrysos, G., Moschoglou, S., Panagakis, Y., Zafeiriou, S.: Polygan: High-order polynomial generators. arXiv preprint arXiv:1908.06571 (2019)
11. Cohen, N., Shashua, A.: Convolutional rectifier networks as generalized tensor decompositions. In: International Conference on Machine Learning (ICML), pp. 955–963. PMLR (2016)
12. Cui, Y., Jia, M., Lin, T.Y., Song, Y., Belongie, S.: Class-balanced loss based on effective number of samples. In: Conference on Computer Vision and Pattern Recognition (CVPR), pp. 9268–9277 (2019)
13. Deng, J., Dong, W., Socher, R., Li, L.J., Li, K., Fei-Fei, L.: Imagenet: A large-scale hierarchical image database. In: Conference on Computer Vision and Pattern Recognition (CVPR), pp. 248–255 (2009)
14. Galassi, A., Lippi, M., Torroni, P.: Attention, please! a critical review of neural attention models in natural language processing. arXiv preprint arXiv:1902.02181 (2019)
15. Gao, S., Cheng, M.M., Zhao, K., Zhang, X.Y., Yang, M.H., Torr, P.H.: Res2net: A new multi-scale backbone architecture. IEEE Transactions on Pattern Analysis and Machine Intelligence (T-PAMI) (2019)
16. Georgopoulos, M., Chrysos, G., Pantic, M., Panagakis, Y.: Multilinear latent conditioning for generating unseen attribute combinations. In: International Conference on Machine Learning (ICML) (2020)
17. Georgopoulos, M., Oldfield, J., Nicolaou, M.A., Panagakis, Y., Pantic, M.: Mitigating demographic bias in facial datasets with style-based multi-attribute transfer. In: International Journal of Computer Vision (IJCV) (2021)
18. Girdhar, R., Carreira, J., Doersch, C., Zisserman, A.: Video action transformer network. In: Conference on Computer Vision and Pattern Recognition (CVPR), pp. 244–253 (2019)
19. Hanin, B.: Universal function approximation by deep neural nets with bounded width and relu activations. Mathematics 7(10), 992 (2019)
20. Hardt, M., Ma, T.: Identity matters in deep learning. In: International Conference on Learning Representations (ICLR) (2017)
21. Hayashi, K., Yamaguchi, T., Sugawara, Y., Maeda, S.i.: Einconv: Exploring unexplored tensor network decompositions for convolutional neural networks. In: Advances in neural information processing systems (NeurIPS) (2019)
22. He, K., Gkioxari, G., Dollár, P., Girshick, R.: Mask R-CNN. In: International Conference on Computer Vision (ICCV) (2017)

23. He, K., Sun, J.: Convolutional neural networks at constrained time cost. In: Conference on Computer Vision and Pattern Recognition (CVPR), pp. 5353–5360 (2015)

24. He, K., Zhang, X., Ren, S., Sun, J.: Deep residual learning for image recognition. In: Conference on Computer Vision and Pattern Recognition (CVPR) (2016)

25. Hornik, K., Stinchcombe, M., White, H., et al.: Multilayer feedforward networks are universal approximators. Neural Netw. **2**(5), 359–366 (1989)

26. Hu, J., Shen, L., Albanie, S., Sun, G., Vedaldi, A.: Gather-excite: Exploiting feature context in convolutional neural networks. In: Advances in neural information processing systems (NeurIPS), pp. 9401–9411 (2018)

27. Hu, J., Shen, L., Sun, G.: Squeeze-and-excitation networks. In: Conference on Computer Vision and Pattern Recognition (CVPR), pp. 7132–7141 (2018)

28. Huang, G., Liu, Z., Van Der Maaten, L., Weinberger, K.Q.: Densely connected convolutional networks. In: Conference on Computer Vision and Pattern Recognition (CVPR), pp. 4700–4708 (2017)

29. Huang, L., Yang, D., Lang, B., Deng, J.: Decorrelated batch normalization. In: Conference on Computer Vision and Pattern Recognition (CVPR), pp. 791–800 (2018)

30. Huang, Z., Wang, X., Huang, L., Huang, C., Wei, Y., Liu, W.: Ccnet: Criss-cross attention for semantic segmentation. In: International Conference on Computer Vision (ICCV), pp. 603–612 (2019)

31. Jayakumar, S.M., et al.: Multiplicative interactions and where to find them. In: International Conference on Learning Representations (ICLR) (2020)

32. Kileel, J., Trager, M., Bruna, J.: On the expressive power of deep polynomial neural networks. In: Advances in neural information processing systems (NeurIPS) (2019)

33. Kim, J.H., Jun, J., Zhang, B.T.: Bilinear attention networks. In: Advances in neural information processing systems (NeurIPS), pp. 1564–1574 (2018)

34. Kolda, T.G., Bader, B.W.: Tensor decompositions and applications. SIAM Review **51**(3), 455–500 (2009)

35. Krizhevsky, A., Nair, V., Hinton, G.: Cifar-100 (canadian institute for advanced research) https://www.cs.toronto.edu/~kriz/cifar.html

36. Krizhevsky, A., Nair, V., Hinton, G.: The cifar-10 dataset. online: https://www.cs.toronto.edu/~kriz/cifar.html 55 (2014)

37. Krizhevsky, A., Sutskever, I., Hinton, G.E.: Imagenet classification with deep convolutional neural networks. In: Advances in neural information processing systems (NeurIPS), pp. 1097–1105 (2012)

38. Li, X., Wang, W., Hu, X., Yang, J.: Selective kernel networks. In: Conference on Computer Vision and Pattern Recognition (CVPR), pp. 510–519 (2019)

39. Li, Y., Wang, N., Liu, J., Hou, X.: Factorized bilinear models for image recognition. In: International Conference on Computer Vision (ICCV), pp. 2079–2087 (2017)

40. Li, Y., et al.: Neural architecture search for lightweight non-local networks. In: Conference on Computer Vision and Pattern Recognition (CVPR), pp. 10297–10306 (2020)

41. Lin, T.-Y., Maire, M., Belongie, S., Hays, J., Perona, P., Ramanan, D., Dollár, P., Zitnick, C.L.: Microsoft COCO: common objects in context. In: Fleet, D., Pajdla, T., Schiele, B., Tuytelaars, T. (eds.) ECCV 2014. LNCS, vol. 8693, pp. 740–755. Springer, Cham (2014). https://doi.org/10.1007/978-3-319-10602-1_48

42. Livni, R., Shalev-Shwartz, S., Shamir, O.: On the computational efficiency of training neural networks. In: Advances in neural information processing systems (NeurIPS), pp. 855–863 (2014)

43. Lokhande, V.S., Tasneeyapant, S., Venkatesh, A., Ravi, S.N., Singh, V.: Generating accurate pseudo-labels in semi-supervised learning and avoiding overconfident predictions via hermite polynomial activations. In: Conference on Computer Vision and Pattern Recognition (CVPR), pp. 11435–11443 (2020)
44. Ma, X., et al.: A tensorized transformer for language modeling. In: Advances in neural information processing systems (NeurIPS), pp. 2232–2242 (2019)
45. Nikol'skii, S.: Analysis III: Spaces of Differentiable Functions. Encyclopaedia of Mathematical Sciences, Springer, Berlin Heidelberg (2013)
46. Parmar, N., Ramachandran, P., Vaswani, A., Bello, I., Levskaya, A., Shlens, J.: Stand-alone self-attention in vision models. In: Advances in neural information processing systems (NeurIPS), pp. 68–80 (2019)
47. Ramachandran, P., Zoph, B., Le, Q.V.: Searching for activation functions. arXiv preprint arXiv:1710.05941 (2017)
48. Reed, S., Sohn, K., Zhang, Y., Lee, H.: Learning to disentangle factors of variation with manifold interaction. In: International Conference on Machine Learning (ICML), pp. 1431–1439 (2014)
49. Rolnick, D., Tegmark, M.: The power of deeper networks for expressing natural functions. In: International Conference on Learning Representations (ICLR) (2018)
50. Roy, A.G., Navab, N., Wachinger, C.: Concurrent spatial and channel 'squeeze & excitation' in fully convolutional networks. In: Frangi, A.F., Schnabel, J.A., Davatzikos, C., Alberola-López, C., Fichtinger, G. (eds.) MICCAI 2018. LNCS, vol. 11070, pp. 421–429. Springer, Cham (2018). https://doi.org/10.1007/978-3-030-00928-1_48
51. Ruan, D., Wen, J., Zheng, N., Zheng, M.: Linear context transform block. In: AAAI, pp. 5553–5560 (2020)
52. Russakovsky, O., et al.: Imagenet large scale visual recognition challenge. Int. J. Comput. Vision (IJCV) 115(3), 211–252 (2015)
53. Shamir, O.: Are resnets provably better than linear predictors? In: Advances in neural information processing systems (NeurIPS), pp. 507–516 (2018)
54. Sidiropoulos, N.D., De Lathauwer, L., Fu, X., Huang, K., Papalexakis, E.E., Faloutsos, C.: Tensor decomposition for signal processing and machine learning. IEEE Trans. Signal Process. 65(13), 3551–3582 (2017)
55. Simonyan, K., Zisserman, A.: Very deep convolutional networks for large-scale image recognition. In: International Conference on Learning Representations (ICLR) (2015)
56. Stone, M.H.: The generalized weierstrass approximation theorem. Math. Mag. 21(5), 237–254 (1948)
57. Styan, G.P.: Hadamard products and multivariate statistical analysis. Linear Algebra Appl. 6, 217–240 (1973)
58. Szegedy, C., Ioffe, S., Vanhoucke, V., Alemi, A.A.: Inception-v4, inception-resnet and the impact of residual connections on learning. In: AAAI Conference on Artificial Intelligence (2017)
59. Szegedy, C., et al.: Intriguing properties of neural networks. In: International Conference on Learning Representations (ICLR) (2014)
60. Vaswani, A., et al.: Attention is all you need. In: Advances in neural information processing systems (NeurIPS), pp. 5998–6008 (2017)
61. Wang, W., Li, X., Yang, J., Lu, T.: Mixed link networks. In: International Joint Conferences on Artificial Intelligence (IJCAI) (2018)
62. Wang, X., Girshick, R., Gupta, A., He, K.: Non-local neural networks. In: Conference on Computer Vision and Pattern Recognition (CVPR), pp. 7794–7803 (2018)

63. Wang, Y., et al.: Sort: Second-order response transform for visual recognition. In: International Conference on Computer Vision (ICCV), pp. 1359–1368 (2017)
64. Warden, P.: Speech commands: A dataset for limited-vocabulary speech recognition. arXiv preprint arXiv:1804.03209 (2018)
65. Won, M., Chun, S., Serra, X.: Toward interpretable music tagging with self-attention. arXiv preprint arXiv:1906.04972 (2019)
66. Xie, S., Girshick, R., Dollár, P., Tu, Z., He, K.: Aggregated residual transformations for deep neural networks. In: Conference on Computer Vision and Pattern Recognition (CVPR), pp. 1492–1500 (2017)
67. Yang, Z., Zhu, L., Wu, Y., Yang, Y.: Gated channel transformation for visual recognition. In: Conference on Computer Vision and Pattern Recognition (CVPR), pp. 11794–11803 (2020)
68. Yin, M., et al.: Disentangled non-local neural networks. In: Vedaldi, A., Bischof, H., Brox, T., Frahm, J.-M. (eds.) ECCV 2020. LNCS, vol. 12360, pp. 191–207. Springer, Cham (2020). https://doi.org/10.1007/978-3-030-58555-6_12
69. Yu, Z., Yu, J., Fan, J., Tao, D.: Multi-modal factorized bilinear pooling with co-attention learning for visual question answering. In: International Conference on Computer Vision (ICCV), pp. 1821–1830 (2017)
70. Zaeemzadeh, A., Rahnavard, N., Shah, M.: Norm-preservation: Why residual networks can become extremely deep? arXiv preprint arXiv:1805.07477 (2018)
71. Zagoruyko, S., Komodakis, N.: Wide residual networks. arXiv preprint arXiv:1605.07146 (2016)
72. Zhang, H., Goodfellow, I., Metaxas, D., Odena, A.: Self-attention generative adversarial networks. In: International Conference on Machine Learning (ICML) (2019)
73. Zhu, Z., Xu, M., Bai, S., Huang, T., Bai, X.: Asymmetric non-local neural networks for semantic segmentation. In: International Conference on Computer Vision (ICCV), pp. 593–602 (2019)

# Learning with Noisy Labels by Efficient Transition Matrix Estimation to Combat Label Miscorrection

Seong Min Kye, Kwanghee Choi, Joonyoung Yi, and Buru Chang$^{(\boxtimes)}$

Hyperconnect Inc., Seoul, South Korea
{harris,kwanghee.choi,joonyoung.yi,buru.chang}@hpcnt.com

**Abstract.** Recent studies on learning with noisy labels have shown remarkable performance by exploiting a small clean dataset. In particular, model agnostic meta-learning-based label correction methods further improve performance by correcting noisy labels on the fly. However, there is no safeguard on the label miscorrection, resulting in unavoidable performance degradation. Moreover, every training step requires at least three back-propagations, significantly slowing down the training speed. To mitigate these issues, we propose a robust and efficient method, *FasTEN*, which learns a label transition matrix on the fly. Employing the transition matrix makes the classifier skeptical about all the corrected samples, which alleviates the miscorrection issue. We also introduce a two-head architecture to efficiently estimate the label transition matrix every iteration within a single back-propagation, so that the estimated matrix closely follows the shifting noise distribution induced by label correction. Extensive experiments demonstrate that our FasTEN shows the best performance in training efficiency while having comparable or better accuracy than existing methods, especially achieving state-of-the-art performance in a real-world noisy dataset, Clothing1M.

**Keywords:** Learning with noisy labels · Label correction · Transition matrix estimation

## 1 Introduction

In the last decade, supervised learning has achieved great success by leveraging an abundant amount of annotated data to solve various classification tasks such as image classification [37], object detection [24], and face recognition [89]. It has been proven both theoretically and empirically that the performance of supervised learning-based classification models steadily improves as the size of annotated data increases [12,21,27]. However, we cannot avoid *noisy labels* due to its coarse-grained annotation sources [40,121], resulting in performance degradation [14].

---

S. M. Kye, K.Choi and J.Yi—Equal contribution.

---

**Supplementary Information** The online version contains supplementary material available at https://doi.org/10.1007/978-3-031-19806-9_41.

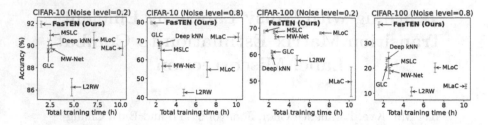

**Fig. 1.** Plotting accuracy (%) **(y-axis)** according to total training time (hours) **(x-axis)**. Our proposed method (FasTEN) shows the best performance in training efficiency while having comparable or better accuracy on both CIFAR-10/100 with various noise levels.

Many methods have been proposed to build a classifier that is robust to noisy labels. Unlike traditional methods [2,68,75,94] which assume that all the given labels are potentially corrupted, recently proposed methods utilize an inexpensively obtained small clean dataset to improve performance further. Based on the clean data set, loss correction methods [40,101] reduce the influence of noisy labels by modifying loss functions and re-weighting methods [3,23,80,85] penalize samples that are likely to be noisy labels. Especially, recent label correction methods [105,121] achieve remarkable performance based on model-agnostic meta-learning (MAML) [20]. These methods relabel noisy labels to directly reduce the noise level, raising the theoretical upper bound of the predictive performance (See Appendix A.1).

However, there are two challenges for these MAML-based label correction methods: (1) *The label correction methods blindly trust the already miscorrected labels.* Erroneously corrected labels are often kept throughout the training, which causes the model to learn the miscorrected labels as ground-truth labels. Several studies [67,105] attempt to tackle this through training techniques such as soft labels, whereas it does not fundamentally solve the problem. (2) *MAML-based methods are inherently slow in training, resulting in excessive computational overhead.* The inefficiency comes from multiple training steps per single iteration of MAML-based methods, including virtual updates with inner optimization loops.

To alleviate these issues, we propose a robust and efficient method called *FasTEN* (**Fas**t **T**ransition Matrix **E**stimation for Learning with **N**oisy Labels). FasTEN efficiently estimates a transition matrix to learn with noisy labels while continuously correcting them on-the-fly. It is theoretically proven that the correctly estimated label transition matrix is useful to obtain a statistically consistent classifier from noisy labels [108,113] (See Appendix A.2), i.e., more robust to noisy labels. To efficiently estimate the transition matrix, we adopt a two-head architecture that consists of two classifiers, a noisy and a clean classifier, with a shared feature extractor. For every iteration, the noisy classifier estimates the label transition matrix shifted by the label correction. On the other hand, the clean classifier is trained to be statistically consistent by leveraging the estimated transition matrix. Using the output of the clean classifier, Fas-TEN relabels noisy labels to reduce the noise level. Our proposed FasTEN has a safeguard for the miscorrected labels since it adaptively estimates the transition matrix on every iteration, so that the clean classifier stays equally skeptical towards all the corrected labels. Furthermore, our efficient method jointly optimizes the two-head architecture with only a single back-propagation for each iteration, boosting training speed. In this paper, we focus on solving the problem of *class-dependent* noisy labels [25, 76, 119] (i.e., $p(\bar{y}|y, x) = p(\bar{y}|y)$), although the problem of instance-dependent noisy labels [16, 107, 123] remains an important problem to be addressed.

Experimental results show that our method achieves state-of-the-art performance by a large margin on both the synthetic and real-world noisy label datasets, various noise levels of *CIFAR* [49] and *Clothing1M* [109], respectively. We demonstrate the exceptional training speed of our proposed FasTEN while achieving better performance compared to baselines, as shown in Fig. 1. Especially, although our FasTEN assumes only class-dependent noisy labels, it also achieves state-of-the-art performance in the Clothing 1M dataset which contains instance-dependent noisy labels. This experimental result supports recent observations that leveraging the accurately estimated transition matrix with small clean data is helpful for alleviating instance-dependent noise [40, 45, 66, 123] (See Appendix A.2). Finally, we conduct a thorough analysis to understand the inner mechanisms of our proposed method.

Our contribution in this paper is threefold: (1) We propose a robust and efficient method that learns a transition matrix to learn with noisy labels while continuously correcting them on the fly. To the best of our knowledge, this is the first attempt to improve the label correction with the transition matrix estimation. (2) Our proposed method boosts training speed by employing a two-head architecture so that the label transition matrix can be learned with a single back-propagation. (3) Extensive experiments validate the efficacy of our proposed method in terms of both training speed and predictive performance.

## 2    Related Work

Learning with noisy labels assumes that labels in all the training samples are potentially corrupted. They can be further categorized as follows: *various loss functions* [22, 45, 57, 61–63, 71, 75, 94, 94, 99, 112, 120], *regularizations* [2, 10, 35, 36, 38, 39, 42, 46, 53, 55, 57, 59, 62, 64, 65, 73, 74, 87, 117], *re-weighting training samples* [14, 43, 44, 60, 67, 77, 80, 93, 100, 102, 104, 104], and *correcting noisy labels* [30, 34, 47, 86, 90, 106, 114, 119, 122]. However, different losses or regularizations yield inferior performance to state-of-the-art methods [42, 55, 67, 117], and re-weighting methods often filter out noisy but helpful samples for extracting features to show sub-optimal performance [11, 58, 67, 84, 86, 105, 121]. *Label correction* methods circumvent their shortcomings by relabeling so that the feature extractor leverage the corrected labels. However, label correction methods also have a limitation in that they are prone to propagate the error when miscorrected labels are continuously accumulated [67,105,121]. Others *correct the training loss* by estimating a label transition matrix [7,25,68,76,79,88,108,111,113] to build a statistically consistent classifier, where the methods need multiple training stages; e.g., include a separate pretraining stage. In this paper, we join a simple label correction method with estimating the label transition matrix to alleviate the miscorrection issue caused by miscorrected noisy labels, which only requires a single training stage.

**Learning with Noisy Label via Small Clean Dataset.** Unlike traditional methods that use noisy datasets only [56,76,113], several recent studies argue that a small clean dataset is easily obtained by techniques such as image retrieval [78]; hence one can further devise a method that effectively leverages it. Many studies have successfully adapted the idea and shown massive performance improvement compared to the traditional methods. Early methods [3,40,118] require multiple training stages where it hinders the training efficiency. Recent studies widely adopt MAML [20] to various strategies discussed above: sample re-weighting [44,50,54,80,85,97], label correction [105,121], and label transition matrix estimation [101]. These approaches first perform a virtual update with the noisy dataset, find optimal parameters using the clean dataset, and update the actual parameters by the found parameters. This virtual update process requires three back-propagations per iteration, leading to at least three times the computational cost. Our proposed label correction method estimates the label transition matrix using a batch drawn from the clean small dataset in a single back-propagation, greatly enhancing the training speed while showing comparable or better performance to existing state-of-the-art methods. Additional related works are described in Appendix D.

## 3 Methodology

Existing label correction methods try to find and fix noisy labels to utilize them as clean samples in model training, where they can improve the classification performance by reducing the noise level of the whole training samples. However, erroneously corrected samples, i.e., clean samples deemed noisy, or vice versa, are often kept throughout the model training. Since current label correction methods blindly trust these miscorrected labels, this behavior degrades the classification performance under the noisy label situation (Sect. 4.4).

In this section, we show that the accurately estimated label transition matrix with the clean dataset alleviates the miscorrection problem of existing label correction methods. Further, we describe our efficient method estimating the label transition matrix for every training iteration while correcting noise labels. Our proposed method is illustrated in Fig. 2 and summarized in Algorithm 1.

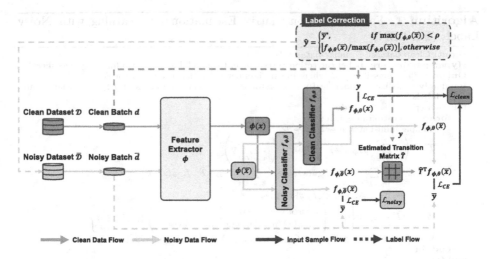

**Fig. 2.** Summarization of our proposed method (FasTEN).

## 3.1   Batch Formation

We estimate the transition matrix to track the shifted noisy label distribution caused by label correction using a clean batch. To ensure the effective estimation of the label transition matrix, we formulate the batch to have the same number of samples per class. We first compose the clean batch $d$ with randomly chosen $K$ samples for the entire $N$ classes in the clean dataset $\mathcal{D}$ to get benefits from having a certain amount of clean samples for each class, as follows $d = \{(x_n, y_n)\}_{n=1}^{KN}$ where $x$ is an input and $y \in \mathbb{R}^N$ is the clean label of $x$. A noisy batch $\bar{d}$ is randomly sampled from the noisy dataset $\bar{\mathcal{D}}$, as follows $\bar{d} = \{(\bar{x}_n, \bar{y}_n)\}_{n=1}^{M}$ where $\bar{y} \in \mathbb{R}^N$ is the noisy label of $\bar{x}$ and $M$ is the size of the noisy batch which we set as $M = KN$ for simplicity. It is different from other methods [80, 85, 105, 121] based on meta-learning which randomly compose the clean batch.

## 3.2   Transition Matrix Estimation

Each element $T_{ij}$ of the label transition matrix $\boldsymbol{T} \in \mathbb{R}^{N \times N}$ is defined as the probability of a clean label $i$ to be corrupted as a noisy label $j$, i.e. $T_{ij} = p(\bar{y} = j | y = i)$. It is well-known that a robust classifier can be obtained with the accurately estimated label transition matrix [40, 76, 88, 108, 113]. We choose a simple but accurate method that directly estimates the posterior with a clean dataset [40, 108, 113], whereas there are other more sophisticated methods that estimate the label transition matrix [7, 25, 68, 76, 79, 88]. Following the assumption of the previous work [8, 15, 40, 107], we also assume conditional independence of $\bar{y}$ and $y$ given $x$:

$$p(\bar{y}|y) = p(\bar{y}|y) \int p(x|\bar{y}, y) dx = \int p(\bar{y}|y, x) p(x|y) dx = \int p(\bar{y}|x) p(x|y) dx. \tag{1}$$

**Algorithm 1. Fast Transition Matrix Estimation for Learning with Noisy Labels (FasTEN)**

---

**Input:** Clean dataset $\mathcal{D}$, noisy dataset $\bar{\mathcal{D}}$.
**Hyper-parameters:** Label correction threshold $\rho$, Controllable loss ratio for noisy classifier $\lambda$.
**Output:** Clean classifier $f_{\phi,\theta}$ where linear classifier $\theta$ and feature extractor $\phi$.
Randomly initialize common feature extractor $\phi$, linear classifiers $\theta$, and $\bar{\theta}$ for clean labels and noisy labels.
**for** each epoch $i = 0, \cdots$ **do**
  **for** each iteration in epoch $i$ **do**
    Sample mini-batch $d \sim \mathcal{D}$, $\bar{d} \sim \bar{\mathcal{D}}$.

$$\hat{T} \leftarrow \left( \sum_{(x,y) \in d} y f_{\phi,\bar{\theta}}(x)^\top \right) \mathrm{diag}^{-1} \left( \sum_{(x,y) \in d} y \right)$$

$$\mathcal{L}_{\mathrm{clean}} \leftarrow \sum_{(x,y) \in d} \mathcal{L}_{\mathrm{CE}} \left( f_{\phi,\theta}(x), y \right) + \sum_{(\bar{x},\bar{y}) \in \bar{d}} \mathcal{L}_{\mathrm{CE}} \left( \hat{T}^\top f_{\phi,\theta}(\bar{x}), \bar{y} \right)$$

$$\mathcal{L}_{\mathrm{noisy}} \leftarrow \sum_{(\bar{x},\bar{y}) \in \bar{d}} \mathcal{L}_{\mathrm{CE}} \left( f_{\phi,\bar{\theta}}(\bar{x}), \bar{y} \right)$$

$$\bar{\mathcal{D}} \leftarrow (\bar{\mathcal{D}} - \bar{d}) \cup \left\{ \left( \bar{x}, \begin{cases} \bar{y}^*, & \text{if } \max(f_{\phi,\theta}(\bar{x})) < \rho \\ \lfloor f_{\phi,\theta}(\bar{x})/\max(f_{\phi,\theta}(\bar{x})) \rfloor, & \text{otherwise} \end{cases} \right) \Big| (\bar{x},\bar{y}) \in \bar{d} \right\}$$

    Update $\phi, \theta, \bar{\theta}$ using $\nabla_{\phi,\theta,\bar{\theta}} \left( \mathcal{L}_{\mathrm{clean}} + \lambda \mathcal{L}_{\mathrm{noisy}} \right)$ with a single back-propagation.
  **end for**
**end for**

---

We design the transition matrix to be *class-dependent*, i.e., $p(\bar{y}|y,x) = p(\bar{y}|y)$, following recent state-of-the-art methods [60,82,108,113]. By parameterizing a feature extractor $\bar{\phi}$ and a linear classifier $\bar{\theta}$, we obtain $p(\bar{y}|x) = f_{\bar{\phi},\bar{\theta}}(x)$ where $f_{\bar{\phi},\bar{\theta}}$ is the noisy classifier that consists of the linear classifier and the feature extractor trained only with the noisy labels. If the noisy classifier $f_{\bar{\phi},\bar{\theta}}$ gives a perfect prediction for the noisy data, we can estimate the transition probability $p(\bar{y}|y)$ using the clean samples $(x,y) \in d$ as follows (See Appendix A.3 for details):

$$\hat{T} \leftarrow \left( \sum_{(x,y) \in d} y f_{\bar{\phi},\bar{\theta}}(x)^\top \right) \mathrm{diag}^{-1} \left( \sum_{(x,y) \in d} y \right). \tag{2}$$

We emphasize the importance of the transition matrix estimation, as its accuracy determines the bounds of the generalization error of the classifier [108]. However, the limited number of clean samples inside a single batch may yield an inaccurate transition matrix, even with the ideal $f_{\bar{\phi},\bar{\theta}}$. We analyze the upper bound of the estimation error as follows:

**Theorem 1.** *Assume the Frobenius norm of the weight matrices $\bar{\phi}_1, ..., \bar{\phi}_{H-1}, \bar{\theta}$ are at most $\bar{\Phi}_1, ..., \bar{\Phi}_{H-1}, \bar{\Theta}$ for $H$-layer neural networks $f_{\bar{\phi},\bar{\theta}}$. Let the loss function be $L$-Lipschitz continuous w.r.t. $f_{\bar{\phi},\bar{\theta}}$. Let the activation functions be 1-Lipschitz, positive-homogeneous, and applied element-wise (such as ReLU). Let $x$ be upper bounded by $B$, i.e., for any $x \in \mathcal{X}$, $\|x\| \leq B$. Then, for $\epsilon \geq 0$*

$$p\left( \left| \hat{T}_{ij} - T_{ij} \right| > \epsilon \right) \leq \frac{NLB(\sqrt{2H \log 2} + 1)\bar{\Theta} \Pi_{h=1}^{H-1} \bar{\Phi}_i}{\sqrt{|\bar{\mathcal{D}}|}}$$

$$+ \frac{\sqrt{-\log(\epsilon)}}{\sqrt{2|\bar{\mathcal{D}}|}} + 2 \exp\left( -2\epsilon^2 K \right). \tag{3}$$

*Proof.* See Appendix A.4.

Although the upper bound of the estimation error of the transition matrix is affected by the batch size $K$, we empirically verify that small $K$ does not necessarily harm the classification performance (See Appendix C.7).

## 3.3   Learning with Estimated Transition Matrix

A clean classifier $f_{\phi,\theta}$ is trained with the estimated transition matrix $\widehat{T}$:

$$\mathcal{L}_{\text{clean}} = \sum_{(x,y)\in d} \mathcal{L}_{\text{CE}}\left(f_{\phi,\theta}(x), y\right) + \sum_{(\bar{x},\bar{y})\in \bar{d}} \mathcal{L}_{\text{CE}}\left(\widehat{T}^{\top} f_{\phi,\theta}(\bar{x}), \bar{y}\right), \qquad (4)$$

given the cross-entropy loss function $\mathcal{L}_{\text{CE}}$, where the feature extractor $\phi$ and the linear classifier $\theta$ form the clean classifier $f_{\phi,\theta}$ which estimates clean labels. If $\widehat{T}$ is correctly estimated, the clean classifier $f_{\phi,\theta}$ becomes statistically consistent [40,76,88,108,113]. This approach makes the clean classifier skeptical towards corrected labels, hence avoiding the miscorrection issue.

On the other hand, the noisy classifier $f_{\bar{\phi},\bar{\theta}}$ is trained to model the noisy label distribution.

$$\mathcal{L}_{\text{noisy}} = \sum_{(\bar{x},\bar{y})\in \bar{d}} \mathcal{L}_{\text{CE}}\left(f_{\bar{\phi},\bar{\theta}}(\bar{x}), \bar{y}\right) \qquad (5)$$

We emphasize that updating the noisy classifier $f_{\bar{\phi},\bar{\theta}}$ every iteration is critical as it can adaptively model the ever-changing noisy label distribution on the fly, where the distribution constantly shifts as the noisy labels are actively corrected to reduce the noise level (See Sect. 3.5).

## 3.4   Efficient Training

Similar to [44,98], we propose an efficient training scheme through weight sharing via two-head architecture, as shown in Fig. 2. Where the architecture closely resembles the ones of [44,98], our two-head architecture only shares the feature extractor $\phi = \bar{\phi}$. Unlike the shared feature extractor, our architecture does not share the linear classifier since modeling both noisy and clean data distribution with a single linear classifier is impractical. Based on the two-head architecture, the given samples require only a single inference on the feature extractor for (1) training classifiers, (2) estimating the transition matrix, and (3) correcting labels, which makes model training highly efficient. Thus, we define the clean and noisy classifier as $f_{\phi,\theta}$ and $f_{\phi,\bar{\theta}}$, respectively, to produce our final objective function $\mathcal{L}$:

$$\mathcal{L} = \mathcal{L}_{\text{clean}} + \lambda \mathcal{L}_{\text{noisy}} \qquad (6)$$

where $\lambda$ is a loss balancing factor. In order to prevent over-fitting on $\bar{d}$, we introduce $\lambda$ to the final objective function. We search for the optimal hyperparameter $\lambda$ for all of our experiments (See Appendix C.7).

**Efficiency Analysis.** Compared to the vanilla training scheme, which assumes that all labels are clean, we only add a single linear classifier $\bar{\theta}$ with only $N$

additional parameters. Also, our loss only requires a single back-propagation, where the added linear classifier has a negligible computational burden. Our training scheme stands out even more compared to the existing MAML-based methods [105, 121] or multi-stage training [3, 40] (See Sect. 4.2 and Fig. 1).

### 3.5   Label Correction

In this paper, we focus on the efficient, on-the-fly estimation of the label transition matrix to combat label miscorrection. To further demonstrate the effectiveness of our method, we employ a nave label correction strategy where we feed each noisy set sample $x \in \bar{d}$ to the clean classifier $f_{\phi,\theta}$ to produce a probability vector. If the maximum probability $\max(f_{\phi,\theta}(x))$ is bigger than the threshold $\rho$, we correct its label to a more probable label. This strategy relies only on the most recent prediction of the model mid-training, so the decision is prone to change. Formally, we can describe the relabeled $\hat{y}$,

$$
\hat{y} = \begin{cases} \bar{y}^*, & \text{if } \max(f_{\phi,\theta}(\bar{x})) < \rho \\ \lfloor f_{\phi,\theta}(\bar{x})/\max(f_{\phi,\theta}(\bar{x}))\rfloor, & \text{otherwise} \end{cases} \tag{7}
$$

where $\lfloor \cdot \rfloor$ denotes floor function and $\bar{y}^*$ denotes the original label from $\bar{d}$. $\bar{y}^*$ differs from $\bar{y}$; the former denotes the original label from the noisy dataset, whereas the latter is continuously corrected by the above strategy. Even with this simple strategy, our model shows better performance compared to the state-of-the-art methods. The experimental results suggest that replacing this strategy may further improve the model performance.

## 4   Experiments

In this section, we evaluate our proposed learning method, FasTEN, in terms of predictive performance (Sect. 4.1) and efficiency (Sect. 4.2). We also validate the label correction performance to demonstrate that our method is better in correcting noisy labels (Sect. 4.3 and Appendix C.6) and experimentally show the robustness of our proposed method towards miscorrected labels. (Sect. 4.4). We further analyze whether our method successfully estimates the label transition matrix in the case where the label correction shifts the true label transition matrix (Sect. 4.5) or not (Sect. 4.6). Additional experimental results and further analyses are described in Appendix C. We provide the source codes[1] for the reproduction of the experiments conducted in this paper.

---

[1] https://github.com/hyperconnect/FasTEN.

**Table 1.** Performance comparison on CIFAR-10/100 datasets under various noise level. Test accuracy (%) with 95% confidence interval of 5-runs is provided.

| | Method | Symmetric noise level | | | | Asymmetric noise level | |
|---|---|---|---|---|---|---|---|
| | | 20% | 40% | 60% | 80% | 20% | 40% |
| CIFAR-10 | L2RW | 88.26 ± 0.79 | 83.76 ± 0.54 | 74.54 ± 1.54 | 42.60 ± 1.71 | 88.79 ± 0.63 | 85.86 ± 0.87 |
| | MW-Net | 89.76 ± 0.31 | 86.52 ± 0.28 | 81.68 ± 0.25 | 56.56 ± 3.07 | 91.31 ± 0.25 | 88.69 ± 0.37 |
| | Deep kNN | 90.02 ± 0.35 | 87.27 ± 0.39 | 82.80 ± 0.55 | 68.30 ± 1.21 | 89.97 ± 0.48 | 84.56 ± 0.87 |
| | GLC | 89.66 ± 0.10 | 85.30 ± 0.73 | 80.34 ± 0.73 | 67.44 ± 1.50 | 91.56 ± 0.66 | **89.76 ± 0.89** |
| | MLoC | 90.50 ± 0.71 | 87.20 ± 0.35 | 81.95 ± 0.44 | 54.64 ± 4.04 | 91.15 ± 0.16 | 89.35 ± 0.45 |
| | MLaC | 89.75 ± 0.62 | 86.63 ± 0.56 | 82.20 ± 0.81 | 71.94 ± 2.22 | 91.45 ± 0.32 | **90.26 ± 0.48** |
| | MSLC | 90.94 ± 0.45 | 88.36 ± 0.80 | 83.93 ± 1.21 | 64.90 ± 4.84 | **91.45 ± 1.35** | 89.26 ± 0.52 |
| | FasTEN (ours.) | **91.94 ± 0.28** | **90.07 ± 0.17** | **86.78 ± 0.31** | **79.52 ± 0.78** | **92.29 ± 0.10** | **90.43 ± 0.31** |
| CIFAR-100 | L2RW | 57.79 ± 1.88 | 44.82 ± 4.30 | 30.01 ± 1.74 | 10.71 ± 1.79 | 59.11 ± 2.74 | 55.12 ± 3.40 |
| | MW-Net | 66.73 ± 0.78 | 59.44 ± 0.91 | 49.19 ± 1.57 | 19.04 ± 1.21 | 67.90 ± 0.78 | 64.50 ± 0.34 |
| | Deep kNN | 59.60 ± 0.97 | 52.48 ± 1.37 | 39.90 ± 0.60 | 23.39 ± 0.75 | 57.71 ± 0.47 | 50.23 ± 1.12 |
| | GLC | 60.99 ± 0.64 | 49.00 ± 4.33 | 33.38 ± 4.09 | 20.38 ± 1.35 | 64.43 ± 0.43 | 54.20 ± 0.86 |
| | MLoC | **68.16 ± 0.41** | 62.09 ± 0.33 | **54.49 ± 0.92** | 20.23 ± 1.86 | 69.20 ± 0.59 | 66.48 ± 0.56 |
| | MLaC | 49.81 ± 5.59 | 35.15 ± 5.75 | 20.15 ± 2.81 | 12.85 ± 0.87 | 56.46 ± 3.54 | 49.20 ± 3.23 |
| | MSLC | **68.62 ± 0.60** | 63.30 ± 0.49 | 53.83 ± 0.70 | 21.07 ± 5.20 | **70.86 ± 0.30** | 66.99 ± 0.69 |
| | FasTEN (ours.) | **68.75 ± 0.60** | **63.82 ± 0.33** | **55.22 ± 0.64** | **37.36 ± 1.15** | 70.35 ± 0.51 | **67.93 ± 0.53** |

**Baselines Using the Small Clean Dataset.** We deliberately choose the baselines that utilize the small clean dataset in learning with noisy labels. These baselines are categorized in the following three types. *Re-weighting*: **L2RW** [80] learns to assign weights to training samples based on their gradients. **MW-Net** [85] trains an explicit weighting function with the training samples. **Deep kNN** [3] applies the k-nearest neighbor algorithm to the logit layer of classifiers to find noisy samples. *Label transition matrix estimation*: **GLC** [40] estimates the label transition matrix using the small clean dataset. **MLoC** [101] considers the label transition matrix as trainable parameters to be obtained through meta-learning. *Label correction*: **MLaC** [121] trains a label correction network as a meta-process to provide corrected labels. **MSLC** [105] uses soft labels with loss balancing weight through meta-gradient descent step under the guidance of the clean dataset.

### 4.1 Predictive Performance Comparison

**CIFAR-10/100 with Synthetic Noise.** CIFAR-10/100 [49] have been widely adopted to assess the robustness of the methods to noisy labels. Since CIFAR-10/100 are known as clean datasets, labels are synthetically manipulated to contain noisy labels, injecting two types of noise: symmetric and asymmetric.

**Table 2.** Test accuracy (%) comparison on Clothing1M dataset with real-world label noise. Rows with † denote results directly borrowed from [121] and * denotes the result directly borrowed from [56]. All the other results except L2RW [80] are taken from original papers.

|              | Method         | Top-1 accuracy    |
|--------------|----------------|-------------------|
| Clean set X  | Forward*       | 69.91             |
|              | T-Revision*    | 70.97             |
|              | casualNL       | 72.24             |
|              | IF             | 72.29             |
|              | VolMinNet*     | 72.42             |
|              | DivideMix      | 74.76             |
|              | AugDesc        | 75.11             |
| Clean set O  | MLoC           | 71.10             |
|              | L2RW           | 72.04 ± 0.24      |
|              | GLC†           | 73.69             |
|              | MW-Net†        | 73.72             |
|              | MSLC           | 74.02             |
|              | MLaC†          | 75.78             |
| Ours         | FasTEN w/o LC  | 77.07  ± 0.52     |
|              | **FasTEN**     | **77.83 ± 0.17**  |

**Symmetric:** The labels are randomly flipped with uniform distribution. **Asymmetric:** the labels are flipped with class-dependent distribution, following the evaluation protocol of [76,111]. We claim that most studies report the performance highly overfitted to the test set without hyperparameter tuning on the validation set [53,73,74,105]. Moreover, baseline models employ different backbone networks, making it challenging to dissect the performance improvement whether it originated from each method or the backbone networks. Therefore, we first extract 5K samples as the validation set from the training set containing 50K samples and further extract 1K samples as the clean dataset. Then, we unify the backbone network as ResNet-34 [37], which is widely adopted in various baselines [59,105]. Note that we do our best to maintain the experimental settings of each method, including the hyperparameters written in the original paper. Detailed settings are deferred to Appendix B.

**Results.** Table 1 summarizes the evaluation results on CIFAR-10/100. For both CIFAR-10/-100, our proposed FasTEN achieves state-of-the-art performance on various noise levels within 95% confidence intervals. Especially, under a high noise level (80%), our FasTEN considerably outperforms the baselines with small variance on performance, which implies the robustness of our method [51,52]. These results demonstrate that our proposed method performs well in learning with noisy labels, especially considering its training efficiency (See Sect. 4.2).

**Clothing1M with Real-World Noise.** Clothing1M [109] is a noisy real-world dataset that consists of one million samples with additional 47K human-annotated clean samples. We use its original splits of clean and noisy data. For a fair comparison, we employ ResNet-50 architecture pretrained with the ImageNet dataset [18] for the initial backbone architecture. Evaluation results on Clothing1M are summarized in Table 2.

**Table 3.** Training time comparison on CIFAR-10 dataset with 80% symmetric noise. Time (hours) per total training on a single RTX 2080Ti GPU are provided with the relative ratio compared to our method.

| Method | L2RW | MW-NET | Deep kNN | GLC | MLoC | MLaC | MSLC | FasTEN |
|---|---|---|---|---|---|---|---|---|
| | [80] | [85] | [3] | [40] | [101] | [121] | [105] | (Ours.) |
| Total training time | 4.78 | 2.63 | 2.32 | 2.29 | 7.13 | 10.2 | 2.51 | **1.54** |
| (Relative to ours.) | (3.11x) | (1.71x) | (1.51x) | (1.49x) | (4.64x) | (6.64x) | (1.64x) | |

**Further Baselines.** We further compare our proposed FasTEN with additional baselines that have already reported their performance on Clothing1M dataset. Since the data split of Clothing1M dataset is the same for all the baselines, we simply obtain the performance of the baselines from their original papers and report the performance in Table 2. **DivideMix** [53] and **AugDesc** [73] leverages semi-supervised learning with various data augmentation strategies. **Forward** [76], **T-Revision** [108], **IF** [45], and **causalNL** [112], and **VolMin-Net** [56] are transition matrix estimation methods that use certain data points without clean data points.

**Results.** As shown in Table 2, our proposed FasTEN achieves remarkable performance on Clothing1M which contains instance-dependent noisy labels, beating the baselines by a large margin. This evaluation result indicates that our proposed FasTEN is more applicable in real-world problems where label corruption frequently occurs, although it does not directly target to address the problem of instance-dependent noisy labels. Similar to previous observations [40,66], we suspect that using the transition matrix seems to combat instance-dependent noise to some extent. Also, not only that our method shows superior performance over all the baselines that use the small clean set, but it also surpasses the semi-supervised learning-based methods (DivideMix and AugDesc) without any complex augmentation techniques. Finally, FasTEN shows better performance than T-Revision, causalNL, IF, and VolMinNet, which estimate the transition matrix without the small clean data (this is not a fair comparison). This result indicates that using the small clean data is effective in estimating the transition matrix accurately, leading to performance improvement eventually.

## 4.2   Training Time Comparison

**Setup.** To verify the efficiency of our proposed FasTEN, we compare it with the baselines in terms of accuracy by total training time. Total training time is measured on CIFAR-10/-100, respectively, with a single RTX 2080Ti GPU. Test accuracy shows the predictive performance on CIFAR-10/-100 with 20% and 80% symmetric noise ratios, the mildest and most severe noise conditions, respectively. Since Deep kNN and GLC require multiple training stages, the summation of all the hours needed for each training phase is provided.

**Results.** Figure 1 shows that our FasTEN, which learns the label transition matrix with the single back-propagation in the single-training stage, makes model training more efficient than other baselines that need multiple back-propagation or multiple training stages while showing better performance. Table 3 shows the total training hours of each baseline, including our FasTEN. Our method provides the training time speedup of minimum ×1.49 to maximum ×6.64.

## 4.3   Label Correction Performance Comparison

**Table 4.** Label correction performance comparison on CIFAR-10 with symmetric 80% noise. Accuracy (%) and Negative Log Likelihood (NLL) loss are calculated using the true labels before the synthetic noise is injected. Performance of the trained model on all training samples (Overall) and incorrectly labeled training samples (Incorrect) is measured. † denotes performance extracted from the meta model.

| | Method | L2RW [80] | MW-Net [85] | Deep kNN [3] | GLC [40] | MLoC [101] | MLaC [121] | MLaC† | MSLC [105] | MSLC† | FasTEN w/o LC | FasTEN (Ours.) |
|---|---|---|---|---|---|---|---|---|---|---|---|---|
| Acc. | Overall | 0.4450 | 0.6024 | 0.6471 | 0.6900 | 0.6261 | 0.7567 | 0.7672 | 0.6762 | 0.2821 | 0.7559 | **0.7847** |
| | Incorrect | 0.4447 | 0.6024 | 0.6483 | 0.6903 | 0.6257 | 0.7569 | 0.7382 | 0.6755 | 0.2836 | 0.7560 | **0.7861** |
| NLL | Overall | 1.6684 | 1.6961 | 1.6085 | 1.3904 | 1.7492 | 0.9868 | 1.7004 | 1.2694 | 1.5989 | 1.0057 | **0.8889** |
| | Incorrect | 1.6674 | 1.6957 | 1.6084 | 1.3881 | 1.7493 | 0.9851 | 1.7299 | 1.2722 | 1.5990 | 1.0033 | **0.8877** |

We analyze the predictive performance of the baseline methods on all the training samples (Overall) and the wrongly labeled subset of them (Incorrect), respectively. Table 4 demonstrates that our method can successfully correct the noisy labels, where using the label correction further improves the correction performance. This also implies that our FasTEN may be helpful in further cleansing the noisy training set.

We also compare the performance between Overall and Incorrect cases. Reweighting (L2RW, MW-Net, Deep kNN) and transition matrix estimation-based methods (GLC, MLoC) show similar performance between two cases: Overall and Incorrect. However, the performance of the meta-model of MLaC is worse for the Incorrect case, which indicates that the correction from the meta-model is less effective where the labels are wrong. Also, notable underperformance of the meta-model of MSLC may indicate the inefficacy of the meta-model. We also analyze the meta-model of the re-weighting methods in the Appendix C.6, where they do not distinguish the wrongly labeled samples well.

### 4.4  Robustness to Miscorrection: What Happens if Labels Are Wrongly Corrected?

This subsection illustrates the robustness of our label correction method to mis-corrected labels by comparing it with other label correction methods (MLaC and MSLC) which blindly trust the miscorrected labels as the ground-truth, where we verify the imperfect corrections (See Sect. 4.3). We examine how much this behavior deteriorates the predictive performance.

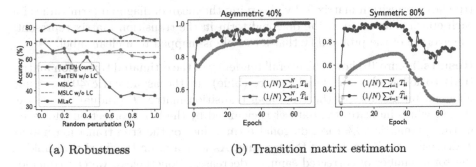

(a) Robustness                    (b) Transition matrix estimation

**Fig. 3.** (a) Robustness to miscorrected labels on CIFAR-10 with various perturbation strength. Test accuracy (%) of baselines and baselines without the label correction is provided. (b) The plot for the mean of the diagonal term in true transition matrix $T$ and our estimated transition matrix $\widehat{T}$ according to the epoch on CIFAR-10 dataset with symmetric 80% and asymmetric 40% noise. (Color figure online)

**Setup.** We experiment on CIFAR-10 with symmetric 80% noise where there are a maximum number of noisy labels to correct. To simulate the miscorrection, we perturb the corrected labels by injecting artificial noise. We control the degree of random perturbation to observe the robustness of each method on various levels of miscorrection. We further assess the robustness of our FasTEN and MSLC by comparing it with the performance obtained without label correction.

**Results.** Figure 3a shows our proposed FasTEN outperforms MLaC and MSLC on all the degrees of the random perturbation. MLaC shows steep performance degradation when perturbation worsens, i.e., there are more miscorrected labels. This observation reveals the susceptibility of MLaC. MSLC shows trivial perfor-mance gains when labels are corrected, implying that it is not using the full bene-fits of label correction. Furthermore, when highly perturbed, MSLC performance worsens if it attempts to correct the labels. In contrast, the label correction of our FasTEN improves performance even in harsh situations. FasTEN does not degrade performance even if the correction becomes useless (100% perturbation). These observations show that our FasTEN builds a more robust classifier to miscorrected labels through its efficient estimation of the label transition matrix, acting as a safeguard combating the miscorrected labels.

## 4.5   On-the-Fly Estimation of the Label Transition Matrix

Our proposed FasTEN newly estimates the label transition matrix on every iteration, where the matrix is constantly shifted by label correction. To assess the matrix estimation quality, we compare it with the true label transition matrix.

**Setup.** We train FasTEN on CIFAR-10 with symmetric 80% and asymmetric 40% noise, which are harsh conditions on symmetric and asymmetric noise injection, respectively. We compare the estimated label transition matrix $\hat{T}$ with the true label transition matrix $T$ by observing the mean of diagonal term values for each epoch. The mean of the diagonal term in the transition matrix represents the average of the probability that a sample is mapped to a clean label.

**Results.** Figure 3b shows the overall tendency of the estimated transition matrix (red) to follow the true label matrix (blue). In the asymmetric 40% setting, diagonal term values of the true label transition matrix $T$ gradually increases (blue), which indicates the dataset is cleansed by the label correction. However, in the symmetric 80% case, diagonal term values of the true transition matrix $T$ decreases at the middle of the training. As we maintain the fixed threshold $\rho$, the total number of corrected samples decreases. Nonetheless, we can conclude that the transition matrix is successfully estimated on shifting noise levels.

Additionally, we observe that the estimated transition matrix $\hat{T}$ shows higher mean values, i.e., being overconfident on the clean dataset samples. Theoretically, $f_{\phi,\bar{\theta}}$ should correctly approximate the noisy label distribution given enough number of clean samples (See Appendix A.4), but it seems to be overfitting to the clean dataset in practice. This observation is consistent with the popular belief that neural networks tend to learn clean samples first and noisy samples later [1]. For better matrix estimation to yield a more robust classifier [31,67,108,113], it appears that we need to address the overfitting through additional components.

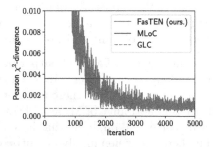

**Fig. 4.** Plot of transition matrix estimation error for every iteration. Pearson $\chi^2$-divergence of our FasTEN, MLoC and GLC is provided.

## 4.6 Empirical Convergence Analysis on Estimating the Label Transition Matrix

**Setup.** This section analyzes the convergence of estimation error between the true label transition matrix $T$ and the estimated transition matrix $\widehat{T}$, comparing our FasTEN to other methods, MLoC and GLC, which learn the transition matrix. For fair comparison, we exclude the label correction for our method.

**Results.** Figure 4 shows the difference between the probability distribution of the true label transition matrix $T$ and the estimated transition matrix $\widehat{T}$ for each iteration, where Pearson $\chi^2$-divergence is used to measure the discrepancy between the two matrices. GLC error remains fixed (dotted line) as it estimates the transition matrix only once in the entire learning process. The decrease of MLoC error is extremely slow (blue line), implying the high dependence of the initialization of $\widehat{T}$ and its ineffectiveness on estimation. Although our FasTEN does not require multiple stages of training and produces the single mini-batch-based estimate every iteration, it shows fast convergence with a similar estimation error to GLC, which uses all the available data.

## 5 Conclusion

In this work, we propose a robust and efficient method, FasTEN, which efficiently learns a label transition matrix that mitigates the label miscorrection problem of existing label correction methods. Our proposed FasTEN accurately estimates the label transition matrix using a small clean dataset even if the samples are miscorrected. Moreover, our FasTEN is highly efficient compared to existing methods since it requires single back-propagation through two-head architecture and needs only a single training stage. Extensive experiments show that our method is the fastest and the most robust classifier. Especially, our method achieves remarkable performance on both the real-world noise dataset (Clothing1M) and the synthetic dataset on various noise levels (CIFAR). The detailed analysis shows that our method is robust to miscorrected labels by efficiently estimating the transition matrix shifted by the label correction.

## References

1. Arpit, D., et al.: A closer look at memorization in deep networks. In: International Conference on Machine Learning, pp. 233–242. PMLR (2017)
2. Azadi, S., Feng, J., Jegelka, S., Darrell, T.: Auxiliary image regularization for deep CNNs with noisy labels. arXiv preprint arXiv:1511.07069 (2015)
3. Bahri, D., Jiang, H., Gupta, M.: Deep k-NN for noisy labels. In: International Conference on Machine Learning, pp. 540–550. PMLR (2020)
4. Bartlett, P., Foster, D.J., Telgarsky, M.: Spectrally-normalized margin bounds for neural networks. arXiv preprint arXiv:1706.08498 (2017)
5. Bartlett, P.L., Jordan, M.I., McAuliffe, J.D.: Convexity, classification, and risk bounds. J. Am. Stat. Assoc. **101**(473), 138–156 (2006)

6. Bartlett, P.L., Mendelson, S.: Rademacher and Gaussian complexities: risk bounds and structural results. J. Mach. Learn. Res. **3**(Nov), 463–482 (2002)
7. Bekker, A.J., Goldberger, J.: Training deep neural-networks based on unreliable labels. In: 2016 IEEE International Conference on Acoustics, Speech and Signal Processing (ICASSP), pp. 2682–2686. IEEE (2016)
8. Berthon, A., Han, B., Niu, G., Liu, T., Sugiyama, M.: Confidence scores make instance-dependent label-noise learning possible. arXiv preprint arXiv:2001.03772 (2020)
9. Boucheron, S., Lugosi, G., Massart, P.: Concentration Inequalities: A Nonasymptotic Theory of Independence. Oxford University Press, Oxford (2013)
10. Cao, K., Chen, Y., Lu, J., Arechiga, N., Gaidon, A., Ma, T.: Heteroskedastic and imbalanced deep learning with adaptive regularization. arXiv preprint arXiv:2006.15766 (2020)
11. Chang, H.S., Learned-Miller, E., McCallum, A.: Active bias: training more accurate neural networks by emphasizing high variance samples. arXiv preprint arXiv:1704.07433 (2017)
12. Charikar, M., Steinhardt, J., Valiant, G.: Learning from untrusted data. In: Proceedings of the 49th Annual ACM SIGACT Symposium on Theory of Computing, pp. 47–60 (2017)
13. Chawla, N.V., Bowyer, K.W., Hall, L.O., Kegelmeyer, W.P.: Smote: synthetic minority over-sampling technique. J. Artif. Intell. Res. **16**, 321–357 (2002)
14. Chen, P., Liao, B.B., Chen, G., Zhang, S.: Understanding and utilizing deep neural networks trained with noisy labels. In: International Conference on Machine Learning, pp. 1062–1070. PMLR (2019)
15. Chen, P., Ye, J., Chen, G., Zhao, J., Heng, P.A.: Robustness of accuracy metric and its inspirations in learning with noisy labels. arXiv preprint arXiv:2012.04193 (2020)
16. Cheng, H., Zhu, Z., Li, X., Gong, Y., Sun, X., Liu, Y.: Learning with instance-dependent label noise: a sample sieve approach. In: ICLR (2021)
17. Cheng, J., Liu, T., Ramamohanarao, K., Tao, D.: Learning with bounded instance and label-dependent label noise. In: International Conference on Machine Learning, pp. 1789–1799. PMLR (2020)
18. Deng, J., Dong, W., Socher, R., Li, L.J., Li, K., Fei-Fei, L.: Imagenet: a large-scale hierarchical image database. In: 2009 IEEE Conference on Computer Vision and Pattern Recognition, pp. 248–255. IEEE (2009)
19. Drory, A., Avidan, S., Giryes, R.: How do neural networks overcome label noise. arXiv Preprint (2018)
20. Finn, C., Abbeel, P., Levine, S.: Model-agnostic meta-learning for fast adaptation of deep networks. In: International Conference on Machine Learning, pp. 1126–1135. PMLR (2017)
21. Floridi, L., Chiriatti, M.: GPT-3: its nature, scope, limits, and consequences. Mind. Mach. **30**(4), 681–694 (2020)
22. Ghosh, A., Kumar, H., Sastry, P.: Robust loss functions under label noise for deep neural networks. In: Proceedings of the AAAI Conference on Artificial Intelligence, vol. 31 (2017)
23. Ghosh, A., Lan, A.: Do we really need gold samples for sample weighting under label noise? In: Proceedings of the IEEE/CVF Winter Conference on Applications of Computer Vision, pp. 3922–3931 (2021)
24. Girshick, R., Donahue, J., Darrell, T., Malik, J.: Rich feature hierarchies for accurate object detection and semantic segmentation. In: Proceedings of the IEEE Conference on Computer Vision and Pattern Recognition, pp. 580–587 (2014)

25. Goldberger, J., Ben-Reuven, E.: Training deep neural-networks using a noise adaptation layer (2016)
26. Golowich, N., Rakhlin, A., Shamir, O.: Size-independent sample complexity of neural networks. In: Conference On Learning Theory, pp. 297–299. PMLR (2018)
27. Goodfellow, I., Bengio, Y., Courville, A.: Deep Learning. MIT Press, Cambridge (2016). http://www.deeplearningbook.org
28. Guan, M., Gulshan, V., Dai, A., Hinton, G.: Who said what: modeling individual labelers improves classification. In: Proceedings of the AAAI Conference on Artificial Intelligence, vol. 32 (2018)
29. Guo, C., Pleiss, G., Sun, Y., Weinberger, K.Q.: On calibration of modern neural networks. In: International Conference on Machine Learning, pp. 1321–1330. PMLR (2017)
30. Guo, J., Gong, M., Liu, T., Zhang, K., Tao, D.: LTF: a label transformation framework for correcting label shift. In: International Conference on Machine Learning, pp. 3843–3853. PMLR (2020)
31. Han, B., et al.: SIGUA: forgetting may make learning with noisy labels more robust. In: International Conference on Machine Learning, pp. 4006–4016. PMLR (2020)
32. Han, B., et al.: Masking: a new perspective of noisy supervision. arXiv preprint arXiv:1805.08193 (2018)
33. Han, B., et al.: Co-teaching: robust training of deep neural networks with extremely noisy labels. arXiv preprint arXiv:1804.06872 (2018)
34. Han, J., Luo, P., Wang, X.: Deep self-learning from noisy labels. In: Proceedings of the IEEE/CVF International Conference on Computer Vision, pp. 5138–5147 (2019)
35. Han, K., Wang, Y., Xu, Y., Xu, C., Wu, E., Xu, C.: Training binary neural networks through learning with noisy supervision. In: International Conference on Machine Learning, pp. 4017–4026. PMLR (2020)
36. Harutyunyan, H., Reing, K., Ver Steeg, G., Galstyan, A.: Improving generalization by controlling label-noise information in neural network weights. In: International Conference on Machine Learning, pp. 4071–4081. PMLR (2020)
37. He, K., Zhang, X., Ren, S., Sun, J.: Deep residual learning for image recognition. In: Proceedings of the IEEE Conference on Computer Vision and Pattern Recognition, pp. 770–778 (2016)
38. Hendrycks, D., Lee, K., Mazeika, M.: Using pre-training can improve model robustness and uncertainty. In: International Conference on Machine Learning, pp. 2712–2721. PMLR (2019)
39. Hendrycks, D., Mazeika, M., Kadavath, S., Song, D.: Using self-supervised learning can improve model robustness and uncertainty. arXiv preprint arXiv:1906.12340 (2019)
40. Hendrycks, D., Mazeika, M., Wilson, D., Gimpel, K.: Using trusted data to train deep networks on labels corrupted by severe noise. Adv. Neural Inf. Process. Syst. 31 (2018)
41. Hong, Y., Han, S., Choi, K., Seo, S., Kim, B., Chang, B.: Disentangling label distribution for long-tailed visual recognition. arXiv preprint arXiv:2012.00321 (2020)
42. Hu, W., Li, Z., Yu, D.: Simple and effective regularization methods for training on noisily labeled data with generalization guarantee. arXiv preprint arXiv:1905.11368 (2019)
43. Huang, L., Zhang, C., Zhang, H.: Self-adaptive training: beyond empirical risk minimization. Adv. Neural Inf. Process. Syst. 33 (2020)

44. Jiang, L., Zhou, Z., Leung, T., Lif, L.J., Fei-Fei, L.: MentorNet: learning data-driven curriculum for very deep neural networks on corrupted labels. In: International Conference on Machine Learning, pp. 2304–2313. PMLR (2018)

45. Jiang, Z., et al.: An information fusion approach to learning with instance-dependent label noise. In: International Conference on Learning Representations (2022). https://openreview.net/forum?id=ecH2FKaARUp

46. Jindal, I., Nokleby, M., Chen, X.: Learning deep networks from noisy labels with dropout regularization. In: 2016 IEEE 16th International Conference on Data Mining (ICDM), pp. 967–972. IEEE (2016)

47. Kim, T., Ko, J., Choi, J., Yun, S.Y., et al.: Fine samples for learning with noisy labels. Adv. Neural Inf. Process. Syst. **34** (2021)

48. Kingma, D.P., Ba, J.: Adam: a method for stochastic optimization. arXiv preprint arXiv:1412.6980 (2014)

49. Krizhevsky, A., Hinton, G., et al.: Learning multiple layers of features from tiny images (2009)

50. Lee, K.H., He, X., Zhang, L., Yang, L.: CleanNet: transfer learning for scalable image classifier training with label noise. In: Proceedings of the IEEE Conference on Computer Vision and Pattern Recognition, pp. 5447–5456 (2018)

51. Li, D., Chen, C., Liu, W., Lu, T., Gu, N., Chu, S.M.: Mixture-rank matrix approximation for collaborative filtering. In: Proceedings of the 31st International Conference on Neural Information Processing Systems, pp. 477–485 (2017)

52. Li, D., Chen, C., Lv, Q., Yan, J., Shang, L., Chu, S.: Low-rank matrix approximation with stability. In: International Conference on Machine Learning, pp. 295–303. PMLR (2016)

53. Li, J., Socher, R., Hoi, S.C.: DivideMix: learning with noisy labels as semi-supervised learning. arXiv preprint arXiv:2002.07394 (2020)

54. Li, J., Wong, Y., Zhao, Q., Kankanhalli, M.S.: Learning to learn from noisy labeled data. In: Proceedings of the IEEE/CVF Conference on Computer Vision and Pattern Recognition, pp. 5051–5059 (2019)

55. Li, M., Soltanolkotabi, M., Oymak, S.: Gradient descent with early stopping is provably robust to label noise for overparameterized neural networks. In: International Conference on Artificial Intelligence and Statistics, pp. 4313–4324. PMLR (2020)

56. Li, X., Liu, T., Han, B., Niu, G., Sugiyama, M.: Provably end-to-end label-noise learning without anchor points. In: International Conference on Machine Learning. PMLR (2021)

57. Lienen, J., Hüllermeier, E.: From label smoothing to label relaxation. In: Proceedings of the 35th AAAI Conference on Artificial Intelligence, AAAI, Online, 2–9 February 2021. AAAI Press (2021)

58. Lin, T.Y., Goyal, P., Girshick, R., He, K., Dollár, P.: Focal loss for dense object detection. In: Proceedings of the IEEE International Conference on Computer Vision, pp. 2980–2988 (2017)

59. Liu, S., Niles-Weed, J., Razavian, N., Fernandez-Granda, C.: Early-learning regularization prevents memorization of noisy labels. arXiv preprint arXiv:2007.00151 (2020)

60. Liu, T., Tao, D.: Classification with noisy labels by importance reweighting. IEEE Trans. Pattern Anal. Mach. Intell. **38**(3), 447–461 (2015)

61. Liu, Y., Guo, H.: Peer loss functions: learning from noisy labels without knowing noise rates. In: International Conference on Machine Learning, pp. 6226–6236. PMLR (2020)

62. Lukasik, M., Bhojanapalli, S., Menon, A., Kumar, S.: Does label smoothing mitigate label noise? In: International Conference on Machine Learning, pp. 6448–6458. PMLR (2020)
63. Ma, X., Huang, H., Wang, Y., Romano, S., Erfani, S., Bailey, J.: Normalized loss functions for deep learning with noisy labels. In: International Conference on Machine Learning, pp. 6543–6553. PMLR (2020)
64. Ma, X., Wang, Y., Houle, M.E., Zhou, S., Erfani, S., Xia, S., Wijewickrema, S., Bailey, J.: Dimensionality-driven learning with noisy labels. In: International Conference on Machine Learning. pp. 3355–3364. PMLR (2018)
65. Menon, A.K., Rawat, A.S., Reddi, S.J., Kumar, S.: Can gradient clipping mitigate label noise? (2020)
66. Menon, A.K., Van Rooyen, B., Natarajan, N.: Learning from binary labels with instance-dependent corruption. arXiv preprint arXiv:1605.00751 (2016)
67. Mirzasoleiman, B., Cao, K., Leskovec, J.: Coresets for robust training of deep neural networks against noisy labels. Adv. Neural Inf. Process. Syst. **33** (2020)
68. Mnih, V., Hinton, G.E.: Learning to label aerial images from noisy data. In: Proceedings of the 29th International Conference on Machine Learning (ICML-12), pp. 567–574 (2012)
69. Mohri, M., Rostamizadeh, A., Talwalkar, A.: Foundations of Machine Learning. MIT Press, Cambridge (2018)
70. Montgomery-Smith, S.J.: The distribution of Rademacher sums. Proc. Am. Math. Soc. **109**(2), 517–522 (1990)
71. Natarajan, N., Dhillon, I.S., Ravikumar, P., Tewari, A.: Learning with noisy labels. In: NIPS, vol. 26, pp. 1196–1204 (2013)
72. Neyshabur, B., Bhojanapalli, S., Srebro, N.: A PAC-Bayesian approach to spectrally-normalized margin bounds for neural networks. arXiv preprint arXiv:1707.09564 (2017)
73. Nishi, K., Ding, Y., Rich, A., Höllerer, T.: Augmentation strategies for learning with noisy labels. arXiv preprint arXiv:2103.02130 (2021)
74. Ortego, D., Arazo, E., Albert, P., O'Connor, N.E., McGuinness, K.: Multi-objective interpolation training for robustness to label noise. arXiv preprint arXiv:2012.04462 (2020)
75. Patrini, G., Nielsen, F., Nock, R., Carioni, M.: Loss factorization, weakly supervised learning and label noise robustness. In: International Conference on Machine Learning, pp. 708–717. PMLR (2016)
76. Patrini, G., Rozza, A., Krishna Menon, A., Nock, R., Qu, L.: Making deep neural networks robust to label noise: a loss correction approach. In: Proceedings of the IEEE Conference on Computer Vision and Pattern Recognition, pp. 1944–1952 (2017)
77. Pleiss, G., Zhang, T., Elenberg, E.R., Weinberger, K.Q.: Identifying mislabeled data using the area under the margin ranking. arXiv preprint arXiv:2001.10528 (2020)
78. Radford, A., et al.: Learning transferable visual models from natural language supervision. In: International Conference on Machine Learning, pp. 8748–8763. PMLR (2021)
79. Reed, S., Lee, H., Anguelov, D., Szegedy, C., Erhan, D., Rabinovich, A.: Training deep neural networks on noisy labels with bootstrapping. arXiv preprint arXiv:1412.6596 (2014)
80. Ren, M., Zeng, W., Yang, B., Urtasun, R.: Learning to reweight examples for robust deep learning. In: International Conference on Machine Learning, pp. 4334–4343. PMLR (2018)

81. Rodrigues, F., Pereira, F.: Deep learning from crowds. In: Proceedings of the AAAI Conference on Artificial Intelligence, vol. 32 (2018)

82. Scott, C.: A rate of convergence for mixture proportion estimation, with application to learning from noisy labels. In: Artificial Intelligence and Statistics, pp. 838–846. PMLR (2015)

83. Scott, C., et al.: Calibrated asymmetric surrogate losses. Electron. J. Stat. **6**, 958–992 (2012)

84. Shrivastava, A., Gupta, A., Girshick, R.: Training region-based object detectors with online hard example mining. In: Proceedings of the IEEE Conference on Computer Vision and Pattern Recognition, pp. 761–769 (2016)

85. Shu, J., Xie, Q., Yi, L., Zhao, Q., Zhou, S., Xu, Z., Meng, D.: Meta-weight-net: learning an explicit mapping for sample weighting. arXiv preprint arXiv:1902.07379 (2019)

86. Song, H., Kim, M., Lee, J.G.: Selfie: refurbishing unclean samples for robust deep learning. In: International Conference on Machine Learning, pp. 5907–5915. PMLR (2019)

87. Song, H., Kim, M., Park, D., Lee, J.G.: How does early stopping help generalization against label noise? arXiv preprint arXiv:1911.08059 (2019)

88. Sukhbaatar, S., Bruna, J., Paluri, M., Bourdev, L., Fergus, R.: Training convolutional networks with noisy labels. arXiv preprint arXiv:1406.2080 (2014)

89. Taigman, Y., Yang, M., Ranzato, M., Wolf, L.: DeepFace: closing the gap to human-level performance in face verification. In: Proceedings of the IEEE Conference on Computer Vision and Pattern Recognition, pp. 1701–1708 (2014)

90. Tanaka, D., Ikami, D., Yamasaki, T., Aizawa, K.: Joint optimization framework for learning with noisy labels. In: Proceedings of the IEEE Conference on Computer Vision and Pattern Recognition, pp. 5552–5560 (2018)

91. Tanno, R., Saeedi, A., Sankaranarayanan, S., Alexander, D.C., Silberman, N.: Learning from noisy labels by regularized estimation of annotator confusion. In: Proceedings of the IEEE/CVF Conference on Computer Vision and Pattern Recognition, pp. 11244–11253 (2019)

92. Thekumparampil, K.K., Khetan, A., Lin, Z., Oh, S.: Robustness of conditional GANs to noisy labels. arXiv preprint arXiv:1811.03205 (2018)

93. Thulasidasan, S., Bhattacharya, T., Bilmes, J., Chennupati, G., Mohd-Yusof, J.: Combating label noise in deep learning using abstention. arXiv preprint arXiv:1905.10964 (2019)

94. Van Rooyen, B., Menon, A.K., Williamson, R.C.: Learning with symmetric label noise: the importance of being unhinged. arXiv preprint arXiv:1505.07634 (2015)

95. Vapnik, V.: The Nature of Statistical Learning Theory. Springer, New York (2013). https://doi.org/10.1007/978-1-4757-3264-1

96. Vapnik, V.N.: An overview of statistical learning theory. IEEE Trans. Neural Netw. **10**(5), 988–999 (1999)

97. Veit, A., Alldrin, N., Chechik, G., Krasin, I., Gupta, A., Belongie, S.: Learning from noisy large-scale datasets with minimal supervision. In: Proceedings of the IEEE Conference on Computer Vision and Pattern Recognition, pp. 839–847 (2017)

98. Vinyals, O., Blundell, C., Lillicrap, T., Kavukcuoglu, K., Wierstra, D.: Matching networks for one shot learning. arXiv preprint arXiv:1606.04080 (2016)

99. Wang, Y., Ma, X., Chen, Z., Luo, Y., Yi, J., Bailey, J.: Symmetric cross entropy for robust learning with noisy labels. In: Proceedings of the IEEE/CVF International Conference on Computer Vision, pp. 322–330 (2019)

100. Wang, Y., Kucukelbir, A., Blei, D.M.: Robust probabilistic modeling with Bayesian data reweighting. In: International Conference on Machine Learning, pp. 3646–3655. PMLR (2017)
101. Wang, Z., Hu, G., Hu, Q.: Training noise-robust deep neural networks via meta-learning. In: Proceedings of the IEEE/CVF Conference on Computer Vision and Pattern Recognition, pp. 4524–4533 (2020)
102. Wang, Z., Zhu, H., Dong, Z., He, X., Huang, S.L.: Less is better: unweighted data subsampling via influence function. In: Proceedings of the AAAI Conference on Artificial Intelligence, vol. 34, pp. 6340–6347 (2020)
103. Wei, J., Zhu, Z., Cheng, H., Liu, T., Niu, G., Liu, Y.: Learning with noisy labels revisited: a study using real-world human annotations. In: ICLR (2022)
104. Wu, P., Zheng, S., Goswami, M., Metaxas, D., Chen, C.: A topological filter for learning with label noise. arXiv preprint arXiv:2012.04835 (2020)
105. Wu, Y., Shu, J., Xie, Q., Zhao, Q., Meng, D.: Learning to purify noisy labels via meta soft label corrector. arXiv preprint arXiv:2008.00627 (2020)
106. Xia, X., et al.: Sample selection with uncertainty of losses for learning with noisy labels. arXiv preprint arXiv:2106.00445 (2021)
107. Xia, X., et al.: Part-dependent label noise: Towards instance-dependent label noise. Adv. Neural Inf. Process. Syst. **33** (2020)
108. Xia, X., Liu, T., Wang, N., Han, B., Gong, C., Niu, G., Sugiyama, M.: Are anchor points really indispensable in label-noise learning? arXiv preprint arXiv:1906.00189 (2019)
109. Xiao, T., Xia, T., Yang, Y., Huang, C., Wang, X.: Learning from massive noisy labeled data for image classification. In: Proceedings of the IEEE Conference on Computer Vision and Pattern Recognition, pp. 2691–2699 (2015)
110. Yang, F., Koyejo, S.: On the consistency of top-k surrogate losses. In: International Conference on Machine Learning, pp. 10727–10735. PMLR (2020)
111. Yao, J., Wu, H., Zhang, Y., Tsang, I.W., Sun, J.: Safeguarded dynamic label regression for noisy supervision. In: Proceedings of the AAAI Conference on Artificial Intelligence, vol. 33, pp. 9103–9110 (2019)
112. Yao, Y., Liu, T., Gong, M., Han, B., Niu, G., Zhang, K.: Instance-dependent label-noise learning under a structural causal model. Adv. Neural Inf. Process. Syst. **34** (2021)
113. Yao, Y., et al.: Dual t: reducing estimation error for transition matrix in label-noise learning. arXiv preprint arXiv:2006.07805 (2020)
114. Yi, K., Wu, J.: Probabilistic end-to-end noise correction for learning with noisy labels. In: Proceedings of the IEEE/CVF Conference on Computer Vision and Pattern Recognition, pp. 7017–7025 (2019)
115. Yu, X., Liu, T., Gong, M., Tao, D.: Learning with biased complementary labels. In: Ferrari, V., Hebert, M., Sminchisescu, C., Weiss, Y. (eds.) ECCV 2018. LNCS, vol. 11205, pp. 69–85. Springer, Cham (2018). https://doi.org/10.1007/978-3-030-01246-5_5
116. Zhang, C., Bengio, S., Hardt, M., Recht, B., Vinyals, O.: Understanding deep learning requires rethinking generalization. arXiv preprint arXiv:1611.03530 (2016)
117. Zhang, H., Cisse, M., Dauphin, Y.N., Lopez-Paz, D.: mixup: Beyond empirical risk minimization. arXiv preprint arXiv:1710.09412 (2017)
118. Zhang, X., Wu, X., Chen, F., Zhao, L., Lu, C.T.: Self-paced robust learning for leveraging clean labels in noisy data. In: Proceedings of the AAAI Conference on Artificial Intelligence, vol. 34, pp. 6853–6860 (2020)

119. Zhang, Y., Niu, G., Sugiyama, M.: Learning noise transition matrix from only noisy labels via total variation regularization. In: International Conference on Machine Learning, pp. 12501–12512. PMLR (2021)
120. Zhang, Z., Sabuncu, M.R.: Generalized cross entropy loss for training deep neural networks with noisy labels. arXiv preprint arXiv:1805.07836 (2018)
121. Zheng, G., Awadallah, A.H., Dumais, S.: Meta label correction for noisy label learning. In: Proceedings of the 35th AAAI Conference on Artificial Intelligence (2021)
122. Zheng, S., Wu, P., Goswami, A., Goswami, M., Metaxas, D., Chen, C.: Error-bounded correction of noisy labels. In: International Conference on Machine Learning, pp. 11447–11457. PMLR (2020)
123. Zhu, Z., Liu, T., Liu, Y.: A second-order approach to learning with instance-dependent label noise. In: Proceedings of the IEEE/CVF Conference on Computer Vision and Pattern Recognition, pp. 10113–10123 (2021)

# Online Task-free Continual Learning with Dynamic Sparse Distributed Memory

Julien Pourcel[1(✉)], Ngoc-Son Vu[1], and Robert M. French[2]

[1] ETIS - CYU, ENSEA, CNRS, Paris, France
`julien.pourcel@ensea.fr`
[2] LEAD - UBFC, CNRS, Paris, France

**Abstract.** This paper addresses the very challenging problem of online task-free continual learning in which a sequence of new tasks is learned from non-stationary data using each sample only once for training and without knowledge of task boundaries. We propose in this paper an efficient semi-distributed associative memory algorithm called Dynamic Sparse Distributed Memory (DSDM) where learning and evaluating can be carried out at any point of time. DSDM evolves dynamically and continually modeling the distribution of any non-stationary data stream. DSDM relies on locally distributed, but only partially overlapping clusters of representations to effectively eliminate catastrophic forgetting, while at the same time, maintaining the generalization capacities of distributed networks. In addition, a local density-based pruning technique is used to control the network's memory footprint. DSDM significantly outperforms state-of-the-art continual learning methods on different image classification baselines, even in a low data regime. Code is publicly available: https://github.com/Julien-pour/Dynamic-Sparse-Distributed-Memory.

## 1 Introduction

Although having obtained impressive performance on many different individual tasks, current static deep neural networks (DNNs) must be trained on batches of independently and identically distributed (i.i.d) data samples. These batch learning algorithms distinguish between the processes of knowledge training and knowledge inference, and require restarting the full training process each time new data becomes available. Indeed, they need to access all of the training data within multiple epochs (offline training).

Continual learning (CL) considers the scenario of learning from a non i.i.d data stream where different data and tasks are presented to the model in a sequential manner. While humans can continually observe and learn new knowledge, DNNs have been shown to suffer from catastrophic forgetting (CF) - they are not able to perform well on previously seen data after being updated with recent data. Because their learned knowledge is stored in a single set of weights and learning new information modifies that set of weights, sometimes drastically,

© The Author(s), under exclusive license to Springer Nature Switzerland AG 2022
S. Avidan et al. (Eds.): ECCV 2022, LNCS 13685, pp. 739–756, 2022.
https://doi.org/10.1007/978-3-031-19806-9_42

new learning frequently causes the networks to forget all, or most of, what they have previously learned.

Catastrophic forgetting was actively studied in the late 1980s and 1990s, mainly in neuro-scientific literature, and numerous solutions were adopted in an attempt to overcome the problem [41]. A more general problem, referred to as the stability-plasticity dilemma, where the trade-off between the ability of retaining previous knowledge and fast learning a new task, was studied as well [8]. CF is a direct consequence of the overlap of distributed representations. Indeed, highly distributed representations with significant interaction among them are able to generalize but suffer from CF while very local representations with little or no interaction among them do not suffer from CF but lack generalization ability or storage capacity.

Many early algorithms involved reducing the distributed nature of the network's internal representations, thereby creating relatively sparse representations to reduce the representational overlap. This was done in several ways, either by gradually nudging the network's internal representations into largely non-overlapping clusters [49] or by orthogonalizing the input representations [15,33,35]. Other solutions have involved the network learning "pseudo-patterns" that reflected the previously learned patterns [50]; using dual networks in which the old information was transferred to a second, independent network and then interleaved with the new information being learned [4,16], creating an approximation of the error surface of the previously learned patterns and integrating that error surface with the error surface associated with the new patterns [18], and so on. See [17] for a review of early work on CF, dating from the early 1990's through the mid-2000's. A large number of recent continual learning methods have been proposed in the literature and many of them are built on those early solutions.

**Sparse Distributed Memory:** the standard Kanerva Sparse Distributed Memory (SDM) is a content-addressable memory model developed in the 1980's [26,27]. In its development, SDM respected fundamental biological constraints and is considered to be a generalization of the original Hopfield network [28,46]. Recent work [6] has shown mathematically that SDM closely approximates Attention, the core of widely used Transformer models. SDM was used as semi-distributed representations that allowed it to be robust to CF. In SDM, input content is stored in hyperspheres in a very high-dimensional space around hard locations that are largely, but not completely, independent and, thus, do not significantly interfere with one another. At the same time, the size of the hyperspheres is large enough that generalization is not significantly impaired. In this way, the representational overlap causing CF is avoided, while, at the same time, the generalization capacities of the system are not overly affected.

Taking into account these advantages of SDM, we propose a novel algorithm called Dynamic Sparse Distributed Memory (DSDM) that performs excellently on the most challenging setting of continual learning, namely, online task-free scenario. Figure 1 gives a brief overview and the difference between SDM and

DSDM. Experiment results of DSDM on a number of image classification bench-marks under different scenarios demonstrate its excellent ability to eliminate catastrophic forgetting.

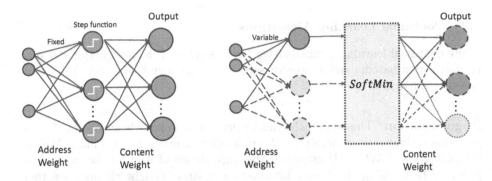

**Fig. 1.** SDM (left) vs. DSDM (right). While in SDM, the number of neurons is fixed, their addresses are randomly distributed and fixed, and the radius of reading and writing patterns are predefined, in DSDM all these factors are data-driven and dynamically learnt. The dashed/dotted lines/states mean that these connections and nodes will be added or removed as needed.

## 2    Related Work

We first briefly discuss different scenarios of CL in Sect. 2.1 and then present several existing CL methods in Sect. 2.2. We provide an overview of the standard SDM on which our algorithm is based in Sect. 2.3.

### 2.1    Continual Learning Settings

Continual learning has been studied under different scenarios that are often divided into three categories of increasing difficulty [57]: **task, domain**, and **class-incremental**. In task-incremental learning, there is a single classification head assigned to each task, whereas in class-incremental learning, there is a single head for all tasks. Models doing domain-incremental learning use a single classification head and do not have to infer the identity of the task.

Online learning requires each image or item to be seen only once during learning, whereas in offline learning, the input data may be seen repeatedly, as is necessary. Additionally, continual learning can be task-based or task-free, depending on whether boundaries between different tasks are known or not. Recently, the **data-incremental learning** paradigm has been introduced [11] to facilitate learning from any data stream, without any assumption regarding task identity, task boundaries or the order of observing the data.

The work presented here studies the most challenging scenario of continual learning in an **online, completely task-free and class-incremental** (data incremental) setting where learning and evaluating can be carried out at any point of time.

## 2.2   Continual Learning Algorithms

Many continual learning methods have been developed in three major streams: regularization-based, architecture-based, and memory-based (or rehearsal-based) approaches.

**Regularization.** This approach aims to preserve the knowledge acquired from previous tasks, while maintaining the plasticity of every node. Elastic Weight Consolidation (EWC) [31] estimates the importance of each of the weights on previous tasks using the Fisher information matrix. Weight changes are then based on the degree of importance of particular weights. Another regularization method penalizes each weight change according to a measure of synaptic intelligence (SI) [63]. An attempt is made to estimate the task specificity for each parameter and penalize changes of parameters with high task specificity. This ensures that the parameter stays close to its present value, a value that ensured good performance on learning the initial task.

Knowledge Distillation (KD) is an efficient manner of transferring the knowledge between networks. It was initially introduced for network compression by using the teacher-student mechanism [24] and widely adopted for CL methods [36,52] and is considered to be one of regularization techniques.

However, it has been shown [57] that methods based on only regularization such as EWC and SI completely fail in a class-IL setting.

**Architecture.** These methods are often based on architectural modifications. They introduce task-specific parameters that dynamically increase the capacity of the model by adding a new layer to the network, as in [58]. Other methods of this kind dynamically add new layers to the network [51]. Other strategies developed by [39,53] attempt to freeze weights that are judged by the system to be the most important to a particular task and that will, therefore, not be updated by future back-propagation. Similar strategies use a mask for each previous task to protect parameters during the backward pass or to choose which parameters to use during the forward pass.

**Memory-based Approaches.** The key idea is to choose a strategy to store specific exemplars. It can be a strategy as simple as random selection or a more complex method, as in [48]. Some models can replay the exemplars stored in memory with the stream of data from the current task or they can be used as a regularization term, as in GEM [38], or in A-GEM [10], by computing the scalar product of the loss gradient vectors of previous examples stored in memory and the current data gradient vector. The parameters of the model are then only updated if the scalar product is positive.

To overcome the necessity of an external memory to store data from previous tasks, as in memory-based approaches, certain architectures integrate a generative model able to generate exemplars from previous tasks. These models include the use of a Generative Adversarial Network (GAN) [19] as in [44,60] or a Variational AutoEncoder [29,30] as in [56]. These methods are also called *Generative Replay* methods. The main drawback is that generative models are themselves prone to catastrophic forgetting. Moreover, methods which use a GAN to generate new samples, such as GDM [43] and ILUGAN [61], are both offline and task-based.

The proposed DSDM, a dynamic memory, can be considered to be a hybrid model that combines architecture-based and memory-based approaches.

## 2.3   Sparse Distributed Memory (SDM)

SDM is a content-addressable memory capable of both auto-associative and hetero-associative operation. It typically consisting of one million 1000-bit memory locations which are randomly distributed (i.e., fixed addresses) [26]. Using only a million locations out of possible $2^{1000}$ locations ($10^6 \ll 2^{1000}$), it is 'sparse'. SDM is mapped to a two-layer feed-forward neural network (without counting the input layer). The input units convey data patterns to the memory units (i.e., the address nodes). A pattern has two components: the pattern address is the vector representation of a memory point; and the pattern content. The weights to the address nodes represent a 'hard locations' and the weights to the output units store the memory contents.

**Storing Patterns.** When storing a pattern, the network computes the Hamming distance between the input address vector and each hard address. Address nodes within a preset Hamming distance will be activated (i.e., set to 1). In other words, if the fixed fan-in weight-vector associated with an address node is similar to the input vector, the address node will be activated; otherwise, it will remain inactive. The content weights that will be modified are those that fan-out from an active address nodes.

**Retrieving Patterns.** Reading is the operation of retrieving a data pattern from the memory at a particular address pattern. The input pattern is used to select a certain number of hard memory locations. The retrieved content is the average of the contents (i.e. fan-out weights) at the selected locations, followed by a fixed thresholding step.

## 3   Dynamic Sparse Distributed Memory

Conventional SDM networks have a fixed number of memory nodes whose 'hard' addresses are randomly distributed in a binary memory space. This

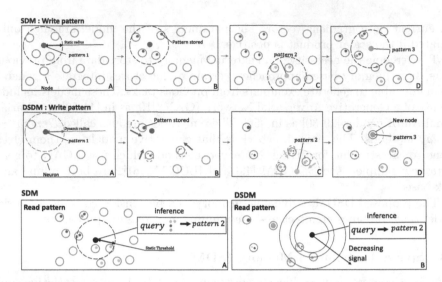

**Fig. 2.** The read and write operations of SDM and DSDM. **Top row, SDM write:** A+B+C. Two patterns are stored inside nearby fixed neurons within a fixed write radius; D. Writing a third pattern and neurons storing a superposition of multiple patterns. **Middle row, DSDM write:** A. Writing the first pattern that is close enough to its best matching unit with respect to a dynamic write radius; B. Neurons in space will move toward the pattern address while their content is sharpened with the pattern content; C. Writing the second pattern being close enough to its BMU; D. The third pattern is far from its BMU with respect to a dynamic radius, so a new neuron in memory is created. **Bottom row, Read operation:** A. SDM read: the query content reading from nearby neurons within a fixed radius using a majority vote; B. DSDM read: the query content is retrieved from multiple neurons according to its distance to the query address using a softmin function.

tends to lower performance when dealing with correlated, i.e., nonrandom, input data [23]. In our algorithm, we start with an empty memory space, and new address nodes are incrementally added depending on the considered input patterns and the current state of memory space. In other words, we dynamically grow new address nodes as a function of the input. DSDM models the distribution of the input patterns much better than SDM where certain fixed neurons are too far from the current input distribution and therefore are never activated, meaning that our memory has a higher storage capacity. We show experimentally in Sect. 4.2 that DSDM considerably outperforms SDM with far fewer neurons. Moreover, while a predefined Hamming distance is crucial in SDM, we propose to use a dynamic threshold, a so-called recursive temperature (RT) mechanism as a means of dynamically deciding whether a new memory unit is created.

In our work on image classification, we use DSDM network almost as a backend to a deep encoder and each address-content association consists of a feature vector, extracted from inputs by the encoder and a category label vector, coded in a one-hot manner.

---

**Algorithm 1.** DSDM training

---

1: **Init:** Address matrix $A = \{a_1 = x_1\}$, content matrix $C = \{c_1 = y_1\}$ with capacity $Q$, $RT = 0$; $K = 1$;
2: **Require:** $\beta$, $\lambda_{RT}$, $\lambda$. $\lambda_{RT}$ and $\lambda$ are the different learning rates, one for updating the dynamic threshold, one for sharpening the address and content.
3: **Input:** Consider each sample $(x_t, y_t)$ from the data stream $\{(x_2, y_2), (x_3, y_3), ...\}$.
4: $BMU = \operatorname{argmin}_{i \in [\![1,K]\!]} \|x_t - a_i\|$
5: $d_{BMU} \leftarrow \|x_t - a_{BMU}\|$
6: **if** $d_{BMU} > RT$ **then**
7:     $A \leftarrow A \cup (x_t)$
8:     $C \leftarrow C \cup (y_t)$
9:     $K \leftarrow K + 1$
10: **else**
11:     $A \leftarrow A + \lambda \times softmin(\|A - x_t\|/\beta) \times (A - x_t)$
12:     $C \leftarrow C + \lambda \times softmin(\|A - x_t\|/\beta) \times (C - y_t)$
13: **end if**
14: $RT \leftarrow \lambda_{RT} \times RT + (1 - \lambda_{RT}) \times \|x_t - a_{BMU}\|$
15: **if** $K > Q$ **then** # if memory is full
16:     LOF-based pruning
17: **end if**

---

## 3.1   Training Phase

As can be seen in Fig. 2, DSDM carries out two different types of learning, competitive and supervised learning, within its two layers respectively. The pseudo-code of DSDM training phase is described in Algorithm 1.

Our memory $M$ is represented by two matrices $A$ and $C$ that are initialized with the first input pattern, denoted by $(x_1, y_1)$, presented to the model. Our algorithm is online, each data sample is considered only once. It is also completely task-free, no assumption on task boundaries or the order of data presentation is required. Consider the pattern $\{(x_t, y_t)\}$ in the never-ending data stream $\{(x_2, y_2), (x_3, y_3), ...\}$ progressively presented to the model, we first find its nearest memory node, i.e., the best matching unit - BMU, in the memory space with respect to the location (address). For simplicity, we denote the index of BMU as "BMU":

$$BMU = \operatorname{argmin}_{i \in [\![1,K]\!]} \|x_t - a_i\| \tag{1}$$

where $\|a_i - a_j\|$ is distance between two memory locations; $K$ is the number of neurons created so far; $a_{BMU}$ is then the nearest neuron of $x_t$; $\|x_t - a_{BMU}\|$ is hereafter called "to-BMU distance" $(d_{BMU})$.

In the literature, there exist several expandable architectures [14,40,62] and they compare the to-BMU distance or similar metric to a *pre-defined* threshold to decide whether a new node or layer is added. While other methods can add a new layer, our DSDM by design has only two layers (excluding the input layer) and we only add/remove nodes. Since the to-BMU distance changes depending on the order of observing data, using a static threshold cannot be optimal and this often leads to an inadequate trade-off between the memory performance and size. To overcome this problem, we define a dynamic threshold as a means of dynamically deciding on whether a new node is created. This is achieved by using an exponential moving average of the last to-BMU distances. We call this mechanism *recursive temperature* (RT) since its value tends to increase when DSDM starts to learn a new task and then gradually decreases (see Sect. 4.6). The recursive temperature is dynamically updated as:

$$RT = \lambda_{RT} \times RT + (1 - \lambda_{RT}) \times \|x_t - a_{BMU}\| \tag{2}$$

where $\lambda_{RT}$ is the learning rate.

At this step, two possible cases can occur:

• If the to-BMU distance is lower than RT, meaning that the input sample is "close enough" to its BMU, the information for the input sample (address and content) will be distributedly stored across multiple nodes already created in memory. The address and content weights of these existing nodes are sharpened proportionally with respect to their distance to the considered input pattern's address, as follows:

$$A = A + \lambda \times softmin(\|A - x_t\|/\beta) \times (A - x_t) \tag{3}$$

$$C = C + \lambda \times softmin(\|A - x_t\|/\beta) \times (C - y_t) \tag{4}$$

where $\lambda$ is the learning rate for sharpening the address and content.

This update strategy is similar to that of competitive learning proposed by [28] to adapt models to the current data distribution.

• If the to-BMU distance is higher than RT, a new memory node is created and added into the memory space: $A \leftarrow A \cup (x_t)$, $C \leftarrow C \cup (y_t)$, $K \leftarrow K + 1$.

**Memory Pruning.** Besides using a recursive temperature mechanism to dynamically expand the memory space, we also propose using a density-based algorithm as a means of controlling memory size. In order to estimate the local density of patterns, we use in this work the Local Outlier Factor LOF algorithm [5], which is widely used for anomaly detection. However, we did not remove boundary samples as is done in LOF-based anomaly detection. Instead, we removed address nodes with high density, along with their associated content weights, until the desired number of address nodes has been reached. The intuition is that the removed patterns can still be retrieved by DSDM. We will continue to study different pruning techniques and threshold criteria.

### 3.2   Inference Phase

Consider the input query with address $x_q \in \mathbb{R}^m$, to obtain the model output, we first compute its $L_2$ distance to every patterns in the memory space: $d(A, x_q) = [\|a_1 - x_q\|, \|a_2 - x_q\|, ..., \|a_K - x_q\|]$.

We then compute the activation vector of the first layer, denoted by $W = [w_1, w_2, ..., w_K]$, using a softmin function:

$$\forall j \in [\![1, K]\!], w_j = \frac{e^{-d_j/\beta}}{\sum_{i=1}^{K} e^{-d_i/\beta}} \tag{5}$$

where $\beta$ is a temperature parameter which has the same role as the fixed threshold in the original SDM. If we increase $\beta$, nodes being far from the query pattern will have higher contribution in the final decision. If $\beta$ decreases, these nodes being far from the query pattern will have less contribution. In the extreme case with $\beta$ close to zero, only the content of the nearest address to the query is considered.

The final output $y_q$ is finally obtained by:

$$y_q = \sum_{i=1}^{K} w_i * c_i \tag{6}$$

where $c_i$ is the content of $i^{th}$ node, and $*$ is the element-wise multiplication.

## 4  Experiments

### 4.1  Experiment Setting

**Evaluation Metrics.** We consider the commonly used evaluation metrics - namely, average accuracy (Avg) and last step accuracy (Last) where Avg is the average of accuracy obtained after learning of each task, and Last is the final performance once all tasks/classes have been learned one after the other. We ran each experiment five times on a computer with one NVIDIA RTX 2060 GPU and report the average Top-1 classification results.

**Datasets.** We evaluated our algorithm under an online class-incremental setting on five commonly used image classification datasets:

**MNIST dataset** [13] is a handwritten digit recognition dataset with 60k training samples and 10k testing samples.

**CIFAR-10 dataset** [32] contains 10 classes and each class is composed of 6k images. They are divided into 50k images for training and 10k for testing.

**CIFAR-100 dataset** [32] consists of 100 mutually exclusive classes. Within each class, there are 500 training images and 100 testing images.

**CUB-200 dataset** [59] includes 200 fine-grained bird species. There are 5994 images for training and 5794 images for testing. For each category, there are about 29–30 training images and 11–30 testing images.

**CORE-50 dataset** [37] consists of 164,866 128 × 128 color images. It has for each class around 2400 training images and 900 testing images. For the class-incremental setting, it is divided into nine tasks and has a total of 50 classes with 10 classes in the first task and 5 classes in the other eight tasks.

In our experiments on all five datasets, we randomly arrange the class order. For each dataset (except CORE-50), other authors often report their results on different incremental step values. For a dataset of 10 classes in total (MNIST or CIFAR-10), when the incremental step is set to 2, the dataset itself is divided into five tasks with two class labels each (with step = 2, we will call Split MNIST and Split CIFAR-10 respectively). Those algorithms have different performances for different step sizes since they are not completely task-free. By contrast, DSDM is data-incremental learning, i.e., online (training with batch size = 1) and completely task-free. In this data configuration, we invariably obtained excellent performance, meaning that our results do not depend on the order of observing data.

Our model has three hyperparameters, i.e., $\beta$, $\lambda_{RT}$, and $\lambda$, where $\beta$ is the temperature parameter of the softmin function being used during inference phase and has the same role as the fixed threshold in the original SDM, $\lambda_{RT}$ and $\lambda$ are the different learning rates, one for updating the dynamic threshold, the other for sharpening the addresses and contents. The model performed similarly for a wide range of parameter values: $\beta \in [0.5, 6]$, $\lambda, \lambda_{RT} \in [0.001, 0.01]$ when an encoder is used (see details in Sects. 4.2, 4.3). Without an encoder (for the MNIST dataset only), we report the accuracies with $\beta = 0.5$, $\lambda = 0.0022$, $\lambda_{RT} = 0.0025$. In order words, for the moment these values are fixed. Future work will involve updating these values dynamically. One idea is to dynamically update $\beta$ as $K$ increases. We also consider having several BMUs, rather than only one BMU.

## 4.2   Advantage of DSDM over SDM

This section mainly aims at showing the advantage of DSDM over SDM. To this end, we consider the split MNIST benchmark and we do not use any encoder. The pattern address component of our memory is the original MNIST image vector, $x_t = I_t$. We modified the SDM to handle vectors of integers for multiple gray levels by replacing the Hamming distance with the city-block and $L_p$ distances. While it is theoretically shown in [1] that for SDM, the city-block distance can slightly outperform the $L_2$ distance (by 1–2%), it is not the same for our DSDM. Indeed, we evaluated DSDM with these two distances and found that DSDM performs better with the $L_2$ distance.

As can be seen in Table 1, DSDM significantly outperforms SDM (we set the DSDM model size to 5k that is the half of SDM). Their last accuracies of 94.0±0.2 and 74.2 ± 3.5, respectively, are *surprisingly* good. DSDM achieved the SOTA performance without any encoder. Our associative memory model is much simpler than other competing algorithms and no gradient flow was even considered. By comparison, other methods in Table 1 (except the Ensemble method) used a multi-layer perceptron with two hidden layers of 400 nodes each and ReLU non-linearities were used in all hidden layers. To achieve 91.0 ± 0.4, the Ensemble algorithm used a variational autoencoder where the encoder half comprises two convolutional layers followed by two linear layers and the decoder has two linear layers followed by two transpose convolutional layers. The results of CURL [47],

CN-DPM [34] and Ensemble [54] methods are taken from their original work while other ones are from [11].

**Table 1.** Last accuracy on split MNIST (step=2). Without any encoder and gradient-based update, the shallow DSDM model outperforms SOTA deep methods.

| Shallow | | Deep | | | | | |
|---|---|---|---|---|---|---|---|
| SDM | DSDM | Finetune | CURL [47] | CN-DPM [34] | Ensemble [54] | MIR [2] | CoPE [11] |
| $74.2 \pm 3.5$ | $\mathbf{94.0 \pm 0.2}$ | $19.7 \pm 0.05$ | $92.6 \pm 0.7$ | $93.2 \pm 0.1$ | $91.0 \pm 0.4$ | $93.2 \pm 0.4$ | $93.9 \pm 0.2$ |

### 4.3 Comparison with Online SOTA Methods

We compare our method with existing online approaches including A-GEM [10], GSS [3], MIR [2], ASER [55], GDUMB [45] and Candidates Voting (CV) [21]. Similar to the very recent work of CV [21], we report the average and last accuracies on Split CIFAR-10 and CORE-50. A small version of ResNet-18 [22] pretrained on ImageNet [12] is used as the backbone for all of the methods compared. In DSDM, the address component of a pattern is the feature extracted from the image produced by ResNet-18: $x_t = ResNet18(I_t)$. CV and DSDM freeze the parameters of the backbone network, while others do not. We vary the buffer size $Q \in \{1k, 2k, 5k\}$ for comparisons.

On CORE-50, the dataset that is specifically designed for continual learning, DSDM significantly outperforms existing online approaches on all considered buffer sizes $Q$ with the single exception of CV with buffer sizes of 1k when measured by the average accuracy. As for the last accuracies, DSDM is on average 50% better than the second-best results. On the split CIFAR-10 benchmark, DSDM outperforms all other methods with a limited storage capacity $Q = 1k$ and its performance is essentially the same as the best algorithm (CV). Moreover, only our algorithm is completely task-free, the learning and evaluating can be carried out at any point in time. The CV algorithm is online but it is not task-free during training with the use of task boundaries.

Several methods like MIR and GSS in Table 2 can perform reasonably well in both task-based and task-free settings. Their performance in the latter is worse than in the former. Their performance on the CIFAR10 dataset under these settings are respectively 52.2% and 42.8% (–19.6% for MIR) and 56.7% and 38.4% (–18.3% for GSS).

### 4.4 Comparison with Offline SOTA Methods

We also compare our method with offline continual learning approaches that update the model in multiple epochs on the CIFAR 100 and CUB-100 benchmarks with different incremental steps. Similar to FearNet [29] and ILUGAN

**Table 2.** Average and last accuracy on CIFAR-10 (step=2) and CORE-50. Best results marked in bold; second best results are underlined. **Only our algorithm is completely task-free.** Several methods like MIR and GSS can perform reasonably well under both task-based and task-free settings. We report here their best performance when task boundaries are known. The lines from "A-GEM" to "CV" are from [21].

| Datasets | CIFAR-10, step = 2 | | | | | | CORE-50 | | | | | |
|---|---|---|---|---|---|---|---|---|---|---|---|---|
| Buffer size $Q$ | 1k | | 2k | | 5k | | 1k | | 2k | | 5k | |
| Accuracy | Avg | Last | Avg | Last | Avg | Last | Avg | Last | Avg | Last | Avg | Last |
| A-GEM [10] | 43.0 | 17.5 | 59.1 | 38.3 | 74.0 | 59.0 | 20.7 | 8.4 | 21.9 | 10.3 | 22.9 | 11.5 |
| MIR [2] | 67.3 | 52.2 | 80.2 | 66.2 | 83.4 | 74.8 | 33.9 | 21.1 | 37.1 | 24.5 | 38.1 | 27.7 |
| GSS [3] | 70.3 | 56.7 | 73.6 | 56.3 | 79.3 | 64.4 | 27.8 | 17.8 | 31.0 | 18.9 | 31.8 | 21.1 |
| ASER [55] | 63.4 | 46.4 | 78.2 | 59.3 | 83.3 | 73.1 | 24.3 | 12.2 | 30.8 | 17.4 | 32.5 | 18.5 |
| GDUMB [45] | 73.8 | 57.7 | 83.8 | 72.4 | 85.3 | 75.9 | 41.2 | 23.6 | 48.4 | 32.7 | 54.3 | 41.6 |
| CV [21] | <u>76.0</u> | 62.9 | **84.9** | **74.1** | **86.1** | **77.0** | **45.1** | <u>26.5</u> | <u>50.7</u> | <u>34.5</u> | <u>56.3</u> | <u>43.1</u> |
| DSDM | **80.2** | **67.0** | <u>83.8</u> | <u>72.5</u> | <u>85.6</u> | <u>76.0</u> | <u>43.9</u> | **43.3** | **53.2** | 50.8 | 66.3 | **57.1** |
| DSDM/CV (%) | | 107 | | 98 | | 99 | | 163 | | 147 | | 132 |

([61]), Resnet-50 backbone pre-trained on ImageNet is used as the feature extractor in DSDM: $x_t = ResNet50(I_t)$. On these benchmarks, we set $Q = 3k$. We consider SOTA offline approaches including EWC [31], LWF [36], iCaRL [48], End-to-End [9], FearNet [29] and ILUGAN [61]. The reported results are from [61]. Although it is widely acknowledged that performance in the online scenario is worse than offline, our DSDM still outperforms those SOTA offline approaches with important margins, as can be seen in Table 3(a). Table 3(b) presents the training batch size and epoch number of different algorithms and clearly shows the advantages of DSDM.

**Table 3.** (a) Comparison of average accuracy on CIFAR-100 and CUB-200. (b) Comparison of training batch size (BS) and epochs (Ep). **Only DSDM can carry out learning and evaluating at any point in time.**

| Datasets | **CIFAR-100** | | **CUB-200** | |
|---|---|---|---|---|
| Step | 2 | 5 | 2 | 5 |
| EWC [31] | 15.4 | 17.9 | 15.9 | 18.2 |
| LwF [36] | 32.8 | 37.9 | 29.8 | 36.1 |
| iCaRL [48] | 52.8 | 57.2 | 44.3 | 49.6 |
| End-to-End [9] | 50.3 | 49.7 | 44.5 | 49.9 |
| FearNet [29] | 56.9 | 62.5 | 47.8 | 52.7 |
| ILUGAN [61] | 58.0 | 63.1 | 49.7 | 54.9 |
| **DSDM** | **63.3** | **63.2** | **55.5** | **55.2** |

(a)

| Datasets | **CIFAR-100** | | **CUB-200** | |
|---|---|---|---|---|
| Training | BS | Ep | BS | Ep |
| iCaRL | 450 | 70 | 450 | 70 |
| End-to-End | 128 | 70 | 128 | 70 |
| FearNet | 450 | 250 | 200 | 100 |
| ILUGAN | | 90 | | 90 |
| CV | 10 | 1 | 10 | 1 |
| DSDM | 1 | 1 | 1 | 1 |

(b)

## 4.5    Completely Task-Free and Few-Shot Settings

**Completely Task-Free:** As mentioned above, other authors often reported different results with different incremental step sizes since their algorithms distinguish tasks that have clear task boundaries, at least during the training phase. By contrast, our model operates in the completely task-free setting (DSDM achieved similar performances as can be seen in Tables 1, 2). We demonstrate this capability by evaluating DSDM under the Gaussian schedule benchmarks, recently proposed in [54]. A schedule defines how a data distribution evolves over training. In the Gaussian schedule, there are no task boundaries. Each label appears in the data with a probability that follows a Gaussian distribution, and each label's probability peaks at a different time.

**Table 4.** Comparison of last accuracy of different methods under the challenging scenarios. Best results marked in bold; second best results are underlined. Our algorithms works well on limited-data regimes.

| Dataset | CIFAR-10 | | | CIFAR-100 | | |
|---|---|---|---|---|---|---|
| step | 1 | 2 | Gaussian | 1 | 5 | Gaussian |
| CoPE [11] | – | 48.90 | – | – | 21.60 | – |
| CN-DPM [34] | – | 45.21 | – | – | 20.10 | – |
| Vanilla classifier [54] | $10.6 \pm 2.2$ | $23.2 \pm 4.8$ | $11.4 \pm 2.4$ | $1.0 \pm 0.2$ | $3.8 \pm 0.5$ | $6.9 \pm 2.9$ |
| Ensemble [54] | $78.3 \pm 0.4$ | $79.0 \pm 0.4$ | $50.1 \pm 9.5$ | $54.1 \pm 0.5$ | $55.3 \pm 0.4$ | $39.0 \pm 1.4$ |
| **DSDM+CNN, low data** | $\underline{79.4 \pm 0.5}$ | $\underline{79.6 \pm 0.5}$ | $\underline{78.7 \pm 1.1}$ | $\underline{54.9 \pm 1.4}$ | $55.3 \pm 1.3$ | $\underline{55.5 \pm 1.2}$ |
| **DSDM+ViT, low data** | $\mathbf{85.5 \pm 0.7}$ | $\mathbf{85.6 \pm 0.6}$ | $\mathbf{84.9 \pm 0.6}$ | $\mathbf{61.1 \pm 0.5}$ | $\mathbf{60.8 \pm 0.9}$ | $\mathbf{61.4 \pm 1.1}$ |

**Few-shot CL:** We further study the data efficiency of our model. We report the results on CIFAR-10 and CIFAR-100 when using only 10% and 30% of the training samples from these datasets respectively. We use here two different feature extractors. We use two different feature extractors, ResNet50 pretrained on ImageNet in a supervised manner and a vision transformer encoder pretrained with self-supervised learning (SSL) [7]). (The simplest version ViT8 was used). We denote these methods as 'DSDM + CNN' and 'DSDM + ViT' respectively. For 'DSDM + CNN', we used a buffer size $Q = 2k, 6k$ for CIFAR-10 and CIFAR-100, respectively. For 'Ours ViT', we used a buffer size $Q = 1k, 3k$ for CIFAR-10 and CIFAR-100, respectively.

Table 4 compares the last accuracies under different scenarios. To the best of our knowledge, only the Ensemble architecture using a fixed ResNet50 pretrained in a SSL manner on ImageNet reports its performance with a Gaussian schedule (other results of Table 4 come from [54]). DSDM outperforms Ensemble while requiring much less data. Under the challenging scenario of a Gaussian schedule, DSDM's gain is highly significant. The performance accuracies of 'DSDM + ViT' are respectively 69% and 57% better than those of Ensemble on CIFAR-10 and CIFAR-100, respectively.

### 4.6   Impact of a Dynamic Threshold

This section shows the importance of using a dynamic threshold. Figure 3 shows the evolution of recursive temperature and to-BMU distances on the Core-50 training dataset. The to-BMU distances change when new data is seen.

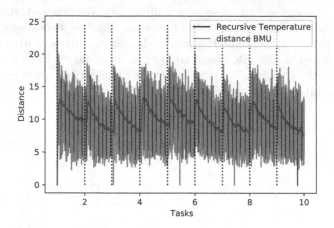

**Fig. 3.** The evolution of recursive temperature and to-BMU distance on the training set of Core-50.

## 5   Conclusion

This work introduces DSDM, an online and completely task-free algorithm called DSDM for class-incremental learning. DSDM is an associative content-addressable memory model that evolves dynamically and continually to model the distribution of non-stationary data streams. With DSDM, learning and eval-uating can be carried out at any point in time. DSDM outperforms SOTA meth-ods on many image classification benchmarks, including MNIST, CIFAR-10, CIFAR-100, CUB-200 and Core-50 under different challenging scenarios, even without an encoder front-end and with limited training data.

Modifying or eliminating the use of DSDM's fixed encoder is currently under study. [20] has shown that an SSL encoder can be trained in online learning with random images. Moreover, [42] showed that features learned by an SSL encoder on a subset of the visual experiences of developing children led to high accuracy in non-trivial downstream categorization tasks. Further, the capacity to generalize under these circumstances was shown in [7]. This potentially means that our algorithm could generalize to new data that is very different from the initial pre-training data. In future work we will explore training a combination of an encoder and our DSDM architecture in an online and continual manner with a scenario corresponding to that of developing children. Indeed, we could first learn good representation features with SSL, followed by the continual learning phase with supervised learning. This scenario would arguably simulate real human learning more realistically than most current CL scenarior that start directly with incremental learning without any pretraining. We will, in addition, study how to apply DSDM to other tasks, such as regression or anomaly detection, as in [25].

# References

1. Aggarwal, C.C., Hinneburg, A., Keim, D.A.: On the surprising behavior of distance metrics in high dimensional space. In: Van den Bussche, J., Vianu, V. (eds.) 8th International Conference on Database Theory, pp. 420–434. Springer (2001)
2. Aljundi, R., et al.: Online continual learning with maximal interfered retrieval. In: Advances in Neural Information Processing Systems, vol. 32 (2019)
3. Aljundi, R., Lin, M., Goujaud, B., Bengio, Y.: Gradient based sample selection for online continual learning. Adv. Neural Inf. Process. Syst. **32** (2019)
4. Ans, B., Rousset, S., French, R.M., Musca, S.: Self-refreshing memory in artificial neural networks: learning temporal sequences without catastrophic forgetting. Connection Sci. **16**(2), 71–99 (2004)
5. Breunig, M.M., Kriegel, H.P., Ng, R.T., Sander, J.: LOF: identifying density-based local outliers, p. 12 (2000)
6. Bricken, T., Pehlevan, C.: Attention approximates sparse distributed memory. Adv. Neural Inf. Process. Syst. **34**, 15301–15315 (2021)
7. Caron, M., Touvron, H., Misra, I., Jégou, H., Mairal, J., Bojanowski, P., Joulin, A.: Emerging properties in self-supervised vision transformers. In: 2021 IEEE/CVF International Conference on Computer Vision (ICCV), pp. 9650–9660 (2021)
8. Carpenter, G., Grossberg, S.: ART 2: self-organization of stable category recognition codes for analog input patterns. Appl. Opt.**26**, 4919–4930 (1987)
9. Castro, F.M., Marín-Jiménez, M.J., Guil, N., Schmid, C., Alahari, K.: End-to-end incremental learning. In: Ferrari, V., Hebert, M., Sminchisescu, C., Weiss, Y. (eds.) Proceedings of the European conference on computer vision (ECCV), pp. 233–248 (2018)
10. Chaudhry, A., Ranzato, M., Rohrbach, M., Elhoseiny, M.: Efficient lifelong learning with A-GEM. In: International Conference on Learning Representations (2018)
11. De Lange, M., Tuytelaars, T.: Continual prototype evolution: learning online from non-stationary data streams. In: Proceedings of the IEEE/CVF International Conference on Computer Vision, pp. 8250–8259 (2021)
12. Deng, J., Dong, W., Socher, R., Li, L.J., Li, K., Fei-Fei, L.: ImageNet: a large-scale hierarchical image database. In: 2009 IEEE Conference on Computer Vision and Pattern Recognition, pp. 248–255 (2009)
13. Deng, L.: The MNIST database of handwritten digit images for machine learning research. IEEE Sign. Process. Mag. **29**(6), 141–142 (2012)
14. Fahlman, S.E., Lebiere, C.: The cascade-correlation learning architecture. In: Touretzky, D.S. (ed.) Advances in Neural Information Processing Systems 2, [NIPS Conference, Denver, Colorado, USA, November 27–30, 1989], pp. 524–532. Morgan Kaufmann (1989). http://papers.nips.cc/paper/207-the-cascade-correlation-learning-architecture
15. French, R.M.: Dynamically constraining connectionist networks to produce distributed, orthogonal representations to reduce catastrophic interference. In: Proceedings of the 16th Annual Cognitive Science Society Conference, pp. 335–340 (1994)

16. French, R.M.: Pseudo-recurrent connectionist networks: an approach to the sensitivity-stability dilemma. Connection Sci. **9**(4), 353–380 (1997)

17. French, R.M.: Catastrophic forgetting in connectionist networks. Trends Cogn. Sci. **3**(4), 128–135 (1999)

18. French, R.M., Chater, N.: Using noise to compute error surfaces in connectionist networks: a novel means of reducing catastrophic forgetting. Neural Comput. **14**(7), 1755–1769 (2002)

19. Goodfellow, I.J., et al.: Generative Adversarial Networks. arXiv:1406.2661 (2014)

20. Goyal, P., et al.: Self-supervised Pretraining of Visual Features in the Wild. arXiv:2103.01988 (2021)

21. He, J., Zhu, F.: Online continual learning via candidates voting. In: 2022 IEEE/CVF Winter Conference on Applications of Computer Vision (WACV), pp. 3154–3163 (2022)

22. He, K., Zhang, X., Ren, S., Sun, J.: Deep residual learning for image recognition. In: 2016 IEEE Conference on Computer Vision and Pattern Recognition (CVPR), pp. 770–778 (2016)

23. Hely, T.A., Willshaw, D.J., Hayes, G.M.: A new approach to Kanerva's sparse distributed memory. IEEE Trans. Neural Netw. **8**(3), 791–794 (1997). https://doi.org/10.1109/72.572115

24. Hinton, G., Vinyals, O., Dean, J.: Distilling the Knowledge in a Neural Network. arXiv:1503.02531 (2015)

25. Jezequel, L., Vu, N., Beaudet, J., Histace, A.: Efficient anomaly detection using self-supervised multi-cue tasks. CoRR arXiv:abs/2111.12379 (2021)

26. Kanerva, P.: A cerebellar-model associative memory as a generalized random-access memory. In: Thirty-Fourth IEEE Computer Society International Conference: Intellectual Leverage, pp. 770–778 (1989)

27. Kanerva, P.: Sparse distributed memory and related models. Tech. Rep. NASA-CR-190553, keeler (1992)

28. Keeler, J.: Capacity for patterns and sequences in Kanerva' s SDM as compared to other associative memory models. In: Neural Information Processing Systems. American Institute of Physics (1988)

29. Kemker, R., Kanan, C.: FearNet: Brain-inspired model for incremental learning. In: International Conference on Learning Representations (2018)

30. Kingma, D.P., Welling, M.: Auto-Encoding Variational Bayes. arXiv:1312.6114 (May 2014)

31. Kirkpatrick, J., Pascanu, R., Rabinowitz, N., Veness, J., Desjardins, G., Rusu, A.A., Milan, K., Quan, J., Ramalho, T., Grabska-Barwinska, A., Hassabis, D., Clopath, C., Kumaran, D., Hadsell, R.: Overcoming catastrophic forgetting in neural networks. Proc. Natl. Acad. Sci. **114**(13), 3521–3526 (2017)

32. Krizhevsky, A.: Learning Multiple Layers of Features from Tiny Images (2009)

33. Kruschke, J.K.: Human category learning: implications for backpropagation models. Connection Sci. **5**(1), 3–36 (1993)

34. Lee, S., Ha, J., Zhang, D., Kim, G.: A neural dirichlet process mixture model for task-free continual learning. In: 8th ICLR 2020. OpenReview.net (2020). https://openreview.net/forum?id=SJxSOJStPr

35. Lewandowsky, S.: Gradual unlearning and catastrophic interference: a comparison of distributed architectures. In: Relating theory and data: Essays on human memory in honor of Bennet B. Murdock, pp. 445–476. Lawrence Erlbaum Associates Inc, Hillsdale, NJ, US (1991)

36. Li, Z., Hoiem, D.: Learning without forgetting. In: 14th European Conference on Computer Vision, ECCV 2016. Computer Vision - 14th European Conference, ECCV 2016, Proceedings, pp. 614–629 (2016)
37. Lomonaco, V., Maltoni, D.: CORe50: a new dataset and benchmark for continuous object recognition. In: CoRL, pp. 17–26 (2017)
38. Lopez-Paz, D., Ranzato, M.A.: Gradient episodic memory for continual learning. Adv. Neural Inf. Process. Syst. **30**(2017)
39. Mallya, A., Lazebnik, S.: PackNet: adding multiple tasks to a single network by iterative pruning. In: 2018 IEEE/CVF Conference on Computer Vision and Pattern Recognition, pp. 7765–7773 (2018)
40. Marsland, S., Shapiro, J., Nehmzow, U.: A self-organising network that grows when required. Neural Netw. 15(8-9), 1041–1058 (2002)
41. McCloskey, M., Cohen, N.J.: Catastrophic interference in connectionist networks: the sequential learning problem. In: Bower, G.H. (ed.) Psychology of Learning and Motivation, vol. 24, pp. 109–165 (1989)
42. Orhan, A.E., Gupta, V.V., Lake, B.M.: Self-supervised learning through the eyes of a child. Adv. Neural Inf. Process. Syst. (2020)
43. Ostapenko, O., Puscas, M., Klein, T., Jähnichen, P., Nabi, M.: Learning to Remember: A Synaptic Plasticity Driven Framework for Continual Learning. arXiv:1904.03137 [cs] (2019)
44. Ostapenko, O., Puscas, M.M., Klein, T., Jähnichen, P., Nabi, M.: Learning to remember: a synaptic plasticity driven framework for continual learning. In: IEEE Conference on Computer Vision and Pattern Recognition, CVPR 2019, Long Beach, CA, USA, June 16–20, 2019, pp. 11321–11329. Computer Vision Foundation/IEEE (2019). https://doi.org/10.1109/CVPR.2019.01158
45. Prabhu, A., Torr, P.H.S., Dokania, P.K.: GDumb: a Simple approach that questions our progress in continual learning. In: Vedaldi, A., Bischof, H., Brox, T., Frahm, J.M. (eds.) Computer Vision - ECCV 2020, vol. 12347, pp. 524–540 (2020)
46. Ramsauer, H., et al.: Hopfield Networks is All You Need. arXiv:2008.02217 (2021)
47. Rao, D., Visin, F., Rusu, A.A., Teh, Y.W., Pascanu, R., Hadsell, R.: Continual unsupervised representation learning. CoRR arXiv:abs/1910.14481 (2019)
48. Rebuffi, S.A., Kolesnikov, A., Sperl, G., Lampert, C.H.: iCaRL: incremental classifier and representation learning. In: 2017 IEEE Conference on Computer Vision and Pattern Recognition (CVPR), pp. 2001–2010 (2017)
49. R.M, F.: Semi-distributed representations and catastrophic forgetting in connectionist networks. Connection Sci. **4**(3-4), 365–377 (1992)
50. Robins, A.: Catastrophic forgetting, rehearsal and pseudorehearsal. Connection Sci. **7**(2), 123–146 (1995)
51. Roy, D., Panda, P., Roy, K.: Tree-CNN: a hierarchical deep convolutional neural network for incremental learning. Neural Netw. (2019)
52. Schwarz, Jet al.: Progress & compress: a scalable framework for continual learning. In: Proceedings of the 35th International Conference on Machine Learning, pp. 4528–4537 (2018)
53. Serrà, J., Surís, D., Miron, M., Karatzoglou, A.: Overcoming catastrophic forgetting with hard attention to the task. Int. Conf. Mach. Learn. 4548–4557 (2018)
54. Shanahan, M., Kaplanis, C., Mitrović, J.: Encoders and Ensembles for Task-Free Continual Learning. arXiv:2105.13327 (2021)
55. Shim, D., Mai, Z., Jeong, J., Sanner, S., Kim, H., Jang, J.: Online class-incremental continual learning with adversarial shapley value. In: Proceedings of the AAAI Conference on Artificial Intelligence **35**(11), 9630–9638 (2021)

56. van de Ven, G.M., Siegelmann, H.T., Tolias, A.S.: Brain-inspired replay for continual learning with artificial neural networks. Nat. Commun. **11**(1), 1–14 (2020)
57. van de Ven, G.M., Tolias, A.S.: Three scenarios for continual learning. arXiv:1904.07734 (2019)
58. Wang, Y.X., Ramanan, D., Hebert, M.: Growing a brain: fine-tuning by increasing model capacity. In: Proceedings of the IEEE Conference on Computer Vision and Pattern Recognition, pp. 2471–2480 (2019)
59. Welinder, P., Branson, S., Mita, T., Wah, C., Schroff, F., Belongie, S., Perona, P.: Caltech-UCSD birds 200 (2010)
60. Wu, C., Herranz, L., Liu, X., wang, y., van de Weijer, J., Raducanu, B.: Memory replay GANs: learning to generate new categories without forgetting. Adv. Neural Inf. Process. Syst. **31** (2018)
61. Xiang, Y., Fu, Y., Ji, P., Huang, H.: Incremental learning using conditional adversarial networks. In: 2019 IEEE/CVF International Conference on Computer Vision (ICCV), pp. 6619–6628 (2019)
62. Yoon, J., Yang, E., Lee, J., Hwang, S.J.: Lifelong learning with dynamically expandable networks. In: International Conference on Learning Representations (2018)
63. Zenke, F., Poole, B., Ganguli, S.: Continual learning through synaptic intelligence. In: Proceedings of the 34th International Conference on Machine Learning, pp. 3987–3995 (2017)

# Author Index

Printed in the United States
by Baker & Taylor Publisher Services